DATE DUE

			PRINTED IN U.S.A.

Literature Criticism from 1400 to 1800

Guide to Gale Literary Criticism Series

For criticism on	Consult these Gale series
Authors now living or who died after December 31, 1959	*CONTEMPORARY LITERARY CRITICISM (CLC)*
Authors who died between 1900 and 1959	*TWENTIETH-CENTURY LITERARY CRITICISM (TCLC)*
Authors who died between 1800 and 1899	*NINETEENTH-CENTURY LITERATURE CRITICISM (NCLC)*
Authors who died between 1400 and 1799	*LITERATURE CRITICISM FROM 1400 TO 1800 (LC)* *SHAKESPEAREAN CRITICISM (SC)*
Authors who died before 1400	*CLASSICAL AND MEDIEVAL LITERATURE CRITICISM (CMLC)*
Authors of books for children and young adults	*CHILDREN'S LITERATURE REVIEW (CLR)*
Dramatists	*DRAMA CRITICISM (DC)*
Poets	*POETRY CRITICISM (PC)*
Short story writers	*SHORT STORY CRITICISM (SSC)*
Black writers of the past two hundred years	*BLACK LITERATURE CRITICISM (BLC)*
Hispanic writers of the late nineteenth and twentieth centuries	*HISPANIC LITERATURE CRITICISM (HLC)*
Native North American writers and orators of the eighteenth, nineteenth, and twentieth centuries	*NATIVE NORTH AMERICAN LITERATURE (NNAL)*
Major authors from the Renaissance to the present	*WORLD LITERATURE CRITICISM, 1500 TO THE PRESENT (WLC)*

ISSN 0740-2880

Volume 46

Literature Criticism from 1400 to 1800

Critical Discussion of the Works
of Fifteenth-, Sixteenth-, Seventeenth-, and
Eighteenth-Century Novelists, Poets, Playwrights,
Philosophers, and Other Creative Writers

Jelena O. Krstović
Marie Lazzari
Editors

The Gale Group

DETROIT • SAN FRANCISCO • LONDON • BOSTON • WOODBRIDGE, CT

Riverside Community College
 Library
4800 Magnolia Avenue
Riverside, CA 92506

STAFF

Jelena O. Krstović, Marie Lazzari, *Editors*
Suzanne Dewsbury, Ira Mark Milne, *Associate Editors*
Janet Witalec, *Managing Editor*

Maria Franklin, *Permissions Manager*
Kimberly F. Smilay, *Permissions Specialist*
Kelly A. Quin, *Permissions Associate*
Sandra K. Gore, *Permissions Assistant*

Victoria B. Cariappa, *Research Manager*
Patricia T. Ballard, Tamara C. Nott, Tracie A. Richardson,
Corrine Stocker, Cheryl L. Warnock, *Research Associates*

Gary Leach, *Graphic Artist*
Randy Bassett, *Image Database Supervisor*
Mike Logusz, Robert Duncan, *Imaging Specialists*
Pamela A. Reed, *Imaging Coordinator*

This book is printed on acid-free paper that meets the minimum requirements of American National Standard for Information Sciences—Permanence Paper for Printed Library Materials, ANSI Z39.48-1984.

Library of Congress Catalog Card Number 94-29718
ISBN 0-7876-2415-2
ISSN 0740-2880
Printed in the United States of America

10 9 8 7 6 5 4 3 2 1

Contents

Preface vii

Acknowledgments xi

Preface

*L*iterature Criticism from 1400 to 1800 (LC) presents critical discussion of world literature from the fifteenth through the eighteenth centuries. The literature of this period is especially vital: the years 1400 to 1800 saw the rise of modern European drama, the birth of the novel and personal essay forms, the emergence of newspapers and periodicals, and major achievements in poetry and philosophy. *LC* provides valuable insight into the art, life, thought, and cultural transformations that took place during these centuries.

Scope of the Series

LC provides an introduction to the great poets, dramatists, novelists, essayists, and philosophers of the fifteenth through eighteenth centuries, and to the most significant interpretations of these authors' works. Because criticism of this literature spans nearly six hundred years, an overwhelming amount of scholarship confronts the student. *LC* organizes this material concisely and logically. Every attempt is made to reprint the most noteworthy, relevant, and educationally valuable essays available.

A separate Gale reference series, *Shakespearean Criticism,* is devoted exclusively to Shakespearean studies. Although properly belonging to the period covered in *LC,* William Shakespeare has inspired such a tremendous and ever-growing body of secondary material that a separate series was deemed essential.

Each entry in *LC* presents a representative selection of critical response to an author, a literary topic, or to a single important work of literature. Early commentary is offered to indicate initial responses, later selections document changes in literary reputations, and retrospective analyses provide the reader with modern views. The size of each author entry is a relative reflection of the scope of criticism available in English. Every attempt has been made to identify and include the seminal essays on each author's work and to include recent commentary providing modern perspectives.

Volumes 1 through 12 of the series feature author entries arranged alphabetically by author. Volumes 13 through 47 of the series feature a thematic arrangement. Each volume includes an entry devoted to the general study of a specific literary or philosophical movement, writings surrounding important political and historical events, the philosophy and art associated with eras of cultural transformation, or the literature of specific social or ethnic groups. Each of these volumes also includes several author entries devoted to major representatives of the featured period, genre, or national literature. With Volume 48, the series returns to a standard author approach, with occasional entries devoted to a single important work of world literature. One volume annually is devoted wholly to literary topics.

Organization of the Book

Each entry consists of a heading, an introduction, a list of principal works, annotated works of criticism, each preceded by a bibliographical citation, and a bibliography of recommended further reading. Many of the entries include illustrations.

- The **Author Heading** consists of the most commonly used form of the author's name, followed by birth and death dates. Also located here are any name variations under which an author wrote, including transliterated forms for authors whose native languages use nonroman alphabets. Uncertain birth or death dates are indicated by question marks. Topic entries are preceded by a **Thematic Heading,** which simply states the subject of the entry. Single-work entries are preceded by the title of the work and its date of publication.

- The **Introduction** contains background information that concisely introduces the reader to the author, work, or topic that is the subject of the entry.

- The list of **Principal Works** is ordered chronologically by date of first publication. The genre and publication date of each work is given. In the case of foreign authors whose works have been translated into English, the title and date (if available) of the first English-language edition is given in brackets following the original title. Unless otherwise indicated, dramas are dated by first performance, not first publication. Lists of **Representative Works** by different authors appear with topic entries.

- Reprinted **Criticism** is arranged chronologically in each entry to provide a useful perspective on changes in critical evaluation over time. The critic's name and the date of composition or publication of the critical work are given at the beginning of each piece of criticism. Unsigned criticism is preceded by the title of the source in which it appeared. All titles by the author featured in the text are printed in boldface type. Footnotes are reprinted at the end of each essay or excerpt. In the case of excerpted criticism, only those footnotes that pertain to the excerpted text are included. Criticism in topic entries is arranged chronologically under a variety of subheadings to facilitate the study of different aspects of the topic.

- Critical essays are prefaced by brief **Annotations** explicating each piece.

- A complete **Bibliographical Citation** of the original essay or book precedes each piece of criticism.

- An annotated bibliography of **Further Reading** appears at the end of each entry and suggests resources for additional study. In some cases, significant essays for which the editors could not obtain reprint rights are included here.

Cumulative Indexes

Each volume of *LC* includes a series-specific cumulative **Nationality Index** in which author names are arranged alphabetically by nationality. The volume or volumes of *LC* in which each author appears are also listed.

Each volume of *LC* includes a cumulative **Author Index** listing all of the authors that appear in a wide variety of reference sources published by The Gale Group, including *LC*. A complete list of these sources is found facing the first page of the Author Index. The index also includes birth and death dates and cross references between pseudonyms and actual names.

LC includes a cumulative **Topic Index** that lists the literary themes and topics treated in the series as well as in *Nineteenth-Century Literature Criticism*, *Twentieth-Century Literary Criticism*, and the *Contemporary Literature Criticism* Yearbook.

Each volume of *LC* also includes a cumulative **Title Index,** an alphabetical listing of all the literary works discussed in the series. Each title listing includes the corresponding volume and page numbers where criticism may be located. Foreign-language titles that have been translated into English followed by the tiles of the translation—for example, *El ingenioso hidalgo Don Quixote de la Mancha (Don Quixote)*. Page numbers following these translated titles refer to all pages on which any form of the titles, either foreign-language or translated, appear. Titles of novels, dramas, nonfiction books, and poetry, short story, or essay collections are printed in italics, while individual poems, short stories, and essays are printed in roman type within quotation marks.

A Note to the Reader

When writing papers, students who quote directly from any volume in the Literary Criticism Series may use the following general format to footnote reprinted criticism. The first example pertains to material drawn from periodicals, the second to material reprinted from books.

Eileen Reeves, "Daniel 5 and the *Assayer*: Galileo Reads the Handwriting on the Wall," *The Journal of Medieval and Renaissance Studies,* Vol. 21, No. 1, Spring, 1991, pp. 1-27; reprinted in *Literature Criticism from 1400 to 1800,* Vol. 45, ed. Jelena O. Krstović and Marie Lazzari, Farmington Hills, Mich.: The Gale Group, 1999, pp. 297-310.

Margaret Anne Doody, *A Natural Passion: A Study of the Novels of Samuel Richardson*, Oxford University Press, 1974, pp. 17-22, 132-35, excerpted and reprinted in *Literature Criticism from 1400 to 1800,* Vol. 46, ed. Jelena O. Krstović and Marie Lazzari. Farmington Hills, Mich.: The Gale Group, 1999, pp. 20-2.

Suggestions Are Welcome

Readers who wish to suggest new features, topics, or authors to appear in future volumes, or who have other suggestions or comments are cordially invited to call, write, or fax the editor:

Editor, *Literature Criticism 1400-1800*
The Gale Group
27500 Drake Road
Farmington Hills, MI 48133-3535
1-800-347-4253
fax: 248-699-8049

Acknowledgments

The editors wish to thank the copyright holders of the excerpted criticism included in this volume and the permissions managers of many book and magazine publishing companies for assisting us in securing reproduction rights. We are also grateful to the staffs of the Detroit Public Library, the Library of Congress, the University of Detroit Mercy Library, Wayne State University Purdy/Kresge Library Complex, and the University of Michigan Libraries for making their resources available to us. Following is a list of the copyright holders who have granted us permission to reproduce material in this volume of *LC*. Every effort has been made to trace copyright, but if omissions have been made, please let us know.

COPYRIGHTED EXCERPTS IN *LC*, VOLUME 46, WERE REPRODUCED FROM THE FOLLOWING PERIODICALS:

Cultural Critique, v. 1, Fall, 1985. © 1985. Used by permission of Oxford University Press, Inc. —*Eighteenth-Century Fiction*, v. 3, October, 1990 for "Patterns of Property and Possession in Fielding's Fiction" by James Thompson; v. 4, 1992; v. 6, January, 1994; v. 6, April, 1994. Reproduced by permission. —*Eighteenth-Century Studies*, v. 25, Winter, 1991/92. © 1991/92. Reproduced by permission of The Johns Hopkins University Press. —*ELH*, v. 35, 1968 for "Fielding's Definition of Wisdom: Some Functions of Ambiguity and Emblem" by Martin Battestin. Reproduced by permission of The Johns Hopkins University Press. —*Essays in Literature*, v. X, Spring, 1983; v. XXIII, Fall, 1996. Reproduced by permission. —*Studies in English Literature*, v. XXIII, 1988; v. 37, Summer, 1997. (c) 1988, 1997 William Marsh Rice University. Reproduced by permission of *SEL: Studies in English Literature 1500-1900*. —*Studies in Scottish Literature*, v. XXIII, 1988. Copyright © G. Ross Roy 1988. Reproduced by permission of the editor. —*The Dalhousie Review*, v. 62, 1982 for "The Physiology of Deceit in Fielding's Works" by Alan T. McKenzie. Reproduced by permission of the publisher and the author.

COPYRIGHTED EXCERPTS IN *LC*, VOLUME 46, WERE REPRODUCED FROM THE FOLLOWING BOOKS:

Penguin Books, 1974. Copyright © Penguin Books, 1974. Reproduced by permission of the Peters, Fraser & Dunlop Group Ltd. —Jack, R. D. S. From "Appearance and Reality in 'Humphry Clinker'" in *Smollett: Author of the First Distinction*. Edited by Alan Bold. Vision/Barnes & Noble, 1982. © 1982 Vision Press Ltd. All rights reserved. Reproduced by permission. —Kettle, Arnold. From *An Introduction to the English Novel, Vol. 1*. Hutchinson University Library, 1967. Reproduced by permission. —Kraft, Elizabeth. From *Character and Consciousness in Eighteenth-Century Comic Fiction*. The University of Georgia Press, 1992. © 1992 by The University of Georgia Press. All rights reserved. Reproduced by permission. —Mace, Nancy A. From *Henry Fielding's Novels and the Classical Tradition*. University of Delaware Press, 1996. © 1996 Associated University Presses, Inc. All rights reserved. Reproduced by permission. —McKeon, Michael. From *The Origins of the English Novel, 1600-1740*. The Johns Hopkins University Press, 1987. © 1987 by The Johns Hopkins University Press. All rights reserved. Reproduced by permission of The Johns Hopkins University Press. —Paulson, Ronald. From *Satire and the Novel in Eighteenth-Century England*. Yale University Press, 1967. Copyright © 1967 Yale University Press. All rights reserved. Reproduced by permission. —Paulson, Ronald. From *Satire and the Novel in Eighteenth-Century England*. Yale University Press, 1967. Copyright © 1967 by Yale University. All rights reserved. Reproduced by permission of the author. —Price, Martin. From "The Comedy of Forms: Low and High" in *Henry Fielding*. Edited by Harold Bloom. Chelsea House, 1987. © 1987 by Chelsea House. All rights reserved. Reproduced by permission of the author.

Francis Coventry

1725-1754

English novelist, poet, and essayist.

INTRODUCTION

In the mid-eighteenth century Coventry's only novel, *The History of Pompey the Little; or, The Life and Adventures of a Lap-Dog* (1751), was a great popular success. In an era when low literacy rates made for small potential audiences and high publication costs made books luxury items, *Pompey the Little* appeared in two authorized editions in less than a year and an extensively revised third edition in 1752. By 1800 at least eight authorized editions and two pirated editions had been printed. *Pompey the Little* is a text from a transitional stage in the novel's development—when the genre was regarded as the height of fashion, but at the same time individual novels were regarded as passing products of popular culture.

Biographical Information

The nephew of William, the fifth Earl of Coventry, William Francis Walter Coventry was the son of a wealthy merchant from Buckinghamshire. Born in mid-July 1725, he was most likely educated at home by private tutors before enrolling at Eton in 1742, where he studied until 1744. In 1746 he was admitted to Magdalene College, Cambridge, where he excelled, distinguishing himself with a B.A. *in Comitiis Prioribus* (among the best in his class) in 1749. While still at Cambridge, he made the acquaintance of Thomas Gray and showed the poet a comedy (now lost) he had written, parts of which served as the basis of *Pompey the Little*. Having been ordained as a cleric, he accepted the position of perpetual curate of the parish of Edgware, Middlesex, in 1751. A year later Coventry received his M.A. from Cambridge. He died, reportedly of smallpox, in January 1754.

Major Works

Coventry's earliest published work was the poem *Penshurst* (1750), a text in the *genius loci* tradition (which strives to describe the atmosphere and spirit of a particular place) that owed something to both Ben Jonson's well known "To Penshurst" and the popular topographical tradition of mid-eighteenth-century poetry. It was printed by Robert Dodsley, a bookseller of some fame who was connected with Mary Cooper, the printer of the first edition of *Pompey the Little*. A pamphlet entitled *An Essay on the New Species of Writing Founded by Mr. Fielding*, which appeared in the same year as the first edition of *Pompey*, is commonly attributed to Coventry, as is an essay on the English garden that appeared in the periodical *The World*, also published by Dodsley, in 1753. Also in that year, Coventry edited and published *Philemon to Hydaspes*, a collection of dialogues written by his late cousin Henry Coventry.

Critical Reaction

Critical reception of Coventry's work has focused almost exclusively on *Pompey the Little*. Like many of the novels of its time, it first suffered from its reading public's ambivalence regarding prose fiction. Thomas Gray, who may have seen an early version at Cambridge, called the novel a "hasty production" in a letter to Horace Walpole. In contrast, the author John Cleland wrote that Coventry's novel was "painted with great humour, fancy, and wit" in his review for the February 1751 *Monthly Review*. More universally popular with readers, the novel was in print until the early nineteenth century, but following an 1824 edition, *Pompey* was not published again until 1926, and then only in a limited reprint of the fourth edition. Interest in the development of the English novel as a genre and in contemporaries of the early novelists Samuel Richardson and Henry Fielding has spurred new critical attention to Coventry in the latter half of the twentieth century. In general, critics have seen *Pompey* as largely derivative of Fielding's works, yet unique for its use of a non-human character, Pompey the lap-dog, to unify its otherwise disparate sections. Most commentators who have undertaken to study Coventry's novel in the twentieth century have been primarily interested in what the changes introduced in the third edition imply about the novel genre in the Augustan era.

PRINCIPAL WORKS

Penshurst (poem) 1750
An Essay on the New Species of Writing Founded by Mr. Fielding (essay) 1751
The History of Pompey the Little (novel) 1751

CRITICISM

Francis Coventry (essay date 1752)

SOURCE: *Novel and Romance, 1700-1800: A Documentary Record,* edited by Ioan Williams, Routledge & Kegan Paul, 1970, pp. 176-79.

[*In the following preface from the third edition of* The History of Pompey the Little, *Coventry attributes his contemporaries' disdain for prose fiction to an attempt by educated males to maintain their privileged place within society.*]

To Henry Fielding, Esq.;

Sir,

My design being to speak a word or two in behalf of novel-writing, I know not to whom I can address myself with so much propriety as to yourself, who unquestionably stand foremost in this species of composition.

To convey instruction in a pleasant manner, and mix entertainment with it, is certainly a commendable undertaking, perhaps more likely to be attended with success than graver precepts; and even where amusement is the chief thing consulted, there is some little merit in making people laugh, when it is done without giving offence to religion, or virtue, or good manners. If the laugh be not raised at the expence of innocence or decency, good humour bids us indulge it, and we cannot well laugh too often.

Can we help wondering, therefore, at the contempt, with which many people affect to talk of this sort of composition? they seem to think it degrades the dignity of their understandings, to be found with a novel in their hands, and take great pains to let you know that they never read them. They are people of too great importance, it seems, to mispend their time in so idle a manner, and much too wise to be amused.

Now, tho' many reasons may be given for this ridiculous and affected disdain, I believe a very principal one, is the pride and pedantry of learned men, who are willing to monopolize reading to themselves, and therefore fastidiously decry all books that are on a level with common understandings, as empty, trifling and impertinent.

Thus the grave metaphysician for example, who after working night and day perhaps for several years, sends forth at last a profound treatise, where *A.* and *B.* seem to contain some very deep mysterious meaning; grows indignant to think that every little paltry scribbler, who paints only the characters of the age, the manners of the times, and the working of the passions, should presume to equal him in glory.

The politician too, who shakes his head in coffee-houses, and produces, now and then, from his fund of observations, a grave, sober, political pamphlet on the good of the nation; looks down with contempt on all such idle compositions, as lives and romances, which contain no strokes of satire at the ministry, no unmannerly reflections upon *Hanover,* nor any thing concerning the balance of power on the continent. These gentlemen and their readers join all to a man in depreciating works of humour: or if they ever vouchsafe to speak in their praise, the commendation never rises higher than, 'yes, 'tis well enough for such a sort of a thing;' after which the grave observator retires to his news-paper, and there, according to the general estimation, employs his time *to the best advantage.*

But besides these, there is another set, who never read any modern books at all. They, wise men, are so deep in the learned languages, that they can pay no regard to what has been published within these last thousand years. The world is grown old; mens geniuses are degenerated: the writers of this age are too contemptible for their notice, and they have no hopes of any better to succeed them. Yet these gentlemen of profound erudition will contentedly read any trash, that is disguised in a learned language, and the worst ribaldry of *Aristophanes* shall be critiqued and commented on by men, who turn up their noses at *Gulliver* or *Joseph Andrews.*

But if this contempt for books of amusement be carried a little too far, as I suspect it is, even among men of science and learning, what shall be said to some of the greatest triflers of the times, who affect to talk the same language? these surely have no right to express any disdain of what is at least equal to their understandings. Scholars and men of learning have a reason to give; their application to severe studies may have destroyed their relish for works of a lighter cast, and consequently it cannot be expected that they should approve what they do not understand. But as for beaux, rakes, petit-maitres, and fine ladies, whose lives are spent in doing the things which novels record, I do not see why they should be indulged in affecting a contempt of them. People, whose most earnest business is to dress and play at cards, are not so importantly employed, but that they may find leisure now and then to read a novel. Yet these are as forward as any to despise them; and I once heard a very fine lady, condemning some highly finished conversations in one of your works, sir, for this curious reason:—'because,' said she, ''tis such sort of stuff as passes every day between me and my own maid.'

I do not pretend to apply anything here said in behalf of books of amusement, to the following little work, of which I ask your patronage: I am sensible how very imperfect it is in all its parts, and how unworthy to be ranked in that class of writings, which I am now defending. But I desire to be understood in general, or more particularly with an eye to your works, which I take to be master-pieces and complete models in their kind. They are, I think, worthy the attention of the greatest and wisest men, and if any body is ashamed of reading them, or can read them without entertainment and instruction, I heartily pity their understandings.

The late editor of Mr. *Pope's* works, in a very ingenious note,[1] wherein he traces the progress of romance-writing, justly observes, that this species of composition is now brought to perfection by Mr. *De Marivaux* in *France,* and Mr. *Fielding* in *England.*

I have but one objection to make to this remark, which is, that the name of Mr. *De Marivaux* stands foremost of the two: a superiority I can by no means allow him. Mr. *Marivaux* is indeed a very amiable, elegant, witty, and penetrating writer. The reflections he scatters up and down his *Marianne* are highly judicious, *recherchés,* and infinitely agreeable. But not to mention that he never finishes his works, which greatly disappoints his readers, I think, his *characters* fall infinitely short of those we find in the performances of his *English* contemporary. They are neither so original, so ludic[r]ous, so well distinguished, nor so happily contrasted as your own: and as the characters of a novel principally determine its merit, I must be allowed to esteem my countryman the greater author.

There is another celebrated novel writer, of the same kingdom, now living, who in the choice and diversity of his characters, perhaps exceeds his rival Mr. *Marivaux,* and would deserve greater commendation, if the libertinism of his plans, and too wanton drawings of nature, did not take off from the other merit of his works; tho' at the same time it must be confessed, that his genius and knowledge of mankind are very extensive.[2] But with all due respect for the parts of these two able *Frenchmen,* I will venture to say they have their superior, and whoever has read the works of Mr. *Fielding,* cannot be at a loss to determine who that superior is. Few books of this kind have ever been written with a spirit equal to *Joseph Andrews,* and no story that I know of, was ever invented with more happiness, or conducted with more art and management than that of *Tom Jones.*

Notes

[1] William Warburton, *Works of Pope* (1751), IV, 169. See above, No. 28, headnote, and below, No. 62, nn. 5 and 6.

[2] Probably Coventry is referring to Claude-Prosper Jolyot de Crebillon (1707-1777), author of the light-hearted and licentious novels, *L'Ecumoire* (1734) and *Le Sopha* (1745), for which he was banished from Paris.

Lady Mary Wortley Montagu (letter date 1752)

SOURCE: *The Complete Letters of Lady Mary Wortley Montagu,* edited by Robert Halsband, Clarendon Press, 1967, p. 2-7.

[*In the following excerpt from a letter to her daughter, Lady Bute, Lady Montagu expresses her appreciation for* Pompey the Little *and draws parallels between the novel's characters and her contemporaries.*]

. . . Candles came, and my Eyes grown weary I took up the next Book meerly because I suppos'd from the Title it could not engage me long. It was **Pompey the Little,**[2] which has realy diverted me more than any of the others, and it was impossible to go to Bed till it was finish'd. It is a real and exact representation of Life as it is now acted in London, as it was in my time, and as it will be (I do not doubt) a Hundred years hence, with some little variation of Dress, and perhaps Government. I found there many of my Acquaintance. Lady T[ownshend] and Lady O[rford] are so well painted, I fancy'd I heard them talk, and have heard them say the very things there repeated.[3]

I also saw my selfe (as I now am) in the character of Mrs. Qualmsick. You will be surpriz'd at this, no English Woman being so free from Vapours, having never in my Life complain'd of low spirits or weak nerves, but our ressemblance is very strong in the fancy'd loss of Appetite, which I have been silly enough to be persuaded into by the Physician of this place.[4] . . .

Notes

. . . [2] *The History of Pompey the Little: or, The Life and Adventures of a Lap-Dog* (1751) by Francis Coventry. LM's copy remains in her library (Sotheby Catalogue, 1 Aug. 1928, p. 84).

[3] Lady Tempest has married a foolish man for his money and cuckolded him (or pretended to); she is 'the greatest Female Wit in *London*' (1751 ed., p. 45). Lady Sophister, full of affected wisdom, is divorced from her husband and has travelled abroad; she has read Hobbes, Malebranche, Shaftesbury, Wollaston, and especially Locke, and argues with her physicians 'at the Expence only of Christianity and the Gospel' (p. 66).

[4] 'Do you eat, Madam?' Mrs. Qualmsick's physician asks her. 'Not at all, Sir, . . . not at all; I have neither Stomach, nor Appetite, nor Strength, nor any thing in the World; and I believe verily, I can't live a Week

longer—I drank a little Chocolate yesterday Morning, Sir, and got down a little Bason of Broth at Noon, and eat a Pigeon for my Dinner, and made a shift to get down another little Bason of Broth at Night—but I can't eat at all, Sir; my Appetite fails me more and more every Day, and I live upon mere nothing' (p. 226). . . .

Robert Adams Day (essay date 1974)

SOURCE: An introduction to *Pompey the Little*, by Francis Coventry, Oxford University Press, 1974, pp. ix-xxiii.

[*In the following introduction to his edition of* Pompey the Little, *Day argues that Coventry's novel was an anomaly among anomalies—an unusual novel in an era when the novel was a non-traditional literary genre.*]

On 16 February 1752, Lady Mary Wortley Montagu wrote from her Italian exile at Brescia to give her daughter, Lady Bute, the latest news and to thank her for a box of the latest books from London. Lady Mary had begun to read avidly, but was not entirely pleased with her first choices, *Peregrine Pickle* and *The History of Charlotte Summers*. Then,

> Candles came, and my Eyes grown weary I took up the next Book meerly because I suppos'd from the Title it could not engage me long. It was ***Pompey the Little***, which has really diverted me more than any of the others, and it was impossible to go to Bed till it was finish'd. It is a real and exact representation of Life as it is now acted in London, as it was in my time, and as it will be (I do not doubt) a Hundred years hence, with some little variation of Dress, and perhaps Government. I found there many of my Acquaintance. Lady T[ownshend] and Lady O[rford] are so well painted, I fancy I heard them talk, and have heard them say the very things here repeated.[1]

Other books followed, but Lady Mary returned in her remarks to ***Pompey the Little***: 'I also saw my selfe (as I now am) in the character of Mrs. Qualmsick. . . . I am now convinc'd I am in no danger of starving, and am oblig'd to little Pompey for this discovery.'[2]

The book which had so delighted Lady Mary, no mean critic, was the first and only essay in fiction of a young man named Francis Coventry, a recent graduate of Cambridge who had taken holy orders and was 'perpetual curate' (or vicar) of Edgware, within convenient distance of London. Nephew of the fifth earl of Coventry and cousin of the sixth, he was no stranger to 'Life as it is now acted in London', and his education had given him the insouciant grace of expression and the aristocratic bias that made Lady Mary

admire Fielding, while its absence forced her to be ashamed of her partiality for Richardson.[3] This background made Coventry something of an anomaly among the creators of a form of literature that was winning only slow acceptance in the mid-eighteenth century. Yet another anomaly was equally striking. The 'hero' of the book was not a castaway or a Newgate bird, neither a foundling nor a lady's maid, but a Bologna lapdog.

These two extraliterary novelties doubtless had much to do with the book's initial success, as can be seen from the favourable notice given it in the *Monthly Review* for February 1751, shortly after its publication, by John Cleland, author of *Memoirs of a Woman of Pleasure* ('Fanny Hill'), who was no mere pornographer, but a cultivated if impecunious man of letters:

> There are, to the great disgust of the public, too many productions of the press, beneath giving a character of: This one is, however, so far of a different kind, that it is not easy to do justice to the merit of it. The author, whose name is not to the work, takes for his subject, a *Bologna* lap-dog, brought from *Italy* to *England*, where he often changes masters, by several accidents, which furnish the writer with a handle to introduce a variety of characters and situations; all painted with great humour, fancy, and wit: and, indeed, he every where displays a perfect knowledge of the world, through all its ranks, and all its follies. These he ridicules, with a fineness of edge, unknown to the sour satyrist, or the recluse philosopher. Even his negligences are pleasing. The gentleman, in short, breathes throughout the whole performance, and the vein of pleasantry, which runs through it, is every where evenly upheld, from the beginning to the end. He laughs at the world, without doing it the honour to be angry with it. His lashes, however smart, carry with them rather the marks of a benevolent correction, than of the spleen of misanthropy. All his characters are natural. His language easy and genteel.[4]

But writing like a gentleman is no guarantee of literary merit, as hundreds of feeble poems and essays by the noble and gentle authors of the eighteenth century can attest. Coventry, on the other hand, wrote like a minor Fielding. The urbane, intrusive author, the shapely, balanced sentences, the classical learning, the irony which is fully perceived only after a split-second's reflection—these hallmarks of Fielding's manner, though intermittent and not under full control, give ***Pompey*** an artistic force that almost raises it to the category of major satire.

But apart from its own worth, the circumstances of ***Pompey***'s introduction to the world were more than usually auspicious. Whether Ralph Griffiths, the founder and editor of the influential *Monthly Review,* and Cleland, his second-in-command during its first few years, wished to do Coventry a personal favour or were genuinely struck by the book's merit, is unknown; but circumstances combined to give it a publicity campaign unprecedented for such a work at the time. The favourable review quoted above (the *Monthly* had been far less kind to *Peregrine Pickle* and *Charlotte Summers*) appeared as we have seen in the February 1751 number; lack of space forced a series of extracts from it (not uncommon practice in the early days of periodical reviewing) into the March number, where they made up the second article; and an error caused the reprinting of yet more extracts, which had been omitted, in the April number, so that the reading public was reminded of the book for three consecutive months, with samples of its contents totalling three entire chapters and part of a fourth, and occupying sixteen of the *Monthly*'s pages.[5] Griffiths' interest in the book is further evinced by the fact that in marking up his master copy of the *Monthly* for a possible reprinting, he indicated that the passages appearing in the April number should be moved back into their proper place, and gave *Pompey* a cross-reference in the table of contents.[6]

Whether because of this puffing or not, it appears that the book rapidly became, if not the talk of the town, at least a subject of considerable interest among those who corresponded on literary matters. The first edition was anonymous, as befitted the maiden effort of a novelist who was not a hack; but at least one reader, and probably more, was sure that Fielding was its author. By May, Shenstone had heard of it and wanted to borrow it of Lady Luxborough; in replying she remarked that 'Fielding you know cannot write without humour.'[7] Other admirers included Mrs. Delany, who from Ireland inquired after the book's reception in England only a month after its publication (though she thought it a mere trifle),[8] Richardson's friend Lady Bradshaigh, who found it 'both well designed and well executed,'[9] and the erudite printer William Bowyer, who wrote to a friend on 1 August 1751: 'You do me much honour in ascribing "Pompey the Little" to me. I am obliged to you; and shall be glad never to be suspected of a worse thing.'[10] Horace Walpole purchased a copy of the first edition,[11] and evidently wrote to his friend Thomas Gray at Cambridge to ask for details, since the latter part of the book is set in Cambridge and includes portraits of a seclusive scholar, a do-nothing don, and a frivolous undergraduate, among other Cambridge characters. Gray, hardly an indiscriminate snapper-up of unconsidered trifles, may have been attracted to *Pompey* by hearing of its merits; but he was personally acquainted with its author and with his cousin Henry Coventry, who had been a Fellow of Magdalene College since 1730 and a close friend of Walpole when the latter was an undergraduate.[12] He therefore wrote to Walpole, only a few weeks after *Pompey* was first published: '*Pompey* is the hasty production of a Mr. Coventry (cousin to him you knew), a young clergyman: I found it out by three characters,

which once made part of a comedy that he showed me of his own writing.'[13] And it is thought that nearly two years later Arthur Murphy was counting on the associations which the name Pompey would arouse when, satirizing the hack writer and physician 'Sir' John Hill in the *Gray's Inn Journal*, he converted him into Lady Fidget's lapdog Pompey, who has a sanguinary encounter in the park with five other dogs.[14]

At any rate, the 'more favourable reception than its writer had any reason to expect'[15] led to a revised third edition, which was prepared in the autumn of 1751, and for which the bookseller Dodsley paid Coventry the amazing fee (for a mere work of fiction by a new author) of thirty pounds.[16] Now sure of himself, and not unaware of the advantage of enrolling himself among the followers of such a literary lion, Coventry affixed his name to the third edition's laudatory dedication to Fielding. Here he clearly indicated his admiration for the manner of writing which Fielding represented by classing him as first among living novelists.

English fiction in the second half of the eighteenth century, if we except the late 'Gothic' romance and the whimsical imitations of Sterne, can be seen as deriving ultimately from the influence either of Richardson or of Fielding—that is, to put it crudely, having a bias toward either satire or sentiment. The taste of readers was divided in like manner, and the initial success of *Pompey the Little* was lasting. It had the honour of being twice pirated in Dublin; it ran to at least ten English editions by 1824. It was translated into French in 1752 and Italian in 1760, and in 1753 it was even mentioned (albeit inaccurately and unfavourably) in the literary newsletter which Friedrich Melchior von Grimm circulated among the crowned heads of Europe. . . .

But the most significant measure of *Pompey*'s success, and its importance to the history of fiction, lies in the fact that it may be said to have originated, or at least prepared the public to receive, a sub-genre of fiction which flourished for fifty years or more—the satirical story in which a non-human 'hero' (a dog, cat, hackney-coach, flea, banknote, rupee, monkey, and many more) passed rapidly from hand to hand and underwent as many varied adventures as the author was disposed to invent. Perhaps the most famous example in its day was the notorious *Chrysal* (1760-5) of Charles Johnstone, in which a golden guinea fell into the hands of a galaxy of characters including George II himself, and in which the 'secret histories' of many well-known persons were scandalously revealed. Several dozen such works appeared, and various comments toward the end of the century indicate that this form of satire was taken for granted, however much it might be deplored. Even Smollett, almost certainly established as the author of the anonymous *History and Adventures of an Atom* (1769), would seem to have sensed the value of the device in constructing a savage and all-inclusive attack on the conduct of public affairs in the last years of George II. *Pompey* had started a fashion, but it had also established a literary technique.

Pompey the Little is very much a young man's book; if the comparison is admissible, he came to it like Swift to *A Tale of a Tub*, 'his invention at the height, and his reading fresh in his head.' His prejudices have not had time to mellow, the collegian's desire to display his classical attainments is all too obvious, and the giddy alterations in style between the sublime and the ridiculous have not been smoothed over by a concern for overall symmetry. The narrative is totally episodic; scenes are finished either by being brought to a natural outcome or by mere accident—whatever first comes to the author's mind. The text bristles with learned quotations and allusions, but no less with the slang and the local allusions of London in 1750. (It is remarkable how many nonce-words of the time in the *Oxford English Dictionary* give *Pompey* as their sole source.) But it is precisely this 'unfinished' quality of *Pompey* that conveys the flavour of its time and place, elements which would have been subdued in a more polished work. The point is easily established by comparing *Pompey* as to specific details with the far greater novels of Fielding which it professedly imitates. If the comparison lowers our estimation of Coventry's work, it also points up *Pompey*'s ability to achieve a legitimate end of fiction (what Mary McCarthy indeed has called its most essential quality, Diderot's 'petites choses' or her own 'thinginess') which Fielding, by the classical requirements of his art, was forced to renounce. Dr. Johnson's famous comparison of Fielding as a man who could tell time by the face of a watch to Richardson as a man who understood its interior mechanisms is relevant here: the works of the watch (though Johnson of course meant the subtle shadings of emotion and thought displayed in Richardson's novels) are laid open in *Pompey*'s linguistic texture and knowing references as they cannot be on the larger, more generalized surfaces of *Tom Jones*.

But pointing out this fact serves only to give Coventry the virtues of his defects. If one were asked to sum up the furniture of his mind as he commenced . . ., the task would be simple—it is not too reductive to say, 'Swift, Pope, and Fielding'. Coventry alludes constantly to the three, he continually quotes or perhaps merely lifts passages from them (and in the context of his literary milieu it is impossible to decide which—Pope was not plagiarizing from Addison when he modified one of the latter's well-known couplets with a satirical effect that would not be lost on his audience). Like all three Coventry is firmly oriented politically with the Tory or Country party (though this, considering his family background and ecclesiastical hopes, is the reverse of astonishing). But it is Fielding in particular on whom Coventry seems to be consciously modelling himself.

The larger virtues of Fielding were and are perhaps inimitable, but Coventry showed himself fully aware of his master's idiosyncrasies. The archaic 'hath' and 'doth' that Fielding (and Swift) affected, the addressing of the reader as 'thou', the false-innocent irony, the author's intrusive reflections on life and manners in his own voice, the constant comment on the fact that the writer is constructing a story and manipulating the reader, all are consciously adopted. Likewise the ironic, impudent, or tantalizing chapter-titles ('What the Reader will Know if he Reads it') represent an attempt to proceed in the manner of Fielding. In fact, the only aspect of Fielding's art which is intensively rather than generally examined and evaluated in the anonymous *Essay upon the New Species of Writing* (1751; generally attributed to Coventry) is the handling of chapter titles (pp. 21-7). The author comments on the damage done to the vital quality of suspense by giving too much away in chapter titles, and this discussion is the best reason for ascribing the pamphlet to Coventry. Fielding, who had a copy of *Pompey* in his library, must have been pleased by the compliment of imitation.

But clearly *Pompey the Little* is no *Tom Jones;* and while Coventry could hardly have chosen better contemporary models to form his thought than Swift, Pope, and Fielding, literary mimicry is not originality. There remains the central device of the novel—the use of a non-human protagonist. Most of Coventry's readers, to be sure, would have found this a striking novelty, though modern scholars would quickly cite among English occurrences the medieval *Owl and the Nightingale*, Chaucer's *Nun's Priest's Tale*, William Baldwin's satirical prose tale *Beware the Cat* (1561) and many more. But a University man of Coventry's day would have known other works ready to hand and more to the purpose. There existed as model the *Metamorphoses* (or *'Golden Ass'*) of Apuleius, in which the narrator-turned-ass is bandied about by a congeries of rascals in high and low life and of both sexes; there was *Le Diable boiteux* of Le Sage, translated early in the century, in which a demon flits about Madrid, unroofing houses to reveal vice. One of the *Tatlers* had used the idea of narrating the adventures of a shilling to hold together several satirical portraits,[18] and an anonymous novel called *The Tell-Tale* (1711) had introduced a spirit who darted from one boudoir to another to report on amorous intrigues. The 'secret history' was of course nothing new; the undeservedly infamous Mrs. Mary Manley and Mrs. Eliza Haywood were among many who had enlivened the first third of the century with their reports on the alleged misbehaviour of the great. But these fictions, most of which Coventry undoubtedly knew, could have furnished him only with the general direction of his satire. There were, nevertheless, direct ancestors of *Pompey*. In 1741 Robert Goadby had published his translation of *Two Humorous Novels* of Cervantes (republished 1747); one of these was 'A Diverting Dialogue between Scipio and Berganza', two dogs which have been granted the power of speech for a night. Scipio, sententious and garrulous, loves to quote the classics (he has accompanied his young master to a Jesuit academy), and he laments the treatment he has undergone from various masters, including shepherds, beggars, a butcher, and a sorceress. The novella, in short, is a picaresque tale with a dog as *picaro*. Even closer to **Pompey** were two works of fiction by the hack writer and opponent of Pope, Charles Gildon: not novels, but rather narrative satires. In the first, *The Golden Spy* (1709) a golden *louis d'or* exemplifies the proverb 'money talks' in a manner indicated by the full title,

> The Golden Spy: or, a Political Journal of the British Nights Entertainments of War and Peace, and Love and Politics: Wherein are laid open, The Secret miraculous Power and Progress of Gold, in the Courts of Europe. Intermix'd with Delightful Intrigues, Memoirs, Tales, and Adventures, Serious and Comical.

In the second, *The New Metamorphosis* (1724), the 'editor' presents a 'Vatican manuscript . . . of *Fumoso de la Fantasia,*' and speaks of the latter's

> transformation into a *Bologna* Lap-Dog; a Form more opportune for the Discovery of the Secrets and Intrigues of Ladies and great Men, than that of an Ass, who could not be admitted beyond the very Stable, or at most to a nearer View of the Affairs of the Mob.[19]

Gildon made little and feeble use of the device, and we cannot know whether Coventry knew the book, but authors are not prone to take their inventions out of the air.

The mere use of a dog as hero, however, would have mattered little if Coventry had not made it in a sense organic to the conduct of his novel. It clearly occurred to him at a very early stage, as his first chapter shows, that the use of a dog (and a toy dog at that) offered an admirable vehicle for the mock-heroic mode that was so central to the satire of his models, Swift, Pope, and Fielding. The text of **Pompey** shows that Coventry knew *The Rape of the Lock* very well, and there we find

> Now Lap-Dogs give themselves the rouzing
>   Shake,
> And sleepless Lovers, just at Twelve, awake.
> (i, 15-16)

> Not louder Shrieks to pitying Heav'n are cast,
> When Husbands, or when Lap-Dogs, breathe
>   their last.
> (iii, 157-8)

> Nay, *Poll* sate mute, and *Shock* was most
>   Unkind!
> (iv, 164)

> Sooner let Earth, Air, Sea to Chaos fall;
> Men, Monkies, Lap-Dogs, Parrots, perish all!
> (iv, 119-20)

The lapdog is as much a citizen of the belle's toy-world of inverted humane values as is the man (who is not a man, but a 'husband' or a 'beau'). Here certainly is the principal *reason* for the use of little Pompey in the novel; Coventry is writing the 'life' of a lapdog, just as Conyers Middleton wrote the life of Cicero and Colley Cibber the life of himself; the author will be just as precisely pedantic about minute facts, just as eloquent in describing the data of character, as they (it should be remembered that both are attacked in *Joseph Andrews* and by Pope), and the inversion of values and wasted effort revealed in the painstaking dating of Pompey's birth and death will point up the waste and inversion of Christian and humanistic values that Coventry sees in the life and letters of his day. In the world of Pompey, a dog is of course more important than a man, or should be, and Coventry could not foresee a time when humanitarianism should have eroded humanism to such an extent that a critic could in effect complain that the 'character' of Pompey was not handled in the manner of Black Beauty or Greyfriars Bobby.[20] The fact that Lady Tempest, and perhaps the lady of fashion she stood for, and her friends, could and did place dogs above men was for Coventry, a late Augustan and a son of Pope, a sufficient symptom of the decay of values in society to be used as a pivot around which his satire could circle.

But Coventry was no Swift or Fielding, and he did not make the dog-man inversion the centre of his book. (Indeed, at several points there are as eloquent pleas against the mistreatment of animals as any modern crusader for the prevention of cruelty to animals could wish.) Coventry does not attempt to create a unified fiction, and throughout most of the book the 'character' of Pompey serves merely as a string on which the satiric episodes can be threaded. And this point brings one to a final question: what can be said of **Pompey the Little** as a work of art; what is its value for the reader of today?

Pompey is not a novel, if by 'novel' one means anything more than a fictional prose narrative of a certain length. It is certainly not a novel about a dog in the manner of Jack London. The question of complex characterization in the protagonist cannot be raised except paradoxically; there are no minor characters, only portraits. There is no unification of tone or point of view, at least in the demanding modern sense. As for plot, Pompey's loose skein of episodes cannot be mentioned in the same context as, for instance, *Pamela,* to say nothing of the elaborate symmetries of *Tom Jones.* It is these 'deficiencies', no doubt, that have brought about the almost total absence of comment on the book in the older standard histories of fiction, oriented as they have been to a concept of the 'rise of the novel' borrowed from the somewhat misapprehended theory of biological evolution. But more recent treatments of fiction have been led to discard the idea of its painful development in the direction, say, of George Eliot and Henry James in favour of an attempt to see what authors were trying to do in their own times and their own terms. Notable among these is that of Ronald Paulson,[21] who examines certain eighteenth-century fictions as though they were offshoots in narrative prose of the formal poetic satire in the tradition of Juvenal. Such a scheme offers a perfect characterization of *Pompey*—the problems of handling the Juvenalian protagonist as a believable human being are solved by making him non-human; the catalogue of vices is metamorphosed into a journey with its incidents and adventures; the fact that formal satire is essentially 'the middle of a story' is rendered less troublesome by making the story that of a dog, whose life can have no plot; the unconventional or shocking approaches of satire to its subjects, and its concrete detail, fit easily into the succession of vivid unrelated scenes permitted by the dog's random movements from master to master.

Here is an adequate accounting for what *Pompey* does; the question of what it *is* involves the idea of genre. Although as we have seen it may be regarded as the work that established a briefly flowering sub-genre, the humorous narrative with a non-human protagonist, this sub-genre has been given no name. But it might be regarded historically as the fusion of two already well established forms—the secret history or 'spy' novel and the picaresque narrative. Like the spy novel (examples would be Montesquieu's *Lettres persanes* and the *Turkish Spy*) *Pompey* offers a protagonist who is in some way detached from uncritical acceptance of the life around him, and through whom the author can criticize the mores, politics, religious practices, or personal eccentricities he encounters. The picaresque novel carried its protagonist through all levels of society, but often failed in the attempt to make him believable, a sympathetic human being who would engage the reader, as Smollett's criticism of Le Sage's *Gil Blas* pointed out.[22] Such a novel as *Pompey* eliminated certain artistic liabilities of its predecessors, but incurred others: the 'spy' could have infinite and rapid social mobility and did not have to be characterized in detail; but on the other hand the author's richness of humour and satire would suffer if he set himself the problem of conscientiously representing how a non-human spectator of society might think and react. Thus *Pompey the Little* can be regarded, if one wishes, as almost an

inevitable development from several forms of fiction that had arisen before it, an attempt to rectify several of their literary shortcomings by compromise, though clearly at the expense of warm humanity. But then satire, narrative or not, has seldom been noted for its human warmth.

The modern reader, unless his interests include the scholarly, will first be interested in *Pompey,* or any novel, as merely something to read; and its value as entertainment should not be in question after a few pages. Though its comedy flickers in intensity it never goes out. But the reader who desires something beyond entertainment to justify his interest may reflect that *Pompey* is perhaps the best example of a form of English fiction that is at the very least historically important, and that deserves to be better known. Its verbal texture affords a more authentic and wide-ranging voice of its era than can be found in the more impressive contemporary novels that were polished either by an artistic conscience or in a mistaken pursuit of gentility and delicacy. Its satire, *mutatis mutandis,* is applicable to the social climbers, the adherents of gurus, the fashionable swindlers, and the well-heeled delinquents of our own day. Its scenes of both high and low life are filled with the specific details that inform as well as amuse. Lastly, and by no means the worst recommendation for a novel, it still gives the reader what it gave Lady Mary Wortley Montagu two hundred and twenty years ago: 'Life . . . as it was in my time, and as it will be . . . a Hundred years hence.'

Notes

[1] *Complete Letters,* ed. Robert Halsband (1967), iii. 4.

[2] Ibid., pp. 4-5.

[3] See Robert Halsband, 'Lady Mary Wortley Montagu and Eighteenth-Century Fiction', *English Studies Today* (Rome, 1966), pp. 330-6.

[4] *Monthly Review,* iv (article XLV), 316-17. The authorship of the review was indicated by Ralph Griffiths, the editor, in his own marked copy (preserved in the Bodleian Library). See Benjamin C. Nangle, *The Monthly Review: First Series* (1934), p. 125.

[5] *Monthly Review,* iv (Articles XLVIII and LXVI), 329-37, 457-65.

[6] MS annotations in the Bodleian copy, pp. 11, 321, 329.

[7] *Letters written by the Late Right Honourable Lady Luxborough, to William Shenstone, Esq.* (1775), p. 265 (27 May 1751).

[8] *The Autobiography and Correspondence of Mary*

Granville, Mrs. Delany, ed. Lady Llanover (1861), iii. 26 (16 March 1751).

[9] *The Correspondence of Samuel Richardson,* ed. Anna L. Barbauld (1804), iv. 159 (c. March 1752).

[10] John Nichols, *Biographical and Literary Anecdotes of William Bowyer, Printer, F. S. A.* (1782), p. 326n.

[11] See Allen T. Hazen, *A Catalogue of Horace Walpole's Library* (1969), i. 411.

[12] John Nichols, *Literary Anecdotes of the Eighteenth Century* (1815), v. 564-9; ix. 801. Many years before as a Cambridge freshman Gray had sent Walpole a humorous description of Cambridge characters, reminiscent of Coventry's; see *Horace Walpole's Correspondence with Thomas Gray* (Yale Edition, ed. W. S. Lewis, *et al.,* 1948), i. 58-60 (letter of 31 October 1734).

[13] *Horace Walpole's Correspondence with Thomas Gray,* ii. 48 (letter of 3 March 1751).

[14] *The Gray's Inn Journal,* No. 7 (2 December 1752). Hill had satirized Mountefort Brown, who retaliated by caning and kicking him at Ranelagh. Hill published an account in which he represented himself as having been set upon by five bullies, and grossly exaggerated his injuries. See Gerard E. Jensen, ed., *The Covent Garden Journal* (New Haven, 1915), i. 73-4, 81.

[15] See p. xlv [of Robert Adams Day, An introduction to *Pompey the Little,* by Francis Coventry, Oxford University Press, 1974.]

[16] See p. xxvi [of Robert Adams Day, An introduction to *Pompey the Little,* by Francis Coventry, Oxford University Press, 1974.]

[18] No. 249 (11 November 1710).

[19] P. 3 (copy in the Houghton Library, Harvard University).

[20] See Arundell del Re's introduction to the Golden Cockerel edition of *Pompey* (1926), p. xii.

[21] *Satire and the Novel in Eighteenth-Century England* (New Haven, 1967), pp. 21-3.

[22] In the introduction to *Roderick Random.*

Susan G. Auty (essay date 1975)

SOURCE: "Fielding's Followers" in *The Comic Spirit of Eighteenth-Century Novels,* National University Publications, Kennikat Press, 1975, pp. 55-65.

[In the following excerpt, Auty explores the differences between the first and third editions of Pompey the Little, *demonstrating that Coventry was attempting to follow Fielding's example and differentiate the type of satire afforded by the novel from the satire of the earlier picaresque narratives.]*

Admiration for the spirit of *Joseph Andrews* and the happy inventiveness of *Tom Jones,* along with a hearty contempt for those who scorned novels as being "empty, trifling and impertinent," led Francis Coventry to offer his unashamedly mirthful (though anonymously published) work to the public in 1751. The welcome reception accorded **The History of Pompey the Little, or, The Life and Adventures of a Lap-Dog,** reflects the growing number of readers who were willing to accept a book merely for the hours of enjoyment it promised them. The *Monthly Review* was disposed to treat the novel with the respect usually reserved for more substantial volumes, even devoting a portion of the following issue to additional extracts. A total of seventeen pages of choice bits was finally printed for the amusement of regular readers, and the critical content of the review was given over entirely to praise, especially for the benevolence of the wit:

> The author, whose name is not to the work, takes for his subject, a *Bologna* lap-dog, brought from *Italy* to *England* where he often changes masters, by several accidents, which furnish the writer with a handle to introduce a variety of characters and situations; all painted with great humour, fancy, and wit: and, indeed, he every where displays a perfect knowledge of the world, through all its ranks, and all its follies. These he ridicules, with a fineness of edge, unknown to the sour satyrist, or the recluse philosopher. Even his negligences are pleasing. The gentleman, in short, breaths throughout the whole performance, and the vein of pleasantry, which runs through it, is every where evenly up-held, from the beginning to the end. He laughs at the world, without doing it the honour to be angry with it. His lashes, however smart, carry with them rather the marks of benevolent correction, than of the spleen of misanthropy. All his characters are natural. His language easy and genteel.[1]

Though the form of Coventry's little work resembles that of the classic picaresque novel, *Lazarillo de Tormes,* being comprised of casually linked episodes each with its own object of attack, the spirit of the lapdog's adventures is, as the reviewer points out, benevolent and cheerful, closer to the works of Coventry's idol, Henry Fielding, than to the picaresque satires. Like *Peregrine Pickle,* which has essentially the same structure as *Roderick Random* but is a happier work than the earlier novel, **Pompey** retains the elements of satire while manifesting a new leniency towards society's shortcomings.

Coventry does not seek to arouse indignation; in his Dedication to Fielding in the third edition he makes it quite clear that he will be pleased to raise a mere laugh:

> To convey instruction in a pleasant manner, and mix entertainment with it, is certainly a commendable undertaking, perhaps more likely to be attended with success than graver precepts; and where amusement is the chief thing consulted, there is some little merit in making people laugh, when it is done without giving offence to religion, or virtue, or good manners. If the laugh be not raised at the expence of innocence or decency, good humour bids us indulge it, and we cannot well laugh too often.

> (1752: iv)

Indeed, the extensive changes that Coventry made in this 1752 edition seem to be primarily in the interest of even greater amusement, though one may question in some instances the basis of his judgment. William Scott, one of the few modern critics to do more than mention Coventry's work—which in its heyday was regularly linked with Fielding's[2]—feels that "improvement" involved no more than the omission of several interesting chapters and the addition of some "fresh ones which are in general neither better nor worse than those they replace."[3]

A more generous conclusion is possible, however, if one examines the two editions for the quality of pleasure they arouse. Indeed, while considering the narrator still to be essentially satiric in outlook, "a speaker with a bitter and sardonic tone," Toby Olshin finds evidence of Coventry's increasing maturity: "He no longer considers his model [Fielding] a simple satirist who shows his sardonic views on human nature through the use of a picaresque hero."[4] This change is reflected in the narration: there is little reason to distinguish the author from the narrator. The morals that close many chapters in the early editions, a crude satiric device at best, are often shortened or removed in the later. Whereas in the third edition Coventry merely begs the reader's pardon for digressing from the hero's history, in the original version he does not have the confidence to allow a conversation between Lady Sophister and the Doctors Kildarby and Rhubarb to stand without comment. He feels it necessary to conclude with a clarifying note and apologies to Locke. Yet, as he recognized in the later edition, Lady Sophister's sophistry would be evident even to her prototypes among contemporary readers and is far more effectively presented without comment:

> 'Pardon me, Madam,' said Rhubarb; 'Roses, and peach-trees, and elephants, and lions! I protest I remember nothing of this nature in Mr. Locke.'— 'Nay, Sir,' cried she, 'can you deny me this? If the soul is fire, it must be extinguished; if it is air, it must be dispersed; if it be only a modification of

matter, why then of course it ceases, you know, when matter is no longer modified—if it be anything else, it is exactly the same thing, and therefore you must confess—indeed Doctor, you must confess, that 'tis impossible for the Soul to be immortal.'

> (1752: 60)

Similarly, increased liveliness is the result of Coventry's decision to recast an episode so that a factual account formerly given by the narrator emerges instead in the course of a conversation between servants, which is occasioned by Pompey's careless upset of a dish while in search of food.

> Scarce had this happened, when my lady's maid appeared below stairs, and began to scream out in a very shrill accent, 'why who has done this now? I'll be whipped if this *owdacious* little dog has not been and thrown down my lady's backside's breakfast;' after which she fell very severely on the cook, who now entered the kitchen and began to reprimand her in a very authoritative tone, for not taking more care of her dressers; 'but let the 'pothecary, added she, come and mix up his nastiness himself an' he will, for deuce fetch me if I'll wait on her ladyship's backside in this manner: If she will have her clysters, let the clyster-pipe doctor come and minister them himself, and not put me to her filthy offices—O Lord bless us! well, rather than be at all this pains for a complexion, I'd rather be as brown as a berry all my life-time!'

> (1752: 77-78)

The lady's inconsiderate attention to her person is at once made more actively real to the reader's imagination and a good deal funnier in the colorful language of the rightfully annoyed maid than the factual sentences of the original narrator, who does not back up his material with the force of Pompey's accident. In addition, Coventry's eye for human frailty has more scope for observation in the tirade that results: the maid who drops the burden of her annoyance on the cook gets an oblique glance cast upon her; the apothecary's part in the business of vanity is disparagingly hinted at.

These little glances are found throughout both versions, but in the later one they seem to be directed more against affectation and less on vicious human beings, in keeping with Fielding's teachings. The man who encourages the untimely death of his first three wives and who appears in the first edition as one of the suitors of Aurora (a worthy young lady) is absent from her drawing-room in the third. Newly developed characters include a "blind" beggar who likes lemon on his sweetbreads (a figure similar to Lazaro's sly, blind master, whose inventiveness supports his avarice) and various members of the scribbling trade. However, one cannot make a positive statement about Coventry's intentions; in one instance a previously humane ostler is turned into an insensitive brute.

Moreover, as much as Coventry softened the general satire, expunging incidental remarks on flatterers, ministers, and the like, the second version includes some new lampoons, including a highly ludicrous and very cutting portrait of Mr. Whitefield, that object of so many eighteenth-century attacks (especially Graves's). The incident is not without humor, but it is humor in the manner of Pope's lampoons, splenetically motivated and outrageously belittling:

> All the former part of the time, our hero sat very composed and quietly before the fire; but when they began to chant their hymns, surprized and astonished with the novelty of this proceeding, he fell to howling with the most sonorous accent, and in a key much higher than any of the screaming sisters. Nor was this all; for presently afterwards, Mr. Wh——d attempting to stroke him, he snarled and bit his finger: which being the self-same indignity that Lucian offered to the hand of a similar imposter, we thought it not beneath the dignity of this history to relate it. To say the truth, I believe he had taken some disgust to the exceeding pious gentleman; for besides these two instances of ill-behaviour, he was guilty of a much greater rudeness next day to his works.
>
> (1752: 97)

Today we may laugh at the liberties taken with the normally dignified figure, but in 1810 Mrs. Barbauld still felt compelled to soften some of the remarks for her British Novelists editions.[5] Coventry's offhand attitude towards the dog's impertinence, the casual reference to Lucian and the "imposter," and the flippant suggestion of Pompey's additional crimes are what make the description of the event stinging, yet at the same time funny: the author's amusement both shocks and amuses us in turn. Yet however funny Pompey's rudenesses are, the mirth is paid for with the benevolence that otherwise characterizes the final version of the book.

Inevitably Coventry had to sacrifice some moments of liveliness in excising the satiric episodes that gave rise to them. Thus Pompey no longer gets to demonstrate his masticatory talents or to show off another instance of his admirable sense of occasion:

> They were no sooner gone, than his Lordship returned to his Closet, and fell a laughing at the Folly and Impertinence of his Petitioners. 'Curse the Boobies, cries he, do they think I have nothing to do but to make Mayors and Aldermen?' and so saying, he threw down the Petition to the Dog and began to make him *fetch and carry* for his Diversion. Pompey very readily entered into the Humour of

> this Pastime, and made such good use of his Teeth, that the Hopes of a new Corporation were soon demolished, and the Lord knows how many Mayors and Aldermen in the Moment perished by the unmerciful Jaws of a *Boulogna* Lap-dog.
>
> (1751: 207-08)

One can do without this passage if one must, but the image of Chance that one sees in the description of Pompey's active jaws is typical of the wit that distinguishes Coventry's work from the usual mass of satirically motivated novels.

Unfortunately, too, the little old lady who bore the brunt of the Methodist satire in the 1751 edition takes her cat with her when she departs into oblivion. The brief friendship between Pompey and Mopsa is the only event in Pompey's life, apart from his accidental separation from Lady Tempest, that the reader is likely to regard with human interest. Regrettably, some of Coventry's most charming descriptive writing shares the fate of the cat:

> From this Time their Friendship grew stricter every Day; they used to go upon little Parties of Innocent Amusement together, and it was very entertaining to see them walking Side by Side in the Garden, or lying Couchant under a Tree to surprize some little Bird in the Branches. Malicious Fame no sooner observed this Intimacy than with her usual Malice she published the Scandal of an Amour between them; but I am persuaded it had no Foundation, for *Mopsa* was old enough to be *Pompey's* Grandmother, and besides he always behaved to her, rather with the Homage due to a Parent than the ardent Fondness of a Lover.
>
> (1751: 92)

The serious tone is perfectly maintained and made to seem appropriate to the animal relationship. Meanwhile the reader is forced to see likenesses to human behavior and to mock society while feeling compassion for the creatures. The balance between fable and satire is so delicately held that the ludicrousness of the *amour* does not make it any less touching.

Because Coventry does not confine his inventiveness to introductory chapters—indeed, his one rather dull imitation of Fielding's prefaces does not survive his second thoughts—because he does not simply dress a stock novel in the trappings of comedy, as the anonymous writer of *The History of Charlotte Summers* must be accused of doing (his claim to be the natural son of Fielding is not borne out by any demonstrable relationship), one may agree with Edmund Gosse's judgment: "Francis Coventry had gifts of wit and picturesqueness which deserved a better fate than to amuse a few dissipated women over their citron-waters, and then to be forgotten."[6] Even more, one may see that it is his understanding of these very women, his perception of the petrified emotions that pass for human feeling in polite society, and his ability to reveal the foibles of that society at once succinctly and sympathetically that call his novel to our attention.

Coventry knew well that "spleen is the daughter of mortified vanity," and rather than further mortify the sensitive vanities of his readers he set out to ease the affliction by making everyone seem equally afflicted and equally absurd—even the lovely Aurora—in the eyes of a lap-dog. When Aurora's fantasy world, in which only pleasing things can happen, is rudely imposed upon by the frisky puppy, she shows the nature of her vanity by strenuously objecting to the real world and punishing its representative for the destruction of her satisfying dream. One can imagine Pompey's shrug at Aurora's typically human irrationality: "To be interrupted in so critical a minute, while she was dreaming of her beloved peer, was an offence she knew not how to pardon. She darted a most enraged look at him, and resolved never to see him any more; but disposed of him that very morning to her milliner, who attended with a new head-dress" (1752: 196).

Though contributing no more than the occasional bark to the book's action, Pompey has a more unifying effect on the work than a statistical account of his activities would suggest. In spite of his underdeveloped personality and his lack of an animal life of his own, we are conscious of the little creature as a separate character, as a continuous observer in his own right. As one of its most common frivolous possessions, Pompey is a fitting commentator on the artificial society and, as the victim of its frivolity, becomes emblematic of the shiftlessness, the emptiness, and the selfishness that subvert the values of domestic life and turn the faithful hearthside animal into a nomadic beggar. Rather like Dickens's little Jo, whose life is only seemingly tangential to the business of Chancery Lane, little Pompey accepts the world as it is thrust upon him, and in so doing, forces the reader to consider the state of that world. Unlike Jo, however, he is frivolous himself, and dies of old-age after a full and varied life having managed to survive all the comical elevations and depressions in his fortune. In this respect he is a picaresque hero, demonstrating his resiliency and strength as he goes along, either by gnawing through a thick wooden board to escape dissection (by Cambridge students) or simply by adapting matter-of-factly to new and different masters. Even the accidental separation from Lady Tempest, who has fed him on fricassees for a large part of his life, does not affect his equanimity: "He had no sooner dined, and felt himself snug in his new apartment, than he entirely forgot his former mistress" (1752: 71-72).

If Pompey himself cannot express his even-tempered

attitude towards life, his creator does it for him in the urbanity of his tone. Though Pompey's eyes are not, for the most part, the medium through which we view society, his presence encourages us to see things with the dispassionate concern of a different species. Coventry's tone is always one of faint amusement, such as we would expect if Pompey were endowed with rational faculties and a speaking voice:

> [O]f all the people, who composed this illustrious assembly, Lady *Bab* came the last. They took care to inform the company from time to time, that she was expected, by making the same observation on the arrival of every fresh coach, and, still persisting, that they knew her footman's rap, tho' they had given so many proofs to the contrary. At length, however, Lady *Bab Frightful* came; and it is impossible to express the joy they felt on her appearance; which revived them on a sudden from the depth of despair to the highest exaltation of happiness.

> Her ladyship's great toe engrossed the conversation for the first hour, whose misfortune was lamented in very pathetic terms by all the company, and many wise reflections were made upon the accident which had happened; some condemning the ignorance, and others the carelessness of the surgeon, who had been guilty of such a trespass on her ladyship's flesh.

> (1752: 221-22)

That the joy of the whole company should rest on a title and be hung in suspense by the condition of a large toe is a fact that takes on all its ludicrous implications when set out in simple sentences. Coventry need not try to express their "exaltation": his slightly ironic overstatement of the facts conveys the absurdity of the emotion. His laughter is evident in such phrases as "a trespass on her ladyship's flesh," which at once mimics the tone of the ladies' speech and lowers the diction considerably. Indeed, Mrs. Barbauld was distressed by the unsavory image presented by the word "flesh" and among her many other changes quietly substituted "person."

Even in a clause Coventry's gentle irony works effectively, as when he describes a fastidious gentleman as one "whose embroidery gave a peculiar poignancy to his wit." The use of "peculiar" to modify "poignancy" and "poignancy" to mean a transferable quality of embroidery may be easily appreciated by substituting "polish" for both words. One then loses the sense of this gentleman's immaculate refinement, his complete mastery of polite and meaningless conversation, which one gets from the narrator's overly fastidious choice of words.

When Coventry can refrain from unsubtle sermonizing, which unfortunately he is not always able to do, his style comes close to Smollett's at its most vigorous and cleverly ironic:

> A resolution was immediately taken, to make a sally into the streets, and drink champaigne upon the horse at Charing-Cross. This was no sooner projected than executed, and they performed a great number of heroical exploits, too long to be mentioned in this work, but we hope some future historian will arise to immortalize them for the sake of posterity. After this was over, they resolved to scour the streets, and perceiving a light in a cellar under ground, our two heroes magnanimously descended into that subterranean cave, in quest of adventures. There they found some hackney-coachmen, enjoying themselves carousing with porter and tobacco, whom they immediately attacked, and offered to box the two sturdiest champions of the company. The challenge was accepted in a moment, and whilst our heroes were engaged, the rest of the coachmen chose to make off with their cloaths, which they thought no inconsiderable booty. In short, these gentlemen of pleasure and high-life were heartily drubbed, and obliged to retreat with shame from the *cellar* of battle, leaving their cloaths behind them, as spoils, at the mercy of the enemy. Soon after they were taken by the watch, being too feeble to make resistance, and conducted to the round-house; where they spent their night in the manner already described. The next morning, they returned home in chairs, dressed themselves, and then took their seats in parliament, to enact laws for the good of their country.

> (1752: 121-22)

Coventry does not quite achieve Smollett's atmosphere of activity, mainly because he parcels the actions into separate sentences. But the contrast between the hurly-burly of the night's escapades and the very quiet mention of the morning's business has a startling effect nevertheless: the narrator's restraint in the face of all the excesses he is describing is sufficiently ironic for his remarks to stand without further comment.

The control that this young and largely inexperienced writer could exercise over his material is epitomized nowhere better than in the final chapter of Pompey's history,[7] which in mock-conformity to similar works gives a general account of the hero's notable qualities:

> Let it be remembered, in the first place, to his credit, that he was a dog of the *most courtly manners,* ready to fetch and carry, at the command of all his masters, without ever considering the service he was employed in, or the person from whom he received his directions: He would fawn likewise with the greatest humility, on people who treated him with contempt, and was always particularly officious in his zeal, whenever he expected a new collar, or stood candidate for a ribbon with other dogs, who made up the retinue of the family.

. . . . .

> [W]hoever considers that he was born in the house of an Italian courtesan, that he made the grand tour with a young gentleman of fortune, and afterwards lived near two years with a lady of quality, will have more reason to wonder that his morals were not entirely corrupted, than that they were a little tainted by the ill effects of such dangerous examples.

> (1752: 288-89)

The mingling of satire and fable is consummately carried out here (as in the earlier description of his relationship with Mopsa). Now Pompey is a fawning dependant, no better than a dog; now he is a dog, no better than a typically debauched human. However, by insulting neither humanity nor caninity, Coventry avoids the sinister implications that the *Modest Proposal* so subtly exudes: unlike Swift, he does not suggest that the identification between man and dog (in Swift's case, baby and pig) is frighteningly true and shockingly horrible. Rather, he shows them both to be simply weak and excusably helpless creatures, misled by society and innocently unaware of their own absurdity.

The description of Pompey's death is also applicable to the human event, yet without real sorrow; one cannot expend much pity on creatures who are untouched by their own misery:

> For the latter part of his life, his chief amusement was to sleep before the fire, and indolence grew upon him so much, as he advanced in age, that he seldom cared to be disturbed in his slumbers, even to eat his meals: his eyes grew dim, his limbs failed him, his teeth dropped out of his head; and, at length, a pthisic came very seasonably to relieve him from the pains and calamities of long life.

> (1752: 290-91)

Only insofar as Pompey's fate is the universal fate can one grieve, for the image of the lazy old dog in retirement from an adventurous life is pleasingly unpathetic.

The scale of the reader's sorrow or outrage is similarly reduced throughout the work: Pompey's misfortunes are a dog's misfortune's, not a young boy's—Lazaro's for instance. The creature's role may be tangential to the major business of the novel, which is to focus on the artificial life of the genteel classes, yet things happen to him which would be intolerable, especially in reference to human life, were he not so able to manage. In turn we would be forced to despise rather than laugh at the unthinking Cambridge scholars who want to mutilate the cheerful animal or the beggar who is addicted to luxury. Only an exceptionally sturdy human hero can soften the satiric blows of a picaresque work and turn bitterness into bitter-sweet. A dog need only be himself, naturally sturdy and nonhuman, to make the crimes against him seem laughable.

An inanimate hero will not do so well: Charles Johnstone's *Adventures of a Guinea,* one of the many imitations to appear in the following twenty years, lacks the warmth of a happily living creature. The passage of the guinea from hand to hand is not reassuring, for the adaptability of the object is never in question, and its relation to human survival is never established. Pompey, on the contrary, tells us as much about the flexibility of individuals as he does about the artificiality of society: marriage may be a financial arrangement and nothing more, but couples come to terms with the fact in their own ways—indeed, the wife may take to lap-dogs. Pompey shares the attitude of his "acceptance world," digesting fricassees and scraps alike, as much as he reveals the essential boredom of its inhabitants simply by being one of the playthings that helps to make acceptance possible.

Coventry puts forth his novel as another kind of plaything, another way of breaking down the artifact by provoking honest mirth. That the "Beaux, rakes, petit-maitres and fine ladies, whose lives are spent in doing the things which novels record," should spurn these works as too low or too familiar is something he laments in his Dedication. His implication is that these people are depriving themselves for reasons of pride of the very amusement that might make their lives as bearable as it seems in comic novels.

Because Coventry is interested in and entertained by his characters, he is able to cancel out the dullness he attributes to them. Using the little animal to convey his interest and amusement, he makes their emptiness seem paradoxically full of life, and invites his readers to enrich their own disappointing realities with the cheerful result. One must not be unduly surprised that the only two novels to be found among Fielding's books after his death in 1754 were *Pompey the Little* and *The Female Quixote:*[8] both authors can fairly claim their own shares of liveliness and imagination, and no doubt were able to provide Fielding with as much mirthful pleasure as he sought.

Notes

[1] *The Monthly Review,* III (1751), 316-17.

[2] As late as 1772, a reviewer in *The Monthly Review* (XLVI, 263), included Coventry in the "first Rank" of humorous novelists. A fifth edition of *Pompey* was printed in 1773.

[3] Scott, p. 218.

[4] Olshin, pp. 118, 123.

[5] Volume XXIII in the series. Mrs. Barbauld butchered the work to her taste, frequently changing words and omitting clauses and sentences. Scott draws attention to several of these alterations.

[6] Gosse, p. 211.

[7] Very little is known about Coventry's life. A letter from Gray to Walpole, 3 March 1751, is one of the few sources of information: "Pompey is the hasty production of a Mr. Coventry . . . a young clergyman; I found it out by three characters which once made part of a comedy that he showed me of his own writing [when they were together at Cambridge]." Gray, *Correspondence,* I, 344.

[8] According to Ethel Thornbury, p. 8. The catalogue of the sale of Fielding's library has, however, been missing from the shelves of the British Museum since 1955. . . .

Jerry C. Beasley (essay date 1982)

SOURCE: "Fiction in the 1740s: Backgrounds, Topics, Strategies" in *Novels of the 1740s,* University of Georgia Press, 1982, pp. 1-2.

[*In the following excerpt, Beasley notes that Coventry was among the first critics to argue that the novel genre had literary merit.*]

During the earlier decades of the eighteenth century, the problem of public acceptance faced by the aspiring writer of fiction was truly a formidable one. In an age still under the powerful influence of Locke, Descartes, Newton, and the seventeenth-century Puritan apologists, an age which placed so much intellectual and moral emphasis on the value of empirically verifiable "truth," fiction was "false."[2] In an atmosphere charged with the presence of the great Augustans Pope and Swift, fiction rested on no solid and respectable foundations of quality, literary tradition, or critical theory. Even quite able works by avowed novelists like Jane Barker, Penelope Aubin, and Mary Davys suffered from lack of recognition of their real though limited worth. Only two years after the publication of *Tom Jones* an important admirer of Fielding, the novelist Francis Coventry, severely blamed the class of literati and certain aristocratic dilettantes for the hollow contempt with which prose fiction was characteristically treated. Coventry sneered at the "pride and pedantry of learned men, who are willing to monopolize reading themselves, and therefore fastidiously decry all books that are on a level with common understandings, as empty, trifling, and impertinent." And he despised as "some of the greatest triflers of the times" those "beaux, rakes, *petit-maîtres,* and fine ladies, whose lives are spent in doing the things which novels record," but whose professed disdain for the fiction they so avidly read was no less forward than that of the puritanical or the genuinely learned.[3] Coventry's burst of anger expresses his very acute sense of the low estate of the novel in his day. . . .

Notes

. . . [2] It is one of the ironies of literary history, however, that the intellectual movements of the seventeenth century actually converged with the social currents of the early eighteenth century, enabling prose fiction to develop its narrative modes and thus to become the apparent chronicler of real life. See chapter I of Ian Watt, *The Rise of the Novel: Studies in Defoe, Richardson, and Fielding* (London: Chatto and Windus, 1957), for the best available discussion of this subject.

[3] Francis Coventry, *The History of Pompey the Little; or, The Life and Adventures of a Lap-Dog*, 3rd ed. (London, 1752), dedication. For a full and detailed account of the reputation of eighteenth-century English fiction, see John Tinnon Taylor, *Early Opposition to the English Novel: The Popular Reaction from 1760 to 1830* (New York: King's Crown Press, 1943). . . .

FURTHER READING

Barbauld, Mrs. [Anna Letitia], ed. *The British Novelists.* London, 1810.
    Includes a brief introductory essay on Coventry.

Booth, Wayne C. "The Self-Conscious Narrator in Comic Fiction before *Tristam Shandy.*" *PMLA* 67 (March 1952): 163-85.
    Important essay on narrative technique in mid-eighteenth-century novels which suggests that none of Fielding's followers equaled his expertise.

Cleland, John. Review of *Pompey the Little. Monthly Review* 4 (February 1751): 316-17.
    An overwhelmingly positive review of Coventry's novel, approving its humor and uncritical satire.

del Re, Arundell, ed. *The History of Pompey the Little,* by Francis Coventry. Waltham St. Lawrence, England: Golden Cockerel Press, 1926.
    A reprint of the fourth edition, with a largely biographical introduction.

Gosse, Edmund. *Gossip in a Library.* London, 1891.
    Includes a brief essay on *Pompey the Little* and its place in Fielding's library.

Haywood, Ian. "Chatterton's Lady Tempest." *Notes and Queries*, Vol. 30, No. 1, February, 1983, 63-4.
    Suggests that the character of Lady Tempest from *Pompey the Little* was the inspiration for a character of the same name in two short works by Thomas Chatterton.

Olshin, Toby A. "*Pompey the Little*: A Study in Fielding's Influence." *Revue des Langues Vivantes*, Vol. 36, 1970/2, pp. 117-24.
    Examines both editions of *Pompey the Little* and uses evidence from both texts to demonstrate Coventry's increasing grasp of literary device with artistic function, particularly in his evident imitation of the novelistic devices of Henry Fielding.

William Scott, "Francis Coventry's *Pompey the Little*: 1751 and 1752." *Notes and Queries* Vol. 15, No. 6, June, 1968, pp. 215-19.
    Compares different editions of *Pompey the Little*, noting differences between them

Mary Davys

1674-1732

English novelist, dramatist, and poet.

INTRODUCTION

Mary Davys was one of the first English novelists to be concerned with bringing lifelike detail and realistic character psychology to the novel. She rejected both the improbabilities of the French-style romance and the episodic nature of the picaresque novel. Drawing on her knowledge of dramatic structures to build narrative, and finding subject matter in the private world of women's lives, Davys pushed the novel in new directions. Like Henry Fielding, she dealt predominantly with English rural life; like Richardson, she experimented with the epistolary form and helped establish the unmarried, independent heroine as a prominent figure in eighteenth-century fiction. Davys also took important first steps in articulating a theory of the novel when few writers yet accepted the genre as a serious form of literature.

Biographical Information

The details of Davys' life are scant. She was born in Dublin and was married at 20 to the Reverend Peter Davys, a respected schoolmaster and college friend of Jonathan Swift. Apparently happy in her marriage, Davys was widowed in 1698, after just four years. In 1700 she went to England, later settling in York and struggling to make a living. She received some occasional, if grudging financial assistance from Swift during these early years and turned to writing to support herself. Her earliest published works were not profitable, and women writing was seen as a morally questionable activity, an opinion she challenged in one of her prefaces. But in 1716 her play *The Northern Heiress* was produced in London to some success. The proceeds enabled her to move to Cambridge where she established a coffeehouse and continued her literary endeavors with the encouragement of local students and intellectuals. With their support, her next novel, *The Reform'd Coquet* was sold by subscription in 1724. Notable subscribers included Alexander Pope and John Gay. The novel was fairly well received and enabled her to bring out an edition of collected works the following year. Her last novel, *The Accomplish'd Rake,* considered her finest, was published in 1727. She continued to run the coffeehouse until her death in 1732.

Major Works

While Davys is generally regarded as a minor novelist, her work was influential in the development of the novel. Many of the genres and techniques Davys employed in her fiction—the epistolary novel, fictionalized autobiography, comedy, and dramatic structure—influenced her contemporaries and helped advance novelistic forms beyond the picaresque and the romance. Her best novels, *The Reform'd Coquet* (1724) and *The Accomplish'd Rake* (1727), treat the subject of moral development and reform for the heroine and hero respectively. More carefully written, *The Accomplish'd Rake* has been cited as a rare example of a mature English novel from the period. With a skillful combination of realism, light comedy, subtle didacticism, and narrative complexity, the novel provides a psychologically compelling portrait of the stock figure of the rake. *The Reform'd Coquet* uses similar techniques and demonstrated a sophistication and skill at characterization that were missing in her earlier efforts. In a then unusually effective example of character development, the heroine Amoranda grows and changes through the action of the novel. Davys effectively blended didactic purpose and moral themes with comic elements and characters borrowed from the stage. *Familiar Letters Betwixt a Gentleman and a Lady* (1725) a love story in letters, is also regarded as an important work, a sophisticated epistolary novel that is a precursor to Richardson. *The Fugitive* (1705) a loosely autobiographical novel based on her arrival and early travels in England, sheds light on the lives of eighteenth-century women and marks a stage in the era's developing notions about fact and fiction. While many novelists presented their stories as strictly factual, Davys explicitly acknowledged and highlighted authorial adaptations of real experience. In the prefaces to her work, Davys made a final contribution to literary history with her short but astute comments on the theory of the novel which called for realism and outlined a unified structure for the genre.

Critical Reception

Davys achieved only modest recognition in her own day and, like other women writers of the period, was attacked and criticized for her work, and for writing at all. Shortly after her death, her work went out of print until the middle of the twentieth century. With renewed critical interest in the origins of the novel, and later, attention to the development of women's literary traditions, Davys work came to have a new importance. For some critics, Davys' most important contribution to English literature is to be found in the critical preface she wrote for her collected works. In this essay she argued that the novel must be grounded in real life. Davys thus became the first writer of the eighteenth-century to establish a realistic theory for fiction. Moreover, she outlined a basic structure for the novel and determined the properties of plot development. Her novelistic works make significant contributions to an understanding of the genre and are valuable for their insights into gender relations and the lives and thoughts of eighteenth-century women. She remains an interesting figure in the history of English literature—the first to theorize the novel, to use realistic comedy, to emphasize character and setting over plot, and the first to draw on English rural settings. Her work is generally held as an influence on Henry Fielding, Samuel Richardson and later novelists.

PRINCIPAL WORKS

*The Amours of Alcippus and Lucippe (novel) 1704
†*The Fugitive* (novel) 1705
The Northern Heiress; or the Humours of York (drama) 1716
The Reform'd Coquet; or the Memoirs of Amoranda (novel) 1724
§*The Cousins* (novel) 1725
‡*Familiar Letters Betwixt a Gentleman and a Lady* (novel) 1725
‡*The Self-Rival* (drama) 1725
The Works of Mrs. Mary Davys 2 vols. (novels, drama, poetry) 1725
The Accomplish'd Rake; or Modern Fine Gentleman. Being an Exact Description of a person of Distinction (novel) 1727

* This work was revised and published as *The Lady's Tale* in the *Works* in 1725.

† This work was revised and published as *The Merry Wanderer* in the *Works* in 1725.

‡ These titles were first published in the *Works* in 1725.

§ This work was revised as *The False Friend; or the Treacherous Portugueze* and published in 1732.

CRITICISM

Mary Davys (essay date 1725)

SOURCE: Preface to *The Works of Mrs. Davys, 1725,* in *Eighteenth-Century British Novelists on the Novel,* edited by George L. Barnett, Appleton-Century-Crofts, 1968, pp. 38-39.

[*In the following essay, Davys comments on the methods and motivations of her own work.*]

'Tis now for some time that those sort of writings called

novels have been a great deal out of use and fashion and that the ladies (for whose service they were chiefly designed) have been taken up with amusements of more use and improvement—I mean History and Travels, with which

the relation of probable feigned stories can by no means stand in competition. However, these are not without their advantages, and those considerable, too. And it is very likely the chief reason that put them out of vogue was the world's being surfeited with such as were either flat and insipid, or offensive to modesty and good manners, or that they found them only a circle or repetition of the same adventures.

The French, who have dealt most in this kind, have, I think, chiefly contributed to put them out of countenance, who, tho' upon all occasions and where they pretend to write true History, give themselves the utmost liberty of feigning, are too tedious and dry in their matter, and so impertinent in their harangues that the readers can hardly keep themselves awake over them. I have read a French Novel of four hundred pages without the least variety of events, or any issue in the conclusion either to please or amuse the reader, yet all fiction and romance, and the commonest matters of fact, truly told, would have been much more entertaining.

Now this is to lose the only advantage of invention, which gives us room to order accidents better than Fortune will be at the pains to do, so to work upon the reader's passions, sometimes keep him in suspense between fear and hope, and at last send him satisfied away. This I have endeavoured to do in the following sheets. I have in every Novel proposed one entire scheme or plot, and the other adventures are only incidental or collateral to it, which is the great rule prescribed by the criticks, not only in tragedy and other heroick poems but in comedy too. The adventures, as far as I could order them, are wonderful and probable; and I have with the utmost justice rewarded virtue and punished vice.

The **Lady's Tale** was writ in the year 1700 and was the effect of my first flight to the Muses. It was sent about the world as naked as it came into it, having not so much as one page of preface to keep it in countenance. What success it met with I never knew, for, as some unnatural parents sell their offspring to beggars in order to see them no more, I took three guineas for the brat of my brain and then went a hundred and fifty miles northward, to which place it was not very likely its fame should follow. But meeting with it some time ago, I found it in a sad ragged condition and had so much pity for it as to take it home and get it into better clothes, that, when it made a second sally, it might with more assurance appear before its betters.

My whole design, both in that and the **Cousins,** is to endeavour to restore the purity and empire of love and correct the vile abuses of it, which, could I do, it would be an important service to the publick. For, since passions will ever have a place in the actions of men, and love a principal one, what cannot be removed or subdued ought at least to be regulated. And if the reformation would once begin from our sex, the men would follow it in spite of their hearts, for it is we have given up our empire, betrayed by rebels among ourselves.

The two plays I leave to fight their own battles; and I shall say no more than that I never was so vain as to think they deserved a place in the first rank, or so humble as to resign them to the last.

I have been so anxious for the credit of my **Modern Poet** that I shewed it to several of my friends and earnestly begged their impartial opinion of it. Everyone separately told me his objection, but not two among them agreed in any one particular; so that I found to remove all the faults would be to leave nothing behind, and I could not help thinking my case parallel with the man in the fable whose two wives disliking, one, his grey hairs, and the other, his black, picked both out, till they left him nothing but a bald pate.

Perhaps it may be objected against me, by some more ready to give reproach than relief, that, as I am the relict of a clergyman and in years, I ought not to publish plays, &c. But I beg of such to suspend their uncharitable opinions till they have read what I have writ, and, if they find anything there offensive either to God or man, anything either to shock their morals or their modesty, 'tis then time enough to blame. And let them farther consider that a woman left to her own endeavours for twenty-seven years together may well be allowed to catch at any opportunity for that bread which they that condemn her would very probably deny to give her.

Robert A. Day (essay date 1955)

SOURCE: Introduction to *Mary Davys: Familiar Letters Betwixt a Gentleman and a Lady,* Augustan Reprint Society, Vol. 54, Clark Memorial Library, University of California, 1955, pp. i-iv.

[*In the following excerpt, Day discusses Davys's* Familiar Letters Betwixt a Gentleman and a Lady *in the context of early epistolary fiction.*]

Although students of Restoration and Augustan literature are aware that letters were used as a fictional device before Richardson's *Pamela* appeared, the minor fiction of these periods has been little studied. The authors of these "novels" were mostly unknown and industrious hacks; the books are now excessively rare, found only in the largest libraries; and their frequently poor quality and the stilted conventions which dominated them make them of little interest except to the specialist.

In the period 1660-1740 there appeared in England nearly 200 works, original, translated, and revived, in which letters figured largely or entirely as the narrative medium; many of these passed through numerous editions. Moreover, the ill-paid authors were often not content

with merely chopping a narrative into sections arbitrarily called "letters," but showed an appreciation of the technical adventages of a framework of correspondence which would have done credit to Richardson.[1] Indeed, the brevity and informality of many of these imitated correspondences, the concentration on letters rather than on novel, gave them an air of realism which Richardson, with his incredibly prolix *épistoliers,* was unable to maintain. The writers frequently placed an emphasis on "sensibility" and the minute analysis of the emotions which, though briefly sustained, was little inferior to that in the works which made Lady Mary Wortley Montagu weep like a chambermaid.

The "novel" reproduced here is principally remarkable not for *beaux sentiments,* the technical manipulation of correspondence, or tearing a passion to tatters (many of its predecessors had accomplished one or more of these feats much better);[2] but for its atmosphere of British middle-class realism, its characterization, its breezy humor, and its conduct of a plot that is simple, credible, and carefully omits romantic fripperies.[3] Although it retains the high-flown names of worn-out tradition, "Artander" and "Berina" are obviously Thomas and Jane. And this realism of furniture, food, and the difficulties of day-to-day life is as rare as a sense of humor in the early English novel. This refreshing innovation—a pair of lovers who manage to be witty instead of passionate while conveying the impression that they entertain tender feelings—together with her eye for physical detail, gives Mrs. Davys a claim to be a pioneer in the approach to fiction improved by Fanny Burney and perfected by Jane Austen.

Little is known of Mrs. Mary Davys (1674-1732),[4] but in her day she was nearly unique in being a female author of unblemished reputation. The widow of the Reverend Peter Davys, a friend of Swift, she came to England from Ireland after her husband's death in 1698. She wrote for a living (her novel **The Reform'd Coquet** and her play **The Northern Heiress** had some success) and established a coffee-house in Cambridge, where she had some acquaintance in intellectual circles. The **Familiar Letters** appeared in her **Works** of 1725, which she published by subscription, indicating a fair expectation of success in the university town. She shows the influence of Congreve and the *Spectator,* and all her work shows a talent which, while slight, is marked by dry wit, realism, satire, and careful avoidance of immorality and old-fashioned romantic absurdity. A remark from her preface shows how far author and public had advanced toward Richardson's sobriety:

> . . . if [censurers] find any thing there offensive either to God or Man, any thing either to shock their Morals or their Modesty, 'tis then time enough to blame. And let them further consider, that a Woman left to her own Endeavours for Twenty-seven Years together, may well be allow'd to catch at any Opportunity for that Bread, which they that condemn her would very probably deny

to give her.[5]

Familiar Letters, although it shows that epistolary fiction of considerable merit had been produced long before *Pamela,* fails to convey a notion of the variety and importance of the works in that field, or of their significance to the history of English prose fiction and of the development of taste. It will be seen from the bibliography appended to this introduction that they fall into three groups, receiving their impetus from popular translations from the French. The enormously popular *Lettres Portugaises* gave rise to imitations which analyzed the emotions of lovers at length and in detail, sometimes with high-flown heroics, sometimes realistically—primitive "psychological" novels. Scandal-chronicles and journey-narratives explored humor and descriptive technique, while epistolary sequences of varying length sometimes developed great skill in the use of letters in plotting.

This "no-man's-land" in the history of English fiction offers valuable material for the student. These haphazardly-produced works showed a real concern with such problems as point of view, a primitive "stream-of-consciousness" technique, and subjective narration as opposed to the unadorned tale. The public response to them, seen in prefaces, advertisements, and journalistic comment, suggests that the cult of sensibility, so pronounced after Richardson, had a vigorous existence long before. The minor fiction of this period deserves more attention than it has had; and its serious study may throw new light on the whole literary history of the time, besides uncovering important "missing links" in the evolution of English fiction. . . .

Notes

[1] For an excellent and detailed study of Richardson's technique, see Alan D. McKillop, "Epistolary Technique in Richardson's Novels," *Rice Institute Pamphlet,* XXXVIII (1951), 36-54.

[2] See, for example, Nos. 25, 36, 43, 70, 94, 151, 153, and 175 in the bibliography which follows.

[3] Mrs. Davys, in the preface to her *Works,* indicates her great concern with these points in plotting.

[4] Our knowledge comes mainly from Swift's correspondence and from incidental remarks in her works; but see also the (inaccurate) entry in *DNB.*

[5] *Works* (2 vols., 1725), II, viii.

George L. Barnett (essay date 1968)

SOURCE: "Mrs. Mary Davys" in *Eighteenth-Century British Novelists on the Novel,* edited by George L. Barnett, Appleton-Century-Crofts, 1968, pp. 37-38.

[*In the following essay, Barnett offers a brief introduction to Davys and the "Preface" to her* Works.]

As *The Works of Mrs. Davys,* published in two volumes in 1725, noted in the subtitle—*Consisting of Plays, Novels, Poems, and Familiar Letters*—this author's literary efforts attained variety. But fame, in spite of her diverse efforts, never came, and today she is forgotten. Still, the Preface to her *Works* "is valuable as one of the few detailed statements by a practicing novelist of the pre-Fielding period" (W. H. McBurney, "Mrs. Mary Davys: Forerunner of Fielding," *PMLA,* LXXIV, 1959, 350).

Born in Dublin, married to the Rev. Peter Davys, and widowed in 1698, Mrs. Davys was the recipient of some small charities from Swift, a friend of her husband. Needing to supplement her income, she turned to writing and, like Mrs. Aphra Behn and Mrs. Mary Manley, decided to write fiction only after a period of writing plays. Their realism and paucity of imagination reflect her limited middle-class experience, but this apprenticeship established the terms in which her fiction was later conceived.

Perhaps the success of Mrs. Haywood and of Defoe in narrative fiction prompted Mrs. Davys to try this new genre, for she was obviously writing for money. In any case, *The Reformed Coquet: A Novel* appeared in 1724 and saw at least eight editions by the end of the century. Published for the first time in her *Works* were: *The Lady's Tale, The Cousins: A Novel, Familiar Letters Betwixt a Gentleman and a Lady,* and *The Merry Wanderer*—a revision of *The Fugitive* (1705). *The Accomplished Rake: or, Modern Fine Gentleman* (1727) "stands out as one of the few mature English novels to appear between 1700 and 1739" (W. H. McBurney, ed. *Four Before Richardson,* 1963, Intro., p. xxix).

Like the *Incognita* of Congreve, her favorite playwright, Mrs. Davys' stories are plays in narrative form. The influence of the theater on her attempts to apply dramatic rules to prose fiction is obvious. Some realism, humor, individualization of character, and foreshadowing of Fielding's use of the English country scene are about the most one can say in her favor. Also noteworthy is some departure from the artificial and formalized prose that had characterized fiction since the advent of the heroic romance. Writing before the general adoption of chapter division, Mrs. Davys occasionally utilizes authorial intervention to effect changes of scene. Employing a superlative to praise her mediocre achievement, a modern critic labels her the best of the well-meaning women writers of the time who "wrote tediously proper fiction" (Lionel Stevenson, *The English Novel,* 1960, p. 77).

In spite of her shortcomings, her Preface sets forth a conscious theory of the novel at a time when few writers of fiction had turned their attention to theory.

Margaret Anne Doody (essay date 1974)

SOURCE: *A Natural Passion: A Study of the Novels of Samuel Richardson,* Oxford University Press, 1974, pp. 17-22, 132-35.

[*In the following excerpt from a study of Samuel Richardson, Doody discusses Davys and other women novelists of his day.*]

After writers like Mrs. Aphra Behn and Mrs. Manley had shown that it was possible for women to write and be read, even to earn money by the exercise of the pen, a host of minor writers had taken up the love novel or novella. The teens and twenties of the century show a proliferation of such works by authors with whose names the veriest dunce of a sorcerer's apprentice would not attempt to conjure: Mrs. Penelope Aubin, Mrs. Jane Barker, Mrs. Mary Davys. Eliza Haywood is the only feminine novelist of the period to achieve any slight degree of lasting fame, and that, the result of Pope's reference in *The Dunciad,* is largely ill repute. Their works have very few claims to recognition, but they are better than one might expect. No English female author achieved a novel of the classic stature of Mme de Lafayette's *La Princesse de Clèves* (1678), although that novel, the French romances, and most notably the *Lettres Portugaises* (1669), had a decided influence upon the English female novel. In the first quarter of the eighteenth century the English writers were moving cautiously away from the more sensational *novella-fabliau* which had dependably saleable, and were depending more and more upon psychological interest.

Broadly speaking, the female novel of love can be divided into two types: the seduction/rape tale and the courtship novel. The tale of seduction or rape could ostensibly be justified as serving a moral purpose. . . .

The heroines of such novels have reactions and emotions rather than a defined personality, but the flux of emotion is often, given its context, well described. The development of female character emerges more fully in the novels of courtship. Marriage in a recognizable (if not clearly defined) contemporary social situation is the subject, and love is seen in relation to marriage. These novels place their emphasis, not upon unbridled passion, but upon correct relationships with the family and upon proper social behaviour. Although the main setting is vague, and there is still some lack of vivid detail, the atmosphere is different from that of the Utopia of gallantry wherein the heroines of the seduction/rape stories seem to dwell. The novelists who dealt with courtship did not entirely forsake the old sensational events of earlier fiction, but the treatment of emotion is in many respects realistic, and more of the practical problems of a young lady's life in the Georgian era are taken into account—problems such as the parental right to choose a daughter's husband, the difficulties in family relationships, problems about mon-

ey and dowries, the trials of being better educated and more intelligent than is fashionable. Many of the new novels were trying to fulfil some of the functions of the conduct books, by imparting direct or implied advice to women about behaviour. The precepts of the conduct books on duty, obedience, and so on, are examined in relation to the heroine.[1]

Most of these novels intentionally bear out the precepts of the conduct books. In one of the most influential of these novels, Mrs. Mary Davys's **The Reformed Coquet: or, Memoirs of Amoranda** (1724), the spoiled and vain heroine is reformed in a course of surprising adventures which serve to reduce her vanity and instruct her heart. Her guardian, Mentor, who is also in love with her, supervises the process and educates her principles and heart together.[2] The tone of the novel is gentler than its theme might promise; it is the instruction of the heart, the experience of love on the part of a girl who is not very aware of emotion, which makes her a person, not dry precepts. If the courtship novels are conduct books, they are conduct books with a difference, applying judgement and standards with some delicacy. However old the standards of conduct may be, they have to be realized freshly by the young heroine who is, in the most ordinary courtship, dealing with a circumstance new to her. The female novelists' perception, however limited, that the interest of conduct described in fiction must depend on full realization of the exact case in hand led them to particularize more in the courtship novel than in the novel of passion and seduction. In Mrs. Mary Davys's **The Lady's Tale** (1725), which illustrates the trials of filial obedience in a courtship, the domestic setting is credible (although vague as to detail); the heroine is witty enough to be entertaining, and the state of her heart is not uninteresting. The heroine of Mrs. Jane Barker's *Love's Intrigues; or, The Amours of Bosvil and Galesia* (1713) and of its sequel, *A Patch Work Screen for the Ladies* (1723), is a real personality, and in the first part of her story the author has developed a good novel out of the slightest of plots. Galesia has fallen in love with a young man who, she fears, may not return her feeling. The action is mainly interior; Galesia recounts her own fluctuating emotions, her speculations about how she should behave in her situation, about the feelings of Bosvil on the occasion of their various meetings. The main question, which provides the point of interest, is one which she is never able, even in retrospect, fully to answer: has she let her love for Bosvil show too much, or not enough? She is a consistently drawn character, impetuous, loving, yet reserved and slightly bookish; she seeks solace in intellectual exercise, studying her brother's medical texts. She is able to enjoy her own thoughts, a quality which no English male novelist of the period would attribute to a young lady of her sort. (It might be said that Defoe's Moll Flanders and Roxana enjoy thinking, but these businesslike women enjoy cogitations of strategy, not thought for its own sake. As for Marivaux's Marianne, 'La Paysanne Parvenue', her thoughts, if she can be said to have

any, appear to be reflexes of cunning; psychological subtlety is the attribute of the author, not of his character.)
The first-person narration of Mary Davys's Abaliza or
Jane Barker's Galesia is different from that found in masculine picaresque novels. The emphasis is placed upon
the inner feelings of the central character in relation to
an event; she is no detached observer, but the centre of
emotional conflict, of mental and emotional life. The
female novelist, like Jane Austen a century later, understood the heroines' need for leisure to think and be
wretched. Even the sensational Mrs. Haywood's Anadea
(heroine of what is really a courtship novel) desires solitude rather than 'Company, Noise, and Hurry' when shak-
en by emotional perplexity.

The female novelists were not attempting to institute a
rebellion against masculine domination or the accepted
position of women. What they did was quietly to transform the accepted role of woman, not by claiming it
should be something else, but by seeing it in a different
way. In presenting woman and her reception of experience, her knowledge, her moral choice, her attempt to
understand the nuances of situation and her own fluctua-
tion of feeling—her endeavour, in short, to comprehend
experience—they implicitly denied an attitude which
implicitly held women incapable of important experience.
They also brought to the level of literary consciousness
material which was to become the stuff of the novel,
psychological analysis for which the novel is peculiarly
suited, as well as certain modes of presenting this material.

Modes of narration, novelistic devices, had been developed by some of these minor novelists. The first-person
narration in the past tense was the best-developed mode,
and it is in this kind of narrative, requiring a personal
voice, that one is most likely to find attention to style
and language, more especially in the courtship novel. Mrs.
Davys, for instance, preserves the conversational tone by
having Abaliza tell her story to a confidante and interloc-
utor, and within her retrospective account of her courtship there are lively passages of description and quoted
dialogue. The characters occasionally use homely idiom:
Abaliza is afraid she might 'make a Botch of my Story'.[3]
The language of Mrs. Barker's Galesia is easy without
vulgarity, often with a touch of humour: 'the only Syntax
I study'd was how to make suitable Answers to my Father
and him, when the long'd-for Question should be proposed . . .'[4]
Richardson's age was ready for a complex novel in letters; it had been accustomed to the letter form, either as
substance or ornament, in stories dealing with love. The
public was also prepared to read tales dealing with the
problems of conduct encountered in courtship because
of family opposition. The conflict between duty and inclination in the matter of marriage, which is the basis of
the plot of *Clarissa,* and is dealt with for about a quarter
of the whole novel, was already a staple of domestic fiction.

In the period before Richardson's work appeared, Mrs.
Mary Davys had skilfully introduced the theme of filial
obedience in conflict with the heart's inclination into a
dramatically realized situation in a novel. *The Lady's
Tale* has a more developed and believable heroine than is
usually the case in such prose fiction, and the setting is
recognizably middle-class—there is a solidity about Abaliza's home and family that we often search for in vain
in the novels of Mrs. Davys's contemporaries. The basis
of the story, and the arguments presented, bear a strong
resemblance to those in the first part of *Clarissa.* The
usually untroubled relationship between Abaliza and her
parents is established at the beginning of the story, with
their affectionate reunion on her return home. When they
tell her a marriage is being arranged for her, she is a
trifle appalled at the prospect of matrimony. As she tells
her mother: 'I think it is a State that requires more Se-
dateness and Gravity than is usually found in Eighteen . .
. I do assure you Madam . . . it wou'd have been more
agreeable to my temper, had you injoin'd me to Celibacy
for Life . . .'[5] When she meets her proposed suitor, Adrastus, she finds him stupid and disgusting, and is unwilling
to give her hand where she cannot give her heart.[6] She
pleads with her father not to make her marry:

> Can that Parent love a Child, that would sacrifice its
> worldly Happiness to its own Caprice? Beside, what
> can be more solemn than the Charge given us in the
> Marriage Ceremony, where we are commanded in the
> Presence of Heaven to declare we have no Impediment,
> and can there be a greater, than to give my self to a
> Man I hate?[7]

Her father says she should learn prudence and consult
her own good. She endeavours to reassure him, promising 'I will never dispose of myself while you live, without your Approbation and Consent; for I can with much
more pleasure deny the Man I love, than take the Man I
loath.'[8] In this novel, it is moving to find Abaliza pleading
with her father in such a manner, because the relationship
between them has been shown to be affectionate, and
their conversation is usually a pleasant exchange of rail-
lery. The reader is reminded, as is Abaliza, that her father
does possess a serious authority over her, which he could
exercise to make her life miserable. . . .

It is worth remarking that both Mrs. Davys's Abaliza and
Mrs. Haywood's Anadea express, like Clarissa, a desire
to live single rather than marry. By the time Richardson
wrote his novels, it would appear that the preference for
the single life had become a convention, particularly in
descriptions of a heroine faced with unwelcome suitors.
(Harriet, in *Sir Charles Grandison,* has the same attitude when she is pressed by other suitors before she
meets Sir Charles.) Some modern critics have seen in
Clarissa's wish indications of frigidity, or worse; the
vulgarized psychology of this type of criticism shows a
disregard for the conventions from which *Clarissa* is
derived, as well as for the intent and structure of the
novel. The heroine's wish to live single is an expression

of her innocence, modesty, and chastity—qualities which the eighteenth century thought excellent things in a woman. The desire for the single life can also be an expression of youthful ignorance of the power of love, a power which the heroine is shortly to experience, as Harriet does. More than that, the wish is an expression of the heroine's independence. In the novels of female writers such as Mrs. Davys, the character of the heroine is beginning to be established as that of an individual in her own right, who does not desire to live merely as the adjunct of a man, at least not of any man. It is this right which Richardson championed so strongly in the delineation of his female characters.

In Mrs. Davys's **The Lady's Tale** Abaliza's distress is realistically and dramatically presented. When she pleads against an enforced betrothal, she is not in love with anybody else; her protestation that she cannot marry a man whom she dislikes is, like Clarissa's, completely genuine. It is not an excuse made because she loves another man, as is usually the case with stage heroines, from Juliet onwards. Complications do arise when Abaliza falls in love with the young Alcipius, but Mrs. Davys refuses to allow her heroine to abandon the sacred duty of filial obedience. Since her father is a kind and understanding parent, Abaliza's situation resolves itself happily.

In this novel, Mrs. Davys endeavours to create a system of relationships in which both filial duty and the force of love are allowed their full weight. The sprightly style of the narrative allows no moral pontification, but the characters are shown to be virtuous and responsible in social duties. In traditional stage comedy, rules of conduct and of social duty can be flouted with impunity. A father's choice can be brushed aside: 'Fathers seldom chuse well', remarks Hipollita in *The Gentleman Dancing-Master.*[9] In some of the sentimental plays, such as Steele's *The Conscious Lovers* (1722), family duty is presented with exaggerated seriousness, but it is more usual for the father to be presented as comically or repellently short-sighted, and for young love to triumph by somewhat disingenuous means, as in Steele's *The Tender Husband* (1705), or Mrs. Centlivre's *The Busybody* (1708). The novelists were more realistic in presenting the problems of behaviour within the family in a manner neither exaggeratedly sentimental nor comic. The codes of behaviour, and the family, were there to be recognized in ordinary life. In the eighteenth century, the father possessed enormous power to dispose of his daughter's hand in marriage as he saw fit. . . .

Notes

[1] Katherine Hornbeak has pointed out the relation of the conduct books to Richardson's novels in their treatment of family rights and duties ('Richardson's Familiar Letters and the Domestic Conduct Books', *Smith College Studies in Modern Languages*, xix (Jan. 1938)), but she does not mention that such points had already been presented in prose fiction.

[2] The novel is partly a feminine version of *Télémaque.* This is probably the first appearance in English prose fiction of the lover-mentor, a character type to be found in some degree in Sir Charles Grandison, very definitely in Fanny Burney's Edgar Mandlebert in *Camilla* (1796), and (improved beyond recognition) in Jane Austen's Mr. Knightley and Edmund Bertram. . . .

[3] Mary Davys, *The Works of Mrs. Davys,* 2 vols., 1725, vol. ii, *The Lady's Tale,* p. 125.

[4] Jane Barker, *The Entertaining Novels of Mrs. Jane Barker,* 2nd. ed., 2 vols., 1719, vol. ii, *The Amours of Bosvil and Galesia,* p. 19. . . .

[5] Davys, *Works,* vol. ii, *The Lady's Tale,* p. 126.

[6] Ibid., p. 140.

[7] Ibid., pp. 141-2.

[8] Ibid., p. 142. . . .

[9] William Wycherley, *The Gentleman Dancing-Master,* 1673, 1, i, p. 2. . . .

Jean B. Kern (essay date 1983)

SOURCE: "Mrs. Mary Davys as a Novelist of Manners" in *Essays in Literature,* Vol. X, No. 1, Spring, 1983, pp. 29-38.

[*In the following essay, Kern analyzes Davys as a novelist of manners in and against the tradition of women's romance writing.*]

Mrs. Mary Davys (1674-1732), playwright, novelist, and occasional poet, has not fared well from biographers, literary historians, or critics. The *DNB* is inaccurate about her dates; she is not mentioned in the *Oxford Companion to English Literature* although her contemporaries Mary Manley and Elizabeth Haywood are; Ian Watt's *Rise of the Novel* does not even include her name, but his omission is more understandable than the inaccuracies of Ernest A. Baker's ten-volume *History of the English Novel,* which is wrong both about her life, calling her the widow of a schoolmaster of York, and about her novels, which he seems not to have read with care.[1] Charlotte E. Morgan does give her credit for creating a male prig in Formator *(The Reform'd Coquet)* "of which Sir Charles Grandison is the consummate example,"[2] but ignores her other considerable contributions to the novel of manners. Robert Adams Day, who edited her **Familiar Letters Betwixt a Gentleman and a Lady**[3] and expanded his discussion of her contribution to the epistolary novel in his *Told in Letters,* evalutes her *Familiar Letters* . . . as "a true epistolary novel, a humble foreshadowing of the approach to fiction improved by Fanny Burney and perfected by Jane Austen."[4] Such praise of her single letter-novel is almost as distorting of Mrs. Davys's contribution to the novel of manners as the inaccuracies of Baker, the omissions of Watt and others, or the eccentric praise of one character by Charlotte E. Morgan.

William H. McBurney was the first to assess all of her fiction.[5] He points out correctly her relation to the Restoration comedies of Wycherley, Etherege, and Congreve, as well as the influence of drama on her theories of plot construction for her novels. He also gives her credit for using realism rather than romance in both characterization and setting, and for a "dexterous blending of dual dramatic trends of manners and sentiment."[6] While he could have pushed further her parallels to Fielding in learning from the stage, especially in her use of irony, his assessment, plus his reissue of her last novel, *The Accomplished Rake* (1727),[7] first led me to investigate her novels more closely. What caught my attention was McBurney's comment about her "hearty, somewhat masculine temperament."[8] It was this comment which caused me to look more closely at her six novels.[9] Was she a realist because she had a "hearty, somewhat masculine temperament"? Or was it because she was a poor widow (she came to England after the early death of her husband, Peter Davys, who ran the school attached to Swift's church in Dublin) trying to make a living by her pen? What was her attitude toward men, women, and manners in the early eighteenth century? The purpose of this paper is to examine her fiction in order to reassess her as an early novelist of manners.

Briefly, her writing career was as follows: she came to England without any money, after the death of her husband in 1698, and published her first barely disguised autobiographical account of her efforts to collect small debts and live independently (though she often wrote Swift asking for loans), *The Fugitive* (1705), which she dedicated to Mrs. Esther Johnson, Swift's friend. She revised *The Fugitive* extensively for her *Works* (2 vols., 1725) as *The Merry Wanderer,* and it is to this revised version that I shall refer. It is difficult to tell whether this or *The Merry Wanderer* in its 1705 version was first in composition.[10] Her other four novels are *The Reform'd Coquet,* first printed in 1724; its companion piece *The Accomplished Rake* (1727); *The False Friend: or, The Treacherous Portuguese* (1732) which appeared in an earlier version in her *Works* as *The Cousins;* and *Familiar Letters Betwixt a Gentleman and a Lady.* In order of composition, her fiction seems to range as follows: *The Merry Wanderer; The Lady's Tale; The Reform'd Coquet; The False Friend; Familiar Letters* . . . ; and *The Accomplished Rake.* Her canon also includes two plays: *The Northern Heiress: or, The Humours of York,* performed in 1716, and *The Self-Rival,* never performed; both appear in the *Works* along with an incomplete satir-

ic poem, "The Modern Poet." Apparently, after her first "Wanderer" period in England, she lived in York; her first comedy, *The Northern Heiress,* testifies to this by its exploitation of York manners and speech. When she failed to get her second comedy performed in London, she settled in Cambridge by 1718, where she ended her career running a coffee house for Cambridge undergraduates. It was these young gentlemen at Cambridge, whom she knew to be "Men of Taste," that she mentions in the Preface to her *Works* as encouraging her to publish by subscription her collected fiction, plays, and poem after she had shown them "a few pages." While this clergyman's widow was thus able to generate enough interest among the customers of her Cambridge coffee house to enlist subscribers sufficient to publish the collected *Works* in 1725, her subscription list had also included three duchesses, five ladies, John Gay, Martha Blount, and Alexander Pope, when she brought out *The Reform'd Coquet* in 1724 (See *Works,* I, 215-17). All of her fiction except *The False Friend,* which is Spanish, is English in setting and manners despite the foreign names of her characters.

By what methodology can I reassess the novels of Mary Davys? Annette Kolodny has recently suggested one in the following statement: "To the feminist critic, then goes the task of insisting that what may appear as impossibly freaky and neurotic at first reading, is, in reality, *the tentative process of discovering—in literary terms— what the world looks and feels like to that segment of the population which is taught the 'only one way . . . to control her future is to choose her man.'"*[11] Certainly Mary Davys could never be described as freaky or neurotic either by the conduct of her own life or by the lives of her fictional heroines. However, a line from her Prologue to her comedy *The Northern Heiress* did strike me with considerable force: "'Tis Women's Duty Women to Protect." Protect from what? Obviously she was aware that women are in some sense victims. And as an impoverished widow (Swift somewhat grudgingly and only occasionally sent her small sums in response to her many letters) without patrons or wealthy relatives, she must have been conscious of her vulnerability throughout her writing career. The irony and wit with which McBurney credits her is not necessarily, then, a sign of a hearty, masculine temperament but a kind of protective insulation for a widow to examine "what the world looks and feels like."

Patricia Meyer Spacks has suggested that some later women such as Hester Thrale and Fanny Burney wrote because writing "generates psychic mobility and escape," which helped them to avoid desperate social oppression.[12] Her article concludes, "In their precise, though often indirect, recording of the inner life they establish women's claim for attention as individuals."[13] The observation seems also applicable to Mary Davys at the beginning of the century. She started her writing career with *The Merry Wanderer* to record her experience as a widow entering a new environment without financial resources or male protection. She insists throughout her novels that she is writing fact, not fantasy or romance, as she calls it, and that her account is "almost exactly true, to the greatest part whereof I am a Witness"; she is also self-consciously aware that her realism is new: "I had a Mind to make an Experiment, whether it was not possible to divert the Town with real Events just as they happen'd" (Preface to *The Fugitive*). This first record of her travels around the English countryside, where she met with rural curiosity about the Irish and encountered bad housekeepers who never changed the bed linen, as well as unmannerly suitors who sought brides only for their dowry, is told with enough detail to give her fiction the verisimilitude of Moll Flanders' London described by Defoe twenty years later.[14]

Davys's experience as a stranger in England also carried over into *The Lady's Tale* in the humor with which she describes Abaliza's inablity to communicate with her Dutch landlady when she goes in search of Alcipus. After Davys notes that the two women "had gaped and baul'd at one another to no manner of purpose," her authorial comment is revealing of her own experience: "which put me in mind that there were other parts of *Europe* besides *England,* that know how to be rude to Strangers" (*The Lady's Tale,* II, 389). This comment recalls the first episode in *The Merry Wanderer* when a country boor bursts in upon the newly arrived Irish travelers and offers a shilling to see these wild Irish "wi' long Tails, that have no Clothes on, but are cover'd laik my brown Caw a whom with their own Hair" (I, 125). No wonder the Irish widow played a trick on the rustic. Notice that from this first autobiographical fiction the leading female character keeps the upper hand by her wit.

The theme which runs throughout her portrayal of manners, "'Tis Women's Duty Women to Protect," is, then, an appropriate command from a widow speaking out of her "inner experience" when she had to rely on her wit and her pen to survive and remain independent in her new surroundings. What was her alternative? Accumulating debts, which might lead to debtor's prison? Prostitution? Unthinkable as a clergyman's widow, although she might have gone into domestic service as a housekeeper, but that would have left her no time for writing. Instead she used the few guineas she earned by her pen and her one Benefit night for *The Northern Heiress* and opened a coffee house in Cambridge.

The pattern of manners which emerges from her novels is appropriate to her feminine viewpoint. Mary Davys's heroines never question the fact that they must "choose a man" and marry, but they consistently resist the authority of fathers to make the choice for them. Abaliza in *The Lady's Tale,* for example, begs her father to "let Reason and Filial Pity stand my Friends" when he urges her to accept an unwanted suitor. She pursues her argument that reason should govern the passions, and when he

will not admit that he has failed to use reason, she concludes with an even stronger appeal to make her independent choice, by acknowledging that "Nature has given you a superior Power over your Child; and if the Power be not back'd by love and an indulgent Pity, every wretched Child that falls into contrary Hands, must expect nothing but Misery, unless they happen to have the same Taste with an inexorable Father" (II, 360).[15]

However, Davys's heroines not only argue for their right to veto a suitor in an arranged marriage; they also explode the notion of men as romantic lovers. Amoranda, once she becomes *The Reform'd Coquet,* says, "Love is a Subject every Man of Mode is ashamed of. It has been so long exploded, that our modern Wits would no more be seen in Cupid's Toils, than in a church; and would as soon be persuaded to say their Prayers, as tell a Lady they love her" (I, 323). Abaliza *(The Lady's Tale)* distrusts her favorite admirer in a sharper image: " . . . I have known some Men of your Age and Gallantry, who have kept one Speech like a standing Dish, to be served up to every Female they converse with" (II, 372). Thus, whether they are being cured of vanity like Amoranda or holding off a desired suitor like Abaliza, avoiding a rape like Belinda *(The Accomplished Rake)* or masking their inclinations behind political views like Berina *(Familiar Letters),* Mrs. Davys's women all regard their suitors as insincere in love because of the way men are raised. Her most ironic definition of a "fine Gentleman" is from Teachwell, the tutor of Sir John Galliard *(The Accomplished Rake):*

> You are to kill your man before you can be reckoned brave. You must destroy your constitution with diseases ere you are allowed a man of gallantry; unman yourself by immoderate drinking, to qualify you for a boon companion; blaspheme your Maker by execrable oaths and curses to avoid all show of sneaking religion. And if fortune forgets to be your friend while the dice are in your hand, you must fling away your estate to some winning bully, lest you should pass for a man of prudence and thought—which brings you to the last degree of misery, and you are a beggar before you know your danger. And thus, Sir John, I have described the modern man of honour, which in my opinion is the most dishonourable man upon earth, from which character, as from the plague, may Heaven always keep you. (p. 262)

The men in Davys's novels avoid marriage as long as possible even when they have signed a written pledge, as Lord Lofty does in *The Reform'd Coquet* in order to seduce a woman. Marriage, Lord Lofty insists, kills love: "The Marriage-Bed is to love what a cold Bed is to a Melon-Seed, it starves it to death infallibly" (I, 237). Occasionally Davys motivates the cynicism of her male characters. In *The Accomplished Rake,* for example, it is his mother's misalliance with her footman which shocks Sir John Galliard into distrust of female honor. But even honorable men (Alcipus in *The Lady's Tale* or Formator in *The Reform'd Coquet*) show excessive and unwarranted jealousy—Alcipus when he sees his beloved Abaliza sitting on the knees of her uncle—or flaws in their apparent disinterest in sexual attraction: Formator, that noble elderly savant whom Charlotte E. Morgan called an early Sir Charles Grandison, stood "leering" at Amoranda as she tried to pump the messenger of Alanthus, the disguised Formator, about his master's whereabouts (I, 316). Thus with an act or a word Davys undermines the stuffiness and didacticism of her presumably good heroes. Ideally lovers should be friends; Abaliza uses the term when she and Alcipus are reconciled: "We are now Friends again" (II, 395). But the real problem is that men think women perfect only in "Levity, Vanity, Dress, and now and then a little Beauty" (II, 371).

Davys's men have both the strength of their own physical aggressiveness and social approval. Sir John Galliard *(The Accomplished Rake),* who divides men into coxcombs like Sir Combish, fools like Squire Cockahopp, knaves and men of sense (p. 355), is divided himself between the last two categories. He is capable of bribing servants, of drugging Nancy Friendly in order to rape her, and of pursuing a married Lady of fashion until the tables are turned on him in a trap set by the Lady's husband so that Sir John's clothes are set on fire and he is forced into social retirement. With that episode his rakish London career comes to an end and he returns to his country estate. Whenever he is foiled in his advances to women, he acknowledges that "women are riddles," but his pity for Nancy Friendly's ruin and her father's disgrace because of it comes only after his humiliation; then, at the end of the novel, he offers to marry Nancy. Yet he wants a quick marriage before he changes his mind: "And sir John, who had for many years indulged in an aversion to a settled state of life, was now resolved to hasten his new design lest a returning qualm should rise to stop his generous and honorable intentions" (p. 372). Thus the shadow of knave remains even when his good sense prevails in this most completely drawn of Davys's male characters. At the end of the novel, what one remembers is Sir John's curious religious imagery of heaven as satisfied passion and purgatory as frustrated passion in his pursuit of women (p. 343) or his declaration that "women were made to be enjoyed" (p. 324). Small wonder that his lecture to his wayward mother early in the novel rang with the avowal of a double standard for the conduct of both sexes: "Women are naturally modest, man naturally impudent, and, in short, there is no comparing the actions of one with the other" (p. 309) Mary Davys redeems the accomplished rake, but our confidence that he will stay redeemed after his marriage to Nancy is never reinforced.

Because Mrs. Davys often states that her purpose in writing of the passions is to "restore the Purity and the Empire of Love and correct the Vile abuses of it,"[16] it is clear that it is men she would correct while she is protecting women. She acknowledges that "Passions will ever have a place in the Actions of Men and Love a principal one," and then argues that "what cannot be removed or subdued, ought at least to be regulated"; and that the reformation must be begun by women, "for it is we who have given up our Empire, betray'd by Rebels among ourselves" (II, 409). What, then, are the qualities of her women characters?

In the dedication addressed to "Mrs. Esther Johnson of Dublin" in her 1705 version of her own experience, *The Fugitive,* she celebrates what she remembers of Esther Johnson in mixed company: "I observ'd in you all the Decencies of Behaviour and Conversation that I could ever conceive in my Mind, much Knowledge, true Judgment, lively inoffensive Wit, Modesty without Constraint, and perfect Good Humour, and all without the least inclination to Censure" (II, Append. D, 558-59). Wit, modesty, and good humor are, of course, the opposite of the levity, vanity, dress, and a little beauty that she stated as what men value in women (*The Lady's Tale,* II, 371). Not surprisingly, they are the positive qualities repeated in all her female heroines with the possible exception of *The False Friend,* where her Spanish setting produces the least realistic heroine. Yet even in the Dedication of that novel to Lady Slingsby, she again celebrates modesty, good humor, and humility, and describes her Spanish heroine Elvira thus: "Her wit was great, and her Humour good" (II, 416-17). Certainly her other female heroines all have wit, including the *I* of *The Merry Wanderer.* They spar verbally with their suitors; they are not above playing jokes and encouraging men in misapprehensions which are later resolved; they are not given to morose periods of weeping or soul-searching; and they are at ease in mixed company. Apparently she found wit the best accommodation women could make to their inferior social position. Since she tried her hand at writing comedies, undoubtedly some of these qualities are carried over from the witty repartee and epigrammatic dialogue of the women in Restoration plays which she echoes, as McBurney rightly pointed out.[17] Nancy Friendly's wit is even acknowledged by Sir John Galliard in their first London encounter. When she resists his aggressive courtship, Sir John complains, "You are grown so very witty I fear I shall lose you indeed for want of spirit to keep up with your repartee" (p. 282). Abaliza holds off Adrastus, her unwanted suitor, by turning his compliments into insincere stock phrases, and the vain Amoranda outtalks both Lord Lofty and her other suitors such as Froth and Callid. While Amoranda's wit stems from her vanity, encouraged by her overindulgent parents, most of Davys's female characters use wit to defend themselves from predatory males. Occasionally they sustain the wit so long, as Berina does in *Familiar Letters . . . ,* that they are in danger of losing the suitor they prefer. Is it true, Berina asks Artander, after admitting that she has encroached on the prerogative of wit of another woman, that he is engaged to her rival (II, 520)? Thus she unwittingly reveals her own emotional involvement. While this is a turning point in the novel, Berina's wit and well-turned phrases continue. Apparently it is easier to curb a tongue than a pen.

Such examples as I have cited might well stem from the dialogue of the comedies. However, the sharpest female wit in Davys's novels is in her authorial voice as she comments on action and characters, particularly in her last novel, *The Accomplished Rake,* where both verbal and situational irony abound. "Surely unjustly are we called the weaker vessels," she, as author, says in describing how quickly Lady Galliard conquered her grief over the death of her husband by taking her footman Tom as her lover (p. 243). After being once dismissed, Tom later returns with a new wife to take up the positions of footman and housekeeper. Here the authorial comment is "I saw Tom and his wife arrive, one to take possession of a new place and the other of his old one" (p. 269)—in Lady Galliard's bed. Such flashes of wry humor give a unique quality of irony to Davys's style.

Her best situational irony is found in her one epistolary novel, *Familiar Letters . . . ,* where there is no authorial voice. Twenty-two letters are exchanged by Artander, from his estate in the country, and Berina, in London, reporting "The Town goes on as it used to do, full of Party, Pamphlets, Libels, Lampoons, and scurrilous Ballads" (II, 518). The pair has agreed to write only of friendship and to limit themselves to one sheet of paper. Thus Davys sets careful limits on the length of the letters while establishing a situation for subtle nuances as the correspondents drift into deeper emotional attachment. They begin by arguing their political views; Artander is a Tory suspicious of the new Hanoverian monarch while Berina is a Whig who delights to report the birth of an heir to the King. Both write scornfully of marriage by citing examples of mismatches in age, marriages of convenience, or arranged marriages; once Artander reports a gentleman who tried "to bespeak me for his Daughter" (II, 511). But Davys shows impressive control of style when the tone of their letters changes gradually as their emotions shift from friendship to love. As I indicated earlier, it is Berina who begins the shift in Letter 14 when she has won a battle of wits with another woman but then fears that that woman is loved by Artander whose "friendship" she will lose. Artander is quick to protest, "Lose your Friends! *Berina,* that's impossible"; then, referring to their pact to write only in friendship, he adds, "And if Artander shou'd chance to stumble out of the Road he has so long walk'd in, *Berina* will be so far from losing a Friend, that she will gain a Lover too" (II, 523). Her previous urging that he resist the God of Love who "makes mere idiots of Mankind" only aids the situational irony because she had already given herself away and thus unwittingly provoked his open declaration. How? She reported dreaming that Artander was blind, and when she would have led him, "He pull'd out my Eyes too" (II, 522). It is her dream which stimulates her verbal play that love is blind, Cupid is blind, the God of Love "makes mere idiots of Mankind." Mrs. Davys's style is rarely more successful than in playing upon this ironic situation in the remaining six letters which end with Berina protesting that he overacts his part: "The next time you put on the Lover, do it with

an easier Air; 'tis quite out of fashion to talk of Dying, and Sighing, and Killing Eyes, and such Stuff; you shou'd say, Damn it, Madam, you are a tolerable sort of Woman, and, if you are willing, I don't much care if I do you the Honour to marry you" (II, 529). Thus she both puts down conventional courtship and encourages a forthright proposal. Since he has hinted he will soon come to London, she closes by adding,

> Whenever Artander comes, or in whatever Shape, he shall always find a kind Reception from his
>
> Real Friend,
>
> Jan. 12 BERINA

and the novel ends with a note from Artander that he is on his way "by tomorrow Morning." Thus Davys uses well the wit she values in women to improve the texture of her style.

Her other female values—modesty, humility, common sense, and good humor—are equally consistent in her heroines. Amoranda must learn such values in *The Reform'd Coquet* because she lacked proper parental guidance when she was left an orphan at fifteen and, as the author ironically tells us, "it was not possible for one single Fault to be joined to three thousand Pounds a year" (I, 225). But even Amoranda has the common sense to see through the seduction plots of Lord Lofty, Froth, and Callid (with a little help from lost letters and overhead conversations), and it takes only a hint from Formator, her advisor, to make her distrust the fondling of Berintha, a disguised libertine in women's clothing. Near the end of the novel, she rejects Jenny's lower-class, self-indulgent definition of an ideal husband who would hire a nurse to bring up his children: "if ever I have a Child," Amoranda replies, "I will not think it a trouble to nurse it" (I, 318), thus giving evidence of what Mrs. Davys undoubtedly considered as her gradually acquired good judgment.

None of Davys's heroines is sexually promiscuous, which I take to be another proof of their common sense, since this author well understood that society permitted indiscretions by men but not by women. Lady Galliard is, after all, not a heroine; in fact, her promiscuity is used to motivate both her son's awareness of a double standard for sexual conduct and his own later rakish behavior. However, many minor female characters in Davys's novels are forced into sex before marriage, like the servant Betty who is raped by her future husband's employer on the eve of her wedding *(The Accomplished Rake),* or the luckless Altimira who allows Lord Lofty to "satisfy his passion" because he has given her a written promise of marriage *(The Reform'd Coquet).* The most bizarre example of extramarital sex in these novels is the mysterious Stranger who allows Sir John to rape her in the bagnio where he had first planned to take advantage of Nancy Friendly; after the act, the woman tells Sir John that her marriage of eight years has been a disaster because she failed to produce an heir to her husband's estate: "And there lies the bitter pill that takes away the sweets of life; that is the cutting blow, the smarting wound my husband always feels" (*The Accomplished Rake,* p. 288). That a woman married to a man "of great estate" should take so bold an action as to disguise herself as a man, attend a masquerade, follow the sexually aroused Sir John to a bagnio, and allow herself to be raped is a measure of the importance of children for an eighteenth-century woman's role to be fulfilled in marriage. Perhaps it is a bitter testimony to the widow Davys's own disappointment of children. However, her heroines, unlike the mysterious Stranger, equate their virtue, i.e., chastity, with their honor as thoroughly as Pamela would. When Nancy Friendly loses her chastity after being drugged at an inn, she retires in disgrace until Sir John's repentant offer of marriage at the end of the novel; she accepts the offer only on the condition that their illegitimate child be made his legal heir: "I know it must be an Act of Parliament, and you must expose yourself on such an occasion, but as you are the only aggressor, you must be the sufferer too. These are the conditions, Sir John, if ever you and I are to meet again" (*The Accomplished Rake,* p. 372).

In a very real sense, then, Davys's heroines are young women of good judgment and common sense. They know that they are destined for marriage, but prefer not to marry the men their fathers choose unless they love them. They parry male sexual aggression with only their wit to protect them. Once ruined, they know that only an Act of Parliament can make their children legitimate. It is only Berina in *Familiar Letters . . .* whose head does not know where her heart lies, and her situation is exploited for its irony rather than as proof that she lacks good judgment.

The consistency of the female experience recorded in Mary Davys's novels of manners appears to stem from her own observations as *The Merry Wanderer* when she first arrived in England at the beginning of the century. Whether writing of herself or of other fictional women, she achieved a realism of voice, tone, and event because she avoided the sensationalism of Manley and Haywood and limited herself to events "just as they happen'd,"[18] managing her invention with English characters and English settings "which gives us room to order Accidents better than Fortune will be at Pains to do" (I, 3). Her style also improved in spite of her apology for her lack of learning and the fact that "Alas, she knows no Languages but one" (Prologue to *The Northern Heiress,* I, 57).

Finally I do not agree that it was her "hearty, somewhat masculine temperament" that distinguished Mary Davys as a novelist. Rather, it was because she wrote as a woman "with the peculiar clarity of vision which is the special gift of the underdog"[19] who uses her inner experience as a basis for claiming the attention of the outer world.

Notes

[1] *The Merry Wanderer,* Baker says, recounts experiences like those in Mrs. Mary Manley and Mrs. Haywood, "but with a stronger flavor of the picaresque" (III, 126), which is patently inaccurate. He describes *Familiar Letters Betwixt a Gentleman and a Lady,* despite its content of arguments about English Whigs and Tories, as being in "the Portuguese fashion" (III, 127). One wonders whether he reads Davys carefully when her best novel, *The Accomplished Rake,* is not even mentioned.

[2] Charlotte E. Morgan, *The Rise of the Novel of Manners* (1913; rpt. New York: Russell and Russell, 1963), p. 70.
[3] Augustan Reprint No. 54 (1955).

[4] Robert Adams Day, *Told in Letters: Epistolary Fiction Before Richardson* (Ann Arbor, MI: Univ. of Michigan Press, 1966), p. 190.

[5] William H. McBurney, "Mrs. Mary Davys: Forerunner of Fielding," *PMLA,* 74 (1959), 348-55.

[6] McBurney, p. 352.

[7] *The Accomplished Rake* appears in McBurney's edition of *Four Before Richardson, Selected English Novels, 1720-27* (Lincoln, NE: Univ. of Nebraska Press, 1963).
[8] "She was the widow of a schoolmaster and a clergyman, a woman of some literary aspirations, and, to judge by her later work [her novels], a person of hearty, somewhat masculine temperament," McBurney, p. 350.

[9] Fortunately, in 1971 a critical edition of "The Works of Mary Davys," 2 vols., appeared as a doctoral dissertation at the University of Iowa, edited with a good introduction by Donald H. Stefanson. Because of Stefanson's careful selection of copy-texts, all page references in this paper are from this critical edition.

[10] In the Preface to her *Works,* Davys says that *The Lady's Tale,* her frame novel, of an experience narrated by the main character Abaliza four years after it happened, was written in 1700 although no copy of the novel is extant before that in the 1725 *Works.*

[11] Annette Kolodny, "Some Notes on Defining a 'Feminist Literary Criticism,'" *Critical Inquiry,* 2 (1975), 84-85. The italics are mine; the interior quote is from a contemporary novel by Alix Kates Shulman, *Memoirs of an Ex-Prom Queen* (1972).

[12] Patricia Meyer Spacks, "Reflecting Women," *Yale Review,* 63 (1973), 40.

[13] Spacks, p. 42.

[14] See McBurney, "Mrs. Mary Davys: Forerunner of Fielding," p. 355, who calls her one of the few writers before

1740 "to show how realistic comedy might be adapted to the new genre."

15 Lawrence Stone, *The Family, Sex and Marriage in England 1500-1800* (London: Weidenfeld and Nicolson, 1977), p. 280. Stone dates the veto of parental authority in arranged marriages, as reflected in novels by women, after 1780. Davys's novels antedate his estimate by more than half a century.

16 See the Preface to *The False Friend* (II, 409) and also the Preface to her *Works* (I, 4).

17 See his Introduction to *Four Before Richardson,* pp. xxx-xxxii. Stefanson also evaluates her indebtedness to stock characters from the stage in his Introduction to his edition of the *Works,* p. ix.

18 Dedication to *The Fugitive,* II, Append. D, 562. In *The Lady's Tale* she patently rejected sensationalism by describing Abaliza's journey with her uncle across the English Channel as mere statement of fact: "It would be superfluous, to give you an account of our Voyage, since nothing worth repeating happen'd to us; for we were neither taken by Pirates, nor swallow'd by Waves; we escaped both Storms and the *Grand Signior's Seraglio,* and with full sails of a fair Wind we reach'd our wish'd for Harbour" (II, 388).

19 Spacks, p. 41.

Nancy Cotton (essay date 1980)

SOURCE: "Minor Women Playwrights 1670-1750," in *Women Playwrights in England c. 1363-1750,* Bucknell University Press; Associated University Presses, 1980, pp. 156-60.

[*In the following excerpt, Cotton discusses Mary Davys' work as a dramatist.*]

Mary Davys (1674-1732),[7] born in Dublin, was happily married to the Reverend Peter Davys, headmaster of the free school at St. Patrick's and a friend of Swift. When he died young in 1698, she was widowed and without means at the age of twenty-four. She went to England and tried writing. In 1700 she made an unsuccessful "first Flight to the Muses" (*Works,* 1:v) with a novel, *The Lady's Tale,* for which she received three guineas. She then settled in York for fifteen years. Although she was helped occasionally by Swift, it is not known how she eked out a living during this period. About the age of forty-one, this "Female Muse, from Northern Clime" (Prologue, *The Northern Heiress*) took her first play to London and got it performed at Lincoln's Inn Fields.

The Northern Heiress; or, The Humours of York (1716) has many features conventional to prose intrigue comedy—two sets of lovers, an heiress who pretends to lose her fortune in order to test her suitor's affection, a foolish country squire, a fop tricked into marrying a maid, the familiar opening scene of a beau reading, in this case "Humble Cowley" (p. 9). The unusual features give the play its interest. It is set in the country, in a boardinghouse in York. The country characters who display the humours of York are an egregious trio of wives of former lord mayors who insist on being addressed as "lady": Lady Swish, a brewer's wife, Lady Cordivant, a glover's wife, and, chief among them, a chandler's widow, Lady Greasy, who is landlady to the upper-class characters of the main plot. These three breakfast together, waxing nostalgic over former graft as they put away "four Quarts of Country Ale" and "one of strong Beer" (p. 28), and then insist on paying their hostess and tipping her maid. Lady Greasy is given to malapropisms, warning her daughter's suitor "to come no more salivating [i.e., serenading] under our windows" (p. 20). The lively, vigorous prose of the play is characterized by homely diction and specific details of domestic life—teakettles, sciatica, muslin aprons, and rolling pins.

This vein of comic country realism, popular in her later novels, took Davys to a profitable author's benefit. Her preface expresses her pleasure: "The Success it met with the third Night, was (considering the Time of Year, and my own want of Acquaintance) infinitely above what I had Reason to expect; and as the Town, and the Ladies in particular, have been pleas'd to favour my first Attempt, it will make me more industrious to promote their Diversion at a more convenient Season." Her success came in spite of

> how industrious some of the York Gentlemen were to damn this Play. . . . The first Night, in which lay all the Danger, was attended with only two single Hisses; which, like a Snake at a Distance, shew'd a Resentment, but wanted Power to do Hurt. The one was a Boy, and not worth taking Notice of; the other a Man who came prejudic'd, because he expected to find some of his Relations expos'd. But both his Fears, and his ill Nature, were groundless. . . . I think this angry Gentleman would have shewn a greater Contempt, had he said, This is a Woman's Play, and consequently below my Resentment.

Presumably with the profits from this play, Davys opened a coffeehouse in Cambridge, where she lived until her death in 1732. In 1725, encouraged by gentlemen in Cambridge, she printed her *Works* in a two-volume subscription edition. In addition to six novels, her *Works* included, as she had promised in the preface to *The Northern Heiress,* a second play, ***The Self Rival: A Comedy. As it should have been Acted at the Theatre-Royal In Drury-Lane.*** This second play is also written in lively prose, although it is weaker than her first in characterization and humor. The hero, Colonel Bellamont, in order to foil the mercenary objections of his sweetheart's father, woos Maria disguised as his rich old uncle, Lord Pastall. He is forced to be his own rival when Maria pretends not to recognize him through his disguise and accepts the suit of the supposed uncle. An unusual character is Mrs. Fallow, a "good-natur'd old Maid" (dramatis personae), who is contrasted with the more predictable sour old maid, Lady Camphire Lovebane. Mrs. Fallow believes that people should marry young; she is a "Predestinarian" about marriage, having astutely observed "so many Men and Women go together, that, in all probability, could never have met" (p. 51). Although the play is set in London, Davys makes some slight use of her Cambridge experience for details. The second male lead is a student at Cambridge, also Bellamont's alma mater. Barnaby, the colonel's servant, is an adept at quoting poetry because while his master drank his way through Cambridge, Barnaby studied his master's books. These details, however, are peripheral. It is a pity that Davys did not depict the comic humours of university life as she had done before of York.

The prefatory material in the **Works** shows Davys's attitudes toward her writing. In spite of her coffeehouse trade, her "Purse is (by a thousand Misfortunes) grown wholly useless to every body" (**Works,** 2:6). She writes from need and is angry at criticism for doing so:

> Perhaps it may be objected against me, by some more ready to give Reproach than Relief, that as I am the Relict of a Clergy-man, and in Years, I ought not to publish Plays, &c. But I beg of such to suspend their uncharitable Opinions, till they have read what I have writ, and if they find any thing there offensive either to God or Man, any thing either to shock their Morals or their Modesty, 'tis then time enough to blame. And let them consider, that a Woman left to her own Endeavours for Twenty-seven Years together, may well be allow'd to catch at any Opportunity for that Bread, which they that condemn her would very probably deny to give her.

> (**Works,** 1:vii-viii)

Davys estimates her plays accurately: "I never was so vain, as to think they deserv'd a Place in the first Rank, or so humble, as to resign them to the last" (**Works,** 1:vii). . . .

Notes

7 Biographical information is taken from William H. McBurney, "Mrs. Mary Davys: Forerunner of Fielding," *PMLA* 74 (1959): 348-55; Jonathan Swift, *Journal to Stella,* ed. Harold Williams, 2 vols. (Oxford: Clarendon Press, 1948), 1: 264, 2: 625; and from her own comments in *The Northern Heiress* and in her collected *Works,* 2 vols. (London: H. Woodfall, 1725). In-text citations refer to volume and page number in the *Works.* McBurney discusses Davys's anticipation of Fielding in her transference of stage conventions to the novel and

her vignettes of comic country types. Her *Familiar Letters Betwixt a Gentleman and a Lady,* a highly developed pre-Richardsonian epistolary novel, is available in a facsimile edition, with an introduction by Robert A. Day, published by the Augustan Reprint Society, No. 54 (Los Angeles, Calif.: William Andrews Clark Memorial Library, University of California, 1955). Day discusses this novel further in *Told in Letters* (Ann Arbor, Mich.: University of Michigan Press, 1966), pp. 187-90. . . .

Jane Spencer (essay date 1986)

SOURCE: "Reformed Heroines: The Didactic Tradition: The Lover-Mentor: Mary Davys's *The Reform'd Coquet* (1724)," in The *Rise of the Woman Novelist from Aphra Behn to Jane Austen,* Basil Blackwell, 1986, pp. 145-7.

[*In the following excerpt from a study of the development of women's novels in English, Spencer analyzes the portrayal of a reformed heroine in Davys'* The Reform'd Coquet.]

The Lover-mentor: Mary Davys's The Reform'd Coquet (1724)

We might expect that a novel tradition based on the woman writer's role as moral guide to her sex would present stories of a heroine's reform through the advice of a more experienced woman; and in fact, wise women often appear as mentors in didactic novels. Frances Sheridan's Sidney Bidulph is guided by her mother, and later guides her own daughters.[9] In Clara Reeve's *School for Widows* (1791), Mrs Strictland and Mrs Darnford exchange life-histories and promise to monitor each other's conduct; and Mrs Strictland has preserved wifely duty in a difficult marriage with the help of a motherly housekeeper's admonitions.[10] In Jane West's *The Advantages of Education* (1793) Maria Williams learns to reject an attractive rake and accept worthy Mr Herbert under her mother's wise tuition; and the importance of the female mentor is further emphasized by the fact that Mr Herbert's mother was once an equally necessary guide to Mrs Williams herself.[11] A female teacher is not always central, however. Often she plays a subordinate part while a male teacher—the heroine's lover and her mentor—takes the dominant role. The relationship between a faulty heroine and her lover-mentor conveniently combines love story and moral lesson, and reflects the sexual hierarchy established in society; not surprisingly, then, it provides the didactic novel with its central fable.

The prototype of this relationship can be found in the century's comedies, with their coquettes and serious-minded suitors,[12] but it is only fully developed in the novel. The first novel to do this thoroughly is Mary Davys's **The Reform'd Coquet** (1724), the title of which provides an apt designation for many a heroine in the didactic tradition. Davys is at the beginning of a long line of women writers who create coquettish heroines and lover-mentors to reform them.

Davys's Amoranda, pretty and clever, spends her childhood as the centre of an admiring circle of parents and visitors, and is spoiled by indulgence. When her parents die, she is a rich, beautiful and foolish coquette, rather similar in situation and character to a later, more famous heroine, Austen's Emma Woodhouse, who begins as a spoilt young woman with 'the power of having rather too much her own way, and a disposition to think a little too well of herself'.[13]

Amoranda's dangerous independence is curbed by Alanthus, a young man who shows his love for her by disguising himself as Formator, a wise old guardian appointed by her uncle. Alanthus only reveals his true identity at the end of the story, but the reader has guessed it before. Amoranda is instructed, not wooed, by this lover-mentor, and her first sight of him as a young man is calculated to link the idea of lover and stern tutor firmly in her mind. He makes his appearance when her coquetry has placed her in the power of Berinthius, who means to rape her. Instead of rescuing her at once, Alanthus scolds her:

> I presume, Madam, you are some self-will'd, headstrong Lady, who, resolved to follow your own Inventions, have left the Care of a tender Father, to ramble with you know not who. Oh Sir! *said she,* some part of your guess is true; but Father I have none. Nor Mother? *said the Stranger;* nor Guardian? Nor Mother, *said she,* but a Guardian, a good one too, I have; and were I but once again in his possession, I wou'd never leave him while I live.
>
> Well, Madam, *said the Gentleman,* I am sorry for you, but am no Knight-Errant, nor do I ride in quest of Adventures; I wish you a good Deliverance, and am your humble Servant. Saying this, he and his Servants rode away.[14]

He does return and rescue her from harm, but the lesson has been a severe one. Soon after this it is revealed that Alanthus and Formator are the same person, and the heroine, cured of self-will, eagerly accepts her mentor as her husband and guardian for life.

The ideological implications of this novel are clearly very different from those of the seduction tale. We only have to compare **The Reform'd Coquet** with Manley's tale of Charlot in *The New Atalantis*. There are wicked ravishers in Davys's novel as there are in Manley's, but this does not mean, as it does in Manley's, that men are not to be trusted, but that the heroine must find an honest man, submit to his authority, and gain his protection. Whereas Manley portrays the guardian as corrupt, the abuser of his patriarchal authority, Davys makes the guardian the lover and supports his programme of courtship-by-reform. The father substitute, instead of being a quasi-incestuous ravisher, is the legitimate mate for a thoughtless young heroine. His advice is wisdom, and his lifelong control is necessary for a woman who, though basically virtuous, is inevitably subject to vanity, that 'Foible of . . . [her] Sex' (II, 71). The story of Charlot is a protest against male domination: the story of Amoranda is an apology for it. This message of conformity is found in most novels where the heroine's lover is her mentor. It is built into the very structure of the 'reformed coquette' tradition. The heroine's basic fault is usually identified as the natural concomitant of her femaleness—her vanity, her coquettishness are nearly always specifically described as female foibles. The fact that she is a virtuous and sensible woman apart from her little follies only underlines the distrust of femininity implied in her creation. Even the best of women, it would appear, cannot escape the moral weaknesses of her sex. Masculine guidance and protection are the answer to the heroine's problems, and she is given a substitute father to guard her from other men, from the evil of the world, and from her own female nature. . . .

Notes

[9] See *Memoirs of Miss Sidney Bidulph, Extracted from Her Own Journal, And now First Published* (Dublin, 1761). Sidney's daughters appear in the sequel, *Conclusion of the Memoirs of Miss Sidney Bidulph* (1767).

[10] See *The School For Widows* (Dublin, 1791).

[11] See *The Advantages of Education,* by 'Prudentia Homespun' (London: Minerva Press, 1793).

[12] The comedy of the coquette finally cured of frivolity and won by a serious-minded man has been dated from Crowne's *The English Friar* (1690): see John Harrington Smith, *The Gay Couple in Restoration Comedy* (Harvard University Press, 1948) pp. 142-3. A similar pattern is found in the subplot of Cibber's *The Careless Husband* (1715) which Betsy Thoughtless goes to see in Haywood's novel.

[13] Jane Austen, *Emma, The Novels of Jane Austen,* ed. R. W. Chapman, IV 3rd edn (London: Oxford University Press, 1966), p. 5.

[14] *The Reform'd Coquet,* in *The Works of Mrs. Davys* (London, 1725), II, pp. 83-4. . . .

Mary Anne Schofield (essay date 1990)

SOURCE: "Mary Davys," in *Masking and Unmasking the Female Mind: Disguising Romances in Feminine Fiction, 1713-1799,* University of Delaware Press; Associated University Presses, 1990, pp. 79-90.

[In the following excerpt from a study of women's romance writing, Schofield analyzes Davys' response to the romance tradition, arguing that her work becomes more conservative over the course of her career.]

Mary Davys (1674-1732) more than any of the other pre-1740 novelists is concerned with examining the nature of fiction. Specifically, she is concerned with the viability of the romance genre, and she carefully scrutinizes its present state to ascertain how much she can subvert the form. She insists throughout her numerous prefaces that she is writing fact, not fantasy or romance. She provides a picture of the "truth," especially endeavoring "to restore the Purity and Empire of Love."[1] Although Aubin and Barker also study the romance form, it is Davys who takes the most critical view of the genre, realizing, indeed, the innovativeness of the form. "I had a Mind to make an Experiment whether it was not possible to divert the Town with real events just as they happen'd," she writes.[2]

Like her colleagues, Davys buries her radicalism in her scrupulous following of the established male tradition. In the preface to *The Reform'd Coquet,* she clarifies the men's position in her work by observing: "When I had written a Sheet or two of this Novel, I communicated my Design to a couple of young Gentlemen, whom I knew to be Men of Taste, and both my Friends; they approved of what I had done, advised me to proceed, then print it by Subscription."[3] According to this observation, male approval is necessary, if male patterns are followed. Yet, in the preface to *The Accomplish'd Rake,* echoing Defoe and Richardson, Davys argues for an independent use of the imagination: "Now this is to lose the only advantage of invention, which gives us room to order accidents better than Fortune will be at the pains to do, so to work upon the reader's passions, sometimes keep him in suspense between fear and hope, and at the last send him satisfied away."[4]

The prefaces also stress the importance of moral values (a prefiguration of Richardson), and it is as a moral instructor that the female novelist can succeed. Thus, to rescue the romance from the insipid state into which it has fallen and to justify the imagination is the author's goal. In her effort to reinterpret the male text, she concludes: "since Passions will ever have a place in the Actions of Men, and love a principal one, what cannot be removed or subdue'd, ought at least to be regulated."[5] Perceptively, Davys concludes that "if the Reformation would once begin from our Sex, the Men would follow it in spite of their Hearts."[6] In addition, she says: "My Pen is at the Service of the Publick, and yet it can but make some impression upon the young unthinking Minds of some of my own Sex, I shall bless my Labour, and reap an unspeakable Satisfaction."[7]

Thirty years ago William McBurney argued that Davys was a "forerunner" and "influence" on the accepted, canonical, eighteenth-century male novelist and his works with her rejection of the sensational, her support of the unconventional, and with love and marriage as the usual outcome of the romance. He concludes:

> Mrs. Davys is interesting as one of the few writers before 1740 to formulate a conscious theory of the novel, to show how realistic comedy might be adapted to the new genre, to place emphasis upon characterization and setting rather than upon simple variety of action, and to bring sturdy commonsense and humor to a literary form which had been dominated by the extravagant, the scandalous, and the sensational.[8]

McBurney presents the view of the female novelist that has been the accepted one until the last seven or eight years. Although his assessment of her literary endeavors is accurate, he is unaware of the extraordinary ambiguity that exists in the works themselves. Without a contemporary sensibility he is oblivious to her rebelliousness and hostility. Her prefaces speak to the controlling ideologies of the age; her novels offer rebellious alternatives to these ideologies.

Davys's first venture, *The Lady's Tale* (1700),[9] is Abaliza's account of her love affair with Alcipus to her friend, Lucy. By recounting her amorous tale, she "unmasks" for her friend and displays her true self. Further, by having the beloved herself tell the tale, Davys is able to unmask the romance form, as she can be both participator and commentator on the action, for it is the oppressed-suppressed voice that speaks and reveals itself.

The story unfolds as Abaliza recounts her first meeting with the beloved stranger. Interestingly enough, their initial discussion concerns masks. Alcipus teases her:

> I see by that cruel Cloud, with which you have eclipsed your fine face, you thought me too happy when I gazed upon it bare. How many Advantages have you Ladies above our Sex, who can screen your beauties from Sun and Sight, whilst we are forced by Custom to expose ours to both, tho' sometimes, perhaps, we wou'd be glad to hide them? (2:354)

Abaliza is only superficially masked; her interchange with her father about his proposed lover clearly indicates that she is well aware of her heart—"for I shou'd think myself weak indeed, shou'd I give a Heart to one who never offer'd his" (2:356).

Abaliza forthrightly chooses not to disguise herself as the romantic heroine when she declares to Alcipus: "to let you see how industrious I am to secure you from broken Vows, I will never make you any, and then you will be sure that I at least shall never deceive you" (2:371). Rather, it is Alcipus who plays the disguised romance hero, for he has Adrastus initially pursue Abiliza and present his suit to her.

Alcipus continues his blind masquerade when he rushes off supposing Abaliza to be in love with the man on whose lap she is sitting. Unaware it is her uncle, he disguises himself as a wretched, scorned lover and "he [who] was once reckon'd one of the finest Men in a hundred Miles, is . . . now grown pale and lean, and one of the most melancholy" (2:389). Davys has reversed the usual romance expectation of the disguised heroine, and, instead, offers the reader both the masked hero and the sometimes disguised heroine, Abaliza. Even this early in the century, Davys is cognizant of the woman's position, and has her protagonist adopt disguises to suit her purposes and her search for fulfillment and self-identity.

At the conclusion of the tale, when she has been able to locate him, she "clapp'd on [a] Mask and then went towards him" (2:392), now she adopts the aggressor's role, declares her love, and minces no words as she describes her emotional state and commitment. By using the expected disguise at her discretion, Abaliza has been able to expose her own aggressive thoughts and thus invert the romance form.

Davys' ambivalence to the romance is evident in the conclusion. Abaliza is put in her place by her friend Lucy, who judges that both Abaliza and her conduct were "a little whimsical," "too pat"; her arguments "too weak"; "in fine, your whole Behaviour was a little too forward, which . . . is a fault in our Sex" (2:402). When she discards the submissive, subservient, feminine mask, she is condemned. So, although permitted to cast off the mask for a time and be aggressive, Davys's ambivalent feelings reassert themselves with the romance's happy ending.

Davys's **The Merry Wanderer** (1725),[10] a revised version of **The Fugitive** (1705), continues this sense of extreme ambiguity; in fact, its existence encapsulates and underscores the ambivalent position of the novelist herself. When the novel first existed as **The Fugitive**, it was a rebellious text; it displayed Davys's uncertainty about the future, her exile and isolation in Britain as an Irish person, and her general discontent with her position as a female author. This tone of dislocation and disenfranchisement is greatly altered with the revision as **The Merry Wanderer** (even the title change indicates the change in focus and theme).

Rather than a tale of isolation and dislocation, **The Merry Wanderer** is a story about masking, but it is disguise that leads to frustration and deceit. The male protagonist is frequently taken in by the disguise, at one time even discovering his mother beneath the prostitute's mask! Pregnant women disguise themselves and try to seduce him; women ridden with disease also try to abduct him. **The Merry Wanderer** shows that disguise is a nasty game women play to trap men. Unable to be themselves, women have hidden their true natures. Davys reveals this ubiquitous ploy in the novel.

Coming so early in her career, **The Fugitive** is a troublesome piece though. Not only is the disguise motif revealed in all its ambiguities, but the piece itself that purports to be about unmasking is actually an example of masking; the later version, **The Merry Wanderer**, is a disguise of the discontent and unhappiness explored and

vocalized in the earlier **Fugitive.** Further, the novel involves several men disguised as women—a tactic not frequently used by female novelists—with a "message" that seems to be that men think it safer to be women in this unstable world. Yet the feminocentric text reveals that it is unsafe to be a woman.

In the female-centered texts of **The Familiar Letters, the Reform'd Coquet,** and **The Cousins** Davys continues to explore this turmoil by examining the romance fiction that masquerades as reality, thus supporting the controlling ideology of the age. In all three works, Davys systematically strips the disguise from the romance fiction in an effort to get at the true female self.

Regarding Davys's **The Reform'd Coquet** (1720)[11] and **The Familiar Letters** (1718),[12] Josephine Grieder observes that "What makes both novels admirable is Mrs. Davys' understanding that psychology, not sensationalism, gives fiction its substance."[13] It is just this understanding that allows Davys to unmask the ever-popular romance form, review it, and revise it to make it her own. The promise displayed in her earlier works, reaches full maturity here as she uncovers the fatuous romance form while presenting a rich study of the masking necessary and still undertaken by women.

The Familiar Letters provides, at first glance, a nonprovocative, nonbiased examination of the correspondence between a male and female friend. Much political cajolery is exchanged: she is a Whig; he, a Tory. Comments are made about the foolishness of people in love. The first series of letters is heavy-handed with political matters, and finally Artander writes that he thinks their friendship so firm that "you will comply, when I beg of you to put a stop to this sort of Correspondence; and let your Letters for the future, be fill'd with the innocent Diversions of the Town: 'tis a pity Berina's Temper shou'd be ruffled with Politicks" (278). Berina's answer is direct:

> If Artander's Heart were not as hard as the Rock he has been scrutinizing into, he wou'd never have laid such strict Injunctions on my Pen, and robb'd me of my darling Pleasure; but to let you see how ready I am to relinquish every thing that gives you uneasiness, I have, in compliance with my friendship, laid by the Subject you dislike, and will, for the future, entertain you with something else. (280)

Davys here unmasks only to recover her female side. Berina will comply: she will mask her true inclinations and observations to please the man, but not before or without telling him what is truly on her mind. She will record the mildly soporific tale that he wishes, but she makes it clear that such tale telling is not her predilection.

Artander sends mixed signals. At first, he seems to want to know everything about her and develop a love relationship, but then he retreats and asks only for friendship; Artander masks his feelings. Berina, in my reading, seems to be clearer in her understanding of her true emotions;

she is honest about stating her case: "Love is a thing so much against my grain, that tho' it be dressed up in a disguise of Wit, I see it thro' the Mask, and hate the base Imposture" (289). Berina indicates her nonpredilection for love as she remarks: "there is none so silly as this blinking God of Love: he makes mere Idiots of Mankind" (296). But it is really only a mask that she adopts to get Artander to declare his intentions, which he does in his letter of 1 January. He questions: "And is it sufficient Reason to withdraw your Friendship, because mine grows stronger? Don't Berina give me Cause to think you lie upon the Catch for an Opportunity to throw Artander off?" (301). Berina has it both ways. Although she wants romance to result (that is, marriage), she is unwilling to play the romance game.

The correspondence is refreshing, unguarded. For not only does Artander outline his steps of falling in love, thus unmasking this mysterious male process, but unlike the usually disguised, submissive woman, Berina speaks her mind as well. Perhaps *Familiar Letters* is the most important of Davys's works because of this clear-cut anti-romantic attitude and feminine declaration. Berina is aware, though, that she must declare this state by masking her strong feminism in terms of masculine reference. As she writes:

> I shou'd despise a Husband as much as a King who wou'd give up his own Prerogative, or unman himself to make his Wife the Head: We Women are too weak to be trusted with Power, and don't know how to manage it without the Assistance of your Sex, tho'we oftenest shew that Weakness in the Choice of our Advisers. The Notion I have always had of Happiness in Marriage, is, where Love causes Obedience on one side, and Compliance on the other, with a View to the Duty Incumbent on both. (303)

Further, Berina is able to outline clearly what should be done concerning the mask that surrounds life. As she instructs Artander in one of the closing letters:

> But me thinks you are like a half-bred Player; you over act your Part: Then next time you put on the Lover, do it with an easier Air; 'tis quite out of fashion to talk of Dying, and Sighing, and killing Eyes, and such Stuff. (306)

Berina appears as the more rational and objective, more clear-sighted of the two; she is able to strip all the romances' conventions to their essential points, and yet once this reduction has occurred, she slips back into the mask of compliance. *The Familiar Letters,* in the final analysis, is as bothersome as *The Lady's Tale* and *The Merry Wanderer,* for Berina, and through her Davys, ceases to mouth revolutionary statements at the end, and comes to support the male closure of the romantic, integrated ending. Yet she capitulates to such an ending only after she has subverted the form through the outspokenness of the heroine.

Still attempting to unmask the romance and find a voice,

Davys begins *The Reform'd Coquet* ambitiously by declaring she will examine "the art of disguising" (2). The plot begins with the story of Callid and Froth, two would-be suitors to Amoranda, who plan to kidnap her to get her fortune. Their scheme is discovered by her maids, and Amoranda begins her own counterplot. In the meantime, she is directed by her uncle, E. Traffick, to attach herself to his old friend, Formator, who will serve as her guardian; he helps foil the plot to abduct her. Formator disguises himself as a toady to catch the culprits; they are dispatched and ultimately kill each other in a duel.

Formator takes over as her chief guide; "he made no doubt but one day he should see her the most accomplish'd of her Sex: in order to which, he provided a choice Collection of books for her, spent most of his time with her, diverted her with a thousand pleasant Stories" (53). His name should announce his role: he is the "forming" agent, the molder, the hero in disguise.

As the hero in disguise it is generally assumed that he will get the woman at the end. What is more important in this romance is the movement of the heroine: from foolish, excluded, asexual maid, "giddy, thoughtless, inconsiderate . . . fit only for the company of those coxcombs I too frequently convers'd with" (160) to a mature, rational, marriageable woman. *The Reform'd Coquet* provides one of the earliest attempts at a female *bildungsroman* in the period that forthrightly traces the woman's romance journey of self-identity.

Davys's approach vis-à-vis the romance is different from her work in *The Familiar Letters.* Rather than discredit the romance by talking about it, expressing attitudes antithetical to its very raison d'être, she examines the form by placing a three-dimensional heroine against the typically romantic one-sided one. Amoranda is the new heroine.

To highlight her own role, Davys tells the "whinning romantick" (56) tale of Altemira, who has disguised herself as "a poor, thin, pale, meagre young Creature, hardly able to sit [a] Horse" (55), because she is running away from the advances of her brother. She is also duped by Lord Lofty, who tricks her into losing her maidenhead. He is helped in his schemes by the false Kitty. After he has had his way with her and absconds with Kitty for London, Altemira remarks: "my cruel Disquiet of Mind made so great an alteration in my Face, that when I came to look at it, I could not believe that I was *Altemira*" (74). To get her revenge, Altemira conspires with Amoranda to unmask Lord Lofty. Contrary to the expected passivity of the romance heroine, Amoranda takes affairs into her own hands and arranges an assignation for the summer house, carefully orchestrating the unmasking scene. Amoranda disguises Altemira as herself and arranges for a "marriage" to take place between "Amoranda" and Lord Lofty. In point of fact, he marries Altemira disguised as Amoranda, thus making Altemira an honest woman and right-ing his wrongs.

One treacherous plot is unmasked and is metamorphosed into something better. Unfortunately, the story does not end there. Berintha and an old school friend are introduced to Amoranda's household, and again the plot depends on disguise, for "Berintha" is a man who has fallen in love with Amoranda. She berates his "clandestine means" and by so doing presents Davys's own views on this surreptitious male method:

> Do you think, Sir, *said she, turning to him,* I am so fond of my own Sex, that I can like nothing but what appears in Petticoats? Had you come like a Gentleman, as such I would have received you; but a disguised Lover is always conscious of some Demerit, and dares not trust to his right Form, till by a false appearance he tries the Lady: if he finds her weak and yielding, the day's his own; and he goes off in triumph; but if she has Courage to baffle the Fool, he sneaks away with his disappointment, and thinks nobody will know any thing of the matter. (108)

Davys continues: "Biranthus, for that was his True Name, was stung to the very Soul to hear Amoranda so smart upon him, but was yet resolved to disguise his Mind as well as his body" (108-9). Unable to cope with the new forthright woman, he can only resort to brute force: he kidnaps her and takes her to a deep woods. In good romantic fashion, she is rescued by Alanthus, the disguised Formator, her guardian and teacher, who subsequently reveals himself.

Masking here is used as a truth revealer, for she would accept the advice better from the "older" man, just as Amoranda would reveal herself, tell more of her love, to the man not loved. The conclusion brings about complete revelations and all the principals live happily ever after.

Davys's use of disguise is straightforward here. Because she does not have her heroine disguise herself, no great revelations of the interior female self can occur. Instead, we are privy to the machinations that the man adopts to gain and control the woman. Not only did Formator attempt to form her mind, but as Alanthus, he forms her love and emotional life as well. The coquet is reformed because that is the only way that the man can deal with her. Although Amoranda practices control—she engineers Altimira's wedding—it is a control carefully executed by the man.

The Reform'd Coquet displays Davys's great dismay with the eighteenth-century feminine world. The woman is trapped and controlled by the man who is the disguiser; she can only decipher as much as he permits. When the masks are discarded at the conclusion, it is to reveal a world that still forces the woman to hide her true self. Amoranda has been a pawn throughout the game played by the disguised men in the plot. She has only been allowed to react to them and their disguises; she has never been the instigator of the masquerade. (Even the "wed-

ding" is a reaction to a male plot.) Yet great ambivalence exists here, for though the heroine must remain dumb to all the masquerading, the reader and author are allowed to see the face and motives beneath the mask.

Davys's preoccupation with unmasking is further exploited in her use of her critical prefaces and forewords; in them, she attempts to strip the disguise from the novelist's art and reveals the true state of romance writing. In the preface to **The Cousins** (1725) (revised in 1732 as **The False Friend**),[14] for example, she examines the state of the romance and tries to rescue it from the disuse and disfavor into which it has fallen. The romance, the relation of "probably feigned Stories," has fallen out of favor, she observes, because "the World's being surfeited with such as were either flat and insipid, or offensive to Modesty and good Manners; that they found them only a Circle and Repetition of the same Adventures" (407); "the commonest Matters of Fact, truly told, would have been much more entertaining" (408), she concludes, and so Davys tries to expose this romance mystique and tell the true adventures of love. This goal recurs in **The Lady's Tale, The Merry Wanderer, Familiar Letters,** and **The Reform'd Coquet.** In **The Cousins,** Davys once more strips away the mask of male hypocrisy as she tells the story of Elvira.

The doubting father, Gonsalvo, places his daughter Elvira in the care of his closest friend, Alvaro. When Gonsalva is forced to go away on business, "the other began his Wickedness; and, pulling off the Mask, he appeared barefac'd to the innocent Elvira, who had never defil'd her Thoughts with any thing so base as his Designs. He began by degrees to insinuate himself into her Favour, and first by one Stratagem, and then another, strove to work her into a liking of him" (418). But Elvira "was wholly unskill'd in the Art of Dissembling her self, and that made it the harder for her to find out [the] old Practitioner" (418). Her father returns, stops the rape, rescues her, and sends her off with her sister for a period of time. Then her aunt tries to engineer a love attraction with Sebastian, but Elvira falls in love with Emila's son, Lorenzo, instead. Many plot complications arise, but the final resolution finds Elvira united with Lorenzo and Octavio with his Clara; the unfaithful and deceitful, "false friend," Alvaro is punished for his ungenerousness, and the treacherous Portuguese, Sebastian, is equally punished. Unfortunately, Davys relies more and more in the final pages of her text on just working out the love stories; her initial interest in eschewing the romance element is lost, and she is forced into telling a story that is similar to the French romance but with fewer plot complications. The promise offered to the reader in the preface does not seem to be fully justified in the text proper.

With her last novel, **The Accomplish'd Rake: or, Modern Fine Gentleman,** Davys attempts, once and for all, to unmask the ambiguity of her age. On the surface, however, this story bears little resemblance to the romance. Davys is, in the last analysis, unable to achieve her goal, and the complex, feminine ideologies created by the male remain.

In her effort to uncover all the male mystique that governs her concepts of femininity, Davys creates a male protagonist, Sir John Galliard, and traces the making of him into a "modern fine gentleman," thus promoting the theology of the novel and the restoration of Sir John. Even this task is fraught with ambiguity, however. The first paragraph of the tale pleads for authorial license and imagination with the intermixing "now and then a pretty little lie" (241). Teachwell, Sir John's tutor, defines this new man:

> You are to kill your man before you can be reckoned brave. You must destroy your constitution with diseases ere you are allowed a man of gallantry; unman yourself by immoderate drinking to qualify you for a boon companion; blaspheme your Maker by execrable oaths and curses to avoid all show of sneaking religion. And if fortune forgets to be your friend, while the dice are in your hand, you must fling away your estate to some winning bully, lest you should pass for a man of prudence and thought. . . . and thus Sir John, I have described the modern man of honor. (262)

Yet it is an image that neither the characters nor Davys can comprehend. All he must do, it seems, is dress the part. When Teachwell dies, Sir John "is now left at London, sole master of his own actions" (277). In addition, "The first progress he made in modern gallantry was to get into the unimproving conversation of the women of the town, who often took care to drink him up to a pitch of stupidity, the better to qualify him for having his pockets picked" (277).

Sir John's education into the misrepresented role of modern fine gentleman continues as he romances Miss Friendly, the niece of his friend. He takes Miss Friendly and Miss Wary to the masquerade, where Miss Friendly tells him: "For my part, I intend to personate a sea nymph and dress in moss and shells. You, sir John, may appear like Neptune, because you know he is as much obliged to take care of the ladies of his own dominion as you are to protect me" (284). The masquerade, typically, allows the woman to exercise her hidden nature. Here, for example, Miss Friendly and Miss Ware exchange costumes to enjoy Sir John to the fullest. They indulge in a "double masquerade" (286). When he absconds with the supposed Miss Friendly to the bagnio, however, the deceit is revealed, and Miss Wary is dismissed summarily. While at the bagnio, Sir John encounters the masked "man" from the masquerade only to find that it is a woman in disguise, and a married one at that. She is retreating from a husband who cannot father an heir after eight years of marriage. Although they enjoy each other's company for the evening, Sir John is still intent on Miss Friendly. He continues to mask his lecherous designs on her, conveys an opiate to some macaroons, and quietly waits the most auspicious moment to give them to her. She is undone but totally unaware of the violation.

The story continues until Sir John is willing to claim the paternity of the son he begot with the drugged Miss Friendly. He is motivated to do so by Belinda, the only woman who is able to make him ashamed of his actions. He finally begins to think about his treatment of Miss Friendly, and the denouement of *The Accomplish'd Rake* quickly finds Sir John unmasking and becoming the "man of honour" (373) he was born to be. His villainy has been unmasked as shame, and the happy ending has been restored.

As is typical with these early eighteenth-century works, when confronted with the formidable male text, rhetorical strategy, and ideology, *The Accomplish'd Rake* supports the dominant power. The ambivalence that might have predominated in the novel's pages is reconciled, and male closure is assumed. The ideology of romantic love usurps its place, and the myth of female powerlessness is once more ensconced.

As a novelist of the early decades of the eighteenth century, Davys demonstrates the complexity and the extreme ambiguity of these years. Within her novels, the clash between the two conflicting male ideologies—romantic love and female powerlessness—display themselves in all their ambivalence. Her early pieces, like *The Lady's Tale* and *The Familiar Letters,* define a position and a rebelliousness that Davys was unable to maintain in her later years. She makes clear statements that she is out to challenge the established, accepted romance ideology that sees each novel as a courtship story with the denouement predetermined as a marriage choice. Here the woman has no choice but is merely moved through a series of adventures until it is time for the hero to rescue her; she is left powerless. This type of resolution is not the case with Davys's early heroines, most especially Berina *(Familiar Letters).* She controls their correspondence to a large extent and is vocal in expressing her likes and dislikes; she disrupts the typical narrative with her aggressive remarks that do not suit the ideology of the powerless woman. Davys herself is challenging enough initially to make statements about the value of the female life. Initially she attempts to unmask the pervasive and dominant romantic mode, but finds herself, as her career continues, trapped and hedged in by its conventions. Her last novel, *The Accomplish'd Rake,* is almost a complete reversal, as it tells and supports the "male text." The protagonist, Sir John Galliard, uses masks throughout the work, as he seduces and rapes numerous women who all remain in a position of powerlessness to him. Davys tells *his* story and is hesitant to present Miss Friendly's tale, the unwitting victim of his greatest hoax; therefore, the reader ultimately views the tale from the male perspective: the powerful, romantic viewpoint.

Surprisingly enough for an early novelist, Davys was interested, then, not in perpetuating the fatuous, oftentimes frivolous romantic trappings of the popular form, but, like her contemporary Jane Barker, in unmasking the unrealistic, romanticized presentations found in most popular fiction. In contrast to the scandal novels and the cloying courtship novels, she presents unmasked heroines and undisguised romances. Yet, her earlier tone of defiance sounded with *The Familiar Letters* by the end has been translated into the more popular and predominant voice of the all-powerful man. In the earlier works, the female text had been able to insert itself within the pervasive male story. But Davys solidifies herself as her work continues, and the initial avant-garde position becomes more conservative. This new position is marked in the text by her more standard use of the masquerade until, in her last piece, she uses the conventional masquerade as part of the plot advancement technique in the story itself.

Considering her entire corpus, then, one finds that Davys does not live up to the promise displayed in her earlier pieces, for the rebellion announced in *The Familiar Letters* is finally masked in *The Accomplish'd Rake* until little of the true feminocentric text is left exposed. Her work, in actual fact, demonstrates exactly what the masquerade and romance disguise are all about: capitulation to the controlling and all-powerful male world.

Notes

[1] Mary Davys, *The Works of Mrs. Mary Davys: Consisting of Plays, Novels, Poems, and Familiar Letters* (London: H. Woodfall, 1725), "Preface."

[2] Davys, *The Fugitive,* in *Works,* "Preface."

[3] Mary Davys, *The Reform'd Coquet* (1720; reprint, New York: Garland Publishing, 1975), x.

[4] Davys, *The Accomplish'd Rake: or, Modern Fine Gentleman,* in *Four Before Richardson,* ed. William H. McBurney (Lincoln: University of Nebraska Press, 1963), 235. Subsequent citations are noted parenthetically in the text.
[5] Davys, "Preface," in *Works,* 2:vi.

[6] Ibid.

[7] Davys, "Preface," *Reform'd Conquet,* ix-x.

[8] William H. McBurney, "Mrs. Davys: Forerunner to Fielding," *PMLA* 74 (1959): 355.

[9] Davys, *The Lady's Tale,* in *Works,* 2:121-204. Subsequent citations are noted parenthetically in the text.

[10] Davys, *The Merry Wanderer,* in *Works,* 1:162-272.

[11] Another edition of *The Reform'd Coquet* is found in vol. 2 of *Works.*

[12] Davys, *The Familiar Letters Betwixt a Gentleman and a Lady,* in *Works,* 2:265 to end. Subsequent citations are noted parenthetically in the text.
[13] Josephine Grieder, "Introduction," *The Reform'd Coquet and the Familiar Letters Betwixt a Gentleman and a Lady* (1718, 1720: reprint, New York: Garland Publishing, 1975.

Natasha Sajé (essay date 1996)

SOURCE: "'The Assurance to Write, the Vanity of Expecting to be Read': Deception and Reform in Mary Davys's *The Reform'd Coquet.*" in *Essays in Literature,* Vol. XXIII, No. 2, Fall, 1996, pp. 165-77.

[*In the following essay, Sajé analyzes the theme of the "coquette" and the historical dilemma of the marriageable female in Davys' life and novel,* The Reform'd Coquet.]

Since its coinage in mid seventeenth-century France, "coquette" labels a woman who gains power over others by manipulative verbal and body language, a skill referred to as her "art."[1] Etymologically, the word "coquette" comes from "cock," a male animal which controls its hens and is known for feisty aggression; the word, however, refers to a woman, whose passivity and subordination have long been assumed. The coquette figure appears in literature at the moment when the novel as we know it was being invented, also the moment when women started writing in greater numbers, first in France and then in Britain. The reification of "coquette" at this time reflects the anxiety caused by women writing; the coquette figure provides a site for the critique and regulation of women's self-expression and economic power.

Women novelists absorbed the regulatory strictures of conduct books which aimed to make women predictable, transparent, and readable, but chose the highly dialogic genre of the novel as the form for their response, enabling the alternative logic of narrative art to undermine the project of reforming women's coquetry. Mary Davys's 1724 novel *The Reform'd Coquet* (hereafter *TRC*) is the first of several novels, including Eliza Haywood's *The History of Miss Betsy Thoughtless,* Fanny Burney's *Camilla,* Elizabeth Inchbald's *A Simple Story,* and Jane Austen's *Emma,* in which the coquette heroine's "reform" is initiated and monitored by a male character who loves and subsequently marries her, which Jane Spencer calls the "reformed coquette" plot.[2] The "reformed coquette" plot addresses the decline of arranged marriage in Britain. Once a woman was married, of course, her property was legally her husband's and she no longer posed an economic threat. Consequently, in Anglo-American fiction, until the last half of the nineteenth century when divorce becomes an acceptable topic for fiction, the coquette is usually a young unmarried female. Mary Davys makes the male character in *TRC* a dual figure—virile lover disguised as aged guardian—and thus mediates marriage for love and marriage for money. Formator/Alanthus, the male character, ostensibly "reforms" the coquette heroine Amoranda into a happy bride-to-be. The novel's subtext, however, suggests that a reformed coquette is a woman whose will, voice, and financial power have been expunged.

Mary Davys (1674-1732) came to England from Ireland as a young widow, wrote six novels to earn a living, and ran a coffeehouse in Cambridge.[3] When *TRC* was published, subscribers included John Gay, Martha Blount, and Alexander Pope as well as many members of the nobility, no doubt because her husband had been a subordinate of Jonathan Swift's. The novel's dedication to the "Ladies of Great Britain" speaks of "expunging" the "Blots" of vanity and levity in young women: "If I have touch'd a young Lady's Vanity and Levity, it was to show her how amiable she is without those Blots, which certainly stain the Mind and stamp Deformity where the greatest Beauties would shine, were they banish'd" (v). In fact, the heroine loses her vanity and levity only at the cost of her will and self-expression. Consequently the novel reveals that when women marry, they lose their property, and so their ability to act independently, and that men require this loss as a condition of marriage.

Davys herself, however, is an unreformed coquette, one whose ink deceives the reader most pleasurably. In her preface, Davys admits the same vanity she expunges in her heroine: "She who has the assurance to write, certainly has the vanity of expecting to be read . . ." (iv). Davys's vanity and pride—"Only I am accountable for every Fault of my Book; and if it has any Beauties, I claim the Merit of them, too" (xi)—contrast not only with the modesty prescribed by conduct books, but with the modesty her own heroine must learn. The author, like the coquette, transgresses notions of the feminine by her will to power.[4]

In keeping with the other entertainments mentioned in the preface, "Masquerades, Operas, New Plays, Conjurers, Monsters, and feign'd Devils" (iv), the novel depends on deceptions worked on the heroine and reader to provide narrative tension and suspense. Its romance elements—disguise, cross dressing, and coincidence—also provide the key to recognizing the suppressed other story. These narrative deceptions betray the patriarchally approved project of reform. As Mary Jacobus has shown in her reading of *Villette*, "the relationship between [gothicism and realism] points to what the novel cannot say about itself—to the real conditions of its literary possibility" (54). In *TRC* the relationship between romance and realism has a similar function. The romance elements of *TRC* undermine the realistic reform plot, the one that Mary Anne Schofield thinks "forthrightly traces a woman's . . . journey of self-identity." What *TRC* cannot say about itself is that reforming coquettes is a sham, and that such a project is as impossible as constructing fiction that mirrors the world.

Fictional construction of character entails having the character appear to make choices which propel the plot. The character must seem to be making the choice freely, which hides the fact that the author drives the plot; this promotes the novel as a believable world. When the events seem arbitrary, that is, not deriving from the consciousness of the characters, we call the novel "implausible" and dismiss the fiction-making abilities of its author, as has been the case to some extent with *Moll Flanders* and *Pamela*.[5]

Romance, a form that both antedates the novel and is absorbed by it, is not held to the same standard of plausibility as the novel. Coincidence and disguise are traditional elements of romance; although these figure importantly as late as the mid-nineteenth century in the work of novelists like Charlotte Bronte, later in the nineteenth century, novelists, in general, relied less on coincidences of plot than construction of character to make their novels interesting. Novels that contain romance elements are often criticized for their differences from realism. Fielding and Richardson, like Henry James one hundred years later, battle romance in an effort to endow their works with "manly" realism. Romance and women, Laurie Langbauer argues, are "yoked together" as part of a system that privileges men and the novel, though ultimately even the latter terms are undermined by problems of definition and identity. Mary Davys's use of romance facilitates cracking the smooth surface of representation.

Eliminating the "vices" of dissimulation and vanity curtails a woman's self-expression, independence, and creativity, but Davys goes even further, suggesting that "reform" expunges the subjectivity of the coquette, turning her into a transparent object "readable" by the man who controls her. This process is at odds with Davys's project of creating characters: once the coquette is reformed, she loses the mechanisms that make her a believable, rounded character. She is no longer able to think, speak, or act for herself. When the "blots" represented by her coquetry are removed, they do not reveal "truth" or a "genuine" woman; rather they leave a question. Thus Mary Davys represents reform as requiring the silence and disappearance of women.

TRC is a courtship novel in which the heroine Amoranda's fate does not stem from her actions, and in which she shrinks instead of grows. The narrator advises "chusing a Man with fine Sense, as well as a fine Wigg" (viii), but Amoranda is faced with only unsavory choices (men who want her for her money) that she recognizes as such.

When her uncle appoints the white-bearded Formator as her guardian, he is also giving this man—merely disguised as old, in reality the young Alanthus and suitor for Amoranda's hand—a chance to watch her and "re-form" her into a good wife—a docile and quiet one.

> Her Heart was like a great Inn, which finds room for all that come, and she could not but think it very foolish to be belov'd by five hundred, and return it only to one; she found herself inclin'd to please them all, and took no small pains to do so; yet had she been brought to the Test, and forc'd to chuse a Husband among them, her particular Inclinations were so very weak, that she would have been at the greater loss where to fix, tho' her general Favors gave every Man hopes, because she artfully hid from one what she bestow'd upon another. (18)

Davys exposes the contradiction of chastising a woman for pleasing men while asking her to please them in a more modest and self-effacing way.[6] Amoranda bides her time, during her period of power, because there's no man worth forsaking it. "Hiding her general Favors" increases her power over her suitors because they might presume that she intends to marry them, but Davys suggests that Amoranda's wit and her situation as a marriageable girl inevitably produce "coquetry": If a woman talks and she has suitors, then she will talk to them, and thus be labeled a coquette.

Another way to assess Davys's relationship to the project of reforming women is to ask if Formator really "forms" Amoranda. In fact, Amoranda "reforms" the instant he appears—not much of a process. Immediately allowing Formator to replace her own judgment, Amoranda does not rationally come to recognize it as superior, as Austen's Emma does Knightly's for example. The very day of Formator's arrival, she concedes, "I am no longer my own mistress, but am now to live under your restrictions" (33). She admits, "we foolish Girls are not to be trusted with ourselves, and [Formator] has taught me to believe we are the worst Guardians we can possibly have" (97). Despite his name, Formator doesn't form the grown Amoranda so much as simply prevent her inheritance from being seized by another man because Formator's own "eyes [are] always open to [her] actions" (91); he allows Amoranda to be abducted, and then rescues her from being raped in the nick of time. This has ominous overtones for her impending marriage to him, positing marriage as a regression to childhood.

Wit makes Amoranda an appealing heroine, giving her what readers perceive as "personality." For example, she receives a rake by saying,

> how are we to construe those early Sallies of yours? Not to love, I suppose; because Congreve tells us, "A contemplative Lover can no more leave his Bed in the morning, than he can sleep in it." (13)

She begins with a provocative question, answers it herself, and quotes Restoration comedy instead of the Bible—all transgressive verbal acts. Amoranda's awareness of sex, revealed by her teasing, gives Lofty the "courage" (13) to renew his conquest. She "errs" by taking a light tone and *by discussing love,* as suggested by La Rochefoucauld's maxim #418: "Young women who don't want to seem like coquettes and old men who don't want to seem ridiculous should never discuss love as something they are capable of." Even if women *are* innocent, they must make sure they *seem* that way, a prescription that points to the paradox of conduct literature which simultaneously claims to see through women and warns against deception.

Amoranda's precarious period of freedom is the result of her being cut loose from parental authority; Nancy K. Miller points out in *The Heroine's Text* that the novel defined heroines by their sexual vulnerability. In her fifteenth year, a "finish'd beauty and coquet" (9), Amoranda becomes an orphan. However, Amoranda is also an heiress, making her "prey to every designing Rascal" (25). During the early eighteenth century, parental consent was not necessary for marriage, and children could block the arranged marriage preferred by their parents by revealing evidence of a secret precontract. It was easy to get married, as neither the church nor state kept records (the 1604 canons which required the announcing of banns were not enforced). In addition to the ease of marriage, children's inheritance was protected by the notion of "strict settlement," which reduced the arbitrary control of the father to distribute his wealth. Thus, property holders were especially perturbed by the ability of their daughters to pass on family property to men of lesser fortune or social standing.

Amoranda's "Uncle Traffick" understands her vulnerability but prefers to remain in London to see to his (other) investments.[7] The book's central joke is that Uncle Traffick chooses a surrogate guardian, bearded old Formator, who is really young Lord Alanthus, the man her uncle has chosen as Amoranda's husband. Perhaps an eighteenth-century reader heard repetitions of the word "old" describing Formator as a stage whisper calling attention to itself, but I, for one, was as fooled as Amoranda—though for not quite as long. The implausible situation works as a plot device because, rather than being asked to suspend belief, the reader is not even caused to doubt it until the last third when Alanthus is introduced. The only evidence that Formator is Alanthus consists of a reference to "his veins filling with young blood" (38) and the coincidence that the two men are never in the same place at the same time.

Davys's trick is an example of reader entrapment, a strategy especially favored by Swift and Behn.[8] While irony divides the audience—some know the "truth," others do not—reader entrapment works on everyone. All novels can be said to entrap their readers in fictional worlds, but in *TRC,* disguised identity makes the reader question what constitutes identity in the first place. Davys has Formator play his role so well that no one guesses it is a role, one which situates fiancés and husbands as women's guardians. However, because readers figure out the trick sooner than Amoranda (154), they also participate in the scurrilous pleasure of fooling Amoranda.[9] Therefore, Davys's use of a grand deception to cure Amoranda of deception might also suggest Davys's skepticism about reform.

Introducing Amoranda to a suitor this way is like the parental maneuver: never tell a child she's eating liver until she admits that she likes it. The irony, of course, is that Amoranda falls in love with dashing Lord Alanthus, a Marquis, self-described as "a Man of Worth, of Wealth, of Quality" (145) rather than plodding old Formator. Alanthus is an appropriate husband for an heiress and daughter of a baronet; in fact, Amoranda "trades up" because a marquis is three notches above a baronet. Davys supports class distinctions, in keeping with her Tory affiliations. (Her husband was headmaster of a school attached to St. Patrick's Cathedral in Dublin.) Further evidence for her Tory views, along with her subscription list, is her metaphor for Amoranda's period without a guardian as an unruly "interregnum" ended by Formator's "reign." Davys supports nobility even to the point of recuperating Lord Lofty simply because he is a Peer (his rank is not specified). Two other suitors, Callid and Froth, are "vermin"—the word Swift uses to describe the rising class—partly because they lack titles and land.

That Amoranda "waits" to fall in love with Alanthus instead of Formator also suggests writers' and readers' expectations for romance novels. By the time of Inchbald's *A Simple Story* (1791) and Austen's *Emma* (1816), a heroine falling in love with a much older man was something for readers to take seriously. Conversely, a clue that in this period's novels young women rarely fell in love with old men is embedded in Alanthus's comment to Amoranda's cousin: "I believe you are the first Woman under Thirty that ever fell in love with a grey Beard" (165). However, although Amoranda's falling in love with the suitor who is appropriate in class and age signals Davys's adherence to convention, Davys's creation of Alanthus as hero and prig is more open to question, and more potentially subversive.

"Prig" was a synonym for coxcomb, a man who paid too much attention to dress, but it also referred to someone who applied the letter of religious law too precisely. Prigs and coxcombs, like prudes and coquettes, share an attention to surfaces, to the appearance of morality, and to the appearance of its absence. This attention to surfaces interrogates the boundaries between interiors and exteriors, and between the genuine and the artificial, making the reader aware that such distinctions are constructed rather than essential. Lord Lofty calls Formator "a queer old prig" (42), and Formator's own statements lead the

reader to agree. For instance, he "inveighs against an immoderate Love of Pleasure," adding, "I call everything Pleasure that pleases us" (35). Most important, the narrator's stated aim of pleasing her readers (1) rebuts Formator's disapproval of pleasure, but the novel gives other, mixed signals as to whether Davys uses Formator as her spokesman or holds him up as an ironic figure. The controversy of recent readings of Fanny Burney and Hannah Webster Foster also applies to Davys's novel: the male prig and guardian becomes a litmus test of critics' interpretations. Those who believe that Davys resists patriarchy see Formator as an ironical construct; others insist that he is the author's spokesman, advising proper behavior. Davys gives both sides ample ammunition. The prig makes a useful nod to patriarchy, satisfying readers who expect the novel to affirm the status quo. The narrator's rare speeches from the pulpit side with Formator, but the more subtle and also more frequent notes sound an ironic tone.[10]

Amoranda's willingness to hand over responsibility for herself and her actions to Formator is a regression to childhood. Ironically, at nine, she "thrusts [a boy] from her with the utmost Contempt," raging, "I scorn the unmannerly Brat, he shall never be my Spouse!" (7). Instead of educating Amoranda—imparting knowledge and skill—Formator takes away knowledge and skill. The two passages (53) which actually refer to reform are silent as to the nature of Formator's improvements:

> His constant care was to divert her from all the Follies of Life, and as she had a Soul capable of Improvement, and a flexible good Temper to be dealt with, he made no doubt but one day he should see her the most accomplish'd of her Sex: in order to which, he provided a choice Collection of Books for her, spent most of his time with her, diverted her with a thousand pleasant Stories, possibly of his own making, and every moment was lost to Formator, that was not spent with Amoranda. (53)

The sentence structure—he provided books, spent time—makes Amoranda into a passive recipient, but we don't see evidence of "improvement," anything like, for instance, a reference as specific as the earlier mention of Congreve. Note also that Formator tells "stories *possibly* of his own making"; the element of doubt suggests that his stories contrast unfavorably with the very story we are reading. Unlike Formator, Davys *is* "accountable for every Fault [and] . . . Beauty" (xi) of her book. The focus on Formator suggests that Davys is politically unwilling rather than narratologically unable to show us Amoranda's process of reform.

> Formator had, by daily application, endeavor'd to form Amoranda's mind to his own liking; he try'd to bring her to a true Taste of that Behavior, which makes every Woman agreeable to every Man of Sense. A Man, *said he,* of true Judgment and a good Understanding, has the greatest Contempt in the World, for one of those

Creatures commonly call'd a Coquet. (94-95)

The contradiction between forming Amoranda "to his own liking" and the standardization implied in "which makes every Woman agreeable to every Man of Sense" is sarcastic. Similarly, the echo of "true" suggests the opposite. Formator's reference to his "true Judgment" indicates his hubris in thinking that he can raise a woman's character or vindicate her conduct. While the passage expends considerable detail on the "before" stage—coquetry, fire, spirit—and on the "Man of Sense," it is silent as to the admirable lady's character because the project of reforming Amoranda in fact erases her character.

Davys posits Formator as an avatar of truth, but his very position in Amoranda's life is based on deceit. His young male virility hidden under a beard—the only evidence of his age—leads to a twofold tension: (1) (when) will he be exposed? and (2) will he take advantage of his disguise by some impropriety? Davys deals with the latter possibility by making Formator a prig, who, once revealed, tells Amoranda, "I hope you remember what a long time of self-denial I have had, and that during Formator's Reign, I never durst so much as touch your Hand" (170). Still, his mental toying with Amoranda is another sort of impropriety—she is denied knowledge of his motives which might cause her to act differently. He justifies his disguise by saying, "I thought you would be more open and free, in declaring your real Sentiments of every thing to me" (159), but his concealment of known motive constitutes a kind of mental rape. If Amoranda at the beginning of the novel concealed her suitors from each other in order to prolong her period of power, Formator conceals his status as suitor for the same reason: in fact, though he's a coquet too, Amoranda is the one that's "re-formed." The difference is that Formator's power is institutionalized, accorded to him by virtue of his gender and rank by Uncle Traffick, a fact that highlights marriage as a system of kinship between men.

Davys's use of disguise and cross dressing, a standard feature of drama and a convention of romance, also reveals the novel's relation to patriarchal ideology. The deceptions practiced on Amoranda by men are far greater than the deceptions she practices, interesting in light of the fact that it is women (coquettes) who are supposed to be masters of artifice. The protean power of disguise is accorded to men in the novel, while Amoranda is made transparent and readable. Moreover, she is denied the access to information that would enable her to exercise choice. The reader shares in reading Amoranda, while Uncle Traffick and Formator as purveyors of "truth" and "right" remain disguised. In fact, Uncle Traffick, having fueled the major deception, appears only briefly at the end.

Like Formator's beard, instances of disguise in the novel hide male power so that it can work more efficiently. Men disguise themselves in order to abduct Amoranda, and their disguise increases the reader's titillation. Men who adopt women's clothes in **The Reform'd Coquet** do not diminish their power, but rather they increase it, because their superior strength is hidden. Although Amoranda plans to foil Callid and Froth's plot to "gagg" and abduct her (23) by substituting "two sturdy Footmen" for herself and her maid, Formator ends up "personating" Amoranda during the scheme, claiming the right to act simultaneously as her and as himself, as he would were he her husband. The disguise helps him exact physical vengeance against the two "Vermin," but it is also part of Formator's erasure of Amoranda. He not only speaks and acts *for her,* he speaks and acts *as her.* As Shoshana Felman points out, this kind of appropriation is especially pernicious because speaking from "the place of the Other" is never possible (4). The power of males to disguise themselves physically in the novel is ancillary to their power to disguise their motives, as acknowledged by Biranthus, who "resolves to disguise his Mind as well as his Body" (109) in yet another attempt to abduct Amoranda.

Except for Amoranda, female characters can also disguise themselves: Altemira pretends to be Amoranda to marry Lofty; Arentia pretends to be Amoranda's friend to help abduct her. According to La Bruyèe, the worst kind of deception practiced by a woman is not the masquerade, where her wish is to "conceal her personality and remain unknown," but rather, the cases "where a woman pretends to pass for what she seems to be" (35). The distinction, then, is the subtlety of the disguise and consequently its chances of success. In allowing other female characters to assume disguises, Davys points to the heroine's singular position as the object of reform. Amoranda is the only major character who does not disguise herself—because her suitability as a wife for Alanthus depends on her transparency, on her being what she seems to be.

Usually, when a woman dresses as a man, it is to gain the power, authority, and freedom of—and from—men. But the only woman who dresses as a man in *TRC* is so weak that she has no power, despite her masculine attire: she is "a poor, thin, pale meagre young Creature, hardly able to sit his Horse, who look'd as if he wanted a Doctor more than a Mistress" (55). In other words, the male disguise doesn't work; it doesn't imbue Altemira, who comes to warn Amoranda about Lofty, with male virility. Presumably it does protect her from the world that has already harmed her. If a woman is ruined like Altemira, then there's no harm in her disguise, because her virginity, her "true self" is gone. Altemira takes on the appearance of Amoranda's virginity and wealth to trick Lord Lofty into marriage, and the disguise works, suggesting that a "righteous" deception can correct a previous one. This recalls the moral paradox of the bed trick in *All's Well That Ends Well* that "wicked meaning in a lawful deed / and lawful meaning in a lawful act, / where both not sin, and yet a sinful fact" (V,iii,307-8). The Shakespeare play also questions women's power to choose marriage partners, and in both scenarios, it is women who concoct deceptive schemes to correct the infamy of men.

However, while in Shakespeare the bed trick implies the interchangeability of sexual partners, in *TRC* the trick implies that one wife is as good as another. When women marry, they lose their subjectivity, and men demand this loss as a condition of marriage. Once Lofty is forced into marriage, his only concern is marrying someone with money. Women impersonating each other cannot change their shared vulnerability. Like that of the Shakespeare play, Altemira's "happy ending" is tainted. The narrator struggles to justify why Lofty accepts being duped, calling him a "man of Honour at last," but is silent about why Altemira wants to marry someone who has betrayed her. Lofty's recuperation stems partly from his wealth and standing, judging from the admiring reference to his "whole Equipage" (90) and house. But the gap around Altemira's motive indicates how completely marriage was taken for granted as a woman's high-est goal. Davys's readers would have understood that being married to a scoundrel is better than being single and having 10,000 pounds. Amoranda's incapacity for disguise distinguishes her from Shakespearean heroines such as Portia, or from Rosalind who, though initially disguised for safety, opportunistically uses it to extract Orlando's feelings about her from him—much in the way that Formator manipulates Amoranda. Neither do disguise and cross dressing in *TRC* represent the freedom offered by eighteenth-century carnivals and masquerades, which in literature, as Terry Castle has shown, take on a "symbolic role as the exemplary site of mutability, incongruity, and mystery . . . a liberating escape from the status quo" (903-4). Rather, the isolated country of *TRC* helps restrict Amoranda's access to men.

I have argued that cross dressing underscores gender roles in Davys's novel because the viewer always knows the "real gender" underneath the clothes and because narrative suspense centers on the moment of revelation.[11] However, Marjorie Garber argues that cross dressing also always reveals the constructedness of gender: everyone's in drag. In fact, the "third space of representation," the space of the transvestite (Garber 356), is also the space of the novel. Amoranda's virginity prevents her from deceiving or telling stories, but the widow, who has neither the burden of virginity nor the invisibility of the married woman, can trick the readers of her novel. In order to write a novel or invent a persona one has to know enough to be believed—to be plausible. Cross dressing likewise rests on knowledge of how gender is constructed. To be believed as an author, Davys must reflect the patriarchal ideology of reforming coquettes, yet she simultaneously undermines it.

In contrast to Davys's covert authority, Formator's fund of information rests on a base of male privilege accorded to him by Uncle Traffick. He knows "all about" Amoranda, and in addition, he trusts his powers of observation while at the same time demanding that Amoranda not rely on hers. If the "debauch'd wicked age" (80) increases a young woman's fear, the result is not her developing shrewdness and strength, but rather her resorting to her male guardian. Thus, when faced with a man dressed as a woman, Amoranda cannot recognize him. Or when fire threatens the house, Amoranda "durst do nothing without Formator" (55).

Other instances of violence and horror in the novel show Davys to be as much a successor of Aphra Behn as a forerunner of Jane Austen. A violent world lurks right outside the guarded woman's door: not only are Callid and Froth badly beaten in the summer house by Formator and the servant, but they kill each other afterward (52). Arentia, the friend of Amoranda who betrays her, is stung by an adder and dies (113). The servants who betray Amoranda on the barge are manacled and sent to jail. Biranthus is "run quite thro' the body" (116). A fire burns the stables and kills all the horses (154). However, linking the novel's violence only to gender would be reductive. Jerry Beasley has argued that this era's alignment of feminine virtue in a rotten and violent world should be seen as a reflection of the political corruption rampant under the administration of Robert Walpole. Davys's Tory affiliations position the novel as a critique of this political corruption.

If men know more than women, they also take pleasure in so doing. Formator/Alanthus rubs in his superiority. For example, rescuing Amoranda from rape, his first words to her are, "I presume, Madam, you are some self-willed, head-strong Lady, who resolv'd to follow your own Intentions, have left the Care of a tender Father, to ramble with you know not who" (114). His greater knowledge "teaches her a lesson" but the lesson is cruel indeed—not only are women hindered from access to information, but they will be the brunt of jokes because of their ignorance.

Only men have access to information; when women try to usurp them, they are punished, as we see when Amoranda tries to withhold the fact that she has met Alanthus's sister. Formator displays one-up-manship in responding, "but, Madam, as you have found out one Secret, I must tell you another: your Uncle, before I left him, had provided a Husband for you" (145). He exploits her distress until a page later when he reveals that her uncle's choice is Alanthus. Amoranda is also infantilized by being placed in situations where physical violence is required. Scenarios which stress women's physical weakness, a stock feature of the period, highlight the fact that women's bodies are not "enough" to protect them; in fact their bodies are the cause of their insecurity. As Amoranda laments during her brush with abduction, "Why has Nature denied us Strength to revenge our own Wrongs?" (111). In light of the fact that Davys and many other women (Aphra Behn comes to mind) could and did take care of themselves, the novel here points to patriarchal ideology's construction of the female gender as weak. Not nature, but society prevents a woman from carrying a sword, which is what Alanthus uses to save Amoranda.

Amoranda loses the ability to think for herself and act independently, making her only recourse doglike fidelity and duty, even when they offer conflicting avenues. Faced with the possibility that Alanthus may not be the choice of her uncle, Amoranda proclaims, "I will die to oblige my dearest Uncle, but I cannot cease to love Alanthus" (145). Her coquetry has been "reformed" by loving one man only until death, but her malleability to the designs of her guardian eclipses even love; she'll either marry or die. Davys suggests they amount to the same thing. Like Alanthus's sister who says "there is not one Circumstance of my Life worth Knowing" (136), the Countess in *The Female Quixote,* and Lady O'Leary in *Camilla,* a married woman must be so untalked about and so silent herself that she virtually disappears. Characters who achieve this state become extremely minor characters by necessity, footnotes of a sort. Heroines who achieve this state lose what made them heroines in the first place, the reader's perception of them as thinking persons.

Formator relishes his power over Amoranda, "leering" and "laughing" at her ignorance (130). If we recall that in the preface Davys mentions having shown a draft of her novel to "young gentlemen" in Cambridge for their approval, we might well read Formator's mocking superiority under the light of Davys's position as a relatively unlettered woman author. Women's lack of access to the source of male learning—the university—lasts well into the twentieth century, as Virginia Woolf laments in *A Room of One's Own.*

If, as J. Paul Hunter suggests, "novels are an easy place . . . to sort out the ways of the world, to crack the code of adulthood and social expectation" (92), then what might have the young woman reader of *TRC* sorted out? Certainly a grim portent of what it means to be a *feme covert,* for whom a husband thinks, speaks, and acts. She might also have learned that marriage to an autocratic and mean-spirited prig like Alanthus would mean being dominated to the point where she is unsure of her own desires. Finally, she might have understood that information about the world is denied her in a myriad of ways, causing her to turn to more novels. At that point she might have realized that while men disguise themselves in order to dominate her, she had open to her at least one disguise of her own—that of writing.

Women's "art"—their manipulativeness, deceit, opaqueness—is an age-old reason for disciplining them. But these "faults" also represent the difficulty of language in general, the human desire for transparency in a medium that thwarts this desire. By reinscribing the dynamic coquette figure in their novels, women writers like Davys produced plots whose implausibilities tell us about the conditions of their own writing lives. By its gaps, fissures, incomplete resolutions, and contradictions, *TRC* acknowledges differences between the coquette and the woman writer. The novel opposes the writer of the preface—who has "vanity" and the "assurance of being read"—with the silenced protagonist, a contradiction that highlights both the dilemma of the marriageable female and the hubris of the woman writer. Davys, as a widow writing for money, had a freedom that her character Amoranda does not, a difference surely not lost on her readers. Davys's art produced a body of work while Amoranda's body *is* her art; one endures, the other cannot.

Notes

[1] In France the masculine form, "coquet," was rarely used and short lived. In England "coquet" was used to refer to both sexes, though to men only rarely and only until about 1700; the feminine ending "ette" became common after 1750.

[2] Schultz also mentions the "reform" plot.

[3] The two articles devoted to Davys have recovery of her work as their aim. McBurney stresses that her tone antedates that of Fielding, and more recently, Kern "examines her fiction in order to reassess her as an early novelist of manners" (30). In addition, Schofield provides summaries of her novels.

[4] Poovey treats the paradox of authorship for the eighteenth-century woman.

[5] Miller's "Emphasis Added" reads *The Princess of Cleves* against its critics' notions of what is "plausible" for women's lives.

[6] Spacks argues that "Heart" should be read as code for "sex" in this era.

[7] His name refers to the Augustan era's financial revolution, with its development of credit, stocks, and speculation. Davys takes a satirical view of these developments, implicitly disparaging also the Abolition of Feudal Tenure (1646, 1656, 1661), which meant that land could be bought, sold, and mortgaged. Amoranda's grandfather, whose "vicious inclinations led him into a thousand Extravagancies . . . whoring . . . drinking . . . and gaming" (3), dies a beggar, having mortgaged his land. However, it is Uncle Traffick, through his East Indian investments, who repurchases the land and restores the elder brother to wealth. *The Reform'd Coquet* points to marriage as a system of kinship between men and a traffic *in* women. See Rubin for a classic study of the way kin-ship ties between men make women the objects of commerce.

[8] See Kropf.

[9] Formator also fools Amoranda's cousin Maria, a woman "past her first Spring," who is attracted to him and sorely disappointed when he turns out to be Alanthus.

[10] Kern leans in this direction: "Thus with an act or word Davys undermines the stuffiness and didacticism of her presumably good heroes" (33).

[11] For an essay which argues that cross dressing in Shakespeare supports patriarchal ideology, see Howard. See also Kuhn.

Works Cited

Austen, Jane. *Emma.* (1816). New York: Norton, 1972.

Backscheider, Paula. "Women's Influence." *Studies in the Novel* 11 (1979): 3-22.

Beasley, Jerry C. "Politics and Moral Idealism: The Achievement of Some Early Women Novelists." In *Fetter'd or Free: British Women Novelists 1670-1815.* Ed. Mary Anne Schofield and Cecilia Macheski. Athens, OH: Ohio UP, 1986.
Burney, Fanny. *Camilla.* (1796). Oxford: Oxford UP, 1972.

Castle, Terry. "The Carnivalization of Eighteenth-Century English Narrative." *PMLA* 99 (1984): 903-16.

Davys, Mary. *The Reform'd Coquet.* (reprint of 1724 edition). New York: Garland, 1973.

Felman, Shoshana. "Women and Madness: The Critical Phallacy." *Diacritics* 5.4 (Winter 1975): 2-10.

Garber, Marjorie. *Vested Interests: Cross Dressing and Cultural Anxiety.* New York: Routledge, 1992.

Howard, Jean E. "Crossdressing, The Theatre, and Gender Struggle in Early Modern England." *Shakespeare Quarterly* 39 (1988): 418-40.

Hunter, J. Paul. *Before Novels.* New York: Norton, 1990.

Inchbald, Elizabeth. *A Simple Story.* Oxford: Oxford UP, 1967.

Kern, Jean B. "Mrs. Mary Davys as a Novelist of Manners." *Essays in Literature* 10 (1983): 29-38.

Kropf, Carl R., ed. *Reader Entrapment in Eighteenth-Century Literature.* New York: AMS Press, 1992.

Kuhn, Annette. *The Power of the Image: Essays in Representation and Sexuality.* London: Routledge, 1985.
Langbauer, Laurie. *Women and Romance: The Consolations of Gender in the English Novel.* Ithaca: Cornell UP, 1990.

La Rouchefoucauld, François. *Maximes.* (1678 edition) Paris: Editions Garnier, 1967. (Translations in the text are mine.)

Lennox, Charlotte. *The Female Quixote.* (1752). Oxford: Oxford UP, 1970.

McBurney, William H. "Mrs. Mary Davys: Forerunner of Fielding." *PMLA* 74 (1959): 348-55.

Miller, Nancy K. *The Heroine's Text.* New York: Columbia UP, 1980.

————. "Emphasis Added: Plots and Plausibilities in Women's Fiction." *PMLA* 96 (1981): 35-48.

Poovey, Mary. *The Proper Lady and the Woman Writer: Ideology as Style in the Works of Mary Wollstonecraft, Mary Shelley, and Jane Austen.* Chicago: U of Chicago P, 1984.

Rubin, Gayle. "The Traffic in Women: Notes on the 'Political Economy' of Sex." *Toward an Anthropology of Women.* Ed. Rayna R. Reiter. New York: Monthly Review P, 1975.

Schofield, Mary Anne. *Masking and Unmasking the Female Mind.* Newark: U of Delaware P, 1990.

Schulz, Dieter. "The Coquette's Progress from Satire to Sentimental Novel." *Literatur in Wissenschaft* 6 (1973): 77-87.

Spacks, Patricia Meyer. "Every Woman is at Heart a Rake." *Eighteenth Century Studies* 8 (1974-75): 27-46.

FURTHER READING

Ballaster, Ros. *Seductive Forms: Women's Amatory Fiction from 1684 to 1740.* Oxford: Clarendon Press, 1992, 225 p.
> Critical study of the role of female reader and writers in the development of the eighteenth-century novel.

Beasley, Jerry C. *Novels of the 1740s.* Athens: University of Georgia Press, 1982, 238 p.
> Detailed study of the novel form in the mid eighteenth-century, with several references to Davys.

Davis, Lennard J. *Factual Fictions: The Origins of the English Novel.* New York: Columbia University Press, 1983, 245 p.
> Comprehensive analysis of the development of the English novel. Scattered references place Davys as a transitional figure.

Day, Robert Adams. *Told in Letters: Epistolary Fiction Before Richardson.* Ann Arbor: University of Michigan Press, 1966, 273 p.
> Study of the popular genre and its relation to the novel with a discussion of Davys' *Familiar Letters.*

Greider, Josephine. Introduction to *The Reform'd Coquet* and *Familiar Letters* by Mary Davys and *The Mercenary Lover* by Eliza Haywood (reprint). New York: Garland Publishing, 1973.
> Overview and comparison of the three works.

McBurney, William H. *Four Before Richardson: Selected English Novels 1720-1727.* Lincoln: University of Nebraska Press, 1963, 373 p.
> Contains an edition of Davys' *The Accomplish'd Rake,* with Introduction and Davys' commentary on the work.

————. "Mrs. Mary Davys: Forerunner of Fielding" *PMLA* 74 (4) part 1, September 1959, 348-355.
> Argues that Davys' work was a forerunner to and an influence upon Fielding's fiction, with its light, comic tone.

McLaren, Juliet. "Presumptuous Poetess, Pen-Feathered Muse: The Comedies of Mary Pix." in *Gender at Work: Four Women Writers of the Eighteenth Century.* Detroit: Wayne State University Press, 1990.
> Compares Davys to Pix and suggests influence of Pix on Davys.

Schofield, Mary Anne and Macheski, Cecelia. *Fetter'd or Free? British Women Novelists, 1670-1815.* Athens: Ohio University Press. 1986.
> Collection of essays on the development of women's fiction; several of the essays discuss Davys' work as examples.

Spacks, Patricia Meyer. "Ev'ry Woman is at Heart A Rake" *Eighteenth-Century Studies 8 (1),* Fall 1974, 27-46
> Discusses gender relations in the eighteenth century with Davys' *Familiar Letters* as an example of women's ambivalence about love and marriage.

Turner, Cheryl. *Living by the Pen: Women Writers in the Eighteenth Century.* New York: Routledge, 1992.
> Compares Davys success as a businesswoman with her limited earnings as a writer.

Williamson, Marylin. *Raising Their Voices: British Women Writers 1650-1750.* Detroit: Wayne State University Press, 1990.
> Includes discussion of Davys's novels.

Additional coverage of Davys's live and works is contained in the following sources published by The Gale Group: *Literature Criticism 1400-1800*, Vol. 1, and *Dictionary of Literary Biography*, Vol. 39.

Henry Fielding

1701-1754

(Also used pseudonyms of Conny Keyber and Scriblerus Secundus) English novelist, dramatist, essayist, journalist, and poet.

INTRODUCTION

Fielding is often considered one of the most significant contributors to the development of the English novel. His nearly seamless incorporation of drama, satire, romance, and epic into his works helped distinguish the novel as a new and unique genre quite distinct from its early influences. Fielding's long and bitter feud with rival novelist Samuel Richardson also contributed to the development of the novel form: opposed to the didactic tone and unrealistic characters and situations of his contemporaries, Fielding infused the novel with compassion, comedy, and a heightened sense of realism. Although Fielding's lasting reputation rests on his major novels, he was also a popular and important playwright, an influential journalist, and one of England's leading judicial reformers. In all of his writing, Fielding demonstrated a concern with social and moral hypocrisy, attacking not only Richardson but also dramatist and Poet Laureate Colley Cibber and Prime Minister Robert Walpole for what he considered their failure to deal openly with serious social issues, whether in literary works or as a government official.

Biographical Information

Fielding was born in Somersetshire to aristocratic parents. He had three sisters, including the novelist Sarah Fielding, whose first novel, *The Adventures of David Simple,* appeared while she lived with his family. He was educated at Eton, from which he graduated in 1725. Afterwards he moved to London and began a career as a playwright. His first effort, *Love in Several Masques,* was produced in 1728, and during the next nine years over twenty of his plays were performed. These burlesques and farces, which met with great success, satirize various literary, social, and political trends and figures. In 1734 Fielding married Charlotte Cradock, who later served as the model for the heroines of *Tom Jones* (1749) and *Amelia* (1751). A year or two after his marriage, Fielding became the manager and chief playwright of the Little Haymarket Theatre; some of his noted plays from this period of his career include *Tom Thumb* (1730) and *The Grub-Street Opera* (1731). His career as a playwright ended abruptly after two of his political satires, *Pasquin* (1736) and *The Historical Register for the Year 1736* (1737) induced Prime Minister Robert Walpole to impose the Licensing Act, an ordinance that allowed government censorship of the stage, on the Little Haymarket. Fielding then studied law at the Middle Temple and became a lawyer in 1740. According to biographers, he was an honest lawyer with a solid but modest practice. To supplement his income, Fielding wrote and edited several periodicals, including *The True Patriot* and *The Covent-Garden Journal.* Shortly thereafter he published his first satire, *An Apology for the Life of Mrs. Shamela Andrews* (1741), under the name of Conny Keyber; in it he parodied both the popular Richardson novel *Pamela; or Virtue Rewarded* and the autobiography of his theatrical rival, *An Apology for the Life of Mr. Colley Cibber.* The book was a sort of preview for Fielding's first novel, *The History of the Adventures of*

Joseph Andrews, which appeared a year later. Fielding published a variety of *Miscellanies,* including the satire *Jonathan Wild,* in the next few years which were distinguished more by professional achievement and personal tragedy than by his creative output. In 1744 his wife Charlotte died; he caused a scandal in 1747 by marrying her maid, Mary Daniel. In 1748 he was appointed a London magistrate and as a justice of the peace for Westminster. During this time he wrote several essays on criminal justice and social reform, including *An Enquiry into the Causes of the Late Increase of Robbers* and *A Proposal for Making an Effectual Provision for the Poor;* his legal experience may also have provided source material for prison and trial scenes in *Tom Jones.* Shortly after he completed his final novel, *Amelia,* in 1751, Fielding became seriously ill. He resigned his judicial posts and traveled to Portugal to recover. He recorded the details of his journey in *The Journal of a Voyage to Lisbon* (published posthumously in 1755) before dying in 1754.

Major Works

The extreme topicality of most of Fielding's essays and dramatic works made most of them seem dated rather quickly. As a result, his novels *Joseph Andrews, Tom Jones,* and *Amelia* are generally considered his major works. In contrast to *Shamela,* his parody of the self-centered virtue of the heroine of Richardson's novel *Pamela, Joseph Andrews* is a full-fledged novel of manners that did not directly parody the plot and characters of Pamela, but which attacked Richardson's sanctimonious values and sentiments. Andrews is introduced as Pamela's brother, and, like Richardson's heroine, he is determined to remain chaste until marriage. But where Fielding saw Pamela's virtue as a facade calculated to advance her social standing, he portrays Joseph's as sincere, founded on Christian ethics rather than social mores. In *Joseph Andrews,* Fielding advanced one of the first theories of the English novel, distinguishing it from the pastoral romances and epic poems which had been its major influences. His second novel, however, is generally considered to be his greatest achievement. *The History of Tom Jones, a Foundling,* is often called the quintessential comic novel. This work is renowned for its artistic unity, memorable characters, and vivid portrayal of life in the eighteenth century. The book chronicles the adventures of a well-intentioned but imprudent orphan, Tom Jones, after he is banished from his kind but misguided guardian's estate. Throughout the novel, Tom pursues his beloved Sophia, the daughter of the memorable Squire Western, who owns the neighboring estate. As in *Joseph Andrews,* a number of interpolated episodes thread through the main narrative, but in *Tom Jones* Fielding succeeds in integrating these stories into the main plot, contributing to a sense of greater coherence.

In contrast to his earlier novels, *Amelia* is regarded as one of Fielding's most overtly serious works. The novel evokes a world in cultural and spiritual decline, recounting the corruption of a weak but basically good man, Captain Booth, by social, political, and legal forces. Lacking the narrative interruptions and interpolated stories that mark his first novels, *Amelia* is considered Fielding's most coherent work, but it suffers from its didactic tone and stilted rhetoric. Some critics suggest that *Amelia* reveals Fielding's exploration of new possibilities for the novel form.

Critical Reception

Commentators on the novel generally preferred Richardson's serious, unambiguous piety to Fielding's comic moral vision throughout the eighteenth and nineteenth centuries. His sympathy with the lower classes and his critical depiction of the justice system won him the scorn of most of his contemporaries, who found his writing coarse and his characters base. Not until early in the twentieth century did critics begin to appreciate Fielding's literary skill, which had in part been overshadowed by inaccurate biographies portraying Fielding as a licentious drunkard. More recent criticism has explored Fielding's complex value system: Martin Price suggests that Fielding's so-called low characters contribute to his definition of virtue, and Martin Battestin examines the character of Sophia Western as an example of Fielding's nuanced moral code. The influence of Fielding's theatrical training has also been the subject of scholarly inquiry. Alan T. McKenzie examines the theatrical displays of passion in Fielding's novels and in *Jonathan Wild,* and Sheridan Baker describes in some detail how plot devices and themes from Fielding's plays were transplanted into his fiction. The rich realism of Fielding's fiction has encouraged scholars to examine his work in its cultural context, as exemplified both in Michael McKeon's study of Fielding's work and in James Thompson's essay on *Tom Jones* and economic history. Critics continue to debate the influences and effects of Fielding's innovative narrative techniques; some focusing on his connection to classical traditions, others emphasizing Fielding's skillful exploitation of the developing novel genre which he himself helped bring into being.

PRINCIPAL WORKS

Love in Several Masques (drama) 1728
The Author's Farce and The Pleasures of the Town (drama) 1730
The Temple Beau (drama) 1730
Tom Thumb (drama) 1730; also published as *The Tragedy of Tragedies; or, The Life and Death of Tom Thumb the Great* [enlarged edition] 1731

The Welsh Opera, or, The Grey Mare the Better Horse [as Scriblerus Secundus] (drama) 1731; also published as *The Grub-Street Opera*, 1731

The Covent-Garden Tragedy (drama) 1732

The Modern Husband (drama) 1732

Don Quixote in England [adaptor; from the novel *Don Quixote* by Miguel de Cervantes] (drama) 1734

Pasquin: A Dramatick Satire on the Times; Being the Rehearsal of Two Plays, viz. a Comedy Called "The Election" and a Tragedy Called "The Life and Death of Common Sense" (drama) 1736

The Historical Register for the Year 1736 (drama) 1737

An Apology for the Life of Mrs. Shamela Andrews. In Which, the Many Notorious Falsehoods and Misrepresentations of a Book Called "Pamela" Are Exposed and Refuted; and All the Matchless Arts of That Young Politician, Set in a True and Just Light [as Conny Keyber] (satire) 1741; also published as *Shamela* in *Joseph Andrews and Shamela*, 1961

The History of the Adventures of Joseph Andrews, and of his Friend Mr. Abraham Adams. Written in Imitation of Cervantes, Author of "Don Quixote" (novel) 1742; also published as *Joseph Andrews*, 1935

A Journey from This World to the Next (satire) 1743; published in *Miscellanies, Vol. II*

The Life of Mr. Jonathan Wild the Great (satire) 1743; published in *Miscellanies, Vol. III*; also published as *Jonathan Wild*, 1932

Miscellanies. 3 vols. (essays, satires, dramas, and poetry) 1743

The History of Tom Jones, a Foundling (novel) 1749; also published as *Tom Jones*, 1896

Amelia (novel) 1751

An Enquiry into the Causes of the Late Increase of Robbers, & c., with Some Proposals for Remedying This Growing Evil (essay) 1751

A Proposal for Making an Effectual Provision for the Poor (essay) 1753

The Journal of a Voyage to Lisbon (journal) 1755

The Works of Henry Fielding, Esq; With the Life of the Author. 4 vols. (dramas, novels, satires, and essays) 1762

The Complete Works of Henry Fielding, Esq. 16 vols. (novels, satires, dramas, essays, journalism, and poetry) 1903

———

CRITICISM

Martin Price (essay date 1964)

SOURCE: "The Comedy of Forms: Low and High," in *Henry Fielding*, edited by Harold Bloom, Chelsea House, 1987, pp. 43-50. Originally published in Martin Price, *To the Palace of Wisdom:*

Studies in Order and Energy from Dryden to Blake (Price, 1964; Feffer & Simons, 1970).

[*In the following excerpt, originally published in 1964 and reprinted in 1970 and 1987, Price maintains that the low social status of Fielding's virtuous characters subverts both social and generic expectations.*]

> *It would have been useless for our Lord Jesus Christ to come like a king, in order to shine forth in His kingdom of holiness. But He came there appropriately in the glory of His own order.*
>
> *It is most absurd to take offence at the lowliness of Jesus Christ, as if His lowliness were in the same order as the greatness which He came to manifest. It we consider this greatness . . . we shall see it to be so immense that we shall have no reason for being offended at a lowliness which is not of that order.*
>
> *—Pensées*

These are solemn words to bring to Fielding's novels; yet their import is essential to an understanding of his lowness. I have argued for his constant subversion of forms, his deliberate overturning of rigid stances or systematized attitudes. Even the attitudes he espouses and the characters he admires submit to this untiring alertness to pretense. It is not simply the hypocritical or affected he attacks but the insensible conversion of active feeling into formal structure. The lowness of Fielding's heroes—the fact that in one sense or another they are dispossessed or disinherited—thrusts them into a situation where they have no props of status. The nakedness of Joseph, as he lies at the roadside after the robbery, is itself an extreme instance of the unprotectedness of these characters.

Not only are the characters without recourse to position; they are, by their nature, unable to foresee the malice of others. This inability is both worldly folly and the wisdom of charity. Parson Adams, we are told, "never saw farther into people than they desired to let him." Hypocrites like Peter Pounce were "a sort of people whom Mr. Adams never saw through." Allworthy, of course, carries on the pattern, and Dr. Harrison is no more beyond it than Booth and Amelia. In contrast, the selfish count on finding their own deviousness in others and often as a result overshoot their mark, like Fainall and Mrs. Marwood in *The Way of the World*. Fielding is insisting upon the fact that goodness cannot be recognized unless it is first felt within. This is a counterpart of the traditional Christian view that one cannot know God until one loves Him. Until that love is felt, one's knowledge remains fixed in categories of another order. There is no way of grasping the order of charity, one might say, with the categories of the order of mind. The kind of awareness upon which characters act seems deficient when it is interpreted in the terms of another order.

Dr. Harrison charges Booth with abusing him by calling him wise: "You insinuated slily," says the doctor, "that I was wise, which, as the world understands the phrase, I should be ashamed of; and my comfort is that no one can accuse me justly of it" (*Amelia,* 9, 4). Characters speak to each other in foreign tongues, although the words they use are the same. It is Fielding himself who can entertain all these levels of discourse at once, who can perceive how men think in each order of being, and who can embody a harmony of orders within himself.

Fielding's strategy is to dissociate orders—to give us figures who upset our conventional expectations of "goodness and innocence." In the preface to *Joseph Andrews* he sets forth a doctrine of the "comic epic in prose" that steers a course between the conventional high heroism of romance and the monstrous parodies of burlesque. He offers us "low" characters, and among them, "the most glaring in the whole," Parson Adams, "a character of perfect simplicity" whose goodness of heart "will recommend him to the good-natured." As Stuart M. Tave has shown (in *The Amiable Humorist,* Chicago, 1960), Fielding's profession to write "in imitation of the manner of Cervantes, author of *Don Quixote*" is deceptive to the modern reader, for Fielding is one of the pioneers in the gradual recognition of the dignity of the foolish Quixote. Parson Adams is a challenge to the reader to discern an essential goodness within a sententious, vainly bookish, shortsighted country clergyman. It is only near the close of the novel that he can rise to the dignity of self-assertion in his reply to Lady Booby:

> Madam . . . I know not what your ladyship means by the terms master and service. I am in the service of a master who will never discard me for doing my duty. . . . Whilst my conscience is pure, I shall never fear what man can do unto me. (4, 2)

The contrasts that run through *Joseph Andrews* are less sharp than those of *Jonathan Wild,* the dissociations less overtly satirical and emphatic. The strain of pastoral allows Fielding to use his setting as commentary; it reaches its culmination in Mr. Wilson's garden, where the freshness and vitality of the country (already so evident in Joseph and Fanny) take on dignity and serenity:

> No parterres, no fountains, no statues, embellished this little garden. Its only ornament was a short walk, shaded on each side by a filbert-hedge, with a small alcove at one end; whither in hot weather the gentleman and his wife used to retire and divert themselves with their children, who played in the walk before them. But though vanity had no votary in this little spot, here was variety of fruit, and every thing useful for the kitchen; which was abundantly sufficient to catch the admiration of

Adams, who told the gentleman, he had certainly a good gardener. Sir, answered he, that gardener is now before you: whatever you see here is the work solely of my own hands. (3, 4)

When the visitors leave, Adams declares "that this was the manner in which the people had lived in the golden age," an echo of his obsession with classical learning, but also of Pope on pastoral poetry: "pastoral is an image of what they call the golden age. So that we are not to describe our shepherds as shepherds at this day really are, but as they may be conceived then to have been, when the best of men followed the employment." What gives *Joseph Andrews* its striking quality is that Fielding mixes this Virgilian note with the Theocritean of Gay's mock pastorals. The low energies of nature are given their animal vigor (though carefully distinguished from the urgencies of Lady Booby or Slipslop, let alone Beau Didapper), but they are made continuous with the warmth and generosity of a pastoral golden age and of the Christian charity that has drawn so much of its imagery from the life of the shepherd.

In *Tom Jones* the pastoral motive is also present, with the mock pastoral centering in Molly Seagrim and Squire Western. Western is the most startling creation in the novel; perhaps the finest English comic character to have emerged after Falstaff. He is a great baby, frankly selfish and uncontrolled, imperious in his whims, cruelly thoughtless, with the tyranny of a demanding child but none of the capacity to spin out of his appetites subtle schemes of domination or revenge, like Blifil and Lady Bellaston. When he bursts into the London scene, he brings with him the simplicity of the flesh at its most fleshly. He breaks through the code of honor, that most elaborate and attractive of worldly substitutes for goodness, as he breaks through the delicate modesty of Sophia ("To her, boy, to her, go to her"). Early in the novel we see his simplicity achieve the same ends as real astuteness. Thwackum and Square compete in praising Blifil, who has maliciously released Sophia's bird; Square sees in him another Brutus, Thwackum an exemplary Christian. "I don't know what you mean, either of you," Western breaks in, "by right and wrong. To take away my girl's bird was wrong in my opinion" (4, 4). And it is he who defends Tom's effort to recapture the bird for Sophia. "I am sure I don't understand a word of this," he says to Square and Thwackum, still debating their moral doctrine.

> It may be learning and sense for aught I know; but you shall never persuade me into it. Pox! you have neither of you mentioned a word of that poor lad who deserves to be commended; to venture breaking his neck to oblige my girl was a generous-spirited action; I have learning enough to see that. D——n me, here's Tom's health! I shall love the boy for it the longest day I have to live. (4, 4)

It is only to be expected that Squire Western cannot sustain this noble intention. He has as little mind as any man can have; he lives in bursts of enthusiasm, maudlin affection, barbarous willfulness, sheer physicality. He pairs off with his sister—she all Whig politics and would-be townish smartness, he the typical hard-drinking Tory country squire. But Fielding does more with him than that. He uses him to embody animal energy without either the selfish cunning that builds upon appetites in some or the generous charity that fuses with appetite (and transforms it) in others. Tom stands between Western and Allworthy, able to participate in the worlds of both—an innocent carnality in Western and a rational charity in Allworthy— and to bring them together. It would be hard, in fact, to conceive of Tom without the presence of both Allworthy and Western in the novel.

One should observe as well how Jenny Jones, who is something of a prig at the outset, mellows into the generous, if irregular, Mrs. Waters of the later parts— in marked contrast to the vain and shallow Harriet Fitzpatrick. The progression of Tom's temptresses is significant. Molly Seagrim is coarse but pretentious, Lady Bellaston is refined and vindictive. Mrs. Waters strikes a balance between Molly's unmitigated (and slightly corrupt) low and Lady Bellaston's inverted high. She is capable—in the case of Tom—of a robust and unfastidious appetite:

> The beauty of Jones highly charmed her eye; but as she could not see his heart, she gave herself no concern about it. She could feast heartily at the table of love, without reflecting that some other already had been, or hereafter might be, feasted with the same repast. (9, 6)

But she is also capable—in the case of Northerton—of "that violent and apparently disinterested passion of love, which seeks only the good of its object" (9, 7). Fielding allows her only a strong sensuality in her relations with Tom, but he makes her a woman who squares her passions with her conscience more boldly than the hypocrites around her. She defends, in Allworthy's presence, an attachment that has constancy without legal sanctions, and she values Tom's virtue at a greater rate than his freedom from vices. And, all the while, she retains her deep gratitude to Allworthy and recognizes in his goodness something that "savored more of the divine than human nature" (18, 8). Fielding discriminates carefully between moral laxity and moral obliviousness—or, as Coleridge puts in, between what a man does and what he is.

Amelia is a weaker novel than *Tom Jones,* but it is clearly moving in a new direction. The fact that Billy Booth has a family depending upon him makes his irregularities less appealing than Tom's. His only sexual infidelity takes place at the opening of the novel, before our concern for his family has grown too strong.

For the rest of the story he is suffering from remorse and the threat of Miss Matthews's revenge; we see more of the hangover than the intoxication. He is guilty of less attractive vices than Tom's; he is vain about keeping a coach, and he gambles disastrously when his family is near starvation. He is also older and shabbier than Tom; and he can do little for himself in the course of the novel. The center of attention is Amelia, his wife. Fielding makes their marriage the object of the world's attack, and Booth's moral dependence upon Amelia gives the marriage all the more significance. Amelia is as close as Fielding comes to a pure embodiment of the order of charity; she has traces of vanity, and she is sometimes handled with irony, but she is never made so ridiculous as Mrs. Heartfree. Still, Fielding seems to have gone back to the Heartfrees, that "family of love," reworked them in a new way, and perhaps offered them finally as a further qualification of the ethical doctrines of *Tom Jones.*

It is Amelia's Christian goodness—selfless, warm, readily forgiving—that sets the tone of the book. We hardly see Booth acting well on his own—except on the battlefield—as we see Tom Jones refuting the Gulliver-like misanthropy of the Man of the Hill, keeping Partridge in check, advising Nightingale, resisting the kind proposal of Mrs. Hunt. In this novel the generosity of goodness is much more strictly limited to the forgiveness of Amelia and the benevolence of that harsher, less amiable version of Adams, Dr. Harrison. And goodness is heavily beleaguered; under the stress of difficulties, Amelia tells her children hard truths. Good people will show love, "but there are more bad people, and they will hate you for your goodness" (4, 3).

More than this, Fielding brings to the surface and faces what he cannot escape in the Heartfrees; the sentimentalism of Booth and Amelia in their innocence. The book opens with the savage injustices perpetrated by Justice Thrasher and the moral chaos of the prison itself. But it moves on at once to the two narratives of Miss Matthews and Booth. Miss Matthews is a brilliant instance of sentimental vanity; she is capable of stabbing her betrayer, and we have few doubts about her strength of will, but she voluptuates in a vision of herself as the creature of helpless passion. She can describe her method quite coolly in the case of her father. The kind old man had once caused Miss Matthews to miss a ball, and she fanned this memory until it could be revived at will in full strength. "When any tender idea intruded into my bosom, I immediately raised this phantom of an injury in my imagination, and it considerably lessened the fury of that sorrow which I should have otherwise felt for the loss of so good a father, who died within a few months of my departure from him" (1, 9). As Booth tells his own story, with torrents of tears, he inflames Miss Matthews's passion for him; and it bursts out in her brilliantly funny interruptions. But he is totally involved in his tale of how Amelia recovered from the accident wherein "her lovely nose was beat all to pieces."

Amelia's nose has become famous because Fielding failed, in the first edition of the novel, to make explicitly clear that it was restored, and the image of a noseless Amelia danced before critics' eyes. Even if we allow for an unfortunate oversight, the choice of a nose seems singularly inept. Amelia's suffering consists of having to hear false friends say that "she will never more turn up her nose at her betters"; and surely no author of Fielding's skill brought this kind of difficulty upon himself unintentionally. We can pity Amelia, but we cannot take her accident with quite the solemnity that Booth does. There is an undernote of laughter in more than Miss Matthews's sublime remarks ("a cottage with the man one loves, is a palace"). And there is surely laughter as well as pathos in Booth's account of his departure from Amelia:

> clinging round my neck, she cried, "Farewell, farewell forever; for I shall never, never see you any more." At which words the blood entirely forsook her lovely cheeks, and she became a lifeless corpse in my arms.
>
> Amelia continued so long motionless, that the doctor, as well as Mrs. Harris, began to be under the most terrible apprehensions; so they informed me afterwards, for at that time I was incapable of making any observation. I had indeed very little more use of my senses than the dear creature whom I supported. At length, however, we were all delivered from our fears; and life again visited the loveliest mansion that human nature ever afforded it. (3, 2)

Booth's sentimentalism helps explain his belief that man could act only "from the force of that passion which was uppermost in his mind, and could do no otherwise" (1, 3). Just as his sister Nancy dies, he learns that he may lose Amelia to someone else. "I now soon perceived how superior my love for Amelia was to every passion; poor Nancy's idea disappeared in a moment; I quitted the lifeless corpse, over which I had shed a thousand tears, left the care of her funeral to others, and posted, I may almost say flew, back to Amelia. . . ." (2, 5). It is necessary for Colonel James, his superior officer, to warn him—when he seems dangerously wounded—against going back to Amelia. James can appreciate "the comfort of expiring in her arms," but he points out the cruelty, too: "You would not wish to purchase any happiness at the price of so much pain to her" (2, 5). The danger of Booth's temperament is obvious; as Fielding says, he is "in his heart an extreme well-wisher to religion . . . yet his notions of it [are] very slight and uncertain." He comes close to the error Dr. Johnson found in his friend Savage: "he mistook the love for the practice of virtue, and was indeed not so much

a good man as the friend of goodness."

Amelia, far more than Booth, grows stronger under the stress of suffering. Fielding has designed the novel so that, at each point, we see Amelia—so much a human embodiment of pure charity—assailed by those who cannot understand her nature. She lives with a landlady who is little more than a procuress. She is tried by the designs of two rakes who have no comprehension of the sanctity of "wedded love." When Booth, too, seems to have lost all sense of the meaning of Amelia's love, she is close to despair. Amelia can, however, be freed from the temptations of sentimentality by devoting herself to others. When she joins Booth "she could not so far command herself as to refrain from many sorrowful exclamations against the hardships of their destiny; but when she saw the effect they had upon Booth she stifled her rising grief [and] forced a little cheerfulness into her countenance" (12, 2).

Fielding allows Amelia's purity of character to emerge from the test of ridicule. Amelia is constantly seen in contrast with Mrs. Atkinson, who is good but vain and touchy, and whose story of her life exhibits a certain amount of partiality and self-justification. The angelic selflessness of Amelia is her primary quality, and it can afford to be seen in lights that make others ridiculous. Amelia's pathos is heightened by the very kind of extended simile that was once used to overwhelm a Deborah Wilkins or to mock a naïve Tom Jones; Amelia's quiet goodness can wear it with grace.

Ronald Paulson (essay date 1967)

SOURCE: "Fielding the Anti-Romanticist," in his *Satire and the Novel in Eighteenth-Century England,* Yale University Press, 1967, pp. 100-31.

[*In the following chapter from his book-length study* Satire and the Novel in Eighteenth-Century England, *Paulson argues that the works of Fielding represent a transition between satire and the early English novel. Focusing mainly on* Joseph Andrews, *Paulson discusses Fielding's subversions of the romance genre and his disagreement with Samuel Richardson's* Pamela.]

Fielding vs. Richardson

In the context of his earlier work it would appear that when Fielding came to write the first of his novels his intention was to correct the unhealthy tendencies of the Richardsonian novel in the same spirit in which he had earlier corrected the excesses of the pantomimes and operas. *Pamela* (1740), in one sense, represented the culmination of the forces of bad writing and fraudulent morality that Swift had attacked in *A Tale of a Tub* and Pope in *The Dunciad.* Like Swift, Fielding may have seen the new literary forms as dangerous because of their aggressive abandonment of classical models or any formal standards of excellence, their exaltation of the new and disordered, and their effect of raising the ego to an unprecedented prominence.[1]

Of course the same discrepancy resulted between intended meaning and the meaning communicated by the action itself which Fielding had explored in the hack writing that drew his attention before 1737. *Pamela* was "the first novel," the final anti-romance, in that it produced an ultimate in formal realism through the immediacy, prolixity, and verisimilitude of the letter form, which expresses the inner workings of a mind and effectively immerses the reader in its simulacrum of the real world. But if *Pamela* was the prototype of the modern novel as defined by Ortega y Gasset and others, it was also a descendant of the romance and, in a sense, the prototype of the popular or romantic novel of the fleeing heroine, the interrupted seduction, and the happy marriage.[2] Although the novel's main concern seemed to be with the momentary and ephemeral, Richardson was very much concerned with eternal verities; he had a great moral to convey about virtue and vice, with his subtitle "Virtue Rewarded." This moral imposed certain conditions on the narrative that were not met by Richardson's account of the immediate workings of his heroine's mind. What led contemporaries to attack *Pamela* was, besides its immense and enviable success, the unstable compound Richardson created by mixing conventions of realism, romance, and morality play.

The romance convention probably caused the most trouble, requiring that the girl and the seducer be united at the end and thus preordaining the nature of virtue's reward. Since Richardson combined the figures of the lover and the ogre (we should also notice traces of fairy-tale romance, Cinderella, Beauty and the Beast, etc.), Mr. B. became such a monster that Pamela's ultimate acceptance of him seemed hypocritical self-advancement. Moreover, Richardson further tended to subvert his paragon by keeping her in a situation of pursuit and defense—the basic plot of romance—while at the same time granting her pious knowledge of Mr. B.'s nefarious intention and plentiful opportunity to leave his service. At his best Richardson used these contradictions to create a convincing picture of divided minds, both Pamela's and Mr. B.'s, struggling between conscious and unconscious drives—between Pamela's ideal of chastity and her love for Mr. B.; between his notion that a servant girl should be his for the asking and his growing love for Pamela as an ideal woman. At worst the jumbled conventions created the impression of double-dealing on the part of Pamela and her creator.

When *Pamela* came into Fielding's sights he seems to have sensed—certainly before his contemporaries—the peculiar danger of Richardson's hold over his readers.

The effect of *Pamela's* particularity, piled-up minutiae, repetitions, and prolixity was to draw the reader as close as possible to the heroine's immediate experience and mind, in fact to suck the reader in and immerse him in her experience. "Such a record," A. D. McKillop writes of Pamela's letters, "gives the reader a continuous and cumulative impression of living through the experience, and thus creates a new kind of sympathy with the character whose experiences are being shared."[3]

Immersion may lead to a sinister titillation in *Pamela's* erotic scenes, but more serious, it allows the reader to identify himself so much with the character that he tends to lose a sense of relationships, the wholeness of the moral design, and his moral perspective on the character. The reader becomes uncritical, a "friend" of the character, and having accepted Pamela's rationalizations as completely as he would his own, he emerges ready to modify his own conduct accordingly. The situation, as Fielding evidently saw it, was analogous to the blindness inflicted upon people by fashion and the conventions of "greatness" and "great men," all of which hindered not only the judgment of other people's actions but the decisions by which one takes one's own actions. Identification with a character was, of course, a prime ingredient of romance, the same danger that Cervantes perceived in *Amadis de Gaula*. But Fielding sensed that in this bourgeois story, laid in contemporary England with all the realism that particularity of description and immediacy of the letter form can give, immersion was much stronger than in a chivalric romance laid in the Middle Ages.

Samuel Johnson, writing in 1750 (*Rambler*, No. 4), also recognized this phenomenon at work, but his solution was more conservative—and perhaps more realistic—than Fielding's. He simply argued that the novelist, recognizing the power he wielded over his reader, must make his protagonist a virtuous man:

> if the power of example is so great as to take possession of the memory by a kind of violence, and produce effects almost without the intervention of the will, care ought to be taken, that, when the choice is unrestrained, the best examples only should be exhibited; and that which is likely to operate so strongly, should not be mischievous or uncertain in its effects.

In the right hands, Johnson thought, the novel could be a transcendent force for moral reform; the reader, sympathizing with the good man, would then go out and behave in the same way. But Fielding, seeing more danger than Johnson did in the example of Pamela, believed that with such an instrument in the hands of a bourgeois like Richardson, a man with enormous talent for "writing to the moment" but with a narrow, uncertain, even obtuse morality, the only answer was an alternative form that never for a moment left the reader in doubt about the author's intention as to who was good and who evil.

Seeing *Pamela* as a moral chaos in which the reader was invited to wallow self-indulgently, Fielding began his alternative, **Shamela,** by adding the objective commentator that *Pamela* lacked. Richardson, however good his intentions, could only appear as a sententious editor, a lone voice in an occasional note which was effectually outside the fiction and could be ignored. The reader had only Pamela and himself; almost everything was seen through Pamela's eyes, and she (Fielding believed) carried Richardson and the reader away with her.

Fielding's initial response was the Swiftean solution—letting the Pamelian speaker condemn herself. But even when he has made the dramatic irony unmistakable, if not coarse and obvious, and simplified the action, he surrounds Shamela's letters with commentary, offering viewpoints other than the heroine's which place her actions in clearer perspective. **Shamela** still uses the farce's approach to parody, surrounding the action with comment and not allowing it to stand by itself, and thus it remains halfway between the plays and *Joseph Andrews.* In the latter, however, Fielding replaces the directly imitated voices of the heroine and the commentators (Parsons Oliver and Tickletext) with one voice which controls and conveys the whole action.

While Medley was as close as Fielding came in the farces to a normative commentator, in *Joseph Andrews* the narrator is in temperament close to the persona of the periodicals—like him, an arbiter of morals and manners. He is, to begin with, a creator and/or historian, who sets before the reader an object that can be accepted as objectively true. The effect is evident if we compare the portraits of two ill-favored women:

> [Mrs. Jewkes] is a broad, squat pursy, *fat thing,* quite ugly, if any thing human can be so called; about forty years old. She has a huge hand, and an arm as thick as my waist, I believe. Her nose is flat and crooked, and her brows grow down over her eyes; a dead spiteful, grey, goggling eye, to be sure she has. And her face is flat and broad; and as to colour, looks like as if it had been pickled a month in saltpetre.

> [Mrs. Slipslop] was not at this time remarkably handsome, being very short, and rather too corpulent in body, and somewhat red, with the addition of pimples in the face. Her nose was likewise rather too large, and her eyes too little; nor did she resemble a cow so much in her breath as in two brown globes which she carried before her; one of her legs was also a little shorter than the other, which occasioned her to limp as she walked. This fair creature had long cast the eyes of affection on Joseph.[4]

While Richardson undoubtedly intended his portrait of

Mrs. Jewkes to arouse our contempt if not ridicule, even drawing upon satiric conventions to do so, he put the description into the mouth of a character, Pamela, and thus made it subjective. When Pamela describes Jewkes, we see a portrait distorted by fear and apprehension. Almost at once, as if to make sure that there is no mistake, Richardson has Pamela add: "This is poor helpless spite in me:—But the picture is too near the truth notwithstanding." Her nightmare fantasies are collected in her portraits of Jewkes and Colbrand ("great staring eyes . . . a monstrous wide mouth; blubber lips; long yellow teeth, and a hideous grin"), and all the evil she is unwilling to see in her master is transferred to his underlings, as in another instance it is transferred to a bull (who turns out to be a harmless cow). But when Fielding describes Slipslop, we know that, however fantastic, in the context of his fiction she looked that way.

Second, Fielding's commentator is a manipulator. When an appalling event like the abduction of Fanny by the squire's men takes place, the narrator juggles scenes so that the reader does not lose sight of the overall structure of meaning in his concern for Fanny. Instead of closely following her fate in the Richardsonian manner, he switches to "a discourse between the poet and the player; of no other use in this history but to divert the reader" (Bk. III, Chap. 10; *1,* 293). The poet and player, sycophants of the squire who wants Fanny, and participants themselves in the abduction, casually discuss drama. This scene is followed by a dialogue between Joseph and Adams concerning Fanny, in which Joseph's anguish is counteracted by Adams' insistence on stoic acceptance. Only then is the reader returned to Fanny herself and her predicament. This diversion and the various parodic devices that follow set off the narrative and the characters from immediate contact with the reader and keep the reader aware of the author's controlling presence and his message. The juxtaposition also dramatizes the total unconcern of the poet and player about Fanny or any moral issue, as well as Fielding's favorite analogy between the shoddiness of art and morals, between the stage and life. The effect of the pause after the abduction is therefore essentially to allow contemplation. Beginning in *Joseph Andrews,* the important formal elements in Fielding's novels are the scene and the relationship between scene and commentary and between one scene and another.

In the third place, the commentator is an ironist. His ironic mask produces the impression necessary to Fielding's conception of the novel—the impression of neutrality and authority, as opposed to the disreputable, prejudiced, and limited vision of a Pamela. The ironic attitude implies a contrast between a limited and conventional view and a more generous, inclusive one. The effect is very different from Richardson's inclusiveness—gathering a great mass of minutiae and particulars within a narrow compass in order to submerge the reader. Irony holds the reader at some distance from the action; as Rebecca Parkin has noted, it "implies a sophisticated reader and a sophisticated poet, together with an awareness and acceptance, on the part of both, of their sophisticated status."[5] This is the old poet-audience relationship assumed and fostered by Dryden, Swift, and Pope. With them Fielding accepts the assumption that the air of artifice is compensated for by the sanity of the exposition, the clarity and, in that sense, realism of the picture—the impression that the author is aware of more than one aspect of his subject.

If Richardson's realism is one of plenitude, Fielding's is one of opposite and larger reference; if Richardson achieves verisimilitude by an oppressive intimacy, Fielding does the same by polarizing his views of people, his kinds of people, and their experiences and motives. The analogues he introduces in *Joseph Andrews* have the effect of suggesting both the complexity and the interrelations of life; ironic similes thus connect Slipslop and a tiger, Adams and Colley Cibber, Lady Booby and Cupid, Joseph and the biblical Joseph. The effect is exactly like that of Fielding's earlier satires, to extend the behavior of a Lady Booby to the outside world of art, politics, religion, and the reader's own behavior. When Fielding wants to show how passion transforms sensible people, he compares it to Rich transforming (in his pantomimes) men into monkeys or wheelbarrows and to Cibber transforming the English language into something new and strange (Bk. I, Chap. 7). The implications involve not only the theatrical quality of Lady Booby's passion but the irrationality that is at the bottom of Rich's and Cibber's behavior.

The "reality" generated by Fielding's irony is a kind of control or discrimination, a depth of understanding—what Ian Watt has called "realism of assessment."[6] We might distinguish between reality as placement of something in a proper or true relationship to everything else in the world (Fielding's type), and reality as exposition of the authenticity of something (Richardson's). It follows that by reality Fielding means moral or factual truth apprehended by the reader, whereas he sees in Richardson a reality that means the true workings of a character's mind, without any concern for the truth or falseness of apprehension in relation to the external world.

Irony also serves Fielding as a controllable equivalent of Richardson's presentation of the workings of a mind. He puts mock-heroic speeches in his characters' mouths: Lady Booby cries, "Whither doth this violent passion hurry me! What meanness do we submit to from its impulse!" and reveals that she sees herself as a tragedy queen and her lust for Joseph as a grand passion.[7] But the narrator's ironies, in the manner of Dryden and the

mock-heroic poets, also expose Lady Booby's mind. As soon as she is alone,

> the little god Cupid, fearing he had not yet done the lady's business, took a fresh arrow with the sharpest point out of his quiver, and shot it directly into her heart: in other and plainer language, the lady's passion got the better of her reason. (Bk. I, Chap. 7; *1*, 45)

This passage tells how Lady Booby would describe her feelings about Joseph (in terms of Cupid and hearts) and what actually happened ("passion got the better of her reason"); the passage not only sets her lust in perspective but also demonstrates her self-delusion, revealing an unhappy, misguided woman who rationalizes her petty affair into a great Didoesque love. Its effect in the larger context of Lady Booby's character is to suggest that her hypocrisy (calling her lust virtue) may be only a means to an end that is beyond her control.

Mrs. Slipslop "at last gave up Joseph and his cause, and with a triumph over her passion highly commendable" went off to get drunk. The author's ironic praise is obvious, but what it says in context is that she *felt* that she had triumphed and should be commended. Fielding's irony almost consistently, whether in speech or the author's comment, suggests the character's rationalization, just as Pamela's moral interpretations of her actions do (less self-consciously) in the novel he is criticizing. The mock-heroic of *Jonathan Wild* works in the same way, except that the self-delusion is mixed with aspiration to a false ideal, "greatness." Whether from the character's own lips or from those of the commentator, the irony tends to become an expression of the character's psychology.

Fielding does not call *Joseph Andrews* a satire; he infrequently refers to the word "satire" and holds firmly to the designation "comic epic in prose." Comedy, of course, still contained the idea of the satiric in the early eighteenth century and, by this time, had better connotations. But Fielding had other reasons as well for using the broader term.

To begin with, he specifically rules out certain kinds of satire he had used in the earlier part of his career as unsuited to the comic epic in prose. By the word "burlesque" he means, first, literary parody: he is not writing a parody of *Pamela* or of anything else, a strategy he had already handled in *Shamela*. His second meaning of "burlesque" is the more general one, "the exhibition of what is monstrous and unnatural"—a Shamela, a Pistol in *The Author's Farce,* or a Queen Ignorance in *Pasquin.* This meaning, the literary equivalent of caricature, applies to a particular kind of satire, travesty or mock-heroic, "appropriating the manners of the highest to the lowest, or *è converso*." Although *Joseph Andrews* betrays unmistakable elements of parody and high and low burlesque, they are, as Fielding claims, incidental and decorative rather than essential; they help to determine our attitude toward a character but do not ordinarily alter the character himself and certainly do not caricature him.

Fielding intends to set up not an exaggerated image of what he detests, in the manner of *The Dunciad* or his own *Shamela,* but rather an alternative of his own. This is, I think, the basic reason for his avoiding reference to satire. Throughout all three of his major novels he continues to refer to the importance of the new form he has created, but though he connects this form at various times with comedy, epic, and history, he never does with satire. His intention is not finally satiric. Although he may include the idea of satire, he means by "comedy" a more general imitation of reality or what he calls a "just imitation" of nature. Since satire remains an important part of his point of view, however, he wishes to dissociate himself from the particular kind of satire he had written a few years earlier in *Pasquin* and *The Historical Register* and more recently in *Shamela.* In one of the few occurrences of the word "satire," he gives us the *Spectator's* view that the preference of the general to the particular in subject "distinguishes the satirist from the libeller," and that in *Joseph Andrews* "we mean not to lash individuals, but all of the like sort" (Bk. III, Chap. 1; *1,* 216). This was a conventional definition, but Fielding would have to do some explaining to apply it to some of his earlier satires.

Fielding's analogy between his novel and the works of Hogarth makes his point clear. Hogarth's prints, which had become enormously popular after the publication of *A Harlot's Progress* in 1732, offered the best example of what Fielding himself wished to do: replace the fantasy of traditional, emblematic, and Augustan satire with a more restrained delineation, closer to experience, and reliant on "character" rather than "caricature," on the variety rather than the exaggeration of expression. Both, moreover, sought a more secure place in the classical hierarchy of genres than satire, the grotesque, or even the comic by itself could command (or, for that matter, than the rootless Richardsonian form could lay claim to). As Hogarth steered a course between the flatulent history painting of his time and the popular forms of satire and burlesque, Fielding sought to establish a genre between the romance he discerned in Richardson's *Pamela* and the grotesquerie of travesty.

The point that Fielding makes by bracketing *Joseph Andrews* between romance on one side and burlesque on the other is that he intends to write according to his own definition of realism. Both romance and burlesque are used by Fielding in this connection to show the different ways in which reality may be distorted—to glamorize and to vilify. He equates *Pamela* with the romances of Jack the Giant Killer and Guy of Warwick as he equates his own early work (though perhaps not so wholeheartedly) with burlesque and caricature. But his claim, like that of Defoe and Richardson, is to seek truth and reality; he says—and this is an important contribution of his preface—that the novel is a search for the real.

Fielding's idea of reality is, of course, quite different from Richardson's, and while he claims to be following a middle way, his realism is largely (like anti-romance realism) a contrary to Richardson's. Richardson sees life as a single-minded conflict between two people, one good, the other evil. He is interested only in the sensibility of one woman, alone in a closet with her daydreams and wish fantasies. His setting is usually indoors, in drawing rooms, hallways, and bedrooms—the "close, hot, day-dreamy" world Coleridge noted.[8] To what he considered the narrow world of *Pamela* Fielding opposes the wide world of epic with all classes and all manner of locales. His settings are out-of-doors, on roads, in inns, in coaches, on horseback, as well as in the places used by Richardson. Life is not a private relationship between a man and a woman but a journey on which one passes through all kinds of experiences and meets a great variety of people.

The analogy between epic and novel was a conventional one made by critics when attempting to justify the new fiction in terms of classical genres.[9] In his preface to *Joseph Andrews,* Fielding claims that to present true reality the novelist must correct his personal bias with reference to the larger view of tradition, developing the novel's affinities with the classical genres and in particular those genres associated with broad scope and objectivity of attitude. His preference for the *Odyssey* was natural, as he explains in the preface to the second edition of his sister Sarah's novel, *David Simple* (1744). The *Iliad* and *Odyssey* "differ principally in the action, which in the Iliad is entire and uniform; in the Odyssey, is rather a series of actions, all tending to produce one great end." He argues that "those who should object want of unity of action here, may, if they please, or if they dare, fly back with their objection in the face even of the Odyssey itself." He also implies the distinction he feels between this form and satire. The comic epic in prose should not "set before us the odious instead of the amiable." By this he means that the central character should not be subject to attack on any serious grounds; he should be neither a villain like Milton's Satan nor a mock-hero like Shadwell or Cibber. Thus *Joseph Andrews* would be a comic epic; *Jonathan Wild* would not.

In *Joseph Andrews* Fielding inserts the action of the *Odyssey* or the *Aeneid* (the uprooting of a protagonist and his attempts to find his way home) in the middle of the seduction scene of the Richardsonian novel. As if to point out that one must break free from that small room and narrow relationship, he allows Joseph to escape and follows his flight. Each of the subsequent actions moves Joseph toward his final goal.

The action of *Joseph Andrews,* with its movement toward a positive goal and a happy ending, is clearly not satiric, but the picaresque novel, the contemporary equivalent of the *Odyssey*-type epic, naturally influenced Fielding's conception. By placing the emphasis on the various incarnations of Lady Booby that block or delay the hero's return, without sacrificing the generally epic intention, Fielding renders a greater part of the overall effect satiric. For his alternative to Richardson's novel he turned to the epic, but in practice he drew upon the conventions and techniques, the externalizing and expository forms with which he was most familiar in satire.

Anti-Romance

In *Shamela* Fielding parodied the formal conventions of the Richardsonian novel in the heroine's letters, in her circumstantial lists of wearing apparel and books, and in her furious scribbling "to the moment": "Odsbobs! I hear him just coming at the door. . . . Well, he is in bed between us, wc both shamming a sleep; he steals his hand into my bosom."[10] Fielding's strategy is to travesty the Richardsonian style, dramatis personae, and, in an abbreviated form, plot, shifting it downward toward cruder and more extreme situations. *Shamela* is the simplest kind of anti-romance, the "true history" that travesties romance by revealing the real schemer beneath the pious phrases and coyness of Richardson's heroine. Thus Fielding reveals Mrs. Jervis to be a bawd, Parson Williams to be Pamela's lover, and "our old friend Nanny Jewkes" to be a rival for the love of Parson Williams. Mr. B. becomes the Booby he appeared to be in his bungling attempts to seduce Pamela, and Pamela becomes the designing slut that Mr. B. occasionally suspected her of being and that she appeared to be in such slips as when, with her pursuer close upon her, she recalls: "I found his hand in my bosom; and when my fright let me know it, I was ready to die; and I sighed and screamed, and fainted away. And still he had his arms about my neck."[11] Fielding simply gives us the *true* Pamela: "I thought once of making a little Fortune by my Person. I now intend to make a great one by my Vartue" (Letter 10; p. 325).

Shamela is conceived in the tradition of Jonathan Wild and Fielding's early villains, a central symbol of vice. But she is also, like some of them, a surrogate or apprentice, and in this sense *Shamela* is related to the *Don Quixote* kind of anti-romance. The hero acts according to a romantic ideal ("greatness") that is external and not entirely appropriate to him. Just as Quixote reads his romances, Shamela reads Whitefield and listens to Parson Williams' sermons advocating faith over works. Fielding's point is not only that these sermons are used as hypocritical masks but that they contain the code of hypocrisy that Shamela is teaching herself to follow. Worst of all, however, are her mother's letters, which continually exhort her to pursue her calculating end and capture Mr. Booby. Like Wild she is shown stretching to reach a mark held up to her by a hard taskmaster; her mother keeps urging her on and she, in her own way, always falls a little short.[12]

Her trouble is that she cannot control her passion for Parson Williams, and in spite of her mother's warnings this leads to her downfall; Mr. Booby catches them in bed together and the whole scheme comes to nothing. The obverse of Wild's failure at personal relationships, Shamela's passion is her tragic flaw. Love as a lack, Fielding seems to say, helps to characterize the bad man and foretell the disintegration of his designs; but love as a positive force, even in so crude a form as Shamela's lust, must destroy hypocrisy and calculation, just as Shaftesbury's ridicule must destroy sham. It is not certain whether Shamela's love affair with Parson Williams is supposed to be more important as an act of hypocrisy or as a sign of her passion that obtrudes to destroy her hypocritical fabrication. What should appear to be vice punished may be interpreted as Shamela's one sincere action discovered. The Shamelian context admittedly warrants a less positive construction; but whatever the emphasis in *Shamela,* the love-profit contrast is central to *Joseph Andrews.*

Here Fielding creates an action that is roughly parallel to *Pamela*'s but at a remove. The death of Sir Thomas Booby, like the death of Mr. B.'s mother, sets the plot going, but Lady Booby is not simply a parody of Mr. B. She is a distinct person, a relative of Booby's, just as Joseph is (or rather appears to be) a relative of Pamela's, and the two sets of characters, Fielding's and Richardson's, carry on their own stories in *Joseph Andrews.* They are connected only by the reader's memory, Joseph's two letters to his sister, and the eventual meeting at Booby Hall. By that time Mr. Booby has married Pamela and Lady Booby has begun her last concentrated effort to corrupt Joseph. The Mr. Booby-Pamela action is not travestied, except perhaps in Pamela's insistent snobbery that is a sequel to her marriage.

As we have seen, Fielding conceives *Joseph Andrews* less as a parody, like *Shamela,* than as an alternative.[13] He starts with Colley Cibber's *Apology* and Richardson's *Pamela,* just as Cervantes started with the romances of chivalry; here, says Fielding, we are shown an "ideal" male and female, models for their respective sexes. But they, like those knights and ladies, are neither real people nor real ideals; *Joseph Andrews* will show what a true ideal is and what real people are like. This involves, first, an adjustment of values. Self-seeking that uses chastity as a means to an end (Pamela) and vanity that calls unchastity a virtue (Cibber) are offered their opposites, chastity and natural goodness (Joseph and Parson Adams). Second, it involves stripping off what appear to be virtues in most people and revealing the self-interest underneath. The latter, only half of the intention, corresponds to the travesty of *Shamela.*

In one of the many epic similes attached to Parson Adams, we are told that

> he did not more than Mr. Colley Cibber apprehend any such passions as malice and envy to exist in mankind; which was indeed less remarkable in a country parson, than in a gentleman who hath passed his life behind the scenes,—a place which hath been seldom thought the school of innocence, and where a very little observation would have convinced the great Apologist that those passions have a real existence in the human mind. (Bk. I, Chap. 3; *1*, 30)

Adams' inability to detect malice and envy is compared to Cibber's, and the audience notes the irony—that Adams is unable (from simplicity and goodness) to recognize malice when it appears, while Cibber (all too aware of it) is unwilling to admit that it *is* malice. The parallel continues to be enforced from time to time, as in the chapter heading, "A curious dialogue that passed between Mr. Abraham Adams and Mr. Peter Pounce, better worth reading than all the works of Colley Cibber and many others" (Bk. II, Chap. 13).

In much the same way, Lady Booby and Joseph are contrasted in a crucial scene with the further analogue of Potiphar's wife and the biblical Joseph.[14] Slipslop, whose pretended gentility and literacy recall Pamela's, is contrasted with Adams, whose shabbiness hides his true learning; a high churchman is contrasted with a low, a bad with a good. Whenever Fanny is in trouble at least two people come along, one to react selfishly and one (for either good or bad motives) to save her. When Adams asks a favor of two men, the first is rude, the second kindly.

Thus the novel begins with a discussion of examples (Bk. I, Chap. 1) and a comparison of the examples of worldly wisdom, Pamela and Cibber, and the examples of simple goodness, Joseph and Adams. Once this comparison has been set up, Fielding takes the examples he has presupposed into the world of experience as Richardson and Cibber took theirs. By inference, Pamela and Cibber would have come through far differently. When Joseph maintains his virtue against Lady Booby's advances he is discharged; Pamela, for neither surrendering nor protecting hers, receives her master's hand in marriage. Adams is hardly an example for ambitious young Cibbers to follow: at forty he is still a curate; when he had the influence of his nephew at his disposal he did not know how to use it. We

are told from time to time what a different sort would have done in the same circumstances: the men who have captured him and Fanny, thinking them robbers, are so busy arguing among themselves over the reward "that a dexterous nimble thief, had he been in Mr. Adams' situation, would have taken care to have given the justice no trouble that evening." Adams, however, makes no attempt to escape, trusting "rather to his innocence than his heels" (Bk. II, Chap. 10; *1*, 165-66).

True virtue is repeatedly rewarded by abuse, blows, or even imprisonment in place of the vicious. Joseph is beaten by robbers and left naked in a ditch and is then subjected to equally brutal treatment at the hands of several decent citizens who pass him in a coach. The progress of Joseph and Adams from London to Booby Hall is one long succession of such violent encounters: Adams is brained with a blood pudding, chased (as a substitute hare) by a pack of hounds, tormented with practical jokes, and dropped into a tub of water. The punishers, it is made abundantly clear, are the Cibbers and Pamelas.

Joseph Andrews is similar to *Shamela* in that it treats the "romances" of *Pamela* and Cibber's *Apology* not as the reading of an isolated Quixote, but as a pernicious ideal to which most people aspire. Fielding has ironically shown that the romance world is the real (in the sense of practical) world. The Quixote parallel, introduced on the title page, is enforced from time to time, as when Adams and his friends have difficulty getting away from an inn where they owe the reckoning: "they had more reason to have mistaken [this inn] for a castle than Don Quixote ever had any of those in which he sojourned, seeing they had met with such difficulty in escaping out of its walls" (Bk. II, Chap. 16; *1*, 196-97). The imaginary world of Quixote is quite real here: these innkeepers and clergymen *are* monsters.

In the romance world characters' virtues are miraculously synchronized with their surroundings, and so Pamela saves her virtue and wins a fortune. Joseph and Adams, put into a real world where Pamela's virtues are as inappropriate as Quixote's delusions about chivalry, are notably unsuccessful. The explanation, Fielding insists, is that Pamela's virtue is feigned for self-interest; this, he implies, accounts for the strange synchronization of her "virtue" and her world. Appear virtuous and act viciously: this is the Pamelian formula for success. Neither vice nor virtue can finally succeed, only pseudo-virtue.

The romance in the old Quixotic sense then is embodied in Joseph and Parson Adams. They have a true ideal that does not agree with the world around them, which behaves according to the code of the Cibbers and Pamelas. The romance values are chastity and charity, Christian virtues, all ironically exposed as inappropriate to eighteenth-century England. In short, Fielding has adopted the interpretation of *Don Quixote* that attacks the accepted morality and criticizes it by the standard of an absolute. His interpretation of Quixote always carries this emphasis, sensing that in this world Richardson and Cibber, the innkeepers and merchants, express the real and Quixote the romance.

One effect of making both sides of the reality-romance contrast forms that are imitated or codes of conduct is to suggest that the characters act not independently or by storybook conventions but in terms of divergent sets of manners.

The Alternative Hero: Quixote

Although Richardson presents an unromantic, bourgeois milieu, Fielding detects beneath the psychological and sociological realism the old outlines of the romance heroine, knight, and dragon. The heroine, taken at her own and her author's valuation, is much too good, and the villain much too bad; moreover, the subject is the pursual of the angelic by the diabolic (Mr. B. is frequently called Lucifer), the latter extending downward into the sexual and sadistic.

For Fielding, the middle area between the romance and the burlesque is the "ridiculous," still a satiric domain where no man is above censure. "Great vices," Fielding tells us, explaining his meaning, "are the proper objects of our detestation, smaller faults, of our pity; but affectation appears to me the only true source of the Ridiculous." This area excludes the noncomic experience—the absolutely good and absolutely evil. Within this middle area, however, are worse kinds of affectation: people who take pride in their real or supposed virtues, their folly being evident to others but unknown to themselves (vanity); and people who, practicing a vice, consciously pretend to virtue (hypocrisy).

Fielding's earlier villains in the farces and *Jonathan Wild* were, despite their vicious acts and employment of incidental hypocrisy, essentially of the first type. In these characters Fielding avoided the detestable by dealing with those who imitated without attaining it; they differed from the vain mainly in their conscious effort to be "great," but like the vain they were always falling short. Pamela's particular vice, however, leads Fielding in *Joseph Andrews* to deal with those who pursue selfish ends while affecting virtue. In one key scene he contrasts the robbers who waylaid Joseph with the respectable folk who came upon him in their stagecoach. The robbers simply robbed and beat Joseph, making no excuses for their villainy and taking the risk of hanging; they are contrasted with the fine gentlemen and ladies who are just as ruthless and brutal but in no danger of being called robbers and hanged. The admitted villain is followed by the woman who is appalled at the idea of being asked for a dram but later, when held up by a highwayman, is shown to carry a flask.

Beyond the comedy of hypocrisy is the plain wickedness of the robbers and the malignant, melodramatic evil of the rapist and murderer. The latter appear only occasionally—in the squire who pointlessly kills the little dog of Wilson's daughter, in the man who tries to rape Fanny, or in the squire who torments Adams and attempts to abduct Fanny. Though sometimes appearing as threats, these acts are ordinarily averted. Such true villains, Fielding adds in his preface, recalling the Satanic villain, "never produce the intended evil." The mistreatment of Joseph and Adams, for example, stops after it passes a certain degree of brutality, and the squire himself is ducked; knavery is present in life, incidental to follies, but is carefully placed in relation to the more universal area of the ridiculous. Furthermore, all of the typically satiric situations are resolved happily. Having drawn out the full effect of the satire, Fielding cancels it with a happy ending. One example is the nightmare situation in which Adams finds himself when he saves Fanny from a rapist and is then accused of robbery and attempted murder by the would-be rapist. He is brought before a justice and remanded to prison until the next assizes; having reached its satiric climax, after which only pathos could follow, the scene is suddenly interrupted, someone recognizes Adams, and all is saved, except that in the confusion the real culprit slips away. The ending does not cancel the effect of the scene (it preserves the good without altering the fact of the evil), but it does restrain satire from becoming melodrama.

A more difficult problem for Fielding was how to create a good character. I wish to approach his solution from two directions, both somewhat tentative but, I think, illuminating for the development of satiric conventions into novelistic ones. The first is through the surrogate villains of the early satires, and the second is through one particular form of this villain, Don Quixote.

Following Gay's example, Fielding had begun by dividing evil into the general and the particular. The general was abstract "greatness," pure drive for power; the particular was an ordinary imitator of the general, a Peachum or Lockit, a below-stairs type, and thus a comic reflection of the more serious, but only implied, upper plot. Only occasionally, as in *The Modern Husband,* was the plot played out on its higher level, and then it failed dismally, perhaps because it had to be taken too seriously. The hero of the early works was all love or feeling, contrasted to the fools who sacrificed their real selves to an imaginary and delusive ideal. Much of the sympathy the reader may have felt for the surrogate villains resulted from the fact that, in terms of the types of affectation listed in the preface to *Joseph Andrews,* vanity, not hypocrisy, was the predominant vice—a character merely follows fashion, aspires to be something he is not, without any intent to deceive (indeed, quite the opposite). Even the hypocrite Wild, who pretended to be Heartfree's friend while ruining him, was, in terms of the theatrical metaphor, wearing as his mask the "great man's" face.

The hero of Fielding's novel, as a reaction to Pamela the "paragon," has to be complex—in the sense that appearing bad or foolish, he is good or wise, and that he is also a mixture of these qualities. Thus if the bad character was complex in the early works (in the sense of being two things at once), in the later works the complexity is transferred to the good character. The bad character can be said to derive from the Wild who pretends to be Heartfree's best friend while betraying him; but the good derives from the Wild who is striving for an ideal of greatness but is betrayed by his own humanity.

Both hypocrisy and vanity appear on the spectrum of the "ridiculous" in *Joseph Andrews,* part of that middle area where there are neither paragons nor Satanic villains; the evil characters tend toward the hypocrisy end, and the good, aspirers to inappropriate ideals, tend toward the vanity end. At the outset, Joseph is ridiculous as an imitator of London fashion and, over a more extended period, an imitator of his sister Pamela's ideal of chastity, which is being imparted to him by her letters (cf. Shamela and her mother's letters). The abstraction of chastity is soon dropped, and Joseph's love for Fanny is substituted as his motive for remaining intact. By then Parson Adams, whose vanities are his conviction of his great knowledge of the world, his classical learning, his abilities as a schoolmaster, and his sermons, especially the one on "Vanity," has entered the story. In terms of fashion, Adams, though naturally a good, charitable man, is ridiculous because he conforms to certain doctrines of the Stoics and the Church Fathers, which, whether good or bad in themselves, are at odds with his own natural goodness.

In a very real sense, Fielding approaches Adams, his great comic creation, through ridicule. Arthur Murphy, analyzing the scene in which Adams assures a stranger that he is rich by showing his half-guinea, experienced "an Emotion of Laughter attended in this Instance with a Contempt for *Adams's* Want of Knowledge of the World."[15] We may not agree, but the point, of course, is that Adams' innocence is accompanied by claims that he *is* knowledgeable. In the scenes after Fanny and Joseph are joined, he is juxtaposed in scene after scene with Joseph, and in each case a judgment has to be made against Adams.

However, if Fielding approached Adams through ridicule, it is important to note the peculiar effect that renders the word inadequate. Fielding's hero, contrast-ed to Pamela as hypocrite, had to be a representative of feeling over form; contrasted to Pamela as paragon, he had to be a mixed or middling character. Fielding chose a hero who expressed the virtue of feeling so completely that he was somewhat ridiculous on that account; part of the point, of course, was that heroes, in order to escape being paragons, have to be slightly ridiculous. Don Quixote offered Fielding his prototype for the man who reacts to stimuli from his basic good nature, often in complete opposition to custom, convention, and even prudence.

The paradigm Cervantes introduced in *Don Quixote* is a remarkable satiric device which Fielding was quick to grasp and exploit, presumably as early as 1729, when he wrote the first version of *Don Quixote in England.* Quixote, as he saw, can offer a satire either on the visionary who wished to change the world, or on the innkeepers who will not be changed, or on both. Quixote is too impractical, too inward; the innkeepers are too practical, too much of the world; since both are excesses, they act as criticisms of each other.

English satirists recognized the usefulness of one or both of these aspects of Quixote as early as the Civil War, when Samuel Butler made a Quixote out of a hypocritical Puritan enthusiast. Fielding explored one aspect when he made his early villians Quixotic—obsessive characters like Politic, Justice Squeezum, Sir Avarice Pedant, Sir Simon Raffler, even Jonathan Wild, pursuing his chimera of "greatness" as Quixote pursued his chimera of chivalry. The second possibility which informs Fielding's novels is to see Quixote as representative of idealism and simplicity, of a dedication to unfashionable and inward ideals that makes him the opposite of all the conformists or pretenders to conventional and fashionable immorality. His idealism, by comparison, makes the crassness of the world stand out in strong satiric relief.

The Quixotic hero is opposed by the officiousness of innkeepers, the crude reality of windmills and sheep, and the cruelty of masters and the officers of the law. Though Cervantes at the time condemns Quixote, there remains something noble about his freeing the prisoners on their way to the galleys—something deeper and more real, as well as more generous, than the officialdom that sent them there. In short, Quixote's madness is socially and prudentially bad, but spiritually good. His motive is always the best, whatever his action. In fact if one were to look for an example of feeling at odds with form, or motive at odds with action (in the opposite sense from Pamela), he could not find a better one than Quixote.

The emphasis of disapproval in a Fielding hero falls more decidedly on the society through which he moves than on the impractical hero himself, but there is just enough of the visionary in him to make us wish for some of the Pamelian prudence that would keep him on his guard, ready for assaults with more than a crab-stick or his fists. Adams is given the obsession of charity and Joseph the obsession of chastity. Joseph's is the more Quixotic in its origin, having been learned from his sister Pamela's letters, and also the more easily outgrown. By the time he is reunited with Fanny he has become the passionate lover—an equally Quixotic figure in this economically oriented society. Adams' basic obsession, seemingly natural but perhaps learned from the works of the Church Fathers, is a belief in the tenets of Apostolic Christianity, which, like Quixote's chivalry, no one else believes any more. Adams sees the world differently from most people, acts according to his vision, and sometimes tries to convert the people he meets. He argues the true nature of charity with Barnabas, Trulliber, and Pounce; he argues the necessity of truth-telling with the innkeeper; and he instructs Joseph in what he considers to be Christian submission to providence. Unlike the Swiftean version of Quixote, however, he never imposes physical coercion on those he tries to convert. There is no action and response, only response—from the wicked whom he meets.

As many critics have pointed out, Adams is the first great comic hero of the English novel. He is comic because of the constant jangling of the spiritual and physical in his makeup. He is wholly the parson, and yet he is hindered and jostled (dragged down in the Quixotic sense) by his ragged, unpriestly clothes, his physical grossness and athletic prowess, his bout with Parson Trulliber's pig, and so on. He is comic in the same sense as Dr. Johnson, the great lexicographer and moralist who, aroused in the middle of the night, is always willing to come down and frolic. Adams goes trotting ahead of the coach carrying the rest of his party: "Mrs. Slipslop desired the coachman to overtake him, which he attempted, but in vain; for the faster he drove, the faster ran the parson, often crying out, 'Aye, aye, catch me if you can'" (Bk. II, Chap. 7; *1,* 150). It is this Quixotic incongruity that makes him comic *and* sympathetic, a completely new combination and precisely what Fielding must have been seeking as the center of his comic epic in prose.

The Touchstone Structure

If the general effect of Fielding's comic epic in prose is indeed comic, the detail is drawn from the satiric forms and devices he knew so well. His particular use of scenic juxtaposition consists most often of a profession followed by an action in which the profession is exposed. To show that appearances or professions like Pamela's can be misleading, he fills his novel with situations in which a character speaks in high-flown terms, such as Lady Booby rationalizing her passion for Joseph, or in heroic terms, such as the gentleman discoursing "on courage, and the infamy of not being ready at all times to sacrifice our lives to our Country"

(Bk. II, Chap. 9; *1,* 158). Shortly thereafter the character's words are belied by his actions: Lady Booby's self-control dissolves and her lecherously leering face appears, or the gentleman runs away at the first sound of a woman's cry of rape. A conventional pose gives way to reveal the real person through his action—whether it be a worse person or occasionally a better. A third element is often present, which makes satiric judgment obligatory—an Adams, a quiet sort who makes no professions, but who rescues the girl who is being attacked or translates the Latin correctly, and thus gives us a norm by which to judge the other performers. With the most important unit of exposition established, Fielding launches into the elaboration of the central part of the novel—the adventures of the road. Throughout this section punishment of the innocent acts as the central structural device, keeping the reader's attention focused on the Trullibers and Tow-wouses, whose unamiable qualities are exposed by contact with Joseph and Adams.

Around the central touchstone of Joseph or Adams flock a series of characters, each classified and judged by his response. While the continental picaresque often employs its protagonist as a touchstone, nowhere does one find the device used so schematically and extensively as in *Joseph Andrews.* The most famous instance takes place in the scene where Joseph, robbed and left naked in a ditch, is met by the coachload of respectable folk. Here is Joseph, the prototypical touchstone, suffering humanity stripped of everything, but instead of stimulating charity, he reveals various forms of selfishness in the passengers: prurient prudery in the lady; greed in the coachman who wants his fare; in the lawyer, fear that the passengers will be called to account if Joseph dies; and in the old gentleman, fear that the robbers may still be about but eagerness for an opportunity to show off his wit in front of the lady. In this satiric structure the ideal is indicated by the poorest, most un-Pamelian of the group, the postilion who lends Joseph his coat (and is later transported for robbing a hen roost). The whole scene, in typical Augustan fashion, carries overtones of the parable of the good Samaritan (*Luke* 10:25-37), preparing the reader for the long series of similar scenes that follows.

This fan-shaped structure can be discrete, as in the stagecoach episode, or it can spread over several chapters. Joseph continues as a touchstone when he is taken to the Tow-wouses' inn, and reactions follow in quick succession. (1) The doctor, learning that Joseph is not a gentleman, goes home to bed. When he does get to Joseph the next day he reveals his professional incompetence (or his desire to gain credit for healing a hopeless case) by claiming that Joseph is as good as dead. (2) Mr. Tow-wouse shows charity, wishing to send Joseph one of his own shirts. (3) Mrs. Tow-wouse, however, will not let him ("Common charity, a f——!"); she is concerned because if Joseph dies they will have to pay for his funeral. (4) The servant girl Betty, another un-Pamelian character, secures Joseph a shirt from one of her lovers. A normative character like the postilion, she is later caught in a compromising situation and punished by her "betters." (5) Mr. Barnabas, the clergyman, though informed that Joseph is dying, spends his time guzzling punch. Chapter Thirteen describes Barnabas' circuitous route to Joseph's room, his haste to be finished and back at the punch bowl ("For no one could squeeze oranges till he came"). The chapter ends with Mrs. Tow-wouse refusing Joseph the tea he desires, and Betty buying him some herself (it should be added, however, that Betty is much attracted physically to Joseph). When Joseph's situation has been thoroughly exploited, Fielding turns to the highwayman who has been taken prisoner (one of those who nearly killed Joseph). The prisoner—or rather his loot—calls forth the constable's dishonesty, the legal arguments of the surgeon and Barnabas, Mrs. Tow-wouse's blame of her husband, and Tow-wouse's fear that he might be held liable.

Each new inn, each new encounter, presents a new "stagecoach" and a new set of characters to be met, tested, and judged. When the story of Leonora jilting Horatio for the richer Bellarmine is told (and it too is made up of such situations), the listeners react automatically:

> "Poor woman!" says Mrs. Slipslop; "what a terrible quandary she must be in!" "Not at all," says Miss Grave-airs; "such sluts can never be confounded." "She must have then more than Corinthian assurance," said Mr. Adams; "ay, more than Lais herself." (Bk. II, Chap. 4; *1*, 130)

Every action is capable of revealing its observers— Slipslop's lust, Graveairs' prudery, Adams' moralizing, naïveté, and vanity in his classical learning. Some situations catch Adams and even Joseph, but the first purpose of such scenes is to contribute to the gauntlet run by the heroes on their way back to Booby Hall and to pit against these innocents the Cibbers and Pamelas. When Fanny appears before the justice, the whole gamut of reactions is run through:

> the justice employed himself in cracking jests on poor Fanny, in which he was seconded by all the company at table. One asked, "Whether she was to be indicted for a highwayman?" Another whispered in her ear, "If she had not provided herself a great belly, he was at her service." A third said, "He warranted she was a relation of Turpin." To which one of the company, a great wit, shaking his head, and then his sides, answered, "He believed she was nearer related to Turpis." (Bk. II, Chap. 11; *1*, 168)

With the good Samaritan echoes now building to unmistakable echoes of the trial and punishment of Christ (Adams and Fanny condemned; the real criminal re-

leased), Fielding presents the irresponsible justice, the lecher, the vicious-minded, and the great wit revealing themselves as they collect about the helpless innocents. The tricks played on Adams by the squire and his hangers-on, leading to the attempted rape of Fanny, are only the climax of these encounters.

In terms of the profession-performance form, which is central in a work concerned with hypocrisy, the touchstone becomes the second half, the exposing action, with the profession either assumed (these are often pious-seeming folk) or implicit in the pompous terms they use to cover up the brutality of their reactions. These satiric structures do not disappear in the beginning and end of the novel but are subordinated to the story of Lady Booby's passion for Joseph. Yet even here, when all that is necessary is for Lady Booby to corrupt a corruptible lawyer, the reader is treated to a small anatomy of the unethical lawyer in his speeches and plans for thwarting the Joseph-Fanny marriage. Nor is it sufficient for Mr. Booby to rescue Joseph from the court; the reader is also presented with lawyer Scout's deposition, which demonstrates the shiftiness, illiteracy, and legal jargon of the justice who wrote it. The most conventional of all satiric expository forms appears in the narrative of Mr. Wilson, who simply recites a list of the evils of London, ending with his withdrawal to an Eden (or Golden Age) in the country. But here the form has not been absorbed, and the purely satiric piling up of vice upon vice, crowding of incident upon incident, carries an imitative effect that is closer to Richardson than to Fielding.

The profession-performance and touchstone forms, on the other hand, support the initial and sustaining point of the novel about Pamelian appearance and reality. More than satire, these forms represent Fielding's image of the way life operates, and they demonstrate his continuing concern with the meaning of an action. In the *Champion* (Dec. 11, 1739), he argues that

> The only Ways by which we can come to any Knowledge of what passes in the Minds of others, are their Words and Actions; the latter of which, hath by the wiser Part of Mankind been chiefly depended on, as the surer and more infallible guide.[16]

Faces, he adds, are no more reliable than words. This discussion, which is used to introduce a hypocrite's letter-to-the-editor, is transformed into the theme of *Shamela.* Reminiscent of Pamela, Shamela tells us "That to go to church, and to pray, and to sing psalms, and to honour the clergy, and to repent, is true religion; and 'tis not doing good to one another." And in Parson Williams the maxim is "That 'tis not what we do, but what we believe, that must save us."[17] In *Joseph Andrews,* where Josephs and Shamelas are placed in the same world, the central fact is that actions alone can be relied on as tests of men's character or inner being. In the ***Essay on the Knowledge of the Characters of Men,*** published in the ***Miscellanies*** of 1743, Fielding goes into more detail on the subject, which clearly interests him more and more. Here he argues in the typically satiric vein that "the actions of men seem to be the justest interpreters of their thoughts, and the truest standards by which we may judge them. By their fruits you shall know them." He then examines the various factors that obscure a proper judgment of actions: "when we take their own words against their actions" and "when we take the colour of a man's actions, not from their own visible tendency, but from his public character: when we believe what others say of him, in opposition to what we see him do" (*14,* 289-90). The first of these is the subject of ***Joseph Andrews;*** the second, anticipating a new phase of Fielding's career, becomes the subject of ***Tom Jones,*** where the reputations of Tom and Blifil render judgment difficult.

It is important to see that the touchstone structure is a logical development of the multiple commentators of Fielding's satiric farces. The normative aspect of these commentators led to the Fielding narrator: their apparently different points of view in the farces resolved into a single one that unambiguously explained the action they observed. In the *Champion* essays, where Fielding again began with a group of commentators, the Vinegar family tended to narrow into one person, the normative speaker, who subsequently became the narrator of ***Joseph Andrews.*** But the suggestion of multiple opinions and their reflection back on the commentators remained to some extent throughout the *Champion* and leads in ***Joseph Andrews*** to the multiple reactions to an action that is unambiguous (perhaps made so by the normative narrator) and by which the spectators are judged.

Already the device begins to imply the difficulty of judging an action, but as yet the difficulty lies in the observers, not in the action itself. The device may also, in the generally epistemological context of the anti-*Pamela,* suggest a range of attitudes rather than a group of different kinds of vice. Finally, as part of an anti-romance situation, it brings together a number of people from different professions and social classes and records their reactions to a social situation or crisis, something out of the ordinary routine that will reveal their true selves and (the crucial element) juxtapose the social appearance and the animal reality. In short, it suggests that revelation of character through an action is the point in question rather than the proof of a satiric theorem.

We cannot accept these forms as exactly what Fielding claims them to be or what they may appear to be. They are not in fact honest searches for truth or reality. Even if their extremely schematic anatomy-like structure did not argue against their objectivity, it would be clear that their purpose is a satiric one—to support Fielding's general premise about the relationship between his heroes and Cibberian and Pamelian society. As A. D. McKillop puts it, in Fielding's novels the discrepancy between appearance and reality "is not treated as an ultimate metaphysical problem, as in *Don Quixote.* Fielding is not trying to present or to pluck out the heart of a mystery; he is continuously corroborating a position which he has made clear from the first."[18] Nevertheless, Fielding's basic unit became a basic unit of the novel and, in his next novel, outgrew its satiric origin. The sense of a test and a judgment emerges, as does the leisurely pace, which as much as anything creates the mood of the novel as it developed in his hands.

The Debt to Pamela

Joseph Andrews is an anti-*Pamela,* but in more ways than one it verges on being a pro-*Pamela.* The most important element of *Pamela* and, later, *Clarissa* was the portrait of the individual defending her personal integrity, her very identity against threats from outside. Since Coleridge, however, readers reacting to Richardson's hot, stuffy sickroom tend to forget what a moral intention meant to Richardson, Pope, Bishop Slocock, and other conservative contemporaries who went on record in praise of *Pamela.* It meant, on the one hand, presenting an ideal of conduct, a Christian passing through trials and tribulations; on the other hand, it meant showing the evil threats to this virtue in their true colors. The most effective method for the latter was, of course, satire.

Mrs. Jewkes and Colbrand, both epitomes of the malevolent guardian, are presented by conventional satiric portraits, emblematic and perhaps derived from the picaresque. They are domesticated in Richardson's novel because they are seen through Pamela's eyes and thus thoroughly assimilated to her psychologically convincing situation. She is satirizing a particular enemy, with only her own fear as motive and with no sense of exposing a general vice. Nevertheless, it is interesting that embedded in such a work should be fragments of the old satiric conventions.

More significant for Fielding is the touchstone form with which Richardson begins his novel—the treatment of a helpless servant girl at the hands of a wicked master, self-seeking servants, and the master's self-satisfied relatives and neighbors. A central character in a difficult situation is reacted to by a series of good and bad people. The vague outlines of this form occasionally emerge in a structure very much like that of ***Joseph Andrews,*** as in Parson Williams' letter recounting his failure to secure aid from the neighboring gentry. Lady Jones does not care to make an enemy of B.; Lady Darnford puts the responsibility on her husband, who sees nothing wrong with a young gentleman's seducing his waiting-maid ("He hurts *no family* by this"); Mr. Peters, the minister of the parish, sees ulterior motives in Williams' defense of Pamela, says it is "too common and fashionable a case to be withstood by a private clergyman or two," claims that any action on his part might turn B. against him, and, besides, "'tis what all young gentlemen will do"; even Williams has some doubts, since "the gentleman is dying, whose living Mr. B. has promised me" (*1,* 168-70).

The novel, however, changes direction when B. arrives at his Lincolnshire estate: the touchstone structure and the anatomy are replaced by the simple battle of wills, a contest between B. and Pamela. The domain of satire, as Frye has pointed out, is the time *after* the forces of evil have defeated those of good; this precludes any active conflict between good and evil which is not one-sided. If Richardson had included letters from B. as well as from Pamela (as he did with their equivalents in *Clarissa*), his whole novel might have taken on the form of a battle of wills. The single point of view renders the larger part of the novel the pursuit of an innocent. Richardson is drawing in a vague way on Mrs. Manley's *chroniques scandaleuses* (even in the sense that he began with a true story); while his form is conventional, however, his conclusion and general effect are not.[19]

Once Pamela and B. are married, she again becomes a persecuted maiden and touchstone. This time she runs the gauntlet of the outraged reaction of Lady Davers, the foppish one of her nephew Jackey, and the jealous one of Lady Davers' maid. Pamela's confrontation of Lady Davers is less a conflict between strong-willed characters than the high point in the introduction of the new wife to a satiric portrait gallery of snobbish relatives. First she is the virtuous person tormented by these unfeeling, snobbish boors, and then she is the female satirist goaded into rebuke—the same figure who appeared occasionally in Lincolnshire. In his efforts to make the reader aware of Pamela's biting retorts, Richardson has Jackey point to her satiric strength whenever she completes a sally. Her remarks, however, are too direct, too prolix and realistic, too much a result of her situation to create a genuine feeling of satire.

Thus whenever the possibility of a dramatic conflict is past and the situation becomes relatively static, Richardson slips into popular conventions, which are sometimes satiric, although to him they were probably less specifically satiric than a way to the moral tone of denunciation through ridicule. The greatest force working against any possibility of sustained satire, as well as moral doctrine, is the character of Pamela. In the usual moral work the central character is not so central as she is, so closely felt, so absorbing as far as the reader is concerned. When she describes someone as vicious, he is only vicious through her eyes, to her way

of thinking; when she explains one of her own actions, it is only from her point of view. This unreliability of the narrator, of course, notoriously destroys the intended direction of Richardson's structure, which is to contrast Pamela's angelic flight to the evil pursuit of Mr. B. and with the good and bad people who react to her during flight. But it does create, among other things, a new scene based on satiric conventions, in which one character satirizes another without reference to anything outside their own private situation. This is a scene to which we shall return later.

Joseph Andrews is an alternative to Pamela, and yet Fielding places him in a situation roughly parallel to hers. Fielding has taken from Richardson the satiric situation of the innocent pursued and punished by the guilty and turned it into an obviously satiric principle of structure. It is even somewhat unfair of Fielding to contrast Joseph repulsing Lady Booby's advances and being discharged with the consequence of Pamela's less unequivocal repulses; after all, Pamela is threatened and put upon for a long time before she arrives at her happy ending. In a sense Fielding is merely showing that interim period, though extending the scope of Joseph's experience beyond sexual attack. Attacks on Joseph begin with his virtue but go on to more general and physical assaults and finally extend to Adams and even Fanny—to all the good, innocent people. The point is that this is how a virtuous Pamela would be treated in this real world, but it is also very close to the treatment accorded to the actual Pamela during the first and best-known part of Richardson's novel.

The influence is largely formal, since Fielding never dwells on Joseph's or Fanny's feelings; most of the time the reader is not allowed sympathy for the victim (as in *Pamela*) but indignation at the persecutor. Richardson is not a more important source for the persecuted hero than Cervantes; but from Richardson, the "enemy," Fielding was able to pick up an older strain of the picaresque, in which the low social status of the protagonist contributes to his troubles (not one of Quixote's problems) and in which the servant-master relationship plays some part.[20] Joseph, however, like Richardson's second heroine Clarissa, refuses to come to terms with his corrupt society and in this sense derives from the Quixote tradition.

Parson Adams is another of Fielding's original and brilliant contributions to this compromise form. By a weird logic Adams corresponds to Parson Williams, as Joseph and Fanny correspond to Pamela; Fielding gives his hero a clergyman, like Pamela's, to assist him to escape. Adams is as effective in preserving Joseph as Williams was in preserving Pamela (an irony Fielding had already explored in **Shamela**). By shifting the focus, on the one hand, to the pursuers and, on the other, to the figure of the comic clergyman-helper, Fielding has created a result not too far from Richardson's, yet comic and satiric. He has both the moral truth and the psychological truth Richardson attempted to join. Richardson's mistake may have been attempting both in the same figure, Pamela.

It is from *Pamela* (novel *and* character) that Fielding took his immediate inspiration. Looking at Richardson's novel he could see both strains of the potential novel; he could see the one he was interested in, the moral commentary, perverted and ruined, and so he set about correcting it, naturally following to some extent the basic situation of Richardson's novel. He changed the focus from the pursued to the pursuers, particularly in the middle part of his novel, but not so much as to deny the connection with Pamela or the alternative version he was presenting. But like Pamela, Adams and Joseph are positive, fully explored proposals for the good; they have to be, as alternatives to Pamelian virtue. Figures so fully developed were not common in satire prior to this. It is, in fact, in the development of these good characters that Fielding establishes *Joseph Andrews* as a transition between satire and the novel.

Joseph Andrews is the great watershed of Fielding's career. In all of his work the evil character appears either as the protagonist or as the persecutor of the protagonist: as the spider at the middle of a web dotted with trapped flies or as the cutthroat lying in wait along dark streets for the good man to pass. In *Jonathan Wild* both situations appear—Wild by himself and Heartfree and his wife being waylaid by Wild. In the satires that can best be called Augustan the evil agent is a larger-than-life symbol of man's perversity attempting to engross, amoeba-like, all that comes within reach. Certain mitigations accompany his portrait, but he remains bad and more or less in the center of the canvas. In *Joseph Andrews,* however, the evil agent receives much attention and even in the aggregate is still the subject of the satire, but he is no longer in the center, no longer dwelt on so lovingly, and is in fact less interesting than Parson Adams. His pride and swagger have been reduced to hypocrisy, and his exposure is that of a coward who affects bravery or a slut who affects gentility. So long as the character aspired to "greatness," a fashionable ideal, hypocrisy was secondary—one might use it as a way to achieve "greatness." But when Fielding turned from opera heroes and politicians to Pamela, who aspired not to "greatness" directly but disguised this quality by the term "virtue," he became concerned primarily with hypocrisy. Evil is no longer the adhering to a fashionable but wrong standard, but adhering to this standard while making loud protestations of a morally right standard; the character's motive has now become the subject of exposure.

With *Pamela* goodness became a problem for Fielding. The relative complexity of the evil man is transferred to the good man who is in the center of the narrative. It is altogether possible that *Pamela* may have made Fielding conclude that a hero could be as interesting as a villain. His moral essays, though assisting him, could not have shown him the way. His reaction against *Pamela* did show him that if the ordinary evil man is a mixed lot, so is the ordinary good man.

Notes

[1] Cf. Swift's "Dedication to Prince Posterity" in *A Tale of a Tub* and Fielding's *Covent-Garden Journal,* No. 40, ed. Jensen, *1,* 362.

[2] See Ian Watt, *The Rise of the Novel* (Berkeley and Los Angeles, University of California Press, 1956), and Leslie Fiedler, *Love and Death in the American Novel* (New York, Criterion Books, 1960).

[3] *The Early Masters of English Fiction* (Lawrence, University of Kansas Press, 1956), p. 57.

[4] *Pamela* (London, Chapman and Hall, 1902), *1,* 141; *Joseph Andrews,* Bk. I, Chap. 6; *1,* 40.

[5] *The Poetic Workmanship of Alexander Pope* (Minneapolis, University of Minnesota Press, 1955), p. 31.

[6] Watt, *Rise of the Novel,* p. 288.

[7] Maynard Mack has pointed out this effect in his introduction to *Joseph Andrews* (New York, Rinehart, 1948), p. 6.

[8] Samuel Coleridge, *The Complete Works,* ed. W. C. T. Shedd (New York, 1853), *4,* 380.

[9] See André Le Breton, *Le Roman au XVIIIeme siècle* (Paris, n.d.), and Dorothy Frances Dallas, *Le Roman Français de 1660 à 1680* (Paris, 1932), Chap. 1.

[10] Letter VI; *Joseph Andrews* and *Shamela,* ed. Martin C. Battestin (Boston, Riverside Editions, 1961), p. 313.

[11] *Pamela, 1,* 72.

[12] The situation is perhaps even more reminiscent of *The Beggar's Opera* with the Peachum-Polly-Macheath relationship repeated in Mrs. Andrews-Shamela-Parson Williams. Gay offered Fielding a model for the interpretation of the middle-class mind that must have contributed to Fielding's interpretation of Pamela as Shamela. Mrs. Peachum sounds like Mother Andrews when she explains that "the first time a woman is frail, she should be somewhat nice, methinks, for then or never is the time to make her fortune. After that, she hath nothing to do but to guard herself from being found out, and she may do what she pleases" (II.8). Polly herself puts it this way: "A girl who cannot grant some

things, and refuse what is most essential, will make but a poor hand of her beauty, and soon be thrown upon the common" (I.7).

[13] Cf. Martin C. Battestin, *The Moral Basis of Fielding's Art: A Study of "Joseph Andrews"* (Middletown, Conn., Wesleyan University Press, 1959), pp. 8-9.

[14] Another sort of parallel may also be present. Battestin believes that Fielding uses a mock-heroic structure similar to Pope's, but with the *Bible* instead of the *Aeneid* as the second term. Abraham Adams and Joseph, he argues, should suggest to us overtones of the biblical Abraham and Joseph (see *The Moral Basis,* pp. 41, 48).

[15] *The Gray's-Inn Journal,* No. 96, Aug. 17, 1754.

[16] *Champion, 1,* 79.

[17] *Shamela,* p. 319.

[18] "Some Recent Views of Tom Jones," *College English, 21* (1959), 19.

[19] This is not to deny anticipations and analogues in France that were strictly amorous. Prévost employs pursued heroines, and Mlle. de Theville is pursued by the wicked comte de Versac in Crébillon fils' *Egarements du Coeur et de l'Esprit* (1736); the heroine of Duclos' *Histoire de Mme. de Lux* (1741) is forced to give herself to a blackmailer and is also subsequently drugged and raped. While these carry *Pamela's* erotic theme, they do not carry the other un-French qualities that distinguish Richardson's novel—its echoes of satiric and picaresque forms.

[20] The idea of the servant girl probably came to Richardson from the large conduct book literature of his time, but consciously or not, he has connected his book with the basic servant-master relationship of the early picaresque novels, though characteristically narrowing his focus to only one episode. In the first third of *Pamela,* during the assaults on her virtue, he constantly refers to the proper relationship between Pamela and B. and B.'s perversion of it. "Well may I forget that I am your servant," Pamela tells B., "when you forget what belongs to a master"; she accuses him of "demeaning" himself "to be so free to a poor servant" (*1,* 18). "When a master of his honour's degree demeans himself to be so free as *that* to a poor servant as me, what is the next to be expected?" Pamela talks on and on, referring to "the distance between a master and a servant" (*1,* 33-34). Pamela of course derives less directly from the Spanish picara like Justina than from Defoe's heroes and heroines whose final goal, however disguised by moral platitudes, is simply survival.

Glenn W. Hatfield (essay date 1968)

SOURCE: "'Words and Ideas': Fielding and the Augustan Critique of Language," in his *Henry Fielding and the Language of Irony,* University of Chicago Press, 1968, pp. 28-53.

[*In the following excerpt from his book* Henry Fielding and the Language of Irony, *Hatfield examines Fielding's moral vision in the context of early eighteenth-century concerns about the increasing discontinuity between words and the things they were intended to represent. Taking into account Fielding's occasional prose as well as his major novels, Hatfield focuses on Fielding's pessimism with respect to the potential for clear and coherent communication.*]

The idea of the "corruption of language" is as old, perhaps, as the study of language itself. It takes cognizance of an obvious fact—the phenomenon of linguistic change—and it was in this sense that the phrase was most often used in the seventeenth and eighteenth centuries. For Fielding, however, it meant this and something more. He was not interested, so far as we know, in linguistic change as such, and there is little evidence that he was worried, in the manner of Pope,[1] over the possibility that such as Chaucer is would Fielding be. The kind of corruption he was concerned about was that which had already infected and rendered suspect the language of the day, the language which he, as a writer, had no choice but to use.

He was not, then, a reformer of the tongue in the sense that Dryden and Swift would have liked to be, with their visions of an English Language Academy for the purpose of "settling" usage and arresting change,[2] and he was probably more skeptical than Dr. Johnson himself of the aspirations of eighteenth-century lexicographers to "fix" the English language. He did not live to see the publication of Johnson's *Dictionary* (1755), but he was familiar with Nathan Bailey's *Universal Etymological English Dictionary* (1721) and, though the evidence is slim, seemed little impressed with its pretensions of settling the proper meanings of words. A witness for Colley Cibber, on trial in the *Champion* "for the Murder of the English Language," testifies before the Court of Censorial Enquiry that she saw the defendant "often . . . look in a Book [called] *Bailey's Dictionary. At which there was a great Laugh*"[3]— though whether at the expense of Cibber or Bailey (or both) it is not clear. In an earlier *Champion* paper about the "arcana" of politics he quotes with apparent approval Bailey's definition of the word "Mystery," but refers to the lexicographer himself as "the learned Mr. *Bailey*,"[4] the kind of "corrupt" epithet which in Fielding is always suspect of irony[5] And in *Tom Jones,* Sophia's blunt statement of her objection to Blifil as a suitor—"I hate him"—elicits from Aunt Western the recommendation that if she is ever to "learn a proper use of words," she "should consult Bailey's Dictionary" and learn that "it is impossible you should hate a man from whom you have received no injury" (III, 339-40). Mrs. Western, of course, is the most dubious of advocates, but it is interesting, both as evidence of Fielding's concern for detail and as an indication of why he may have distrusted the lexicographer's claims to authority, that Bailey's definition of the word in question supports her quibble. "To hate," according to Bailey (in the original version of his *Dictionary* which Fielding must have had in mind), meant "To bear an ill-Will to"—a sense which would indeed make the word inappropriate to describe the feelings of the determined but generous-spirited Sophia. And though Bailey's addition of a second meaning in a later (1730) expanded edition of the *Dictionary* would accommodate Sophia's sense of the word ("To have an Aversion to"), the limitations of the lexicographer's methods are clear, particularly in the case of a word such as "hate" which could not be referred back to a respectable Latin or Greek "original" and which had therefore to be defined according to the compiler's own knowledge of current usage. Even Dr. Johnson, the first dictionary-maker who tried systematically to register all the various senses of words, would probably not have satisfied Fielding's apparent objections to a method which so conspicuously failed to reflect the subtlety and variety of living speech. Fielding would have agreed, no doubt, with Johnson's own self-deprecating caveat in his Preface to the *Dictionary* that "to enchain syllables, and to lash the wind, are equally the undertakings of pride, unwilling to measure its desires by its strength."

Nor is it likely that the man who sometimes called himself Scriblerus Secundus approved any more than did the original Scriblerians of the program of the Royal Society for "improving the English tongue" by bringing it, in Bishop Sprat's famous words, "as near the Mathematical plainness" as possible so as to enable scientific and philosophical writers to state "so many *things* almost in an equal number of *words*." [6] The special liability of abstract words to perversion and multiplicity of meaning was recognized by nearly all of the seventeenth- and eighteenth-century critics of the tongue. But the orthodox assumption that language was (or ought to be) the exact mirror of objective nature gave more comfort in a materialistic age to those reformers who wished to banish abstractions from the language altogether on the grounds that they could not be assigned concrete referents [7] than to the humanists who saw in the shifting meanings of such words a threat to traditional immaterial values which must be resisted, they believed, not by substituting the mechanistic vocabulary of a Hobbesian materialism in which the great ethical and spiritual truths of man and nature would be inexpressible, but rather by shoring up the abstract words themselves. There is no such direct attack in Fielding on the Royal Society's supposed wish

to purge the language of abstractions as Swift's description in Part III of *Gulliver's Travels* of the School of Languages at the Grand Academy of Lagado, whose professors manage to dispense with words altogether and to discourse entirely by means of "things" which they clumsily carry about with them for that purpose. But, like Pope in Book IV of *The Dunciad,* Fielding ridiculed the preoccupation of the Royal Society *virtuosi* with meaningless trivia like the polyp which is the overt subject of **Some Papers To Be Read before the Royal Society** (1743) and curious anomalies like the pullet in **Tom Jones** "with a letter in its maw," which "would have delighted the Royal Society" (V, 210)—at the expense, it is always implied, of universal principles of nature and intangible human values; and in the *Champion* for April 27, 1740, he refers in passing to "such as we generally say can hardly write and read, or, in other Words, a Man qualified to be a Member of the R——S——y." [8]

Of grammarians, the most flourishing breed of language reformers in his own time, Fielding was perhaps more tolerant, though again the evidence of his views is rather slight. Against the legal "Art of Tautology" in the *Champion* essay on the abuse of words he cites the authority of William Lily, whose Latin grammar was the standard work on that subject throughout the seventeenth and eighteenth centuries and the probable source of many of the rules which English grammarians sought (as Fielding does here) to import into English. [9] The examples in the turncoat essay of "corrupted" words (tyrant, villain, knave) were apparently borrowed by Fielding from Michael Maittaire's *English Grammar* (1712), a work which avowedly set out to "draw a Parallel between [the English] Language and the Learned ones" and which offered the same three words as instances of "how powerful and arbitrary is Use and Custom in abusing . . . the true and original signification of words." [10] The grammarian James Harris was a friend of Fielding and may have been an occasional contributor to the *Covent-Garden Journal*. His *Hermes* (1751), the classic eighteenth-century statement of the theory of universal grammar, was in Fielding's library at the time of his death. [11]

At most, then, we can conclude that Fielding was acquainted with the grammatical reformers of his time and may have sympathized with some of their aims. He associated himself, in another *Champion* paper, with Quintilian's pronouncement "that Grammar is the Foundation of all Science" [12] and included in the indictment against Colley Cibber the charge "that you, not having the Fear of Grammar before your Eyes, . . . in and upon the *English* Language an Assault did make." But Fielding's actual assessment of the relative importance of grammar is probably reflected in the testimony of the critic who, in support of Cibber's claim "that other *Literati* have used the said Language more barbarously than I have," produces enough examples of sheer meaninglessness in the works of a certain "very great and Eminent Physician" that the hapless Cibber's share in the crime seems small by comparison. For "it may be more properly called the Murder of the Language to bring Sentences together without any Meaning, than to make their Meaning obscure by any Slip in Grammar or Orthography." [13]

The grammarians, like the advocates of a Language Academy, the Royal Society theorists, and the other would-be reformers of the age, believed that the rule of language could be imposed from above. "Corruption" for them was mere change, whether in morphology, pronunciation, spelling, or meaning, and so long as this process could be either arrested or directed by some external authority, the language, they believed, was safe. It could be fixed; it could even be improved. But there is no evidence that Fielding shared this assumption. For all his concern about the condition of the language he was not a reformer in this sense because he was too conscious of the fact that language is, above all else, the words which men *use,* whether they are responsible citizens of the Republic of Letters like himself, ignorant hacks like Cibber, or obfuscating pedants like the "very great and Eminent Physician" who shares Cibber's responsibility for the murder of the English language. Corruption was change, to be sure, but not merely the historical process which distinguished the modern Dryden from the archaic Chaucer and which threatened, by the same token, the immortality of all writers. Corruption for Fielding was more significantly the change which was going on in his own time—the change from meaning to meaninglessness, the change from grandness of import to triviality, the change which was contaminating the vocabulary of sincerity with the suspicion of hypocrisy, the change which rendered "very great" and "eminent" into ironic words not simply by means of a conscious understanding with the reader that their senses should be reversed, but by virtue of the current irresponsible use in society which had already made this reversal implicit in the words themselves.

In a passage already quoted from the *Covent-Garden Journal,* Fielding declares that the moralists and theologians "offend" by using words "in a Sense often directly contrary to that which Custom (the absolute Lord and Master, according to Horace, of all the Modes of Speech) hath allotted them." The deferential tone, of course, is ironic, and "Custom" is the real object of attack. But the effectiveness of the Modern Glossary depends on our recognizing that the definitions of the terms in question *are* an accurate reflection (allowing, as always, for satiric distortion) of popular usage—not what the words *used* to mean, or *ought* to mean, but what they actually *do* mean in common use. The serious point of the essay, then (as of Fielding's other statements of the corruption theme and of much of his irony of "corrupted" words), lies in the juxtaposition

of two kinds or levels of usage. One level (represented here by the "Divines and moral Writers") is traditional and responsible; the other (represented in this instance by the "polite Part of Mankind") is popular, current, and irresponsible. But even more basically, perhaps, the point of the essay lies in an unresolved tension between a recognition of the power of popular usage and a denial of its right to that power, a belief on the one hand that the meaning of words is inviolable, and a recognition on the other that in practice meaning is arbitrary, inconstant, and frequently nonexistent, the product not of inherited culture and wisdom but only of social whim and chance, the mirror not of the permanent ideals of religion, morality, and civilization, but only of the shabby and shifting values of the moment.

The idea that usage (or "Custom") was the ruler of language was by no means new. There was classical authority for it in Horace and Quintilian, and the former's dictum on

$$\text{Quem penes arbitrium est et jus et norma} \overset{\text{usus}}{} \text{loquendi,}^{[14]}$$

which Fielding cites, was a special favorite of English writers on language. The biblical accounts of the origin and evolution of language, to which most of the language theorists paid lip service at least, tended to the same conclusion. Language was the gift of God to Man, the special power given Adam to "name" all the creatures of the earth. These names were at first, by the grace of God, constant and universal, mirroring exactly the things which they described. But at Babel, God's wrath brought down upon Man the curse of dispersal and multiplicity of tongues, and thereafter His blessing on the marriage of words and things was withdrawn. The arbitration of language was left to Man alone, and the result was the mutability and confusion of all modern tongues.

The corruption of language was the inevitable result of its government by a corrupt humanity, and English theorists of language from the early seventeenth century on were well aware of it. "Words are formed at the will of the generality," wrote Bacon, "and there arises from a bad and inapt formation of words a wonderful obstruction to the mind." [15] Bacon himself offered no remedies for this situation, but the implications were clear: if learning is ever to advance beyond the vague and cumbersome formulations of the present, steps must be taken either to remove the existing language from the control of "the generality" or else to devise a new medium of discourse altogether free (like poetic diction) of their influence. John Wilkins' *Essay towards a Real Character and a Philosophical Language* (1668), for example, was predicated on the assumption that human reason could construct a "universal" tongue close to, if not identical with, the original language invented by the divinely inspired Adam. The belief of such eighteenth-century grammarians as James Harris and Robert Lowth in a "universal grammar" rested on a similar faith but with less reliance on the biblical underpinnings. Even Sprat conceived of the ideal scientific medium as a kind of reconstruction of a perfect original: a "return back to the primitive purity and shortness" of language.[16]

But whether the ideal was regarded as a past perfection to be recovered or as a pattern of future excellence to be reached by a gradual process of "refinement," the appeal was always to an authority above current usage—reason, "the nature of things," universal grammar, etymology.[17] Even Dr. Johnson, who endeavored in the *Dictionary*, so he said, merely "to discover and promulgate the decrees of custom," could not suppress his doubts as to whether "the sovereignty of words" belonged to custom "by right or by usurpation,"[18] and in his actual definitions he decided, as often as not, in favor of the latter by utterly excluding current meanings which he felt were "incorrect." He defined the word "journal," for example, as D. Nichol Smith has pointed out, as "any paper published daily," even though at the time he wrote and for a considerable period before nearly all of the English newspapers so entitled were weeklies.[19] "Every dictionary," observed Anselm Bayly in *An Introduction to Languages* (1758), "is more or less formed upon the principle, that names were imposed from some reason, and that language is ideal."[20] In the eighteenth century, at least, this was probably true, and not only of dictionaries but of any approach to the problems of language which appealed to some "original" standard of purity or to some "universal" principle of language. The doctrine of usage as the arbiter of language was everywhere acknowledged, but the whole effort of the reform movement was bent on repudiating its final implications: that authoritative control was impossible for any medium which took its life from the active principle of use. It was perhaps the needs of the new science for a more precise medium, as R. F. Jones has maintained,[21] or the reaction against the rhetorical excesses of Puritan and "metaphysical" "enthusiasts," as George Williamson has argued,[22] which first gave impetus to the campaign to reform the English language. But it was the common struggle to wrest control away from "the generality" which gave it its real unity of purpose.

Fielding, in his appeals to etymology and in his ironic invocations of the "original" meanings of words, was at one with his age in denying the *right* of current usage to the rule of language. But he was too much of a realist to underestimate its power and too conscious of the ground the enemy had already won to have much faith in the more sanguine plans of reform. The campaigns to reform the tongue, however successful they

may have been by Fielding's time in the formalization of spelling, pronunciation, and grammar, had failed dismally in their attempts to arrest semantic change, or to "settle the significations of words." The vocabulary of the eighteenth century, says Joan Platt, a modern historian of the language, was "remarkable for having adopted a great number of new senses for words already existing, rather than in having acquired many completely new words." The process of "degradation," whereby a word passes out of standard "good English" and is relegated to use by lower, ignorant classes only, was much more common in this period, she notes, than "amelioration," or the process of a word's rising in respectability, and one aspect of this degradation was an inevitable "deterioration" in meaning. In the course of decline, a word once powerful and serious often became weak and facetious as semi-educated middle-class speakers, trying to imitate their "betters," succeeded only in dragging the word in question down from the level of respectability. Another cause she isolates for this "deterioration" is the "rise of journalese" in the early eighteenth century. But the most prevalent kind of semantic change Miss Platt discovers in the period is the process of "specialization," the change of a word's meaning (as in the classic case of "wit") from a general or abstract primary sense to a more concrete, specific, or particular one. The process, of course, could work the other way too, and "generalization" was also a factor in the changing meanings of the time. But "the eighteenth century was peculiarly the period in which the restrictive tendency worked in preparation for modern colloquial English."[23] Lord Chesterfield, always a shrewd observer of his times, noticed the same tendencies, though he was inclined to place the blame particularly on the ladies: "Not content with enriching our language by words absolutely new, my fair countrywomen have gone still further, and improved it by the application and extension of old ones to various and very different significations. They take a word and change it, like a guinea into shillings for pocket money, to be employed on the several occasional purposes of the day."[24]

These are the kinds of "corruptions," it is clear, with which Fielding was concerned, and there was good reason for fearing that the forces of popular usage were getting the upper hand. "Great" and "eminent," for all their original power and seriousness, seemed to have been reduced not only in social status but also, as a consequence, in meaning as well, and insofar as they still conveyed any "ideas," these were as likely as not to have a facetious edge, or at least to lend themselves readily to facetiously ironic usage. "Honor," narrowed in popular application to such senses as "dueling," was a great abstraction broken down into the small change of specialized meanings; and "virtue" and "religion," the victims of similar forces, had been reduced, according to Fielding, to the condition of sheer meaninglessness.

Nor was Fielding alone in singling out such words as the products of debilitating semantic change. "No one in the eighteenth century," remarks Ian Watt, "seems to have spoken about great men . . . without irony."[25] Gay's use of the term, in *The Beggar's Opera* (1728), as a noble word fallen among thieves, is almost identical with Fielding's in **Jonathan Wild;** and Steele, in the *Spectator,* strikes off a parenthetical qualification which is pure Fielding in its identification of the ironic word with its corrupt usage: Louis of France and Peter of Russia, he says, are "the two greatest Men now in *Europe* (according to the common acceptation of the Word Great)."[26] Again, in the *Tatler,* Steele lists among his achievements as the "Censor of Great Britain" the separation he has made of "Duellists from Men of Honour," referring, apparently, to the *Tatler* No. 25, in which, anticipating Fielding's formulation of the same point in **The Temple Beau,** he declares that "as the matter now stands, it is not to do handsome actions denominates a man of honour, it is enough if he dares to defend ill ones."[27] Similarly, Robert South (whose *Sermons* Fielding owned and much admired[28] and who is doubtlessly among those "Divines and moral Writers" whom he regularly takes as the standard of proper usage) complained in one of his series of sermons on "The Fatal Imposture and Force of Words" of the "outrageous, ungoverned violence and revenge, . . . passing by the name of *sense of honour,* . . . which is as much the natural result, as it is the legal reward of virtue. And yet, in spite of nature and reason, and the judgment of all mankind, this high and generous thing must be that in whose pretended quarrel almost all the duels of the world are fought." South is aware, too, of the corruptive influence on the word of so-called titles of honor: "Princes, indeed, may confer honours, or rather titles and names of honour; but they are a man's or woman's own actions which make him or her truly honourable, . . . Honour being but the reflection of a man's own actions."[29] Pope, in his Scriblerian role of the mock rhetorician who recommends "to our Authors the Study of the *Abuse of Speech*" as the surest means to literary success, is another witness to the corrupting title when, in *The Art of Sinking in Poetry* (1728), he ironically reminds would-be authors that "Every Man is honourable who is so by *Law, Custom,* or *Title.*"[30]

Fielding was conscious also of the "generalizing" process in language, which works not to shrink the grand old abstract words but to inflate formerly restricted and trivial terms into false new abstractions, reflecting once again the shabbiness of modern values. In "A Dissertation Concerning High People and Low People" in **Joseph Andrews,** he defines the former as "people of fashion," thus distinguishing them from low people, who are "those of no fashion." But, as so often, he pauses to examine the key word of his definition: "Now, this word of fashion hath by long use lost its original meaning, from which at present it gives us

a very different idea." Formerly, he says, it referred only to "dress," but now it has come to mean birth, accomplishment, social status, and a whole complex of superficial aristocratic values. Yet "the word really and truly signifies no more [than dress] at this day" (I, 180). Again, in the *Covent-Garden Journal* for May 9, 1752, he returns to the same phrase and speculates ironically about how the "Term, PEOPLE OF FASHION . . .first acquired its present Meaning, and became a Title of Honour and Distinction," defending his mock derivations against "those who have not much considered the barbarous Corruption of Language." But plainly it was the process of specialization which Fielding was most seriously alarmed about, particularly when it threatened to narrow words to the point of meaninglessness or to splinter their meanings so finely that the same word would mean radically different things, covering the whole range, perhaps, from greatness to pettiness, to different speakers and writers and, more seriously yet, to speakers and their hearers or to writers and their readers.

Fielding's interest in language, then, was characterized by his preoccupation with semantic instability in the language of the present, particularly as it affected the great ethical and spiritual abstractions, by his sensitivity to the power of popular usage, and by his distrust of authoritative programs of reform. It was for these reasons, probably, that he was attracted by the linguistic theory of John Locke. For Locke was pre-eminently in the eighteenth century the philosopher of semantics as well as the first of the major theorists of language really to deal adequately with the idea of usage as the matrix and arbiter of speech. An effective use of language, he taught, depended not on rules and methods of control but on an understanding of the psychology of communication. He recognized the desirability of a dictionary compiled on scientific principles, but he thought such a project not feasible and emphasized instead the *personal responsibility* of each serious *user* of the language to purify, as it were, his own language. But Locke was also, for all his affinities to the Royal Society and for all his distrust of metaphysics, no enemy of abstractions, and he gave their defenders a philosophy of abstract words which was at once true to the modern experience and expectations of language and loyal to the traditional values which such words were believed to represent.

The main thesis of the *Essay Concerning Human Understanding* (1690), it will be remembered, is that the human understanding is imperfect and our knowledge limited. Book I develops the basic proposition that ideas are not innate in the mind. Book II establishes that all ideas have their source in either sensation or reflection (the mind's perceptions of its own operations on the ideas received from sensation), and are either simple (proceeding directly from sensation), complex (produced by reflection), or relations (comparisons of two or more ideas). Book IV exposes the weaknesses and limitations of the human mind, especially the "disease" of the association of ideas. There are no certain truths available to man, but only probability and faith—except in morality, which is "amongst the sciences [along with mathematics, etc.] capable of demonstration" (IV, iii, 18)[31] and therefore certain. Thus man's understanding and knowledge, though limited by his dependence on sensation and the imperfect workings of the mind, are adequate for his conduct in this world and sufficient for the duties of life.

This, so Locke informs us, was his original plan, and it was not until he had already written the first two books of the *Essay* that he was struck with the realization that words "interpose themselves so much between our understandings, and the truth which it [*sic*] would contemplate and apprehend, that, like the medium through which visible objects pass, the obscurity and disorder do not seldom cast a mist before our eyes, and impose upon our understandings" (III, ix, 21). The result of this afterthought was Book III, "Of Words."

A consideration of the nature and function of language was particularly essential to Locke's design because one of his basic assumptions was the reality in objective nature of "particulars" only and the unreality of "universals." Such concepts as "essence" and "species" have no counterparts in nature. They exist only in the minds of men and are built up out of their perceptions of "particulars" in the outer world. But this situation is not, according to Locke, grounds for despair or cynicism, nor is it a reason for spurning abstractions. It is merely one of the conditions of human understanding—the peculiarly human (but not therefore contemptible) way of looking at the world. Far from despising abstract universals, in fact, Locke values them as the highest reaches of human thought, and language occupies a crucial place in his system because it supplies the agency whereby the process of abstraction is carried out: "In mixed modes [i.e., abstract ideas] it is the name that seems to preserve essences, and give them their lasting duration. For, the connexion between the loose parts of those complex ideas being made by the mind, this union, which has no particular foundation in nature, would cease again, were there not something that did, as it were, hold it together, and keep the parts from scattering" (III, v, 10).

We do not know whether Fielding subscribed to Locke's view that abstract ideas have no foundation in nature. He was simply not enough of a philosopher to make the point clear. The notion might be suggested by a passage in his early poem, ***Of True Greatness:***

Tis strange, while all to greatness homage pay,
So few should know the goddess they obey;

That men should think a thousand things the
    same,
And give contending images one name.

. . . . .

To no profession, party, place confined,
True greatness lives but in the noble mind.
                                                    (XII, 249-57)

But he is more likely thinking of the *quality* of greatness than of the *idea,* and probably he believed, in accordance with the Neo-platonic and antinominalistic traditions of Christian humanism, that abstract terms were the audible and visible symbols (however imperfect) of "real" values, independent of any thinking mind. "What we look on as *Power, Honour, Wisdom, Piety,* etc.," he wrote in the *Champion* for November 22, 1739, "are often not the Things themselves, but the Appearance only." But the assumption underlying such a statement is that "the Things themselves" do have a "real" existence. Again his view of the relationship of words and ideas seems close to that of Robert South: "Honour is indeed a noble thing, and therefore the word which signifies it must needs be very plausible. But as a rich and glistening garment may be cast over a rotten, fashionably diseased body, so an illustrious, commending word may be put upon a vile and an ugly thing; for words are but the garments, the loose garments of things. . . . But the body changes not, though the garments do."[32]

Still, Locke was not preaching a cynical nominalism of the kind Fielding attributed to Mandeville, who "proves religion and virtue to be only mere names."[33] He did not attempt to reduce the great moral and spiritual questions to a simple affair of words. The ideas words stood for were still important to him, however little foundation they might have in objective nature, and if Fielding could not follow him in rejecting "real" universals, there was yet no reason why he could not accept the proposition that it was words which gave these ideas form and permanence in human thought. He may have rejected the notion of nominal essence, but he could still recognize the practical validity of the idea that words "preserve essences and give them their lasting duration" in the cultural tradition, and this was reason enough why they should be valued and preserved intact. Sophia, we are told, "honored Tom Jones, and scorned Master Blifil, *almost as soon as she knew the meanings of those two words"* (III, 157; my italics).

The emphasis, so Fielding probably thought, was where it belonged: on the connection between words and ideas in the human mind, for here was where corruption (or "abuse," to use Locke's own term) originated and was perpetuated, and only here could it be effectively resisted. "I am apt to suspect," he wrote in his essay on good nature, "when I see sensible Men totally differ in

Opinion concerning any general Word, that the complex Idea in their several Minds which this Word represents is compounded of very different Simples. . . . I will venture to illustrate this by a familiar Instance: Suppose an Apothecary (as perhaps they often do) after mixing up a most pleasant Cordial, and a most nauseous Potion for different Patients, should write the same hard Word (*Haustipotiferous Draught* for Example) on each of the Bottles, would not these two Patients ever after conceive very different Ideas of *Haustipotiferous?*"[34] What Fielding "took" from Locke, as we have already suggested, was not a systematic philosophy of words so much as a working rationale of his own intuitive concerns about language, and these were all directed to the practical questions of its imperfections and abuse.

Locke's analysis was eminently useful in this respect because it provided an explanation not only of how words and their ideas were united but also of how, in the normal give and take of communication, they often became separated and confused. For though he assigned words a high purpose in the system of human knowledge, Locke's concept of language as a man-made structure (as opposed to the traditional view of a divinely ordained institution) also made him acutely aware of its limitations. He seemed to believe of language (as he did of civil government) that it was the artificial result of a contract or agreement among the members of a given society. The connection between "words and things," therefore, is purely illusory. Nor is there any *necessary* connection "between particular, articulate sounds and certain ideas . . . but by a voluntary imposition, whereby such a word is made arbitrarily the mark of such an idea" (III, ii, I). Words do not mean something by divine *fiat* or natural law, but are mere "signs" of ideas in the mind of the speaker. The principal "imperfection" (i.e., inherent defect) of language, then, is simply that words have "naturally no signification." Even those standing for simple ideas refer to a standard in nature which is imperfectly known, while those standing for abstract ideas have "no settled standard anywhere in nature existing, to rectify and adjust them by" (III, ix, 5).

Yet for purposes of communication this connection between words and ideas must be respected and, if possible, preserved. For "there comes, by constant use, to be such a connexion between certain sounds and the ideas they stand for, that the names heard, almost as readily excite certain ideas as if the objects themselves . . . did actually affect the senses" (III, ii, 6). It is this arbitrary connection, institutionalized by usage, which makes communication possible in language, and "unless a man's words excite the same ideas in the hearer which he makes them stand for in speaking, he does not speak intelligibly" (III, ii, 8). The liberty which the originators of language enjoyed "of affixing any new

name to any idea," we have still today. But there is this difference:

> that, in places where men in society have already established a language amongst them, the significations of words are very warily and sparingly to be altered. Because men being furnished already with names for their ideas, and common use having appropriated known names to certain ideas, an affected misapplication of them cannot but be very ridiculous. He that hath new notions will perhaps venture sometimes on the coining of new terms to express them: but men think it a boldness, and it is uncertain whether common use will ever make them pass for current. But in communication with others, it is necessary that we conform the ideas we make the vulgar words of any language stand for to their known proper significations, . . . or else to make known that new signification we apply them to. (III, vi, 51)

At its best, then, "common use" is the expression of the original compact or "tacit consent" of society which makes communication possible. It is the lawgiver of language and the principle of its continuity. But at the same time it is the lawless force of revolution and chaos, for the constancy of language depends on its individual users, each of whom retains the power to ignore the "agreed" connections between words and ideas and to rearrange them as he pleases. The more abstract the word, the more complex is the combination of ideas it expresses and the more liable it is to be used in private and unusual senses. The result is that the traditional connections are broken down and the words cut adrift from their established meanings. They become, at worst, literally meaningless because the social contract which made their meanings generally available has been violated and the word is reduced to its "natural" state of mere sound. Hence Fielding's frequent assertions that such terms as "virtue" and "religion" were "words of no meaning" or "no more than a sound" were more than just satiric exaggerations. There was a sense, founded on the Lockean theory of language, in which this was the simple truth.

The first obligation of the responsible speaker or writer, therefore, is to established usage, and when Locke comes to consider the "abuses of words" (those "*wilful* faults and neglects," above and beyond the natural imperfections of language, "which men are guilty of in the way of communication, whereby they render those signs less clear . . . than naturally they need to be" [III, x, I]), he gives special prominence to the vice of applying "the words of any language to ideas different from those to which the common use of that country applies them . . . without defining [one's] terms" (III, x, 29); and his specific examples of this abuse recall not only Fielding's attacks on the verbal corruptions of hypocrisy but also Pope's ironic recommendation, in *The Art of Sinking in Poetry,* of "the method [of] converting Vices into their *bordering* Virtues." ("A man who is a

Spendthrift and will not pay a just Debt, may have his Injustice transform'd into Liberality; Cowardice may be metamorphos'd into Prudence; Intemperance into good Nature and good Fellowship, Corruption into Patriotism, and Lewdness into Tenderness and Facility."[35] "I may have the ideas of virtues or vices," says Locke, "and names also, but apply them amiss: v.g. when I apply the name *frugality* to that idea which others call and signify by this sound, *covetousness*" (III, x, 33).

But once traditional usage has been violated by enough individual users of a word to make its "agreed" sense uncertain, the appeal to "common use" is no longer valid, particularly for purposes of "Philosophical Discourses," "there being scarce any name of any very complex idea (to say nothing of others) which, in common use, has not a great latitude, . . . and even in men that have a mind to understand one another, [does] not always stand for the same idea in speaker and hearer" (III, ix, 8). This abuse, originating with individuals, is perpetuated by the haphazard way in which words are learned, "especially the most material of them, *moral words*." For "the sounds are usually learned first; and then, to know what complex ideas they stand for, [men] are either beholden to the explication of others, or (what happens for the most part) are left to their own observation and industry; which being little laid out in search of the true and precise meaning of names, these moral words are in most men's mouths little more than bare sounds; or when they have any, it is for the most part but a very loose and undetermined, and, consequently, obscure and confused signification" (III, ix, 9).

One "great abuse of words," therefore, is "*inconstancy* in the use of them." This is a "plain cheat, . . . the wilful doing whereof can be imputed to nothing but great folly, or greater dishonesty" (III, x, 5). Another is "an *affected obscurity,*" (III, x, 6) which may take the form of old words used in new and unusual senses, new words introduced without good reason and clear definition, or ordinary words brought together in ambiguous combinations—the "learned gibberish" (III, x, 9) which Fielding satirizes in the disputes of Thwackum and Square (ironically recalling Locke in Square's assertion that "It was a mere abuse of words to call those things evil in which there was no moral unfitness") (III, 211), in his Scriblerian burlesques of literary criticism (whose practitioners "have very confused Ideas, and but few Words to express them"),[36] and in his tireless attacks on professional jargon ("to which it will be very difficult to assign any certain Idea").[37] Still another abuse—which Locke allows may not be accepted as such by many of his readers—is the use of figurative language. For "all the artificial and figurative applications of words eloquence hath invented, are for nothing else but to insinuate wrong ideas, move the passions, and thereby mislead the judgment; and so indeed are perfect cheats" (III, x, 34).

This was a principle which Fielding, like any imaginative writer (and like Locke himself, whose most famous passage, perhaps, is the one involving the figure of the *tabula rasa*) could not follow implicitly. But his habit of "translating" his more florid metaphors into "plain English" indicates that he is conscious of the obfuscation figurative language can lead to. This distrust of the metaphor, moreover, is at least partly Lockean in its rationale. As we have seen in the instance of "turncoat," Fielding's objection is not to the device of analogy as such but only to the loss of meaning which occurs when the metaphorical usage of a word becomes habitual and its "original idea" is forgotten. In the chapter of **Tom Jones** entitled "A Comparison between the World and the Stage," he explains this objection. He has nothing against the classic comparison of the world and the stage in itself; in fact, he goes on to develop the idea in his own way in the same chapter. But he does feel that "This thought hath been carried so far, and is become so general, that some words proper to the theatre, and which were at first metaphorically applied to the world, are now indiscriminately and literally spoken of both; thus stage and scene are by common use grown as familiar to us, when we speak of life in general, as when we confine ourselves to dramatic performances; and when transactions behind the curtain are mentioned, St. James's is more likely to occur to our thoughts than Drury Lane" (III, 331). As always, of course, one must not overlook the satiric intent of such a passage (here the cut at the covert political manipulations which make these terms appropriate to St. James's), but the satire rests on Fielding's exposure of the abuse of metaphorical language: the words in question have been cut loose from their original ideas, and what he asks of his readers is not that they should stop using the words of the theater in connection with St. James's, but rather that they should remain fully alive to the normative implications of this transference of terms.

For the most basic and iniquitous abuse of language, according to Locke, is simply "the using of words without clear and distinct ideas; or, which is worse, signs without anything signified" (III, x, 2). "The whole mischief which infects . . . our [political] economy," Fielding writes in **The Journal of a Voyage to Lisbon,** "arises from the vague and uncertain use of a word called Liberty, of which, as scarce any two men with whom I have ever conversed, seem to have one and the same idea, I am inclined to doubt whether there be any simple universal notion represented by this word" (XVI, 239). And of the word "Humour," in the *Covent-Garden Journal* No. 19: "perhaps there is no Word in our Language of which Men have in general so vague and undeterminate an Idea. To speak very plainly, I am apt to question whether the greater Part of Mankind have any Idea at all in their Heads, when this Word drops (perhaps accidentally) from their Tongue." But Fielding does not agree with Locke that this abuse is serious only on the level of philosophical discourse and that it is of small consequence in the "ordinary occurrences of life" (III, x, 4). He is being facetious when, in *Tom Jones,* he applies the test of "clear and distinct ideas" to the words uttered by Mrs. Waters in the comic scene at the inn, but once again there is a serious edge to his mockery. The occasion is the one in which the jealous Fitzpatrick, searching for his wife, bursts into Mrs. Waters' room and discovers her with Jones. As the two men struggle in the dark, she sits up in bed and begins "to scream in the most violent manner, crying out murder! robbery! and more frequently rape! which last, some, perhaps, may wonder she should mention, who do not consider that these words of exclamation are used by ladies in a fright, as fa, la, la, ra, da, etc., are in music, only as the vehicles of sound, and without any fixed ideas." But the serious implications of such an empty use of words are suggested a moment later when Mrs. Waters, fearful now for her reputation rather than for her safety, continues to scream the same words and, when help arrives, pretends to believe that both Jones and Fitzpatrick had entered the room "with an intent upon her honor" (IV, 199-200). Perhaps Fielding, as a magistrate, had had experience with the loose way some women could use the language of accusation—not to mention that much abused word "honor."

He is also, however, more conscious than Locke of the emotional content of words and of the question of sincerity involved in their use. Locke is inclined to attribute most abuse of words to sheer negligence, and when he turns, in the final chapter of Book III, to a consideration of the "Remedies" for these abuses he is therefore confident that, on the level of the individual speaker or writer, all that is needed is greater care in using words with clear and distinct ideas, more attention to consistency of meaning, and more frequent use of definitions, synonyms, and examples. Fielding . . . is less optimistic than Locke regarding these remedies, and one of the reasons for his pessimism is his sensitivity to the nonrational elements of language. We have already seen how Fielding's awareness of these elements causes him, in *An Essay on Conversation,* to defend words and phrases which "have in a philosophical sense no meaning" (i.e., which have been separated from their original ideas) on the grounds that they convey impressions of esteem necessary to the conduct of society. We have also seen, however, that he more often attacks these same words and phrases for their insincerity and that even in *An Essay on Conversation* his defense is grudging and ambivalent. Mrs. Waters' use of words is another case in point. The cry "Rape!" is not the sign of an "idea," but, in the first instance, a way of summoning aid and, in the second, a means of safeguarding her reputation. Such "ideas" as the word conveys are to her purely secondary and accidental; her primary objective is not the communication of thought but the conveyance of emotional attitudes

important to her own self-interest. In short, in the second instance at least, she is a hypocrite, and her use of the word is a lie.

But again the "common use" of such words in such contexts is corrupting because it separates the words from their proper ideas and infects them with the suspicion of insincerity. If enough boys cry "Wolf!" when there is no wolf, it is not only the liars who will fall under suspicion but the word itself, and this is also true of ladies who cry "Rape!" Even on the simplest levels of speech this can have serious consequences when the wolf or the rape are real, and on the higher levels of discourse the principle is the same. "Honor," "virtue," "religion," and the other words Fielding identifies as "corrupt" have been reduced in efficacy not only by the process of specialization but also by the erosions of insincere usage, and however much this sincere speaker may try to apply Locke's rationalistic remedies he cannot be certain that his words will be accepted at their face values, he cannot be sure that they have been purified of the associations of insincerity. Certain terms, as a result, are all but removed from the vocabulary of truth: "The Words *curious, eminent, learned,*" for example, are according to Fielding like the false labels which unscrupulous merchants use to pass off cheap wine as champagne: "all of them certain Marks of Perry."[38] The word "grace" (which Locke himself, in a passage quoted by Fielding, identifies as an "abused" word)[39] was similarly contaminated by insincerity. Charles DeLoach Ashmore has observed that "The word *grace,* as used by the Methodist pickpocket [at the beginning of *Amelia*] was particularly offensive to the novelist. Not only in the mouths of sectarians, but also on the lips of orthodox clergymen, the word seemed to have an ugly sound in Fielding's ears. . . . Apparently he felt that *grace* was at best used by men to throw upon God responsibilities that they themselves ought to shoulder. At worst, it was a cant word used by hypocrites as a substitute for Christian virtue in action."[40] The hypocritical Parson Barnabas uses the word in *Joseph Andrews,* as does Joseph's sister Pamela (repeatedly) at the end of that novel (I, 72, 343). In *Tom Jones,* Captain Blifil attempts to persuade Allworthy to abandon the infant Jones by arguing that grace is more important than good actions; and it is surely no accident that the easy-virtued chambermaid, at the inn where the puppet show is given, is named Grace (III, 82; IV, 324)—a living symbol, like Mrs. Honour in the same novel (and like Jonathan Wild's three sisters, Grace, Charity, and Honour) of the corruption of words.

Fielding, in fact, is nearly always conscious of the "ideas" conveyed by proper names. "Whatever sour Ideas may be annexed to the Name of *Vinegar,*" writes the irascible *persona* of the *Champion,* Captain Hercules Vinegar, "no Family hath been more remarked for Sweetness of Temper than ours; and as for myself, those who know me thoroughly, agree in calling me the best natured Man in the World."[41] And in another *Champion* paper an explanation of how names acquire "ideas" foreign to their original significations serves Fielding as a sort of paradigm of one of the processes of linguistic corruption. The reason, he says, why some names are regarded as lucky or unlucky, foolish or grave, good or bad, is not "as some think, from any greater Agreement, that certain Sounds bear [to certain ideas], nor from any of the other chimerical Reasons ludicrous Persons assign; but it is, indeed, because the Name hath been made odious by some Person who hath borne it, *and hath transformed it to Posterity with his Iniquity annexed*"[42] (my italics). This is the same process, clearly, which makes it necessary for Fielding to apologize, in the *Jacobite's Journal* for January 23, 1748, for using the words "Patriot" and "Critic": "The Persons who have, without any just Pretensions, assumed these Characters, must answer for the disadvantageous Light in which they have placed these Words."

It is also very close to the kind of contamination by "the grossness of domestick use" (in Dr. Johnson's phrase)[43] from which poetic diction was supposed to protect the language of poetry,[44] the process whereby a word, according to Addison, may "contract a Kind of Meanness by passing through the Mouths of the Vulgar," and thus become "debased by common Use."[45] "The best expressions," explained a seventeenth-century rhetorician, "grow low and degenerate, when profan'd by the populace, and applied to mean things. The use they make of them, infecting them with a mean and abject Idea, causes that we cannot use them without sullying and defiling those things, which are signified by them."[46] The difference, of course, is that Fielding, who ridiculed the pretensions of poetic diction in *The Tragedy of Tragedies* and in innumerable burlesque passages in the novels and who had to defend himself throughout his career against the charge of being a "low" writer, was not troubled by "domestick" use so much as by *hypocritical* use. But the effect is strikingly similar: the word so contaminated is no longer fit, in the one case, for poetry, in the other, for truth.

But if Fielding was more pessimistic than Locke about the condition of the language, if he used the charged word "corruption" where Locke invariably employed the more neutral "abuse," it was not entirely because he was more sensitive to the emotional content of words. Locke's optimism, for all his emphasis on individual responsibility for effective communication, rested finally on a faith in the basic solidarity of society. The contract theory of language presupposes a society homogeneous enough to have an "agreed" standard of meaning and responsible enough to observe it. For Locke, it is clear, such a society still existed. He had witnessed social upheaval in his time—much more than Fielding was to experience in his—but his belief in the

Revolutionary Settlement of 1689 was supreme. Here, so he thought, was the social contract of civil government affirmed in actual fact, palpable evidence of the fundamental unity of English society under the unalterable laws of reason. The laws of language, he realized, were neither so reasonable nor so unalterable. In their original framing, in fact, they were quite arbitrary, and men still possessed their original power to use words in an arbitrary fashion. But for practical purposes they no longer had the *right* to do so, not only because arbitrary tampering with the "agreed" meanings of words would lead to confusion in communication but also because language was itself "the great bond that holds society together" (III, xi, 1), and widespread violation of the linguistic contract could only result in eventual breakdown of the social contract. But Locke, though he recognized the threat of this eventuality, clearly did not see it as present and immediate. He believed that the reasonableness of men would cause them to respect "agreed" meanings and that his "remedies" would suffice for those cases in which "agreed" meanings had already been lost or were otherwise inadequate.

To Fielding, however, a generation later, the situation looked different. He believed as devoutly as Locke in the Settlement of 1689, but he did not find it so easy to believe in the solidarity and reasonableness of English society on which this setlement must rest. Everywhere he looked he saw not homogeneity but factionalism, "interest," and party, not a sense of social responsibility but crass opportunism, not reasonableness but fatuous "enthusiasm." And nearly always he saw the effect of these forces on language and, conversely, the effect of "corrupted" language on society. From Locke, Fielding took a method and terminology of linguistic criticism, but his interest in the problems of communication was not, like Locke's, epistemological so much as social and moral, and his sense of the corruption of words was deeply rooted in his own experience of the language and society of his day . . .

Notes

[1] Our sons their fathers' failing language see, / And such as Chaucer is, shall Dryden be. *An Essay in Criticism,* lines 482-83.

[2] Dryden proposed a language academy in the dedicatory epistle of his *Rival Ladies* (1664), Swift in his *Proposal for Correcting, Improving, and Ascertaining the English Tongue* (1712).

[3] May 17, 1740.

[4] Feb. 14, 1739/40.

[5] See [*Henry Fielding and the Language of Irony,* by

Glenn W. Hatfield (Chicago: The University of Chicago Press, 1968)], p. 77.

[6] Thomas Sprat, *History of the Royal Society* (London, 1667), Part II, Sec. 20.

[7] See A. C. Howell, "*Res et Verba:* Words and Things," *ELH,* 13 (1946): 131-42.

[8] See also *The Mock Doctor,* scene xvii; *Champion,* Apr. 29, 1740; *True Patriot* Nos. 5 and 22; *Covent-Garden Journal* Nos. 2 and 70; and *An Attempt toward a Natural History of the Hanover Rat,* attributed to Fielding by Jensen in "Two Discoveries," *Yale University Library Gazette,* 10 (1935); 23-32.

[9] "I need not mention that Custom so notorious among Gentlemen of the Law, of taking away from Substantives, the Power given them by Mr. *Lilly* of standing by themselves, and joining two or three more Substantives to shew their Signification." *Champion,* Jan. 17, 1739/40. Lily's rule is "A Noun Substantive is that standeth by himself, and requireth not another Word to be joined with him to shew his Signification." Lily's grammar appeared in numerous editions from the time of its publication in 1527 until well into the nineteenth century, and under various titles. The edition I have used is *A Short Introduction to Grammar* (London, 1742). The noun substantive rule appears on p. 1.

[10] *The English Grammar, or An Essay on the Art of Grammar Applied to and Exemplified in the English Tongue,* pp. vii, 213.

[11] See Cross, 1: 247, 374, 379; and "A Catalogue of the . . . Library of the Late Henry Fielding," reprinted in Appendix to Ethel M. Thornbury's *Henry Fielding's Theory of the Comic Prose Epic* (Madison: University of Wisconsin Press, 1931). Fielding inserted an abstract of *Hermes* in *Covent-Garden Journal,* Mar. 14, 1752.

[12] Apr. 29, 1740.

[13] *Champion,* May 17, 1740.

[14] *Ars Poetica,* lines 71-72.

[15] *Novum Organum* (London, 1620), Aphorism 43.

[16] *History of the Royal Society,* Part II, Sec. 20.

[17] See S. A. Leonard, *The Doctrine of Correctness in English Usage,* p. 14 and *passim.*

[18] *Plan of an English Dictionary, The Works of Samuel Johnson,* ed. Arthur Murphy (London, 1792), 2: 23.

[19] D. Nichol Smith, "The Newspaper," *Johnson's England* (Oxford: Clarendon Press, 1933), 2: 339.

[20] P. 76.

[21] See especially "Science and English Prose Style in the Third Quarter of the Seventeenth Century," *The Seventeenth Century,* pp. 75-110.

[22] See especially "The Restoration Revolt against Enthusiasm," *Studies in Philology,* 30 (1933): 571-603.

[23] "The Development of English Colloquial Idiom during the Eighteenth Century," *Review of English Studies,* 2 (1926): 70, 194. On the changing meaning of "wit," see Stuart M. Tave: "The word was sinking [from the mid-seventeenth century] into common, trifling, and narrow usages—mere quickness and sharpness in the making of similitudes, the odd metaphor, the lucky simile, the wild fetch, epigrammatic turns and points, quibble, conceit." By the early eighteenth century, it had "become so degraded by its association with the unimportant and even the profane that it was more and more difficult to use it with grave connotation." *The Amiable Humorist* (Chicago: University of Chicago Press, 1960), pp. 58, 63. See also J. E. Spingarn, ed., *Critical Essays of the Seventeenth Century* (Oxford: Clarendon Press, 1908-9), 1: lviii-lxiii; and Edward Niles Hooker, "Pope on Wit," *The Seventeenth Century,* p. 23. Fielding's contributions to the traditional discussion of the meaning of "true wit" may be seen in the *Covent-Garden Journal* Nos. 18 and 19.

[24] *World* No. 101, 1754. Cited by William Matthews, "Polite Speech in the Eighteenth Century," *English,* 1 (1937): 500. Cf. Boswell's statement that Dr. Johnson "was very much offended at the general licence, by no means 'modestly taken' in his time, not only to coin new words, but to use many words in senses quite different from their established meaning, and those frequently very fantastical." *Life of Johnson,* ed. G. B. Hill, rev. L. F. Powell (Oxford: Clarendon Press, 1934), 1: 221.

[25] "The Ironic Tradition in Augustan Prose from Swift to Johnson," *Restoration and Augustan Prose: Papers Delivered by James R. Sutherland and Ian Watt at the Third Clark Library Seminar, 14 July, 1956* (Los Angeles: University of California Press, 1957), p. 38.

[26] No. 139, Aug. 9, 1711, Everyman ed. (London: Dent, 1958), 1: 418-19.

[27] *Tatler,* Everyman ed. (London: Dent, 1953), pp. 33, 186. This is also one of the themes, of course, of Steele's *The Conscious Lovers* 1722). . . .

28 "A Catalogue of the . . . Library of the Late Henry Fielding." For Fielding's knowledge of South's sermons, see Martin C. Battestin, *The Moral Basis of Fielding's Art.*

29 *Sermons Preached upon Several Occasions* (Philadelphia, 1844), 3: 3-4.

30 *The Art of Sinking in Poetry,* ed. Edna Leake Steeves (New York: Columbia University Press, 1952), p. 77.

31 All references to Locke are to *An Essay Concerning Human Understanding,* ed. Alexander Campbell Fraser (Oxford: Clarendon Press, 1894). Citations are to book, chapter, and section.

32 *Sermons Preached upon Several Occasions,* 3: 3.

33 See [*Henry Fielding and the Language of Irony*], p. 21.

34 *Champion,* Mar. 27, 1740.

35 Steeves ed., p. 79.

36 *Covent-Garden Journal,* Feb. 15, 1752.

37 *Champion,* Jan. 17, 1739/40.

38 *Covent-Garden Journal,* Mar. 3, 1752.

39 See [*Henry Fielding and the Language of Irony*], pp. 22-23.

40 "Henry Fielding's 'Art of Life': A Study in the Ethics of the Novel" (Ph.D. diss., Emory University, 1957), p. 257.

41 Mar. 27, 1740.

42 June 7, 1740.

43 *The Life of Dryden.* Cited by James Sutherland, *A Preface to Eighteenth-Century Poetry* (Oxford: Clarendon Press, 1948), p. 131.

44 A concept almost exactly contemporaneous in its development with the Restoration and eighteenth-century critique of language. See Thomas Quale, *Poetic Diction* (London: Methuen, 1924), p. 6; F. W. Bateson, *English Poetry and the English Language* (Oxford: Clarendon Press, 1934), pp. 69-70; and Geoffrey Tillotson, "Eighteenth-Century Poetic Diction," *Essays and Studies by Members of the English Association,* 25 (1939; Oxford: Clarendon Press, 1940): p. 76.

45 *Spectator,* Jan. 26, 1712, Everyman ed. (London: Dent, 1958), 2: 349-50.

46 [Bernard Lamy], *The Art of Speaking,* 2d ed. (London, 1708), pp. 50-51. Translated from a French treatise of *ca.* 1668.

Martin C. Battestin (essay date 1968)

SOURCE: "Fielding's Definition of Wisdom: Some Functions of Ambiguity and Emblem in *Tom Jones,*" in *Henry Fielding: "Tom Jones": The Authoritative Text, Contemporary Reactions, Criticism,* 2d ed., edited by Sheridan Baker, Norton Critical Edition, W.W. Norton, 1995, pp. 733-49. Originally published in *ELH,* Vol. 35, 1968, pp. 188-217.

[*In the following excerpt, originally published in 1968 and reprinted in 1995, Battestin, one of Fielding's most important modern biographers and critics, examines Fielding's treatment of the virtues of prudence and wisdom in* Tom Jones. *Battestin focuses on the character of Sophia, arguing that the novel's heroine and protagonit's love interest both embodies and portrays an idealized representation of Fielding's complex moral vision.*]

To alter the terms of his own simile for the ancient authors, Fielding's novels may be considered as a rich common, where every critic has a free right to fatten his bibliography. As the number of commentaries in recent years attests, **Tom Jones** offers an ample field for critical investigation, with many aspects requiring a variety of approaches. At present I wish to explore only two of these: the substance and the form of the novel's most important theme, the definition of Wisdom.

In dedicating the book to Lyttelton, Fielding himself provides the clue both to his moral purpose in **Tom Jones** and (in part at least) to his method of implementing that purpose. He declares

> that to recommend Goodness and Innocence hath been my sincere Endeavour in this History. This honest Purpose you have been pleased to think I have attained: And to say the Truth, it is likeliest to be attained in Books of this Kind; for an Example is a Kind of Picture, in which Virtue becomes as it were an Object of Sight, and strikes us with an Idea of that Loveliness, which *Plato* asserts there is in her naked Charms.

> Besides displaying that Beauty of Virtue which may attract the Admiration of Mankind, I have attempted to engage a stronger Motive to Human Action in her Favour, by convincing Men, that their true Interest directs them to a Pursuit of her.[1]

The dominant ethical theme of **Tom Jones** turns upon the meaning of "Virtue" and of the phrase, our "true

Interest"—what Squire Allworthy calls "the Duty which we owe to ourselves" (XVIII.x). One method Fielding chooses to present this theme is implicit in the Platonic figure of Virtue's irresistible "Charms" and in the metaphor of the "Pursuit of her." Fielding's statement, then, is schematic, pointing both to the doctrine of the novel and to the means, which may be described as iconomatic, by which the novelist transforms the abstraction of his theme into "an Object of Sight."

Tom Jones, in a sense, is an exercise in the fictive definition of Virtue, or moral Wisdom—just as Fielding's earlier novels, *Joseph Andrews* and *Jonathan Wild,* may be regarded as attempts to represent through word and action the true meaning of such concepts as Charity, Chastity, and Greatness. To achieve this purpose, Fielding employs many devices—characterization, for one, by which certain figures in the novel become "Walking Concepts," as Sheldon Sacks has observed,[2] acting out the meaning of various virtues and vices. At present, however, I am concerned with only two of these techniques: Fielding's exploitation of verbal ambiguity—the power of the word, as it were, to define the moral vision or blindness of character and reader alike—and his attempt to delineate emblematically the meaning of true Wisdom. The problem for the critic, fundamentally, is to ascertain the nature of that Wisdom which Fielding, together with the philosophers and divines of the Christian humanist tradition, wished to recommend. For this we may conveniently recall Cicero's distinction in *De Officiis* (I.xliii) between the two kinds of wisdom, the speculative and the practical, *sophia* and *prudentia:*

> And then, the foremost of all virtues is wisdom—what the Greeks call όϊϋßá; for by prudence, which they call öñüíçóéò, we understand something else, namely, the practical knowledge of things to be sought for and of things to be avoided.[3]

The apprehension of *sophia* was the goal of Plato's philosopher; the acquisition of *prudentia*—which begins with the intimation that the Good, the True, and the Beautiful are one—is the quest of the *vir honestus.* Fielding's intention in *Tom Jones* is to demonstrate the nature, function, and relationship of these correlative ethical concepts.

I. Prudence: The Function of Ambiguity

Prudence (together with the more or less synonymous word *discretion*) is the central ethical concept of *Tom Jones.*[4] The term recurs and reverberates throughout the novel, acquiring something of the quality and function of a musical motif. Yet its meanings are curiously ambivalent: according to the context, which Fielding carefully controls, prudence is either the fundamental vice, subsuming all others, or the essential virtue of the completely moral man. It exists, as the exegetical tradition might express it, *in malo et in bono.* At the

very start of the narrative Bridget Allworthy, the prude of easy virtue, is said to be remarkable for "her Prudence" and "discreet . . . in her Conduct" (I.ii); but on the last page of the novel Tom Jones himself is represented as a fit partner for Sophia only because he has "by Reflexion on his past Follies, acquired a Discretion and Prudence very uncommon in one of his lively Parts." In one sense, prudence is the summarizing attribute of Blifil, the villain of the piece, and it is the distinguishing trait of a crowded gallery of meretricious and self-interested characters from every rank of society—of Deborah Wilkins (I.v, vi), Jenny Jones (I.ix), Mrs. Seagrim (IV.viii), Mrs. Western (VI.xiv), Partridge (VIII.ix), Mrs. Honour (X.ix), Lady Bellaston (XIII.iii, XV.ix). Antithetically, however, the acquisition of prudence is recognized by the good characters of the novel—by Allworthy, Sophia, and ultimately by Jones—as the indispensable requisite of the moral man. "Prudence," Allworthy maintains, "is indeed the Duty which we owe to ourselves" (XVIII.x). Sophia alone, of all the characters in the novel, is possessed of prudence in this positive sense (XII.x). And the lack of it in Jones is the source of all his "Calamities" (XVII.i), all his "miserable Distresses" (XVIII.vi).

References to prudence, understood in either the positive or pejorative sense, may be found elsewhere in Fielding's writings; but only in *Tom Jones* does the word recur with such frequency and insistence. Indeed, as I wish to suggest, Fielding's intention to recommend this virtue affected the very shape and character of *Tom Jones:* the choice and representation of the principal characters, the organization of the general movement of the narrative, and the content of particular scenes were determined in significant ways in accordance with a broadly allegorical system designed both to define the virtue of prudence and to demonstrate its essential relevance to the moral life. Unfortunately for modern readers, the passage of time has obscured the meaning of this concept in the novel.

One of the fullest contemporary expositions of this virtue occurs in an article "On Prudence" appearing in Sir John Hill's *British Magazine* for March 1749, one month after the publication of *Tom Jones.* This essay, Number XLI in the series called "The Moralist," begins by celebrating the dignity and antiquity of the concept.

> PRUDENCE is at once the noblest and the most valuable of all the qualifications we have to boast of: It at the same time gives testimony of our having exerted the faculties of our souls in the wisest manner, and conducts us through life with that ease and tranquility, that all the boasted offices of other accomplishments can never give us. The ancient Moralists with great reason placed it in the first rank of human endowments, and called it the parent and guide of all the other virtues. Without prudence,

nothing in our lives is good, nothing decent, nothing truly agreeable or permanent: It is the rule and ornament of all our actions; and is to our conduct in this motly world of chances, what physick is to the body, the surest means of preventing disorders, and the only means of curing them.[5]

To further define the nature and function of this virtue, "the Moralist" invokes the traditional metaphor of sight, opposing the unerring perspicacity of the rational, to the blindness and brutishness of the passionate man: "Prudence is the just estimation and trial of all things; it is the eye that sees all, and that ought to direct all, and ordain all: and when any favourite passion hood-winks it for the time, man ceases to be man, levels himself with the brutes, and gives up that sacred pre-rogative his reason, to be actuated by meanest [*sic*] of all principles."[6] The special provinces of prudence are the judgment and the will: seeing what is right and how to attain it, the prudent man translates this knowl-edge into action—deeds "which will make ourselves and our fellow-creatures most happy, and do the great-est honour in our power to our nature, and to the great creator of it."[7] Again, the prudent man looks to the past (memory), the present (judgment), and the future (foresight); his own and others' past experiences in-form his perception of present exigencies and enable him to predict the probable consequences of actions and events.[8] The prudent man alone is equipped to survive in a world of deceitful appearances and hostile circumstances, for only he "sees things in their proper colours, and consequently expects those things from them which ruin others by the surprize of their coming on"; only he "is guarded against what are called the changes and chances that undo all things."[9] Although, as Tillotson and William Sherlock observed,[10] not even prudence can always foresee the improbable casualties which occur under the direction of Providence, yet she is, however fallible, our only proper guide.

Prudence in this positive sense is indeed, as Allworthy insists, "the Duty which we owe to ourselves," that self-discipline and practical sagacity which Fielding's open-hearted and impetuous hero must acquire. But as Tom Jones has his half-brother Blifil, or Amelia her sister Betty, so every virtue has its counterfeit, its kindred vice which mimics it. The result is a kind of sinister parody of excellence. Thus Cicero warns against confusing false prudence and true, a vulgar error by which the clever hypocrite, bent only on pursuing his own worldly interest, passes for a wise and upright man. Such are the scoundrels of this world who—practised in what Fielding liked to call "the *Art of Thriving*"[11]—wear the mask of prudence, separating moral rectitude from expediency.[12] It is "wisdom [*prudentia*]," Cicero writes, "which cunning [*malitia*] seeks to counterfeit,"[13] so as the better to dupe and use us.

The concept of prudence in **Tom Jones** is deliberately complex, as significant yet as elusive as the meaning of wisdom itself. The single term carries with it at least three distinct meanings derivative from the ethical and historical contexts we have been exploring: (1) it may signify *prudentia,* the supreme rational virtue of the Christian humanist tradition, that practical wisdom which Tom Jones, like the *vir honestus,* must acquire; (2) it may signify the shadow and antithesis of this virtue—reason in the service of villainy—that malevo-lent cunning which characterizes the hypocrite Blifil; or (3) it may signify that prostitute and self-protective expediency, that worldly wisdom, which, owing to the influence of Gracian, De Britaine, Fuller, and the other pious-sounding perpetrators of a middle-class morali-ty, replaced the humanist concept of *prudentia* in the popular mind. These are the basic variations on the theme. According to the context in *Tom Jones,* one of these meanings will be dominant, but the others echo in the reader's memory effecting a kind of ironic coun-terpoint and ultimately, as it were, testing his own sense of values, his own ability to make necessary ethical distinctions between goods real or merely apparent.

In Book XII, Chapter iii, Fielding protests: "if we have not all the Virtues, I will boldly say, neither have we all the Vices of a prudent Character." The vices of the prudent characters in **Tom Jones**—of Blifil, Bridget Allworthy, Lady Bellaston, and their kind—should now be sufficiently evident. The positive meaning of pru-dence in the novel, however, is perhaps less obvious, for the virtue which Fielding recommends is essential-ly synthetic, combining the *prudentia* of the philoso-phers with certain less ignoble features of the modern version. What Tom Jones fundamentally lacks, of course, is *prudentia:* moral vision and self-discipline. Although he intuitively perceives the difference be-tween Sophia and the daughters of Eve, he is too much the creature of his passions to be able to act upon that knowledge. He moves through life committing one good-natured indiscretion after another, unable to learn from past experiences or to foresee the future conse-quences of his rash behavior. Only in prison, at the nadir of his misfortunes, does the full meaning of his imprudence appear to him. To Mrs. Waters, Jones "la-mented the Follies and Vices of which he had been guilty; every one of which, he said, had been attended with such ill Consequences, that he should be unpar-donable if he did not take Warning, and quit those vicious Courses for the future," and he concludes with a "Resolution to sin no more, lest a worse Thing should happen to him" (XVII.ix). When, moments later, he is informed that Mrs. Waters, the woman he had slept with at Upton, is his own mother, Jones arrives at last at the crucial moment of self-awareness toward which the novel has been moving. Rejecting Partridge's sug-gestion that ill luck or the devil himself had contrived this ultimate horror, Fielding's hero accepts his own responsibility for his fate: "Sure . . . Fortune will never have done with me, 'till she hath driven me to Distraction. But why do I blame Fortune? I am myself the Cause of all my Misery. All the dreadful Mischiefs which have befallen me, are the Consequences only of my own Folly and Vice" (XVIII.ii). Here is at once the climax and the resolution of the theme of *prudentia* in the novel—a theme to which Fielding would return in **Amelia,** where, in the introductory chapter, he propounded at length the lesson Tom Jones learned: "I question much, whether we may not by natural means account for the Success of Knaves, the Calamities of Fools, with all the Miseries in which Men of Sense sometimes involve themselves by quitting the Directions of Prudence, and following the blind Guidance of a predominant Passion; in short, for all the ordinary Phenomena which are imputed to Fortune; whom, perhaps, Men accuse with no less Absurdity in Life, then a bad Player complains of ill Luck at the Game of Chess."[14] Prudence in this sense is the supreme virtue of the Christian humanist tradition, entailing knowledge and discipline of the self and the awareness that our lives, ultimately, are shaped not by circumstances, but by reason and the will. This, Fielding concludes, echoing Cicero, is "the Art of Life."

Although this is the fundamental positive meaning of prudence in **Tom Jones,** Fielding extends the concept to accommodate a nobler, purified version of that worldly wisdom so assiduously inculcated by the moderns. Since the business of life was a matter not simply of preserving the moral health of one's soul, but also of surviving in a world too quick to judge by appearances, it was necessary to have a proper regard to one's reputation. In Maxim XCIX Gracian warned that "THINGS are not taken for what they really are, but for what they appear to be. . . . It is not enough to have a good Intention, if the Action look ill" (see also CXXX), and Fuller's apothegms (for example, Nos. 1425 and 1590) similarly emphasize that "a fair Reputation" is necessary to all men. Fielding, however, is careful to distinguish his own version of prudence from that of the cynical proponents of a self-interested dissimulation—those who cared not at all for virtue, but only for the appearance of virtue. Good-nature and charity are the indispensable qualifications of Fielding's heroes—of Parson Adams, Heartfree, Tom Jones, Captain Booth—who demand our affection despite their naïveté, their foibles and indiscretions. But Fielding was concerned that the good man preserve his good name; otherwise he became vulnerable to the malicious designs of his enemies and subject to the disdain of his friends. The difficulty of distinguishing truth from appearances is Fielding's constant theme: the classical *prudentia* enables us to make these crucial discriminations; prudence in the modern sense, on the other hand, is in part the awareness that such distinctions are rarely made by the generality of men, that we are judged by appearances and must therefore conduct ourselves with discretion. As early as *The Champion* (22 November 1739) Fielding had insisted on this point:

"I would . . . by no Means recommend to Mankind to cultivate Deceit, or endeavour to appear what they are not; on the contrary, I wish it were possible to induce the World to make a diligent Enquiry into Things themselves, to withold them from giving too hasty a Credit to the outward Shew and first Impression; I would only convince my Readers, *That it is not enough to have Virtue, without we also take Care to preserve, by a certain Decency and Dignity of Behaviour, the outward Appearance of it also."*[15] This, too, is the "very useful Lesson" Fielding sets forth in *Tom Jones* for the benefit of his youthful readers, who will find

> . . . that Goodness of Heart, and Openness of Temper, tho' these may give them great Comfort within, and administer to an honest Pride in their own Minds, will by no Means, alas! do their Business in the World. Prudence and Circumspection are necessary even to the best of Men. They are indeed as it were a Guard to Virtue, without which she can never be safe. It is not enough that your Designs, nay that your Actions, are intrinsically good, you must take Care they shall appear so. If your Inside be never so beautiful, you must preserve a fair Outside also. This must be constantly looked to, or Malice and Envy will take Care to blacken it so, that the Sagacity and Goodness of an *Allworthy* will not be able to see thro' it, and to discern the Beauties within. Let this, my young Readers, be your constant Maxim, That no Man can be good enough to enable him to neglect the Rules of Prudence; nor will Virtue herself look beautiful, unless she be bedecked with the outward Ornaments of Decency and Decorum. (III.vii)

Like Virtue herself, Sophia is concerned to preserve her good name, the outward sign of her true character (XIII.xi). And Allworthy more than once echoes his author's sentiments in advising Jones that prudence is "the Duty which we owe to ourselves" (XVIII.x), that it is, together with religion, the sole means of putting the good-natured man in possession of the happiness he deserves (V.vii).

As the recommendation of Charity and Chastity is the underlying purpose of Fielding's first novel, **Joseph Andrews,** the dominant ethical concern of **Tom Jones** is the anatomy of Prudence. It is a process as essential as the discrimination of vice from virtue, of selfishness from self-discipline, and as significant to life as the pursuit of wisdom. Lacking prudence, Tom Jones is a prey to hypocrites and knaves and too often the victim of his own spontaneities, his own generous impulses and extravagancies. For Fielding in this his greatest novel, virtue was as much a matter of the understanding and the will as of the heart. Prudence, he implies, is the name each man gives to that wisdom, worldly or moral, which he prizes. This is the fundamental paradox of the novel as of life. Fielding's rhetorical strategy—his ironic use of the same word to convey antithetical meanings—forces the reader to assess his own sense of values, to distinguish the true from the false. We, too, are implicated, as it were, in Tom Jones' awkward progress toward that most distant and elusive of goals—the marriage with Wisdom herself.

II. Sophia and the Functions of Emblem

Since it is a *practical* virtue, Fielding may thus define prudence, negatively and positively, by associating the word with various examples of moral behavior chosen to illustrate those disparate meanings of the concept which he meant either to ridicule or recommend. In action the "prudence" of Blifil or Mrs. Western may be distinguished from the "prudence" of Sophia; the deed to which the word is applied controls our sense of Fielding's intention, whether ironic or sincere. The nature of *speculative* wisdom, on the other hand, is less easily and effectively conveyed by means of the counterpoint of word and action: *sophia* was a mystery even Socrates could describe only figuratively—a method to which Fielding alludes in the Dedication to *Tom Jones* when he invokes the Platonic metaphor of the "naked Charms" of Virtue imaged as a beautiful woman.[16] In *Tom Jones* the meaning of *sophia* is presented to the reader as "an Object of Sight" in the character of Fielding's heroine.

Although it has apparently escaped the attention of his critics, the emblemizing technique Fielding here employs—which it is our present purpose to consider in its various manifestations in *Tom Jones*—is one of the most distinctive resources of his art as a novelist. More than any other writer of his day—unless, perhaps, one accepts J. Paul Hunter's provocative interpretation of Defoe's method in *Robinson Crusoe* [17]—Fielding organized his novels schematically, choosing his characters and shaping his plots so as to objectify an abstract moral theme which is the germ of his fiction. There is what may be called an iconomatic impulse behind much of Fielding's art: many of his most memorable episodes and characters, and the general design and movement of such books as *Joseph Andrews* and *Tom Jones,* may be seen to function figuratively as emblem or allegory, as the embodiment in scene or character or action of Fielding's themes. *Tom Jones* is not of course an allegory in the same sense or in the same way that *The Faerie Queene,* let us say, is an allegory; nevertheless, both these works have certain schematic intentions and certain narrative and scenic techniques in common. *Tom Jones* differs from the conventional allegory in that Fielding's *story* is primary and autonomous: characters, events, setting have an integrity of their own and compel our interest in and for themselves; they do not require, at every point in the narrative, to be read off as signs and symbols in some controlling ideational system. Whereas Una is "the One," Sophia Western is the girl whom Tom Jones loves and her family bullies. Spenser's heroine engages our intellect; Fielding's our affection and sympathy.

Yet at the same time Fielding shares with the allegorist the desire to *render* the abstractions of his theme—in this instance, to find the particular shape and image for the complementary concepts of Providence and Prudence, of divine Order and human Virtue, which were the bases for his comic vision of life. What Charles Woods observed of Fielding's plays, invoking a favorite term of the critic Sneerwell in *Pasquin,* pertains as well to the novels, where Fielding deserts the "realistic" mode for the "Emblematical."[18]

The general figurative strategy in *Tom Jones* is implicit in the passage from Fielding's Dedication comparing "Virtue" (i.e., *sophia*) to a beautiful woman and our "true Interest" (i.e., *prudentia*) to the "Pursuit of her." Although Sophia Western is first of all a character in Fielding's novel, she is also the emblematic redaction of the Platonic metaphor. After his expulsion from Paradise Hall, Tom Jones' journey is at first aimless and uncertain: "*The World,* as *Milton* phrases it, *lay all before him;* and *Jones,* no more than *Adam,* had any Man to whom he might resort for Comfort or Assistance" (VII.ii). After the crisis at Upton, however, his pursuit of Sophia will symbolize his gradual and painful attainment of *prudentia,* of self-knowledge and clarity of moral vision. The marriage of Tom and Sophia is thus the necessary and inevitable culmination of Fielding's theme: it is a symbolic union signifying the individual's attainment of true wisdom.

To illustrate this quasi-allegorical dimension of *Tom Jones,* we may consider, first of all, the ways in which Fielding renders the Platonic metaphor of Virtue—in which the idea of *sophia* becomes associated with the girl Sophy Western. Without forgetting his heroine's role and function in the story itself, from time to time in the course of the narrative Fielding makes the reader aware that Sophia's beauty is ultimately the physical manifestation of a spiritual perfection almost divine, that she is for him as for Tom Jones, the Idea of Virtue incarnate. Like much of his comedy Fielding's introduction of Sophia *"in the Sublime"* style (IV.ii) is both playful and serious, mocking the extravagancies of romance while at the same time invoking the old values of honor and virtue which romance celebrates. By a process of allusion—to mythology, art, poetry, and his own more immediate experience—Fielding presents his heroine as the ideal woman, the representative of a beauty of form and harmony of spirit so absolute as to be a sort of divine vitalizing force in man and nature alike. She is like "the lovely *Flora,*" goddess of springtime, whom every flower rises to honor and who is the cause of the perfect harmony of the birds that celebrate her appearance: "From Love proceeds your Music, and to Love it returns." Her beauty excels that of the Venus de Medici, the statue considered by Fielding's contemporaries to be "the standard of all female beauty and softness."[19] She is the idealization in art of his dead wife Charlotte, "whose Image never can depart from my Breast." But what is clear above all is that her beauty is only the reflection of her spiritual nature: "the Outside of *Sophia* . . . this beautiful Frame," is but the emblem of her "Mind," which diffuses "that Glory over her Countenance, which no Regularity of Features can give." Like Elizabeth Drury, Donne's ideal woman in *The Anniversaries,* to whom Fielding here expressly compares her, Sophy Western is also the image and embodiment of "*Sophia* or the *Divine Wisdom.*"[20]

For Jones, of course, Sophia *is* the perfection of beauty and virtue that her name implies: she is "my Goddess," he declares to Mrs. Honour; "as such I will always worship and adore her while I have Breath" (IV.xiv). And he can scarcely think of her except in terms of divinity itself: he stands in awe of her "heavenly Temper" and "divine Goodness" (V.vi); she is his "dear . . . divine Angel" (XVIII.xii). Such sentiments are, to be sure, the usual effusions and hyperbole of the adolescent lover, but they work together none the less to reinforce the reader's sense of Sophy's perfections. In answer to the landlady's insipid description of his mistress as "a sweet young Creature," Jones supplies a truer definition, applying to Sophia alone Jaffeir's apostrophe to Woman in *Venice Preserved* (I.i):

> 'A sweet Creature!' cries *Jones,* 'O Heavens!
>
> *Angels are painted fair to look like her.*
> *There's in her all that we believe of Heaven,*
> *Amazing Brightness, Purity and Truth,*
> *Eternal Joy, and everlasting Love.'* (VIII.ii)

Like his author, Jones insists that Sophia's physical beauty is only the imperfect manifestation of her essential spiritual nature. It is her "charming Idea" that he doats on (XIII.xi). Thus, when his friend Nightingale inquires if she is "honourable," Jones protests that her virtues are so dazzling as to drive all meaner considerations from his thoughts; it is not her body but the spiritual reality it expresses which demands his love:

> 'Honourable?' answered *Jones* . . . 'The sweetest Air is not purer, the limpid Stream not clearer than her Honour. She is all over, both in Mind and Body, consummate Perfection. She is the most beautiful Creature in the Universe; and yet she is Mistress of such noble, elevated Qualities, that though she is never from my Thoughts, I scarce ever think of her Beauty; but when I see it.' (XV.ix)

Twice during the novel Fielding symbolically dramatizes the distinction he wishes his readers to make between the girl Sophy Western and her "Idea"—that is, in a Platonic sense, the mental image or form of that essential spiritual Beauty of which his heroine's lovely face is but an imperfect manifestation.[21] As

Socrates had regretted that mortal eyes were able to behold only the shadow of *sophia,* reflected as in a glass darkly,[22] so Fielding uses the conventional emblem of the mirror to dramatize the nature of his allegory, to demonstrate that what is ultimately important about Sophia is not her physical charms, but her spiritual reality. The use of the mirror as an emblem of the mind's powers to conceptualize and abstract was common among iconographers. "The Glass," writes a commentator upon Ripa's emblems, "wherein we see no real Images, is a Resemblance of our *Intellect;* wherein we phancy many Ideas of Things that are not seen"; or it "denotes *Abstraction,* that is to say, by Accidents, which the Sense comprehends; the Understanding comes to know their Nature, as we, by seeing the accidental Forms of Things in a Glass, consider their Essence."[23] Fielding introduces this emblem at the moment when his hero, having pursued Sophia from Upton, is reunited with her in Lady Bellaston's town house (XIII.xi). The first sight the lovers have of each other is of their images reflected in a mirror:

> . . . *Sophia* expecting to find no one in the Room, came hastily in, and went directly to a Glass which almost fronted her, without once looking towards the upper End of the Room, where the Statue of *Jones* now stood motionless.—In this Glass it was, after contemplating her own lovely Face, that she first discovered the said Statue; when instantly turning about, she perceived the Reality of the Vision. . . .

The vision in the mirror that has momentarily turned Jones to a statue is the visible projection of the ideal image of Sophia he has carried in his mind. Whatever his indiscretions, he assures her that his "*Heart* was never unfaithful": "Though I despaired of possessing you, nay, almost of ever seeing you more, I doated still on your charming Idea, and could *seriously* love no other Woman."

Still clearer, perhaps, is Fielding's use of the mirror emblem toward the close of the novel (XVIII.xii), in a scene designed both to stress the allegorical identity of Sophia and to dramatize Socrates' declaration in the *Phaedrus* (250D) that "wisdom would arouse terrible love, if such a clear image of it were granted as would come through the sight." But, as Fielding observed in *The Champion* (5 July 1740), few there are "whose Eyes are able to behold Truth without a Glass." Protesting that "No Repentance was ever more sincere," and pleading that his contrition "reconcile" him to his "Heaven in this dear Bosom," Jones attempts to overcome Sophia's doubts as to his sincerity by making her confront the vision of her own beauty and virtue reflected in a mirror. To behold and possess not the image merely, but the reality itself, would, as Socrates had said, convert even the most inveterate reprobate to the love of virtue:

[Jones] replied, 'Don't believe me upon my Word; I have a better Security, a Pledge for my Constancy, which it is impossible to see and to doubt.' 'What is that?' said *Sophia,* a little surprized, 'I will show you, my charming Angel,' cried *Jones,* seizing her Hand, and carrying her to the Glass. 'There, behold it there in that lovely Figure, in that Face, that Shape, those Eyes, that Mind which shines through these Eyes: Can the Man who shall be in Possession of these be inconstant? Impossible! my *Sophia:* They would fix a *Dorimant,* a Lord *Rochester.* You could not doubt it, if you could see yourself with any Eyes but your own.' *Sophia* blushed, and half smiled; but forcing again her Brow into a Frown, 'If I am to judge,' said she, 'of the future by the past, my Image will no more remain in your Heart when I am out of your Sight, than it will in this Glass when I am out of the Room.' 'By Heaven, by all that is sacred,' said *Jones,* 'it never was out of my Heart.'

Such passages demand to be read on more than one level: Sophy Western's image in the glass is the literalizing of the Platonic metaphor, the dramatization of Fielding's meaning in the broadly allegorical scheme of the novel. Ultimately, her true identity is ideal, an abstraction.

Within the paradigmatic universe of **Tom Jones**—in which the values of Fielding's Christian humanism are systematically rendered and enacted—Sophy Western is both cynosure and avatar, the controlling center of the theme of Virtue and its incarnation. Though she is, above all, the woman that Tom loves, she is also, as Fielding's Dedication implies, the emblem and embodiment of that ideal Wisdom her name signifies. Without her Paradise Hall and the country from which Tom has been driven are unbearable, meaningless (XII.iii)—an Eden empty of grace. To win her in marriage is the supreme redemptive act, a divine dispensation which for Jones, as for every man, restores joy and order to a troubled world: "To call *Sophia* mine is the greatest . . . Blessing which Heaven can bestow" (XVIII.x). But for one of Jones' passionate nature the conditions upon which she may be won are exacting, nothing less, indeed, than the acquisition of *prudentia:* Tom must perfect his "Understanding," as Sophia herself insists (XI.vii), must learn not only to distinguish between the values of the spirit and those of the flesh, between the true and the false, but to discipline his will so that this knowledge may govern his life. Having learned this lesson at last, Jones is able to withstand the blandishments of such sirens as Mrs. Fitzpatrick, for, as the narrator observes, "his whole Thoughts were now so confined to his *Sophia,* that I believe no Woman upon Earth could have now drawn him into an Act of Inconstancy" (XVI.ix). On the eve of their wedding, as the company of brides and grooms convenes, Sophia is revealed presiding over the feast of virtuous love, eclipsing the beauty of the women, adored by every man:

she "sat at the Table like a Queen receiving Homage, or rather like a superiour Being receiving Adoration from all around her. But it was an Adoration which they gave, not which she exacted: For she was as much distinguished by her Modesty and Affability, as by all her other Perfections" (XVIII.xiii). In its way not unlike the banquet of Socrates, the wedding dinner of Tom and Sophia celebrates the power of Beauty and Virtue. In the light of such passages, Jones' "Quest" for "his lovely *Sophia*" (X.vii) takes on a symbolic dimension: it is the dramatization of Fielding's expressed concern in the novel to convince "Men, that their true Interest directs them to a Pursuit of [Virtue]."

Fielding's method of projecting the abstractions of his theme in image and action is comparable, in a way, to the poet's device of personification. It is also the correlative in fiction of the graphic artist's use of emblem and allegorical design. Following Horace, Fielding recognized the sisterhood of the two art forms.[24] In this respect, as in others, he may be compared with Pope, many of whose descriptions—that of the triumph of Vice in the *Epilogue to the Satires. Dialogue I* (ll.151 ff.), for example, or of Dulness holding court in *The Dunciad* (IV.17 ff.)—have the effect of allegorical *tableaux,* pictorially conceived and composed in order to carry the poet's meaning before the visual imagination. Fielding himself more than once observed the relationship between his own satiric art and that of his friend Hogarth, the "comic History Painter," who well understood the use of symbolic detail to render and characterize abstractions.[25] Particularly "Hogarthian" in conception and effect, for instance, is the image Fielding presents of the philosopher Square after his hilarious exposure in Molly Seagrim's bedroom (V.v). At the critical moment the rug behind which he has concealed himself falls away, and the august metaphysician—who has made a career of denouncing the body—is revealed in the closet, clad only in a blush and Molly's nightcap and fixed "in a Posture (for the Place would not near admit his standing upright) as ridiculous as can possibly be conceived":

> The Posture, indeed, in which he stood, was not greatly unlike that of a Soldier who is tyed Neck and Heels; or rather resembling the Attitude in which we often see Fellows in the public Streets of *London,* who are not suffering but deserving Punishment by so standing. He had a Night-cap belonging to *Molly* on his Head, and his two large Eyes, the Moment the Rug fell, stared directly at *Jones;* so that when the Idea of Philosophy was added to the Figure now discovered, it would have been very difficult for any Spectator to have refrained from immoderate Laughter.

The distinctive quality of this passage is graphic. It is as close to the pictorial as the artist in words can bring it: the sense of composition, of attitude is there; the subject has been frozen at the critical moment in time, his chagrin economically defined by the two features, the night cap and the astonished stare, which explain and characterize it. What is more, the scene has an emblematic effect: it serves as the pictorial projection of an *idea*—namely, of the theory of "the true Ridiculous," which, as the Preface to **Joseph Andrews** makes clear, Fielding thought to consist principally in the comic disparity between what we are and what we profess to be. As the literal revelation of the naked truth behind the drapery of pretension, the exposure of Square is the quintessential scene in Fielding's fiction.

Other scenes in the novel are pictorially conceived, and for a variety of effects. Most obvious of these is Fielding's ironic imitation of one of the most celebrated historical *tableaux* of the period: Plate VI of Charles Le Brun's magnificent series depicting the victories of Alexander.[26] As Le Brun had represented the vanquished King Porus being carried before the magnanimous conqueror, so Fielding, with due regard to the arrangement and attitudes of his figures, describes the scene after Jones' and Western's bloody victory over the forces of Blifil and Thwackum (V.xii):

> At this time, the following was the Aspect of the bloody Field. In one Place, lay on the Ground, all pale and almost breathless, the vanquished *Blifil*. Near him stood the Conqueror *Jones*, almost covered with Blood, part of which was naturally his own, and Part had been lately the Property of the Reverend Mr. *Thwackum*. In a third Place stood the said *Thwackum*, like King *Porus*, sullenly submitting to the Conqueror. The last Figure in the Piece was *Western the Great*, most gloriously forbearing the vanquished Foe.

Analysis of Fielding's mock-heroicism must clearly extend beyond his burlesque allusions to Homer and Virgil to such skillful imitations of specific masterpieces of historical art.

Certain other scenes in **Tom Jones** recall the art of the painter of "prospect" pieces, wherein, however, Fielding has chosen and arranged the features of the landscape for their allegorical or emblematic suggestiveness. Such are the descriptions, almost iconological in effect, of Allworthy's estate and of the view from Mazard Hill. The prospect at Paradise Hall (I.iv), while apparently a static landscape, is carefully organized so as to carry the reader's eye, and hence his imagination, from the immediate and local outward to the distant and infinite, thereby implicitly presenting the characteristic quality and intention of Fielding's art in the novel, which is a continual translation of particulars into universals: the spring, gushing from its source at the summit of the hill, flows downward to a lake in the middle distance, from whence issues a river which the eye follows as it meanders for several miles before it empties itself in the sea beyond. The scene takes on yet another significant dimension once we are aware that it is composed of elements associating Paradise Hall, the place of Tom Jones' birth and the home of his spiritual father, both with the estates of Fielding's patrons, George Lyttelton and Ralph Allen, and with Glastonbury Tor, which rises fully visible from the threshold of Sharpham Park, Fielding's own birthplace and the seat of his maternal grandfather.[27] Paradise Hall is very much the product of Fielding's symbolic imagination; it is his own, as well as his hero's, spiritual home. Equally suggestive, and more obviously emblematic, is the subsequent description of Allworthy walking forth to survey his estate as dawn breaks, bathing the creation in light. The glory of this good man—who is, more than any other character except Sophia herself, the center of the novel's moral universe—is rendered in terms of the sun, traditional symbol of the deity.[28]

> It was now the Middle of *May,* and the Morning was remarkably serene, when Mr. *Allworthy* walked forth on the Terrace, where the Dawn opened every Minute that lovely Prospect we have before described to his Eye. And now having sent forth Streams of Light, which ascended the Blue Firmament before him, as Harbingers preceding his Pomp, in the full Blaze of his Majesty up rose the Sun; than which one Object alone in this lower Creation could be more glorious, and that Mr. *Allworthy* himself presented; a human Being replete with Benevolence, meditating in what Manner he might render himself most acceptable to his Creator, by doing most Good to his Creatures.

A final illustration of Fielding's emblematic art in **Tom Jones** will serve to return us to the theme of Wisdom. As in presenting the "Idea" of *sophia,* Fielding, at one significant moment in the novel, also drew upon conventional iconological techniques in order visually to project the meaning of *prudentia.* The scene occurs at the opening of Book IX, Chapter ii, as Tom Jones contemplates the prospect from atop Mazard Hill. Structurally, the scene holds a crucial position between the narrative of the Old Man of the Hill and the pivotal events at Upton; thematically, it is the emblematic statement of the nature of true prudence and of Tom's progress along the way to acquiring that virtue. Fielding's basic device was entirely familiar. We will recall that it was conventional for poets and philosophers alike to translate the notion of the prudent man's intellectual apprehension of past, present, and future into physical and spatial terms: to look in the direction from whence one has come is to contemplate the meaning of the past; to look in the direction one is going is to consider what the future holds in store. The iconology of Prudence traditionally represented this virtue in the likeness of a figure with two (or three) faces—one, often the face of an old man, looking to the left or behind; the other, that of a young man or woman, looking to the right or ahead. Titian's *Allegory of Prudence*—the symbolism of which Professor Panofsky has brilliantly explicated[29]—depicts a head with three faces and bears a Latin inscription reading: "The prudent man of today profits from past experience in order not to imperil the future."[30] Following the design by Caesar Ripa, whose *Iconologia* (1593) was the standard work well into the eighteenth century, most emblematists represented Prudence with two faces, while retaining the sense of Titian's symbolism. George Richardson explains the significance of the design as follows: "The ancients have represented this virtue with two faces, the one young, and the other old, to indicate that prudence is acquired by consideration of things past, and a foresight of those to come."[31] The persistence of this metaphor, associating Prudence with the vision of distant things, is further suggested by Pope's personification of this virtue in *The Dunciad* (I.49), where the image of Prudence with her perspective glass was drawn from a different, but obviously related, iconological tradition.

As we have already remarked, what Tom Jones must acquire before he is ready to marry Sophia and return to the country of his birth is prudence—the ability to learn from past experience, both his own and others', so as to distinguish the true from the false and to estimate the future consequences of his present behavior. To invoke the Aristotelian notion of the "Three Ages of Man,"[32] at this juncture in Tom's progress toward maturity he is presented with the extreme alternatives of youth and age—the rashness and passion which characterize his own adolescence, and which define all that is most and least admirable about him, as opposed to the cowardly cynicism of the Old Man of the Hill. Having heard the wretched history of the Old Man and rejected his misanthropy, Tom has profited from one lesson that experience has to teach him; but, as events in Upton will soon prove, he has not yet mastered the more difficult test of his own past follies. As Upton represents the apex of the rising action of the novel and the turning point in Tom's progress, so at this stage in the narrative Fielding's hero stands literally at the summit of a high hill, from which he can survey the vast terrain that separates him from his home and mistress, and, by facing in the opposite direction, regard the obscure and tangled wood which, it will appear, contains the woman who will abruptly dislodge Sophia from his thoughts and involve him in the near fatal consequences of his own imprudence. The prospect Fielding describes, with a warning that we may not fully "understand" it, allegorizes the theme of prudence in the novel, rendering spiritual and temporal matters in terms of physical and spatial analogues: the view southward toward "Home" representing the meaning of the past, the view northward toward the dark wood imaging the problem of the future. As the Old Man shrewdly remarks to his young companion: "I perceive now the Object of your Contemplation is not within your Sight":

> *Aurora* now first opened her Casement, *Anglicè*, the Day began to break, when *Jones* walked forth in Company with the Stranger, and mounted *Mazard* Hill; of which they had no sooner gained the Summit, than one of the most noble Prospects in the World Presented itself to their View, and which we would likewise present to the Reader; but for two Reasons. *First*, We despair of making those who have seen this Prospect, admire our Description. *Secondly*, We very much doubt whether those, who have not seen it, would understand it.
>
> *Jones* stood for some Minutes fixed in one Posture, and directing his Eyes towards the South; upon which the old Gentleman asked, What he was looking at with so much Attention? 'Alas, Sir,' answered he with a Sigh, 'I was endeavouring to trace out my own Journey hither. Good Heavens! what a Distance is *Gloucester* from us! What a vast Tract of Land must be between me and my own Home.' 'Ay, ay, young Gentleman,' cries the other, 'and, by your Sighing, from what you love better than your own Home, or I am mistaken. I perceive now the Object of your Contemplation is not within your Sight, and yet I fancy you have a Pleasure in looking that Way.' *Jones* answered with a Smile, 'I find, old Friend, you have not yet forgot the Sensations of your youth.—I own my Thoughts were employed as you have guessed.'
>
> They now walked to that Part of the Hill which looks to the North-West, and which hangs over a vast and extensive Wood.
>
> Here they were no sooner arrived, than they heard at a Distance the most violent Screams of a Woman, proceeding from the Wood below them. *Jones* listened a Moment, and then, without saying a Word to his Companion (for indeed the Occasion seemed sufficiently pressing) ran, or rather slid, down the Hill, and without the least Apprehension or Concern for his own Safety, made directly to the Thicket whence the Sound had issued.

Occurring midway through Jones' journey—and through his progress toward maturity, toward the acquisition of prudence—the scene atop Mazard Hill is the emblematic projection of Fielding's theme. The past and its meaning are plain and clear to Jones, but not plain and clear enough; the future is obscure and tangled, fraught with sudden and unforeseen dangers. Sophia is abruptly supplanted in his thoughts by the more immediate appeal of another woman, in whose arms at Upton Tom will forget, for the moment at least, the lesson of his past follies and the claims of his true mistress. It is his affair with Jenny Jones at Upton that will result in his estrangement from Sophia and, eventually, in the anxious knowledge that his behavior, however generous and gallant, has apparently involved him in the sin of incest. What Tom sees looking south from Mazard Hill reassures us about his essential health of spirit, about those values he ultimately cherishes. His precipitous descent, however, reflects those qualities of character which are both his greatest strength and his weakness: on the one hand, courage and selflessness, prompting him to the assistance of injured frailty; on the other, that rashness which is the source of his vulnerability as a moral agent.

Despite the number of illuminating studies in recent years, the technical resources of Fielding's art as a novelist have not yet been fully disclosed, nor have we as yet adequately appreciated the degree to which Fielding applied the devices of his craft to the communication of his serious concerns as a moralist. If the structure of *Tom Jones* is organic in an Aristotelian sense—as Professor Crane has shown it to be—it is also schematic, the expression through emblem, parable, and significant design of Fielding's controlling themes. If *Tom Jones* is the playful celebration of the feast of life—as Andrew Wright has insisted—it is also the expression in art of Fielding's Christian vision. The ways in which such devices as ambiguity, allegory, and emblem function together to define the theme of Wisdom in the novel may be taken as one more measure of Fielding's intention and his achievement.

Notes

[1] Quotations from *Tom Jones* are from the 4th edition (1750).

[2] See *Fiction and the Shape of Belief* (Berkeley and Los Angeles, 1964).

[3] Walter Miller, trans. (Loeb Classical Library, 1913).

[4] Only recently have critics begun to direct serious attention to this theme in the novel: see Eleanor N. Hutchens, "'Prudence' in *Tom Jones:* A Study of Connotative Irony," *PQ,* XXXIX (1960), 496-507, and the excellent discussion by Glenn W. Hatfield in Chapter V of his forthcoming book, *Henry Fielding and the Language of Irony* (University of Chicago Press).

[5] *The British Magazine,* IV (March 1749), 77.

[6] *Ibid.,* IV, 78.

[7] *Loc. cit.*

[8] *Ibid.,* IV, 78-79.

[9] *Ibid.,* IV, 79.

[10] See John Tillotson, Sermon XXXVI, "Success not always Answerable to the Probability of Second Causes," *Works* (1757), III, 28-29; and William Sherlock, *A Discourse Concerning the Divine Providence,* 9th ed.

(1747), p. 43.

[11] "An Essay on the Knowledge of the Characters of Men," in *Miscellanies* (1743), I, 183.

[12] Cicero, *De Officiis,* II.iii, III.xvii.

[13] *Ibid.,* III.xxv; trans. W. Miller (Loeb Classical Library, 1913).

[14] Quoted from the 1st ed. (1752).

[15] Quoted from the 1741 reprint, I, 23.

[16] Cf. *Phaedrus,* 250D: "wisdom would arouse terrible love, if such a clear image of it were granted as would come through sight" (trans. H. N. Fowler, Loeb Classical Library, 1914). See also Cicero, *De Finibus,* II.xvi, and *De Officiis,* I.v; and Seneca, *Epistulae Morales,* CXV.6. The specific notion of the naked charms of Virtue, imaged as a beautiful woman, is only implicit in Plato. Fielding was especially fond of this commonplace: see, for example, *The Champion* (24, 26 January 1739/40), and "An Essay on Conversation" and "An Essay on the Knowledge of the Characters of Men"—both published in the *Miscellanies* (1743), I, 159, 217. For a discussion of this image and its relation to the moral theme of Fielding's last novel, see Alan Wendt, "The Naked Virtue of Amelia," *ELH,* XXVII (1960), 131-148.

[17] See Hunter, *The Reluctant Pilgrim: Defoe's Emblematic Method and Quest for Form in 'Robinson Crusoe'* (Baltimore, 1966).

[18] Fielding, *The Author's Farce,* ed. Charles B. Woods (Lincoln, Neb., 1966), p. xvi.

[19] Joseph Spence, *Polymetis* (1747), p. 66.

[20] The quotation is from Jacob Boehme, *The Way to Christ* (Bath, 1775), p. 56, as given in Frank Manley, ed., *John Donne: The Anniversaries* (Baltimore, 1963), p. 38. On the identification of "the noble Virgin Sophia" with the biblical figure of Wisdom, see Manley's Introduction, pp. 37-38.

[21] The definition of *idea* given in George Richardson's *Iconology: or, A Collection of Emblematical Figures, Moral and Instructive* (1778-79), is as follows: "In general, [Idea] is the image of any thing, which, though not seen, is conceived in the mind. Plato defines it, the essence sent forth by the divine spirit, which is entirely separated from the matter of created things" (I,82).

[22] *Phaedo,* 99D-E.

[23] See Isaac Fuller and Peirce Tempest, *Iconologia: or, Moral Emblems, by Caesar Ripa* (1709), Figures 229

and 269, folios 57 and 67.

[24] For an excellent discussion of the relationship between poetry and painting in the eighteenth century, see Jean H. Hagstrum, *The Sister Arts: The Tradition of Literary Pictorialism and English Poetry from Dryden to Gray* (Chicago, 1958).

[25] For Fielding's compliments to Hogarth, see, among many other references, the Preface to *Joseph Andrews* and *Tom Jones* (I.xi, II.iii, III.vi, VI.iii, X.viii), where Fielding refers the reader to particular Hogarth prints to clarify the description of Bridget Allworthy, Mrs. Partridge, and Thwackum.

[26] Done at the command of Louis XIV, Le Brun's series depicting the victories of Alexander now hangs in the Louvre. Copies of the official engravings by the Audrans were commissioned in England and published by Carington Bowles. The series was much admired: see, for example, Farquhar's *Beaux' Stratagem* (1707), IV, and Charles Gildon, *The Complete Art of Poetry* (1718), I, 230. When Louis Laguerre was commissioned to commemorate Marlborough's victories over the French, he looked to Le Brun's *tableaux* for a model (see Margaret Whinney and Oliver Millar, *English Art, 1625-1744* [Oxford, 1957], pp. 305-306).

[27] In describing Allworthy's seat, Fielding's intentions are as much allusive and symbolic as they are chorographical. The description is based upon elements associated primarily with Sharpham Park and secondarily with Hagley Park and Prior Park, the estates of Lyttelton and Allen respectively. From the doorway at Sharpham Park Fielding would have looked daily across the moors at Glastonbury and Tor Hill. The prospect from Allworthy's Paradise Hall corresponds in general with the view westward from Tor Hill (see Wilbur L. Cross, *The History of Henry Fielding* [New Haven, 1918], II, 165). The "Style" of Paradise Hall itself is doubtless in honor of a mutual friend of Fielding's and Lyttelton's, Sanderson Miller (1717-80), amateur architect and pioneer of the Gothic revival. In 1747-78 and 1749-50 Lyttelton erected a ruined castle and a rotunda of Miller's design at Hagley Park; indeed, until his second wife disapproved, he had wanted Miller to build him a Gothic house. Like Allworthy's mansion, furthermore, Hagley Hall is situated on the south side of a hill, nearer the bottom than the top, yet high enough to command a pleasant view of the valley. And many of the details in Fielding's description echo Thomson's celebration of Hagley Park in "Spring," ll. 900-958 (*Seasons,* 1744 ed.). At the same time, in the third paragraph of the chapter, Fielding does not forget Ralph Allen, whose house, an example of "the best *Grecian* Architecture," he had praised earlier in *Joseph Andrews* (III.i, vi) and *A Journey from This World to the Next* (I. v): Allen's Palladian mansion stands on the summit of a hill down which a stream falls into a lake which is visible "from every Room in the Front."

[28] For an elaborate gloss on the sun as *"A fit Emblem, or rather Adumbration of God,"* see William Turner's *Compleat History of the Most Remarkable Providences* (1697), pp. 14-19. The sun, according to Turner (and many others), is "the *Eye of Heaven*" (p. 14) and a symbol of God's "Benignity and Beneficence" (p. 18). It is with this latter attribute of the Deity that both Barrow and Fielding particularly associated the sun. Wrote Barrow: "Such is a charitable man; the sun is not more liberal of his light and warmth, than he is of beneficial influence" (Sermon XXVII, "The Nature, Properties and Acts of Charity," *op. cit.,* I, 261). In the verse epistle "Of Good-Nature," Fielding, recalling Matthew V:45, exclaims: "Oh! great Humanity, whose beams benign,/Like the sun's rays, on just and unjust shine."

[29] Erwin Panofsky, *Meaning in the Visual Arts,* Doubleday Anchor Books (Garden City, N.Y., 1955), pp. 146-168.

[30] Because she regards past, present, and future, Prudence is represented in Dante's *Purgatorio,* XXIX, as a figure with three eyes. See also Francisco degli Allegri, *Tractato Nobilissimo della Prudentia et Iustitia* (Venice, 1508): British Museum, Prints and Drawings. 163*.a.23.

[31] Richardson, *op. cit.,* II, 23-24. For earlier emblems of Prudence, based on Ripa and representing a figure with two faces, see the following: Jacques de Bie and J. Baudoin, *Iconologie* (Paris, 1644), pp. 160, 164, and Fuller and Tempest, *op. cit.,* Figure 251 and folio 63.

[32] See Aristotle, *Rhetoric,* II.xii-xiv.

Alan T. McKenzie (essay date 1982)

SOURCE: "The Physiology of Deceit in Fielding's Works," in *The Dalhousie Review,* Vol. 62, No. 1, 1982, pp. 140-52.

[*In the following essay, McKenzie examines Fielding's use of physiology in each of his major novels, arguing that Fielding's depictions of theatrical displays of passion offer keys to interpreting the actions of his characters.*]

As unwilling to be imposed upon as the most sceptical of his contemporaries, and with an eye for deceit sharpened both behind the stage and upon the bench, Henry Fielding developed one of the general concerns of his age into high art. He equipped many of his characters with certain passions and their attendant physiology—

just enough to generate deceit, discomfort, and, eventually, discovery. The mechanism of the passions is not, I need hardly add, something Fielding invented; he relied on the tradition of faculty psychology originated by Aristotle and modified by the stoics, Galen, Descartes, and many others. These passions came to him as thoroughly analyzed and intricately systematic components of character. He instilled them in his characters as responses to actions and objects, and by way of distillations from the blood. In passage after passage the vital spirits go about their business, carrying messages of satisfaction or distress within the body and producing indications of these sensations without. I propose to demonstrate, by both citation and analysis, that Fielding turned to the physiology of deceit at crucial moments in every book, and that he relied far more on physiology than has been previously suggested. The psychological tradition in which he chose to work provided sufficient intricacy to suit his genius and his integrity, and to fulfill both artistic and moral purposes.[1]

I shall argue that Fielding found the physiology of passion dramatic and that he rendered it forensic. Alert, in his earliest works, to the dramatic possibilities inherent in the changes passion induced in both voice and countenance, he made the display of passion highly, perhaps excessively, theatrical. He sometimes overdrew the passions for comic effect, as in the "agonies" of Lady Booby, the "Ebullience" of Parson Adams, and the sudden humours of Squire Western, and he sometimes overdid the blushing of his heroines. Nevertheless, as his discursive treatments of passion and deceit in the "Preface" to *Joseph Andrews* and the **"Essay on the Characters of Men"** indicate, he understood very well both the passions and their potential for his art. The most thorough and effective exploitation of his doctrine is evident, as we might expect, in *Tom Jones,* but passion and deceit are hard at work in several crucial passages in *Jonathan Wild.* The concern lingers, perhaps a little feebly in *Amelia* and the *Journal of a Voyage to Lisbon.*

In all his works those characters who can simulate or suppress their displays of passion are always to be distrusted by the narrator, as well as by those characters and readers who wish to thrive in the world Fielding creates. In characters with a capacity for evil the connections between the heart within and the face and voice without can (for a while) be interrupted at will, enabling those characters to perpetrate much imposition. Then, without fail, some passion that begins on the outside, in response to external circumstances, grows so overwhelming that it restores the severed connections, and informs the bad heart of something it does not wish to know. The working of passion in these characters is usually accompanied by considerable, but comic, internal discomfort, implicit in figures of speech suggesting boiling, chagrin, pangs, struggles, and

flame—all figures derived from the physiology of passion, and most used with some sense of that derivation by Fielding. In the good characters, on the other hand, the physiological connections are easy and regular, and the attendant sensations pleasant. What goes on in the heart is readily and agreeably communicated to the face, and never distorts the voice. Thus Fielding employs the passions to send signals from one character to another, from some characters to themselves, and from all of his characters to some of his readers. Sometimes the passions send messages of character, sometimes they send hints of plot, and sometimes they make moral statements. In every case, they bend the precepts of Eighteenth century physiology to Fielding's wise and humorous purposes.

Jonathan Wild was blessed by mother nature and the generic requirements of rogue biography with many attributes that qualified him for greatness—among them ingenuity, ambition, dexterity, avarice, and insatiability, together with "a wonderful knack of discovering and applying to the passions of men . . ." and, most applicable to the present purposes, that great art which the vulgar call "dissembling" and great men call "policy". His ability to render his own passions impenetrable, frequently remarked upon by Fielding and never, as far as I can see, made much of by critics, underlies all of Wild's success. It must have made that success most alarming in an age unwilling to be imposed upon.

This skillful severing of the connections between a passion within and the display without concludes Wild's fifteen maxims for the attaining of greatness: "15. That the heart was the proper seat of hatred, and the countenance of affection and friendship" (pp. 202-203). It reappears in the passage from which I have taken my title: "Thus did our hero execute the greatest exploits with the utmost ease imaginable, by means of those transcendent qualities which nature had indulged him with, viz. a bold heart, a thundering voice, and a steady countenance." [2]

I isolate that phrase because it implies the physiological interdependence among three parts of the body, one hidden (except from an omniscient narrator), and the other two quite conspicuous. The heart is the seat of the passions; it communicates, and often betrays, their presence and identity by altering the flow of the vital spirits. These vital spirits, distillations from the blood, course about in direct response to a passion, altering the muscles, and thus the face, and the vocal chords, and thus the voice. The unnatural few who can prevent or simulate these effects are wonderfully equipped to impose upon the rest of us, and wonderfully equipped to act as villains in Fielding's works. He comments on Wild's talents in this respect again and again, using phrases like "with wonderful greatness of mind and steadiness of countenance," "with the notable presence of mind and unchanged complexion so essential to a great character," and "He was greatly superior to all mankind in the steadiness of his countenance, but this undertaking seemed to require more of that noble quality than had ever been the portion of a mortal" (pp. 69, 70, and 108-109). Wild summons up all of his unnatural prowess in a scene in which he discovers that his pocket has been picked by the sister of his beloved:

> However, as he had that perfect mastery of his temper, or rather of his muscles, which is as necessary to the forming a great character as to the personating it on the stage, he soon conveyed a smile into his countenance, and, concealing as well his misfortune as his chagrin at it, began to pay honourable addresses to Miss Letty. (p. 63)

Fielding's knowledge of what goes on both on and off the stage is implicit in the notion of "forming" a great character, while the hint in "or rather of his muscles" is taken up in the friction and discomfort implicit in "chagrin" in this passage.

The most intriguing incident in which Fielding manipulates Wild's management of the display of his passions is one in which Wild loses his characteristic "assurance." He has just been set adrift in a small boat, "without oar, without sail," and with only "half-a-dozen biscuits to prolong his misery." He resorts first to blasphemy, then to a posturing defiance, and finally to what he thinks will be suicide:

> At length, finding himself descending too much into the language of meanness and complaint, he stopped short, and soon after broke forth as follows: "D——n it, a man can die but once! what signifies it? Every man must die, and when it is over it is over. I never was afraid of anything yet, nor I won't begin now; no, d——n me won't I. What signifies fear? I shall die whether I am afraid or no; who's afraid then, d——n me?" At which words he looked extremely fierce, but, recollecting that no one was present to see him, he relaxed a little the terror of his countenance, and, pausing a while, repeated the word, d——n! (pp. 88-90)

The effect of this wonderfully theatrical passage depends on the absence of an audience and the presence of the vital spirits. (I pass over the theological implications of all that "Damning" in the face of death and omnipotence.) As I read it Wild begins confidently enough, with much boldness in his voice. Then, as his words find no audience to convince, they succeed only in unconvincing their speaker. Finally, his facial expression begins to fail, also for lack of an audience. And Wild needs his facial expressions to help him to stimulate within the passion he has simulated without. As he relaxes a little the terror of his countenance, his vital spirits dissolve his spurious inner strength, and imperil his soul. As his voice falters and his

countenance slackens, his heart grows much less bold. The "wonderful resolution" with which he casts himself headlong into the sea is really only confusion mingled with despair.

Wild survives, but he lives "under a continual alarm of frights, and fears, and jealousies," (p. 138) until his transgressions grow too evident even for the Eighteenth-century judicial system. His transgressions eventually find their way, quite naturally, into his countenance.

> . . . but, when one of the keepers . . . repeated Heartfree's name among those of the malefactors who were to suffer within a few days, the blood forsook his countenance, and in a cold still stream moved heavily to his heart, which had scarce strength enough left to return it through his veins. In short, his body so visibly demonstrated the pangs of his mind, that to escape observation he retired to his room, where he sullenly gave vent to . . . bitter agonies. . . . (pp. 157-58)

I regard that passage as a triumph of physiology over deceit, and perhaps also over art. Nonetheless, it would be unfortunate if we were to allow the contrivance and the melodrama to obscure the deft theatrical awareness (in both character and narrator) in "to escape observation" and the hint of physiological discomfort in "bitter." Fielding soon developed formal and stylistic subtleties not evident here, but he never abandoned his concern with either physiology or deceit or his assumption, both moral and aesthetic, that the connections between the two were strong and exploitable. We will come shortly to two comparable passages from *Tom Jones*—one even more theatrical, and also set in a prison, and the other comparable in administering a strong dose of well-deserved and self-inflicted bitterness to a villain. Both passages will draw additional strength from a much more sophisticated plot and a much more penetrating narrator.

Jonathan Wild is certainly an early work, written well before its publication in 1743. And while this convenient (but still impressive) manipulation of passion suggests as much, the play of passion both on and behind the face had always struck Fielding as a source of drama and humour. He exploits several other possibilities in his plays, all of them earlier than *Jonathan Wild.* In them he works often and well with one manifestation of passion he had little occasion for in Jonathan Wild—blushing. This coursing of the blood and the vital spirits toward the skin in response to the passions of shame or embarrassment is usually reserved for his female characters, and was, I suppose, rendered more noticeable by the decolletage then very much in style. Indeed, I suspect that the fashion was a response to the social demand for frequent evidence of modesty. Thus Huncamunca, when "The burning Bridegroom" hints at his intentions toward "the blushing Bride" (notice the physiology at work in the participles): "O fie upon you, Sir, you make me blush." To which Tom Thumb in tiny voice replies: "It is the Virgin's sign, and suits you well—".[3] I pass over several other passages, most notably in **The Modern Husband,** to mention the auction scene in **The Historical Register for the Year 1736,** a scene in which Fielding goes beyond, as well as behind, the fan and the mask as instruments of imposition to suggest that those demireps who have rendered themselves *unable* to blush ought to employ these devices to hide that inability. As we shall see, Fielding believed in blushing, and required it, perhaps a little too often, in his heroines. It proved them physically incapable of deceit.

The passions in **Joseph Andrews** are all so straightforward that there is much physiology and little deceit. Lady Booby's passions are so potent that she cannot control them, much less dissemble them. She usually takes her passions to bed, where their failure to secure an object becomes all the more comic, comedy echoed in the physiology lurking behind their "boiling": "She then went up into her Chamber, sent for *Slipslop,* [and] threw herself on the Bed, in the Agonies of Love, Rage, and Despair; nor could she conceal these boiling Passions longer, without bursting."[4] Joseph's passion and nature are so innocent that concealment is out of the question. When he visits "her in whom his Soul delighted" (p. 295) the whole world knows of, and shares, that delight. Fanny blushes so convincingly that she brings out that lamentable propensity for priggishness in her lover:

> . . . an Admiration at his Silence, together with observing the fixed Position of his Eyes, produced an Idea in the lovely Maid, which brought more Blood into her Face than had flowed from *Joseph's* Nostrils. The snowy Hue of her Bosom was likewise exchanged to Vermillion at the instant when she clapped her Handkerchief round her Neck. *Joseph* saw the Uneasiness she suffered, and immediately removed his Eyes from an Object, in surveying which he had felt the greatest Delight which the Organs of Sight were capable of conveying to his Soul. (p. 305; IV.vii)

It is, of course, the vital spirits that convey Joseph's delight from his eyes to his soul. Whether Fielding meant wickedly to imply that another organ might one day convey greater delight to Joseph's soul I cannot say, but only a prig would overlook the possibility.

Parson Adams's heart is so pure, and his physiology in such good order, than when he finds himself yet again indebted to an old pedlar, he cannot conceal his gratitude: " . . . he felt the Ebullition, the Overflowings of a full, honest, open Heart towards the Person who had conferred a real Obligation, and of which if thou can'st not conceive an Idea within, I will not vainly endeavour to assist thee" (p. 310; IV.viii).

Because of the goodness of his heart, Parson Adams feels that response throughout his system. Stimulated by an object ("the Person who had conferred . . .") his heart, "full" and "open", sends forth an "Ebullition" of vital spirits, which makes its appearance in his countenance and his manner. Here again, the fullness and openness of the heart and its Ebullition and overflowing are drawn, even overdrawn, from the realm of the physiology of passion. And again, it is only the bad characters who manage, for a while, to redeploy their vital spirits. When Leonora, is caught by her fiance with a rival, she greets him with "A long Silence." "At length *Leonora* collecting all the Spirits she was Mistress of, addressed herself to [Horatio], and pretended to wonder at the Reason of so late a Visit" (p. 113; II.iv). Her ability to become Mistress of her spirits signals Leonora's decline; now she can impose on those around her—but not on the narrator. Similarly, the "roasting" Squire, "having first called his Friends about him, as Guards for the Safety of his Person, rode manfully up to the Combatants, and summoning all the Terror he was Master of, into his Countenance, demanded with an authoritative Voice of *Joseph,* what he meant by assaulting his Dogs in that Manner" (p. 242; III.vi). The commas make it clear that the Squire's heart is by no means bold. As Horatio has already proven to Bellarmine: "the Seat of Valour is not the Countenance, and many a grave and plain Man, will, on a just Provocation, betake himself to that mischievous Metal, cold Iron; while Men of a fiercer Brow, and sometimes with that Emblem of Courage, a Cockade, will more prudently decline it" (p. 115; II.iv). The cockade is an emblem of courage in the same way that the fan is an emblem of modesty. It can be displayed, but it is separate from the body and therefore not validated by physiology.

To these scattered indications of an underlying and continuous attention to physiology and deceit Fielding adds the consideration of the subject in the "Preface" to **Joseph Andrews.** The passages, excessively well known, wherein he announces that "The only Source of the true Ridiculous . . . is Affectation" and that "Affectation proceeds from one of these two Causes, Vanity or Hypocrisy: for as Vanity puts us on affecting false Characters, in order to purchase Applause; so Hypocrisy sets us on an Endeavour to avoid Censure by concealing our Vices under an Appearance of their opposite Virtues" (pp. 7-8) are followed by two others, less well known, but very much to the present purpose, as they address themselves to the physiology underlying both kinds of deceit. The innocent kind of affectation, vanity, "hath not that violent Repugnancy of Nature to struggle with, which that of the Hypocrite hath," so that the affectation of liberality "sits less awkwardly on [a vain man] than on the avaricious Man, who *is* the very Reverse of what he would *seem* to be" (p. 8). It is, I take it, physiology that makes affectation sit awkwardly on one in whom it provokes a struggle.

The vital spirits can be more readily summoned to displays of vain passions than hypocritical ones.

Fielding extended his discursive treatment of this concern in his penetrating **"Essay on the Knowledge of the Characters of Men"**. Written, as he says, to champion "the innocent and undesigning, and . . . to arm them against Imposition," it asserts that "the Passions of Men do commonly imprint sufficient Marks on the Countenance; and it is owing chiefly to want of Skill in the Observer, that Physiognomy is of so little Use and Credit in the World."[5] The marks that physiology imprints are so faint, and skilled observers so rare, that most of us are better advised to watch men's actions than their faces, and to watch their private actions, rather than those they perform in public (as in the public-private displays that betrayed Jonathan Wild). Even then, it will never be easy to avoid imposition: " . . . but while Men are blinded by Vanity and Self-Love, and while artful Hypocrisy knows how to adapt itself to their Blind-sides, and to humour their Passions, it will be difficult for honest and undesigning Men to escape the Snares of Cunning and Imposition . . ." (p. 174).

The engaging and penetrating analysis to which Fielding subjects the generous provision of human nature provided in **Tom Jones** relies extensively and cunningly on the treatment of physiology. The leisurely unfolding of character into the sophisticated leverage of plot confirms the analysis of passion as an essential, fruitful, and revealing component of humanity. The confusion engendered by the deceptive display of passion generates much of the novel's intricacy, providing hints for the alert reader and significance to the understanding one. For example, the reader who understands a little physiology will appreciate the cleverness of the "hearty" in: "the good Lady [Bridget Allworthy] could not forbear giving [the foundling] a hearty Kiss, at the same time declaring herself wonderfully pleased with its Beauty and Innocence."[6] This passage uses the physiology implicit in that "hearty" as subtly as another one on the same page uses the subjunctive: "Her Orders were indeed so liberal, that had it been a Child of her own, she could not have exceeded them. . . . "

Squire Western, the least deceitful character in the novel, "had not the least Command over any of his Passions; and that which had at any Time the Ascendant in his Mind, hurried him to the wildest Excesses" (p. 296; VI.vii). It is just this direct response of his passions that makes Squire Western so impetuous, so troublesome, so undeceitful, and so endearing.[7] The connections between his body and his passions are emphasized in his maxim *"that Anger makes a Man dry"* (p. 304; VI.ix), drawn from the lore of the four humours (choler being the one that is hot and dry). The passions had only recently outgrown this doctrine,

and Western is surely the most humorous, in the original sense of the word, character in the novel. Conversely, his sister Di, to whom he is constantly opposed, temperamentally and artistically, feels only the passions of pride and its concomitant, contempt, and she manifests these passions in her language rather than in her body. The fair Parthenissa remains, as always, untouched. Yet there is one passage in which she gets the better of her contempt by using her digestive juices as a solvent on her vital spirits: "'Hold a Moment', said she, 'while I digest that sovereign Contempt I have for your Sex; or else I ought to be angry too with you. There—I have made a Shift to gulp it down" (p. 276, VI.ii). This triumph of physiology over good manners and good sense is Di Western's only meal in a very festive novel. It also, I might add, precedes her triumphant announcement that Sophia must be in love with the unspeakable Blifil.

With Lady Bellaston the physiology of passion, but not of deceit, grows most intriguing. The convenient and controllable detachment of her heart from her body is expressed in everything that Lady Bellaston does and everything that Fielding says about her. Her occasional "hurries of spirit" are never occasioned by love, and the only real manifestation of passion that the reader sees comes not from her heart, but her purse, in the form of the "wages" she bestows on Tom. Only once is the flame in her heart conveyed into her countenance and her voice. It is in a passage rendered theatrical by the display of passion, in both face and voice, in front of a curtain. It is anger rather than love that is being displayed, and it is being displayed because *she* has been deceived:

> Lady *Bellaston* now came from behind the Curtain. How shall I describe her Rage? Her Tongue was at first incapable of Utterance; but Streams of Fire darted from her Eyes, and well indeed they might, for her Heart was all in a Flame. And now as soon as her Voice found Way . . . she began to attack poor *Jones*. (p. 747; XIV.ii)

Sophia has not detached her heart from her body. Indeed, she blushes in nearly every appearance she makes in the novel. Perhaps it is the readiness with which her heart fires her blood and dispatches her vital spirits toward her epidermis that makes her so charming, so amiable, and sometimes so tedious? It is probably this hurry of spirit, doubtless inherited from her father, that lies behind her convenient fainting spells. I cite but one passage from the dozen or so available:

> He then snatched her Hand, and eagerly kissed it, which was the first Time his Lips had ever touched her. The Blood, which before had forsaken her Cheeks, now made her sufficient Amends, by rushing all over her Face and Neck with such Violence, that they became all of a scarlet Colour. She now first felt a Sensation to which she had

been before a Stranger, and which, when she had Leisure to reflect on it, began to acquaint her with some Secrets which the Reader, if he doth not already guess them, will know in due Time. (p. 168; Iv.v)

Sophia's physiology conveys messages from the outside in, confirming and assisting the work of the omniscient narrator as it does so. Moreover, the contrast in their physiologies evident in these two passages in which Tom is the object of their respective passions figures in most of the scenes between Sophy and Lady Bellaston, underlying, explaining, and dramatizing each of their conflicts (see, for example, XIII.xi and XV.iii).

Parson Supple, quoting, as is his wont, Juvenal, tells us all there is to be told about the manifestation (in the sense in which I have been discussing it) of Tom's passions: "'I wish, indeed, he was a little more regular in his Responses at Church; but altogether he seems *Ingenui vultus puer ingenuique pudoris.* That is a classical Line . . . and being rendered into *English* is, A Lad of an ingenuous Countenance and of an ingenuous Modesty . . . '" (pp. 189-190; IV.x). Tom's spirits, always violent, and always evident, give him away in each of his (well-intended) attempts at deceit; they prevent him from concealing his goodness from Allworthy, his love from Sophia, and his change of heart from Lady Bellaston. She comes to visit him in what she expects to be a sickbed, but he forgets "to act the Part of a sick Man," and greets her with "good Humour," instead of "Disorder," in his countenance (p. 810; XV.vii). The many connections between Tom's mind, heart, and body are precisely those connections that Lady Bellaston has so successfully and repellently interrupted in herself.

I conclude this discussion of **Tom Jones** with two scenes that take us back, each in its own way, to much that has already been said. The first exploits the theatricality of the passions, and the second employs them as tools of jurisprudence. Together they evoke Fielding's apprenticeship behind the stage and his career upon the bench. But while both scenes reproduce elements we encountered in **Jonathan Wild,** these scenes both depend on and contribute to the plot, making more than merely theatrical use of the elements in them: the prison, the despair, the reversals of passion and fortune, and the passionate responses in voice and countenance. Fielding has come a considerable artistic distance from that early work, yet he has brought the passions and their physiology with him.

In the first scene Partridge reveals to Tom, already in prison for murder, an even more disturbing offense. The scene is played as a very tragic one with Terror, Fear, Horror, and Amazement on the faces, in the voices, and in the hearts of both men. It is a clever

parody of the way such scenes were played in those days, and it includes several sly references back to the scene (XVI.v) where Tom watches Partridge watch Garrick as Hamlet start at his father's ghost.[8] There is no boldness, thunder, or steadiness in this scene; the only deceit is in Fielding's plot. Indeed, it is the Narrator's studied attention to the theatricality of the passions in this scene that makes it bearable, even pleasurable, to read. If Fielding is playing with us, he is at least doing so honorably and consistently:

> While *Jones* was employed in those unpleasant Meditations . . . *Partridge* came stumbing into the Room with his Face paler than Ashes, his Eyes fixed in his Head, his Hair standing an [sic] End, and every Limb trembling. In short, he looked as he would have done had he seen a Spectre. . . .
>
> *Jones,* who was little subject to Fear, could not avoid being somewhat shocked at this sudden Appearance. He did indeed himself change Colour, and his Voice a little faultered
>
> . . . . .
>
> '. . . as sure as I stand here alive, you have been a-Bed with your own Mother.'
>
> Upon these Words, *Jones* became in a Moment a greater Picture of Horror than *Partridge* himself. He was indeed, for some Time, struck dumb with Amazement, and both stood staring wildly at each other. (p. 915; XVIII.ii)

As Fielding says near the end of this scene: "The Pencil [i.e., the brush, and probably Hogarth's brush], and not the Pen, should describe the Horrors which appeared in both their Countenances."

In the other scene that seems to me to continue the excellence and confirm the maturity of Fielding's attention to the physiology of passion and deceit, Blifil, who has always used "the sober and prudent Reserve of his own Temper" (p. 253; V.ix) to control the manifestations of his own (quite manageable) passions, is finally betrayed by his own physiology. Is not this the perfect agent to undo the impositions of a young man as selfish as Blifil has always been?

> There is nothing so dangerous as a Question which comes by Surprize on a Man, whose Business it is to conceal Truth, or to defend Falshood. . . . Besides, the sudden and violent Impulse on the Blood, occasioned by these Surprizes, causes frequently such an Alteration in the Countenance, that the Man is obliged to give Evidence against himself. And such indeed were the Alterations which the Countenance of *Blifil* underwent from this sudden Question, that we can scarce blame the Eagerness of Mrs. *Miller,* who immediately cry'd out, 'Guilty,

upon my Honour! Guilty, upon my Soul!' (p. 932; XVIII.v)

Whereas, earlier in the novel the passions gave rise to the plot, here, in both these scenes from its conclusion, plot and passion are perfectly fused—a fusion effected by physiology and manifested in the voice and the countenance.

I pass quickly over *Amelia,* in which the physiology figures occasionally, but without the regularity, the subtlety, or the effect we have seen previously. The passions that prevail in this novel lend themselves a little too readily to analysis, even by a booby like Booth, who insists that the doctrine of the passions has always been his favorite study (III.iv). Sometimes the physiology gives rise only to melodrama: "'There lodged in the same house—O Mrs. Booth! the blood runs cold to my heart, and should run cold to yours, when I name him. . . .'"[9] In an earlier passage, equally physiological and even more melodramatic, the spirits that desert Booth seem already to have failed his creator: "A deep melancholy seized his mind, and cold damp sweats overspread his person, so that he was scarce animated; and poor Amelia, instead of a fond warm husband, bestowed her caresses on a dull, lifeless lump of clay" (VI, 184; IV.iii). In passages like these the passions are no longer clear and distinct ideas in the narrator's mind. They have become mere sensations in the character's body. They are confirmed by physiology, but they are no longer validated by a forceful tradition.

I conclude with a passage from Fielding's last work, the posthumous *Journal of a Voyage to Lisbon.* In this work Fielding asserts that:

> . . . nature is seldom curious in her works within, without employing some little pains on the outside; and this more particularly in mischievous characters. . . .

> This observation will, I am convinced, hold most true, if applied to the most venomous individuals of human insects. A tyrant, a trickster, and a bully, generally wear the marks of their several dispositions in their countenances; so do the vixen, the shrew, the scold, and all other females of the like kind.[10]

While Fielding is here discussing permanent temperament instead of fleeting passions, and is therefore concerned with settled manifestations, the venom that settled these marks on the countenance was distilled from physiology, it was put there by nature, and, presumably, it causes discomfort and inconvenience to the character through whom it courses as well as to those on whom it is brought to bear. Here, as elsewhere, physiology provides a warning to those who attend to it, and as always in Fielding's works, an opportunity for artistic comment.

From his earliest work until his very last piece, then, Fielding saw fit to attend to physiology, and to urge his readers to do likewise. He seems to have found the vital spirits exactly that, a convenient and potent device for bringing characters, and the books in which they figure, to life. They do the work of an omniscient narrator, conveying into the countenance and the voice the nature and intensity of internal responses. Those who manage to interrupt or dissemble these conveyings eventually undo themselves. The inattentive and uninformed, whether reader or character, will be imposed upon. The rest of us might well be impressed with the skilfulness and ingenuity with which Fielding manipulates the passions.

Notes

[1] There are numerous accounts of this intricate tradition, among them: Geoffrey Bullough, *Mirror of Minds: Changing Psychological Beliefs in English Poetry,* London: Athlone Press, 1962, and George S. Rousseau, "Nerves, Spirits, and Fibres: Towards Defining the Origins of Sensibility," in *Studies in the Eighteenth Century, III: Papers Presented at the Third David Nichol Smith Memorial Seminar,* ed. R. F. Brissenden and J. C. Eade, Toronto: University of Toronto Press, 1973, pp. 137-57. For Fielding and faculty psychology see Martin Battestin, *The Moral Basis of Fielding's Art: A Study of Joseph Andrews,* Middleton [Conn.]: Wesleyan University Press, 1959, pp. 58-74; Morris Golden, *Fielding's Moral Psychology,* Amherst [Mass.]: University of Massachusetts Press, 1966, pp. 20-41; and Henry Knight Miller, *Essays on Fielding's Miscellanies: A Commentary on Volume One,* Princeton: Princeton University Press, pp. 189-228.

[2] *The Complete Works of Henry Fielding, Esq.,* ed. William Ernest Henley, New York: Croscup & Sterling, 1902, II, 28, 73. Hereafter cited as "Hentley Edition."

[3] Henry Fielding, *Tom Thumb and the Tragedy of Tragedies,* ed. L. J. Morrissey, Berkeley: University of California Press, 1970, p. 35 (II.viii).

[4] Henry Fielding, *Joseph Andrews,* ed. Martin C. Battestin, The Wesleyan Edition of the Works of Henry Fielding, Middletown [Conn.]: Wesleyan University Press, 1967, p. 326 (IV.xiii). For Joseph's priggishness see J. Paul Hunter, *Occasional Form: Henry Fielding and the Chains of Circumstance,* Baltimore: The Johns Hopkins University Press, 1975, pp. 95-100.

[5] *Miscellanies by Henry Fielding, Esq.; Volume One,* ed. Henry Knight Miller, The Wesleyan Edition of the Works of Henry Fielding, Oxford: Wesleyan University Press, 1972, pp. 153, 157.

[6] Henry Fielding, *The History of Tom Jones, A Foundling,* ed. Martin C. Battestin and Fredson Bowers, The Wesleyan Edition of the Works of Henry Fielding, Middletown [Conn.]: Wesleyan University Press, 1975, pp. 45-46 (I.v).

[7] For this aspect of Squire Western see Robert Alter, *Fielding and the Nature of the Novel,* Cambridge: Harvard University Press, pp. 91-94.

[8] See Alan T. McKenzie, "'The Countenance You Show Me': Reading the Passions in the Eighteenth Century," *The Georgia Review,* 32, (1978), 758-73.

[9] Henley Edition, VII, 41 (VII.vi); the next quotation is from VI, 184 (IV.iii). For the passions in *Amelia* see Tuvia Bloch, "*Amelia* and Booth's Doctrine of the Passions," *SEL [Studies in English Literature, 1500-1900],* 13 (1973), 461-73 and Frederick G. Ribble, "The Constitution of the Mind and the Concept of Emotion in Fielding's *Amelia,*" *PQ [Philological Quarterly],* 56 (1977), 104-22.

[10] Henley Edition, XVI, 236.

Sheridan Baker (essay date 1985)

SOURCE: "Fielding: The Comic Reality of Fiction," in *The First English Novelists: Essays in Understanding,* edited by J. M. Armistead, Tennessee Studies in Literature, Vol. 29, University of Tennessee Press, 1985, pp. 109-42.

[*In the following essay, noted scholar and Fielding editor Sheridan Baker offers a thorough account of Fielding's approach to quixotic comedy in both his drama and his fiction. Calling the theater "Fielding's apprenticeship," Baker demonstrates that Fielding's early comic plays provided the groundwork for his didactic use of comedy in the novel.*]

Fielding's achievement in his four novels is immense. *Joseph Andrews* (1742) is not only the first English comic novel but the Declaration of Independence for all fiction. *Jonathan Wild* (1743), though imperfectly, turns Augustan satire into a novel. *Tom Jones* (1749) supersedes and absorbs the drama as the dominant form and, more significantly, culminates the Augustan world of poetry and Pope in the new poetics of prose. *Amelia* (1751) signals the eighteenth century's sombre midday equinox as its undercurrent of sentiment and uncertainty wells up through the cool neoclassic crust. *Amelia* is the first novel of marriage, and it explores a new and modern indeterminacy of character. Notwithstanding Defoe's and Richardson's achievement in fictionalizing the lonely struggle of modernity, Fielding proclaimed the truth of fiction as he gave the novel

form. He also gave it mystery with the romantic, and psychic, discovery of identity, acceptance, and success. He gave it its omniscient narrator and comprehensive scope.

Fielding is not of Defoe's and Richardson's rising middle class, where the individual makes himself and the future, where the underdog's struggles are no longer comic. Fielding is a young aristocrat down on his uppers.[1] His is the Augustan perspective, a sophisticated detachment that staves off evils and passionate dogmas through satire and irony, seeking a rational balance between violent extremes. His allegiance is to hierarchy in orderly rank. Like Swift, he prefers Ancients to Moderns. Like Pope, he perceives God's providential creation with calm optimism, and amusement.

He elects himself a Scriblerian. His first major effort, his anonymous *The Masquerade* (1728), a satire in Swiftian tetrameters, is "By LEMUEL GULLIVER, Poet Laureate to the King of *Lilliput.*" Soon, with his eminent cousin, Lady Mary Wortley Montagu, he is writing a burlesque of Pope's recent *Dunciad* (1728). His first stage satire and ballad opera, *The Author's Farce* (1730), is "Written by *Scriblerus Secundus,*" emulating the *Dunciad* in a trip to the underworld of the Goddess of Nonsense. *Tom Thumb* (1730), which imitates Swift's Lilliputian-Brobdingnagian contrasts and, in its final form, Pope's mock-scholarly preface and footnotes, is also by *Scriblerus Secundus,* who becomes *H. Scriblerus Secundus,* with Fielding's initial, in the expanded *Tragedy of Tragedies* (1730). *The Grub-Street Opera* (1731) is by *Scriblerus Secundus* in all three versions. In short, Fielding set out to emulate the three Augustan masterpieces, all deriving from the brief heyday of the Scriblerus Club (February to June 1714): Swift's *Gulliver's Travels* (1726), Gay's *Beggar's Opera* (1728), Pope's *Dunciad* (in three books, 1728). As Sherburn suggests *("Dunciad"),* Pope confirmed the alliance by borrowing back from Fielding's farces the kaleidoscopic court of Dulness in his fourth book (1742, 1743).

The theater was Fielding's apprenticeship.[2] It gave him stock characters and situations, repeated until they became universal types. It gave him a knack for scene and dialogue, the balanced structural arch of *Tom Jones,* and the long, downward comic slant of fortune that thrusts suddenly upward like a reversed check mark. It gave him social satire and comedy of manners aimed at a serious point.

Fielding's first play, *Love in Several Masques* (1728), written at twenty-one, forecasts *Tom Jones* in surprising detail. It is intricately plotted. Its hero is Tom Merital, a meritorious rake, a preliminary Tom Jones. Tom's wealthy lady love is an orphan guarded by an aunt and uncle—a stock preliminary Sophia, to be married against her will to save her from the rake. The heroines speak up for the hero, and the aunts respond.

> Lady Trap: I have wondered how a creature
>   of such principles could spring
>   up in a family so noted for the
>   purity of its women. (II.vi)
>
> Mrs. Western: You are the first—yes, Miss
>   *Western,* you are the first of
>   your Name who ever entertained
>   so groveling a Thought. A Family
>   so noted for the Prudence of its
>   Women. . . . (VI.v)

Lady Trap is also an Amorous Matron—the first Lady Booby, Mrs. Slipslop, Mrs. Waters, and especially Lady Bellaston, who, like Lady Trap, has bad breath: "Brandy and Assafoetida, by Jupiter," cries kissing Tom.

Here, at the play's mathematical center, the heroine catches Tom just as Sophia will discover her Tom and Mrs. Waters at central Upton. We also have the stock comic maid, saucy and ingenious, who will become Mrs. Honour. Finally, we have Wisemore, a junior and sourer Allworthy, a virtuous young country squire who introduces Fielding's perpetual contrast with the wicked city and represents the play's moral center, a book-read idealist whom his mistress twice calls Don Quixote. Wisemore will also transform comically into Parson Adams.

In his six rehearsal-farces—no one else wrote more than one—Fielding discovered himself as parodic satirist. In *The Author's Farce* (1730), he also discovered his autobiographical authorship of comic romances, a comic double self-portraiture in hero and author alike. Harry Luckless, the "author," is young playwright Harry Fielding, luckless with Mr. Colley Cibber of Drury Lane, who appears in no less than two comic versions and two more allusive thrusts. Harry loves Harriot, in the twinnish way of romance, whom his nonentity denies him—courtly love in a London rooming-house. Then Harry stages his show in the Popean realm of Nonsense and becomes Fielding commenting on his work as it goes. In the giddy finale, a pawned jewel proves Luckless a farcical foundling, lost heir of a fabulous kingdom, who may now marry and live happily ever after as Henry I. Fielding's blithe comedy distances his wish for recognition, the universal yearning typical of romance, as we simultaneously fulfill and recognize our fancies in the way of *Joseph Andrews* and *Tom Jones.*

Fielding eventually put nine commenting authors on the stage—seven in the rehearsal-farces (two in *Pasquin*) plus two authorial inductors like Gay's in *The Beggar's Opera*—breaking the bonds of drama to reach for narration. Many of their comments Fielding will repeat less facetiously in his novels. Medly, in *The Historical Register* (1737), Fielding's last, comes particularly close:

> Why, sir, my design is to ridicule the vicious and foolish customs of the age . . . I hope to expose the reigning follies in such a manner, that men shall laugh themselves out of them before they feel that they are touched.

Fielding says of *Tom Jones* (in the Dedication):

> I have employed all the Wit and Humour of which I am Master in the following History; wherein I have endeavoured to laugh Mankind out of their Favourite Follies and Vices.

But *The Historical Register* brought down Sir Robert Walpole's wrath, and the Licensing Act (1737) shut Fielding from the stage. He made himself a lawyer and followed the circuits along the roads of his future novels. He turned to journalism with the *Champion,* the opposition newspaper backed by Lord Chesterfield and Lord Lyttelton, Fielding's Eton school-friend. He is now "Capt. Hercules Vinegar, of Hockley in the Hole," slaying the Hydras of political corruption like the popular cudgel player and boxing promoter of that name. Like Pope, who had declared himself "TO VIRTUE ONLY AND HER FRIENDS, A FRIEND" in his first *Imitation of Horace* (1733), Fielding is the champion of England against Walpole's government, the future essayist as novelist who will dedicate *Tom Jones* to Lyttelton, believing that it will serve as "a Kind of Picture, in which Virtue becomes as it were an Object of Sight."

Fielding's religious concern deepens in the *Champion.* We can almost see *Shamela* and *Joseph Andrews* accumulating. In the spring of 1740, Fielding pauses in his political championship to write four thoughtful essays about the materialism and vanity of the clergy and the necessity of humble charity. The first (March 29) is untitled. Then in the next issue (April Fool's Day, by luck or design), he satirizes Walpole, along with a new book by "the most inimitable Laureat," none other than *An Apology for the Life of Mr. Colley Cibber, Comedian, Written by Himself.* Cibber had been a standing joke as political sycophant and bad writer ever since Walpole had made him poet laureate in 1730. Moreover, Cibber, from his side of the political fence, had in his *Apology* called Fielding a mudslinger and failed writer. So Fielding interrupts his religious meditation here and returns in several papers to ridicule the vanity and grammar of his old personal and political opponent, whom he will enthrone as an egotistical fraud in *Shamela* and *Joseph Andrews,* as Pope would also in the *Dunciad.* Fielding then continues with his religious essays under the ironic title "THE APOLOGY FOR THE CLERGY,—*continued.*"

As Cibber and the clergy mix in Fielding's mind, another new book appears: *A Short Account of God's Dealings with the Reverend Mr. George Whitefield* (1740), written by himself in what would seem Cibberian conceit at God's personal attention. It stirred a controversy between the new Methodist (and old Calvinist) belief that only faith and God's grace warranted Heaven as against the doctrine that "Faith without works is dead" (Battestin, *Moral Basis,* 18), which Fielding had asserted in the *Champion.* Whitefield's *Dealings* would become Shamela's favorite reading, as Fielding mocks Pamela's egotistical piety, and Parson Williams espouses spiritual grace to release the body for pleasure.[3] Fielding turns these negatives positive when he transforms Williams into Adams, who, with Methodist John Wesley, prefers a virtuous Turk to a tepid Christian (Woods, "Fielding," 264). Adams is a lovingly comic portrait of a Whitefieldian enthusiast, who shames the fatness of orthodoxy and nevertheless condemns Whitefield's enthusiastic grace:

> "Sir," answered *Adams,* "if Mr. *Whitfield* had carried his Doctrine no farther . . . I should have remained, as I once was, his Well-Wisher. I am myself as great an Enemy to the Luxury and Splendour of the Clergy as he can be." (I.xvii)

But selfless charity was the center of Fielding's religion, and Whitefield stood ready with Cibber to coalesce with pious Pamela, when she arrived in the fall, as symbols of meretricious vanity and hypocrisy.

Pamela: Or, Virtue Rewarded, the "real" letters of a serving girl, prefaced by twenty-eight pages of letters praising its moral excellence, is really *An Apology for the Life of Mrs. Shamela Andrews* (1741)—so proclaims Fielding's title page in the typography of Cibber's *Apology,* with "Conny Keyber" as author: *Keyber* being the standard political slur at Cibber's Danish ancestry. Parson Tickletext, who can dream of nothing but Pamela undressed, sends a copy of the new best seller to Parson Oliver so that he too can preach it from the pulpit (as had actually been done in London). Oliver tells Tickletext the book is a sham, doctored by a clergyman who can make black white. The girl is really Shamela, a calculating guttersnippet from London working in a neighboring parish. Richardson's Mr. B. is really Squire Booby, his busybody Parson Williams is really an adulterous poacher of Booby's hares and wife. He sends Tickletext the real letters—Fielding's breezy parodies of Richardson's, which concentrate on his two bedroom scenes, now lifted to peaks of hilarity as Fielding brilliantly condenses two volumes to some fifty pages.

Fielding's title page tells us immediately that something has happened to fiction, now allusively declaring and enjoying in the Augustan way the fictive pretense Defoe and Richardson had pretended real. English fiction has become literate. Here, suddenly, is a book that—like Joyce's *Ulysses,* let us say—generates its being, and its meaning, from other literature as it gets its hold on life. By declaring his letters true to tell us ironically they are not—precisely the comic pose Cervantes shares with his readers—Fielding asserts both the validity and power of fiction, which he will proclaim in *Joseph Andrews. Shamela* is probably the best parody anywhere, but it is also a broadly Augustan burlesque of social ills—moral, political, religious, philosophical—in the true Scriblerian mode (Rothstein, 389).

In naming "Conny Keyber" the author, Fielding concentrates his inclusive satire in a bawdy sexual symbol. "Conny" merges Cibber's first name with that of the Rev. Mr. Conyers Middleton, whose dedication to his *Life of Cicero* (February 1741, less than two months before *Shamela*) Fielding closely parodies as a dedication by Conny Keyber to "Miss Fanny, &c." Middleton had dedicated his *Cicero* to John, Lord Hervey, Walpole's propagandist; and Hervey, an effeminate bisexual, had acquired the epithet "Fanny" from Pope's first *Imitation of Horace* (1733), where Pope had saucily Anglicized Horace's Fannius, a bad poet and a homosexual. Now, as Rothstein notes (387), *Conny, coney,* and *cony* (for "rabbit") were all pronounced "cunny"—a version of the still-prevailing obscenity for the female pudendum, and *Fanny* and *et cetera* were both slang terms for the same (382).

In parodying one of Richardson's introductory letters praising Pamela, Fielding writes, "it will do more good than the C——y have done harm in the World," wherein one may read both the *clergy* and the *cunny* of Fielding's satirical attack. Later, Shamela reports that her husband gave her a toast so wicked she can't write it and that Mrs. Jewkes then "drank the dear *Monysyllable;* I don't understand that Word, but I believe it is baudy." Williams and Booby likewise drink to and joke about her *"et cetera."* In short, Cibber, Hervey, Middleton, Richardson, and Pamela, "that young Politician" named on the title page, are all moneysyllabic prostitutes in their various ways. Fielding's slyest touch is in quoting directly another introductory letter telling Richardson he had "stretched out this diminutive mere Grain of Mustard-seed (a poor Girl's little, innocent, Story) into a resemblance of Heaven, which the best of good Books has compared it to." Fielding alters only the parenthesis of this extravagant Biblical allusion (Matt. 13:31): "has stretched out this diminutive mere Grain of Mustard-seed (a poor Girl's little, &c.) into a Resemblance of Heaven."

Shamela sharpened Fielding's belief, to be formulated in *Joseph Andrews,* that comedy can be both realistic and morally instructive. No serving maid was ever named Pamela, after the romantic princess in Sidney's recently republished *Arcadia,* nor wrote such letters, if she could write at all. The realistic idiom of Shamela and the housekeepers, and even their calculating morality, amusingly point up the falsity in Richardson's idea of virtue. Tearful Pamela, proud of her dead mistress's clothes, becomes Shamela, wanting to set herself up with Parson Williams, since "I have got a good many fine Cloaths of the Old Put my Mistress's, who died a whil ago." Her language rings colloquially true and yet mimics Richardson at every turn. Shamela actually seems more honest, and Mrs. Jewkes more wholesome, than their prototypes. Nothing seems more typical of Fielding's realistic countryside than Booby riding in his coach with Shamela and catching Williams poaching. Yet as Williams rides off in the coach with Booby's bride, we realize that this is all a mime of an episode in *Pamela* where we find Williams walking, book in hand, at the meadowside; he is met, reconciled, and finally taken into the coach by Mr. B. with his Pamela.

The close parody of Richardson's bedroom scenes taught Fielding the high comedy of sex. The amorous scenes in his plays are heavy. The ladies know what's what. But *Shamela* shimmers with the comic hypocrisies of civilized sex. Pamela wants—not simply for prestige—to submit to her master, but everything she believes in prevents her desire from even breaking surface. Richardson, simply to keep his story going, has her stay when she wants to go, writing into his tale this elemental sexual hypocrisy that gives it the mystic dimension of Beauty and the Beast. In burlesquing it, Fielding learned what it was. His stage ladies wish to appear proper only in the eyes of others; Lady Booby and Mrs. Slipslop of *Joseph Andrews* wish to appear proper in their own eyes as well. A great deal of the comedy in Fielding's novels comes from the universal struggle of hidden passion against propriety or, on the masculine side, of passion against the best of intentions. *Shamela,* more than anything before, brought this to the center of Fielding's comic vision.

Parson Oliver, another step toward Fielding's commenting author, decrying Richardson's lascivious images and meretricious rewards, spells out the moral. He declares the future lesson of *Tom Jones:* Prudence must rule. *Pamela,* he says, encourages young men to impetuous matches that will "sacrifice all the solid Comforts of their Lives, to a very transient Satisfaction of a Passion." In *Tom Jones,* Fielding will seek "to make good Men wise" by instilling in them "that solid inward Comfort of Mind, which is the sure Companion of Innocence and Virtue." Oliver writes of "the secure Satisfaction of a good Conscience, the Approbation of the Wise and Good . . . and the extatick Pleasure of contemplating, that their Ways are acceptable to the Great Creator of the Universe." "But for Worldly Honours," Oliver continues, "they are often the Purchase of Force and Fraud." Tom Jones cries out concerning Blifil, who has defrauded him:

What is the poor Pride arising from a magnificent House, a numerous Equipage, a splendid Table, and from all the other Advantages or Appearances of Fortune, compared to the warm, solid Content, the swelling Satisfaction, the thrilling Transports, and the exulting Triumphs, which a good Mind enjoys, in the Contemplation of a generous, virtuous, noble, benevolent Action? (XII.x)

Shamela's success made Fielding a novelist; he gives *Pamela* another parodic turn in *Joseph Andrews* (1742) and also finally brings Cervantes to English life. At last, Fielding finds his authorial voice in the playful ironies of Cervantes and Scarron:

Now the Rake *Hesperus* had called for his Breeches. . . . In vulgar Language, it was Evening when *Joseph* attended his Lady's Orders. (I.viii)

And now, Reader, taking these Hints along with you, you may, if you please, proceed to the Sequel of this our true History. (III.i)

He now ironically holds up Pamela and Cibber as consummate models for the kind of biography he is writing. He extends the joke of *Shamela* in its next inevitable mutation, transposing the sexes for the more ludicrous effect. Pamela Andrews, who had become Shamela Andrews, will now become Pamela's equally virtuous, and hence more comically prudish, brother: a footman named Joseph, after the biblical hero who resisted Potiphar's wife. Lady Booby now pursues *her* servant—Squire Booby is her nephew—as Mr. B. pursued his. Richardson's Mrs. Jewkes, "a broad, squat, pursy, *fat thing*" who drinks, becomes Mrs. Slipslop, who also reflects Cervantes's grotesque chambermaid, Maritornes,[4] a libidinous little dwarf with shoulders somewhat humped and a breath with "a stronger *Hogoe* than stale Venison" (I.iii.2). Mrs. Jewkes's salacious lesbianism becomes Slipslop's comic passion for Joseph.[5] Fielding even dares to name his heroine after the obscene "Miss Fanny" of *Shamela,* rinsing the name clean without losing all of its comic pubic potential. In fact, Fielding's Beau Didapper, who attempts to rape the purified Fanny, is none other than Lord Hervey again (Battestin, "Hervey"), the original "Miss Fanny," as if everything of *Shamela* must be converted to new uses. Finally, Mr. B.'s curate Williams becomes, through the wringer of *Shamela,* Lady Booby's curate Adams.

Adams is Fielding's triumph. At twenty-one, as a student at Leyden, Fielding had tried to naturalize Cervantes in his *Don Quixote in England*—eventually a ballad opera (1734). Now, in *Joseph Andrews* ("Written in Imitation of the Manner of Cervantes") he finally creates a thoroughly English Quixote, a country parson drawn from the very life—from Fielding's friend from childhood, the absent-minded parson William Young. Like Cervantes, Fielding comically confronts the ideal quest of romance with the satiric picaresque tour of society. Adams is his comic knight, a quixotic Christian benevolist embodying the virtues outlined in the *Champion*. Like Quixote, he is book-blinded, but by the New Testament and classics alike. His tattered cassock replaces Quixote's patchwork armor. His borrowed horse, soon abandoned, a Christian Rosinante, frequently stumbles to its knees. He rescues "Damsels" (Fanny) and stands up for the innocent with his crabstick against the selfish world's windmills. Andrews travels the English roads and inns as realistic squire to the daft idealist and, like Sancho Panza, grows in wisdom.

Fielding's parody becomes *paradiorthosis,* as the Greeks would say, an emulative borrowing and bending of a master's words, well loved by Augustans, except that Fielding finds creative joy in allusively reapplying whole characterizations, episodes, and dramatic arrangements. Richardson furnishes his major structure—two wild bedroom episodes at beginning and end, followed by the discovered truth of identity and social elevation of romance, which Pamela had also enacted. It is almost as if Fielding had cut **Shamela** down the middle and pulled the halves apart to accommodate his Cervantic roadway. The first bedroom scenes (I.v-vi), in which first Lady Booby and then Mrs. Slipslop try to possess Joseph—"Madam," says Joseph, "that Boy is the Brother of *Pamela*"—are probably the most hilarious chapters in the English novel. The second and concluding bedroom episode (IV. xiv) is more broadly comic, a reworking of the old picaresque fabliau about a wrong turn into bed that simultaneously parallels two versions from Cervantes and three from Scarron, as critics from Cross to Goldberg have detected, and primarily into the bed of Mrs. Slipslop, that caricature of Mrs. Jewkes, in whose bed Richardson's second scene of attempted rape is laid, if one may use the term. Even Lady Booby must laugh at the universal selfish scrambling of sex to which intrinsic virtue is impervious (Spilka, 403).

Fielding's central Cervantic journey is linear and episodic, as Joseph becomes both romantic hero and practical companion to idealistic Christianity. When Lady Booby dismisses him, he heads not for home (as Pamela longs to do) or for "his beloved Sister *Pamela*," but to Lady Booby's country parish to see the girl he loves. Fielding's genius is nowhere more blithely evident than in his ability to change his lighting and reveal the young man within the parodic abstraction— this very funny male Pamela—without losing his hero, or his readers. Joseph matures, as Taylor notes, and clearly becomes the romantic hero at an inn, very near the center of the novel (II.xii), which reunites the major characters (except Lady Booby) in much the way the inn at Upton will do at the central climax of **Tom Jones.**

Fielding is reworking an episode from Cervantes he had already used for the whole of **Don Quixote in England,** where the lovers, as Tom and Sophia will be at Upton, are under the same roof unbeknownst to each other. Adams has brought the rescued Fanny, who, like Dorothea in the play and Sophia in **Tom Jones,** has set out across country in search of her lover. Mrs. Slipslop in her coach has picked up Joseph along the road and brought him in "Hopes of something which might have been accomplished at an Ale-house as well as a Palace" (II.xiii). As in Cervantes, our heroine hears a beautiful voice singing. But realism renders romance comic. Joseph's pastoral song ends in sexual climax, with Chloe "expiring." Fanny, only recognizing the voice, cries "O Jesus!" and faints. Adams, to the rescue, throws his beloved Aeschylus into the fire, where it "lay expiring," and enraged Slipslop rides off in disappointment.

Balancing this comic juxtaposition of ideal and sexual love is another structuring episode Fielding will also elaborate in **Tom Jones.** This is Mr. Wilson's story, just on the other side of the central divide between Books II and III, which is, as Paulson ("Models," 1202) and Maresca (199) have noted, Fielding's realistic version of the *descensus Averno* (*Aeneid* VI.126), the trip to the underworld for truth.[6] Our travelers descend a hill in spooky darkness, cross a river, and find Elysium in the country Eden of Wilson, who tells them the truth about the wicked world of London. Wilson's straightforward account fills out Fielding's social panorama, and Wilson, in the end, neatly fits into Fielding's comic romance as the long-lost father of cradle-switched Joseph, whose white skin (which, as with Tom Jones to come, a lady discovers in succoring the wounded hero) has already disclosed to the reader of romances his unknown nobility.

Fielding comically fulfills the romantic dream of Harry Luckless. He opens his preface by assuming that his readers will have "a different Idea of Romance" from his, never before attempted in English, which will be "a comic Romance." He takes his term from Paul Scarron's *Romant Comique* (1651), the *Comical Romance* in Tom Brown's translation (1700) recently read, which augments Cervantes's authorial facetiousness and claims of "this true History,"[7] and sends its lovers chastely down the picaresque road disguised as brother and sister, in the amusingly incestuous twinship of romance that Fielding will exploit with Joseph and Fanny, the almost identical foundlings of romance from *Daphnis and Chloe* onward. His identical portraits gently parody those typical of Scudéry's romances (Shesgreen, 33-34; Maresca, 200-201), especially in their noses "inclining to the Roman" (I.viii; II.xii). In Joseph's nose and brawny physique, Fielding has again pictured himself both accurately and comically as romantic hero.

"Now a comic Romance," he writes, "is a comic Epic-Poem in Prose." From his bows toward the epic, the twentieth century has largely ignored his, and his readers', context: the vast French romances—which he names, and which had virtually shaped the fancies, manners, and idiom of English elegance—and the new romance of princess Pamela, the serving maid. He is not writing the high life of epic, which can live among modern realities only in mock heroics: "Indeed, no two Species of Writing can differ more widely than the Comic and the Burlesque," touches of which he has indulged here and there to amuse his classical readers. In his conclusion he insists again on distinguishing his realistic comedy from "the Productions of Romance Writers on the one hand, and Burlesque Writers on the other." His new "Species of writing . . . hitherto unattempted in our Language" avoids both the impossibilities of "the grave Romance" and the absurdities of the comic mock-epic. His comic romance will draw from the realities of ordinary life, as his friend Hogarth has done pictorially, to illustrate the vanity and hypocrisy everywhere and eternally evident.[8]

This comic realism he outlines in III.i, which, most likely written before his preface, stands as his Declaration of Independence for fiction. Unlike actual historians, he says, Cervantes has written "the History of the World in general," as have Scarron, Le Sage, Marivaux, and other authors of "true Histories," including the *Arabian Nights*. Fiction is truer than history. It illustrates the typical, the perennially true in human nature in all time and every country: "I describe not Men, but Manners; not an Individual, but a Species." One might add only that typicality is the very stuff of comedy, along with the celebration of life (which Wright and Langer point to)—that central romantic thread on which the comic typicalities are strung, and which *Pamela* seriously exploits: the unknown nobody's becoming somebody in happy marriage. Fielding keeps the wish fulfillment of all us Harry Lucklesses playfully comic, letting us know in his affectionate irony that our deep-seated yearning is real enough, but with no Richardsonian guarantee. Romance encapsulates the central psyche: one's secretly noble self, whom no one appreciates, crying for recognition and riches, especially in the classless world emerging as Fielding wrote, and surely representing his own déclassé impulse. His comic-romantic perspective acknowledges the comic impossibility of the ideal and romantic glories of life, yet affirms their existence and value.

Adams, like Quixote, comically embodies the romantic struggle of the ideal against the cruel realities. As with Quixote, we begin in laughter and end in admiration. For the Duke and Duchess who amuse themselves at Quixote's expense, Fielding gives us an actual practical-joking country squire—son-in-law of the Duchess of Marlborough, indeed (Wesleyan ed., xxiv)—who

cruelly abuses Adams for a laugh, and we uncomfortably discover ourselves in company with the laughers at the noble in spirit. In fact, Fielding goes beyond Cervantes, first with Adams and then even with Slipslop, as true nobility rises within the comic bubble without bursting it. When Lady Booby threatens Adams with losing his livelihood if he proceeds to marry Joseph and Fanny, he answers: "I am in the Service of a Master who will never discard me for doing my Duty: And if the Doctor (for indeed I have never been able to pay for a Licence) thinks proper to turn me out of my Cure, G——will provide me, I hope, another." If necessary, he and his numerous family will work with their hands. "Whilst my Conscience is pure, I shall never fear what Man can do unto me" (IV.ii). Adams's comically honest parenthesis deepens the effect as it sustains the amusing characterization, and the scene returns to amusement as Adams awkwardly bows out, mistakenly thinking Lady Booby will understand.

Fielding never again equals this. Neither Quixote, his model, nor Jones to come must stand up for others against tyranny with all they have. And Fielding repeats this feat, in which comedy contains the feeling that would destroy it, when funny old never-to-be-loved Slipslop, the image of the selfish world, turns selfless in Joseph's defense—"I wish I was a great Lady for his sake"—and a chastened Lady Booby mildly bids her goodnight as "a comical Creature" (IV.vi). Evans well illustrates how in *Joseph Andrews* and *Tom Jones* comedy necessarily absorbs the tragic in its broader rendering of the "whole truth" ("World," "Comedy"). *Tom Jones* is the masterwork, of course—bigger, richer, wiser, more Olympian—but because of Adams and his comic depth here achieved, along with the very neatness of the parody, its enduring comic realism, and its joyous energy, *Joseph Andrews* achieves a perfection of its own.

In *Jonathan Wild* (1743), Fielding turns from comic romance for an uneven experiment in sardonic satire. As Digeon suggests, he patched it together for his *Miscellanies* (1743), during a time of sickness and trouble, from previous satirical attempts perhaps beginning as early as 1737, the bitter year when Walpole drove him from the stage. Indeed, a dialogue between Wild and his wife, little suiting them, carries a stage direction: *"These Words to be spoken with a very great Air, and Toss of the Head"* (III.viii).[9] Fielding takes his tone from Lucian, as he had in the dreary *Journey from This World to the Next*, also published in the *Miscellanies.* Although Fielding's Booth calls Lucian "the greatest in the Humorous Way, that ever the World produced" (*Amelia*, VIII,v), and although Fielding claims to have "formed his Stile upon that very Author" (*Covent-Garden Journal*, 52), his Lucianic writings are among his least attractive, uncongenial in a way he could not see.[10]

In *Jonathan Wild,* Fielding tries in a Lucianic-Swiftian way to emulate Gay's *Beggar's Opera* without the Scriblerian verve. Gay had already animated the standing Opposition parallel between Walpole, the "Great Man" of public power, and Wild (executed 24 May 1725), the "Great Man" of London's underworld. As Fielding says in his Preface, "the splendid Palaces of the Great are often no other than *Newgate* with the Mask on."

Defoe's pamphlet on Wild (1725), one of Fielding's sources (Irwin, 19), indicates the difficulty. Defoe "does not indeed make a jest of his story . . . which is indeed a tragedy of itself, in a style of mockery and ridicule, but in a method agreeable to fact." Life down here is tragic, not to be viewed from Fielding's comic heights.[11] The vicious life of Newgate is too real for comedy, too dark for Fielding's satire on human foibles. It rises again in *Amelia,* after Fielding's exposure as magistrate, again to cloud his comic optimism.

Nevertheless, *Jonathan Wild* constantly reflects Fielding's characteristic situations, turns of style and thought, as it exposes his uncertainty. His real hero is Wild's victim, Thomas Heartfree, an older merchant-class Thomas Jones, innocently trusting hypocritical avarice; a Booth, married, with children, jailed for debt by the mighty to seduce his wife. Like Adams, Heartfree believes that "*a sincere* Turk *would be saved*" (IV.i). Like Jones, he extols a good conscience, "a Blessing which he who possesses can never be thoroughly unhappy" (III.v). Not harming others brings him "the Comfort I myself enjoy: For what a ravishing Thought! how replete with Extasy must the Consideration be, that the Goodness of God is engaged to reward me!" (III.x).[12] Fielding has idealized Heartfree from his honest friend, the jeweler and playwright George Lillo (Digeon, 121). But this is the serious middle-class world of Defoe and Richardson, essentially alien to Fielding, in spite of his generous condescension.

Fielding distinguishes "Greatness" from "Goodness" in his preface and opening chapter. The "*true Sublime in Human Nature*" combines greatness with goodness, but the world associates greatness only with the powerful rascal, the "Great Man." Fielding hopes to tell the world that greatness is not goodness (cf. Hatfield, "Puffs," 264-65). But as Dyson remarks (22), no one can believe Wild's great roguery generally typical enough to be of much interest, and Heartfree's goodness is both unconvincing and sentimental.

Of course, Fielding manages some genuine comedy here and there, especially in Mrs. Heartfree's disclaimer of pleasure in repeating compliments to herself (IV.xi). But all in all, *Jonathan Wild* strains at ideas already overworked—Walpole had fallen from power the previous year. Fielding, in ill health and with his wife desperately ill, has tried to clear his desk for his

Miscellanies, make some badly needed money, and end his career as writer:

> And now, my good-natured Reader, recommending my Works to your Candour, I bid you heartily farewell; and take this with you, that you may never be interrupted in the reading these Miscellanies, with that Degree of Heart-ache which hath often discomposed me in the writing them. (Preface, *Miscellanies*)

A year later, in his preface to his sister's *David Simple* (July 1744), Fielding reiterated his farewell. But before long (Wesleyan ed., xxxviii), Lyttelton prompted *Tom Jones,* with financial support. "It was by your Desire that I first thought of such a Composition," writes Fielding in his Dedication. Lyttelton evidently had proposed something new, a novel recommending "Goodness and Innocence" and the "Beauty of Virtue." Fielding adds its rewards: "that solid inward Comfort of Mind," the loss of which "no Acquisitions of Guilt can compensate." He also adds the lesson most likely to succeed, the one taught Tom Heartfree, "that Virtue and Innocence can scarce ever be injured but by Indiscretion." Prudence is the theme, because "it is much easier to make good Men wise, than to make bad Men good."

Again Fielding's hero, handsome, impetuous, generous, is comically romantic self-portraiture, amusing but now admonitory, played opposite an affectionate version of his dead wife. Again, a Cervantic idealist and realist, now reversed as young Jones and old Partridge, travel English roads in picaresque satire. The story is again the essence of romance: the mysterious unknown foundling, with the qualities and white skin of noble knighthood, discovers identity, paternity, riches, and marriage. Fielding called his new book *The History of a Foundling* as late as six months before publication, and others continued to call it *The Foundling* after it appeared (Wesleyan ed., xliii-xlvi). Indeed his title, usually foreshortened, is actually **The History of Tom Jones, a Foundling.** To keep the comic-romantic expectation before us, across the tops of its pages marches not "The History of Tom Jones," but "The History of a Foundling." But Fielding nevertheless seems to find this generally different from *Joseph Andrews,* with its comically positive Christian championship. **Tom Jones,** though philosophically positive, is morally cautionary. Be wary, or your goodness comes to naught. The old Adam should grow wise before he is old. In this cautionary balance and wiser view, Fielding culminated the Augustan perspective.

Martin Price epitomizes (3) the neoclassic period in the concepts of *balance* and *the detached individual.* Irony and satire stake out for the individual the ground on which he dare not dogmatize. Any stand is extreme, smacking of Commonwealth enthusiasm and bloody fanaticism. With orthodoxy shattered, the emerging individuals of either the middle-class Defoes or the shaken aristocrats must regain their footing, the Defoes in engagement, the aristocrats in detachment. *Tom Jones* embodies the detached Augustan's vision. As Pope in his *Essay on Man* (1733-34) surveyed the cosmic maze in gentlemanly ironic detachment, balancing deism and orthodoxy in a synthesis of divine immanence and contemporary psychology, so Fielding works out the ways of Providence in this conflicting world.

Battestin well makes "The Argument of Design."[13] This evidently unjust and accidental world has really a Providential order. The mighty maze has a plan, comically and affectionately fulfilled. Fielding had declared Pope "*the inimitable Author of the* Essay on Man," who "*taught me a System of Philosophy in* English *Numbers*" (Fielding's preface to *Plutus, the God of Riches*, 1742). Fielding's literary creation reflects the providential order beyond our limited vision:

> All Nature is but Art, unknown to thee;
> All Chance, Direction, which thou canst not see;
> All Discord, Harmony, not understood;
> All partial Evil, universal Good. . . .
> (Pope, *Essay,* I:289-92)

Fielding illustrates this *concordia discors,* the Horatian harmony of discords (*Ep.* I.xii.19) that one finds repeatedly echoed in Pope and other Augustans, with a superbly comic "as if," which reflects both the ultimate resolution and its daily dissonance. Chance is really direction: a stupid guide misdirects Jones from the sea toward the army and Upton; Sophia chances upon the same guide to change her direction toward Jones; Blifil's betrayal works out Jones's identity and marriage with Sophia, the name of the "wisdom" he is to obtain (Powers, 667; Battestin, "Wisdom," 204-205; Harrison, 112). Fielding's very sentences reflect the balancing of opposites, the ordered containment of discords, of Pope's couplets as well as of his serenely balancing philosophy (Alter, 61; Battestin, "Design," 297).

All the thorny vines of Nature are really God's Art. And art, in its providential ordering, reflects God's universe. Providence orders the macrocosm; Prudence (semantically linked in Latin) orders the microcosm, man (Battestin, "Design," 191). Fielding the novelist plays God to the world of his creation, illustrating God's ways to man. Fielding sums this in a crucial passage, pausing with ironic detachment in the architectural middle of his comic confusion. He warns the reader not to criticize incidents as "foreign to our main Design" until he or she sees how they fit the whole, for "This Work may, indeed, be considered as a great Creation of our own," of which any fault-finder is a "Reptile" (X.i), a proud and imperceptive Satan in the creator's garden. The analogy, he says in ironic humility, may be too great, "but there is, indeed, no other."

The artist brings order out of chaos and reflects God's providential order. Form symbolizes meaning (Battestin, "Design," 301).

Fielding's remarkable ironic balancing of opposites, first comically coupled for him in Cervantes, illustrates both the universal harmonizing of discords and the Augustan sense that opposites mark the norm without defining it: the principle "of Contrast," says Fielding, "runs through all the Works of Creation" (V.i). Everyone notices the contrasting pairing: Tom and Blifil, Allworthy and Western, each with a comically learned spinster sister; Sophia and Mrs. Fitzpatrick, as well as Sophia contrasted successively with her worse and worse opposites, Molly, Mrs. Waters, Lady Bellaston; Thwackum and Square; even the two brothers Blifil and Nightingale. Everything balances as formal artifice ironically orders daily chaos: six books for the country, six for the road, six for the city, as Digeon first noted (175, n.2). Hilles diagrams the remarkable structural balances on the scheme of a Palladian mansion, of which Ralph Allen's at Bath furnished one of the models for Allworthy's—a wing of six rooms angled up to the central six, a wing of six rooms angled down.[14]

For his architectural reflection of providential order, Fielding has heightened the linear episodic structure of *Joseph Andrews* into the arch of formal comedy. The episodic scene from *Don Quixote in England* now becomes the centerpiece. The high hurly-burly of sex and fisticuffs in the inn at Upton spans Books IX and X at the novel's mathematical center. As in the play, our heroine, running off in pursuit of her lover on the eve of forced marriage, arrives at the inn where he is, both lovers unaware of the other's presence. Fielding again comically contrasts sex and love, as Mrs. Slipslop's purpose with Joseph climaxes with Mrs. Waters and Tom, and bedrooms are scrambled as wildly as those concluding *Joseph Andrews.* As in the play, a foxhunting squire with his hounds rides up in pursuit, now converted from the unwanted suitor into Western, the heroine's father. The actual name *Upton* coincides with Fielding's peak of comic complexity (Wright, 89-90). It even seems the top of a geographical arch, as Sophia pursues Tom northward and then Tom pursues Sophia southward.

Fielding combines his favorite dramatic plot of the worthy rake and the heiress with the basic romantic story of the foundling, both in hopeless courtly love. *Love in Several Masques* has proliferated into a novel, complete with the country lover pursuing his mistress into the wicked city, an element repeated in three other plays (*The Temple Beau,* 1730; *The Lottery,* 1732; *The Universal Gallant,* 1735). In fact, four plays from Fielding's burgeoning year of 1730 awaken in *Tom Jones* nineteen years later. Here again is the wicked brother bearing false witness to defraud the hero of his birthright *(The Temple Beau),* the threat of inadvertent incest through unknown identity (*The Coffee-House Politician, The Wedding Day,* written c. 1730), and especially the comic pattern of discovered identity already borrowed from romance for *The Author's Farce.*

As readers have frequently noticed, Fielding balances two retrospective stories precisely on either side of his central theatrical peak: a lesson for Tom, a lesson for Sophia. The first is another *descensus Averno,* as if Fielding had lifted Wilson's account of wasted youth from the middle of *Joseph Andrews,* put it before his Cervantic inn, and also put it on Mazard Hill to suggest the greater peak to come. In *Joseph Andrews,* our travelers descend "a very steep Hill"; now Jones and Partridge, their quixotic counterparts, ascend "a very steep Hill" because Jones wants to cultivate his romantic "melancholy Ideas" by the "Solemn Gloom which the Moon casts on all Objects" (VIII.x). Partridge fears ghosts. They see a light and come to a cottage. Jones knocks without initial response, and Partridge cries that "the People must be all dead." Like Wilson, the Man of the Hill has retired from the world of debauchery and betrayal, which he describes for Jones and the reader. But Wilson, with wife and children, lives like people "in the Golden Age," as Adams remarks (III.iv); the Man of the Hill is an embittered recluse. Young Jones rejects his misanthropy and urges Fielding's lesson of prudence—the old man would have continued his faith in humanity had he not been "incautious in the placing your Affection" (VIII.xv). In his *descensus,* Jones has learned the truth. On the other side of Upton, Sophia hears from her cousin Mrs. Fitzpatrick a tale of elopement and amours that illustrates what she should not do with Jones.

Upton emphasizes the balanced theatrical architecture of *Tom Jones.* And many have noticed the theatricality of the city section (Cross, II:202; Haage, 152). Two scenes—with Lady Bellaston behind the bed, then Honour, then both—are pure theater (XIV.ii, XV.vii). Moreover, Lady Bellaston descends directly from Fielding's versions of Congreve's Lady Wishfort, beginning with Lady Trap in his first play. Tom Jones courts her to get at her ward, just as Mrs. Fitzpatrick urges him to court Mrs. Western (XVI.ix), the very ruse of her own ruin (XI.iv), as Fielding thrice deploys Tom Merital's strategem, acquired from Congreve. But Fielding shapes the whole novel in the abstract pattern of five-act comedy: Act I, exposition; Act II, intrigue; Act III, climactic complications; Act IV, unraveling toward disaster; Act V, depression shooting upward into triumph—the playlike ending already traced in Joseph's reprieve from Platonic celibacy and Heartfree's from the gallows.

If we treat the central six books as Act III, dividing the first and the last six books in halves, we find startling references to the theater at each break, except the in-

vocation to Fame that begins the London section, or "Act IV." At "Act V," where the stage expects the final darkness before dawn, Fielding talks, first about the playwright's problem of prologues (XVI.i) and then, in the next Book, most facetiously about the playwright's problem of concluding a comedy or tragedy, and about his own in extricating "this Rogue, whom we have unfortunately made our Heroe," whom he may have to leave to the hangman, though he will do what he can, since "the worst of his Fortune" still lies ahead (XVII.i). "Tragedy is the image of Fate, as comedy is of Fortune," says Susanne Langer (p.333). Indeed, the formal structure of comedy, superimposed on the novel's more realistic vagaries, comments more quizzically on Fortune than a simple affirmation. It sustains with an ironic detachment Fielding's demonstration that the partial evils, the accidents that happen (in his frequent phrase), interweave fortunately in "universal Good." As "we may frequently observe in Life," says Fielding, "the greatest Events are produced by a nice Train of little Circumstances" (XVIII.ii). The author, like the Craftsman of Creation, is shaping our near-sighted joys and blunders, the realities of life.

Life does have odd coincidences. Apparent evils do often prove blessings as life flows on. For Fielding, as Stevick shows, history has meaning, just as his comic "true History" reflects a meaningful actuality. There are people, who, like Jones, have in fact accidentally taken the right road. Possessions, like Sophia's little book with a £100 bill in its leaves, have in fact been lost and luckily recovered—perhaps have even changed a course of life, as when Jones turns from the army to find Sophia. Acquaintances do turn up in restaurants and airports, like Partridge, Mrs. Waters, or Dowling, who seems to dowl his way through apparently random events to conclude the mystery. Accident, bad and good, which Ehrenpreis finds a weakness (22ff.), is actually the very stuff in life from which comedy creates its mimesis.

Fielding's third-person detachment, on which comedy also depends, may seem to deny the inner life that Defoe and Richardson opened for the novel with first-person narration (Watt, *Rise*). But actually, we are perceiving psychic complexities exactly as we do in life—from the outside, from what people do and say. Dowling, apparently only a comically busy lawyer, proves a complex rascal in blackmailing Blifil and keeping Tom from his birthright, yet he is affable and even sympathetic. Bridget, the sour old maid, actually attracts all eligible males. Her secret passions, simmering toward forty, not only beget the illegitimate Tom but thwart her plans for him (Crane, 119) as, again pregnant, she rushes to marry Blifil, whom she has evidently trapped—with his calculated concurrence. She takes a sly pleasure in having Thwackum whip her love-child, when Allworthy is away, for the psychic strain he has caused her, but never her legitimate son, whom she hates, as Fielding tells us directly. She later attracts not only Thwackum but Square, with whom (now that she is past the threat of pregnancy) she has an affair—from which Fielding turns our eyes even as he ironically confirms it, attributing it to malicious gossip with which he will not blot his page (III.vi). Before Tom is eighteen, he has openly replaced Square in her affections, with a hint of the incest that plays comically through Tom's affairs (Hutchens, 40), incurring Square's hatred and his own expulsion from Paradise.[15] Fielding's psychological realism abounds in little self-deceptions: Sophia's about Jones is neatly symbolized in her muff, which appears when love blooms, turns up in Jones's empty bed at Upton, and accompanies him to London, an amusingly impudent visual pun in public slang (Johnson, 129-38). Jones has put his hands into it, as Honour reports: "La, says I, Mr. *Jones,* you will stretch my Lady's Muff and spoil it" (IV.xiv).

But Fielding's implied psychology fails with Allworthy. From the first, readers have found him bland if not unreal: the ideal benevolist and ultimate judge, taken in by duplicity, throwing out the good. Fielding seems to have intended a more dignified comic Adams. Allworthy talks "a little whimsically" about his dead wife, for which his neighbors roundly arraign him (I.ii). And we first meet him indeed in a bedroom, absentmindedly in his nightshirt, contemplating "the Beauty of Innocence"—the foundling sleeping in his bed—while Fielding wonderfully suggests that Mrs. Wilkins, "who, tho' in the 52d Year of her Age, vowed she had never beheld a Man without his Coat," believes she was summoned for another purpose (I.iii). Had Fielding sustained this comic view of the imperceptive idealist—he must make him imperceptive at any rate—his book would have fulfilled the perfection it very nearly achieves. But except for some touches about Thwackum's piety and Square's "Philosophical Temper" on his misperceived deathbed (V.viii), Allworthy fades from comic view.

As Hutchens says, Fielding takes an ironic and "lawyerlike delight in making facts add up to something unexpected" (30), and he does the same with the facts that convey personality. Mrs. Western, the comic six-foot chaperone, proud of her little learning and political misinformation, is also the superannuated coquette. Fitzpatrick has fooled her; she treasures in her memory a highwayman who took her money and earrings "at the same Time d———ning her, and saying, 'such handsome B———s as you, don't want Jewels to set them off, and be d———nd to you'" (VII.ix). To avoid forced marriage with Lord Fellamar, Sophia slyly flatters her with the many proposals she claims to have refused. "You are now but a young Woman," Sophia says, one who would surely not yield to the first title offered. Yes, says Mrs. Western, "I was called the cruel *Parthenissa,*" and she runs on about "her Conquests and her

Cruelty" for "near half an Hour" (XVII.iv). And Western, with his vigor, his Jacobite convictions, his Somerset dialect, his views as narrow as the space between his horse's ears, who has cruelly driven his wife to the grave, yet stirs our compassion as Fielding reveals the feeling that threatens and heightens the comic surface in a Falstaff or Quixote, as he had done with Adams and Slipslop. Western's comic limitations reveal their pathos in London, where—lonely, beaten by Egglane, bewildered—he pleads with Sophia:

> 'Why wout ask, *Sophy?*' cries he, 'when dost know I had rather hear thy Voice, than the Music of the best Pack of Dogs in *England.*—Hear thee, my dear little Girl! I hope I shall hear thee as long as I live; for if I was ever to lose that Pleasure, I would not gee a Brass Varden to live a Moment longer. Indeed, *Sophy,* you do not know how I love you, indeed you don't, or you never could have run away, and left your poor Father, who hath no other Joy, no other Comfort upon Earth but his little *Sophy.*' At these Words the Tears stood in his Eyes; and *Sophia,* (with the Tears streaming from hers) answered, 'Indeed, my dear Papa, I know you have loved me tenderly'. . . . (XVI.ii)

And the scene soon returns to full comedy as Western leaves in his usual thunder of misunderstanding.

This is the comic irony of character, the comedy of limited view, of the *idée fixe,* which plays against our wider perception and the narrator's omniscience, and in turn makes us part of the human comedy as we think we see all but learn that we do not.[16] Fielding's omniscience guides and misguides us constantly; in his lawyerlike way, he presents the evidence and conceals the mystery, tempting our misunderstandings along with those of his characters, whom we believe less percipient than ourselves, or pretending ironically not to understand motives to guide our understanding: "Whether moved by Compassion, or by Shame, or by whatever other Motive, I cannot tell," he will write of a landlady who has changed her hostile tune when Jones appears like an Adonis and a gentleman (VIII.iv). This is Cervantes's mock-historian elevated to mock-psychological ignorance in the ironic service of psychology. This is Fielding's Cervantic omniscience, which delights us by showing in comic fiction life as it is, comic in selfish imperception, comic in providential blessing.

Fielding's commenting authorship has reached its full ironic power and elegance, and much more pervasively than in *Joseph Andrews.* The earlier twentieth century scorned this kind of "intrusive author." But McKillop (123) and, especially, Booth have well certified the central impact and necessity of Fielding's authorial presence. He has become his own most worthy character, amiable, wise, benevolent, literate, balanced between extremes, engaging us constantly through a long and pleasant journey until "we find, lying beneath our amusement at his playful mode of farewell, something of the same feeling we have when we lose a close friend, a friend who has given us a gift which we can never repay" (Booth, 218). He has shown us the world of Sophias and Toms, Blifils and pettifoggers, but he has also shown us that it contains a wonderfully ironic and compassionate intelligence we have come to know, which is something very like the wisdom of a benevolent God surveying our selfish vices and romantic yearnings.

Booth, of course, insists on the "implied author," a fictive creation clear of biographical irrelevancies. When the author refers to himself as infirm, Booth says that it "matters not in the least" whether Fielding was infirm when he wrote that sentence: "It is not Fielding we care about, but the narrator created to speak in his name" (218). But I dare say readers do care about Fielding as Fielding—Keats as Keats, Whitman as Whitman, Joyce as Joyce—else why our innumerable researches? Booth also oddly implies that Fielding's introductory chapters, which we can read straight through "leaving out the story of Tom," comprise all the narrator's "seemingly gratuitous appearances" (216). But Fielding actually "intrudes" on every page as the authorial voice ironically displaying life's ironies or commenting earnestly, with or without the "I."[17]

Fielding clearly considers that he himself addresses his readers, however much he may pretend, in the Cervantic way, that his history is true, that Allworthy may still live in Somerset for all he knows, or that he has given us "the Fruits of a very painful Enquiry, which for thy Satisfaction we have made into this Matter" (IX.vii). He is playful or straight, facetiously elevated or skeptically glum, exactly as he would be in conversation or anecdote, writing as if he were actually present—as indeed he was when he read his book aloud to Lyttelton and others before publication. He hopes that some girl in ages hence will, "under the fictitious name of *Sophia*," read "the real Worth which once existed in my *Charlotte*," and that he will be read "when the little Parlour in which I sit this Instant, shall be reduced to a worse furnished Box," and all this in a wonderfully mock-heroic invocation conveying his actual aims and beliefs as a writer (XIII.i). As Miller says ("Style," 265), "he is Henry Fielding all right." As with Pope—who characteristically begins by addressing a friend, who refers to his garden, his grotto, his ills, his aims, and concludes again in autobiography—the "implied author" seems unnecessary, or irrelevant. Fielding is projecting himself, playing the kind of role we all must play in whatever we do, as teacher, citizen, neighbor, fellow trying to write a scholarly essay, or whatnot. He dramatizes himself, of course, but in a way quite different from those partial versions of himself

he comically (or guiltily) dramatized in Harry Luckless, Andrews, Jones, and Billy Booth.

As Miller well says, Fielding in his comic romance gives us a seamless weave of the real and ideal with life inhering "down to the smallest particle" ("Rhetoric," 235). Many have admired these verbal particles that reflect the universe. Take his "solid comfort." Here is the common reality of life, verbally and emotionally. *Shamela's* Oliver upholds "all the solid Comforts of their Lives." In his preface to the *Miscellanies,* Fielding says that his wife, dangerously ill, gives him "all the solid Comfort of my Life." In *Tom Jones,* he writes to Lyttelton of the "solid inward Comfort of Mind" that will reward benevolence and that Tom will aver as "solid Content" (XII.x). Yet Fielding acknowledges the universal ambiguity even in sincere belief, playing ironically with his favorite term in an extended passage revealing the motives of Bridget and Captain Blifil, who—bearded to the eyes, built like a plowman—bristles virility: Bridget expects a solid phallic comfort; Blifil, the comfort of hard cash.

> She imagined, and perhaps very wisely, that she should enjoy more agreeable Minutes with the Captain, than with a much prettier Fellow; and forewent the Consideration of pleasing her Eyes, in order to procure herself much more solid Satisfaction. . . .
>
> The Captain likewise very wisely preferred the more solid Enjoyments he expected with his Lady, to the fleeting Charms of Person. (I.xi)

That "Minutes" speaks sexual volumes. [18]

With *Amelia* (1751), the realities darken beyond comic affirmation. [19] The Augustan certainties, earned in irony, have faded into the doubts and sentimentalities of the century's second half. Free will now enters the providential scheme (Knight, 389), infinitely more chancey than the happy accidents of comedy. Individual responsibility replaces comic Fortune, now only an "imaginary Being." Each must shape his own luck in an "Art of Life" that resembles the cagey and protective maneuvering of chess. What we blame on Fortune we should blame on "quitting the Directions of Prudence," now active as well as cautionary, for "the blind Guidance of a predominant Passion" (I.i). The world of *Tom Jones,* which had darkened from country to city, reversing the progress of *Joseph Andrews,* now opens in the Newgate of *Jonathan Wild,* with a diseased and vicious Mrs. Slipslop, no longer funny, as Blear-eyed Moll. The subject is the "various Accidents which befel a very worthy Couple," as the husband redeems "foolish Conduct" by "struggling manfully with Distress," which is "one of the noblest Efforts of Wisdom and Virtue"—a struggle and virtue the hero hardly exhibits. In his Dedication, Fielding says that he also wants to expose "the most glaring Evils," public and private, that "infest this Country," and here, at least, he succeeds.

Fielding has attempted another new species of writing. For the first time, he adopts an epic, the *Aeneid,* for his "noble model" as he tells us in the *Covent-Garden Journal* (Jensen, ed., I.186). His serious subject can now sustain the epic parallel his comic romance had prohibited as burlesque mock-heroics. In his Court of Censorial Inquiry, "a grave Man" stands up to defend "poor Amelia" from "the Rancour with which she hath been treated by the Public." He avows "that of all my Offspring she is my favourite Child," on whom he has "bestowed a more than ordinary Pains" (186). Fielding's strange favoritism doubtless owes to his loving fictionalization of his dead wife, complete with scarred nose, whom he elevates to his title and make the virtuous lodestone (Wendt, "Virtue"):

> H. Fielding [writes Lady Mary Wortley Montagu] has given a true picture of himself and his first wife, in the characters of Mr. and Mrs. Booth, some compliments to his own figure excepted; and, I am persuaded, several of the incidents he mentions are real matters of fact. (Cross, II.328)

Fielding is clearly working out some remorse, perhaps for the same infidelities both religious and sexual through which Booth suffers.

Powers demonstrates how closely Fielding parallels the *Aeneid.* Like Virgil, Fielding begins *in medias res* with the long, retrospective first-person accounts of the central action that are typical of epic and new in Fielding. [20] Powers matches characters and actions throughout the book, beginning with Miss Matthews (Dido), who seduces Booth (like Aeneas, separated from his wife with a new order to establish), though Powers omits remarking how starkly the chamber in Newgate reflects Virgil's sylvan cave. Fielding's masquerade at Ranelagh matches Aeneas's *descensus,* though moved from *Aeneid* VI to *Amelia* X, where Aeneas meets the resentful shade of Dido and Booth the resentful Miss Matthews. The masquerader's conventional "Do you know me?" in "squeaking Voice" (*Tom Jones,* XIII.vii; *The Masquerade,* 190) now becomes Miss Matthews's caustic "Do'st thou not yet know me?" (X.ii). In the end, Fielding replaces the pious Aeneas's defeat of violent Turnus with Booth's escaping a duel and affirming a new order in his Christian conversion.

As Cross notes, however (II.325), Fielding also characteristically reworks his plot from three of his plays. From *The Temple Beau* (1730), he had already taken the evil brother defrauding the good of his inheritance, with an accomplice, as models for Blifil and Dowling. He feminizes this for *Amelia.* In the play, a father dies and disinherits his heir, abroad in Paris. His brother, through a false witness, had blackened the heir's character "and covered his own notorious vices under the appearance of innocence" (*Works,* VIII.115). Amelia's older sister likewise vilifies her while abroad. She learns in Paris of her mother's death and her disinheritance. But now sister Betty and her accomplices forge a new will reversing the mother's decree to leave her and not Amelia penniless, as Fielding adds a touch from actuality. Four years after the play, Fielding eloped to marry against a mother's wishes, as does Booth. Similarly, his wife's mother died soon after, but nevertheless left her estate to his wife, cutting off her elder sister with a shilling (Cross, II.330).

In *The Coffee-House Politician* (1730), Fielding also foresketches his and Booth's elopement, and introduces the good magistrate who untangles things in *Jonathan Wild* and becomes another self-portrait in *Amelia* (Cross, II.322): the unnamed justice who, about to dine, hears the evidence and resolves, "Tho' it was then very late, and he had been fatigued all the Morning with public Business, to postpone all Refreshment 'till he had discharged his Duty" (XII.vi). Fielding concludes his play with his justice: "Come, gentlemen, I desire you would celebrate this day at my house." Similarly, the justice in *Amelia:*

> Whether *Amelia's* Beauty, or the Reflexion on the remarkable Act of Justice he had performed, or whatever Motive filled the Magistrate with extraordinary good Humour, and opened his Heart and Cellars, I will not determine; but he gave them . . . hearty Welcome . . . nor did the Company rise from Table till the Clock struck eleven. (XII.vii)

The Coffee-House Politician indeed frames *Amelia's* plot, with the instrumental justice at the end, and at the beginning a half-pay army captain, on his way through London streets at night to a rendezvous for elopement who aids a person attacked and is jailed as attacker by a venal judge through false witness—exactly as Booth lands in Newgate at the outset.

The Modern Husband (1732) furnishes Fielding's central matter, already worked in *Jonathan Wild:* two influential men, one a lord, ruin and jail a husband in order to seduce his virtuous wife. The husband has an affair and suffers a painful conscience. His extravagance becomes Booth's addictive gambling. His wife's fear of a duel, which keeps the lord's advances secret, becomes the actual challenge Amelia keeps secret. In play and novel, the wife's constancy inspires contrition, confession, and reform. The play's contrasting "modern" couple, who collude in adultery for extortion, become the Trents of *Amelia.* [21]

Except at beginning and end, Fielding's sustained epic parallel has no force, as it would have in the comic contrasts of a mock-epic or a *Ulysses.* It passes unnoticed into Fielding's romance motifs, now similarly forsaken by comedy and indeed more prevalent. Booth has himself smuggled into his lady's hostile household in a basket straight from the flowery thirteenth-century romance of *Floris and Blancheflour.* [22] As Maurice Johnson commented to me in a letter (26 April 1965), this smuggled entry midway in Book II matches precisely the Grecian warriors' entry into the enemy's citadel inside the Trojan horse, midway in *Aeneid* II. But implausible romance obliterates the epic.

Indeed, in spite of the book's seamy realism (Sherburn, *"Amelia,"* 2; Butt, 27), Fielding's first instance of comic self-portraiture, **The Author's Farce,** now lends surprising and uneasy touches of romance to this more extended autobiographical fiction, no longer comic. Lady Mary, noting the autobiography, complained of *Amelia,* along with **Tom Jones:** "All these sort of books . . . place a merit in extravagant passions, and encourage young people to hope for impossible events . . . as much out of nature as fairy treasures" (*Letters,* III.93, quoted in Blanchard, 102). The burlesque of wonderful endings, which Fielding initiated in his **Farce** and continued playfully in **Joseph Andrews** and **Tom Jones,** now indeed becomes the fairytale strained by realism. In the play, Harry Luckless has pawned a jewel. His servant's return to the pawnshop enables a bystander to find him and disclose his identity and his kingdom far from London's unjust indifference.

In *Amelia,* this hero's jewel has multiplied. Fielding modifies an episode from Ariosto's *Orlando Furioso*—the story of Giocondo (Canto 28), the same that gives Spenser his Squire of Dames—in which the hero, departing reluctantly from his wife, forgets a little jeweled cross, a farewell gift. Booth, on his departure for war, forgets a little casket, similarly given, which should have contained a jeweled picture of Amelia, lost a month before. Her foster brother and silent courtly adorer—in the submerged incestuous way of romance, which is no longer comic as with Joseph and Fanny—has stolen it. Nothing so clearly illustrates Fielding's fall from comedy as the contrast between this scene and that with Lady Booby in bed and Joseph Andrews beside it. Now, the new noble servant Joseph Atkinson is abed, visited by Mrs. Booth. Fielding's instinctive self-revision—the Josephs, the As, the Bs—here turns romance lugubrious. Atkinson, tears gushing, returns the picture to his lady, who has come to her poor lovesick knight, with words widely adapted—in fiction and actuality both, one suspects—from that famous and monstrous romance so prominent on Fielding's early blacklist, La Calprenède's *Cassandra:* "that Face which, if I had been the Emperor of the World . . ." (XI.vi.) [23] Later, Amelia pawns the picture; a second visit to the pawnshop discloses that a bystander has identified her by it, and his information leads to her long-lost inheritance and an estate far from London's unjust indifference.

Harry Luckless's ancient dream of the disinherited and the happy accidents of comedy dissolve into pathos and implausibility in the tragic world of *Amelia.* As Rawson says (70), Amelia's despairs carry the novel's conviction: "There are more bad People in the World, and they will hate you for your Goodness," wails Amelia to her "poor little Infants"; "There is an End of all Goodness in the World"; "We have no Comfort, no Hope, no Friend left" (IV.iii, VII.x, VIII.ix). This is the modern existential woe of Clarissa:

> What a world is this! What is there in it desirable? The good we hope for, so strangely mix'd, that one knows not what to wish for: And one half of Mankind tormenting the other, and being tormented themselves in Tormenting! (Richardson's *Clarissa* II, Letter vii)

Augustan detachment becomes sentimental involvement. The ironic providential overseer has departed, leaving a less frequent sociologist:

> . . . I myself (remember, Critic, it was in my Youth) had a few Mornings before seen that very identical Picture of all those ingaging Qualities in Bed with a Rake at a Bagnio, smoaking Tobacco, drinking Punch, talking Obscenity, and swearing and cursing with all the Impudence and Impiety of the lowest and most abandoned Trull of a Soldier. (I.vi)

The reader, as Coley notes (249-50), has likewise diminished from the "ingenious" to the "good-natured" who enjoys a "tender Sensation." Goodness must demonstrate its sensitivity in faintings and tears (Ribble). Parson Harrison, a realistic Adams, replaces the author as evaluative intelligence, and yet in his uncomic blindness, which drives Amelia to despair, he becomes one of Fielding's most plausible characters in this new indeterminacy of characterization (Coolidge). The quixotic Adams, upholding virtue, now also becomes Colonel Bath, the swordsman upholding only the passé code of honor—pistols were to be the weapons of James's duel. [24] The type no longer represents the comic universals in humanity. The limited view is no longer comically typical but painfully characteristic of human imperfection.

Indeterminacy replaces comic truth in typicality. The psychological complexities authorially implied in a Bridget now become the unreliable testimony of a Mrs. Bennet. Booth agonizes and develops, as against the characteristic comic changelessness of Andrews and Jones (Coley, 251). This is a new age; subjective consciousness breaks through Augustan order and objectivity. Human nature is no longer everywhere the same. Hume's solipsistic feeling has overturned reason, and Hume is clearly Fielding's unmentioned antagonist as he attempts to adjust the new philosophy to the providential Christianity it so profoundly unsettled (Battestin, "Problem").

Booth's Epicurean fatalism wavers toward atheism. Chance is no longer providential direction nor a "blind Impulse or Direction of Fate." Man acts as his uppermost passion dictates and can "do no otherwise" (I.iii; cf. Thomas). Booth is a prisoner, psychically and physically, throughout the book—limited at best to the Verge of Court (Lepage; Wendt, "Virtue," 146; Battestin, "Problem," 631). In the end, Barrow's sermons free Booth from his passional fatalism, as Harrison frees him from custody for his providential reward. But Fielding's demonstration contradicts his theory that the will can shape the passions and one's fate. Hume's emotive philosophy has persuaded him more than he recognizes. Dr. Harrison bases his strongest argument for religion on Hume's passional doctrine, which Fielding had set out to refute (Battestin, "Problem," 632-33). Harrison asserts that men act from their passions, and that "the strongest of these Passions; Hope and Fear," support the truth of religion (XII.v). Booth converts, and Providence fulfills the dream of escape to Eden with the affluent lady, in the line of Luckless's Harriot, Wilson's Harriet Hearty, Heartfree's Mrs. Heartfree, and Jones's Sophia.

From the first play to last novel, Fielding repeats himself perhaps more than any major writer, working and reworking literary conventions as living paradigms. Even amid the sentimentalities in **Amelia,** his fictive truth persuades us that life is like this: selfish, conceited, agonized, wishful, looking for philosophical certainty. The primordial foundling of romance lives in our dreaming self-pity. The noble Quixote lives in our ideals. When Fielding insulated aspiration in comedy, ironically acknowledging both its truth and probable unfulfillment, he achieved the incomparable **Joseph Andrews** and **Tom Jones.**

Abbreviations

ECS   *Eighteenth-Century Studies*

ELH   *English Literary History*

MLR   *Modern Language Review*

PMLA *Publications of the Modern Language Association*

PQ   *Philological Quarterly*

RES   *Review of English Studies*

TSLL *Texas Studies in Literature and Language*

Notes

[1] Genealogists deny his family's connection to the royal Hapsburgs (Cross, 1.2-3), but Fielding and his contemporaries assumed it. "Most members of the family . . . have uniformly added the quartering of Hapsburg and displayed their arms upon the double headed eagle of the Holy Roman Empire" (Henley, ed., XVI.xlvi). Fielding used the double eagle as his seal on at least one letter. Oddly, Hogarth's portrait of Fielding shows an unmistakable Hapsburg lower lip. Battestin has recently identified another probable portrait ("Pictures").

[2] I borrow extensively throughout from my essays listed in "Works Cited." Historical details and many other points originate in Cross. Texts are Henley for plays; Wesleyan for *Joseph Andrews* and *Tom Jones;* first editions for *Shamela, Jonathan Wild,* and *Amelia.*

[3] See Evans on the *Whole Duty of Man,* a book central to Fielding's charitable Christianity since childhood. Shamela, like Pamela, approves it but with the major duty of charity missing, and Whitefield condemned it as useless for the Grace of being born again.

[4] Paulson, *Satire,* 103-04; Brooks, 161; my "Irony," 142-43; Goldberg, 146-47, 232-33.

[5] Golden sees in Fielding's older women assaulting the heroes "the same stuff as the witches of child lore"; the aggressive males are ogres, "grotesques of adults in the child's fantasy" (145). But this wholly ignores the comic, adult perspective.

[6] Originating in the *Odyssey* and taken over by Lucian and the romances as well—Ariosto sends Rinaldo to the moon; Cervantes sends Quixote down the cave of Montesinos and both Sancho and his ass down another cavern—the *descensus* became an Augustan favorite: Swift's Glubbdubdrib, Pope's Cave of Spleen *(Rape)* and Elysian shade *(Dunciad),* Fielding's *Author's Farce* and *Journey from This World to the Next.* For the long prevalence of the *descensus,* see Boyce.

[7] Lucian also wrote a satiric *Vera historia,* a "true history," and, like Fielding, claimed a new way of writing (Coley, 241). But Fielding's phrase and manner comes directly from Cervantes, underlined by Scarron's more frequent reiteration; see my "Comic Romances."

[8] The twentieth century takes "comic epic in prose" as Fielding's generic category, ignoring his defining term, "comic romance," as it also overlooks his romantic plot and Cervantic perspective. Neither he nor his contemporaries thought of his novels as epics, or even as "comic epics" like the *Dunciad,* from which he borrows his remarks on Homer's mock-heroic *Margites,* now "entirely lost." Pope's "Martinus Scriblerus of the Poem" in turn borrows, tongue in cheek, from Aristotle (*Poetics,* IV.12). But Aristotle does not mention loss. Pope says "tho' now unhappily lost." Fielding's similar reference in his preface to *David Simple* has "tho' it be unhappily lost," indicating Pope as his

source. As Goldberg (7) and Miller (*Romance*, 8, 16) indicate, *epic* for Fielding means simply "extended narrative." This, for the eighteenth century, was indeed the primary meaning. Johnson's primary definition of *epic* in his *Dictionary* (1755) is: "Narrative; comprising narrations, not acted, but rehearsed." In fact, Fielding has taken "comic epic in prose" from Cervantes's defense of romances (I.iv.20): "Epicks may be well writ in Prose as Verse." Cervantes's discussion clearly indicates that he takes *epic* to mean "any significant narrative," whether history, classical epic, or romance. Fielding also borrows his reference to the *Telemachus* from the Ozell-Motteux translator's footnote to this passage: "The *Adventures of Telemachus* is a Proof of this." J. Paul Hunter errs particularly in a fanciful derivation of *Tom Jones* from the *Télémaque*. See my two articles on this head, esp. "Fielding's Comic."

[9] In 1754, Fielding revised this to *"These Words were spoken . . . ,"* along with changing "Prime Minister" (Walpole) to the innocuous "Statesman" (Digeon, 120). Miller sees this passage as imitating Lucian's dialogues (*Essays,* 367n).

[10] Saintsbury claims that "Fielding has written no greater book . . . compact of almost pure irony" (vii-viii). Digeon finds it "profound and rich in various lessons" (127); Shea, "a highly complex satire" (73). Wendt argues that Fielding deliberately made Heartfree "imperfect" ("Allegory," 317); Hopkins (passim), that the sentimentality is really comic irony; Rawson rightly disagrees with both (234ff., 253-54), and extends his perceptive analysis through the latter half of his book (101-259). Miller observes that Fielding's confident and skeptical perspectives simply reflect different moods, with the usual human inconsistency (*Essays,* 75).

[11] Hopkins (225-27) points out that Fielding satirizes Defoe's *The King of Pirates* in Mrs. Heartfree's travels and (less convincingly) Defoe's matrimonial dialogue in his *Family Instructor.*

[12] Fielding changed this to read (1754) "that Almighty Goodness is by its own Nature engaged. . . . " Hopkins takes this passage as rendered intentionally ridiculous by *ravishing,* already punned upon sexually in Wild's addresses to Laetitia, and in *ecstasy.* But this is exactly the serious language of Parson Oliver and Tom Jones; see the foregoing discussion of *Shamela.*

[13] Battestin, "Design," 290; see also Work and Williams. Preston, Knight, Poovy, Vopat, Braudy, and Guthrie resist the providential reading in various ways. Snow finds Battestin's providential equation "intriguing but ultimately a misreading of the teasing, obfuscating narrator and his story" (50). But she herself misreads Fielding's reference to secrets that "I will not be guilty of discovering" till the muse of History "shall give me leave" (II.vi). Snow believes that Battestin

posits "Fielding's belief in a benevolent deity who, in effect, works like a detective in a murder mystery, perceiving the pattern of cause and effect, discovering the innocent and guilty, and distributing the rewards and punishments" (40). She takes *discover* to mean "find out" (39-40). But this is not Fielding's (or Battestin's) conception of an omniscient deity who eventually *reveals* ("discovers" in the eighteenth-century sense) the benevolent design behind apparently haphazard events.

[14] Hilles elaborates Van Ghent's architectural suggestion ("Art," 81). Battestin quotes Palladio himself (pref., bk. IV) on how "these little Temples we raise, ought to bear a resemblance to the immense one of (God's) infinite goodness," in which all "parts . . . should have the exactest symmetry and proportion" ("Design," 300).

[15] Knight well notices the imperfections in this country Paradise Hall, which Tom's restoration redeems. E. Taiwo Palmer and Combs work out the implication of Fielding's Miltonic expulsion, though this, like Fielding's naming of Allworthy's estate, seems a happy afterthought to authenticate his grand providential design.

[16] Stephanson well describes this process in *Joseph Andrews.* See also McKenzie and McNamara.

[17] See my "Narration"; Stevick: "Every word is 'told,' nothing is impersonally rendered" ("Talking," 119).

[18] Alter also analyzes this passage (42). See also my "Cliché," 358. Hutchens demonstrates the similar ironic shadings in *prudence,* Fielding's central word and concept (101-18). Also see Hatfield *(Irony).*

[19] From the first, readers have found *Amelia* a "failure" (Cross, II:328ff.; Sherburn, *"Amelia,"* 1). See Wolff, Eustace Palmer, Hassall, Osland, Donovan, among others cited passim.

[20] Cross, II:326; Digeon, 195-96; Sherburn, *"Amelia,"* 4.

[21] Fielding had introduced to the stage a situation aired in two contemporary lawsuits (Cross, I:121; Woods, "Notes," 364).

[22] Only this romance, and Boccaccio's version, *Filocopo,* where Fielding probably read it, have the lover carried past hostile guardians in a basket. Dudden calls it a device from the comic stage (811), probably thinking of Falstaff's basket: a means of escape, not of entrance. The chest in *Decameron* II.ix and in *Cymbeline,* and the jars in *Ali Baba,* all serve hostile intentions.

[23] Miss Matthews responds to Booth's *"Scene of the*

tender Kind" (III.ii), describing his emotional departing from Amelia, with a sigh (nicely leading to his seduction): "There are Moments in Life worth purchasing with Worlds." In *Cassandra,* Statira, widow of Alexander, "emperor of the world," says that she prefers death to "the Empire of the whole World with any other Man" (V.106; also IV.109, IV.204). Lady Orrery classed "the works of the inimitable Fielding" with "*Cassandra, Cleopatra,* Haywood's novels" and "a thousand more romantick books of the same kind" (quoted in Foster, 102). Watt points out that "Amelia" and "Sophia" were the most popular romance names ("Naming," 327).

[24] Atkinson's nocturnal "wineskin" battle with his wife, a poor attempt at the bedroom fisticuffs in *Joseph Andrews,* is another remnant from Cervantes, which he had derived from Apuleius (Becker, 146-47; Putnam, I:483n).

Works Cited

Alter, Robert. *Fielding and the Nature of the Novel.* Cambridge, Mass.: Harvard Univ. Press, 1968.

Baker, Sheridan. "Bridget Allworthy: The Creative Pressures of Fielding's Plot." *Papers of the Michigan Academy of Science, Arts, and Letters* 52 (1967), 345-56.

———. "Fielding and the Irony of Form." *Eighteenth-Century Studies* 2 (1968), 138-54.

———. "Fielding's *Amelia* and the Materials of Romance." *PQ* 41 (1962), 437-49.

———. "Fielding's Comic Epic-in-Prose Romances Again." *PQ* 58 (1979), 63-81.

———. "Henry Fielding and the Cliché." *Criticism* 1 (1959), 354-61.

———. "Henry Fielding's Comic Romances." *Papers of the Michigan Academy of Science, Arts, and Letters* 45 (1960), 411-19.

———. "The Idea of Romance in the Eighteenth-Century Novel." *Papers of the Michigan Academy of Science, Arts, and Letters* 49 (1964), 507-22.

———. Introduction to *An Apology for the Life of Mrs. Shamela Andrews.* Berkeley: Univ. of California Press, 1953.

———. Introduction to *Joseph Andrews and Shamela.* New York: Crowell, 1972.

———. "Narration: the Writer's Essential Mimesis." *Journal of Narrative Technique* 11 (1981), 155-65.

Battestin, Martin C. "Fielding's Definition of Wisdom: Some Functions of Ambiguity and Emblem in *Tom Jones.*" *ELH* 35 (1968), 188-217.

———. "Lord Hervey's Role in *Joseph Andrews.*" *PQ* 42 (1963), 226-41.

———. *The Moral Basis of Fielding's Art: A Study of Joseph Andrews.* Middletown: Wesleyan University Press, 1959.

———. "Pictures of Fielding." *Eighteenth-Century Studies* 17 (1983), 1-13.

———. "The Problem of Amelia: Hume, Barrow, and the Conversion of Captain Booth." *ELH* 41 (1974), 613-48.

———. "'Tom Jones': The Argument of Design." In Miller, Rothstein, and Rosseau, 289-319. Reprinted as "Fielding: The Argument of Design," ch. 5, in Battestin's *The Providence of Wit: Aspects of Form in Augustan Literature and the Arts.* Oxford: Clarendon Press, 1974.

Becker, Gustav. "Die Aufnahme des Don Quijote in die englische Literatur." *Palaestra* 13 (1906), 122-57.

Blanchard, Frederic T. *Fielding the Novelist: A Study in Historical Criticism.* New Haven, Conn.: Yale Univ. Press, 1927.

Booth, Wayne C. *The Rhetoric of Fiction.* Chicago: Univ. of Chicago Press, 1961.

Boyce, Benjamin. "News from Hell: Satiric Communications with the Nether World in English Writing of the Seventeenth and Eighteenth Centuries." *PMLA* 58 (1943), 402-37.

Braudy, Leo. *Narrative Form in History and Fiction: Hume, Fielding, and Gibbon.* Princeton, N.J.: Princeton Univ. Press, 1970.

Brooks, Douglas. "Richardson's *Pamela* and Fielding's *Joseph Andrews.*" *Essays in Criticism* 17 (1967), 158-68.

Butt, John. *Fielding.* Writers and Their Work, no. 57. London: Longmans, Green, 1954.

Coley, William B. "The Background of Fielding's Laughter." *ELH* 26 (1959), 229-52.

Combs, William W. "The Return to Paradise Hall: An Essay on *Tom Jones.*" *South Atlantic Quarterly* 67 (1968), 419-36.

Coolidge, John S. "Fielding and 'Conservation of Character.'" *Modern Philology* 57 (1960), 245-59.

Crane, R.S. "The Plot of *Tom Jones.*" *The Journal of General Education* 4 (1950), 112-30.

Cross, Wilbur L. *The History of Henry Fielding.* 3 vols. New Haven: Yale Univ. Press, 1918.

Digeon, Aurélien. *The Novels of Fielding.* London: Routledge, 1925.

Donovan, Robert Alan. *The Shaping Vision: Imagination in the English Novel from Defoe to Dickens.* Ithaca: Cornell Univ. Press, 1966.

Dudden, F. Homes. *Henry Fielding, His Life, Works, and Times.* London: Oxford Univ. Press, 1952.

Dyson, A.E. *The Crazy Fabric: Essays in Irony.* London: Macmillan; New York: St. Martin's Press, 1966.

Ehrenpreis, Irvin. *Fielding: Tom Jones.* London: Arnold, 1964.

Evans, James E. "Comedy and the 'Tragic Complexion' of *Tom Jones.*" *South Atlantic Quarterly* 83 (1984), 384-95.

———. "Fielding, *The Whole Duty of Man, Shamela,* and *Joseph Andrews.*" *PQ* 61 (1982), 212-19.

———. "The World According to Paul: Comedy and Theology in 'Joseph Andrews.'" *Ariel* 15 (1984), 45-56.

Fielding, Henry. *Amelia.* London: A. Millar, 1752.

———. *An Apology for the Life of Mrs. Shamela Andrews.* London: A. Dodd, 1741.

———. *The Complete Works of Henry Fielding, Esq.* Ed. William Ernest Henley. 16 vols. New York: Croscup & Sterling, 1902.

———. *The Covent-Garden Journal.* Ed. Gerard Edward Jensen. 2 vols. New Haven, Conn.: Yale Univ. Press; London: Oxford Univ. Press, 1915.

———. *The History of the Adventures of Joseph Andrews.* Wesleyan ed. Ed. Martin C. Battestin. Oxford: Clarendon Press, 1967.

———. *The History of Tom Jones, a Foundling.* Wesleyan ed. Ed. Martin C. Battestin and Fredson Bowers. [Middletown, Conn.]: Wesleyan Univ. Press, 1975.

———. *The Life of Mr. Jonathan Wild the Great.* In *Miscellanies,* Vol. III.

———. *Miscellanies.* 3 vols. London: A. Millar, 1743.

Foster, James R. *History of the Pre-Romantic Novel in England.* New York: Modern Language Association, 1949.

Goldberg, Homer. *The Art of Joseph Andrews.* Chicago: Univ. of Chicago Press, 1969.

Golden, Morris. *Fielding's Moral Psychology.* Amherst: Univ. of Massachusetts Press, 1966.

Guthrie, William B. "The Comic Celebrant of Life in *Tom Jones.*" *Tennessee Studies in Literature* 19 (1974), 91-106.

Haage, Richard. "Charakterzeichnung und Komposition in Fieldings *Tom Jones* in ihrer Beziehung zum Drama." *Britannica* 13 (1936), 119-70.

Harrison, Bernard. *Henry Fielding's* Tom Jones: *The Novelist as Moral Philosopher.* London: Sussex Univ. Press, 1975.

Hassall, Anthony J. "Fielding's *Amelia:* Dramatic and Authorial Narration." *Novel* 5 (1972), 225-33.

Hatfield, Glenn W. *Fielding and the Language of Irony.* Chicago: Univ. of Chicago Press, 1968.

———. "Puffs and Politricks: *Jonathan Wild* and the Political Corruption of Language." *PQ* 46 (1967), 248-67.

Hilles, Frederick W. *The Age of Johnson: Essays Presented to Chauncey Brewster Tinker.* New Haven, Conn.: Yale Univ. Press, 1949.

———. "Art and Artifice in *Tom Jones.*" In Mack and Gregor, 91-110.

Hopkins, Robert H. "Language and Comic Play in *Jonathan Wild.*" *Criticism* 8 (1966), 213-28.

Hunter, J. Paul. *Occasional Form: Henry Fielding and the Chains of Circumstance.* Baltimore: Johns Hopkins Univ. Press, 1975.

Hutchens, Eleanor. *Irony in Tom Jones.* University: Univ. of Alabama Press, 1965.

Irwin, William Robert. *The Making of Jonathan Wild.* New York: Columbia Univ. Press, 1941.

Johnson, Maurice. *Fielding's Art of Fiction.* Philadelphia: Univ. of Pennsylvania Press, 1961.

Knight, Charles A. "*Tom Jones:* The Meaning of the 'Main Design.'" *Genre* 12 (1979), 379-99.

La Calprenède, Gaultier. . . . *The Famous History of Cassandra,* tr. abridged. London: Cleave et al., 1703.

Langer, Susanne K. *Feeling and Form: A Theory of Art,* New York: Scribner, 1953.

Le Page, Peter V. "The Prison and the Dark Beauty of 'Amelia.'" *Criticism* 9 (1967), 337-54.

Mack, Maynard, and Ian Gregor, eds. *Imagined Worlds: Essays on Some English Novelists in Honour of John Butt.* London: Methuen, 1968.

McKenzie, Alan T. "The Process of Discovery in *Tom Jones.*" *Dalhousie Review* 54 (1974), 720-40.

McKillop, A.D. *Early Masters of English Fiction.* Lawrence: Univ. of Kansas Press, 1956.

McNamara, Susan P. "Mirrors of Fiction within *Tom Jones:* The Paradox of Self-Reliance." *ECS* 12 (1979), 372-90.

Maresca, Thomas. *Epic to Novel.* Columbus: Ohio State Univ. Press, 1974.

Miller, Henry Knight. *Essays on Fielding's Miscellanies: A Commentary on Volume One.* Princeton, N.J.: Princeton Univ. Press, 1961.

————. *Henry Fielding's Tom Jones and the Romance Tradition.* ELS Monograph Series, no. 6. Victoria: *English Literary Studies,* 1976.

————. "Some Functions of Rhetoric in *Tom Jones.*" *PQ* 45 (1966), 209-35.

————. "The Voices of Henry Fielding: Style in *Tom Jones.*" In Miller, Rothstein, and Rousseau, 262-88.

Miller, Henry Knight; Eric Rothstein; and G.S. Rousseau, eds. *The Augustan Milieu: Essays Presented to Louis A. Landa.* Oxford: Clarendon Press, 1970.

Montagu, Lady Mary Wortley. *Letters and Works,* 2d ed., ed. Wharncliffe. London: Tentley, 1837.

Osland, Dianne. "Fielding's *Amelia:* Problem Child or Problem Reader?" *Journal of Narrative Technique* 10 (1980), 56-67.

Palmer, E. Taiwo. "Fielding's Tom Jones Reconsidered." *English* 20 (1972), 45-50.

Palmer, Eustace. "*Amelia*—The Decline of Fielding's Art." *Essays in Criticism* 21 (1971), 135-51.

Paulson, Ronald. "Models and Paradigms: *Joseph Andrews,* Hogarth's *Good Samaritan,* and Fénelon's *Télémaque.*" *Modern Language Notes* 91 (1976), 1186-1207.

————. *Satire and the Novel in Eighteenth-Century England.* New Haven, Conn.: Yale Univ. Press, 1967.

Poovy, Mary. "Journies from This World to the Next: Providential Promise in *Clarissa* and *Tom Jones.*" *ELH* 43 (1976), 300-315.

Powers, Lyall H. "The Influence of the *Aeneid* on Fielding's *Amelia.*" *Modern Language Notes* 71 (1956), 330-36.

Preston, John. *The Created Self: The Reader's Role in Eighteenth-Century Fiction.* London: Heinemann, 1970.

Price, Martin. *The Restoration and the Eighteenth Century.* New York: Oxford Univ. Press, 1973.

Putnam, Samuel. *The Ingenious Gentleman Don Quijote de la Mancha.* New York: Viking, 1949.

Rawson, C.J. *Henry Fielding and the Augustan Ideal Under Stress.* London and Boston: Routledge & Kegan Paul, 1972.

Ribble, Frederick G. "The Constitution of Mind and the Concept of Emotion in Fielding's *Amelia.*" *PQ* 56 (1977), 104-22.

Rothstein, Eric. "The Framework of *Shamela.*" *ELH* 35 (1968), 381-402.

Saintsbury, George. Introduction to *Jonathan Wild,* Everyman ed. New York: Dutton, 1932.

Shea, Bernard. "Machiavelli and Fielding's *Jonathan Wild.*" *PMLA* 72 (1957), 55-73.

Sherburn, George. "The *Dunciad,* Book I." *University of Texas Studies in English* 24 (1944), 174-90.

————. "Fielding's *Amelia:* An Interpretation." *ELH* 3 (1936), 1-14.

Shesgreen, Sean. *Literary Portraits in the Novels of Henry Fielding.* DeKalb: Northern Illinois Univ. Press, 1972.

Snow, Malinda. "The Judgment of Evidence in *Tom Jones.*" *South Atlantic Review* 8 (1983), 37-51.

Spilka, Mark. "Comic Resolution in Fielding's *Joseph Andrews.*" *College English* 15 (1953), 11-19.

Stephanson, Raymond. "The Education of the Reader

in Fielding's *Joseph Andrews*." *PQ* 61 (1982), 243-58.

Stevick, Philip. "Fielding and the Meaning of History." *PMLA* 79 (1964), 561-68.

———. "On Fielding Talking." *College Literature* 1 (1974), 119-33.

Taylor, Dick, Jr. "Joseph as Hero in *Joseph Andrews*." *Tulane Studies in English* 7 (1957), 91-109.

Thomas, D.S. "Fortune and the Passions in Fielding's *Amelia*." *MLR* 60 (1965), 176-87.

Van Ghent, Dorothy. *The English Novel: Form and Function*. New York: Rinehart, 1953.

Vopat, James B. "Narrative Techniques in *Tom Jones*: The Balance of Art and Nature." *Journal of Narrative Technique* 4 (1974), 144-54.

Watt, Ian. "The Naming of Characters in Defoe, Richardson, and Fielding." *RES* 25 (1949), 322-38.

———. *The Rise of the Novel*. Berkeley: Univ. of California Press, 1957.

Wendt, Allan. "The Moral Allegory of *Jonathan Wild*." *ELH* 24 (1957), 306-20.

———. "The Naked Virtue of Amelia." *ELH* 27 (1960), 131-48.

Williams, Aubrey. "Interpositions of Providence and Design in Fielding's Novels." *South Atlantic Quarterly* 70 (1971), 265-86.

Wolff, Cynthia. "Fielding's *Amelia*: Private Virtue and Public Good." *TSLL* 10 (1968), 37-55.

Woods, Charles. "Fielding and the Authorship of *Shamela*." *PQ* 25 (1946), 248-72.

———. "Notes on Three of Fielding's Plays." *PMLA* 52 (1937), 359-73.

Work, James A. "Henry Fielding, Christian Censor." In Hilles, *Age of Johnson*, 137-48.

Wright, Andrew. *Henry Fielding, Mask and Feast*. Berkeley: Univ. of California Press, 1965.

Michael McKeon (essay date 1987)

SOURCE: "The Institutionalization of Conflict (II): Fielding and the Instrumentality of Belief," in his *The Origins of the English Novel, 1600-1740*, Johns Hopkins University Press, 1987, pp. 382-409.

[*In the following excerpt, McKeon examines the representation of truth and the foundation of knowledge in Fielding's fiction, especially* Jonathan Wild *and* Joseph Andrews. *McKeon's book is an early and important major revision of Ian Watt's history of the eighteenth-century novel,* The Rise of the Novel; *in this chapter and throughout the book, McKeon emphasizes both cultural and philosophical movements as essential context for analyzing the development of this generic form.*]

1

In the Richardson-Fielding rivalry of the 1740s it is easy to be reminded of the more tacit opposition between Defoe and Swift several decades earlier. The similarities are temperamental as well as cultural. Richardson's transparent vanity, masking a persistent sensitivity to his lack of "the very great Advantage of an Academical Education," seems a natural foil to the serene diffidence and careless superiority of the graduate of Eton and Leyden, who counted the Earl of Denbigh among his blood relations. But Fielding's mastery of a certain aristocratic hauteur belies a social background—and social attitudes—of considerable complexity. His father was the younger son of a younger son and a military man under Marlborough. His mother came from a family of established professional standing, and after her death when Henry was eleven, there ensued a custody suit that consumed the remainder of his youth, and enforced on him an alternation between city and country pursuits and between culturally divergent expectations of how his own way was to be made in the world.[1]

Until the Licensing Act of 1737, Fielding made his way most successfully as a playwright, a profession in which many of the narrative preoccupations with which we will be concerned underwent an important development. The highly reflexive quality of much of Fielding's drama suggests that he was both fascinated and impatient with an artistic mode so obligated to the evidence of the senses that its illusions fairly cried out for an easy disconfirmation. In *The Historical Register for the Year 1736,* for example, Fielding toys with the literalistic, pseudo-Aristotelian "unity of time," and its requirement of a strict correspondence between time represented and time elapsed in its representation, in a way that presages his later play with the naive claim to historicity and its pretense to an unselective completeness of narrative detail. These farces are also Fielding's first laboratory for the experimental juxtaposition of questions of truth and virtue. It was not hard to see, in the popular theater of the period, a connection between the epistemological ingratiation of the senses evident in the wholesale reliance on theatrical "spectacle," and the shameless commercial pandering that was entailed in such theatrics. Moreover Fielding often seized the occasion to specify the traditional analogy of the world and the stage to a self-conscious critique of political manipulation and corruption under the Whig "management" of the 1730s. Even the old dramatic device of discovery and reversal takes on (at least with hindsight) a characteristically Fieldingesque exorbitance. Thus, in *The Author's Farce* (1730), we follow the fortunes of a platitudinously progressive hero who, "thrown naked upon the world . . . can make his way through it by his merit and virtuous industry," and who nevertheless turns out, in a riot of romance revelations of parentage, to be heir apparent to royalty.[2]

Given the energy with which he pushed against the conventions of dramatic representation, it is scarcely surprising that, once obliged to turn to narrative, Fielding adopted the skeptical stance of the "historian." His earliest work of this sort, *The History of the Life of the Late Mr. Jonathan Wild the Great* (1743), was substantially complete before *Pamela* appeared at the end of 1740. Its satiric response to the problem of how to tell the truth in narrative therefore owes less to the instigations of Richardson than to Fielding's wide reading in ancient and modern historiography. And the difficult complexity of that response can be explained by the way the parodic mode of his skepticism both does and does not coordinate with the ironic mode of his mock-heroic.[3]

What is shared by these modes is the familiar pattern of "double reversal." Fielding's parodic "history" is first of all a critique of the idealizing, "romancing" method of traditional biographies, with their near-immemorial lineages, premonitions of greatness, frankly supernatural deliverances, fabricated speeches, and the like. Yet the parody of traditional history can also implicitly subvert the modern and rationalizing standard of historicity, from which it is incompletely separated. On this second level of formal satire, Fielding parodies the distinctively modern form of criminal biography, its characteristic devices of authentication, and especially the proliferation of documents on which its claim to historicity depends—ordinary's accounts, authentic letters and journals, convincingly fragmentary shorthand transcriptions, and painstaking ear-witness testimony. Thus the critique of the old, romancing histories is supplemented by a critique of the "new romance" of naive empiricism and its modernized methods of imposing on the credulity of the reader.[4] By the same token, Fielding's mock-heroic is first of all an ironic reduction of the unheroic rogue by the normative standards of genuine heroism and its conventional panegyric forms; but it is then also an unstable and self-subverting movement against the heroic standard itself. Jonathan Wild is like Alexander and Caesar in evincing the "imperfection" of "a mixture of good and evil in the same character." But Fielding is

different from the ancient biographers in knowing—and in letting us know—that these qualities are morally incompatible: that precisely what we call "heroism" is the essence of evil in such figures, and that it entirely overshadows whatever small goodness they may also exhibit (I, i, 3-5; IV, xv, 175-76). Modern heroes are rogues; but so are ancient heroes, and on this recognition Fielding bases his sincere claim "to draw natural, not perfect characters, and to record the truths of history, not the extravagances of romance" (IV, iv, 135). So the critique of modern roguery is supplemented by a critique of ancient roguery and of the romancing historians who call it heroism.[5]

The self-subversive instability of Fielding's mock-heroic, which he shares with his age, is parallel to that of naive empiricism and an expression of the same implacable process. Once launched, the skeptical critique might assume a force of its own and overturn its original premises. What makes Fielding's satire notoriously difficult here is that the same element, traditional historiography, occupies opposed positions in the two parallel reversals. In Fielding's strategy of extreme skepticism, Plutarch and Suetonius are the negative examples that are attacked by the normative standard of empirical history, even as naive empiricism itself is subjected to parody. But in the mock-heroic movement, it is the modern example that is negative; the positive norm by which it is criticized is ancient history, which in turn becomes vulnerable to a similar attack. What is achieved by this remarkable interweaving of satiric strategies that are structurally parallel but asymmetrical in substance? The major effect of the asymmetry—the confusing conflation of terms (positive and negative, ancient and modern, hero and rogue) that have been posited in opposition to each other—is to emphasize what is a dominant feature of each strategy as it operates on its own: the sense of the collapse of categories. At the same time, the structural parallel between the skeptical and mock-heroic strategies is solid enough to suggest that what is at issue here is not only questions of truth. For the latter movement mediates us from the epistemological concerns of the former to an analogous realm of ethical and social concerns, from questions of truth to questions of virtue.

Fielding's central term in the critique of heroism—the slippery notion of "greatness"—bears a close relation to the equally slippery notion of Machiavellian *virtù*. Machiavelli is the modern historian most responsible for extending and transforming the Roman "ideal" of amoral heroism, and Fielding's Jonathan Wild is a classic Machiavellian "new man" who rises by force and fraud and even learns to purvey his own Machiavellian "maxims" (IV, xv, 173-74). Like his epistemology, Fielding's ideology is the issue of a double critique: first of aristocratic ideology by progressive, then of progressive ideology by conservative. The slipperiness of "greatness" is vital to this dialectical movement. To the progressive mentality, the greatness of a newly risen "Great Man" like Sir Robert Walpole is a matter of social stature that implies a correspondent moral elevation. But Fielding shows that progressives are the unconscious and stealthy heirs of ancient aristocratic assumptions about the congruity of inner and outer states. The moral proximity of great men like Walpole and Alexander the Great (who might with justice end their days by hanging), and rogues like Wild (who actually do), argues the conservative truth that status inconsistency yet reigns in the modern world of progressive "social justice" as surely as it did in ancient, aristocratic culture, when "greatness" and "goodness" were taken to be coextensive (IV, xii, 168, xiv, 170, 171).[6]

Yet if Fielding's major purpose in *Jonathan Wild* is clearly a conservative critique of the progressive upstart, the narrative retains the coherent, if schematic, imprint of its enabling progressive premise, the skeleton of a progressive plot satiric of aristocratic honor. Of course, the progressive foundation is evident elsewhere in Fielding's work as well. Earlier, in the *Miscellanies*, he is outspoken in his contempt for the way that

> the least Pretensions to Pre-eminence in Title, Birth, Riches, Equipage, Dress, &c. constantly overlook the most noble Endowments of Virtue, Honour, Wisdom, Sense, Wit, and every other Quality which can truly dignify and adorn a Man . . . That the fortuitous Accident of Birth, the Acquisition of Wealth, with some outward Ornaments of Dress, should inspire Men with an Insolence capable of treating the rest of Mankind with Disdain, is so preposterous, that nothing less than daily Experience could give it Credit.

And to the "infamous worthless Nobleman" who claims that his inherent worth has descended to him with his title, Fielding makes the empiricist retort "that a Title originally implied Dignity, as it implied the Presence of those Virtues to which Dignity is inseparably annexed; but that no Implication will fly in the Face of downright positive Proof to the contrary."[7]

In *Jonathan Wild,* the dominant conservative satire is supported by the scaffolding of a progressive satire against aristocratic values. Like Fielding's worthless nobleman, Jonathan Wild is convinced of the genealogical powers of "the blood of the Wilds, which hath run with such uninterrupted purity through so many generations," and he passionately believes honor to be "the essential quality of a gentleman" (IV, x, 156; I, xiii, 37). To appreciate Wild's story as a progressive satire on aristocratic ideology we must isolate that discontinuous but palpable strain of "greatness" which consists in a genealogical gentility distinguished by nothing so much as petty viciousness and bumbling incompetence. We begin with "the fortuitous accident

of birth" memorialized in the Wild lineage (I, ii). His father educates "the young gentleman" in "principles of honour and gentility" and sends him on his own version of the Tour (I, iii, 11, vii, 21-22). Wild soon learns to socialize with aristocratic types like Count la Ruse, whose status as "men of honour" is firmly established by their apparent willingness to duel at the drop of a glove (see I, iv, 11-12, viii, 25-26, xi, 31, xiii, 36-37). And his later career is broadly marked by a succession of dupings—generally receiving worse than he gives—that confirm in the "gentleman" an absence both of virtue and of dignity.[8]

In a truly progressive plot, the dominant corollary of this negative example would be the positive story of the rise of industrious virtue.[9] In *Jonathan Wild* we have the problematic shadow of such a corollary in the figure of Heartfree (to whom I will return). But the more fundamental—and characteristically conservative—tendency is to collapse the very distinction between positive and negative, on which progressive plots thrive, by making "industrious virtue" itself a highly suspect category. Thus the "progressive" critique of the "aristocratic" Wild is constantly neutralized by the demonstration that the legitimate and successful man of virtue, against whom he has putatively been judged, is essentially no different from Wild himself. As we are relentlessly compelled to attend to the leveling analogy between rogue and statesman, Fielding's progressive plot dissolves before our eyes. The insistent proximity of Wild and Walpole forces us to identify the trappings of "honor" as the hypocritical aggrandizements of the assimilationist upstart; and the status inconsistency of aristocratic culture, so far from being resolved by the rise of the new men of "virtue," is seen to be aggravated by it.[10]

Echoing his conservative predecessors, Fielding sometimes makes the relation between rogue and statesman intelligible as one not simply of similarity but of contiguity, as the plot of doing well enough in the world to be called no longer the former but the latter:

> Can there be a more instructive Lesson against that abominable and pernicious Vice, Ambition, than the Sight of a mean Man, rais'd by fortunate Accidents and execrable Vices to Power, employing the basest Measures and the vilest Instruments to support himself; looked up to only by Sycophants and Slaves and sturdy Beggars, Wretches whom even he must in his Heart despise in all their Tinsel; looked down upon, and scorned and shunned by every Man of Honour . . . without Dignity in his Robes, without Honour from his Titles, without Authority from his Power [?]

Here is the classic conservative reduction. Progressive "virtue" only recapitulates the old arbitrariness of aristocratic "honor": if inherited nobility owes its ascendancy to "the fortuitous accident of birth," the self-made upstart is similarly "raised by fortunate accidents and execrable vices." But in **Jonathan Wild** the rise of rogue to statesman is less crucial than the riveting fact of their similarity. A "great man and a great rogue are synonymous," Fielding writes, and in this conjunction he focuses on the internal quality of "greatness" that is essential to the new aristocracy of upstarts, cutting across the old social categories (in a parody of progressive virtue and Protestant grace) by uniting "high and low life" (IV, xv, 176; I, v, 17). By this means he conflates the several villains of conservative imagination—the scheming rogue of criminal biography, the Whiggish "public servant," the industrious parvenu of improving parables, the enthusiastic convert of spiritual autobiography—into a single resonant figure of corruption.[11]

As the Newgate debtors discover, to be "great" is to be "corrupted in their morals" (IV, xii, 161), a character trait that qualifies the petty London gangleader for legitimate and distinguished professional careers in the (scarcely separable) fields of politics and high finance. As Wild observes at one point, not only robbery but even murder is comfortably carried on "within the law" (III, iii, 91). If fraud is a "courtier's" accomplishment, then the policy of the "statesman" and the "prime minister" elevates petty theft and the betrayal of friends to an engagement with the "public trust" itself (I, vi, 19, v, 16, 18; II, viii, 69). "Greatness," the unifying element in "prigs," "statesmen," and "absolute princes" (I, xiv, 42; II, iv, 58), depends not upon the nature or scope of one's sphere of influence but on one's will to exercise "absolute power" there (III, xiv, 120-22; IV, xv, 175). Fielding's argument resists the customary restriction of "absolutism" to the sphere of princely "authority," radically modernizing it as a psychological and moral capacity to engross power, whose egalitarian servant, willing to work for any man and to corrupt all others, "is indeed the beginning as well as the end of all human devices: I mean money" (I, xiv, 43).

It is not surprising that Fielding propounds the familiar parallel between theft and financial investment, or that Wild passes "for a gentleman of great fortune in the funds" (I, vi, 21; see also I, xiv, 43-44). At the heart of the parallel that ties the absolute politician to the absolute possessive individualist is the unlimited indulgence of the appetites, which here are arranged in a characteristically conservative hierarchy. When Fielding observes that "the truest mark of greatness is insatiability," it is clear at once that he refers most of all to the desire for material goods (II, ii, 51). Wild's "most powerful and predominant passion was ambition . . . His lust was inferior only to his ambition . . . His avarice was immense, but it was of the rapacious, not of the tenacious kind" (IV, xv, 172-73). Avarice and lust are reciprocal signs of corruption, but unlike the case of the progressive villain, here the lust for money

predominates. Thus, although Wild is inflamed by the very sight of Mrs. Heartfree, the ruin of Mr. Heartfree has a clear priority over the rape of his wife (II, i, 47, viii, 71). Only when both have been arranged does Wild, "secure . . . of the possession of that lovely woman, together with a rich cargo," anticipate the satisfaction of both appetites in language that renders them well-nigh interchangeable: "In short, he enjoyed in his mind all the happiness which unbridled lust and rapacious avarice could promise him" (II, viii, 74). By the same token, Wild's beloved Laetitia knows that of her "three very predominant passions; to wit, vanity, wantonness, and avarice," she can implicitly rely on Jonathan to satiate the third in particular (II, iii, 55). We, at least, are left in no doubt that theirs is a "Smithfield" match—a marriage for money—and soon after it Laetitia informs her insulted husband that she married him not for love but "because it was convenient, and my parents forced me" (III, vi, 98, viii, 105; see also vi, 99-100, 103).[12]

So despite the intimations that, as in Richardson's progressive ideology, "honor" may be purged of aristocratic poisons and realigned with "virtue," the more compelling argument in **Jonathan Wild** is that the term has been so corrupted by progressive assimilationism as to be completely and unredeemably arbitrary. "A man of honour," says Wild, "is he that is called a man of honour; and while he is so called he so remains, and no longer" (I, xiii, 38). Fielding's "preoccupation with semantic instability"[13] expresses an insight into the analogous relation between linguistic and socioeconomic corruption, an insight he shares with Swift and other utopian travel narrators. The attack on modern cant terms is a microscopic version of the attack on modern narrative, which has only devised, through the pretense of telling an antiromance truth, a more efficient method of imposing on the credulity of the innocent. For corruption to operate successfully in these several spheres it is essential that the two principals, not only the knaves but also the fools, faithfully perform in their respective roles: "Thus while the crafty and designing Part of Mankind, consulting only their own separate Advantage, endeavour to maintain one constant Imposition on others, the whole World becomes a vast Masquerade." "Constant imposition" is crucial both for *"The Art of Politics"* and for *"the Art of thriving."* In an allegorical satire on the Whig establishment, Fielding depicts monetary corruption not as naked opportunism but as a credulous religious rite, the worship of a deity called MNEY and of its ambitious high priest, whose creed includes the maxim that "All Things Spring from Corruption, so did MNEY, and therefore by Corruption he is most properly come at." As in other conservative writers, the model is of an artfully constructed, quasi-religious social fiction whose greatest power is to impose upon the credulity of the many.[14]

Throughout Fielding's narratives, the law provides an

especially persistent example of such a social fiction. Jonathan Wild's main weapon against his enemies is not brute force but the law, which he is able to turn to his own ends only because it depends so fully on procedures of witness, testimony, and evidence that enjoin an earnest empiricist belief and are highly subject to falsification. But Fielding's most explicit articulation of the analogy between sociopolitical and epistemological imposition—between questions of virtue and questions of truth—in *Jonathan Wild* invokes the fictions not of the law but of the stage, and it recalls the analogy of world and stage that had earlier preoccupied him in the farces. Wild is about to enact the supreme betrayal of his friend Heartfree. A great man such as he, Fielding observes, is best compared to a puppet master, for the effectiveness of his manipulations depends entirely upon his inaccessibility to sense perception:

> Not that any one is ignorant of his being there, or supposes that the puppets are not mere sticks of wood, and he himself the sole mover; but as this (though every one knows it) doth not appear visibly, i.e. to their eyes, no one is ashamed of consenting to be imposed upon . . .

> It would be to suppose thee, gentle reader, one of very little knowledge in this world, to imagine thou has never seen some of these puppet-shows which are so frequently acted on the great stage . . . He must have a very despicable opinion of mankind indeed who can conceive them to be imposed on as often as they appear to be so. The truth is, they are in the same situation with the readers of romances; who, though they know the whole to be one entire fiction, nevertheless agree to be deceived; and, as these find amusement, so do the others find ease and convenience in this concurrence. But, this being a subdigression, I return to my digression. (III, xi, 114)

The passage suggests a three-part analogy of impositions: Wild is to Heartfree as Walpole is to the people, and as the romance writer is to his readers. The willingness of those on the receiving end to be deceived in these relationships is that of the audience at a puppet show. The tenor of the comparison, however, is not art but political exploitation. The effect of the analogy is to oblige us to see the posture of the audience not in the positive light of an "aesthetic response" but in the negative light of political bad faith. And of course the analogy strikes close to home. If we "gentle readers" seek no more than a passive "ease and convenience" in this narration—if we resist Fielding's self-conscious reference to his own digressive manipulations, for example, preferring a comfortable belief in his claims to historicity—then we are really no different from Heartfree.

But what does it mean to be no different from Heartfree? Critics have recognized Heartfree's inadequacy

as a positive norm in *Jonathan Wild,* but they have disagreed about Fielding's awareness of this inadequacy and hence about its role in the narrative's moral and social program.[15] Heartfree's several soliloquies on the comforts of a good conscience, the satisfactions of Christian behavior, and the anticipated rewards of the world beyond are indistinguishable from Fielding's "own" precepts, which he occasionally delivers in this homiletic mode, but they also bespeak, in the face of worldly injustice, a comprehensive passivity (III, ii, 88-89, v, 97-98, x, III). A jeweler by trade, Heartfree is (not surprisingly) a remarkably fair dealer who would never impose on his customers (II, i, 46), and Fielding encourages us to associate the Heartfrees' willingness to "credit" the lies by which Wild and the Count impose upon them with their willingness to extend these villains financial "credit" (e.g., II, iii, 52, viii, 70). There are limits to this credence. When Wild persuades Mrs. Heartfree to flee the country for her husband's sake, Mr. Heartfree soon overcomes his initial doubts about his wife's fidelity (III, i, 85, v, 95-96); but of Wild's account of the affair he cannot help wondering "whether the whole was not a fiction, and Wild . . . had not spirited away, robbed, and murdered his wife" (III, ix, 109). But it is not until Mrs. Heartfree returns from her travels, and is called upon to tell her own story, that Fielding fully illuminates the function of Heartfree in posing the multifaceted problem of imposition and "convenient" fictions.

Even in the absence of the "wonderful chapter" that Fielding deleted after the first edition, Mrs. Heartfree's interpolated tale is replete with events and devices—storm, shipwreck, pirates, attempted rapes, a hermit castaway, a curious native culture—that contemporaries would have associated with the related marvels of romance mutability and travel-narrative historicity. Fielding expressed his contempt for the naive empiricism of romancing travel narratives at several points in his career, most lucidly in his own, posthumously published travel journal. There he distinguishes ancient and modern travel "romances" from the "true history" he himself has composed, "the former being the confounder and corrupter of the latter." Vanity, he claims, leads these travel romancers both to describe things that have never happened and, on the contrary, to record minute trivialities whose only distinction is that they happened to the author. The good traveler must be highly selective. The worth of his character will be reflected not in any spurious, quantitative completeness of detail or observation but in the success of his selection in "diverting or informing" the reader.[16]

Judged by these standards, Mrs. Heartfree's credibility is impugned not only by the conventionalized wonders of her narration but by its patent self-interest. After all, it is the story of how she managed, despite a succession of threats that include the ravenous lust of half a dozen men, not only to preserve her chastity but to miraculously recover the jewels that had been stolen from her husband. Like Robinson Crusoe and Pamela, Mrs. Heartfree attributes all her good fortune to the power of providence, and she ends her narrative with the cheerful lesson that virtue gets rewarded in the end—"THAT PROVIDENCE WILL SOONER OR LATER PROCURE THE FELICITY OF THE VIRTUOUS AND INNOCENT" (IV, xi, 161; see also IV, vii, 145, 146, viii, 147, ix, 153, xi, 160). Yet her self-reliance reminds us of no one so much as Wild himself. Her adaptive mastery of nautical terminology is striking enough for her husband to comment upon, and she lingers over the romance compliments of her suitors as though they were vital to her story rather than to her self-love (IV, vii, 143, ix, 155, xi, 157). She fends off would-be seducers by pretending to comply with their desires (e.g., IV, vii, 146), a technique of imposture at which she is so accomplished that in the crucial exchange—when she obtains the jewels—we experience some doubt as to just how it has been done. To be sure, Mrs. Heartfree's official story is one of providential repossession (IV, ix, 153). But it is she herself who plants in her persecutor's mind the idea that her virtue might be vulnerable to a bribe, and before she is providentially rescued she energetically attempts "to persuade him of my venality" (IV, ix, 151). The supposed imposture has the ring of plausibility, for the pragmatic and business-like exchange of one "jewel" for another may seem by now more likely than the earnest narrator's account of one more wonderful event. The play on words itself becomes explicit at the very end of Mrs. Heartfree's narrative, when yet another suitor is said to give her "a very rich jewel, of less value, he said, than my chastity" (IV, xi, 160).

Most important, our mounting skepticism at the circumstances of these windfalls is greatly strengthened by our wish to dissociate ourselves from the credulity of our surrogate audience, Mr. Heartfree, whose acute anxiety at the recurrent threats to his wife's virtue during her narration is exceeded only by the ease with which he credits her persuasions "that Heaven had preserved her chastity, and again had restored her unsullied to his arms" (IV, vii, 145; see also IV, vii, 144, ix, 152). And the general instability of this marital interaction is heightened when it is interrupted all at once by its mock-heroic reduction. Mrs. Heartfree has been narrating her story in Newgate, and suddenly Wild creates an uproar because he has caught his wife Laetitia with his confederate Fireblood. For the improbably delicate Wild, it is as much his own fastidious "honor" that is offended as it is hers, and he reiterates the word with a manic insistence (IV, x, 155-57). Coming as it does in the middle of another tale of imperiled honor, Wild's absurdly elevated outrage provides a perspective on both Heartfrees: a reflection of the wife's false idealism, and a foil for the husband's easy agreement to be deceived. But the episode is also an artful interpolation within an interpolation, and like Fielding's earlier "sub-

digression," it amounts to a formal reminder of the manipulative and "political" power of the narrator, affording us an opportunity to distinguish ourselves from the good Mr. Heartfree by doubting the accuracy of his wife's story. In this way Fielding transforms her, if only for the space of her travel narrative, from the constant female lover of romance into the scheming rogue of conservative ideology, whose claim to truth is imposture and whose protestation of inner virtue masks an essential avarice. And her husband, because he will not be a knave like Wild, tends to be his wife's ideal audience—that is, a willing fool.[17]

Thus *Jonathan Wild* reflects, like *Gulliver's Travels* before it, the analogous and interlocked asperities of extreme skepticism and conservative ideology. And like Swift, Fielding is impelled to reverse the implacable momentum of his critique by guardedly reaffirming the old values. As in his predecessors, this amounts not to an unmediated act of faith but to a defense of the instrumentality and utility of belief, a tactic whose repercussions are not easily controlled. Thus, when in other contexts Fielding the latitudinarian refutes deist arguments against the reality of future rewards, his earnest insistence that the "Delusion" (if such it be) affords a "Spring of Pleasure" recalls not only Tillotson and South but also his own rather silly Heartfree. And when he defends the old social forms and titles—"His Grace," "Right Honourable," "Sir"—not because they have any substantial "philosophical" meaning but because, "being imposed by the Laws of Custom," they have become "politically essential," we are reminded as much of Jonathan Wild as of Jonathan Swift.[18]

If the "instrumentality of belief" argument seems even more volatile and contradictory in Fielding's hands than in those of his predecessors, it is partly because his commitment to some of the basic institutions of conservative ideology is less profound than theirs. His family background tied him securely to the "upstart" Marlborough's war, to the system of financial investment by which it was funded, and to the reality of nonlanded property. Moreover Fielding seems to have been sufficiently comfortable with the modern system of political management to have accepted a bribe from Walpole in exchange for delaying publication of *Jonathan Wild*—by Swiftian lights surely an act of "corruption." Because Fielding does not fully share Swift's comprehensive aversion to progressive institutions, he cannot share Swift's circumspect dedication to the utopian idea of a preprogressive culture. As a result, his advocacy of an instrumental belief in institutions whose authority may be fictional—social deference, custom, the law—can sound less like a parabolic intuition of a better dispensation than like a hearty and forward-looking justification of this one. Thus, in *Jonathan Wild* the figure of the "good magistrate" (IV, vi, 141, xv, 176) benevolently beckons our saving faith in a legal system whose viciousness—"politically essential" to the corruptions of great upstarts—Fielding has been at great pains to document from the outset.[19]

Yet the good magistrate is a persistent personage in Fielding's narratives, increasingly a model for the author's own stance as the benevolent narrator. And the example of this dual function—the external institution internalized as an authorial capacity—suggests how Fielding makes the "instrumentality of belief" argument more adequately his own. Whereas in Swift the argument is most explicit in the realm of ideology and sociopolitical institutions, in Fielding the major emphasis modulates to the epistemological "institution" of narrative form, to the reclamation of specifically literary fiction as a mode of telling the truth. Buttressing Fielding's extreme skepticism is a critique of empiricist objectivity (and of the allied belief that the instrument of verification is separable from the object verified) that would make a deist proud. On the basis of this powerful critique, Fielding implicates narrative in the fictionalizing deceptions of the political puppeteer. The question, then, is not how to avoid the inevitable condition of fictionality (of "romance"), but how to avoid the ethical pitfalls that seem to be an inevitable part of it: the impositions of the puppeteer and the bad faith of his audience. What is required is a fiction so palpable, so "evident to the senses," that its power to deceive even a "willing" audience becomes neutralized.[20]

Indeed, Fielding has this requirement in view when, instead of seeking the quantitative completeness of the naive empiricists, he explicitly insists on the necessity of narrative selection and the qualitative discrimination between the virtuous and the vicious, the important and the trivial. In *Jonathan Wild* we have already seen an example of this insistence in Fielding's advocacy of "mixed characters" and his critique of the notion, among both ancients and moderns, of a perfect "uniformity of character" (I, i, 4). He makes a similar point less explicitly, and with respect to plot rather than character, when he apologizes for the shortness of a chapter that covers eight years in Wild's life. The problem is that the period "contains not one adventure worthy the reader's notice"; and unlike experiential time, narrative time is selective (I, vii, 21-22). Relatively programmatic passages like these should be seen as part of the more general phenomenon of Fielding's highly distinctive self-consciousness, an epistemological strategy that is entirely familiar from his best-known narratives but already effective in *Jonathan Wild.* Undoubtedly (in the words of the title page of *Joseph Andrews*) more in "the manner of Cervantes" than of Swift, this narrative reflexiveness aims to enclose its object in a shell of subjective commentary. Its ideal and unstated function is simultaneously to demystify fiction ("romance," "history") as illusion and to detoxify it, to negate its negation, to empower it by ostentatiously enacting, even announcing, its impotence to tell an immediate truth.[21] Two brief examples from *Jonathan Wild* will help clarify the "theory" of this dialectical technique.

Late in Book II, Jonathan, having cast himself into the sea, is "miraculously within two minutes after replaced in his boat," and the narrator promises to explain how this escape occurred by natural means, without the traditional aid of dolphin or sea horse. Rejecting all "supernatural causes," he personifies Nature, describes her power, depicts her working her purposes on Wild—who obligingly changes his mind and leaps aboard again—and thereby demonstrates the naturalness of his "history" (II, xii, 79-81). Proudly disowning artifice ("romance") at the outset, Fielding makes abundantly clear that what he calls "nature" ("true history") is only art by another name. But to show that all is art is to vindicate its vices by acknowledging their inevitability, and we accept Fielding's manipulations (at least in theory) precisely because they are so ingenuous and obtrusive. In a similar fashion, Fielding's narrator boasts of spurning the romance convention whereby the story ends with a happy marriage, and instead we are treated to Jonathan and Laetitia's marital dispute in the middle of Book III (vii-viii, 103-7).[22] Yet the episode is introduced by conventionalized claims to historicity and then conveyed, in a "dialogue matrimonial," as a page from the script of a bedroom farce. And by the end of the narrative, Fielding is content to close very much according to convention, histrionically rewarding the good and punishing the great (IV, xv, 176-77).

How does this differ, we may ask, from Mrs. Heartfree's dubious invocations of providential reward at the end of her own story? Presumably in the fact that here there is no imposition, because there is no belief: unlike Heartfree, the knowing reader agrees not to be deceived but to be "diverted" (in the language of the *Voyage to Lisbon*) by Fielding's reclamation of fictionality. But we may sense that Fielding would wish to acknowledge this state, too, as a species of belief, if only he could disentangle its mysterious, knowing innocence from the moral opprobrium of the agreed-upon deception. We are close here to the realm of the aesthetic and its own peculiar rationalization of the reader's commitment and response. But the sizable distance yet to be traversed is suggested by the fact that it will entail a rethinking of the other half of the Horatian dictum—not only to be "diverted" but also to be "informed"—which is more fundamental than anything Fielding and his contemporaries are willing to undertake.

2

Thus, by the time *Pamela* was printed in the fall of 1740, Fielding's future course in narrative had already been charted in the unpublished drafts of *Jonathan*

Wild. Within the space of a year Fielding wrote **Shamela** and **Joseph Andrews.** In both works it is clear that he is continuing what he had begun and that his target is by no means simply Richardson. But *Pamela* provided an occasion for the emergence into public controversy—for the "institutionalization"—of that characteristically dialectical relation of action and reaction in which the origins of the English novel had thus far less obtrusively consisted. And in this important respect, **Shamela** and **Joseph Andrews** are quite accurately seen as a reactive response to *Pamela,* a negation and a completion of its achievement.[23] In the remainder of this chapter I will attempt to show how the most significant ties of these works both to *Pamela* and to **Jonathan Wild** are also significant for the origins of the novel.

The fact that **Shamela** negates *Pamela* by fully extending its premises can be seen clearly in the way Fielding parodically subverts Richardson's epistolary form. It is not that narrative empiricism is inherently naive, but that, on the contrary, *Pamela*'s claim to historicity is not authentic enough. The events themselves possess a reality, but the documents of which *Pamela* consists (according to Fielding's parodic premise) were fabricated by a hired pen and completely misrepresent her true history. Luckily her mother has communicated the "authentic" "originals" to Parson Oliver. He in turn has sent copies of these to his ingenuous colleague Parson Tickletext, whose former enthusiasm for *Pamela*'s truth and virtue is memorialized in the correspondence that precedes the printing of these truly authentic documents. Tickletext's name itself ties him to the vanity and credulousness of Protestant self-documentation. But having read Oliver's "authentic copies," he is much abashed at having endured so easily the "imposition" of *Pamela,* and it is he who is responsible for publishing (in the words of the title page) these "exact Copies of authentick Papers delivered to the Editor."[24]

Tickletext is like a Heartfree who has ceased to agree to be deceived. And it is easy to see why, since everything is altered, in this truer history, by the candor of the narrator. It is not entirely clear whether the name change—Shamela's parodic rebirth into the romance gentility of a Pamela—is due to the ingenuity of the protagonist or to that of the hack author of *Pamela* (cf. 308, 309, 337). But the restoration of the authentic name aptly encapsulates Fielding's central strategy, which is to restore the crucial access to Pamela's inner motives, whose absence rendered the historicity of *Pamela* (we can now appreciate) fatally incomplete. Even Richardson's Pamela is obliged to engage in the occasional subterfuge, to counterplot against Mr. B.'s plotting. And Mrs. Heartfree carries this extenuated duplicity further. But Shamela's character consists in nothing but the will to impose herself upon Mr. Booby, to misrepresent herself as what she is not. Fielding

makes good use of those episodes in *Pamela,* like the pretended drowning (321), in which Shamela's deceit can be seen to have a basis in Pamela's. But he also makes Shamela a complete "Politician" (299), as Pamela never was. Thus her master's excitement at seeing her dressed like a farmer's daughter clearly becomes, as Mr. B. had charged, the result of a deliberate "stratagem" on Shamela's part (315). Yet even here, the barely plausible effect is that of, not a different person but the same person unbowdlerized, carelessly and candidly reporting the whole truth back home to her mother. And the whole truth requires not a greater quantity of details but a critical selection of the most vital ones concerning her own conniving state of mind. In this context, "writing to the moment" can only appear suspect, one more instance of supposedly "innocent" activity hilariously betrayed by the intimately self-conscious reflex of reporting (e.g., 313). Pamela's "virtue" becomes Shamela's "vartue," like Machiavelli's *virtù* a corrupted term that embodies its own contradictory negation. Moving from *Pamela* to **Shamela** is like hearing Mary Carleton's story retold as a rogue's tale by her husband John and posterity—except that here the transformation is achieved simply by letting the protagonist speak in her own person.[25]

Shamela is a rogue because she is a scheming, ambitious upstart. Fielding leaves us in no doubt as to the moral both of his own work and of its model. *Pamela* teaches "young gentlemen . . . to marry their mother's chambermaids" and "servant-maids . . . to look out for their masters as sharp as they can" (338, 307). By disclosing the real Pamela in action, **Shamela** reverses this moral. We see her profiting from the subversive loyalty of the "family of servants"; we observe her "betraying the secrets of families"; we watch her plot her progress from one family to the other; and we end up convinced of Parson Oliver's prediction that "the character of Shamela will make young gentlemen wary how they take the most fatal step both to themselves and families, by youthful, hasty and improper matches" (316, 338, 337). Six years after the publication of **Shamela** Fielding himself was content to marry his first wife's maid. But for the moment this kind of social mobility, at least in Richardson's rendition of it, could resonate for Fielding with the culturally fraught effrontery of the rise of the undeserving. Fielding's ostensible target in **Shamela** is not only the anonymous author of *Pamela* but also Colley Cibber's autobiographical *Apology* of 1740 and Conyers Middleton's *Life of Cicero* (1741). And as Hugh Amory has observed, the attack is unified by the fact that all three works "explain the success of *parvenus* by their superior moral merit and all three substantiate this contention from the very mouths of their *parvenus,* whose naive candor seems unquestionable."[26]

Shamela's status as a conservative villainess is solidified by the predominance of her avarice. Of course her lubricity is never in doubt either, at least when Parson Williams is around. But her first lust is the lust for money. Like her mother and Mrs. Jervis, Shamela is at heart a whore (308-9). Advised by the former early on to make "a good market" with her "rich fool" of a master (311), she is pleased to find in Lincoln-shire that Mrs. Jewkes also will help "sell me to my master" (317). But as in all such roguery, the success of the transaction depends upon the hypocritical dis-guise of financial ambition as the outer mark of inner virtue. Shamela tells Booby that "I value my vartue more than all the world, and I had rather be the poorest man's wife, than the richest man's whore" (324). And in a certain sense she is quite sincere. Presented with the possibility of being a whore—of a sham-marriage "settlement" as Mr. Booby's "mistress"—Shamela, like Pamela, rejects the offer (313, 321). But her reasons are rather different. Whereas Pamela fears the loss of (what is admittedly a complex entity) her virtue, Shame-la simply fears the loss of the more lucrative settle-ment of a genuine marriage. "No, Mrs. Jervis," she insists, "nothing under a regular taking into keeping, a settled settlement, for me, and all my heirs, all my whole lifetime, shall do the business" (313). To be a wife is a financial improvement on being a whore; "virtue" is eminently profitable. Indeed, this is the meaning of Shamela's famous Machiavellian maxim: "I thought once of making a little fortune by my per-son. I now intend to make a great one by my vartue" (325). The corruption of virtue culminates in the cor-ruption of marriage.

After the wedding Shamela allows the mask to slip somewhat. She engages in a bit of desultory charity. But unlike Pamela, who exults, "Oh how I long to be doing some Good!" Shamela only complains: "I long to be in London that I may have an opportunity of laying some out, as well as giving away. What signi-fies having money if one doth not spend it." "It would be hard indeed," she adds, "that a woman who marries a man only for his money, should be debarred from spending it" (331, 332). In the presence of such con-summate presumption, even the fatuous Booby takes on some dignity, and in the final scenes of the narra-tive he affords us fleeting glimpses of a normative type in conservative ideology: the Tory squire, natural ruler of the besieged English countryside. To Shamela he vents his just irritation at Parson Williams, "whose family hath been raised from the dunghill by ours; and who hath received from me twenty kindnesses, and yet is not contented to destroy the game in all other places, which I freely give him leave to do; but hath the im-pudence to pursue a few hares, which I am desirous to preserve, round about this little coppice" (333). That night Booby rails against the ignorant politics of Wil-liams and the rest of the company that presumes upon his hospitality until all hours, "a parcel of scoundrels roaring forth the principles of honest men over their cups" (335).[27]

As we might expect, the opportunistic parson is of "the court-side," holding that "every Christian ought to be on the same with the bishops" (336). But Williams becomes a rather complicated satirical butt in Field-ing's conservative treatment. As a proponent of "what we believe" over "what we do" (319), Williams repre-sents for Fielding the Methodist reawakening of the old Puritan individualism and self-indulgence. The historical continuity had a real basis, and Fielding's association of the renovated doctrine of faith not only with progressive notions of "virtue" but also with empirical standards of truth is clear in the deep appre-ciation expressed by the credulous Parson Tickletext for "the useful and truly religious doctrine of *grace*" that Williams preaches (304). But Williams advocates at least a certain species of "works" as well, contend-ing "that to go to church, and to pray, and to sing psalms, and to honour the clergy, and to repent, is true religion" (319). Fielding's additional target here is, in part, the nominal observance promoted by complacent Anglican opponents of the Methodist revival. Yet much else about Shamela's favorite clergyman—doctrinal points like the conviction that a multitude of sins can "be purged away by frequent and sincere repentance," but also the haughty ease of his general manner and address—carries the cavalier associations of High Church Laudian and crypto-Jacobite culture (317-18).[28]

In this respect there is a Swiftian economy to Will-iams's overdetermination as a satiric butt, for he dem-onstrates, like Jack in *A Tale of a Tub,* how the radical subversion of Anglican orthodoxy involuntarily and stealthily recapitulates the original Roman enemy. But Fielding's Anglicanism is not Swift's, and it is not entirely clear that his two-pronged attack through the serviceable figure of Williams leaves any room for his own middle way. Like the latitudinarian divines he admired, Fielding is eloquent on the preferability of actions to words as a guide in ethical judgments. But so is the Puritan Bunyan, who excoriates Talkative for ignoring that "the soul of religion is the practice part." Whatever Fielding's contemporaries wished to believe, Puritanism and latitudinarianism are not simply antag-onists; they are closely parallel Protestant strategies for confronting the problem of mediation, and they necessarily reflect a similar instability. No less than Puritan discipline, Fielding's hearty and no-nonsense embrace of good works places a large instrumental faith in the power of worldly institutions and achievements to make a moral signification, an investment whose ideological implications could only be uncertain. The greatest commitment of this sort in *Joseph Andrews* is to the institutional practice of charity.[29]

3

As Martin Battestin has shown most fully, *Joseph Andrews* is dedicated to promulgating the two Chris-tian virtues that are embodied in its two principal characters, Joseph and Abraham Adams. Chastity and charity may be understood, respectively, as analogous private and public modes of moral restraint, the Christian capacity to limit the power of the selfish and destructive human passions. Joseph's early resistance to Lady Booby, which is the narrative's most declaratory reaction against Richardsonian example, broadly represents to us the triumph of chastity as such. If Shamela is Pamela as she really is, stripped of her feigned innocence, Joseph is Pamela as she should have been, stripped of her self-indulgence. Joseph is a reproach to Richardson's progressive protagonist because, unlike her, he masters both his sexual and his social appetites. Although he deferentially models his behavior on his older sister's, we are made to sense the unwitting and ironic contrast when he writes to her, "I never loved to tell the Secrets of my Master's Family," instantly reconciling himself to leaving Lady Booby's service so as to "maintain my Virtue against all Temptations."[30] But despite Fielding's easily insinuated parallel between the social servitude of Joseph the footman and that of Pamela the lady's maid, the sexual difference is all-important. It is not just that, as Fielding admits, a man's "Chastity is always in his own power" (I, xviii, 87). By making the issue one of male chastity, he slyly avoids all the social ramifications of female chastity.

For Richardson's Pamela, the "religious" injunction to remain chaste is overlaid by a complex "political" requirement, and she has both more to lose and more to gain—a social transformation—as the potential consequence of a liaison with her better. For Fielding's Joseph the situation is, despite appearances, much simpler. Already in love with Fanny, he must do no more than control his momentary sexual desire (I, x, 46-47). Although to Lady Booby he implies that he is chaste by virtue of being "the Brother of *Pamela*," to Pamela he writes that it is as much from Parson Adams's religious instruction as from her that he has learned "that Chastity is as great a virtue in a Man as in a Woman" (I, viii, 41, x, 46; see also xii, 53). And for Adams the principle of chastity, devoid of any social complexities, has the simple moral purpose of guarding against "the Indulgence of carnal Appetites" (IV, viii, 307). Of course succumbing to Lady Booby would bring some material reward. Adams knows that with the proper encouragement and education, Joseph might rise up the ladder of domestic service as his sister did (I, iii, 26). But the final great elevation, from service to gentility, is not within the power of Lady Booby to engineer. This is the lesson Mr. B. teaches his sister, Lady Davers, in *Pamela*. In *Joseph Andrews* Lady Booby ends up the counterpart, in this respect, of Lady Davers rather than of Mr. B., prevented from doing what Mr. Booby has done with Pamela not only by Joseph's resistance but also by her own obsessive fear that so far from raising him to her level, she has the power only "to sacrifice my Reputation, my Character, my Rank in Life, to the Indulgence of a mean and vile

Appetite" (IV, xiii, 328). Lady Booby's echo of Parson Adams's religious teachings here clearly is not a sign that she, too, believes in chastity. Instead it suggests how effectively Fielding has managed, not to refute Richardson's progressive social ethics in the great contest between "industrious virtue" and "aristocratic corruption," but to defuse its social volatility through the stealthy reversal of sexes. Adrift from its moorings in female experience, Joseph's heroically passive resistance soon becomes rather silly,[31] and in a characteristically conservative turn, neither "virtue" nor "corruption" comes off very well in the contest. In fact, so far from occupying the center stage that it has in *Pamela*, in *Joseph Andrews* the encounter quickly shrinks into an attenuated frame within which questions of virtue are most efficiently propounded in terms of the problem not of chastity but of charity.

An English Quixote obsessed with the rule of Apostolic charity, not of romance chivalry,[32] Abraham Adams reminds us of both the madness of the *hidalgo* estranged from reality and the conservative wisdom of the utopian social reformer. Traversing the circuit to London and back again, he upholds the standard of good works against a cross-section of humanity whose complacency, hypocrisy, and downright viciousness announce, again and again, the absence of charity in the modern world. The traditional proponents of charity—clergymen like Barnabas and Trulliber—abhore Methodist reform for the wrong reasons and jealously defend their own material comforts against the needs of the poor (I, xvii; II, xiv). The inheritors of the feudal obligation of charity, the country gentry, are, if possible, even worse. One squire specializes in entrapping the needy with false promises of munificence. Having been tricked himself by this man, Adams then listens in horror to "true Stories" of how the squire has ruined several local youths, among them a Pamela figure and a hopeful younger son, by feeding their expectations of upward mobility and withdrawing his support only after they have become fully dependent upon it (II, xvi-xvii). Another squire is so corrupted in sensibility and education that he has become addicted to victimizing those who have come into his care. Adams protests that "I am your Guest, and by the Laws of Hospitality entitled to your Protection" (III, vii, 247), but the practical jokes culminate in a serious attack upon his traveling party and the abduction of Fanny as a prospective "Sacrifice to the Lust of a Ravisher." The rape is foiled by Lady Booby's steward, Peter Pounce, a "Gentleman" and burlesque progressive "gallant"—the chivalric protector as monied man—who "loved a pretty Girl better than any thing, besides his own Money, or the Money of other People" (III, xii, 268-69). But needless to say, the monied man soon evinces his own species of corruption, and the adventure ends on a conservative note with Pounce replicating the sins of the selfish gentry, reviling the poor laws and asserting that charity "does not so much consist in the Act as in the Disposition" to relieve the distressed (III, xiii, 274).

The paradigmatic instance of failed charity in *Joseph Andrews* is the early stagecoach episode, in which an entire social spectrum of respectable passengers refuses to relieve Joseph's distress until the lowest of them all, the postilion, gives him his greatecoat (I, xii). Later confirmed by the humble goodness of Betty the chambermaid and the mysterious pedlar (I, xii, 55; II, xv, 170; IV, viii, 309-10), this episode establishes the basic paradox that if charity involves giving something for nothing, only those with nothing are likely to be charitable. And the traveling lawyer is of course no more compassionate than anyone else. Throughout *Joseph Andrews* the law is seen as the secularizer of traditional institutions, possessed of at least the potential to civilize their social functions for the modern world. In the progressively oriented "History of Leonora," for example, the symbolic supplanting of sword by robe nobility is intimated by the rivalry between the dishonorable fop Bellarmine, an accomplished "Cavalier," and the sober Horatio, who, "being a Lawyer . . . would seek Revenge in his own way" (II, iv, 115). Most often, however, the authority of the law in the settlement of modern disputes works only to aggravate the old thirst for "revenge" by making it financially profitable. This Adams learns when the interpolated tale of Leonora is itself interrupted by the fistfight at the inn, and a litigious bystander advises the parson's antagonist that "was I in your Circumstances, every Drop of my Blood should convey an Ounce of Gold into my Pocket" (II, v, 121). Later on Mrs. Trulliber, seeing that her husband is about to strike Adams for calling him uncharitable and un-Christian, advises him instead to "shew himself a true Christian, and take the Law of him" (II, xiv, 168).

It is a typically conservative reversal that in *Joseph Andrews* the modern institution of the law tends not to civilize the bloody passions of anger and revenge but to corrupt them, to replace physical with financial violence. And in this respect the law is a distinct deterioration from the traditional peacekeeping institutions—like Christianity—that it is quickly displacing in the modern world. When Adams delivers Fanny from her highway ravisher, he does it in the chivalric spirit of a stout "Champion" in defense of an innocent "Damsel" (II, ix, 139). But when the case is brought before the justice it is quickly corrupted by the ambitions of everyone involved for some portion of the reward. The innocents are libeled as "Robbers," "Highwaymen," and "Rogues," and they escape only through the chance intervention of a local squire and the justice's extreme obsequiousness to gentility (II, x-xi, 142-43, 145, 148-49). And when Lady Booby wishes to foil the match between Joseph and Fanny, she has no trouble persuading Lawyer Scout and Justice Frolick to help her in circumventing the settlement laws. As Scout puts it,

"The Laws of this Land are not so vulgar, to permit a mean Fellow to contend with one of your Ladyship's Fortune" (IV, iii, 285).

But if the modern purveyors of charity and justice are riddled with corruption, we are also justified in being skeptical about the efficacy of Adams's anachronistic ideals, and not simply because the parson's own means of fulfilling them are severely limited. As a comprehensive moral imperative, the rule of charity does not readily admit of fine ethical distinctions as to relative obligations and deserts, a problem of which the growing popularity of benevolist philosophies was making contemporaries aware.[33] The innkeeper Mrs. Tow-wouse is surely discredited when she exclaims to her husband, "Common Charity, a F——t!" (I, xii, 56). But her real point here is suggestively echoed later on by Adams's wife and daughter. Book IV opens with a sharp contrast between the reception of Lady Booby and that of Parson Adams on their return to their respective country seats. We are well aware of the total absence of feudal care in her ladyship, and Fielding's ironic portrait of her entry into "the Parish amidst the ringing of Bells, and the Acclamations of the Poor" is quickly followed by a sincere account of how the parson's parishioners "flocked about" him "like dutiful Children round an indulgent Parent, and vyed with each other in Demonstrations of Duty and Love" (IV, i, 277). As Mrs. Adams tells Lady Booby, her husband does indeed say "that the whole Parish are his Children," but there are children of his own on whose career prospects the parson has exercised less patriarchal care than on those of Joseph and Fanny. "It behoved every Man to take the first Care of his Family," she complains to her husband. However, Adams is oblivious, Fielding adds, persisting "in doing his Duty without regarding the Consequence it might have on his worldly Interest" (IV, xi, 321, viii, 307). There is certainly no calculation on the part of the parson, but is his virtue always untainted by his interest? Even the innocent Joseph knows how "an Ambition to be respected" can inspire acts of goodness, and Fielding has allowed us to observe how Adams's vanity can be manifested in the very denunciation of vanity (III, vi, 233, iii, 214-15). Fielding's latitudinarian beliefs are very close to the Mandevillian argument that the autonomous purity of virtue is a pleasing fiction. And although we clearly are not encouraged to see the parson's undiscriminating love of his neighbor as a stealthy self-love, nevertheless, to a real degree, the Apostolic and feudal role of charity is itself demystified in *Joseph Andrews* as a Quixotic social fiction.

By the same token, although Fielding surely strips modern institutions like the law and the gentry of their authority, at times the assault is moderated and the reigning fictions are allowed a certain instrumental utility. We have already seen this to be true of the law in *Jonathan Wild* and of gentility in *Shamela.* When

Mr. Booby discovers that his brother-in-law has been ordered to Bridewell for, in Justice Frolick's sage words, "a kind of felonious larcenous thing," he is shocked by the triviality and brutality of the law. But the justice is happy to commit Joseph and Fanny to Booby's benevolent custody instead, easily discerning now, with the kindly lechery that often distinguishes Fielding's basically good-natured men, that Fanny's beauty deserves better than Bridewell (IV, v, 289-91). And at the end of the narrative, Booby calls to mind his own briefly normative incarnation in **Shamela,** becoming the true representative of feudal gentility by dispensing gifts of "unprecedented Generosity" and by entertaining the assembled company "in the most splendid manner, after the Custom of the old *English* Hospitality, which is still preserved in some very few Families in the remote Parts of *England*" (IV, xvi, 343, 341).

At such moments of affirmation, customary noblesse oblige and the hallowed system of the English law seem able to redeem themselves as the best scheme of social justice available, if also the only one. But this is not to say that they are also able to counter the endemic condition of status inconsistency—perhaps the more precise term for Fielding would be "status indeterminacy." In a central chapter of **Joseph Andrews,** Fielding characteristically affirms that social distinctions are merely formal, being determined neither by birth nor by accomplishments but by fashion (II, xiii, 156-58). "*High* People" are distinguished from "*Low* People" by the way they dress, and the great "Ladder of Dependance," of which social hierarchy consists, is a closely articulated chain of employments, each of which attends upon its next-highest neighbor and is attended upon, in turn, by the next-lowest one. The function of attendance is essentially the same; what differs is the level at which it is done. Thus social station is arbitrary: the relative placement of a Walpole or a Wild— of a Booby or a Slipslop (I, vii, 34)—is quite accidental. But if the ladder is a fiction in that its rungs are placed arbitrarily, the ladder itself is systematic and functional. And if there is no basis for affirming the justice of the present arrangement, there is no reason to suppose that any systematic alteration would be an improvement. To be sure, there are exceptions to the rule of status inconsistency. Fielding "could name a Commoner raised higher above the Multitude by superior Talents, than is in the Power of his Prince to exalt him," but he also "could name a Peer no less elevated by Nature than by Fortune" (III, i, 190-91; cf. III, vi, 235). The very ease with which exceptions to all rules can be enumerated seems to strengthen the implacability of the system itself, which continues remorselessly to grind out the present dispensation, certainly no better, but probably no worse, than any replacement for it might do.

Something akin to this quiet desperation must be the issue of any direct attempt to distill Fielding's stance on matters of social justice and reform—on questions of virtue—in **Joseph Andrews.** And it is strikingly discordant with the genial and confident exuberance of the voice that self-consciously suffuses so much of the narrative. How does his stance on questions of truth help palliate Fielding's social vision? Calling itself, on the title page and at various points throughout the narrative, a true and authentic history, **Joseph Andrews** deploys the range of authenticating devices and claims to historicity with which we have become familiar not only in Fielding's predecessors but also in his own earlier efforts.[34] His extreme skepticism is never really in doubt, but it is conveyed to us through a characteristic combination of parodic impersonation and self-subversive definition that undertakes the positing of a form by a series of contradictory negations. In Chapter I, for example, Fielding specifies his "History" as a biographical life; yet after a brief allusion to ancient Roman biographies, his chief instances of this form are several late-medieval redactions of chivalric romance (I, i, 17-18).[35] Moreover, two eminent modern examples are autobiographies that work, "as the common Method is, from authentic Papers and Records"; but these are none other than Cibber's *Apology* and *Pamela* (I, i, 18).

In the first chapter of Book III (185-91) Fielding picks up, where this early discussion left off, the account of what he means by "history," and now he is prepared to be more explicit in his epistemological reversals. Whatever "Authority" they may be accorded by the vulgar, books that bear the title "the History of *England,* the History of *France,* of *Spain,* &c." are really the work of "Romance-Writers." The skeptical reader is correct to judge them "as no other than a Romance, in which the Writer hath indulged a happy and fertile Invention," for it is in biography "that Truth only is to be found." Of course no one would deny that the aforementioned "histories" can be relied upon for the quantitative and topographical recording of isolated "Facts." "But as to the Actions and Characters of Men," the very same facts can be "set forth in a different Light." Biography is concerned with this more qualitative sort of truth. The "Facts we deliver may be relied on" because their truth is understood to be fully dependent upon the interpretive "light" in which they are "set forth." Biography aims at the truth of general nature and of universal types. A good example is the "true History" of Gil Blas or Don Quixote: the "Time and Place" of Cervantes' characters may well be questioned, but "is there in the World such a Sceptic as to disbelieve the Madness of *Cardenio,* the Perfidy of *Ferdinand . . . ?*"

It is clear enough that Fielding is seeking here to distinguish between a naively empiricist and a more "imaginative" species of belief. But he is also at pains to emphasize the crucial degree to which he is in accord with the empiricist perspective, and to distinguish his preferred sort of belief also from the sheer creativity of romance.[36] For he quickly adds, "I would by no means be thought to comprehend" in this preferred category "the Authors of immense Romances" or of *chroniques scandaleuses,* "who without any Assistance from Nature or History, record Persons who never were, or will be, and Facts which never did nor possibly can happen: Whose Heroes are of their own Creation." Both romancers and romancing historians, in other words, rely too much on a "happy and fertile invention." As a biographer, Fielding is "contented to copy Nature" and to write "little more than I have seen," aiming not at all to repudiate the evidence of the senses but to do full justice to its complexity. And the category "true History," in which he places *Joseph Andrews* at the conclusion of the chapter, provides a positive term for the complicated dance of double negation—neither romance nor history—in which his extreme skepticism has thus far consisted.

Another such category, of course, is "comic romance." Fielding's "Preface" to *Joseph Andrews* is as celebrated as it is in part because it so explicitly announces the fact that this is a project in epistemological and generic categorization, an effort to describe a "kind of Writing, which I do not remember to have seen hitherto attempted in our Language," and which "no Critic hath thought proper to . . . assign . . . a particular Name to itself" (3). Fielding's taxonomic procedure in the "Preface" is self-consciously imitative of Aristotle's, but only up to a point. For given the normative meaning of "history" in Fielding's redefinition of the term, the invidious Aristotelian distinction between "history" and "poetry" can hold no attraction for him. So despite its crucial importance in most of his other generic considerations, in what has become the most famous of all the term "history" makes no appearance whatsoever. Even so, "comic romance" is an appropriate substitute for "true history." Together these terms resuscitate the two generic categories Fielding's extreme skepticism has decisively discredited, and the adjectival addition in each case signifies that the naiveté of the original category has been corrected by (a Cervantic procedure) conjoining it more closely with its supposed antithesis.[37]

How does "romance" correct "history" in the body of *Joseph Andrews?* Most obviously, in the parodic and self-subversive deployment of the claim to historicity that I have already noted. But as in *Jonathan Wild,* all modes of self-conscious narration work here to subjectify the objective historicity of the narrative line. On the micronarrative level these reflexive intrusions are everywhere, and they are most amusing when Fielding's ostensible purpose is not to frankly advertise his control of the plot but on the contrary to underwrite a self-effacing authenticity.[38] On the macronarrative level, authorial intrusion amounts to a quite palpable in-terruption of the main action by apparently unrelated episodes. On such occasions, the challenge to the historical criterion of truth involves replacing the linear coherence of contiguity by—not chaos, but the alternative coherence of relations of similarity, which are simply too neat to be "natural." The most complex instance of this in *Joseph Andrews* occurs in Book III, when the "authentic History" of Fanny's rape (ix, 255) is interrupted by two successive chapters of static dialogue, first between the poet and the player and then between Joseph and Adams (x, xi). The first discourse, disclaimed as "of no other Use in this History, but to divert the Reader" (x, 259), concerns the power of actors to affect for good or ill the material that authors give them to work with. The second discourse, acknowledged as "a sort of Counterpart of this" (x, 264), debates the proper degree of human submission to "the Dispensations of Providence." And when at last we irritably return to Fanny's plight, we find that the "main plot" has really been continued rather than suspended by these analogous "episodes," since she was destined all along to be delivered by Peter Pounce (had we only had patience enough to submit ourselves to Fielding's narrative dispensations).[39]

Because *Joseph Andrews* is periodically punctuated by coincidental meetings that increasingly seem too neat to be natural—Joseph with Adams (I, xiv, 64), Adams with Fanny (II, x, 143), Joseph with Fanny (II, xii, 154-55), Fanny with Peter Pounce (III, xii, 269)—its entire plot gradually takes on the air of a "historical" line that has been charmed, by the magical intrusions of "romance," into a circle. Yet there is one coincidental discovery, Joseph's meeting with Mr. Wilson, that is different from these in that our intrusive author denies us the crucial knowledge needed to distinguish it from the random ongoingness of everyday history—the knowledge that Mr. Wilson is Joseph's father. (Thus our ignorance of our hero's lineal descent at this point preserves the impression of linear contingency.) We cannot say that we have not been warned—although the early clues are rather ambiguous. True, there have been "romance" intimations of Joseph's genealogical gentility in what we have heard of his external appearance (I, viii, 38-39, xiv, 61). But readers have long since become used to hearing such things said of progressive protagonists who possess "true," as distinct from inherited, gentility, especially in narratives that progressively insist, as here, that their heroes are capable "of acquiring Honour" even in the total absence of ancestry (I, ii, 21). In other words, Fielding's "romance" conventions are equally parodic, antiromance conventions, and they create in us the erroneous expectation of an empiricist and a progressive ending.[40]

So as his long-lost child, innocently returned to his place of birth, sits listening, Mr. Wilson concludes the history of his life with the only episode for which he cannot gratefully thank "the great Author," the theft of his eldest son by gypsies. Shortly thereafter the three travelers renew their journey. Joseph and Adams are soon lost in discourse about the rival claims of nature and nurture, until they find themselves all at once in "a kind of natural Amphitheatre," nature reworked by art, whose trees "seemed to have been disposed by the Design of the most skillful Planter . . . [And] the whole Place might have raised romantic Ideas in elder Minds than those of *Joseph* and *Fanny,* without the Assistance of Love" (III, iii, 224, v, 232). Here the travelers rest, and here our own author, as though encouraging us to rest in his analogous design, informs us that Mr. Wilson plans to pass through Parson Adams's parish in a week's time, "a Circumstance which we thought too immaterial to mention before." And as a pledge of his good will Fielding ends this chapter by letting the reader in on what the next contains, "for we scorn to betray him into any such Reading, without first giving him Warning" (III, v, 233). Thus the narrative power of imposition is defused by being made explicit, and the incredibility of "romance" coincidence is gently softened into a benign and watchful disposition of the author. When Mr. Wilson's visit later turns out to coincide remarkably with other events to which it is intimately related, Fielding will remind us that we knew it was going to happen (IV, xv, 338), as though now encouraging us toward an instrumental belief in a palpable fiction in which, after all, we are already to this degree knowingly invested. The last chapter heading—"In which this true History is brought to a happy Conclusion"—finely balances the claims of history and romance contrivance, and its closing words pleasantly insist upon the present historicity of Fielding's characters, as if counting on us to know the sort of belief with which to honor that claim (IV, xvi, 339, 343-44).

It is tempting to say that questions of truth and virtue merge with the climactic discovery of Joseph's parentage. Certainly it is a scene of contrivance calculated enough to permit the ghosts of romance idealism and aristocratic ideology to be raised simultaneously. But the effect depends so fully on the delicate balance of our liaison with our author that the relation is most accurately seen not as a merging but as a subsumption of questions of virtue by questions of truth. Not that Fielding does anything now to discourage our (highly provisional) belief in the benevolent authority of the gentry and the law. Thus far he has led us to associate Joseph's social elevation—the overcoming of his status inconsistency—with the interested goodness of Mr. Booby, who not only improves the law of Justice Frolick but immediately thereafter has Joseph "drest like a Gentleman" (IV, v, 292). If anything, Mr. Booby's charity increases in the last episodes of the narrative. But of course the real agent of Joseph's upward mobility, Fielding's narrative procedure insists, is not noblesse oblige at all; it is the good will of our benevolent author. Social justice and the rule of charity are most dependably institutionalized not in the law or the gentry but in the patriarchal care of the narrator, who internalizes the charity of an imagined "old English hospitality."

The representatives of the archaic feudal order that one finds among Fielding's characters are plentiful enough, but they are hedged about with a suppositional aura that we detect also in the power of providence—in some respects analogous to the power of the old gentry in Fielding—largely because of the perpetual association of providence with the more manifest power of the author. Not that he would have us doubt for a moment the reality of divine justice. But the belief in it that Fielding argues for most energetically tends to be a well-rationalized and instrumental one. And meanwhile we are able to experience the palpable poetic justice of the narrator—why not call it providence?—who periodically intrudes into the daily life of story so as to ensure there what divine and human justice manifestly do not ensure in the world outside.[41] Fielding's subsumption of questions of virtue by questions of truth transfers the major challenge of utopian projection from the substantive to the formal realm. And a central reason for this, we may speculate, is the relative uncertainty of his commitment to the utopian institutions and communities envisioned by conservative ideology. Attracted, on the other hand, to the energy of the career open to talents, Fielding was appalled by the vanity and pretension of those who enacted that career with any success or conviction. Accordingly, what "happens" at the end of *Joseph Andrews* (and *Tom Jones*) is less a social than an epistemological event; not upward mobility but—as in the invoked model of *Oedipus* (IV, xv, 336)—the acquisition of knowledge.

The subsumption is anticipated in *Joseph Andrews* in its two most extended discussions of formal strategy, the "Preface" and the first chapter of Book III. In both discussions Fielding's extreme sensitivity to the analogous relation between questions of truth and questions of virtue leads him to exemplify the former by the latter. Thus we are told in the "Preface" that comic romance works through the discovery of affectation, as when we find someone "to be the exact Reverse of what he affects." And the exemplary cases of affectation are also cases of status inconsistency: a "dirty Fellow" who "descend[s] from his Coach and Six, or bolt[s] from his Chair with his Hat under his Arm"; or a "wretched Family" in whose presence we find an "Affectation of Riches and Finery either on their Persons or in their Furniture" (9). Later on Fielding qualifies his technique of representing universal types in biography by acknowledging that life admits of exceptions to the rule. And the exceptions singled out for comment are those elevated individuals whose social status is, surprisingly enough, consistent with their "superior Talents" and "Mind" (III, i, 190). The ease with which formal argument comprehends the substantive social problem in both of these passages, by treating as an exemplary case, prefigures the increasing facility with which Fielding's charitable narrator will tacitly compensate for the failure of social—and providential—mechanisms to justify our provisional credence, by mobilizing narrative's own more perfect versions of them. Fielding's reflexive narration permits the discursive argument of the instrumentality of a belief in what cannot be shown to be credible to infiltrate narrative form itself. And once acclimatized, it becomes an automatic and all-purpose gesture of reconciliation, an invisible thread of affirmation that is as unconditional as the fact of the narrative form into which it has been woven. Approaching it from a very different direction, Fielding meets Richardson at the nexus where moral and social pedagogy hesitate on the edge of their transformation into something else entirely, aesthetic pleasure. . . .

Notes

[1] During Henry Fielding's lifetime the family was thought to derive from the Hapsburgs, a spurious genealogy that was concocted once Denbigh's main line had been raised to the peerage after his marriage to the Duke of Buckingham's sister in 1622. On Fielding's lineage and on the custody suit, see Wilber L. Cross, *The History of Henry Fielding*, 3 vols. (New Haven: Yale University Press, 1918), vol. I, chap. 1. On the inflation of honors under Buckingham and James I, see [*The Origins of the English Novel, 1600-1740*, by Michael McKeon (Baltimore: The Johns Hopkins University Press, 1987); hereafter cited as *Origins*,] chap. 4, n. 31. For Richardson's sensitivity see Samuel Richardson to David Graham, May 3, 1750, in *Selected Letters of Samuel Richardson*, ed. John Carroll (Oxford: Clarendon Press, 1964), 158.

[2] Henry Fielding, *The Author's Farce*, ed. Charles B. Woods, Regents Restoration Drama Series (Lincoln: University of Nebraska Press, 1966), II, x, 15-17 (the speaker is the hero's beloved). For the unity of time see idem, *Historical Register*, ed. William W. Appleton, Regents Restoration Drama Series (Lincoln: University of Nebraska Press, 1967), I, 58-59, 66-69, where Sourwit wonders "how you can bring the actions of a whole year into the circumference of four-and-twenty hours," and Medley replies, "My register is not to be filled like those of vulgar news-writers with trash for want of news, and therefore if I say little or nothing, you may thank those who have done little or nothing." See Fielding's *Jonathan Wild* (1743), I, vii, and *Tom Jones* (1749), II, i, for a similar comparison and argument. Ronald Paulson, *Satire and the Novel in Eighteenth-Century England* (New Haven: Yale University Press, 1967), 52-53, observes the affinity between Pope's and Fielding's satire on the spectacles of "the

Smithfield Muses." On the analogy of world and stage see J. Paul Hunter, *Occasional Form: Henry Fielding and the Chains of Circumstance* (Baltimore: Johns Hopkins University Press, 1975), 57-67; see also Hunter's suggestive discussion of reflexiveness in Fielding's drama (69-74). On the formal relations between drama and narrative see [*Origins*], chap. 3, nn. 81-86.

[3] *Jonathan Wild* was published in 1743 as Volume III of the *Miscellanies*. On its composition see F. Homes Dudden, *Henry Fielding: His Life, Works, and Times* (Oxford: Clarendon Press, 1952), I, 480-483; Bertrand A. Goldgar, *Walpole and the Wits: The Relation of Politics to Literature, 1722-1742* (Lincoln: University of Nebraska Press, 1976), 197-98. On the extent and character of Fielding's historiographical reading see Robert M. Wallace, "Fielding's Knowledge of History and Biography," *Studies in Philology*, 44, no. 1 (Jan., 1947), 89-107.

[4] For the primary critique of traditional biography see Henry Fielding, *Jonathan Wild*, ed. A. R. Humphreys and Douglas Brooks (London: Everyman's Library, 1973), I, ii-iii, 5-9; II, xii, 79-81; III, vi, 100-01 (hereafter cited as *Jonathan Wild* [Everyman's ed.]). All parenthetical references in the text are to this edition and include book, chapter, and page numbers. In these examples, the second-level critique occurs where the supernatural intrusion of dolphins and sea horses is disowned only to be replaced by the ostentatiously "natural" intrusion of authorial rationales, and the eloquence of modern heroes also is shown to be an invention. For parody of the authenticating devices of criminal biography see ibid., I, vii, 22, xiii, 36; II, vii, 67-68; III, vi, 100, vii, 103; IV, xii-xiii, 163-65, xiv, 169. On the form of criminal biography see [*Origins*], chap. 3, nn. 16-24. Among the several models available to Fielding for the writing of this particular life was Daniel Defoe's *True and Genuine Account of the Life and Actions of the late Jonathan Wild; not Made up out of Fiction & Fable, but Taken from his own Mouth, and Collected from Papers of his own Writing* (1725). On Wild's contemporary notoriety see William R. Irwin, *The Making of Jonathan Wild: A Study in the Literary Method of Henry Fielding* (New York: Columbia University Press, 1941), chap. 1. Maximillian Novak observes in Fielding and Swift a similar distrust of the materials of criminal biography as conducive to a "wrong kind of art"; see his *Realism, Myth, and History in Defoe's Fiction* (Lincoln: University of Nebraska Press, 1983), 122.

[5] For *Jonathan Wild* as a normatively stable mock-heroic, see William J. Farrell, "The Mock-Heroic Form of *Jonathan Wild*," *Modern Philology*, 63, no. 3 (Feb., 1966), 216-26. On its formal instability see John M. Steadman, *Milton and the Renaissance Hero* (Oxford: Clarendon Press, 1967), 173; and C. J. Rawson, *Henry*

Fielding and the Augustan Ideal under Stress (London: Routledge and Kegan Paul, 1972), 158. On the relation between the critique of ancient heroes and that of ancient historians in *Jonathan Wild,* see ibid., 148-55.

[6] On the Machiavellian connection see, generally, Bernard Shea, "Machiavelli and Fielding's *Jonathan Wild,*" *PMLA* [*Publications of the Modern Language Association*], 72, no. 1 (March, 1957), 54-73. Shea argues that Fielding was indebted to the 1695 translation of Machiavelli by the republican Henry Neville, and he sees an especially close parallel between Fielding's version of Wild's career and the *Life of Castruccio Castracani of Lucca* (ibid., 66-73). On Machiavellian *virtù* see [*Origins*] chap. 5, nn. 16-18. On the common application of the term "great man" to Walpole for purposes of both praise and blame, see John E. Wells, "Fielding's Political Purpose in *Jonathan Wild,*" *PMLA,* 28, no. 1 (1913), 14-19.

[7] Henry Fielding, "An Essay on Conversation," in *Miscellanies by Henry Fielding, Esq;* (1743), vol. I, ed. Henry K. Miller (Oxford: Clarendon Press, 1972), 138, 140; Henry Fielding, "An Essay on Nothing," ibid., 186. In his imaginary voyages of Job Vinegar, Fielding satirizes the belief of the Ptfghsiumgski or "Inconstants" that the virtues of the nobility "descend in a perpetual Line to their Posterity"; see *Champion,* no. 106 (July 17, 1740), in "The Voyages of Mr. Job Vinegar," ed. S. J. Sackett, *Augustan Reprint Society,* no. 67 (1958), 7.

[8] Compare Henry Fielding, *The Covent-Garden Journal,* ed. Gerard E. Jensen (New Haven: Yale University Press, 1915), no. 4 (Jan. 14, 1752), I, 156, where Fielding defines "Honour" simply as "Duelling." For other instances of Fielding's ironic subversion of gentility and aristocratic honor see Glenn W. Hatfield, *Henry Fielding and the Language of Irony* (Chicago: University of Chicago Press, 1968), 19-20, 117-18, 163-65, 168-73. Rawson is particularly sensitive to the comic oafishness of Fielding's protagonist; see his *Henry Fielding,* especially chap. 4.

[9] The corollary is explicit in Fielding's diatribes against hereditary honor. E.g., see Henry Fielding, *The Champion,* 2 vols (1741), Nov. 17, 1739, I, 8, 10-11: "This Esteem for hereditary Honour was at so high a Pitch among [the ancient Romans], that they looked on the *Plebians* as Persons of almost a different Species, which may, I think, be collected from the Appelation they gave to what we call an Upstart, namely, *Novus Homo, a new Man* . . . I have often wondered how such Words as *Upstart, First of his Family, &c.* crept into a Nation, whose Strength and Support is Trade . . . For my Part, I am at a Loss to see why a Man, who has brought 100,000 *l.* into his Country by a beneficial Trade, is not as worthy and honourable a Member of

the Community, as he who hath spent that Sum abroad, or sent it thither after *French* Wines and *French* Foppery."

[10] Paulson, *Satire and the Novel,* 75, argues that John Gay's *The Beggar's Opera* (1728) "was Fielding's most important source for the use of the heroic level as a parallel instead of a contrast to his subject." Fielding's own *Don Quixote in England* (1734) uses the wise madness of the Cervantic protagonist to discern the rogue in the statesman or vice versa; see Paulson, *Satire and the Novel,* 89. On the assimilationism of rogues and statesmen compare Fielding's account of *Jonathan Wild* in the "Preface" to the *Miscellanies,* ed. cit., I, 13: "This Bombast Greatness then is the Character I intend to expose . . . [which takes] to itself not only Riches and Power, but often Honour, or at least the Shadow of it." In his *Brief and true History of Robert Walpole and his Family From Their Original to the Present Time* . . . (1738), William Musgrave spends thirty-eight pages tracing Walpole's lineage up from the Norman Conquest. Among his sources are "several ancient Charters in the Custody of the Right Honourable Sir *Robert Walpole,* who out of Regard to Literature, and the Memory of his Ancestors, favoured me with the Perusal of them" (2).

[11] Fielding is not the only writer to see the possibilities of this sort of generic conflation. *The Statesman's Progress* . . . (1741), an anonymous parodic fusion of *The Pilgrim's Progress* and *The Life and Death of Mr. Badman,* narrates the allegorical journey of a rogue figure toward "Greatness Hill"; see Irwin's discussion in *The Making of Jonathan Wild,* 46-47. For the classic conservative reduction see *Champion,* June 10, 1740, II, 318. On the fortuitous accident of birth see [*Origins*], n. 7. Compare *Champion,* Dec. 6, 1739, I, 66, 67, where Fielding gives a characteristically conservative account of Oliver Cromwell's career as exemplifying the Juvenalian maxim that *"Fortune often picks a great Man, in Jest, out of the lowest of People."* Cromwell is the Machiavellian "new prince" who owes his power "principally to Chance; namely, to the Death of those great Men whom the long Continuance of the Civil War had exhausted; those who begun [sic] that War would have disdained to have seen the Nation enslaved to the absolute Will of a Subject, in Rank very little above the common Level." For related conservative accounts of the macronarrative of the English Revolution see [*Origins*], chap. 6, n. 18.

[12] Conservative ideologues were able to understand marriages of convenience as an institution of aristocratic culture given new life by the culture's supposed, progressive antagonist. For another context in which Fielding clearly associates such marriages with the new monied culture, see *Champion,* no. 114 (Aug. 5, 1740), in "Voyages of Mr. Job Vinegar," ed. cit., 15-17. Paulson, *Satire and the Novel,* 80, remarks on the charac-

teristic inadequacy of Fielding's "great" villains as lovers, in contrast to their political and financial success; cf. Justice Squeezum in Fielding's *Rape upon Rape; or, The Coffee-House Politician* (1730). For the parallel between theft and financial investment, and for the conservative hierarchy of appetites, see [*Origins*], chap. 6, nn. 31, 53-54.

[13] Hatfield, *Henry Fielding,* 40.

[14] Henry Fielding, "An Essay on the Knowledge of the Characters of Men," in *Miscellanies,* ed. cit., I, 154-55; *Champion,* no. 98 (June 28, 1740), in "Voyages of Mr. Job Vinegar," ed. cit., 5. In a parody of the Royal Society's *Philosophical Transactions,* Fielding combines the critique of naive empiricism with the critique of the naive progressive enchantment with money; see "Some Papers Proper to be Read before the R——l Society, Concerning the Terrestrial Chrysipus, Golden-Foot or Guinea," in *Miscellanies,* ed. cit., I, 191-204. (For other satirical allusions to the Royal Society by Fielding see ibid., p. xl, n. 1; and Hatfield, *Henry Fielding,* pp. 30-31 and n. 8.). With Fielding's cult of MNEY compare Eliza Haywood's cult of Lust and Pecunia in her *Memoirs of a Certain Island* (1725), [*Origins*], chap. 6, n. 53.

[15] E.g., cf. Allan Wendt, "The Moral Allegory of *Jonathan Wild,*" ELH [English Literary History], 24 (1970), 302-20; and Rawson, *Henry Fielding,* chap. 7.

[16] Henry Fielding, *The Journal of a Voyage to Lisbon* (1755), printed with *Jonathan Wild* (Everyman's ed.), "Author's Preface," I, 187; see, generally, 183-88. The deleted chapter is IV, ix of the 1743 edition. Its subtitle invokes the maxim "strange, therefore true": "A very wonderful chapter indeed; which, to those who have not read many voyages, may seem incredible; and which the reader may believe or not, as he pleases" (*The Life of Mr Jonathan Wild the Great* [London: Shakespeare Head, n.d.], IV, ix, 196). For a parody of the self-advertising mode in travel narratives see *Champion,* no. 112 (July 31, 1740), in "Voyages of Mr. Job Vinegar," ed. cit., 12-15. Fielding precedes this parodic political allegory by complaining that "there are a sort of Men so sceptical in their Opinions, that they are unwilling to believe any Thing which they do not see . . . Several excellent Accounts of *Asia* and *Africa* have been look'd on as little better than fabulous Romances. But if a Traveller hath the good Fortune to satisfy his Curiosity by the Discovery of any new Countries, any Islands never before known, his Reader allows him no more Credit than is given to the Adventures of *Cassandra,* or the celebrated Countess *Danois's Fairy Tales.* To omit *Robinson Cruso,* and other grave Writers, the facetious Capt. *Gulliver* is more admired, I believe, for his Wit than his Truth" (*Champion,* no. 55 [March 20, 1740], in "Voyages of Mr. Job Vinegar," ed. cit. 1). See also Fielding's imaginary voyage,

which opens with the discovered manuscript topos and has been refused by the Royal Society (according to its discoverer) because "there was nothing in it wonderful enough for them": *A Journey from This World to the Next* (1743), ed. C. J. Rawson (London: Everyman's Library, 1973), 2. As Rawson observes (viii-xiii), the formal self-consciousness of the *Journey* seems to be aimed both at a Lucianic or Scriblerian satire of "learned" works and at a parody of the modern claim to historicity. Fielding much admired the works of Lucian, among them the *True History;* see the discussion in Henry K. Miller, *Essays on Fielding's Miscellanies: A Commentary on Volume One* (Princeton: Princeton University Press, 1961), 366-86.

[17] With Mrs. Heartfree's tale compare the first account of Bavia's adventures in W. P., *The Jamaica Lady; or, The Life of Bavia* (1720), in which Bavia refuses the advances of the ship's captain on the grounds "that her honor was dearer to her than her life," but promises him, in exchange for her deliverance, "one rich jewel of a very great value, which she brought with her by accident." The skeptical audience to this account, Captain Fustian, "believed it (as he afterwards found it) all a romance." See William H. McBurney, ed., *Four before Richardson: Selected English Novels, 1720-1727* (Lincoln: University of Nebraska Press, 1963), 100, 102. For the common "jewel/jewel" metaphor see, e.g., Samuel Richardson, *Pamela* (1740), ed. T. C. Duncan Eaves and Ben D. Kimpel (Boston: Houghton Mifflin, 1971), 166.

[18] See *Champion,* Jan. 22, 1740, I, 208-9 (cf. Heartfree on the same subject, *Jonathan Wild* [Everyman's ed.], III, ii, 88-89); Fielding, "An Essay on Conversation," in *Miscellanies,* ed. cit., I, 127-28.

[19] On the political significance of Fielding's family background see Brian McCrea, *Henry Fielding and the Politics of Mid-Eighteenth Century England* (Athens: University of Georgia Press, 1981), chap. 2. For documentation of Fielding's great admiration for Marlborough see ibid., 217n.19. Contrast Swift and other conservative authors, [*Origins*], chap. 5, n. 55; chap. 6, nn. 24-25. McCrea's useful argument nevertheless ignores some important evidence of Fielding's profound distaste for monied culture. For a review of the evidence for the general proposition that Fielding took money from Walpole, and for the particular role of *Jonathan Wild* in this relationship, see Martin C. Battestin, "Fielding's Changing Politics and *Joseph Andrews,*" *Philological Quarterly,* 39, no. 1 (Jan., 1960), 39-55; Goldgar, *Walpole and the Wits,* 197-98, 205-7. Goldgar (219) summarizes how most of the men of letters contemporary with Fielding "sought some accommodation with the administration." Fielding later defended a writer's changing sides for money; see *The Jacobite's Journal,* ed. W. B. Coley (Oxford: Oxford University Press, for Wesleyan University Press, 1975),

no. 17 (March 26, 1748), 215.

[20] For Fielding's extreme skepticism, compare *Champion*, March 1, 1740, I, 322: "Writing seems to be understood as arrogating to yourself a Superiority (which of all others will be granted with the greatest Reluctance) of the Understanding . . . *The Understanding, like the Eye* (says Mr. *Lock*) *whilst it makes us see and perceive all other Things, takes no Notice of itself; and it requires Art and Pains to set it at a Distance and make it its own Object.* This Comparison, fine as it is, is inadequate: For the Eye can contemplate itself in a Glass, but no *Narcissus* hath hitherto discovered any *Mirrour* for the Understanding, no Knowledge of which is to be obtained but by the Means Mr. *Lock* prescribes, which as it requires Art and Pains, or in other Words, a very good Understanding to execute, it generally happens that the Superiority in it, is a Cause tried on every dark and presumptive Evidence, and a Verdict commonly found by self Love for ourselves." On Lockean epistemology and the analogy between knowledge and visual sense perception see [*Origins*], chap. 2, nn. 31-32, 36. On the parallel between magistrate and narrator see the discussion in Paulson, *Satire and the Novel*, 96.

[21] For a related argument concerning what he calls Fielding's "language of irony" see Hatfield, *Henry Fielding*, esp. chap. 6.

[22] The device was common in the French antiromance: cf. [Charles Sorel], *The Extravagant Shepherd* . . . (1654), trans. John Davies, 193; and [Antoine Furetière], *Scarron's City Romance* . . . (1671) (a translation of Furetière's *Roman Bourgeois*), 19. See also Samuel Richardson, "Hints of Prefaces for Clarissa," 2, in *Clarissa: Preface, Hints of Prefaces, and Postscript*, ed. R. F. Brissenden, *Augustan Reprint Society*, no. 103 (1964).

[23] The unity is artificial, however, if limited to this interchange. Part II of *Pamela*, which was begun two weeks after the publication of *Shamela* in April, 1741, may be at least in part a counterdefense against it; see Owen Jenkins, "Richardson's *Pamela* and Fielding's 'Vile Forgeries,'" *Philological Quarterly*, 44 (Oct., 1965), 200-210.

[24] Henry Fielding, *An Apology for the Life of Mrs. Shamela Andrews* . . . (1741), in *Joseph Andrews and Shamela*, ed. Martin C. Battestin (Boston: Houghton Mifflin, 1961), 299, 306-8, 337, 339; all parenthetical citations to *Shamela* in the text are to this edition. A source for Fielding's credulous clergyman may be found in the Mr. Tickletext of Aphra Behn's *The Feign'd Curtezans; or, A Night's Intrigue* (1679) (see [*Origins*], chap. 3, n. 55). Fielding refers to Behn's character in discussing the absurdities of the claim to historicity in travel journals; see "Author's Preface," *Voyage to Lisbon*, 187-88. Behn's Tickletext as a source for Fielding's has been overlooked by editors of *Shamela*; see, e.g., Fielding, *Joseph Andrews and Shamela*, ed. Sheridan Baker (New York: Thomas Y. Crowell, 1972), 9-10n.9. Fielding was not the only critic of *Pamela* who used the strategy of claiming to possess the truly authentic papers; see [*Origins*], chap. 11, n. 3.

[25] See [*Origins*], chap. 6, nn. 32-34.

[26] Hugh Amory, "*Shamela* as Aesopic Satire," *ELH*, 38, no. 2 (June, 1971), 241. On Fielding's second marriage see Cross, *History of Henry Fielding*, II, 60; his first wife had died three years earlier. The parallel with Mr. B. and Pamela did not escape the notice of Fielding's critics (ibid., II, 61).

[27] With Fielding's Booby compare Swift's Lord Munodi, [*Origins*], chap. 10, n. 7. For Pamela's exultation see *Pamela*, 315.

[28] On Fielding's satire of complacent, and of High Church, Anglicanism see, respectively, Hunter, *Occasional Form*, 78-80, and Amory, "*Shamela* as Aesopic Satire," 245-46. On Methodist satire—and the relation of Methodism to Puritanism—see Eric Rothstein, "The Framework of *Shamela*," *ELH*, 35, no. 3 (1968), 389-95. On the continuity between seventeenth-century radical Protestantism and eighteenth-century Methodism see, generally, Umphrey Lee, *The Historical Backgrounds of Early Methodist Enthusiasm* (New York: Columbia University Press, 1931). For a discussion of pious, and specifically Methodist, journals, lives, and spiritual autobiographies of the 1730s and 1740s that reflect many features of their seventeenth-century predecessors, see Jerry C. Beasley, *Novels of the 1740s* (Athens: University of Georgia Press, 1982), 128-34. On the provenance of Tickletext's credulity see [*Origins*], n. 24.

[29] On the relationship between "latitudinarian" liberal Anglicanism and capitalist ideology see [*Origins*], chap. 5, nn. 42-43. Compare *Champion*, Jan. 24, 1740, I, 213: "Virtue is not . . . of that morose and rigid Nature, which some mistake her to be . . . she has been known to raise some to the highest Dignities in the State, in the Army, and in the Law. So that we find Virtue and Interest are not . . . as repugnant as Fire and Water." For the defense of actions over words see *Champion*, Dec. 11, 1739, I, 79; and Fielding, "An Essay on the Knowledge of the Characters of Men," in *Miscellanies*, ed. cit., I, 162-63 (cf. *Jonathan Wild* [Everyman's ed.], IV, xv, 174). On the stealthy recapitulation in Swift's *Tale*, and its relation to the double reversal of extreme skepticism, see [*Origins*], chap. 5, n. 36.

[30] Henry Fielding, *The History of the Adventures*

of Joseph Andrews And of his Friend Mr. Abraham Adams. Written in Imitation of The Manner of Cervantes, Author of Don Quixote (1742), ed. Martin C. Battestin (Oxford: Clarendon Press, 1967), I, v, 29-30, x, 47 (hereafter cited as *Joseph Andrews*). All parenthetical citations in the text and in the notes of this chapter are to this edition, and include book, chapter, and page numbers. While still in her service, Joseph hopes "your Ladyship can't tax me with ever betraying the Secrets of the Family, and I hope, if you was to turn me away, I might have the Character of you" (ibid., I, v, 29). When he later learns that Lady Booby "would not give him a Character," Joseph says that he will nonetheless always give her "a good Character where-ever he went" (ibid., IV, i, 279). On the importance of these matters of "character" in *Pamela,* see [*Origins*], chap. 11. n. 18. On Joseph and Abraham as embodiments of chastity and charity, see Martin C. Battestin, *The Moral Basis of Fielding's Art: A Study of Joseph Andrews* (Middletown, Ct.: Wesleyan University Press, 1959), chaps. 2, 3, and passim.

[31] Many critics have observed this. However, it is worth noting that what is ludicrous is not male chastity itself but the spuriously social resonance it acquires in this particular encounter. On male chastity see [*Origins*], chap. 4, n. 40.

[32] See the observations of Paulson, *Satire and the Novel,* 120.

[33] E.g., see Samuel Johnson, *Rambler,* no. 99 (Feb. 26, 1751), in *The Rambler,* ed. W. J. Bate and Albrecht B. Strauss, Yale Edition of the Works of Samuel Johnson (New Haven: Yale University Press, 1969), II, 164-69.

[34] E.g., see *Joseph Andrews,* I, ii, 20, xvi, 71-72; II, xv, 168; III, vi, 235, vii, 246, ix, 255; IV, v, 289, xvi, 339.

[35] In *Jacobite's Journal,* ed. cit., no. 13 (Feb. 27, 1748), 177-78, Fielding attacks Thomas Carte's *General History of England* as a "great Romance," compares it to these same popular romances, and advises that if published serially as they are, it should have as good a sale as "the inimitable Adventures of *Robinson Crusoe.*"

[36] The difficulty of the exercise is suggested by the fact that in another context Fielding used the story of Cardenio, Ferdinand, Dorothea, and Lucinda as an example of how Cervantes "in many Instances, approaches very near to the Romances which he ridicules": *Covent-Garden Journal,* ed. cit., no. 24 (March 24, 1752), I, 281. In the absence of a stable critical theory, to reject naive empiricism inevitably risks a return to its antagonist, romance idealism.

[37] Thus, just as Fielding distinguishes his own "true history" from the naive claim to historicity that he discredits, so here he distinguishes the "comic Romance" from the serious "Romance." And we would seem to be justified in identifying the latter with "those voluminous Works commonly called *Romances*" (*Joseph Andrews,* "Preface," 3-4), that is, with the French heroic romances that he later alludes to as those "immense Romances" and that he discredits for their idealist detachment from both nature and history (see [*Origins*]). As Sheridan Baker has argued, and despite modern critical practice, the significant generic term in the "Preface" is "comic Romance" and not the pedantically exhaustive synonym "comic Epic-Poem in Prose"; see Baker's "Henry Fielding's Comic Romances," *Papers of the Michigan Academy of Science, Arts, and Letters,* 45 (1960), 441.

[38] Contrast the following passages from *Joseph Andrews:* "to which likewise he had some other Inducements which the Reader, without being a Conjurer, cannot possibly guess; 'till we have given him those hints, which it may be now proper to open" (I, x, 47); and "Indeed, I have been often assured by both, that they spent these Hours in a most delightful Conversation: but as I never could prevail on either to relate it, so I cannot communicate it to the Reader" (II, xv, 168).

[39] Compare the technique of Cervantes [*Origins*], chap. 7, sec. 1). The invasion of "historical" contiguity by "romance" similarity is especially pleasing when it occurs within an interpolated tale, which is already itself an interruption of the linear plot and which nonetheless may lay claim to being integral with it. A good example of this in *Jonathan Wild* is the disruption of Mrs. Heartfree's travel narrative by Wild's marital outrage. The best instance in *Joseph Andrews* is the progressive plot of Leonora (II, iv-vi), which is accompanied by claims to historicity but interrupted by the conservative themes that arise during Adams's fistfight at the inn.

[40] In *Joseph Andrews* Fanny also has a "natural Gentility" (II, xii, 153), so much so that once on the road she is more than once taken to be a young lady of quality either run or stolen away from her parents (III, ii, 199-200, ix, 257).

[41] Thus the status of Fielding's narratives as expressions of a belief in a providentially ordered universe seems to me far more problematic—or, at its simplest level, far less interesting—than it does to Aubrey Williams, "Interpositions of Providence and the Design of Fielding's Novels," *South Atlantic Quarterly,* 70, no. 1 (Spring, 1971), 265-86; see also Martin C. Battestin, *The Providence of Wit: Aspects of Form in Augustan Literature and the Arts* (Oxford: Clarendon Press, 1974), chap. 5. See [*Origins*], chap. 3, nn. 75-

80. For Fielding's instrumental belief in divine justice see, e.g., [*Origins*], n. 18.

James Thompson (essay date 1990)

SOURCE: "Patterns of Property and Possession in Fielding's Fiction," in *Critical Essays on Henry Fielding,* edited by Albert J. Rivero, G.K. Hall & Co., 1998, pp. 112-30. Originally published in *Eighteenth-Century Fiction,* Vol. 3, 1990, pp. 21-42.

[*In the following essay, originally published in 1990 and reprinted in 1998, Thomspon examines the importance of money and other valued objects in the context of eighteenth-century economic history. Focusing primarily on* Tom Jones, *Thompson suggests that Fielding's work reflects the instability of money—specifically cash—as a mode of social relations, responding by valorizing land and estates as true and lasting forms of wealth.*]

Henry Fielding's **Tom Jones** (1749) tells the history of a number of lost objects which range from the foundling protagonist and his patrimony to wives, daughters, a muff, and several bank notes. The most prominent story of errant money begins with the £500 Squire Allworthy gives to Tom (p. 310), which he subsequently loses (p. 313).[1] Black George appropriates the money (p. 314), and passes it on to Old Nightingale, in whose hands Squire Allworthy recognizes it (p. 920), and so it is presumably restored to Tom, the natural or rightful owner (p. 968). We are treated in similar detail to the fortunes of the £200 which Squire Western gives to Sophia (p. 359), who also loses her money (p. 610). Her wallet is found by a beggar who passes it on to Tom (pp. 631-35), and who, in turn, restores it to its proper owner: "I know the right Owner, and will restore it her . . . the right Owner shall certainly have again all that she has lost" (p. 634)—a promise which emblematizes the narrative of lost property in the novel. Partridge, of course, repeatedly urges Tom to spend the hundred pounds (pp. 675-76, 679, 711), but Tom restores it to Sophia whole: "I hope, Madame, you will find it of the same Value, as when it was lost" (p. 731).

In good Aristotelian fashion, the peripeteia in this tale of economic wandering coincides with Allworthy's recognition of his original bills: Old Nightingale, the financier or broker, announces:

> "I have the Money now in my own Hands, in five Bank Bills, which I am to lay out either in a Mortgage, or in some Purchase in the north of *England.*" The Bank Bills were no sooner produced at Allworthy's Desire, than he blessed himself at the Strangeness of the Discovery. He presently told *Nightingale,* that these Bank Bills were formerly his, and then acquainted him with the whole Affair. (p. 920).

This scene is one in a long series of recognitions, of Mrs Waters, Partridge, Tom's ancestry, his goodness, each in its own way a classic anagnorisis. But this recognition of money is by far the most curious, for it is difficult to say what, exactly, is being recognized here. Is it some true identity, ownership, or value which these bills reflect or retain and which, in the economy of plot, must be revealed and recognized? How does Allworthy recognize his notes, and, moreover, why has Fielding interpolated these little tales of monetary loss and restoration? The monetary subplot in **Tom Jones** reflects a conservative desire to stabilize cash and paper credit, and to represent and contain currency within traditional patterns of property and possession; a desire which is determined by a specific stage in the development of money. That is to say, in a view we could characterize as "late feudal" (following Ernest Mandel), Fielding domesticates cash transactions and commodities by inscribing them in a traditionally fixed, hierarchical (and agricultural) economy, where real property is the essential model for all other types of property, especially currency.[2]

Another way to put this is to say that Fielding represents cash transactions in the traditional comic form of the "lost and found": objects, characters, and values are lost, temporarily separated from their rightful owners, so that the comic plot can eventually reassert order by restoring lost objects to their owners, as if possession were a transcendent relation, unaffected by the vicissitudes of time, accumulation, and profit.[3] *The History of Tom Jones, a Foundling* opens with the discovery of a "lost" object, an infant, and the plot of the novel is concerned with the process of restoration, returning the infant to his family and thereby restoring the heir to his inheritance.[4] But the protagonist is only one of a multitude of objects lost and found in the novel; children, estates, wives, jobs, reputations, even a kingdom follow the same lost and found pattern, in which a temporary, unworthy claimant is foiled and the object is inevitably returned to its rightful owner: nothing is finally lost in **Tom Jones**.[5] Here we will focus on one representative example of this ordering pattern, the loss and restoration of money, for Fielding observes a kind of comic rule of conservation, under which it is finally impossible to lose anything.[6] The story of money in **Tom Jones** is bound up with the nature of currency in the period and its inherent instability, and so we need to understand the situation of currency in eighteenth-century English society before we can understand its function in Fielding's fiction.

The monetary system in eighteenth-century England was far more unstable than anything we are accustomed to now. To conservative observers such as

Alexander Pope, Jonathan Swift, and Henry Fielding, this instability must have accentuated their hostility to a cash nexus, the growing dependence on short-term credit and public debt.[7] In Pope's *Epistle to Bathurst,* for example, paper credit exacerbates all of the dangerously changeable, movable, fluid qualities of money, as opposed to the stability and constancy represented by land and the hereditary estate, a metonym for genealogical and possessive continuity.[8]

> Blest paper-credit! last and best supply!
> That lends Corruption lighter wings to fly!
> Gold imp'd by thee, can compass hardest things,
> Can pocket States, can fetch or carry Kings;
> A single leaf shall waft an Army o'er,
> Or ship off Senates to a distant Shore;
> A leaf, like Sibyl's, scattered to and fro
> Our fates and fortunes, as the winds shall blow.
>
> (lines 69-76)

Pope's and Fielding's hostility must be understood in the context of the social impact of paper money in early modern Europe, the significance of which Fernand Braudel explores: "If most contemporaries found money a 'difficult cabbala to understand,' this type of money, money that was not money at all, and this interplay of money and mere writing to a point where the two became confused, seemed not only complicated but diabolical. Such things were a constant source of amazement."[9] More suggestively, Marc Shell explores the correlation between language and money as representation:

> money, which refers to a system of tropes, is also an "internal" participant in the logical or semiological organization of language, which itself refers to a system of tropes. Whether or not a writer mentioned money or was aware of its potentially subversive role in his thinking, the new forms of metaphorization or exchanges of meaning that accompanied the new forms of economic symbolization and production were changing the meaning of meaning itself.[10]

The purpose of this paper is not simply to identify the notes in Nightingale's hands, but rather to explore one dimension of the historicity of Fielding's discourse by focusing on his representation of money and value; that is, to connect Fielding's narrative with a particular stage in the development of money.[11] Tracing similar forms of representation of value through Fielding's fiction, we can discern a consistent resistance to capital.

The story of eighteenth-century English currency, in terms of both economic practice and economic theory, turns on three interrelated factors: the rapid expansion of the economy; the establishment of mechanisms for credit on which that expansion was predicated; and the shortage of government-issued currency—copper, silver, and gold coins. Until 1797 coin was the only legal tender in England, and yet a vast number of financial transactions had to be carried on by other means. Because silver fetched a higher price in the Far East and on the continent than the price established by statute for the English Mint, newly minted silver coins, and later gold and copper as well, were culled from circulation, melted down, and shipped abroad as bullion— an illegal, but profitable and therefore common practice. The long-term history of a coinage always follows an endless cycle of issue, eventual debasement from wear, clipping, and counterfeiting, leading to the necessity of large scale recoinage. In this period, however, recoinage (in 1696-98 and 1773-74, as well as the devaluation of the guinea in 1717) had little or no effect on the number of coins in circulation, precisely because the new, heavier coins were the readiest targets for melting, following Gresham's Law that "bad money drives out good." The result of such culling and melting was a severe and chronic shortage of coin of the realm throughout the century.[12] What coin remained in circulation was disastrously debased: in 1777, the government found that a sampling of £300 in silver, which ought to have weighed 1200 ounces, weighed 624 ounces.[13]

In theory, currency was based on its "intrinsick" value as precious metal, but this theory bore little or no relation to practice because the silver coinage was both severely debased and entirely inadequate to the volume of circulation. Lord Lowndes claimed in *A Report containing an Essay for the Amendment of the Silver Coins* (1695) that "the Moneys commonly currant are Diminished near one Half, to wit, in a Proportion something greater than that of Ten to Twenty two." Light silver "when offered in Payments, is utterly Refused, and will not Pass, and consequently doth not serve the end or Purpose for which it was made." He goes on to describe the social disruption caused by inadequate coinage, a disruption which is essentially a crisis in the concept of value:

> In consequence of the Vitiating, Diminishing and Counterfeiting of the Currant Moneys, it is come to pass, That great Contentions do daily arise amongst the King's Subjects, in Fairs, Markets, Shops, and other Places throughout the Kingdom, about the Passing or Refusing of the same, to the disturbance of the Publick Peace; many Bargains, Doings and Dealings are totally prevented and laid aside, which lessens Trade in general; Persons before they conclude in any Bargains, are necessitated first to settle the Price or Value of the very Money they are to Receive for their Goods; and if it be in Guineas at a High Rate, or in Clipt or Bad Moneys, they set the Price of their Goods accordingly, which I think has been One great cause of Raising the Price not only of Merchandizes, but even of Edibles, and other Necessaries for the sustenance of the Common People, to their great Grievance.[14]

The monetary system maximized instability and as a

consequence suffered chronic shortages and periodic crises, with increasing frequency towards the end of the century.[15] In all senses, this was a transitional system, neither realist nor nominalist, or both realist and nominalist, based neither on bullion nor on paper money. Such contradictions are evident everywhere in the pamphlet literature, much of which argues against lowering the value of money—recoinage by way of debasement—by insisting on the "intrinsick" value of precious metal. Locke's influential argument in *Some Considerations of the Consequences of the Lowering of Interest and the Raising of the Value of Money* encapsulates all the contradictions of eighteenth-century monetary theory: silver has both real and imaginary value, and intrinsic and extrinsic value. Silver coins are indistinguishable in value from an equal amount of bullion, for value is based solely on quantity, but value is also based on quality (fineness), and both quantity and quality are in turn guaranteed by the authoritative stamp which functions as a pledge to insure its weight and fineness. In short, silver money is a physical, material object that has value, but that value is based on conventional agreement: precious metals have no real inherent value, but are accepted only by custom and contract:

> Now Money is necessary to all these sorts of Men as serving both for Counters and for Pledges, and so carrying with it even Reckoning, and Security, that he, that receives it, shall have the same Value for it again, of other things that he wants, whenever he pleases. The one of these it does by its Stamp and Denomination; the other by its intrinsick Value, which is its *Quantity*.
>
> For mankind, having consented to put an imaginary Value upon gold and Silver by reason of their Durableness, Scarcity, and not being very liable to be Counterfeited, have made them by general consent the common Pledges, whereby Men are assured, in Exchange for them to receive equally valuable things to those they parted with for any *quantity* of these Metals. By which means it comes to pass, that the intrinsick Value regarded in these Metals made the common Barter, is nothing but the *quantity* which Men give or receive of them. For they having as Money no other Value, but as Pledges to procure, what one wants or desires; and they procuring what we want or desire, only by their *quantity*, 'tis evident, that the intrinsick Value of Silver and Gold used in commerce is nothing but their *quantity*.[16]

The inherent value of silver is a point which Locke never tires of repeating: "*Silver, i.e.* the *quantity* of pure Silver separable from the alloy, makes the real *value* of Money. If it does not, coin Copper with the same Stamp and denomination, and see whether it will be of the same value" (p. 145). And then, in answer to the question, why then do we not simply exchange in bullion, by weight, he answers simply that it would be inconvenient, for it is hard to tell the difference between fine and mixed silver.[17] Despite its function as pledge, in *Short Observations on a Printed Paper Intituled, For encouraging the Coining Silver Money in England, and after for keeping it here* (1695), Locke dismisses the value of the stamp: "the Stamp neither does nor can take away any of the intrinsick value of the Silver, and therefore an Ounce of Coined standard Silver, must necessarily be of equal value to an Ounce of uncoined standard Silver" (p. 2). The fundamental argument here is a tautology—silver is silver: "it will always be true, that an Ounce of Silver coin'd or not coin'd, is, and eternally will be of equal value to any other Ounce of Silver" (p. 10). In 1757, eight years after Fielding's **Tom Jones** appeared, we find the same insistence on permanence and immutability of silver coins, and the same language of real, inherent and intrinsic worth in Joseph Harris's *An Essay upon Money and Coins*: "Money . . . differs from all commodities in this, that, as such, its value is permanent or unalterable; that is, money being the measure of the values of all other things, and that, like all other standard measures, by its quantity only; its own value is to be deemed invariable." Along with the emphasis on immutability, we find the same hostility to paper: after a consideration of the physical properties money should have—scarcity, immutability, easy divisibility, ability to be tested for fineness, resistance to wear—he argues against experimentation with paper money:

> We see that some of our plantations, make a shift without any money, properly so called; using only bits of stamped paper, of no real value. But, wherever that material, which passeth as or instead of money, hath not intrinsic value, arising from its usefulness, scarcity, and necessary expence of labour in procuring it; there, private property will be precarious; and so long as that continues to be the case, it will be next to impossible for such people, to arrive at any great degree of power and splendour.[18]

Yet a mere twenty years later, Adam Smith could claim that "the substitution of paper in the room of gold and silver money, replaces a very expensive instrument of commerce with one much less costly, and sometimes equally convenient. Circulation comes to be carried on by a new wheel, which costs less both to erect and to maintain [*i.e.*, as fixed capital, which he has been examining] than the old one." When he writes of bank notes, paper and silver specie, it is to assert their fundamental equivalence: "these notes come to have the same currency as gold and silver money, from the confidence that such money can at any time be had for them."[19]

> The gold and silver which circulates in any country, and by means of which the produce of its land and labour is annually circulated and distributed to the proper consumers, is, in the same manner as the ready money of the dealer, all dead stock. It is a

very valuable part of the capital of the country, which produces nothing to the country. The judicious operations of banking, by substituting paper in the room of a great part of this gold and silver, enables the country to convert a great part of this dead stock into active and productive stock; into stock which produces something into the country. The gold and silver money which circulates in any country may very properly be compared to a highway, which, while it circulates and carries to market all the grass and corn of the country, produces itself not a single pile of either. The judicious operations of banking, by providing, if I may be allowed so violent a metaphor, a sort of wagon-way through the air; enable the country to convert, as it were, a great part of its highways into good pastures and cornfields, and thereby to increase very considerably the annual produce of its land and labour. The commerce and industry of the country, however, it must be acknowledged, though they may be somewhat augmented, cannot be altogether so secure, when they are thus, as it were, suspended upon the Daedalian wings of paper money, as when they travel about upon the solid ground of gold and silver.[20]

There is not a simple continuum of monetary theory from Locke to Smith; rather, Locke, Harris, and Smith exemplify positions taken throughout the century. And even if Smith's view appears to be sharply divergent from those of the earlier two writers, the seeds of that view are implicit in the deep contradictions found throughout Locke's economic theory.

The suspicion and hostility to nominal or paper currency evident in Locke and Harris were shared by other writers throughout the century. But, as a consequence of the constant dearth of coin, merchants, manufacturers, bankers, and employers regularly had to resort to the use of various forms of scrip or symbolic money, from metallic tokens stamped with the emblem of a shop's guild to elaborate systems of paper money, all issued by small, private institutions.[21] (In order to protect the monopoly of the Bank of England, banking laws limited banks to no more than six partners.) Business was transacted in negotiable, interest-bearing securities in addition to coin of the realm.[22] Of the various forms of paper credit—the bill of exchange, promissory note, and the cheque—bills of exchange were the most common. Bills of exchange had been used in foreign trading since the thirteenth century, but they come into use in the second half of the seventeenth century in inland trade and with third parties as the bearer.[23] Many of these changes can be traced to the increased volume of commerce, and the need for new methods of payment and, in turn, new mechanisms of banking. English banking followed Italian and then Dutch innovations, starting with goldsmiths who paid interest on money deposited with them, in turn lending it to others, often the Crown, at a higher interest.[24] Credit currency develops from these practices, as gold-

smith's receipts eventually become negotiable notes payable to an anonymous bearer, and as goldsmiths take on what we now consider to be bankers' functions. Bank bills derive from bills of exchange: the Bank of England issued bills under their seal (their sealed bills were discontinued in 1716), and cash notes, signed by the cashier, with blanks for names and amounts. Bank notes were engraved forms with blanks for amount and bearer. Often part was drawn off, and noted on the back, but the note could still be endorsed off to a third party or discounted by a broker; that is, the broker would buy the bill before it was due at a price less than its face value. It is the bill brokers who become the first commercial bankers, discounting bills for provincial customers. By and large, money circulated from agricultural districts, through London, to manufacturing districts by means of bills of exchange, not bank notes. Country bank notes or cash notes circulated in the agricultural districts, while bills of exchange circulated in the manufacturing districts.[25]

To return to Henry Fielding's **Tom Jones,** what are the notes which Allworthy recognizes? They are referred to at one point as "five bank bills" and as "bank bills" (p. 920), and at another point as "the 500*l.* Bank-Notes" (p. 968). According to the *Oxford English Dictionary,* "bank-note" and "bank bill" were used synonymously, though it is clear from the dictionary's examples that both referred to interest-bearing bills. Under "bank bill," the first definition is "bank note," and the second is "a bill drawn by one bank upon another payable at a future date, or on demand, synonymous with *banker's draft.*"[26] Allworthy's notes cannot, of course, be government-issued currency, which was not issued until well into the nineteenth century. His notes are unlikely to be a country bank's notes, for there were very few provincial banks in operation in the first half of the eighteenth century. They are unlikely to be bills of exchange, for those circulated largely in manufacturing districts, and less commonly in agricultural districts. Rather, they are more likely to be bank notes or bills drawn on a London bank. (In sending him off to make his fortune, Allworthy presumably would have given Tom his most negotiable paper.) They are unlikely to be Bank of England notes, for those circulated almost exclusively in London and not in the provinces. The best guess is that they are in the form of a cash note, from a smaller, West End bank of the sort that catered to the gentry, such as Hoare's or Child's.[27]

Unlike the anonymous and interchangeable paper money issued by the post-absolutist state, bills in Fielding's day would be individually identifiable as a consequence of the individualized nature of paper money in the eighteenth century, which not only held the name of the drawer and the bearer, but often a number of intermediary bearers who had endorsed it.[28] It is entirely possible to read the history of a bill or note in its endorsements—the various hands through which it passed. Paper money is not government issued, neither anonymous nor impersonal in this period, but is something which can be "told" and narrated. These are identifiable, distinguishable objects whose history can be read from their surfaces, much like a novel. This fact gives a significant clue to the function of money in Fielding's fiction.[29] A readable bank note has obvious uses in Fielding's romance plot of discovery, a plot which asks if money can (re)make the man.

The threat of the transformative or generative power of money runs throughout Fielding's novels, particularly in the anonymity promoted by journeys, during which strangers are trusted on the strength of their money. Parson Trulliber is a prominent example of trust contingent upon cash in *Joseph Andrews,* as is the first landlady in *Tom Jones:* "this was one of those Houses where Gentlemen, to use the Language of Advertisements, meet with civil Treatment for their Money" (p. 407); those who have money are assumed to be gentlemen.[30] Peter Pounce in *Joseph Andrews* is Fielding's archetypal money man, the servant turned master, all by means of credit and interest. Pounce's fortune is accumulated by usury (legally defined at the time as any rate of interest above 5 percent):

> [Pounce] used to advance the Servants their Wages: not before they were due, but before they were payable; that is, perhaps, half a Year after they were due, and this at the moderate *Premiums* of fifty *per Cent,* or a little more; by which charitable Methods, together with lending Money to other People, and even to his own Master and Mistress, the honest Man had, from nothing, in few Years amassed a small Sum of ten thousand Pounds or thereabouts. (p. 38)

Old Nightingale is Peter Pounce's counterpart in *Tom Jones:* "He had indeed conversed so entirely with Money, that it may be almost doubted, whether he imagined there was any other thing really existing in the World; this at least may be certainly averred, that he firmly believed nothing else to have any real Value" (pp. 771-72). These hostile portraits of Pounce and Nightingale serve to deny the generative power of money. In like manner the money which Lady Bellaston gives Tom (p. 718) cannot change his nature even though it may temporarily transform him into a town beau. Much the same thing may be said of charity: when Tom gives money to Mr Enderson, the "highwayman" (p. 680), the money enables Enderson to live up to his natural class or station—it does not transform him into something he is not. Enderson may be said to exemplify for Fielding the worthy poor, those whose lot is improved by charity. Black George, on the contrary, exemplifies the unworthy poor, those on whom Tom's charity is wasted, leaving them in unimproved squalor. Either way, money cannot change the nature of the individual; rather the cash nexus is invariably

pictured by Fielding in such a way as to deny its efficacy.

In all these scenes of exchange in *Tom Jones,* Fielding expresses a traditionally conservative hostility to the potential of liquid assets, to their dangerously enabling capacities, to which Marx later also draws attention:

> Do not I, who thanks to money am capable of all that the human heart longs for, possess all human capacities? Does not my money, therefore, transform all my incapacities into their contrary? . . . The overturning and confounding of all human and natural qualities, the fraternization of impossibilities—the *divine* power of money—lies in its *character* as men's estranged, alienating and self-disposing *species nature.* Money is the alienated *ability of mankind.* That which I am unable to do as a man, and of which therefore all my essential powers are incapable, I am able to do by means of *money.* Money thus turns each of these powers into something which in itself it is not—turns it, that is, into its *contrary.*[31]

It is just these alchemical properties of money that Fielding is at such pains to negate, and the negation points to a curious, if not contradictory, conjunction of two languages or two stories in *Tom Jones.* As Braudel observes: "uneasiness [with new systems of bank notes and paper credit] was the beginning of the awareness of a new language. For money is a language . . . it calls for and makes possible dialogues and conversations; it exists as a function of these conversations."[32] Fielding's purpose in *Tom Jones* is to transform this new language, these new dialogues and conversations of accumulation and profit, and the transformations which result from them, back into the old dynastic language of the stable hereditary estate.

One way to account for this fundamental difference in the representation of credit is *not* simply in terms of political affiliation, that is, by seeing Fielding as a conservative Whig, allied by family to the landed aristocracy and their agricultural interests,[33] rather, we need to see Fielding responding to a highly transitional or contradictory stage in the currency system and in the English economy itself. In the *Grundrisse,* Marx argues that money passes through three stages of development, in which it functions first as a measure of value, and secondly as price or a universal equivalent or medium of exchange. In the second stage, money comes to represent accumulation or treasure, that is to say, wealth itself. Finally, in the most complex system of development, money comes to be posited in exchange *per se,* not merely as the measure of accumulated wealth, but rather as a means of wealth, as capital. The following passage encapsulates the complex dialectical relation among these three successive but interrelated stages and functions of money:

Only with the Romans, Greeks, etc. does money appear unhampered in both its first two functions, as measure and as medium of circulation, and not very far developed in either. But as soon as either their trade, etc. develops, or, as in the case of the Romans, conquest brings them money in vast quantities—in short, suddenly, and at a certain stage of their economic development, money necessarily appears in its third role, and the further it develops in that role, the more the decay of their community advances. In order to function productively, money in its third role, as we have seen, must be not only the precondition but equally the result of circulation, and, as its precondition, also a moment of it, something posited by it. Among the Romans, who amassed money by stealing it, from the whole world, this was not the case. It is inherent in the simple character of money itself that it can exist as a developed moment of production only where and when *wage labour* exists; that in this case, far from subverting the social formation, it is rather a condition of its development and a driving wheel for the development of all forces of production, material and mental.[34]

At issue, then, is Fielding's response to and representation of a stage in the development of money, specifically capital—what Marx calls "money in process" for "capital is a not a thing but a social relation between persons, established by the instrumentality of things."[35] In order to see this instrumentality in *Tom Jones,* we need to look at Fielding's earlier and later fiction, first *Jonathan Wild* and then *Amelia,* both narratives with considerably more economic detail than Fielding's master work.

Like many Augustan satirists, in *Jonathan Wild* (1743), Fielding shows his central character as a parodic or inverted capitalist. Wild and his gang are presented as capital and labour, the gang leader exploiting the labour of others. In such a scheme, money is the motor of human activity: "Having thus preconceived his scheme, he [Wild] saw nothing wanting to put it in immediate execution but that which is indeed the beginning as well as the end of all human devices: I mean money" (p. 80). Wild is a successful exploiter: as the narrator puts it, "a prig [thief] to steal with the hands of other people" (p. 168). Fielding also plays with the other dimension of capital, its capacity to make money from money, so that Wild cheats a whole series of people one after another, profiting from each of them. Theft then serves Fielding as a kind of laboratory economy, a miniaturization of an exchange system. It also serves as the ironic frustration of capitalist exchange, for theft is a zero-sum game, one in which money moves around, through various forms of thieving, cheating, and pickpocketing, but the value remains constant (as in the card-sharking scene, pp. 72-76). In this microeconomic system, thieves prey upon one another in daisy-chain fashion, all cheating one another and negating each other's effects: "Bagshot and the

gentleman intending to rob each other; Mr Snap and Mr Wild the elder meditating what other creditors they could find out to charge the gentleman then in custody with; the count hoping to renew the play, and Wild, our hero, laying a design to put Bagshot out of the way, or, as the vulgar express it, to hang him with the first opportunity" (p. 76).[36] Like *Tom Jones,* this narrative comically traces the return of goods to their rightful owners, though here it is Wild who plays the role of an inverted providence by orchestrating the return of possessions to their original owners: "Wild, having received from some dutiful members of the gang a valuable piece of goods, did, for a consideration somewhat short of its original price, re-convey it to the right owner" (p. 169). As a fence, Wild deals in commodities and exchange value, for stolen objects are of no use either to thief or fence: their only value lies in exchange. The perpetual frustrations of Wild present the criminal/capitalist as the essence of unproductive labour, involved in an elaborate but useless exchange system which ultimately produces no increase in value.

Many of the narrative functions of loss and recovery work in the same way here as in *Tom Jones;* the central objects purloined and eventually returned are the jewels which Wild steals from Heartfree.[37] In *Amelia,* the casket which Amelia gives to Booth has the function of the muff or wallet in *Tom Jones* (that is, it is both a possession and a kind of romance love-token). Like *Tom Jones* again, in *Amelia* the plot turns on the theft of an inheritance by a sibling. In its representations of economic exchange, *Amelia* is Fielding's most interesting novel, for it portrays a world almost totally ruled by money; Amelia's is a world where money talks and where the most basic needs and rights are denied to the poor. In *Tom Jones* we watch the movement of bills, but in *Amelia* we trace the journey of debts, in particular the climactic use of Booth's gambling debt to Trent, which is sold to the lecherous Lord (pp. 432, 438, 472, 492). In Fielding's last novel desire and justice are caught in a cash nexus, for "justice" is bought and sold with perjured witnesses, and bodies are for sale in prostitution; in short things are for sale here that should not be for sale, just as there is no equal access to basic human rights (as is the case with Mrs Bennet's first husband, denied burial rights by his creditors). Booth before the Justice of the Peace and in Newgate is powerless without money: injustice *per se* is thematized in *Amelia.* The negotiations with various suitors over Amelia's hand in marriage illustrate the point—precious things are to be had for money. These issues come to the fore early on when Miss Mathews announces that she has not enough money in her pocket to pay the lawyer Murphy to save her life: life itself in the form of life-saving service is available only for money.

Furthermore, money and the power it represents are inevitably exploitive here, where the rich prey upon the poor; as Dr Harrison puts it, where they "prey upon the Necessitous" (p. 355), or, as the narrator puts it, where "a Set of Leaches are permitted to suck the Blood of the Brave and Indigent; of the Widow and the Orphan" (p. 477). The narrator says of the nobleman who is promoting Booth's commission in the army in order to gain sexual access to Amelia, "This art of promising is the Oeconomy of a great Man's Pride, a sort of good Husbandry in conferring Favours, by which they receive ten-fold in Acknowledgments for every obligation, I mean among those who really intend the Service: for there are others who cheat poor Men of their Thanks, without ever designing to deserve them at all" (p. 203). Exploitation functions as a gross inversion or parody of the deference and obligation which Harold Perkin called the glue that held the Old Society together.[38] When a "great man" receives "ten-fold," we can see a kind of capitalization of hierarchical obligation; similarly, the political satire at work throughout *Jonathan Wild* of course indicates that Robert Walpole has capitalized political patronage, turning political deference and obligation into a cash nexus. Colonel Bath, Booth says, "hath oppressed me, if I may use that Expression, with Obligations" (p. 368), while Booth defines "Obligations, as the worst kind of Debts" (p. 236).[39] In Fielding's attack on the decadent aristocracy in *Amelia,* social obligation has become explicitly financial, transformed into a kind of social capital deployed to oppress the lower classes.[40]

In the first half of the eighteenth century Defoe recognized and celebrated money as capital, as an instrument for creating wealth, not just as wealth itself, but Fielding refuses to show the reproduction of accumulated capital in criminal hands. Black George has instructed Old Nightingale to "lay out [the £500] either in a Mortgage, or in some Purchase in the North of England" (p. 920), but Fielding has constructed his story so as to resist or repress the possibility of turning cash into capital. The notes remain inert and nontransformative, and Black George's act does not lead to accumulation but remains simple theft. Recognized and recovered by Allworthy, the notes remain safe, stable, unchanging property, much like a landed estate, suspended within the patriarchal system of continuity. The new language of money has its analogue in the language of the new form of the novel; Defoe's novels are stories of new dialogues, social mobility, and personal development, individual changes that are achieved by way of financial accumulation, profit, and class transgression. The conjunction of these two languages of real and monetary property, then, can be understood in generic terms. It has been argued that *Tom Jones* is a hybrid form, a comic epic in prose, a romance, a satire; its mixed form can be seen most clearly in relation to the economic base of the culture.[41] In his *The Theory of the Novel* Georg Lukács distinguished between the epic, which tells the history of an unchanging community, and the novel, which takes the outward biographical form of the history of a problematic individual. *Tom Jones* combines the residual with the emergent, vestiges of the epic with elements of the new form of the novel, for it concerns the story of Squire All-worthy's estate just as much as the story of the titular hero.[42] From the Lukácsian point of view, the title and outward biographical form mask the fact that the true protagonist of *Tom Jones* is Paradise Hall.[43] Tom's becoming a worthy steward to the estate is but part of the larger history, the possessive and genealogical continuity represented by the dynastic estate itself.[44]

To the very end of his life Fielding displayed a consistent resistance to the notion of free-flowing capital. In his Introduction to *The Journal of a Voyage to Lisbon,* Fielding observed of his income as Bow Street Magistrate:

> I will confess to him [the reader], that my private affairs at the beginning of the winter had but a gloomy aspect; for I had not plundered the public or the poor [in his capacity as magistrate] of those sums which men, who are always ready to plunder both as much as they can, have been pleased to suspect me of taking: on the contrary, by composing, instead of inflaming, the quarrels of porters and beggars (which I blush when I say hath not been universally practised) and by refusing to take a shilling from a man who most undoubtedly would not have had another left, I had reduced an income of about £500 a year of the dirtiest money on earth, to little more that [*sic*] £300. (pp. 189-90)

The taint of dirty money here is adduced from the immoral conditions of the job, the *Amelia*-like conditions of bribery and exploitation, and such immorality adheres to the money. Such a persistence of immorality, even after the money changes hands, is quite unlike the laundering of money that goes on in Defoe's novels where money is rootless, without meaningful genealogy, and so is always "clean." Stolen objects, such as the bank note in *Colonel Jack* or the watch in *Moll Flanders,* carry no taint of their history: giving her son a gold watch at the close of her story, Moll adds, "*I did not indeed tell him* that I had stole it from a Gentlewomans side, at a Meeting-House in *London,* that's by the way."[45] In *Tom Jones,* Jacobite rebellions, runaway wives, daughters, rogue nephews, and the cash nexus of London[46] momentarily threaten the stability of landed property, but the transcendence of possession extends beyond land to cash itself in Fielding's epic, harnessing, domesticating, or declawing the threat of cash, paper credit, unbridled accumulation, and universality of exchange value—in short, early market capitalism and commodity. Those intermediate systems of sealed bills and bills of exchange, with their assertively individualized appearance, similarly can be seen as provisional mechanisms which evolved to control the treacherously fluid capacity of paper money. After anonymous Bank of England notes become legal tender in 1797, rightful possession would never again be so easily recognized or so easily restored.

Notes

[1] Quotations from Fielding's fiction are from the *Wesleyan Edition of the Works of Henry Fielding,* ed. Martin Battestin: *Tom Jones* (1975, reprinted Middletown, CT: Wesleyan University Press, 1983); *Joseph Andrews* (1967); *Amelia* (1983, reprinted 1984); *Jonathan Wild,* ed. David Nokes (Harmondsworth: Penguin Books, 1982); *The Journal of a Voyage to Lisbon* in *The Works of Henry Fielding,* ed. William Ernest Henley (1902, reprinted New York: Barnes and Noble, 1967), vol. XVI. Page references are to these editions.

[2] Ernest Mandel, *Late Capitalism,* trans. Joris de Bres (London: Verso, 1978). Samuel L. Macey characterizes Fielding's attitude towards money as "aristocratic" (*Money and the Novel: Mercenary Motivation in Defoe and his Immediate Successors* [Victoria, B.C.: Sono Nis Press, 1983], p. 122.) Michael McKeon writes of "Fielding's profound distaste for monied culture" (*The Origins of the English Novel* [Baltimore: Johns Hopkins University Press, 1987], p. 503).

[3] Fielding's comic order has been discussed in terms of Providence. See Aubrey Williams, "The Interpositions of Providence and the Design of Fielding's Novels," *South Atlantic Quarterly* 70 (1971), 265-86 and Martin Battestin, *The Providence of Wit* (Oxford: Clarendon Press, 1974). Henry Knight Miller connects the persistence of romance form (cycle and return) with providential thematics (*Henry Fielding's "Tom Jones" and the Romance Tradition* [Victoria, B.C.: University of Victoria, 1976], especially chap. 2, pp. 22-41). What appears as transhistorically romantic to Miller I argue has peculiar historic specificity, for the comic interpositions of providence work to support a late aristocratic concept of property. On the differences between Fielding's and earlier providential plots, see Leopold Damrosch, Jr, "*Tom Jones* and the Farewell to Providential Fiction," in *Henry Fielding, Modern Critical Views,* ed. Harold Bloom (New York: Chelsea House, 1987), pp. 221-48, reprinted from *God's Plot and Man's Stories* (Chicago: University of Chicago Press, 1985). See also John Bender, *Imagining the Penitentiary* (Chicago: University of Chicago Press, 1987), pp. 186-87.

[4] Homer O. Brown, in "*Tom Jones:* The Bastard of History," *boundary* 2 7 (1978), 201-33, observes that Tom remains a bastard and therefore ineligible to inherit the estate. He is a "genealogical aberration" (p. 207), a disruption of the dynastic narrative. Similarly, Brown sees the allegorical or metonymic function of the Jacobite rebellion of 1745 in *Tom Jones* as "history

as order" (p. 224). From Coleridge to its most classic statement in R. S. Crane ("The Plot of *Tom Jones*" [1950], reprinted in *Essays on the Eighteenth-Century Novel,* ed. Robert D. Spector [Bloomington: Indiana University Press, 1965], pp. 92-130), the favourite word used in all sorts of descriptions of the novel and its plot is "order" or "ordered." Studies of Fielding's thematics are similarly filled with concern for the "whole," as in Damrosch: "Fielding's poetics finds significance in the whole, and is committed to showing how everything is interconnected. This narrative epistemology is reflected in the world of social relationships" (p. 236). So too, Paul Hunter opens his discussion of Fielding's elaborate patterns of symmetry with the observation that "Viewing *Tom Jones* is a little like viewing the eighteenth century as a whole" (*Occasional Form* [Baltimore: Johns Hopkins University Press, 1975], p. 167). The fragility of this totalizing order, at least for the later Fielding, is explored by C. J. Rawson in *Henry Fielding and the Augustan Ideal under Stress* (London: Routledge and Kegan Paul, 1972). Terry Castle also explores the subversion of apparent order in *Amelia* in *Masquerade and Civilization* (Stanford: Stanford University Press, 1986), pp. 177-252. Here, I am interested in exploring both the economic dimensions of the fictional order, and the historical forces it is arrayed against.

[5] A similar conservation or continuity is apparent in Fielding's psychology: see John S. Coolidge, "Fielding and 'Conservation of Character,'" in *Modern Philology* 57 (1960), 245-59. Similarly, Patricia Meyer Spacks argues that Fielding's characters are not subject to transformation: "The characters in eighteenth-century fiction show less capacity for essential change than we like to believe is possible in life, and the limited possibilities for change they have depend upon external kinds of learning about the world outside themselves." *Imagining a Self* (Cambridge: Harvard University Press, 1976), p. 7.

[6] Brian McCrea in *Henry Fielding and the Politics of Mid-Eighteenth-Century England* (Athens: University of Georgia Press, 1981) focuses on "the central role of property in Fielding's political and social writings" (p. 201), which he characterizes as Lockean: the purpose of the state is to protect property: "Fielding was unequivocal and unsparing in his defense of property" (p. 203). "His political career is understood, most truthfully, as one instance of the transformation of Whiggism from a revolutionary political philosophy that challenged royal authority to a conservative political philosophy that protected the values and interests of a property-owning elite" (p. 207).

[7] For the history of these developments, see P. G. M. Dickson, *The Financial Revolution in England: A Study in the Development of Public Credit 1688-1756* (London: Macmillan, 1967).

[8] See Earl Wasserman, *Pope's Epistle to Bathurst* (Baltimore: Johns Hopkins University Press, 1960), for a thorough discussion of economics in the poem.

[9] Fernand Braudel, *Capitalism and Material Life 1400-1800*, trans. Miriam Kochan (New York: Harper and Row, 1973), p. 358.

[10] Marc Shell, *Money, Language and Thought: Literary and Philosophical Economies from the Medieval to the Modern Era* (Berkeley: University of California Press, 1982), pp. 3-4.

[11] Fredric Jameson offers a suggestive model for this connection between money form and fiction: "The art-novella, then, may be governed by the experience of money, but of money at a specific moment of its historical development: the stage of commerce rather than the stage of capital proper. This is the stage Marx describes as exchange on the frontiers between two modes of production, which have not yet been subsumed under a single standard of value; so great fortunes can be made and lost overnight, ships sink or against all expectations appear in the harbor, heroic travellers reappear with cheap goods whose scarcity in the home society lends them extraordinary worth. This is therefore an experience of money which marks the form rather than the content of narratives; these last may include rudimentary commodities and coins incidentally, but nascent Value organizes them around a conception of the Event which is formed by categories of Fortune and Providence, the wheel that turns, bringing great good luck and then dashing it, the sense of what is not yet an invisible hand guiding human destinies and endowing them with what is not yet 'success' or 'failure,' but rather the irreversibility of an unprecedented fate, which makes its bearer into the protagonist of a unique and 'memorable' story" ("The Ideology of the Text," in *The Ideologies of Theory, Essays 1971-1986* [Minneapolis: University of Minnesota Press, 1988], I, 52). For other relevant studies of literature and economics, see Max Novak, *Economics and the Fiction of Daniel Defoe* (Berkeley: University of California Press, 1962); Walter Benn Michels, *The Gold Standard and the Logic of Naturalism* (Berkeley: University of California Press, 1987); John Vernon, *Money and Fiction: Literary Realism in the Nineteenth and Early Twentieth Centuries* (Ithaca: Cornell University Press, 1984); and Roy R. Male, *Money Talks: Language and Lucre in American Fiction* (Norman: University of Oklahoma Press, 1981).

[12] T. S. Ashton writes that "in 1773, coin of the realm was hardly obtainable" (*An Economic History of England: The Eighteenth Century* [New York: Barnes and Noble, 1955], p. 186).

[13] C. R. Josset, *Money in Britain: A History of the Currencies of the British Isles* (London: Frederick Warne, 1962), p. 112.

[14] William Lowndes, *A Report containing an Essay for the Amendment of the Silver Coins* (London, 1695), reprinted in John R. McCulloch, ed., *A Select Collection of Scarce and Valuable Tracts on Money* (1856, reprinted New York: A. M. Kelley, 1966), p. 233. Josset confirms Lowndes's picture (pp. 112-13).

[15] "Banking statutes do appear to have maximized instability. . . . English banks remained small, with six partners or fewer, and unincorporated. Yet, in their operation (in great contrast with most continental states) no public control was exerted on the extent of their note issues, their cash ratios, their reserves, cheque transactions or expansionist credit policies. Thus, instability was maximized" (Peter Mathias, *The First Industrial Nation: An Economic History of Britain 1700-1914* [London: Methuen, 1983], p. 36].

[16] John Locke, *Several Papers Relating to Money, Interest and Trade* (1696, reprinted New York: A. M. Kelley, 1968), p. 31. This volume contains: *Some Considerations of the Consequences of the Lowering of Interest and the Raising of the Value of Money* (1691); *Short Observations on a Printed Paper Instituted, For encouraging the Coining Silver Money in England, and after for keeping it here* (1695); and *Further Considerations concerning Raising the Value of Money. Wherein Mr. Lowndes Arguments for it in his late Report concerning "An Essay for the Amendment of the Silver Coins," are particularly Examined* (second edition, 1696). Page numbers refer to this collection of pamphlets.

[17] "The *Stamp* was a *Warranty* of the publick, that under such denomination they should receive a piece of such weight, and such a fineness; that is, they should receive so much silver. And that is the reason why counterfeiting the Stamp is made the highest Crime, and has the weight of Treason upon it: Because *the Stamp is the publick voucher* of the intrinsick value" (Addenda to *Some Considerations,* pp. 146-47).

[18] Joseph Harris, *An Essay upon Money and Coins* Part I, 1757, reprinted in McCulloch, pp. 372 and 374.

[19] Adam Smith, *The Wealth of Nations,* ed. Edwin Cannan (Chicago: University of Chicago Press, 1976), pp. 309, 310.

[20] Smith, p. 341.

[21] As Sir Albert Feavearyear puts it in his history of English money, "Roughly speaking, paper money of all kinds in the first half of the century stayed within the sphere occupied by cheques today. Outside that sphere coin alone was used" (*The Pound Sterling: A*

History of English Money, 2nd ed. [Oxford: Clarendon Press, 1963], p. 160).

[22] According to T. S. Ashton, "Some of these including exchequer bills, navy bills, and lottery tickets (as also the short-term obligations of the East India Company, the Bank of England, and the South Sea Company) could be used to settle accounts between individuals, and may perhaps, therefore, be thought of as falling within the somewhat shadowy boundaries of 'money'" (pp. 177-78). The transition towards "true" paper money in circulation by the end of the century (that is, as we currently understand paper money) involves the gradual purging of the interest-bearing functions of these notes (Feavearyear, pp. 117-18). As Ashton puts it, "By means of a bill, purchasing power could be transferred by one man to another under conditions of repayment plainly set forth and generally understood. Unlike the coin or bank note, the bill could be sent from place to place without danger of theft. It could pass from hand to hand without formality other than endorsement, and each person who put his name to it added to its security. Any holder could get coin or other currency by discounting it: as a security it was highly liquid" (p. 185).

[23] Feavearyear, p. 101.

[24] See Ernest Mandel, *Marxist Economic Theory,* trans. Brian Pearce (London: Merlin Press, 1962), pp. 242-70.

[25] Feavearyear, p. 159. See pp. 161-67 for the circulation of bills of exchange. There is an excellent discussion of the history of bills of exchange in Braudel, pp. 367-70.

[26] Under *bank note,* the definition reads as follows, "a promissory note given by a banker: *formerly* one payable to bearer on demand, and intended to circulate as money." Under *note,* we find, "a bank-note, or similar promissory note passing current as money," from 1696. Under *bill,* we find: "(more fully Bill of Exchange) A written order by the writer or 'drawer' to the 'drawee' (the person to whom it is addressed) to pay a certain sum on a given date to the 'drawer' or to a third person named in the bill as the 'payee.'"

[27] See Dickson, pp. 437-44, for a detailed discussion of Child's Bank, an example of private London bank catering to the aristocracy.

[28] Feavearyear notes that bills under £1 were prohibited in 1775: "in 1777 an Act was passed which provided that all notes of 20s. or of any amount greater than 20s. and less than £5 should specify names and place of the abode of the persons to whom or to whose order they were payable. Further, they were to bear a date not later than the date of issue and to be made payable within twenty-one days, after which period they would cease to be negotiable" (p. 174).

[29] For an intelligent discussion of Fielding's use of detail, see Lennard Davis, *Factual Fictions: The Origins of the English Novel* (New York: Columbia University Press, 1983), p. 205 and note.

[30] See James Cruise, "Fielding, Authority, and the New Commercialism in *Joseph Andrews,*" *ELH* 54 (1987), 253-76 for an extended discussion of Fielding's hostility towards commercialism and the cash nexus.

[31] Karl Marx, *The Economic and Philosophical Manuscripts of 1844,* ed. Dirk J. Struik (New York: International Publishers, 1964), pp. 167-69.

[32] Braudel, p. 328.

[33] For a good overview of politics in Fielding, see Morris Golden, "Fielding's Politics," in *Henry Fielding, Justice Observed,* ed. K. G. Simpson (Totowa: Barnes and Noble, 1985), pp. 34-53. For McCrea, in *Henry Fielding and Politics,* the issue of Fielding's politics is explicitly biographical: how Fielding's family connections mediate his political position and so on. Both these studies focus on the contradictions between praxis and theory, between political patronage and association, between conservative and progressive political stances, inherent in the unstable nature of Whiggism at mid-century, issues that come out of Bertrand Goldgar's influential *Walpole and the Wits* (Lincoln: University of Nebraska Press, 1976). Straightening out the interrelations among political service and patronage, loyalty, and ideology is a continuing project in Fielding studies. The most detailed study is Thomas R. Cleary, *Henry Fielding, Political Writer* (Waterloo: Wilfrid Laurier University Press, 1984).

[34] Karl Marx, *Grundrisse,* trans. Martin Nicolaus (Harmondsworth: Penguin Books, 1973), p. 223. The whole "Chapter on Money" (pp. 113-238) is relevant, particularly pp. 226-38.

[35] Karl Marx, *Capital,* 3 vols. ed. Frederick Engels, trans. Samuel Moore and Edward Aveling (New York: International Publishers, 1967), I, 154 and 766.

[36] Crime as unproductive labour or negation is encapsulated in Fielding's description of Newgate: "all Newgate was a complete collection of prigs, every man behind desirous to pick his neighbour's pocket, and every one was as sensible that his neighbour was as ready to pick his: so that (which is almost incredible) as great roguery was daily committed within the walls of Newgate as without" (pp. 203-4). Compare this with Mrs Heartfree's conclusion: "THAT PROVIDENCE WILL SOONER OR LATER PROCURE THE FELICITY OF THE VIRTUOUS AND INNOCENT" (p. 203).

[37] Fielding's hostility to capital is apparent in the fact that only the disreputable know how to exploit the tricks of credit here (p. 90): the Count obtains one of the jewels, sells it, raises money on that cash, which he then uses as a deposit for the rest of Heartfree's jewels—making money on money: "so he paid him the thousand pound in specie, and gave his note for two thousand eight hundred pounds more to Heartfree." They then attack Heartfree and steal the cash back from him, after which the cash is stolen by the prostitute Molly Straddle. Wild offers the jewels to Lætitia Snap, but they turn out to be paste, substituted by the Count. The jewels reappear with the Count in Africa (pp. 192-93) and are returned eventually to Heartfree (p. 203). So too, Heartfree recognizes a bank note (one of the Count's) stolen from him the previous day, just as in *Tom Jones* (p. 99); Heartfree endorses it over, it is stopped (because the Count has disappeared and will not make good on it) and, as the endorsee, Heartfree is held for the debt and jailed.

[38] Harold Perkin, *The Origins of Modern English Society* (1969, reprinted London: Routledge, 1985), pp. 17-62.

[39] There are negative suggestions of the generative or reproductive capacity of capital, in that Booth cannot borrow money without having some to start with (p. 122). In keeping with Fielding's "late feudal" outlook, money in this novel is still part of a zero-sum game, for it changes hands by theft or misappropriation or coercion (primitive accumulation), but there is no new money produced. It is only old, familiar, known money that appears, disappears, and reappears in the course of the narrative, just as in *Tom Jones*.

[40] It could be argued that Fielding's obsession with prostitution in *Amelia* is connected with capitalization, as in the central contrast between the good wife, Amelia, who protects her virtue at all cost, and Mrs Trent. Amelia is explicitly termed Booth's "Treasure" (p. 382) compared to Colonel Bath's worthless wife or Colonel Trent's wife, who is a commodity to be traded, a prostitute. In this respect, *Jonathan Wild* seems very much like a satiric version of *Amelia,* since the central contrast is also one between honour (a nostalgic aristocratic virtue) and its commodification or capitalization, between the good wife and the whore, Mrs Heartfree and Lætitia Wild. Like Amelia, Mrs Heartfree's adventures consist of a sequence of resisting would-be rapists. For these issues of gender, see April London, "Controlling the Text: Women in *Tom Jones,*" *Studies in the Novel* 19 (1987), 323-33.

[41] Sheldon Sacks, *Fiction and the Shape of Belief* (Chicago: University of Chicago Press, 1964), remains the best discussion of the variety of forms in *Tom Jones*. The issue of form is related to the more general matter of the historicity of his discourse, and the question of how it is inscribed in the cultural field of the 1740s and the 1750s. In other words, what do Fielding's narratives tell us about the dialectic between romance and novelistic discourse? There are at least two senses of "history" as story and reality that need to be worked out here: See John F. Tinkler, "Humanist History and the English Novel in the Eighteenth Century," *Studies in Philology* 85 (1988), 510-37. See also John J. Burke, Jr, "History without History: Henry Fielding's Theory of Fiction," in *A Provision of Human Nature,* ed. Donald Kay (University: University of Alabama Press, 1977), pp. 45-63. McKeon's *Origins of the English Novel* is the fullest and most successful attempt to resolve Fielding's place in both romance and novelistic discourse.

[42] George Lukács. *The Theory of the Novel,* trans. Anna Bostock (Cambridge: MIT Press, 1971). My application of Lukács is dependent upon J. M. Bernstein's excellent study of Lukács's novel theory in *The Philosophy of the Novel* (Minneapolis: University of Minnesota Press, 1984).

[43] The ending sentence of *Tom Jones,* with its emphasis on the estate and its dependents, condenses Fielding's Tory myth of genealogical continuity and economic conservatism: "And such is their Condescension, their Indulgence, and their Beneficence to those below them, that there is not a Neighbour, a Tenant, or a Servant, who doth not most gratefully bless the Day when Mr. Jones was married to his Sophia." It is no accident that in *Pamela* and in *Sir Charles Grandison* Richardson felt obligated to track the newlyweds much further before the family history could be safely and sensibly concluded. *Pamela* ends, not with the marriage of Pamela and Mr B or with the reconciliation of Mr B and his sister Lady Davers; instead, the whole narrative is stretched out in order to end with a triumphant return to the paternal estate. So too, Smollett's *Roderick Random* closes with a return to the dynastic estate and a similar show of affection, deference, and dependence by the servants. As a measure of what has changed by the end of the century, we may compare these endings with Sir Walter Scott's *Waverley,* where the estate returned to at the end is pitifully fragile, only recently recovered, and only partially restored.

[44] By contrast, Defoe's novels speak a completely different economic language, and present the cash nexus, paper money, and credit in an entirely different light. Rather than being threatened by the alchemical, transformative powers of money, Defoe's characters are explicitly made rich by its properties: that is to say, for Moll, Colonel Jack, and Roxana, mastery of the credit system is the *sine qua non* of success in the material world. The most instructive example of paper credit in Defoe's fiction is Colonel Jack's £94 bank note, the accumulation of his early years of theft. Once Jack passes into the New World, that note loses all connec-

tion with its illicit origin; indeed the £94 note becomes a sign of Jack's gentility, surety to his new master that Jack is not, in fact, a transported criminal, but rather an innocent who has been abducted to Maryland by an unscrupulous sea captain (Daniel Defoe, *The Life of Colonel Jack,* ed. Samuel Holt Monk [London: Oxford University Press, 1970]). For the drawing up of the bill see pp. 76-77, and for its function in Maryland, see pp. 124-25. In short, the note in Defoe serves in all its enabling capacity, transforming Colonel Jack from a common criminal into a respectable citizen, which is exactly what Fielding prevents the £500 note from doing for Black George in *Tom Jones.*

[45] *Moll Flanders,* ed. David Blewett (Harmondsworth: Penguin Books, 1989), p. 422.

[46] In Jane Austen's *Mansfield Park* (1814) Mary Crawford recites "the true London maxim, that everything is to be got with money." R. W. Chapman, ed., *The Novels of Jane Austen* (London: Oxford University Press, 1923), III, 58.

Charles A. Knight (essay date 1992)

SOURCE: "*Joseph Andrews* and the Failure of Authority," in *Critical Essays on Henry Fielding,* edited by Albert J. Rivero, G.K. Hall & Co., 1998, pp. 69-82. Originally published in *Eighteenth-Century Fiction,* Vol. 4, 1992, pp. 109-24.

[*In the following essay, originally published in 1992 and reprinted in 1998, Knight examines Fielding's narrative style in* Joseph Andrews, *arguing that the text's heterogeneous construction emphasizes the mutual relationship between author and reader made possible by the emerging genre of the novel.*]

The garrulous narrator of *Joseph Andrews* and his complex novel have been interpreted in terms of implicitly conflicting analogies describable alternatively as religious and political. According to the first, the apparent authority of the narrator stands for the authority of God, especially the Christian and incarnate God who acts in history.[1] The function of Fielding's fictions is thus to reinforce, by their comic conclusion, the reader's confidence in a universe controlled by a benevolent deity. The secular alternative sees narrative authority as analogous to political and legal control. The narrator's control over the actions of characters and the interpretations of readers stands for social control over personal behaviour. The narrator adopts or prefigures techniques like those of civil control. John Bender sees Fielding concerned with "the deployment of narrative as an authoritative resource." Narratives parallel the information systems that organize an urban society, "the densely stored, cross-

referenced informational networks that characterize written accounting in the modern metropolis. . . . I count the realist novel as one of these systems."[2] The epistemic shifts implied by the closely sequential developments of the novel as a canonic genre, of lawyers' roles in presenting and arguing legal cases, and of the reforming penitentiary give particular importance to narratives: "not to possess a story, to be without narrative resources, is to lack a comprehensible character within the metropolitan order and to be subject to a reformation of consciousness."[3] These religious and secular versions of Fielding's narrative authority are both clearly analogies, although of different sorts. Both account for a limited range of material and shape the text to fit the terms of the analogy. My present concern is with a possible misfit between Bender's legal-political analogy and the text of *Joseph Andrews.* The secular analogy proposes suggestive connections (especially for *Jonathan Wild* and *Amelia*), but it represents the critic's assertion of an authority which, like the narrator's, is open to sceptical scrutiny about the limits of its utility.

Authority is the assertion of a claim to power and, because it is an assertion, it is both the subject and product of interpretation: "it is an attempt to interpret the conditions of power, to give the conditions of control and influence a meaning by defining an image of strength. . . . It is an interpretive process which seeks for itself the solidity of a thing."[4] But the urgency that governs this interpretive assertion often derives from the threat to authority or even from its collapse. In Fielding's case the values he could use in addressing a broader audience seemed uncertain, forcing him both to pretend to authority and to mock that pretence. And the new genre of the novel either required an authoritative statement of generic ancestry or served to undermine literary authority altogether. In *Joseph Andrews* the significant collapse of generic clarity portends broader failure. Three elements of *Joseph Andrews* seem to threaten its claim to narrative authority: the instability of its genre, the unreliability of its narrator, and the ironies of its ending.

Generic Instability

Fielding's critical pronouncements on the genre of *Joseph Andrews* manifest his authority in several ways: he parodies Richardson to establish authority through contrast; he asserts the realism of his own material and thus the naturalness of his authority; he articulates generic terms that are familiar to readers and verify his authority by reference to tradition. His useful classical precedents lead to overlapping terms. Hence his Preface asserts that his novel is a "comic Romance" (from Scarron's *Roman comique*) that is in turn "a comic Epic-Poem in Prose," and he goes on to analyse these terms, especially "comedy."[5] His classifications seek to place the novel among the familiar and to account for its novelty. The Preface and the introductory chapters to the first three books trace the relationship of his new form to Homer's *Odyssey* and Fénelon's *Télémaque,* to French romance, and to histories and biographies.

But many readers suggest that the Preface is itself inconsistent and does not fit the novel. Michael McKeon observes that Fielding seeks to redefine genre with a "self-serving skepticism," especially regarding the terms "history" and "romance," which he seeks to recombine into different meanings, a pattern to which I shall return as a tactic of reading.[6] Walter Reed explores various senses of "romance" in European literature (senses which Fielding certainly knew); he notes that Fielding's elaborate generic classifications are themselves affectations (hence proper comic subjects) and that the Preface contradicts the text.[7] Fielding's protestation that "I have no Intention to vilify or asperse any one" (Preface, p. 10) is surely violated on the first pages by his attacks on Cibber and Richardson. The assertion is at odds with the novel's failure to remain circumscribed to a fictional world. Likewise, despite the recent claim that Adams "is designed as a universal type,"[8] early readers recognized him as Fielding's friend William Young, and several specific historical characters, perhaps including Fielding himself, appear by way of fictional representation or direct reference.[9] The character of Adams is certainly comic but not based on affectation, vanity, and hypocrisy, and Fielding's description of him as "a Character of perfect Simplicity" recommended by "the Goodness of his Heart" (Preface, p. 10) may seem too simplistic itself.[10]

Fielding's difficulty in asserting the authority of his genre lies both in the ungeneric nature of novels (the intractable form eluding Fielding's efforts to give it authoritative shape) and in the conflicting implications of the works to which he refers for his authority. For example, the title page proclaims that the novel is "Written in Imitation of the Manner of Cervantes, Author of *Don Quixote.*" But *Don Quixote* attacks "romance" itself in ways that parallel Fielding's attack on Richardson, and its attack has serious implications for the mixture of genres and structures in *Joseph Andrews.*[11]

The reader becomes engaged by Joseph's love for Fanny as the romantic issue which the novel will resolve. The powerful comic narration and the force of Fielding's surprising movement from mockery of Joseph's chastity to sympathy with his real love give the romantic plot particular urgency for the reader, who is metaphorically making the marriage of Fanny and Joseph possible by reading the novel. The satisfaction that attends the fulfillment of their love, despite the manipulation that brings it about, gives the literal boy-girl plot a nearly mystic function.[12] The apparent authority

of the narrator derives in part from his role in providing that comic conclusion.

Pulling against this purposeful romantic plot and the authority it bestows is an open, Cervantic structure that takes the form of a journey and, despite the recurrence of significant topics, includes episodes that make no apparent contribution to the romantic resolution. If Joseph is the hero of the romantic plot, Adams seems the centre of its Cervantic mode. Like Quixote, Adams seems unable to change, and his character shows its ambiguities and shortcomings in the changing contexts of his journey. His progress from London to Booby-Hall is, like the sallies of Don Quixote, built on repetition and variation, rather than on the linear movement of romance. Such a structure may advance primarily local meanings. Unlike the strongly significant romantic plot, it may be indeterminate, as is stunningly shown by the capacity of *Don Quixote* to survive conflicting views of its basic issues.

The Cervantic incidents of ***Joseph Andrews*** carry much of the novel's satire but establish a fragmentary narrative surface, especially in the central books. The reader's instinct, however, is to feel the romantic plot as a governing structure. The usual response to the most egregious interruptions of the novel, the three interpolated stories (II, iv, vi; III, iii; and IV, x), is to link them to the romantic plot by seeing them as related to thematic concerns, to the behaviour of the central characters, or to the reactions of those who hear them.[13] But such links are nearly impossible for the rapid pattern of minor interruptions. The merging of a romantic plot with an open structure may be a major advance on Cervantes,[14] but it presents a central critical problem because Fielding's various generic signals are only approximate rather than authoritative guides.

Although books I and IV of ***Joseph Andrews*** emphasize its romantic and parodic elements and books II and III its Cervantic journey, the romantic plot and open structure overlap. The romantic plot is modified by the opening parody of *Pamela* and by the literary artifices of the conclusion. Joseph becomes realistic by escaping from the romantic into the quixotic. His chastity ceases to be an abstract principle inculcated by Adams and exemplified by Pamela; his return to Fanny becomes the goal of his journey (I, xi). But when the lovers are reunited (II, xii) and Adams persuades them to marry properly (II, xiii), the journey's purpose is again redefined, only to be interrupted when the abduction of Fanny reveals the depth of Joseph's feelings (III, xi). Critics have proposed each event as a turning point, but all are stages in bringing the romance plot to its expected conclusion.[15] Moreover, scenes redefining the journey seem occasional (though they recur regularly near the end of each book), and their striking connection with the romance plot reminds readers that much of journey is not thus connected.

Romance in *Joseph Andrews* parodies the novelistic contrivance of *Pamela* and is an aristocratic answer to the Puritan, middle-class myth that confuses virtue with self-interest. But once this romance response is established, it is rendered problematic by its incapacity to meet the needs of ordinary experience (the need for money, for example). But "ordinary experience" is suspect because its demands are often products of arbitrary institutions or unreasonable conventions. Thus each generic shift is destabilized by the next pattern. The genres question at the moment they assert, and the assertion of power repeatedly seems a compensation for incapacity.

Traditional romance establishes characters by stereotypes. Thus the mixed genres of *Joseph Andrews* produce an inconsistency between stereotypical roles and actual behaviour. This gap is a formal equivalent to the distance between affectation and personality that Fielding identifies as central to his comedy. It allows Adams to appear as a comic character without the negative affectations of Mrs Slipslop, Peter Pounce, and Pamela herself. Adams not only acts in a way that is inconsistent with his professed principles, he also falls into inappropriate roles from romance; as a result romance itself is open to question as a dubious social affectation. (Throughout, the conventions by which readers interpret texts are proposed as equivalents to the social conventions satirized by the novel.) The shifting of generic characters also parallels the shifting of narrative voice that I shall shortly discuss, for its presence is often revealed by the disconcerting presence of stereotypical discourse.

The texture of these shifting stereotypes is shown by one of Fanny's infrequent excursions into speech. In book II, chapter x, after Adams has rescued her from violent attack, she is caught in an unusual lie about her affection for Joseph: "'La! Mr. *Adams,*' said she, 'what is Mr. *Joseph* to me? I am sure I never had anything to say to him, but as one Fellow-Servant might to another.'" Adams accuses her of being dishonest to him or false to Joseph but tells her of Joseph's affection, without further inquiry, for he "never saw farther into People than they desired to let him." The narrator adds several sentences telling how Fanny, hearing of Joseph's misfortune, "immediately set forward in pursuit of One, whom, notwithstanding her shyness to the Parson, she loved with inexpressible Violence, though with the purest and most delicate Passion." The passage shows a quick sequence of readjustments, moving from Fanny's effort to deceive and Adams's failure in perception to the explanation of Fanny's statement by the conflict between her shyness and the violence (though refinement) of her passion. But it shifts again to a sudden consciousness of audience: "This Shyness, therefore, as we trust it will recommend her Character to all our Female Readers, and not greatly surprise such of our Males as are well acquainted with the younger part of the other Sex, we shall not give ourselves any trouble to vindicate." The narrator's intrusion seems designed to tell us that he need not intrude, but since we hope that even an intrusive narrator will supply useful information, we may combine this reference to social practice (which we have learned to regard suspiciously) with our surprise at the Slipslopian archness of Fanny's language to Adams, to conclude that the naturalness of her character does not prevent a significant social artifice (not entirely unbecoming to Pamela's actual sister), but redeemed by her true strength of feeling, much as Adams's naïveté is redeemed by his active goodness.

For much of the novel Fanny appears as the desirable heroine of romance—the worthy reward of Joseph's coming to maturity. Here she has been saved from rape not by the heroics of her lover but by the bravery of the comic parson, indeed the very parson whose sermons have been cited as a source of her lover's chastity. And the incident shows us a realistic Fanny—coy, deceptive, and passionate. Fanny has recognized Adams because he thought of Joseph and "could not refrain sighing forth his Name." The stereotypes of the romantic plot are all askew: Adams, not the hero, rescues Fanny; Adams, not the heroine, sighs out Joseph's name. The action progresses through such shifts among literary and social conventions.

The quixotic patterns of repetition and variation encourage readers to form subjective groupings according to topics. Many groupings are connected with travelling, such as the repetition of inn scenes, of hosts, of Adams's efforts to borrow money, and of debates on the topic of charity. The more such incidents accumulate, the broader seem their implications: for example, the professions (medicine, the church, the law, and innkeeping) function both to make money and to provide necessary human services, but service is repeatedly perverted by the profit motive. Once the reader has elicited this moral (surely early in the novel), it multiplies in its forms and in its impediments to the marriage of Fanny and Joseph. But as parallels extend, they grow complex in their implications and extend beyond the limitations of genre and the patterns of repetition and variation. The conflict of structures, the medley of generic signals, and the interruptions of interpolation, are replicated in narrative shifts that require frequent readjustment of the reader's expectations. *Joseph Andrews* seems not so much an indeterminate novel as a novel of determined instability.

The instability of authority in *Joseph Andrews* may be contrasted with the determination of legal discourse. The fitting analogy between novelistic and legal discourse may be that romantic fictions resemble legal procedures and that realistic ones contrast with them. Because it includes both romantic and realistic modes, *Joseph Andrews* has a dialectic rather than analogical relation to the law. John Bender argues that Fielding's novels parallel a shift in trials from the activist status of a judge who could use them as a devices of inquiry to the role of lawyers not only in cross-examining but organizing and conducting the cases for the prosecution and defence.[16] But legal argument in a trial by jury, whoever makes it, moves from the top downward. The jury is to determine the guilt or innocence of the defendant and must exclude information irrelevant to that determination. The role of detail is to confirm the presupposition that the defendant is innocent or to deny it beyond reasonable doubt.

But in realistic novels the procedure seems reversed. The discoveries made by the reader are not clearly defined but must themselves be discovered, and the text suggests various possibilities, some deliberately misleading. Because romantic plots are highly determined, their pattern is closer to jury deliberations, limited by rules of procedure, by the judge's charge, and by the questions to be answered. Romance resembles the movement of legal argument by defining initially the issues governing its structure. The more realistic and unstable the genre is, the less it resembles this basic process. *Joseph Andrews* is thus legally complex: its authoritative romantic conventions establish the reader's strong expectation that the novel will conclude with the marriage of Joseph and Fanny, but against that expectation it arrays both the uncertainties of interpretation and the dangers that emerge from the random but real world where unhappy endings are more common than happy ones.

Trial by jury assigns the factual determination of guilt or innocence to the jury, whatever the private opinion of the judge might be, and hence the judge's role differs from that of the omniscient narrator. The task of readers is to find out what the narrator already knows, and part of the complexity of *Joseph Andrews* lies in the tension between the narrator's revelations and the author's concealments. That fictions are the creations of authors and that authors overlap with narrators limit the comparability of narrative and judicial roles. These limits pertain even in an epistemology that sees all discourse as mental construct, for the "fiction" of novels differs from the "fiction" of law: judges and narrators, juries and readers know (or construct) evidence in different ways.

Narrative Unreliability

Because of the generic instability of *Joseph Andrews,* the narrator is tentative even when his tone is authoritative. At the beginning of book III, he contrasts unreliable historians with authoritative biographers (whom he equates with novelists). Histories supply contradictory testimony, "where Facts being set forth in a different Light, every Reader believes as he pleases, and indeed the more judicious and suspicious very justly esteem the whole as no other that a Romance, in which the Writer hath indulged a happy and fertile Invention" (III, i, pp. 185-86). "Biographers," in contrast, although unreliable on time and place (the only reliable information of historians), speak truly about people and values. This claim of narrative authority overstates the unreliability of historians and conflates historical fact with the subjective but universal truth of fictitious character, but it distinguishes between historical and fictional discourses, a distinction that the term "narrative discourse" overrides. This distinction points to a further one between the reliability and the authority of the narrator. The narrator takes responsibility for the text composed by the author, but given his unreliability, especially in providing generic terms for his novel, he may be particularly authoritative when irony itself implies meaning. The contrast of the artificial romantic plot of *Joseph Andrews* with its random realism is echoed by the shifting voice of a narrator who is both assertively ironic and disarmingly direct.

He frequently shifts from the surface of his story to reveal information needed to understand a character. The present, Fielding implies, is deceptive, and appearances cannot be deciphered without a narrator's privileged information. In the context of the romantic plot, temporal and causal shifts to the past are ambiguous: because they are shifts, they interrupt the forward movement of the plot; in so far as they are causal, they may contribute to the outcome (which actually does require revelations about the past, significantly not supplied by the narrator). We are encouraged by our trust in the narrator to accept such temporal shifts as unobtrusive and helpful. But shifts that reveal relevant information can easily shade into non-causal shifts where the narrator voices opinions not germane to his plot, and narrative shifts are so common in *Joseph Andrews* that we cannot consistently see them as signals to look for indirect meanings. Hence Fielding adopts a self-conscious irony that alerts us to interpretive caution, as in his description of Adams and Fanny in book II, chapter x. He directly states or ironically hints that narrative shifts require alert reading, and we move from feeling that the romantic plot organizes reading to a sense that it is guided by our conversational relation to the narrator.

But sometimes the text shifts laterally away from the central characters or from the direction of the action without the presence of the narrator. Such lateral shifts, lacking a trustworthy explanation and a reliable explainer, leave readers to their own resources and perhaps in some doubt about the relevance of a narrated incident. Usually the narrative surface is stabilized by the presence of a central character, and movements from one character to another as the centre of attention are plainly marked, often, in the central books, by changes in the mode of travelling or, in book IV, by quasi-dramatic entrances or shifts of scene. But at times the silence of the narrator gives lateral shifts the quality of Joycean epiphanies—sudden flashes of ambiguous revelation.

Despite their remoteness from the romantic plot and their questionable relevance to the characters, lateral shifts open the scope of the novel's satire by commenting on recurrent topics. As Ronald Paulson has pointed out, Fielding's satire uses the central characters as touchstones through whom others reveal their hypocrisy.[17] But, as Paulson goes on to note, the consequent interpretive process is complex: the narrator may be silent; the central characters are not strong interpreters; the explanation, as with the host of book II, chapter iii, may come from a character who fails the novel's satiric test. And some incidents, such as the hunters' conversation of book I, chapter xvi, seem completely random. Even when readers understand the significance of such instances, they are aware that, like the characters, they may be wrong. Occasionally such shifts defy efforts to incorporate them into a larger structure. (Robert Alter comments that the story of Leonard and Paul can be made relevant "only by the most determined overinterpretation.")[18]

Readers concerned about shifting and its relation to structural units may welcome the narrator's discussion of "Divisions in Authors" in book II, chapter i. But Philip Stevick shows appropriate frustration that this chapter is "so arch, so puzzlingly ironic, that it leaves quite unclear what Fielding meant to assert."[19] Walter Reed notes the "politicization of the republic of letters" in book II, chapter i, and its "figurative displacement of literary authority into the realm of commercial enterprise."[20] The most distinct moral of Fielding's playful similes is that frequent division slows the pace of reading, so that one will not "miss the seeing some curious Productions of Nature which will be observed by the slower and more accurate Reader." Since the novel's shifts imply that we must think diversely about our reading, Fielding's consciousness of pace leads one to question whether the structure of chapters suggests proper patterns in our thought. The parallels and contrasts framed by Fielding's manipulation of chapters seem to point towards meanings that we do not find. Fielding's narrative frames heighten gaps as well as connections. Chapters enforce patterns of interpretation without necessarily resolving the questions they create. Their manipulated irresolution may confirm our puzzlement.

The novel's tendency to spread beyond the narrator's explanations parallels the quarrel between reading and experience associated with the learned but credulous Parson Adams and is complicated by the fact that Adams, like Don Quixote, is a questionable reader.[21] His constant companion (until book II, chapter xii, where he accidentally throws it into the fire) is the Greek text of Aeschylus, but his treatment of it speaks more highly of his Greek than of his judgment. Careful reading of Aeschylus ought to correct his Pelagian belief in the goodness of human nature. He may be right that books articulate principles that guide individual perceptions, but he does not derive such awareness from his own reading of Aeschylus, whose companionship seems a whimsy. Yet even if we see Adams's position as dubious, we continue to read (and Fielding to write) a book.

The reading debate between Adams and the host in book II, chapter xvii juxtaposes familiar positions: experience is meaningless unless interpreted through the corporate knowledge expressed in print; learning may appreciate aesthetics regardless of content (as in Adams's reading of Homer) or may fail to apply the relevant generalities to experience (as in his reading of Aeschylus). Fielding sets forth a dichotomy only to contradict it: reading without experience is useless; experience without reading is dangerous. The debate reveals the narrowness of both positions, and truth lies in the unity of their partial truths. A proper reaction (as with the narrator's generic distinctions in the Preface) is to recombine the debated terms.

Trust in a benevolent authority and scepticism about an unreliable narrator imply a distinction of terms that modify each other throughout the novel. The variety of discourses achieved in such comic novels as *Joseph Andrews* depends not only on the dialectic between the narrator's voice and those of his characters but also on his capacity to shift according to the material he articulates, in contrast to the efforts of courts and bookkeepers to reduce disparate evidence to a useful single discourse.[22] Such special discourses as legal proceedings and double-entry bookkeeping were efforts to reduce ambiguity and to make unequivocal action possible. The "heteroglossia" of the novel has the opposite effect of heightening ambiguity to complicate discernment and judgment. Just as the looseness and variety of the novel imply the inadequacy of a single genre to organize human experience, a unified and consistent narrative procedure cannot articulate it. One possible explanation of the difference between Fielding the novelist and Fielding the magistrate lies not in his character or personal intentions but in the discourses through which he acted.

The cacophonies among the various languages adopted by the narrator and between the voice of the narrator and those of his characters echo the discordancies between the author's narrative roles and his personal intentions and the disharmonies among the various genres subsumed by the text or proposed as models for its readers. The noisy disorder is not merely random, for the same author is responsible both for the garrulous and shifting narrator and for the material that eludes his strategies of control. The narrator's struggles to control his text further replicate the author's ultimate difficulty in controlling its readers. The novel's resemblance to the Panopticon prison is rather different from that suggested by Bender.[23] While visual transparency allows guards to keep prisoners under surveillance and supervision, such openness also allows prisoners to communicate with one another. The simultaneous dialogues of many voices subvert the transforming purpose of impersonal and physical isolation.

Endings and Conclusions

The openness that permeates the narrator's efforts to erect controlling structures for his fiction and that threatens to render his authority local and tentative is reinforced by the conscious manipulations that make the ending of the novel ambiguous. Fielding has been blamed for the aristocratic idyll that blesses the marriage of Fanny and Joseph by making Boobies of them.[24] But the ending concludes a plot that emphasizes the power of personal affection to engage characters in a world of risk. By the novel's end they have identified protected centres of experience, only to have them disappear. Mr Wilson has withdrawn from London to tend a farm. From that vantage point he is initially sceptical of Adams, Joseph, and Fanny and able to narrate the past from which his scepticism derives. But the "tragic" death of his daughter's dog (III, iv) reminds him that injustice is inescapable. Adams's counsels of Christian stoicism are undercut by his grief at the "death" of his son and by his wife's testimony that he is more caring than his doctrines imply. Indeed, Adams is preeminently the character whose activity derives from his commitment to others. But Joseph himself fails a similar test when the Pedlar who saved Jacky brings the news that Fanny is his sister.

Our discovery that the report of Jacky's death is false surely prepares us for a similar discovery in this case, but the news sets off a conversational sequence on Platonic love that nearly equals the poet-player and Adams-Joseph pairings (III, x-xi) in its elaboration; the Platonic-love conversations frame the "curious night-adventures" (IV, xiv) that are the novel's comic apogee. At the end of book IV, chapter xiii (p. 330), Pamela

> chid her Brother *Joseph* for the Concern which he exprest at discovering a new Sister. She said, if he loved *Fanny* as he ought, with a pure Affection, he had no Reason to lament being related to her.— Upon which Adams began to discourse on *Platonic* Love; whence he made a quick Transition to the Joys in the next World, and concluded with strongly asserting that there was no such thing as Pleasure in this. At which Pamela and her Husband smiled on one another.

The night adventures begin with Didapper pretending to be Joseph and proclaiming to what he thinks is Fanny that they are not siblings and can be lovers; it concludes with the innocent Adams explaining that he does not know whether Fanny is man or woman.

> As soon as *Fanny* was drest, *Joseph* returned to her, and they had a long Conversation together, the Conclusion of which was, that, if they found themselves to be really Brother and Sister, they vowed a perpetual Celibacy, and to live together all their Days, and indulge a *Platonick* Friendship for each other. (IV, xv, p. 335)

"Platonick Friendship" sounds suspiciously like the language of seduction ("vowed . . . to live together . . . and indulge"), even as it yokes Joseph and Fanny directly to Adams's Christian stoicism. Here the readers rather than Pamela and her husband smile. The perpetual celibacy of the lovers denies the force of their sexual passion. Joseph's brief but striking link with the naïveté of Adams on the issue of Platonic friendship makes it difficult to read the novel as an *Erziehungsroman* in which Joseph replaces Adams as moral guide. The evaluation of Adams's Christian stoicism now applies to Joseph's: for all its worthiness, it denies powerful and deeply human passions.

It seems a mistake to read the ending of *Joseph Andrews* simply as an aristocratic cop-out or as an affirmation of providence. The interpretive task imposed by the recombination of apparent opposites is the difficult reconciliation of the harsh real world to the romantic one concocted by the comic artist. "The rhetorical method of *Joseph Andrews* is a negative one—taking away comfortable alternatives rather than offering any really plausible ones."[25] The novel's shifting narrative makes the reader account for the conflicts manifested by its consciously constructed gaps. To argue that the comic artifice of the ending displaces the discordant reality of the middle books is to simplify the complexities of Fielding's art.

A proper understanding of Fielding's outlandishly happy conclusion may depend on a distinction between fiction and truth rather than a distinction between fiction and reality. Because fiction is not measured by the usual criteria of truth, the opposing elements of a fictional contradiction can both be affirmed, and their opposition remains as an implication of meaning. Fictional affirmation can imply statements that avoid the restrictions of ordinary language. A problem of discourse, as the reading debate between Adams and the host shows, is that speakers overstate their cases to make narrow points or to feed their vanity or to put down their antagonists. And individual speakers lack the variety and breadth of perspective that is possible in Fielding's fiction by virtue of its narrative shifts. As a satire of discourse *Joseph Andrews* repeatedly demonstrates the superiority of its own fictionality, which can simultaneously affirm truths and express reservations about them. The openness of the affirmative fictional structure allows conflicting statements to retain their meanings and provides an alternative to the confining tyranny of discourse. If the authority of the narrator derives from his responsibility for the romantic and comic plots, it also derives from his openness to the multiple meanings that undermine the conclusiveness of the ending itself. Ultimately the narrator's authority derives from his failure to be authoritative.

The difficulty of the analogy between novels and history lies in its literalness, in its tendency to deny the fictional nature of one of its terms. Fiction is itself a genre of uncertainty where each of the relationships that it subsumes—between what characters say and what they do, between the narrator's generic claims and his actual material, between the author's intentions and the readers' interpretations—is unstable and open to question. Hence it can be used only tentatively and approximately to locate cultural analogies. Rather than reflecting the connected roles of Fielding as both narrator and magistrate (a connection plausibly argued for *Amelia*),[26] *Joseph Andrews* may emphasize the difference. At the moment when Fielding's narrative authority reflects the need for social control, his parodic discourses proclaim his distrust of the vehicles of control and of the motives of those who seek it.

What makes the failure of narrative authority comfortable is the naturalness and universality of readers. Even if Fielding had not read book III of Hume's *Treatise of Human Nature* (1740), his narrative process shares its sense of moral sentiments, "so rooted in our constitution and temper, that without entirely confounding the human mind by disease or madness, 'tis impossible to extirpate and destroy them."[27] This sense of universal sentiment means that individual readers, however their interpretations differ in detail, share what is important in Fielding's novel (and do not find Joseph and Fanny unattractive or Adams hateful). It allows broad scope for an irony circumscribed by a belief that author and readers share a natural moral feeling—a belief that distributes authority between judicious readers and a judicial author.

Notes

[1] Martin Battestin, *The Moral Basis of Fielding's Art* (Middletown, CT: Wesleyan University Press, 1959), as well as several articles on *Tom Jones* reprinted in *The Providence of Wit* (Oxford: Clarendon Press, 1974); see also Aubrey J. Williams, "Interpositions of Providence and the Design of Fielding's Novels," *South Atlantic Quarterly* 70 (1971), 265-86.

[2] John Bender, *Imagining the Penitentiary: Fiction and the Architecture of Mind in Eighteenth-Century England* (Chicago: University of Chicago Press, 1987), especially pp. 139-98 (the quotations appear on pp. 139 and 140); John Richetti compares the narrative procedure of *Tom Jones* to "the workings of the Ha-

noverian-Whig oligarchy" in "The Old Order and the New Novel of the Mid-Eighteenth Century: Narrative Authority in Fielding and Smollett," *Eighteenth-Century Fiction* 2 (1990), 190.

[3] Bender, p. 160.

[4] Richard Sennett, *Authority* (New York: Vintage, 1981), p. 19.

[5] Henry Fielding, *Joseph Andrews*, ed. Martin C. Battestin (Middletown, CT: Wesleyan University Press, 1967, p. 4. References are to this edition.

[6] Michael McKeon, *The Origins of the English Novel 1600-1740* (Baltimore and London: Johns Hopkins University Press, 1987), pp. 404-5.

[7] Walter Reed, *An Exemplary History of the English Novel: The Quixotic versus the Picaresque* (Chicago and London: University of Chicago Press, 1981), pp. 117-23; cf. Sheridan Baker, "Fielding's Epic-in-Prose Romances Again," *Philological Quarterly* 58 (1979), 63-81.

[8] David Nokes, *Henry Fielding: Joseph Andrews*, Penguin Critical Studies (Harmondsworth: Penguin Books, 1987), p. 30.

[9] Martin C. Battestin, with Ruthe R. Battestin, *Henry Fielding, A Life* (London and New York: Routledge, 1989), pp. 329-36.

[10] For a reading of Adams as a character free of affectation, see, for example, J.B. Priestley, *The English Comic Characters* (London: Lane, 1925), pp. 106-27.

[11] Discussions of the Cervantic characteristics of *Joseph Andrews* include Leon Gottfried, "The Odyssean Form: An Exploratory Essay," in *Essays on European Literature in Honor of Liselotte Dieckmann*, ed. Peter Uwe Hohendalh, Herbert Lindenberger, and Egon Schwartz (St Louis: Washington University Press, 1972), pp. 19-43; also Stephen Gilman, "On Henry Fielding's Reception of *Don Quijote*," in *Medieval and Renaissance Studies in Honor of Robert Brian Tate*, ed. Ian Michael and Richard A. Cardwell (Oxford: Dolphin, 1986), pp. 27-38; and Reed, pp. 123-32.

[12] See Jeffrey M. Perl, "Anagogic Surfaces: How to Read *Joseph Andrews*," *The Eighteenth Century—Theory and Interpretation* 22 (1981), 249-70.

[13] I.B. Cauthen, Jr, "Fielding's Digressions in *Joseph Andrews*," *College English* 17 (1956), 379-82; Douglas Brooks, "The Interpolated Tales in *Joseph Andrews* Again," *Modern Philology* 65 (1968), 208-13; J. Paul Hunter, *Occasional Form: Henry Fielding and*

the Chains of Circumstance (Baltimore: Johns Hopkins University Press, 1975), p. 152.

[14] Reed, p. 130.

[15] Dick Taylor, Jr, Joseph as Hero of *"Joseph Andrews," Tulane Studies in English* 7 (1957), 91-109, regards II, xii as the central scene, where Joseph becomes more independent as a character, and Robert Alter sees Joseph's song as recapitulating "the action of the whole novel" (*Fielding and the Nature of the Novel* [Cambridge: Harvard University Press, 1968], p. 105); Joseph's emotional depth in III, xi is the turning point for Dianne Oslund, "Tied Back to Back: The Discourse between the Poet and Player and the Exhortations of Parson Adams in *Joseph Andrews,*" *Journal of Narrative Technique* 12 (1982), 191-200.

[16] Bender, pp. 174-80.

[17] Ronald Paulson, *Satire and the Novel in Eighteenth-Century England* (New Haven: Yale University Press, 1967), pp. 121-26.

[18] Alter, p. 110.

[19] Philip Stevick, *The Chapter in Fiction: Theories of Narrative Division* (Syracuse: Syracuse University Press, 1970), p. 25.

[20] Reed, p. 134; James Cruise sees the displacement as sinister, in "Fielding, Authority, and the New Commercialism in *Joseph Andrews,*" *ELH* 54 (1987), 268-69.

[21] Reed describes Adams as "a Quixote who is deluded by classical literature" and by a "neoclassical culture" (p. 126), but Adams fails to comprehend the potential conflicts between classical texts and his own principles, and hence is never informed by his reading of the classics.

[22] "The comic style demands of an author a lively to-and-fro movement in his relation to language, it demands a continual shifting of the distance between author and language, so that first some, then other aspects of language are thrown into relief" (M.M. Bakhtin, *The Dialogic Imagination: Four Essays,* ed. Michael Holquist; trans. Caryl Emerson and Michael Holquist [Austin: University of Texas Press, 1981], p. 302).

[23] For Bender "the penitentiary stages impersonal, third-person presence . . . so as to represent actual character and conscience as fictions capable of alteration" (p. 203).

[24] This point is intriguingly made by Cruise (pp. 271-72), who finds the ending a narrative compromise undertaken to avoid moral compromise.

[25] Hunter, p. 114.

[26] Bender, pp. 180-96.

[27] David Hume, *A Treatise of Human Nature,* ed. L.A. Selby-Bigge, 2nd edition; revised by P. H. Nidditch (Oxford: Clarendon Press, 1978), p. 474.

Elizabeth Kraft (essay date 1992)

SOURCE: "Narrative Authority and the Controlling Consciousness in Fielding's *Tom Jones*," in her *Character and Consciousness in Eighteenth-Century Comic Fiction,* University of Georgia Press, 1992, pp. 65-82.

[*In the following chapter from her book* Character and Consciousness in Eighteenth-Century Comic Fiction, *Kraft examines the way in which authorial narrative interrupts and replaces the representation of the characters' consciousness in* Tom Jones.]

No one has ever seriously argued that there is no evidence of consciousness in **Tom Jones.** The narrator is clearly a thinking being, and throughout the introductory chapters we find ourselves as readers actively involved with the process of his thought.[1] When, in chapter 1 of book 11, Fielding says, "The Slander of a Book is, in Truth, the Slander of the Author" (2: 569), we are quite prepared to admit the personal identification. The personality of the "narrator" author so dominates the text that his imposing presence continually inserts itself between us and the characters of the novel, and not only, as noted before, in his generic self-consciousness. He is simply always there, and we are simply too aware of him to experience the psychological realities of his characters.[2] We feel their consciousnesses necessarily remain remote, available only in the most general of senses, perceptible in the isolated moment in time and not throughout the contiguous, ongoing moments of time that produce what Locke refers to and what empirical fiction celebrates as the train of ideas.[3]

Quite often, the momentary reflections to which we are privy do suggest psychological complexity of character. For example, when Jones receives Sophia's letter promising never to marry another man, though she will not be able to correspond further with Tom himself, his mind reels, we are told, under the conflicting emotions of "Joy and Grief." However, the immediacy of Tom's confusion is quickly deflected by a narrative flourish: a comparison of Tom's emotions to those that "divide the Mind of a good Man, when he peruses the Will of his deceased Friend, in which a large Legacy, which his Distresses make the more welcome, is bequeathed to him" (2: 851).[4] In this case, and in others like it, pause and stasis replace contiguity. In other words, reflection is by and large the narrator's province; during moments of reflection, the character's time is suspended in favor of the teller's time. The moment of consciousness—that is, the present moment as it emerges from the past and precipitates the future—is the narrator's moment and not the characters'.[5]

However, to say that *Tom Jones* is concerned with the consciousness of the narrator admittedly seems to require a special definition of consciousness; for a thinking being of this narrator's stamp and a being of consciousness, as we generally understand him or her to be, seem two entirely different things.[6] While we have a fairly complete understanding of the narrator's thoughts about the novel, about character, about truth, and about morality, and while we even see development in this thought, a certain "working through" of the problem of aesthetic distance and an expounding of the problematics of aesthetic response, what we miss is his ordering of his own experience into a story. Sometimes—as in his description of Sophia as resembling "one whose Image never can depart from my Breast" (1: 156)—we are momentarily reminded of the story of Fielding's own life; but these glimpses, like the brief forays into the reflections of the characters, are disruptive and disrupted. They constitute pause and stasis rather than contiguity.[7] They set up the characters as a source of narrative mediation. The story of Tom and Sophia is conceived in terms of, and is therefore momentarily displaced by, the history of Henry and Charlotte Fielding in much the same way that Fielding's thoughts about the mind experiencing joy and grief displace Tom's emotional response to Sophia's letter.

In short, *Tom Jones* does not seem like a novel of consciousness on any level because we find disjunction where we expect conjunction. As the very organization of the work suggests, narrative and reflection seem to occupy two different and irreconcilable planes in this fictional world.[8] In fact, everywhere in *Tom Jones* is contrast; on every level opposition seems to define meaning. Reflection alternates with narrative; the serious clashes with the comic; and a character makes his or her way through the narrative in contrastive alliance with or overt defiance of others: Sophia and Molly, Thwackum and Square, Tom and Blifil, Allworthy and Western, Partridge and Tom, Nightingale and Tom, the Man of the Hill and Tom. Such pairings establish and elaborate character through implicit or explicit points of differentiation.[9] In fact, it is our awareness of the disjunctive property of this work that has encouraged our practice of reading the narrative as allegory.[10] However, allegory is, we must admit, a conjunctive form of disjunctive expression, for the literal is simply put aside in favor of the symbolic, and, while *Tom Jones* might call upon allegory in the end to achieve a semblance of fusion as the history draws to a close, if we try to read the entire novel as symbol we involve ourselves in a task of little certainty or, for that matter, usefulness.[11] *Tom Jones* revels in disjunction, contrast, and polarization, not merely to define meaning, truth, or essence, but to defy it as well.

The principle of contrast "runs through all the Works of the Creation," Fielding tells us, seemingly advancing a notion that meaning is worked out through dichotomous categorization or binary oppositions, a notion characteristic—we might think—of a mind in search of fixed principles. Fielding's definition of beauty, for example, seems to suggest a highly authoritative habit of mind. As he defines it, beauty means beauty only as it is suggested by an awareness of its opposite. Were it "possible for a Man to have seen only" day and summer, for example, "he would have a very imperfect Idea of their Beauty" (1: 212). The beauty of day and summer is perceived, even perceptible, only through an awareness of the terrors of night and winter. The insidiousness of conceptualizations that posit definition of one thing through devaluation of another is clear, as is the means by which such conceptualizations support the order of hierarchy, patriarchy, and authority in general.

With relation to *Tom Jones,* however, we cannot stop here, because Fielding does not do so. He shifts subject and tone to disjoin and defuse the very idea of perceptual certainty even as he establishes it: "But to avoid too serious an Air: Can it be doubted, but that the finest Woman in the World would lose all Benefit of her Charms, in the Eye of a Man who had never seen one of another Cast? The Ladies themselves seem so sensible of this, that they are all industrious to procure Foils; nay, they will become Foils to themselves: for I have observed (at *Bath* particularly) that they endeavour to appear as ugly as possible in the Morning, in order to set off that Beauty which they intend to shew you in the Evening" (1: 212). In asserting experientiality and in finally shifting the locus of contrast to the selfsame entity, Fielding ironically undercuts the notion of essential differentiation that he has asserted in the preceding passage. Further, he introduces an example of mastery and manipulation that seems to challenge his own claim to be opening "a new Vein of Knowledge, which, if it hath been discovered, hath not, to our Remembrance, been wrought on by any antient or modern Writer" (1: 212). He may be *explicating* the principle of contrast for the first time, but, by his own admission, women have long been basing their creative acts upon the principle, which they seem to understand better than he. Finally, in the implied satirical thrust of such a comment, the whole idea of contrast as an index of order is so severely undermined, it begins to break apart under the strain. The disintegration is completed by a discussion of the way dullness sets off brilliance in "great" works of literature: "Soporific Parts are so many Scenes of *Serious* artfully interwoven, in order to contrast and set off the rest; and this is the true Meaning of a late facetious Writer, who told the Public, that whenever he was dull, they might be assured there was a Design in it" (1: 215).

With this, we are almost ready to abandon the notion of contrast altogether, when Fielding closes with a reminder of the subject with which he began: the difference between the serious and the comic—that is, his prefaces and his narrative—a difference we must admit, though not so clearly any more a difference articulable in polarized language, in terms of opposition or blatant contrast. We are finally left concluding, at least tentatively, what he said we would *not* have to conclude: that "there are sound and good Reasons at the Bottom, tho' we are unfortunately not able to see so far" (1: 210).

As Eric Rothstein has explained it, ***Tom Jones*** insists that we accept the authority of Fielding by leaving us no other authority upon which to depend. The narrative voice, Rothstein maintains, systematically undermines all rival authorities, from Lyttelton to Allworthy to Prudence to expectations founded on the recognition of generic conventions and themes:

> ***Tom Jones*** frees itself from the tyranny of the preestablished, whether the authority of prior literary works, the conditions of narrative that make prudence possible, or figures of social power. Fielding proffers his own world alone as the "real," the measure of propositions about ethics and "human nature" (in that his readers, so his didactic claims insist, can project its patterns of action to their everyday lives). As a work of art, it dispels the rule of rules in favor of the rule of taste, in keeping with much aesthetic thought of its time. And taste, a matter of finesse and connoisseurship in judgment, requires a tone of urbanity, of a wisdom filtered from much experience, of a nice balance between involvement and distance. . . . Fielding must affirm social, moral, and literary canons so that we trust him and he must also exploit or transcend these canons so that we have nothing to trust unmediated by him. ("Virtues of Authority" 123)

Of course, such a center is less stable than we would like, for the narrator is as unreliable as he is authoritative. He is all we have, but not necessarily all we would wish.[12]

Both our uncertainty about character and our dependence on the narrator in ***Tom Jones*** seem to derive from the self-containment, the self-referentiality, of the text. In spite of allusions to historical reality, or maybe in part because of these allusions, which have the effect of heightening fictionality rather than establishing

credibility, ***Tom Jones*** resists textual transcendence. The characters are part of the narrative and do not have reality apart from the narrative. Of course, the same must be said, and has been said, of all novelistic characters: they are constructs of language, existing, not in time, but in text. Yet I would argue that, for ***Tom Jones,*** "text" or narrative is not merely the written word; it is also conceptualization, the ordering of experience, here no less fictional than either the texts of our own lives or the stories we tell of others.

In fact, the one very real sense in which the narrator of ***Tom Jones*** can be said to have a conscious life is insofar as that life is characterized by his preoccupation with the history of ***Tom Jones*** and with the narrative (if we, like Wayne C. Booth, want to see it as such) of his relationship with his readers.[13] Narrative in ***Tom Jones*** is consciousness: that is, it is a consciousness of character, a definition of interiority as interest and involvement in the lives of others. What Fielding's novel seeks to do is establish an awareness of both the degree of certainty and the kind of uncertainty that such narrative represents.

The novel is full of narrative moments, present moments that fuse past and future in a pattern revealing the character of the ordering consciousness even while interpreting the characters of others. In these moments, it is clear that the act of narrative is an act of reading, that the reader is in fact a writer as well.[14] Upon meeting Jones on the road to London, Partridge listens to Tom's narration of his story, and he responds by an imaginative rendering of circumstances neither authored nor authorized by Tom himself:

> When *Partridge* came to ruminate on the Relation he had heard from *Jones,* he could not reconcile to himself, that Mr. *Allworthy* should turn his Son (for so he most firmly believed him to be) out of Doors, for any Reason which he had heard assigned. He concluded therefore, that the whole was a Fiction, and that *Jones,* of whom he had often from his Correspondents heard the wildest Character, had in reality run away from his Father. It came into his Head, therefore, that if he could prevail with the young Gentleman to return back to his Father, he should by that Means render a Service to *Allworthy,* which would obliterate all his former Anger; nay, indeed he conceived that very Anger was counterfeited, and that *Allworthy* had sacrificed him to his own Reputation. (1: 426-27)

Partridge's "reading" of events differs profoundly from Tom's, from the narrator's, and from ours, partly because Tom has omitted "a Circumstance or two, namely, every thing which passed on that Day in which he had fought with *Thwackum*" (1: 419). Of course, in this situation Partridge is markedly like us, for we, too, are constantly being told by the narrator that some circumstance or other has been passed over silently until he thinks it "proper to communicate it" (1: 230). The principle this episode avowedly illustrates is the following: "Let a Man be never so honest, the Account of his own Conduct will, in Spite of himself, be so very favourable, that his Vices will come purified through his Lips, and, like foul Liquors well strained, will leave all their Foulness behind" (1: 420). A man's narration of his own story, the narrator continues, is so different from the account his enemy would give "that we scarce can recognize the Facts to be one and the same" (1: 420). Partridge's response, however, suggests that listeners respond so differently to a tale that the same could also be said of them.[15]

Tom Jones is replete with examples of what we might call the other as self. In fact, characters are more often defined by their responses to others than by the narrator's "objective" commentary.[16] This is true of major characters as well as minor characters: Jones's treatment of Black George, his attitude toward Allworthy, and his behavior toward Molly so clearly establish his generosity, loyalty, and impetuosity that the narrator's remarks become corroboratory rather than informative, and Sophia's judgment about Blifil, her responsiveness to Tom, and her respect for her father serve to characterize her more significantly than anything the narrator ever says. In fact, throughout *Tom Jones,* character is customarily established through relational descriptions that at once define individual psychology and assert social identity. The synthetic brilliance of the novel resides in the deceptively casual narrative merging of the individual and the others with whom he lives.

Consider, for example, the narrative moment wherein Mrs. Wilkins discovers "the Father of the Foundling." It is a typically Fieldingesque moment, characterized as it is by an elaborate and elaborated pause in the flow of the narrative to "trace [the discovery] from the Fountain-head," a movement backward in time to "lay open . . . previous Matters," as Fielding "shall be obliged to reveal all the Secrets of a little Family, with which my Reader is at present entirely unacquainted" (1: 81). This is how Fielding describes his narrative strategy, and, in fact, it is the strategy of all four narrative acts that define the moment.

Wilkins's discovery is itself a narrative act, and it is about a narrative act as well. In Wilkins's story, Mrs. Partridge is the focal character, for her belief in her husband's guilt is what ultimately establishes his paternal responsibility. The story of Partridge's conviction is, as it were, the story of his wife's conviction, *her* narrative about her husband and Jenny Jones and about her growing belief in their complicity. As we learn the events of the story, Wilkins is displaced as narrator by Fielding, who begins by establishing the character of the more important narrator, Mrs. Par-

tridge. She is a shrew, Fielding tells us, one of the "Followers of *Xantippe,*" a woman possessed of a jealous disposition (1: 86). She expects her personal domestic history to include conjugal betrayal. Her narrative expectations yield the particular configuration her personal history acquires, both in her active organization of the events of her life (her refusal to hire a pretty female servant) and in her response to those events over which she feels she has no control (her reading of Jenny Jones's supper-table smile as one of romantic complicity rather than intellectual derision).

In fact, both active and passive behaviors are interpretative and reflect Mrs. Partridge's psychology, her individual way of ordering information and interpreting experiential reality. Fielding makes it quite clear that Mrs. Partridge's narratology is causal, comprehensive, and cumulative. When she hears at the chandler's shop that Jenny Jones had been "brought to bed of two Bastards," she mentally arranges the events of the past, as she sees them, into a pattern consistent with the outcome:

> Nothing can be so quick and sudden as the Operations of the Mind, especially when Hope, or Fear, or Jealousy to which the two others are but Journeymen, set it to work. It occurred instantly to her, that *Jenny* had scarce ever been out of her own House, while she lived with her. The leaning over the Chair, the sudden starting up, the Latin, the Smile, and many other Things rushed upon her all at once. The Satisfaction her Husband expressed in the Departure of *Jenny,* appeared now to be only dissembled; again, in the same Instant, to be real; but yet to confirm her Jealousy, proceeding from Satiety, and a hundred other bad Causes. In a Word, she was convinced of her Husband's Guilt, and immediately left the Assembly in Confusion. (1: 88)

"In Confusion" is rather deceptive, however; for Mrs. Partridge is now less confused than she has been for quite a while. By selecting carefully, she has been able to fit the details of her husband's behavior toward Jenny Jones into the narrative she had planned to write all along. Further, to achieve coherence and to clarify causality, she must ignore certain details that cast doubt on her interpretation. There is, for example, the most salient matter of the young "Lad near Eighteen" who also lived in the Partridges' house and who enjoyed with Jenny "sufficient Intimacy to found a reasonable Suspicion." Interestingly, when Fielding offers this detail, we compose our own narrative. At least on first reading, we join to the idea of Jenny as mother the notion of her compeer as father, solving (we think) the mystery of Tom's birth within the first hundred pages of the novel. Of course, our narrative, in its causal logic, its cumulative completeness, its delimiting finality, is as self-deceptive as Mrs. Partridge's narrative.

Mrs. Wilkins's involvement in the narrative act also

illustrates the way events can be—indeed, must be—recalled and restructured when the need to incorporate new narrative details arises. When she first hears the story of the Partridges' quarrel, Mrs. Wilkins does not recognize in it the "Father of the Foundling." A crucial piece of information has been obscured: the cause of the quarrel has been misreported by the chandler-shop (or some such) gossips.[17] When, "by Accident," Mrs. Wilkins gets "a true Scent of the . . . Story, though long after it had happened, [she] failed not to satisfy herself thoroughly of all the Particulars" (1: 92). As a consequence, she revises the narrative, which has become, to her mind, a tale worth telling.

Narrative is interpretation, Fielding insists; it is the ordering of that which cries out for order but which rejects order as soon as it is imposed. Narrative acts in **Tom Jones,** of which Mrs. Partridge's is a representative sample, have the effect of questioning narrative authority, even in the act of asserting it. The fictionality of the narrative itself is thus underscored; but, at the same time, the narrative speaks to the perceptual truth of the ordering consciousness. It is a momentary truth, in a sense, for further information might lead to a reordering, yet it is also an enduring truth, for it proceeds from habitual modes of conceptualization which, even if they lack the permanence of essence, speak to a kind of predictability. There is, however, another dimension to the relationship between character and consciousness, and that dimension has to do with audience. While Mrs. Partridge is a reader of events, Allworthy is a reader of narrative; and, like ours, his knowledge is confined to what the narrator—first Mrs. Wilkins and later Mrs. Partridge—is willing to tell. And while it may be true, as Rothstein says, that he should not admit a wife's evidence against her own husband, his confusion is really a result of Jenny's earlier admission of maternity, which no magistrate would be likely to discount.[18] To seek further for the father, assuming Jenny to be the mother, would have been to find another innocent party and believe his guilt, as we do for a time on first reading. While the reader may be aware at all times of the discreteness of his or her own consciousness, this discreteness is somewhat undermined by the inability to refer to any but the narrator for the facts. In other words, we are virtually forced to share the perceptual bias of the narrator: what he tells us is all we know.

Fielding makes it quite clear that Mrs. Wilkins's motivation as a storyteller is self-interest and that she, like Mrs. Partridge, tells the story that suits her. Expecting Captain Blifil to outlive Allworthy and recognizing the "no great Good-will" the captain has for Tom, "she fancied it would be rendering him an agreeable Service, if she could make any Discoveries that might lessen the Affection which Mr. *Allworthy* seemed to have contracted for this Child" (1: 91). That the revelation does not have that effect suggests that the reader

has some control over the narrative moment and that his authority is ultimately the only way narrative interpretation can gain currency. Scandal thrives on the indiscriminate reader who credits everything he or she hears; other listeners, such as Allworthy, in this case, refuse to draw the expected conclusion. Instead of dismissing "little Tommy," Allworthy "grew every Day fonder" of him, much to Captain Blifil's disgust. Allworthy, it seems, has his own version of the story of Tom Jones.

What Fielding suggests is that each individual is commonly a reader of action and character and a maker of narrative, and, as he asserts in **"An Essay on the Knowledge of the Characters of Men,"** what we think of others does emerge from and determine our definition of self. His aim in this essay, he says, is to "arm [the innocent] against Imposition," "against those who can injure us . . . by obtaining our good Opinion" (153, 164). Imposition can be of two sorts, Fielding acknowledges: not only might others misrepresent themselves to us, but we might also misapprehend others by imposing what we know to be true of ourselves on them. As Fielding notes, the honest and upright are easy to deceive, because they believe others to be like them: "That open Disposition, which is the surest Indication of an honest and upright Heart, chiefly renders us liable to be imposed on by Craft and Deceit" (156). Most of Fielding's essay is devoted to countering this sort of imposition: he warns the innocent to beware of the other, to develop a skeptical awareness of the telling disjunctions between appearance and reality, word and deed. Although Fielding argues, for example, that the austerity of countenance that passes for wisdom hides pride, ill-nature, and cunning, that there is, in other words, a disjunctive relationship between physiognomy and personality, he also asserts that interpretation resolves the seeming contradiction: "The Passions of Men do commonly imprint sufficient Marks on the Countenance; and it is owing chiefly to want of Skill in the Observer, that Physiognomy is of so little Use and Credit in the World" (157). A skilled, penetrating interpreter will read correctly. He or she will have no trouble recognizing "that a constant, settled, glavering, sneering Smile in the Countenance, is so far from indicating Goodness, that it may be with much Confidence depended on as an Assurance of the contrary" (160).

Interpretation, however, can be hampered. Many lack the skills to read the denotative meaning of the sneer, the smile, the look of solemnity. Fielding acknowledges the difficulty of interpreting another's physical appearance and seeks to offer surer guidelines for recognizing behavior that signals danger. Again, the point is imposition. Flattery, professions of friendship on short acquaintance, profuse promises, prying curiosity, and slander of others are signs of an individual whose behavior might well endanger the ease and happiness of others. The most dangerous character, the one that illustrates most clearly the threatening aspects of life in society, is the hypocrite whose self, in effect, is other and who approaches all others as self: "The Business of such a Man's Life is to procure Praise, by acquiring and maintaining an undeserved Character; so is his utmost Care employed to deprive those who have an honest Claim to the Character himself affects only, of all the Emoluments which could otherwise arise to them from it" (170).

Finally, narrative must be based on probability, and stories must be expected to follow predictable patterns. Although possibility is allowed, one must not count on it: "Nothing . . . can be more unjustifiable to our Prudence, than an Opinion that the Man whom we see act the Part of a Villain to others, should on some minute Change of Person, Time, Place, or other Circumstance, behave like an honest and just Man to ourselves" (176). While repentance is possible, judging its sincerity is difficult; therefore, it is safest to assume "that a Man whom we once knew to be a Villain, remains a Villain still" (176).

The narrative expectations implicit in Fielding's advice to the innocent reveal a tragic, not a comic, perception, a fear of narrow definition by another that is personally threatening and probably ruinous. The importance of the individual is acknowledged and decried as social relationships are presented in terms of the subsuming of one identity in another. Fielding does hold out the possibility of objectivity, of being able to avoid imposition by recognizing the disjunction of self and other through interpretation that admits the possibility of multiple meanings. In discussing the hypocrite, for example, Fielding cites the description of this character from the Gospel of Saint Matthew, quoting it thus: *It strains off a Gnat, and swallows a Camel"* (168). In a note, Fielding explains that this is a correction of the more usual translation "*strain at a Gnat, i.e.* struggle in swallowing"; and he goes on to explain that the Greek word actually refers to a "Cullender," the idea being "that though they pretend their Consciences are so fine, that a Gnat is with Difficulty strained through them, yet they can, if they please, open them wide enough to admit a Camel" (168 n. 3). Speaking both to the inside (conscience) and the outside (behavior), yet not in the same translation (disjunction), the phrase itself becomes a metaphor for individual personality, for social relationship, for narrative as interpretation. The synthesizing force is the interpreter, who admits both possibilities, though interpretation requires choice, preference, meaning, at least of a transitory nature.[19]

Still, narrative authority is never really objective, though it aims for objectivity, and never fully knowledgeable, though it values and seeks truth. In **"A Clear State of the Case of Elizabeth Canning,"** Fielding demon-strates the full range of tensions that inform the relationship between an individual consciousness, the character of another, and narrative authority. The document is in a sense a personal justification, a defense of the ruling Fielding had given in favor of eighteen-year-old Elizabeth Canning's claim that she had been kidnapped and held by Mary Squires. Her story had been called into question by commentators to whom certain aspects of her self-defense seemed improbable. In establishing their probability, Fielding offers a defense, answers objections, includes two first-person, corroboratory accounts, and reminds readers of the difficulty of attaining a guilty verdict in the "admirable" and "amiable" judicial system he represents (223). Interestingly, however, throughout his justification runs a self-portraiture that admits the possibility of error. Fielding, for all practical purposes, credits Elizabeth Canning's narrative, yet he includes as a kind of counterpoint another narrative that he fully credits as he cannot fully credit hers. That narrative is the narrative of his own growing conviction of the guilt of Mary Squires.

Fielding's self-portrait in **"The Case of Elizabeth Canning"** emphasizes his fallibility in such a way that it establishes his objectivity. When he introduces himself into the narrative, after reviewing the Canning story from the point of view of those who disbelieve her and answering their objections, we find him in a domestic setting and about to take tea with his wife, who lays aside the papers on the case when they first arrive and then retrieves them when the solicitor comes to discuss the case. Fielding emphasizes his exhaustion, "almost fatigued to death, with several tedious examinations at that time," and his desire to "refresh myself with a day or two's interval in the country, where I had not been, unless on a Sunday, for a long time" (239). After first declining the case, he yields because of "the importunities of Mr. Salt," "curiosity," and "compassion" (239). His conviction is born of the corroboratory evidence of Canning and Virtue Hall, whose narratives, differing in point of view, agree in point of fact.

The final three pages of Fielding's defense are composed of self-assessment and a recognition of the difficulty of judging another: "The only error I can ever be possibly charged with in this case is an error in sagacity. . . . In this case . . . one of the most simple girls I ever saw, if she be a wicked one, hath been too hard for me. . . . To be placed above the reach of deceit is to be placed above the rank of a human being; sure I am that make no pretension to be of that rank; indeed I have been often deceived in my opinion of men, and have served and recommended to others those persons whom I have afterwards discovered to be totally worthless" (252-54). The essay concludes with an open-endedness ("This is the light in which I see this case at present"), with a desire that "the government . . . authorise some proper persons to examine to the very bottom, a matter in which the honour of our national justice is so deeply concerned," and with a postscript presenting further evidence, some that Fielding had forgotten and some new evidence that has cemented Fielding's conviction by "corroborating the whole evidence of Canning, and contradicting the *alibi* defence of the gipsy woman" (254-55). Although in the end Fielding remains convinced of his interpretation of the events of the Canning case, he takes care to distinguish himself from those who "though . . . , perhaps, heard the cause at first with the impartiality of upright judges, [but who] when they have once given their opinion, . . . are too apt to become warm advocates, and even interested parties in defence of that opinion" (226). Fielding's own interpretation, for all its consistency, insists on its inconclusiveness, partiality, and temporality.

Like **"An Essay on the Knowledge of the Characters of Men," "A Clear State of the Case of Elizabeth Canning"** speaks to a tension between narrative and identity that narratives of causality, narratives of consciousness, customarily elide. Yet both essays proceed from the seductiveness of such elision, the desire to believe, to find coherence, to close up, to regard interpretation as truth. Resisting the temptation involves, not a denial of consciousness, but an admission of consciousnesses, alternative interpretations, other narratives. The truly objective point of view must admit its partiality, present other possibilities, and defer to a higher authority, which, in Fielding's world, of course, is ultimately God. As the creative act of fictionalizing in a sense mocks the creative act of the Godhead, we might assume the analogy to obtain, thereby making the narrator the final authority of *Tom Jones,* as Rothstein and others have suggested. But the creative act of fictionalizing is shared by narrator, characters, and readers, so that ultimate authority seems to be denied even the author here, whose focus on others and whose self-conscious portrayal of self as other establishes identity as temporal and temporary rather than eternal and enduring. In other words, while *Tom Jones* values essence over existence, it, like **"Characters of Men"** and **"The Case of Elizabeth Canning,"** finds expression for the latter only.

In *Tom Jones,* Fielding does not so much struggle with the tension between self and other, essence and expression, as he celebrates it, exploits it, and explodes it. He loves a paradox, and, in the process of creating his well-made, tightly ordered narrative, he undermines the whole notion of order and narrative. There are broad hints throughout the novel that a healthy skepticism toward language representation, particularly metaphor, is advisable if truth is in any way the aim of expression. Take, for example, the narrator's examination of the world-as-a-stage metaphor. "The World hath been often compared to the Theatre," Fielding observes, so often, in fact, that "some Words proper to the Theatre, and which were, at first, metaphorically applied to the World, are now indiscriminately and literally spoken of both" (1: 323). As Fielding notes, figure has supplanted meaning, and all the more ludicrously, as the meaning that has been supplanted was figural in the first place: "The theatrical Stage is nothing more than a Representation . . . of what really exists." But, then again, what *does* really exist? "The larger Part of Mankind . . . [are but] Actors . . . personating Characters no more their own, and to which, in Fact, they have no better Title, than the Player hath to be in Earnest thought the King or Emperor whom he represents." Interestingly, Fielding concludes, "Thus the Hypocrite may be said to be a Player; and indeed the *Greeks* called them both by one and the same Name" (1: 324), pointing to the conclusion that representation, whether in art, language, or life, should be regarded with some skepticism.

Having illustrated that the dichotomy with which he began is in fact no dichotomy at all, as art and life are equally representational, bearing equal claims to truth and sharing the same propensity to fiction, Fielding adds another twist. The representational world, the world of figure, whatever that figure may be, while itself an other with relation to the essence it represents, also finds itself defined by other and in danger, as is all essence, of being defined solely by other. Fielding cautions against this danger, using the story of Black George to do so. The audience will interpret Black George's behavior according to their own various predilections, he asserts: the upper gallery is vociferous, the boxes polite, the pit divided. Of course, Fielding is having great fun here expressing himself figuratively and revealing his own assessment of society through analysis and classification based on his own experience. For the individual, however, he seems to recommend narrative, the suspended moment that admits of contiguous action and the possibility of change. On Black George's behalf, he pleads that we realize a "single bad Act no more constitutes a Villain in Life, than a single bad Part on the Stage" (1: 328). Of course, Black George is not in life. He is in art. He is not an actor in the world but a character in a narrative. The analogy breaks down by ignoring the authorial presence, on the one hand, and by usurping it, on the other. Fielding alone is qualified to judge the behavior of Black George; he alone is admitted "behind the Scenes of this great Theatre of Nature," a fact, he claims, that should be true of all authors of anything but "Dictionaries and Spelling-Books" (1: 327). We are back once more to language. While Fielding's point is clearly that interpreters should be possessed of the truth while list makers need only fact, we might ask ourselves just what author finds himself or herself backstage in life. The reason Fielding can condemn Black George's behavior without censuring the man is that he has contrived the narrative.

Representation is in some ways all we have of reality, *Tom Jones* asserts; it is and should be recognized as an interpretation of reality, but it is an interpretative stance that should be regarded as important, not simply dismissed as incomplete. One of the great comic scenes of *Tom Jones* invokes Partridge's response to *Hamlet*. Unable to keep in view the distinction between the play and life, Partridge, in his confusion, is a figure of fun. He has not the sophisticated distance of a playgoer such as Tom, who brings to the performance an aesthetic sensibility capable of judging the actors, the staging, the audience response. In other words, Tom's is a metadramatic sensibility of such sophistication that he finds little or no interaction between the play and his own emotional reality. Partridge, on the other hand, responds quite naturally, as he is "unimproved . . . , but likewise unadulterated by Art" (2: 852); he affords great pleasure to the rest of the audience, for whom the play appears to have lost its significance. Partridge is the evening's entertainment, as Tom had known he would be all along.

Rothstein reads this scene as challenging the authority of dramatic representation and predictable (tragic) plot in favor of the narrative authority that creates chaotically ("Virtues of Authority" 119-23). The parallels and differences he points to certainly establish destabilization. But the challenge is analogous as well as exclusive. Any representation can lose its validity and vitality and does so when it becomes or is perceived too clearly as artifice. For Partridge, the best actor is the one who most seems to be acting, the one who makes the audience ever aware of the difference between himself and his role. The actor who really seems to be the character is, of course, the most skilled, but Partridge, who confuses representation and reality at this point, cannot so judge him. While we laugh at his judgment, we also recognize that we do so because we possess the disjunction he requires of his actors. And his fear of ghosts suggests the danger of our ever conjoining what our imaginations can so readily, in this instance, distinguish.

Tom Jones is about the threat inherent in things that seem other than what they are and the inevitability, even the desirability, of their doing so. While the narrative places much emphasis on getting to the bottom of, discovering, seeing behind the scenes, revealing, and pursuing, just as often we have diversion, deferral, and distraction, a supplanting of the chain of causality with a validity of its own. Partridge, who diverts attention from the play, becomes himself the evening's entertainment; the actors, rather than the action or the characters, become the subject of discourse about the play; the play, rather than the reality upon which it is based, is the audience's concern; legend orders and then supplants fact.[20]

Deferral or distraction is most readily recognized in all eighteenth-century novels in the interpolated narrative, where a character generally usurps narrative authority in self-representation. *Tom Jones,* of course, has the Man of the Hill and Mrs. Fitzpatrick, whose stories provide us with alternative narratives for Tom's and Sophia's histories. In general, we regard these alternatives as less attractive, largely because of the narrative authority that has determined that Tom and Sophia be the center of the narrative. Yet the histories, by focusing on the self as other, reveal the main narrative to be the narrator's own deferral to Tom, Sophia, Allworthy, and the rest. They represent the other as self, and, as such, they, like the narrator's representation of himself, are legitimately authorized but of limited and dubious reliability.

For all the questioning of the validity of narrative representation, however, *Tom Jones* argues its value. To entertain—to hold between—to divert, to please, is the narrator's primary concern. And, in the final analysis, the other by which the consciousness of the narrator is largely defined is the reader—not the critic, who maintains a distance between himself and the narrative, looking more at how than at what, but the reader, who shares with the author responsibility for the narrative. This responsibility arises from the impulse to narrate, to piece together a story largely causal, largely definitive, but at the same time subject to revision, reinterpretation, new combinations as new information presents itself. What Fielding does through his structuring of the narrative is allow us to participate in the writing of the story and the understanding of the characters.

Of course, in the end we discover how many of the narratives and the characters we created are not Fielding's narratives and characters. We learn that to interpret is to risk misinterpretation, for events and people lend themselves to variant readings. We see, if we look again to the beginning of the novel, that Bridget, for example, always behaved toward Tom as a loving mother, a mother who loved her son's father, would behave, though her actions were variously interpreted as jealousy or even lust (1: 92, 139-40). Upon a second reading, of course, the latter misinterpretation, encouraged by the narrator's sly speculations and reporting of the theories of others, anticipates the ending of Tom's story. It is a significant foreshadowing, for, in bracketing the novel, incest serves as a metaphor for narrative itself.[21] In its self-reflexivity, its confusion of other and self, its dangerous inability to separate identity and experience, and its fundamental self-absorption, narrative is like incest. The act of narrating, like consciousness, is inescapable, and whether the self or another is the focal point of the narration, the same limitations obtain. The individual perception is colored by emotions, desires, idiosyncrasies that govern the narrative structure. Momentary in nature, open-ended, arising from and existing in the present alone, narrative can seem continual, delimiting, and temporally comprehensive. But, as **Tom Jones** illustrates, it is not often what it seems.

Notes

1 Henry James was an early celebrant of the mind of the narrator; see his preface to *The Princess Casamassima*. Seminal studies by Wayne Booth, Henry Knight Miller, and John Preston have made treatment of the narrator as thinking being a critical commonplace; see, respectively, *The Rhetoric of Fiction* (215-18), "The Voices of Henry Fielding," and *The Created Self* (114-32).

2 Ian Watt complains about the narrator's intrusions producing "a distancing effect which prevents us from being . . . fully immersed in the lives of the characters" (285), and others, including Alan Dugald McKillop (129) and Bernard Harrison (45-49), make similar observations, though with less rancor.

3 See Locke, *Essay,* bk. 2, ch. 14 (184).

4 For discussions of the way other moments in the novel speak to the complexity of character, see Bernard Harrison's analysis of Blifil's conduct concerning Sophia's bird in book 4, chapter 3, and William Empson's discussion of Black George's behavior toward Tom in books 6 and 15 (44-46).

5 See chapter 7 [*Character & Consciousness in Eighteenth-Century Comic Fiction*, by Elizabeth Kraft (Athens: University of Georgia Press, 1992)] for a more thorough discussion of the present, the novel, and consciousness.

6 See Henry Knight Miller ("Voices"), who sees the narrator as the hero of *Tom Jones,* "not because he displays for our delectation the intimate operations of a self-absorbed psyche, but rather because he has a unique view of objective reality" (267). See also Thomas Lockwood, who argues that "Fielding's presence in *Tom Jones* acts as a screen through which we see the story he calls the history of a foundling" (230).

7 Both F. Holmes Dudden (1: 145-48) and Wilbur L. Cross (208-9) use *Tom Jones*'s description of Sophia as a fundamental source of information about Charlotte Craddock Fielding. On the critical tendency to try to match the characters of *Tom Jones* with real people, see J. Paul Hunter's remarks on the "Salisbury Tradition" (*Occasional Form* 124-29).

8 Many critics argue for connections between the narrative and the commentary, ranging from Lockwood and his assertion that the shifts are so rapid and frequent that the effect is one of unification (233) to Paulson and his exploration of thematic unity (95-99). Many readers, however, would agree with Henry Knight Miller's passing comment that the narrator and his characters seem to reside in different dimensions ("Voices" 262).

9 Rothstein describes the pre-1750 English novel as one that "moved by muted contrasts" to express an epistemology of plenitude: "What we see before us is a heterocosm, various and uncertain. The structure is loose, without a hierarchy implicit in the individual experiences. Our progress through it is tied to the order of mind, in that association of ideas binds event to event, character to character. Different casts of mind, sometimes those of different characters and sometimes those of the same character in different stages of enlightenment, regard the same (repeated, analogous) phenomena so as to provide a range of possibilities for the particulars we encounter" (*Systems of Order* 245). See also Hunter's discussion of the use of character groupings in his *Occasional Form* (169-72).

10 The most important proponent of the allegorical reading is, of course, Martin C. Battestin. See his introduction to the Wesleyan edition of the novel (xvii-xix) and his *"Tom Jones:* The Argument of Design."

11 On the matter of the allegorical significance of Paradise Hall, however, Battestin himself has noted that the name "Paradise," "which I had always taken to be mere allegory, . . . is actually the name of that part of the Gould estate that lay closest to St. Benedict's Church, in which Fielding was baptized" ("Fielding's Muse" 53). An illustration of the problem with allegorical readings of the novel is the difficulty over Allworthy, whose "all-worthiness" is, and I imagine always will be, a matter of debate. For varying points of view, see Preston 124-28, Wright 159-62, Empson 37, and Rothstein, "Virtues of Authority" 100-107.

12 See Preston's argument that Fielding posed as a bad writer "in order to unseat the bad reader" (116).

13 See Georges Poulet, "Criticism and the Experience of Interiority." In this essay, he refers, of course, to the act of reading, but the extent to which narrating and reading are analogous in *Tom Jones* will, I hope, be clear soon. On the narrative of the prefaces, Booth finds "a running account of the growing intimacy between the narrator and the reader, an account with a kind of plot of its own and a separate denouement" (*Rhetoric* 216).

14 See Norman N. Holland, "UNITY IDENTITY TEXT SELF," for the argument that "all of us, as we read, use the literary work to . . . replicate ourselves" (816) in what he goes on to describe (following Whitehead, Langer, Husserl, and others) as "an in-gathering and in-mixing of self and other" (820).

15 Alter comments on the discrepancies in Fielding's

own readership: "At some points one almost wonders whether Fielding's popular following and modern detractors, on the one hand, and the more sophisticated of his admirers, on the other hand, have really read the same novelist" (*Fielding* 5).

[16] See J. Paul Hunter on Squire Western (*Occasional Form* 178-79), Sheridan Baker on Bridget Allworthy, and William Empson on Tom Jones himself, though Empson's point has more to do with Sophia's and Allworthy's readings of Jones (43-44).

[17] As the narrator tells us, "The Cause of this Quarrel was . . . variously reported; for, as some People said that Mrs. *Partridge* had caught her Husband in Bed with his Maid, so many other Reasons, of a very different Kind, went abroad. Nay, some transferred the Guilt to the Wife, and the Jealousy to the Husband" (1: 91).

[18] Rothstein, "Virtues of Authority" 103.

[19] As Fielding continues to discuss the scriptural portrayal of hypocrisy, he illustrates the multivalency of language in his literal, then figural, readings of certain passages (see especially 169).

[20] On the theme of pursuit, see Dorothy Van Ghent, who reads it as encouragement to the reader's perception of unity of design (71-72), and John Preston, who sees it as a suggestion of the instinctive but irrational impulses of man (105-6). On play and diversion, see especially Wright 74-104 and Damrosch 263-65.

[21] The role of incest in *Tom Jones* has troubled some critics, most notably Empson, who concludes that it is just a "trick . . . to heighten the excitement at the end of the plot" (138-39). See Battestin's discussion of the biographical significance of incest as a motif in the works of both Sarah Fielding and Henry Fielding ("'Sin of Incest'").

Works Cited

. . . Alter, Robert. *Fielding and the Nature of the Novel.* Cambridge, MA: Harvard UP, 1968. . . .

Baker, Sheridan. "Bridget Allworthy: The Creative Pressures of Fielding's Plot." *Papers of the Michigan Academy of Science, Arts, and Letters* 52 (1966): 345-56. Rpt. in Fielding, *Tom Jones.* Norton Critical Edition. New York: Norton, 1973. 906-16. . . .

Battestin, Martin C. "Fielding's Muse of Experience." *Henry Fielding in His Time and Ours.* Intro. Andrew Wright. Los Angeles: William Andrews Clark Memorial Library, 1987. 31-61.

————. "Henry Fielding, Sarah Fielding, and 'the Dreadful Sin of Incest.'" *Novel* 13 (1979): 6-18. . . .

————. "*Tom Jones:* The Argument of Design." *The Augustan Milieu: Essays Presented to Louis A. Landa.* Ed. Henry Knight Miller, Eric Rothstein, and G. S. Rousseau. Oxford: Clarendon, 1970. 289-319. . . .

Booth, Wayne C. *The Rhetoric of Fiction.* Chicago: U of Chicago P. 1961. . . .

Cross, Wilbur L. *The History of Henry Fielding.* 3 vols. New Haven: Yale UP, 1918. New York: Russell and Russell, 1963.

Damrosch, Leopold. *God's Plots and Man's Stories: Studies in the Fictional Imagination from Milton to Fielding.* Chicago: U of Chicago P, 1985. . . .

Dudden, F. Holmes. *Henry Fielding: His Life, Works, and Times.* 2 vols. 1952. London: Archon, 1966. . . .

Empson, William. "Tom Jones." *Fielding: A Collection of Critical Essays.* Ed. Ronald Paulson. Englewood Cliffs, NJ: Prentice-Hall, 1962. 123-45. . . .

Fielding, Henry. "A Clear State of the Case of Elizabeth Canning." *The Legal Writings.* Vol. 13 of *The Complete Works.* 16 vols. Ed. William Ernest Henley. New York: Croscup and Sterling, 1902. 223-55. . . .

————. "An Essay on the Knowledge of the Characters of Men." *Miscellanies.* Ed. Henry Knight Miller. Middleton, CT: Wesleyan UP, 1967. 153-78.

————. *The History of Tom Jones, a Foundling.* Introduction and commentary by Martin Battestin. Ed. Fredson Bowers. 2 vols. Oxford: Clarendon, 1974. . . .

Harrison, Bernard. *Henry Fielding's "Tom Jones": The Novelist as Moral Philosopher.* London: Sussex UP, 1975. . . .

Holland, Norman N. "UNITY IDENTITY TEXT SELF." *PMLA* 90 (1975): 813-22. . . .

Hunter, J. Paul *Occasional Form: Henry Fielding and the Chains of Circumstance.* Baltimore: Johns Hopkins UP, 1975. . . .

Langer, Susanne K. *Feeling and Form: A Theory of Art.* New York: Charles Scribner's Sons, 1953. . . .

Locke, John. *An Essay concerning Human Understanding.* Ed. Peter H. Nidditch. Oxford: Clarendon, 1975.

Lockwood, Thomas. "Matter and Reflection in *Tom Jones.*" *ELH* 45 (1978): 226-35. . . .

McKillop, Alan Dugald. *Early Masters of English Fic-*

tion. Lawrence: U of Kansas P, 1956. . . .

Miller, Henry Knight. "The Voices of Henry Fielding: Style in *Tom Jones.*" *The Augustan Milieu: Essays Presented to Louis A. Landa.* Ed. Henry Knight Miller, Eric Rothstein, and G. S. Rousseau. Oxford: Clarendon, 1970. 262-88. . . .

Paulson, Ronald. *Satire and the Novel in Eighteenth-Century England.* New Haven: Yale UP, 1967. . . .

Poulet, Georges. "Criticism and the Experience of Interiority." Trans. Catherine Macksey and Richard Macksey. *Reader-Response Criticism: From Formalism to Post-Structuralism.* Ed. Jane P. Tompkins. Baltimore: Johns Hopkins UP, 1980. 41-49.

Preston, John. *The Created Self: The Reader's Role in Eighteenth-Century Fiction.* New York: Barnes and Noble, 1970. . . .

Rothstein, Eric. *Systems of Order and Inquiry in Later Eighteenth-Century Fiction.* Berkeley: U of California P, 1975. . . .

———. "Virtues of Authority in *Tom Jones.*" *Eighteenth-Century: Theory and Interpretation* 28 (1987): 99-126. . . .

Van Ghent, Dorothy. *The English Novel: Form and Function.* New York: Rinehart, 1953. . . .

Watt, Ian. *The Rise of the Novel: Studies in Defoe, Richardson, and Fielding.* Berkeley: U of California P, 1957. . . .

Wright, Andrew. *Henry Fielding: Mask and Feast.* London: Chatto and Windus, 1965. . . .

Jill Campbell (essay date 1995)

SOURCE: "The Meaning of a Male Pamela," in her *Natural Masques: Gender and Identity in Fielding's Plays and Novels,* Stanford University Press, 1995, pp. 67-89.

[*In this chapter from her book* Natural Masques: Gender and Identity in Fielding's Plays and Novels, *Campbell argues that* Joseph Andrews *not only compels us to examine assumptions about gender roles but also demonstrates the potential of the novel as a new genre to offer new modes of characterization.*]

Even in the opening scenes of **Joseph Andrews,** Fielding's substitution of a man for a woman in Richardson's plot does not function as simply as it might seem to at first glance. The inversion it creates is comic and strikes us as a kind of parodic reduction of Richardson's high drama; but it also confronts us with the question of what has been reduced in the act of substitution—why what is virtue in one sex comes off as triviality in the other. If, as Schilling says, Joseph's assumption of his sister's virtue looks as ridiculous as "dressing a man in woman's clothes," Fielding reminds us of a surprising similarity between virtues and clothing by showing us chastity worn out of fashion, out of character, on the wrong occasion. In the auction scene in **The Historical Register** Fielding expressed a clearly satiric view on the externality and adventitiousness of virtues by presenting them for sale in the form of clothing and cosmetics, whose prices reflect fashion's whim. In the opening scene of **Joseph Andrews,** he only raises our awareness that a virtue's value depends on its bearer, implying that Pamela's virtue might itself be "assumed," but not clearly guiding our conclusions about whether virtue *should* look ridiculous when it appears as cross-dressing.[1]

A male Pamela reminds us of assumptions about gender roles by defying them, though we are free to laugh at him or reconsider them. More specifically, he makes visible the conventional analogizing of class and gender structures by standing in different relations to the two. When Fielding replaces Richardson's woman with a man in the position of sexually embattled servant, he not only displaces the defense of chastity from its traditional female preserve but also breaks the correspondence between socioeconomic and sexual disempowerment in Richardson's protagonist. Pamela could become a virtually mythic representative of the culturally disentitled because her age, gender, and class position all coincide in powerlessness; the mythologizing of her powerlessness serves complex ideological functions in Richardson's novel, a vehicle for both progressive and conservative suggestion.[2] The very associations between class and gender positions employed by critics when they liken Richardson to a woman writer are explored by Fielding when he replays Richardson's scenario in a different key, separating the part of masculinity from the position of social and economic power. The scenes between Lady Booby and Joseph especially foreground the tension between hierarchies of class and of gender in Fielding's narrative, expressed by the mistress Lady Booby as a titillating form of sexual tension:[3]

> "La!" says she, in an affected Surprize, "what am I doing? I have trusted myself with a Man alone, naked in Bed; suppose you should have any wicked Intentions upon my Honour, how should I defend myself? . . . But then, say you, the World will never know any thing of the Matter, yet would not that be trusting to your Secrecy? Must not my Reputation be then in your power? Would you not then be my Master?" (30)

When Lady Booby voices astonishment at Joseph's reference to his own virtue in the second interview between them—"Your Virtue! Intolerable Confidence! Have you the Assurance to pretend, that when a Lady demeans herself to throw aside the Rules of Decency, . . . your Virtue should resist her Inclination?"— Joseph's defense oddly aligns his masculinity and his poverty. "'Madam,' said *Joseph,* 'I can't see why her having no Virtue should be a Reason against my having any. Or why, because I am a Man, or because I am poor, my Virtue must be subservient to her Pleasures'" (41). Pamela must resist the assumption that because she is doubly powerless as a woman and a poor one her virtue should be subservient to her master's pleasures; Joseph must defend his right to control his own virtue against a more complicated pairing of assumptions—his disentitlement as a servant limits his power to act on his own virtue while his sexual entitlement as a man limits the dramatic *authority* of his desire to do so. Lady Booby had reminded Joseph in their first interview of the greater physical vulnerability of women, even socially superior women, to sexual attack ("how should I defend myself?"), and her outrage at Joseph's resistance when she voluntarily invites sexual advances reflects a sense that the relative invulnerability of male chastity to coercion makes it less valued, less available as a privileged symbol of self-determination—the symbol on which Pamela's story centered.[4]

These early scenes of *Joseph Andrews* contain some suggestion of an inquiry into the deep cultural assumption (made explicit in Lady Matchless and Vermilia's remarks in *Love in Several Masques*) that the interior realm of private virtue belongs to woman, and that the greater physical (and social) power of a man makes any claim he might assert to personal or sexual virtue a misplaced pretense. These scenes do not foreclose the possibility that we should take a man's chastity more seriously than we do, or that a masculine version of private virtue might be conceived; but they also include the possibility that a man's claim to private virtue can *only* be modeled on a woman's and will necessarily involve him in a laughable kind of cross-dressing of identity.[5] After asserting his right to his own virtue, though poor and a man, Joseph immediately goes on to reject Lady Booby's incredulity about a boy's virtue by declaring that "that Boy is the Brother of *Pamela*"—his virtue taken from his sister's wardrobe. In the first book of *Joseph Andrews* Joseph is feminized by his economic vulnerability (the "defenseless" Lady Booby deprives him of his employment, has him stripped of his livery, and denies him the "character" that would have allowed him to find other employment), by his appearance in the conventionally female role of embattled chastity, and by his reliance on his sister's example in conceiving the importance of his own virtue. With Pamela as the immediately proximate representative of femininity, Joseph's connection with female identity in the novel's opening scenes works predominantly to render him ridiculous.

But a connection between Joseph and female identity will prove crucial to the end of the novel as well, when Joseph has left his initial appearance as parodic reduction far behind him. In the scene that provides a comic resolution to the novel's plot, Gammar Andrews reveals the key to Joseph's obscured birth, history, and true family relations: he came into the Andrews family as a sick boy substituted in the cradle by gypsies for a healthy girl. The long-ago exchange of Joseph and Fanny that emerges in *Joseph Andrews*' recognition scene reasserts as the identifying feature of Joseph's character the substitution of boy for girl that we were aware of in the novel's inaugural joke. Though he is not interested in the exchange of genders involved, Homer Obed Brown comments that this secret event in Joseph's past "might perhaps be allegorized as part of the shifting and substitutional nature of the relationship between Fielding's text and Richardson's,"[6] and we can give that allegory more specific content when we see it repeat the relation between Joseph and a female character in the novel's opening. It repeats it with a difference, however: the substitution has now come inside Fielding's own narrative, as plot device rather than as an allusive relation to a prior text, and it now places Joseph in a physical space previously occupied by a girl rather than in her feminine role.

The literalizing of the substitution removes it from its earlier parodic purpose and satiric reflection on Joseph's character—although, suggestively, Gammar Andrews implies that the gypsies left Joseph in Fanny's place because he was such "a poor sickly Boy, that did not seem to have an Hour to live" (337). The sickliness that motivated this exchange might be said to feminize Joseph the way his reliance on Pamela's example did. But in an aside, Gammar Andrews at once asserts the identity between the past and present Josephs and marks the change between them: "the poor Infant (which is our *Joseph* there, as stout as he now stands) lifted up its Eyes upon me so piteously, that to be sure, notwithstanding my Passion, I could not find in my heart to do it any mischief." Though the infant Joseph's self-protection through piteous appeal is reminiscent of Pamela's, the girl with whom he is associated through the exchange in the cradle turns out to hold a relation to the grown Joseph quite different from Pamela's in the novel's first book. At the beginning of the novel, Joseph has replaced a female character to whom he claims a genealogical tie and family resemblance, and with whom he is mimetically identified, modeling himself on her through the notion of moral "example"; the end of the novel reveals that Joseph has occupied the same space as a female character with whom he will eventually be erotically rather than mimetically united.

The ending of the novel cancels its opening's version of Joseph's relation to female identity not only through repetition with a difference but through the details of its plot resolution: the story of the gypsies' exchange is also what establishes that Joseph is *not* Pamela's brother (or Fanny's, for that matter). As Joseph is released from a genealogical relation to Richardson's heroine by the revelations of the novel's conclusion, so Fielding's work itself has gained a kind of autonomy from its predecessor in the course of the novel, finally insisting that an accurate identification of its main character can only be made within the perimeter of its own narrative.[7] And still, when the novel comes to providing its own history for the character of Joseph, it concludes by creating an alternative, narrative version of that same fluid relation to feminine identity in which Joseph first appeared—by making Joseph, again, a changeling of gender, though perhaps of another kind.

Before Joseph's history is revealed, a series of what Fielding calls "curious Night-Adventures" occur among those spending the night at Lady Booby's, and provide one last deferral of plot resolution. The content of these adventures prepares us for the importance of gender substitutions in the news that arrives in the morning, confirming that that feature of Joseph's history is not a narrative accident. The adventures occupy all of book 4, chapter 14, and begin with Beau Didapper's plan to impersonate Joseph and to seduce Fanny by taking Joseph's place in her bed. His plan goes awry immediately, however, when he enters Slipslop's bedroom rather than Fanny's; and when Slipslop cries out for help and Adams runs to her rescue, the confusions in identity that create the farcical upheaval of the chapter become confusions specifically of gender identity:

> [Adams] made directly to the Bed in the dark, where laying hold of the Beau's Skin (for *Slipslop* had torn his Shirt almost off) and finding his Skin extremely soft, and hearing him in a low Voice begging *Slipslop* to let him go, he no longer doubted but this was the young Woman in danger of ravishing, and immediately falling on the Bed, and laying hold on *Slipslop's* Chin, where he found a rough Beard, his Belief was confirmed; he therefore rescued the Beau. (331-32)

This scene anticipates the interchanging of genders in a bed that will be revealed the next morning as the hidden secret of Joseph's identity; it also recalls the comic recasting of the embattled chastity story of the novel's opening, imagining a man rather than a woman as in need of rescue—but here only as the characters of the drama are misrecognized by Adams. When we place the revelation of the gypsies' replacement of Fanny with Joseph in the context of the night-adventures that precede it, we might broaden the allegory Brown finds in it, and see it as one emblematic moment in a sustained investigation of the "shifting and substitutional nature" of the relationship not only between Fielding's and Richardson's texts but also between the two sexes.

Lady Booby soon arrives on the scene of Adams, Slipslop, and Didapper's struggle and straightens out the story, sending Adams back to his room. But all paths lead to confusion on this night before the novel's plot is resolved, and Adams makes a wrong turn and enters Fanny's room—the room Didapper had been seeking to start with—and sleeps, oblivious, beside her for hours. All paths lead specifically, that is, to gender confusion: when awakened by a surprised Joseph in the morning, Adams protests repeatedly, "I know not whether she is a Man or Woman"; he insists that his male clothes have been "bewitched away too, and *Fanny's* brought into their place"; and he is only convinced of the truth of the situation when Joseph points out that "the Women's Apartments were on this side Mrs. *Slipslop's* Room, and the Men's on the other," and that "it was plain he had mistaken, by turning to the right instead of the left" (334-35). Gender structures even the physical space in which these characters reside, and in the comic entr'acte through which they must pass before Joseph's identity is revealed, the possibility of wrong turns in gender identification is underscored with all the literalizing insistence and extremity of farce.

The burlesque treatment of gender inversions and confusions in this scene may remind us of the farcical inversions and slapstick action centering on gender in Fielding's *Tom Thumb, Pasquin,* or *The Author's Farce.* Early in the novel, Joseph's assumption of feminine roles potentially grouped him with the effeminate men satirized repeatedly in Fielding's plays, but in this scene he stands notably on the sidelines of theatrical role-confusions—he is even instrumental in sorting out the last of the confusions.[8] It is Beau Didapper, instead, whose gender is comically compromised in this scene; and in several ways Didapper's character is imported so directly from the comic repertoire of Fielding's theatrical days as to make it appear incongruous in the pages of *Joseph Andrews.* Not only do Fielding's choice of a name for the beau, his references to him as a Hylas rather than a Hercules (303 and 333), and his description of his physical appearance place him among the sexually ambiguous beaux of Fielding's dramatic satires; but the echoes of Conyers Middleton's dedication of his *Life of Cicero* in Fielding's description of Didapper's "qualifications" identify him with Lord Hervey in particular, a frequent butt of the political/sexual satire in his plays (312-13, 313 n. 1).

While the world of Fielding's plays was filled with characters that suggested themselves as versions of one or more offstage actors, Beau Didapper, entering the novel quite late, seems oddly anomalous as the one character in *Joseph Andrews* with a pointed historical referent. His presence reminds us that in the largely political context of Fielding's plays, figures of compromised gender were usually clearly negative ones, implicated in compromises of political, moral, or literary categories as well. Beau Didapper's character also shadows Joseph's own—at least in broad outline. Both of them replay, in different ways, the story of Potiphar's wife: Fielding alerts us to that story as the source of Joseph's name when he begins to call him Joseph rather than Joey (29 and 47),[9] but he in fact recalls the biblical story in more detail (the woman's self-serving accusations of rape, the piece of the man's garment left behind serving as evidence) in Didapper's encounter with Slipslop than in Lady Booby's interviews with Joseph. Taking over the allusive context that had provided Joseph's very name, Beau Didapper might seem to present a dark mirror to the character of Joseph, as a satiric doubling of the theme of compromised gender.

To invoke Lord Hervey as the original of Beau Didapper has the effect of making Didapper a kind of self-conscious cliché of gender problems within the corpus of Fielding's own works, the easily recognizable sign of the negative possibilities of gender compromise; and Fielding's treatment of Didapper identifies him with both the theatrical forms and some of the recurrent satiric subjects of his early writings. Robert Alter notes that some of the Beau's actions "read like comic stage directions translated into the idiom of the novel." He observes that Fielding also "appl[ies] in new ways techniques he had learned in his years of writing for the theater" in the dialogue he writes for Lady Booby: in her defense of her virtue, "Lady Booby's hypocrisy confesses itself with such splendidly lucid theatricality that it is entirely appropriate for Fielding to include actual stage directions, properly italicized."[10] Within the novel, the theatricality of Lady Booby's manner of expression is acknowledged in Joseph's first letter to Pamela: "and she held my Hand, and talked exactly as a Lady does to her Sweetheart in a Stage-Play, which I have seen in *Convent-Garden,* while she wanted him to be no better than he should be" (31).

The theatrical thus appears within *Joseph Andrews* not only as a literary mode, but as a characterizing manner of self-expression, and even a style of sexuality for both Lady Booby and her "distant relation," Beau Didapper (303)—one that Joseph recognizes and specifically rejects. The little we learn of Didapper's sexuality establishes its similarity to the purely mimetic and mediated desire, concentrated upon display and "reputation," which Fielding had represented in the beaux and castrato-lovers of his dramatic satires (and which he touches upon in Wilson's story of his life as a London fop, 203-4). In his ironic description of Didapper's "Qualifications" he tells us that he was "no Hater of Women; for he always dangled after them; yet so little subject to Lust, that he had, among those who

knew him best, the Character of great Moderation in his Pleasures" (312); and the Beau confirms this character when, after being routed from the wrong bed in his attempt at a sexual adventure, "he was far from being ashamed of his Amour, and rather endeavoured to insinuate that more than was really true had past between him and the fair *Slipslop*" (336).

Beau Didapper's plan to seduce Fanny, which sets all of the "curious Night-Adventures" in motion, relies on the fact that "he was an excellent Mimick." We have heard something of this earlier when he frightened the members of Adams's household with a display of his wit in announcing his party's arrival at Adams's cottage by "mimicking" with his cane "the rap of a *London* Footman at the Door" (312).[11] The role Didapper mimics at Adams's door is one Joseph has actually filled earlier in the novel—we meet him first, in action, as a London footman—and when we see Didapper practice mimicry for the second time, it is Joseph in particular that he impersonates: "he groped out the Bed with difficulty; for there was not a Glimpse of Light, and opening the Curtains, he whispered in *Joseph's* Voice (for he was an excellent Mimick), '*Fanny,* my Angel . . . '" (330). Through his emphasis on Beau Didapper's reliance on mimicry, especially as focused on Joseph, Fielding suggests one possible relation between the two male figures of compromised gender in this novel: that the Beau is just a poor dramatic impersonation of something more complicated in Joseph's character.

Didapper's doubling of aspects of Joseph's identity may function, then, not to reflect badly on Joseph but to split Fielding's initially ambiguous treatment of him into a pair of linked characters, one clearly satirically conceived and the other positive. Occurring on the brink of the revelation of Joseph's true identity, Beau Didapper's appearance seems to work to free Joseph of some of the dangers or satiric potential of his compromised gender position by embodying them in someone else, locating the negative version of mixed gender identity specifically in someone also implicated in play-acting. Didapper's very anomalousness within the novel provides a measure of how far Fielding has moved, in creating Joseph, from the satiric treatment of the effeminate man in his plays.

Much earlier in the novel, Fielding associated Joseph with another standard satiric figure from his plays: the Italian castrato singers so popular in the London opera at this time. The decision to associate his romantic hero with the figure of the castrato is surely a bold one, and in examining Fielding's treatment of that association we can begin to explore to what end he might create a hero of ambiguous gender to start with—what positive purposes such a design might hope to achieve—and by what means he works, gradually, to disengage his hero from the expected negative burden of such a role.[12]

At the beginning of *Joseph Andrews,* Abraham Adams first notices Joseph in church, where "his Voice gave him an Opportunity of distinguishing himself by singing Psalms" (22). Later in the novel, Joseph is recognized by the sound of his voice (see, for example, 154 and 295). We are told that Joseph distinguished himself particularly in music while in London, so that "he led the Opinion of all the other Footmen at an Opera, and they never condemned or applauded a single Song contrary to his Approbation or Dislike" (27). Lest the reader forget the focus of Fielding's satiric concern with the opera in his plays, soon after Joseph's success at the opera is reported, Slipslop reminds us of it, sharply responding to Lady Booby's censure of "lewdness" in her house: "'If you will turn away every Footman,' said *Slipslop,* 'that is a lover of the Sport, you must soon open the Coach-Door yourself, or get a Sett of *Mophrodites* to wait upon you; and I am sure I hated the Sight of them even singing in an Opera'" (43). But the Joseph she calls "a strong healthy *luscious* Boy enough" (35) has already been more pointedly associated by the narrator with those "hermaphrodites" she abhors. In summarizing the brief and rather uneventful history of Joseph's life before the action of the novel opens, the narrator explained the vicissitudes of his employment in the Booby household:

> the young *Andrews* was at first employed in what in the Country they call *keeping Birds.* His Office was to perform the Part the Antients assigned to the God *Priapus,* which Deity the Moderns call by the Name of *Jack-o'-Lent:* but his Voice being so extremely musical, that it rather allured the Birds than terrified them, he was soon transplanted from the Fields into the Dog-kennel, where he was placed under the Huntsman, and made what Sportsmen term a *Whipper-in.* For this Place likewise the Sweetness of his Voice disqualified him: the Dogs preferring the Melody of his chiding to all the alluring Notes of the Huntsman. (21-22)

Fielding refers to the humble task Joseph is given of scaring off birds from the fields as "the Part of Priapus," introducing into the English landscape the image of this ancient figure, a daimon of fertility often represented as a grotesquely misshapen man with a huge and erect phallus, and sometimes represented simply as the phallus itself, "the other human attributes being incidental."[13] Joseph is found unfit for this part by the sweetness of his voice—like the castrati, he combines an alluringly sweet voice with a disqualification from phallic office.[14]

Why would Fielding want to link the man who will gradually emerge as the hero of his novel to the castrati he had so satirized in his plays? In those works the figure of the castrato serves not only as an object of ridicule but as an occasion to defend the very practice of ridicule: Fielding's satire of him involves an account of satire itself, imagined as threatened directly by the castrato's popularity. The allusions to this satiric subject within *Joseph Andrews,* then, may function not just to adapt the humor of his dramatic satires to the novel form but to reexamine the nature of that humor, and to reflect on his old and new forms. As we saw in Chapter I, Fielding had repeatedly associated the castrati's popularity with a moral decline, making explicit an assumption that moral rigor resides in a specifically phallic authority, and that such rigor is enforced specifically by the instrument of satire. For example, in his epilogue to *The Intriguing Chambermaid* (1733), he opposes the "soft Italian warblers" who "have no sting" and "no harm within" to satire, which "may wound some pretty thing" and "gives the wounded hearer pain." He concludes the epilogue by expressing sympathy with his female audience's choice of opera over other forms of drama, but his sympathy and approval are only ironic: although he describes the phallic satire that "soft Italian warblers" lack as aggressive and wounding, as a lashing rod, he defends it as a necessary aggression in the service of moral correction, like the disciplines of the schoolmaster and the preacher. In *Joseph Andrews* Fielding allows himself to explore more openly some of the negative dimensions of phallic satire, the possibility that its aggression is at times primary and the moral purpose of its application not assured. Though Fielding pokes fun at Joseph's compromised gender identity in the passage quoted above by showing his failure in the part of phallic enforcement—his office of chasing the birds off—he also pokes fun at the image of a more adequate masculinity by choosing to imagine it in the figure of the grotesque Priapus, all phallus and no form.

Two books later, Fielding will give more extended and serious treatment to the negative dimensions of conventional masculine identity that Joseph may be created to evade: the Roasting-Squire who bursts upon the scene in book 3, chapter 6, and dominates the chapters that follow provides a dark embodiment of irresponsible satiric impulses allied with the misuse of masculine power. Associated, too, with drama, the Roasting-Squire requires us to understand *Joseph Andrews* as a complicated reflection not only on Richardson's *Pamela* but on Fielding's own most popular early works, his dramatic satires. By the time we meet the Roasting-Squire, however, Fielding's characterization of Joseph has evolved to make him a more viable alternative to the portrait of masculinity we find there; and before we turn in Chapter 3 to the problem represented by the Squire, we must trace the way Fielding gradually redefines Joseph's compromised gender. He begins by superimposing the figure of the castrato, familiar from his dramatic satires, onto Joseph, and then separates Joseph in certain ways from that figure to free him from its negative associations—he thus uses the old figure in a new way to explore some of the more positive possibilities represented by the castrato's escape from monolithic phallic identity.

Fielding's description of Joseph's physical appearance early in the novel offers a simple example of his construction of Joseph's gender in equivocal terms, but an example in which we can already see the value given to that equivocation becoming less strictly negative. Indeed, Fielding provides his description of Joseph's appearance when he does so that we may better understand the temptation Joseph is about to present to Lady Booby. Schilling comments that Fielding makes Joseph's assumption of feminine virtue "seem the more outlandish by a glowing description of Joseph's physical beauty," but as Fielding sketches the features of Joseph's body and face for us, we find that his particular form of physical beauty combines the feminine with the masculine.[15] Fielding introduces the special nature of Joseph's attraction by alluding to "the uncommon Variety of Charms, which united in this young Man's Person"; what is uncommon about them is that they bring together, in his person, beauties traditionally granted to each gender. The systematic way in which Fielding surveys the separate features of Joseph's appearance is itself reminiscent of descriptive techniques conventionally applied to women:[16]

> [Joseph Andrews] was of the highest Degree of middle Stature. His Limbs were put together with great Elegance and no less Strength. His Legs and Thighs were formed in the exactest Proportion. His Shoulders were broad and brawny, but yet his Arms hung so easily, that he had all the Symptoms of Strength without the least clumsiness. His Hair was of a nut-brown Colour, and was displayed in wanton Ringlets down his Back. His Forehead was high, his Eyes dark, and as full of Sweetness as of Fire. His Nose a little inclined to the Roman. His Teeth white and even. His Lips full, red, and soft. His Beard was only rough on his Chin and upper Lip; but his Cheeks, in which his Blood glowed, were overspread with a thick Down. His Countenance had a Tenderness joined with a Sensibility inexpressible. (38)

The first sentence of the description establishes a rhythm of assertion followed by qualification which serves to characterize Joseph throughout the passage: his height is of the highest degree—of middle stature. Repeatedly, the syntax of the description creates hinges between assertions and their modification which either pair disparate characteristics, providing a balanced weighting of qualities associated with masculine and feminine beauty ("great Elegance and no less Strength," "as full of Sweetness as of Fire"), or insist on the distinction between a positive masculine characteristic assigned to Joseph and some negative extension of it ("His Shoulders were broad and brawny; but yet his Arms hung so easily, that he had all the Symptoms of Strength with-

out the least clumsiness"). The description of Beau Didapper that Fielding will provide in book 4, chapter 9, not only mockingly echoes Middleton's praise of Hervey, but parallels, in its balanced weighting of qualities, the syntax of this earlier description of Joseph. The "moderation" achieved by the balanced weighting there is handled, however, as Fielding acknowledges, "negatively": "He had lived too much in the World to be bashful, and too much at Court to be proud . . . No Hater of Women; for he always dangled after them; yet so little subject to Lust, that he had, among those who knew him best, the Character of great Moderation in his Pleasures" (312). While Fielding emphasizes what's lacking from Didapper's body—he is four feet five inches tall, scarce of hair, "thin and pale," with "very narrow Shoulders, and no Calf"—the balance of qualities in Joseph is not achieved negatively, by absence. Though the description of Joseph immediately precedes the interview in which Joseph declares himself "the brother of Pamela," Fielding does not broaden his parody of a "male Pamela" in it by denying him the strength and brawn of a traditionally masculine body.

At the same time, though, Fielding carefully negotiates Joseph's particular relation to expectations about the masculine body. He emphasizes the presence of a "Tenderness" and a "Sensibility" in Joseph's countenance that is "inexpressible"; along with his male massiveness, there is something elusive here that is traditionally associated with female beauty.[17] Even Joseph's beard equivocates: it is rough below, but downy above, in a way that allows the flush of his blood to appear. Finally, if his facial hair presents us visually with some kind of vertical distribution of Joseph's complex sexual identity, Fielding's description of his "Ringlets" complicates Joseph's gender identification in another direction, in the relation between narrative foreground and the background of literary echo, where it again crosses into association with a woman.

The display of Joseph's hair in "wanton Ringlets down his Back" seems an apparently insignificant flourish in the description of his pretty-boy good looks, but the phrase "wanton Ringlets" connects Fielding's description of Joseph's physical appearance to the passage in *Paradise Lost* that first introduces a structuring principle of gender into the poem's cosmos. Traveling with Satan in his approach to the Garden of Eden, the reader of *Paradise Lost* first glimpses Adam and Eve when Satan does, in book IV. Milton presents him and us with the "two of far nobler shape erect and tall" among God's new creatures, saying that "the image of their glorious Maker shone" in them both.[18]

> though both
> Not equal, as thir sex not equal seem'd;
> For contemplation hee and valor form'd,

For softness shee and sweet attractive Grace,
Hee for God only, shee for God in him:
His fair large Front and Eye sublime declar'd
Absolute rule; and Hyacinthine Locks
Round from his parted forelock manly hung
Clust'ring, but not beneath his shoulders broad:
Shee as a veil down to the slender waist
Her unadorned golden tresses wore
Dishevell'd, but in wanton ringlets wav'd
                          (IV.295-306)

Though Joseph's hair is just one of a number of features of his appearance that Fielding describes, the passage from *Paradise Lost* that he recalls by referring to Joseph's "wanton Ringlets" gives hairstyle a singular importance. Milton chooses it, rather than the more obvious differences of bodily parts or shape or size, to represent the difference in identity created by sex in the first man and woman.[19] But not only does Fielding echo Milton's reference to Eve's hair rather than to Adam's; he specifies that Joseph's hair hangs "down his Back," while Milton insists that Adam's "manly" locks hung "not beneath his shoulders broad." Elaborating on his physical emblem of the two sexes' different statuses, Milton glosses its figurative significance with a simile. Eve's hair

          in wanton ringlets wav'd
As the Vine curls her tendrils, which impli'd
Subjection, but requir'd with gentle sway,
And by her yielded, by him best receiv'd,
Yielded with coy submission, modest pride,
And sweet reluctant amorous delay.
                          (IV.306-11)

When, in placing Joseph against the backdrop of this first description of our first parents, Fielding aligns him with Eve, he implicates him, then, not just in feminine appearance but in the feminine position of "subjection" and "submission" which Milton says her curling, pendant locks fittingly picture. The adjective "sweet," repeated twice to characterize Eve in the seventeen-line passage, appears in the description of Joseph's eyes, as the "softness" given to Eve in contrast to Adam appears in Joseph's lips. Suggestively, Milton's account of Adam's and Eve's hair and of the primal nature of "hee" and "shee" ends on a note about female sexuality: the "sweet reluctant amorous delay" afforded by Eve's "coy submission" and "modest pride" brings the passage to a close. While the meanings "undisciplined," "natural," or "profuse" seem denoted by "wanton" in the description of Eve's long hair, as Milton interprets all that that hair represents about female identity, the sexual meaning of "wanton" surfaces as well, and her hair comes to express the need created, even by Eve's gorgeous plenitude and luxuriance, for masculine "sway," a need shaping the sexual relations between the first man and woman.

In its relation to *Pamela,* Fielding's novel has from the first placed Joseph in a position held earlier by a woman, the position of a young servant defending her chastity; in its relation to the passage from *Paradise Lost,* the novel again places Joseph in a position held earlier by a woman, linking Joseph to Eve through a phrase that specifically figures both her subjection and her sexuality. The force of this gender-inverting allusion is complex: as it appears in the context of a description of Joseph's attractions, its force would not seem to fall so clearly against Joseph himself as the inversion of Richardson's scenario does. The interpretive tensions created by the crossing of gender categories within the allusion raise questions about the relevance of Milton's Eden to a modern "history" and about the authenticity of Richardson's version of gender difference, as well as about the character of Joseph. The incongruity with which Fielding alludes to Eve's "wanton ringlets" might remind us of the distance between Joseph's world and Adam and Eve's: Joseph exists in a historical world, one where power is structured by changing class distinctions as well as by the gender categories which represent stable, naturalized hierarchies of authority in timeless Eden. Replacing Pamela momentarily with Eve as Joseph's female counterpart, the allusion also historicizes notions of gender, shifting the content of Joseph's feminine sexual role from the eighteenth-century identification of woman with chastity to a more complex picture of feminine sexual luxuriance and compliance—a "modest pride" and "coy submission" that are not without desire.

As Ian Watt has argued, notions of female identity changed dramatically between the appearance of Milton's Eve and Richardson's Pamela. Indeed, following R. P. Utter and G. B. Needham, Watt asserts that the publication of *Pamela* itself "marks a very notable epiphany in the history of our culture: the emergence of a new, fully developed and immensely influential stereotype of the feminine role," an ideal of womanhood characterized by youth, inexperience, passivity, extreme mental and physical delicacy, and the absence of sexual passion. By conjuring the older tradition represented by Milton, which was "prone to lay more emphasis on the concupiscence of women than of men,"[20] Fielding reminds us that Richardson's portrait of female nature is not the only one (as he does also through the characters of Lady Booby and the more appealing Betty, the innkeepers' chambermaid). But his use of Milton within the parody of Richardson, suggesting a competing version of the feminine sexual role, also destabilizes Milton's own mythologized gender oppositions, not only reversing the characteristics assigned by Milton to the two sexes but explaining them in terms of fashion.

If we look back to an earlier passage in *Joseph Andrews,* we recognize that Joseph's ringlets, unlike Eve's, are not a natural outward expression or emanation of his inner identity. Though Joseph remains uncorrupted by vice while living in London, he is reshaped by fashion, having his hair cut, we are told, "after the newest Fashion" and learning to curl it in curling papers (27). Fashion has shaped the appearance of Fanny's hair too, and has shaped it in a way that makes it actually less like Eve's than Joseph's is. Although "Nature" has given Fanny "extremely lavish" hair, she too has had it cut; and on Sundays she arranges it in curls that, unlike Joseph's, reach only "down her Neck" in what Fielding calls "the modern Fashion" (152). Even the powerful physical attractions of Fielding's romantic hero and heroine are not entirely untouched by artifice, although fielding emphasizes, for example, that in Fanny's skin "a Whiteness appeared which the finest *Italian* Paint would be unable to reach" and that "she had a natural Gentility, superior to the Acquisition of Art" (152-53).

Fielding concentrates the influence of fashion on his hero and heroine in the treatment of their hair, and the glancing allusion to *Paradise Lost* in his description of Joseph's hair recalls a context in which a natural difference in hair length is to express the whole order of relations between the sexes. The quiet echo of Milton early in the novel, with the discontinuities between its original and new contexts, suggests a contrast between the constructed nature of gender in Joseph's world and the stable, "natural" hierarchy of gender in Milton's Eden. We will see that this is not an isolated or entirely fragmentary echo: further echoes of *Paradise Lost* in **Joseph Andrews** sustain and develop a relation between the two works that provides one form of commentary on the later work's aims. Indeed, in these echoes, the very act of invoking Milton will assume a special force and significance within the novel.

The Eve of "wanton ringlets," despite her distance from Joseph's world, provides a more complex and appealing version of the feminine sexuality with which he is identified than the initial model of Pamela; and the allusion to her within a description of Joseph's physical charms begins the novel's movement beyond a strictly parodic treatment of him. As Joseph advances toward the chapters in which we will meet the Roasting-Squire (and encounter a cluster of Miltonic allusions) he passes through a number of situations that progressively reformulate his relation to the feminized man as a butt for Fielding's satire. In his travels, he will literally pass through a series of inns that house different scenarios from Fielding's satiric repertoire about domestic and sexual relations.

In book 1, Joseph sets out from Lady Booby's house, is severely beaten by highwaymen, and first comes to rest in the outside world (returning, according to his doctor, from the very threshold of death) in a stronghold of "petticoat government." As we have seen, Fielding had satirized the inversion of domestic power relations in a number of plays, including *The Tragedy of*

Tragedies, The Grub-Street Opera, Pasquin, and *Eurydice,* and the innkeepers at the Dragon establish their familiar roles of browbeaten husband and domineering wife in their first piece of dialogue. "'Well,' says he, 'my Dear, do as you will when you are up, you know I never contradict you.' 'No,' says she, 'if the Devil was to contradict me, I would make the House too hot to hold him'" (56). The name the two innkeepers share expresses the domination of their marriage by the woman: Mr. and Mrs. Tow-wouse are named with a slang word for the female genitals.[21] While staying in their inn, Joseph is physically weak and vulnerable, penniless, and at the mercy of Mrs. Tow-wouse's notions of charity ("'Common Charity, a F——t!' says she, 'Common Charity teaches us to provide for ourselves, and our Families'"). Going out into the world, the "male Pamela" has turned up in the scene that King Arthur described with his maxim:

> when by Force
> Or Art the Wife her Husband over-reaches
> Give him the Peticoat, and her the Breeches.
> ***The Tragedy of Tragedies*** (I.iii)

And Joseph seems to be aligned within this scene with the ineffective husband, Mr. Tow-wouse, who wishes to do him well but has little will or way.

The next time we see Joseph he is at an inn quite decisively ruled by a husband. In this scene, however, Joseph appears grouped with the tyrannized wife. Again, Joseph is injured and helpless—this time Adams's horse has suddenly knelt, crushing his leg—and has retreated to the woman's realm of the kitchen, where he is tended by the innkeeper's wife (118-19). Her husband chastises her for attending to a mere footman's leg and proposes that Joseph "find a Surgeon to cut it off"; in the brawl that follows, the offended Adams exchanges blows with the host and hostess, while Joseph sits helplessly by, scarce able to "rise from his Chair" (120). Fielding's thrice-repeated emphasis on the hostess's rubbing, "with a warm Hand," of Joseph's leg, the strength of her husband's objection, and his nasty recommendation that the leg be cut off, all hint at a metonymic association of Joseph's leg with his genitals, his injury signifying as a figurative castration that keeps him out of the masculine physical struggle even after the hostess and Slipslop have joined in. Moving between the two inns, each representative of one extreme in domestic arrangements, Joseph passes through identification with several different satiric versions of the feminized man—from the weak-willed husband overreached by his aggressive wife to the dephallicized man adored and attended to by someone else's alienated wife. When we again meet up with Joseph at an inn, he will be more directly implicated in that role of the castrato opera singer recalled by the description of his bird-keeping in 1.2 and distantly evoked in this injury to his leg.

We enter the inn that is the scene of book 2, chapter 12, with Adams and Fanny, and share their surprise at the revelation of Joseph's presence there as well. In this chapter the three characters are reunited on the road for the first time. Both Dick Taylor and Maurice Johnson see this chapter as a crucial turning point in Joseph's development from a parodic to a serious and sympathetic character.[22] And yet the chapter does not begin by freeing Joseph from association with satiric figures. The preceding chapter has ended on a note that might prepare us for satiric allusions to opera. Meditating upon the "litigious Temper" in men, Adams rather gratuitously tells a story about two men, contending for the place of clerk, whose fierce competition in the singing of psalms at church eventually breaks forth into fighting (150-51); this story seems less arbitrary if we see it as modeled on one of the standard jokes in send-ups of the Italian opera—the bitter rivalry between the sopranos Faustina Bordoni and Francesca Cuzzoni (which led to their aggressively competitive singing while together on stage and even to an exchange of blows there).[23] Our introduction to Joseph in the chapter that follows recalls his association early in the novel with an even more frequent target in jokes about the Italian opera—for Joseph appears here singing an extended song with "one of the most melodious [voices] that ever was heard."

To be more precise, he doesn't *appear* here singing the song: if the bird-keeping passage somehow imagined him as deprived of his phallus, disqualified, like the castrato singers, for the part of Priapus by the sweetness of his voice, this chapter momentarily disembodies him altogether, returning him to his friends first *only* as a voice, overheard singing "from an inner Room." He is recognized by, and overwhelmingly present to, Fanny (who, like an opera fan, swoons) simply through the sound of his voice. Yet although the song he sings tells a story of passionate sexual desire and eventual fulfillment, Joseph's own body has been temporarily removed from that story. Fielding's dramatic satires ridiculed the notion of the castrato celebrities who sought romantic affairs for reputation's sake,[24] and the first stage of Joseph's reunion with Fanny acts out the absence of the phallus, and of real sensual contact, from the fashionable appearance of "Intrigues"—here generalized to the absence of the whole body.

The description of Fanny that leads up to it and the content of the song itself pose, in a variety of ways, the question of the place of "images" in the physical experience of sexual desire. Introducing his description of Fanny's physical beauties with a warning to readers of an "amorous Hue," Fielding alludes to the fates of Pygmalion and Narcissus as versions of the frustration he fears for us. The words of Joseph's song, given on the next page, return us to the reflection of Narcissus. The speaker of its pastoral love story first laments that he can't escape the remembrance of Chloe's beauties; then reasons with rapture that he is "thus of *Chloe* possest," as, "Nor she, nor no Tyrant's hard Power, / Her Image can tear from my Breast"; but next uncovers the limits of this consolation:

> But felt not *Narcissus* more Joy,
> With his Eyes he beheld his lov'd Charms?
> Yet what he beheld, the fond Boy
> More eagerly wish'd in his Arms. (153)

Explaining the frustrations of fixing on the image rather than the substance of the loved one with the example of Narcissus, the speaker implies that there is something self-enclosed or even self-loving about such a fixation; and the insularity of Joseph's performance of the love song, alone in another room, evokes another side of this reflective relation—the self-enclosure of a desire to turn *oneself* into an image of love, like Wilson writing love-letters to himself to acquire the reputation of intrigues (203).[25] Joseph, however, has turned himself not exactly into an image, but into a disembodied voice: Joseph's absent presence when overheard at the inn takes the theatricality of this kind of desire to an odd, even paradoxical, extreme. His offstage performance is at once somehow stagey (the "inner Room" from which he sings might suggest the "inner stage" or "discovery space" of the theater) and decidedly untheatrical; the personal body that is flattened by the theater into an image is here so attenuated that it disappears. The effect of Joseph's song on Fanny recalls both classical allusions used by Fielding in the chapter's opening: its performance turns her momentarily into the Echo figure of Narcissus's story ("'Bless us,' says Adams, 'you look extremely pale.' 'Pale! Mr. Adams,' says she, 'O Jesus!'"), and then into Pygmalion's statue. After her stunned repetition of Adams's last word, Fanny faints, unceremoniously falling "backwards in her Chair." It is only when Joseph enters the room and clasps her in his arms that, like Pygmalion's statue softening and blushing at his touch, she comes (back) to life with "Life and Blood returning into her cheeks" (154-55).[26]

For Joseph *has* suddenly appeared in the room—not as insular as he has seemed, he responds to Adams's call for help at Fanny's distress—and now enacts a physical passion so far from mere theatricality that he embraces and kisses Fanny "without considering who were present" as witnesses. Fanny and Joseph meet here in the flesh for the first time in the novel, and one effect of Joseph's disembodiment on the threshold of that meeting is to make his entrance almost an act of materialization, his passion given flesh in this scene, his body conjured more strongly as a physical presence after being pointedly withheld, except as it manifested itself in voice. The scene that Taylor and Johnson identify as a turning point in the presentation of Joseph does, among other things, establish his difference from the castrati with whom he'd been identified—at least with respect to the ironic relation they represent for Fielding between public passion and bodily reality, which this scene confronts by staging and then reversing it. Suggestively, we learn in the following chapter that the next morning Joseph finds "his Leg surprisingly recovered" (161).[27]

From this point in the novel on, Fielding is increasingly straightforward and firm about Joseph's physical strength and self-possession. He shows him carrying Fanny in his arms, beating a pack of hounds off Adams with his cudgel, drubbing (as Taylor notes) the Roasting-Squire's captain, defeating Beau Didapper's servant in a fistfight, and giving the Beau himself a box on the ear. In the first of these events, when Joseph carries Fanny down a hill in the dark, Fielding uses the occasion explicitly to distinguish Joseph from the beaux whose questionable gender Joseph's role as a male Pamela and his mixed masculine and feminine charms might at first have seemed to mirror. Fielding moralizes,

> Learn hence, my fair Countrywomen, to consider your own Weakness, and the many Occasions on which the strength of a Man may be useful to you; and duly weighing this, take care, that you match not yourselves with the spindle-shanked Beaus and Petit Maîtres of the Age, who instead of being able like *Joseph Andrews,* to carry you in lusty Arms through the rugged ways and downhill Steeps of Life, will rather want to support their feeble Limbs with your Strength and Assistance. (194)

Joseph is here actually exhibited as the alternative to the gender role reversals in which he at first seemed to be implicated. Even before Joseph has met up with Fanny at the inn, the novel's "embattled chastity" theme has begun to shift its focus from Joseph to Fanny, a more conventional object of sexual aggression; and once they have been reunited, Joseph not only ceases to appear as a male Pamela, defending his own chastity, but takes up the proudly masculine role of the defender of that of a woman. Is the body that the reunion scene in 2.12 seems dramatically to award Joseph, after all the equivocations and negotiations about Joseph's gender that lead up to it, the simply and conventionally masculine one that the first portion of the novel had denied him? Does Joseph turn out to be "something entirely, almost diametrically different" from what he'd first appeared, as Hunter eloquently argues,[28] or does something of his initial appearance remain crucial to what he has to offer as the novel's central character?

The addresses to his reader that Fielding places on either side of Joseph's song and sudden materialization in book 2, chapter 12, suggest that the reunion scene plays out the ambiguities not only within theatrical modes of behavior but within the promise offered by Fielding's new form, the novel. Fielding's comments at both the beginning and the end of the scene tease us about what *our* relation to the actions and passions of the scene could be: "if it should happen to us or to thee to be struck with this Picture, we should be perhaps in as helpless a Condition as *Narcissus;* and might say to ourselves, *Quod petis est nusquam.*" "But, O Reader, when this Nightingale, who was no other than *Joseph Andrews* himself, saw his beloved *Fanny* in the Situation we have described her, can'st thou conceive the Agitations of his Mind?" (152, 154). Within the scene, Adams's position as an onlooker might allegorize ours. Fielding comments that "Some Philosophers may perhaps doubt, whether he was not the happiest of the three; for the Goodness of his Heart enjoyed the Blessings which were exulting in the Breasts of both the other two, together with his own"; but he then debunks the thought as "Metaphysical Rubbish," and provides a sobering emblem of the reader's fate. Adams has flung the book of Aeschylus he's been studying into the fire when Fanny faints, and "as soon as the first Tumults of *Adams's* Rapture were over, he cast his Eyes towards the Fire, where *Æschylus* lay expiring; and immediately rescued the poor Remains, to-wit, the Sheepskin Covering of his dear Friend, which was the Work of his own Hands, and had been his inseparable Companion for upwards of thirty Years" (155).

Adams's relation to "the Work of his own Hands," "his inseparable Companion," suggests the attachments of Pygmalion and of Narcissus as much as Joseph's theatricality might; and the reduction of his book to sheepskin covers pictures a kind of emptying out of the reader's experience in the face of the demands of human events. In some ways, of course, a novel's characters are quite literally disembodied, while the drama functions precisely by giving its characters body. But then, the book Adams was reading was not a novel: it was a copy of the plays of the first tragic dramatist, itself referred to by that dramatist's name. This episode, described by Taylor and Johnson as a turning point in the presentation of Joseph's character—and which we read as a crisis in the depiction of Joseph's gender identity—also plays out with some urgency issues of literary representation and reception, bringing into a kind of associational circulation questions about theater, theatricality, opera, voice, and reading. In the present chapter, while focusing on Fielding's changing treatment of the problem of Joseph's gender, we have repeatedly come across a loose and sometimes mysterious network of connections between definitions of gender, alternative forms of sexual desire, and matters of generic convention and literary echo (as Didapper's inadequate masculinity and suspect forms of desire are linked by Fielding to the theater, as the castrato is placed in opposition to masculinized satire, as Richardson's new novel form and Milton's Christian epic offer competing accounts of female character). In the chapter below, we will focus more directly on a specific example of an interplay between genre, allusion, and contending definitions of gendered identity. Despite its warnings to the reader, the episode in 2.12 at the inn, and *Joseph Andrews* more generally, do not simply throw textually dependent forms of feeling and identity into the fire.

If Joseph has earlier rejected Lady Booby's theatrical expressions of sexual desire—and if, in the course of 2.12, he is carefully separated from a theatricalized desire centered on images—he nonetheless remains implicated, as Chapter 4 shows, in what we might term echoic emotion, or in desire and feeling that are dependent upon conventionalized acts of voice and upon prior texts. Indeed, before we arrive at Chapter 4, in the first section of Chapter 3 we will study Fielding's suggestion in *Joseph Andrews* that echo itself evokes the materiality of words, so that the opposition I have been using above between "images" and the physical reality of the body breaks down before the bodylike presence of words. What Fielding seems to highlight about echo in his direct narrative treatment of it in several scenes is the way that echo (unlike Didapper's "mimicry") can become dynamic rather than mechanical as it overlays recollections of *multiple* prior texts. The specific verbal echoes of Milton in the scenes analyzed in Chapter 3 can only be heard amid the simultaneous redounding of echoes from a variety of prior texts. The multiplicity of the texts recalled seems itself to be essential to the effect Fielding seeks in these scenes.

Notes

[1] Without exploring it at length, Hunter addresses this issue in his discussion of *Joseph Andrews,* commenting on Joseph's second letter to Pamela: "The burlesque context makes it unlikely that we will be in a mood to notice, but alongside the foolish posturing and mindless canting is a certain amount of solid sense, for beyond the absurd example-mongering and exclamatory effusions about 'fine things' is the point, repeated from chapter 1, about a single standard for both sexes" (*Occasional Form,* 100).

[2] At times the convergence of class and gender structures in Pamela allows her resistance to oppression to speak for all those without social authority and power, as when she asserts the equal value of her soul; at times it works to naturalize or rationalize her different forms of powerlessness by explaining them in terms of each other. As Pamela's letters approach the event of her wedding, for example, and the gradual domestication of her spirit, they recur frequently to her fear of the "happy, yet awful moment" of her sexual union with Mr. B. The only explanation she can find for her apprehension about her wedding night has to do with her class identity: "My heart, at times, sinks within me; I know not why, except at my own unworthiness,

and because the honour done me is too high for me to support myself under, as I should do. It is an honour . . . I was not born to. . . . But I suppose all young maidens are the same, so near so great a change of condition, though they carry it off more discreetly than I" (357; and see 357-72 generally).

Pamela's train of thought overlays her own specific cause to feel "lacking," unworthy, afraid—her social and economic inferiority to her husband—onto the conventional expectation that a woman's sexual desire is necessarily adjoined to dread and awe—presumably, in the face of the phallus. The effect seems to me to be to naturalize her class inferiority as analogous to biological gender identity, and to rationalize conventional constructions of her gender as analogous to lesser possession of wealth and social position. The cliché of the "blushing bride," then, serves to bring together Pamela's positions as female and as lower-class and to conceive and accept them in terms of each other—just at that point in the novel when it makes its crucial transition toward domesticating its potentially subversive message.

[3] Alter describes well the particular erotics of Lady Booby's imagination in this scene as "her eager prurient anticipation of 'submitting' herself to her own foot-boy, the mistress deliciously mastered by a servant" (73).

[4] McKeon discusses the different social functions of female and male chastity in eighteenth-century England (*The Origins of the English Novel,* 148-49 and 156-58); and he discusses chastity in *Pamela* and *Joseph Andrews* specifically, 366-68 and 398-400.

[5] Hunter suggests both possible readings of the seduction scenes, allowing at one point that Joseph's assertion of "individual rights" shows him to be more sensible and dignified than we might have thought, while remarking casually at another that in these scenes "the laughter is altogether at Joseph's expense" (*Occasional Form,* 100, 95).

[6] Homer Obed Brown, 202.

[7] Even Richardson's own two main characters are brought within the perimeter of Fielding's narrative in the final book of the novel and reconstituted as parodic, flat versions of themselves, peripheral now to the main thrust of the action.

[8] Taylor comments on Fielding's treatment of Joseph in the "night-adventures": "He holds Joseph from participating in the hurly-burly to keep him from being ridiculous, because he wants to maintain Joseph's dignity—Joseph is definitely out of the frame of either the Pamelian burlesque or picaresque high jinks. When Joseph does come into the episode the next morning in

Fanny's room where Adams is discovered slumbering peacefully, he is . . . quite positive and dominating. . . . it is Joseph who comprehends what has actually happened and how Adams made his mistake" (107-8).

[9] Both Battestin and Hunter discuss the biblical significance of Joseph's name. See *The Moral Basis of Fielding's Art* and *Occasional Form,* especially 103-5.

[10] Alter, 50-51.

[11] The thrust of Didapper's crude wit seems to be the incongruity of the practice he mimics at the Adamses' humble and rural door, making the object of any humor attached to its violent noise simply poverty and lack of pretensions. These are objects Fielding has specifically excluded from the force of legitimate ridicule in his preface, but objects of severe and violent ridicule from the Roasting-Squire and his men . . . .

[12] I am indebted to Hunter for his discerning account of the importance of expectation (and its subversion) in Fielding's unfolding of character (see both "Fielding and the Disappearance of Heroes" and *Occasional Form*).

[13] Stapleton, 182-83.

[14] Hunter too, notes the phallic allusion in the reference to Priapus in this passage, but he interprets it as a leering suggestion of Joseph's "sexual potential" and "promising future" as a "sexual object" (*Occasional Form,* 96-97). If the allusion functions on some level to make this suggestion, on the surface at least its context works to assert Joseph's failure as a sexual object.

[15] As several critics have observed, this combination characterizes Tom Jones's beauty as well, though with a somewhat different emphasis. . . .

[16] As in the Renaissance rhetorical convention of the *blazon,* or item-by-item enumeration of a woman's beauties. See Lanham's *Handlist of Rhetorical Terms.*

[17] Remarking on Fielding's reference to Joseph's "tenderness joined with a sensibility inexpressible," Jean Hagstrum notes that "the parallel portrait of Fanny endows her with a countenance 'in which, though she was extremely bashful, a sensibility appeared almost incredible; and a sweetness, whenever she smiled, beyond either imitation or description' (II. 12)" (179). Thomas E. Maresca, too, notes the shared phrasings in the two descriptions and comments that they make Fanny "the female counterpart of Joseph," though he also argues for important differences between the two characters (200-201). Hagstrum identifies the sensibility Fielding grants to both Joseph and Fanny as femi-

nine, observing that he grants it to Tom Jones as well, and commenting: "once again, as if to avoid the implication of effeminacy that sensibility could obviously carry with it, Fielding insists that Tom also possesses a 'most masculine person and mien.' The whole of *Tom Jones* illustrates abundantly both the vigorously masculine and the delicately feminine qualities of the hero. . . . As the ingredient of delicacy became more prominent in love, the drive towards forms of unisexuality also became more prominent. It may be worth considering that in the spirit of so robustly a heterosexual man as Fielding delicate sensibility loomed larger than we have hitherto realized" (179-80).

Hagstrum's brief discussion of Fielding in *Sex and Sensibility* (178-85) draws attention to aspects of Fielding's work that have not been adequately recognized; and his historical study of changing notions of sex and sensibility in this period provides an illuminating context for our study of the interest in gender in Fielding's work in particular.

[18] All quotations of *Paradise Lost* will be from the Odyssey Press edition, ed. Hughes; book and line numbers for further citations from the poem will be given parenthetically in the text.

[19] In their notes to this passage of *Paradise Lost,* editors John Carey and Alastair Fowler cite St. Paul's similar treatment of hair length as an expression of the hierarchic relation of the sexes (I Corinthians 11: 7, 15). But they also comment that "the elaborateness of the present passage lends some support to the theory that Milton had a special interest in hair" (*The Poems of John Milton* [New York: Longman Group of W. W. Norton, 1968], 631).

[20] Watt, *Rise of the Novel,* 160-63.

[21] See Eaves and Kimpel, 408-9.

[22] Taylor remarks that book 2, chapter 12, "marks the point of change in the appearance of Joseph in the thought and action so that he is treated on more serious levels of meaning, and it initiates a line of action which is to carry him to a dignity and a stature and an elevation of personality far beyond the original limitations imposed by the burlesque mode" (97). See also Johnson, 53-55.

[23] Faustina and Cuzzoni's rivalry was burlesqued, for example, in the struggle between Gay's Polly and Lucy in *The Beggar's Opera* (1728) and in the farcical competition of the two sopranos in the anonymous *The Contretemps; or, Rival Queans* (1727). On the satirical referents of the scene between Polly and Lucy (II.xiii), see the notes to *The Beggar's Opera,* ed. Lewis, 120-21; and Erskine-Hill in Axton and Williams, 157-58.

The burlesque struggle between Fielding's own Glum-dalca and Huncamunca in *The Tragedy of Tragedies* may also glance at operatic rivalries, reduced to the level of personal insult (II.vii). Fielding's footnotes to the scene between them also confirm its parallels to the famous "Altercative Scene between Cleopatra and Octavia" in Dryden's *All for Love* (Act III). Fielding completes the same collocation of associations in *Joseph Andrews* when, just on the other side of the re-union scene at the inn, he tells us that Slipslop cast a look at Fanny as she flung herself into the chaise "not unlike that which *Cleopatra* gives *Octavia* in the Play" (159).

24 See, for example, *Eurydice* and *The Author's Farce*. I take the word "intrigues" from Wilson's description of his desire for the mere reputation of sexual con-quest: "Nothing now seemed to remain but an Intrigue, which I was resolved to have immediately; I mean the Reputation of it" (203). The puzzle of a castrato's sexual relations represents for Fielding the wider phenome-non of the beau's desire for the empty appearance of sexual engagement.

25 Several critics have pursued this problem of narcis-sism in *Joseph Andrews*—here not done justice—in more depth, and have suggested its relation to other important matters in the novel. Pointing out that Fan-ny's name in *Joseph Andrews* strangely repeats Field-ing's satiric name for Lord Hervey in the frame mate-rials for *Shamela,* and that Lord Hervey reappears in *Joseph Andrews* as Beau Didapper, Hunter interprets the beau's attempts to ravish Fanny as the expression of a confused kind of narcissistic desire: "as he tries to ravish Fanny, [Didapper] confronts for a moment his own self-love. . . . He sees not the Fanny we have by then come to know, but some idealized vision of himself" (*Occasional Form,* 106). Hagstrum discusses the meaning of both narcissism and incest in *Joseph Andrews* and *Tom Jones;* and my awareness of this issue in *Joseph Andrews* has been informed by a paper presented by William Jewett about the relation be--tween the principle of "exemplarity" and the problem of narcissism in Fielding's implicit critique of Rich-ardson (graduate course presentation at Yale Universi-ty, 1984).

26 On the awakening of Pygmalion's statue, see Ovid, *Metamorphoses,* X.280-95.

Pygmalion's statue would be evoked more easily by Fanny's faint because of the network of references to people turning into statues in *Joseph Andrews.* Hunter highlights Fielding's description of Lady Booby as a *"Statue of Surprize"* (*Occasional Form,* 40) and com-ments, "The statue becomes an important mark on the Fielding landscape, and the rhetoric of *Joseph Andrews* often honors it, not only to avert seduction for his characters but to engineer ours" (95).

27 The question of Joseph's injury arises again when the False Promiser offers to lend the travelers a horse and a servant: "a very fierce Dispute ensued, whether *Fanny* should ride behind *Joseph,* or behind the Gen-tleman's Servant; *Joseph* insisting on it, that he was perfectly recovered, and was as capable of taking care of *Fanny,* as any other Person could be. But *Adams* would not agree to it, and declared he would not trust her behind him; for that he was weaker than he imag-ined himself to be" (174). The dispute concerns how fully recovered Joseph's leg is (Adams has mentioned Joseph's "lame Leg" the page before), but Taylor as-sumes it has to do with Joseph's sexual self-control. He summarizes: "Adams demands [that Fanny ride] behind the gentleman's servant, since he says that Jo-seph is not to be trusted, 'being weaker than he imag-ined himself to be'—Adams has not forgotten Joseph's fiery haste to have the marriage ceremony performed on the spot without benefit of banns" (101). I think that the passage does, in some general way, encourage a confusion between Joseph's leg and his sexual abil-ities and vulnerabilities, gently extending the kind of metonymic association suggested earlier by his injury.

28 Hunter, "Fielding and the Disappearance of Heroes," 136.

Works Cited

. . . Alter, Robert. *Fielding and the Nature of the Novel.* Cambridge: Harvard University Press, 1968.

———. "Fielding and the Uses of Style." *Novel: A Forum on Fiction* 1 (1967): 53-63.

Axton, Marie, and Raymond Williams, eds. *English Drama: Forms and Development: Essays in Honour of Clara Bradbrook.* With an Introduction by Raymond Williams. Cambridge: Cambridge University Press, 1977. . . .

Battestin, Martin C. *The Moral Basis of Fielding's Art: A Study of Joseph Andrews.* Middletown, Conn.: Wes-leyan University Press, 1959. . . .

Brown, Homer Obed. "Tom Jones: The 'Bastard' of History." In *Boundary 2: A Journal of Postmodern Literature* 7, No. 2 (1979): 201-33. . . .

Eaves, T. C. Duncan, and Ben D. Kimpel. "Two Names in Joseph Andrews." *Modern Philology* 72 (1975): 408-09. . . .

Hagstrum, Jean H. *Sex and Sensibility: Ideal and Erot-ic Love from Milton to Mozart.* Chicago: University of Chicago Press, 1980. . . .

Hunter, J. Paul. "Fielding and the Disappearance of Heros." In *The English Hero, 1660-1800,* edited with an introduction by Robert Folkenflik, pp. 116-42. Newark: University of Delaware Press; Associated University Presses, 1982.

———. *Occasional Form: Henry Fielding and the Chains of Circumstance.* Baltimore: Johns Hopkins University Press, 1976. . . .

Johnson, Maurice. *Fielding's Art of Fiction.* Philadelphia: University of Pennsylvania Press, 1961. . . .

Lewis, Peter Elfed. *John Gay: "The Beggar's Opera."* London: Edward Arnold, 1976. . . .

Maresca, Thomas E. *Epic to Novel.* Columbus: Ohio State University Press, 1974. . . .

McKeon, Michael. *The Origins of the English Novel, 1600-1740.* Baltimore: Johns Hopkins University Press, 1987. . . .

Milton, John. *Paradise Lost.* Edited by Merritt Y. Hughes. New York: The Odyssey Press, Inc., 1935.

Milton, John. *The Poems of John Milton.* Edited by John Carey and Alastair Fowler. New York: Longman Group of W. W. Norton, 1968. . . .

Taylor, Dick, Jr. "Joseph as Hero in *Joseph Andrews.*" In *Tulane Studies in English* 7 (1957): 91-109. . . .

Watt, Ian. *The Rise of the Novel: Studies in Defoe, Richardson and Fielding.* Berkeley: University of California Press, 1964. . . .

Nancy A. Mace (essay date 1996)

SOURCE: "Classical Epic and the 'New Species of Writing,'" in her *Henry Fielding's Novels and the Classical Tradition,* University of Delaware Press; Associated University Presses, 1996, pp. 61-76

[*In the following chapter from her book* Henry Fielding's Novels and the Classical Tradition, *Mace details the specific classical influences on Fielding's major novels and his use of the epic tradition. Mace includes a special section on Fielding's* Amelia *as a revision of Virgil's* Aeneid.]

> Now a comic Romance is a comic Epic-Poem in Prose;
>
> —Preface to *Joseph Andrews*

> when any kind of Writing contains all its other Parts, such as Fable, Action, Characters, Sentiments, and Diction, and is deficient in Metre only; it seems, I think, reasonable to refer it to the Epic,
>
> —Preface to *Joseph Andrews*

> I have attempted in my Preface to *Joseph Andrews* to prove, that every Work of this kind is in its Nature a comic Epic Poem, of which *Homer* left us a Precedent, tho' it be unhappily lost.
>
> —Preface to *The Adventures of David Simple*

The generic sources of Fielding's "new species of writing" have generated a lively critical debate over the last seventy years because they affect our understanding of his originality, his use of and place in literary tradition, and his affinities with other eighteenth-century authors. Like his contemporaries, Fielding could have drawn from several different literary models, among them classical epic, satire, romance, history, and spiritual autobiography. What he chose to imitate and which genres he invoked in his critical prefaces reveal both his purpose in writing fiction and the authors with whom he wanted his audience to identify him.

Although some scholars have argued that Fielding drew primarily on satire, the essay, and history, most of the discussion has centered on the importance of the epic and the romance in his concept of the novel. Critics who argue that Fielding wrote firmly in the epic tradition of Homer and Virgil emphasize Fielding's classical background and his ties to Dryden, Addison, Swift, and Pope, who championed the classics in the debate between the ancients and the moderns.[1] But by asserting that Fielding relied heavily on romance—a genre used by such novelists as Richardson and Defoe—other scholars have maintained that Fielding is more "modern" than his classical references suggest and that his concept of fiction is similar to that of many eighteenth-century romance and novel writers.[2] Both of these positions have substantial limitations, however. Because they take Fielding's epic pretensions seriously, epic theorists cannot satisfactorily explain his use of the mock-heroic in *Jonathan Wild, Joseph Andrews,* and *Tom Jones* or the distinction between Fielding's use of the epic in his earlier novels and in *Amelia.* Romance theorists weaken their position by measuring Fielding's work against modern definitions of the epic rather than those familiar to Fielding and his readers; consequently, they have not considered the relationship of the critical essays in both *Joseph Andrews* and *Tom Jones* to eighteenth-century epic theory and have often claimed falsely that Fielding's plot devices, inflated language, and characters are signs of the influence of romance, not epic.

The problems raised by these theories demonstrate that several questions about Fielding's use of other genres remain to be answered. How frequently does Fielding allude to the epic, and how close are his statements to eighteenth-century epic theory? If he does consider his novels part of the epic tradition, why does he use mock-heroics? What connection exists between his use of epic in his earlier novels and in *Amelia?* Because Fielding's classical allusions and quotations indicate the importance of epic—and such genres as satire, romance, and history—to his conception of the novel, they are useful in addressing these issues.

A review of Fielding's references to classical literature reveals that the classical epic more profoundly shaped his theory of fiction than many recent critics have been willing to allow. Albeit at times ironically, he deliberately defines his new genre in terms that would relate it to eighteenth-century discussions of epic familiar to both him and his audience, and, in his introductory chapters, he distances his work from the romance by his repeated attacks on the form. At the same time that Fielding identifies his work with epic in his prefaces, his mock-heroics betray his ambivalence about the epic hero and his concern that the moral values inherent in these ancient poems were not compatible with Christianity. He introduces this theme in **Jonathan Wild, Joseph Andrews,** and **Tom Jones** but develops it most fully in **Amelia,** where he treats the epic analogy seriously in order to dramatize the difference between the heroic and Christian codes. Consequently, the use of epic shows a greater continuity between the early and late works than has been previously recognized.

References to Classical Epic Poets in Fielding's Novels

Two generalizations have long played an important role in discussions of the classical influence on Fielding's "new species." (1) Noting that Fielding seldom uses the term "epic" in his fiction, some critics have argued that his references to epic are too occasional and local to be taken seriously.[3] (2) Because of the reputed influence of Lucian, others have stressed the impact of classical satire on Fielding's theory of the novel.[4] As widespread as such views are, we must reconsider them in the light of Fielding's references to classical writers, which show that both these commonplaces about his use of ancient sources are questionable.

Although Fielding uses the term "epic" very few times, a tabulation of the classical allusions and quotations in the novels reveals that he refers to epic poets and theorists more often than scholars have generally assumed.[5] . . .

. . . [Two] of the three authors Fielding refers to most often in the novels are Homer and Virgil, who account for 98 (or 30 percent) of his 330 allusions and quotations, whereas in the periodicals the two epic poets represent only 84 (or 14 percent) of the 613 references. The numbers suggest that Fielding deliberately added references to these poets to associate his work with the epic genre. These direct references to Virgil are reinforced by the structural parallels between **Amelia** and Virgil's *Aeneid,* which Fielding designated as the model for this novel in the *Covent-Garden Journal,* no. 8 (28 January 1752): 65.[7] Such evidence implies that Fielding conceived of his novels—and wanted his readers to think of his novels—in relation to the epic tradition.

The number of references to Horace and Aristotle, who account for 74 allusions and quotations, or 22 percent of the total, is also important, because both were associated with eighteenth-century epic theory and many of Fielding's quotations and allusions come from their critical works. In **Tom Jones,** where Fielding writes extensively about his theory of fiction, the narrator quotes or alludes to Aristotle 8 times: half of these are to his criticism or the *Poetics;* the other half, to his *Politics.* Of the narrator's 24 references to Horace—many of which appear in the prefatory chapters treating Fielding's theory of the novel—20 are specifically related to the *Ars Poetica* and his other critical works. For example, when he discusses the question of probability in the opening chapter of book 8 of **Tom Jones,** Fielding alludes to Horace's *Ars Poetica* (lines 188, 191) and Aristotle's *Poetics* (24.19, 9.1-3) (**Tom Jones,** bk. 8, chap. 1, 1:397-402).[8] Such allusions and quotations indicate that Fielding wanted his readers to relate his concept of the novel to classical criticism and acknowledge that the rules for his "new species" grew out of those set down by Horace and Aristotle for the epic. His reliance on classical critics also heightens the authority of his pronouncements and encourages his readers to compare his narratives to the ancient epics.

The scarcity of references to Horace's *Satires* and other ancient satires suggests that this classical genre did not play a large role in Fielding's fiction. In the course of all four novels, Fielding mentions Horace's *Satires* only 6 times; when we compare this number to the abundance of references to the Roman writer's critical works, we see that Horace was more important to Fielding as a critical and moral standard than as a satirist. The references to other prominent satiric poets support this conclusion: Fielding quotes or alludes to Lucian, Persius, and Juvenal only 19 times (or 6 percent of the total). As in the journalism, Lucian is unimportant; he is mentioned only twice: once in **Tom Jones** and once in **Amelia,** where Fielding puffs his proposed translation of the Greek writer.[9] This evidence suggests that, while Fielding may have drawn on modern satirists like Cervantes and Scarron, ancient satiric poets had little effect on his fiction.

Clearly, Fielding was thinking of the classical epic poets as he wrote his novels, and he alludes frequently to epic theorists to give his fiction the weight of ancient authority. His use of epic theory as a background for the critical essays in **Joseph Andrews** and **Tom Jones** also shows his ties to eighteenth-century epic theorists and indicates why he wanted his readers to identify his works with epics rather than romances.

Epic Theory and the Critical Discussions of the New Species

While Fielding alluded frequently to Virgil, Homer, and epic theorists, he also derived many of the guidelines for his new genre from eighteenth-century discussions of the epic, which would have been familiar both to him and his audience. Ethel M. Thornbury and James L. Lynch have noted that Fielding drew on eighteenth-century theories of the epic in his preface to *Joseph Andrews,* but they have not discussed the extent to which the prefatory essays at the beginning of each book of *Joseph Andrews* and *Tom Jones* address issues that concerned eighteenth-century epic theorists.[10] These references to contemporary issues align Fielding with such writers as Dryden, Pope, and Addison, who wrote about and translated epics, and they suggest how Fielding conceived of the purpose of his novels and their place in the literary hierarchy.

Nearly all the eighteenth-century critics who wrote about epic used the formal definition taken from René Le Bossu, whose *Treatise of the Epick Poem* (1695) was one of the most influential works on this ancient genre. Le Bossu's description of the epic, derived from Aristotle and Horace, emphasized its didactic purpose rather than its formal elements.

> The *EPOPEA* is a Discourse invented by Art, to form the Manners by such Instructions as are disguis'd under the Allegories of some one important Action, which is related in Verse, after a probable, diverting, and surprizing Manner.[11]

This definition provided a framework for discussions of the epic in the eighteenth century, since epic theorists followed Le Bossu in discussing the fable, action, moral, characters, machines, and language of the epic poem.[12] Fielding and his readers were clearly aware of this definition and the topics usually covered in treatments of epic because many of the critics and writers with whom they were familiar also used it. For example, Dryden structured his entire discussion of the *Aeneid* around Le Bossu's topics, and, in his translation of the *Odyssey,* Pope includes an abbreviated version of Le Bossu, entitled "A General View of the Epic Poem and of the *Iliad* and *Odyssey.* Extracted from *Bossu.*"[13] Addison's famous series of essays on *Paradise Lost* in the *Spectator* also follows Le Bossu topic by topic. In chapter 1, I demonstrated the popularity of Dryden's and Pope's translations of the epic poets; consequently, even if Fielding and his readers had not read Le Bossu's entire treatise in French or in an English translation, they could easily learn indirectly about this author and his critical pronouncements from such well-known sources. Because of their familiarity with Dryden, Pope, and Addison, Fielding's readers also would associate Fielding's critical remarks with this description of the epic, and they would relate the topics discussed by Fielding to the epic genre.

Fielding's critical essays in *Joseph Andrews* and *Tom Jones* reflect the extent of his awareness of epic theory and the key issues that concerned epic theorists. In addition to Aristotle and Horace, the two most important ancient critics related to discussions of the epic, Fielding also refers to seventeenth-and eighteenth-century scholars who wrote treatises on this genre. For example, in *Tom Jones* he lists Le Bossu and Dacier along with Aristotle and Horace as examples of the great critics the world has produced (bk. 11, chap. 1, 2:569-70). Although he does not mention them by name, Fielding comments on the theories of Richard Bentley and René Rapin about the divisions in Homer's epics (*Joseph Andrews,* bk. 2, chap. 1, pp. 90-91).[14] While his use of their names does not guarantee that Fielding had actually read these critics, his detailed comments about their positions indicate more than a passing knowledge of their theories.

Fielding's knowledge of epic theory is important because, in his introductory essays, he applies Le Bossu's definition and his list of topics to his new genre. The statements most closely related to Le Bossu appear in the preface to *Joseph Andrews,* where he initially describes his new form of writing. Although he realizes that some may object to his use of the term epic because he writes prose, not poetry, Fielding says, "[W]hen any kind of Writing contains all its other Parts, such as Fable, Action, Characters, Sentiments, and Diction, and is deficient in Metre only; it seems, I think, reasonable to refer it to the Epic" (preface, 4). Later in the preface, when he distinguishes between his comic work and serious epics or romances, he once again uses Le Bossu's categories (4-5). Because Fielding's narrator is often ironic, some scholars have dismissed the references to epic in this passage, suggesting that Fielding here means no more by the term "epic" than narrative. Fielding may well be parodying serious discussions of the ancient genre; nevertheless, his choice of terms would resonate with readers familiar with the discussion of the epic written by such critics as Le Bossu, Dryden, Pope, and Addison. Thus, the repetition of these criteria establishes a connection between Fielding's novels and this classical genre even as the humor implies a distance between these two forms.[15]

The essays that introduce individual books of *Joseph Andrews* and *Tom Jones* also show that Fielding was aware of epic theory and that he wanted to draw on his audience's understanding of epic to define his new form. For example, his introductory essays reveal his concern with unity, an important concern in treatments of the epic. Le Bossu had prescribed that the action of the epic be one, entire, and great; in other words, the episodes of the story must bear a close relation to the main action.[16] Fielding is clearly thinking of this matter in *Tom Jones* when he advises critics not to condemn any of the incidents in his story as "impertinent and foreign to our main Design" (bk. 10, chap. 1, 2:524-25). He also alludes to this issue when he justifies his right to make rules for this new genre and discusses his decision to select from Tom's early life only those events that are significant to the narrative (*Tom Jones*, bk. 2, chap. 1, 1:75-78; bk. 5, chap. 1, 1:209-10). He invokes this criterion for an epic to contrast his work with loosely organized romantic tales whose complex plots did not revolve around a single great theme.

Although Fielding's adoption of epic terminology ties his work to the best of the classical tradition, his discussions of epic show that he did not believe that his novels should slavishly follow epic conventions or even that such devices were desirable in modern works. His comments about probability are typical of his ambivalence about certain features of epic. Epic critics in the seventeenth and eighteenth centuries hotly debated the extent to which epics could violate the laws of probability by including supernatural beings and fantastic episodes; some theorists argued that fairies and magic did not violate probability, whereas others maintained that works using such devices were no more than romances. Fielding clearly agrees that a work should be probable and that supernatural events have no place in his new species. In *Jonathan Wild* his naïve narrator assures his audience that he would rather have Wild hanged than violate "the strictest Rules of Writing and Probability" (bk. 4, chap. 6, p. 205). In *Joseph Andrews* he relates the probable directly to his objections to the romance:

> for I would by no means be thought to comprehend those Persons of surprising Genius, the Authors of immense Romances, or the modern Novel and *Atalantis* Writers; who without any Assistance from Nature or History, record Persons who never were, or will be, and Facts which never did nor possibly can happen: Whose Heroes are of their own Creation, and their Brains the Chaos whence all their Materials are collected. (Bk. 3, chap. 1, p. 187)

In *Tom Jones* Fielding devotes an entire introductory essay to "the Marvellous," in which he discusses the distinction between the possible and the probable and considers which marvelous events and characters are suitable for novels; he argues that the fictions of romance are contrary to the demands of probability (bk. 8, chap. 1, 1:395-407).[17] Thus, Fielding uses this issue to associate his work with epic and distance it from romance.

At the same time, Fielding cannot take seriously critics' lengthy debates over the use of divine machinery in modern epics, in which some advised their contemporaries to substitute angels and saints for heathen gods and goddesses.[18] He alludes to this controversy both in *Jonathan Wild* and *Tom Jones*, where he asserts that he will not bring in supernatural agents to rescue heroes, as the ancient epic writers frequently did with heathen deities.[19] Fielding underscores his own disdain for the issue when he humorously concludes that the only supernatural agents fit for modern works are ghosts but advises that they be used sparingly, since the writer using them will most likely elicit a "horse-laugh" from his reader (*Tom Jones*, bk. 8, chap. 1, 1:399).

Fielding's remarks about character reveal that he is not slavish in his thinking about this issue either. He readily agrees with epic theorists that a key problem is whether characters should be perfectly good or have some bad characteristics.[20] In *Jonathan Wild* he refers to this issue when he defends the "weakness" that Wild shows towards Heartfree by observing that "Nature is seldom so kind as those Writers who draw Characters absolutely perfect" (bk. 4, chap. 4, p. 200). Later Fielding advises critics who read *Tom Jones* not to condemn characters with some blemishes, citing the authority of Horace (bk. 10, chap. 1, 2:526-27). Although he accepts that novels, like epics, should have consistent characters, he rejects the requirement that the only suitable heroes and heroines are nobles, choosing instead "low" characters, who have noble qualities but with whom his readers can identify more easily. Consequently, Fielding reveals that he shares many of the artistic concerns of epic poets but that he does not think that novelists can, or should, imitate epics in every respect.

Fielding does not simply use these criteria to show to what degree his works resemble epics; he also deliberately invokes epic topoi to distinguish his works from romances. Even though the writers of seventeenth-century heroic romances may have drawn their critical pronouncements from epic theory, many eighteenth-century critics held the form in contempt and used the term "romance" pejoratively. According to writers on epic, romances were written merely for entertainment and lacked the didactic purpose that Le Bossu considered essential to the epic poem. Fielding is thinking of this criticism in *Joseph Andrews* when he ranks his works with Fénelon's *Télémaque* and the *Odyssey* instead of romances, because the latter contain "very little Instruction or Entertainment" (preface, 3-4). Because epic theorists attacked romances for violating the rules of probability, Fielding repeatedly maintains that his works differ from romances, which abandon truth and are the products merely of the fertile imagination of the author. For example, in *Tom Jones* he says that the historian who ignores probability becomes a writer of romance (bk. 8, chap. 1, 1:402).[21] He also alludes to the loose, episodic structure that critics associated with romance when speaking of a brook in *Tom Jones* "which Brook did not come there, as such gentle Streams flow through vulgar Romances, with no other Purpose than to murmur" (bk. 5, chap. 12, 1:264).

Although Fielding used romance plot devices and other features associated with this genre, such were the negative associations of this term that in his critical comments he carefully distanced his work from it.

In his prefaces and the critical essays in *Tom Jones* and *Joseph Andrews,* Fielding clearly tied his new species to the epic genre and demonstrated how the reader should distinguish his work from the romances written in both prose and verse. His use of epic terminology and categories demonstrates that the term "epic" meant more than "prose narrative," the definition used by many modern critics. Drawing on Le Bossu, Aristotle, and Horace, Fielding used the term to indicate to his readers that, unlike romance, his new genre had a didactic purpose, unified organization, realistic characters drawn from ordinary life, and an appropriate mixture of the probable and the surprising. By equating his new genre with the ancient form, Fielding aligned his work with a type of narrative at the top of the literary hierarchy, giving it an aura of respectability the romance lacked. At the same time, Fielding's comments about various issues of interest to epic theorists reveal that he did not think that novelists should adopt epic conventions entirely. While he considered his novels part of the classical tradition, he recognized that the novel was a more appropriate vehicle for eighteenth-century readers than the epic. The allusions to epic criticism also heighten the reader's awareness of the verbal epic devices he used in his novels, which are frequently mock-heroic.

Mock-Heroics and Classical Epic

Although Fielding's mock-heroics have been widely noted, few critics have given them more than a passing comment because of the difficulties they raise both for those who dismiss the influence of epic and for those who regard seriously his allusions to this ancient genre.[22] The number of times Fielding imitates epic conventions in his novels belies the claim that he rarely draws an analogy between his new species and the epic form; at the same time that it reinforces the connections established in the prefaces, the parody of epic convention may undermine its authority.[23] Claude Rawson demonstrates the dual nature of the epic parodies when he asserts that the mock-heroic elements of *Jonathan Wild* demonstrate the interplay between the world of the novel and the past, but he maintains that the epic parallels in Fielding's later novels do not share this quality.[24] When we examine Fielding's mock-heroic diction, however, we find the same attitudes toward epic revealed in the prefaces and critical essays; furthermore, the mock-heroics address some of the liveliest critical debates of his time.

One of the primary functions of the mock-heroics in Fielding's novels is to distance the reader from the story. In addition to mock-heroic battle descriptions,

Fielding uses rhetorical devices associated with classical epic, which are striking because he carefully calls the reader's attention to their artificiality: invocations to the Muses, formulae for dawn and sunset, and epic similes.[25] Sometimes he signals the epic convention with a chapter title, such as "A Battle sung by the Muse in the *Homerican* Stile, and which none but the classical Reader can taste" (*Tom Jones,* bk. 4, chap. 8) or "An Invocation" (*Tom Jones,* bk. 13, chap. 1). He often completes an epic simile with a translation "in vulgar Language" or with a lengthy interpretation that forces the reader to note what has preceded it.[26] He also heightens our awareness of his artificial diction with direct parodies of scenes in Homer and Virgil.[27] For example, the description of Joseph's cudgel in the "battle" involving Joseph, Adams, and the dogs recalls the shield of Achilles in book 18 of the *Iliad* and the armor of Aeneas in *Aeneid* 8.608-731 (*Joseph Andrews,* bk. 3, chap. 6, pp. 238-42).[28] With these allusions and figures, he reminds us that this book is a work of art and not a factual history, thus keeping us from getting too involved with the characters he has created.

Fielding probably chose to rely on epic rather than romance conventions because these devices were probably more effective at distancing readers from the narrative than the romance diction used by so many of his contemporaries. Sheridan Baker has noted that few readers would be especially conscious of the romance elements in novels, for, by the eighteenth century, the real world had adopted romance diction, the ideal of conduct, and the romance success story. Consequently, such elements would strike the reader not as artificial but as realistic.[29] Since it is more consciously contrived, epic diction remains distinct from the real world and keeps the reader continually attuned to the literary form. When Fielding introduces epic invocations before his description of Sophia and the scenes in London, he prevents readers from becoming too involved in the world of the novel. Thus, they will be more likely to question the values of the characters and the world in which they live.

Fielding's calculated use of these rhetorical techniques is also closely related to his attack on romance in both *Joseph Andrews* and *Tom Jones.* As Ronald Paulson and other critics have noted, Fielding was writing an antiromance in the tradition of Cervantes and Scarron.[30] Like Quixote's delusion, Adams's preoccupation with the heroic world makes him a ridiculous figure in contemporary society. Adams interprets his surroundings through the mirror of the heroic past, and his battles with ravishers, dogs, and squires for the honor of Fanny Goodwill are to him akin to the deeds of Achilles, Odysseus, and Aeneas. The juxtaposition of the real and epic worlds reveals how unworkable Adams's values are in modern society, and it suggests that the classical heroic ideal may be unsuitable in the Christian world.

While they demonstrate that Adams's view of the world is unrealistic, the mock-heroics also indicate the short-comings of Adams's opponents, whose behavior is guided by self-interest and ignorance. By engrafting the epic world on the real one, Fielding calls attention to the disparity between ancient and modern values. The epic rhetoric encourages the reader to see that modern society—and such writers as Richardson and Cibber, who glorified it—does not measure up to the standards set by the ancients. The technique is similar to that of *The Tragedy of Tragedies* (1731), in which Fielding elevates a midget to gigantic proportions to underline the limited aspirations of those in his own world.

As in *Joseph Andrews,* the use of epic motifs in *Tom Jones* underscores Tom's unrealistic view of the world and his imprudent actions early in the novel. Unlike Adams, who fights battles for a virtuous young girl, Tom selects inappropriate objects for his chivalry. Neither Jenny Jones nor Molly Seagrim lives up to Tom's idealistic image, and both cause him to abandon his true love, Sophia. Similarly, Tom reveals his heroic code when he chooses to become a soldier after All-worthy sends him away. When Tom abandons his military aspirations and pursues Sophia to London, the epic battle descriptions cease. Although Fielding enno-bles Tom by identifying him with epic heroes, there-fore, he calls into question the morality of the ancient heroic ideal.

Epic diction in *Tom Jones* also reveals the unsavory features of minor characters. When Fielding describes Mrs. Partridge as an Amazon, he suggests her ability to fight with and dominate her husband (*Tom Jones,* bk. 2, chap. 4, 1:89). The predatory natures of Mrs. Deborah Wilkins and Miss Bridget appear in the epic similes that Fielding uses to describe them (*Tom Jones,* bk. 1, chap. 6, 1:47-48; bk. 1, chap. 8, 1:56). Overall, the use of epic, reinforced by the attention Fielding calls to it, makes the reader more aware of the pretenses that lie behind the behavior of such charac-ters.

Although the epic devices enhance the reader's aware-ness of the limitations of the modern world with which the heroic world is compared, then, they indicate a certain ambivalence toward heroic morality that Field-ing shared with his contemporaries. Ian Watt has noted that both Defoe and Richardson objected to the vicious behavior inherent in the Homeric ideal.[31] While valu-ing the epic form above all others and imitating the epics of Homer and Virgil, even Pope and Dryden were uncomfortable with the heroic code of honor, which is distinctly non-Christian. For example, among Homer's defects Pope lists "the vicious and *imperfect Manners* of his *Heroes.*"[32] Thus, Fielding's approach to epic associates him with others in the eighteenth century who were uncomfortable with the epic hero.

The epic devices in *Jonathan Wild, Joseph Andrews,* and *Tom Jones* indirectly reflect this ambivalence to-ward the heroic world. In all three novels nearly all the epic similes disclose the vicious nature of the charac-ters. Although Adams's picture of the heroic world offers an alternative to the sordid values of modern society, Fielding indicates that it hardly enables Ad-ams to deal effectively with the people he encounters on the road. Fielding enunciates the problem with the heroic world more clearly in *Tom Jones,* where Tom's heroic pretensions are associated with imprudent choic-es. Consider the women of questionable virtue or the military life, whose brutality and ignorance is repre-sented by Northerton: only when he abandons the he-roic ideal does Tom develop the restraint that helps him win Sophia. Such uses of heroism are tied to the phenomenon Rawson has noted in *Jonathan Wild.* Fielding's allusions to Virgil and Homer underscore the sordidness of the moral world that Wild inhabits, but the analogy between Wild and Aeneas suggests that epic heroism itself is unacceptable.[33]

Fielding identifies his use of inflated language with epic rather than romance by allusions to and parodies of Homer and Virgil. These devices distance the read-ers from the characters and story and encourage them to contrast the values of the modern and epic worlds. Each comments on the other: the idealism of the epic heightens the readers' awareness of the selfish motiva-tions lying behind the pretensions of many characters, and the limitations of the heroic code become apparent when characters who adopt it prove ineffectual in the modern world.

Amelia *and the* Aeneid

In *Amelia* Fielding abandons the epic devices he relies on in his earlier fiction and draws a deliberate parallel between *Amelia*'s structure and that of the *Aeneid.* Although many scholars have detailed the similarities between these two works, none has been able to ex-plain satisfactorily why Fielding used Virgil's epic. Maurice Johnson claims that the Virgilian framework exalts the modern domestic characters of the novel, implying that epic heroism may show itself in human nature.[34] Lyall Powers suggests that Booth's victory over Bath represents a victory over a passé code of honor, which parallels Aeneas's victory over Turnus, the victory of *pietas* over *violentia,* and that, like Ae-neas, who triumphed by submitting to the will of the gods, Booth succeeds by yielding to providence.[35] While each theory is partially true, neither considers eigh-teenth-century objections to the heroic code and con-cern with its applicability in a Christian world.

To account for the differences in the endings of *Ame-lia* and the *Aeneid,* scholars imply that the heroic code is a positive ideal, thus ignoring the ambiguity of the *Aeneid's* closing scene, which is implicit both in the original and in Dryden's version of the epic. As I have already shown, many eighteenth-century critics and writers questioned the validity of the Homeric concept of heroism, and Virgil's epic shares this ambivalence. Aeneas's murder of Turnus at the end of the *Aeneid* is not simply the victory of a pious man over a violent one; when Aeneas refuses to grant his opponent mercy, he violates the injunction laid upon him by his father Anchises in book 6: "tu regere imperio populos, Romane, memento / (hae tibi erunt artes), pacique imponere morem, / parcere subiectis et debellare superbos" (6.851-53) [Remember to rule the people in your empire, Roman (this will be your skill), and to impose law in peace, to spare those who have been subjugated, and to make war on the proud] (my translation). In his final confrontation with Turnus, he does not show him mercy, killing him violently. Thus, Virgil suggests that Aeneas has succumbed to his own rage and is little better than the man he defeated.

Although Dryden asserts in his dedication that Aeneas's defeat of Turnus is a victory for *pietas,* the ambivalence of the heroic ideal is apparent in his translation of the final lines of book 12.

> In deep Suspence the *Trojan* seem'd to stand;
> And just prepar'd to strike repress'd his Hand.
> He rowl'd his Eyes, and ev'ry Moment felt
> His manly Soul with more Compassion melt:
> When, casting down a casual Glance, he spy'd
> The Golden Belt that glitter'd on his side:
> The fatal Spoils which haughty *Turnus* tore
> From dying *Pallas,* and in Triumph wore.
> Then rowz'd anew to Wrath, he loudly cries,
> (Flames, while he spoke, came flashing from his Eyes:)
> Traytor, dost thou, dost thou to Grace pretend,
> Clad, as thou art, in Trophees of my Friend?
> To his sad Soul a grateful Off'ring go;
> 'Tis *Pallas, Pallas* gives this deadly Blow.
> He rais'd his Arm aloft; and at the Word,
> Deep in his Bosom drove the shining Sword.
> The streaming Blood distain'd his Arms
>   around:
> And the disdainful Soul came rushing thro'
>   the Wound.
>
> (Lines 1360-77)[36]

Dryden's emphasis on Aeneas's wrath and the blood of Turnus links the gory death of Aeneas's opponent to the violent behavior of Achilles when he slaughters Hector in the *Iliad.* Aeneas's violation of Anchises' injunction enhances the reader's sense of discomfort with the ending.[37] Thus, Dryden's version demonstrates that Fielding and his readers undoubtedly knew this interpretation of the final scene of Virgil's epic.

Fielding shares Dryden's concern about the epic hero. The connection between greatness and the violence of war is apparent in the poem **"Of True Greatness,"** where he derives the image of the plain drenched with

gore from the battle scenes in Dryden's *Aeneis* and Pope's *Iliad.*[38] In *Jonathan Wild* he draws the parallel between Homer's heroes and the behavior of Alexander when Wild expresses his admiration for both at the same time (bk. 1, chap. 3, pp. 12-13). Clearly Fielding associated the heroic ideal with greatness, which he repeatedly condemns for its violence and cruelty. In *Tom Jones* he acknowledges that women love men because they are glorious, citing Penelope in the *Odyssey* as an example (bk. 4, chap. 13, 1:202). When Lady Bellaston tries to persuade Lord Fellamar to rape Sophia, she uses the example of Paris's behavior towards Helen and the Romans to the Sabine women (bk. 15, chap. 4, 2:794-95). Again, Fielding associates the heroic code with violence and cruelty.

In *Amelia* Fielding underscores the relationship between the soldier's concept of honor and the heroic code in his allusions to the *Aeneid* and Homer's epics. When Dr. Harrison and Colonel Bath discuss the conflict between honor and Christianity, Harrison denies that the Greeks and Romans dueled. But Bath cites examples from both Homer and Virgil that implicitly establish a connection between the code of honor that he follows and that of the Greeks and the Trojans (bk. 9, chap. 3, pp. 365-66). Fielding reinforces the connection between Bath and the Homeric hero at the masquerade when Bath pulls off his mask before the bucks, who flee "as the *Trojans* heretofore from the Face of *Achilles*" (bk. 10, chap. 2, p. 416). Clearly, Fielding associates the military code of honor followed by Booth, Bath, and Colonel James with the heroic code of classical epic.

Dr. Harrison returns to the conflict between the Christian and the heroic ideal after Amelia reveals that Colonel James has challenged Booth to a duel. He argues with Amelia that her concern for her husband's military honor is wrong. He relates this concept to classical heroism by observing that in Homer Helen criticizes Paris for unheroic behavior after he fights Menelaus (bk. 12, chap. 3, p. 504). When she again mentions the importance of Booth's "reputation," Harrison replies, "*Virgil* knew it a great While ago. The next Time you see your Friend Mrs. *Atkinson,* ask her what it was made *Dido* fall in Love with *Aeneas*" (bk. 12, chap. 3, p. 505). Even in his discussions with Mrs. Atkinson, he remarks that Homer's *"Pollemy"* is "the true Characteristic of a Devil" (bk. 10, chap. 4, p. 427). While Harrison consistently maintains that his favorite classical writers were critical of the heroic ideal, he and other characters establish a connection between the epic heroes and the soldier's code of honor that is unmistakable.

Within the context of this conflict between Christianity and Homeric morality, Fielding's use of the *Aeneid* and his departure from Virgil's ending are understandable. As a soldier, Booth is bound to the traditional military code of honor. Early in his marriage to Amelia, his honor dictates that he abandon his wife and follow his regiment to Gibraltar, undermining the domestic happiness that Fielding designates as the main subject of the novel. Later Booth threatens his marriage again when he must fight a duel with Colonel Bath. His preoccupation with obtaining a military position distracts him from the threats to his wife's virtue offered by the Peer and Colonel James, which nearly destroy his marriage. Finally, after Booth recognizes the value of Christianity, Amelia is able to avert the duel between him and Colonel James, providing the novel with a Christian rather than a heroic ending. Significantly, at the end of *Amelia,* Booth abandons the military life in order to live happily, surrounded by his family.

Although it uses epic structure and avoids the burlesque diction of mock epic, Fielding's *Amelia* offers his final comment on the heroic code of behavior. In *Joseph Andrews* Fielding views the Homeric hero as an ideal against which to measure the sordid values of the modern world, but he suggests that such a hero cannot be an effective guide to modern life. The perception of the epic world reflected in both *Jonathan Wild* and *Tom Jones* is more ambivalent: while the heroic world represents an ideal that offsets the sordidness of reality, its connection with that reality throws its values into question. Finally, in *Amelia* Fielding seriously considers the viability of the heroic ethic in the domestic and Christian world and finds it completely lacking.

Although Fielding probably did not consider his novels "epics" in the traditional sense, he drew plentifully on his audience's familiarity with epic theory and the translations of Pope and Dryden to define his new form and heighten the reader's awareness of the conflict between the ancient and modern worlds, between the world of romance and reality, and between the heroic and Christian ideals. He also used epic effectively as a thread that unites his novels from *Jonathan Wild* through *Amelia.* He exploits the associations aroused by epic as part of a strategy to make his readers more discerning about the story. . . .

Notes

[1] Ethel M. Thornbury, *Henry Fielding's Theory of the Comic Prose Epic,* University of Wisconsin Studies in Language and Literature 30 (1931; rpt., New York: Russell and Russell, 1966); Martin C. Battestin, *The Moral Basis of Fielding's Art: A Study of Joseph Andrews* (Middletown: Wesleyan University Press, 1959), 40-41, 86-88, 104, 151-52; E. T. Palmer, "Fielding's *Joseph Andrews:* A Comic Epic in Prose," *English Studies* 52 (1971): 331-39; Leon Gottfried, "The Odyssean Form," in *Essays on European Literature in Honor of Liselotte Dieckmann,* ed. P. Hohendahl, H.

Lindenberger, and E. Schwarz (St. Louis: Washington University Press, 1972), 19-43; J. Paul Hunter, *Occasional Form: Henry Fielding and the Chains of Circumstance* (Baltimore: Johns Hopkins University Press, 1975), 16-17, 130-40, 185.

[2] For detailed discussion of the position of the "romance" theorists, see Homer Goldberg, "Comic Prose Epic or Comic Romance: The Argument of the Preface to *Joseph Andrews,*" *Philological Quarterly* 43 (1964): 193-215; and Sheridan Baker, "Fielding's Comic Epic-in-Prose Romances Again," *Philological Quarterly* 58 (1979): 63-81. These articles give useful, though biased, summaries of the previous criticism on this issue. The only recent addition to this debate is James Lynch, *Henry Fielding and the Heliodoran Novel: Romance, Epic, and Fielding's New Province of Writing* (Rutherford, N.J.: Fairleigh Dickenson University Press, 1986), which covers much of the same ground as Baker, Goldberg, and Henry Knight Miller, *Henry Fielding's Tom Jones and Romance Tradition,* University of Victoria English Literary Studies 6 (Victoria: University of Victoria Press, 1976).

[3] See Baker, "Fielding's Comic," 64-67; Hunter, *Occasional Form,* 131; J. Paul Hunter, *Before Novels: The Cultural Contexts of Eighteenth-Century Fiction* (New York: W. W. Norton, 1990), 18-21; Ian Watt, *The Rise of the Novel: Studies in Defoe, Richardson and Fielding* (Berkeley: University of California Press, 1957), 257-59; and Claude Rawson, *Henry Fielding and the Augustan Ideal under Stress* (London: Routledge and Kegan Paul, 1972), 147-70.

[4] For example, see Paulson's discussion of the influence of Lucian and other classical satirists in *Satire and the Novel in Eighteenth-Century England,* 132-41, 161-64.

[5] I have not included *Shamela* in this tabulation. Because it is a close parody of Richardson, *Shamela* has very few references to classical authors; most are Williams's miscitations of Latin writers, the significance of which I will discuss in chapter 4. I have chosen to use the second edition of *Jonathan Wild,* published in 1754, rather than the first edition, which appeared in volume three of the *Miscellanies* (1743); Fielding added several references to classical authors in the second edition, but the first edition has no references that are unique to it.

[6] For a complete list of authors, see appendix C [of *Henry Fielding's Novels and the Classical Tradition,* by Nancy A. Mace (Newark: University of Delaware Press, 1996)].

[7] See George Sherburn, "Fielding's *Amelia:* An Interpretation," *ELH* 3 (1936): 1-14; Lyall Powers, "The Influence of the *Aeneid* on Fielding's *Amelia,*" *Mod-*

ern Language Notes 71 (1956): 330-36; and Maurice Johnson, *Fielding's Art of Fiction: Eleven Essays on Shamela, Joseph Andrews, Tom Jones, and Amelia* (Philadelphia: University of Pennsylvania Press, 1961), 139-56. Although Joseph F. Bartolomeo argues that Fielding makes the analogy to the *Aeneid* to mount a clever defense of "a tepidly received novel," the parallels that other critics have outlined between *Amelia* and Virgil's epic suggest that Fielding's remarks were more than just a rhetorical device. See Joseph F. Bartolomeo, *A New Species of Criticism: Eighteenth-Century Discourse on the Novel* (Newark: University of Delaware Press, 1994), 71.

[8] Fielding also cites Horace and Aristotle when discussing epic theory in the following: the title page, which quotes Horace's comment in the *Ars Poetica* about Homer (lines 141-42); bk. 11, chap. 1, 2:569-70, where they are listed with epic theorists Le Bossu and Dacier; bk. 5, chap. 1, 1:210, in which Fielding alludes to Horace's rules about the five-act structure of plays in connection with unity; bk. 9, chap. 1, 1:490 and 491, where Fielding supports his comments about the need for genius and learning in authors with allusions to Horace (*Ars,* lines 408-18); and bk. 10, chap. 1, 2:527, where Fielding justifies the mixed character with a quotation from Horace (*Ars,* lines 352-53). Other references are connected with Horace's critical pronouncements in the *Ars:* bk. 4, chap. 14, 1:208, and bk. 7, chap. 6, 1:344, where Fielding mentions Horace's strictures on what material is suitable for description (*Ars,* lines 149-50); and bk. 9, chap. 2, 1:494, where Fielding says that the author who makes his reader weep, must first weep himself (*Ars,* lines 102-3).

[9] See *Tom Jones,* bk. 13, chap. 1, 1:686, where Fielding groups Lucian with Aristophanes, Cervantes, Rabelais, Molière, Shakespeare, Swift, and Marivaux; and *Amelia,* bk. 8, chap. 5, pp. 325-26.

[10] See Thornbury, *Henry Fielding's Theory,* and Lynch, *Henry Fielding and the Heliodoran Novel,* 17-19. Arthur L. Cooke, "Henry Fielding and the Writers of Heroic Romance," *PMLA* 62 (1947): 984-94, mentions Fielding's concern with probability, unity, characters, and moral purpose, but he suggests that Fielding and the writers of seventeenth-century heroic romances share these interests. As I will show, Fielding repeatedly argued that these are the very areas in which the romance and his new genre differed.

[11] René Le Bossu, *Treatise of the Epick Poem* (1695), in *Le Bossu and Voltaire on the Epic,* introduced by Stuart Curran (Gainesville, Fla.: Scholars' Facsimiles and Reprints, 1970), 6.

[12] For a detailed discussion of the theory of the epic in the eighteenth century, see A. F. B. Clark, *Boileau and the French Classical Critics in England, 1660-1830* (Paris: Librarie Ancienne Edouard Champion, 1925), 232-55, 286-88; and H. T. Swedenberg Jr., *The Theory of the Epic in England, 1650-1800,* University of California Publications in English 15 (1944; rpt., Milwood, N.Y.: Kraus Reprint Co., 1977), 16-27, 43-57.

[13] See John Dryden, dedication of the *Aeneis,* in *The Works of John Dryden* (Berkeley: University of California Press, 1987), 5:267-341; Alexander Pope, preface to *The Iliad of Homer,* ed. Maynard Mack, in *The Poems of Alexander Pope* (London: Methuen, 1967), 7:3-25 and *The Odyssey of Homer,* ed. Maynard Mack, in *The Poems of Alexander Pope* (London: Methuen, 1967), 9:3-24.

[14] For a discussion of the critical theories of these men, see A. F. B. Clark, *Boileau,* 275-79; and M. L. Clarke, *Greek Studies in England, 1700-1830* (1945; rpt. Amsterdam: Adolf M. Hakkert, 1986), 136-38.

[15] For a discussion of the meaning of "comic epic" in this passage, see W. L. Renwick, "Comic Epic in Prose," *Essays and Studies* 32 (1946): 40-43; and Claude Rawson, *Satire and Sentiment, 1660-1830* (Cambridge: Cambridge University Press, 1994), 146-47. Bartolomeo (*New Species of Criticism,* 70-71) discusses the interpretive problems created by the narrative voice in this passage. See also Abraham Adams's discussion of the *Iliad* in *Joseph Andrews,* bk. 3, chap. 2, pp. 196-99, where he uses categories similar to those of Le Bossu.

[16] See Swedenberg, *Theory of the Epic,* 216-19.

[17] See also *Tom Jones,* bk. 4, chap. 1, 1:150, where Fielding refers to "those idle Romances which are filled with Monsters, the Productions, not of Nature, but of distempered Brains."

[18] See A. F. B. Clark, *Boileau,* 308-10; Swedenberg, *Theory of the Epic,* 266-70.

[19] *Jonathan Wild,* bk. 2, chap. 12, p. 112; *Tom Jones,* bk. 17, chap. 1, 2:875-76.

[20] See Swedenberg, *Theory of the Epic,* 306-8.

[21] See also *Jonathan Wild,* bk. 3, chap. 11, p. 167, where Fielding argues that the readers of romance like to be deceived; bk. 4, chap. 4, p. 198, where he talks about the extravagancies of romance; *Joseph Andrews,* bk. 3, chap. 1, p. 185, where he equates historians with romance writers who are not concerned with the truth; pp. 185-86, in which he refers to works that readers justly consider romances because "the Writer hath indulged a happy and fertile Invention"; and *Tom Jones,* bk. 9, chap. 1, 1:489, where he says that he has avoided the term romance because he wants to make sure

that his readers understand that his novels have some truth.

[22] See, for example, Paulson, *Satire and the Novel,* 106-7; Hunter, *Occasional Form,* 130. Although Thornbury discusses the mock-heroic description of the fight involving Molly Seagrim, she argues that it is not mock-heroic but comic; she maintains that the battle is fitted to the importance of the characters and reflects their seriousness about the fight (*Henry Fielding's Theory,* 128-30).

[23] For a discussion of the mock-heroic as imitation and critical parody, see Ulrich Broich, *The Eighteenth-Century Mock-Heroic Poem,* trans. David Henry Wilson (Cambridge: Cambridge University Press, 1990), 1-6, 50-67. Although Broich observes that the serious epic is never consciously mocked in mock-heroics as in a critical parody, he concludes by admitting that such parodies often have the inadvertent effect of putting the classical epic in a "comic light" (66-67).

[24] Rawson, *Henry Fielding and the Augustan Ideal Under Stress,* 147-70, esp. 159-60.

[25] See *Joseph Andrews,* bk. 1, chap. 12, pp. 55-56; bk. 1, chap. 8, pp. 37-38; and bk. 3, chap. 4, p. 225; and *Tom Jones,* bk. 9, chap. 2, 1:495.

[26] See, for example, *Joseph Andrews,* bk. 1, chap. 8, pp. 37-38; *Tom Jones,* bk. 1, chap. 6, 1:47-48; bk. 4, chap. 2, 1:154-55; bk. 5, chap. 11, 1:259; and bk. 9, chap. 2, 1:495.

[27] *Joseph Andrews,* bk. 2, chap. 9, pp. 138-39, the battle between Adams and Fanny's intended ravisher; bk. 3, chap. 6, pp. 237-43, between Joseph, Adams, and the dogs; bk. 3, chap. 10, pp. 256-59, between Joseph and Adams and the emissaries of the Squire; *Tom Jones,* bk. 2, chap. 4, 1:89-90, between Mr. and Mrs. Partridge over Jenny Jones; bk. 4, chap. 8, 1:177-84, involving Molly Seagrim and the townspeople; bk. 5, chap. 11, 1:259-63, involving Tom, Thwackum, and Blifil over Molly; and bk. 9, chap. 3, 1:501-4, involving Partridge, Jones, the Innkeeper, and his wife over the honor of Mrs. Waters.

[28] See also the parody of the libation in the *Iliad* in *Tom Jones,* bk. 9, chap. 4, 1:508.

[29] Sheridan Baker, "The Idea of Romance in the Eighteenth-Century Novel," *Papers of the Michigan Academy of Science, Arts, and Letters* 49 (1964): 507-22. For a detailed discussion of the adoption of courtly language in *Pamela* and *Clarissa,* see Carey McIntosh, *Common and Courtly Language: The Stylistics of Social Class in 18th-Century English Literature* (Philadelphia: University of Pennsylvania Press, 1986), 77-78, 118-30.

[30] See Paulson, *Satire and the Novel,* 22-41, 89-92, 111-21.

[31] See Watt, *Rise of the Novel,* 240-47.

[32] Alexander Pope, preface to *The Iliad of Homer,* 13-14.

[33] Rawson, *Henry Fielding and the Augustan Ideal Under Stress,* 150-61.

[34] Johnson, *Fielding's Art of Fiction,* 155-56.

[35] Powers, "Influence of the *Aeneid,*" 334-36.

[36] Dryden, *Aeneis,* 6:806.

[37] For a full discussion of Dryden's ambivalence towards the Homeric hero, see William Frost, *Dryden and the Art of Translation,* Yale Studies in English 128 (New Haven: Yale University Press, 1955), 62-69; and Judith Sloman, *Dryden: The Poetics of Translation* (Toronto: University of Toronto Press, 1985), 126-36.

[38] See *Miscellanies,* 1:21-22, lines 67-90, and Miller's note.

FURTHER READING

Baker, Sheridan. "Bridget Allworthy: The Creative Pressures of Fielding's Plot." In *Tom Jones: The Authoritative Text, Contemporary Reactions, Criticism,* edited by Sheridan Baker, pp. 778-786. New York: W.W. Norton, 1995. Originally published in *Papers of the Michigan Academy of Science, Arts, and Letters* 52 (1967): 345-56.

    Argues that an examination of the little-studied character of Bridget reveals something of Fielding's technique in creating *Tom Jones.*

Bartschi, Helen. "Character's Speeches: Transparence and Intertextuality." In her *The Doing and Undoing of Fiction: A Study of Joseph Andrews,* pp. 72-115. Berne: Peter Lang, 1983.

    Focuses on the characters of Slipslop and Lady Booby, with attention to the use of language.

Campbell, Jill. "Fielding and the Novel at Mid-Century." In *The Columbia History of the British Novel,* edited by John Richetti, pp. 102-126. New York: Columbia University Press, 1994.

    Examines Fielding's drama and fiction to demonstrate his contribution to the development of the English novel.

Cruise, James. "Precept, Property, and 'Bourgeois' Practice in *Joseph Andrews.*" *Studies in English Literature 1500-1900* 37, 3 (1997): 535-552.

Maintains that Fielding is not altogether successful in his attempt to render the novel Joseph Andrews into a source of sound moral instruction for his readers.

Evans, James E. "The Social Design of Fielding's Novels." *College Literature* 7, 2 (1980): 91-103.

Claims that Fielding's novels can be better understood by examining the complex social relationshipsbetween the characters, rather than analyzing the allegorical nature of the characterizations.

Foster, James R. "Sensibility Among the Great and Near Great." In his *History of the Pre-Romantic Novel in England,* pp. 104-138. New York: MLA, 1949.

Discusses Fielding's *Amelia* in the context of more sentimental novels by Richardson, Goldsmith, Smollet, and Sterne.

Goldgar, Bertrand A. *"Jonathan Wild."* In *Critical Essays on Henry Fielding,* edited by Albert J. Rivero, pp. 35-56. New York: G.K. Hall & Co., 1998. Originally published in General Introduction, *Miscellanies by Henry Fielding, Esq.,* Vol. 3 (Oxford University Press, 1997).

Discusses the sources, cultural influences, and textual history of *Jonathan Wild.*

Harrison, Bernard. *Henry Fielding's Tom Jones: The Novelist as Moral Philosopher.* London: Sussex University Press, 1975.

Defends Fielding's reputation as a moral philosopher. The concluding chapter offers extensive analysis of *Jonathan Wild.*

Irwin, Michael. "Didacticism in Fielding's Plays." In his *Henry Fielding: The Tentative Realist,* pp. 24-20. Oxford: Clarendon Press, 1967.

Describes Fielding's efforts to incorporate several genres into his plays, arguing that Fielding was largely unsuccessful as a dramatist.

Michaelson, Patricia Howell. *"The Wrongs of Woman* as a Feminist *Amelia." The Journal of Narrative Technique* 21, 3 (1991): 250-261.

Compares Mary Wollenstonecraft's posthumously published work *The Wrong of Women; or, Maria* with Fielding's *Amelia,* and proposes the theory that the later work is an intentional revision of Fielding's last novel.

Ortiz, Ricardo L. "Fielding's 'Orientalist' Moment: Historical Fiction and Historical Knowledge in *Tom Jones." Studies in English Literature 1500-1900* 33,3 (1993): 609-628.

Discusses the "Gypsy Episode" in *Tom Jones* to analyze Fielding's various approaches to realism and history.

Plank, Jeffrey. "The Narrative Forms of *Joseph Andrews."*

Papers on Language and Literature 24, 2 (1988): 142-158.

Links Fielding's use of interpolated episodes in *Joseph Andrews* to the conventions of Augustan poetry.

Preston, John. "Plot as Irony: The Reader's Role in *Tom Jones."* In *Tom Jones: The Authoritative Text, Contemporary Reactions, Criticism,* edited by Sheridan Baker, pp. 778-786. New York: W.W. Norton, 1995. Originally published in *ELH* 35 (1968): 365-80.

Suggests that the irony and plot structure of *Tom Jones* function to educate the reader in comprehending Fielding's innovations of form.

Rothstein, Eric. "Virtue and Authority in *Tom Jones."* In *Critical Essays on Henry Fielding,* edited by Albert J. Rivero, pp. 141-163. New York: G.K. Hall & Co., 1998. Originally published in *The Eighteenth Century* 28 (1987): 99-126.

Discusses Fielding's attempt to create model readers through narrative authority in *Tom Jones,* arguing that the visibility of the narrator's intention may undercut his efforts.

———— *"Amelia."* In his *Systems of Order and Inquiry in Later Eighteenth-Century Fiction,* pp. 154-207. Berkeley: University of California Press, 1975.

Argues that Fielding returns to a theatrical mode in his last novel; finds it flawed but nonetheless a good example of the epistemological concerns of the era.

Scheuermann, Mona. "Henry Fielding: *Tom Jones* and *Amelia."* In her *Her Bread to Earn: Women, Money, and Society from Defoe to Austen,* pp. 96-133. Lexington: University Press of Kentucky, 1993.

Examines Fieldings ambiguous presentation of women characters in the cited novels. Scheuermann concludes that Fielding's unrealistically idealized heroines set an impossibly high standard.

———— *"Amelia."* In her *Social Protest in the Eighteenth-Century Novel,* pp. 13-40. Columbus: Ohio State University Press, 1985.

Discusses Fielding's portrayal of political and legal corruption in *Amelia.* The critic suggests that in this novel Fielding explores a variety of interactions between the individual and society, noting especially where societal expectations are difficult for the average person to meet.

Smallwood, Angela J. *Fielding and the Woman Question: The Novels of Henry Fielding and Feminist Debate 1700-1750.* New York: St. Martin's Press, 1989.

Argues that gender roles and the social position of women are important, unrecognized themes in all of Fielding's works.

Wilner, Arlene Fish. "Henry Fielding and the Knowledge of Character." *Modern Language Studies* 18, 1 (1988): 181-194.

Suggests that Fielding may be more skeptical about

the proper interpretation of character than earlier scholarship allows.

Wilputte, Earla A. "Ambiguous Language and Ambiguous Gender: The 'Bisexual' Text of *Shamela.*" *Modern Language Review* 89, 3 (1994): 561-71.
    Advocates a more serious examination of the use of language in *Shamela,* arguing that the text reveals Fielding's attraction to the ambiguity of language.

Additional coverage of Fielding's life and works is contained in the following sources published by The Gale Group: *Literature Criticism 1400-1800,* Vol. 1, *DISCovering Authors, DISCovering Authors: British, DISCovering Authors: Canadian, DISCovering Authors Modules: Dramatists,DISCovering Authors Modules: Most-Studied, DISCovering Authors Modules: Dramatists, World Literature Criticsm, Dictionary of Literary Biography,* Vol. 39, 84, 101, **and** *Concise Dictionary of British Literary Biography 1660-1789.*

Tobias (George) Smollett

1721-1771

Scottish novelist, satirist, travel writer, historian, journalist, translator, poet, and dramatist.

INTRODUCTION

Smollett is regarded as one of the major British novelists of the eighteenth century, the era when the novel as a genre emerged and became established as an important new form of literary expression. His experiments in satire and caricature, as well as his manipulation of the picaresque and epistolary forms, helped establish the novel as an appropriate means for attacking social vices and criticizing the absurdities of humanity. Before his reputation declined during the Victorian period, Smollett's writings exerted a considerable influence over the work of a number of nineteenth-century authors, among them Sir Walter Scott and Charles Dickens, both of whom borrowed from his methods of comic characterization and picaresque realism. Although today, many critics rank Smollett below Samuel Richardson in his methods of characterization and far beneath Henry Fielding in dramtic presentation, they still find his novels—particularly his first, *Roderick Random,* and his last, *Humphry Clinker*—significant and enjoyable. In the words of Robert Donald Spector, these two works "remain among the finest novels written in English."

Biographical Information

Smollett was born in Dumbartonshire, Scotland. His father died when Smollett was only two years old. Smollett was supported well into his teens by his grandfather. At fifteen, Smollett was sent to Glasgow, first to attend the university there and then to be apprenticed to a surgeon and apothecary. Although he received no degree from the university, three years later Smollett left it as a qualified surgeon. Meanwhile, he had been working in his spare time on a drama entitled *The Regicide; or, James the First of Scotland.* In 1739 he moved to London, where he hoped to secure the production of this, his first literary effort. An immature play filled with inflated rhetoric, *The Regicide* was turned down by everyone who read it, including the actor David Garrick and the literary patron George, Lord Lyttelton. Smollett never forgave any of his potential producers for their rejection. Unable to support himself as a writer, Smollett was forced to accept an appointment as a surgeon for the British Navy. In 1740 he sailed to the West Indies. He participated in the battle of Cartagena, a brutal experience he later vividly portrayed in his first novel, *Roderick Random.* When the fleet reached Jamaica, Smollett abandoned both the ship and the navy. He remained in Jamaica until 1744. while there, he met a woman named Anne Lascelles. Smollett returned to London and opened a medical practice; Lascelles joined him there and the two were married in 1747, and Smollett began work on *Roderick Random.* Published in 1748, the novel was a great popular and financial success, the one such success that Smollett would experience in his lifetime. In 1750 he received his degree in medicine and tried again to establish a medical practice. He published two more novels, *Peregrine Pickle* and *Ferdinand, Count Fathom,* neither of which won critical or public acclaim. In need of money, Smollett began what was to be the first English "literary factory," employing a dozen or so writers to produce all kinds of literary hackwork, such as translations, travelogues, and brief histories. It was also during this period that Smollett composed most of his nonfictional works and undertook his translations of *Gil Blas* and the works of Voltaire. In the 1760s

Smollett tried unsuccessfully to launch a career as a journalist. He also traveled through Europe to improve his failing health. He returned to England in better health, but soon became ill again. In 1769 he and his wife moved to Italy, where he began work on what was to be his last and what many consider his greatest novel, *The Expedition of Humphry Clinker*. This novel appeared just shortly before his death in 1771.

Major Works

Smollett's first novel, *The Adventures of Roderick Random*, was a major success. The novel is a combination of picaresque narrative and social satire that strings together a series of often-unrelated episodes and ends with the hero's reformation and marriage to the heroine. The stock ending has put off many modern readers—just as Roderick's selfishness and brutality repelled some of Smollett's contemporaries. Nevertheless, there is much in the novel that is regarded as both powerful and unique, particularly the description of shipboard life and the vivid account of the disastrous attack on Cartagena by the British fleet. In fact, several scholars consider *Roderick Random* among the earliest literary protests against abuses in the Royal Navy. Smollett's next novel, *The Adventures of Peregrine Pickle* (1751), was based on material he collected while living in Paris. Although not as well received as his first work (probably the result of its savagery and its ruthless, womanizing hero), *Peregrine Pickle* has since been commended for its excellent prose and a number of brilliant scenes. Many literary historians consider *Peregrine Pickle* as significant as *Roderick Random* because it demonstrates Smollett's growing ability to direct his satire toward a specific end, and because it helped broaden the scope of the English novel by including events and characters from European countries other than England. The plot of *Peregrine Pickle* is similar to that of *Roderick Random* although Peregrine is more despicable as a character than Roderick and thus his transformation to goodness is even less probable. Both novels share Smollett's facility for comic characterization and graphic realism. *Peregrine Pickle* was followed two years later by *The Adventures of Ferdinand, Count Fathom* (1753), a complete failure during its time and still regarded by many as one of Smollett's weaker novels, principally because its central character, Count Fathom, is a portrait of villainy. For nearly a decade afterward, most of Smollett's writing was nonfictional. Then in 1762 he published *The Adventures of Sir Launcelot Greaves*. Modeled on Cervantes' Don Quixote, Greaves is from start to finish the only morally upright and sentimental hero in all of Smollett's works. Unfortunately for Smollett, *Sir Launcelot Greaves* enjoyed little popularity with its contemporary audience, and its reputation has not improved significantly over time. By contrast, Smollett's last novel, *The Expedition of Humphry Clinker* (1771) was an immediate success and is today regarded by many as one of his greatest works. *Humphry Clinker* is an epistolary rather than a picaresque novel. It is based on a family's tour of the British Isles and includes a cast of humorous characters who through their letters provide different points of view of their travels and of each other. While it is considered one of Smollett's funniest and most enjoyable novels, it shares with his other works a detailed account of the more sordid aspects of the eighteenth century, in this case illness and hygiene. Variously interpreted as a creative work of political propaganda, an autobiographical account of Smollett's travels through Britain, a commentary on the breakdown of traditional values in the eighteenth century and the movement toward religious, social, and moral reform, and a mythical-psychological quest, *Humphry Clinker* remains the most praised, as well as the most controversial of Smollett's canon.

Critical Reception

Smollett, like many other English novelists of the eighteenth century, had the misfortune of competing against such writers as Henry Fielding and Samuel Richardson. Although numerous eighteenth- and nineteenth-century critics judged him according to the accomplishments of these two novelists, Smollett has since been regarded as of a temperament far different from either Fielding or Richardson. Smollett saw the world as a "vicious and sordid place," and most twentieth-century critics agree that this perception of society and humanity shaped all of his work. During the century after his death, the established opinion of Smollett was that he was a talented caricaturist and a master of realistic presentation, but that he lacked the psychological insight of Fielding and, most signifcantly, his work suffered from indecency. Gradually, a more tolerant view of Smollett's coarseness has evolved, with most critics attributing it to the nature of his age or of the picaresque tradition, rather than as something inherently wrong with his personality. Other eighteenth- and nineteenth-century views of Smollett's work have also been challenged in the present century. For example, the argument that his novels (with the exception of *Humphry Clinker*) lack any sense of structure has been contradicted today by numerous critics. And the long-standing belief that Smollett's moral conclusions to his stories were simply tacked on in order to avoid censorship has increasingly come under attack by critics who argue that Smollett's early picaresque novels follow a pattern similar to the German *Bildungsroman* and, therefore, must depict the eventual education and reformation of their protagonists. In fact, most modern critics agree that Smollett was more aware of his craft than previous commentators understood. Although he still lacks the stature of Fielding, Richardson, or Sterne, Smollett nevertheless must be included among the group as a significant contributor to the development of the English novel.

PRINCIPAL WORKS

"The Tears of Scotland" (poetry) 1746

Advice (poetry) 1746

Reproof (poetry) 1747

The Adventures of Roderick Random (novel) 1748

* *The Regicide; or, James the First of Scotland* (drama) 1749

The Adventures of Peregrine Pickle: In Which Are Included Memoirs of a Lady of Quality (novel) 1751

The Adventures of Ferdinand, Count Fathom (novel) 1753

A Compleat History of England, Deduced from the Descent of Julius Caesar to the Treaty of Aix-la-Chapelle, 1748. 4 vols. (history) 1757-58

The Reprisal; or, The Tars of Old England (drama) 1757

The Adventures of Sir Launcelot Greaves (novel) 1762

Continuation of the Compleat History of England. 5 vols. (history) 1763-65

The Present State of All Nations: Containing a Geographical, Natural, Commercial, and Political History of All the Countries in the Known World (history) 1764

Travels through France and Italy (epistolary essays) 1766

The History and Adventures of an Atom [as Nathaniel Peacock; attributed to Smollett] (satire) 1769

The Expedition of Humphry Clinker (novel) 1771

Ode to Independence (poetry) 1773

The Works of Tobias Smollett. 12 vols. (novels) 1885-1903

The Letters of Tobias Smollett (letters) 1970

*This work was written in 1739.

CRITICISM

Holbrook Jackson (essay date 1908)

SOURCE: "Tobias Smollett," in *Great English Novelists,* George W. Jacobs & Co., 1908, pp. 87-107.

[*In the following essay, Holbrook surveys Smollett's life and career, concluding that Smollett, while neither essential to the development of English literature nor particularly original as a writer, nevertheless did contribute somewhat to the growth of the novel as a genre.*]

Of the early masters of the English novel, Tobias Smollett is the least original and on the whole the least satisfying. But his work was by no means without some considerable influence on the literary taste of his time. His novels are entirely derivative, harking back to the picaresque mode of narrative, whose greatest English exemplar was Defoe, and admittedly based upon the finest of all specimens of this particular form of fiction—the satirical narratives of Spain. Into the framework thus adopted Smollett contrived to instill the restless and combative qualities of his own nature, and an individual, if not a penetrating power of observation.

He was born in the year 1721 at Dalquhurn House, in the parish of Cardross, Vale of Leven Dumbartonshire. His people were gentlefolk, known pretty familiarly in Scotland as the Smolletts of Bunhill, and latterly chiefly engaged in law and medicine. Tobias George Smollett, the novelist, was the younger son of Archibald Smollett, who, himself a younger son, was not in the position to endow the lives of his children in such a way as to have encouraged idleness. So, after some school experience at Dumbarton, where he was noted for his Latin, Tobias was apprenticed to a medical practitioner named Gordon. There is scant record of his life after this until we hear of his arrival in London in 1739, with his first literary work, a tragedy called the *Regicide*, dealing with the murder of James I of Scotland at Perth, in his pocket.

His life as an apprentice is largely a blank, so far as history is concerned; but Campbell has put it on record, with probably some truth, that he was "a restive apprentice and a mischievous stripling." This description is borne out by an anecdote preserved by his friend and disciple, Dr. John Moore, who had a brief fame as the author of a romance called *Zeluco:*—

On a winter evening, when the streets were covered with snow, Smollett happened to be engaged in a snowball fight with a few boys of his own age. Among his associates was the apprentice of that surgeon who is supposed to have been delineated under the name of Crab in *Roderick Random*. He entered his shop while his apprentice wa in the heat of the engagement. On the return of the latter the master remonstrated severely with him for his negligence in quitting the shop. The youth excused himself by saying that while he was employed in making up a prescription a fellow had hit him with a snowball, and that he had been in pursuit of the delinquent.

"A mighty probablestory, truly," said the master, in an ironical tone; "I wonder how long I should stand here before it would enter into any mortal's head to throw a snowball at me?" While he was holding his head erect, with a most scornful air, he received a very severe blow in the face by a snowball.

Smollett, who stood concealed behind the pillar at the shop-door, had heard the dialogue, and perceiving that his companion was puzzled for an answer, he extricated him by a repartee equally smart and *apropos*.

In starting out to capture London, the young Smollett was armed, besides his tragedy, with a number of letters of introduction to people of eminence. And he was in full hopes of getting the Regicide placed upon the stage with little delay. Through the influence of his friends he got to know such useful men as Lyttelton and Garrick. But in spite of such opportunities as acquaintanceship with the leading patron of letters and the leading actor of the day gave him, the tragedy, which he considered a masterpiece of the first order, but which in reality was very second-rate stuff, was never performed. But not to be entirely defeated he printed the rejected play some years later, in 1749, with a lively preface in which he rated in good round terms all those eminent people who had failed to recognise its hazy merits.

With the failure of his first literary ambitions he turned round for some other means of subsistence, and, as a fleet of warships was on the point of sailing from Spithead for the West Indies, to rap the knuckles of Spain, who had become more than usually annoying in the region of the American colonies, he was fortunate, in so far as useful experience goes, in obtaining an appointment as surgeon's mate on one of His Majesty's ships. England had made up her mind in the matter and was determined to give her ancient enemy and then present irritant a final lesson. Her best ships were gathered together, and in October, 1740, under Sir Chaloner Ogle, they sailed to conquer the marauding armadas of the Far West. It is uncertain which of the line-of-battleships was joined by Tobias Smollett, but it is certain that his experiences on this memorable expedition, which came to so unlucky an end at Carthagena, gave him material for his first notable work, **Roderick Random**, and incidentally made him the first characteriser of seamen in English fiction.

The navy at this period was perhaps at its lowest point of organisation and efficiency. The hopeless muddle into which things had fallen, coupled with the abominable treatment of the sailors, particularly during active engagements, gave Smollett a theme for his habitual indignation with men and their ways. So excellent are his descriptions of life in the navy during this campaign, that had he written no other book, **Roderick Random** would have been memorable for this alone. There was a deep-seated irascibility of temper in Smollett, which on more than one occasion militated against his own comfort, but it also served him as the fuel of an indignation, which was quickly aroused in the face of cruelty, treachery, and incompetence. He was one of those who would not suffer fools gladly, and the misery following the reverse of Cathagena, which was brought about by the muddling of officers who were

perpetually at loggerheads one with another, was a subject worthy of his steel. He describes with satiric detail the whole series of disastrous events, including the differences of the leaders. Here is his appalling description of the treatment of the wounded during the battle:—

> As for the sick and wounded, they were next day sent on board the transports and vessels called hospital ships, where they languished in want of every necessary comfort and accommodation. They were destitute of surgeons, nurses, cooks, and proper provision; they were pent up between decks in small vessels, where they had not room to sit upright; they wallowed in filth; myriads of maggots were hatched in the putrefaction of their sores, which had no other dressing than that of being washed by themselves with their own allowance of brandy; and nothing was heard but groans, lamentations, and the language of despair, invoking death to deliver them from their miseries. What served to encourage this despondence was the prospect of those poor wretches who had strength and opportunity to look around them, for there they beheld the naked bodies of their fellow-soldiers and comrades floating up and down the harbour, affording prey to the carrion crows and sharks, which tore them in pieces without interruption, and contributing by their stench to the mortality that prevailed.

This frank exposure of the condition of things in the navy went some distance towards bringing about that awakening of public feeling which sought by various means to improve the management and organisation of the fleet. Carlyle, in his caustic way, said that the only noticeable thing about the Spanish expedition was the presence of Tobias Smollett; perhaps, in the light of after reforms, it would have been nearer the truth to have said that the most useful member of the expedition was Tobias Smollett.

After the fall of Cathagena the crippled fleet returned to Jamaica, where Smollett retired from the service and settled for a while at Kingston, where he fell in love with and married Nancy Lassells, a lady of some means, whose portrait is drawn in the person of Narcissa, the adored one of Roderick Random. He left Jamaica with his wife in 1744 and set up as a doctor in Downing Street, Westminster. He took his M.D. degree from Marischal College, Aberdeen, in 1750. For a time he practised medicine but gradually drifted into a life of letters. His first literary work after his return from the Indies was satire. It was a satirical age, and satirists, since a taste for their wares had been created by the masterpieces of Swift and Pope, grew "plentiful as tabby-cats—in point of fact too many." But Smollett saw possible profit in the prevailing fashion, and, nothing loth, he joined the dance with three satirical poems, **The Tears of Caledonia** and **The Advice: a Satire**, in 1746, and with **The Reproof: a Satire**, in 1747. But it was not until the next year that he made any serious bid for fame, when he made a lasting name for himself with *Roderick Random*.

This long picaresque novel is based on his own life, but how far it would be safe to accept the story as fact, apart from the admirable passages of certain biographical authenticity, dealing with the Spanish War, is more than doubtful. Smollett, as we have seen, was by no means the inventor of this form of fiction, and, in the preface to *Roderick Random*, he owns his indebtedness to Le Sage, whose light touch and happily comic sense of human foibles, however, Smollett has not succeeded in catching. Indeed, this was not his aim. His aim was more purposeful, for, like all the notable novelist before Sterne and Scott, he was a moralist, and sought to set his fellows in the right path. His method, like that of a later teacher-novelist, Zola, was not so much to point to the moral of any particular action as to depict human delinquencies in their most lurid colours, and by so doing help the reader to draw his own conclusions.

This treatment had at least the chance of promoting the illusion of reality, fir its users were free of the fatal tendency among moralist and theorists to construct characters in order to wear the garments of abstract ideas. The pitfalls of this sort of realism, on the other hand, were an equally dangerous tendency towards gross frankness. It all, of course, depended upon the novelist. Smollett succeeded in so far as he steered clearly between his desire to please his public and his desire to teach them, and he created quite a number of really life-like people. But there was a coarser strain in his temperament which never permitted him to go far without exaggerating the more material sides of human nature. This wa a matter entirely within the taste of the eighteenth century, but it has gone far towards keeping Smollett out of the modern home or confining him to the locked cabinet.

He conceived the novel as, in his own words, "a large diffused picture, comprehending the characters of life, disposed in different groups and exhibited in various attitudes, for the purposes of an uniform plan." And his novels come will within this idea. They are crowded canvases, full of characters and teeming with a coarse vitality. Smollett neither possesses the minute sense of the movement of emotion peculiar to Richardson, nor the jovial and healthy naturalness of Fielding; and it was not until he had read *Tristram Shandy* (1759-67) that he had any sense of the more subtle, to say nothing of the gentler, forms of humour. The fun in *Roderick Random* too often becomes mere horse-play, and the action of the volumes is too much in the nature of a carnival of brutality to be entirely pleasing. Yet it is imaginable from what we know of the times that Smollett did not exaggerate over much, or at any rate not deliberately. The brutality of his books is a fault of his realism. He was a quarrelsome, combative person him-

self, and this characteristic gave colour to his vision of men. He was on the look out for such things, and so got more of them into his books than most people are in the habit of seeing.

He, again, often raises laughter by exhibition of merely brute strength, or by depicting the whims and oddities of people. And his habit of thus depicting eccentricity rather than interpreting character has the effect, whether he is actually guilty of exaggeration or not, of giving his readers the impression that he overstates his case. It is quite natural that such a writer should find little sympathy in France, where people have been long used to a daintier wit, a wit of the rapier, rather than of the broadsword. And when Taine says that "the generous wine of Fielding, in Smollett's hands, becomes brandy of the dram-shop," we feel that he is after all not only speaking for his own nationality, but at the present day, at least, for the majority of novel readers. Smollett was a barbarian in *Roderick Random*; he had no reticences and no consideration for the feelings of anyone but himself. He satirises and caricatures in bold uncompromising strokes, which are so convinced of their own truth that they cause doubt in the eyes of all who behold them. They lack that little touch of psychology which makes all art kin. If Fielding was the Hogarth, Smollett was the Gilray of novelists.

The success of *Roderick Random* gave Smollett a more promising means of livelihood than the medical profession, although he did not burn his medical boats with undue haste, in fact, he turned an honest penny by exploiting his professional reputation with his pen in a tract entitled *An Essay on the External Use of Water, with Particular Remarks on the Mineral Waters of Bath* (1752). In 1751 he published his second novel, *The Adventures of Peregrine Pickle*, and in 1753, his third, *The Adventures of Ferdinand Count Fathom*. In the first of these he imitated his first success but only succeeded in becoming tedious. *Peregrine Pickle* has all the faults of *Roderick Random*, with few of its good qualities, and besides this it lacks the cohesion which distinguished his earlier book whilst *Count Fathom* is poorer still, it being nothing more than a feeble hotch-potch of *Jonathan Wild* and *Don Quixote*. The barbarisms of his first book which are generally made at least tolerable by the skill with which they are held together, become nothing short of an uncalculating savageness in the disjointed pages of these later novels.

Smollett, although now famous, was not well known in literary circles and seems never to have come into the charmed circle of Samuel Johnson. He was not by any means without friends or even a circle of his own, and there are anecdotes left by some of his boon fellows which show him in a pleasant and even convivial light. But he was an ostentatious and dominant man, preferring, as is often the case, the slavish admiration of his inferiors rather than the friendship of his equals. His temperament was strong and self-reliant in so far as equals and superiors went, but he liked to lean on his dependents. In some respects this reminds one of the feudalism of Scott, who loved nothing better than to be surrounded by retainers, but in Smollett this love was not always free from mercenary ends. His retainers and dependents were only too often his literary hacks and slaves.

In this respect Smollett was not an artist, but a business man. Like Defoe he became a busy and productive journalist. But his journalism never approached genius, as it did in the case of the founder of the *Review*. He edited various journals, among which were *The Critical Review*, a forerunner of the literary reviews of our own day; and from May, 1762, to February, 1763, he had a brief spell of political journalism in the editorship of *The Briton*, a journal founded to support the Bute administration. But Smollett's politics proved so unstable that the paper was stopped when Bute found that its methods were making him more enemies than friends. Smollett's other political venture was his pamphlet attacking Pitt, *The History of the Adventures of an Atom* (1769), one of the bitterest and most offensive lampoons in the language.

Under the term journalism, for the sake of convenience, may be classed all that ephemeral work which he did for the money it would bring in, such as the *Compendium of Voyages*; the *Universal History*; *The Present State of All Nations*; and his *History of England*. Besides this there were translations, the most notable being that of *Don Quixote*; and in 1757 a play called *The Reprisal: or, The Tars of Old England*, which was produced by David Garrick at Drury Lane. The more enduring *Travels through France and Italy* was issued in 1766, and his last book, *The Expedition of Humphry Clinker*, which with *Roderick Random* are the two books on which his claim upon the future depends, was issued just before he died in 1771.

In 1752 Smollett took a house named Monmouth House, in Lawrence Street, and now devoted himself entirely to literature, and employed that weird band of hacks who aided him in the manufacture of his histories and other bibliographical wares. There is a famous description of this circle in *Humphry Clinker* which reminds one of Edgar Poe.

> At two in the afternoon, I found myself one of ten messmates seated at a table; and I question if the whole world could produce such another assemblage of originals. Among their peculiarities I do not mention those of dress, which may be purely accidental. What struck me were oddities originally produced by affectation, and afterwards confirmed

> by habit. One of them wore spectacles at dinner, and another his hat flapped; though as Ivy told me, the first was noted as having a seaman's eye when a bailiff was in the wind, and the other was never known to labour under any weakness or defect of vision, except about five years ago, when he was complimented with a couple of black eyes by a player with whom he had quarrelled in his drink. A third wore a laced stocking, and made use of crutches, because once in his life he had been laid up with a broken leg, though no man could leap over a stick with more agility. A fourth had contracted such an antipathy to the country, that he insisted on sitting with his back towards the window that looked into the garden; and when a dish of cauliflower was set on the table, he snuffed up volatile salts to keep him from fainting. Yet this delicate person was the son of a cottager, born under a hedge, and many years had run wild with asses on a common. A fifth affected distraction. When spoken to he always answered from the purpose: sometimes he suddenly started up and rapped out a dreadful oath; sometimes he burst out a laughing; then he folded his arms, and sighed; and then he hissed like fifty serpents.

This is obviously a caricature, and incidentally it is a good specimen of Smollett's leaning towards the revelation of eccentricity; but it is founded upon the fact of the strange members of his intimate circle of workers. His idiosyncrasy for living a retired busy life among curious nonentities perhaps fostered the querulousness of his nature and often got him into scrapes, which he rather enjoyed than otherwise. He liked a fight, and this was probably the basis of his satire, more than any sense of outraged feelings or crossed convictions. These satires also got him into trouble, and on one occasion he was fined £100 and imprisoned for three months in the King's Bench prison for criticising Admiral Knowles. But this incident throws rather a pleasant light upon Smollett. The criticism was anonymous and appeared in the *Critical Review*, and the prosecution was, of course, drawn against the printer. But the Admiral said that it was not a legal revenge he wanted, much less against a beggarly printer, but rather did he want to know who the writer of the article was, so that, if the culprit proved to be a gentleman, another form of satisfaction could be taken. Smollett, immediately upon hearing this, declared himself the author of the incriminating criticism. Whereupon the doughty Admiral retreated behind the letter of the law and contented himself with legal revenge. The King's Bench was no trial, for Smollett was treated as a prisoner of State with no other punishment but that entailed by confinement.

In 1755 he went to Scotland and saw his mother, and about this time he visited the Continent. Besides this, he often went from his Chelsea home to Bath, for which town he had a great liking. All this travel does not seem to suggest impoverished conditions, but at this period of his life it would seem he was often in straitened circumstances. The novelist was never a man of robust health, and the failure of his editorship of *The Briton* worried him and preyed upon his mind at a time when his strength was on the decline, and when, in 1763, he lost his only daughter, the shock so overcame him that he had to go abroad, where he stayed until 1765, visiting France and Italy and publishing his impressions in the book of travels issued in the following year. On his return to England he lived for a while in Bath and went again to Scotland, but his health grew worse, and in 1768 he left England for ever. He hoped to obtain a consulship at Nice or Leghorn, but failed in his attempt to get an appointment. He settled at the latter place, where he finished his **Universal History** and **Humphry Clinker**, and there he died in September, 1771.

He met his death with a grim courage which reminds one of a similar courage pervading the death-bed of Tom Hood, who suggested to a sorrowing friend that he would have "to apologise to the worms for offering them nothing but bones." A day or two before Smollett died, in a like spirit, he wrote to a friend:—

> With respect to myself I have nothing to say but that, if I can prevail upon my wife to execute my last will, you shall receive my poor carcase in a box after I am dead, to be placed among your rarities. I am already so dry and emaciated that I may pass for an Egyptian mummy, without any other preparation than some pitch and painted linen.

Tobias Smollett was not a novelist whose work was essential to English literature, and yet coming at the time it did, his work, albeit not original in form, was a link of no small importance in the evolution of the novel. The picaresque novel wanted the modern note, such a note as fielding and Richardson and Sterne had put into their own works, and this Smollett gave to it. In many ways he was more modern to his day than either of the other novelist, and perhaps the very note in his work, the gross barbarism of his atmosphere which shocks us now, is a truer picture of the colour and feeling of his environment than anything in the earlier novelists.

Because, after all, Smollett was freer than the other novelist; they all had moral axes to grind, and they let you hear the scraping of the axe as it touched the wheel of imagination. Smollett had an axe to grind also, but it is not so easy to hear it scraping on the wheel of his art. Fielding's realism was a reaction against the sentimentalism of Richardson; the realism of Smollett is an extension of that of Fielding into more material regions. It is more like photography.

His pictures of seamen are masterpieces, and they prepared the way for Marryat. Yet Marryat never drew more vital people than Lieutenant Bowling, Captain Oakum, Commodore Trunnion, or Hatchway. Fielding is undoubtedly a more profound writer; his characters have something more than form—they have psychology; but the best of Smollett's characters can hold their own even in such good company. Humphry Clinker and Winifred Jenkins; Matthew Bramble, Lismahago, and Tabitha Bramble; Strap, the little French friar, and other delightful people are actual creations, and if not always quite so convincing as the realities of *Tom Jones* and *Tristram Shandy*, they are worthy and companionable additions to the orders of the imagination.

His novels, said Hazlitt,

> always enliven, and never tire us: we take them up with pleasure, and lay them down without any strong feeling of regret.

That is quite true. Smollett is never an inseparable friend, inspiring a deep attachment and the responsibilities of friendly relations. He is an entertaining acquaintance. One of those good and pleasant fellows who are known and forgotten, met casually and passed easily in the procession of life, yet giving colour and interest to the show, and supplying a need no less necessary and inevitable than the great friendships.

Ronald Paulson   (essay date 1967)

SOURCE: "Smollett: The Satirist As a Character Type," in his *Satire and the Novel in Eighteenth-Century England,* Yale University Press, 1967, pp. 186-208.

[*In the following excerpt, Paulson focuses on Smollett's later novels, arguing that while earlier works like* Roderick Random *define what it is to be a satirist, later novels, such as* Ferdinand Count Fathom *and, ultimately,* Humphry Clinker, *represent Smollett's greatest maturity as a writer and contain his most realistic character portrayals.*]

The Search for a Satirist

After **Peregrine Pickle** each of Smollett's novels is to some extent a search for a satirist, an exploration into the function and meaning of the satirist, just as each contains a solution of some kind to the problem of a satiric form. Roderick, Peregrine, and Crabtree [a character in **Peregrine Pickle**] offer three solutions to the problem of the satirist and his function: beginning his career with a mechanical adaptation, Smollett ends with a rather searching inquiry into the nature of satire in relation to the individual who practices it. Peregrine and Crabtree are useful satirists (in the sense that their attacks are "true"), but before they can be useful human beings as well, they have to be cured of their misanthropy. The distinction between man and satirist, private and public roles, runs through the rest of Smollett's fiction, receiving its definitive treatment in his last novel, **Humphry Clinker.**

This distinction arose, one suspects, as part of Smollett's attempt to square his Juvenalian satirist first with the current doctrine (Steele, *Tatler,* No. 242) that satire, and so the satirist, must be good-natured, and second with the picaresque form. His solution is related to the Jonsonian one, the theory of humoring and dehumoring. Both Ben Jonson and Smollett recognized that satirizing is not the normal state of man and has to be explained. Smollett requires Peregrine to be cured of his pride and misanthropy, as Jonson did his malcontent satirists, when there is no longer any need for the envy and dissatisfaction that brought them into being. The return of his money, the timely inheritance of his estate, the love of Emilia, and revenge on his old enemies free Peregrine from the need for misanthropy; under Emilia's loving smile even Crabtree has become cheerful as the book ends.

There are also suggestions of dehumoring in the case of Roderick. All the important characters along the way gravitate back to the hero at the end; the evils have been repaid—Captain Oakum is dead and the loathsome Mackshane is in prison; the good have been rewarded—Morgan with a rich wife, Bowling with success, Roderick with father, wife, and fortune. There is no further need for revenge: "The impetuous transports of my passion are now settled and mellowed into endearing fondness and tranquility of love" (Chap. 69; *3,* 260). It is clear that the satiric function is a sort of mask, assumed when the hero is dispossessed and discarded when his estate is returned to him, for both Roderick and Peregrine have streaks of good nature in them, invariably of a sentimental or benevolent kind; opposed to Roderick's passionate rages are his "sympathy and compassion" for the unfortunate and his "tender passion" for the good, and Peregrine's generosity, compassion, good nature, and "natural benevolence" are insisted on from time to time. By making misanthropy a mask for a tender heart Smollett suggests the idea that one is not simply a satirist but a man who is for a time forced into the role by intolerable circumstance.

This seems to be a general idea behind the character of Ferdinand Fathom, who is the malcontent satirist carried to its furthest implication. In his preface to **Ferdinand Count Fathom** (1753), Smollett says that Fathom is himself the evil that is being exposed; but running just below the novel's surface is a recognition of (or an unwillingness to pass up) the connection between the satirist and the criminal: both exploit and punish the folly of mankind. Take for example the

seduction of Celinda. "Perhaps such a brutal design might not have entered his imagination," the reader is told, if Fathom had not noticed "certain peculiarities":

> Besides a total want of experience, that left her open and unguarded against the attacks of the other sex, she discovered a remarkable spirit of credulity and superstitious fear . . . so delicate was the texture of her nerves, that one day, while Fathom entertained the company with a favourite air, she actually swooned with pleasure.

(Chap.34; *8,* 274-75)

With aeolian harps and old wives' tales Fathom seduces Celinda; in sections like this it is problematic whether the satire is more on Fathom's viciousness or on Celinda's folly. In his commentary on the episode, Smollett shifts his authorial emphasis from the victim's gullibility to Fathom's evil.[28] But one wonders whether by pointing out that Celinda thereafter "grew every day more sensual and degenerate," ending in a life on the streets, Smollett is not presenting both the evil example of Fathom and the punishment Celinda deserves for her romantic illusions.

Fathom is to some extent that traditional figure of the English picaresque, the criminal who unwittingly serves to reveal the folly of his dupes as well as his own knavery. An example is his cheating of Don Diego de Zelos, who reveals in his discourse to Fathom a great fund of pride, vanity, and intolerance, as well as a tempting overconfidence in his own judgment. As if enough functions had not been heaped upon him, Fathom is also one of the dupes, more often than not gulled by the party he intended to gull.[29] Finally, he has maintained all along an "ingredient in his constitution" which, though not exactly a tincture of goodness, will ultimately "counteract his consummate craft, defeat the villainy of his intention"; thus, like Smollett's other satiric figures, he is permitted to return to a normal life at the end—this time by repentance (Chap. 43; *9,* 37).[30]

In Smollett's next novel, **Sir Launcelot Greaves** (1760-61), he uses the favorite solution of the Elizabethan dramatists who wanted to give their heroes license to rail—madness. Madness as a mask is very different from madness as a commentary on the protagonist. The essential difference between Sir Launcelot and Don Quixote, his prototype, is that Quixote goes out to attack imaginary wrongs while the real world of less spectacular but more dangerous wrongs lies all about him; Sir Launcelot attacks real wrongs which in his (and Smollett's) world cannot be cured in any way other than by the intervention of a madman. Sir Launcelot contrasts himself with Quixote: "I see and distinguish objects as they are discerned and described by other men. . . . I quarrel with none but the foes of virtue and decorum" (Chap. 2; *10,* 19). "It was his opinion," we are told, "that chivalry was an useful institution while confined to its original purposes of protecting the innocent, assisting the friendless, and bringing the guilty to condign punishment" (Chap. 18; *10,* 245-46). Smollett here proves the integrity of his satirist without concealing the fact of his madness—having his "truth" as well as his rage. Sir Launcelot is forced to revert to an older, nobler code by the sorrow he feels at losing his beloved Aurelia and the outrage he feels at her guardian's conduct; all combine to unhinge his mind and turn him into a foe of all injustice.

Unlike Quixote, he is not allowed to be mocked, however eccentric his appearance and actions; for that there is his Sancho Panza, Crabshaw (as there was Strap in *Roderick Random*). When Sir Launcelot finds himself among the unregenerate, he simply lays about him with his lance and disperses them. Confronting Justice Gobble, he is able to cow the ex-tailor and his wife by producing his name and rank. Like Peregrine and Crabtree, he fancies himself a higher justice. When all the prisoners flock around him "in accusation of Justice Gobble," he is reminded of the "more awful occasion, when the cries of the widow and the orphan, the injured and oppressed, would be uttered at the tribunal of an unerring Judge against the villainous and insolent authors of their calamity" (Chap. 11; *10,* 140).[31] In short, he thinks of himself as God's right hand, and with madness as a mask Smollett can accept him as such without having to postulate a set of psychological traits like Peregrine's to explain him. At the end, when order has been restored and Aurelia is safe, Greaves returns to his normal pursuits. Having put off his armor, he appears at his wedding in "a white coat and blue satin vest" (Chap. "The Last"; *10,* 339).

From the radical metaphor of this novel it appears that satire to Smollett is a vocation or a quest, and for eighteenth-century Englishmen like Greaves it must be a throwback of some sort to an earlier, simpler, or more sensible world. It is not an entirely admirable occupation, and even Greaves learns that recourse to law is the only answer. And so the pattern established in *Peregrine Pickle* is followed in the subsequent novels, although the satirists themselves represent different areas of exploration and experiment. They have in common a dislocation of some sort—whether a criminal mind like Fathom's or a sort of madness like Greaves', and they use these infirmities (Fathom unconsciously, Greaves consciously) to reveal the hidden corruption around them; finally, in one way or another, they are returned to a normal equilibrium when the satiric role is no longer required. One can distinguish between Smollett's treatment of the cause of the humor and his treatment of the humor itself. He early sensed what causes would be acceptable (loss of estate, loss of Aurelia), but two sorts of humor were available to him, an internal and an external one. It could be internal like rage, which is peculiarly individ-

ual and needs explaining; or it could be external like madness or sickness, which is beyond the individual's control and responsibility. The latter, which most clearly delimits the areas of the observer and the observed, as well as private and public experience, will be the method of Smollett's final works.

The Sick Satirist

Smollett returns in his last work to the connection between satire and abnormality established in *Sir Launcelot Greaves,* exploring its possibilities, both technical and moral. The satiric observers of his *Travels Through France and Italy* (1766) and *History and Adventures of an Atom* (1769) act as a bridge between the demented Greaves and the physically ill Matthew Bramble of *Humphry Clinker* (1771).

In the *Travels,* Smollett sees his journey in terms of the conventions of Juvenalian satire. His departure is the prototypical exile of the Juvenalian idealist, and this "Smollett" coincidentally has all the characteristics of the figure: he rails, threatens to cane rogues, and smells out evil beneath the fairest disguises. He is driven to travel the road of moral censure like the Juvenalian, first, by personal defeat (he is "traduced by malice, persecuted by faction, abandoned by false patrons, and overwhelmed by the sense of a domestic calamity"); second, by the general situation in England ("a scene of illiberal dispute, and incredible infatuation, where a few worthless incendiaries had, by dint of perfidious calumnies and atrocious abuse, kindled up a flame which threatened all the horrors of civil dissension"); and, third—the original touch that sets him off from the conventional Juvenalian—by the poorness of his health (he hopes "the mildness of the climate" in southern France will "prove favorable to the weak state of [his] lungs").[32] Although all of these motives for travel have their foundation in biographical fact, I suspect that Smollett sensed the connection between his own illness and his travels and Sir Launcelot Greaves' madness and his quest. The sick Smollett looking for health becomes the satirist seeking a place in which he can morally survive, and the sickness itself gradually develops into a satiric metaphor of man's condition.

Smollett's frail health and his background as a physician make up a central fact of his point of view. The chicanery and selfishness of the people who meet the friendless traveler are translated into the physical effect they have on him. The roguery of a ship's captain is dramatized by the effect on a delicate man of being put into a rough sea in an open boat and then having to walk a mile to an inn; the roguery of an innkeeper, by the effect of poor diet or of having to sit up in a cold kitchen until a bed is emptied in the morning. It is always the physical that Smollett attacks—inns, sanitation, even the white sand used on the paths of Versailles which hurts his eyes by the reflection of the sun. The physical sensation in his bones or lungs tells him to look for a moral corruption in his surroundings; garbage in the streets connects with indecency in behavior and finally with a perverted morality.

The *Travels* is thus as much a guidebook to conduct as to the sights of France and Italy. It is related less significantly to travel books than to the imaginary visits made by Orientals to Paris and London, as in the *Lettres persanes* of Montesquieu and Goldsmith's *Citizen of the World.* Smollett's work shares with these a satiric intention and the convenience of the epistolary form, which is easily adaptable to the cumulative catalogue of formal verse satire. As Smollett must have recognized in writing the *Travels,* the letter form offered as striking an opportunity to the satirist as to the Richardsonian writer-to-the-moment. The letter lends itself not only to emotional crises but also to other moments of great intensity, from which indignation as well as sentiment may issue. As the Duchess of Newcastle wrote in her preface to *CCXI Sociable Letters* (1664), "The truth is they are rather scenes than letters, for I have endeavored under cover of letters to express the humors of mankind and the actions of man's life." Thus as a satire the *Travels* has an advantage over Smollett's satiric explorations in his novels: there is no need for either plot or character development, the emphasis being neatly balanced between the sight seen and the commentary. But the *Travels* is also a true memoir and so lacks the emphasis, the coherence, and the point, as well as the complexity, of Smollett's fictions.

The moral-physical parallel that underlies the satiric use of sickness in the *Travels* becomes the structural principle of Smollett's political satire, *The History and Adventures of an Atom.* The device of an object that passes from person to person making satiric observations on what it witnesses was probably taken from Charles Johnstone's *Chrysal* (1760, 1765), in which the object is a coin and the episodes are held together by the theme of man's lust for and dependence on gold.[33] Smollett follows Johnstone in combining the idea of the coin that passes from pocket to pocket (as in *Tatler* No. 249) with the idea of metamorphosis (as in *Spectator* No. 343 and Fielding's *Journey from This World to the Next*). Johnstone makes Chrysal not only a guinea but, at the same time, the *spirit* of gold, which can enter into the possessor's mind. Smollett's satirist is the indestructible atom whose travels from organ to organ, from body to body (via digestion, dysentery, and disease), give a moral history of the Newcastle, Pitt, and Bute ministries. Thus his point of view is, like Chrysal's, internal as well as external.

Smollett allegorizes the humiliating relations between

George II and his prime ministers by a daily kick in the posteriors. In his earliest writings, the verse satires **"Advice"** and **"Reproof,"** he uses such physical equivalents as sexual perversion as metaphors for corruption in political and social morality. So too in the early novels moral instruction is accompanied by practical jokes and beatings, and a character's villainy is suggested by his twisted shape. The terror that is expressed in Newcastle by defecation appears in Commodore Trunnion in similarly physical terms—the knocking of his knees, the bristling of his hair, and the shattering of his teeth. The difference between the allegory of Newcastle's fear and the objectification of Trunnion's is mainly in the degree of extravagance.

In the *Adventures of an Atom,* however, the moral-physical parallel is not only more obtrusive (and consistent) but more explicitly involved with sickness. One senses behind the atom a medical intelligence asking exactly what is wrong with Newcastle and Pitt, what makes them act the way they do? Like a dissector the atom examines the inside as well as the outside of bodies to discover the secret source of evil: inside Muraclami (the Earl of Mansfield) it finds a "brain so full and compact, that there was not room for another particle of matter. But instead of a heart, he had a membranous sac, or hollow viscus, cold and callous, the habitation of sneaking caution, servile flattery, griping avarice, creeping malice, and treacherous deceit" (p. 309). The mixing of anatomical and moral terms (with the latter enlivened by adjectives of movement) creates a vivid picture of destructive and parasitic evil. But the result is quite different from that of the *Travels* and of less use in Smollett's search for an effective satirist. Here the satirist has access to the bodies of others and investigates them as vehicles of moral squalor; in the *Travels* the satirist's own body is the one under scrutiny. Smollett's use of disease in the *Adventures of an Atom* is still conventional. The disease is an image of Mansfield's evil or, as seems likely from the passage above, the cause of his evil. The atom is looking for "the motives by which the lawyer's [Mansfield's] conduct was influenced."[34] It describes the organs in terms which suggest a disease preying on Mansfield; and if Mansfield is diseased, one might argue, he bears less responsibility for his villainy. Even taken merely as an equivalent of his abstract evil, disease must be regarded as reductive decoration; there is no *necessary* connection between sickness, perversion, and erratic behavior and the Pitt Ministry (except perhaps in Newcastle's physical peculiarities).

Smollett's original touch in the *Travels* is to attach the physical disorder not to the evil but to the good man. Sickness is a reflection of the evil and filth that affect an ordinary decent man, rather than a descriptive image of the evil itself. The evil person is not sick, Smollett says, but sick-making. As always, Smollett is finally more interested in the evil as it is reflected in the consciousness of an observer than as it exists in itself. He has advanced from portrayals of villainy that is punished by a hero to villainy that is reflected in the punishment of the hero. But when he turns to this second use of punishment, he qualifies it by making it sickness. People do not, as in *Joseph Andrews,* merely meet "Smollett" and abuse or cheat him; he does not need to have violent contact with people—merely by observing them he suffers the punishment of illness. Moreover, medical and anatomical imagery is not merely decorative when it is involved with a central character who is sick, and the result is a fiction of more compelling belief. On a naturalistic level it is credible that a sick man should be sensitive to his surroundings, and it is the matter of belief, or credibility, that holds the *Travels* within the area of the memoir, as it holds *Humphry Clinker* within the area of the novel.

In *The Expedition of Humphry Clinker* Smollett takes the idea of the valetudinarian traveler from his *Travels* and uses it to explain Matthew Bramble as a satiric observer and to relate him to the satiric objects that surround him. Bramble's reactions to his environment are more immediate, startling, and emotional than "Smollett's." In the *Travels* poor accommodations endanger "Smollett's" frail health; in *Humphry Clinker* Bramble has only to be in the presence of the morally corrupt for his body to react involuntarily: "his eyes began to glisten, his face grew pale, and his teeth chattered" (Apr. 24; *11, 45*);[35] this is followed by railing and sometimes by physical chastisement. Bramble's sickness is Smollett's most effective equivalent to Juvenal's "Difficile est saturam non scribere," the claim that merely confronted by vice he reacts much as Pavlov's dogs salivated at the ringing of a bell. In a crowded ballroom of Bath, when things got too bad, his "nerves were overpowered, and [he] dropped senseless upon the floor" (May 8; *11, 98*). In short, as he says at one point, "my spirits and my health affect each other reciprocally—that is to say, everything that discomposes my mind, produces a correspondent disorder in my body" (June 14; *11,* 234); his travels record a search for health which is a search for moral standards in a chaotic world. As Jery notes, "He is as tender as a man without a skin, who cannot bear the slightest touch without flinching" (Apr. 30; *11,* 73). Bramble is a man without defenses upon whom the least deviation from normal acts as upon a thermometer. In certain areas, the cities and spas of England, he is sick; the Scottish air brings improvement. Upon leaving Scotland Jery writes, "I never saw my uncle in such health and spirits as he now enjoys" (Sept. 21; *12,* 129). And, as the sick man who knows sickness at first hand, Bramble recognizes false cures and sickness in others who do not recognize the symptoms; when he is well, he knows that others must be too.

The analogy between moral and physical sickness does not end with the invalid Bramble. The chief images he applies to the conditions he sees are drawn from the vocabulary with which he is most familiar. Bath, "which nature and providence seem to have intended as a resource from distemper and disquiet," has now become "the very centre of racket and dissipation" (Apr. 23; *11,* 49). London is "a dropsical head, [which] will in time leave the body and extremities without nourishment and support" (May 29; *11,* 131). Under London's glittering exterior the sick Bramble can detect "steams of endless putrefaction"; its people have "languid sallow looks, that distinguish [them] from those ruddy swains that lead a country life" (June 8; *11,* 181). Beginning with disease, he extends his imagery to imbalance, disorder, and collapse of other kinds. Starting with the unhealthy fumes of the waters at Bath, he goes on to see the new constructions as "the wreck of streets and squares disjointed by an earthquake," the houses "built so slight, with the soft crumbling stone found in this neighbourhood," that you can push a foot through the walls (Apr. 23; *11,* 53). Bodies, houses, cities, and the whole nation are organisms that are sick or conducive to sickness.

Bramble's diatribes take the form of letters written, appropriately, to his doctor (his first words are "The pills are good for nothing"). I have said that the epistolary form in the *Travels* accommodates the catalog form, the static scene, and the cumulative effect of the formal satire Smollett liked to write. Bramble's search for health is similarly compartmentalized. Each of his letters, reporting his condition to Dr. Lewis, is a self-contained satire, and together they produce a powerful cumulative effect. The most impressive of these units are the two tirades on Bath (one on its luxury, the other on its sanitation) and, more fully developed, the two great tirades on London (again, one on its luxury, the other on its unhealthfulness). The latter, reminiscent of Johnson's "London" (or Juvenal's third satire), gives an idyllic picture of the naturalness of Bramble's home in Wales, followed by a nightmarish, kaleidoscopic vision of London's perversion of nature: bread is turned into "a deleterious paste" in order to make it whiter, veal is bleached, greens are colored, soil is produced artificially, and the poultry is more quickly fattened "by the infamous practice of sewing up the gut" (June 8; *11,* 182, 183). Both London and Bath are described in terms of a terrible proliferation, with millions of shabby, crumbling, but new houses spreading in all directions, choking and stifling, crowding and crushing out value and even life itself; and paralleling the houses are the great aimless crowds of people. Bramble's descriptions of these cities, piling detail upon frightful detail, are reminiscent of the satires of Juvenal, Swift, and Pope, in which a chaos is described as moving ever outward to engulf all that remains of value and order.

But the general pattern of a formal satire presupposes not only an apocalyptic vision of the multiplicity and complete ruin to come, but also a glimpse of unity in the traditional ideas that are being defeated; this can be a picture of a golden age in the past, as in Juvenal's sixth satire, or simply a reference to the poet's own past, as in Pope's "Epistle to Arbuthnot." Smollett presents the two visions as contemporary in time, and spatially the vision of ruin in England precedes the vision of the golden age in Scotland—a more hopeful progression than is usual in satire. Scotland is still, however, the past in the sense that, because of its backwardness, its feudalism and traditionalism, it is not strictly contemporary with England; its people live (as do Bramble and Sir Launcelot Greaves) according to the standards of an older, simpler time. Bramble's search for health causes the novel to fall into the traditional two-part structure of formal verse satire. The thesis-antithesis contrast is apparent both on the level of the individual letters (as in the opposition of good Wales and vicious London in the satire on London) and on the more general level of the novel's action, in the journey from unhealthy England to healthy, invigorating Scotland.

But with the pattern of a satire apparent, and the bitter denunciations of London and Bath, one might ask why the overall effect of the novel is not so disturbing as that of *The Dunciad* or *Gulliver's Travels*. One answer is that Smollett softens the force of his satire by delivering his criticisms of society through a mouthpiece whose habit of criticism he attributes to disease. A second answer is that Smollett, in various ways, subordinates Bramble to the larger plan of his novel. We shall take up others later.

It is clear that Smollett was conscious of the implications of Bramble's position. He balances the accuracy—or the truth—of Bramble's satire against the sickness of the man. Bramble's niece Lydia, for one, substantiates the truth of his observations. To her Bath appears to be "a new world. All is gaiety, good-humour, and diversion." Nevertheless the noise, heat, smells, and conversation give her "the head-ache and vertigo the first day" (Apr. 26; *11, 57, 58*). Even Tabitha Bramble's dog Chowder gets sick in these surroundings. So much for Bramble's accuracy; the sickness of the man—as opposed to the satirist—is closely bound up with the figure of Humphry Clinker. Humphry too is a reformer, though of an altogether different sort from Bramble: his proposal for stopping "profane swearing . . . so horrid and shocking, that it made my hair stand on end" is to "Make them first sensible that you have nothing in view but their good, then they will listen with patience, and easily be convinced of the sin and folly of a practice that affords neither profit nor pleasure" (June 2; *11, 151, 152*). However inadequate this is as persuasion, it offers a revealing contrast to Bramble's misanthropic railing, particularly when one notices that it takes Humphry to budge Bramble into action on the notorious Chowder, and that it is Humphry who more than once rescues Bramble from drowning. Near the end, when the coach overturns a second time (the first time occasions the introduction of Humphry), Humphry hauls Bramble out of the river onto the bank nearest Dennison's property; this leads, with Dennison's arrival and the use of Bramble's former name "Loyd," to Humphry's being revealed as his son. With the baptism in the river Bramble loses his misanthropy and takes upon himself the responsibility for his past actions by acknowledging Humphry as his son. Humphry, in fact, offers a commentary on satirists of Bramble's type. His enthusiasm and visionary quality are necessary to get Bramble successfully through his travels, and the reader may recall, by contrast, the more usual role of the servant in holding down to earth the fancies of his master. Smollett has reversed the Quixote-Sancho Panza roles, giving the master the skepticism and the servant the enthusiasm, in order to emphasize the incompleteness of the sceptical character.

Bramble's sickness betrays a certain weakness in his position: however much his satire reveals about his surroundings and other people, it is really only a concern for his own comfort; the people he rails at are keeping him from being well. Thus, finding a simpler, more congenial countryside relieves only the symptoms of his disease. Ultimately he must find the cure in himself by turning from railing at others to recognizing the disorder within himself. His railing (we finally see) is a luxury roughly analogous to the one he secured from Humphry's mother, passing on (as he does from Bath to London) without accepting any responsibility for his pleasure.

Observation as Theme

Second, Bramble is only one of five letter writers (though he is the most important one). Their points of view qualify his own and contribute significantly to the novel's overall form and theme.

In **Peregrine Pickle** Smollett introduced at least one other satirist—Cadwallader Crabtree—as a contrast to Peregrine. In **Sir Launcelot Greaves** he again included other satirists along the way for comparison. Most reprehensible is the political lampooner, the misanthropic Ferret, who looked "as if his sense of smelling had been perpetually offended by some unsavoury odour; and he looked as if he wanted to shrink within himself from the impertinence of society" (Chap. 1; *10, 2*). A Hobbesian, he believes that all men and laws are corrupt, but instead of seeking to correct them he tries to exploit their corruption to his own ends. After a speech reviling quacks he shows that he himself is one by selling an "Elixir of Long Life" to the crowd. Throughout the novel he questions the whole idea of the knight-errant and his efficacy. At the very beginning, at the Black Lion, he argues that a knight-errant is ridiculous, mad, and no more than a vagrant, and he stands face to face with Greaves—the satirist as cynic vs. the satirist as corrector of wrongs, the two figures who were one in Peregrine. At the end of the novel Sir Launcelot provides an apartment for Ferret at Greavesbury Hall (which Ferret leaves, however, disgusted with seeing his fellow creatures too happy).

Dick Distich, another satirist, is confined to a madhouse; he "reviled as ignorant dunces several persons who had writ with reputation, and were generally allowed to have genius." Confining Greaves in an asylum with an insane satirist has the same effect as putting him in Greavesbury Hall with Ferret. Then there is the secondary Quixote, Captain Crowe, who is closer to Quixote than Sir Launcelot because he is older, madder, and more often defeated. He attacks coaches containing beautiful maidens he fancies are in distress and (like Quixote) is beaten down by the realities of their servants. But, since he is a Smollettian satirist, however wrong or mad he may be, his satiric instinct is correct. It turns out that the lady *is* in distress, for she is Sir Launcelot's beloved Aurelia who is held captive by her evil guardian Antony Darnel.

Greaves himself, the crusading satirist, an ideal by which the passive or foolish satirists are tested, is only one aspect of a larger theme. The novel, Smollett's most thoughtful if not most successful to this time, is about the individual's relation to society, with its crux the question of justice in reality vs. justice in law. At the beginning justice and law are separate entities. Civil laws do not accord with real justice, and even natural law appears to be unjust in Greaves' loss of Aurelia. The most potent contrast is between the people in prison or the madhouse and the people who put them there. Distich explains of the madhouse "That it contained fathers kidnapped by their children, wives confined by their husbands, gentlemen of fortunes sequestered by their relations, and innocent persons immured by the malice of their adversaries" (Chap. 23; *10,* 310).

The satirist and the knight-errant are the traditional punishers of crime unreached by the law, and Greaves is both. Smollett uses Greaves to show that the situation is so bad that a madman is necessary to demonstrate exactly how bad. But while Greaves is an improvement and does set some things right, he is lawless. On the one hand there is the idealist Greaves, and on the other the exploiter of the law, Justice Gobble; in the middle is the honest lawyer Tom Clarke—at first another Quixote with his legal terminology, but ultimately sensible. He acts as a restraining influence on Greaves, interposing when the knight lifts a bench to dash open the cell door and "assuring him he would suggest a plan that would avenge himself amply on the

Justice Gobble, without any breach of the peace" (Chap. 10; *10,* 138). Near the end Greaves, locked in the madhouse, comes to the realization that knight-errantry is futile against the legal chicanery that put him there and returns to his senses; he is released by Clarke's careful legal work. Once free, Greaves uses legal means to extricate Aurelia; to get Sycamore and Dandle he "practiced a much more easy, certain, and effectual method of revenge [than the satirist's], by instituting a process against them" (Chap. "The Last"; *10,* 332). Sad as it may be, Smollett says, legal restitution is the only true kind. Satire then has become part of a larger theme concerning the law, and the good and bad satirists become examples along a spectrum of judges running from the unjust Gobble to the good justice who frees Aurelia.

In **Humphry Clinker,** within the frame of an extremely conventional plot concerning the reunion of lovers and the reunion of a father and son, Smollett presents letters from five observer-correspondents visiting a series of cities—Bristol Hot Well, Bath, London, Edinburgh—which are the occasions for their meditations. He takes the device of the multiple letter writers from Christopher Anstey's verse satire, *The New Bath Guide,* published in 1766.[36] As in his earlier adaptations, however, Smollett's own intention is made clear by a look at the radical changes he makes in Anstey's form. Anstey employs a series of rather bland poetic epistles written by the members of a family sojourning in Bath; the chief letter writer is Sim B-n-r-d, a young man bothered with the wind, but there are also letters (hardly distinguishable from his) by his sister, their "Cousin Jenny," and their maid Tabby Runt. Perhaps the most obvious difference between the two books, in terms of what we have already seen of Smollett's satiric method, is that Sim quickly becomes a part of Bath and is absorbed into the satiric object. Smollett's commentators in **Humphry Clinker** are in varying degrees outside the object and remain critical. The second difference between the two books is that Smollett has grouped his letters around central incidents and locations. The characters move from Bristol Hot Well to Bath to London to Harrogate to York, and they give their separate comments about each city. This form is an improvement on the picaresque novel as a vehicle for Smollett's satire because the emphasis is of necessity shifted from the protagonist as actor to the object satirized and his opinion of it. Third, in terms of his interest in the nature and function of the satirist, Smollett's use of the collection of letters brings a number of different points of view (in varying degrees satiric) to bear on each situation; unlike Anstey, Smollett does not let slip the opportunity for utilizing grotesquely various temperaments in his letter writers. Their different views of an object act as spotlights on the various aspects of the evil. This is also a more economical solution to the problem of the satiric anatomy than presenting a long series of adventures that reveal the object's different aspects, as Smollett had done earlier in **Roderick Random.**

In contrast to the Juvenalian spirit of Bramble, there is the Horatian satire of his nephew Jery Melford (the Sim B-n-r-d of **Humphry Clinker**).[37] After describing his uncle's violent reaction to a situation Jery adds, "But this chaos is to me a source of infinite amusement. . . . These follies, that move my uncle's spleen excite my laughter" (Apr. 30; *11, 73*).[38] While his uncle scourges, Jery lets folly speak for itself and condemn itself. But with his objectivity he lacks his uncle's moral purpose and the personal involvement occasioned by his ill health; thus such an object of satiric contemplation as Lieutenant Lismahago he finds merely "a high-flavoured dish. . . . It was our fortune to feed upon him the best part of three days" (July 13; *12, 18*). As Bramble expresses the seriousness of his concern in his choice of a correspondent, so Jery characteristically corresponds with an Oxford chum who merely wishes to be entertained.

The other letter writers have considerably less to say. Lydia Melford is the naïve, impressionable young girl whose instincts (physical reactions) tell her that Bath is appalling, but whose sense of fashion makes her adjust to it. Winifred Jenkins, representing the servant's point of view, is all eager acceptance, to the extent that appearances dupe her fearfully. Tabitha Bramble, on the other hand, reflects her environment as much as a stone wall; her only concern as a letter writer is back at Brambleton-hall in her belongings, the price of flannel, and the affairs of her servants (she corresponds with her housekeeper). When she happens to mention Bath or Hot Well it is only as it affects Brambleton-hall. As a character (as opposed to a letter writer) Tabby's railing (reminiscent of her brother's) is directed toward getting a husband. In short, she rejects all the world but the narrow demesne of her current prospect (who again has reference only to her concerns back at Brambleton-hall).

Tabby's total rejection is one end of the spectrum, the other end of which is Win Jenkin's total acceptance of Bath and London. Between these extremes are the various degrees of acceptance and rejection of Jery and Bramble. Also along this spectrum are the points of view registered by the characters whom Bramble and Jery meet in their travels. Many of them have satiric inclinations—some bad, like Bulford, who exposes his guests' weaknesses with practical jokes; and some good, like S——t (Smollett himself), whom Jery meets in London. S——t simply invites the fools and knaves to dinner, observes their follies, and privately draws their attention to them; he suggests a resignation that is perhaps closest to the feelings of Smollett the author—at least those Smollett wishes associated with himself.[39] The most important of these satirists-within-the-action is Lismahago, the Scot who has lost a scalp to the

American Indians, has his wisdom entirely from the experience of bloody deeds in the wilderness, and takes pains to qualify every apparent truth. Refusing to make a choice between England and Scotland, he acts as a corrective to Bramble, the seeker of health and comfort, and broadens the sick man's perspective during the crucial Scottish tour. But looking at the scenes between Bramble and Lismahago (reported by Jery) one has to conclude not that Lismahago is simply seeing a truth Bramble does not see, but that he is a disputatious malcontent, as Jery says. Lismahago, like Bramble, tells the truth or an important part of it, but for the wrong reasons: they are both incomplete men, only less so than others like Holder and Bulford or even Paunceford. Both have to be cured at the end of the book; once Lismahago is married and has the security he seeks, "His temper, which had been soured and shrivelled by disappointment and chagrin, is now swelled out and smoothed like a raisin in plum-porridge" (Nov. 8; *12, 260*).

The relation of points of view and satiric objects thus creates a reciprocal theme—the moral significance of the scene and the moral significance of the observer. Because the focus is usually on the scene rather than on the characters, the questions the reader tends to ask about the characters are in relation to the scene he observes; for example, what is X's reaction and what does it reveal about him qua observer? One character's point of view acts as a commentary on another's. Jery's Horatian attitude shows up an inadequacy in Bramble's Juvenalian; Bulford with his practical jokes and Jack Holder, who manufactures satiric situations for his own amusement, point up Jery's shortcomings; Tabby's self-centered railing is the most damaging commentary on her brother's.

The characters analyze not only the situations, but each other. Jery follows his uncle's every reaction with disapproval or admiration, and Bramble anatomizes all of the characters: Jery is "a pert jackanapes, full of college-petulance and self-conceit, proud as a German count, and as hot and hasty as a Welsh mountaineer"; Lydia "has got a languishing eye, and reads romances"; and sister Tabby, "that fantastical animal," is "the devil incarnate come to torment me for my sins" (Apr. 17; *11, 15*). Even when one character is contemplated in action by another, both maintain their roles of observers: ensnared by the romantic Wilson, Lydia (according to Bramble) is "a simple girl utterly unacquainted with the characters of mankind" (Apr. 17; *11, 18*); the nature of her reaction is the main thing in question.

Smollett has presented in **Humphry Clinker** a dramatic essay on the values of various kinds of satire, much as Ben Jonson did with Asper, Macilente, and Carlo Buffone, the objective satirist, the envious malcontent, and the mere buffoonish railer in *Every Man Out of His Humour*. But Smollett has also included many characters whose reactions fall outside the satiric range. The satiric attitude toward the world is simply the most critical; it is one end of the spectrum I have postulated; the other end is total acceptance or, worse, affected acceptance.

As in Roderick Random's satirizing, Bramble's diatribes are closely related to a theme concerning ways of looking at the world. "Sophistication" is the word he applies to all he hates in England: it is "a vile world of fraud and sophistication," to which he opposes "the genuine friendship of a sensible man" (like Dr. Lewis, Apr. 23; *11,* 55) or the time "about thirty years ago" when Bath was a healthy, simple spa, and the most crowded parts of London were "open fields, producing hay and corn" (Apr. 23, May 29; *11,* 49, 130). Sophistication for Bramble involves the change from a genuine, true form to something that may appear good but is really false, useless, and harmful. He attacks the fantastic shapes that are replacing the ordinary, functional houses of Bath; the idea that ordure can, if called perfume, be pleasant to smell; that Harrogate water owes "its reputation in a great measure to its being so strikingly offensive" (June 26; *11,* 247); that sickness requires so many doctors and so many elaborate (and actually unhealthful) cures. The theme extends beyond Bramble's and Jery's commentary. Because the indefatigable Wilson disguised himself in the first place he is not accepted as a suitor for Lydia. He is doing what he thinks is expected of a lover, according to the sophistication of London and Bath: part of this is disguise; part is the idea of elopement and the flowery letter that starts, "Miss Willis has pronounced my doom," and continues, "tossed in a sea of doubts and fears" (Mar. 31; *11,* 20). If Wilson had simply gone up to Bramble and announced his true name and intentions he would have had Lydia at once, and there would have been no novel (just as there would have been no novel if Bramble had given his true name to Humphry's mother).

The antithesis of British sophistication is the underdeveloped Scottish land and the old-fashioned Scottish customs; and so Bramble finds the immediate antidote to England in Scotland. But it is also the naked Humphry, without clothes or parents; Lismahago, scalped and exposed in his nakedness by Bulford; and, of course, Bramble himself, who is "a man without a skin."[40] Thus far Smollett is developing a conventional satiric contrast between false and true, affected and sincere, artificial and natural, apparent and real.[41] His originality lies in his noticing that, if the opposite of sophistication is the bare forked animal Bramble, it is also his act of stripping off the illusions of others. The sophisticate and the satirist are thesis and antithesis.

There is still some question, however, as to the exact value attached to the satiric attitude within *Humphry*

Clinker. The word "original," which is applied both to satirists like Bramble and to some of the fools he observes, gives an idea of Smollett's intention. Applied to Bramble and the people he admires, "original" has the meaning of having existed from the first or of being "a thing (or person) in relation to something else which is a copy" *(OED).* This meaning connects "original" with that other key word "sophistication," a change from the genuine to something that appears good but is false.[42] Since the evil anatomized in *Humphry Clinker* is the conforming to a false standard and form, being what one is not, an original is at least a more valuable person than the sophisticates of Bath and London. Bramble admires S——t as an original because he "had resolution enough to live in his own way in the midst of foreigners; for, neither in dress, diet, customs, or conversation, did he deviate one tittle from the manner in which he had been brought up" (July 4; *12,* 5). In this sense an original is true to himself, and Bramble, Humphry, and Lismahago are all originals. Gradually, however, it becomes apparent that whatever its meaning in a particular context, "original" in general refers to an eccentric or an oddity, and whatever the emphasis intended, it does not designate an ideal.[43] This is clear enough from the inclusion of Tabitha Bramble or Micklewhimmen or Newcastle within its ranks. Those to whom the word is not applied are, significantly, very bad or very good; noticeably missing are the affected and sophisticated, such as the Pauncefords, the Burdocks, and the Oxmingtons, as well as the unmistakably good people like Moore, Captain Brown, Dennison, the Admiral, and S——t.

Primitivism is not the ideal of *Humphry Clinker.* Bramble's misanthropy is as extreme a state as sophistication. Humphry is "innocent as the babe unborn," "a great original" (May 24, June 8; *11,* 128, 162), but that this is not altogether an ideal situation becomes obvious when we see that it has left Humphry open to the influence of Whitefield's sermons and to exploitation by the Tabitha Brambles and Lady Griskins of this world. Similarly, Lismahago, however free of illusions, has to compromise and find a wealthy wife and security for his old age. Even Scotland itself, which is "original" in the old sense and which has usually been taken as Smollett's ideal in *Humphry Clinker,* does not receive unstinted praise from either Bramble or Lismahago. Bramble tells the story of the stones that mar the fields in Scotland: the peasants leave them and grow their scanty crops; the philosopher has them removed, whereupon his crops decrease; when he returns the stones to his fields the crops again grow. The point seems to be that things should be left as they are. When the philosopher offers his rational explanation for the effectiveness of the rocks—that they restrain the perspiration of the earth and act as protectors from the winds or reflectors of the sun—Bramble adds:

But surely this excessive perspiration might be more effectually checked by different kinds of manure. . . . As for the warmth, it would be much more equally obtained by enclosures; one half of the ground which is now covered would be retrieved; the cultivation would require less labour; and the ploughs, harrows, and horses would not suffer half the damage which they now sustain. (Aug. 28; *12*, 103)

This procedure of showing the virtue of originality, which now comes to mean primitivism, and then qualifying his admiration is employed by Bramble throughout the Scottish sections. The virtue and limitation of primitivism is shown in Bramble's discussion of the clans. He admires the patriarchal system, the solidarity of the family, and the loyalty to a clan chief on purely family grounds which cannot be destroyed by passing laws that free the family from legal ties, but he regrets the clans' lack of property and independence. Jery, a few pages earlier, while admiring the same qualities ("the simplicity of ancient times") and even claiming he had never slept so well as on the rush-strewn floor of the Campbells' great hall, laughs at the useless and unpleasant traditions of the bagpiper (Campbell, the clan chief, stuffs his ears with cotton) and the carousing funeral. Bramble's praise of Scottish naturalness is balanced by his praise of the progress of cities like Lieth and Glasgow.

If we notice that the travelers, having visited the bracing air of Scotland and being improved in health by the contrast, return to England and there encounter examples of the true ideal, we will see that, instead of employing the thesis-antithesis mode of formal verse satire, Smollett goes one step further and, presenting two extremes, ascertains the golden mean.[44] In **Humphry Clinker** he offers a progression from sophistication in Bath and London to an opposite primitivism in Scotland and finally to a compromise in northern England. The ideal estate, Dennison's, was put in order by Englishmen who withdrew from the city to a traditional home and "restored" it, and the chaos of Baynard's estate is being repaired by the same Englishmen. Running parallel to the progression of the journey are three kinds of people: the good, hospitable, wise people, scattered along the way (for contrast) but concentrated in the scenes at the end; the "originals," eccentric but better than the third group; and finally the affected, the poor hosts, the ungrateful, and those who affect originality. Members of the second group can, by losing their eccentricity, become members of the first, the most obvious example being Bramble with the recovery of his health.

Bramble's Juvenalian satire falls with Bramble into the second group (as does Jery's Horatian). Satire is one reaction to a sophisticated, corrupt world, and a useful one, but not sufficient in itself. It is needed as a jolt back to reality, as an extreme like Scotland. When this

extreme has been seen, however, it must be qualified into a useful, livable reality like the Bramble or Lismahago at the end of the novel. Thus, in his last novel, Smollett has placed the satiric temperament in a world of various other attitudes and temperaments. . . .

Notes

[28] For other examples of the author's overemphasis of evil in his hero's actions, see [The Works of Tobias Smollett, ed. G. H. Maynadier (12 vols. New York, Sully & Kleinteich, 1903)], Chaps. 42, 49; 9, 32, 107-08. [References to Smollett's works are based on this text.]

[29] The possibilities of the criminal as satiric observer were glimpsed near the beginning of *Roderick Random,* where the highwayman Rifle recounts his latest robbery: "I likewise found ten Portugal pieces in the shoes of a Quaker, whom the spirit moved to revile me with great bitterness and devotion" (Chap. 8; *1*, 65). The source of this episode, incidentally, is probably the robbery in *Joseph Andrews* in which the highwayman reveals the prudish lady's secret penchant for alcohol (Bk. 1, Chap. 12). Smollett explored the possibilities of the confidence man as satirist in *Peregrine Pickle* in the fortune-telling hoax set up by Peregrine and Crabtree and in the figure of Peregrine himself.

[30] This sentimental use of the tincture of goodness, ending in regeneration, should be contrasted with Fielding's use of Wild's "weaknesses."

[31] In this respect he is related to the Quixote who claims he "was born, by Heaven's will, in this our age of iron, to revive what is known as the Golden Age" (Cervantes, *Don Quixote,* trans. Putnam, 1, 146). Cf. Samuel Butler's observation, "A Satyr is a Kinde of Knight Errant," etc. (*Characters,* ed. A. R. Waller [Cambridge, Cambridge University Press, 1908], p. 469).

[32] *Travels* (London, 1766), *1*, 1-2. Smollett's complaints do, of course, like the journey itself, have a basis in facts: his work for the Bute ministry involved him in attacks and counterattacks, and his only child Elizabeth died in April 1763. When he reaches the general situation of England, however, he may be indulging in the pathetic fallacy. In spite of what he says about England as he sets out, his homeland remains a standard by which he judges the other countries he visits; every unsatisfactory place is "inconvenient, unpleasant, and unhealthy," and when he returns to England at the end he praises it as "the land of liberty, cleanliness, and convenience" (*1*, 33; *2*, 254).

[33] The tradition in which both *Chrysal* and the *Adventures of an Atom* are written probably owes more to the French descendants of the *chronique scandaleuse,* Crébillon fils' *Sopha* (1740) and Diderot's *Bijoux in-*

discrets (1748), than to the English specimens of Addison and Fielding.

[34] *The History and Adventures of an Atom,* in *Works,* ed. Saintsbury, *12, 252.*

[35] Cf. Commodore Trunnion, whose "eye glistened like that of a rattlesnake" when his indignation rose (*Pickle,* Chap. 2).

[36] The *Travels* is a series of letters written by one man, while *Humphry Clinker* is a series of letters written by five different people. As a satiric device, however, the difference is more apparent than real. The singleness of a series of letters from one correspondent is dissipated in the *Travels* by addressing the letters to different audiences—to a woman for a satiric description of French fashions, to a man for a discussion of French politics, and so on.

[37] It is interesting that the figure in *The New Bath Guide* who may possibly have suggested to Smollett the role Bramble plays is the object of Sim's amused scrutiny. Sim and his companions dance in his room, disturbing "Lord Ringbone, who lay in the parlour below, / On account of the gout he had got in his toe." They hear him beginning "to curse and swear," sounding very much like Bramble. In *Humphry Clinker* the same situation is seen from the point of view of Jery Melford, whom Bramble sends up to quiet the dancers (as Ringbone sends his French valet); and it is Bramble who, a few pages later, rails. In short, Ringbone may have suggested to Smollett the possibility of his own favorite kind of satiric persona in this situation, the possibility of using the valetudinarian of the *Travels,* as well as the need for keeping this figure one of a group of observers.

[38] Jery's connection with a Fielding commentator like Medley is suggested by his frequent use of the stage metaphor. After Humphry's appearance in court, Jery writes that "the farce is finished, and another piece of a graver cast [is] brought upon the stage" (June 23); after describing Lishmahago at some length (in two letters), he remarks, "I suppose you are glad he is gone off the stage for the present" (July 18; *12,* 45). At the end he calls the journey a comedy on which the curtain has at last fallen (Nov. 8; *12,* 259).

[39] Smollett is following the practice of Pope, Swift, Prior, and other eighteenth-century satirists by inserting a self-portrait (a "good-humoured and civilized" man Jery calls him), which represents a norm of behavior from which the deviations of the other characters can be measured.

[40] For a fuller discussion of nakedness, and a slightly different interpretation of it, see M. A. Goldberg, *Smollett and the Scottish School* (Albuquerque, University of New Mexico Press, 1959), pp. 171-75.

[41] Sophistication is also attacked in Smollett's *Travels:* women's paint and dress; vanity that makes a soldier wear fashionably long hair in spite of the inconvenience to fighting; the "absurd luxury" of having fifty scullions to cool an army meal; the empty and pernicious forms of dueling; false honor and gallantry.

[42] See Jery's remark to his correspondent Watkins that "I was much pleased with meeting the original of a character, which you and I have often laughed at in description" (Apr. 18; *11,* 28); also, "perusing mankind in the original" (Oct. 14; *12, 239).*

[43] The *OED* cites *Humphry Clinker* for the sense of "original" as "oddity," perhaps because in at least two cases "original" appears in close proximity to "oddity" (June 8, 10; *11,* 186, 188). There also appears to be a distinction between kinds of "original" in Smollett's novel: Bramble speaks of "Those originals [the authors who praise themselves and damn others, who] are not fit for conversation" (June 2; *11,* 161), and on the next page Humphry "turns out a great original." The difference between good and bad originals is again implicit in Bramble's comment, "if you pick up a diverting original by accident, it may be dangerous to amuse yourself with his oddities. He is generally a tartar at bottom" (June 8; *11,* 186).

[44] Smollett uses the dialectical structure elsewhere in details, but *Greaves* is his only novel that anticipates *Humphry Clinker* in its general structure. The failure of law and Graves' lawless corrective are both shown to be excesses that must be resolved in the proper administration of law.

Paul-Gabriel Boucé (essay date 1971)

SOURCE: "The Representation of the Real," in his *The Novels of Tobias Smollett,* translated by Antonia White in collaboration with the author, Longman, 1976, pp. 255-301.

[*In the following excerpt from a translation of Boucé's book, originally published in French in 1971, Boucé focuses closely on* Roderick Random *to prove his assertion that Smollett did in fact make use of the "real" or "truthfulness" as he saw it to expose the wrongs of eighteenth-century life and that "realism" is a modern term by which Smollett's works have been unfairly criticized.*]

Right from the beginning of his literary career, Smollett was aware of the problems posed by the representation of the real in the novel. His preface to **Roderick Random** expresses in very clear terms this prime concern of the author confronted with the choice between a fantastic and fictitious version of life and, at the opposite extreme, a deliberate concentration on everyday existence at its most commonplace, not to say vulgarest. In the first phase, Smollett contemptuously rejects this fallacious vision of humanity and hails with joy the liberating work of Cervantes, whose satirical attacks on it permitted literature to return to the paths of reality and ordinary life (I, lxi). In the second part of this preface, he adopts a tone at once aggressive and defensive. Fortified by the example set by Lesage, Smollett is going to dare to describe scenes which will undoubtedly shock certain readers. The adjectives 'mean' and 'low' (I, lxii) formed part of the critical arsenal of those who were roused to indignation by the liberties taken by Fielding, and even by Richardson, who had the literary courage to be interested in the tribulations of heroes of slender means and humble birth. In his desire to represent reality, the *whole* reality, without omitting the least pleasant aspects of a too often corrupt society, or the physiological necessities of mankind, Smollett declares, in the tone of defiance which is typical of his character: 'Every intelligent reader will, at first sight, perceive I have not deviated from nature in the facts, which are all true in the main, although the circumstances are altered and disguised, to avoid personal satire' (I, lxiii).

Two features are noteworthy in this rough outline, still crude and incomplete, of a literary theory. For Smollett, the representation of the real cannot be dissociated from satire and his moralising purpose. . . . Already, Smollett comes up against this problem which, in the nineteenth century, obfuscates all critical discussions on realism. The 'realist' writer, in his overwhelming passion for total objectivity, is led to treat subjects which the aristocratic or bourgeois tradition of aesthetic criticism, based on the taste of the ruling class, regards with contempt or even horror. Louis XIV detested the humble domestic subjects treated by Flemish painters. Did he not, according to Voltaire, say 'Remove those monstrosities', one day when a Teniers had been hung in one of his apartments?

Smollett's adoption of a literary standpoint in favour of describing far from elevated persons and milieux without repugnance, and his refusal to transform man romantically into pure spirit without imperious and sometimes sordid physical needs, arise, as often in his work, more from a spontaneous and instinctive practice than from a deliberate critical intention elaborated into a rigid theory. In *Peregrine Pickle* he almost contradicts his preliminary statements in *Roderick Random* when he derides this obsession with repulsive pictorial detail of that Dutch painter who has taken great trouble to reproduce an enormous flea on a beggar's shoulder. By taking a satirical line over Pallet's absurd enthusiasm for this picture in which flies are battening on a piece of carrion, he implicitly condemns

this meticulous insistence of the artist on a mimicry reduced to the most disgusting detail. In fact, the contradiction is only apparent. Smollett, in this brief passage[1], has foreseen the dangers of a slavish reproduction of reality, in which the search for an unusual detail takes the place of genuine inspiration. More important on the theoretical plane is the furious reaffirmation, in *Ferdinand Count Fathom,* of his adherence to a concept—free of social or aesthetic constraints and inhibitions—of the novelist faced with contemporary reality. The auto-dedication of *Ferdinand Count Fathom* presents the same mixture as the preface to *Roderick Random*. Its defensive aggressiveness gives a somewhat strident tone to this personal apologia. Smollett replies straightaway in advance to possible (and probable) detractors, that their indignant objections to the 'obscene objects of low life' (p. 7) or to the 'lowest scenes of life' (p. 8) tend to turn literature into an insipid dish. A certain cantankerous unfairness with regard to illustrious foreign predecessors (from Petronius to Lesage via Rabelais and Cervantes) and English ones (Swift and Pope) gives an unpleasantly polemical tone to this satirical, although courageous, defence of the novelist's aesthetic freedom. Smollett reaffirms his liking for characters of humble origin, in spite of the disapproving snobbery of readers who thoroughly enjoy, in foreign works, what they so strongly condemn in the writings of their English contemporaries. He shows himself fiercely resentful of the criticisms made of his *Peregrine Pickle* and speaks of them with bitterness in his preface to the second edition (1758). . . .

All through the nineteenth century and even the twentieth, critics have attacked, with the wearisome monotony of inveterate literary spleen, the picture given by Smollett in his novels of a violent world, in which mischievous deeds, gratuitous brutality, debauchery and scatological coarseness appear as so many caustic caricatures of deliberately travestied reality. Smollett, accused of distorting reality by his satirical bias, is rebuked, in the same breath, for the vulgarity, or indecency, of incidents or characters he does not hesitate to include in his novels. The moral aim of his satirical representation of reality is compromised by the literary methods he adopts in the choice and description of subjects banned, at least in theory, by good taste and decency, according to the aesthetic and literary standards of that time.

Any examination of the representation of the real in an eighteenth-century novelist comes up against a problem of literary terminology. How can one speak of the representation of the real without using the word 'realism', that paltry critical counter which is almost entirely worthless when applied to the eighteenth century? Used for the first time at the beginning of the nineteenth century in France (1826) and about the middle in England[3], this term cannot account for the satirical and moral purpose inherent in all representation of the real by Smollett and the other eighteenth-century novelists. A few critics have had the courage to denounce the illicit and noxious use of 'realism'. C. E. Jones, in his *Smollett Studies* (1942), puts modern readers of **Roderick Random** or other novels on their guard. He emphasises that 'realism' is 'not only a modern term, but represents a distinction neither considered by the creative artist nor accepted by the critic in the eighteenth century' (p. 74). The same critical prudence is displayed all through the first chapter ('Realism and the novel form') of Ian Watt's book, *The Rise of the Novel,*[4] in which the author denounces the almost automatic implication of social and verbal vulgarity which removes a great part of this term's critical utility: 'the novel's realism does not reside in the kind of life it presents, but in the way it presents it' (p. 11). As a general rule, 'realism' will appear little in this study. After the example of Barbara Hardy in her work *The Appropriate Form*[5], who substitutes 'truthfulness' for 'realism', the terms 'faithfulness to reality', 'authenticity' and even 'veracity' will be used. If perchance 'realism' (or the adjective 'realist') slip into these pages, what must be understood, according to René Wellek's definition, and with the reserves indicated above, is: 'the objective representation of contemporary social reality'[6]. It is necessary to recall that Smollett's objectivity varies according to the degree of satire, more or less visible and virulent, but hardly ever absent in his representation of reality? For this reason—the indissociability of the satirical and 'realistic' elements—it has seemed artificial to conduct two separate studies. On the one hand, many (and indispensable) references have already been made to Smollett's satirical methods in the particular study of each novel. On the other, satire, either in general or in the work of Smollett, has for some years been the subject of a vast number of works. Conversely, there exists no attempt at a synthetic appreciation of the relationship of Smollett's work to the reality of the eighteenth century[7].

Finally, by 'representation', one must beware of understanding a photographic reproduction of reality in its smallest details. This notion, often implicit in the popular concept of 'realism', in the end confines the role of the author to the passivity of a sensitive plate on to which the external world is projected. Now all representation of reality can only be partial and incomplete. This is what Joyce Cary expresses, with the vehemence of an author who had himself to endure, *mutatis mutandis,* somewhat the same accusations as Smollett:

> It is not valid to charge a writer with falsification because he emphasises one truth rather than another. As for saying that he does not give the whole, that is absurd because the whole truth cannot be known. It would have to include not only events which are happening all the time and changing the phenomenal

world while I speak, but the valuation of events. The most important part of truth is what humanity is suffering, is feeling and thinking at any moment, and this cannot be known, as a totality to any person[8].

Lukács also emphasises this resigned modesty when confronted with the shifting complexity of the real in his attempt to define the novel as

> a form of mature virility, as opposed to the normal infantility of the epic—that means that the closed character of his world is, on the objective plane, imperfection, and on the subjective plane of the lived, resignation[9].

The representation is not a simple (!) *transcription* but well and truly a *construction,* indeed creation, according to a critic like Robbe-Grillet:

> Fictional writing does not aim at giving information as does the chronicle, the eye-witness account or the scientific report, but it constitutes reality. It never knows what it is looking for, it has no idea what it has to say. It is invention, invention of the world and of man, constant and perpetually inconclusive invention[10].

But this modern view, however intellectually attractive, cannot give a satisfactory vision of Smollett's novels in which, very definitely, the part played by social testimony, conscious or unconscious, cannot be neglected. Robbe-Grillet's theory has the merit of suggesting that reality is not an amorphous *datum* pre-existent to all literary creation. On the contrary, the novelist, by the creative magic of his word *gives* life to reality. The hellish world of English warships had existed for several centuries, but Smollett was the first who gave it solid dimensions, in a word, the vitality which made it known to the public. Literature and reality are not entities strange to one another and mutually exclusive because of a negative relationship of exteriority. On the contrary, it is necessary to place them on the plane of equivalence, identification or superposition. For Raymond Jean, literature, and the novel in particular, is not mediation but contact, the points of contact between literature and the real being the same as those of our senses with the real:

> There is not the written thing on one side and the real thing on the other: there is a constant dialectical transcendence of this opposition in the act of reading as in the act of writing and this transcendence is a continual creation which enriches life and culture, but also modifies reality and makes it 'advance'[11].

These critical prolegomena will make it easier to grasp what must be understood by 'representation of the real'. If Smollett has left us, consciously or not, a testimony (whose veracity it is the critic's business to assess) regarding the English world about the middle of the eighteenth century, he was also able to create a fictional universe which by very reason of its exaggerations and its satirical distortions seems more real and *is* more real than a flat, didactic type of description. In Volume III of the *Present State,* Smollett (or an amanuensis) gives a description of Bath and London. But these are dead towns beside those which appear, swarming with life, in *Humphry Clinker.* So, in a first critical survey, the testimony of Smollett on his age will be examined, and in a second complementary one, the limits, characteristics, strengths and weaknesses of the Smollettian universe.

The terms 'witness' and 'testimony' also leave something to be desired: nothing in Smollett's work or in his letters really warrants the supposition that he was conscious of his role of 'witness'. But Smollett, whose manifold activities brought him into contact with the most diverse specimens of humanity, even when he was occupied in the historical examination of civilisation and events, nevertheless fulfilled the role of 'witness' by the richness of his observations, even fleeting, on everyday life in the eighteenth century. In a way, the first thing with which Smollett provides his modern readers is an involuntary testimony, that is to say a whole series of particulars which retrospectively acquire a historical or sociological value as 'facts of civilisation'. Often these are hidden details which only a slow, thorough reading, backed by an indispensable knowledge of the civilisation, will cause to emerge from the literary text. Of no particular importance for Smollett's contemporary readers, except as proof of his knowledge of the life of that day, these details constitute for the modern reader, whether English or foreign, a very dense network of historical, sociological, not to mention economic, indications of which it is impossible to analyse more than a few samples.

Thus, when Roderick Random is carried off by the press-gang, he is, according to the heading of Chapter xiv, on Tower Hill. The specification of place is not without historical interest, for this spot, dangerous for the solitary pedestrian without social protection or official pass, was the oldest and most popular rallying point of the men whose job was to impress men for the fleet. Moreover in that vicinity there were always plenty of disembarked sailors—the favourite prey of the press-gang—who had just collected their back pay from the Navy Office, situated quite nearby[12]. To stay in the nautical realm, Smollett, at the end of *Roderick Random* (Chapter lxvii), makes Morgan, the Welsh ex-surgeon's mate on board the *Thunder,* settle down as an apothecary in Canterbury. This professional transformation is not just a fanciful idea of the novelist's but corresponds to the fact that it was legally possible for naval surgeons, once they were back on land, to obtain an apothecary's licence. . . .

This involuntary testimony cannot be regarded as an absolutely faithful copy of historical events. Smollett transposes, rather than transcribes. The rebellion led by Peregrine at Winchester (pp. 87-92) does not seem, according to the chroniclers of that respectable public school, to have a factual counterpart, at least at the time when *Peregrine Pickle* was written, though, about 1750, this school was going through a difficult period[14]. On the contrary, Eton had six revolts between 1728 and 1832[15]. So it is not impossible that Smollett attributed the sins of Eton to Winchester, unless the agitation fomented by the real models of Peregrine and his band of mutineers was too usual and commonplace an occurrence at Winchester to merit the name of 're-bellion'. But it is quite natural for Peregrine to go up to Oxford from Winchester (p. 113), in view of their historical and administrative links[16], Wykeham having founded New College in 1379 and Winchester School in 1394. But Smollett does not say whether Peregrine went to New College. The reader of *Humphry Clinker* knows from Jery's very first letter that the latter went to Jesus College, Oxford. There again, the choice is not arbitrary, for this college was founded by a Welshman for Welsh students, as John Macky recalls in the second edition (1722) of his *Journey Thro' England.* . . .

Smollett's testimony, even accidental, does not always bear the stamp of absolute originality; on the contrary it sometimes belongs to a socio-literary tradition both anterior and posterior to his work. At the beginning of his stay in London, Roderick is the victim of a 'money dropper', who, with the complicity of his confederates, fleeces him of all his money (I, 98-101). Now this dirty trick, the character of the swindler, and even his technique, were no novelty to eighteenth-century readers. Gay (to go back no further) already writes in Book iii of his *Trivia* (1716):

> Who now the Guinea-dropper's bait regards,
> Tricked by the sharpers dice, or juggler's
>   cards?

Is Gay being unduly optimistic or is he taking refuge in rhetorical irony? A year before *Roderick Random* there appeared a pamphlet, *The Tricks of the Town Laid Open: or a Companion for Country Gentlemen,* whose seventeen letters were a scarcely altered repetition of another pamphlet entitled *The Country Gentleman's Vade-Mecum; or his Companion for the Town,* published in 1699[18]. Letter xiii (pp. 75-8) is summarised thus in the table of contents: 'The Villany of MONEY DROPPERS is expos'd, and the Roguish Methods they take to impose on Countrymen'. In less than four pages, the anonymous author retraces the history of this swindle which had been practised for sixty years, its favourite places, and its technique, which, with a few slight variations, corresponds with the one used to fleece Roderick. Smollett thus invents nothing new, he is content to adapt a well-known trick and to insert it, without much difficulty, into the plot of his novel, Roderick, as an innocent young Scot newly arrived from his distant homeland, being a readymade victim. But the career of the 'money-dropper' (or 'guinea-dropper') does not end with **Roderick Random.** This booby-trap of urban warfare turns up again in the *Extracts from such of the Penal Laws as particularly relate to the Peace and Good Order of the Metropolis* (1768) by John Fielding, the blind magistrate and half-brother of the novelist, who sums it up in a few succinct lines (p. 256). It reappears in a highly instructive pamphlet dedicated to John Fielding, *Thieving Detected* (1777). The author devoted ten pages (pp. 28-38) to the subtleties of the operation he calls 'The Drop' in thieves' slang. The three confederates are called the 'Picker-up', the 'Kid' and the 'Cap', the victim being referred to as 'a Flat'. No doubt about the same date[19], Richard King wrote *The Frauds of London Detected,* which also gives an exact description of the 'money-droppers' (pp. 53-5) and their malpractices. Smollett's testimony therefore links up with a series of writings, of very unequal merit, which enable one to appreciate his fidelity to contemporary social reality. He did not write of this form of swindling from any morbid taste for low life or in order to decry his era, but simply because such fraudulent practices were still common in 1748, and long after.

These few examples of an involuntary testimony which can be drawn from Smollett's work raise the more general problem of the novelist's objectivity. In other words, what part is to be attributed to the observation of real life and what part to satirical distortion? To attempt to solve this problem it was necessary to find a collection of scenes in these novels, sufficiently concrete in detail to provide firm ground for analysis and for which there might also exist irrefutable proofs, warranted by the author's actual participation in the events he describes. It was also necessary to be fairly amply documented on the period in order to compare Smollett's version with that of his contemporaries. Only the chapters in **Roderick Random,** where Smollett, through the medium of Roderick, describes life on board the *Thunder* comply with all these critical imperatives. The purpose of the following pages is not to make yet another systematic study of the British Navy as it appears in *Roderick Random.* It would be futile to repeat the labours of Robinson, Watson, Knapp, Martz, Jones and Kahrl[20] to mention only the most important. The aim of this study is more limited: to analyse the picture Smollett gives of life on board in Chapters xxiv-xxxvii inclusive (over 100 pages) of **Roderick Random.** According to the degree of concordance with contemporary documents it will then be possible to appreciate the discrepancy due to satirical distortion on the triple plane of discipline, living conditions and medical treatment.

Roderick's first contact with naval discipline is characterised by the brutality and gross injustice of Crampley the midshipman (I, 200, 204) who spits on him, belabours him with blows and has him put in irons. But Crampley himself soon replaces Roderick in the same decidedly uncomfortable situation, which at least testifies to a rudimentary justice, when the master-at-arms deigns to exercise it (I, 204-5). Smollett emphasises straight away the difference between the naval officer risen from the ranks, like his uncle Bowling, and those who owe their rapid promotion to high-placed and influential patrons. The honest tar Jack Rattlin says of Bowling: 'None of your Guinea pigs, nor your freshwater, wishy washy, fair weather fowls' (I, 200). It is not certain to which of the two categories Captain Oakum belongs. Rumour has it that he is the brother of a nobleman (I, 202), but there is nothing to prove that he owes his rank to favouritism. Although he shows himself an ignorant and cantankerously vindictive tyrant when Roderick and Morgan are put on trial, he behaves courageously during the murderous and futile engagement with the French ships. Bowling—and in **Peregrine Pickle,** Trunnion, another officer who has risen to his rank 'by creeping up through the hawsehole' as eighteenth-century English sailors used to say— is the moral and social antithesis of the effeminate Captain Whiffle who replaces Oakum. Bowling and Trunnion belong sociologically to that generation of about 1755, described by a naval officer in his *Sailor's Letters,* published in 1766: 'The last war, a chaw of tobacco, a ratan, and a rope of oaths, were sufficient *qualifications* to constitute a lieutenant' (second edition, 1767, p. 144). There must also be added, no doubt, for Bowling, Trunnion and Crowe (although the two latter appear only on land) the technical competence of these men for whom ships and the sea constituted their sole horizon, sometimes from the age of twelve or thirteen.

That Whiffle, with his sartorial elegance and his homosexual tendencies, represents a type current in the Navy of that time is highly unlikely, and, after all, difficult to verify. On the other hand, this character belongs to a dramatic and satirical tradition: the predecessor and perhaps the original of Whiffle, is the sea-dandy Mizen, created by Charles Shadwell in 1710 in the play *The Fair Quaker of Deal.* Edward Thompson altered this play which was acted at Drury Lane on November 11th 1773[21]. More than half a century after Shadwell, he only emphasised the fundamental difference between 'Commodore Flip', an officer of the old school, a coarse, heavy-drinking but worthy man, and one of his officers 'Beau Mizen'. Flip loathes Mizen with all his might and maintains—but he is the only one among the group of officers to hold this opinion— that the sailor's profession is incompatible with the status of a gentleman. Dissolute, cowardly and incompetent, the worst thing about these foppish officers, in Flip's eyes, is their wanting to live on board in the same luxurious comfort as on shore:

I hate a fop; it is impossible a fop can be a good sailor, and therefore I hate my lieutenant; the fellow boasts that he does not know the name of one rope in the ship; the puppy too, lies in chicken-skin gloves to make his hands white, and washes them in almond-paste (1773 edn, p. 5).

Mizen defends himself and it is certain that his arguments met with more sympathy in 1773 than the satirical accumulation of sartorial, cosmetic and olfactory details with which Smollett loads the caricature that Whiffle is (I, 279-86). Here is how he replies to his commanding officer's accusations: 'Why, commodore, won't you permit a man to be clean! will nothing please you, but what stinks of tar and tobacco!' (I, 6). Finally Worthy, the officer who embodies common sense, condemns the opponents: 'Mizen is as great an extreme of absurdity as the commodore' (I, 8). A dated fact will make one realise how slowly the British Navy developed in the direction Mizen desired: soap did not make its official appearance on board warships until 1795. In their excessive refinement, Mizen and Whiffle were the distant literary precursors of an indispensable hygienic measure.

The tyranny of Oakum, absolute master on board, especially at sea when he had to render no account to any higher authority, was not a new feature, either in literature or in the pamphlets of those who had been complaining from the beginning of the eighteenth century of the flagrant abuses of this autocratic discipline. The satirist Edward Ward (1667-1731) does not spare ship's captains, either in his *London Spy* (1698-1709) or, above all, in his virulent and burlesque pamphlet *The Wooden World Dissected* (1707), in which all ranks, from captain to seaman, are ruthlessly lampooned. Ned Ward insists on this tyrannical absolutism of the Captain: 'He is a *Leviathan,* or rather a Kind of Sea-God, whom the poor Tars worship as the *Indians* do the Devil, more through Fear than Affection; nay, some will have it, that he is more a Devil than the Devil himself'[22]. More caustic still is the accusation of one Barnaby Slush, the probable and appropriate pseudonym of a cook whose indignation impelled him to write *The Navy Royal: or a Sea-Cook turn'd Projector* (1709). Slush attacks pell-mell the incompetent officers, the system of bounties for voluntary enlistment, the unfair sharing-out of prize money, the conditions of life on board, and most of all the intolerable reign of terror established on board by certain authoritarian skippers

who debauch their Power and use it so Tyranically; Tyranically, I call it, since no Slavery is greater than impositions upon the Mind and Temper of a Gentleman. To be ty'd up to a Servile compliance with any Fantastick, Hare-brained injunction, which Pride, or Liquor, shall kindle in the Noddle of a Haughty Blunderbuss, is worse than shackles (p. 9).

After Smollett, Fielding, in his *Voyage to Lisbon* (1755) does not display any tenderness for the various officers he meets and the words 'tyrant' and 'bashaw' recur with indignant regularity to describe their conduct as soon as they feel themselves absolute masters on board. But, unlike Smollett in the **Travels through France and Italy,** Fielding never fulminates, and despite his desperate state of health does not collapse into morbid erethism. His portrait of Captain Veal, a petty tyrant terrified, just like Trunnion in **Peregrine Pickle,** at the thought of having a bone to pick with the lawyers, does not want a certain indulgent sympathy which is lacking in Smollett.

It is obvious that Smollett has condensed the defects both of the system of recruitment and of the various officers he may have met during his time in the Navy. Satire cannot have any impact unless the faults it condemns are concentrated in a limited number of characters, who consequently lose most of their specific individuality and become types. So it is fatal that Smollett's implicit judgment of superior officers such as Oakum and Whiffle should have been guided by his satirical purpose. The appreciation of his objectivity is rendered all the more difficult because the testimonies of his contemporaries on ship's captains by no means agree with each other. A specialist in British naval history arrives at this balanced conclusion: 'Some ships were lax in their discipline, others taut, some officers were humane and considerate, others were sadists and capricious tyrants'[23]. Thus, apart from the punishment of the cat-o'-nine-tails inflicted by command of the Captain (I, 226-7) and which was never officially abolished in the British Navy, there were informal corporal punishments on board which could make life hellish for the members of the crew if a choleric boatswain or midshipman let themselves go in raining blows with a rattan cane. This is what happens to Roderick (I, 204), who gets several stinging slashes from Crampley. This punishment was called 'starting' and was the subject of one of the most usual complaints of ill-treated crews. This practice was only abolished in 1806 but it continued long after[24]. In the case of shipwreck, this brutal discipline completely broke down. Watson (pp. 166-8) and, after him, Kahrl (pp. 15-16) have noticed the similarities between the shipwreck of the *Wager* one of the ships in Anson's expedition, and that of the *Lizard* (I, 300-2). Kahrl suggests (p. 16) that Smollett, without being directly inspired by the account given by Bulkeley and Cummins in their *Voyage to the South Seas* (1743) may well have heard the circumstances from the lips of Captain Cheap, the commander of the *Wager*. John Bulkeley, the gunner, and John Cummins, the carpenter, condemn the looters, who, as soon as the ship runs aground, fling themselves on the ship's provisions and the officers' chests:

we had several in the ship so thoughtless of their Danger, so stupid and insensible of their misery, that upon the principal officers leaving her they fell into the most violent outrage and disorder; They began with broaching the wine in the lazaretto: then to breaking open Cabbins and Chests, arming themselves with swords and pistols, threatning to murder those who should oppose or question them: Being drunk and mad with liquor, they plunder'd Chests and Cabbins for money and other things of value, cloath'd themselves in the richest apparel they could find, and imagined themselves lords paramount (pp. 14-15).

It is difficult not to compare this passage with the pages in which Smollett describes the same incident on board the *Lizard* (I, 300-31). As Smollett remarks, this was a customary proceeding, which John Byron, 'Foul-weather Jack', the grandfather of Lord Byron, mentions in his own account of the events which took place on May 14th 1741. This immediate breakdown of discipline in the case of shipwreck is explained not only by obvious psychological causes, but most of all by the following maritime regulation: as soon as a ship is wrecked, the crew's pay is immediately stopped, and, at the same stroke, the authority of the officers and the captain vanishes. In his *Narrative of the Honourable John Byron* published in London in 1768, which furnished Lord Byron with the factual sources for the shipwreck described in *Don Juan,* the author confirms the statements of Bulkeley and Cummins about the behaviour of the crew and lays particular stress on the drunkenness which caused some of them to be drowned in the flooded holds and 'tween-decks[25]. Even before the belated testimony of John Byron, another midshipman in the *Wager,* Alexander Campbell, had published, as early as 1747, a pamphlet less well known than the other two, *The Sequel to Bulkeley and Cummins's Voyage to the South Seas* which also confirms[26] the observations of his predecessors on the behaviour of the crew. Campbell complains of the injustice of Captain Cheap, a choleric man who shot dead another midshipman, Cozens, for insubordination when those who had escaped were trying to survive after running aground on a hostile shore. Cheap, who had arrived in Britain a few weeks before Campbell accused the latter (wrongly) of having defected to the service of the Spaniards, when all he had done was to embark on a Spanish ship. Like the gunner who saved the abandoned *Lizard,* Campbell received neither reward for his loyalty to his Captain nor promotion and even lost his position in the Navy. Confronted with so many concordant accounts, one is forced to conclude that Smollett's description of the scene of the shipwreck of the *Lizard* is in no way exaggerated.

As to the living conditions, right from Roderick's first rude contact with them in the tender which served as a floating headquarters of the press-gang, they are characterised by a persistent impression of vile stench which greets the unlucky Roderick wherever he goes (I, 200, 214-15, 216, 273). Tainted provisions, in particular rotten cheese, are the main basic olfactory ingredients of life on board ship. L. M. Knapp's discovery of the diary kept on board the *Chichester* by Lieutenant Robert Watkins states on December 22nd 1740, this officer 'condemnd Eighteen Hundred and Ninety five pounds of cheese' (Knapp, p. 32). But this might be just an isolated incident. Such does not seem to be the case, if one is to believe William Thompson's pamphlet *An Appeal to the Public in Vindication of Truth and Matters of Fact* (1761). This former cooper and inspector of the Pickle-Yard, dismissed for the abuses which he indignantly denounced, tried to draw the public's attention to the deplorable quality of the victuals destined for the British war fleet. He reveals in particular

> that seamen in the King's fleet have made *buttons* for their *Jackets* and *Trowses,* with the *Cheese* they were served with, having preferred it by reason of its *tough* and *durable* quality, to buttons made of *common metal;* and that Carpenters in the Navy-service have made *Trucks* to their Ship's flagstaffs with whole *Cheeses,* which have *stood* the *Weather equally with any timber* (p. 18).

On the following page he denounces the ship's biscuit, swarming with black-headed maggots, and the beer which stinks like foul water, which does not surprise the reader of **Roderick Random** (I, 266-7). As early as 1757 the same author had vigorously denounced, in *The Royal Navy—Men's Advocate,* a sixty-page pamphlet respectfully dedicated to William Beckford, the rottenness of the meat (beef and pork) destined for the sailors, the bad quality of the pickling, the dirtiness of the casks and the corruption of those responsible who ordered the workmen to salt down even stinking carrion. The film director Bunuel could find in William Thompson's pamphlet those horrifying gory details for which he has such a passion, like the piglets escaping from the disembowelled sow in the slaughterhouse, reared by hand and then bled to death in their turn. Another film director, Eisenstein, in *The Cruiser Potemkin,* nearly two centuries after **Roderick Random,** managed to recreate this medley of filth and violence with his shots of meat swarming with maggots, his depiction of the men huddled together in the crew's quarters, and the gratuitous brutality of the leading seaman. There is a direct line of continuity from Smollett to Eisenstein, running through Melville, the reformer Melville of *White Jacket* (1850).

Faecal stenches are added to the odours of putrefaction. It is easy to accuse Smollett of enjoying displaying his olfactory and scatological obsessions, for example in the incident in the sickberth (I, 214-15). But once again he is faithful to reality, even in its most malodorous details. This soil-tub, unluckily overturned, is a necessity anticipated in the regulations as early as 1731 and appears in the third section of *Rules for the Cure of Sick or Hurt Seamen on board their Own Ships:*

The Cooper may, by the Captain's Direction, make out of any old Staves and Hoops, Buckets with Covers, for the necessary Occasions of the sick Men; and if any of them have fractured Bones, or such Ailments as requite their lying in Cradles, the Carpenter may make such a number as shall be necessary (2nd edn, 1734, p. 55).

This mixture of prudent economy and solicitous foresight did not, however, take into account such possible accidents as a sudden heavy roll. It is very difficult to know whether Captain John Blake had ever read ***Roderick Random*** but, in his very serious *Plan for Regulating the Marine System of Great Britain* (1758), he does not disdain, unlike Smollett's disgusted but futile and narrow-minded detractors, to touch on this problem of general hygiene. Stopping one's nose in the name of a pseudoaesthetic criticism is no doubt a very refined reaction, but it is not of the slightest practical use. Blake, as a man of experience, knew living conditions on board really well, and proposed the following improvements for the sick:

> That the hospital-room be provided with one or more strong-armed chairs, which may be lashed to the deck, each having in its bottom a close stool-pan made of metal, which may be more easily emptied and washed clean than the wooden buckets directed by the present regulation of the navy to be used, which always retain a smell, though washed ever so clean, and are very inconvenient for a sick man to sit on, frequently overset with him, by the sudden rolling of the ship, and produce very offensive and unwholesome consequences; and on such occasions fill the ship with a stench, which not only annoys the whole company, but retards the cure of the sick, and even contributes to infect those who are well (p. 53).

Captain John Blake's pamphlet was very well received in the *Critical Review* of May 1758 (v, 437-8). In view of such a document which explicitly confirms *all* the details of the scene in the sick-bay of the *Thunder,* can one still talk of satirical exaggeration or excremental obsession? Only the insincerity (or smug ignorance) of a criticism full of contempt for the facts of civilisation can explain such opinions, though not justify them.

The bad ventilation in these ships with superimposed decks and no air shafts constituted a problem all the graver because the health of the crew suffered in these appalling living conditions, especially in tropical zones. When Roderick realises that he has caught the fever, his first care is to find a berth where he can benefit from a little air, for the cockpit where the surgeons lodged was generally situated in the bowels of the ship, often on the orlop deck well below the waterline (I, 273). This problem of proper ventilation attracted the attention of the inventor Stephen Hales, who in 1743 published *A Description of Ventilators,* to wit

enormous bellows which would permit the air to be changed in prisons, hospitals and ships of the fleet and the merchant navy. Like many scientists and doctors of the time, Hales was convinced that breathing noxious air was one cause of contagion. In his *Treatise on Ventilators* (1758), he summarises the experiments made on ships in which his cumbrous apparatus had been installed; as early as 1748, on the *Captain,* of seventy guns, the *Blandford,* a slavetrader of twenty guns, the *Laura,* and in 1749 on five Nova-Scotian ships. Another inventor, Samuel Sutton, criticises Hales's bellows in his *Historical Account of a New Method for Extracting the Foul Air out of Ships* (1757). He had got in touch with the Admiralty as early as 1739:

> In the Year 1739, I was informed that the sailors on board the fleet at Spithead were so dangerously ill, for want of fresh air, that they were put ashore to recover their health; and the ships to which they belonged, stunk to such a degree, that they infected one another[27]

Sutton's system was a collection of pipes which went right down to the hold where a fire was lit to make the air circulate. Sutton received the support of Dr Richard Mead right from the beginning, but, as always, the resistance due to the inertia of ship's captains and officers was hard to overcome. A letter from Rear-Admiral Boscawen to Corbett, dated April 9th 1748, nevertheless shows that, at the very moment when ***Roderick Random*** came out (January 1748), reforms were already afoot in the British Navy: 'I cannot help thinking, the air-pipes fixed in the men of war have been of great service in this particular [i.e. of preserving the health of seamen], by purifying the air between decks, and thereby preventing the scurvy.'

Even if the conclusion, which conformed with the medical theories of the day, is erroneous, the effects of this invention, soon followed by other improvements[28] were beneficial, but obviously it was not installed in Smollett's *Chichester.* So Smollett, far from distorting reality in the interests of satire, appears as the literary pioneer of a technological reform vital for the health of thousands of men on board ship.

The details given by Smollett on the food (I, 201, 206, 212), abundant but monotonous and ill-balanced, are confirmed by modern scientific studies by such specialists as Lloyd and Coulter, and D. A. Baugh.[29] The rations fixed by the regulations of 1734 provided between 4,000 and 4,500 calories a day, but the purser had the right to reduce them by an eighth to compensate for his losses. Moreover there were a great many pursers who cheated over the quantity and reduced the rations still more, not to mention the custom which allowed the men to sell them back part of their rations in order to make a little money, or to get credit for tobacco or clothes. For bedding space, the fourteen inches which made Roderick so indignant (I, 213) was exactly the width prescribed by the regulations. In such conditions fleas, lice and bedbugs could only increase and multiply, as Roderick quickly learns from bitter experience (I, 216-17). It is strange that Smollett makes no mention of the rats which infested these wooden ships, rich in inaccessible hiding-holes. In 1783, a curious character, Thomas Swaine who entitled himself 'Ratcatcher to his Majesty's Royal Navy' could boast, in his *Universal Directory for Taking Alive or Destroying, Rats and Mice, by a Method hitherto Unattempted,* of having caught (it was his record!) 2,475 rodents on board the *Duke,* thanks to a preparation based on powdered arsenic, sugar and wheat flour.

Before touching on Roderick's medical activities, it should be remembered that, even in his first novel, Smollett did not indulge in a systematic pessimism. However black the general picture of life on board, the author has brightened it here and there with some touches of human warmth and kindness. Opposed to the 'baddies'—Crampley, Oakum and Mackshane—there are the 'goodies'—Jack Rattlin, Morgan, Thomson, and later, on board the *Lizard,* Tomlins, the surgeon who dies as a result of Crampley's sadistic persecution (I, 299). Atkins (I, 223) Mackshane's predecessor, befriends Roderick after his forced arrival on board and helps him to procure a surgeon's mate's warrant. It is therefore incorrect to accuse Smollett of depicting only the darker side of life. In this perpetual strife between the forces of Good and Evil to which Smollett returns in all his novels, he relies on the support of characters who are sound at heart but not devoid of human weaknesses, like Morgan with his choleric arrogance or Thomson with his inability to stand firm under strain.

The cockpit which served as the hospital and whose space was restricted enough in normal times (I, 205-6) became, during a naval battle, a kind of human slaughterhouse 'where legs and arms were hewed down without mercy' (I, 263). Floundering in blood and human debris, the surgeons and their assistants looked more like infernal killers than doctors. Long after Smollett, surgeons like Edward Ives, about 1755, and Robert Young, in 1797[30], described the bloody horror of this naval butchery, with a wealth of details, before which the same scene in **Roderick Random** (I, 261-4) pales. Once again, the analysis of these pages makes one realise how skilfully Smollett blends his factual knowledge of the navy with fictitious elements. Before the bombardment of the forts of Cartagena, Mackshane, the cowardly surgeon 'insisted upon having a platform raised for the convenience of the sick and wounded in the after-hold, where he deemed himself more secure than on the deck above' (I, 260). Oakum, who detests any manifestation of cowardice, refuses. Mackshane then invokes the regulation which authorises such a

transfer. He is referring to Article IX of the instructions to surgeons (*Regulations and Instructions Relating to His Majesty's Service at Sea,* 2nd edn, 1734) which provides:

> In an Engagement, he is to keep himself in the Hold, where a Platform is to be prepared for the Reception of the Wounded Men; and himself, and his Mates and Assistants, are to be ready and have every thing at Hand, for stopping their Blood, and dressing their Wounds (p. 133).

Smollett uses a real fact in order to bring out more clearly the cowardly nature of his character, who, in turn, makes the fact seem a more living reality. The exchange between the real and its representation is therefore not a one-way transaction, like the mere reflection of an object in a mirror. This comparison has obsessed critics ever since Stendhal used it, first in his preface to *Armance* and later in *Le Rouge et le Noir* where he wrote: 'A novel is a mirror that one carries along a road', as an epigraph to Chapter xiii. But the mirror is not lifeless: the reflection of the real object illuminates the latter and gives it a new dimension.

Another example will enable one to appreciate Smollett's fidelity to medical facts. During the storm, Jack Rattlin has fallen from the mast and is suffering from an open fracture of the tibia (I, 233). After a consultation with Mackshane, who is in favour of immediate amputation, Morgan and Roderick decide to take the responsibility on themselves and not to proceed with the removal of the wounded limb. This incident reveals the surgeon's ignorance and his lack of compassion for his patients. Moreover, Smollett relies on his medical knowledge for the treatment given to Rattlin, which saves his leg. The treatment (I, 235) follows the advice given by John Atkins in his *Navy Surgeon* (1734, pp. 37-52). In cases of open fracture Atkins prescribes three operations, extraction of foreign bodies, reduction and bandaging, which Morgan and Roderick perform *secundum artem*. Smollett even specifies that they use 'the eighteen-tailed bandage' which Atkins recommends in these words: 'We always chuse that of eighteen Tails, for the Conveniency and Ease of daily dressing the Wound' (p. 42). And, to leave nothing to chance, Atkins gives, on the same page, two ways of obtaining these bandages, of which this is one: 'It is made of three Doubles of strong Linnen sown in the Middle, and divided at each End with two Cuts of your Scissors, a fit Depth.'

But the efficiency of the nursing care lavished on Rattlin cannot hide the scandalous contempt for the life of the sick and wounded. Even the worthy Morgan refuses to go and tend a dying sailor until he has eaten and drunk his fill (I, 208). No doubt the habit of rubbing elbows with death must have hardened the ebullient Welshman, but even he is shocked by the inhuman order (I, 225) given by Oakum, to wit an inspection of the sick on the quarter-deck. This new kind of medical visitation promptly resulted in the death of several of the sick. Smollett denounces 'the inhumanity and ignorance of the captain and surgeon, who so wantonly sacrificed the lives of their fellow-creatures' (I, 227). The same waste of human life before the forts of Cartagena is even worse in the emergency hospital ships which are so understaffed with surgeons and nurses that they soon become floating charnel-houses (I, 268). There again, Smollett used the adjective 'inhuman' and the word 'barbarity' to describe the abominable behaviour of Crampley (I, 268, 299). It is difficult to estimate the number of victims of the Cartagena expedition:

> Because of the numbers that were hastily buried at sea, it is impossible to compute the total casualties. Smollett says that 1,500 out of 8,000 survived, but he is evidently speaking of the army only. Another estimate puts the sick at 8,431 out of 12,000[31].

At the beginning of the Seven Years' War, the great naval doctor James Lind could write in his *Essay on the Most Effectual Means of Preserving the Health of Seamen in the Royal Navy* (1757):

> The number of seamen in time of war, who died by shipwreck, capture, famine, fire, or sword, are but inconsiderable, in respect of such as are destroyed by the ship diseases, and by the usual maladies of intemperate climates[32]

The following figures published in the *Annual Register* of 1763, can only justify Lind, and, retrospectively, Smollett too: during the Seven Years' War, the British Navy lost 133,708 men through disease or desertion, but only 1,512 in battle. The horrors in **Roderick Random** were less than they were in reality. In view of the statistics, how can one doubt Smollett's veracity?

Nevertheless, it would be unfair not to express some reservations. Smollett's satirical temperament, his youth at the time of the Cartagena expedition, his total lack of contact with the general staff, especially with Admiral Vernon, made him commit errors which his cantankerous spirit soon built up into injustices. Smollett blames Vernon in very harsh terms and makes him responsible, because of his inflexible character, for the death of thousands of men whose loss could have been avoided if the Admiral had consented to put the naval surgeons available in each ship at the disposition of General Wentworth. And he adds, not without satirical malice: 'but, perhaps, the general was too much of a gentleman to ask a favour of this kind from his fellow chief, who, on the other hand, would not derogate so much from his own dignity, as to offer such assistance unasked' (I, 269). Now the publication

of the *Vernon Papers* (1958) reveals a very different man:

> The general picture that emerges from these documents is that of an efficient administrator, with an eye for the smallest detail, but always looking and planning ahead, and with a full appreciation of the importance of logistics and humane leadership as essential ingredients of success in battle[33].

Vernon himself complained of the lack of surgeon's mates, and asked the 'Navy-Board' to send out a supplementary contingent with all speed (pp. 346-7). Vernon, throughout his letters, orders of the day and other administrative circulars, appears as a man who cared about the health of his men and their food and clothing. Even in instituting the obligatory diluting of their daily half-pint of rum with two pints of water by his famous order of August 21st 1740, Vernon was trying to fight against the endemic vice of his seamen, drunkenness. (Smollett alludes to this measure of Vernon's, but does not seem to realise its anti-alcoholic purpose: I, 232.) Vernon was also very well aware of the defects of his ships and complains, in particular of the *Chichester* and the *Torbay* which are among the crankiest of the ships, which explains the formidable pitching and rolling of the *Thunder,* as also the panic of the crew during the storm described by Smollett (I, 232). Published two years before **Roderick Random,** Vernon's long pamphlet (170 pages) entitled *Some Seasonable Advice from an Honest Sailor* (1746) presents a fervent plea in favour of more humane treatment of seamen and an indirect condemnation of the press-gang. Vernon *prescribes* (without immediate success), Smollett *describes,* but, in fact, both were animated by the same humanitarian concern.

Conversely, the total absence of pity for the black slaves bought and resold at the end of **Roderick Random** (II, 270-3) shocks the modern reader of Smollett. Roderick speaks only of an epidemic (typhus no doubt) which breaks out on board his slaver; and consequently, once the slaves are sold at a good price, he says he is glad to see the ship 'freed from the disagreeable lading of negroes' (II, 273). On several occasions Smollett, too, sold slaves to Jamaica, without a single trace of humanitarian feeling appearing in the correspondence (legal documents quoted by Knapp, pp. 326-8). This insensitiveness is all the more inexplicable since other naval surgeons and officers, before and after the publication of **Roderick Random** expressed (sometimes very fleetingly, but showing the beginnings of an awakened consciousness) their disapproval and horror at this treatment of the negroes. This is the case with Atkins, who, in his *Voyage to Guinea* (1735), deplores seeing their masters regarding the slaves 'only as Beasts of Burthen; there is rather Inhumanity in removing them from their Countries and Families' (pp. 61-2). This sentiment is already expressed in *The Sea-Surgeon or the Guinea Man's Vade Mecum* (1729) by Thomas Aubrey who denounced the brutal behaviour of the crew to the cargo of slaves, the bad food, the lack of water, the inhuman cruelty of the captain and the ignorance of the ship's surgeon (pp. 128-30, 132). Finally, Commodore Edward Thompson, who was not yet even a lieutenant at the time, in a letter from Barbados dated December 5th 1756, writes of his indignation at seeing daily examples of this 'cruel tyranny exercised over the slaves . . . shocking to humanity' (*Sailor's Letters,* 1767 edn, II, 29).

At the end of this analysis of naval scenes, one is compelled to admit that Smollett has not exaggerated the blackness of the reality. Specialists in naval medicine and naval history like R. S. Allison, Lloyd and Coulter, and D. A. Baugh[34], with a few slight reservations, confirm this opinion. Smollett is occasionally unjust, as his prejudiced and ill-informed attacks on Vernon prove. But one is seldom able to catch him out, especially in the medical realm, in some flagrant inexactitude. It is even strange that the scenes in which Smollett describes the horrors of the naval battle, the injustice of the Captain and the incredibly harsh living conditions on board are not more conspicuously animated by the spirit of satire. Attention has already been drawn to a certain callousness in Smollett's attitude to slavery. This is certainly an ethical flaw in his passionate but also puritanical character; the generous indignation of satire must not hinder commercial transactions. In Smollett, as in his contemporaries, there is a certain hardness, due to being more accustomed than nowadays to the daily proximity of death, disease, poverty, dirt and corruption. Thus William Cockburn, an extremely rich quack doctor and a friend of Swift's, in his *Account of the Nature, Causes, Symptoms and Cures of the Distempers that are Incident to Seafaring People* (1696) is not unduly outraged by the living conditions on board warships. The food, the beer, and even the crew's quarters seem perfectly all right to him. The great jurist Sir Michael Foster, in *The Case of the King against Alexander Broadfoot* (Oxford, 1758), relates the famous trial in which Broadfoot was sentenced for having killed a press-gang crimp who had boarded his ship in April 1743 without a search warrant. While admitting that there were extenuating circumstances for the accused, Foster nevertheless firmly defends the principle of the press-gang and supports the theory of its being a national necessity in time of war:

> War itself is a great Evil, but it is chosen to avoid a greater. The Practice of Pressing is one of the Mischiefs War brings with it. But it is a Maxim in Law, and good Policy too, that all private Mischiefs must be borne with Patience, for preventing a National Calamity (p. 6).

Foster is only expressing in lofty legal terms the same hardened resignation as Jack Rattlin, when obliged to allow his hand to be amputated. But Foster was *decreeing* and Jack Rattlin *submitting*. Charles Butler, in *An Essay on the Legality of Impressing Seamen* (1777), was still defending Foster's arguments and even backing them on the grounds of the existence of social inequalities which he regards as inevitable, not to say desirable:

> We shall attempt to shew that an inequality of rank is inseparable from society; that in the distribution of the duties of society, those which are offensive and disagreeable public duties (among which we reckon service in the armies and navies of the State), must fall to the lot of that part of mankind which fills the lower ranks of life; that this mode of distribution, however hard or unjust it may appear to the human eye is necessarily incident to society in all it's states (pp. 6-7).

After all, why should the riffraff on board complain if King and Country demanded that it should die in defence of them? Some of the callousness for which one can blame Smollett, if not for the brutality of the details, at least for the absence of shuddering sensitiveness, is also explained *a posteriori* by the progress of medical and surgical science. The instructions to the surgeons of 1731 laid down that, if their instruments were not adequate for amputations, they should have recourse to carpenter's saws (with no anaesthetic, of course). It is possible, in this case, to talk of insensitiveness? What must also be borne in mind is the incredible inertia displayed by the entire British Navy, from the First Sea Lord to the lowest cabin-boy, towards any attempt at reform. Anson, in *A Voyage Round the World* (1748), complains that nothing had been done to improve living conditions on board, in particular the ventilation. But he realises the obstinate prejudices that exist in the navy against any form of progress. He denounces 'an obstinate, and in some degrees superstitious attachment to such practices as have been long established and . . . a settled contempt and harred of all kinds of innovations, especially such as projected by landmen and persons residing on shore' (p. 37).

This illogical obstinacy is the hallmark of closed conservative worlds. Although it may be amusing when it is a matter of affectations of speech or manners, it becomes tragic if the refusal of all innovation involves contempt for (or indifference to) medical discoveries. Such is the tragic history of the fight against scurvy, that scourge which ravaged the navy all through the eighteenth century[35]. As early as 1617, in *The Surgeon's Mate,* John Woodall already empirically recommends, among other and useless remedies, lemon juice: 'the use of the juice of Lemons is a precious medicine and well tried, being sound & good, let it have the chiefe place, for it will deserve it' (p. 185). James

Lind's decisive experiment dates from May 1747. Yet the Admiralty did not recognise the antiscorbutic value of lemon juice until 1795, when it ordered regular distributions of it. Smollett seems to have realised the importance of fresh victuals for the soldiers and sailors of the expedition. He even reproaches the commanding officers for not having used the available transport ships to procure provisions from the neighbouring islands (I, 267). His absence of emotion, his apparent callousness in the face of the most painful sights is here again only a mask. Given the psychological and physical induration of the period, the mere fact of daring to describe, even with a few satirical exaggerations, incidents in which men were treated almost like brute beasts, is already a courageous challenge to the system of social oppression and a cry of hope for the future. . . .

Smollett introduces his readers to a world swarming with rogues, crooks, thieves, prostitutes and highwaymen. The critic may be shocked by this display of the more or less sordid sides of the eighteenth century. But Smollett does not show any *complacency* in this description of the underworld, which he surveys in general rather than systematically exploring it. Moreover, he was haunted by the fascinating problem of the interplay of Good and Evil in life and its literary expression. He had already realised that it is impossible to make good literature with good sentiments alone. Conversely, the modern critic who is shocked by Smollett's choice of subjects could (and should) ask himself the following question: in two or three centuries, what idea would these then engaged in research on the twentieth century form after having ransacked the columns of *France-Soir* or the *News of the World* which wallow ambiguously in the depravities of our era? The flat, everyday, commonplace life of Mr So-and-So is a recent literary discovery which Smollett has foreshadowed in **Humphry Clinker** by offering his readers the activities and thoughts of a group of letter-writers who, by their connections and occupations, constitute an analytical cross-section of English society about 1765-70.

He runs no risk, however, of becoming bogged down in the boring morass of what, in the nineteenth century, was called the 'slice of life', cut from some monstrous, highly indigestible cake. The omnipresent leaven of satire contributes to making his literary pastry more digestible without always avoiding an excess of acidity. The moral preoccupations of satire partly explain why the fresco painted by Smollett in his five novels is not complete, and at least as rich as that of Balzac or Dickens. Smollett suffers not only from the almost inevitable but rather fruitless comparison of his work with Fielding's, but also with the massive work of his openly avowed admirer, Dickens. In fact, it would be fairer to place Smollett among the painters, halfway between Hogarth and Rowlandson. Satire of a

personal character (literary and political) belongs henceforth to the abstruse world of erudition. It has lost its brilliance and most of its interest (first and foremost in **The History and Adventures of an Atom**) and shares the same fate as *Le Canard Enchaîne, Punch,* or *Private Eye* a few weeks after their publication; this kind of satire is a dish which needs to be eaten piping hot: the slightest delay renders it flat and tasteless. On the contrary, satire allied to the representation of the real, thanks to the curative virtues of its acidity, presents the occasionally aggressive, but always very lively éclat of a world where social and economic tensions were at once to disappear and revive in the profound unheaval which precedes the Industrial Revolution. Thanks to this mixture, the representation of the real in Smollett's novels has not aged and occasionally even retains a surprising ring of actuality. . . .

Abbreviations

CL   *Comparative Literature*

ELH   *English Literary History*

JEGP   *Journal of English and Germanic Philology*

MLN   *Modern Language Notes*

MLQ   *Modern Language Quarterly*

N & Q *Notes and Queries*

PLL   *Papers on Language and Literature*

PMLA   *Publications of the Modern Language Association*

SNL   *Satire Newsletter*

YR   *Yale Review*

Notes

[1] PP, p. 335.

[2] P. J. Klukoff, 'Smollett as the reviewer of *Jeremiah Grant*', *N & Q,* ccxi (Dec. 1966), 466.

[3] See René Wellek's study of 'The concept of realism in literary scholarship', in his *Concepts of Criticism,* Yale U.P., paperback edn, 1963, pp. 222-55. For a critical analysis and various attempts to define this term, one may consult G. H. Gerould, *How to Read Fiction* (1937); George J. Becker, 'Realism: an essay in definition', *MLQ,* x (June 1949), 184-97; D. S. Savage, *The Withered Branch,* Eyre & Spottiswoode, 1950, the preface: 'Truth and the art of the novel'; 'A Symposium on Realism', *CL,* iii (Summer 1951), in particular the articles by Harry Levin, 'What is realism?', pp. 193-9, and Robert Gorham Davis, 'The sense of the

real in English Fiction', pp. 200-17; K. Lever, *The Novel and the Reader,* Methuen, 1961; C. S. Lewis, *An Experiment in Criticism,* Cambridge U.P., 1961; G. Lukács, *La Théorie du Roman,* Paris, edn, 1963, as also the following studies: *Studies in European Realism,* London, 1950 and *The Meaning of Contemporary Realism,* Merlin Press, 1963. These indications are by no means exhaustive. Eric Auerbach, in *Mimesis,* Doubleday Anchor Books, 1957, touches on the problem of the representation of the real in western literature with an erudite subtlety which does not exclude debatable prejudices; see also Damian Grant, *Realism,* Methuen, 1970.

[4] Ian Watt, *The Rise of the Novel,* Chatto, 1957, Peregrine, 1963.

[5] Barbara Hardy, *The Appropriate Form,* Athlone Press, 1964.

[6] *Concepts of Criticism,* p. 253.

[7] For general studies, see the celebrated articles by Louis I. Bredvold, 'A note in defence of satire', *ELH,* vii (Dec. 1940), 2-13 and Maynard Mack, 'The muse of satire', *YR,* xli, no. 1 (1951), 80-92, both reproduced in Boys, ed., *Studies in Literature of the Augustan Age;* the books by Robert C. Elliott, *The Power of Satire,* Princeton U.P., 1960; Gilbert Highet, *The Anatomy of Satire,* Yale U.P., 1962; Alvin B. Kernan, *The Plot of Satire,* Yale U.P., 1965; R. Paulson, *The Fictions of Satire,* 1967. Studies on satire in Smollett's work: Earl R. Wasserman, 'Smollett's satire on the Hutchinsonians', *MLN,* lxx (May 1955), 336-7; Kelsie B. Harder, 'Genealogical Satire in *Humphry Clinker', N & Q,* cc (Oct. 1955), 441-3; Mohammed Awad Al-Usaily, 'Satire in the Novels of Smollett', unpublished Edinburgh PhD thesis, 1963, in which the laborious accumulation of details and the barely disguised paraphrase overwhelm any faint attempt at synthesis; Mary Wagoner, 'On the satire in *Humphry Clinker', PLL,* ii (1966), 109-16; Grant T. Webster, 'Smollett's microcosms: a satiric device in the novel', *SNL,* v (Fall 1967), 34-7; Ronald Paulson, *Satire and the Novel in XVIIIth Century England,* Yale U.P., 1967, pp. 165-218 (devoted to Smollett repeat in part *verbatim* in a former article by the same author, "Satire in the early novels of Smollett', *JEGP,* lix, Jan. 1960, 381-402); R. D. Spector, *Tobias Smollett,* Twayne, 1968, *passim.*

[8] Joyce Cary, *Art and Reality,* Cambridge U.P., 1958, p. 115.

[9] G. Lukács, *La Théorie du Roman,* Paris, 1963, p. 66. The first edition dates back to 1920. Lukács repudiated it and refused any reprinting until 1962 (trans.).

[10] Alain Robbe-Grillet, *Pour un Nouveau Roman,* Paris, NRF, 1963, p. 175; see the article 'Du réalisme à la realité' (trans.).

[11] Raymond Jean, *La Littérature et le Réel: de Diderot au 'Nouveau Roman',* Paris, 1965, p. 17 (trans.).

[12] See C. Lloyd, *The British Seaman,* Collins, 1968, p. 127.

[13] See C. Lloyd and J. L. S. Coulter, *Medicine and the Navy,* 4 vols, E. & S. Livingstone, 1961, iii, *1714-1815,* 49.

[14] See Arthur F. Leach, *A History of Winchester College,* London, 1899, the author speaks of rebellions under the reign of Dr Warton in 1770, 1774, 1778, 1793, but reports nothing before 1770.

[15] See *Winchester: its history, building and people,* 3rd edn revised, London, 1933, by the Winchester College Archaeological Society.

[16] See *The History of the Colleges of Winchester, Eton, and Westminster . . .* published by R. Ackermann, London, 1816, pp. 44-6. The greater part of this history was written by W. Combe.

[17] 17 Geo. II, c. 5. See Sir Frederic Morton Eden, *The State of the Poor,* London, 1797, I, 307-8, concerning the 'Vagrant Act' of 1744.

[18] See Ralph Straus, ed., *Tricks of the Town,* London, 1927, pp. xiv-xvi; this edition will be used for all references to this pamphlet.

[19] The British Museum Catalogue gives 1770, with a questionmark. This date is unlikely, as the author alludes on p. 88 to the activities of smugglers in 1778.

[20] C. N. Robinson, *The British Tar in Fact and Fiction,* London, 1909, see in particular Ch. xiii 'Smollett and the naval novel', pp. 266-83: this very anecdotal book can still be read with profit, but lacks order and pays no heed to literary accuracy; more serious is H. F. Watson's book, *The Sailor in English Fiction and Drama 1500-1800,* New York, Columbia Univ. Studies in English, 1931, in which pp. 156-7 are devoted to *The Reprisal,* 164-9 to *RR;* see also L. M. Knapp, 'The naval scenes in *Roderick Random', PMLA,* xlix (June 1934), 593-8; L. L. Martz, 'Smollett and the Expedition to Carthagena', *PMLA,* lvi (June 1941), 428-46; C. E. Jones, *Smollett Studies,* University of California Press, 1942; 'Smollett and the Navy', pp. 31-75 gives the most complete study; G. M. Kahrl, *Tobias Smollett Traveler-Novelist,* Chicago U.P., 1945, pp. 1-27. The biographies of David Hannay (1887) pp. 29-41, and of Knapp, 1949, pp. 29-38, also contain useful details about life on board an English warship about 1740. See also Nathan Comfort Starr,

'Smollett's Sailors', *American Neptune,* xxxii, no. 2 (1972), 81-99.

[21] For a nautical study of *The Fair Quaker of Deal* and the alterations made by Thompson, see Robinson, op. cit., pp. 204-24.

[22] Edward Ward, *The Wooden World,* The Society for Nautical Research, 1929 reprint, p. 15.

[23] Lloyd, *The British Seaman,* p. 230.

[24] See Lloyd, op. cit., pp. 210, 241-2.

[25] *Narrative of the Honourable John Byron,* London, 1768, account of the shipwreck, pp. 10-16, the absurd appearance of the sailors decked out in the officers' clothes they had stolen, p. 25. See also Peter Shankland, *Byron of the Wager,* London, Collins, 1975, pp. 42-52.

[26] See the account of the shipwreck, p. 12 onwards; the behaviour of the looters and drunks who stayed on board the wreck, pp. 14-16.

[27] See vol. II of the *Medical Works of Dr. Richard Mead,* Edinburgh, 1763, in which Sutton's *Historical Account* is reproduced in part; quotations p. 210 and 237.

[28] See on this subject Lloyd and Coulter, op. cit., supra, n. 13, pp. 72-7, 'Ventilation and fumigation'.

[29] Lloyd and Coulter, op. cit., Ch. 7, 'Victualling', pp. 81-93; Daniel A. Baugh, *British Naval Administration in the Age of Walpole,* Princeton U.P., 1965, an indispensable work for understanding the naval background of *RR:* see in particular Ch. viii, 'Victualling', pp. 373-451.

[30] See Lloyd and Coulter, op. cit., n. ii, all Ch. 5, 'The cockpit, the sick-berth and hospital ship', pp. 57-69. The unpublished evidence of Robert Young (pp. 58-60), shows that fifty years after Cartagena the operating conditions had in no way changed on board. The same surgical nightmare resurrected in the midst of the horrors of Biafra: see *Le Monde,* of May 7th 1969, pp. 1, 12.

[31] Lloyd and Coulter, op. cit., n. ii, p. 106.

[32] See the edition of this work in *The Health of Seamen* (vol. CVII of the Publications of the Navy Records Society, edited by Christopher Lloyd, 1963), p. 27.

[33] B. M. Ranft, *The Vernon Papers,* Navy Records Society, 1958, p. 304; information concerning the *Chichester,* p. 348.

[34] See R. S. Allison, *Sea-Diseases,* London, J. Bale Medical Publications, 1943, pp. 65, 117-19 on Smollett; Lloyd and Coulter, op. cit., n. ii, pp. 25-8, in particular p. 28: 'The description of the hospital ships . . . rings horribly true'; Baugh, op. cit., n. 27, pp. 225, 396.

[35] See Lloyd and Coulter, op. cit., Ch. 18, 'Scurvy', pp. 293-328.

Douglas Brooks (essay date 1973)

SOURCE: "Smollett: *Roderick Random, Peregrine Pickle, Ferdinand Count Fathom,*" in his *Number and Pattern in the Eighteenth-Century Novel: Defoe, Fielding, Smollett, and Sterne,* Routledge and Kegan Paul, 1973, pp. 123-43

[*In the following excerpt, Brooks examines the numerological patterns of certain events and chapters in Smollett's first three satirical novels as well as the meaning behind such symmetry, observing that Smollett's use of numerological symmetry improves with each succeeding novel.*]

I Roderick Random

Form mattered to Fielding. Even in *Amelia,* its iconographical implications can still be detected, if only faintly. In Smollett's first novel, published in 1748, on the other hand, the overriding impression is one of disorder and fragmentation, in subject-matter and in structure. Robert Alter has justly remarked on the way it reflects the phrenetic and neurotic quality of life in the period;[1] and it does so with a fidelity and awareness of the grotesque and the chaotic that has, once again, its visual counterpart in the middle and late works of Hogarth. But to concentrate on this aspect of *Roderick Random* is to do Smollett an injustice by ignoring his attempts to impose arithmetical schemes on his material, attempts which make his novels structurally very different from their picaresque antecedents.[2] I use the word 'impose' advisedly, however: the young Smollett was too much a man of the transitional mid-century to achieve, or even want to achieve, at this stage of his development, the kind of formal complexity manifested in, say, *Joseph Andrews.* Nevertheless, before writing *Roderick Random* he had obviously studied Fielding's novel with some care, as the several echoes of it in his own work attest,[3] and doubtless one of his reasons for reading *Joseph Andrews* was to seek guidance on the structuring of a long prose fiction.

Like *Joseph Andrews,* *Roderick Random* was published in two volumes. This format obviously assisted Smollett in working out his narrative symmetries, as it assists the reader in grasping them. It should be recorded here, then, that vol. I contains thirty-six chapters, and vol. II, thirty-three chapters. The chapter numbering is continuous (i.e., running from 1 to 69), though in later eighteenth-century editions there seems to have been a tendency to number each volume separately.[4]

The novel's fundamental circularity is announced in chapter 1 with the sage's interpretation of Roderick's mother's dream as meaning that he 'would be a great traveller, that he would undergo many dangers and difficulties, and at last return to his native land, where he would flourish with great reputation and happiness'. It is also in this first chapter that Roderick's father mysteriously disappears, 'and notwithstanding all imaginable inquiry, could not be heard of, which confirmed most people in the opinion of his having made away with himself in a fit of despair'. Both Roderick and his father return to Scotland and regain the family estate in the final chapter.

Such a balancing of beginning and end is elementary enough. More interesting is the way Smollett prepares us for the rediscovery of Roderick's father. Don Rodrigo is, it will be recalled, encountered in chapter 66, living in Buenos Aires. No sooner have he and his son been reunited than they sail from the Rio de la Plata to Jamaica where they meet Roderick's former shipmate Thomson (ch. 67). Leaving Thomson they set off for England and almost immediately lose a man overboard:

> About two hours after this melancholy accident happened . . . I heard a voice rising, as it were, out of the sea, and calling, 'Ho, the ship, ahoy!' Upon which one of the men upon the forecastle cried, 'I'll be d——n'd, if that an't Jack Marlinspike, who went over-board!' Not a little surprised at this event, I jumped into the little boat that lay along-side, with the second mate and four men, and rowing towards the place, from whence the voice (which repeated the hail) seemed to proceed, we perceived something floating upon the water; when we had rowed a little farther, we discerned it to be a man riding upon a hen-coop. . . .

The man turns out to be from another ship; but this apparent resurrection of the drowned sailor is a clever retrospective analogue to the unexpected discovery of Roderick's father, thought to be dead long since. The incident makes full structural sense, however, only if we remember what happened to Thomson earlier on in the novel. Because of Mackshane's brutality (Thomson mentions Mackshane at the beginning of chapter 67) he had thrown himself overboard from the ship in which he and Roderick were serving together (ch. 29). Nothing more is heard of him (and he is presumed dead) until chapter 36, when Roderick goes ashore at Morant and notices a horseman who turns out to be 'the very person of my lamented friend'. Thomson then

explains how he comes to be alive: once in the water he had 'hailed a large vessel' but her crew had not wanted 'to lose time, by bringing to; however, they threw an old chest over-board, for his convenience, and told him that some of the ships a-stern would certainly save him. . . . '

The parallel could scarcely be closer. And this episode itself has been prepared for by Roderick, who, in chapter 34, after nearly dying of a fever, pretends to be dead and suddenly to come to life in order to startle Morgan. We might say, then, that ***Roderick Random***'s basic structure is planned round the disappearance and rediscovery of Don Rodrigo, and that the 'resurrections' noted here, but especially that of Thomson at the very end of the first volume, have a deliberate anticipatory function—a function that is made the more explicit by Thomson's reappearance in chapter 67 immediately after Roderick's reunion with his father, and by the echo of his original plight by the sailor on the hen-coop.

If the end of the first volume looks forward, the first chapter of the second (37) looks back and also marks a new beginning for Roderick. Returning to England with wealth and clothing and seeing himself 'as a gentleman of some consequence' (ch. 36), it is suddenly apparent that his quest for gentility[5] has reached only a contrived, not a genuine, conclusion. For in chapter 37 there is a storm, and Roderick, who tells us 'I cloathed myself in my best apparel', fights with his enemy Crampley and is left destitute on a Sussex beach, where 'I cursed the hour of my birth, the parents that gave me being', and so on.[6] This curse is important; for it is clearly intended to take us back to chapter 1. And as a further reminder that the novel is, in a sense, beginning again, Roderick finds himself a surrogate mother in Mrs Sagely (chapter 38; his own mother had died in chapter 1): the old woman 'drew a happy presage of my future life from my past sufferings' (recalling the sage's prediction in chapter 1)[7] and Roderick 'contract[s] a filial respect for her', but only after he has heard her life history: she had married beneath her and without her parents' consent, and they had disinherited her. The story echoes that of Roderick's own father, who had married 'a poor relation' without parental consent and had again been disinherited. Mrs Sagely then leaves the novel until near the end (chaps 65 and 67);[8] and in chapter 67 she alludes to her words in chapter 38: 'she thanked heaven that I had not belied the presages she had made, on her first acquaintance with me. . . . ' Beginning, middle, and end of the novel are thus closely bound together as they are also by the disappearance of Roderick's father, the disappearance and reappearance of Thomson, and the reappearance of Don Rodrigo.

Miss Williams provides another link between the two halves of the novel. Roderick, already in his eyes 'a gentleman in reality' (ch. 20), had first encountered her when he pursued her as a supposed heiress, and had met her again as an abandoned prostitute in the following chapter. This hints at a theme that is developed in more detail in vol. II with the courtesan picked up by the deluded Roderick in chapter 45 and Melinda (chaps 47ff.). Miss Williams's function is therefore proleptic: she acts as a warning of the sexual and social temptations that will confront him on his return to London, though the relevance of her 'history' (chaps 22, 23) becomes apparent only after Roderick has met his beloved Narcissa in the second volume. As a girl Miss Williams had been attacked by a drunken squire in a wood and rescued by a young man who 'was the exact resemblance of' Roderick. He had seduced her and then 'left [her] without remorse'. The parallel (with a difference) with the main narrative emerges in chapter 41, when Roderick rescues Narcissa from an indecent attack by Sir Timothy Thicket. Moreover, the link thus forged between the two women is strengthened when Miss Williams appears as Narcissa's maid in chapter 55 (acting as a warning to him once more: he had pursued her unsuccessfully as an heiress in Part I and had nearly married her; now she brings Roderick and Narcissa together when he is again on a false trail by chasing another heiress, Miss Snapper). Roderick first met Miss Williams in chapter 20; chapter 55 is the nineteenth chapter of vol. II.

Miss Williams's story is interrupted at the beginning of chapter 23 by her wrongful arrest. She is driven off to the Marshalsea, but is released when the mistake is realized. The interruption is as much a structural matter as anything else; for Roderick hears the second interpolated story, that of Melopoyn, in chapters 62 and 63, when he has been arrested for debt and is himself imprisoned in the Marshalsea. Both narratives last for two chapters, and although the Marshalsea provides the only substantive link between them, and their relative positions in their respective volumes by no means correspond, we have here yet another indication, I think, of Smollett's anxiety to give his first novel all the trappings of formal unity even if, in his treatment of the interpolated narrative, he was unable to live up to the examples of Fielding and Fielding's own model, Cervantes.

The symmetries created by the appearances of Bowling are also worth comment. We last hear from him in the first volume in chapter 6; Roderick then encounters him in France in chapter 41, and he departs in chapter 42 (i.e., the sixth chapter of vol. II), to reappear to rescue his nephew from the Marshalsea in chapter 64 (the sixth chapter from the end of the novel). Strap, too, is involved in analogous symmetries: he and Roderick meet and decide to travel together in chapter 8, and they meet up again in France in chapter 44, the eighth chapter of vol. II.

If we now turn from large-scale patterns to the internal organization of the individual volumes, an interesting contrast is apparent. There is an undeniable arithmetical patterning in vol. I, since its thirty-six chapters are clearly divided into three sets of twelve by Roderick's arrival in London (ch. 13) and his being press-ganged into the navy (after the beginning of chapter 24, which is therefore transitional). Smollett was obviously working to the following scheme:

1-12	Scotland; Journey
13-24	London
25-36	Navy

[Editor's note: the source reproduced this diagram in a linear format. The columnar format of *LC* did not allow it to be reproduced in the same way.]

While in addition, the following subdivisions may be detected: chapters 1 to 6, Scotland, and 7 to 12, journey (i.e., the first block falls into two sets of six chapters); chapters 13 to 15, various London matters; 16 to 18, the navy office; 19 to 21, Lavement; 22 to beginning of 24, Miss Williams (four sets of three). The third block is similarly divided: nearly four chapters (24 to 27) are devoted to Roderick's initial experiences on board ship; three chapters (28 to 30) recount events on the voyage to Carthagena, and Carthagena itself takes up three chapters (31 to 33); finally, the last three chapters of the volume (34 to 36) form a single unit centring round Captain Whiffle and Crampley.

But the second volume lacks such a precise individual arithmetical structure, though it does contain the few symmetries already noted. Of *Roderick Random* as a whole, it can be said that Smollett here reveals no firm sense of structural direction, and that the patterns I have described lack any real iconographical import despite the lip service paid to the power of Providence in the novel.[9] I suspect, in fact, that they are little more than mere scaffolding.

II Peregrine Pickle

The symmetries in Smollett's much longer second novel, however, possess more symbolic significance. Indeed, we might anticipate a little here, and say that from the structural point of view at least Smollett's development is the exact opposite to that of Defoe and of Fielding, in that it manifests an increasing concern with architectonics and such numerological details as mid-point symbolism. As we shall see, this concern coincides with a move towards greater thematic and moral clarity.

The question of structural schemes in *Peregrine Pick-*

le (1751) is complicated by the considerable revisions made for the second edition (1758). For the time being, therefore, I shall consider the first edition, and since the volume divisions once again have an important part to play, I supply the following table:[10]

Volume	Chapters	Total
I	1-38	38
II	39-78	40
III	79-93	15
IV	94-114	21

Only with this information before us can we appreciate, for example, how carefully Trunnion's death at the garrison at the beginning of the third volume (ch. 79), together with his warning to Peregrine not to abuse Emilia, is balanced by the death of Peregrine's aunt at the beginning of vol. IV (ch. 94), which again brings Peregrine to the garrison. And chapter 94 can also serve as a useful introduction to the kind of less symmetrical repetitive structuring that we encounter in **Peregrine Pickle.** For Peregrine here meets Emilia, whom, despite his uncle, he has abused, and with whom he is on bad terms. He asks Sophy to be his advocate with her, and in so doing he draws the parallel with her previous identical role in vol. I (ch. 26) by remembering 'that fond, that happy day, on which the fair, the good, the tender-hearted Sophy became my advocate, though I was a stranger to her acquaintance, and effected a transporting reconciliation between me and that same inchanting beauty, that is now so implacably incensed'. The parallel here has both a moral and a structural function. The first incident, caused by the letter fabricated by Pipes, had been a comic misunderstanding. But the second involves a much more serious alienation between the two, brought about by Peregrine's pride and his failure to recognize and live up to the virtue embodied in Emilia. And just as Pipes, because of the letter, had had a major part in chapter 26, so he does in chapter 94, trying to help Peregrine's case by pretending that his master has 'hanged himself for love'. Again, Peregrine draws the parallel: 'this is the second time I have suffered in the opinion of that lady by your ignorance and presumption; if ever you intermeddle in my affairs for the future, without express order and direction, by all that's sacred! I will put you to death without mercy.'

The parallel deaths of Peregrine's uncle and aunt are not the only way in which Smollett has linked the last two volumes: the third volume, beginning as it does with Trunnion's death, sees Peregrine in possession of his uncle's estate and his initiation into the fashionable world; at the end of vol. IV (ch. 111) Peregrine's father, Gamaliel, dies. Having squandered his first inheritance, Peregrine can handle with temperance the 'more ample' fortune he now receives. The point is made explicitly: Peregrine has 'a stock of ex-perience that [will] steer him clear of all those quick-sands among which he had been formerly wrecked' (ch. 112).

Further instances of such patterning abound. For example, the series of misunderstandings and reconciliations between Peregrine and Godfrey near the end of the first, second, and fourth volumes: in chapter 30 (ninth from the end), chapter 73 (sixth from the end) and chapter 109 (also sixth from the end); or the satirical adventures of the two at the end of the first volume (chaps 34ff.) and of the second volume (chaps 73ff.), where they have a more moral aim and are not mere practical jokes as they were earlier). It is here (ch. 76) that Peregrine becomes acquainted with Crabtree, and near the end of vol. III (chaps 89ff.) occur several satirical *exposés* in which Peregrine and Crabtree engage together (including Peregrine's unmasking of 'a couple of sharpers' in chapter 92—compare the *'Scheme'* in chapter 74 *'by which a whole Company of Sharpers is ruined'*).

Similarly, towards the end of vol. I, in chapter 35, Peregrine's sister Julia is alienated from her family because of her affection for her brother. In a corresponding position in vol. II (ch. 72) she is married to a Mr Clover who, at the end of the fourth volume, is instrumental in seeing that Peregrine gets his rightful inheritance (ch. 111); while a couple of chapters from the end of vol. III Peregrine claims to have seen an apparition of 'the commodore . . . , in the very cloaths he wore at [Julia's] wedding' (ch. 92). Finally, there is the repetitive pattern created by Godfrey's military promotions: in chapter 33 Trunnion discovers that he knew Godfrey's father, and he and Peregrine give Godfrey money which enables him to purchase an ensigncy; in chapter 73 Peregrine, again unknown to Godfrey, helps him to a lieutenancy, and in chapter 92 he gets him 'a captain's commission'. The sequence is completed when, in the fourth volume, Godfrey is again seeking promotion and discovers who his benefactor has been (ch. 109). At this point Pipes refers Godfrey to the first event in the sequence: 'That same money you received from the commodore, as an old debt, was all a sham, contrived by Pickle for your service. . . .' (In the first, second, and last instances the relevant event occurs in the sixth chapter from the end of the volume.)

I suggested that **Roderick Random** begins again, as it were, with the opening of the second volume. We have already seen Defoe (in *Robinson Crusoe*) and Fielding (in *Tom Jones* and *Amelia*) using the centres of their novels in a similar way, and, as I said earlier, I regard this preoccupation with the centre as deriving (in part at least) from the rich tradition of mid-point symbolism in seventeenth-century poetry. Interestingly, though, in **Peregrine Pickle** Smollett's concern for the thematic possibilities of the centre is much more evident than in his first novel: it is here that we sense him, however tentatively, beginning to explore the iconographical implications of pattern. In fact, he places Trunnion's death exactly in the middle, that is, in the first chapter of vol. III (in Clifford's edition, on p. 394 out of a total of 781). The volume divisions are essential in directing us to the symmetry for we are prepared to take on trust that, as we open the third volume, we have reached the half-way stage in a four-volume work. (Though in terms of chapter-totals, of course, chapter 79 is considerably beyond the mid-point; this is because of the imbalance created by Lady Vane's 'Memoirs', which occupy the greater part of vol. III.) The counting of pages, therefore, merely confirms what the external (i.e., volume) divisions have already made explicit. The death of Trunnion is, of course, crucial to Peregrine's career and moral development. Significantly, then, Smollett underlines the event and its centrality with the traditional image of elevation which is here invoked to affirm Peregrine's pride: 'The possession of such a fortune, of which he was absolute master, did not at all contribute to the humiliation of his spirit, but inspired him with new ideas of grandeur and magnificence, and elevated his hope to the highest pinnacle of expectation.'[11]

Moreover, vols I, II, and IV themselves possess symbolic centres. Of the first volume's thirty-eight chapters, the first nineteen narrate (among other matters) Peregrine's schoolboy pranks and practical jokes. His Winchester rebellion fails in chapter 20, and at this point 'he plunged into a profound reverie that lasted several weeks, during which he shook off his boyish connections, and fixed his view upon objects which he thought more worthy of his attention.' He is, Smollett tells us, 'in the utmost hazard of turning out a most egregious coxcomb', and there are hints of unstable equilibrium and potential fall: 'While his character thus wavered between the ridicule of some, and the regard of others, an accident happened, which, by contracting his view to one object, detached him from those vain pursuits that would in time have plunged him into an abyss of folly and contempt.' This 'accident' is his meeting with Emilia; so that the second half of vol. I is concerned with Peregrine and Emilia, the transition coming in the centre with Peregrine's character change and the appearance of Emilia. An element of chiastic patterning reinforces the symmetry:

17 Trunnion (sends Peregrine away from
    garrison to Winchester)
  18
    19 Insurrection (leaves school)
      20 Failure of insurrection; Emilia
    21 Elopes from school (because of Emilia)
  22
23 Trunnion (summons Peregrine to garrison)

Like Sophia in *Tom Jones,* Emilia represents that virtue to which Peregrine is aspiring as he journeys through the novel. He is especially forgetful of her (and hence of her symbolic significance) during his travels in vol. II, and returns from France prepared to violate her. His attempt to do so, which occurs in chapters 80 to 84, is Smollett's profoundest comment on his hero's moral decadence; and, it is essential to note, the episode has been carefully prepared for by the pattern of sexual encounters in the second volume. First of all frustrated in his attempts on Mrs Hornbeck (chaps 40ff.), Peregrine meets up with her again and finally enjoys her 'without restraint' (ch. 64). But this successful amatory adventure frames an unsuccessful one with an unknown girl whom Peregrine dubs his 'Amanda'. The Amanda episode resolves itself into a series of frustrations at the very moment of consummation, the last frustration being the most important for the comment it elicits from Amanda: 'she hoped last night's adventure would be a salutary warning to both their souls; for she was persuaded, that her virtue was protected by the intervention of heaven; that whatever impression it might have made upon him, she was enabled by it to adhere to that duty from which her passion had begun to swerve . . . ' (ch. 62).

In other words, 'the intervention' is to be read as a Providential warning to Peregrine, which he fails to heed.[12] And its function in this respect is reinforced structurally in a way that should by now come as no surprise: for Amanda occupies the centre of the second volume and is thus implicitly contrasted with Emilia, who, as we have seen, is introduced in the centre of vol. I (the central chapters of vol. II are 58 and 59, twentieth and twenty-first out of a total of forty). The whole episode is, in addition, symmetrical in itself: Peregrine meets Amanda in a coach (ch. 56) and parts from her in a coach (62); in the central chapter of the group and of the volume Peregrine arranges a coach accident so that he might seduce her at an inn:

  56 A and P meet in coach
    57 A and P interrupted by Jolter and Jew
      58 A and P interrupted by Pallet
        59 Coach accident
      60 A and P interrupted by Pallet
    61 A and P interrupted by Jolter and Pallet
  62 A and P part in coach

Two other symmetries in this volume are worth noting. First, in the seventh chapter (45) Peregrine receives a letter from Godfrey and fails 'to honour the correspondence which he himself had sollicited' and also begins 'to conceive hopes of [Emilia] altogether unworthy of his own character and her deserts'; in chapter 71 (eighth from the end) Peregrine, now in England, 'remembred, with shame, that he had neglected the correspondence with her brother, which he himself had sollicited', and we are told that 'Tho' he was deeply enamoured of miss Gauntlet, he was far from proposing her heart as the ultimate aim of his gallantry. . . .' Second, Peregrine dismisses Pipes in chapter 56 (just before the Amanda affair begins); and in chapter 64—shortly after its conclusion—Pipes reappears.

As I have said, the Amanda episode, far from being a

warning to Peregrine, seems rather to act as an incitement. He returns to England intent on seducing Emilia, and, significantly, his attempt on her contains several echoes of the earlier attempts on Amanda. Thus, the failure of his attempted seductions leads to a fit of rage and madness ('he raved like a Bedlamite, and acted a thousand extravagancies' (ch. 82)) which recalls the 'distraction', 'delirious expressions', 'agitation', and 'extasy of madness' that are the result of Amanda's refusal to see him any more (ch. 62); he chases unsuccessfully after Emilia (ch. 84) as he does after Amanda (ch. 66); and, as if to confirm the parallel, Emilia has already been referred to as 'his Amanda' at the beginning of chapter 84. It takes 'a dangerous fever'—the consequence of his passion—to bring 'him to a serious consideration of his conduct' (chaps 84, 85). But again, Smollett's attention to structural detail ensures that the point is made more subtly. For in chapter 85 Peregrine returns to the garrison—always associated with integrity and right thinking in the novel—not only to assist in Hatchway's courtship of Mrs Trunnion but also 'to give orders for erecting a plain marble monument to the memory of his uncle' (the chapter begins with Peregrine writing a letter to Mrs Gauntlet expressing his sense of shame at having abused Emilia). Now immediately before Peregrine's attempt on Emilia, the dying Trunnion had warned his nephew, 'if you run her on board in an unlawful way, I leave my curse upon you . . . ' (ch. 79); and since the actual seduction attempt on Emilia occurs in the central chapter (82) of the group of five devoted to Peregrine's scheme against her (80 to 84), we get the following symmetry: garrison / two chapters // attempt on Emilia // two chapters / garrison. Peregrine's involvement in the erection of the commodore's tombstone thus functions as a tacit, symbolic, reminder of his abuse of Emilia and of his uncle's trust, his abandonment of Trunnion's values.

The mid-point of vol. IV has even more obviously iconographical implications than those in the first two volumes. Here, in chapter 104 (eleventh out of twenty-one), we see Peregrine disappointed in his expectations of preferment from Sir Steady Steerwell, and his resultant despair. Just as, at the mid-point of the novel as a whole, Peregrine was 'elevated' in pride and fortune, so now, with that fortune squandered, he has reached his nadir: he has undergone a 'reverse of fortune' and 'such a gush of affliction would sometimes rush upon his thought, as overwhelmed all the ideas of his hope, and sunk him to the very bottom of despondence' (ch. 104)—the inversion of the traditional central image of elevation again. And at the end of the chapter the 'lady of quality' calls upon him to redirect his attentions to Emilia ('it is now high time for you to contract that unbounded spirit of gallantry, which you have indulged so long, into a sincere attachment for the fair Emilia . . .'), who thus occupies the centre of this last volume as of the first. Moreover, chapter 104 is framed in such a way as to affirm unequivocally its median position. The preceding chapter concludes with a squabble between the fly-fancier and mathematician whom Peregrine has encountered at the virtuoso's public breakfast—a squabble that is announced with a comic balance-image: 'the engineer proceeded to the illustration of his mechanicks, tilting up his hand like a ballance, thrusting it forward by way of lever, embracing the naturalist's nose like a wedge betwixt two of his fingers. . . .' The function of this as a numerological pointer is reinforced by a complementary passage in chapter 105, where Peregrine is imprisoned in the Fleet and 'in this microcosm' discovers a concern with justice that puts the greater world to shame: 'Justice is here impartially administered, by a court of equity, consisting of a select number of the most respectable inhabitants, who punish all offenders with equal judgment and resolution, after they have been fairly convicted of the crimes laid to their charge.'

And in between we have the blatant injustice of the minister Sir Steady Steerwell, whose name, which graces the heading of the 104th chapter, parodies that ideal of just government which it so manifestly expresses.[13] Deflated on the one side by the *Dunciad* world of the college of authors (itself a transparent comment on hierarchy and preferment in the political sphere) and of the virtuosi, Sir Steady is shamed on the other by the just world of the Fleet and—the irony is a manifestly numerological one—by the 'just' division of the volume itself into two equal halves with Sir Steady maintaining the mean.[14]

There can be no doubt, it seems to me, that these patterns are deliberate on Smollett's part. And their effectiveness is both a symptom and a result of *Peregrine Pickle*'s moral and thematic clarity. In *Roderick Random* Narcissa had been introduced too late to act convincingly as a moral cynosure; but, as Rufus Putney showed long ago,[15] in Smollett's second novel the Emilia-Peregrine relationship is crucial: we measure Peregrine's growth in terms of his attitudes to Emilia, who is thus given the central positions of sovereignty. *Peregrine Pickle* quite literally revolves round her.

In addition to these exact symmetries, as I have already suggested, *Peregrine Pickle* reveals the less significant repetitions and episode-parallelisms that we are familiar with from the novels discussed in earlier chapters, and there is no need to cite further examples. But before going on to consider how the revisions for the second edition affected the symmetries outlined above, a word or two should be said about the long interpolated narratives, '**The Memoirs of a Lady of Quality**' (ch. 88), and the history of MacKercher and the Annesley case (ch. 106). It is evident from the facts that, although it is possible to detect links between the 'Memoirs' and the story of Peregrine, they were included in the novel for extra-literary reasons. It would be a mistake, therefore, to attempt to isolate every possible parallel; and the Annesley case has only slightly more relevance: together with Peregrine's tale at the end of chapter 106 of a child deprived of an estate which is subsequently restored to him, it obviously anticipates the restoration to Peregrine of his family estate at the end of the novel.[16] Clearly, Smollett's concern for a tighter, symbolic, structure in his second novel did not extend to the interpolated tale, which he had handled with more sensitivity in **Roderick Random**.

The revisions for the 1758 text have been analysed in detail by Howard S. Buck.[17] In effect, they amount to the omission of various personal attacks (against Fielding and Garrick, etc.) and of episodes regarded by Smollett in retrospect as being in bad taste—the homosexual episode in chapter 49 and Pallet's urinating at the masquerade, the business between Peregrine and the nun in chapter 66, and so on. These changes considerably reduced the length of the novel and entailed the renumbering of chapters, the total now being 106 instead of 114. Inevitably, some of the symmetries that I have noticed in connection with the first edition disappear: looked at from one point of view, they had been the novel's scaffolding which could now be dismantled without incurring structural collapse. Thus, Peregrine's Winchester rebellion is omitted, and with it the chiasmus at the centre of vol. I; but Smollett ensures that Emilia still occupies the volume's midpoint (she is introduced in the seventeenth chapter of a total of thirty-four). And although certain alterations to vol. II mean that the Amanda episode is no longer exactly central in that volume (it is narrated in chapters 52 to 58; chapters 53 and 54 mark the middle of the revised total of thirty-eight), its slight shift in position is a trifling matter and in no way affects its central 'feel'. Moreover, the position of Trunnion's death is unaffected at the beginning of vol. III; and since the chapter-total for the final volume stays at twenty-one, its symmetries, too, remain intact.

III Ferdinand Count Fathom

Ferdinand Count Fathom (1753) manifests a stark simplicity of structure which is a fitting complement to the novel's moral schematism as announced in the Dedication.[18] Smollett here exploits the tradition of midpoint symbolism in which, as we have seen, he had shown increasing interest, with full awareness of its iconographical implications (its association with sovereignty, the midday sun, elevation, and the triumph), and once again utilizes the volume-divisions to direct attention to the novel's symmetries. In addition, the Dedication contains an explicit authorial statement to the effect that this novel—and presumably the others—

was conceived of in visual and spatial terms by defining 'A Novel [as] a large diffused picture, comprehending the characters of life, disposed in different groupes, and exhibited in various attitudes, for the purposes of an uniform plan, and general occurrence, to which every individual figure is subservient. . . . '

The novel, like poetry, is *ut pictura.* And as we read **Ferdinand Count Fathom,** taking note of the symbolism of the centre, it is worth recalling Hogarth's preoccupation with the mid-point in the *Election* (1755-58), which I have discussed above (ch. iv): a glance at the allusive structures which Hogarth incorporated in even his popular prints leaves one in little doubt as to the contemporary reader's ability to detect and interpret spatial schemes of considerable complexity. In the mid-eighteenth century literature and painting were still very much sister arts.

Fathom appeared in two volumes, vol. I containing the first thirty-five chapters and vol. II containing chapters 36 to 67 (i.e., thirty-two chapters). The first volume traces Fathom's rise in fortune and reputation, and the climax occurs in chapter 35 with the heading's explicit allusions to sovereignty and elevation: *'He repairs to Bristol spring, where he reigns Paramount during the whole season.'* The opening paragraph of this chapter, by again hinting at centrality ('Fathom, as usual, formed the nucleus or kernel of the beau monde'), confirms that he has built on the success that was his in chapter 32 where, we are told (presumably as an early directive to the iconography of the centre), 'he . . . shone in the zenith of admiration.'

Fathom arrives at Bristol claiming knowledge of medicine, and this is the beginning of his downfall.[19] For as vol. II opens (ch. 36) he becomes involved with one of his patients, Mrs Trapwell, 'the young wife of an old citizen of London'. He is betrayed by her, prosecuted, and imprisoned: 'Thus, he saw himself, in the course of a few hours, deprived of his reputation, rank, liberty and friends; and his fortune reduced from two thousand pounds, to something less than two hundred, fifty of which he had carried to gaol in his pocket.' And the second half of the novel abounds in references to Fathom's decline, speaking of it specifically in terms of 'eclipse': the heading to chapter 54 announces *'His eclipse, and gradual declination',* and in chapter 63 Madame Clement has 'traced him in all the course of his fortune, from his first appearance in the medical sphere to his total eclipse'.

There is, incidentally, an important ironic comment on this imagery in chapter 40, where the just imprisonment of Fathom is contrasted by Smollett with the unjust treatment of the historical figure of Theodore, King of Corsica, whom Fathom meets in gaol. The heading reads: *'He contemplates majesty and its satellites in eclipse';* so that for once in the novel the solar imagery is used seriously with the full significance that it had long enjoyed in the iconography of kingship.[20] And Smollett's belief in Theodore's rightful sovereignty emerges clearly from the following passage: he 'actually possessed the throne of sovereignty by the best of all titles, namely, the unanimous election of the people over whom he reigned. . . .' Theodore plays a minimal part in the plot. Nevertheless, this piece of political propaganda functions thematically to illustrate by contrast the villainy of Fathom, who is Theodore's antithesis, and who, as we have seen, *'reigns Paramount'* over the beau monde at the structural centre. The contrast is expressed emblematically at the beginning of chapter 40 when Theodore greets Fathom 'with a most princely demeanour' and 'seat[s] him on his right hand, in token of particular regard'.

There can be no doubt, then, that Smollett exploited the numerological device of mid-point symbolism in **Fathom** to illustrate the rise and fall of the count's fortunes, since the break—from good to bad fortune—comes unequivocally in the centre as marked by the volume divisions. Moreover, the individual volumes are themselves divided exactly into two. In vol. I a change of scene and subject-matter is announced in the heading to chapter 18 (central out of a total of thirty-five): *'Our hero departs from Vienna, and quits the domain of Venus for the rough field of Mars'*; and the central chapters of the second volume, 51 and 52 (sixteenth and seventeenth out of a total of thirty-two), echo his moment of triumph at the middle of the novel as a whole. For he is again a physician, and *'Triumphs over a medical rival'* (heading to chapter 51); but in chapter 52 he moves to London, becomes well known and (ch. 53) seduces one of his patients, a clergyman's wife, and is prosecuted by her husband (as he was prosecuted by Trapwell at the beginning of the volume). Chapter 50 has already reminded us that his second appearance as a physician, this time not as a nobleman who knows about medicine but as a man who 'professed himself one of the faculty', is an indication of 'the decline of his fortune'. And it is now, once the mid-point of the second volume, with its echoes of his earlier triumph, is past, that the images of decline and overthrow increase apace. Chapter 54—as we have seen—proclaims *'His eclipse, and gradual declination'* and tells us that 'our hero was exactly in the situation of a horseman, who, in riding at full speed for the plate, is thrown from the saddle in the middle of the race. . . .' He has a coach accident ('Then was his chariot overturned with a hideous crash . . .'), and it is finally revealed that he has, all the time, been enlisted under the banner of capricious Fortune: 'Fathom, finding himself descending the hill of fortune, with an acquired gravitation, strove to catch at every twig, in order to stop or retard his descent.'[21] It is impossible to read these substantive references to physical falls and to being 'thrown . . . in the middle of the race' without relating them to the novel's

physical structure—its observance of mid-point symbolism—especially when we notice that the sentence immediately succeeding the one just quoted ('the hill of fortune', etc.) reminds us of Fathom's former glory in terms that should by now be familiar: 'He now regretted the opportunities he had neglected, of marrying one of several women of moderate fortune, who had made advances to him, in the zenith of his reputation. . . .'

In chapter 56 he suffers a further 'torrent of misfortunes' which induces him for the first time to recognize his guilt and to invoke Providence: 'Shall the author of these crimes pass with impunity? Shall he hope to prosper in the midst of such enormous guilt? It were an imputation upon providence to suppose it— Ah, no! I begin to feel myself overtaken by the eternal justice of heaven! I totter on the edge of wretchedness and woe, without one friendly hand to save me from the terrible abyss.' And Fathom's fall is complemented, as we might expect, by an increasing number of allusions to Providence, especially in connection with the reappearance of Monimia: 'Mysterious powers of providence! this is no phantome!', etc. (ch. 63).[22] However, before we can see how the concepts of Fortune and Providence (the former relating to Fathom, the latter to Renaldo and Monimia) are inter-related in the novel, it is necessary to look at its structure even more closely.

In the foregoing analysis I have regarded the division between volumes I and II as marking the novel's mid-point which, to all intents and purposes, it does. But in fact the arithmetically central chapter is the thirty-fourth (out of a total of sixty-seven), and this, significantly, contains yet another instance of Fathom's iniquity, his seduction of Celinda, whom he leaves an alcoholic. This means, then, that Fathom is only *apparently* elevated at the centre, because his triumph at Bristol occurs at the centre as marked by the division between the two volumes; and that the exact—arithmetical—centre is dedicated to stripping away appearances and conveying, to quote the chapter heading, *'a true idea of his gratitude and honour'*. And with this structural subtlety established, further symmetries are revealed. The Celinda episode harks immediately back to Fathom's treatment of Elinor, whom he has left deranged in the madhouse in chapter 31; and it also has affinities with Don Diego's narrative in chapter 26: just as Fathom destroys Celinda and Elinor, so does Diego think he has killed his wife and daughter. Furthermore, it functions proleptically by anticipating Fathom's most heinous piece of villainy, the alienation of Monimia from Renaldo and his attempted seduction of her, which leads to her illness and apparent death.

If **Fathom**'s symmetries are now reassessed by taking the arithmetical centre (ch. 34) as the starting point, it emerges that they are designed to bring Renaldo and

Monimia, the novel's symbols of virtue, into prominence, and, simultaneously, to accentuate the count's vices. For Don Diego's story of his daughter Serafina and her lover Orlando is narrated to Fathom in chapter 26. In chapter 42 Renaldo arrives at the gaol where Fathom is imprisoned, arranges his release, and tells him that

> he was captivated by the irresistible charms of a young lady on whose heart he had the good fortune to make a tender impression: that their mutual love had subjected both to many dangers and difficulties, during which they suffered a cruel separation; after the torments of which, he had happily found her in England, where she now lived entirely cut off from her native country and connexions, and destitute of every other resource but his honour, love, and protection. . . .

She is introduced in the next chapter with a clear hint that her real identity will be announced later: 'It was not without reason he had expatiated upon the personal attractions of this young lady, whom (for the present) we shall call Monimia. . . . ' And in chapter 64 we discover, if we haven't guessed already, that Monimia is Serafina; so that Diego's story in chapter 26 and Renaldo's brief *résumé* in chapter 42 are about the same person. I reproduce in diagrammatic form the pattern thus created:

1-25	25 chapters
26	Don Diego, Serafina
27-33	7 chapters
34	Celinda
35-41	7 chapters
42	Reynaldo, Monimia
43-67	25 chapters

[Editor's note: the source reproduced this diagram in a linear format. The columnar format of *LC* did not allow it to be reproduced in the same way.]

There are, finally, additional symmetries which link the beginning and end of the novel. Chapter 57 is recapitulatory, narrating Renaldo's journey to Vienna and his preparations there for regaining his rightful inheritance from his stepfather, Count Trebasi. Renaldo travels to Vienna in company with a Major Farrel, who had served under the old Count Melvile and who 'owed his promotion' to him. Farrel is a symbol of gratitude as Fathom, who again owes everything to the old count, is an arch-symbol of ingratitude. This journey to Vienna—in chapter 57—occurs in the eleventh chapter from the end of the novel; and it was in chapter 10 that Renaldo had made his first journey to that city, accompanied by Fathom. In chapter 59 Renaldo's sister, Mlle de Melvile, is released from the Viennese convent in which she had been confined by Trebasi, and reveals Fathom's treachery, including his alliance with Teresa, which had been dedicated to systematic theft. Smollett

writes: 'She then explained their combination in all the particulars, as we have already recounted them in their proper place. . . . ' If we turn to the beginning of the novel, we find that the thefts occurred in chapters 9 and 10; and chapter 59 is the ninth from the end. It will be recalled that Fathom had devised the plan for stealing from Renaldo's sister because he had been unsuccessful in his attempts to possess her fortune by marrying her (chaps 6 to 8). Once again there is a structural relationship with, and moral contrast to, Major Farrel, who explains openly to Renaldo in chapter 60 that he has contracted some debts, that he is attracted to Mlle de Melvile, and that he would like to marry her, in part for her fortune. Renaldo agrees and the marriage takes place. The major's frankness contrasts with Fathom's deception; and just as Fathom's last attempt on Mlle de Melvile had occurred in chapter 8, so is chapter 60 the eighth chapter from the end of the novel.

Fathom, then, possesses an elaborate symmetrical structure, which clearly fulfils a symbolic function by exalting the forces of good (Renaldo, Monimia, Farrel, etc.) over Fathom, the embodiment of evil. We do Smollett and the 'uniform plan' of his work a gross injustice if we fail to detect the patterns outlined above and to note how Fathom's rise and fall, with its apparent observance of the mid-point as marked out by the volume divisions, is undercut by the numerically exact symmetries revolving round the story of Celinda in chapter 34. Fathom's story, as Smollett indicates, is that of a child of Fortune; but Monimia's and Renaldo's is just as explicitly Providential. The asymmetry of the one is overridden by the precise balance of the other to create, for the first time in Smollett's fiction, a compelling Providential paradigm.

Notes

[1] *Rogue's Progress: Studies in the Picaresque Novel* (Cambridge, Mass., 1964), pp. 62-3.

[2] Smollett does, of course, mention his indebtedness to *Don Quixote* and *Gil Blas* in the Preface to *Roderick Random,* though, so far as I can see, the debt is not in any significant sense a formal one. Paul-Gabriel Boucé gives a detailed discussion of the influence of these works on Smollett's novels in *Les Romans de Smollett: Étude Critique* (Publications de la Sorbonne; Littératures, I (Paris, 1971)), Pt. II, ch. 1.

[3] E.g., the bedroom mix-ups in ch. 11; the business over Roderick's diary (which is written in Greek characters) in ch. 30; and the hospitality given to the destitute Roderick by Mrs Sagely in ch. 38. Compare *Joseph Andrews,* IV. 14; II. 11 (where Adams's Æschylus is mistaken for 'a Book written . . . in Ciphers'; a passage added in the second edn), and I. 12 respectively. Tuvia Bloch, 'Smollett's Quest for Form', *MP*

[*Modern Philology*], 65 (1967-8), 103-13, incidentally, argues for Fielding's formal influence on Smollett. She concentrates mainly on *Ferdinand Count Fathom* and *Launcelot Greaves,* however, and her discussion is limited largely to plot patterns and Smollett's attempts to imitate Fielding's detached, ironic, narrator. Her concept of form does not include the kind of structural parallelisms that I am concerned with.

[4] This is the case with the text printed in *The Novelist's Magazine,* II (1780). In quoting from the novel I have used the first edn, since Smollett's subsequent revisions had no effect on its structure as outlined in this section. For a collation of textual variants, see O. M. Brack, Jr, and James B. Davis, 'Smollett's Revisions of *Roderick Random*', *Papers of the Bibliographical Society of America,* 64 (1970), 295-311.

[5] An important theme here as in *Colonel Jack,* though not so consistently sustained. As early as ch. 20 Roderick has rejected Strap as an unworthy companion and has told us 'I now began to look upon myself as a gentleman in reality.'

[6] M. A. Goldberg, *Smollett and the Scottish School* (Albuquerque, New Mexico, 1959), pp. 39-42, detects five main catastrophes or reversals in *Roderick Random* of which this is the central one, though he fails to note the significance of its position at the novel's approximate structural centre. Also worth mentioning is P.-G. Boucé's analysis of the novel in terms of a capital 'W', with the three top points representing Roderick's birth, encounter with Narcissa at Bath, and marriage, and the two bottom points his shipwreck and fight with Crampley, and his imprisonment in the Marshalsea: see his *Les Romans de Smollett,* pp. 169 and 193-4. Boucé makes no comment on its arithmetical structure, however.

[7] Boucé also notices the parallel, ibid., p. 159.

[8] Where her maternal relationship with Roderick is again insisted on: in ch. 65 Roderick calls her 'Dear mother' and she 'received me with a truly maternal affection'; in ch. 67 her 'maternal affection' is divided between Roderick and Narcissa.

[9] In ch. 41 (where Mrs Sagely and Bowling mention Providence); ch. 43 ('I could not comprehend the justice of that providence, which after having exposed me to so much wretchedness and danger, left me a prey to famine at last in a foreign country . . . '); ch. 44 ('providence or destiny acted miracles in their behalf'); ch. 66 (Roderick's father cries out 'Mysterious Providence!', and refers to 'this amazing stroke of providence'); and ch. 67 (Narcissa 'observed that this great and unexpected stroke of fate seemed to have been brought about by the immediate direction of providence').

[10] This has been prepared from a copy of the 4-vol. first edn, though for ease of reference all quotations are from James L. Clifford's OEN edn (1964), which reprints the 1751 text but without indicating the volume divisions.

[11] Crabtree, who has made his appearance at the end of the preceding volume, is clearly a replacement for the commodore: Trunnion presides over the more carefree first half of the novel, the misanthrope over the darker second half.

[12] Though he has already been 'almost persuaded, that so many unaccountable disappointments must have proceeded from some supernatural cause, of which the idiot Pallet was no more than the involuntary instrument' (ch. 61).

[13] The notion, in connection with self-government, recurs in ch. 112, with its reference to Peregrine's 'stock of experience that would steer him clear of all those quicksands among which he had been formerly wrecked'.

[14] In view of the allusion to Fielding in ch. 105 ('I might here, in imitation of some celebrated writers, furnish out a page or two, with the reflections [Peregrine] made upon the instability of human affairs . . . '), the balance, etc., in vol. IV might, in part, be a parody of the mid-point symbolism in *Tom Jones;* though Smollett is clearly more interested in its serious, iconographic, function.

[15] Rufus Putney, 'The Plan of *Peregrine Pickle*', *PMLA [Publications of the Modern Language Association],* 60 (1945), 1051-65.

[16] The 'Memoirs' are discussed in detail by Howard S. Buck, *A Study in Smollett, Chiefly 'Peregrine Pickle'* (New Haven, Conn., 1925), ch. 2, and, together with MacKercher, by Lewis M. Knapp in *Tobias Smollett: Doctor of Men and Manners* (Princeton, N.J., 1949), pp. 121ff. See also Clifford's Introd., pp. xxvi-xxvii, and Boucé, *Les Romans de Smollett,* pp. 188-90 and 192. On the 'Memoirs' Boucé follows Putney, 'The Plan of *Peregrine Pickle*', p. 1064, to the effect that they confirm Smollett's 'thesis that the life of the upper classes was often vicious and immoral'.

[17] His *A Study in Smollett* contains a collation of the first and second edns.

[18] 'That the mind might not be fatigued, nor the imagination disgusted by a succession of vitious objects, I have endeavoured to refresh the attention with occasional incidents of a different nature; and raised up a virtuous character, in opposition to the adventurer, with a view to amuse the fancy, engage the affection, and form a striking contrast which might

heighten the expression, and give a *Relief* to the moral of the whole.' Quotations are from the OEN edn, ed. Damian Grant (1971), which reproduces the text of the first edn, 2 vols, 1753.

[19] Boucé analyses the novel in similar fashion, noting that Fathom enjoys his 'apogee' in ch. 35, from which he then declines (op. cit., p. 210, and cf. p. 239).

[20] For a detailed discussion, see Ernst H. Kantorowicz, 'Oriens Augusti—Lever du Roi', *Dumbarton Oaks Papers,* 17 (1963), 117-77.

[21] Compare the antithetical image in the first half of the novel, where we are told that Fathom 'surveyed the neighbouring coast of England, with fond and longing eyes, like another Moses reconnoitring the land of Canaan from the top of mount Pisgah' (ch. 27): and cf. also ch. 19, where England is alluded to as 'the Canaan of all able adventurers'.

[22] Cf. ch. 61 ('Sure Providence hath still something in reserve for this unfortunate wretch . . . '; this is Don Diego speaking of himself), and ch. 62, Renaldo on Fathom's treatment of Monimia: 'Sacred heaven! why did providence wink at the triumph of such consummate perfidy?'

R. D. S. Jack (essay date 1982)

SOURCE: "Appearance and Reality in *Humphry Clinker,*" in *Smollett: Author of the First Distinction,* edited by Alan Bold, Vision and Barnes and Noble, 1982, pp. 209-27.

[*In the following essay, Jack contends that Smollett uses the epistolary form in* Humphry Clinker *to provide a picture of reality that is truer because it is seen from a "variety" of viewpoints rather than simply through the eyes of a single narrator.*]

It was Robert Giddings who suggested that the one moral point made in *Humphry Clinker* concerned the difference between appearance and reality. He did not himself develop upon this thesis and indeed indicated that Smollett 'seems for the most part unaware of it'.[1] But an overtly didactic approach to the theme would have been completely out of place in a work which makes its comments much more subtly.[2] I believe that various possible oppositions between appearance and reality are explored in *Humphry Clinker,* and that while they do not form the thematic core of a novel which self-evidently does not have a thematic core, an examination of this topic does lead to a more thorough understanding of the work.

To begin with, the two central narrative lines in the novel are examples of this opposition. Wilson who appears to be a poor actor and therefore wholly unsuitable socially as a marriage partner for Lydia is actually the son of a respected family and so an ideal husband! Humphry, the unwanted derelict, turns out to be Matthew's natural child. The novel contains two 'discovery' plots and in the simplest terms we move from appearance to reality; illusion to truth. But Smollett goes to some trouble to develop these basic situations and he does so in contrasting ways.

With Wilson, the audience is let in on the secret from the outset. In his own letter he indicates that he is concealing his true identity, while Lydia at an early stage writes, 'I am still persuaded that he is not what he appears to be' (p. 37).[3] The various disguises he chooses strengthen the idea of a man who is sustaining an illusion. He initially makes his living as an actor (a creator of illusions). He passes himself off as a seller of spectacles, thus keeping others in darkness by pretending to improve their sight. In short, he accepts that in order to gain his genuine ends he must adapt to a world which worships appearance. He does this so successfully that poor Lydia at the fancy dress party faints at the sight of a man dressed up as one of the characters Wilson had portrayed in the theatre and later when he actually rides past, she thinks he is a ghost, 'Good God! did he really appear? or was it only a phantom, a pale spectre to apprise me of his death?' (p. 349). On the one hand, therefore, he draws sincere characters into his world of illusion and deception. Lydia, after all, deceives her family in order to maintain the liaison. But more importantly he shows up a society which in many ways is anxious to accept the appearance and blind itself to the reality due to social prejudices. His subterfuge is occasioned by his refusal to go along with an 'arranged' marriage. Its success is largely sustained because people are guided in their judgements by preconceptions of class. Who would look for a man of respectable family among a company of players? The most extreme and most comic example of this sort of blindness is, of course, Jerry. So long as Wilson is an actor, he is beneath contempt—'I know not what to call him' (p. 36). As soon as he is a prospective landowner, he becomes 'one of the most accomplished young fellows in England' (p. 374). Wilson's answer, then, is actively to use the weapons of a prejudiced society against that society. His energetic embracing of his world of illusion serves to highlight a variety of more pernicious illusions harboured by others.

Humphry Clinker's situation is entirely different. As readers we are given no earlier hints of his true pedigree. We therefore accept him as the simple servant he believes himself to be. And Humphry's simplicity, even more than Wilson's acting, condemns the society around him as one which worships appearance and denies true worth. Admittedly it also makes him act foolishly as when he tries to rescue Matthew from a non-existent drowning but generally he stands out as a figure of simple virtue lost in a world which cannot understand honest values. Smollett uses a variety of techniques to underline this point. Most obviously there are direct character contrasts. His simple appearance and hypocritical wooing of Dutton. His honest (if naïve) Christianity is set beside Tabitha's egocentric brand of the same creed. ('God forbid that I should lack christian charity; but charity begins at huom', p. 190.) At other times his oppressed situation provides Matthew Bramble with the opportunity to expatiate on the way in which men pay lip service to ideals which in practice their every action contradicts. Such an instance occurs when first we meet Clinker and Matthew castigates the landlord as a 'Christian of bowels' (p. 113). This is a technique which works in reverse, for occasionally the straightforward vision of Clinker is used to reveal Bramble's own besetting prejudice—his rigidly hierarchical vision of society. Thus when the master orders his servant to cease preaching on the grounds that such an occupation ill befits one of the lower orders, Clinker, with apparent naïvety, counters:

> May not the new light of God's grace shine upon the poor and ignorant in their humility, as well as upon the wealthy and the philosopher in all his pride of human learning? (p. 170)

From the moment he appears, rejected as a man because of his poverty and as a postilion because his trousers split, Clinker is relentlessly used to indicate the hypocrisy and the superficiality of those values which permeate society—that is, both the appearance which conceals a directly contradictory reality and the appearance, overconcern with which, causes false, prejudiced attitudes. The two combine in the scene where Humphry is arrested, an incident which reminds one of the Morality dramas at the stage where Vice rules and Dame Chastity is confined to the stocks as a whore. What society is this in which the most honest of men can be convicted as a thief? What degree of prejudice must have existed in the minds of those spectators who see sure signs of villainy in a face which is 'the very picture of simplicity'? (p. 178) What double standards exist in a court of law whose presiding judge sends to jail a man whom he knows innocent? What hope is there for integrity when the hesitation of simplicity is construed as prevarication and religious reservations on man's generally sinful nature seized upon as proof of particular guilt? This is a court of justice in appearance only. It is also a microcosm of that larger society which is characterized by prejudice, the worship of externals, deceit and hypocrisy. In their different ways the passive Humphry and the ingenious Wilson underline this fact.

In terms of the initial distinction between reality and appearance, we have three rather different levels. There is first of all the simple dramatic opposition we have just been discussing. But this 'discovery' element on the narrative level has introduced two further approaches to the theme. There is the level of hypocrisy and deceit in which the truth is known and a 'mask' consciously created in order to make others accept that 'mask' for the 'face'. The perpetrators of such situations inevitably feed on the folly of another group who see only the surface and accept it with no desire to probe deeper. Their dedication to worldly values obscures their vision, leaving them a prey both to the trickery of the manipulators and to the surface attractions of the new, luxurious, town society which Smollett appears to have distrusted so much. One group deserves the other. One presents a false appearance in order to obscure the reality; the other accepts false appearances sometimes wilfully, sometimes due to folly. Clearly Smollett is arguing that such behaviour characterizes much of British society in the later eighteenth century. The next portion of this study will be concerned with this, ultimately moral, argument and I shall be arguing that he sees falsity of this sort in individual characters, in a wide variety of institutions and in the deepest human relationships of friendship and love.

The third level is the most complex of all and in a sense it may appear to go beyond the opposition between reality and appearance. There are five letter writers in *Humphry Clinker*.[4] Each writer views life and frequently identical situations in life very differently. If Matthew, Jerry, Lydia, Win and Tabitha each observes Bath and paints for us a picture which bears no resemblance to that presented by the others, where then is the reality, where the appearance? In the final part of this article I shall endeavour to show first of all how Smollett does introduce this idea of 'appearance' as vision—people, events, countries viewed through the prejudices and preconceptions of a variety of observers. But I shall also, through an analysis of his literary techniques, prove that he usually guides us towards a more balanced overview, using our knowledge of the characters, their social positions, their agreements and disagreements to achieve this end.

The novel is, of course, full of hypocrites. Many of the most memorable prove to be Tabitha's suitors. Sir Ulic Mackilligut feigns an extreme passion for her, but his true motives are perceived by Bramble early on. 'He is said to be much out at elbows; and, I believe, has received false intelligence with respect to her fortune' (p. 77). This is indeed the case[5] and on discovering the true state of her purse the ingenious knight extricates himself from the situation by kicking her beloved dog Chowder, a sin for which there is no possible forgiveness. The Scottish advocate Micklewhimmen is an even more extreme example of the hypocritical suitor.

He begins by learning her governing obsession of the moment and professes to share it:

> As for Mrs. Tabitha, his respects were particularly addressed to her, and he did not fail to mingle them with religious reflections, touching free grace, knowing her bias to methodism, which he also professed upon a calvinistical model. (p. 207)

If Mackilligut was a hypocrite in love, Micklewhimmen's whole life is based on hypocrisy. His addresses to Tabitha have no serious intentions beyond making his life in Scarborough more comfortable. He feigns lameness so that people will cater for his every need. He drinks medicine which proves to be claret and generally fools the majority of the company into a spirit of sympathy and servitude. The complete falsity of his position is ludicrously revealed during the fire. The supposed invalid is one of the first to escape, 'running as nimble as a buck along the passage' (p. 208). And when Tabitha seeks his aid, he just pushes her down, ironically in so doing uttering one of her own favourite phrases, 'Na, na, gude faith, charity begins at hame' (p. 209). Despite his later desperate, sophistic attempts to justify his behaviour, he is finally seen by all in his true colours.

It is, however, undeniably the case that Tabitha attracts such hypocrites because her all-consuming desire for marriage blinds her to their true natures. She sees them as she wants them to be and so is the perfect gull. She also indulges in her own brand of hypocrisy. Once the possibility of matrimony emerges, she will forsake all her apparent principles. As Bramble puts it:

> Though she is a violent church-woman, of the most intolerant zeal, I believe in my conscience she would have no objection, at present, to treat on the score of matrimony with an Anabaptist, Quaker, or Jew; and even ratify the treaty at the expense of her own conversion. (p. 94)

Even the freethinking Lismahago's direct questioning of Christian tenets meets with little opposition from the pious spinster, who has decided *a priori* that he is 'a prodigy of learning and sagacity' (p. 232). Primarily, however, Smollett presents her as the sort of person who accepts 'appearances' if they are pleasing to her and has no desire to probe deeper. Indeed, she goes further and interprets the most obvious situations in an entirely fallacious manner, albeit consistent with her ruling passion. It does not need a hypocrite to mislead Tabitha. She is quite capable of misleading herself when faced with honesty. The most obvious instance of this occurs when Barton begins his rather timid wooing of Lydia. Both Matthew and Jerry see clearly the true nature of the young man's desires. Both also see the malicious role being played by Lady Griskin. But poor Tabitha errs at the outset:

> she mistakes, or affects to mistake, the meaning of his courtesy, which is rather formal and fulsome; she returns his compliments with hyperbolical interest. (p. 127)

and remains entirely deluded until the ludicrous/pathetic finale.

It is no coincidence that Win, who has largely modelled herself on Tabitha, can also be misled by appearance in matters of the heart. The flamboyantly dressed, glib-tongued Dutton, by appealing to her desire to rise above her station, briefly wins her away from Clinker. In situations of this sort Smollett is not only attacking those who, for selfish purposes, present a false mask to the world; he is also satirizing those whose prejudices, ruling passions or even simple naïvety make them overanxious to accept illusion for fact.

That said, the hypocrites in **Humphry Clinker** outnumber the gulls. Often too their hypocrisy is not set against folly but integrity. Serle may have been over-generous to Paunceford initially but his quiet stoicism in the face of his erstwhile protégé's complete ingratitude can only arouse admiration. Smollett skilfully contrasts the two characters. The one, once wealthy now poor; the other rising from poverty to riches. The one solitary; the other surrounded by gay company. The one even now refusing to denounce his friend; the other proclaiming his gratitude in words to others but staunchly avoiding any private confrontation or any practical return for all the benevolence he has been shown. The world of **Humphry Clinker** is one in which deviousness triumphs with great regularity, leaving honesty to suffer.

On a broader level, the worlds of law, politics and literature are shown to be false; further clear symptoms of a society in which appearance belies reality. Clinker's court case has already been mentioned but it deserves more detailed treatment because in it Smollett mounts a brief but powerful satire on the state of the law in England.[6] Everything is the opposite of what it appears to be. The innocent Clinker is accused of robbery by a man who himself turns out to be a thief. He is defended by Martin, the highwayman who is guilty of the very crime for which Clinker is being tried. The judge, with all his appearance of power, is in fact powerless. Legally he cannot deny the sworn evidence of the postilion. He cannot even grant Clinker bail but must send him to jail. This is in spite of the fact that he and everyone else with any influence in the court KNOW his innocence, the postilion's knavery and the true identity of the guilty party. What we are seeing is a grotesque charade, but one which could conceivably result in wrongful execution.

We are also told that the Judge and Martin who oppose each other in the court room and should be sworn enemies, given the conflicting nature of their chosen professions, are in fact on quite intimate terms:

> Sometimes they smoke a pipe together very lovingly, when the conversation generally turns upon the nature of evidence. (p. 182)

There is a sense in which the image of the 'club' which this evokes, applies to the court situation generally. There are those (like Martin) who are members and know the rules. There are others (like Clinker) who are not and do not. The former argue and manipulate; the latter are bewildered and oppressed. For the first group the 'rules' sometimes seem to become an end in themselves, the whole activity is a sort of game in which rhetorical skills are valued above the facts of the case. For the second group everything is much more grave for in the end it is their lives which may be at stake.

Thus the opposition between appearance and reality in the court of Justice Buzzard could scarcely be more clearcut nor the implied satire more damning. An uninitiated observer would suppose the honest Clinker dishonest, the roguish postilion an earnest upholder of the law, the actual highwayman a clever lawyer expertly handling a difficult case, and the inffectual judge all-powerful. As he observed the knowing looks passing from judge to defender, from thief-taker to thief-taker or heard the matter of fact, sometimes even light-hearted, tones of the major participants, he might be forgiven for thinking he was involved in some complex but essentially enjoyable game rather than watching a serious trial. But above all he would take a cynical act of complete injustice for the fair verdict which, on the most superficial level, it appears to be.

When Smollett turns his attention to politics, the opposition between reality and appearance is no less stark. Bramble and Jerry are taken to a levee arranged by the Duke of N——.[7] The whole event is itself a facade; a repetition of the sort of occasion held by the Duke when he possessed real power. Now, however, he is rejected and despised by the government of the day. His few remaining friends go through the motions as before 'to support the shadow of that power, which he no longer retains in substance' (p. 142). What appears to be a momentous political occasion is in fact a meaningless assembly.

Jerry and Bramble go there at the invitation of Barton, whose political and personal naïvety serves to highlight the deviousness of his fellow politicians. Their main companion is Captain C——, whose character and career reintroduce the theme of appearance and reality in highly complex fashion. To Barton, he is 'a man of shrewd parts' (p. 142), highly valued by the government. More reliable sources suggest that he was a fraudulent merchant who then became a spy in the English cause. Disguised as a Capuchin he hazarded his life in both France and Spain, gaining important information for the government. Jerry's letter, however, strongly suggests that he is a double agent; that he really is a priest and that his true allegiance lies with France. Their guide, therefore, is a man whose whole livelihood depends on deception and it would appear that he is in fact deceiving the very people who believe he is deceiving on their behalf.

But the major point stressed by Smollett in this vignette of British politics is that where one would expect wisdom, folly rules. He emphasizes this in a variety of ways, all bearing on the theme of reality and appearance. The Duke of N——proves himself a complete buffoon, mistaking the identity of nearly everyone at his own gathering:

> So saying, he wheeled about; and going round the levee, spoke to every individual, with the most courteous familiarity; but he scarce ever opened his mouth without making some blunder, in relation to the person or business of the party with whom he conversed; so that he really looked like a comedian, hired to burlesque the character of a minister. (p. 145)

So idiotic is he that a Turkish guest actually mistakes him for a professional fool, holding it a great marvel that Britain is ruled by a 'counsel of ideots' (p. 144).

The comments of Captain C—— strengthen this impression. He explains at great length how the government in their planning for war proved themselves unaware that Cape Breton was an island. In his opinion:

> They are so ignorant, they scarce know a crab from a cauliflower; and then they are such dunces, that there's no making them comprehend the plainest proposition. (p. 143)

For only one contemporary politician does he have any respect and that is C——T——.[8] But while the others appear wise yet are in fact foolish, Townshend belies truth in another way:

> There's no faith to be given to his assertions and no trust to be put in his promises. (p. 146)

In the legal world Bramble and his friends were faced with a facade of justice behind which lurked bribery, corruption and inadequate laws. In the political world they visit a man who clings to the appearance of power. They do this in the company of someone who appears to be a loyal Englishman but who is in all probability a double agent. They learn that behind the appearance of wisdom lies folly; behind promises and protestations of friendship lie falsity and political opportunism. Once more, briefly and poignantly, Smollett has indicated the great gap that exists between the appearance and the reality; the mask and the face.

The situation proves to be very much the same in the world of letters. Matthew and Jerry discover at least five different ways in which writers and scholars present a vision of themselves which is at odds with reality. There is first of all the conflict between the vision of the writer presented in his works and his private personality. Matthew in particular is upset to discover that one writer whose works he had read with particular pleasure, proves to be a dogmatic idiot, who can find reasons to condemn every other author except himself. And the more widely he mixes with men of letters, the more disillusioned he becomes. Fine ideas on paper may originate from petty, spiteful individuals intent only on self-advancement. As he writes to Dr. Lewis, 'For my part, I am shocked to find a man have sublime ideas in his head, and nothing but illiberal sentiments in his heart' (p. 138).

Related to this is the opposition between reputation and ability. In London Jerry is invited to meet the leading wits and professors of the day. The wits he finds insipid, confessing that he had 'never passed a duller evening in (his) life' (p. 149). The professors parade their love for argument and tedious long-winded explanations, but in so doing also reveal their ignorance. Wherever he and Matthew go it is the same story. Men of reputed genius prove boring companions and generally where they have been led to expect intelligence, open discussion and generosity of sentiment, they find ignorance, superficial conversation and intense personal jealousies.

Another and more glaring example of reality and appearance in conflict is uncovered at the lunch given by S——.[9] There, a number of minor writers are assembled. Almost without exception they have devised glaring eccentricities, hoping in this manner to draw attention to themselves. Each of these eccentricities is completely at odds with the true character of the individual concerned. Thus one wears spectacles despite having particularly fine eyesight; another affects crutches 'though no man could leap over a stick with more agility' (p. 157); a third pretends to hate the country, although he was brought up there. They do these things because they are aware that without idiosyncrasies they would be revealed for the ordinary, boring people they are. As such they are perfect representatives of a literary society, which the novel presents as second-rate and hypocritical.

This falsity extends to their work. We learn that a book which deals with the niceties of the English language has been written by a Piedmontese; that a treatise on practical agriculture has been completed by a man who 'had never seen corn growing in his life' and

that another mastermind has just finished a study of his travels through Europe and Asia without himself venturing out of London. All of these studies bear the appearance of long research and serious thought. They turn out to be mere fantasies dreamt up by men whose own lives are as deceitful as the literature they produce.

On a personal level too they prove as expert as either lawyers or politicians at pretending friendship, while nursing envy or hatred in their hearts. This is most fully explored in Jerry's description of S——'s party. We learn that every one of his literary visitors is indebted to him in some way. As he talks with them, the relationships appear to be uncomplicated and generous. Yet Jerry is soon to learn that a high proportion of the critical abuse S—— has suffered in fact originated from the pens of these very men.[10] His companion attributes such behaviour to one source above all others. 'Envy (answered Dick) is the general incitement' (p. 164). This is to echo a judgement made earlier by Matthew, whose first encounter with the London literati had led him to ponder on the same subject:

> I am inclined to think, no mind was ever wholly exempt from envy; which, perhaps, may have been implanted as an instinct essential to our nature. (p. 138)

The literary world in *Humphry Clinker* is indeed a world of jealous factions, where minor criticisms lead to lifelong enmities; writers cannot bear to hear others praised and boost themselves by denigrating their rivals. Also, from a whole variety of angles, it is a world of appearance, peopled by men who create false images of themselves, show no integrity in their writing and gain reputations wholly at odds with their true ability. In letters, in politics and in law it is the image which is all important. True values are of secondary importance.

It is, I believe, because Smollett was so concerned with the theme of reality and appearance in *Humphry Clinker* that he devoted so much of the later part of the novel to a series of visits at which his central characters received starkly contrasting examples of hospitality. Hospitality is the outward, the social sign of friendship and love. In Scotland the group had uniformly received warm receptions. Indeed the only criticism proffered was that perhaps the Scots prided themselves too much on their hospitality.[11] Now in England between 30 September and 8 October, Bramble visits four different households. At the first, Lord Oxmington's, all is appearance. The meal is 'served up with much ostentation' (p. 321), but his Lordship only uses the event to demonstrate his own affluence and influence. He dismisses his guests as unfeelingly as he had treated them throughout the meal. There is no trace of real friendship here, as Bramble's furious reaction underlines.

The second visit, to Baynard, is in many ways similar. Once more the meal is ostentatious. It is composed almost entirely of foreign dishes; lacqueys stand behind the chairs and there is a veritable 'parade' of plate and china. Yet the rudeness shown by Mrs. Baynard, her aunt and son is even more extreme than Oxmington's. The difference lies in the disposition of poor Baynard. Crying, 'Friendship is undoubtedly the most precious balm of life!' (p. 333), he endeavours, despite his henpecked position, to make his old comrade welcome. But his infatuation for his wife has led him into a world in which 'appearance' is all. His house, once pleasant, has been extravagantly re-modelled according to her fashionable (if exccrable) architectural tastes. His estate, once profitable, has been turned into walks, shrubberies and an economic disaster. The number of servants has been dramatically increased solely to impress others. And the poorer Baynard in fact becomes, the richer he must appear to be. His own genuine feelings remain but the world into which he invites Bramble and his company is false in every other particular as the ostentatious, friendless hospitality underlines.

The third visit, to Sir Thomas Bullford, in many ways represents an advance on the earlier ones. The pervading spirit is one of mirth; the meal appears to be more than adequate and his wife proves as friendly and genuine as Mrs. Baynard had been offhand and false. Yet we are still not in a world of genuine love and friendship. Bullford's guests are there primarily to promote his own enjoyment. He is more concerned with making them sources of laughter through his talent for practical joking than caring for their needs. It is, in this context, important that the meal, though good, is used as a practical joke, which convinces one guest that he is about to die. It is true that when Lismahago turns the tables on Bullford, the latter takes it in good spirit, but basically we have an egocentric host and, once more, the appearance of friendship rather than the genuine thing. After all, as Jerry points out, 'the greatest sufferer' (p. 346) of the baronet's wit is likely to be Bramble, whose health is not robust enough to stand the shocks and 'night-alarms' in which Bullford glories. A true friend would have understood this and desisted from self-indulgence.

Thus, before introducing the novel's three marriages, Smollett has used three contrasting visits to highlight the various false forms friendship and love may take. He has done this by continuing to examine, although in a different context, the opposition between appearance and reality. In the fourth and last visit, to Dennison, he presents the positive vision. Dennison's lifestyle contrasts in particular with that of Baynard. He is married to a loving wife completely lacking in preten-

tiousness. Instead of ruining a flourishing estate, he has turned one on the verge of ruin into a profitable enterprise. Instead of living beyond his means in order to keep up with the neighbours, he lives within his means and scorns their opinion of his household.[12] Now at last Bramble and his companions find hospitality, friendship and love free from pretence of any sort.

So far the oppositions between appearance and reality have seemed quite clear and I think there is no doubt that Smollett intended to satirize eighteenth-century Britain, and in particular eighteenth-century England, as a land dominated at every level by false or superficial values. But he does choose to do this by presenting the opinions of five clearly contrasted characters. Of these at least three present misleading visions of themselves to society. Bramble's affected misanthropy conceals the heart of a sentimental philanthropist. Tabitha's prudery and extreme religious enthusiasm hide the passions born of long frustration. And Win in her letters depicts herself as a tight-lipped confidante before revealing to Molly every detail of gossip known to her. Each of the five sees his own 'reality' and often the definitions of that reality differ sharply. This is most obvious when they are visiting towns and passing comment on them. For Lydia, Bath is a place of wonder and romance:

> an earthly paradise. The Square, the Circus, and the Parades, put you in mind of the sumptuous palaces represented in prints and pictures; and the new buildings, such as Prince's row, Harlequin's row, Bladud's row, and twenty other rows, look like so many enchanted castles, raised on hanging terraces. (p. 68)

For Jerry, it is primarily an exciting social centre:

> I am, on the contrary, amazed to find so small a place so crowded with entertainment and variety. (p. 78).

For Bramble, viewing it with the eye of aged cynicism, it is 'the very centre of racket and dissipation' (p. 63), a gaudy show, signifying primarily the breakdown of a society in which everything and everybody had its appointed place. For Win it is where she dropped her petticoat and achieved a new worldly vision which places her in a position of superiority to Molly Jones: 'But this is all Greek and Latten to you, Molly' (p. 73). Tabitha's comments suggest that Bath as such makes no impression on her at all. She is more concerned with the practicalities of running the home in Wales and curbing the generosity of her brother to his servants. Yet she is writing formally to her housekeeper and the letters of the others strongly suggest that Bath, like any other place on earth, is merely a source of hypothetical husbands.

Each of these visions is the truth for its creator and on one level reality is what any individual chooses to believe. Smollett is, therefore, exploring a rather different aspect of the reality/appearance problem. In a sense there are as many Baths as people to view them. What is the truth about the town for Lydia is almost exactly the antithesis of the truth for Matthew. Smollett even introduces in Lismahago a character whose nature drives him to believe that the most evident truths are falsities, arguing his paradoxical convictions with great energy and ingenuity:

> I believe in my conscience he has rummaged, and read, and studied with indefatigable attention, in order to qualify himself to refute established maxims, and thus raise trophies for the gratification of polemical pride. (p. 237).

Yet Lismahago's sincerity is never seriously called into question. He is the most extreme example of the relativity of vision; one for whom each apparent truth must be, *a priori*, a falsity. The more obvious a situation appears to be, the more emphatically will Lismahago argue the contrary case.

But does Smollett leave us there? Does he simply say there is no absolute truth, just a number of perspectives? I do not think his position is as extreme as that, although he does patently argue that Bramble's Bath is as real for him as Lydia's for her. Perhaps a second comment on Lismahago will help to explain his position. Jerry also sums up the man's nature:

> The lieutenant was, by this time, become so polemical, that every time he opened his mouth out flew a paradox, which he maintained with all the enthusiasm of altercation; but all his paradoxes favoured strong of a partiality for his own country. (p. 237)

In each case (as here) we are given careful outlines of the prejudices, education and nature of the characters whose opinions dominate the book. Lismahago, as a man who questions 'appearances' in a society which fosters falsity in so many forms must and does strike the note of truth with some frequency. When he argues against Bramble that the Union has done nothing but ill for the Scots, we sense that he is in many instances right. But we know his love of paradoxicality and his intense patriotism and so realize that he is probably over-stating.[13] In a similar way we know Lydia's confined upbringing and the romantic novels on which she has been nurtured. We consider her vision of Bath in that light. Bramble's ill-health and defensive misanthropy; Win's superficiality and Tabitha's governing obsession—all these are made clear to the reader and his judgements are tempered by that knowledge.

But such breadth of vision combined with the knowledge of individual idiosyncrasies can also work in the opposite way, arguing for incontrovertible truths as well as conditioned responses. When Bramble nearly dies everyone is overcome with relief at his recovery. Here the disparity of character argues for the fact that undeniably he is a good and lovable man. If Tabitha and Lydia, Jerry and Win (not to mention Humphry) all lament then the ultimate benevolence of this self-styled misanthropist can be in no doubt. The case is the same with Clinker. Everyone, although for different reasons, vouches for his worth and integrity. For Jerry, he is 'honest Humphry' (p. 185), a man for whose courage and loyalty he has the highest esteem. For Matthew, his 'character is downright simplicity, warmed with a kind of enthusiasm, which renders him very susceptible of gratitude and attachment to his benefactors' (p. 186). He wins over Tabitha after making such a bad impression initially. In her opinion, he is 'a sober civilized fellow; very respectful, and very industrious; and . . . a good Christian into the bargain' (p. 132). Even Lydia terms him 'a deserving young man' (p. 297), while Win expresses her admiration in the most extreme fashion possible by marrying him. The very different personalities of the letter writers guarantee that when they do agree on any topic, the reader is unlikely to arrive at a different conclusion.

If Smollett sometimes uses unanimity of vision to guide his readers' reactions, he also uses what I shall, for convenience, term 'inversion of vision', for the same purpose. If someone's most confirmed prejudices are overturned, this is strong evidence that the influence upon him or her is real. It is in this sense that I believe **Humphry Clinker** to be, on balance, a book written with a bias in Scotland's favour. Not because Lismahago argues so ingeniously, for Lismahago's character is built on ingenuity and paradoxicality. Nor because Smollett drops any pretence at narrative continuity to focus on the country's characteristics.[14] But because in Scotland, Bramble the cynic at times begins to sound like Lydia in his romanticism and enthusiasm:

> I should be very ungrateful, dear Lewis, if I did not find myself disposed to think and speak favourably of this people, among whom I have met with more kindness, hospitality, and rational entertainment, in a few weeks, than ever I received in any other country during the whole course of my life. (p. 267)

He sees Loch Lomond and finds it 'romantic beyond imagination' (p. 286). These reactions contrast so markedly with his jaundiced opinions of Bath, London and Scarborough that we feel Scotland must really possess the qualities he attributes to it.

Sometimes too, we are faced with comments which,

although apparently opposed, are in fact complementary. Both Win and Tabitha, for example, discuss the position of servants in Scotland. Here we have an initial inclination to believe the former. For the most part she is presented as foolish and impressionable but she is herself a servant. Just as we might be prepared to accept Jerry's assessment of University life or Bramble's comments on estate management in preference to the views of the others, so in this case we know that she alone has first-hand experience of the situation. And for Win, although the Scots are 'civil enuff' (p. 257), she is horrified by their treatment of menials: 'the sarvants of the country . . . are pore drudges, many of them without shoes or stockings' (p. 257). Her horror is only matched by Tabitha's enthusiasm. She finds the whole situation admirable and wonders why their enlightened approach is not more widely practised:

> I don't see why the servants of Wales shouldn't drink fair water, and eat hot cakes and barley cale, as they do in Scotland, without troubling the botcher above once a quarter. (p. 313)

We know, however, that one of Tabitha's principal aims in life is to keep the lower orders existing on the most minimal expense account possible. Paradoxically, therefore, her approbation serves to strengthen rather than oppose Win's evidence. Given the social situation of the one and the known prejudices of the other, it becomes clear that Scots treat visiting gentry with overpowering kindness but that their servants are resolutely kept in penury.

To 'unanimity of vision', 'inversion of vision' and 'opposed but complementary visions', we might add finally the 'development of vision'. It is true that most of the characters in **Humphry Clinker** do not change much throughout the novel despite the many experiences which befall them.[15] The major exception to this rule is Lydia. Naïve, idealistic and easily led at the outset, she becomes gradually more forceful and realistic as the journey progresses:

> There is such malice, treachery and dissimulation even among professed friends and intimate companions, as cannot fail to strike a virtuous mind with horror; and when Vice quits the stage for a moment, her place is immediately occupied by Folly, which is often too serious to excite anything but compassion. (p. 348)

These words were not penned by Bramble, as one might have supposed, but by Lydia towards the end of her travels. Her opinion confirms the viewpoints of her uncle and brother but it is more striking because it comes from one who, at the outset, saw romance and sincerity everywhere. It is her experience of society which has transformed her outlook and we sense that she cannot be wrong.

If we apply all this evidence to the topic of reality and appearance, we may say that on one level Smollett does argue that everyone's perception of reality differs. As Donald Bruce notes, 'Much of **Humphry Clinker** is a bland statement of the subjectivity of human outlook.'[16] At the same time, using the techniques I have analysed, Smollett gives the reader an 'overview'. This 'overview' is not imposed. The reader is invited to enter and sympathize with the opinions of each letter writer. They are all, in their own ways, lovable. But he is given insights into their strengths and limitations; their visions and prejudices. In any situation, therefore, he can weigh up the comparative authority of each writer's evidence. In this way Smollett uses the breadth of his chosen epistolary form to guide us towards the truth as he sees it. By drawing together a variety of limited outlooks he provides us with a varied and convincing picture of British life in the late eighteenth century. Behind all the 'appearances' we perceive a reality.

Notes

[1] Robert Giddings, *The Tradition of Smollett* (London, 1967), p. 149.

[2] I cannot agree with the allegorical interpretation of the work advanced by M. A. Goldberg in *Smollett and the Scottish School* (Albuquerque, 1959): 'But symbolically, the expedition is a moral journey which culminates in the *expediting* or *freeing* of Humphry Clinker from the fetters of poverty, hunger, nakedness, and anonymity', p. 153.

[3] All quotations and page references are taken from *Humphry Clinker,* ed. Angus Ross (Harmondsworth, 1978).

[4] This excludes the single letter written by 'Wilson' to Lydia from Gloucester.

[5] Win is the conveyor of this false information as she reveals in her letter to Molly (Bath, 26 April).

[6] Later he deals much more favourably with the legal system in Scotland.

[7] Thomas Pelham-Holles (1693-1768), Duke of Newcastle.

[8] Charles Townshend (1725-67), Chancellor of the Exchequer in Pitt's second ministry.

[9] Smollett himself.

[10] Much of Smollett's unpopularity derived from the fact that for some time he was director of the influential literary journal *The Critical Review*.

[11] 'I am afraid that even their hospitality is not quite free of ostentation' (Matthew to Lewis; Edinburgh, 8 August).

[12] Laurence Brander, *Tobias Smollett* (London, 1951), notes, 'Matthew Bramble, in his letters about Dennison and Baynard, expresses the eighteenth-century nostalgia for the ideal country life, the craving for a well-ordered society based on the perennial round of toil on the good earth.' It is a nostalgia which Smollett appears to have shared to some degree.

[13] Louis L. Martz, *The Later Career of Tobias Smollett* (Yale, 1942), argues persuasively that 'The satire of England and encomium of Scotland may well represent Smollett's attempt to reconcile himself with those of his countrymen who were offended with *The Present State of All Nations*' (p. 130). But Smollett does find much to criticize in Scotland in *Humphry Clinker* and he is careful to make its most voluble protagonist (Lismahago) a man whose views are suspect for the reasons noted above.

[14] See M. A. Goldberg, *op. cit.*, p. 163.

[15] See Robert Giddings, *op. cit.*, p. 144. 'There is one important aspect of character lacking, however, and this is development. Matthew Bramble's character does not develop as, for example, Peregrine's does.'

[16] Donald Bruce, *Radical Doctor Smollett* (London, 1964), p. 55. But he also comments that 'since it allows for the variations of prejudice and opinion, the book is all the more valid as a survey of England [*sic*] in the late eighteenth century.'

Jerry C. Beasley (essay date 1985)

SOURCE: "Smollett's Art: The Novel As 'Picture,'" in *The First English Novelists: Essays in Understanding*, edited by J. M. Armistead, The University of Tennessee Press, 1985, pp. 143-58.

[*In the following excerpt, Beasley compares the vivid, episodic, and grotesque world of* Roderick Random *with Hogarth's serial engravings, and observes that Smollett's narratives possess great visual power and impact.*]

"A Novel," remarked Tobias Smollett in the mock-dedication (to himself) introducing *The Adventures of Ferdinand Count Fathom* (1753), is "a large diffused picture, comprehending the characters of life, disposed in different groupes, and exhibited in various attitudes, for the purposes of an uniform plan."[1] These comments represent, in part, the only extended statement Smollett ever made concerning a theory of fiction, and they have usually been dismissed by critics as conventional

and trite or as irrelevant to any meaningful understanding of his work. But actually they are quite crucial, for they exactly describe the intentions with which their author approached each of his five novels, different as they all are from one another.

The brief analogy to painting was, in other words, no mere exercise in metaphor. Smollett's conception of his novelistic art may in fact be best illustrated by reference, not to the works of a writer like his contemporary Henry Fielding, whose *Tom Jones* has been so justly praised for the beauties of its organic design, but to such famous series of dramatic paintings as William Hogarth's *Industrious Apprentice* and *Rake's Progress*.[2] In any case, Smollett was a deliberately experimental storyteller whose imagination apprehended experience directly in the scattered fragments by which it presented itself to his observing eye. In composing his narratives he sought always for meaningful forms, but he cared little for the conventional laws of causality and process. Instead, he turned his fertile genius enthusiastically to the creation of self-contained episodes occurring in hurried succession, each rendered as a separate dramatic picture of assorted and often wonderfully eccentric character types engaged in abrasive interaction with a fast-moving central personage or (in *Humphry Clinker*) group of personages.[3]

One of the chief pleasures in reading Smollett's stories arises from the continual surprises made possible by the fragmentation of their structures. The individual parts of a seemingly erratic Smollett plot, like the scenes in a Hogarth series, do eventually add up to a whole, but by a method more cumulative than linear. There is always resolution at the end, the fulfillment of a "uniform plan." Roderick Random gets his beloved Narcissa; Matt Bramble goes home happy and healthy to Wales. Resolution occurs, however, only after passage through the entire gallery of pictorial episodes has been completed, when what has been observed and powerfully felt is at long last made fully intelligible to reader and protagonist alike. With understanding comes redemption and, finally, the reward of happiness and repose. The endings of Smollett's novels are always providentially contrived and thus fanciful in some degree, though never quite gratuitously so. They identify him as a comic writer who subscribed to, and reflected, a generally optimistic Christian interpretation of history, despite an abiding consciousness of human meanness and moral deformity that often drove him to the riotous cynicism of bitter Juvenalian satire.[4]

Smollett began writing novels when he was still young (*Roderick Random* came out just two months before his twenty-seventh birthday), though not as the result of some early ambition. He seems to have dabbled in poetry as a boy in Scotland, but his first and fondest hope was for fame as a playwright. When he left home for London in 1739, he had folded away in his pocket a quite inferior tragedy, *The Regicide,* with which he expected to dazzle the great city. He also carried with him letters of introduction from the two Glasgow surgeons he had served as apprentice, William Stirling and John Gordon. Smollett may have dreamed of literary celebrity, but he needed a livelihood, and surgery was to provide it. Though descended from an old and respected Dumbartonshire family, he was poor. His father, Archibald Smollett, had defied his parents by marrying a penniless woman and had been disinherited. When Archibald died shortly after Tobias's birth in March 1721, he left his wife and children to depend for their livelihood upon the small and uncertain kindnesses of relatives. The future novelist was lucky enough to study at the local grammar school for five or six years and then to attend lectures at Glasgow University. He entered upon his appreticeship in 1737, but a persistent cough determined him to seek a warmer climate, and so he set off for London to pursue a medical career there. And indeed for most of the following decade he did so with some vigor, although with only modest success.

Smollett met with nothing but frustration in his efforts to have *The Regicide* produced upon the stage. The bitterness of this early failure never entirely left him, partly because he kept renewing it over the next several years with periodic fresh assaults upon the good will and judgment of theatrical managers. Finally, after the success of *Roderick Random* had earned him a certain recognition, he simply published the play by subscription in 1749 and thereafter gave up hope of ever seeing it acted. His unhappy adventure with *The Regicide* did, however, furnish him with materials for the story of the poet Melopoyn that occupies Chapters 61-63 of his first novel, where Smollett damned those who (so he believed) had mistreated him. *Roderick Random* draws heavily upon other early experiences of its author, including the vividly remembered misfortunes of his family at the hands of a stingy and hardhearted grandfather. His years with Stirling and Gordon gave Smollett abundant opportunities to observe firsthand the quackery and charlatanism of eighteenth-century medical practice. Stirling and Gordon were themselves gifted and devoted physicians, but many of their colleagues were not. The situation was even worse in London, and Smollett made the deception, hypocrisy, and incompetence of doctors and apothecaries an important subject for satiric treatment in *Roderick Random* and indeed in all of his novels.

In April 1740, probably out of a desperate need for money, Smollett completed the required examinations and shipped as a surgeon's mate on board the *Chichester,* an eighty-gun man-of-war registered with the fleet sent out to prosecute the new war against Spain. He was present at Carthagena, where the British navy suffered a bloody and humiliating defeat, and this

experience was the obvious source for Roderick Random's adventures as one of the crew of the *Thunder.* Smollett devoted a substantial portion of his story (Chapters 24-37) to his hero's shipboard days, and his account of the horrors of eighteenth-century sailing life is still considered one of the most graphic and authentic we possess. By 1744, Smollett was back in London, newly married to the daughter of a Jamaican plantation owner and ready to take up once more his vocation as a surgeon and his avocation as a writer. The latter, it appears, occupied his attention in a share disproportionate to the rewards it brought him, at least during the several years preceding *Roderick Random.* He made no further progress with the fortunes of *The Regicide,* and the four poems he managed to publish earned him little recognition and less money. Two of these poems, *Advice* (September 1746) and *Reproof* (January 1747), are satires in imitation of Alexander Pope. They are negligible things of their kind, but in composing them, Smollett may have gotten the idea for his first novel, which he conceived—as he explained in a letter to his Scottish friend Alexander Carlyle—as a "Satire on Mankind."

This new work was written hurriedly—"begun and finished," Smollett wrote to Carlyle, "in the Compass of Eight months, during which time several Intervals happened of one, two, three and four Weeks, wherein I did not set pen to paper."[6] At the close of all this frenzied activity, *The Adventures of Roderick Random* was published in two duodecimo volumes on 21 January 1748; and it proved an immediate and enduring favorite with the public. Three editions totaling 6,500 copies (a very large number in those days) had appeared by November 1749; thereafter the novel was translated into German (1754) and French (1761), while it continued to be reprinted and read in a dozen English editions throughout the remaining years of the eighteenth century. The most resplendent of these, issued in London in 1792, was adorned by the illustrations of Thomas Rowlandson. Eventually, the fame of Smollett's book spread all over Europe, and indeed only a very few other English novels of its early period (one of them was Smollett's own *Humphry Clinker*) managed to equal or exceed *Roderick Random* in general popularity.

No doubt the extraordinary appeal of Smollett's novel derived in part from his ability to join in a fresh combination the attractions of several different kinds of familiar narrative: rogue or picaresque "biography," the imaginary voyage, the sentimental novel of love and intrigue, the romance of disinheritance and discovery. In its eclecticism, *Roderick Random* closely resembles the work of its author's nearest rivals, Samuel Richardson and Henry Fielding. It is important to remember that in the mid-eighteenth century the modern novel was still in its formative stages, and every major writer of fiction (and some not so major) was engaged in experiments involving the re-creation of conventional materials into what Richardson called a "new species of writing."[7] Like Fielding, Smollett was deeply influenced by Cervantes, whose immensely popular *Don Quixote* he signed on to translate sometime during the year 1748.[8] His most immediate model for the story of **Roderick Random,** however, was the celebrated *History and Adventures of Gil Blas of Santillane,* by Alain René LeSage, an episodic picaresque tale of roguish escapades that had for several decades enjoyed an enthusiastic following in translation from the French. As it happens, Smollet was preparing a brand-new English version of *Gil Blas* while **Roderick Random** was regaling its first readers, and he may actually have begun this task before sending his own book to the printer.[9] We may be sure that LeSage's lively story was in Smollett's mind, along with his own recently published verse satires, during those "Eight months" of furiously sporadic writing in 1747 when he happened upon his real talent as a novelist.

Despite his acknowledged admiration for *Gil Blas,* Smollett makes it plain in the preface to **Roderick Random** that he means to depart significantly from the example of LeSage. Gil Blas, he observes, is hardly credible as a moral agent: the fictional environment through which he travels is projected as too neutral, and there is little in his character to command anyone's sympathetic identification. Or, as Smollett himself puts it, the "conduct" of LeSage's picaro "prevents that generous indignation, which ought to animate the reader, against the sordid and vicious disposition of the world."[10] Roderick struggles through life in a pattern of fits and starts, ups and downs, and seemingly aimless wandering that superficially resembles the course of Gil Blas's adventures, and the two characters are much alike in their raw instincts for survival, their resourcefulness, and their function as outsiders who become instruments of satire. Both Smollett and LeSage seem deeply conscious of the long tradition of picaresque narrative, extending back to the Spanish prototype in *The Life of Lazarillo de Tormes* (1554), as a species of satiric writing against the chaos and destruction with which a corrupt society threatens the individual. Smollett, however, introducs a dimension of moral idealism into his version of the picaresque, which is typically so limited by cynicism as to preclude all possibility of such idealism. Roderick, a "friendless orphan" beset by "his own want of experience" as well as the "selfishness, envy, malice, and base indifference of mankind,"[11] is not only a vehicle of satire but also the object of Smollett's severe judgment for his understandable yet punishable failure to recognize the world's dark "apparitions" for what they are and for his consequent near-descent into self-destruction.[12]

Roderick Random is actually built upon a foundation of paradox, and in its tentative way it anticipates the later *Bildungsroman,* or "education" novel. Experience beleaguers one so violently and mercilessly, it appears, that pain and continual hardship inevitably seem to constitute the only reality that matters, just as a response in indignation and cynicism seems the only alternative to passive submission and thus absorption. Chance governs the world, which is without hope. The episodic structure of **Roderick Random,** with its long pauses over unpredictably disparate incidents and the characters who play them out dramatically with the hero, enforces this sense of things. But unrestrained indignation negates moral identity, for it is the surest means to helpless identification with what is being scourged.[13] Nothing less than reliance on the ideals of love, Roderick must learn, can redeem the self and ensure release from the threat of ensnarement.

The pattern of providential interventions in **Roderick Random** and the final, complete transformation of its fictional world affirm Smollett's belief in the ultimate precedence of a moral reality that provides the only meaningful framework for human happiness, indeed for the preservation of personal integrity. Smollett was no fool; he knew that even the most determinedly pious do not always thrive in real life. There is a strong element of the Christian fable in **Roderick Random,** as there is to one extent or another in all of Smollett's novels—and in many others of his day besides (*Robinson Crusoe,* for example, and *Pamela,* and *The Vicar of Wakefield*). Smollett's story, we may say, is an intricately detailed metaphor defining the very meaning of human redemption from the thralldom of wordly evil. In this respect, **Roderick Random** bears strong resemblances to Fielding's more famous *Tom Jones.*[14] Fielding's world is potentially as dark and perverse as Smollett's, and his wayward hero, like Roderick, must rise into self-knowledge from a nadir of misfortunes and personal failure before he can enjoy the reward of marriage to his beauteous heroine. But there the resemblances end. Fielding provides a buffer against villainy in the voice of his playful ironic narrator, and he never permits the reader to forget that his "history" is a work of careful artifice, a deliberate "Creation" that proclaims in its every device the ordering power of comic and providential vision. Smollett, in effect, turns the imaginary world of a Fielding upside down and inside out. His angle of vision is very different; it does not allow for much protection of his characters or his reader against irruptions of stupidity or meanness or violence in the fictional environment.

Even in **Peregrine Pickle, Ferdinand Count Fathom,** and **Sir Launcelot Greaves**—all of which (like Fielding's novels) employ third-person narrators to relay their respective stories of roguery, villainy, and comic quixotism—the representation of experience focuses on the way it is registered by the consciousness of the character who must live it and eventually arrive at some interpretation of it. Smollett is by no means a psychological novelist in the twentieth-century sense of the term, but he proves much more interested than Fielding in capturing the sometimes crazily textured immediacy of life's felt hardships, perplexities, and rewards. In *Roderick Random* and *Humphry Clinker,* two novels in which he relies on the carefully particularized voices of imagined characters as the instruments of transmission, the effects of immediacy are uncommonly powerful. *Roderick Random,* because it projects so convincingly the illusion of an angry "autobiographical" account of personal suffering and misjudgments, has actually fooled many readers (among them several modern critics) into believing that Roderick is a self-portrait of his author, whose performance in the work (some say) so lacks detachment and so confuses the relationship between narrator and audience that it must be judged at least a partial failure.[15]

There can be no doubt of Smollett's emotional identification with his hero, whose experience does in numerous details exactly coincide with his own; and it is likely that the strength of that identification influenced the course of his narrative, even promoted the improvisational qualities of certain richly textured and extended episodes. But it might be argued from a strictly technical standpoint that in *Roderick Random,* as in Defoe's novels or the epistolary narratives of Richardson, the author has retreated to a position of near-invisibility behind the completed product of his creative energy, whatever its sources, leaving his readers to a difficult process of participation and discovery as the principal means toward understanding the story and their own responses. If Smollett had chosen to preserve the anonymity under which he originally published his first work of fiction, or if we knew even less than we do about the facts of his troubled childhood and youth, then the issue of authorial distance might never have arisen to deflect criticism away from a proper consideration of what the text of *Roderick Random* actually means and what it achieves as an innovative and enduring early example of novelistic art.

In any event, the moral ambiguity and the complications of reader response that Smollett attempted in *Roderick Random* go far beyond anything to be found in picaresque tales like *Gil Blas* and *Lazarillo,* not to mention the hundreds of popular rogue and criminal biographies that also form part of the background for the novel.[16] One generally knows how to take LeSage's rather transparent first-person narrator, or the eponymous Lazarillo, but there is much less certainty with Roderick. His character as a modestly virtuous young fellow of respectable birth and education predisposes the reader in his behalf (or so Smollett hoped, as he said in his preface), but the increasing violence with which he avenges himself upon a world that viciously attacks his idealism and good nature simultaneously promotes a vicarious pleasure and compels judgment.

In Chapter 20, when Roderick so brutally flogs and strips the wretched villain Captain O'Donnell, he does so out of a combination of mischief and uncontrollable fury, and his actions at least verge upon the criminal. What reader, however, does not share in the satisfaction Roderick feels? Yet what reader does not also recognize that by returning O'Donnell's meanness in kind, Smollett's young hero has sunk to his base level and must therefore be righteously repudiated? Righteousness is not always so easy to sustain as it is here, however. Often—during the episodes on board the *Thunder,* for example—Smollett deliberately endangers the members of his audience by trapping them into a unity of feeling with the increasingly cynical Roderick, causing a loss of distance that threatens to implicate the reader in the hero's failings, his desperation, his self-destructive rage. This novel does not make it easy for us to keep our balance.

Much of the dramatic and moral point of *Roderick Random* is to show how perversely seductive the wicked world can be and how awesome its power over the individual will. The price of the modern ideal of individualism, as Smollett and so many of his contemporaries were already beginning to understand, is a condition of lonely insignificance in the midst of a disordered, bewildering, and sometimes terrifying unknown. "I am old enough," Smollett wrote to David Garrick at the age of forty, "to have seen and observed that we are all playthings of fortune."[17] Roderick is a kind of modern Everyman figure, as his generalized last name suggests. But Smollett particularizes his hero's experience and intensifies our sense of his frightened loneliness by making him a Scotsman (like his author, of course) who, deprived early of the stability of a loving family, becomes the victim of ridicule and abuse in the deeply hostile environment of England. London and, later, the scenes of Roderick's naval adventures serve as almost overwhelming images of modern life in all its bustling inhumanity, grotesqueness, and uncertainty. The people in Roderick's world often seem not quite human. They are monstrosities of avarice, pride, and hypocrisy with names like Lavement, Gawky, Quiverwit, Whiffle, Wagtail, Badger, and Straddle; or, just as often, they are bestial figures with grasshopper legs or canine fangs.[18] Small wonder, then, that reality as Roderick encounters it seems not whole and safe but fragmented, portentous and threatening, void of compassion and love, disfigured.

For all his close attentiveness to the real "facts" of eighteenth-century English life, Smollett was no literary "realist." Roderick's experience of the world partakes of nightmare. Smollett projects this quality of his vision on the very first page of the story with a description of the horrid dream that came to the hero's mother just before her son's birth and her own melancholy death. In the dream Mrs. Random was "delivered of a tennis-ball," which the devil (her midwife) instantly knocked into oblivion, leaving her "inconsolable" until suddenly she beheld it return "with equal violence, and earth itself beneath her feet, whence immediately sprung up a goodly tree covered with blossoms."[19] The old sage who interprets the dream sees in it—rightly as it turns out—a happy conclusion, but also predicts the mercurial pattern of "dangers and difficulties" the child will have to live through. The dream is an involuntary act of prophecy on the part of the mother, and its image of the devil slamming her "offspring" so violently about exactly foreshadows not only the subsequent buffetings of the hero in a darkly evil world but also the nightmarish qualities of that world as he will learn to see it.

By this same device of the dream, Smollett establishes the identity of Roderick as a traveler whose motion is to be perpetual until at last it ceases, as the wise sage said it would, with a resolution in "great reputation and happiness." Percy G. Adams has shown, more convincingly than anyone, how the journey was adopted as a paradigm—a powerful metaphor, really—by Smollett and many other eighteenth-century novelists, who used it to organize their own understanding of experience and to shape their imaginative representations of its meaning.[20] Roderick's path of life is to take him through a succession of encounters with nightmarish "apparitions" in a progress that is partly willed but in the main profoundly directionless, simply because circumstance possesses the power to deflect individual volition. If the end of his journey signifies the perfection of understanding and thus of moral will, then the passage toward that conclusion must inevitably be a tortuous one.

Roderick's lack of real direction ensures great diversity in his adventures. It is of course his persistent presence—manifested in his intensive language, in his role as moral agent, in his restless movement toward decline and finally reward—that provides the unifying center of Smollett's novel. We may trace Roderick's movement, and at the same time exemplify the complex and vividly represented disarray of his world, by simply looking at three or four episodes spaced through his story. Roderick's miseries begin in earnest when he is only a boy, as do his outraged reactions to them. Orphaned, he is sent to school by the mean-spirited patriarch of his family in a condition of ragged wretchedness; there he is flogged when not ignored, and provoked into pranks and mischief, but he advances in his studies anyway—and is punished for it. To prevent him from writing letters begging relief from his grandfather, the schoolmaster "caused a board to be made with five holes in it," and, as Roderick tells us out of painful memory, through it "he thrust the fingers and thumb of my right hand, and fastened it by a whipcord to my wrist."[21] Roderick breaks free of this cruel restraint only by using it against the head of a schoolmate who insults his poverty. Daily brutalized at school,

he fares no better on play days at home, where his cousin (now, instead of Roderick, the grandfather's heir) delights in setting his hunting dogs upon him.

With the sudden appearance of the blustering, goodhearted Tom Bowling, one of this novel's more memorable examples of the eccentric sailing man, Smollett inaugurates a pattern that will include several providential interventions in behalf of his hero. The effects of Bowling's rescue and his beneficence are not long felt, however. Roderick thrives for a time at the university where his uncle installs him, but a reversal of fortune casts him upon his own devices. Now comes the first of Smollett's many pictures of grotesque subhumanity in the person of Mr. Launcelot Crab, the corrupt, drunken, and incompetent surgeon who—almost in a parody of Bowling's earlier gesture of avuncular kindness—extricates Roderick from the horrors of approaching want and despair by taking him on as an assistant. The figure of this man, as Roderick describes it, redoubles the suggestiveness of his surname (we may note also the irony carried by his Christian name) and provides an exact definition of his character. He is "about five foot high, and ten around the belly"; his face is fat and round "as a full moon, and much of the complexion of a mulberry," and it is adorned by an enormous nose "resembling a powderhorn" and "studded all over with carbuncles." This remarkable countenance is completed by a pair of "little grey eyes" that reflect the light of day in such an oblique way that when Mr. Crab looks straight ahead, he appears to be "admiring the buckle of his shoe."[22]

The portrait of Crab is a caricature, of course; as such, it succeeds by a strategy of distortion and reduction. What Crab represents, real enough to be sure, is made less dangerous by being thus formed into a ridiculous picture of itself, and Roderick is as able as the reader to laugh at and dismiss him. But as the smug lad is about to find out, nearly the whole world is populated by such grotesques, and they will gradually multiply and surround him. During his progress to London, Roderick meets a sizable collection of misshapen or perverse oddities aboard the wagon on which he hops a ride. His fellow passengers include a "brisk airy girl," obviously a prostitute, oddly dressed and brandishing a whip; a limping, hollow-eyed, wrinkled, toothless old usurer whose long nose and peaked chin approach one another like "a pair of nut-crackers" when he speaks; a thin, small, baboonlike "lady's woman" named Mrs. Weazel; and the amazing captain, her husband, whose bombast masks his cowardice and whose ludicrous appearance Smollett captures in one of the funniest descriptions in the entire novel. Weazel, as Roderick remembers him, was "about five foot and three inches high, sixteen inches of which went to his face and long scraggy neck; his thighs were about six inches in length, his legs resembling spindles or drum-sticks, two feet and an half, and his body, which put me in mind of extension without substance, engrossed the remainder;—so that on the whole, he appeared like a spider or grasshopper erect."[23]

In this cluster of ridiculous and affected characters, Smollett develops a composite portrait of mankind, occasioned by an adaptation from one of the oldest conventions of storytelling and travel narrative, the journey by coach—here, comically, a wagon; and the portrait is presently elaborated by means of the equally ancient convention of riotous misadventures at an inn.[24] For now, Roderick remains capable of amused detachment in his responses, as does the reader; his language is graphic and his vision distorting, but there is no rage because he has not yet entered fully into the utter darkness of the world's troubling reality. The sign that he is approaching it comes during a comic interlude in Chapter 13, when he and his loyal companion Strap lie trembling in their bed as the "terrible apparition" of a tame raven wanders aimlessly through deepest night and into their room at a wayside inn. "I verily believed we were haunted," Roderick recalls; the "violent fright" left him "petrified with fear" and tormented his sleep.[25]

Thus the nightmare begins, and it gathers intensity as Roderick arrives in London, where he encounters meanness and often physical deformity in the face of nearly everyone he meets. The story reaches an early climax during the scenes laid on board the *Thunder*, following Roderick's maddening attempts to fathom the twisted image of the bureaucratic naval establishment. The world of the ship, with its assortment of sick, mutilated, filthy, idiosyncratic, splenetic, depraved, and malicious humanity, is a microcosm, vividly pictured in a hellish version of the convention already employed in the earlier episode of the wagon, its grimness relieved only by the presence of Thomson and Morgan, the latter another of Smollett's unforgettable sailing men. Here the darkness concentrates itself, as do the heartlessness and violence of this world. When Roderick descends below deck to the sick berth, he adjusts his eyes and looks in horrified astonishment upon the putridness, the vileness, the manifestations of unimaginable cruelty and unspeakable indifference he finds there. "Here," he cries out in an almost audible burst of anger,

> I saw about fifty miserable distempered wretches, suspended in rows, so huddled one upon another, that not more than fourteen inches of space was allotted for each with his bed and bedding; and deprived of the light of the day, as well as of fresh air; breathing nothing but a noisome atmosphere of the morbid steams exhaling from their own excrements and diseased bodies, devoured with vermin hatched in the filth that surrounded

them, and destitute of every convenience necessary for people in that helpless condition.[26]

This description throbs with energy and feeling, just as the verbal picture startlingly projects its sensual details. Words like *distempered wretches, suspended, huddled, noisome, morbid steams, devoured,* and *vermin* call direct attention to themselves, and convey for Roderick an emotional response as violent as the scene itself.

Language is for Smollett a tricky but trustworthy, if not always fully conscious, signifier of the inner self. Sometimes its effects are comical or even farcical, as in the case of the inadvertent sexual malapropisms of Tabitha Bramble, the man-hungry but outwardly prudish old spinster of **Humphry Clinker.** Roderick's language, from the beginning of his story, steadily increases the frenzy of its response to multiplying absurdities, outrages, and dangers; it actually registers the process by which the world threatens to re-create him in the image of its own dark, fragmented, scarifying madness. There is a paradox here. Roderick's language makes real, in sometimes painfully detailed pictures, the chaotic nightmare of his life; but it also serves—much more reliably than his actions alone could do—as an index of the progressive disintegration of his moral self, of the gradual and almost total loss of his moral identity.[27]

The shipboard scenes display with ghastly clarity the world's great power to destroy. The officers of the *Thunder,* in collusion with the surgeon Mackshane, have created the scene witnessed in the sick berth, they are moral if not physical grotesques, and they soon make Roderick a victim of their mindless cruelty. On a trumped-up charge of mutiny, they chain him to the poop deck, where he lies in a condition of utter isolation and helplessness during a ferocious bombardment. Bespattered by the brains and entrails of his mates, he loses all discretion, bursts into hysterics, and bellows forth an almost elemental cry of "oaths and execrations."[28] From this point forward, Roderick is no longer capable of detachment. His loneliness grows upon him when he is left beaten and naked upon the shore and at first can find no one to relieve his almost unbearable distress. At last (significantly, it is at the very midpoint of his story) he encounters Mrs. Sagely and then the exemplary Narcissa, but he is by then so broken and embittered that he cannot find the path that would unite him with the ideals of benevolence and beauteous virtue they represent.

The restorative image of Narcissa, "amiable apparition" that she seems when Roderick first looks upon her,[29] does remain with him, and its hold upon his imagination tightens continuously. But his journey into self-absorbing and self-destructive cynicism takes him further and further away from his heroine, until despair finally leaves him prostrate in prison. Meanwhile, Smollett continues to throw his hero into adventures that portray human nature in its progressively more sordid variety. Better acquainted with the "selfishness and roguery of mankind" as a result of his painful experiences at sea, Roderick considers himself no longer very liable to "disappointment and imposition."[30] Yet when he travels to France, he is immediately duped by a lusty, hard-drinking, foul-smelling Capuchin friar—a "thick brawny young man, with red eye-brows, a hook nose, a face covered with freckles; and his name was Frere Balthazar"[31]—who takes all his cash. After spending a few weeks as a soldier in the French army, Roderick luckily runs into Strap, from whom he has been long separated, and accepts his old friend's offer of money to set up as a gentleman; the two companions then return to England in quest of a fortune. In a round of balls and assemblies and excursions to the theater, Roderick is deceived by courtesans, sneered at by dandies, and finally seduced into the company of a set of wild young coffeehouse riffraff—Bragwell, Banter, Chatter, Slyboot, and Ranter.

As he sinks ever deeper into riotous iniquities, Roderick grows more susceptible to the world's false appearances and more desperate in his responses to them. His pursuit of the vapid Melinda Goosetrap and her fortune of £10,000 drives him to the gaming tables to support its costs, nearly involves him in a duel with a crazy rival named Rourk Oregan, and at last leaves him defeated, humiliated, and vengeful. He almost rushes into marriage with a mysterious inamorata—a "wrinkled hag turned of seventy!" whose "tygeress"-like advances when at last they meet set his bowels in a convulsion and his feet in speedy motion.[32] The "lewd and indecent" seductions of the sodomite Earl Strutwell, even more hideously than the garlicky pantings of the lusty spinster, define the world as a place going entirely and everywhere mad in its perversity, in the process (it seems) canceling all possibility of fertile, fulfilling love. At "this day," says the leering Strutwell most alarmingly to Roderick, the practice of pederasty "prevails not only over all the east, but in most parts of Europe; in our own country it gains ground apace, and in all probability will become in a short time a more fashionable vice than simple fornication."[33]

In the midst of such precisely vivified moral darkness, the image of Narcissa increases in its brightness, even while Roderick's desperate course veers from it at a widening distance. His attempt upon the fortune and the person of one Miss Snapper, the sickly, misshapen, conniving daughter of a rich Turkey merchant, almost brings him to permanent misery. Like the grizzled septuagenarian from whom Roderick has very recently fled in revulsion, Miss Snapper is obviously a foil to Narcissa; should he unit with her in marriage, he would symbolically become one with all that she stands for in her physical and spiritual deformity. Roderick meets this remarkable creature during one of his author's finely executed coaching episodes, this time along the road to Bath. The collection of humanity in whose company he finds himself represents yet another close pictorial grouping of varied character types, among them a blustering soldier, a grave matron, and a shifty lawyer. Miss Snapper herself is drawn with great exactness, and her obsessed suitor does not find her entirely displeasing, though her head bears a certain resemblance "to a hatchet, the edge being represented by her face," and though she is both large-breasted and humpbacked.[34] Roderick abandons his schemes against this fair lady only after he accidentally meets Narcissa once again in the assembly rooms at Bath. This is another providential occurrence, but not the reversal a lesser novelist might have made of it. When the two lovers are separated by Narcissa's brother, Roderick dashes headlong into the last extremities of self-destructive despair. Back in London, he casts his lot with Fortune, turns gambler, swindles a tailor to finance his reckless play, and is arrested and flung into prison.

Throughout these long episodes, as Roderick tries repeatedly and always unsuccessfully to create riches from nothing so as to secure a meaningless future, he becomes more and more not only the helpless wanderer but a foolish and guilty one. His actions shift from the physical riotousness of his earliest days to concentrated deviousness; his language, far from losing its energy and intensity, adds density and subtlety as it reflects his increasing entanglement in the cobwebby sordidness of a darkening world. His crony Banter suggests the scheme that ends in his arrest, and the rationalization by which Roderick leads himself to undertake it is couched in the words and rhythms of subdued frenzy. The language here lacks the overt violence that pulses through the passages describing the horrors of life on board the *Thunder,* but in its fitful twistings it reveals an even more troubled and troubling kind of inner conflict. Banter's wickedly clever proposal, Roderick recalls,

> savoured a little of fraud; but he rendered it palatable, by observing, that in a few months, I might be in a condition to do every body justice; and in the mean time, I was acquitted by the honesty of my intention—I suffered myself to be persuaded by his salvo, by which my necessity, rather than my judgment, was convinced; and . . . actually put the scheme in practice.[35]

The blatant criminality of this enterprise, only half acknowledged if at all, is hinted at in Roderick's reversals upon the words *justice, acquitted,* and *honesty,* while his use of the military term *salvo* suggests the brutality of this culminating assault of the world's artillery of evil against him. Conquered at last, he submits.

The prison where Roderick finds himself next, like the city and the microcosm of the ship, is closely particularized as a revealingly bleak image of the world at large, and it completely encloses him along with his fellow criminals—and victims. His energy gone, and his resilience with it, Roderick no longer possesses even the language to express his grief, despair, and loss. The failed and suffering poet, Melopoyn, furnishes the expression he needs by reading aloud one of his elegies in imitation of Tibullus, but the experience leaves Roderick so weakened and distraught that he takes to his bottle, sleeps, and then wakes "in the horrors," his imagination haunted with "dismal apparitions."[36] Later, the interpolated tale of Melopoyn's terrible misfortunes, in an echo of the earlier history of Nancy Williams (Chapters 22-23), calls forth from Roderick a response in generosity and sympathy by reminding him that the troubles of others may be greater than his own. This long interlude, despite its obvious references to Smollett's disappointments with *The Regicide,* is thus not a merely gratuitous intrusion of personal vindictiveness. Roderick's response to Melopoyn helps to justify the redemption that is to follow, though it does not precipitate it. Still hopeless, Roderick grows altogether "negligent of life," loses his appetite, and degenerates into "such a sloven" that by the morning of his deliverance he has been for two months "neither washed, shifted nor shaved."[37] The punishment inflicted upon Roderick for his failings is severe, but it is at last enough. When his uncle reappears miraculously to renew his faith in the power of human affections, he is "transported" at the sight; his relief is as complete as it is sudden, and happy resolution—a new journey toward discovery of his father in the New World, marriage to the constant Narcissa, joyous retirement to idyllic Scotland—follows swiftly. In the end, by an "amazing stroke of providence,"[38] the chaotic, dark, hideously evil world of *Roderick Random* is re-created into an ordered, serene paradise of love, light, and beauty. Roderick proceeds from a language of indignation and self-negating despair to a language of ecstasy, and the reader becomes fully conscious—perhaps for the first time—that this retrospective story, told in the past tense, has achieved its often astonishing effects of immediacy by the contrastive visual faculties of Roderick's memory. The "dismal apparitions" of his nightmare existence, their power to control him dissolved, are like the airy figures of dreams, now receded from the center of his consciousness, which has recovered them in such striking pictures. They are as illusory as the rule of Fortune, or Chance, while the "amiable apparition" Narcissa, emblem of the providential love Roderick had once denied at his peril, represents all that is real and enduring. "Heaven," this faithful girl had knowingly written to Roderick at the crucial moment just prior to his arrest, will surely contrive some "unforeseen event in our behalf,"[39] and she was right.

Smollett's readers have sometimes complained that the providential maneuverings with which he concluded *Roderick Random* weaken the work, wreck its consistency of texture, surprise too much, and finally are just too trivially conventional to be convincing or effective.[40] There is some merit in the objection to the suddenness of the novel's ending, and Smollett may actually have rushed the composition of his last chapters, bestowing upon them less care than he had given to earlier portions of the narrative. Nevertheless, the resolution he provided is vital to his overall design, and it is deliberately anticipated from his very first page, which records the mother's dream. The bright presence of Bowling, Strap, Thomson, Mrs. Sagely, and Narcissa contributes importantly to the preparations for the eventual triumph of all that they represent. Without the comic and providential ending, Roderick's experience would (from Smollett's point of view at least) lack all relevance to the human problem of sustaining moral identity in a worldly context of intensifying and confusing secularity—a context without a center, so to speak. Roderick's autobiographical narrative, taken as a whole, expresses his clear-eyed, full, secure understanding of the accumulated facts of entropic reality and their deeply felt, scarifying threats—now past—to his survival; and the reader knows that his redemption, more suffered for than earned, came in part as a consequence of his fixation upon the transcendent image of the matchless Narcissa. The "picture" of this "lovely creature," Roderick remarks during the account of his prison experiences, "was the constant companion of my solitude."[41] The necessarily radical transformation of Smollett's fictional world and of his Everyman hero proclaims with dramatic urgency the vast distance dividing most of society from restorative idealism, while it also imaginatively adumbrates—in the manner of the Christian fable—the much greater wrenching of the whole creation by which, Smollett believed, Providence would at last redeem the miserable failures of mankind and restore the perfections of Eden.[42]

Roderick Random achieves its striking rhetorical effects precisely because its structure provides so purposefully diffuse a picture of the rampant disorder of life, wrought into order by benevolent authorial interposition. Despite its comic resolution and its echoes of Christian orthodoxy, however, Smollett's novel develops a deep and unmistakable ambiguity in its approach to the nostalgic ideals of faith. By a rapid-fire sequence of scattered episodes portraying the world's harshness, its indifference to moral life, and most of all its shattering uncertainty, *Roderick Random* verges on a vision of existential absurdity and is thus in some ways very modern. Its portrait of a hero who is in important respects an *anti*-hero likewise anticipates conceptions of character made familiar in the works of such recent writers as James Joyce, William Faulkner, Saul Bellow, Joseph Heller, and John Barth.[43] Surely these are among the reasons why Smollett's first novel continues to be read and why it is currently attracting more admiring attention than at any time since the days immediately following its original publication. . . .

Notes

[1] *The Adventures of Ferdinand Count Fathom,* ed. Damian Grant (London: Oxford Univ. Press, 1971), 2.

[2] Space will not permit full development of this point here, but the reader may wish to consult the following for some useful observations concerning Smollett's connections with and interest in the painterly arts: Milton Orowitz, "Smollett and the Art of Caricature," *Spectrum* 2 (1958), 155-67; George M. Kahrl, "Smollett as a Caricaturist," in *Tobias Smollett: Bicentennial Essays Presented to Lewis M. Knapp,* ed. G.S. Rousseau and P.-G. Boucé (New York: Oxford Univ. Press, 1971), 169-200. Hogarth was Smollett's contemporary, and his visual art of caricature was at the time a relatively new thing in England. Smollett and others were keenly interested in appropriating it as a verbal art. Given the striking pictorial qualities of Smollett's novels, it is not surprising that he attracted the enthusiastic attention of great illustrators like Thomas Rowlandson and George Cruikshank, both of whom provided splendid drawings to accompany major editions of his works. In this same general connection, it ought to be mentioned that the dramatic qualities of the pictorial episodes in Smollett's novels, like the many allusions to plays (especially those of Shakespeare) scattered through them, importantly reflect his lifelong interest in the theater. See Lee M. Ellison, "Elizabethan Drama and the Works of Smollett," *PMLA* 44 (1929), 842-62.

[3] I have elsewhere discussed at length the importance of Smollett's theoretical statement in *Ferdinand Count Fathom* and its implications for his narrative structures: see "Smollett's Novels: *Ferdinand Count Fathom* for the Defense," *PLL* 20 (1984), 165-84.

[4] For contrasting but complementary views of Smollett's episodic structures and comic endings, see Philip Stevick, "Smollett's Picaresque Games," in *Tobias Smollett: Bicentennial Essays,* 111-30; Paul-Gabriel Boucé, *The Novels of Tobias Smollett* (London: Longman, 1976), esp. ch. 8.

[5] *The Letters of Tobias Smollett,* ed. Lewis M. Knapp (Oxford: Clarendon Press, 1970), 6. For a full account of Smollett's early years and their importance to the beginnings of his career as a novelist, see Knapp, *Tobias Smollett: Doctor of Men and Manners* (Princeton, N.J.: Princeton Univ. Press, 1949). I have relied on this authoritative biography for many of the details of Smollett's life introduced throughout the present discussion.

[6] *Letters,* 8.

[7] *Selected Letters of Samuel Richardson,* ed. John Carroll (Oxford: Clarendon Press, 1964), 41.

[8] Smollett's Spanish was not fluent, and he was slow to finish this translation, which did not appear in print until 1755.

[9] Smollett's translation of *Gil Blas,* published in October 1748, is still considered the best that has ever been done. The four volumes of LeSage's work were published in France between 1715 and 1735, and English versions followed quickly (from 1716 to 1736, with reprints thereafter).

[10] *The Adventures of Roderick Random,* ed. Paul-Gabriel Boucé (Oxford: Oxford Univ. Press, 1981), Preface, xxxv. I have used this World's Classics paperback edition of *Roderick Random* because it is both reliable and readily available. For the convenience of any reader who may have another text in hand, I refer in subsequent citations to chapter (or, as here, to the preface) as well as page numbers.

[11] Preface, xxxv.

[12] For fuller discussion of Smollett's adaptations from the picaresque, see my essay, "*Roderick Random:* The Picaresque Transformed," *College Literature* 6 (1979-80), 211-20. See also Robert Alter, "The Picaroon as Fortune's Plaything," in *Rogue's Progress: Studies in the Picaresque Novel* (Cambridge, Mass.: Harvard Univ. Press, 1964), 58-79; Alice Green Fredman, "The Picaresque in Decline: Smollett's First Novel," in *English Writers of the Eighteenth Century,* ed. John H. Middendorf (New York: Columbia Univ. Press, 1971), 189-207; Richard Bjornson, "The Picaresque Hero as Young Nobleman: Victimization and Vindication in Smollett's *Roderick Random,*" in *The Picaresque Hero in European Fiction* (Madison: Univ. of Wisconsin Press, 1977), 228-45.

[13] Smollett knew this firsthand. His mock-dedication to *Ferdinand Count Fathom* alludes directly to his personal tendencies toward uncontrollable rage and cynicism, and acknowledges his anxiety over their potential injury to his character; much of his adult life was devoted to restraining these impulses. It is in its echoes of this private struggle, more than in its specific references to Smollett's actual experience, that *Roderick Random* may be meaningfully understood as an autobiographical work. Roderick, of course, is not his author, as Smollett himself makes plain in a letter to Alexander Carlyle written shortly after the book's publication (*Letters,* 7-9).

[14] In Smollett's view, there were other resemblances besides, too striking to be accidental, and they angered

him. *Tom Jones* was published in February 1749, just thirteen months after *Roderick Random,* and Smollett believed that Fielding had plagiarized the character of Partridge from his own Strap. Later, he would be equally convinced that Fielding had stolen the idea for the Miss Matthews of *Amelia* (1751) from *Roderick Random*'s Nancy Williams. Despite superficial similarities, Fielding's characters differ importantly from Smollett's, and there was no real reason for such suspicions except perhaps the younger writer's insecurity over his newcomer's position in the literary world of London.

[15] Ronald Paulson, for example, finds this lack of detachment a source of Smollett's failure to make a successful transition from Augustan satirist to novelist; see *Satire and the Novel in Eighteenth-Century England* (New Haven, Conn.: Yale Univ. Press, 1967), 165-78 and passim.

[16] I have traced this background at considerable length in my *Novels of the 1740s* (Athens: Univ. of Georgia Press, 1982), ch. 4.

[17] *Letters,* 98.

[18] The apologue prefixed to the fourth edition of the novel (1754, dated 1755) is a modified beast fable that emphasizes the subhuman qualities of some of Smollett's characters—and some of his contemporary critics as well.

[19] Ch. 1, p. 1.

[20] See Percy G. Adams, *Travel Literature and the Evolution of the Novel* (Lexington: Univ. Press of Kentucky, 1983). George M. Kahrl, in *Tobias Smollett: Traveler-Novelist* (Chicago: Univ. of Chicago Press, 1945), has demonstrated at great length how deeply Smollett's abiding interest in travel and travel literature affected the style and structure of his novels.

[21] Ch. 2, p. 5.

[22] Ch. 7, p. 26.

[23] Ch. 11, pp. 49-50.

[24] See Adams, *Travel Literature,* ch. 8, for full discussion of these two important conventions or (to use Adams's own term) "motifs."

[25] Ch. 13, p. 61.

[26] Ch. 25, p. 149.

[27] For varied discussion of the general question of Smollett's style, see Albrecht B. Strauss, "On

Smollett's Language: A Paragraph in *Ferdinand Count Fathom,*" in *Style in Prose Fiction: English Institute Essays, 1958,* ed. Harold C. Martin (New York: Columbia Univ. Press, 1959), 25-54; Philip Stevick, "Stylistic Energy in the Early Smollett," *PQ* 64 (1967), 712-19; Damian Grant, *Tobias Smollett: A Study in Style* (Manchester: Manchester Univ. Press, 1977). Strauss finds the failures of Smollett's sentimental language very revealing with respect to his real talent for the language of hyperbole and emotional violence; Stevick and Grant stress Smollett's stylistic exaggerations and virtuosity as chief attractions in his works, though they understate the importance of intensive language as a means of character definition. Grant argues further that in Smollett, style is almost everything; plot, episodes, and characters are in themselves relatively uninteresting.

[28] Ch. 29, p. 168.

[29] Ch. 39, p. 219.

[30] Ch. 41, p. 235.

[31] Ch. 42, p. 240.

[32] Ch. 50, pp. 303, 305.

[33] Ch. 51, p. 310. Earlier, Roderick had described the effeminate Captain Whiffle of the *Thunder* as guilty of a passion "not fit to be named" (ch. 35, p. 199). Robert Adams Day has recently suggested that Smollett's often repeated antagonism to homosexuality, together with his obsessive interest in scatological humor and word play on the subject of bodily functions, gives rise to a suspicion that he himself may have harbored some latent homosexual tendencies; see "Sex, Scatology, Smollett," in *Sexuality in Eighteenth-Century Britain,* ed. Paul-Gabriel Boucé (Manchester: Manchester Univ. Press, 1982), 225-43.

[34] Ch. 54, pp. 326-27.

[35] Ch. 60, p. 372.

[36] Ch. 61, p. 377.

[37] Ch. 64, p. 397.

[38] Ch. 66, p. 416.

[39] Ch. 60, p. 371.

[40] Robert Alter, for example ("The Picaroon as Fortune's Plaything," 76), complains that the conventional happy ending, with its obvious contrivances, defeats the novel's development as an exercise in picaresque satire. The problem with this objection is its failure to acknowledge that Smollett deliberately set out to write

a variation upon the picaresque.

41 Ch. 64, p. 397.

42 Smollett was no orthodox Christian, or so his writings suggest. Actually, we know very little about his personal theology. Still, it is clear that he shared with many of his contemporaries a belief in the providential ordering of the world and in the scriptural guarantee of ultimate redemption for the Christian part of mankind; see Thomas R. Preston, *Not in Timon's Manner: Feeling, Misanthropy, and Satire in Eighteenth-Century England* (University: Univ. of Alabama Press, 1975), 2, 69-120. For fuller treatment of the transformation occurring at the end of *Roderick Random,* see my *Novels of the 1740s,* 122-25.

43 Barth, in fact, provided a most interesting (if unscholarly) afterword for an edition of *Roderick Random* issued some years ago in a popular paperback series (New York: New American Library, 1964). This edition is now regrettably out of print. . . .

R. S. Krishnan (essay date 1988)

SOURCE: "'The Vortex of the Tumult': Order and Disorder in *Humphry Clinker,*" in *Studies in Scottish Literature,* Vol. XXIII, 1988, pp. 239-53.

[*In the following essay, Krishnan contends that not only the images or concepts of order and disorder but also the very terms order and disorder themselves contribute to Smollett's organization and structuring of the novel* Humphry Clinker.]

The various readings of Smollett's **Humphry Clinker**—as a comic romance, as a study of primitivism and progress, or as a satire on eighteenth-century life and scene, just to mention a few—have served only to reconfirm the vitality and variety of Smollett's comic inventiveness in his best and most popular work.[1] Smollett's use of various imagery of heaven and hell, monsters, animals, and his frequent references to excrement and nudity, have also been examined, with interesting results.[2] The novel's basic premise—Matthew Bramble's search of a "cure" to his mental and physical ailments, as he and his entourage make their way through England and Scotland—may be more thoroughly understood by examining yet another pattern of imagery in the novel. Although various critics have suggested the idea of order in the novel, particularly in relation to what they see as the novel's main preoccupation—"to point steadily to the superiority of a peaceful, ordered country life over anything the bustling and wicked city can provide"[3]—no concerted effort has been made to study Smollett's frequent use of the terms "order" and "disorder" in the novel as a *pattern,* which, in its frequency and parallelism, functions both as an organizing principle and a structural component.

Organizationally and structurally this pattern can be viewed, first, in relation to the breakdown in social order which Bramble experiences in a number of places he visits (Bristol Hot Well, Bath, Clifton, London). Second, this pattern parallels Bramble's constant personal struggle to maintain his mental equilibrium and physical health against the noise and tumult and the various ailments that beset him. And, finally, this organizing principle is reinforced in the restoration of order in his own immediate family.

The key to understanding this pattern of order and disorder lies in the development of Matthew Bramble as a character. To the extent that Bramble is both the satiric persona and at times the object of satire—his peevishness and morbid comments are as much a reflection on his own disordered perspective as they are a highly satirical account of his experience—his point of view imposes itself upon, and contrasts with, the views of the other four letter-writers in the novel.[4] As a satirist, Bramble distances himself from the action by deliberately assuming the facade of a misanthrope ("But what have I to do with human species?" he asks, early on in the novel), and his strident social criticism underscores his role.[5] As the object of satire, however, his peculiar excesses, brought about by his hypochondria, are held up to ridicule: "For a man is as apt to be prepossessed by particular favors as to be prejudiced by private motives of disgust. If I am partial, there is, at least, some merit in my conversion from illiberal prejudices which had grown up with my constitution" (III, 231), comments Bramble the man, seemingly unaware of its ironic implication with respect to his own misanthropic behavior.[6] It is this incongruity between Bramble the satirist and Bramble the man that is reconciled toward the end of the expedition, paving the way for the reestablishment of his essential "good humour" and a more balanced view of things. Mary Wagoner notes that "Bramble is obsessed with men, and his experiences are a series of farcical demonstrations to remind him of that fact. He is reduced by horseplay only as his outburst become intemperate . . ."[7]

The search for social order is implied in the gradual progression of the Bramble entourage from city to country, from the disordered and chaotic worlds of Bath and London to the relative placidity of Glasgow and Edinburgh in Scotland. This progression also parallels the gradual tempering of Bramble's character and views as he regains his health and mental equilibrium.

His earlier letters to his close friend and personal physician Dr. Lewis are noteworthy for what they reveal about Bramble's character. His innate system of values is based on the notion of order (his constant ruminations on his own Brambleton-Hall is an indication), and he hides his basically benevolent nature beneath his affected misanthropy. Bramble needs to purge himself of his misanthropy in order that he may move toward a more tolerant view of life and the living. His benevolence is demonstrated, initially, in his detailed instructions to Dr. Lewis to put the affairs of his household and his tenants in good order, including giving the Alderney cow to Morgan's widow and "forty shillings to clothe her children" (I, 5). Even in the midst of his journeyings Bramble does not forget either his obligations as a landed gentry, or the need to maintain order in his household in his absence. As one of the landed gentry, Bramble represents the solid middle order in society—what Donald Greene describes as the "squirearchy," "those who considered themselves . . . the backbone of the nation"—and his innate benevolence is a manifestation of his acknowledged role as a responsible member of this order.[8] At the very outset of his expedition, Bramble is aligned with, and exemplifies, the social order. This concern for the well-being of people, frequently reiterated, is one of Bramble's admirable qualities, and Smollett clearly intends it as a contrast to his satiric pose. It is this sense of benevolence, for instance, that underscores Bramble's charity to the ensign's widow (I, 20-3), and his admiration for the "filial virtue" of Captain Brown (III, 262-5), two of the more moving scenes in an otherwise unsentimental work.

If his concern for his tenant's welfare establishes Bramble's benevolence and preference for an orderly life, his misanthropic pose and hypochondria oftentimes hide his geniality, which only Jery recognizes: "He affects misanthropy, in order to conceal the sensibility of a heart, which is tender, even to a degree of weakness" (I, 28). At the same time, Jery also recognizes his uncle's hypochondria: "Indeed, I never knew a hypochondriac so apt to be infected with good humour" (I, 49). Jery recognizes, as Bramble himself does not or is unable to, that his excesses are not simply the cause, but also the effect of his hypochondria:

> What tickles another would give him torment; and yet he has what we may call lucid intervals, when he is remarkably facetious . . . A lucky joke, or any ludicrous incident, will set him a-laughing immoderately, even in one of his gloomy paroxysms; and, when the laugh is over, he will curse his own imbecillity [sic]. . . . When his spirits are not exerted externally, [says Jery,] they seem to recoil and prey upon himself (I, 49).

If Bramble's hypochondria exacerbates his "spirits," his misanthropic ire and satiric eye take in a perspective that further aggravates his already overwrought sensitivity. He finds in Clifton-Downs "the daemon of vapous descend[ing] in a perpetual drizzle" (I, 11), and his first impression of Bath, viewed as it is, from "the irritable nerves of an invalid" (I, 34), is

a jaundiced one. He is quick to admit to Lewis that his perspective of the city may have been altered since his last visit to Bath thirty years earlier, but now his impression is one of irritation: "This place, which Nature and Providence seems to have intended as a resource from distemper and disquiet, is become the very center of racket and dissipation" (I, 34).

What for Jery is "a source of amusement" that provides for the "humour in the farce of life" (I, 49) is for Bramble a constant source of mental and physical discomfort: "This is what my uncle reprobates," writes Jery, "as a monstrous jumble of heterogeneous principles; a vile mob of noise and impertinence, without decency or *subordination*" (I, 49—emphasis added). Bramble rails against the breakdown of order, but what is particularly vexing to his sensibility is that at Bath "a very inconsiderable proportion of genteel people are lost in a mob of impudent plebians, who have neither understanding nor judgment, nor the least idea of propriety and decorum; and seem to enjoy nothing so much as an opportunity of insulting their betters" (I, 37).

Bramble hears of nothing but woeful tales of shattered lives. His account of the misfortunes of Baldric, "the companion of my youth," now "metamorphosed into an old man, with a wooden leg and a weatherbeaten face," and reduced to receiving "the half-pay of a rear-admiral" as a reward for loyal service (I, 55-6); the Baronet forced to give up his parliamentary seat and sell his estate; and the genteel and "decent" families who had retreated to Bath in the hopes of settling down comfortably, but who are now forced to flee "to the mountains of Wales," are all prime examples of the insidious influence of the disordered and disjointed world of Bath (I, 57). He is mortified that they have to "lead a weary life in this stewpan of idleness and insignificance," where "every day teems with fresh absurdities, which are too gross to make a thinking man merry" (I, 56-7).

Even the architecture of the edifices in Bath is representative of the general disorder and chaotic state of the city:

> The avenues [to the Square] are mean, dirty, dangerous and indirect . . . [and] the great number of small doors belonging to the separate houses, the inconsiderable height of the different orders, the affected ornaments of the architrave, which are both childish and misplaced, and the areas projecting into the street, surrounded with iron rails, destroy a good part of its effect upon the eye; and, perhaps, we shall find it still more defective, if we view it in the light of convenience (I, 34-5).

Inasmuch as it is the delicacy "in all his sensations, both of soul and body" (I, 67), that is responsible for his outburst, the honesty of Bramble's opinion of the general disorder that he experiences cannot be denied. As A.D. McKillop notes, "Like Moliere's Alceste, [Bramble] can be diagnosed as a neurotic, and at the same time admired for the pride and honesty that lead him to talk harsh sense about the world."[9]

In short, Bramble's criticism stems as much from. his measure of human nature as from the excesses of his misanthropic and distempered mind. Bramble's basically benevolent nature and habit of mind revolt at the violation of decorum and propriety, but his distemper and heightened sensitivity exaggerate his experience out of proportion. As Eric Rothstein has accurately observed:

> The sick Bramble and society each reveal and cause the appearance of disease in the other: he reveals to the extent that his satire is accurate, and causes to the extent that it is not; society reveals Bramble's bad temper and raw nerves by prodding them with noxious stimuli, making them worse yet, and so causing further disorder.[10]

Bramble's description of the corruption in Bath, and his condemnation of the "tide of luxury" that has made London an odious place are real enough, and are borne out in contemporary accounts of the time. The social historian Dorothy George, for instance, quotes Shebbeare's description that "in London amongst the lower class all is anarchy, drunkenness and thievery, in the country, good order, sobriety, and honesty . . ."[11] But if Bramble's misanthropy often gives a keen edge to his satiric comments, his self-indulgent hypochondria at times distorts his otherwise accurate judgment of people.

Bramble's misanthropic pose, fueled by his distemper, reveals his intolerance for the mixing of classes, and his misconceived belief that the lack of such distinction and subordination can only lead to the corruption of those who move in the "upper spheres of life." He finds the "mixture of people in the entertainments of this place . . . destructive of all order and urbanity" (I, 51). Bramble's "cure," then, involves not only his health and spirits, but also the disabusement of his misconceived notions on class structure. At Jack Holder's tea-drinking, Jery, watching the activity of the mob below with Bramble and Mr. Quin, postulates that by imitating "the dress and equipage of their superiors" the lower classes "would likewise, in time, adopt their maxims and their manners, be polished by their conversation, and refined by their example" (I, 51). To his consternation, Bramble discovers that the representatives of the upper class are as capable of flouting convention and behaving indecorously as any in the vile mob of "plebians":

> The two amazons who singularized themselves most in the action [in the pell-mell rush to the table "furnished" with "sweet-meats" and "nose-gays"],

did not come from the purlieus of Puddle-dock, but from the courtly neighbourhood of St. James palace. One was a baroness, and the other, a wealthy knight's dowager (I, 52-3).

Bramble's misconception represents an ironic reversal for him. He mistakes apprearance for reality; his entrenched social expectations contradict the nature of things, which he fails to understand, because his hypchondriacal mind refuses to acknowledge this insight: "He hung his head in manifest chagrin, and seemed to repine at the triumph of his judgment—Indeed, his victory was *more complete than he imagined*" (I, 52—emphasis added).

The other revealing incident occurs within Bramble's own family. Bramble violently objects to Clinker's attempts at proselytizing, because he perceives in his new-found "enthusiasm" for Methodism an insidious force designed to destroy the distinction between classes. But Clinker's response, "may not the new light of God's grace shine upon the poor and the ignorant in their humility, as well as upon the wealthy, and the philosopher in all his pride of human learning?" brings only this rejoinder from Bramble: "What you imagine to be the new light of grace . . . I take to be a deceitful vapour, glimmering through a crack in your upper story" (II, 138). Here again, Bramble the satirist is accurate, but Bramble the man fails to see the irony, for it is the "vapour" of his own distemper that prevents Bramble from a clear understanding of Clinker's virtuous, if excessive behaviour—for, as Jery observes, "The first thing that struck him was the *presumption* of his *lacquey* (II, 137—emphasis added). As R. D. Jack indicates, "Clinker is used to reveal Bramble's own besetting prejudice—his rigidly hierarchiacal vision of society."[12] Bramble persists in his obsession with class distinction, when he tells Lydia, "I don't think my *servant* is a proper ghostly director, for a devotee of your sex and character" (II, 187—emphasis added). Ironically, it is Clinker's resourcefulness, and not his "rank," that time and again proves useful—once, when he saves Bramble's life (III, 313), and at another time, when he finds an ingenious way to fix their overturned coach (II, 185-6).

But even in the midst of the general disorder, there are tales Bramble hears that remind him of his ties to humanity. The episode concerning Serle and Paunceford is one such example. Serle's initial generosity to Paunceford, and the latter's subsequent ingratitude, arouse Bramble's admiration for the former; for, even though his predicament is widely known, Serle refuses to condemn his erstwhile "friend" (I, 67-70).

The mist of "vapours" that had clouded Bramble's perspective begin lifting only after his humiliation at the hands of those he had least expected to behave indecorously. The episodes concerning Lord Oxmington's self-indulgence and inhospitality (III, 281-5),

Bullford's practical jokes (III, 297-305), the demeaning behaviour of his Yorkshire cousin's wife (II, 164-8), and the vanity of Baynard's wife (III, 286-97) are on par with the despicable behaviour earlier of Sir Ulic Mackilligut and Mr. Micklewhimmen (I, 60-4; II, 173-8). Furthermore, these episodes are clearly arranged in contrast with each other in order to reinforce the satire of Bramble's misconceptions and diatribes on class distinctions.

In one of his more temperate moments, Bramble admits to Lewis:

> I find my spirits and health affect each other reciprocally—that is to say, every thing that discomposes my mind, produces a correspondent disorder in my body; and my bodily complaints are remarkably mitigated by those considerations that dissipate the clouds of mental chagrin (II, 154).

The correspondence between Bramble's health and his comments also underscores the pattern of order and disorder in the novel. The external stimuli—the attitude and behavior of the people he encounters, and the architecture and stench of the places he visits—act upon Bramble's sensibility to further insulate him from the disordered world in which he finds himself. At the same time, his own excessive reaction to his experience prevents Bramble from attaining the state of mental equilibrium that would allow him to take a more balanced view of things. But as the stimuli decrease, that is, as he and his entourage move further up north, there is a corresponding improvement in Bramble's outlook.

In his letter of June 14, quoted above, Bramble first comes to the realization that his sickness is mostly psychosomatic. Indeed, the very opening lines of the letter hint at his changing attitude: "Thank Heaven! dear Lewis, the clouds are dispersed, and I have now the clearest prospect of my summer campaign, which, I hope, I shall be able to begin to-morrow" (II, 153). It is significant that the "dispersal" of the "cloud" from Bramble's mind comes after Bramble's successful attempt at securing Clinker's release from prison where he had been incarcerated after his false arrest on a robbery charge: "The imprisonment of Clinker brought on those symptoms which I mentioned in my last, and now they are vanished at his discharge" (II, 154). It is not only the environmental disorder in Bath and London, but also his inability to accept reality that had contributed to Bramble's distempered and distorted view of things. It is ironic that perversion of justice—presumably the most impartial class-leveller—is far more insidious than the artificial distinction between classes in society which Bramble had tried to uphold. When Justice Buzzard's "severity to Clinker was no other than a hint to his master to make him a

present in private, as an acknowledgment of his candour and humanity," Bramble finds the proposition so "unpalatable" that "he declared, with great warmth, he would rather confine himself for life to London, which he detested, than be at liberty to leave it to-morrow, in consequence of encouraging corruption in a magistrate" (II, 152).

The physical and mental discomfort that had made Bramble surly, sarcastic, and distempered—in short, that which had contributed to his misconceptions and prevented him from understanding the contradictory impulses within himself—gradually yields to a more balanced view of life. Bramble finds the "pastoral" quality of the river Clyde (III, 269) a fitting antidote to the "abominable discharges of various kinds" of the Hot Well at Bath (I, 46). Whereas the distorted and horrendous noise of the abbey bells at Bath had discomposed Bramble, the melodious peel of the steeple bells in Edinburgh moves him to proclaim it "very striking to the ears of a stranger" (II, 219). In what is clearly a movement from disorder to order, Bramble, who had earlier condemned the architecture in Bath and London, now waxes eloquent on the castle and the palace of Holyrood-house in Edinburgh which, he notes, are "sublime in scite [sic] and architecture" and "a jewel in architecture" (III, 233).

Whereas in his earlier letters Bramble had unequivocally condemned the mercantile nature of London society which had made it a "mishapen and monstrous capital, without head or tail, members or proportion," he views Scotland with approval (I, 90). He has mellowed enough from his previously rather splentic outlook to praise Glasgow as "one of the prettiest towns in Europe" (III, 245-6). Scotland transforms Bramble the curmudgeon into Bramble the poet, and thus begins the process of Bramble's regeneration. There is even a tinge of nostalgia in Bramble's leave-taking of Scotland, which he describes as his "arcadia," his "paradise" (III, 257, 252).

For Bramble, Scotland is the symbol of natural order, not merely in its layout and splendid scenery, in the hospitality of its people, and in the lack of ostentation and vanity in public life, but also in its rejuvenating air, which reminds him of his own Brambleton-Hall. Bramble finds much to commend in Scotland, and even his disapproval, as Louis Martz states, "is judicious and mild—at times even apologetic."[13] Whereas in London he found the commerce and industry contributing to and sustaining the "chaos," in Glasgow he finds the same mercantilism contributing to "a perfect bee-hive in point of industry" (III, 246). Scotland, for Bramble, is the highpoint of his journeyings, culminating in his coming to terms both with his hypochondria and the manifest prejudice he had exhibited earlier, and to a grudging acceptance of his family of "originals." As Linda Pannill suggests, "the progress from a state of bedevilment to heavenly order is reflected both in society through which [Bramble] moves and in the family itself."[14]

In Dennison, Bramble finds the embodiment of that perspicacity, decorum, and orderliness to life that he had missed since leaving Brambleton-Hall. There is much in his friend for Bramble to admire. Both Dennison and his wife are down-to-earth, congenial, unpretentious, and suffused with that spirit of altruism that does not fail to cheer Bramble's spirits. Dennison's success at turning a financially disastrous land into a thriving farm through sheer hard work and diligent application of efficient farming techniques, combined with his cheerful outlook, have contributed to his orderly life. As Bramble writes Lewis, Dennison "has really attained to that pitch of rural felicity, at which I have been aspiring these twenty years in vain" (III, 320). In his frugality, moderation, and lack of ostentation, Dennison is clearly a contrast to Bramble's unfortunate friend Baynard.

When Bramble finds Baynard's estate almost decimated through the latter's misguided indulgence of his wife's frivolous vanity—"the shameful spell by which he seems enchanted" (III, 289)—it is Dennison, in his "goodness of heart," who takes Baynard under his wing and, by teaching him the proper farming method, holds out the hope of eventual reclamation of his estate (III, 343).

Bramble's progress from city to country thus parallels the movement from disorder to order. Correspondingly, Bramble's earlier disorder and the gradual rejuvenation of his health and spirits also come full circle. Whereas in his earlier letters he had railed against the "hell" of Bath and London, complained of "gout" and "rheumatism," Bramble now praises the durability of friendship, the advantage of sheep farming, and the salubrious air of the countryside. If the transformation in Bramble is indicative of his gradually tempering outlook, it is also due to the reaffirmation of order within his own immediate family.

Tabitha, whose "natural austerity [had] been soured by disappointment in love," and whose avarice, primping vanity, and "perverseness of nature" (I, 60-1) had in no small measure contributed to exacerbate Bramble's delicate sensibility, has finally succeeded in landing a husband, a task in which she had wholeheartedly employed herself since leaving Brambleton Hall. She who had earlier been described as "a domestic plague," "the most diabolically capricious," and a "wild cat" (I, 61, 22, 14) has finally met her match in Lismahago. In marrying Lismahago, Tabitha foreswears her excesses, and is "humanized." The *"noli me tangere"* in Bramble's "flesh" (I, 61) has, by assuming the mantle of a housewife, presumably been domesticated, by "alter[ing] her temperment [sic] to

femininely submissive."[15] Or, as Jery says, "the vinegar of Mrs. Tabby is remarkably dulcified" (III, 333).

Lismahago, for his part, is also "cured" of his excesses by being "yoked" to Tabby, and thereby made a responsible member of the Bramble household. Lismahago, who was "so polemical, that every time he opened his mouth out flew a paradox" (II, 201), and whose constant violent, disorderly behavior, and championing of views contrary to his own interests had so exasperated Bramble, and made him an object of satire, is now purged of his "polemical arrogance," and is left with his essential "dignity of an honorable career" intact.[16] He can now look forward to "taking the heath in all weathers" with Bramble (III, 351). In thus aligning himself with the family, he "functions to provoke the metamorphosis in Tabby which opens the way for familial harmony and good health for Matthew."[17] Robert Hopkins has also commented on Lismahago's role in helping Bramble attain a more balanced perspective:

> Lismahago as a therapeutic foil helps to ameliorate Matthew's morbid imagination . . . [by] serv[ing] as a catharsis for Matthew's grotesque views . . . [in the] sense of alleviating the squire's fears and anxieties by bringing them to consciousness and giving them objectivity.[18]

Lydia's character, too, undergoes change. Bramble's earlier condescending opinion of her—"soft as butter, and as easily melted," and as one who "has got a languishing eye, and reads romances" (I, 12)—is overturned in the face of her gradual maturity. Initially naive, idealistic, and impressionable, Lydia becomes more aware, more realistic about life. Whereas her earlier letters had gushed with sentiment unhampered by critical judgment, her last letters are evidence of her tempering outlook:

> There is such malice, treachery and dissimulation even among professed friends and intimate companions, as cannot fail to strike a virtuous mind with horror; and when Vice quits the stage for a moment, her place is immediately occupied by Folly, which is often too serious to excite any thing but compassion (III, 308).

Even her letter to Mrs. Jermyn, requesting her aid in securing the presence of her friend Miss Willis at her wedding, is striking for its restraint, propriety, and decorum (III, 336-7).

Her marriage to Wilson is ideal in more respects than one. Not only is Wilson "her equal in rank and superior in fortune" (III, 332), but the revelation that Wilson is actually Dennison's son provides for a satisfactory and orderly resolution of the novel. Dennison, Bramble's friend and social equal, is now coopted into the Bramble household, the felicity of friendship reinforced by the bond of family ties.

The introduction of Humphry Clinker also reinforces the structural pattern of order and disorder. Clinker joins the Bramble entourage without "a shirt to his back," "shewing his bare posteriors," and with "the rags that he wore . . . hardly conceal[ing] what decency requires to be covered" (I, 81), but his demonstrated loyalty and devotion to Bramble has an ameliorating effect upon the latter:

> So far as I can observe, the fellow's character is downright simplicity, warmed with a kind of enthusiasm, which renders him very susceptible of gratitude and attachment to his benefactors (II, 153).

The discovery of Clinker's parentage—that he is Bramble's long-lost son and the evidence of his "disordered" youth (when, perhaps, Bramble was less cantankerous and distraught)—only reinforces the pattern of order. Clinker's marriage to Tabitha's maid Win, in effect, assures not only his place in the household, but defines his social bounds as well.

The purging of the excesses in the main characters, the triple wedding, the recognition of a long-lost son, and the return of Bramble to good health are all parallel movements conforming to the pattern suggested earlier. Bramble's benevolence is never in doubt, and the end of the novel reinforces this idea: "the amelioration has, with each character, been a movement toward the norm of easier, more tolerant, more reasonable behavior . . ."[19]

The conventional happy ending of **Humphry Clinker,** Sheridan Baker has pointed out, aligns it with the tradition of the comic romance—in this case, "the comic romance of man's social ambitions, the physical fact behind his facade, the limited view he mistakes for universal validity"—a view not inconcomitant with the pattern I have discussed.[20] The prospect of return to Brambleton Hall reinforces and reiterates the order that Bramble had left behind at the start of his expedition. His journeyings through the socially disordered societies of Bristol, Bath, and London, his return to good health in Scotland, and the affirmation of the familial ties through the various marriages, all suggest the pattern of order and disorder in Smollett's **Humphry Clinker.**

Notes

[1] For a discussion of *Humphry Clinker* as a comic romance, see Sheridan Baker, "*Humphry Clinker* as a Comic Romance," *Papers of the Michigan Academy of Science, Arts, and Letters,* 46 (1961), 645-54. M.A. Goldberg discusses the novel as essentially a movement from progress to primitivism (*Smollett and the Scottish School* [Albuquerque, 1959], pp. 143-81).

Walter Allen in *The English Novel* (New York, 1954) views *Humphry Clinker* as a "striking panorama of English life in the 1760's" (p. 68). Louis Martz, however, sees the work as a "satire on England . . . [serving] as a foil for a favorable account of Scotland" (*Later Career of Smollett* [New York, 1967], p. 131).

[2] William Park discusses the imagery of water and excrement in "Fathers and Sons—*Humphry Clinker,*" *Literature and Psychology,* 16 (1966), 166-174. See also Baker, above.

[3] David Daiches, "Smollett Reconsidered," *From Smollett to James,* ed. Samuel I. Mintz (Charlottesville, 1981), p. 15.

[4] For a discussion of Smollett's satiric art, particularly the duality of vision of Bramble, as mirror and icon, see Ronald Paulson, *Satire and the Novel in the Eighteenth Century* (New Haven, 1967), pp. 201-3.

[5] Tobias Smollett *The Expedition of Humphry Clinker,* ed. Lewis M. Knapp (London, 1966), I, 47. All references to the work are from this edition and will be cited by volume and page number in the text.

[6] Bramble's affected misanthropy is discussed in Thomas R. Preston's "Smollett and the Benevolent Misanthrope Type," *PMLA [Publications of the Modern Language Association],* 79 (1964), 51-7.

[7] "On the satire in *Humphry Clinker,*" *Papers on Language and Literature,* 2 (1966), 115.

[8] *The Age of Exuberance* (New York, 1970), p. 36.

[9] *The Early Masters of English Fiction* (Lawrence, 1967), p. 177.

[10] *Systems of Order and Inquiry in Later Eighteenth Century Fiction* (Berkeley, 1975), p. 119.

[11] *London Life in the Eighteenth Century* (New York, 1966), p. 159.

[12] "Appearance and Reality in *Humphry Clinker,*" *Smollett: Author of First Distinction,* ed. Alan Bold (London, 1982), p. 211.

[13] *Later Career of Smollett,* p. 125.

[14] "Some Patterns of Imagery in *Humphry Clinker,*" *Touth,* 12 (Fall 1973), 38.

[15] Pannill, p. 42.

[16] Wagoner, p. 112.

[17] Pannill, p. 42.

[18] "The Function of Grotesque in *Humphry Clinker*," *Huntington Library Quarterly*, 32 (1969), 176.

[19] Wagoner, p. 115.

[20] Baker, p. 654.

Robert Adams Day (essay date 1989)

SOURCE: "Introduction," in *The History and Adventures of an Atom* by Tobias Smollet, edited by O. M. Brack, Jr., The University of Georgia Press, 1989, pp. xxv-lxxi.

[*In the following excerpt, Day examines the sources, politics, influences, and attribution of an obscure and little-studies novel by Smollett:*The History and Adventures of an Atom.*The editors have included only those Abbreviations and Footnotes that pertain to the excerpted portion of the introduction.*]

It is safe to say that no lengthy work by a major British author (if we except their juvenilia) is so little known, or has been so little studied, as Tobias Smollett's *History and Adventures of an Atom* (1769). Only a handful of living persons have read it through; and the scholarship devoted to it, aside from brief mention in books or essays and a few short notes in learned journals, consists of three articles, a single chapter or section in each of three books, a recent American dissertation, and a chapter of another.[1] It may not be inappropriate, then, to begin by telling the reader, as Fielding did with *Tom Jones,* what the *Atom* is like and what it is not like.

In intention the *Atom* is a savage satirical attack by a son of Pope, Swift, and Rabelais who has been "traduced by malice, persecuted by faction, abandoned by false patrons, and overwhelmed by the sense of a domestic calamity,"[2] in which Smollett looks back over the previous fifteen years and lashes English conduct of domestic and foreign affairs, English politics and politicians, and "the whole body of the people . . . equally and universally contaminated and corrupted."[3] In execution, the *Atom* is an allegorical narrative of fantastic events that had taken place in Japan a thousand years previously, dictated to a London haberdasher named Nathaniel Peacock by an all-knowing atom that has resided in the bodies of the greatest figures of the state; the story is interrupted by irrelevant digressions that pour out floods of obscure erudition, couched in a relentlessly helter-skelter style; and it is sauced with imagery that makes it by far the most scatological work in English literature.[4] It is also (in execution) a rewriting of all those works of Tobias Smollett that

had dealt with recent history and (in intention) a release of personal spleen and indignation; it is likewise a turning of his enemies' weapons against them by a man totally freed from the restraints of the historian or the pretended good manners of the polemicist, governed entirely, as he now is, by the desire to destroy through words and by the satirist's savage delight in his own powers.

These last characteristics . . . somewhat impair the *Atom*'s artistic achievement and blunt its impact on its victims. If the coarseness of its imagery has repelled some readers, more have in all likelihood been daunted by the complexity of the events and the obscurity of some of the persons satirized, as is evident from the "keys" that were appended in manuscript to early copies and in print to modern editions, together with the disconcerting fact that no two keys are perfectly in agreement.

The *Atom* nevertheless offers its rewards. One of its earliest reviewers complained of "a mixture of indelicacy which though it cannot gratify the loosest imagination, can scarce fail to disgust the coarsest," yet had to concede "great spirit and humour."[5] The modern reader will be less distressed by the coarseness than by the necessity, if he is to relish the satire, of becoming something of an expert on the history of the Seven Years' War and the personages involved in it. He will be rewarded by discovering anew the extraordinary vigor and fertility of Smollett's comic invention; by the robust enjoyment of knockabout satire; and by the endless variety and richness of the *Atom*'s verbal texture. Smollett wrote the *Atom* with a *saeva indignatio* at least equal to Swift's and with more than a little of his genius. Far duller works have been far more admired.

The Seven Years' War and Its Background

. . . Smollett's views in the *Atom* on politics, foreign policy, and society are consistent with those which he maintained more cautiously in the *Complete History of England,* in its *Continuation,* and (still more cautiously) in the *Critical Review.*[47] In his judgment the attrition of royal prerogative since the Glorious Revolution (at least from the perspective of 1764) has gone too far; ministers should be appointed purely for virtue and ability, without regard to party affiliation; both houses of Parliament are shamefully confused, ignorant, venal, and are constantly manipulated by selfish oligarchs; persons without birth or breeding have engrossed most of the effective power in the realm, while the old aristocracy is weak and decadent; the moneyed interests have virtually obliterated the traditional power of the landed gentry; "luxury" has corrupted the fabric of society from top to bottom; and (worst of all) the "mob," comprising almost all persons below the nobility—cowardly, selfish, fickle, stupid, easily led—

has been weakly allowed to assert, through sheer force of numbers, a power it ought never to have had.[48] On the level of specific evils, George II is the next thing to an idiot; his natural tendency to sacrifice the welfare of England to that of Hanover [i.e. during the Seven Years' War], which has resulted in a wasteful war and a crushing burden of debt and which should have been repressed by all lawful means, has been encouraged as an avenue to power, first by the unspeakably silly and inept Newcastle and next by the able but opportunistic and totally unprincipled Pitt, who also relies on the support of the vile "mob." Nearly all the high officials of government are knaves or fools or both. The wise (such as Lord Granville, lord president of the council) choose to do nothing.[49] Foreign policy is largely concerned with neglecting important matters, wasting money on subsidies to protect Hanover, and supporting the unspeakable Frederick in his wars. Generals and admirals are chosen at random, and are nearly always incompetent; the effective few (such as Wolfe, Clive, Cumming, Hawke, Elliot) are promoted by accident or through influence, and later are often either neglected or ignored, or die in action. George III is amiable but ignorant and inexperienced, Bute is virtuous but foolishly idealistic and conceitedly oblivious to practical politics; the war is ended by bribery (the ratification of the Peace of Paris), and domestic policy has degenerated into a ridiculous tug-of-war between Whigs and Tories, both equally stupid and equally obsessed with personal vanity and vengeance, while Bute, driven out of office, vainly tries to put together a stable government from behind the scenes. Such, in essence, is the *Atom*. . . .

Sources and Influences

The *Atom* is a unique literary work, but it is so in the restricted sense that it is a unique synthesis of ingredients that were far from unique or rare—readily available, in fact, and known to many. The chief strands that form its fabric are these: the narration of the story by an omniscient being that has also been virtually omnipresent; satire handled as "secret history," purporting to reveal the hidden springs and sordid motivations really governing famous persons in happenings known to the public; the narrative placed in a remote country, made to seem verisimilar if fantastic by a wealth of specific detail regarding persons, places, and objects; allegory in which historical events are made ridiculous by reducing them into outlandish or contemptible imagery; irrelevant digressions on esoteric or absurd subjects, involving torrents of obscure pedantry; and ubiquitous scatology.

Identification of the exact sources of these satiric strategies must rest upon conjecture, but Smollett left abundant traces of his working methods as he composed the *Atom*. . . . [the] *Atom* may justly be seen as a vast patchwork of quotations from, versions of, and allu-

sions to passages in the later works of Smollett's career, running from the time when he launched the *Critical Review* in 1756 to the publication, in 1765 and 1766, respectively, of the fifth volume of his *Continuation of the Complete History of England* and of his *Travels.* Smollett had also translated *Don Quixote;* and he may well have been thinking, as he composed his satire, of Cervantes' famous simile of the back side of a fair tapestry, seemingly ugly and distorted with its knots, lumps, projecting threads and grotesque figures, but nevertheless revealing how the tapestry (in this case, Britain 1754-68) is really put together.[56]

Smollett's work during this period, with the single exception of his novel *The Adventures of Sir Launcelot Greaves,* was as an editor, historian, compiler, and polemicist, and his duties obliged him to read and absorb an enormous mass of heterogeneous material on every conceivable subject from patristic theology to snuff. He could not have written more than a portion of the reviews in the *Critical,* but he must at least have skimmed every page of it; and if a given review deals with history, science, medicine, or fiction we are safe in assuming that Smollett wrote it, or carefully checked it if he did not write it. Thus, by invoking Occam's razor and discarding farfetched explanations in favor of the simplest and most obvious ones, we may reliably account for the materials generating Smollett's distinctive forms of satire in the *Atom*. . . .

Attribution

So far as can be determined from the documents that have been preserved, Smollett never acknowledged that he had written the *Atom* and never referred to it in his correspondence. This fact has led to a certain amount of confusion concerning its attribution to him, since scholars are often chary of proceeding in such cases without the firmest evidence, and since, perhaps because of its outrageous tone and ubiquitous scatology, the *Atom* has been given very little detailed study. Thus Lewis Knapp, the leading Smollett scholar of our time, was hesitant to pronounce unequivocally for Smollett's authorship; thus several decades ago a fabricated "Smollett letter" asserted that he had *not* written it; and thus the only extensive study of the question, at about the same time, ventured only to say that it "seems reasonably safe to conclude" that Smollett wrote the *Atom*.[118] But the firmest evidence is not wanting. It is both internal and external; and while we still lack an affidavit of authorship in Smollett's hand, nothing further remains to be desired to corroborate the attribution of the *Atom* to him. . . .

Abbreviations

Knapp Lewis Mansfield Knapp, *Tobias Smollett: Doctor of Men and Manners* (Princeton: Princeton University Press, 1949).

Letters *The Letters of Tobias Smollett,* ed. Lewis M. Knapp (Oxford: Clarendon Press, 1970). . . .

Martz Louis L. Martz, *The Later Career of Tobias Smollett* (New Haven: Yale University Press, 1942)

Sekora John Sekora, *Luxury: The Concept in Western Thought, Eden to Smollett* (Baltimore: Johns Hopkins University Press, 1977). . . .

Notes

[1] These are: James R. Foster, "Smollett and the *Atom,*" *PMLA* 68 (1953): 1032-46; Martz, 90-103; Arnold Whitridge, *Tobias Smollett* (Brooklyn: privately printed, 1925), 56-79; Damian Grant, *Tobias Smollett: A Study in Style* (Manchester, Eng.: Manchester University Press, 1977), 56-59, 175-77; Henry B. Prickett, "The Political Writings and Opinions of Tobias Smollett" (Ph.D. diss., Harvard University, 1952), 308-37; Wayne J. Douglass, "Smollett and the Sordid Knaves: Political Satire in *The Adventures of an Atom*" (Ph.D. diss., University of Florida, 1976). See also two more recent articles by [Robert Adams Day] "The Authorship of the *Atom,*" *Philological Quarterly* 59 (1981): 183-89; "*Ut Pictura Poesis?* Smollett, Satire, and the Graphic Arts," in *Studies in Eighteenth-Century Culture,* vol. 10, ed. Harry C. Payne (Madison: University of Wisconsin Press, 1981), 297-312.

[2] Smollett's words at the opening of his first letter in the *Travels* (p. 2).

[3] Lismahago's words in *Humphry Clinker,* as repeated in a letter from Matthew Bramble to Dr. Lewis, Tweedmouth, July 15.

[4] This statement is made with full knowledge of the poems of Swift and Pope and of Sir John Harington's earlier *Metamorphosis of Ajax* (1596), and of Norman Mailer's *The Naked and the Dead* (nominated for that honor by the London *Times Literary Supplement,* 5 May 1978, p. 493, col. 2), to say nothing of Mailer's *Ancient Evenings.*

[5] *Gentleman's Magazine* 39 (April 1769): 205. . . .

[47] The evidence for this statement is carefully analyzed and discussed in Prickett, "Political Writings," 318-28.

[48] For examples of these opinions in Smollett's works see Sekora, 146-53.

[49] John Carteret became Earl Granville in 1744 on the death of his mother, who was Countess Granville in her own right. On Granville's career see Basil Williams, *Carteret and Newcastle* (London: Frank Cass, 1966). . . .

[56] In reviewing *The Peregrinations of Jeremiah Grant, the West Indian,* CR [Critical Review] 15 (January 1763): 18, Smollett remarks: "We cannot call it a faithful copy, . . . but submit to the reader, whether the likenesses may not be compared to the wrong side of a tapestry, on which the figures do not appear to the best advantage. . . . " See Basker, 228, 271. The image is from the prologue to part 2 of *Don Quixote;* see the translation of Samuel Putnam (New York: Viking, 1949), 1028, n. 29. We should number among those works relevant to the *Atom* large portions of the *Universal History* . . . for which Smollett's editorial effort involved much rewriting—perhaps as much as one-third of the "Modern Part," including the sections on the German Empire and Japan; see Martz, 8, and Martz, "Tobias Smollett and the *Universal History,*" *Modern Language Notes* 56 (1941): 1-14. . . .

. . . [118] See Knapp, 280-83; see also the review (by Allen T. Hazen and Lillian de la Torre) of a book by Francesco Cordasco, *Philological Quarterly* 31 (1952): 299-300; and see Foster, *"Atom,"* 1046. . . .

Elizabeth Kraft (essay date 1992)

SOURCE: "*Peregrine Pickle* and the Present Moment of Consciousness," in her *Character and Consciousness in Eighteenth-Century Comic Fiction,* The University of Georgia Press, 1992, pp. 119-36.

[*In the following excerpt, Kraft examines the historiocity and the sense of the present rather that the past in Smollett's second novel.*]

. . . Tobias Smollett's second novel, **Peregrine Pickle,** like all novels, is interested in the relationship between fictional and historical narrative, and it offers the necessary—that is, the personal—corrective to the historical—that is, the official and public—narrative.[1] Not that **Peregrine Pickle,** or any novel, for that matter, is primarily concerned with the structuring of a historical moment. In fact, the present, not the past, is the novel's moment, for, unlike historical narrative, the novel insists on its own contemporaneity, regardless of its temporal setting.[2] While the novel may recognize its participation in a moment that will become historical, its primary goal is to capture and extend that moment that does not really exist: the present that has no extension, that must, in fact, be past to be spoken at all.

Of course, consciousness, like the novel, is a phenomenon of the present moment—not disconnected from the past, not disconnected from the future, but, just the same, a part of neither. As Sterne recognized, it is *that* present, the moment of consciousness, that fictional narrative is particularly interested in capturing. But what Sterne resists, Smollett exploits. The "presentness" of

Peregrine Pickle is defined by Lady Vane's memoirs, the MacKercher narrative, Smollett's own personal history, and the disconnected, picaresque existence of Peregrine himself. These features of the novel combine to suggest something of the complexity of any given moment in time; in other words, they seek to extend consciousness through a stratification of the moment in which it exists for us, for Smollett, and for the characters.

Paul Ricoeur explains the relationship between time and narrative by combining Saint Augustine's discussion of time and Aristotle's notion of plot or emplotment.[3] Human experience, as Augustine explains, is temporal. We are aware of time—past, present, future; periods of duration; the passing moment itself—through our ability to compare, to intellectually experience temporality. Yet what *is* time? To answer this fundamental question, Augustine invokes the concept of the threefold present: the present of the past, the present of the present, and the present of the future. At any given moment, we are aware of a dialectic between the three aspects of the present through an interplay of memory, attention, and expectation, the means by which we experience the threefold present. Human time thus exists in contrast to eternity. The awareness of slippage from future to present to past, from expectation to attention to memory, is characteristic of the temporal, not the eternal, wherein all is a present that is still, fixed, and firm. The eternal is that toward which the temporal moves; it is that which determines time by intensifying time; but it is, itself, neither a part of temporality nor a part of human experience.

Aristotle's discussion of emplotment, Ricoeur explains, does not mention the idea of time. In narrative plot, which insists on its own completeness, "before," "during," and "after" are not temporal markers but markers of structuration. In fact, Aristotelian narrative would seem to be atemporal were it not for the fact that Aristotle insists upon the cathartic effect of the plot, thereby thrusting narrative into the human time in which it is experienced. This observation leads Ricoeur to develop the notion of threefold mimesis: mimesis 1 refers to the action represented; mimesis 3, to the recipient of the representation—the reader, that is, or the audience; and mimesis 2, to the mediating act of creation. The thesis that emerges from the parallel between temporality as threefold present and narrative as threefold mimesis is "that between the activity of narrating a story and the temporal character of human experience there exists a correlation that is not merely accidental but that presents a transcultural form of necessity." In other words, Ricoeur explains, *"time becomes human to the extent that it is articulated through a narrative mode, and narrative attains its full meaning when it becomes a condition of temporal existence"* (1: 52). As Ricoeur continues, the circularity of this thesis suggests a spiral by which temporality

enjoys hierarchization with respect to eternity, a continual narration of time that figures the eternal itself.

With relation to the eighteenth-century comic novel, Ricoeur's insights prove valuable in that these novels typically foreground the disjunction and conjunction (the discordant concordance) of narrative and human time; they foreground as well the similar difference between the completeness of structuration concerned with the threefold present and the timelessness of eternity, which is all present. Narrative concerns the distension or extension of "now," which is different from both the present of temporality and the present of eternality but which partakes of both.[4] As mediation between the temporal and the eternal, narrative—or any creative act—is bound to fail ultimately because of its very temporality. In other words, the imagination can conceive of eternity only through the experience of time, so what emerges is analogous to the eternal, but it is not eternal—it is an idea of eternity, which must not be mistaken for eternity itself. In his discussion of our finite understanding of infinity, Locke speaks directly to the limits of the imagination. We imagine eternity, according to Locke, through the combining of two ideas: the idea of duration, or "perishing distance," and that of expansion, or "lasting distance"—the ephemerality of passing time and the stability of existence. The experience of time is what distinguishes human existence from the divine:

> Man comprehends not in his Knowledge, or Power, all past and future things: His Thoughts are but of yesterday, and he knows not what to morrow will bring forth. What is once passed, he can never recal; and what is yet to come, he cannot make present. . . . Finite of any Magnitude, holds not any proportion to infinite. God's infinite Duration being accompanied with infinite Knowledge, and infinite Power, he sees all things past and to come; and they are no more distant from his Knowledge, no farther removed from his sight, than the present: They all lie under the same view: And there is nothing, which he cannot make exist each moment he pleases. For the Existence of all things, depending upon his good Pleasure; all things exist every moment, that he thinks fit to have them exist. To conclude, Expansion and Duration do mutually imbrace, and comprehend each other; every part of Space, being in every part of Duration. (204)

This figure of the embrace of opposites suggests volatility, a tension housed in every work of the creative imagination, even in the tools employed by the creative imagination (language, music, color) to build monuments that outlast the builder but that themselves are subject to the ravages of time.

In the eighteenth-century novel, the imaginative union of time and timelessness and the resulting tension focus on the question of individual identity. On the whole, these narratives endorse the Lockean view that identity is built through temporal existence, yet they also struggle to reflect a belief (albeit an increasingly tenuous belief) in eternality, quite overtly recognizing the tension between the world in which identity is formed and the immortal state toward which the individual life moves.[5] The characters of eighteenth-century fiction thereby focus our attention on what is supposed—by eighteenth-century novelists, philosophers, and readers alike—to be the paradoxical condition of human existence: the need to live in time with a view toward timelessness.

The eighteenth-century novel's exploration of the isolated moment—the moment of threefold mimesis, the moment of threefold presentness—reveals the complex nature of this relationship between temporal and eternal. In fact, I think we might even say that the momentary structuration of this fiction derives from a cultural anxiety about the paradox of identity. While each moment is presumed to be one in the order of successive moments in which identity is compiled, it is also potentially the final moment in the temporal sequence, the moment that marks the move into timelessness. In its state of arrested incompleteness, the novel, particularly the comic novel, draws attention to the cataclysmic volatility of the present. Further, when the present moment is arrested and enlarged, when the moment of consciousness attains an expansion that argues its potential eternality, we are struck by the extent to which the individual existence is complexly bound to its time. In other words, even as the present is the moment of identity, so the moment of identity is the present. Perhaps more than any other eighteenth-century novel, *Peregrine Pickle,* in its pandering to this present, reveals much about the nature of this "now." Just as *Tristram Shandy* is the most celebrated example of the unifinishable nature of the novel, *Tom Jones* the most conspicuous example of the authoritative novel, *The Female Quixote* the most notable example of the revisioning of authority, *Peregrine Pickle* is the most striking example of the presentness of the novel.[6]

Smollett's signature as a novelist is his ability to begin a story, although, as in Scarron's work, the initial chapters of Smollett's works seem to promise more, or at least other, than what he actually delivers.[7] He introduces characters who will figure but slightly in the main narrative, or he employs striking metaphors in a narrative flourish uncharacteristic of the narrative voice that continues the story. The beginning of a Smollett novel does not so much initiate a causal sequence (this is true for all of the novels, including *Humphrey Clinker,* the most heavily plotted of Smollett's works) as capture the reader's attention. This stratagem is quite revealing in terms of Smollett's approach to the novel, for it suggests an overt recognition of an aspect of consciousness that we have not yet examined in relation to the comic novel but that is central to the genre

as a whole: communal consciousness, or the coming together of disparate consciousnesses over a subject of general interest and current concern.[8]

The initial scene in *Peregrine Pickle* is self-reflexive. It captures the reader's attention by telling of the capturing of a "reader's" attention. The reader—or, rather, listener—is Gamaliel Pickle. A failed London merchant, he has "a sort of inconsistency in his character," which the narrator describes: "With all the desire of amassing which any citizen could possibly entertain, he was encumbered by a certain indolence and sluggishness that prevailed over every interested consideration"(1). Taciturn, phlegmatic, and conservative, Gamaliel moves into seaside retirement with as few qualifications for community life as he had for the merchant's trade. Yet he finds community—or, rather, community finds him.

The setting is, quite naturally, the local public house. Pickle's first introduction to his new home is provided by Mr. Tunley, the pub's proprietor, who describes the most unusual resident, Commodore Trunnion, in terms that significantly emphasize the relationship between character and narrative: "It will do your honour's heart good to hear him tell a story, as how he lay along-side of the French, yard-arm and yard-arm, board and board, and of heaving grapplings, and stinkpots, and grapes, and round and double-headed partridges, crows and carters" (4). In addition to being a narrator himself—a self historian, as it were—the captain is also the subject of others' narratives, such as the landlord's tale of Trunnion's nocturnal encounter with a pair of jackdaws he mistook for ghosts. Yet the fact of narrative does not itself establish community. As Pickle listens to the publican, his countenance "never altered one feature" (6). In fact, at the close of Tunley's speech, the merchant merely removes his pipe and says, "with a look of infinite sagacity and deliberation, 'I do suppose he is of the Cornish Trunnions'" (6).

At the appearance of the nautical triumvirate—Trunnion, Hatchway, and Pipes—Pickle becomes only slightly more involved, despite the extravagance of their collective mien and behavior. As the three take their customary seats, they begin to squabble; that is, Trunnion and Hatchway do, for Pipes, "knowing his distance, with great modesty took his station in the rear": "'D——n my eyes! Hatchway, I always took you to be a better seaman than to overset our chaise in such fine weather. Blood! didn't I tell you we were running bump ashore, and bid you sit in the lie-brace, and haul upon a wind?' 'Yes, (replied the other with an arch sneer) I do confess as how you did give such orders, after you had run us foul of a post, so as that the carriage lay along, and could not right herself'" (7). The two continue to bicker until Trunnion begins to spout accusations of mutiny whereupon Hatchway desists, raising his cup in a toast "to the health of the stranger" (8). Obviously an invitation to join the conversation, the compliment is returned by Pickle, who then, however, falls silent.

Hatchway is a performer. In his altercation with Trunnion, he functions primarily as a catalyst: not angry himself, he fuels the commodore's irascibility for the sake of the company's entertainment. When that fails to unite the company by drawing Pickle in, Hatchway begins to parody the commander. Sitting on Trunnion's blind side, Hatchway "made wry faces, and (to use the vulgar phrase) cocked his eye at him, to the no small entertainment of the spectators, Mr. Pickle himself not excepted, who gave evident tokens of uncommon satisfaction at the dexterity of this marine panto-mime" (8). Finally, Pickle responds. Made one with Hatchway in a confederacy of humor directed against Trunnion, Pickle finds himself a part of this singular community, joined to it, finally, in the experience of laughter.

As the chapter continues, Trunnion's war story, told earlier by the publican, is repeated by Trunnion himself. Prompted by a newspaper account of the new peerage of an Admiral Bower, Trunnion's dismay and disbelief ("and I, Hawser Trunnion, who commanded a ship before he could keep a reckoning, am laid aside, d'ye see, and forgotten!") force him to "stand . . . [his] own trumpeter": "I once lay eight glasses along-side of the Floor de Louse, a French man of war, tho' her metal was heavier, and her complement larger by an hundred hands than mine." Interrupted by Hatchway, who objects to hearing "the same [tune] you have been piping every watch, for these ten months past," Trunnion turns to Pickle and repeats:

> I lay along-side of the Floor de Louse, yard-arm and yard-arm, plying our great guns and small arms, and heaving in stinkpots, powder-bottles, and hand-grenades, till our shot was all expended, double-headed, partridge and grape: then we loaded with iron crows, marlin spikes, and old nails, but finding the Frenchman took a great deal of drubbing, and that he had shot away all our rigging, and killed and wounded a great number of our men, d'ye see, I resolved to run him on board upon his quarter, and so ordered our grapplings to be got ready; but Monsieur perceiving what we were about, filled his topsails and sheered off, leaving us like a log upon the water, and our scuppers running with blood. (9-10)

As we read the captain's account, and as Pickle hears it, we (and he, we assume) hark back to the landlord's jumbled version. Further, as Hatchway undercuts the heroism of this tale by reference to Trunnion's drunken acquisition of one "war wound" (in his lame foot), we recognize a multiplicity of viewpoints on a single subject. The narrative begins to take on the characteristics of an object—not a temporal entity, but an atemporal form. In fact, toward the end of chapter 2, when Trunnion and Hatchway squabble again, they conclude with a fencing match, using crutch and wooden leg for lances, "to the no small admiration of Mr. Pickle, and utter astonishment of the landlord" (11). We find, however, that the landlord "had expressed the same amazement, at the same feat, at the same hour, every night, for three months before" (11). Smollett's emphasis is on ritual, a formula that transcends both time and individual experience, bringing disparate entities together in the lyric moment of consciousness. The group sings:

> Bustle, bustle, brave boys!
> Let us sing, let us toil,
> And drink all the while,
> Since labour's the price of our joys.

"In short," Smollett concludes, "the company began to understand one another" (12).

This moment of understanding, this fusion of communal attention, is not readily won, and the process of achieving it eschews systematic analysis. It is not a causal sequence but a series of separate moments, each tending as much to the potential breakdown of communication as to its establishment.[9] Narrative and this particular narrative's central character are shown to exist at the center of forces that threaten imminent dissolution; and, what is more, these forces are the very ones employed to secure permanence. Repetition of a narrative keeps it alive, but repetition can also alter narrative beyond recognition. The narrative moment cannot exist without a recipient, a response; but that response may be rejection. Revision may carry a narrative closer to factual truth at the expense of human sympathy, just as ridicule may procure the reader's attention only to have him laugh and forget, a common response to the comic vision. The character—the individual personality—reiterated, rejected, revised, or ridiculed, is like narrative in his or her loss of autonomy and consequently compromised identity. Who is Captain Trunnion, after all, but what we make of him? By the end of chapter 2, has he anything to say for himself that we fully credit? Yet, peculiarly, our experience is also one of understanding.

Consider, for example, what happens when Trunnion marries Gamaliel Pickle's sister. The commodore makes few provisions for his bride's comfort; in fact, his efforts extend no further than widening his hammock "with a double portion of canvas" (43). Not surprisingly, with its first trial, the hammock falls, emptying Mrs. Trunnion and the tar onto the floor; in consequence, morning brings carpenters, whom Trunnion surprises in the act of installing a bed. Armed with a crab-tree cudgel, the old salt orders the workmen, in the words of the narrator, "to desist, swearing he would suffer no bulk-heads nor hurricane-houses to stand where he was master" (45). When the carpenters ignore his outburst, believing "him to be some madman belonging to the family," Trunnion begins to club them (45). It is a valiant effort, but in the end his cause is lost. Already blind in one eye, a blow from one of the workmen renders him completely sightless; and, while he is recovering, his wife, with the assistance of the traitorous Hatchway, renovates their home so thoroughly that, when the old sea dog regains his vision, he is "an utter stranger in his own house" (46). The tone of this episode swings so radically between the ludicrous and the sentimental that it is hard to tell exactly how we are supposed to respond. It is amusing to picture Trunnion clubbing the workmen; we can well understand how they might take him for a lunatic raging and shouting in his barely intelligible nautical slang. On the other hand, we must be fairly insensitive readers if we do not feel the poignancy of Trunnion's fall from power, if we do not sense a bit of his bewilderment at Hatchway's betrayal, if we do not share the shock of displacement the old salt feels when his eyes are unbandaged. In short, we understand Trunnion because (rather than although) we experience the present in all of its contradictions.[10]

The idea of a shared consciousness, or, we might say, the fact of communal attention, is at the heart of *Peregrine Pickle,* which exploits such public events as the scandal of Lady Vane and the case of James Annesley in order to claim for itself a place in the public mind. Celebrity is both subject and object of this novel—egregiously so. That the inclusion of Lady Vane's memoirs has been from the beginning the story of *Peregrine Pickle* continues to cause Smollettians embarrassment, smacking as it does of sensationalism and of courting the salacious scandalmongers one would hope a "serious novelist" would not reckon among his readership.[11] However, we cannot deny that, as a marketing ploy, the memoirs worked. They sold the novel. A number of eighteenth-century readers, in fact, felt it to be the only interesting thing in the book; they did not question its presence in Peregrine's history so much as its propriety in general. What has been for us a structural irregularity seemed to the first readers of the novel a violation of manners. Lady Luxborough wrote to William Shenstone: "The thing which makes the book sell, is the History of Lady V——, which is introduced (in the last volume, I think) much to her Ladyship's dishonour; but published by her *own* order, from her *own* Memoirs, given to the author for that purpose; and by the approbation of her *own* Lord. What was ever equal to this fact, and how can one account for it?"[12] How indeed, we have continued to wonder, but less in regard to Lady V——than to the author of *Peregrine Pickle.* And yet, I would suggest, the answer is the same for both Smollett and the lady. It has to do with celebrity, the comic carnival of notoriety.

As we have seen, Sterne's approach to celebrity was to don the masks of Tristram and of Yorick in antic celebration of the parody of identity fame necessarily involves. Smollett courts it more cautiously, shifting the locus of authority and defining celebrity as a fusion of consciousnesses upon a single entity, that entity being largely defined by all the conflicting attitudes—stories and character assessments—that make up the moment of attention. Yet for Smollett this fusion is a violent one, a wrenching of consensus from disparity, and while consensus may be the basis of social cohesion, the fact that it emerges from the clash of competing individualities documents its momentary nature. Celebrity is a kind of caricature—a violently reductive image—and it is fitting that this novel, which so exploits the famous and the infamous, should also be centrally concerned with the art of satiric reduction.[13]

The eighteenth century itself tended to regard caricature with a disparaging eye. Novelists and critics alike reserved the word for literary or artistic portraits that departed from nature—certainly not a practice to be condoned, though occasionally, in an otherwise rich and "natural" landscape, one to be tolerated.[14] Caricature was popular during the eighteenth century, but it was regarded as a satiric tool, as it is still used, and no one argued for its elevated status on aesthetic grounds. Yet caricature is not simply a low form of portraiture. Strictly speaking, it is not a form of portraiture at all but an overdetermined response to cultural uncertainty. In its distortion it is violent and tendentious. It wrenches a partial truth from a landscape of doubt, and, in doing so, it both honors and derides the means by which it communicates, the satiric victim whose image is distorted not so much for his sake as for the sake of the community to which he belongs.

Ernst Kris has said that "whenever caricature develops to any great extent as a form of artistic expression, . . . we are invariably able to discover the use of effigy magic at some point in its development" (179-80). In fact, the roots of caricature in such magic, he says, account for our hurt at seeing our gestures or features exaggerated in imitation. In other words, part of us still responds to the imitation as magical substitution, and we are wounded by the symbolic disfigurement. Residual response to effigy magic may also account for our more positive reactions to some forms of image distortion (such as celebrity roasts and the *New York Review of Books*'s caricatures); for, as Sir James Frazer notes, although effigies in primitive cultures often represented pain, illness, and evil, they offered the possibility of not only harm but also salvation. Effigies used for the "beneficent spirit of vegetation" were burned or buried as sacrificial victims to ensure a bountiful harvest (755). According to Frazer, the same idea lies behind the use of effigies during a time of illness. Many communities afflicted by illness constructed effigies in hopes that the demons of death and sickness would mistake them for or good-naturedly take them in the place of the people they represented (569-71). Again, the idea is beneficence; therefore, the effigy is honored, not despised. Image magic, from which caricature developed, retains the notion of the communally honorific and beneficent, and caricature itself, which often provokes the sympathetic, rather than the derisive, smile, many times reflects tribute in the act of critical distortion.[15]

Caricature can be seen as the art of sudden compromise that grows out of the momentary awareness of conflict.[16] As a satiric act, it is aimed less toward the exclusion of the victim than toward the inclusion of others in a shared value or system of values. Smollett's own use of the exaggerated image suggests as much. *Peregrine Pickle*'s portrayal of Garrick serves as an example. Presented secondhand, through the observations of one of Peregrine's acquaintances in the College of Authors, the description nevertheless bears the stamp of Smollett's own resentment: "I cannot approve of his refinements in the mystery of dying hard; his fall, and the circumstances of his death, . . . being, in my opinion, a lively representation of a tinker oppressed with gin, who staggers against a post, tumbles into the kennel, while his hammer and saucepan drop from his hands, makes diverse convulsive efforts to rise, and finding himself unable to get up, with many intervening hiccups, addresses himself to the surrounding mob" (651). On the surface, this passage does not suggest either compromise or the honoring of the satiric victim as the locus of communal accord. Certainly, Smollett's intention was to humble Garrick, not to raise him.[17] The ridiculous comparison to a drunk tinker distorts the image of the actor with regard to both his outward appearance and his skill of interpretation. It is true, Peregrine tepidly comes to the actor's defense, objecting mainly to the use of a grotesque figure (the drunk tinker) to describe an already grotesque figure (Garrick), but it is not therein that compromise and honor lie. They lie, instead, in the shared reverence for the moment of death and, more particularly, in the belief that such a moment should be artistically represented with appropriate decorum and restraint.

Of course, "decorum" and "restraint" are words that hardly describe Smollett's own style. In fact, the moment of death is treated as grotesquely by Hatchway as it ever could have been by Garrick or any actor.[18] The difference is that, in the Garrick episode, we are expected to step outside the fiction, to agree with or to take exception to the opinions of the speakers with reference to our own experience, our own awareness of the celebrated Garrick style. Hatchway's similarly grotesque language we understand within the fictional construct—a part of his linguistic habit that adds poignancy to the event described. The values are not set but episodic, occasional, momentary, and circumstantial. If we follow the logic of the fiction, what we learn is to accommodate ourselves to the exigencies of the

moment, to laugh at something that in another circumstance, at a different time, might have moved us to tears.

Smollett's surrogate spokesmen in this novel, like Smollett himself, are all masters of the tendentious art of caricature. Hatchway, Peregrine, and Cadwallader Crabtree forge stability from the momentary and in doing so bring a temporary (or, we might say, a temporal) order to a chaotic (or, we might again say, temporal) world. Hatchway and Crabtree are mentors to Peregrine, whom Smollett describes in an early chapter as having "a certain oddity of disposition for which he had been remarkable even from his cradle" (51-52), a satirical impulse that vents itself primarily against his uncle and his aunt, the commodore and the former Mrs. Grizzle, his wife. Interestingly, although Trunnion is usually Peregrine's preferred target, the old sailor maintains for his nephew an affection that increases as the boy begins to manifest his peculiar talents. With Hatchway as tutor, Peregrine performs such satirical exploits as stepping on his uncle's gouty toe, picking his pocket, calling him names, tweaking his nose, and emptying a snuff box into his ale—all of which Trunnion tolerates, and most of which he enjoys. The society of the garrison is cemented by a recognition—indeed, a celebration—of individual foibles, which are pointed out, not for the purpose of correction, but for the purpose of connection. While Hatchway and Peregrine do undermine Trunnion's dignity, they also yield to his authority. In fact, their art of satirical caricature, aimed as it is at the authoritative presence of Trunnion, anatomizes even as it establishes the community of values by which the initial chapters of the novel are defined.

In the beginning, through the tutelage of Hatchway, we and Peregrine learn to laugh at superstition (the captain's fear of lawyers and ghosts), at personal eccentricity (the captain's house built and maintained as a ship), at bodily functions or misfunctions (the captain's gout, his wife's false pregnancy), and at secret vices (Mrs. Trunnion's fondness for brandy); but through it all we are encouraged to maintain a kind of sympathy for the satiric victim. The community is small, intimate, and bound together by recognition of individual limitations and by mutual respect for one another in spite of these limitations. In a sense, the moment of caricature, the narrative moment, is again revealed to be the eternal present, repeated and ritualistic, cyclical and perennial. But as Peregrine moves from the intimate community of family into the impersonal world, we find caricature and narrative called upon to play a different role in a skeptical and disjunctive society.

It is Cadwallader Crabtree, not Hatchway, who is Peregrine's chosen mentor. Both caricaturists are important to Peregrine and, like all satirists, they share certain techniques of exposure and exaggeration. When they finally meet, however, there is conflict, and Peregrine must choose between them. Their differences arise from the context in which the caricaturists function. Hatchway works in a closed, personal environment: his targets are those whom he knows well, and his satire is directed upward, designed to celebrate the infirmity of those with authority over him, an act that is completely creditable in psychological terms. Crabtree, on the other hand, works in an impersonal environment peopled with such recognizable types as the would-be wit, the fickle coquet, and the cowardly braggart: he targets acquaintances whom he does not know well, and his caricature exposes the reality beneath the appearance, not in a celebratory fashion, but in an accusatory one. He adopts a mask to strip others of their disguises in protection of himself and (later) Peregrine. For Crabtree, caricature is an act of alienation that confirms the inimical nature of the world in which he lives. It does support communal standards, but they are standards that must be articulated because constant violation is wearing them away. The caricaturist again usurps authority, but it is not an authority of "position" in a well-structured, stable social system; rather, it is an urban authority born of the confusion and corruption of social relationship in the modern world.

Crabtree's satire belongs to the destabilized modern world, which must reestablish the terms of its authoritative structures and which cannot depend upon the bonds of affection to hold society together. This kind of world is ephemeral, with success today being followed by failure tomorrow—reality exists only in the current moment. In this context, caricature exposes the lack of stability, the threat of extinction by insignificance, the possibility, even probability, of change so drastic as to change identity altogether.

What fuses in the figure of Crabtree is the cultural expression of this destabilization, and his significant features include his participation in all kinds of underground identities, his antisocial, misanthropic personality, and his status as "keeper of the narrative." In the chapter in which we meet him, all of these qualities are emphasized. The character is introduced by way of explaining Peregrine's social activities in Bath. "What above all other enjoyments yielded . . . [Peregrine] the most agreeable entertainment, was the secret history of characters, which he learn'd from a very extraordinary person" (380). Disinherited because he is a younger brother, Crabtree embarks on adventures that include several stints in prison in England and in France and a period of vagrancy; he has appeared in the world as a hack writer, a beggar, and a lunatic. Having, as he puts it, "weaned [himself] from all attachments," he considers himself "very little obliged to any society whatsoever" (385). Feigning deafness, he now "entertains himself with the grimaces of a jack-pudding, and banquets his spleen in beholding his enemies at

loggerheads" (387). He has "become master of a thousand little secrets, which are every day whispered in . . . [his] presence, without any suspicion of their being overheard." In particular, he enjoys "free admission to the ladies, among whom . . . [he has] obtained the appellation of the Scandalous Chronicle"—the tabloid, the illusion of intimacy in an impersonal world (387).

Crabtree is an emblem of contemporaneity. His rancor is the result of his being disenfranchised by the social order; his revenge is the destruction of the order by which he has been marginalized. During his imprisonment in the Bastille, he becomes fascinated by a colony of spiders, which he studies and guards until, capriciously, in accord with his "natural disposition," he destroys them (385). Defined and cast aside as a lunatic, Cadwallader Crabtree decides to launch his counterattack from this vantage point, and in three months he achieves his delivery from incarceration. In the case of Hatchway and Trunnion, the symbiotic relationship between the powerful and the powerless is shown to be a relationship traditionally maintained by obligatory bonds of affection and trust and celebrated by ritualistic narrative and distortion that reaffirms the relationship it seems to question. With Cadwallader Crabtree, the situation is different. The bonds of society are bonds, not of trust and affection, but of law and custom, which privilege one class and set of values and marginalize or contain others in substructural, countercultural groups.[19] The locus of authority thereby shifts; in fact, the social atmosphere becomes a competition for authoritative status, which is gained, not by position, but by attention. In a large conglomerate environment, which is itself basically asocial in that no one truly depends on anyone else, authority is a matter of gaining attention. This is Crabtree's typical strategy. For instance, when Peregrine first meets Crabtree, a young wit "roasts" the old man: "You look extremely shocking, with these gummy eyes, lanthorn jaws, and toothless chaps." In response to this harangue, which he supposedly cannot hear, Crabtree bows and says, "Gentlemen, as I have not the honour to understand your compliments, they will be much better bestowed on each other." The laugh is thereby "returned upon the aggressor," who, "confounded and abashed," leaves the room. Authority accrues to the one who has the last word (380-81).

Obviously, this sort of social atmosphere is highly volatile. But it is the atmosphere of narrative and of consciousness. For what Smollett's use of caricature uncovers about the novel as a form is its participation in a competitive urban environment, a participation that is not coincidental but essential to the genre. Narrative functions differently in a more strictly and clearly hierarchical environment: there, it maintains the social structure and reinforces cultural and individual identity. In a chaotic environment, it establishes the structure by claiming the attention that grants authority, an authority maintained or altered by repetition.

The inclusion of the memoirs of a **"Lady of Quality"** and the narrative of the Mackercher case speaks not so much to the effort to make order out of chaos as to the fact of chaos itself, a feature of the modern world as a whole and synecdochically of narratives produced in the modern world, particularly the novel. Smollett's perception of the chaos of urban life, the blurring of hierarchical distinctions, and the compromise of social order is most familiar to us in Matt Bramble's irascible description of the "fashionable company" he encounters in Bath, "where a very inconsiderable proportion of genteel people are lost in a mob of impudent plebeians, who have neither understanding nor judgment, nor the least idea of propriety and decorum" (37). In *Peregrine Pickle,* we see the same sort of theme, explored, as later, in terms of character and consciousness, but in a more specifically communal forum, a more specifically public form. That is, in *Peregrine Pickle,* Smollett exploits the volatility of the present moment even in narratives that may seem to present an ennobled, authorized version of event. In fact, their inclusion in *Peregrine Pickle* cannot be explained thematically except in the broadest sense, as each story concerns the unjust treatment of the individual by the social structure.[20] But Smollett makes little enough of this in the narrative at large, and, while Peregrine is represented as betrayed, his equanimity in the face of his ill fortune rather calms the resentment we might feel on his behalf. Structurally, however, the interpolated narratives share much with *Peregrine Pickle,* offering reflexive comment on the nature of the novel.

On the surface, this statement does not seem true. Both the memoirs and the third-person Mackercher narrative are presented as romances, not as satiric, picaresque tales. It is expected that the central figure of each tale will gain our sympathy and that we will come to see Lady Vane as one whose "heart hath always been uncorrupted" and who was "unhappy, *because* [she] . . . *loved, and was a woman*" (433), and Daniel Mackercher as "one of the most flagrant instances of neglected virtue which the world can produce" (692). But to see these tales as mere romances with no dialogic, multivocal subtext is to read them without the assistance of historical imagination. Smollett's first readers would not have been able to read the works thus because of the reverberations that would have naturally attended the subject from, in each case, at least a decade of gossip in assemblies and in print.[21] Not one reader would have taken either Lady Vane's or Smollett's version for anything but that—a version, an interpretation, one in both cases informed by a certain degree of self-interest and by an evenhandedness that suggests at least the possibility of truth. In fact, Smollett did not claim authority: his authorial voice was displaced, at least in theory, by Lady Vane herself in the first case and by a character, a clergyman, in the second.[22] Both speakers, of course, have their own claim to authority. Lady Vane tells her own story, and the clergyman credits Mackercher's. Still, Smollett is aware throughout that he is participating in, rather than giving shape to, a cultural preoccupation. He is in a sense responding to, rather than defining, the object of communal attention. In fact, both the Vane and Mackercher narratives function as the caricatures do. They wrench from the volatility of existence a momentary stability, not in the narrative itself but in the fact of communal attention.

The comic novel, as *Peregrine Pickle* illustrates, is of the present. Its validation, its authority, is transitory. There exists no more telling emblem of this fact than the 1758 excisions in *Peregrine Pickle,* by which Smollett paid homage to a new present.[23] His violence in exposing the defects of his enemies—real or perceived—is not permanent hatred but resentment born of the moment, which may or may not exist in the future. For Smollett, the novel was one way of documenting the present; public fame was another. In fact, one can trace in his own life a tendency to construct narrative moments from the chaos of his own existence.[24] His preoccupation with Garrick's treatment of *The Regicide* is one example, as Melopoyn's story in *Roderick Random* would suggest. Once Garrick finally made amends by producing *The Reprisal* narrative exploitation was dropped. Smollett no longer insisted on the episode of *The Regicide* as a significant part of even his personal history, for what it had been all along was a claim for communal attention, for an awareness that validated his existence and experience. Smollett understood the novel's propensity to occupy the consciousness of the reader, and to fully exploit that propensity, he realized, the novelist must be prepared to acknowledge the other things that occupy that consciousness. Those things, of course, are innumerable, and so the individual consciousness always remains to an extent separate from the communal concerns. However, there is, occasionally, fusion, and that fusion produces the lyric moment of shared consciousness. Such is the moment documented by *Peregrine Pickle.*

Notes

[1] In his review of Isabel Allende's *House of the Spirits,* Enrique Fernandez observes, "Novels are the necessary corrective to history and Latin history needs . . . someone to tell what happened besides the quests of our bold conquerors, brave chiefs, noble patriots, monstrous generals, and feverish rebels" (51).

[2] Bakhtin notes the "low-genre" attraction to contemporaneity as opposed to the epic's commitment to an "absolute past" (19-20). He goes on to describe the

inconclusiveness that characterizes the novel's temporal domain: "Every event, every phenomenon, every thing, every object of artistic representation loses its completedness, its hopelessly finished quality and its immutability that had been so essential to it in the world of the epic 'absolute past,' walled off by an unapproachable boundary from the continuing and unfinished present. Through contact with the present, an object is attracted to the incomplete process of a world-in-the-making, and is stamped with the seal of inconclusiveness. No matter how distant this object is from us in time, it is connected to our incomplete, present-day, continuing temporal transitions, it develops a relationship with our unpreparedness, with our present" (30).

[3] The following discussion is taken from Ricoeur's *Time and Narrative* 1: 3-87.

[4] That is, narrative is a kind of embodiment of now, occupying the space of now as well as the time. Sterne's emphasis on the physicality of his text obviously takes cognizance of its spatiality, as does Smollett's use of violence in his fiction (see Grant; and A. Ross).

[5] This is especially true of midcentury novels. Sarah Fielding's *David Simple* is an example, as is Sarah Scott's *Millenium Hall*. On the way such endings point to the conflict of a man-centered and a God-centered world, see New's "'Grease of God.'"

[6] Of course, *Humphry Clinker* and *Roderick Random*, *Tom Jones* and *Tristram Shandy,* also draw on the reader's knowledge of contemporary people and events. They also contribute to the legends and lore of celebrity. But as *Peregrine Pickle* is disrupted for over a hundred pages by the memoirs of a "lady of quality"—gossip, that is—its extreme commitment to the interests of its present makes a persuasive claim to exemplary status on that count.

[7] Sir Walter Scott early noted the disjunction between Smollett's beginnings and his endings: "Characters are introduced and dropped without scruple, and, at the end of the work, the hero is found surrounded by a very different set of associates from those with whom his fortune seemed at first indissolubly connected" (66).

[8] See Paul-Gabriel Boucé's assertion that Smollett establishes a "conscious complicity" with his reader: "He makes the public share his private jokes" (65). I would change the emphasis slightly and say that, in any event, Smollett assumes his and the public's jokes and experiences are one. See Jerry C. Beasley's *Novels of the 1740s* for a discussion of the way Smollett's novels, like those of Fielding and Richardson, are a response to and reflection of "public tastes" (74-84).

[9] See Paulson 185-86.

[10] On the character of Trunnion, see Kahrl 193; Starr 92; and Moore cxxvi-cxxvii.

[11] For examples of discomfort, see James Clifford's introduction to the Oxford edition of *Peregrine Pickle* (xv-xxvii) and Joel Weinsheimer's more sweeping complaint that "the collective charges leveled against *Peregrine Pickle* may be summed up by saying not that the novel lacks realism but that it is too real" (49).

[12] Quoted in Knapp (*Tobias Smollett* 119-20); he also cites Elizabeth Montagu's approbation of the novel and her comment that "Lady Vane's story is well told" (*Tobias Smollett* 119). In his unsigned review in the *Monthly Review,* John Cleland calls the memoirs interesting because of their "rarity" and "ingenuity" (55).

[13] See Kahrl.

[14] The most familiar denunciation of caricature is Fielding's in his prefatory remarks to *Joseph Andrews:* "[In] the Works of a Comic History-Painter . . . we shall find the true Excellence . . . to consist in the exactest copying of Nature. . . . Whereas in the *Caricatura* we allow all Licence. Its Aim is to exhibit Monsters, not Men; and all Distortions and Exaggerations whatever are within its proper Province" (6).

[15] For further discussion of the relationship between caricature and magic, see Elliott 87-99.

[16] Michael Seidel has defined satire itself as "a kind of perverse neutralization of historical progression, a stop without the guarantee of a new start" (21), a description that reinforces my sense of caricature as an act of the present moment.

[17] On Smollett and Garrick's quarrel stemming from Smollett's efforts to bring *The Regicide* to production, see Knapp, *Tobias Smollett* 49-57; Buck 54-62; and Spector 58-60.

[18] Hatchway writes to Peregrine of Mrs. Hatchway's last illness in this manner: "I hope you are in a better trim than your aunt, who hath been fast moored to her bed these seven weeks, by several feet of underwater logging in her hold and hollop, whereby I doubt her planks are rotted, so as she cannot chuse but fall to pieces in a short time" (583).

[19] On Peregrine himself as an alien, see Giddings (109). A related study is Ian Campbell Ross's "'With Dignity and Importance': Peregrine Pickle as Country-Gentleman."

[20] See Warner 276-79. For the way the memoirs and the MacKercher narrative address the basic picaresque theme of individual versus society, see Spector 63-64; M. Goldberg 67-68; Clifford xxvi; Jeffrey 142; and Flanders 157.

[21] Lady Vane's story was widely known, as evidenced by the epistolary comments of Lady Mary Wortley Montagu (1739), Horace Walpole (1742), and Fanny Russell (1744) (see Clifford nn. 795-800). The memoirs in *Peregrine Pickle* were one of several printed versions of the tale published in the late 1740s and 1750s. These included John Hill's effort to preempt Smollett's audience with his *The History of a Woman of Quality; or, The Adventures of Lady Frail* (1751); *The Adventures of Mr. Loveill, Interspers'd with Many Real Amours of the Modern, Polite World* (1750); *An Apology for the Conduct of a Lady of Quality* (1751); and *A Letter to the Right Honourable the Lady V—— ss V——*. The Annesley case had seen print as well. *The Memoirs of an Unfortunate Young Nobleman* (1743); *The Book of the Chronicle of James, the Nephew, with an Hymn of Thanksgiving on His Deliverance from the Hands of Richeth, his Uncle;* and the trial transcripts of 1742 and 1743 chronicled the inci-dent and Mackercher's role in the case. Smollett himself had referred to Mackercher as "the melting Scot" in his 1747 poem *Reproof.* See Knapp, *Tobias Smollett* 70-71; Knapp and de la Torre; and Lang.

[22] For the argument that Smollett actually wrote the memoirs, see Putney.

[23] For the excisions, see Buck 123-207.

[24] Smollett's letters reveal such a narrative propensity. For instance, from his publication of *Roderick Random,* he projects a narrative sequence in which Garrick is portrayed as the despicable Marmozet. Smollett writes: "I will . . . impart a . . . piece of News which I believe, will surprise you . . . after having perused the Revenge I have taken on the Playhouse Managers in Roderick Random. In short, I have planned a Comedy which will be finished by next winter. Garrick who was inexpressibly galled at the Character of Marmozet, has made some advances towards an Accommodation with me, but hitherto I have avoided a Reconciliation, being determined to turn the Tables on him, and make him court my good Graces in his turn" (*Letters* 8-9).

Works Cited

The Adventures of Mr. Loveill, Interspers'd with Many Real Amours of the Modern, Polite World. 2 vols. London: M. Cooper, 1750. . . .

An Apology for the Conduct of a Lady of Quality, Lately Traduc'd under the Name of Lady Frail. . . . In a Letter from a Person of Honour to a Nobleman of Distinction. London: M. Cooper, 1751. . . .

Bakhtin, Mikhail M. *The Dialogic Imagination: Four Essays.* Ed. Michael Holquist. Trans. Caryl Emerson and Michael Holquist. University of Texas Press Slavic Series 1. Austin: U of Texas P, 1981. . . .

Beasley, Jerry C. *Novels of the 1740s.* Athens: U of Georgia P, 1982. . . .

The Book of the Chronicle of James, the Nephew, with an Hymn of Thanksgiving on His Deliverance from the Hands of Richeth, His Uncle. London: John Warner, 1743. . . .

Boucé, Paul-Gabriel. *The Novels of Tobias Smollett.* Trans. Antonia White. London: Longman, 1976. . . .

Buck, Howard Swazey. *A Study in Smollett: Chiefly "Peregrine Pickle."* New Haven: Yale UP, 1925. . . .

Cleland, John. Rev. of *Peregrine Pickle,* by Tobias Smollett. *Monthly Review* Mar. 1751. Rpt. in *Tobias Smollett: The Critical Heritage.* Ed. Lionel Kelly. London: Routledge and Kegan Paul, 1987.

Clifford, James. Introduction. *The Adventures of Peregrine Pickle.* By Tobias Smollett. London: Oxford UP, 1964. . . .

Elliott, Robert C. *The Power of Satire: Magic, Ritual, Art.* Princeton: Princeton UP, 1960. . . .

Fielding, Henry. *The History of Tom Jones, a Foundling.* Introduction and commentary by Martin Battestin. Ed. Fredson Bowers. 2 vols. Oxford: Clarendon, 1974. . . .

Flanders, W. Austin. "The Significance of Smollett's *Memoirs of a Lady of Quality.*" *Genre* 8 (1975): 146-66. . . .

Frazer, Sir James George. *The Golden Bough: A Study in Magic and Religion.* New York: Macmillan, 1922. . . .

Giddings, Robert. *The Tradition of Smollett.* London: Methuen, 1967. . . .

Goldberg, Milton. *Smollett and the Scottish School: Studies in Eighteenth-Century Thought.* Albuquerque: U of New Mexico P, 1959. . . .

Grant, Damian. "*Roderick Random:* Language as Projectile." *Smollett: Author of the First Distinction.* Ed. Alan Bold. London: Vision, 1982. 129-47. . . .

The History of a Woman of Quality; or, The Adventures of Lady Frail. London: M. Cooper and G. Woodfall, 1751. . . .

Jeffrey, David. "Smollett's Irony in *Peregrine Pickle.*" *Journal of Narrative Technique* 6 (1976): 137-46. . . .

Kahrl, George. "Smollett as Caricaturist." *Tobias Smollett: Bicentennial Essays Presented to Lewis M. Knapp.* Eds. G. S. Rousseau and P.-G. Boucé New York: Oxford UP, 1971. . . .

Knapp, Lewis. *Tobias Smollett: Doctor of Men and Manners.* Princeton: Princeton UP, 1949. Knapp, Lewis, and Lillian de la Torre. "Smollett, Mackercher, and the Annesley Claimant." *English Language Notes* 2 (1963): 28-33. . . .

Kris, Ernst. *Psychoanalytic Explorations in Art.* London: George Allen and Unwin, 1953. . . .

Lang, Andrew, ed. *The Annesley Case.* Edinburgh: Hodge and Company, 1912. . . .

Lennox, Charlotte. *The Female Quixote; or, The Adventures of Arabella.* Ed. Margaret Dalziel. Oxford English Novels. Gen. ed. James Kinsley. London: Oxford Up, 1973. . . .

A Letter to the Right Honourable the Lady V——ss V——Occasioned by the Publication of Her Memoirs in the Adventures of Peregrine Pickle. London: W. Owen, 1751. . . .

Locke, John. *An Essay concerning Human Understanding.* Ed. Peter H. Nidditch. Oxford: Clarendon, 1975. . . .

The Memoirs of an Unfortunate Young Nobleman. London: J. Freeman, 1743. . . .

Moore, John. "The Life of T. Smollett, M.D." *The Works of Tobias Smollett, M.D.* London, 1797. . . .

New, Melvyn. "'The Grease of God': The Form of Eighteenth-Century English Fiction." *PMLA* 91 (1976): 235-44. . . .

Paulson, Ronald. *Satire and the Novel in Eighteenth-Century England.* New Haven: Yale UP, 1967. . . .

Putney, Rufus. "Smollett and Lady Vane's *Memoirs.*" *Philological Quarterly* 25 (1946): 120-26. . . .

Ricoeur, Paul. *Time and Narrative.* Trans. Kathleen McLaughlin and David Pellauer. Chicago: U of Chicago P, 1984. . . .

Ross, Angus. "The Show of Violence in Smollett's Novels." *Yearbook of English Studies* 2 (1972): 118-24. . . .

Ross, Ian Campbell. "'With Dignity and Importance': Peregrine Pickle as Country-Gentleman." *Smollett: Author of the First Distinction.* Ed. Alan Bold. London: Vision, 1982, 148-69. . . .

Scott, Sir Walter. *Lives of the Novelists.* World's Classics. London: Oxford UP, 1906. Seidel, Michael. *Satiric Inheritance: Rabelais to Sterne.* Princeton: Princeton UP, 1979. . . .

Smollett, Tobias. *The Adventures of Peregrine Pickle.* Ed. James Clifford. London: Oxford UP, 1964.

———. *The Expedition of Humphry Clinker. Works of Tobias Smollett.* Gen. ed. Jerry C. Beasley. Athens: U of Georgia P, 1990.

———. *The Letters of Tobias Smollett.* Ed. Lewis Knapp. Oxford: Clarendon, 1970. . . .

Spector, Robert Donald. *Tobias George Smollett.* Ed. Bertram H. Davis. Twayne English Authors Series. Boston: Twayne, 1989. . . .

Starr, Nathan. "Smollett's Sailors." *American Neptune* 32 (1972): 81-99. . . .

Sterne, Laurence. *The Life and Opinions of Tristram Shandy, Gentleman.* Ed. Melvyn New and Joan New. 3 vols. Florida Edition of the Works of Laurence Sterne. Gainesville: U of Florida P, 1978-84. . . .

Warner, John. "The Interpolated Narratives in the Fiction of Fielding and Smollett: An Epistemological View." *Studies in the Novel* 5 (1973): 271-83. . . .

Weinsheimer, Joel. "Defects and Difficulties in Smollett's *Peregrine Pickle.*" *Ariel: A Review of International English Literature* 9 (1978): 49-62. . . .

Robert Mayer (essay date 1992)

SOURCE: "History, *Humphry Clinker,* and the Novel," in *Eighteenth-Century Fiction,* Vol. 4, No. 3, April 1992, pp. 239-55.

[*In the following essay, Mayer argues that Smollett's use of history in* Humphry Clinker *makes it not only his best and most coherent novel, but also the only one of his works that inarguably deserves to be defined as a novel.*]

Smollett's fictional narratives often seem to be texts at odds with themselves. A large literature has grown up around the question of what they are—satires, picaresque tales, and romances being among the most popular, but by no means the only, candidates.[1] For some critics the application of one or more of these generic labels to Smollett's narratives amounts to an assertion that those texts ought not to be considered novels.[2] Critics have also decried the "methodlessness" of Smollett's fiction, and such complaints have often been another way of commenting on the multiform character of his texts.[3] An exception is generally made, however, for *The Expedition of Humphry Clinker.* Robert Folkenflik finds in Smollett's last fiction not "a high-spirited hodge-podge" but a "sense of unity in variety."[4] Scholars have offered various explanations for the greater coherence of *Humphry Clinker,* some of which are discussed below. In what follows I argue that the key to the structural superiority of *Humphry Clinker,* as compared with Smollett's other fictions, is a historical argument about the United Kingdom that is enacted within the text. I also contend that Smollett's use of history in his last fictional narrative—both in the historical argument and in the implicit definition of the novel found in the frame of *Humphry Clinker*— is what makes Smollett's last work his most "novelistic" achievement and his one indisputably canonical novel.[5]

That Smollett had history on his mind when he wrote *Humphry Clinker* is not a new idea. Louis Martz argued that *Humphry Clinker* was "an adaptation to novel-form of the topical and historical interests" of Smollett's various historiographical efforts, and many critics have discussed the political or historical theme in the text.[6] Robert Gorham Davis showed that "in *Humphry Clinker,* the movement through time is also a movement through space, a movement from England into Scotland and back into England again, a movement of reconciliation which ends . . . with symbolic intermarriages of Welsh, Scotch, and English."[7] What I now want to demonstrate is that, while Davis and other like-minded critics have been correct in linking the greater unity of *Humphry Clinker* to its political theme, they have not gone far enough; they have failed to discuss the underlying historical argument in the text that ultimately explains both the superior structural unity of Smollett's last narrative and its greater importance in the canon of eighteenth-century English novels.

. . . . .

Ever since the work appeared in 1771, critics have argued that the text was used by Smollett as a means of denigrating England and praising Scotland; Martz asserted that many important aspects of both the form and the content of *Humphry Clinker* result from Smollett's use of the work as "a vehicle for a denunciation of England."[8] Although the narrative ends in a spirit of reconciliation, much of *Humphry Clinker* seems to constitute a scathing attack upon English society and a celebration of life in Scotland.[9] Matthew Bramble's famous description of Bath typifies the overall view of England that emerges from his letters and those of his fellow travellers, at least before the final section of the novel, when the wanderers return to England.[10] In addition to being an attack upon England, *Humphry Clinker* is also a panegyric on Scotland. Although Bramble has almost nothing good to say about Bath, he tells his friend, physician, and correspondent, Dr Lewis, that "Edinburgh is considerably extended on the south side, where there are divers little elegant squares built in the English manner; and the citizens have planned some improvements in the north, which, when put in execution, will add greatly to the beauty and convenience of this capital" (p. 234). Bramble praises the Scottish city as "a hot-bed of genius," one in which such institutions as the infirmary and the workhouse ensure a healthy social atmosphere (pp. 232-34). There is a negative side to Bramble's representation of Edinburgh and of Scotland in general, but on balance it is not inaccurate to see the letters of the first English section and the Scottish section of *Humphry Clinker* as an attack on the southern kingdom predicated on the view that Scotland embodies an ideal which England falls miserably short of achieving.

At least one critic has argued, however, that the real split in the book is not between England and Scotland, but between city and country or even between new and old. The well-ordered country estate is a social ideal that dominates the final English section of the book, and the projection of this ideal involves, to some extent at least, a rejection of modernity in eighteenth-century Britain.[11] The opposition of England and Scotland may be said to mediate these more fundamental antagonisms. Scotland is, after all, a more pastoral society than England; its cities are smaller and closer to the towns and estates of the country-side. Glasgow is seen by Bramble as "a perfect bee-hive in point of industry . . . [which] stands partly on a gentle declivity . . . in a plain, watered by the river Clyde" (p. 246); he might well be speaking of a country house. Scotland is also preferred because the old ways have been preserved and honoured there much more faithfully than in England. The "Ode to Leven-Water" that Bramble sends to Dr Lewis evokes an "Arcadian" Scotland, one dominated by an "ancient faith that knows no guile" (pp. 249-50). Scotland and England are represented as being at different stages of development, and at times it seems that England's "progress" has been her ruination.

Why then the final English section of the narrative and its harmonious conclusion to the journey, which involves not only Bramble's return to his own well-ordered country seat but also the return of his wards to Bath? Bramble's apparent reconciliation to England and to Bath can be explained by the fact that the views of the other letter-writers are different from those of Bramble. Jery considers Bath society "as decent as any" and thinks "the individuals that composed it, would not be found deficient in good manners and decorum" elsewhere; Liddy sees it as "an earthly paradise" and avers that "the new buildings . . . look like so many enchanted castles" (pp. 51, 39). It is perhaps not surprising, therefore, that the young people return to Bath, while their uncle returns to his home in Wales. But the various correspondents are not as far apart as they sometimes appear to be, and the return of Bramble's wards to Bath seems to have his blessing (p. 351).

Smollett's use of the epistolary technique ensures that no one perspective in the narrative is definitive. As each letter-writer's viewpoint is a necessarily restricted one, a unifying perspective is required, one that encompasses the perceptions of the five correspondents. Ultimately the reader has to make sense of it all: "the multiplicity of concrete—but limited—aspects must 'coalesce' in the reader's imagination."[12] Nevertheless, something like a common perspective does begin to emerge within the narrative towards the end of the journey as the five letter-writers—previously so much at odds with one another—achieve a kind of harmony. Tabitha Bramble, Matthew's sister, marries Lismahago, a Scottish former officer in the British army. A principal source of Tabitha's conflict with her brother—her husband-hunting—is thereby removed. Win Jenkins, formerly Tabitha's maid, marries Matthew Bramble's former servant, Clinker, who turns out to be Bramble's natural son; the servants thus move up the social ladder, closer to the Brambles. Wilson, the apparently shiftless young man who claims to be in love with Liddy, turns out to be the son of Bramble's friends, Mr and Mrs Denison—the exemplars in the text of a happy rural existence—and the young man wins Liddy's hand. Jery exclaims "our society is really enchanting," and Bramble sings the praises of society in general: "a change of company [is] as necessary as a change of air, to promote a vigorous circulation of spirits, which is the very essence and criterion of good health" (pp. 333, 339). At the novel's end, then, an emerging harmonious order is projected in which the characters, whose differences have been thoroughly aired in the letters, will be able to live and prosper together.

This increasingly felicitous personal order is linked in important ways to the public realm, which is apparently dominated by the antagonisms of England and Scotland, new and old, city and country. Public and private converge in the characterization of Lismahago, who, Martz argues, is the principal vehicle for Smollett's praise of Scotland.[13] While it is true that Lismahago's defence of his homeland is important, Bramble commends the northern kingdom almost as much as the Scot does. Their dialogue, nevertheless, is sometimes critical of Scotland. For example, when the captain

defends the Scottish dialect and Scottish law and asserts that oatmeal and poverty are Scottish blessings, Bramble disagrees: "I should be glad to see the day when your peasants can afford to give all their oats to their cattle . . . and indulge themselves with good wheaten loaves" (pp. 275-80). The conversations between Lismahago and Bramble are central to the treatment of Scotland in the text, and the key to understanding the link between the personal and the public is to be found in their last major discussion.

The climactic exchange between these two occasional antagonists, which takes place after the travellers have returned to England, centres upon the issue of the unification of the two nations, achieved by acts of both parliaments in 1707. Lismahago condemns the Union in the strongest possible terms. He denies Bramble's assertion that the recent increase in Scottish material well-being is ascribable to the Union and argues instead that it derives from "the natural process of improvement." According to the captain, the Scots gained one advantage from the Union—"the privilege of trading to the English plantations"—but realized few benefits, and meanwhile lost "the independency of their state, the greatest prop of national spirit; . . . their parliament and their courts of justice." Lismahago asserts that the English reaped the benefits of the Union: political security, territorial expansion, increase of population. But Bramble argues again that material benefits to Scotland justify the Union—"many of them [the Scots] in England, as well as in her colonies, amassed large fortunes, with which they returned to their own country." Lismahago denies that on balance Scotland realized any gain, since so much money leaves the northern kingdom to pay the "grievous impositions" of and to buy "superfluities" from the English. But, while Bramble grants that Lismahago is right to decry "the contempt for Scotland, which prevails too much on this side of the Tweed," he insists upon "the happy effects of the Union" (pp. 275-80).

This exchange between the Welshman and the Scot has its roots in Smollett's own historiographical labours. Lismahago's denunciation of the Union echoes the report in Smollett's *History of England* of the arguments of Scottish noblemen, who, with the loss of their parliament, "found themselves degraded in point of dignity and influence"; of Scottish merchants, who worried about being "saddled with heavy duties and restrictions"; and of "the people in general," who believed "that the independency of their nation had fallen sacrifice to treachery and corruption."[14] Bramble's assertion that "the people lived better, had more trade, and a greater quantity of money circulating since the union, than before" (p. 276) is akin to the arguments in the Scottish parliament of the "noblemen attached to the union," who "magnified the advantages that would accrue to the kingdom from the privileges of trading to

the English plantations, and being protected in their commerce by a powerful navy."[15] More important, Bramble's expression of "satisfaction at the happy effects of the union" (p. 275) is identical with the *British* point of view enunciated by the narrator of the *History of England,* who ends his discussion of these events with the sanguine conclusion that the Union "quietly took effect and fully answered all the purposes for which it was intended."[16]

Lismahago is having none of it, but if the reader looks back upon both the censure of England and the praise of Scotland and ahead to the harmonious ending based ostensibly on three marital unions, the discussion of political union will be seen as a focal point in the narrative, one that effects the convergence of many elements in the text that might otherwise seem disparate and unrelated. To begin with, Bramble's defence of the Union suggests the possibility of harmony between the apparently despised southern kingdom and the beloved northern realm. Indeed Bramble's pro-Union stance undermines the argument that an essentially negative view of England is elaborated in the text. From the perspective of the debate over the Union, one can begin to make sense of the hints at a balanced assessment that we find in the midst of the supposed censure of the southern kingdom.[17]

Throughout the journey Bramble acknowledges one feature of English life that is admirable and deserves to be emulated—England's material progress. John Sena argues that Bramble's praise for Blackfriars Bridge is an exception to the Welshman's generally negative view of English architecture, and Bramble himself thinks the bridge an anomaly: "I wonder how they stumbled upon a work of such magnificence and utility" (p. 87).[18] But elsewhere Bramble, however grudgingly, expresses admiration for other indications of English material well-being. "It must be allowed," he acknowledges, "that London and Westminster are much better paved and lighted than they were formerly. The new streets are spacious, regular, and airy; and the houses are generally convenient" (p. 87). In the north of England, furthermore, Bramble finds between Durham and Newcastle "the highest scene of cultivation that ever I beheld," and he admits that the latter town has been "rendered populous and rich by industry and commerce" (p. 202). Once in Scotland, furthermore, Bramble looks back at England and discovers features of English life to praise. About wheat farming, he tells Dr Lewis: "that agriculture in this country is not yet brought to that perfection which it has attained in England" (pp. 215-16). In Dunbar, although the town is "well situated for trade," he notices that there is "little appearance of business in the place," and, while it is faint praise of England, Bramble admits that "the public inns of Edinburgh, are still worse than those of London" (pp. 216, 219). Bramble also grants that "an Englishman . . . refers every thing he sees to a compar-

ison with the same articles in his own country; and this comparison is unfavourable to Scotland in all its exteriors" (p. 231). The clothing, dwellings, and agricultural theories of peasants, as well as the treatment of servants, all point to the fact that Scotland is woefully behind England in material terms (pp. 244-45, 274). In fact, Brambles's favourable comment on Edinburgh's expansion shows that he uses English towns (possibly even Bath!) as a model to be emulated by the Scots. Bramble also avers that Scotland's "gardens and parks are not comparable to those of England" (p. 234).

Remarks by the other correspondents keep the question of England in suspense even as the country comes in for severe criticism. The other letter-writers remind us both that England may not be as bad as Bramble sometimes suggests and that Scotland may not be as wonderful as Lismahago asserts. Although he has much good to say about the northern kingdom, when Jery compares the farmers of Northumberland and Scotland, he finds the former "lusty fellows, fresh complexioned, cleanly, and well-cloathed" but the latter "lank, lean, hard-featured, sallow, soiled, and shabby" (p. 214). Tabitha holds up Scotland as a model in a way which emphasizes the country's backwardness and poverty: "I don't see why the sarvants of Wales should'n't drink fair water, and eat hot cakes and barley cale, as they do in Scotland, without troubling the botcher above once a quarter" (p. 274). The cumulative effect of the letters dealing with Scotland and its relationship to England—and this becomes clearer if the reader has Bramble's endorsement of the union of the two kingdoms in mind—is to suggest that unqualified praise for Scotland and denigration of England are not justified; a more balanced view is necessary.[19] In political terms, this perspective is the British point of view embraced by Bramble in his clash with Lismahago.

This British perspective, however, is not rooted solely in Bramble's recognition of English superiority "in all exteriors"; it also derives from the Welshman's conviction that Scotland is a repository of ancient and essential values. Scotland's moral superiority becomes apparent in the course of a comparison of English and Scottish versions of hospitality. Not surprisingly, the treatment of guests is one of the central concerns of this travel narrative. With respect to English hospitality, Bramble, at the home of squire Burdock, finds proof that the English are "as a people totally destitute of this virtue." The host is inattentive; the hostess is hateful; the house is "like a great inn." "I would rather dine upon filberts with a hermit, than feed upon venison with a hog," declares Bramble (pp. 164-65). But of Scotland, Bramble tells Dr Lewis, "I have met with more kindness, hospitality, and rational entertainment, in a few weeks, than I ever received in any other country during the whole course of my life" (p. 231).

Another instance of the corrupted relations between quest and host in the southern kingdom—one that also illuminates the ways in which *Humphry Clinker* functions as a fictional record of many aspects of mid eighteenth-century English life—is the Duke of Newcastle's levee. Fallen from grace and in a state of virtual stupefaction, the Duke entertains his guests because he wants them "to support the shadow of that power, which he no longer retains in substance." The quests, for their part, are contemptuous of their host. The leering captain C——says of him: "This wise-acre is still a-bed; and, I think, the best thing he can do, is to sleep on till Christmas; for, when he gets up, he does nothing but expose his own folly." In addition, the nearly total absence of clergymen, noted by Jery ("there was no more than one gown and cassock"), is a sign of the rank ingratitude of the churchmen who enjoyed Newcastle's bountiful patronage for many years (pp. 110-11).[20] England, then, is deficient in hospitality and gratitude—a clear sign of its depravity. Scotland is merely lagging behind in material development: Bramble calls the northern kingdom "a paradise" (p. 252).

The comments upon the two countries by the letter-writers focus our attention, then, upon the quite distinct strengths and weaknesses of the two kingdoms. Bramble argues that Scotland has benefited materially from the union; Lismahago worries about the ill effects of English luxury on the Scottish nation. Their inconclusive exchange—each stubbornly asserts his own view—leaves the reader to decide. Living in a post-Union world, however, and generally disposed to side with Bramble rather than with the "comic grotesque" Lismahago, the reader is likely to view the Union as efficacious and beneficial to both sides, even if not unproblematically so.[21] England may threaten Scotland's comparative moral health even as it holds out the promise of necessary progress. Yet the narrative suggests that influence need not always be baneful; Scotland's moral superiority presents itself as a potential remedy for England's ills. The unity that Folkenflik finds in this narrative is, he argues, the result of "a *discordia concors* in which distinct individuals, like the nations England, Scotland, and Wales, come together in a union which gives health to all."[22] The projected concord arises from Smollett's representation and endorsement within the narrative of a change of great historical significance—the gradual creation of the United Kingdom.

The rejuvenating and healing effects of union are most clearly suggested in Smollett's novel in personal terms, but the personal embodies the social and political. Tabitha Bramble, a Welshwoman and therefore someone from south of the Tweed, marries the Scotsman Lismahago. Both Tabitha and her husband are thus happily settled in life, and Matthew Bramble is closer to finding the peace and comfort that he seeks. This and the other marriages, then, should not be dismissed

as mere "plot contrivances," but, rather, should be seen as images of what Smollett represents as the best hope for Britain.[23] The link between the marriages and the historical destiny of the United Kingdom is unmistakable; in the letter in which Bramble and Lismahago air their views on the Union, Bramble announces the coming marriage of Tabitha and the Scottish veteran. And the other marriages—not just the union of the two grotesques—also reinforce the arguments that Smollett elaborates in the text about the historical importance of the Union, thereby suggesting the real possibility of the future health of both family and polity. In choosing Clinker, Jenkins rejects (English) luxury represented by Jery's foppish manservant in favour of (Scottish) sincerity and fellow-feeling, while Liddy's marriage to Dennison is, given the character of the Dennisons, an embracing of the country and of the old ways.

The Dennison estate is the clearest and the most important representation of the harmonious ideal that Bramble celebrates in the novel. He tells Dr Lewis that Mr Dennison "has really attained to that pitch of rural felicity, at which I have been aspiring these twenty years." Dennison's success, however, is not simply the attainment of peace and simplicity; it is also the achievement of plenty and comfort through industry and the application of scientific principles. Dennison works hard, conducts "experiments in agriculture," reforests and encloses his land. Bramble proposes enclosure as the solution to the problems of Scottish agriculture (p. 245). The Dennison estate is consequently a model of "industry and commerce" in a rural setting (pp. 320-28). It is also, of course, a garden. The Dennisons are city people and residents of England who combine the scientific spirit, industry, and activity of the city, of England, of the new age, with the values of the country, of Scotland, of the past. The garden is an image of the ideal espoused by Bramble in *Humphry Clinker*. But the gardens of Scotland are deficient when compared with those of England, and this deficiency is consonant with the backward state of development of the northern kingdom. The Dennison estate, after all, is in England and is therefore an affirmation that the ideal can be achieved in that country. For this reason, the letter-writers can and indeed must return to England. "Their future is in England," as Davis points out.[24] So too is that of Lismahago. And so too is that of Scotland.

Of course, Lismahago himself does not see it that way and in some ways he has the better of his exchange with Bramble on the Union. Bramble's word, however, is the last one, and it is, for him, a somewhat uncharacteristically English word. Lismahago ends by lamenting the ill effects of unbridled personal freedom and commerce on a society, and Bramble answers that "by proper regulations, commerce may produce every national benefit, without the allay of such concomitant evils" (p. 280). England's commerce can be beneficial

if it is suitably regulated—restrained, that is, by a proper sense of value. In *Humphry Clinker* moral values are represented as Scotland's greatest treasure; England is redeemable if the values of Scotland, the country, and the past are embraced along with the benefits of modernity. Baynard, the Welshman's English friend, who is being destroyed by his surrender to a life of luxury, is rescued by Dennison and Bramble, who urge him to adopt Dennison's ways and apply them to his own estate. Dennison's methods constitute a felicitous mix of English and Scottish strengths. So the union of Liddy and "Young Mr. Dennison" means that Bramble's niece, who was at first dangerously taken by Bath and London, is now joined to the scion of the family which represents social order and personal well-being in the narrative. Liddy is, therefore, safe, and her return to Bath need not make Bramble anxious about her future. Old and new, city and country, Scotland and England are harmonized in the series of unions that Smollett uses to end *Humphry Clinker,* valorizing both union—harmonious, moral human society—and the Union in the process.

Underlying, then, the satirical depiction of England and the loving portrait of Scotland, underlying the familial disputes and love interests, underlying the movement through space (city and country) and time (old and new), underlying all the seemingly disparate elements in *Humphry Clinker* is an historical vision. England is to be admired for its material progress; Scotland, at an earlier stage of development, might well emulate the southern kingdom on that score. But England as it grows and changes is being corrupted and can only be saved by a return to the values that are preserved in Scotland. The Union in all its ramifications, *Humphry Clinker* suggests, is a potential solution to the woes besetting England and the challenges confronting Scotland. This historical argument might well be regarded as an illusion, as Byron Gassman has suggested in a rather different context, but if so, it is an illusion that is rooted in a vision of the joint destiny of the kingdoms on both sides of the Tweed, one that is elaborated and endorsed within the narrative.[25]

. . . . .

If the claim is accepted that *Humphry Clinker* is more satisfying structurally than Smollett's other fiction because of the historical argument that unfolds in the narrative, should this text therefore be called Smollett's most "novelistic" fiction and his one successfully achieved novel? Several critics have, at least implicitly, already made this point. Alan McKillop suggests that *Humphry Clinker* is Smollett's best essay in the novel form because it is "successfully centered about a humorous character." John Warner, too, argues that in earlier works Smollett was unable "to entrust the serious work of the novel to the story of the individual," whereas in *Humphry Clinker* the focus was not

upon "the exterior world for its own sake but upon that scene as it relates to the interior world of character."[26] These essentially Forsterian arguments—that Smollett's greatest accomplishment as a novelist derives from his having centred *Humphry Clinker* on successfully realized characters—lend credence to the proposition that Smollett's use of history makes *Humphry Clinker* his most fully accomplished novel, since the characterization of Matthew Bramble and the enactment of the historical argument in the narrative depend each upon the other.

We first encounter Bramble at odds with his physical, social, and political environment, including the company of his fellow travellers. His complaint to his doctor that "The pills are good for nothing" opens the novel. Bramble is sick and England is sick; the illness of both will become more apparent as the journey unfolds. In his first letter Bramble observes, "I shall set out tomorrow morning for the Hot Well at Bristol, where I am afraid I shall stay longer than I could wish"; he travels in search of a cure, but the places that he initially visits cause his condition to worsen. Not just Bramble's health is in disrepair, however; Bramble also tells Dr Lewis that "A ridiculous incident that happened yesterday to my niece Liddy, has disordered me in such a manner that I expect to be laid up with another fit of the gout" (pp. 5-6). The Welshman's relations with his family also contribute to his discomfiture and ill health. These relations too must be improved in the course of the narrative. Bramble is alienated from his environment, his family, and even from himself. Only when his mind and spirit—troubled by the state of his own health and that of his family and his polity—are given relief will his peevishness subside.

The valetudinarian makes real progress in the course of the journey. At the end of the narrative, Bramble's entire family is "happily settled"; Bramble himself has "laid in a considerable stock of health." And not only is Baynard's estate restored to harmony, but Bramble himself is headed back to the "salutary" Brambleton-hall (pp. 350-51). His achievement of a modicum of well-being is linked to the state of his family and both are suggestive of the possibility of social health. When Bramble praises the benefits of society in his penultimate letter to Dr Lewis, he celebrates the new-found harmony within his own family and Baynard's first steps towards the realization of the social ideal represented by the Dennison estate. Bramble provides a centre for this narrative not only because of his relations with the other characters and the richness of his observations and commentary, but also because his health and the well-being of those around him are achieved, like the envisioned health of his polity, by means of a unifying circuit of the southern and the northern kingdoms. In short, Bramble's fate echoes Britain's fate, and Britain's fate conditions Bramble's; Smollett's most successfully realized character is the efficacious centre of *Humphrey Clinker* in important part because he is crucial to the elaboration of the historical argument enacted within the narrative.

The historical argument in *Humphry Clinker,* then, is a crucial aspect of Smollett's most successful achievement in fictional characterization. Moreover, recognizing that argument also leads to a greater appreciation of Smollett's emplotment of this novel. Sheldon Sacks has argued tellingly that *Humphry Clinker* is "an action with so many digressions of one kind and another that its total effect was somewhat vitiated."[27] Sacks did not indicate what elements in the narrative he regarded as digressions, but Lewis Knapp has commented on "the digressive accounts of the Baynards and the Dennisons" in the latter part of the novel (p. xiv). Having recognized the historical argument of the text, however, one can see that these accounts, as well as the descriptions of Bath, London, Edinburgh, and Loch Leven and the characterizations of Clinker, Lismahago, and the Burdocks, can no longer be regarded as digressive. Elements that heretofore seemed interesting or entertaining, but hardly crucial, in a narrative that seemed to many readers to lack a unifying plan, play an important part in the exacerbation and resolution of the "represented instability" in the relationships of Bramble and the other characters, a relationship that has a public as well as a private, an historical as well as a personal, dimension. In short, recognizing Smollett's elaboration of a historical vision in *Humphry Clinker* makes it clear that the narrative is a better integrated "action" than Sacks allowed.[28]

Having shown why I think awareness of the historical argument in *Humphry Clinker* lends credence to the claim that Smollett's last work is his most novelistic achievement, let me now propose another, and for me a more compelling, reason for attributing Smollett's accomplishment in *Humphry Clinker* to its historical aspect by focusing briefly on Smollett's several attempts to define the kind of fiction he was writing. Smollett classified *Roderick Random* for his readers by placing it within the picaresque tradition, by identifying it as a species of satire, and, finally, by promising that the satire would be "introduced . . . in the course of an interesting story, which brings every incident home to life; and . . . represent[s] familiar scenes." Smollett thus focused his reader's attention on the imaginative and the literary character of the text. Later, in *Ferdinand, Count Fathom,* Smollett spoke of a novel as "a large diffused picture, comprehending the characters of life, disposed in different groups, and exhibited in various attitudes, for the purposes of a uniform plan, and general occurrence, to which every individual is subservient." At the same time, however, he also used analogies drawn from painting and drama, as McKillop has shown.[29] Here he moved away from a definition of the novel as a satire and towards the realism that has often been associated with the emergent nov-

el.[30] Thus he continued to emphasize the imaginative traditions within which his creations were to be comprehended, but he also began to link his own work with a tradition that includes attempts to define the novel as a fictional form that functions as history.[31]

This latter tendency became more pronounced in *Humphry Clinker,* in which the narrative was presented to the public as a genuine collection of letters. Jonathan Dustwich offers the letters to Henry Davis, a bookseller, but informs him that "with reference to the manner in which I got possession of these Letters, it is a circumstance that concerns my conscience only" (p. 2). For the first time, Smollett adopted a device that Barbara Foley calls "pseudofactual imposture," a strategy of presentation that we associate with the fictions of Behn, Defoe, and Richardson.[32] The way in which Smollett's frame for *Humphry Clinker* could function as a definition of the new form was discussed by Richardson in a letter to William Warburton. Somewhat dismayed by Warburton's provision of a preface for the first edition of *Clarissa,* Richardson wrote:

> I could wish that the *Air* of Genuineness had been kept up, tho' I want not the letters to be *thought* genuine; only so far kept up, I mean, as that they should not prefatically be owned *not* to be genuine: and this for fear of weakening their Influence . . . [and] that kind of Historical Faith which Fiction itself is generally read with, tho' we know it to be Fiction.[33]

Richardson wanted his narrative to be understood as something other than "mere fiction" or romance; he wanted his text read with the "Historical faith" of readers of novels. Smollett's reasons for adopting "pseudofactual imposture" are less clear than Richardson's, but, in appropriating that technique in *Humphry Clinker,* it is reasonable to conclude that he was insisting upon the historicity of his fiction. Smollett did not identify his last fiction with literary genres other than the novel because, like Richardson, he wanted to induce a "Historical faith" in his readers.

Not only Richardson, of course, but also Fielding and a host of other writers identified the "new species of writing" which they helped to create as a kind of history. In implicitly designating *Humphry Clinker* as a "historical" narrative, then, Smollett linked his last work with a line of development that stretches backward through Defoe to sixteenth and seventeenth-century anti-romancers and forward to Scott. Smollett's use of his "editor" constitutes an identification of his own work with that tradition. In addition, then, to "the ingredients of the early Scott—humorous realism, precise topographical and social details about remote and interesting places with a romantic context"—which McKillop saw in *Humphry Clinker,* Smollett also looked forward to Scott by invoking a convention that indicates to the reader that this fiction should be read as a kind of history and also acknowledges the paradoxical nature of the novel's claim to historicity.[34]

Thus, the final reason for regarding **Humphry Clinker** as Smollett's most novelistic fictional narrative is because it alone of all Smollett's works presses us to conceive of the novel as a fictional form that does the work of history. In doing so, this novel also suggests that the claimed historicity of the novel should be thought of as a necessary element in any theoretical account of the nature of the form. Like many another early English novel, Smollett's last and best work argues for an undeniably problematic but nevertheless constitutive link between the novel and historical discourse. In *Vanity Fair* Miss Rose tells the stiff Mr Crawley that she is reading Smollett's history, "without, however, adding that it was the history of Mr. Humphry Clinker."[35] The joke, it would seem, was on Miss Rose; she said more than she knew. **Humphry Clinker** is indeed historical, and that is an important reason why we still think of it as one of the handful of crucial English novels written in the eighteenth century.

Notes

[1] See, for example, Sheridan Baker, "*Humphry Clinker* as Comic Romance," *Papers of the Michigan Academy of Science, Arts, and Letters* 46 (1961), 645-54; David K. Jeffrey, "*Roderick Random:* The Form and Structure of a Romance," *Revue Belge de Philologie et d'Histoire* 58 (1980), 604-14; Ronald Paulson, *Satire and the Novel in Eighteenth-Century England* (New Haven: Yale University Press, 1967), pp. 165-218; G.S. Rousseau, "Smollett and the Picaresque: Some Questions about a Label," *Studies in Burke and His Time* 12 (1970-71), 1886-1904; and Robert D. Spector, *Tobias George Smollett* (Boston: G.K. Hall, 1989).

[2] Ronald Paulson argues that the "unmodified satiric conventions" found in *Roderick Random* are at odds with "the realistic world of the post-Richardsonian novel" (pp. 176-79). See also Alan McKillop, *The Early Masters of English Fiction* (Lawrence: University of Kansas Press, 1956), p. 151; and Jeffrey, p. 614.

[3] H.W. Hodges, ed., *Roderick Random* by Tobias Smollett (London: Dent, 1927), p. xiii; see also A.R. Humphreys, "Fielding and Smollett," in *From Dryden to Johnson: Volume 4 of The Pelican Guide to English Literature,* ed. Boris Ford (Harmondsworth: Penguin, 1957), p. 314.

[4] Robert Folkenflik, "Self and Society: Comic Union in *Humphry Clinker,*" *Philological Quarterly* 53 (1974), 204. Others who have asserted the unity of the work include Robert Gorham Davis, ed., *The Expedition of Humphry Clinker* (New York: Holt, Rinehart and Winston, 1967), pp. v-xxiii; and B.L. Reid, "Smollett's

Healing Journey," *Virginia Quarterly Review* 41 (1965), 549-70.

[5] By "history," I mean historiography or historical writing, not historical events; by "historical argument" and "historical vision," I mean a line of reasoning or a set of insights about the evolution of the British nation. I assume, here and elsewhere, even though I recognize the problematic character of my assumption, that "fiction" and "history" are fundamentally different forms of discourse, that the latter is distinguished from the former by "its being submitted as a whole to the control of evidence." See Arnaldo Momigliano, "The Rhetoric of History and the History of Rhetoric: On Hayden White's Tropes," in *Comparative Criticism: A Yearbook,* ed. E.S. Shaffer (Cambridge: Cambridge University Press, 1981), pp. 267-68. I use the word "novelistic" to suggest that *Humphry Clinker,* of all of Smollett's fictions, is his most fully novel-like achievement. I substantiate this claim in the latter half of the essay by considering the text in light of several definitions of the novel, showing how an appreciation of Smollett's use of history in this text helps us to see why *Humphry Clinker* is Smollett's best approximation of the form.

[6] Louis L. Martz, *The Later Career of Tobias Smollett* (1942; reprinted Hamden, CT: Archon, 1967), pp. 11, 13-16. Sekora finds in Smollett's various histories a "political history of luxury" and the source for his later writings on luxury—that "capital crime against British civilization"—including *Humphry Clinker.* Sekora argues that Smollett's final work "is a highly political novel, one of the most politically charged of the century" (pp. 136, 219).

[7] Davis, ed., p. xix.

[8] Fred W. Boege, *Smollett's Reputation as a Novelist* (Princeton: Princeton University Press, 1947), p. 30; Martz, p. 129.

[9] Critics who have argued that the novel concludes in such a spirit include Davis, pp. ix, xxi; Folkenflik, p. 204; and Ried, p. 550.

[10] See *The Expedition of Humphry Clinker,* ed. with introduction, Lewis M. Knapp, revised, Paul-Gabriel Boucé (Oxford: Oxford University Press, 1984), pp. 34-38. References are to this edition.

[11] John F. Sena, "Ancient Designs and Modern Folly: Architecture in *The Expedition of Humphry Clinker,*" *Harvard Library Bulletin* 27 (1979), 113.

[12] Wolfgang Iser, *The Implied Reader: Patterns of Communication in Prose Fiction from Bunyan to Beckett* (Baltimore: John Hopkins University Press, 1974), p. 71; see also R.D.S. Jack, "Appearance and Reality

in *Humphry Clinker,"* in *Smollett: Author of the First Distinction,* ed. Alan Bold (Totowa, NJ: Barnes and Noble, 1982), pp. 212-13.

[13] Martz, pp. 168-70.

[14] Smollett, *The History of England from the Revolution in 1688 to the Death of George II,* 2 vols (Philadelphia: Edward Parker, 1822), 1:381.

[15] *History of England,* 1:384.

[16] *History of England,* 1:385.

[17] Spector, 137-38.

[18] Sena, p. 100.

[19] Jack, p. 226.

[20] See Paul-Gabriel Boucé, "The Duke of Newcastle's Levee in Smollett's *Humphry Clinker,"* *Yearbook of English Studies* 5 (1975), 136-41. That *Humphry Clinker* functions as a work of (fictional) contemporary history has been noted by a number of critics, including Jerry C. Beasley ("Smollett's Novels: *Ferdinand Count Fathom* for the Defense," *Papers on Language and Literature* 20 [1984], 182), who has pointed out that the narrative "fairly hums with historical and topical allusions."

[21] Davis, p. xxi; Robert Hopkins, "The Function of the Grotesque in *Humphry Clinker,"* *Huntington Library Quarterly* 32 (1968-69), 168-70.

[22] Folkenflik, p. 204.

[23] Davis, p. xxii.

[24] Davis, p. xxii.

[25] Gassman, *"Humphry Clinker* and the Two Kingdoms of George III," *Criticism* 16 (1974), 108.

[26] McKillop, p. 172; John M. Warner, "Smollett's Development as a Novelist," *Novel* 5 (1971-72), 154, 158.

[27] Sheldon Sacks, *Fiction and the Shape of Belief* (1964; reprinted Chicago: University of Chicago Press, 1980), p. 271. For Sacks's definition of an "action," see p. 26.

[28] No doubt Sacks was correct about *Humphry Clinker* in the sense that, as he observes, "many readers have felt greater pleasure from the work's parts than from the accomplishment of its artistic ends" (p. 271). This is in part because Sacks's readers were disposed to think of *Humphry Clinker* as seriously deficient in comparison with *Tom Jones,* whereas Smollett's work needs to be seen as something fundamentally different from Fielding's masterpiece. In order to understand how *Humphry Clinker* is different from *Tom Jones,* we may turn to Sacks's fellow Chicagoan, R.S. Crane. Crane identified three possible kinds of plots in novels: those of action, character, and thought. He pointed out that most plots are plots of action and that as a result many critics think of plot in terms of action alone. Indeed, Sacks's definition of a novel as a "represented action" suggests that he identified, to some extent at least, plots of action with novelistic plots. Of Crane's three types, however, clearly it is the third that applies to *Humphry Clinker.* There is no real change in Bramble's situation or in his moral character; but Bramble does feel and think differently at the conclusion of the narrative. Thus *Humphry Clinker* ought to be seen as a successful novel with a plot of thought because the various elements deployed by Smollett in the narrative bear upon the changing views and feelings of the protagonist. Seeing the novel in this light does not, of course, make it any more or less unified, but it may make us more sensitive to the particular unity of Smollett's narrative. See Crane, "The Concept of Plot and the Plot of *Tom Jones"* in *Critics and Criticism: Ancient and Modern,* ed. Crane (Chicago: University of Chicago Press, 1952), pp. 620-21.

[29] *The Adventures of Ferdinand Count Fathom,* introduction and notes by Jerry C. Beasley, ed. O.M. Brack (Athens: University of Georgia Press, 1988), pp. 4, 9-10; McKillop, pp. 164-65.

[30] As in Ian Watt's classic study, *The Rise of the Novel: Studies in Defoe, Richardson and Fielding* (Berkeley: University of California Press, 1957), chap. 1.

[31] See Leo Braudy, *Narrative Form in Fiction and History: Hume, Fielding, and Gibbon* (Princeton: Princeton University Press, 1970), pp. 91-212; Jerry C. Beasley, *Novels of the 1740s* (Athens: University of Georgia Press, 1982), pp. 43-84; Michael McKeon, *The Origins of the English Novel, 1600-1740* (Baltimore: Johns Hopkins University Press, 1987), pp. 25-128; and my "The Reception of *A Journal of the Plague Year* and the Nexus of Fiction and History in the Novel," *ELH* 57 (1990), 529-56. Lennard J. Davis, *Factual Fictions: The Origins of the English Novel* (New York: Columbia University Press, 1983) is also apposite.

[32] Barbara Foley, *Telling the Truth: The Theory and Practice of Documentary Fiction* (Ithaca: Cornell University Press, 1986), p. 118.

[33] *Selected Letters of Samuel Richardson,* ed. John Carroll (Oxford: Clarendon, 1964), p. 85.

[34] McKillop, p. 179; also my "The Internal Machinery

Displayed: *The Heart of Midlothian* and Scott's Apparatus for the Waverly Novels," *CLIO* 17 (1987), 1-20.

[35] William Makepeace Thackeray, *Vanity Fair,* introd. Joseph Warren Beach (New York: Random House, 1950), pp. 87-88.

Daniel Punday (essay date 1994)

SOURCE: "Satiric Method and the Reader in *Sir Launcelot Greaves,*" in *Eighteenth-Century Fiction,* Vol. 6, No. 2, January 1994, pp. 169-88.

[*In the following essay, Punday refutes the prevailing view that* Sir Launcelot Greaves *is a failure as a satire. He asserts instead that in this novel, Smollett deliberatelyly manipulated the romantic literary conventions of his time with satiric intent, and that this would have been recognized by his contemporary readership.*]

Tobias Smollett is best known for his picaresque social satires, such as **Roderick Random, Peregrine Pickle,** and **Humphry Clinker.** Critics have generally considered **Sir Launcelot Greaves** a failed experiment, an unhappy mixture of his characteristic mode with chivalric romance conventions.[1] Although Smollett seems to use his hero as a satiric mouthpiece whose exemplary nature implicitly criticizes the age,[2] critics have considered the clash between romantic and picaresque world views a major fault in the novel and its satiric methods.

This essay will attempt to explain how this clash functions as part of the overall satiric method of the novel. That Smollett both uses and criticizes the romantic conventions embodied by Greaves should not surprise us; interpretive tradition has assumed that **Greaves** is careless because of the conditions under which it was conceived and executed, and consequently critics have failed to investigate the conflict between romantic and picaresque perspectives. Such a clash is, in fact, part of the definition of the picaro; as Ronald Paulson suggests: "In a sense the picaro represents . . . an ironic structure embodied in a character: a prudential awareness is joined to a moral obtuseness. Lazaro does not see the truth, but his peasant cunning makes him see something close to it, and so his observations betray himself and his surroundings simultaneously."[3] While Greaves clearly does not have "peasant cunning," I will suggest below that he does have a dual nature—as critic and as satiric butt in his own right. The critical failure to recognize this dual role and integrate it into interpretation of the novel has led to a perception of the novel and its methods as sloppy and piecemeal.

Greaves's seemingly random adventures reiterate a basic theme—the problematic and antagonistic relationship between social roles and individual personality. By adopting the highly formal code of knight-errantry in order to expose individuals who fail to be socially responsible, Greaves attempts to reaffirm the balance between the social and personal. Greaves's dual nature—as a critic upholding the connection between such external forms and the self, and as a character who is defined by just such a formal role—is a way of obviating a problem central to Smollett's satiric method. For Smollett, the formal relations constituted by the text can, like social roles, seem cut off from their "personal" meaning to the reader. Greaves's dual role partially enables Smollett to collapse the distinction between the satirist and the objects of that satire. Yet Smollett must overcome a far greater barrier—that between the lesson of the text and its application in the real world of the reader. We will see that Smollett finds the solution to this problem in the very writing and publishing context that critics have assumed accounted for the novel's carelessness.

. . . . .

The bulk of the satire in **Greaves** exposes the way in which society fails to live up to the hero's expectations. This focus has led critics to assume that the novel's adventures are a loosely joined collection of Smollett's satiric targets. Even critics who have tried to find unifying strands in the novel's themes and satiric thrusts have presupposed vagueness in Smollett's intention. David Evans, for example, suggests that "Greaves is, from the outset, presented as the representative of two sets of ideals, the spirit of chivalry and benevolent squirearchy."[4] Evans assumes that **Greaves** is at best a loosely cohesive work, and hence open to Smollett's casual inclusion of any material that can be criticized by these general ideals. I will argue throughout this essay, however, that Smollett had a much more specific satiric intention, and that this intention reveals not only consistency of message, but purposeful development of characters and plot, and careful and often subtle integration of satire and narrative method.

Greaves's adventures continually reveal the disjunction between individual personalities and the social roles and positions they have adopted. Greaves himself does not represent an ideal conjoining of individual personality and role, but rather a character whose search for the perfect juxtaposition of the two reveals not only the hypocrisy of many of the characters, but, more important, the problems in the very nature of his quest. Greaves himself explicitly expresses his central concern in what may be the novel's clearest example of this disjunction of personality and role, Justice Gobble: "You have abused the authority with which you were invested, intailed a reproach upon your office, and, instead of being revered as a blessing, you are detested as a curse among your fellow-creatures. This, indeed, is generally the case of low fellows, who are thrust into the magistracy without sentiment, education, or capacity" (pp. 97-98). This passage, which occurs near the end of Greaves's wandering and caps the longest of his adventures, makes explicit much that is merely implied in other episodes. Greaves is not the upholder of virtue in general, nor is he the model of the ideal squire; rather he is preoccupied with chastising those who venture above their social level and generally with asserting that public and social positions must be filled by the proper persons.

Smollett's concern for characters who do not fully conform to the social roles they have adopted is equally evident in Greaves's more minor and seemingly incidental adventures. Greaves's first adventure, that with the army recruits, is a somewhat less obvious manifestation of this general theme:

> The knight's steed seemed at least as well pleased with the sound of the drum as were the recruits that followed it; and signified his satisfaction in some curvettings and caprioles, which did not at all discompose the rider, who, addressing himself to the serjeant, "Friend, said he, you ought to teach your drummer better manners. I would chastise the fellow on the spot for his insolence, were it not out of respect I bear to his majesty's service." "Respect mine a——! (cried this ferocious commander) what, d'ye think to frighten us with your pewter pisspot on your scull, and your lacquer'd potlid on your arm?" (p. 48)

Here Greaves's ideal definition of the army—a definition which specifies both the role and the person proper to it—conflicts with the actual personalities who fill the roles. The same problem lies behind another of what seem to be merely random adventures included for the sake of action: Greaves's encounter with the London haberdashers. Greaves, when told that Crabshaw had fought with these officers because they "insisted upon having for their supper the victuals which Sir Launcelot had bespoke" (p. 107), chastises Crabshaw rather than defending his right to his dinner (p. 108). Soon, however, these officers are revealed as "'prentices to two London haberdashers" (p. 110), whose improper assumption of a higher social role the narrator points out: "In a word, the two pseudo-officers were very roughly handled for their presumption in pretending to act characters for which they were so ill qualified" (p. 111). Again, Greaves's expectation that people should be properly fitted for their public roles and thus deserve respect is confounded, and the passage satirizes the presumption.

Greaves's discomfort with the discrepancy between public role and private self began long before his knight-errantry. From the first Greaves had trouble "fitting into" normal society. Critics often attribute this failure

to Greaves's selflessness and rejection of a corrupt society, but Greaves's dissatisfaction seems to be with the nature of social roles themselves. As Paul-Gabriel Boucé suggests in characterizing Greaves's madness: "The hero is driven by a (potentially) tragic 'Até,' a kind of arrogance of the Good, which leads him to wish to take the law into his own hands."[5] Greaves cannot accept a role in society and function according to its models of behaviour. Sir Everhard Greaves, although pleased by his son's "feeling heart" (p. 23), is angered by his inability to distance himself from the object of his beneficence: "the old knight could not bear to see his only son so wholly attached to these lowly pleasures, while he industriously shunned all opportunities of appearing in that superior sphere to which he was designed by nature, and by fortune" (p. 24). Young Greaves rejects the "superior sphere" not because of his charitable impulses, but because he dislikes those who treat social roles as superficial rather than a matter of personal responsibility and self-definition: "He had no communication with your rich yeomen; but rather treated them and their families with studied contempt, because forsooth they pretended to assume the dress and manners of the gentry. . . . I have heard Mr. Greaves ridicule them for their vanity and aukward imitation; and therefore, I believe, he avoided all concerns with them, even when they endeavoured to engage his attention" (p. 21).

To whatever degree Greaves criticizes such imposters, this example suggests that the problem goes far beyond the case of a few people aspiring above their natural position. As young Greaves's attempt to reject the entire social system suggests, individual personalities inevitably fail to coincide with their social roles. The flaw is in the nature of social roles themselves. The impetus for Greaves's knight-errantry—his frustrated love for Aurelia Darnel—suggests how the nature of social roles problematizes authentic individuality. Greaves tells Aurelia immediately after her rescue from the runaway coach, "What I have done (said he) was but a common office of humanity, which I would have performed for any of my fellow-creatures: but, for the preservation of miss Aurelia Darnel, I would at any time sacrifice my life with pleasure" (p. 32). The distinction Greaves makes here is the one I have pointed out in the examples above—that between the personal and the social self, the genuine identity and the social or public role the individual has adopted. Previously Greaves rejected the entire social system with its formally defined network of roles. With this rejection came a kind of loss of self; among the peasants Greaves submerges his personality to become a generic force of good. Aurelia represents the individual desires rejected in his decision to live among the common people, where he could be benevolent without ever addressing the issue of his own proper place and identity. Aurelia thus has the potential to reintroduce Greaves to the social world and to re-establish his individuality. Yet, exactly at this point the wider problem of social roles becomes apparent. Greaves meets opposition to his romance:

> In the mean time, the mother [of Aurelia] was no sooner committed to the earth than Mr. Greaves, mindful of her exhortations, began to take measures for a reconciliation with the guardian. He engaged several gentlemen to interpose their good offices; but they always met with the most mortifying repulse: and at last Anthony Darnel declared, that his hatred to the house of Greaves was hereditary, habitual, and unconquerable. (p. 35)

At issue here is the validity of Anthony Darnel's generalized hatred of the "house of Greaves"—a hatred which depends solely on Sir Launcelot's social role within his family. Taking up a place in society means accepting a social role; severed from the personal, that role is often defined by the manipulation and play of external social forces beyond the control of the individual.

The asylum and prison exemplify the power of social definition taken to the extreme. In the asylum the capacity of society to thrust an individual permanently into an external role becomes complete. Both Greaves (pp. 186-87) and the narrator note: "The melancholy produced from her confinement, and the vivacity of her resentment under ill-usage, were, by the address of Anthony, and the prepossession of his domesticks, perverted into the effects of insanity; and the same interpretation was strained upon her most indifferent words and actions" (pp. 115-16). As we will see below, language is one of the primary means by which people are reduced to social, external definitions. Aurelia is an asylum inmate and, as such, any personal deviation from this role is read simply as evidence of that role. Mrs Clewlin makes essentially the same point about the degree to which social roles can completely and inescapably define a prison inmate:

> Then Felton, advancing to his opponent, "Madam (said he) I'm very sorry to see a lady of your rank and qualifications expose yourself in this manner.— For God's sake, behave with a little more decorum; if not for the sake of your own family, at least for the credit of your sex in general." "Hark ye, Felton, (said she) decorum is founded upon a delicacy of sentiment and deportment, which cannot consist with the disgraces of jail, and the miseries of indigence." (p. 167)

Here the external requirements of society and its laws render impossible what has been throughout the novel the prime measure of personal quality—sentiment and decorum. Prison, like the asylum, confirms an individual within a role which is inescapable, invalidating the possibility of exposing the personal beneath the external roles and determinants. This nightmarish possibility represents the greatest danger and logical end of the generally destructive social roles and codes.

Greaves's quest responds to this danger and is paradoxically consistent with the problem of social roles underlying it. Greaves adopts the most codified and externally defined role he can find—that of a knight-errant—and fully submerges his identity. While this role seems to validate the personal attraction of Greaves to Aurelia, the code in fact places that affection within a system that strips it of all personality. Greaves says to Crowe, "She [a knight's mistress] must, in your opinion, be a paragon either of beauty or virtue" (p. 106). In a sense, Greaves's knight-errantry simply returns to his pre-Aurelian days of personality-less beneficence. Greaves attempts to make this return, however, with an increased recognition of the impossibility of perfectly conjoining personality and social role. As he says to Ferret early in the novel, "I do purpose (said the youth, eying [Ferret] with a look of ineffable contempt) to act as a coadjutor to the law, and even to remedy evils which the law cannot reach; to detect fraud and treason, abase insolence, mortify pride, discourage slander, disgrace immodesty, and stigmatize ingratitude" (p. 14). All of these evils which Greaves will attempt to remedy are personal ones, and by adopting the knight-errantry code he paradoxically attempts to force the characters he encounters to understand and realize the personal consequences of abstract social rules and roles.

Greaves's two longest adventures—those with Farmer Prickle and Justice Gobble—best exemplify his general method of criticism. All of Prickle's relationships derive directly from social duties or, like his "personal" knowledge of the lawyer, are extensions of social and legal codes. The farmer's position in this society relies solely on a formally constituted role: "Others might be easily influenced in the way of admonition; but there was no way of dealing with Prickle, except by the form and authority of the law" (p. 140). In order to force Prickle to recognize the personal consequences of these roles, Greaves puts Prickle into a situation where he cannot rely on such legal constraints and must instead try to find someone to stand bail for him not through social obligations but from personal feelings:

> Prickle happened to be at variance with the innkeeper, and the curate durst not disoblige the vicar, who at that very time was suing the farmer for the small tythes. He offered to deposit a sum equal to the recognizance of the knight's bail; but this was rejected as an expedient contrary to the practice of the courts. He sent for the attorney of the village, to whom he had been a good customer; but the lawyer was hunting evidence in another county. The exciseman presented himself as a surety; but he not being an housekeeper, was not

accepted. Divers cottagers, who depended on farmer Prickle, were successively refused, because they could not prove that they had payed scot and lot, and parish taxes. (pp. 142-43)

Although Greaves may seem simply to be legally out-manoeuvring Prickle, he is in fact specifically forcing Prickle into a situation where legal duties (and the social roles and codes behind them) do not apply, and in which personal respect operates. In the end Prickle is found to be "so little respected, that [he] cannot find sufficient bail" (p. 144).

A second example, Greaves's encounter with Justice Gobble, makes Greaves's method of dealing with those characters who misuse social roles even more explicit. Evans has suggested that Greaves's action in confronting Gobble is "satiric," since, rather than attempting a kind of "detailed legal argument and recommendations for proper punishment,"[6] it exposes Gobble's failure to measure up to the ideal Greaves represents. Given the relation between language and social roles, however, there may be a different method in Greaves's "satire": Greaves applies the legal terminology and Gobble's polite clichés to personal circumstances. Gobble comments:

> if I had a mind to exercise the rigour of the law, according to the authority wherewith I am wested, you and your companions in iniquity would be sewerely punished by statue: but we magistrates has a power to litigate the sewerity of justice, and so I am contented that you shoulds be mercifully dealt withal, and even dismissed.

Greaves rejoins:

> If I understand your meaning aright, I am accused of being a notorious criminal; but nevertheless you are contented to let me escape with impunity. If I am a notorious criminal, it is the duty of you, as a magistrate, to bring me to condign punishment; and if you allow a criminal to escape unpunished, you are not only unworthy of a place in the commission, but become accessory to his guilt, and, to all intents and purposes, *socius criminis*. (p. 93)

In this passage Greaves does not hold up an ideal, but instead applies Gobble's clichés and abstract role to the practical and personal situation, and assigns Gobble an interpersonal relationship with the criminal, *socius criminis*.

The problematic effect of social roles and the resulting need to stress the personal and individual behind these roles is Smollett's satiric point. Yet, as Greaves's adoption of the knight-errantry code suggests, the hero does not always fully realize or articulate this point. We must now turn to the relation between the hero

and this satiric message, and to the "rhetoric" of this satiric point.

. . . . .

Critics have generally assumed that Greaves is simply a mouthpiece for Smollett. Ronald Paulson, for example, suggests that Greaves, like Roderick Random, is a "satiric observer who recognizes, reacts, and rebukes."[7] Yet Greaves is largely a passive hero, a lightning rod which attracts and sets off the action and a great deal of the satire; as Tuvia Bloch says, Greaves performs an "essentially catalytic function in the episodes."[8] Very rarely does Greaves himself punish anyone; he generally allows his adversaries to bring retribution upon themselves. We might take as an example Farmer Prickle, whose punishment is simply to have "received a broken head, and payed two and twenty guineas for his folly" (p. 145)—neither of which punishments was initiated by Greaves. Similarly, Greaves's "satiric" pronouncements about his various adversaries are made only after they have initiated the encounters and revealed their own flaws. Greaves's comments in the case of Gobble are paradigmatic: although the hero's assertions certainly are "satiric," they derive from Gobble's own statements, and simply reveal the flaws already implicit in them. We might take as another example Greaves's encounter with the London haberdashers or the army recruits: in both cases, his adversaries reveal their abuse of their offices long before Greaves himself comments on the scene. Greaves's adoption of the externally determined role of knight-errantry encourages other characters to reveal their own prejudices: they are willing to rely on external roles and rules which they might suppress in the presence of a less easily defined character. The self-revealing quality of the episodes appears to be central to Smollett's satiric method, and related to his basic methods of characterization and his relationship with the reader.

Character language most clearly and pervasively manifests this self-revealing quality. Throughout the novel characters get "caught up" in language. Tom Clarke's use of legal language exemplifies this tendency: "In other respects, he piqued himself on understanding the practice of the courts, and in private company he took pleasure in *laying down the law;* but he was an indifferent orator, and tediously circumstantial in his explanations" (p. 2). The importance of his circumstantiality becomes clear when we examine its effects on Clarke's general speech:

> "Perhaps (said Tom) I do not make myself understood: if so be as how that is the case, let us change the position; and suppose that this here case is a *tail after a possibility of issue extinct.* If a tenant in *tail,* after possibility, make a *feoffment* of his land, he in reversion may enter for the forfeiture. Then we must make a distinction between *general tail* and *special tail.* It is the word *body* that makes

the *intail*—there must be *body* in the *tail,* devised to heirs male or female, otherwise it is a fee-simple, because it is not limited of what *body.* Thus a corporation cannot be seized in *tail.* For example: here is a young woman—What is your name, my dear?" "Dolly," answered the daughter with a curtsy. "Here's Dolly—I seize Dolly *in tail*—Dolly, I seize you *in tail.*"—"Sha't then," cried Dolly, pouting. (p. 5)

This passage shows Smollett's most important method of revealing the disjunction between the formal and the personal at the heart of *Greaves*'s satiric message. A highly abstract character language is recontextualized within a very physical and even scatological perspective, forcing us to see the social as something imposed on and suppressing the personal.

Timothy Crabshaw, virtually an emblem of physicality, is one of Smollett's primary devices for undermining such languages. Crabshaw enters the novel when he interrupts Greaves's story with a groan (p. 9). Crabshaw immediately translates into very physical terms the medical jargon of Fillet's having "performed the operation of phlebotomy" (p. 9) and Crowe's naval metaphor "for, if so be as he had not cleared your stowage of the water you had taken in at your upper works, and lightened your veins, d'ye see, by taking some of your blood, adad! you had driven before the gale" (p. 11). "What, then you would persuade me (replied the patient) that the only way to save my life was to shed my precious blood? Look ye, friend, it shall not be lost blood to me.—I take you all to witness, that there surgeon, or apothecary, or farrier, or dogdoctor, or whatsoever he may be, has robbed me of the balsam of life" (p. 11). Crabshaw deals similarly with the apothecary later in the novel:

> When [Greaves] inquired about the health of his squire, this retainer to medicine, wiping himself all the while with a napkin, answered in manifest confusion, That he apprehended him to be in a very dangerous way, from an inflammation of the *pia mater,* which had produced a most furious delirium. Then he proceeded to explain, in technical terms, the method of cure he had followed; and concluded with telling him the poor squire's brain was so outrageously disordered, that he had rejected all administration, and just thrown a urinal in his face. (p. 132)

Similarly, Crowe's "involuntary impulse" implies a barely suppressed physicality beneath his nautical dialect.[9]

> He was an excellent seaman, brave, active, friendly in his way, and scrupulously honest; but as little acquainted with the world as a sucking child; whimsical, impatient, and so impetuous that he could not help breaking in upon the conversation, whatever it might be, with repeated interruptions, that seemed to burst from him by involuntary

impulse: when he himself attempted to speak, he never finished his period; but made such a number of abrupt transitions, that his discourse seemed to be an unconnected series of of unfinished sentences, the meaning of which it was not easy to decypher. (p. 2)

As these examples of character language suggest, the resurgence of the physical occurs continuously, forcing the reader to see the social as imposed on the individual. The dialectic between the formality of language (as representative of social roles) and the "deconstruction" or recontextualization of that code by physicality is inescapable. The process by which a character comes to be seen as a complete person by others (and by the reader) entails the dialectic between the assertion and deconstruction of language, between roles and codes. The vivid characterization, for which Smollett is often praised, is partially derived from the "personalization" of a more abstract and informal mode of speech. Personalization comes about through the recontextualizing move from the formal to the physical. Crabshaw is clearly the most physical of *Greaves*'s characters, but that very physicality tends to take him out of contact with other characters; he misses, for example, the reunion with Greaves because of his absorption with the impending death of his horse, Gilbert. Crabshaw is a kind of abstraction, and virtually drops out of the novel and contact with other characters because he is unable to go through this very process of construction and destruction of the formal that leads a character to become "known" both to the other characters and to the reader. Greaves and the reader can know Crowe and Clarke much more intimately because they use (and fail to use) highly formal languages; they thus become Greaves's rescuers and friends.

This general method of personalization is part of Smollett's characterization of Greaves as well. Throughout the novel the hero's formal chivalric role is undermined by his madness; a mental state which, like Crowe's self-destructing language, clearly has overtones of the physical: "These last words were pronounced with a wildness of look, that even bordered upon frenzy" (p. 16).[10] Greaves, Crabshaw, and Crowe have similar animalizing reactions to an attempt to take on completely the "generic" form of knight-errantry. Crabshaw, for example, returns to "Greavesbury-hall, where he appeared with hardly any vestige of the human countenance, so much had he been defaced in this adventure" (p. 47). Similarly Crowe after his first encounter "had no remains of the human physiognomy" (p. 140) and only "regained in some respects the appearance of a human creature" (p. 159) after he had more or less decided to give up knight-errantry. Even Greaves becomes "unnatural" at the mention of Aurelia Darnel, whose love forms the heart of his knightly code (p. 130). In all these cases, adopting knight-errantry entails a correspondingly heightened physicality which deconstructs and recontextualizes that formal role.

Greaves needs to give up his adopted formal role both to succeed in his quest, and for the reader and the other characters to come to know him fully. That the dialectic between establishing and deconstructing a formal role or code is the basis for personal understanding of a character has complex ramifications for the reader's overall interaction with the work of fiction. Smollett avoids presenting Greaves as a character who (like Crabshaw) is simply a figure or ideal by making him grow towards the end of the novel. But another side to Greaves's role in the novel complicates the situation. How can the reader avoid seeing the work's message as a "thing" whose origin is external to any direct personal interaction with the reader, and constituted with the generality of a social law beyond the inescapable barrier between fiction and reality? In a sense, Crabshaw seems impersonal in part because we never see beyond his role in the novel; how does the novel's satiric message transcend its "impersonal" role in the text?

. . . . .

Smollett needs both to unify the satire and, at the same time, to problematize the formal boundaries that can sever the world of the text from the world of the reader. These formal boundaries are analogous to the definitions provided by social roles; Smollett therefore needs to recontextualize his textually produced satiric "point" in the physicality of the reader. This re-contextualization guides the overall satiric methods of *Greaves.*

Smollett realized the importance of having a hero with whom the reader can identify and who can unify the satire:

> A Novel is a large diffused picture, comprehending the characters of life, disposed in different groupes, and exhibited in various attitudes, for the purposes of an uniform plan, and general occurrence, to which every individual figure is subservient. But this plan cannot be executed with propriety, probability or success, without a principal personage to attract the attention, unite the incidents, unwind the clue of the labyrinth, and at last close the scene by virtue of his own importance.[11]

Smollett clearly signals here the degree to which a hero's realizations and experiences help to clarify and summarize the major theme of the novel. Ironically, *Ferdinand Count Fathom,* where this statement is to be found in the Dedication, by and large failed with its popular audience because it did not provide a "principal personage" attractive to the reader. A reviewer for the *Monthly Review* 8 (March 1753, 203-14) complained, "In the recital of such a wretch's exploits, can

the reader be greatly interested? Or can any emotions be excited in his mind, but those of horror and disgust? And therefore of what use, it may be demanded, can such a recital prove?"[12]

We may see *Greaves* as a kind of reaction to this criticism. Yet the review also indirectly suggests the danger of building the satire around a single character: how does the writer make the experiences and realizations of that character relevant to the reader? By the end of the novel, when he throws off his armour and accepts the legal help of Clarke in punishing those running the asylum, Greaves seems to have realized the satirical point—the need to establish personal relations in order to make social and legal forms safe. Yet, as soon as the message of the novel and its application become associated with the hero, the author risks making this point an external "thing." Smollett must tackle this dilemma without ignoring the need for his principal personage and losing the reader's sense of authorial purpose. The problem was exacerbated by the fact that *Greaves* was one of the first novels written for serial publication. Writing in this very new format, Smollett faced a greater need to unify the work, but also an increased consciousness of the medium in which he was writing and the physical circumstances of the readers and the text.[13] To some extent, Smollett addressed these problems by making Greaves into a conventional character type, familiar to his readers. Yet, as critics have noted, Smollett's anticipation and characterization of the reaction of his reader is more effective.[14] In characterizing these reactions, however, he also found a way out of the double bind of the need for and danger of a principal personage. Smollett sensed in this very new publishing method an increased presence and physicality in the reader. Thus Smollett made the reader a kind of gear in the machinery of the plot, and erased the distinction between the fictional message and its application in the real world.

Smollett associates the reader with two distinct elements of the novel: the forces that undermine romance convention or the simple progress of the novel, and the characters who come to know Greaves and who eventually save him. Critics have assumed that title headings and similar devices are meant to involve and sustain reader interest, and to create sympathy for Greaves. While this clearly is one of Smollett's intentions, such an explanation has blinded critics to Smollett's larger designs. The first chapter ends, "But as a personage of great importance in this entertaining history was forced to remain some time at the door, before he could gain admittance, so must the reader wait with patience for the next chapter, in which he will see the cause of this disturbance explained much to his comfort and edification" (p. 7). Critics have noted this as evidence of the fact that we are encouraged to identify with Greaves. Close examination of Smollett's address to the reader throughout the novel suggests, however, that Smollett associates the reader less with Greaves than with interruptions in the story. In the rendition of Greaves's biography, a *mise-en-abîme* of the novel as a whole, chapter breaks are marked by emotional outbursts of impatience from the listeners, a response that Smollett associates explicitly with the reader. For example, after the characters have disturbed Clarke's telling of the story because of his digressions, chapter 3 ends, "But as the reader may have more than once already cursed the unconscionable length of this chapter, we must postpone to the next opportunity the incidents that succeeded this denunciation of war" (p. 30). Similarly, chapter 4 ends with the outburst against Clarke's "definitions . . . and . . . long-winded story" (p. 41), and again turns to the reader: "In like manner we shall conclude the chapter, that the reader may have time to breathe and digest what he has already heard" (p. 41). We may also note that Clarke's emotional reaction to seeing Greaves, which provides the break that ends chapter 2, may serve as Smollett's warning that identifying too closely with the hero will ruin the story, while at the same time, through this possibility, tentatively aligning the reader with that which stops the flow of narration.

These early chapter endings exemplify the novel's larger tendency to associate the reader with any movement away from direct romantic development focused on the hero's adventures. The practical reason is obvious: Smollett needs to encourage patience in the reader and tolerance for the temporary lack of a principal personage. When, for example, Smollett ends chapter 17 by anticipating a shift of focus to Sycamore, he says that he will "give some account of other guests who arrived late in the evening, and here fixed their night-quarters—But as we have already trespassed on the reader's patience, we shall give him a short respite until the next chapter makes its appearance" (p. 145). In another place, when Smollett takes us away from the point of view of Greaves to fill in information about Aurelia Darnel, he makes it particularly obvious that such a shift in the movement of narrative derives from the reader's needs: "Yet, whatever haste he made, it is absolutely necessary for the reader's satisfaction, that we should outstrip the chaise, and visit the ladies before his arrival" (p. 114). And again at the end of the chapter before Greaves's interview with Aurelia (chap. 14), the reader is told "but as the ensuing scene requires fresh attention in the reader, we shall defer it till another opportunity, when his spirits shall be recruited from the fatigue of this chapter" (p. 119). This is Smollett's way of justifying his cliffhanger. Yet, in this association, Smollett also begins to characterize readers in terms of their "physicality," their fatigue. Smollett develops a subtext in the novel that makes readers equivalent to the physicality that interrupts Greaves's romantic quest.

In this pattern the ending to chapter 18 stands out: "But the scene that followed is too important to be huddled in at the end of a chapter, and therefore we shall reserve it for a more conspicuous place in these memoirs" (p. 153). The directness here, while perhaps a reflection of Smollett's growing confidence in his ability to write in a serialized format, comes at a key point in the novel: in this chapter (18) Greaves first rejects knight-errantry. These examples suggest that for Smollett the reader's presence functions very much like the physicality that intrudes into character language. As Greaves repudiates his knight-errantry, the need for this deconstruction of the smooth progression of the conventional romantic/heroic narrative lessens, and the reader's associated role in the novel becomes less wrenching. Because physicality exposes the individual beneath the social role, by implication the reader becomes an important part of the process of Greaves's personalization.

The other element of the narrative that Smollett associates with the reader is somewhat less complex. We have already seen that Smollett identifies the reader with that which breaks away from the simple, romantic progression of the story. As the example of outstripping the chaise suggests, Smollett achieves much of this disruption by decentring the novel from Greaves to the peripheral characters. Essential to this decentring is Smollett's association of the reader not with Greaves, but with the characters who surround him. Unlike any of Smollett's previous novels, *Launcelot Greaves* opens not with the introduction of the hero, but with a description of the community into which the hero will intrude. Throughout the novel Smollett positions readers in so that they are asked not to identify with Greaves, but to react to him. Again, this technique is directly connected to Smollett's use of a new medium. He describes a particularly communal context because he anticipates his readers' increased recognition of, and hence distraction by, the medium. The second chapter establishes the position of the reader by focusing, despite the entrance of Greaves, on the group of minor characters and their perception; Smollett gives the reader no information about Greaves's thoughts or intentions that is not available to the group of fictional characters. More important, Smollett immediately sends Greaves off to bed, leaving these minor characters to join with the reader in assessing him. It is an obvious but little noted fact that Greaves does not "resume his importance" until the seventh chapter, almost a third of the way into the novel. Furthermore, much of the reader's identification with Greaves that might arise from his romantic past is forestalled by the interruptions in Greaves's story and through Crowe's burlesque identification with and imitation of the hero. All these elements help to create the context with which the reader can identify, and in which he or she can read Greaves. In this way the potential distraction which the odd context imposes upon the reader is avoided.

I suggest that this practical technique also has a more subtle application in Smollett's general satiric method. As the novel progresses, the minor characters and the reader come to know Greaves increasingly well. Initially the novel encourages the reader to judge Greaves by a literary model (the characters see Greaves at first only as an imitation of Don Quixote) analogous to social roles; eventually the novel establishes a personal relationship between Greaves, the minor characters, and the reader. That Greaves gives up his armour after he has had his meeting with Aurelia obviously suggests that Greaves has established such relationships. The circumstances of this meeting reflect Smollett's focus on personalization; even though Aurelia is soon lost again after their reunion, Greaves's madness abates because of the relationship that they have established. In order to emphasize that the loss of personal relationships is at the root of Greaves's knight-errantry, Smollett stresses the fact that Greaves believes that Aurelia ended their relationship herself. Once Greaves sees his mistake and no longer feels cut off from Aurelia, he no longer needs his armour and the formal role it provides. While this change is the central one, Greaves's reactions to the minor characters that surround him more subtly manifest this establishment of personal relations. With Clarke, Greaves has one of his first moments of human contact unmediated by role since his assumption of knight-errantry. In their reunion in the madhouse, Clarke's and Greaves's signs of affection are a climax of Greaves's movement towards personal relations:

> Capt. Crowe . . . made no scruple of seizing [Greaves] by the collar, as he endeavoured to retreat; while the tender-hearted Tom Clarke, running up to the knight with his eyes brimfull of joy and affection, forgot all the forms of distant respect, and throwing his arms around his neck, blubbered in his bosom.

> Our hero did not receive this proof of attachment unmoved. He strained him in his embrace, honoured him with the title of his deliverer, and asked him by what miracle he had discovered the place of his confinement. (p. 195)

That the novel climaxes in the madhouse is important; here society can place a person within an inescapable "role." Greaves's rescue proves that he has established the personal relations necessary to help him escape from this formal definition. Readers partake of this growing personal knowledge not only because they have been associated throughout with these peripheral characters, but also because, as contemporary readers, they would have gradually come to know the hero through the two years of the novel's serial publication.[15]

Relying on this implied personal relation between Greaves and the reader, Smollett juxtaposes in the asylum the two roles played by readers in order to implicate them into the satire of the novel. Clarke and

Crowe get information about Greaves's imprisonment though the newspapers. While this may pass as unnoticed by a twentieth-century reader, to Smollett's original audience for whom *Greaves*'s serial publication was a very new format, this must have been a potent metafictional device. This source of information associates Greaves's rescue both with the reader's complete personal knowledge of the hero (in their "willingness" to help retrieve Greaves from the asylum's formal definition), and, more important, with the breaking down of external forms, the crossing of the boundary between fiction and reality. This metafictional turn is only the most explicit example of a general tendency for the novel to use the reader as the "real world" which intrudes into the narrative. The reader's physicality problematizes the hermetic quality of the romantic literary world of Greaves's knight-errantry, and generally destabilizes the distinction between the world of the novel and that of the reader. We can thus see the reader as an embodiment of this deconstructive and recontextualizing physicality that contributes to Greaves's escape from the knight-errantry code and consequently makes possible personal relations. The reader is, therefore, left unable simply to dismiss Smollett's satiric point as formally determined because exactly the opposite—the insinuation of the reader in the fiction—has helped bring about this realization in Greaves.

Modern critics have failed to make the connections that would be realized by contemporary readers, and hence they have failed to understand Smollett's satirical methods. It may well be that *The Life and Adventures of Sir Launcelot Greaves* is a two-hundred-year-old joke on the critic. If, as we saw above, Smollett uses Greaves to ridicule those characters who judge the hero in terms of formal roles and thus expose their own dependence on such social definitions, why have critics consistently denounced the novel as a poor imitation of Cervantes? G.S. Rousseau suggests the problems of Smollett criticism: "I have in the past tried to make out of Smollett's narratives coherent literary forms, and I could not. Nor could others. If the new prophets of literary studies, linguistic critics exploring stylistics and poetics, can forge out of Smollett's narratives a *coherent* (this is not to say Jamesian) literary form replete with organic plots, probable characters, and a credible world, they have accomplished what no other school could. What then is left for criticism with regard to this author?"[16] Forcing Smollett into the simple models of literary form and influence that Rousseau criticizes leads critics to condemn *Greaves* on the grounds of inconsistent wavering between picaresque and romantic world-views. In this essay I have tried to show that a significant part of Smollett's writing analyses such formal systems. We need not thus despair with Rousseau at the impossibility of explicating Smollett's works and methods usefully and validly. We need to turn from the models of narrow formal unity to consider the more reader-oriented methods that I have schematized in this essay. These methods use literary forms and parallels not as templates but as the material for the work's satirical reworking, and in the process demand reconsideration of, and a more complex model for, our understanding of form and unity.

Notes

¹ See in particular Robert Giddings, *The Tradition of Smollett* (London: Methuen, 1967), pp. 127-39. Although Robert Donald Spector defends *Greaves* in a number of ways, he nonetheless censures its satiric method. See Robert Donald Spector, *Tobias George Smollett,* updated ed. (Boston: Twayne, 1989), pp. 85-103, esp. 92-97.

² James Beattie provides an early example of this tendency: "Sir Launcelot Greaves is of Don Quixote's kindred, but a different character. Smollet's [sic] design was, not to expose him to ridicule; but rather to recommend him to our pity and admiration. He has therefore given him youth, strength, and beauty, as well as courage, and dignity of mind, has mounted him on a generous steed, and arrayed him in an elegant suit of armour. Yet, that the history might have a comic air, he has been careful to contrast and connect Sir Launcelot with a squire and other associates of very dissimilar tempers and circumstances." "On Laughter, and Ludicrous Composition," *Essays* (Edinburgh, 1776), pp. 350-51.

³ *The Fictions of Satire* (Baltimore: Johns Hopkins University Press, 1967), p. 58.

⁴ Introduction to *The Life and Adventures of Sir Launcelot Greaves,* ed. David Evans (London: Oxford University Press, 1973), p. xvi. References are to this edition.

⁵ *The Novels of Tobias Smollett,* trans. Antonia White (New York: Longman, 1976), p. 181.

⁶ Evans, p. xviii.

⁷ *Satire and the Novel in Eighteenth-Century England* (New Haven: Yale University Press, 1967), p. 171. Although the phrase refers to Roderick Random, Paulson's discussion of Greaves (pp. 199-200) argues that the characters are similar in this respect. See also Giddings, pp. 129-34.

⁸ "Smollett's Quest for Form," *Modern Philology* 65 (1967), 106.

⁹ Damian Grant suggests this, noting that "passion and energy supply the place of ordinary grammatical connection," *Tobias Smollett: A Study in Style* (Manchester: Manchester University Press, 1977), p. 96.

¹⁰ Cf. Greaves's outburst against Clarke, p. 84, and the innkeeper, pp. 128-29.

¹¹ Tobias Smollett, *The Adventures of Ferdinand Count Fathom,* ed. Jerry C. Beasley (Athens: University of Georgia Press, 1988), p. 4. See also the review of *The Peregrinations of Jeremiah Grant, Esq; the West-Indian* in the *Critical Review* 15 (January, 1763), 13-14, and James G. Basker, *Tobias Smollett: Critic and Journalist* (Newark: University of Delaware Press, 1988), p. 271 for the attribution of this anonymous review to Smollett.

¹² *Tobias Smollett: The Critical Heritage,* ed. Lionel Kelly (New York: Routledge and Kegan Paul, 1987), pp. 92-93.

¹³ James G. Basker suggests that public opinion and readers' reactions might have had a very direct influence on the development of the novel: "It has been established that Smollett composed the novel gradually over the two years, sometimes even dashing off an instalment only as the deadline drew near. Thus he had the opportunity to act on readers' suggestions and comments; his sensitivity to public opinion in other contexts (notably the *Critical*) makes it very unlikely that he would be unaffected by comments from friends or readers who wrote in" (p. 203).

¹⁴ See Robert D. Mayo, *The English Novel in the Magazines 1740-1815* (Evanston, IL: Northwestern University Press, 1962), pp. 276-88.

¹⁵ Critics have generally assumed that Smollett's unwillingness to revise *Greaves* after its initial publication (unlike *Roderick Random* or *Peregrine Pickle*) is evidence of the half-heartedness with which he wrote the novel. Yet, the degree to which Smollett integrated the special circumstances of this publication into his satiric methods explains this lack of interest.

¹⁶ G. S. Rousseau, "Beef and Bouillon: Smollett's Achievement as Thinker," in *Tobias Smollett: Essays of Two Decades* (Edinburgh: T. and T. Clark, 1982), p. 90. Published originally as "Beef and Bouillion: A Voice for Tobias Smollett, With Comments on His Life, Works and Modern Critics," *British Studies Monitor* 7 (1977), 4-56.

David M. Weed (essay date 1997)

SOURCE: "Sentimental Misogyny and Medicine in *Humphry Clinker,*" in *Studies in English Literature,* Vol. 37, No. 3, Summer 1997, pp. 615-36.

[In the following essay, Weed argues that in Humphry Clinker, *Smollett depicts some negative effects of*

commercialism on human society, including rendering men effeminate, causing illness, and the leading to the overall unbalancing of masculine society.]

On one level, *The Expedition of Humphry Clinker* (1771) presents its readers with a cast of scraggly, wryly drawn "originals" roaming Britain, including the tatterdemalion Humphry Clinker himself, the quixotic Obadiah Lismahago, and the curmudgeonly Matthew Bramble. It also, however, provides a rare eighteenth-century portrait of England as a "body politic."[1] The connection between an individual's physical health and moral well-being, for example, an issue often discussed in criticism of the novel, also correlates to the health of the nation's social body, which, in the novel's view, is diseased and in need of a cure.[2] In *Humphry Clinker,* Tobias Smollett's medical and literary knowledge meets his perception of England's cultural and social condition, and the combination holds important ramifications for an analysis of eighteenth-century masculinity. In writing his only novel of sensibility, Smollett may have been yielding to popular taste,[3] but within the form he also discovered a way to extend the meaning of sensibility by constructing a distinctly *masculine* man of feeling who resists infection from the femininity intertwined with England's commercial society. The novel represents commerce as the underlying source of England's social ills. I will argue that England's social body incorporates the ill effects of commercialism into its public institutions and civic and social life, and that it produces effeminate men who participate in an epidemic spread of luxury, bodily waste, consumption, and "cannibalism."

The gendering of the novel's attack on commercial society is not unique to eighteenth-century political discourse. Indeed, eighteenth-century economic man "was seen as on the whole a feminised, even an effeminate being, still wrestling with his own passions and hysterias and with interior and exterior forces let loose by his fantasies and appetites . . . [I]n the eighteenth-century debate over the new relations of polity to economy, production and exchange are regularly equated with the ascendancy of the passions and the female principle."[4] In contrast to eighteenth-century economic man, the virtuous, landowning citizen, who is shaped in particular by the republican discourse that has come to be known as civic humanism, was often criticized by "the polite man of commercial and cultivated society" as resting on an "archaic and restrictive" precommercial foundation.[5] In his debate with this republican, patriot ideal, the advocate of commerce and culture gave names such as "savagery" to his demonstrations that "what had preceded the rise of commerce and culture was not a world of virtuous citizens, but one of barbarism."[6] Interestingly, Smollett's novel intervenes in this debate by applying the notion of the sensible man of feeling to its landowning men, which places a formidably polite face on them: in effect, *Humphry*

Clinker critiques economic man by usurping the terms on which he positions himself as civilized in order to construct a model male landowner who is at once more cultivated and more masculine than his allegedly "modern" counterpart. The novel essentially inverts the terms of the debate between republican "country" ideology and commercial "court" ideology by associating England's commercial society with cannibalistic savagery.[7]

The road in *Humphry Clinker,* then, leads continually farther away from England's corrupt and effeminate commercial culture, in which the stress on modernity occludes a real lack of civility. Divided, self-interested, and self-absorbed, the novel's urban Englishmen, painted especially by Bramble in broad strokes that suggest a general disapproval of all of them (except in a few instances, such as Serle), in particular appear incapable of developing or sustaining the kinds of close male bonds that finally emerge among the men in Wales. Comprised of Bramble, Jery Melford, Charles Dennison, Baynard, and Clinker—and the Scotsman Lismahago, the group of men that dominates the end of *Humphry Clinker* implicitly rejects England as a place in which successful male social and political relations can be maintained. The maladies of English culture—its luxury and effeminacy in particular—lead the expedition inexorably toward Britain's geographical margins, where the novel formulates a model of masculinity based on rational male control of a landed economy and polite manly camaraderie rather than commercial passion and effeminate, vain self-interest.

Just as the novel is perhaps the last full-scale indictment of luxury in the "classical" sense,[8] then, the model of landed, virtuous, republican masculinity that it eulogizes also seems destined for marginalization, forced both geographically and ideologically outside a rapidly expanding commercial English culture that the novel represents as a "monster." The novel rarely compromises its position that men must renounce their ties to commerce, which means, in effect, renouncing their ties to overwhelmingly commercialized England, in order to remain civilized, unified, healthy, and organized around principles of virtuous masculine reason rather than corrupt effeminate passion. Despite the novel's innovative masculinization of the discourse of sensibility and its depiction of the exodus from England as the construction of a civilized, masculine haven in a falsely modern world, *Humphry Clinker* also isolates its men outside civic life. Although land in the eighteenth century generally signifies leisure and independence for its owner, it also assumes the landed man's political engagement. In *Humphry Clinker,* the management of private land—especially the management of strictly demarcated gender roles in the family—becomes such a crucial task that the novel redefines the virtuous man as a privately active rather than a civic-minded individual.

The novel's strategic use of medicine to describe the ills of England's urban culture connects these problems of public and private political economy especially to the question of what it means bodily to be a man in the eighteenth century. The novel locates the problem of managing social waste particularly in Bramble's body and sexuality; I read Bramble's personal expedition as an unconscious discovery of ways that he may safely produce bodily waste and legitimize his production of the bastard Humphry Clinker, who is figured as a waste product in the system of inheritance. Only after "waste" is brought under the control of rational, virtuous, masculine men may Bramble allow himself to become a "man of feeling," triumphing over his misanthropy and his metaphorically violent masculine satire, which he affects during the expedition in reaction to England's effeminate culture.

To be a man of feeling in *Humphry Clinker* especially means regarding friendships between virtuous men as the highest social ideal. While Smollett's novel and Adam Smith's *The Theory of Moral Sentiments* (1759) are at opposite ends of the ideological spectrum regarding the virtue of the commercial man, they share an affinity for classical republican models of masculinity in their estimations that friendships based on "esteem and approbation" can "exist only among men of virtue," which, for Smith, are "by far, the most respectable" attachments a man can make.[9] In *Humphry Clinker,* these virtuous attachments between men are far more closely connected to the English landed republican ethic, which urges men's renunciation of both consumer and sexual desire in the name of virtue and independence. The vocabulary of civic humanist discourse "could describe acquisitive and especially commercial activity in the same terms as it described sexual indulgence (the attractions of both could be termed 'luxury'; their effects on men could both be described as 'effeminacy');"[10] John Barrell argues that this model of republican asexual "virile virtue" in the early eighteenth century begins to compete with a model of bourgeois "virile virtue," which legitimates men's desire for women (and, by extension, for material possessions) as a masculine rather than an effeminate pursuit. While Smith's moral man slips between a masculinized Stoic virtue and a more feminine commercial "prudence" throughout *The Theory of Moral Sentiments,* Smollett's men of feeling in *Humphry Clinker,* curiously, resist indulgent, overly sentimental relations with women in order to bond with other men, which suggests that civic humanist and bourgeois discourses on masculine virtue cross and overlap in specific eighteenth-century texts. Just as Smith's Stoicism in the last instance assures the masculinity of the commercial man, then, Smollett provides the masculine, virtuous republican with civilized and amiable sensibilities.

Of course, because *Humphry Clinker* adamantly disapproves of luxury, indulgence, and desire, the novel dramatizes the eradication of those "feminine" qualities in its major male characters and their suppression by men in the women of the expedition, creating an atmosphere in which the men are able to form virtuous, amiable bonds. In constructing a vision of a world ordered rationally by men, which depends in particular upon limiting both men's and women's "feminine" desires, the novel castigates English culture for its associations, through commerce and luxury, with femininity, and dramatizes the ways that the major male characters restrain the women from their supposedly natural attraction to England's feminized culture. At all levels, whether in culture or through the male and female agents of that culture, the "female principle" in commercial society becomes the underlying cause of corruption in English social life and public institutions; the novel's relegation of women to minor, comic, subordinate roles reflects its urge to discover a corner of the British island in which manly men may manage women's desires and keep England's corrupt public world at bay.

The young, impressionable Lydia Melford provides the novel's primary example of the way men may teach women to reject an attraction to "vanity, expense, and disorder," which *Humphry Clinker* associates with "female nature,"[11] and to reconcile themselves willingly to their subordinate position as women. In the novel's terms, Lydia has the intelligence to understand the requirement that she subordinate herself to men: even though she is "as soft as butter, and as easily melted" because she has "a languishing eye, and reads romances," according to Bramble, she is also not a fool.[12] Lydia in particular has the sense to allow men to protect her from her sexual and consumer desires.

Lydia's brother, Jery, functions as the principal agent of her containment. Bramble's initial reaction to his niece and nephew collapses them into the same category: "I an't in a condition to take care of myself; much less to superintend the conduct of giddy-headed boys and girls" (p. 13). Significantly, his reading of Jery proves to be inaccurate: less "giddy-headed" than Bramble must have been in his libertine youth, Jery, the group's dispassionate observer,[13] seems unmoved by sexual desire and is thus untroubled by any potentially dangerous sentimental entanglements with women. Though Smollett generally provides a "gynophobic . . . critique of the social and economic changes he perceives,"[14] Jery's relationship with Lydia depicts the novel's most effective lesson in the way that men may avoid misogyny. That avoidance, however, depends upon women's willingness to relinquish the power that accrues from their natural desires. In other words, the novel suggests that men are free to love and respect women as long as they agree to remain socially subservient and under men's protection.

Throughout the novel, Jery fulfills his brotherly duties

to his sister by exerting control over her "languishing eye": he confronts Wilson and protects Lydia from the "boldness" of Captain O'Donaghan's "look and manner." He is so keenly observant and anxious about patrolling Lydia's sexual desires, in fact, that he seems able to enter his sister's thoughts: Lydia writes that, to prevent her from having to dance with Captain O'Donaghan, Jery excuses himself "by saying I had got the headach; and, indeed, it was really so, though I can't imagine how he knew it" (p. 41). Jery also knows why Lydia faints at the sight of Mr. Gordon, who resembles the character Lydia had seen George Dennison, disguised as Wilson, play on stage: "the cause of my disorder remained a secret to every body but my brother, who was likewise struck with the resemblance, and scolded after we came home" (p. 250).

Over the course of the novel, Lydia comes to understand the reasons that men restrain women's desires. Lydia particularly learns to see Tabitha, the novel's comically grotesque "domestic dæmon" (p. 74), as frivolously irresponsible in her sexual desires. Indeed, the novel counterpoints the two women in relation to their brothers: while Jery effectively regulates Lydia's desires, Bramble is continually frustrated in his attempts to control Tabitha. Before managing to negotiate one of the novel's "patriarchally approved marriages" between Tabitha and Lismahago,[15] Bramble resorts to tactics such as undeceiving Ulic Mackillgut about the state of Tabitha's fortune, in which "he had been misled by a mistake of at least six thousand pounds" in order to undermine the blossoming affair (p. 61). Tabitha's relentless commodification of herself on the marriage market particularly helps Lydia to position herself finally as a female misogynist: "My dear Willis, I am truly ashamed of my own sex—We complain of advantages which the men take of our youth, inexperience, sensibility, and all that; but I have seen enough to believe, that our sex in general make it their business to ensnare the other; and for this purpose, employ arts which are by no means to be justified—In point of constancy, they certainly have nothing to reproach the male part of the creation" (p. 251).

Rather than being a publicly active citizen engaged in civic concerns, then, the virtuous man who wishes to maintain masculine order must privately prevent women from exercising their indiscriminate desires for sex and luxury. The novel's comparison between the Baynards and Dennisons, which contains "essentially the thesis of the novel in miniature,"[16] particularly exploits the difference between the virtuous, assertive Mr. Dennison and the weak, passive Mr. Baynard to support the argument that only masculine male control of land and the household economy produces rational order and profit. The Baynards' marriage suggests that the husband who does not control his wife's desires in-

vests her with the power to turn his real property into wasteland. Mr. Baynard's sentimentality toward his wife produces an inversion of gendered economic roles. In the name of "taste and connoisseurship," Mrs. Baynard's "improvements" to the estate have turned profitable land into an item that requires costly upkeep. Bramble's initial, impressionistic view of the Baynard estate provides a striking sense of the economic disaster that Mrs. Baynard has wrought:

> when we arrived at the house, I could not recognize any one of those objects, which had been so deeply impressed upon my remembrance . . . The house itself, which was formerly a convent of Cistercian monks, had a venerable appearance; and along the front that looked into the garden, was a stone gallery, which afforded me many an agreeable walk, when I was disposed to be contemplative—Now the old front is covered with a screen of modern architecture; so that all without is Grecian, and all within Gothic—As for the garden, which was well stocked with the best fruit which England could produce, there is not now the least vestige remaining of trees, walls, or hedges—Nothing appears but a naked circus of loose sand, with a dry bason and a leaden triton in the middle.
>
> (p. 275)

Bramble's aesthetic sensibility, of course, is also a gendered political sensitivity to the kinds of ruin that a woman such as Mrs. Baynard produces when given the opportunity: her "naked circus" is immodest, costly, tasteless, and dead. Equally important, Mrs. Baynard's disruption of the landed masculine order robs Bramble of the use of private, aestheticized spaces such as the "stone gallery, which afforded me many an agreeable walk, when I was disposed to be contemplative." In civic humanist theory, the private is "appropriate to the contemplative, not the active life," and art is a primary medium for man's contemplation.[17] The novel suggests, however, that landed men cannot afford to follow "what the citizen *should* do in his private capacity,"[18] because men must be privately active, especially in managing their wives, to prevent losing the objects of their contemplation.

On the other hand, Mr. Dennison is the foremost example of a man who renounces commerce and public life in order to focus his attention on his private land, which becomes the last stronghold of masculine control in *Humphry Clinker*. In this economy, wives become rubber-stamp legislators of their husbands' executive decisions: Charles Dennison, "with the approbation of his wife . . . determined to quit business, and retire into the country" (p. 308). Mr. Dennison controls all aspects of this economy: by entering into "a minute detail and investigation" (p. 309), he saves money on household expenses. The ideal family government, using the Dennisons as the model, is not "patriarchal" in the seventeenth-century sense of the term (so that "the family is established by the enclosure of private property, and that family is under the absolute control of the father"),[19] but the man must certainly circumscribe his wife's economic role. The "uncommon" Mrs. Dennison provides the novel's only example of a woman fit to participate in family government (though we may read Lydia, who marries the Dennisons' son, as a potential future candidate). Rather than the excessive love and tears that mark Baynard's relationship with his wife, the Dennisons' marriage is based on friendship and is marked by its formality and absence of overt sexual desire: Mrs. Dennison is "admirably qualified" to be her husband's "companion, confidant, counsellor, and coadjutrix" (p. 307).

Marriage to the (more common) wife who exercises her desires produces a life that is "expensive and fantastic" (p. 281). The eighteenth-century man who pursues overly sentimental relations with women risks revealing a weakness that allows them potentially devastating power. But what is a man to do when, filled with sensibility and feeling (as is Baynard, who is surrounded by cold servants and a wife who sits "in silence like a statue, with an aspect of insensibility" [p. 283]), he loves the very being that threatens his economic happiness? For the man necessarily tied to such a woman by blood, as is Bramble to Tabitha, the answer is for him to find her a proper husband: the alliance of the brother and the husband then insures that her desires are regulated.[20] But marriage to the female economic tyrant is a seemingly intractable problem. Baynard's excessive tenderness, the "greatest defect of his nature" and "the weak side of his soul" (pp. 277, 278), allows his wife to enlarge her role from titular legislator to tyrannical executive. Within the domestic unit, Baynard abdicates his rule, and the threat to the Englishman's property rights becomes a private drama in which the wife confiscates the husband's land and property, which she controls *de facto* if not *de juris*. Women's economic power inverts family government and places it under the absolute control of the mother: Mrs. Baynard wields an "absurd tyranny" over her husband, whose acquiescence is "unmanly" (p. 281).

Bramble's own propensity toward sentimentality, then, in some measure explains his statements that he will not marry: an attachment to a wife like Mrs. Baynard could unman him and entail his estate, heart, and health in a similar sickening corruption. Indeed, the novel characterizes Bramble and Baynard in the same terms: Bramble has a propensity toward a "sensibility of [the] heart, which is tender, even to a degree of weakness." On the expedition, Bramble conceals his sensibility by using satire and "spleen" to defend against the individuals he meets in England's effeminate culture. In Jery's view, Bramble's satire becomes a particularly brutal, masculine, phallic weapon of defense: when provoked, Bramble will "let fly the shafts of his satire, keen and penetrating as the arrows of Teucer" (p. 29). Mrs. Baynard's death provides Bramble with the opportunity to vent his spleen upon the figure of the economically incompetent woman: "I arrived about four in the afternoon, and meeting the physician at the door, was informed that his patient had just expired.—I was instantly seized with a violent emotion, but it was not grief" (p. 325). Her death also allows her husband to recover from his sentimentality toward her: "His heart . . . was still subject to vibrations of tenderness, which returned at certain intervals, extorting sighs, and tears, and exclamations of grief and impatience: but these fits grew every day less violent and less frequent, 'till at length his reason obtained a complete victory over the infirmities of his nature" (p. 327). Tenderness toward and love of women are the "infirmities" of the sentimental man's "nature" which threaten his mental health and over which he must obtain a "complete victory" if he is to maintain his "reason."

Though generally unrealized in the novel, women's potential to exert power in a feminine culture also threatens men's bodies through scatological language. For Win Jenkins and Tabitha, for example, that power is diverted unconsciously into the malapropisms in their letters. Critics have frequently noted that Win's and Tabitha's language is particularly scatological. Win produces writing filled with unintentional puns, "sexual innuendoes, and . . . scatological suggestiveness . . . Writing 'paleass' for 'palace,' describing the family as being in a 'constipation'; dismissing her unfaithful French lover as not worth a 'farting'; and making a 'turd' of 'third' and 'ass of editida' of 'asafetida,' Win does indeed allow 'her innocent pen [to] pursue its anal fixation.' In the same way, Tabby refers constantly to the hired hands as 'hinds,' declares that she will ignore Dr. Lewis's attempts to conciliate her 'though he beshits me on his bended knees,' and gets a great deal of unintended sexual meaning into her description of Humphry."[21] Importantly, though Win and Tabby produce scatological language, their referents are uniformly men. In this reading of the linguistic effects of the women's letters, the problem of bodies in *Humphry Clinker* becomes principally a problem of men's bodies. For Humphry, the problem appears in his name: as a lump of coal, "Clinker" may refer to his employment as a farrier, but the word also refers scatologically to excrement in the eighteenth century.[22] Bramble's bodily problem relates to his health: as he travels through England, where the excesses of excrement and dead bodies merge with the water to be consumed by others, Bramble is constipated. Bramble's constipation, as we will see, is a physical reaction to England's urban diarrhea, and it particularly counterpoints the urban Englishman, who is unwittingly infected by female nature and cannot produce a "healthy" control over his wasteful, indulgent feminine desires.

The novel constructs the bodily excesses and waste of England's commercial society as the savagery underlying its mask of culture, and the collapse of "the extremes of refinement and of savagery" in the novel is most pronounced in the power of women and the propensity toward bodily excesses, marked at its extreme by cannibalism, in both savage and refined cultures.[23] Among the Miami Indians, for example, the strict gender *and* age distinctions that signify a healthy social body are inoperative. Men, at the apex of the cultural hierarchy in a healthy society, suddenly become victims: "[P]oor Murphy was so mangled by the women and children, who have the privilege of torturing all prisoners in their passage, that, by the time they arrived at the place of the sachem's residence, he was rendered altogether unfit for the purposes of marriage" (p. 188). Worse than Murphy's castration, a sure signifier of his disempowerment, however, the Miamis cannibalize him: the "warriors and matrons" make "a hearty meal upon the muscular flesh which they pared from the victim," and Lismahago's bride distinguishes herself by vying with "the stoutest warrior in eating the flesh of the sacrifice" (p. 188). Smollett envisions the Miami society as one in which men and women are equally cannibalistic, and any culture, savage or refined, that feminizes itself by basing itself on consumption—an ethos that women in the novel naturally and particularly desire—is bound to consume human beings. The refined savages of urban England do not pare and eat the muscular flesh from the victim, but they consume, diluted in the water, the sloughed-off flesh and excrement of their society's members, as well as the microscopic remains of dead bodies.

Bramble recognizes that microscopic body parts float in Bath's waters, and his attempt to find pure water becomes a nightmarish vision in which he cannot seem to escape cannibalizing the living and the dead:

> I can't help suspecting, that there is, or may be, some regurgitation from the bath into the cistern of the pump. In that case, what a delicate beverage is every day quaffed by the drinkers; medicated with the sweat, and dirt, and dandriff; and the abominable discharges of various kinds, from twenty different diseased bodies, parboiling in the kettle below. In order to avoid this filthy composition, I had recourse to the spring that supplies the private baths on the Abbey-green; but I at once perceived something extraordinary in the taste and smell; and, upon inquiry, I find that the Roman baths in this quarter, were found covered by an old burying ground, belonging to the Abbey; thro' which, in all probability, the water drains in its passage: so that as we drink the decoction of living bodies at the Pump-room, we swallow the strainings of rotten bones and carcasses at the private bath.
>
> (p. 45)

The "medicinal" water is diseased, and refinement is covert, cannibalistic savagery; the unruly bodies of the living and dead regurgitate and discharge themselves into the water supply as sacrifices to a luxurious culture.

Bramble figures Thames' water, an "agreeable potation, extolled by the Londoners, as the finest water in the universe," literally as the female bearer of contagion insofar as it is "impregnated with all the filth of London and Westminster." The metaphorically female body of water contains animal corpses, human bodies, and humans' industrial waste: "Human excrement is the least offensive part of the concrete, which is composed of all the drugs, minerals, and poisons, used in mechanics and manufacture, enriched with the putrefying carcases [*sic*] of beasts and men; and mixed with the scourings of all the washtubs, kennels, and common sewers, within the bills of mortality" (p. 119). In the same letter, Bramble contrasts the pregnant and diseased urban female water with the sexually pure female water at Brambleton-hall. Although "she" is pure, rural water provides Bramble with a curiously sexual pleasure: "I drink the virgin lymph, pure and crystalline as it gushes from the rock" (p. 118). He idealizes the country as a haven from the effects of women's physical and sexual corruption, to which both men and women fall victim through a symbiosis between the human body and the drinking water. If Dr. L——n is any indication, female nature is even more dangerous to men than to women. In a novel where the humor centers on grotesque characters and the laughter elicited by impolitely exposing the scatological realities of eighteenth-century life, Dr. L——n is perhaps the most thoroughly corrupted of all Smollett's figures. He proposes implicitly to cannibalize Bramble: "Sir, (said he) you seem to be of a dropsical habit, and probably will soon have a confirmed *ascites:* if I should be present when you are tapped, I will give you a convincing proof of what I assert, by drinking without hesitation the water that comes out of your abdomen." Worse than the woman who collapses refinement into savagery, the man who does so takes cannibalistic excesses to their most disgusting degree, causing even the "ladies" to make "wry faces at this declaration" (p. 19).

Bramble generally succeeds at avoiding London's and Bath's waters, but urban Englishmen consume luxury goods and produce waste, which are consumed again by the urban cannibal in a cycle of disease and corruption. Gail Kern Paster writes that seventeenth-century economic discourse focuses particularly upon the place of women's bodies, which may be understood "as a 'streamlining' of the patriarchal family for the economic efficiency required by emerging capitalist modes of production. Representations of the female body as a leaking vessel display that body as beyond the control of the female subject, and thus as threatening the acquisitive goals of the family and its maintenance of status and power. The crucial problematic was whether women as a group could be counted on to manage their behaviors in response to historically emergent demands of bodily self-rule."[24] In Smollett's novel, on the other hand, the fears about the "body's moisture, secretions, and productions as shameful tokens of uncontrol" are located in urban England's effeminate men.[25] The "acquisitive goals of the family and its maintenance of status and power" are less important to *Humphry Clinker* than *men's* acquisitive goals (particularly of real property) and power, and the figures who prove least able to meet the demands are urban Englishmen. They have been "intoxicated" by finding themselves "suddenly translated into a state of affluence." Besides their dissoluteness and their effeminacy, inscribed particularly in the repeated mention of their vanity, urban Englishmen reproduce their corrupt society by impregnating the diseased urban waters with the "discharge" of their wealth "through every channel of the most absurd extravagance" (p. 36).

Bramble's illness, on the other hand, is caused by a physical reaction against England's social distemper. Refusing to excrete normally, Bramble's body retains its integrity by obstructing its normal, porous intercourse with England's "body." To diagnose Bramble's illness correctly, we must understand that Smollett wrote *Humphry Clinker* at a time of transition involving medicine's older model of bodily "humors": the novel relies on this model to suggest that Bramble's body has sealed itself off from England's troubled culture. Humoral theory envisions the body as "characterized by corporeal fluidity, openness, and porous boundaries."[26] The health of the body depends on a balance in the transfer of liquids between its interior and the world outside it: "Every subject grew up with a common understanding of his or her body as a semipermeable, irrigated container in which humors moved sluggishly. People imagined that health consisted of a state of internal solubility to be perilously maintained."[27] Bramble places gout within a series of diseases that Bath's waters will not affect, using humoral theory to prove his argument: "If these waters, from a small degree of astringency, are of some service in the *diabetes, diarrhœa,* and *night sweats,* when the secretions are too much encreased, must not they do harm in the same proportion, where the humours are obstructed, as in the *asthma, scurvy, gout,* and *dropsy?*" (p. 25). Bramble's gout, therefore, prevents him from being purged and thus cannibalized, but it also places him in a double bind. Though his reaction to the society that threatens his body and, in the novel's connection between physical and psychological illness, his mind, saves him from being cannibalized, his protector also endangers his health.

The passage in which Clinker rescues his father after the coach overturns in the river marks an important resolution to the humoral irregularities of Bramble's body. The crisis forces Bramble, through Clinker's agency, to emit water and bodily fluid. Jery writes that, after Clinker pulls Bramble from the river, "[H]e was laid upon the grass, and turned from side to side, [and] a great quantity of water ran out at his mouth, then he opened his eyes, and fetched a deep sigh—Clinker perceiving these signs of life, immediately tied up his arm with a garter, and, pulling out a horse-fleam, let him blood in the farrier stile.—At first a few drops only issued from the orifice; but the limb being chafed, in a little time the blood began to flow in a continued stream, and he uttered some incoherent words, which were the most welcome sounds that ever saluted my ear" (p. 301). Bramble's body at first will not release its blood, but finally, through the agency of his son and surrounded by a group of male relatives, friends, and servants, he can emit the fluid that he has needed to excrete throughout the expedition. He has found a social structure in which he can safely release fluids within a larger culture in danger of being flooded. In a sense, Clinker's purgation of his father's body also repays Bramble for his earlier rescue of Clinker from the bodily excesses that make the lower classes, a seething background tableau in the novel, a potentially disruptive social force within commercial society. By employing Clinker, Bramble saves him from illness and famine, but he also rescues him from "shewing his bare posteriors" (p. 78), to which poverty and, thus, his identification with the "mob" has led him.[28] Bramble is "conscious of no sins that ought to entail . . . family-plagues upon me" (p. 13), but Clinker, as the unconscious sin that follows Bramble for decades, is in atonement clothed and given the opportunity to exhibit bodily self-rule.

In *Humphry Clinker,* then, men must rescue each other from the excesses of England's corrupt and effeminate culture in order to keep each other healthy, balanced, under control, and masculine. This rescue mission also requires that they prevent women from drowning men. In the same scene in which Clinker purges Bramble, Jery writes that when Lismahago tries to rescue Tabitha from the overturned coach, the couple falls "head and ears in each other's arms. [Lismahago] endeavoured more than once to get up, and even to disentangle himself from the embrace, but [Tabitha] hung about his neck like a mill-stone (no bad emblem of matrimony), and if my man had not proved a staunch auxiliary, those two lovers would in all probability have gone hand in hand to the shades below" (p. 301). Jery recognizes the metaphorical power of the incident's gender politics, and his depiction is "no bad emblem" of the novel's practice of matrimonial regulation through male bonds: men must be staunch auxiliaries to husbands to ensure that their wives do not drown them. In the novel's utopian vision of male relations, however, the servant class generally performs no more than a supernumerary function: like Jery's servant, they act as "auxiliaries," or they lend silent, nameless support, thereby tacitly legitimating both cooperation between men and hierarchy of male power.

Even women's names and legal involvement in property relations threaten to corrupt men and prevent the smooth functioning of masculine order, which we see through Bramble's narration of his own history. As a young man, Bramble involved himself in the world that he now finds contemptible. In the novel, he wonders whether a peevish nostalgia induces him to see the "morals of mankind" as diseased, as having "contracted an extraordinary degree of depravity within these thirty years;" or what is "more probable, the impetuous pursuits and avocations of youth have formerly hindered me from observing those rotten parts of human nature, which now appear so offensively to my observation" (p. 104). Because the novel does not provide us with a thorough portrait of Bramble as a youthful libertine, we do not know precisely the extent to which he was part of the corrupt social body against which he now declaims. We do know, however, that Bramble committed "the sins of youth . . . under his maternal name Lloyd [*sic*], which he later abandoned for his paternal name, Bramble—symbolizing his moral reformation."[29] Maternal lineage, therefore, becomes associated with moral depravity: economic control by women, even after death through their bequeathed property and names, endangers men and, moreover, constitutes a false state of affairs: "I took my mother's name, which was Loyd, as heir to her lands in Glamorganshire; but, when I came of age, I sold that property, in order to clear my paternal estate, and resumed my real name; so that I am now Matthew Bramble of Brambleton-hall in Monmouthshire, at your service" (p. 305). To be a "moral" man, therefore, Bramble must purge the maternal and the female, severing their connection with real property. Like the goods of luxury, the maternal estate becomes a waste product, which is only useful insofar as it is disposable. Maternal inheritance is only useful in upholding and servicing the paternal estate for the man who wishes to meet the moral criteria of masculinity in *Humphry Clinker*. In addition, Bramble's previous nominalization as Matthew Loyd prevents Clinker from recognizing Bramble as his father: the revelation of Bramble's past "fictional" name removes the screen of the maternal from between Bramble and Clinker and unites them as father and son.

Clinker never attains the full standing of a gentleman: not only is he a bastard, but also he takes Bramble's maternal name of Loyd, which signifies his deviance from the "real" Bramble paternal line. Nonetheless, the name change significantly improves his status in that it disinfects him by ending his association with the noisome Clinker name. Clinker's recuperation also signifies Bramble's atonement for the "sins" that have

entailed him in "family-plagues" and the transformation of another of Bramble's bodily fluids (p. 13), sperm, into a legitimate social product, a male heir to his property. Bramble's recognition and validation of Clinker's existence provides him finally with masculine control of the system of inheritance and of the sexual economy that produces Clinker—and offspring like him[30]—in the first place. Crucially, Clinker's identity is revealed and verified in the company of Lismahago, Dennison, and Jery, while Tabitha and Lydia have temporarily left the room. The scene takes the form of a judicial proceeding, an exclusively male ceremonial atmosphere in which Bramble acknowledges and recuperates his youthful production of (a) Clinker: "Then, laying his hand on Clinker's head, he added, 'Stand forth, Matthew Loyd—You see, gentlemen, how the sins of my youth rise up in judgment against me'" (p. 305). The troubling effects of male waste production that pursue and plague a man are nullified within the arena of this informal male legal proceeding. Here Bramble removes the stench of the name Clinker by commanding Humphry to "stand forth" as Matthew Loyd and welcoming him into the community of men. As the model male private citizen and father of "a very hopeful young gentleman" (p. 304), Dennison cannot fully approve of Bramble and Clinker: he only "facetiously" congratulates them. Jery, however, shakes his newfound cousin's hand "heartily," and Lismahago "compliment[s]" Clinker "with the tears in his eyes," although his tears may be "occasioned by the fall of the coal-scuttle upon his foot" (p. 305).

This ceremony, which unites father and son and bonds Clinker to Bramble's nephew and male friends, contrasts in important ways to Bramble's portrait of Englishmen's divisiveness. Englishmen do not make worthy companions because their self-interest fosters duplicity and argument rather than honesty and cohesion.

> A companionable man will, undoubtedly, put up with many inconveniences for the sake of enjoying agreeable society . . . [But all] the people I see, are too much engrossed by schemes of interest or ambition, to have any room left for sentiment or friendship . . . Conversation is reduced to party-disputes, and illiberal altercation—Social commerce, to formal visits and card-playing—If you pick up a diverting original by accident, it may be dangerous to amuse yourself with his oddities—He is generally a tartar at bottom; a sharper, a spy, or a lunatic. Every person you deal with endeavours to over-reach you in the way of business; you are preyed upon by idle mendicants, who beg in the phrase of borrowing, and live upon the spoils of the stranger—Your tradesmen are without conscience, your friends without affection, and your dependants without fidelity.

(p. 121)

Men's individual "schemes and pursuits" lead to broken connections, and political differences lead to "altercation" (p. 121). Most of all, Englishmen have no capacity for affection, sentiment, and friendship because they construct a society based on dispute and division, squabbling in order to attain individual affluence and position. Indeed, the expedition's continual movement away from England and the kinds of male relations Bramble encounters among "[a]ll the people" he sees suggests that commercial society has become powerful and corrupt enough to make coexistence impossible: the virtuous man who attempts to live among and befriend the modern urban Englishman is subject to disappointment, loneliness, and financial loss.

Such is the case, for example, with the goodhearted and honorable Mr. Serle. Bramble and Jery meet him as he sits alone in a coffeehouse, uninvited to the tea in the next room hosted by his friend Paunceford. Serle, who once "rescued Paunceford from the lowest distress, when he was bankrupt, both in means and reputation" by providing him with the assistance that allowed him to embrace "the opportunity, which has raised him to this pinnacle of wealth" (p. 66), has been repaid with gratitude but not money: "Paunceford carefully and artfully avoided particular discussions with his old patron, who had too much spirit to drop the most distant hint of balancing the account of obligation" (p. 67). The virtuous Serle has "hurt" his "originally small fortune" a number of times "by a romantic spirit of generosity, which he has often displayed, even at the expence of his discretion, in favour of worthless individuals" (p. 66). One of the few virtuous urban Englishmen in Smollett's novel, Mr. Serle is recompensed for his generosity and good nature with rejection and isolation. Mr. Serle, representative of a kind of friendship that Paunceford now considers "generally too plain and home-spun" (p. 65), becomes an object of abuse and dishonesty. The ungrateful Paunceford is the novel's most precisely sketched effeminate, social-climbing Englishmen: he "lives in a palace, feeds upon dainties, is arrayed in sumptuous apparel, appears in all the pomp of equipage, and passes his time among the nobles of the land" (p. 67).

The novel generally concludes that the only way for "plain and home-spun" men to avoid the personal and financial losses imposed upon them by the now-dominant urban Englishmen is to make a private haven at the geographical margins in the country. Lismahago, however, articulates a more public solution to England's problems that closely follows the eighteenth century's standard, oppositional "Tory" position. Particularly in his use of water metaphors, Lismahago's rhetorical devices for describing England's corruption match those we have seen elsewhere in the novel. In his discourses on parliament, commerce, and the press, he continually refers to "channeling" public institutions in order to render them manageable. For Lismahago, male law has the potential to restrain the effects of the flood that commerce has produced within England's social body, if only it would exercise its power. For instance, he owns that although he will always consider "liberty of the press" a "national evil . . . under due restrictions, it would be a valuable privilege; but affirmed, that at present there was no law in England sufficient to restrain it within proper bounds" (p. 199). Importantly, Lismahago's generally more conciliatory position toward commerce and English public institutions erases the association between women and water that particularly characterizes Bramble's tirades against luxury in Bath and London: "He affirmed, the nature of commerce was such, that it could not be fixed or perpetuated, but, having flowed to a certain height, would immediately begin to ebb, and so continue till the channels should be left almost dry; but there was no instance of the tide's rising a second time to any considerable influx in the same nation. Mean while the sudden affluence occasioned by trade, forced open all the sluices of luxury and overflowed the land with every species of profligacy and corruption; a total pravity of manners would ensue, and this must be attended with bankruptcy and ruin" (p. 198). Lismahago's political theory remains only theoretical, however, and though Bramble generally agrees with Lismahago, they do not return to England to channel public institutions. The novel as a whole suggests that the eighteenth-century "Country" political position, which envisions trade as a corrupting influence but a "necessary evil," has allowed commerce and its influence in public institutions to spread and nearly overwhelm the landed man, who needs to return to and maintain his land as a local bulwark against the nation's opened sluices of luxury and effeminacy.

Part of the novel's answer to the problem of unrestrained corruption, especially in relation to keeping women in their place, lies instead in Edinburgh's apartment houses. Scots women become the novel's model domestic guardians: they remain (or have been placed) in the home, where they labor to provide a refuge from the public. In Edinburgh's apartment houses, the common stairs are "generally left in a very filthy condition . . . Nothing can form a stronger contrast, than the difference betwixt the outside and inside of the door; for the good-women of this metropolis are remarkably nice in the ornaments and propriety of their apartments, as if they were resolved to transfer the imputation from the individual to the public" (p. 210). Scotland's public spaces may be dirty, but its private environments exclude the filth that contaminates all departments of urban English life.[31] In its representation of Edinburgh, Smollett's novel provides a vision of women's ideal social place, which involves severing their ties to the public and, in turn, marking them as the repositories of cleanliness in private spaces. Rather than being allowed to follow their "natural" luxurious desires in public, as

Tabitha and Lydia threaten to do in Bath and London, Scotland's proprietary private women remain within their apartments keeping commerce, filth, and, presumably, their own desires "outside the door." Bramble learns, then, partly from the Scottish model, that the private functions as the arena in which men most effectively circumscribe women's power.

Despite Lismahago's theories, then, the novel's men finally abandon England's commercial centers as spaces in which all things feminine—including women—may be rendered subservient to rational, virtuous male control. Instead, by the novel's end, Bramble orchestrates a cohesive male "little society" in which men associate amiably while they either divide (p. 324), privatize, and observe women, or exclude them altogether. Sentiment between men becomes the basis of this little society; in fact, Bramble states that it is his highest ideal: "I know nothing of equal value with the genuine friendship of a sensible man" (p. 37). The novel's utopian vision ensures a controlled interchange of male feeling. Bramble plans to acquire "the collector's place" in the neighborhood of Brambleton-hall for Lismahago and Tabitha so that the friendship between the two men may grow: "[Lismahago] seems to mend, upon further acquaintance. That harsh reserve, which formed a disagreeable husk about his character, begins to peel off in the course of our communication . . . I make no doubt but that he will prove a valuable acquisition to our little society, in the article of conversation, by the fire-side in winter" (p. 324). Thus, proper marriage provides *men* with access to each other's sensibilities. Dr. Lewis, that "sensible man," will continue as Bramble's friend and medical adviser, and Bramble acquaints Baynard with Dennison, "whose goodness of heart would not fail to engage his esteem and affection" (p. 328). Baynard in particular is now safe from the "ridiculous pride and vanity of silly women." He is no longer a "sacrifice" to his tyrannical wife (p. 283).

Within the framework of affective male friendship, men happily exclude women from finances, discourse, and the bedroom. Together, Baynard and Bramble erase the memory of Mrs. Baynard and, in turn, create an atmosphere of sentimentality that is both safe and productive because it takes men rather than women as its object. Bramble helps his friend to forget "my dear Harriet" by endeavoring "to beguile his attention by starting little hints and insinuating other objects of discourse imperceptibly." Adding to the sexual undertones of Bramble's beguiling and insinuating discourse, Bramble usurps Mrs. Baynard's physical place in the bedroom: "That he might not, however, relapse into weaknesses for want of company, I passed the night in his chamber, in a little tent bed brought thither on purpose" (p. 326). Bramble and Baynard discover male sensibility through the healing of the psychic trauma caused by a wife.

Baynard, Bramble, and "a reputable attorney" will rebuild Baynard's estate along the lines of utility, "and the pleasure-ground will be restored to its original use of corn-field and pasture" (p. 328). Economic control by men bonded together in virtuous friendship insures production and "use" rather than consumption and frivolity. Under male guidance, Baynard will "find himself perfectly at ease in mind and body, for the one had dangerously affected the other." In addition, now that Baynard's mind and body are undergoing a cure, the kind of society that he helps produce will be free from disease. Such a rescue from the "misery and contempt" caused by Mrs. Baynard is Bramble's "exquisite pleasure" (p. 335). Men's sentimental bonds, therefore, protect their bodies, which, in the collapse of physical, mental, and social health, make them also psychologically and culturally safe. "Feeling for other men" involves men's mutual assurances that bodily—and thus societal-production remains under male auspices. By making the production of bodily fluids and waste, from blood to excrement to bastards, safe for men, *Humphry Clinker* asserts a masculine, homosocial, rational society that restores male prerogative, but it can only do so by marginalizing and privatizing its own economy in order to avoid the dreadful connection between commerce and public institutions that, in the novel's terms, has terminally corrupted English society. Finally, *Humphry Clinker* joins other mid-eighteenth-century texts by connecting the question of men's economic desires to their bodies and sexuality. Through their private bonds, the novel's men create a place in which production and waste—bodily, sexual, and economic—are balanced and harmonized, a masculine utopian vision of a world of possession and production made safe and healthy for men.

Notes

[1] Roy Porter, "The Body Politic: Medicine and Political Cartoons" (paper presented at the Wellcome Institute for the History of Medicine, London, 28 September 1994). Although Porter agrees with historians who argue that the trope of the "body politic" generally loses its importance as a metaphor in the seventeenth and eighteenth centuries, he also notes that it appears frequently in eighteenth-century political cartoons by William Hogarth, James Gilray, Thomas Rowlandson, and others.

[2] I am attempting to broaden the numerous readings that have investigated the medical theme in the novel in terms of Bramble's individual journey to bodily and psychological health. Besides George S. Rousseau's article on the medical background to the novel ("Matt Bramble and the Sulphur Controversy in the Eighteenth Century," *Journal of the History of Ideas* 28 [1967]: 577-99), see B. L. Reid, "Smollett's Healing Journey," *VQR* 41, 4 (Autumn 1965): 549-70; John F. Sena, "Smollett's Matthew Bramble and the Tradition of the

Physician-Satirist," *PLL* 11, 4 (Fall 1975): 380-96; and William A. West, "Matt Bramble's Journey to Health," *TSLL* 11, 2 (Summer 1969): 1197-208. Ronald Paulson, in *Satire and the Novel in Eighteenth-Century England* (New Haven: Yale Univ. Press, 1967), mentions in passing the connection between individual and societal health: "Bodies, houses, cities, and the whole nation are organisms that are sick or conducive to sickness" (p. 196).

3 Robert Donald Spector, *Tobias George Smollett: Updated Edition* (Boston: Twayne, 1989), p. 104.

4 J. G. A. Pocock, "The Mobility of Property and the Rise of Eighteenth-Century Sociology," in *Virtue, Commerce, and History: Essays on Political Thought and History, Chiefly in the Eighteenth Century* (Cambridge: Cambridge Univ. Press, 1985), pp. 103-23, 114; originally published in slightly different form in Anthony Parel and Thomas C. Flanagan, eds., *Theories of Property: Aristotle to the Present* (Waterloo ON: published for the Calgary Institute for the Humanities by Wilfred Laurier Univ. Press, 1979), pp. 141-66.

5 Pocock employs the term "civic humanism," particularly in *The Machiavellian Moment: Florentine Thought and the Atlantic Republican Tradition* (Princeton: Princeton Univ. Press, 1975). For work by John Barrell and civic humanism in the fine arts, see *The Political Theory of Painting from Reynolds to Hazlitt: "The Body of the Public"* (New Haven: Yale Univ. Press, 1986).

6 Pocock, *Virtue,* p. 115.

7 Pocock writes: "When the polite man of commercial and cultivated society looked back into his past, what he necessarily saw there was the passions not yet socialised, to which he gave such names as 'barbarism' and 'savagery': and his debate against the patriot ideal could be far more satisfactorily carried on if he could demonstrate that what had preceded the rise of commerce and culture was not a world of virtuous citizens, but one of barbarism" (*Virtue,* p. 115.)

8 John Sekora, *Luxury: The Concept in Western Thought, Eden to Smollett* (Baltimore: Johns Hopkins Univ. Press, 1977). Sekora's examination of the concept of luxury in Western history ends with Smollett's works, particularly *Humphry Clinker*. "For nearly two decades [Smollett] had used the classical concept of luxury to express a revulsion against certain aspects of historical change. This sense of the concept, infused into *Humphry Clinker,* was becoming increasingly ineffectual by the time the novel appeared in 1771. It was increasingly difficult, that is, for a ruling elite to demand effort and expansion while simultaneously urging restraint and retrenchment" (p. 285).

9 Adam Smith, *The Theory of Moral Sentiments* (Oxford: Oxford Univ. Press, 1976), pp. 224-5.

10 Barrell, "'The Dangerous Goddess': Masculinity, Prestige, and the Aesthetic in Early Eighteenth-Century Britain," *CultCrit* 12 (Spring 1989): 101-31, 103-4.

11 John P. Zomchick, "Social Class, Character, and Narrative Strategy in *Humphry Clinker,*" *ECL,* n. s. 10, 3 (October 1986): 172-85, 185 n. 15.

12 Tobias Smollett, *The Expedition of Humphry Clinker,* ed. O M Brack Jr. (Athens: Univ. of Georgia Press, 1990), p. 13. Subsequent references will be to this edition and appear parenthetically in the text.

13 Paul-Gabriel Boucé makes the case for Jery's role as the observer of the group: "Jery does not *want* to get involved in the problems of the group. The only time he makes an exception to this rule of conduct is when he yields to a blind impulse of social and personal hatred for Wilson . . . Jery's vocation—and mission—is to hold himself aloof from events and human problems in order the better to *observe* them" (*The Novels of Tobias Smollett,* trans. Antonia White [New York: Longman, 1976], p. 205).

14 James P. Carson, "Commodification and the Figure of the Castrato in Smollett's *Humphry Clinker,*" *ECent* 33, 1 (Spring 1992): 24-46, 25.

15 Carson, p. 30.

16 Thomas R. Preston, *Not in Timon's Manner: Feeling, Misanthropy, and Satire in Eighteenth-Century England* (University: Univ. of Alabama Press, 1975), p. 117.

17 Barrell, "'Dangerous Goddess,'" p. 116.

18 Barrell, "'Dangerous Goddess,'" p. 125.

19 Peter Stallybrass, *The Politics and Poetics of Transgression* (Ithaca: Cornell Univ. Press, 1986), p. 131.

20 My argument here about male homosocial bonds, which casts the female character as an intermediary figure between two male characters, is strongly indebted to Eve Kosofsky Sedgwick's *Between Men: English Literature and Male Homosocial Desire* (New York: Columbia Univ. Press, 1985).

21 Spector, p. 112.

22 Sheridan Baker, "*Humphry Clinker* as Comic Romance," *Papers of the Michigan Academy of Science, Arts, and Letters* 66 (1961): 645-54, 653.

[23] Carson, p. 31.

[24] Gail Kern Paster, *The Body Embarrassed: Drama and the Disciplines of Shame in Early Modern England* (Ithaca: Cornell Univ. Press, 1993), p. 15.

[25] Paster, p. 52.

[26] Paster, p. 8.

[27] Ibid.

[28] Of course, Smollett also disassociates Clinker from the mob by placing the blame for Clinker's condition on the landlord of the inn at Marlborough, for whom Clinker had worked until he became ill. Bramble tells the landlord, "So that the fellow being sick and destitute . . . you turned him out to die in the streets" (p. 80).

[29] Preston, p. 109.

[30] Early in the novel, Bramble and Jery discuss the financial problems that arise for men in connection with their alleged production of illegitimate children. Jery must pay a monetary penalty for allegedly producing a child with a woman he says he does not know: "far from having any amorous intercourse with the object in question, I never had the least acquaintance with her person" (p. 28). Bramble tells Jery "with great good-humour, that betwixt the age of twenty and forty, he had been obliged to provide for nine bastards, sworn to him by women whom he never saw" (p. 29).

[31] Zomchick provides an excellent detailed analysis of the differences between England and Scotland: "In Bath, Bramble worries about drinking others' bodily discharges . . . In Edinburgh, on the other hand, the public filth does not enter the private space nor threaten the health and welfare of the polite observer." He does not, however, consider the gender implications (pp. 179-80).

FURTHER READING

Baker, Ernest A. "Smollett." In his *The History of the English Novel, Intellectual Realism: From Richardson to Sterne*, pp. 197-239. London: H. F. and G. Witherby Ltd., 1930, and New York: Barnes and Noble, reprint 1950.
> Provides an overview of Smollett's life and work, describing the author as "rather abnormally sensitive," and observing that this sensitivity appears in his novels.

Beasley, Jerry C. "Introduction." In *The Adventures of Ferdinand Count Fathom* by Tobias Smollett, edited by O. M. Brack, Jr., pp. xix-xli. Athens, GA: The University of Georgia Press, 1988.
> Offers a biographical, historical, and critical history of a novel that has been regarded as one of Smollett's "lesser achievements."

Brack, O. M., Jr. "Smollet's *Peregrine Pickle* Revisited." *Studies in the Novel* XXVII, No. 3 (Fall 1995): 260-72.
> Approaches the novel from a textual editor's point of view, looking at its textual history and the textual variants among its various editions.

Day, Robert Adams. "Sex, Scatology, Smollett." In *Sexuality in Eighteenth-Century Britain*, edited by Paul-Gabriel Boucé, pp. 225-43. Manchester, England: Manchester University Press, 1982.
> Suggests that Smollett is an unexpectedly modern writer with regard to his attitudes toward sexuality, and asserts that Smollett's novels display a fascination with male homosexuality and with scatology.

Foster, James R. "Sensibility among the Great and the Near-Great." In his *History of the Pre-Romantic Novel in England*, pp. 104-38. New York: The Modern Language Association of America, 1949.
> Includes brief discussion of Smollett's prose and compare his novels with those of other writers of his era.

Jacobsen, Susan L. "'The Tinsel of the Times': Smollett's Argument against Conspicuous Consumption in *Humphry Clinker*." *Eighteenth-Century Fiction* 9, No. 1, (October 1996): 71-88.
> Argues that unlike many of the thinkers and writers of his era, Smollett disapproved of the common social preoccupation with commercial consumption. He particularly feared that the desire for material goods among the poor would lead England into chaos, vulgarity, and immorality.

Kelly, Lionel. "Introduction." In his *Tobias Smollett: The Critical Heritage*, edited by Lionel Kelly, pp. 1-28. London: Routledge and Kegan Paul, 1987.
> Overview of Smollett's works, of his relationship with his contemporary writers, and of his influence on later writers. The critic proposes Smollett as an influene especially on Charles Dickens.

Preston, Thomas R. "Introduction." In *The Expedition of Humphry Clinker* by Tobias Smollett, edited by O. M. Brack, Jr., pp. xxi-liv. Athens, GA: The University of Georgia Press, 1990.
> Discusses the critical reception, the sources, the themes and the structure of what is described as Smollett's most closely studied novel.

Price, John Vladimir. "Smollett and the Reader in *Sir Launcelot Greaves*." In *Smollett: Author of the First Distinction*, edited by Alan Bold, pp. 193-208. London: Vision Press Ltd., 1982.
> Examines the critical history surrounding the novel *Sir Launcelot Greaves*. The critic concludes that this novel was an experiment by Smollett which resulted as an "interesting failure."

Rousseau, G. S. "From Swift to Smollett: The Satirical Tradition in Prose Narrative." In *The Columbia History of the British Novel,* edited by John Richetti, pp. 127-53. New York: Columbia University Press, 1994.

> Discusses Smollett's distinction as a writer who combined "diverse strains of satire and picaresque tales into a thoroughly original cast of fiction" in an overview of satirical writing in English fiction from Jonathan Swift through Smollett.

Spector, Robert D. "Shaping Forces: Society, Personality, and Literary Tradition." In *Smollett's Women: A Study in an Eighteenth-Century Masculine Sensibility,* pp. 1-18. Westport, CT: Greenwood Press, 1994.

> Examines the ways women are portrayed in Smollett's novels and relates this to what is known about Smollett's personal attitudes toward women..

Thorson, James L., ed. Tobias Smollett's *Humphry Clinker: An Authoritative Text, Contemporary Responses, Criticism.* New York: W. W. Norton and Company, 1983, 436 p.

> Edited and annotated edition of *Humphry Clinker* that includes illustrations, a bibliography, and both contemporary and modern reactions to the novel.

Zomchick, John P. "Social Class, Character, and Narrative Strategy in *Humphry Clinker.*" *Eighteenth-Century Life* X, No. 3 (October 1986): 172-85.

> Argues that the individual characters in Smollett's last novel express the social problems of the day as well as solutions, and that these problems are still present today.

Additional coverage of Smollett's life and works is contained in the following sources published by Gale Research: *Literature Criticism from 1400 to 1800, Vol. 2; Concise Dictionary of Literary Biography 1660-1789;* **and** *Dictionary of Literary Biography, Vols. 39 and 104.*

Literature
Criticism from
1400 to 1800

Cumulative Indexes

How to Use This Index

The main references

Calvino, Italo
1923–1985 .... CLC 5, 8, 11, 22, 33, 39,
73; SSC 3

---

list all author entries in the following Gale Literary Criticism series:

BLC = *Black Literature Criticism*
CLC = *Contemporary Literary Criticism*
CLR = *Children's Literature Review*
CMLC = *Classical and Medieval Literature Criticism*
DA = *DISCovering Authors*
DAB = *DISCovering Authors: British*
DAC = *DISCovering Authors: Canadian*
DAM = *DISCovering Authors: Modules*
    DRAM: *Dramatists Module;* **MST**: *Most-Studied Authors Module;*
    MULT: *Multicultural Authors Module;* **NOV**: *Novelists Module;*
    POET: *Poets Module;* **POP**: *Popular Fiction and Genre Authors Module*
DC = *Drama Criticism*
HLC = *Hispanic Literature Criticism*
LC = *Literature Criticism from 1400 to 1800*
NCLC = *Nineteenth-Century Literature Criticism*
PC = *Poetry Criticism*
SSC = *Short Story Criticism*
TCLC = *Twentieth-Century Literary Criticism*
WLC = *World Literature Criticism, 1500 to the Present*

The cross-references

See also CANR 23; CA 85-88;
   obituary CA116

---

list all author entries in the following Gale biographical and literary sources:

AAYA = *Authors & Artists for Young Adults*
AITN = *Authors in the News*
BEST = *Bestsellers*
BW = *Black Writers*
CA = *Contemporary Authors*
CAAS = *Contemporary Authors Autobiography Series*
CABS = *Contemporary Authors Bibliographical Series*
CANR = *Contemporary Authors New Revision Series*
CAP = *Contemporary Authors Permanent Series*
CDALB = *Concise Dictionary of American Literary Biography*
CDBLB = *Concise Dictionary of British Literary Biography*
DLB = *Dictionary of Literary Biography*
DLBD = *Dictionary of Literary Biography Documentary Series*
DLBY = *Dictionary of Literary Biography Yearbook*
HW = *Hispanic Writers*
JRDA = *Junior DISCovering Authors*
MAICYA = *Major Authors and Illustrators for Children and Young Adults*
MTCW = *Major 20th-Century Writers*
NNAL = *Native North American Literature*
SAAS = *Something about the Author Autobiography Series*
SATA = *Something about the Author*
YABC = *Yesterday's Authors of Books for Children*

Literary Criticism Series
Cumulative Author Index

20/1631
See Upward, Allen
A/C Cross
See Lawrence, T(homas) E(dward)
Abasiyanik, Sait Faik 1906-1954
See Sait Faik
See also CA 123
Abbey, Edward 1927-1989   **CLC 36, 59**
See also CA 45-48; 128; CANR 2, 41
Abbott, Lee K(ittredge) 1947-   **CLC 48**
See also CA 124; CANR 51; DLB 130
Abe, Kobo 1924-1993**CLC 8, 22, 53, 81; DAM NOV**
See also CA 65-68; 140; CANR 24, 60; DLB 182; MTCW 1
Abelard, Peter c. 1079-c. 1142   **CMLC 11**
See also DLB 115
Abell, Kjeld 1901-1961   **CLC 15**
See also CA 111
Abish, Walter 1931-   **CLC 22**
See also CA 101; CANR 37; DLB 130
Abrahams, Peter (Henry) 1919-   **CLC 4**
See also BW 1; CA 57-60; CANR 26; DLB 117; MTCW 1
Abrams, M(eyer) H(oward) 1912-   **CLC 24**
See also CA 57-60; CANR 13, 33; DLB 67
Abse, Dannie 1923-   **CLC 7, 29; DAB; DAM POET**
See also CA 53-56; CAAS 1; CANR 4, 46, 74; DLB 27
Achebe, (Albert) Chinua(lumogu) 1930-**C L C 1, 3, 5, 7, 11, 26, 51, 75; BLC 1; DA; DAB; DAC; DAM MST, MULT, NOV; WLC**
See also AAYA 15; BW 2; CA 1-4R; CANR 6, 26, 47, 73; CLR 20; DLB 117; MAICYA; MTCW 1; SATA 40; SATA-Brief 38
Acker, Kathy 1948-1997   **CLC 45, 111**
See also CA 117; 122; 162; CANR 55
Ackroyd, Peter 1949-   **CLC 34, 52**
See also CA 123; 127; CANR 51, 74; DLB 155; INT 127
Acorn, Milton 1923-   **CLC 15; DAC**
See also CA 103; DLB 53; INT 103
Adamov, Arthur 1908-1970 **CLC 4, 25; DAM DRAM**
See also CA 17-18; 25-28R; CAP 2; MTCW 1
Adams, Alice (Boyd) 1926-**CLC 6, 13, 46; SSC 24**
See also CA 81-84; CANR 26, 53; DLBY 86; INT CANR-26; MTCW 1
Adams, Andy 1859-1935   **TCLC 56**
See also YABC 1
Adams, Brooks 1848-1927   **TCLC 80**
See also CA 123; DLB 47
Adams, Douglas (Noel) 1952-   **CLC 27, 60; DAM POP**
See also AAYA 4; BEST 89:3; CA 106; CANR 34, 64; DLBY 83; JRDA
Adams, Francis 1862-1893   **NCLC 33**
Adams, Henry (Brooks) 1838-1918 **TCLC 4, 52; DA; DAB; DAC; DAM MST**
See also CA 104; 133; DLB 12, 47, 189

Adams, Richard (George) 1920-**CLC 4, 5, 18; DAM NOV**
See also AAYA 16; AITN 1, 2; CA 49-52; CANR 3, 35; CLR 20; JRDA; MAICYA; MTCW 1; SATA 7, 69
Adamson, Joy(-Friederike Victoria) 1910-1980 **CLC 17**
See also CA 69-72; 93-96; CANR 22; MTCW 1; SATA 11; SATA-Obit 22
Adcock, Fleur 1934-   **CLC 41**
See also CA 25-28R; CAAS 23; CANR 11, 34, 69; DLB 40
Addams, Charles (Samuel) 1912-1988**CLC 30**
See also CA 61-64; 126; CANR 12
Addams, Jane 1860-1945   **TCLC 76**
Addison, Joseph 1672-1719   **LC 18**
See also CDBLB 1660-1789; DLB 101
Adler, Alfred (F.) 1870-1937   **TCLC 61**
See also CA 119; 159
Adler, C(arole) S(chwerdtfeger) 1932-**CLC 35**
See also AAYA 4; CA 89-92; CANR 19, 40; JRDA; MAICYA; SAAS 15; SATA 26, 63, 102
Adler, Renata 1938-   **CLC 8, 31**
See also CA 49-52; CANR 5, 22, 52; MTCW 1
Ady, Endre 1877-1919   **TCLC 11**
See also CA 107
A.E. 1867-1935   **TCLC 3, 10**
See also Russell, George William
Aeschylus 525B.C.-456B.C.   **CMLC 11; DA; DAB; DAC; DAM DRAM, MST; DC 8; WLCS**
See also DLB 176
Aesop 620(?)B.C.-564(?)B.C.   **CMLC 24**
See also CLR 14; MAICYA; SATA 64
Affable Hawk
See MacCarthy, Sir(Charles Otto) Desmond
Africa, Ben
See Bosman, Herman Charles
Afton, Effie
See Harper, Frances Ellen Watkins
Agapida, Fray Antonio
See Irving, Washington
Agee, James (Rufus) 1909-1955 **TCLC 1, 19; DAM NOV**
See also AITN 1; CA 108; 148; CDALB 1941-1968; DLB 2, 26, 152
Aghill, Gordon
See Silverberg, Robert
Agnon, S(hmuel) Y(osef Halevi) 1888-1970 **CLC 4, 8, 14; SSC 30**
See also CA 17-18; 25-28R; CANR 60; CAP 2; MTCW 1
Agrippa von Nettesheim, Henry Cornelius 1486-1535   **LC 27**
Aherne, Owen
See Cassill, R(onald) V(erlin)
Ai 1947-   **CLC 4, 14, 69**
See also CA 85-88; CAAS 13; CANR 70; DLB 120
Aickman, Robert (Fordyce) 1914-1981   **C L C 57**

See also CA 5-8R; CANR 3, 72
Aiken, Conrad (Potter) 1889-1973**CLC 1, 3, 5, 10, 52; DAM NOV, POET; SSC 9**
See also CA 5-8R; 45-48; CANR 4, 60; CDALB 1929-1941; DLB 9, 45, 102; MTCW 1; SATA 3, 30
Aiken, Joan (Delano) 1924-   **CLC 35**
See also AAYA 1, 25; CA 9-12R; CANR 4, 23, 34, 64; CLR 1, 19; DLB 161; JRDA; MAICYA; MTCW 1; SAAS 1; SATA 2, 30, 73
Ainsworth, William Harrison 1805-1882 **NCLC 13**
See also DLB 21; SATA 24
Aitmatov, Chingiz (Torekulovich) 1928-**C L C 71**
See also CA 103; CANR 38; MTCW 1; SATA 56
Akers, Floyd
See Baum, L(yman) Frank
Akhmadulina, Bella Akhatovna 1937-   **C L C 53; DAM POET**
See also CA 65-68
Akhmatova, Anna 1888-1966**CLC 11, 25, 64; DAM POET; PC 2**
See also CA 19-20; 25-28R; CANR 35; CAP 1; MTCW 1
Aksakov, Sergei Timofeyvich 1791-1859 **NCLC 2**
See also DLB 198
Aksenov, Vassily
See Aksyonov, Vassily (Pavlovich)
Akst, Daniel 1956-   **CLC 109**
See also CA 161
Aksyonov, Vassily (Pavlovich) 1932-**CLC 22, 37, 101**
See also CA 53-56; CANR 12, 48
Akutagawa, Ryunosuke 1892-1927 **TCLC 16**
See also CA 117; 154
Alain 1868-1951   **TCLC 41**
See also CA 163
Alain-Fournier   **TCLC 6**
See also Fournier, Henri Alban
See also DLB 65
Alarcon, Pedro Antonio de 1833-1891**NCLC 1**
Alas (y Urena), Leopoldo (Enrique Garcia) 1852-1901   **TCLC 29**
See also CA 113; 131; HW
Albee, Edward (Franklin III) 1928-**CLC 1, 2, 3, 5, 9, 11, 13, 25, 53, 86, 113; DA; DAB; DAC; DAM DRAM, MST; WLC**
See also AITN 1; CA 5-8R; CABS 3; CANR 8, 54, 74; CDALB 1941-1968; DLB 7; INT CANR-8; MTCW 1
Alberti, Rafael 1902-   **CLC 7**
See also CA 85-88; DLB 108
Albert the Great 1200(?)-1280   **CMLC 16**
See also DLB 115
Alcala-Galiano, Juan Valera y
See Valera y Alcala-Galiano, Juan
Alcott, Amos Bronson 1799-1888   **NCLC 1**
See also DLB 1

Alcott, Louisa May 1832-1888 NCLC 6, 58;
DA; DAB; DAC; DAM MST, NOV; SSC
27; WLC
See also AAYA 20; CDALB 1865-1917; CLR
1, 38; DLB 1, 42, 79; DLBD 14; JRDA;
MAICYA; SATA 100; YABC 1
Aldanov, M. A.
See Aldanov, Mark (Alexandrovich)
Aldanov, Mark (Alexandrovich) 1886(?)-1957
TCLC 23
See also CA 118
Aldington, Richard 1892-1962   CLC 49
See also CA 85-88; CANR 45; DLB 20, 36, 100,
149
Aldiss, Brian W(ilson) 1925- CLC 5, 14, 40;
DAM NOV
See also CA 5-8R; CAAS 2; CANR 5, 28, 64;
DLB 14; MTCW 1; SATA 34
Alegria, Claribel 1924-CLC 75; DAM MULT
See also CA 131; CAAS 15; CANR 66; DLB
145; HW
Alegria, Fernando 1918-   CLC 57
See also CA 9-12R; CANR 5, 32, 72; HW
Aleichem, Sholom   TCLC 1, 35
See also Rabinovitch, Sholem
Aleixandre, Vicente 1898-1984   CLC 9, 36;
DAM POET; PC 15
See also CA 85-88; 114; CANR 26; DLB 108;
HW; MTCW 1
Alepoudelis, Odysseus
See Elytis, Odysseus
Aleshkovsky, Joseph 1929-
See Aleshkovsky, Yuz
See also CA 121; 128
Aleshkovsky, Yuz   CLC 44
See also Aleshkovsky, Joseph
Alexander, Lloyd (Chudley) 1924- CLC 35
See also AAYA 1, 27; CA 1-4R; CANR 1, 24,
38, 55; CLR 1, 5, 48; DLB 52; JRDA;
MAICYA; MTCW 1; SAAS 19; SATA 3, 49,
81
Alexander, Samuel 1859-1938   TCLC 77
Alexie, Sherman (Joseph, Jr.) 1966- CLC 96;
DAM MULT
See also CA 138; CANR 65; DLB 175; NNAL
Alfau, Felipe 1902-   CLC 66
See also CA 137
Alger, Horatio, Jr. 1832-1899   NCLC 8
See also DLB 42; SATA 16
Algren, Nelson 1909-1981   CLC 4, 10, 33
See also CA 13-16R; 103; CANR 20, 61;
CDALB 1941-1968; DLB 9; DLBY 81, 82;
MTCW 1
Ali, Ahmed 1910-   CLC 69
See also CA 25-28R; CANR 15, 34
Alighieri, Dante
See Dante
Allan, John B.
See Westlake, Donald E(dwin)
Allan, Sidney
See Hartmann, Sadakichi
Allan, Sydney
See Hartmann, Sadakichi
Allen, Edward 1948-   CLC 59
Allen, Fred 1894-1956   TCLC 87
Allen, Paula Gunn 1939-   CLC 84; DAM
MULT
See also CA 112; 143; CANR 63; DLB 175;
NNAL
Allen, Roland
See Ayckbourn, Alan
Allen, Sarah A.
See Hopkins, Pauline Elizabeth

Allen, Sidney H.
See Hartmann, Sadakichi
Allen, Woody 1935- CLC 16, 52; DAM POP
See also AAYA 10; CA 33-36R; CANR 27, 38,
63; DLB 44; MTCW 1
Allende, Isabel 1942- CLC 39, 57, 97; DAM
MULT, NOV; HLC; WLCS
See also AAYA 18; CA 125; 130; CANR 51,
74; DLB 145; HW; INT 130; MTCW 1
Alleyn, Ellen
See Rossetti, Christina (Georgina)
Allingham, Margery (Louise) 1904-1966CLC
19
See also CA 5-8R; 25-28R; CANR 4, 58; DLB
77; MTCW 1
Allingham, William 1824-1889   NCLC 25
See also DLB 35
Allison, Dorothy E. 1949-   CLC 78
See also CA 140; CANR 66
Allston, Washington 1779-1843   NCLC 2
See also DLB 1
Almedingen, E. M.   CLC 12
See also Almedingen, Martha Edith von
See also SATA 3
Almedingen, Martha Edith von 1898-1971
See Almedingen, E. M.
See also CA 1-4R; CANR 1
Almodovar, Pedro 1949(?)-   CLC 114
See also CA 133; CANR 72
Almqvist, Carl Jonas Love 1793-1866 N C L C
42
Alonso, Damaso 1898-1990   CLC 14
See also CA 110; 131; 130; CANR 72; DLB
108; HW
Alov
See Gogol, Nikolai (Vasilyevich)
Alta 1942-   CLC 19
See also CA 57-60
Alter, Robert B(ernard) 1935-   CLC 34
See also CA 49-52; CANR 1, 47
Alther, Lisa 1944-   CLC 7, 41
See also CA 65-68; CAAS 30; CANR 12, 30,
51; MTCW 1
Althusser, L.
See Althusser, Louis
Althusser, Louis 1918-1990   CLC 106
See also CA 131; 132
Altman, Robert 1925-   CLC 16, 116
See also CA 73-76; CANR 43
Alvarez, A(lfred) 1929-   CLC 5, 13
See also CA 1-4R; CANR 3, 33, 63; DLB 14,
40
Alvarez, Alejandro Rodriguez 1903-1965
See Casona, Alejandro
See also CA 131; 93-96; HW
Alvarez, Julia 1950-   CLC 93
See also AAYA 25; CA 147; CANR 69
Alvaro, Corrado 1896-1956   TCLC 60
See also CA 163
Amado, Jorge 1912- CLC 13, 40, 106; DAM
MULT, NOV; HLC
See also CA 77-80; CANR 35, 74; DLB 113;
MTCW 1
Ambler, Eric 1909-   CLC 4, 6, 9
See also CA 9-12R; CANR 7, 38, 74; DLB 77;
MTCW 1
Amichai, Yehuda 1924- CLC 9, 22, 57, 116
See also CA 85-88; CANR 46, 60; MTCW 1
Amichai, Yehudah
See Amichai, Yehuda
Amiel, Henri Frederic 1821-1881   NCLC 4
Amis, Kingsley (William) 1922-1995CLC 1, 2,
3, 5, 8, 13, 40, 44; DA; DAB; DAC; DAM

MST, NOV
See also AITN 2; CA 9-12R; 150; CANR 8, 28,
54; CDBLB 1945-1960; DLB 15, 27, 100,
139; DLBY 96; INT CANR-8; MTCW 1
Amis, Martin (Louis) 1949- CLC 4, 9, 38, 62,
101
See also BEST 90:3; CA 65-68; CANR 8, 27,
54, 73; DLB 14, 194; INT CANR-27
Ammons, A(rchie) R(andolph) 1926-CLC 2, 3,
5, 8, 9, 25, 57, 108; DAM POET; PC 16
See also AITN 1; CA 9-12R; CANR 6, 36, 51,
73; DLB 5, 165; MTCW 1
Amo, Tauraatua i
See Adams, Henry (Brooks)
Amory, Thomas 1691(?)-1788   LC 48
Anand, Mulk Raj 1905-   CLC 23, 93; DAM
NOV
See also CA 65-68; CANR 32, 64; MTCW 1
Anatol
See Schnitzler, Arthur
Anaximander c. 610B.C.-c. 546B.C.CMLC 22
Anaya, Rudolfo A(lfonso) 1937-   CLC 23;
DAM MULT, NOV; HLC
See also AAYA 20; CA 45-48; CAAS 4; CANR
1, 32, 51; DLB 82; HW 1; MTCW 1
Andersen, Hans Christian 1805-1875NCLC 7;
DA; DAB; DAC; DAM MST, POP; SSC
6; WLC
See also CLR 6; MAICYA; SATA 100; YABC
1
Anderson, C. Farley
See Mencken, H(enry) L(ouis); Nathan, George
Jean
Anderson, Jessica (Margaret) Queale 1916-
CLC 37
See also CA 9-12R; CANR 4, 62
Anderson, Jon (Victor) 1940- CLC 9; DAM
POET
See also CA 25-28R; CANR 20
Anderson, Lindsay (Gordon) 1923-1994C L C
20
See also CA 125; 128; 146
Anderson, Maxwell 1888-1959TCLC 2; DAM
DRAM
See also CA 105; 152; DLB 7
Anderson, Poul (William) 1926-   CLC 15
See also AAYA 5; CA 1-4R; CAAS 2; CANR
2, 15, 34, 64; DLB 8; INT CANR-15; MTCW
1; SATA 90; SATA-Brief 39
Anderson, Robert (Woodruff) 1917-CLC 23;
DAM DRAM
See also AITN 1; CA 21-24R; CANR 32; DLB
7
Anderson, Sherwood 1876-1941 TCLC 1, 10,
24; DA; DAB; DAC; DAM MST, NOV;
SSC 1; WLC
See also CA 104; 121; CANR 61; CDALB
1917-1929; DLB 4, 9, 86; DLBD 1; MTCW
1
Andier, Pierre
See Desnos, Robert
Andouard
See Giraudoux, (Hippolyte) Jean
Andrade, Carlos Drummond de   CLC 18
See also Drummond de Andrade, Carlos
Andrade, Mario de 1893-1945   TCLC 43
Andreae, Johann V(alentin) 1586-1654LC 32
See also DLB 164
Andreas-Salome, Lou 1861-1937   TCLC 56
See also DLB 66
Andress, Lesley
See Sanders, Lawrence
Andrewes, Lancelot 1555-1626   LC 5

See Blish, James (Benjamin)

Atherton, Gertrude (Franklin Horn) 1857-1948 **TCLC 2**
See also CA 104; 155; DLB 9, 78, 186

Atherton, Lucius
See Masters, Edgar Lee

Atkins, Jack
See Harris, Mark

Atkinson, Kate   **CLC 99**
See also CA 166

Attaway, William (Alexander) 1911-1986**CLC 92; BLC 1; DAM MULT**
See also BW 2; CA 143; DLB 76

Atticus
See Fleming, Ian (Lancaster); Wilson, (Thomas) Woodrow

Atwood, Margaret (Eleanor) 1939-**CLC 2, 3, 4, 8, 13, 15, 25, 44, 84; DA; DAB; DAC; DAM MST, NOV, POET; PC 8; SSC 2; WLC**
See also AAYA 12; BEST 89:2; CA 49-52; CANR 3, 24, 33, 59; DLB 53; INT CANR-24; MTCW 1; SATA 50

Aubigny, Pierre d'
See Mencken, H(enry) L(ouis)

Aubin, Penelope 1685-1731(?)   **LC 9**
See also DLB 39

Auchincloss, Louis (Stanton) 1917-**CLC 4, 6, 9, 18, 45; DAM NOV; SSC 22**
See also CA 1-4R; CANR 6, 29, 55; DLB 2; DLBY 80; INT CANR-29; MTCW 1

Auden, W(ystan) H(ugh) 1907-1973**CLC 1, 2, 3, 4, 6, 9, 11, 14, 43; DA; DAB; DAC; DAM DRAM, MST, POET; PC 1; WLC**
See also AAYA 18; CA 9-12R; 45-48; CANR 5, 61; CDBLB 1914-1945; DLB 10, 20; MTCW 1

Audiberti, Jacques 1900-1965 **CLC 38; DAM DRAM**
See also CA 25-28R

Audubon, John James 1785-1851 **NCLC 47**

Auel, Jean M(arie) 1936-**CLC 31, 107; DAM POP**
See also AAYA 7; BEST 90:4; CA 103; CANR 21, 64; INT CANR-21; SATA 91

Auerbach, Erich 1892-1957   **TCLC 43**
See also CA 118; 155

Augier, Emile 1820-1889   **NCLC 31**
See also DLB 192

August, John
See De Voto, Bernard (Augustine)

Augustine, St. 354-430   **CMLC 6; DAB**

Aurelius
See Bourne, Randolph S(illiman)

Aurobindo, Sri
See Ghose, Aurabinda

Austen, Jane 1775-1817 **NCLC 1, 13, 19, 33, 51; DA; DAB; DAC; DAM MST, NOV; WLC**
See also AAYA 19; CDBLB 1789-1832; DLB 116

Auster, Paul 1947-   **CLC 47**
See also CA 69-72; CANR 23, 52

Austin, Frank
See Faust, Frederick (Schiller)

Austin, Mary (Hunter) 1868-1934 **TCLC 25**
See also CA 109; DLB 9, 78

Autran Dourado, Waldomiro
See Dourado, (Waldomiro Freitas) Autran

Averroes 1126-1198   **CMLC 7**
See also DLB 115

Avicenna 980-1037   **CMLC 16**
See also DLB 115

Avison, Margaret 1918- **CLC 2, 4, 97; DAC; DAM POET**
See also CA 17-20R; DLB 53; MTCW 1

Axton, David
See Koontz, Dean R(ay)

Ayckbourn, Alan 1939- **CLC 5, 8, 18, 33, 74; DAB; DAM DRAM**
See also CA 21-24R; CANR 31, 59; DLB 13; MTCW 1

Aydy, Catherine
See Tennant, Emma (Christina)

Ayme, Marcel (Andre) 1902-1967   **CLC 11**
See also CA 89-92; CANR 67; CLR 25; DLB 72; SATA 91

Ayrton, Michael 1921-1975   **CLC 7**
See also CA 5-8R; 61-64; CANR 9, 21

Azorin   **CLC 11**
See also Martinez Ruiz, Jose

Azuela, Mariano 1873-1952 **TCLC 3; DAM MULT; HLC**
See also CA 104; 131; HW; MTCW 1

Baastad, Babbis Friis
See Friis-Baastad, Babbis Ellinor

Bab
See Gilbert, W(illiam) S(chwenck)

Babbis, Eleanor
See Friis-Baastad, Babbis Ellinor

Babel, Isaac
See Babel, Isaak (Emmanuilovich)

Babel, Isaak (Emmanuilovich) 1894-1941(?) **TCLC 2, 13; SSC 16**
See also CA 104; 155

Babits, Mihaly 1883-1941   **TCLC 14**
See also CA 114

Babur 1483-1530   **LC 18**

Bacchelli, Riccardo 1891-1985   **CLC 19**
See also CA 29-32R; 117

Bach, Richard (David) 1936- **CLC 14; DAM NOV, POP**
See also AITN 1; BEST 89:2; CA 9-12R; CANR 18; MTCW 1; SATA 13

Bachman, Richard
See King, Stephen (Edwin)

Bachmann, Ingeborg 1926-1973   **CLC 69**
See also CA 93-96; 45-48; CANR 69; DLB 85

Bacon, Francis 1561-1626   **LC 18, 32**
See also CDBLB Before 1660; DLB 151

Bacon, Roger 1214(?)-1292   **CMLC 14**
See also DLB 115

Bacovia, George   **TCLC 24**
See also Vasiliu, Gheorghe

Badanes, Jerome 1937-   **CLC 59**

Bagehot, Walter 1826-1877   **NCLC 10**
See also DLB 55

Bagnold, Enid 1889-1981 **CLC 25; DAM DRAM**
See also CA 5-8R; 103; CANR 5, 40; DLB 13, 160, 191; MAICYA; SATA 1, 25

Bagritsky, Eduard 1895-1934   **TCLC 60**

Bagrjana, Elisaveta
See Belcheva, Elisaveta

Bagryana, Elisaveta   **CLC 10**
See also Belcheva, Elisaveta
See also DLB 147

Bailey, Paul 1937-   **CLC 45**
See also CA 21-24R; CANR 16, 62; DLB 14

Baillie, Joanna 1762-1851   **NCLC 71**
See also DLB 93

Bainbridge, Beryl (Margaret) 1933-**CLC 4, 5, 8, 10, 14, 18, 22, 62; DAM NOV**
See also CA 21-24R; CANR 24, 55; DLB 14; MTCW 1

Baker, Elliott 1922-   **CLC 8**

See also CA 45-48; CANR 2, 63

Baker, Jean H.   **TCLC 3, 10**
See also Russell, George William

Baker, Nicholson 1957- **CLC 61; DAM POP**
See also CA 135; CANR 63

Baker, Ray Stannard 1870-1946   **TCLC 47**
See also CA 118

Baker, Russell (Wayne) 1925-   **CLC 31**
See also BEST 89:4; CA 57-60; CANR 11, 41, 59; MTCW 1

Bakhtin, M.
See Bakhtin, Mikhail Mikhailovich

Bakhtin, M. M.
See Bakhtin, Mikhail Mikhailovich

Bakhtin, Mikhail
See Bakhtin, Mikhail Mikhailovich

Bakhtin, Mikhail Mikhailovich 1895-1975 **CLC 83**
See also CA 128; 113

Bakshi, Ralph 1938(?)-   **CLC 26**
See also CA 112; 138

Bakunin, Mikhail (Alexandrovich) 1814-1876 **NCLC 25, 58**

Baldwin, James (Arthur) 1924-1987**CLC 1, 2, 3, 4, 5, 8, 13, 15, 17, 42, 50, 67, 90; BLC 1; DA; DAB; DAC; DAM MST, MULT, NOV, POP; DC 1; SSC 10; WLC**
See also AAYA 4; BW 1; CA 1-4R; 124; CABS 1; CANR 3, 24; CDALB 1941-1968; DLB 2, 7, 33; DLBY 87; MTCW 1; SATA 9; SATA-Obit 54

Ballard, J(ames) G(raham) 1930-**CLC 3, 6, 14, 36; DAM NOV, POP; SSC 1**
See also AAYA 3; CA 5-8R; CANR 15, 39, 65; DLB 14; MTCW 1; SATA 93

Balmont, Konstantin (Dmitriyevich) 1867-1943 **TCLC 11**
See also CA 109; 155

Balzac, Honore de 1799-1850**NCLC 5, 35, 53; DA; DAB; DAC; DAM MST, NOV; SSC 5; WLC**
See also DLB 119

Bambara, Toni Cade 1939-1995 **CLC 19, 88; BLC 1; DA; DAC; DAM MST, MULT; WLCS**
See also AAYA 5; BW 2; CA 29-32R; 150; CANR 24, 49; DLB 38; MTCW 1

Bamdad, A.
See Shamlu, Ahmad

Banat, D. R.
See Bradbury, Ray (Douglas)

Bancroft, Laura
See Baum, L(yman) Frank

Banim, John 1798-1842   **NCLC 13**
See also DLB 116, 158, 159

Banim, Michael 1796-1874   **NCLC 13**
See also DLB 158, 159

Banjo, The
See Paterson, A(ndrew) B(arton)

Banks, Iain
See Banks, Iain M(enzies)

Banks, Iain M(enzies) 1954-   **CLC 34**
See also CA 123; 128; CANR 61; DLB 194; INT 128

Banks, Lynne Reid   **CLC 23**
See also Reid Banks, Lynne
See also AAYA 6

Banks, Russell 1940-   **CLC 37, 72**
See also CA 65-68; CAAS 15; CANR 19, 52, 73; DLB 130

Banville, John 1945-   **CLC 46**
See also CA 117; 128; DLB 14; INT 128

Banville, Theodore (Faullain) de 1832-1891

NCLC 9

Baraka, Amiri 1934-**CLC 1, 2, 3, 5, 10, 14, 33, 115; BLC 1; DA; DAC; DAM MST, MULT, POET, POP; DC 6; PC 4; WLCS**
See also Jones, LeRoi
See also BW 2; CA 21-24R; CABS 3; CANR 27, 38, 61; CDALB 1941-1968; DLB 5, 7, 16, 38; DLBD 8; MTCW 1

Barbauld, Anna Laetitia 1743-1825NCLC 50
See also DLB 107, 109, 142, 158

Barbellion, W. N. P. **TCLC 24**
See also Cummings, Bruce F(rederick)

Barbera, Jack (Vincent) 1945- **CLC 44**
See also CA 110; CANR 45

Barbey d'Aurevilly, Jules Amedee 1808-1889 **NCLC 1; SSC 17**
See also DLB 119

Barbusse, Henri 1873-1935 **TCLC 5**
See also CA 105; 154; DLB 65

Barclay, Bill
See Moorcock, Michael (John)

Barclay, William Ewert
See Moorcock, Michael (John)

Barea, Arturo 1897-1957 **TCLC 14**
See also CA 111

Barfoot, Joan 1946- **CLC 18**
See also CA 105

Baring, Maurice 1874-1945 **TCLC 8**
See also CA 105; 168; DLB 34

Baring-Gould, Sabine 1834-1924 **TCLC 88**
See also DLB 156, 190

Barker, Clive 1952- **CLC 52; DAM POP**
See also AAYA 10; BEST 90:3; CA 121; 129; CANR 71; INT 129; MTCW 1

Barker, George Granville 1913-1991 **CLC 8, 48; DAM POET**
See also CA 9-12R; 135; CANR 7, 38; DLB 20; MTCW 1

Barker, Harley Granville
See Granville-Barker, Harley
See also DLB 10

Barker, Howard 1946- **CLC 37**
See also CA 102; DLB 13

Barker, Jane 1652-1732 **LC 42**

Barker, Pat(ricia) 1943- **CLC 32, 94**
See also CA 117; 122; CANR 50; INT 122

Barlach, Ernst 1870-1938 **TCLC 84**
See also DLB 56, 118

Barlow, Joel 1754-1812 **NCLC 23**
See also DLB 37

Barnard, Mary (Ethel) 1909- **CLC 48**
See also CA 21-22; CAP 2

Barnes, Djuna 1892-1982CLC 3, 4, 8, 11, 29; SSC 3
See also CA 9-12R; 107; CANR 16, 55; DLB 4, 9, 45; MTCW 1

Barnes, Julian (Patrick) 1946- **CLC 42; DAB**
See also CA 102; CANR 19, 54; DLB 194; DLBY 93

Barnes, Peter 1931- **CLC 5, 56**
See also CA 65-68; CAAS 12; CANR 33, 34, 64; DLB 13; MTCW 1

Baroja (y Nessi), Pio 1872-1956TCLC 8; HLC
See also CA 104

Baron, David
See Pinter, Harold

Baron Corvo
See Rolfe, Frederick (William Serafino Austin Lewis Mary)

Barondess, Sue K(aufman) 1926-1977 CLC 8
See also Kaufman, Sue
See also CA 1-4R; 69-72; CANR 1

Baron de Teive
See Pessoa, Fernando (Antonio Nogueira)

Baroness Von S.
See Zangwill, Israel

Barres, (Auguste-) Maurice 1862-1923TCLC 47
See also CA 164; DLB 123

Barreto, Afonso Henrique de Lima
See Lima Barreto, Afonso Henrique de

Barrett, (Roger) Syd 1946- **CLC 35**

Barrett, William (Christopher) 1913-1992 **CLC 27**
See also CA 13-16R; 139; CANR 11, 67; INT CANR-11

Barrie, J(ames) M(atthew) 1860-1937 **TCLC 2; DAB; DAM DRAM**
See also CA 104; 136; CDBLB 1890-1914; CLR 16; DLB 10, 141, 156; MAICYA; SATA 100; YABC 1

Barrington, Michael
See Moorcock, Michael (John)

Barrol, Grady
See Bograd, Larry

Barry, Mike
See Malzberg, Barry N(athaniel)

Barry, Philip 1896-1949 **TCLC 11**
See also CA 109; DLB 7

Bart, Andre Schwarz
See Schwarz-Bart, Andre

Barth, John (Simmons) 1930-CLC 1, 2, 3, 5, 7, 9, 10, 14, 27, 51, 89; DAM NOV; SSC 10
See also AITN 1, 2; CA 1-4R; CABS 1; CANR 5, 23, 49, 64; DLB 2; MTCW 1

Barthelme, Donald 1931-1989CLC 1, 2, 3, 5, 6, 8, 13, 23, 46, 59, 115; DAM NOV; SSC 2
See also CA 21-24R; 129; CANR 20, 58; DLB 2; DLBY 80, 89; MTCW 1; SATA 7; SATA-Obit 62

Barthelme, Frederick 1943- **CLC 36, 117**
See also CA 114; 122; DLBY 85; INT 122

Barthes, Roland (Gerard) 1915-1980CLC 24, 83
See also CA 130; 97-100; CANR 66; MTCW 1

Barzun, Jacques (Martin) 1907- **CLC 51**
See also CA 61-64; CANR 22

Bashevis, Isaac
See Singer, Isaac Bashevis

Bashkirtseff, Marie 1859-1884 **NCLC 27**

Basho
See Matsuo Basho

Bass, Kingsley B., Jr.
See Bullins, Ed

Bass, Rick 1958- **CLC 79**
See also CA 126; CANR 53

Bassani, Giorgio 1916- **CLC 9**
See also CA 65-68; CANR 33; DLB 128, 177; MTCW 1

Bastos, Augusto (Antonio) Roa
See Roa Bastos, Augusto (Antonio)

Bataille, Georges 1897-1962 **CLC 29**
See also CA 101; 89-92

Bates, H(erbert) E(rnest) 1905-1974CLC 46; DAB; DAM POP; SSC 10
See also CA 93-96; 45-48; CANR 34; DLB 162, 191; MTCW 1

Bauchart
See Camus, Albert

Baudelaire, Charles 1821-1867 **NCLC 6, 29, 55; DA; DAB; DAC; DAM MST, POET; PC 1; SSC 18; WLC**

Baudrillard, Jean 1929- **CLC 60**

Baum, L(yman) Frank 1856-1919 **TCLC 7**
See also CA 108; 133; CLR 15; DLB 22; JRDA; MAICYA; MTCW 1; SATA 18, 100

Baum, Louis F.
See Baum, L(yman) Frank

Baumbach, Jonathan 1933- **CLC 6, 23**
See also CA 13-16R; CAAS 5; CANR 12, 66; DLBY 80; INT CANR-12; MTCW 1

Bausch, Richard (Carl) 1945- **CLC 51**
See also CA 101; CAAS 14; CANR 43, 61; DLB 130

Baxter, Charles (Morley) 1947- CLC 45, 78; **DAM POP**
See also CA 57-60; CANR 40, 64; DLB 130

Baxter, George Owen
See Faust, Frederick (Schiller)

Baxter, James K(eir) 1926-1972 **CLC 14**
See also CA 77-80

Baxter, John
See Hunt, E(verette) Howard, (Jr.)

Bayer, Sylvia
See Glassco, John

Baynton, Barbara 1857-1929 **TCLC 57**

Beagle, Peter S(oyer) 1939- **CLC 7, 104**
See also CA 9-12R; CANR 4, 51, 73; DLBY 80; INT CANR-4; SATA 60

Bean, Normal
See Burroughs, Edgar Rice

Beard, Charles A(ustin) 1874-1948 TCLC 15
See also CA 115; DLB 17; SATA 18

Beardsley, Aubrey 1872-1898 **NCLC 6**

Beattie, Ann 1947-CLC 8, 13, 18, 40, 63; DAM NOV, POP; SSC 11
See also BEST 90:2; CA 81-84; CANR 53, 73; DLBY 82; MTCW 1

Beattie, James 1735-1803 **NCLC 25**
See also DLB 109

Beauchamp, Kathleen Mansfield 1888-1923
See Mansfield, Katherine
See also CA 104; 134; DA; DAC; DAM MST

Beaumarchais, Pierre-Augustin Caron de 1732-1799 **DC 4**
See also DAM DRAM

Beaumont, Francis 1584(?)-1616LC 33; DC 6
See also CDBLB Before 1660; DLB 58, 121

Beauvoir, Simone (Lucie Ernestine Marie Bertrand) de 1908-1986CLC 1, 2, 4, 8, 14, 31, 44, 50, 71; DA; DAB; DAC; DAM MST, NOV; WLC
See also CA 9-12R; 118; CANR 28, 61; DLB 72; DLBY 86; MTCW 1

Becker, Carl (Lotus) 1873-1945 **TCLC 63**
See also CA 157; DLB 17

Becker, Jurek 1937-1997 **CLC 7, 19**
See also CA 85-88; 157; CANR 60; DLB 75

Becker, Walter 1950- **CLC 26**

Beckett, Samuel (Barclay) 1906-1989 CLC 1, 2, 3, 4, 6, 9, 10, 11, 14, 18, 29, 57, 59, 83; DA; DAB; DAC; DAM DRAM, MST, NOV; SSC 16; WLC
See also CA 5-8R; 130; CANR 33, 61; CDBLB 1945-1960; DLB 13, 15; DLBY 90; MTCW 1

Beckford, William 1760-1844 **NCLC 16**
See also DLB 39

Beckman, Gunnel 1910- **CLC 26**
See also CA 33-36R; CANR 15; CLR 25; MAICYA; SAAS 9; SATA 6

Becque, Henri 1837-1899 **NCLC 3**
See also DLB 192

Beddoes, Thomas Lovell 1803-1849 NCLC 3
See also DLB 96

Bede c. 673-735 **CMLC 20**
See also DLB 146

Bedford, Donald F.
See Fearing, Kenneth (Flexner)

Beecher, Catharine Esther 1800-1878 **N C L C 30**
See also DLB 1
Beecher, John 1904-1980 **CLC 6**
See also AITN 1; CA 5-8R; 105; CANR 8
Beer, Johann 1655-1700 **LC 5**
See also DLB 168
Beer, Patricia 1924- **CLC 58**
See also CA 61-64; CANR 13, 46; DLB 40
Beerbohm, Max
See Beerbohm, (Henry) Max(imilian)
Beerbohm, (Henry) Max(imilian) 1872-1956
TCLC 1, 24
See also CA 104; 154; DLB 34, 100
Beer-Hofmann, Richard 1866-1945 **TCLC 60**
See also CA 160; DLB 81
Begiebing, Robert J(ohn) 1946- **CLC 70**
See also CA 122; CANR 40
Behan, Brendan 1923-1964 **CLC 1, 8, 11, 15, 79; DAM DRAM**
See also CA 73-76; CANR 33; CDBLB 1945-1960; DLB 13; MTCW 1
Behn, Aphra 1640(?)-1689 **LC 1, 30, 42; DA; DAB; DAC; DAM DRAM, MST, NOV, POET; DC 4; PC 13; WLC**
See also DLB 39, 80, 131
Behrman, S(amuel) N(athaniel) 1893-1973
CLC 40
See also CA 13-16; 45-48; CAP 1; DLB 7, 44
Belasco, David 1853-1931 **TCLC 3**
See also CA 104; 168; DLB 7
Belcheva, Elisaveta 1893- **CLC 10**
See also Bagryana, Elisaveta
Beldone, Phil "Cheech"
See Ellison, Harlan (Jay)
Beleno
See Azuela, Mariano
Belinski, Vissarion Grigoryevich 1811-1848
NCLC 5
See also DLB 198
Belitt, Ben 1911- **CLC 22**
See also CA 13-16R; CAAS 4; CANR 7; DLB 5
Bell, Gertrude (Margaret Lowthian) 1868-1926
TCLC 67
See also CA 167; DLB 174
Bell, J. Freeman
See Zangwill, Israel
Bell, James Madison 1826-1902 **TCLC 43; BLC 1; DAM MULT**
See also BW 1; CA 122; 124; DLB 50
Bell, Madison Smartt 1957- **CLC 41, 102**
See also CA 111; CANR 28, 54, 73
Bell, Marvin (Hartley) 1937- **CLC 8, 31; DAM POET**
See also CA 21-24R; CAAS 14; CANR 59; DLB 5; MTCW 1
Bell, W. L. D.
See Mencken, H(enry) L(ouis)
Bellamy, Atwood C.
See Mencken, H(enry) L(ouis)
Bellamy, Edward 1850-1898 **NCLC 4**
See also DLB 12
Bellin, Edward J.
See Kuttner, Henry
Belloc, (Joseph) Hilaire (Pierre Sebastien Rene Swanton) 1870-1953 **TCLC 7, 18; DAM POET; PC 24**
See also CA 106; 152; DLB 19, 100, 141, 174; YABC 1
Belloc, Joseph Peter Rene Hilaire
See Belloc, (Joseph) Hilaire (Pierre Sebastien Rene Swanton)

Belloc, Joseph Pierre Hilaire
See Belloc, (Joseph) Hilaire (Pierre Sebastien Rene Swanton)
Belloc, M. A.
See Lowndes, Marie Adelaide (Belloc)
Bellow, Saul 1915- **CLC 1, 2, 3, 6, 8, 10, 13, 15, 25, 33, 34, 63, 79; DA; DAB; DAC; DAM MST, NOV, POP; SSC 14; WLC**
See also AITN 2; BEST 89:3; CA 5-8R; CABS 1; CANR 29, 53; CDALB 1941-1968; DLB 2, 28; DLBD 3; DLBY 82; MTCW 1
Belser, Reimond Karel Maria de 1929-
See Ruyslinck, Ward
See also CA 152
Bely, Andrey **TCLC 7; PC 11**
See also Bugayev, Boris Nikolayevich
Belyi, Andrei
See Bugayev, Boris Nikolayevich
Benary, Margot
See Benary-Isbert, Margot
Benary-Isbert, Margot 1889-1979 **CLC 12**
See also CA 5-8R; 89-92; CANR 4, 72; CLR 12; MAICYA; SATA 2; SATA-Obit 21
Benavente (y Martinez), Jacinto 1866-1954
TCLC 3; DAM DRAM, MULT
See also CA 106; 131; HW; MTCW 1
Benchley, Peter (Bradford) 1940- **CLC 4, 8; DAM NOV, POP**
See also AAYA 14; AITN 2; CA 17-20R; CANR 12, 35, 66; MTCW 1; SATA 3, 89
Benchley, Robert (Charles) 1889-1945 **T C L C 1, 55**
See also CA 105; 153; DLB 11
Benda, Julien 1867-1956 **TCLC 60**
See also CA 120; 154
Benedict, Ruth (Fulton) 1887-1948 **TCLC 60**
See also CA 158
Benedict, Saint c. 480-c. 547 **CMLC 29**
Benedikt, Michael 1935- **CLC 4, 14**
See also CA 13-16R; CANR 7; DLB 5
Benet, Juan 1927- **CLC 28**
See also CA 143
Benet, Stephen Vincent 1898-1943 **TCLC 7; DAM POET; SSC 10**
See also CA 104; 152; DLB 4, 48, 102; DLBY 97; YABC 1
Benet, William Rose 1886-1950 **TCLC 28; DAM POET**
See also CA 118; 152; DLB 45
Benford, Gregory (Albert) 1941- **CLC 52**
See also CA 69-72; CAAS 27; CANR 12, 24, 49; DLBY 82
Bengtsson, Frans (Gunnar) 1894-1954 **T C L C 48**
See also CA 170
Benjamin, David
See Slavitt, David R(ytman)
Benjamin, Lois
See Gould, Lois
Benjamin, Walter 1892-1940 **TCLC 39**
See also CA 164
Benn, Gottfried 1886-1956 **TCLC 3**
See also CA 106; 153; DLB 56
Bennett, Alan 1934- **CLC 45, 77; DAB; DAM MST**
See also CA 103; CANR 35, 55; MTCW 1
Bennett, (Enoch) Arnold 1867-1931 **TCLC 5, 20**
See also CA 106; 155; CDBLB 1890-1914; DLB 10, 34, 98, 135
Bennett, Elizabeth
See Mitchell, Margaret (Munnerlyn)
Bennett, George Harold 1930-

See Bennett, Hal
See also BW 1; CA 97-100
Bennett, Hal **CLC 5**
See also Bennett, George Harold
See also DLB 33
Bennett, Jay 1912- **CLC 35**
See also AAYA 10; CA 69-72; CANR 11, 42; JRDA; SAAS 4; SATA 41, 87; SATA-Brief 27
Bennett, Louise (Simone) 1919- **CLC 28; BLC 1; DAM MULT**
See also BW 2; CA 151; DLB 117
Benson, E(dward) F(rederic) 1867-1940
TCLC 27
See also CA 114; 157; DLB 135, 153
Benson, Jackson J. 1930- **CLC 34**
See also CA 25-28R; DLB 111
Benson, Sally 1900-1972 **CLC 17**
See also CA 19-20; 37-40R; CAP 1; SATA 1, 35; SATA-Obit 27
Benson, Stella 1892-1933 **TCLC 17**
See also CA 117; 155; DLB 36, 162
Bentham, Jeremy 1748-1832 **NCLC 38**
See also DLB 107, 158
Bentley, E(dmund) C(lerihew) 1875-1956
TCLC 12
See also CA 108; DLB 70
Bentley, Eric (Russell) 1916- **CLC 24**
See also CA 5-8R; CANR 6, 67; INT CANR-6
Beranger, Pierre Jean de 1780-1857 **NCLC 34**
Berdyaev, Nicolas
See Berdyaev, Nikolai (Aleksandrovich)
Berdyaev, Nikolai (Aleksandrovich) 1874-1948
TCLC 67
See also CA 120; 157
Berdyayev, Nikolai (Aleksandrovich)
See Berdyaev, Nikolai (Aleksandrovich)
Berendt, John (Lawrence) 1939- **CLC 86**
See also CA 146
Beresford, J(ohn) D(avys) 1873-1947 **T C L C 81**
See also CA 112; 155; DLB 162, 178, 197
Bergelson, David 1884-1952 **TCLC 81**
Berger, Colonel
See Malraux, (Georges-)Andre
Berger, John (Peter) 1926- **CLC 2, 19**
See also CA 81-84; CANR 51; DLB 14
Berger, Melvin H. 1927- **CLC 12**
See also CA 5-8R; CANR 4; CLR 32; SAAS 2; SATA 5, 88
Berger, Thomas (Louis) 1924- **CLC 3, 5, 8, 11, 18, 38; DAM NOV**
See also CA 1-4R; CANR 5, 28, 51; DLB 2; DLBY 80; INT CANR-28; MTCW 1
Bergman, (Ernst) Ingmar 1918- **CLC 16, 72**
See also CA 81-84; CANR 33, 70
Bergson, Henri(-Louis) 1859-1941 **TCLC 32**
See also CA 164
Bergstein, Eleanor 1938- **CLC 4**
See also CA 53-56; CANR 5
Berkoff, Steven 1937- **CLC 56**
See also CA 104; CANR 72
Bermant, Chaim (Icyk) 1929- **CLC 40**
See also CA 57-60; CANR 6, 31, 57
Bern, Victoria
See Fisher, M(ary) F(rances) K(ennedy)
Bernanos, (Paul Louis) Georges 1888-1948
TCLC 3
See also CA 104; 130; DLB 72
Bernard, April 1956- **CLC 59**
See also CA 131
Berne, Victoria
See Fisher, M(ary) F(rances) K(ennedy)

Bernhard, Thomas 1931-1989 **CLC 3, 32, 61**
See also CA 85-88; 127; CANR 32, 57; DLB
85, 124; MTCW 1

Bernhardt, Sarah (Henriette Rosine) 1844-1923
TCLC 75
See also CA 157

Berriault, Gina 1926- **CLC 54, 109; SSC 30**
See also CA 116; 129; CANR 66; DLB 130

Berrigan, Daniel 1921- **CLC 4**
See also CA 33-36R; CAAS 1; CANR 11, 43;
DLB 5

Berrigan, Edmund Joseph Michael, Jr. 1934-
1983
See Berrigan, Ted
See also CA 61-64; 110; CANR 14

Berrigan, Ted **CLC 37**
See also Berrigan, Edmund Joseph Michael, Jr.
See also DLB 5, 169

Berry, Charles Edward Anderson 1931-
See Berry, Chuck
See also CA 115

Berry, Chuck **CLC 17**
See also Berry, Charles Edward Anderson

Berry, Jonas
See Ashbery, John (Lawrence)

Berry, Wendell (Erdman) 1934- **CLC 4, 6, 8,
27, 46; DAM POET**
See also AITN 1; CA 73-76; CANR 50, 73; DLB
5, 6

Berryman, John 1914-1972 **CLC 1, 2, 3, 4, 6, 8,
10, 13, 25, 62; DAM POET**
See also CA 13-16; 33-36R; CABS 2; CANR
35; CAP 1; CDALB 1941-1968; DLB 48;
MTCW 1

Bertolucci, Bernardo 1940- **CLC 16**
See also CA 106

Berton, Pierre (Francis Demarigny) 1920-
CLC 104
See also CA 1-4R; CANR 2, 56; DLB 68; SATA
99

Bertrand, Aloysius 1807-1841 **NCLC 31**
Bertran de Born c. 1140-1215 **CMLC 5**
Beruni, al 973-1048(?) **CMLC 28**
Besant, Annie (Wood) 1847-1933 **TCLC 9**
See also CA 105

Bessie, Alvah 1904-1985 **CLC 23**
See also CA 5-8R; 116; CANR 2; DLB 26

Bethlen, T. D.
See Silverberg, Robert

Beti, Mongo **CLC 27; BLC 1; DAM MULT**
See also Biyidi, Alexandre

Betjeman, John 1906-1984 **CLC 2, 6, 10, 34,
43; DAB; DAM MST, POET**
See also CA 9-12R; 112; CANR 33, 56; CDBLB
1945-1960; DLB 20; DLBY 84; MTCW 1

Bettelheim, Bruno 1903-1990 **CLC 79**
See also CA 81-84; 131; CANR 23, 61; MTCW
1

Betti, Ugo 1892-1953 **TCLC 5**
See also CA 104; 155

Betts, Doris (Waugh) 1932- **CLC 3, 6, 28**
See also CA 13-16R; CANR 9, 66; DLBY 82;
INT CANR-9

Bevan, Alistair
See Roberts, Keith (John Kingston)

Bey, Pilaff
See Douglas, (George) Norman

Bialik, Chaim Nachman 1873-1934 **TCLC 25**
See also CA 170

Bickerstaff, Isaac
See Swift, Jonathan

Bidart, Frank 1939- **CLC 33**
See also CA 140

Bienek, Horst 1930- **CLC 7, 11**
See also CA 73-76; DLB 75

Bierce, Ambrose (Gwinett) 1842-1914(?)
**TCLC 1, 7, 44; DA; DAC; DAM MST; SSC
9; WLC**
See also CA 104; 139; CDALB 1865-1917;
DLB 11, 12, 23, 71, 74, 186

Biggers, Earl Derr 1884-1933 **TCLC 65**
See also CA 108; 153

Billings, Josh
See Shaw, Henry Wheeler

Billington, (Lady) Rachel (Mary) 1942- **C L C
43**
See also AITN 2; CA 33-36R; CANR 44

Binyon, T(imothy) J(ohn) 1936- **CLC 34**
See also CA 111; CANR 28

Bioy Casares, Adolfo 1914-1984 **CLC 4, 8, 13,
88; DAM MULT; HLC; SSC 17**
See also CA 29-32R; CANR 19, 43, 66; DLB
113; HW; MTCW 1

Bird, Cordwainer
See Ellison, Harlan (Jay)

Bird, Robert Montgomery 1806-1854 **NCLC 1**
See also DLB 202

Birkerts, Sven 1951- **CLC 116**
See also CA 128; 133; CAAS 29; INT 133

Birney, (Alfred) Earle 1904-1995 **CLC 1, 4, 6,
11; DAC; DAM MST, POET**
See also CA 1-4R; CANR 5, 20; DLB 88;
MTCW 1

Bishop, Elizabeth 1911-1979 **CLC 1, 4, 9, 13,
15, 32; DA; DAC; DAM MST, POET; PC
3**
See also CA 5-8R; 89-92; CABS 2; CANR 26,
61; CDALB 1968-1988; DLB 5, 169;
MTCW 1; SATA-Obit 24

Bishop, John 1935- **CLC 10**
See also CA 105

Bissett, Bill 1939- **CLC 18; PC 14**
See also CA 69-72; CAAS 19; CANR 15; DLB
53; MTCW 1

Bitov, Andrei (Georgievich) 1937- **CLC 57**
See also CA 142

Biyidi, Alexandre 1932-
See Beti, Mongo
See also BW 1; CA 114; 124; MTCW 1

Bjarme, Brynjolf
See Ibsen, Henrik (Johan)

Bjoernson, Bjoernstjerne (Martinius) 1832-
1910 **TCLC 7, 37**
See also CA 104

Black, Robert
See Holdstock, Robert P.

Blackburn, Paul 1926-1971 **CLC 9, 43**
See also CA 81-84; 33-36R; CANR 34; DLB
16; DLBY 81

Black Elk 1863-1950 **TCLC 33; DAM MULT**
See also CA 144; NNAL

Black Hobart
See Sanders, (James) Ed(ward)

Blacklin, Malcolm
See Chambers, Aidan

Blackmore, R(ichard) D(oddridge) 1825-1900
TCLC 27
See also CA 120; DLB 18

Blackmur, R(ichard) P(almer) 1904-1965
CLC 2, 24
See also CA 11-12; 25-28R; CANR 71; CAP 1;
DLB 63

Black Tarantula
See Acker, Kathy

Blackwood, Algernon (Henry) 1869-1951
TCLC 5
See also CA 105; 150; DLB 153, 156, 178

Blackwood, Caroline 1931-1996 **CLC 6, 9, 100**
See also CA 85-88; 151; CANR 32, 61, 65; DLB
14; MTCW 1

Blade, Alexander
See Hamilton, Edmond; Silverberg, Robert

Blaga, Lucian 1895-1961 **CLC 75**
See also CA 157

Blair, Eric (Arthur) 1903-1950
See Orwell, George
See also CA 104; 132; DA; DAB; DAC; DAM
MST, NOV; MTCW 1; SATA 29

Blais, Marie-Claire 1939- **CLC 2, 4, 6, 13, 22;
DAC; DAM MST**
See also CA 21-24R; CAAS 4; CANR 38; DLB
53; MTCW 1

Blaise, Clark 1940- **CLC 29**
See also AITN 2; CA 53-56; CAAS 3; CANR
5, 66; DLB 53

Blake, Fairley
See De Voto, Bernard (Augustine)

Blake, Nicholas
See Day Lewis, C(ecil)
See also DLB 77

Blake, William 1757-1827 **NCLC 13, 37, 57;
DA; DAB; DAC; DAM MST, POET; PC
12; WLC**
See also CDBLB 1789-1832; CLR 52; DLB 93,
163; MAICYA; SATA 30

Blasco Ibanez, Vicente 1867-1928 **TCLC 12;
DAM NOV**
See also CA 110; 131; HW; MTCW 1

Blatty, William Peter 1928- **CLC 2; DAM POP**
See also CA 5-8R; CANR 9

Bleeck, Oliver
See Thomas, Ross (Elmore)

Blessing, Lee 1949- **CLC 54**

Blish, James (Benjamin) 1921-1975 **CLC 14**
See also CA 1-4R; 57-60; CANR 3; DLB 8;
MTCW 1; SATA 66

Bliss, Reginald
See Wells, H(erbert) G(eorge)

Blixen, Karen (Christentze Dinesen) 1885-1962
See Dinesen, Isak
See also CA 25-28; CANR 22, 50; CAP 2;
MTCW 1; SATA 44

Bloch, Robert (Albert) 1917-1994 **CLC 33**
See also CA 5-8R; 146; CAAS 20; CANR 5;
DLB 44; INT CANR-5; SATA 12; SATA-Obit
82

Blok, Alexander (Alexandrovich) 1880-1921
TCLC 5; PC 21
See also CA 104

Blom, Jan
See Breytenbach, Breyten

Bloom, Harold 1930- **CLC 24, 103**
See also CA 13-16R; CANR 39; DLB 67

Bloomfield, Aurelius
See Bourne, Randolph S(illiman)

Blount, Roy (Alton), Jr. 1941- **CLC 38**
See also CA 53-56; CANR 10, 28, 61; INT
CANR-28; MTCW 1

Bloy, Leon 1846-1917 **TCLC 22**
See also CA 121; DLB 123

Blume, Judy (Sussman) 1938- **CLC 12, 30;
DAM NOV, POP**
See also AAYA 3, 26; CA 29-32R; CANR 13,
37, 66; CLR 2, 15; DLB 52; JRDA;
MAICYA; MTCW 1; SATA 2, 31, 79

Blunden, Edmund (Charles) 1896-1974 **C L C
2, 56**
See also CA 17-18; 45-48; CANR 54; CAP 2;
DLB 20, 100, 155; MTCW 1

Bly, Robert (Elwood) 1926-CLC 1, 2, 5, 10, 15, 38; DAM POET
See also CA 5-8R; CANR 41, 73; DLB 5; MTCW 1

Boas, Franz 1858-1942   TCLC 56
See also CA 115

Bobette
See Simenon, Georges (Jacques Christian)

Boccaccio, Giovanni 1313-1375 CMLC 13; SSC 10

Bochco, Steven 1943-   CLC 35
See also AAYA 11; CA 124; 138

Bodel, Jean 1167(?)-1210   CMLC 28

Bodenheim, Maxwell 1892-1954 TCLC 44
See also CA 110; DLB 9, 45

Bodker, Cecil 1927-   CLC 21
See also CA 73-76; CANR 13, 44; CLR 23; MAICYA; SATA 14

Boell, Heinrich (Theodor) 1917-1985 CLC 2, 3, 6, 9, 11, 15, 27, 32, 72; DA; DAB; DAC; DAM MST, NOV; SSC 23; WLC
See also CA 21-24R; 116; CANR 24; DLB 69; DLBY 85; MTCW 1

Boerne, Alfred
See Doeblin, Alfred

Boethius 480(?)-524(?)   CMLC 15
See also DLB 115

Bogan, Louise 1897-1970 CLC 4, 39, 46, 93; DAM POET; PC 12
See also CA 73-76; 25-28R; CANR 33; DLB 45, 169; MTCW 1

Bogarde, Dirk   CLC 19
See also Van Den Bogarde, Derek Jules Gaspard Ulric Niven
See also DLB 14

Bogosian, Eric 1953-   CLC 45
See also CA 138

Bograd, Larry 1953-   CLC 35
See also CA 93-96; CANR 57; SAAS 21; SATA 33, 89

Boiardo, Matteo Maria 1441-1494   LC 6

Boileau-Despreaux, Nicolas 1636-1711 LC 3

Bojer, Johan 1872-1959   TCLC 64

Boland, Eavan (Aisling) 1944- CLC 40, 67, 113; DAM POET
See also CA 143; CANR 61; DLB 40

Boll, Heinrich
See Boell, Heinrich (Theodor)

Bolt, Lee
See Faust, Frederick (Schiller)

Bolt, Robert (Oxton) 1924-1995CLC 14; DAM DRAM
See also CA 17-20R; 147; CANR 35, 67; DLB 13; MTCW 1

Bombet, Louis-Alexandre-Cesar
See Stendhal

Bomkauf
See Kaufman, Bob (Garnell)

Bonaventura   NCLC 35
See also DLB 90

Bond, Edward 1934- CLC 4, 6, 13, 23; DAM DRAM
See also CA 25-28R; CANR 38, 67; DLB 13; MTCW 1

Bonham, Frank 1914-1989   CLC 12
See also AAYA 1; CA 9-12R; CANR 4, 36; JRDA; MAICYA; SAAS 3; SATA 1, 49; SATA-Obit 62

Bonnefoy, Yves 1923- CLC 9, 15, 58; DAM MST, POET
See also CA 85-88; CANR 33; MTCW 1

Bontemps, Arna(ud Wendell) 1902-1973C L C 1, 18; BLC 1; DAM MULT, NOV, POET

See also BW 1; CA 1-4R; 41-44R; CANR 4, 35; CLR 6; DLB 48, 51; JRDA; MAICYA; MTCW 1; SATA 2, 44; SATA-Obit 24

Booth, Martin 1944-   CLC 13
See also CA 93-96; CAAS 2

Booth, Philip 1925-   CLC 23
See also CA 5-8R; CANR 5; DLBY 82

Booth, Wayne C(layson) 1921-   CLC 24
See also CA 1-4R; CAAS 5; CANR 3, 43; DLB 67

Borchert, Wolfgang 1921-1947   TCLC 5
See also CA 104; DLB 69, 124

Borel, Petrus 1809-1859   NCLC 41

Borges, Jorge Luis 1899-1986CLC 1, 2, 3, 4, 6, 8, 9, 10, 13, 19, 44, 48, 83; DA; DAB; DAC; DAM MST, MULT; HLC; PC 22; SSC 4; WLC
See also AAYA 26; CA 21-24R; CANR 19, 33; DLB 113; DLBY 86; HW; MTCW 1

Borowski, Tadeusz 1922-1951   TCLC 9
See also CA 106; 154

Borrow, George (Henry) 1803-1881 NCLC 9
See also DLB 21, 55, 166

Bosman, Herman Charles 1905-1951 T C L C 49
See also Malan, Herman
See also CA 160

Bosschere, Jean de 1878(?)-1953   TCLC 19
See also CA 115

Boswell, James 1740-1795 LC 4; DA; DAB; DAC; DAM MST; WLC
See also CDBLB 1660-1789; DLB 104, 142

Bottoms, David 1949-   CLC 53
See also CA 105; CANR 22; DLB 120; DLBY 83

Boucicault, Dion 1820-1890   NCLC 41

Boucolon, Maryse 1937(?)-
See Conde, Maryse
See also CA 110; CANR 30, 53

Bourget, Paul (Charles Joseph) 1852-1935 TCLC 12
See also CA 107; DLB 123

Bourjaily, Vance (Nye) 1922-   CLC 8, 62
See also CA 1-4R; CAAS 1; CANR 2, 72; DLB 2, 143

Bourne, Randolph S(illiman) 1886-1918 TCLC 16
See also CA 117; 155; DLB 63

Bova, Ben(jamin William) 1932-   CLC 45
See also AAYA 16; CA 5-8R; CAAS 18; CANR 11, 56; CLR 3; DLBY 81; INT CANR-11; MAICYA; MTCW 1; SATA 6, 68

Bowen, Elizabeth (Dorothea Cole) 1899-1973 CLC 1, 3, 6, 11, 15, 22; DAM NOV; SSC 3, 28
See also CA 17-18; 41-44R; CANR 35; CAP 2; CDBLB 1945-1960; DLB 15, 162; MTCW 1

Bowering, George 1935-   CLC 15, 47
See also CA 21-24R; CAAS 16; CANR 10; DLB 53

Bowering, Marilyn R(uthe) 1949-   CLC 32
See also CA 101; CANR 49

Bowers, Edgar 1924-   CLC 9
See also CA 5-8R; CANR 24; DLB 5

Bowie, David   CLC 17
See also Jones, David Robert

Bowles, Jane (Sydney) 1917-1973 CLC 3, 68
See also CA 19-20; 41-44R; CAP 2

Bowles, Paul (Frederick) 1910-1986CLC 1, 2, 19, 53; SSC 3
See also CA 1-4R; CAAS 1; CANR 1, 19, 50; DLB 5, 6; MTCW 1

Box, Edgar
See Vidal, Gore

Boyd, Nancy
See Millay, Edna St. Vincent

Boyd, William 1952-   CLC 28, 53, 70
See also CA 114; 120; CANR 51, 71

Boyle, Kay 1902-1992CLC 1, 5, 19, 58; SSC 5
See also CA 13-16R; 140; CAAS 1; CANR 29, 61; DLB 4, 9, 48, 86; DLBY 93; MTCW 1

Boyle, Mark
See Kienzle, William X(avier)

Boyle, Patrick 1905-1982   CLC 19
See also CA 127

Boyle, T. C. 1948-
See Boyle, T(homas) Coraghessan

Boyle, T(homas) Coraghessan 1948-CLC 36, 55, 90; DAM POP; SSC 16
See also BEST 90:4; CA 120; CANR 44; DLBY 86

Boz
See Dickens, Charles (John Huffam)

Brackenridge, Hugh Henry 1748-1816N C L C 7
See also DLB 11, 37

Bradbury, Edward P.
See Moorcock, Michael (John)

Bradbury, Malcolm (Stanley) 1932- CLC 32, 61; DAM NOV
See also CA 1-4R; CANR 1, 33; DLB 14; MTCW 1

Bradbury, Ray (Douglas) 1920-CLC 1, 3, 10, 15, 42, 98; DA; DAB; DAC; DAM MST, NOV, POP; SSC 29; WLC
See also AAYA 15; AITN 1, 2; CA 1-4R; CANR 2, 30; CDALB 1968-1988; DLB 2, 8; MTCW 1; SATA 11, 64

Bradford, Gamaliel 1863-1932   TCLC 36
See also CA 160; DLB 17

Bradley, David (Henry, Jr.) 1950- CLC 23; BLC 1; DAM MULT
See also BW 1; CA 104; CANR 26; DLB 33

Bradley, John Ed(mund, Jr.) 1958- CLC 55
See also CA 139

Bradley, Marion Zimmer 1930-CLC 30; DAM POP
See also AAYA 9; CA 57-60; CAAS 10; CANR 7, 31, 51; DLB 8; MTCW 1; SATA 90

Bradstreet, Anne 1612(?)-1672LC 4, 30; DA; DAC; DAM MST, POET; PC 10
See also CDALB 1640-1865; DLB 24

Brady, Joan 1939-   CLC 86
See also CA 141

Bragg, Melvyn 1939-   CLC 10
See also BEST 89:3; CA 57-60; CANR 10, 48; DLB 14

Brahe, Tycho 1546-1601   LC 45

Braine, John (Gerard) 1922-1986CLC 1, 3, 41
See also CA 1-4R; 120; CANR 1, 33; CDBLB 1945-1960; DLB 15; DLBY 86; MTCW 1

Bramah, Ernest 1868-1942   TCLC 72
See also CA 156; DLB 70

Brammer, William 1930(?)-1978   CLC 31
See also CA 77-80

Brancati, Vitaliano 1907-1954   TCLC 12
See also CA 109

Brancato, Robin F(idler) 1936-   CLC 35
See also AAYA 9; CA 69-72; CANR 11, 45; CLR 32; JRDA; SAAS 9; SATA 97

Brand, Max
See Faust, Frederick (Schiller)

Brand, Millen 1906-1980   CLC 7
See also CA 21-24R; 97-100; CANR 72

Branden, Barbara   CLC 44

BLC 1; DAM MULT; DC 1
See also DLB 3, 50

Browne, (Clyde) Jackson 1948(?)-   **CLC 21**
See also CA 120

Browning, Elizabeth Barrett 1806-1861
NCLC 1, 16, 61, 66; DA; DAB; DAC; DAM
MST, POET; PC 6; WLC
See also CDBLB 1832-1890; DLB 32, 199

Browning, Robert 1812-1889 NCLC 19; DA;
DAB; DAC; DAM MST, POET; PC 2;
WLCS
See also CDBLB 1832-1890; DLB 32, 163;
YABC 1

Browning, Tod 1882-1962   **CLC 16**
See also CA 141; 117

Brownson, Orestes Augustus 1803-1876
NCLC 50
See also DLB 1, 59, 73

Bruccoli, Matthew J(oseph) 1931-   **CLC 34**
See also CA 9-12R; CANR 7; DLB 103

Bruce, Lenny   **CLC 21**
See also Schneider, Leonard Alfred

Bruin, John
See Brutus, Dennis

Brulard, Henri
See Stendhal

Brulls, Christian
See Simenon, Georges (Jacques Christian)

Brunner, John (Kilian Houston) 1934-1995
CLC 8, 10; DAM POP
See also CA 1-4R; 149; CAAS 8; CANR 2, 37;
MTCW 1

Bruno, Giordano 1548-1600   **LC 27**

Brutus, Dennis 1924- CLC 43; BLC 1; DAM
MULT, POET; PC 24
See also BW 2; CA 49-52; CAAS 14; CANR 2,
27, 42; DLB 117

Bryan, C(ourtlandt) D(ixon) B(arnes) 1936-
CLC 29
See also CA 73-76; CANR 13, 68; DLB 185;
INT CANR-13

Bryan, Michael
See Moore, Brian

Bryant, William Cullen 1794-1878 NCLC 6,
46; DA; DAB; DAC; DAM MST, POET;
PC 20
See also CDALB 1640-1865; DLB 3, 43, 59,
189

Bryusov, Valery Yakovlevich 1873-1924
TCLC 10
See also CA 107; 155

Buchan, John 1875-1940   TCLC 41; DAB;
DAM POP
See also CA 108; 145; DLB 34, 70, 156; YABC
2

Buchanan, George 1506-1582   **LC 4**
See also DLB 152

Buchheim, Lothar-Guenther 1918-   **CLC 6**
See also CA 85-88

Buchner, (Karl) Georg 1813-1837 NCLC 26

Buchwald, Art(hur) 1925-   **CLC 33**
See also AITN 1; CA 5-8R; CANR 21, 67;
MTCW 1; SATA 10

Buck, Pearl S(ydenstricker) 1892-1973CLC 7,
11, 18; DA; DAB; DAC; DAM MST, NOV
See also AITN 1; CA 1-4R; 41-44R; CANR 1,
34; DLB 9, 102; MTCW 1; SATA 1, 25

Buckler, Ernest 1908-1984   **CLC 13; DAC;
DAM MST**
See also CA 11-12; 114; CAP 1; DLB 68; SATA
47

Buckley, Vincent (Thomas) 1925-1988CLC 57
See also CA 101

Buckley, William F(rank), Jr. 1925-CLC 7, 18,
37; DAM POP
See also AITN 1; CA 1-4R; CANR 1, 24, 53;
DLB 137; DLBY 80; INT CANR-24; MTCW
1

Buechner, (Carl) Frederick 1926-CLC 2, 4, 6,
9; DAM NOV
See also CA 13-16R; CANR 11, 39, 64; DLBY
80; INT CANR-11; MTCW 1

Buell, John (Edward) 1927-   **CLC 10**
See also CA 1-4R; CANR 71; DLB 53

Buero Vallejo, Antonio 1916-   **CLC 15, 46**
See also CA 106; CANR 24, 49; HW; MTCW
1

Bufalino, Gesualdo 1920(?)-   **CLC 74**
See also DLB 196

Bugayev, Boris Nikolayevich 1880-1934
TCLC 7; PC 11
See also Bely, Andrey
See also CA 104; 165

Bukowski, Charles 1920-1994CLC 2, 5, 9, 41,
82, 108; DAM NOV, POET; PC 18
See also CA 17-20R; 144; CANR 40, 62; DLB
5, 130, 169; MTCW 1

Bulgakov, Mikhail (Afanas'evich) 1891-1940
TCLC 2, 16; DAM DRAM, NOV; SSC 18
See also CA 105; 152

Bulgya, Alexander Alexandrovich 1901-1956
TCLC 53
See also Fadeyev, Alexander
See also CA 117

Bullins, Ed 1935- CLC 1, 5, 7; BLC 1; DAM
DRAM, MULT; DC 6
See also BW 2; CA 49-52; CAAS 16; CANR
24, 46, 73; DLB 7, 38; MTCW 1

Bulwer-Lytton, Edward (George Earle Lytton)
1803-1873   NCLC 1, 45
See also DLB 21

Bunin, Ivan Alexeyevich 1870-1953 TCLC 6;
SSC 5
See also CA 104

Bunting, Basil 1900-1985   CLC 10, 39, 47;
DAM POET
See also CA 53-56; 115; CANR 7; DLB 20

Bunuel, Luis 1900-1983   CLC 16, 80; DAM
MULT; HLC
See also CA 101; 110; CANR 32; HW

Bunyan, John 1628-1688   LC 4; DA; DAB;
DAC; DAM MST; WLC
See also CDBLB 1660-1789; DLB 39

Burckhardt, Jacob (Christoph) 1818-1897
NCLC 49

Burford, Eleanor
See Hibbert, Eleanor Alice Burford

Burgess, AnthonyCLC 1, 2, 4, 5, 8, 10, 13, 15,
22, 40, 62, 81, 94; DAB
See also Wilson, John (Anthony) Burgess
See also AAYA 25; AITN 1; CDBLB 1960 to
Present; DLB 14, 194

Burke, Edmund 1729(?)-1797 LC 7, 36; DA;
DAB; DAC; DAM MST; WLC
See also DLB 104

Burke, Kenneth (Duva) 1897-1993 CLC 2, 24
See also CA 5-8R; 143; CANR 39, 74; DLB
45, 63; MTCW 1

Burke, Leda
See Garnett, David

Burke, Ralph
See Silverberg, Robert

Burke, Thomas 1886-1945   TCLC 63
See also CA 113; 155; DLB 197

Burney, Fanny 1752-1840   NCLC 12, 54
See also DLB 39

Burns, Robert 1759-1796   **PC 6**
See also CDBLB 1789-1832; DA; DAB; DAC;
DAM MST, POET; DLB 109; WLC

Burns, Tex
See L'Amour, Louis (Dearborn)

Burnshaw, Stanley 1906-   CLC 3, 13, 44
See also CA 9-12R; DLB 48; DLBY 97

Burr, Anne 1937-   **CLC 6**
See also CA 25-28R

Burroughs, Edgar Rice 1875-1950 TCLC 2,
32; DAM NOV
See also AAYA 11; CA 104; 132; DLB 8;
MTCW 1; SATA 41

Burroughs, William S(eward) 1914-1997CLC
1, 2, 5, 15, 22, 42, 75, 109; DA; DAB; DAC;
DAM MST, NOV, POP; WLC
See also AITN 2; CA 9-12R; 160; CANR 20,
52; DLB 2, 8, 16, 152; DLBY 81, 97; MTCW
1

Burton, Richard F. 1821-1890   NCLC 42
See also DLB 55, 184

Busch, Frederick 1941-   CLC 7, 10, 18, 47
See also CA 33-36R; CAAS 1; CANR 45, 73;
DLB 6

Bush, Ronald 1946-   **CLC 34**
See also CA 136

Bustos, F(rancisco)
See Borges, Jorge Luis

Bustos Domecq, H(onorio)
See Bioy Casares, Adolfo; Borges, Jorge Luis

Butler, Octavia E(stelle) 1947-CLC 38; BLCS;
DAM MULT, POP
See also AAYA 18; BW 2; CA 73-76; CANR
12, 24, 38, 73; DLB 33; MTCW 1; SATA 84

Butler, Robert Olen (Jr.) 1945-CLC 81; DAM
POP
See also CA 112; CANR 66; DLB 173; INT 112

Butler, Samuel 1612-1680   LC 16, 43
See also DLB 101, 126

Butler, Samuel 1835-1902   TCLC 1, 33; DA;
DAB; DAC; DAM MST, NOV; WLC
See also CA 143; CDBLB 1890-1914; DLB 18,
57, 174

Butler, Walter C.
See Faust, Frederick (Schiller)

Butor, Michel (Marie Francois) 1926-CLC 1,
3, 8, 11, 15
See also CA 9-12R; CANR 33, 66; DLB 83;
MTCW 1

Butts, Mary 1892(?)-1937   TCLC 77
See also CA 148

Buzo, Alexander (John) 1944-   **CLC 61**
See also CA 97-100; CANR 17, 39, 69

Buzzati, Dino 1906-1972   **CLC 36**
See also CA 160; 33-36R; DLB 177

Byars, Betsy (Cromer) 1928-   **CLC 35**
See also AAYA 19; CA 33-36R; CANR 18, 36,
57; CLR 1, 16; DLB 52; INT CANR-18;
JRDA; MAICYA; MTCW 1; SAAS 1; SATA
4, 46, 80

Byatt, A(ntonia) S(usan Drabble) 1936- C L C
19, 65; DAM NOV, POP
See also CA 13-16R; CANR 13, 33, 50; DLB
14, 194; MTCW 1

Byrne, David 1952-   **CLC 26**
See also CA 127

Byrne, John Keyes 1926-
See Leonard, Hugh
See also CA 102; INT 102

Byron, George Gordon (Noel) 1788-1824
NCLC 2, 12; DA; DAB; DAC; DAM MST,
POET; PC 16; WLC
See also CDBLB 1789-1832; DLB 96, 110

See also CA 9-12R; CANR 4, 38, 59; DLB 5, 165; INT CANR-4; MTCW 1; SATA 47

Carson, Rachel Louise 1907-1964 **CLC 71; DAM POP**
See also CA 77-80; CANR 35; MTCW 1; SATA 23

Carter, Angela (Olive) 1940-1992 **CLC 5, 41, 76; SSC 13**
See also CA 53-56; 136; CANR 12, 36, 61; DLB 14; MTCW 1; SATA 66; SATA-Obit 70

Carter, Nick
See Smith, Martin Cruz

Carver, Raymond 1938-1988 **CLC 22, 36, 53, 55; DAM NOV; SSC 8**
See also CA 33-36R; 126; CANR 17, 34, 61; DLB 130; DLBY 84, 88; MTCW 1

Cary, Elizabeth, Lady Falkland 1585-1639 **LC 30**

Cary, (Arthur) Joyce (Lunel) 1888-1957 **TCLC 1, 29**
See also CA 104; 164; CDBLB 1914-1945; DLB 15, 100

Casanova de Seingalt, Giovanni Jacopo 1725-1798 **LC 13**

Casares, Adolfo Bioy
See Bioy Casares, Adolfo

Casely-Hayford, J(oseph) E(phraim) 1866-1930 **TCLC 24; BLC 1; DAM MULT**
See also BW 2; CA 123; 152

Casey, John (Dudley) 1939- **CLC 59**
See also BEST 90:2; CA 69-72; CANR 23

Casey, Michael 1947- **CLC 2**
See also CA 65-68; DLB 5

Casey, Patrick
See Thurman, Wallace (Henry)

Casey, Warren (Peter) 1935-1988 **CLC 12**
See also CA 101; 127; INT 101

Casona, Alejandro **CLC 49**
See also Alvarez, Alejandro Rodriguez

Cassavetes, John 1929-1989 **CLC 20**
See also CA 85-88; 127

Cassian, Nina 1924- **PC 17**

Cassill, R(onald) V(erlin) 1919- **CLC 4, 23**
See also CA 9-12R; CAAS 1; CANR 7, 45; DLB 6

Cassirer, Ernst 1874-1945 **TCLC 61**
See also CA 157

Cassity, (Allen) Turner 1929- **CLC 6, 42**
See also CA 17-20R; CAAS 8; CANR 11; DLB 105

Castaneda, Carlos 1931(?)- **CLC 12**
See also CA 25-28R; CANR 32, 66; HW; MTCW 1

Castedo, Elena 1937- **CLC 65**
See also CA 132

Castedo-Ellerman, Elena
See Castedo, Elena

Castellanos, Rosario 1925-1974 **CLC 66; DAM MULT; HLC**
See also CA 131; 53-56; CANR 58; DLB 113; HW

Castelvetro, Lodovico 1505-1571 **LC 12**

Castiglione, Baldassare 1478-1529 **LC 12**

Castle, Robert
See Hamilton, Edmond

Castro, Guillen de 1569-1631 **LC 19**

Castro, Rosalia de 1837-1885 **NCLC 3; DAM MULT**

Cather, Willa
See Cather, Willa Sibert

Cather, Willa Sibert 1873-1947 **TCLC 1, 11, 31; DA; DAB; DAC; DAM MST, NOV; SSC 2; WLC**

See also AAYA 24; CA 104; 128; CDALB 1865-1917; DLB 9, 54, 78; DLBD 1; MTCW 1; SATA 30

Catherine, Saint 1347-1380 **CMLC 27**

Cato, Marcus Porcius 234B.C.-149B.C. **CMLC 21**

Catton, (Charles) Bruce 1899-1978 **CLC 35**
See also AITN 1; CA 5-8R; 81-84; CANR 7, 74; DLB 17; SATA 2; SATA-Obit 24

Catullus c. 84B.C.-c. 54B.C. **CMLC 18**

Cauldwell, Frank
See King, Francis (Henry)

Caunitz, William J. 1933-1996 **CLC 34**
See also BEST 89:3; CA 125; 130; 152; CANR 73; INT 130

Causley, Charles (Stanley) 1917- **CLC 7**
See also CA 9-12R; CANR 5, 35; CLR 30; DLB 27; MTCW 1; SATA 3, 66

Caute, (John) David 1936- **CLC 29; DAM NOV**
See also CA 1-4R; CAAS 4; CANR 1, 33, 64; DLB 14

Cavafy, C(onstantine) P(eter) 1863-1933 **TCLC 2, 7; DAM POET**
See also Kavafis, Konstantinos Petrou
See also CA 148

Cavallo, Evelyn
See Spark, Muriel (Sarah)

Cavanna, Betty **CLC 12**
See also Harrison, Elizabeth Cavanna
See also JRDA; MAICYA; SAAS 4; SATA 1, 30

Cavendish, Margaret Lucas 1623-1673 **LC 30**
See also DLB 131

Caxton, William 1421(?)-1491(?) **LC 17**
See also DLB 170

Cayer, D. M.
See Duffy, Maureen

Cayrol, Jean 1911- **CLC 11**
See also CA 89-92; DLB 83

Cela, Camilo Jose 1916- **CLC 4, 13, 59; DAM MULT; HLC**
See also BEST 90:2; CA 21-24R; CAAS 10; CANR 21, 32; DLBY 89; HW; MTCW 1

Celan, Paul **CLC 10, 19, 53, 82; PC 10**
See also Antschel, Paul
See also DLB 69

Celine, Louis-Ferdinand **CLC 1, 3, 4, 7, 9, 15, 47**
See also Destouches, Louis-Ferdinand
See also DLB 72

Cellini, Benvenuto 1500-1571 **LC 7**

Cendrars, Blaise 1887-1961 **CLC 18, 106**
See also Sauser-Hall, Frederic

Cernuda (y Bidon), Luis 1902-1963 **CLC 54; DAM POET**
See also CA 131; 89-92; DLB 134; HW

Cervantes (Saavedra), Miguel de 1547-1616 **LC 6, 23; DA; DAB; DAC; DAM MST, NOV; SSC 12; WLC**

Cesaire, Aime (Fernand) 1913- **CLC 19, 32, 112; BLC 1; DAM MULT, POET**
See also BW 2; CA 65-68; CANR 24, 43; MTCW 1

Chabon, Michael 1963- **CLC 55**
See also CA 139; CANR 57

Chabrol, Claude 1930- **CLC 16**
See also CA 110

Challans, Mary 1905-1983
See Renault, Mary
See also CA 81-84; 111; CANR 74; SATA 23; SATA-Obit 36

Challis, George

See Faust, Frederick (Schiller)

Chambers, Aidan 1934- **CLC 35**
See also AAYA 27; CA 25-28R; CANR 12, 31, 58; JRDA; MAICYA; SAAS 12; SATA 1, 69

Chambers, James 1948-
See Cliff, Jimmy
See also CA 124

Chambers, Jessie
See Lawrence, D(avid) H(erbert Richards)

Chambers, Robert W(illiam) 1865-1933 **TCLC 41**
See also CA 165; DLB 202

Chandler, Raymond (Thornton) 1888-1959 **TCLC 1, 7; SSC 23**
See also AAYA 25; CA 104; 129; CANR 60; CDALB 1929-1941; DLBD 6; MTCW 1

Chang, Eileen 1920-1995 **SSC 28**
See also CA 166

Chang, Jung 1952- **CLC 71**
See also CA 142

Chang Ai-Ling
See Chang, Eileen

Channing, William Ellery 1780-1842 **NCLC 17**
See also DLB 1, 59

Chaplin, Charles Spencer 1889-1977 **CLC 16**
See also Chaplin, Charlie
See also CA 81-84; 73-76

Chaplin, Charlie
See Chaplin, Charles Spencer
See also DLB 44

Chapman, George 1559(?)-1634 **LC 22; DAM DRAM**
See also DLB 62, 121

Chapman, Graham 1941-1989 **CLC 21**
See also Monty Python
See also CA 116; 129; CANR 35

Chapman, John Jay 1862-1933 **TCLC 7**
See also CA 104

Chapman, Lee
See Bradley, Marion Zimmer

Chapman, Walker
See Silverberg, Robert

Chappell, Fred (Davis) 1936- **CLC 40, 78**
See also CA 5-8R; CAAS 4; CANR 8, 33, 67; DLB 6, 105

Char, Rene(-Emile) 1907-1988 **CLC 9, 11, 14, 55; DAM POET**
See also CA 13-16R; 124; CANR 32; MTCW 1

Charby, Jay
See Ellison, Harlan (Jay)

Chardin, Pierre Teilhard de
See Teilhard de Chardin, (Marie Joseph) Pierre

Charles I 1600-1649 **LC 13**

Charriere, Isabelle de 1740-1805 **NCLC 66**

Charyn, Jerome 1937- **CLC 5, 8, 18**
See also CA 5-8R; CAAS 1; CANR 7, 61; DLBY 83; MTCW 1

Chase, Mary (Coyle) 1907-1981 **DC 1**
See also CA 77-80; 105; SATA 17; SATA-Obit 29

Chase, Mary Ellen 1887-1973 **CLC 2**
See also CA 13-16; 41-44R; CAP 1; SATA 10

Chase, Nicholas
See Hyde, Anthony

Chateaubriand, Francois Rene de 1768-1848 **NCLC 3**
See also DLB 119

Chatterje, Sarat Chandra 1876-1936(?)
See Chatterji, Saratchandra
See also CA 109

Chatterji, Bankim Chandra 1838-1894 **NCLC 19**

Chatterji, Saratchandra   TCLC 13
See also Chatterje, Sarat Chandra
Chatterton, Thomas 1752-1770 **LC 3; DAM POET**
See also DLB 109
Chatwin, (Charles) Bruce 1940-1989 CLC 28, 57, 59; **DAM POP**
See also AAYA 4; BEST 90:1; CA 85-88; 127; DLB 194
Chaucer, Daniel
See Ford, Ford Madox
Chaucer, Geoffrey 1340(?)-1400 **LC 17; DA; DAB; DAC; DAM MST, POET; PC 19; WLCS**
See also CDBLB Before 1660; DLB 146
Chaviaras, Strates 1935-
See Haviaras, Stratis
See also CA 105
Chayefsky, Paddy   CLC 23
See also Chayefsky, Sidney
See also DLB 7, 44; DLBY 81
Chayefsky, Sidney 1923-1981
See Chayefsky, Paddy
See also CA 9-12R; 104; CANR 18; **DAM DRAM**
Chedid, Andree 1920-   CLC 47
See also CA 145
Cheever, John 1912-1982 CLC 3, 7, 8, 11, 15, 25, 64; **DA; DAB; DAC; DAM MST, NOV, POP; SSC 1; WLC**
See also CA 5-8R; 106; CABS 1; CANR 5, 27; CDALB 1941-1968; DLB 2, 102; DLBY 80, 82; INT CANR-5; MTCW 1
Cheever, Susan 1943-   CLC 18, 48
See also CA 103; CANR 27, 51; DLBY 82; INT CANR-27
Chekhonte, Antosha
See Chekhov, Anton (Pavlovich)
Chekhov, Anton (Pavlovich) 1860-1904 TCLC 3, 10, 31, 55; **DA; DAB; DAC; DAM DRAM, MST; DC 9; SSC 2, 28; WLC**
See also CA 104; 124; SATA 90
Chernyshevsky, Nikolay Gavrilovich 1828-1889 **NCLC 1**
Cherry, Carolyn Janice 1942-
See Cherryh, C. J.
See also CA 65-68; CANR 10
Cherryh, C. J.   CLC 35
See also Cherry, Carolyn Janice
See also AAYA 24; DLBY 80; SATA 93
Chesnutt, Charles W(addell) 1858-1932 **TCLC 5, 39; BLC 1; DAM MULT; SSC 7**
See also BW 1; CA 106; 125; DLB 12, 50, 78; MTCW 1
Chester, Alfred 1929(?)-1971   CLC 49
See also CA 33-36R; DLB 130
Chesterton, G(ilbert) K(eith) 1874-1936 **TCLC 1, 6, 64; DAM NOV, POET; SSC 1**
See also CA 104; 132; CANR 73; CDBLB 1914-1945; DLB 10, 19, 34, 70, 98, 149, 178; MTCW 1; SATA 27
Chiang, Pin-chin 1904-1986
See Ding Ling
See also CA 118
Ch'ien Chung-shu 1910-   CLC 22
See also CA 130; CANR 73; MTCW 1
Child, L. Maria
See Child, Lydia Maria
Child, Lydia Maria 1802-1880   NCLC 6, 73
See also DLB 1, 74; SATA 67
Child, Mrs.
See Child, Lydia Maria
Child, Philip 1898-1978   CLC 19, 68

See also CA 13-14; CAP 1; SATA 47
Childers, (Robert) Erskine 1870-1922 **T C L C 65**
See also CA 113; 153; DLB 70
Childress, Alice 1920-1994 CLC 12, 15, 86, 96; **BLC 1; DAM DRAM, MULT, NOV; DC 4**
See also AAYA 8; BW 2; CA 45-48; 146; CANR 3, 27, 50, 74; CLR 14; DLB 7, 38; JRDA; MAICYA; MTCW 1; SATA 7, 48, 81
Chin, Frank (Chew, Jr.) 1940-   DC 7
See also CA 33-36R; CANR 71; DAM MULT
Chislett, (Margaret) Anne 1943-   CLC 34
See also CA 151
Chitty, Thomas Willes 1926-   CLC 11
See also Hinde, Thomas
See also CA 5-8R
Chivers, Thomas Holley 1809-1858 NCLC 49
See also DLB 3
Chomette, Rene Lucien 1898-1981
See Clair, Rene
See also CA 103
Chopin, Kate TCLC 5, 14; **DA; DAB; SSC 8; WLCS**
See also Chopin, Katherine
See also CDALB 1865-1917; DLB 12, 78
Chopin, Katherine 1851-1904
See Chopin, Kate
See also CA 104; 122; DAC; DAM MST, NOV
Chretien de Troyes c. 12th cent. -   CMLC 10
Christie
See Ichikawa, Kon
Christie, Agatha (Mary Clarissa) 1890-1976 **CLC 1, 6, 8, 12, 39, 48, 110; DAB; DAC; DAM NOV**
See also AAYA 9; AITN 1, 2; CA 17-20R; 61-64; CANR 10, 37; CDBLB 1914-1945; DLB 13, 77; MTCW 1; SATA 36
Christie, (Ann) Philippa
See Pearce, Philippa
See also CA 5-8R; CANR 4
Christine de Pizan 1365(?)-1431(?)   LC 9
Chubb, Elmer
See Masters, Edgar Lee
Chulkov, Mikhail Dmitrievich 1743-1792 LC 2
See also DLB 150
Churchill, Caryl 1938-   CLC 31, 55; DC 5
See also CA 102; CANR 22, 46; DLB 13; MTCW 1
Churchill, Charles 1731-1764   LC 3
See also DLB 109
Chute, Carolyn 1947-   CLC 39
See also CA 123
Ciardi, John (Anthony) 1916-1986 **CLC 10, 40, 44; DAM POET**
See also CA 5-8R; 118; CAAS 2; CANR 5, 33; CLR 19; DLB 5; DLBY 86; INT CANR-5; MAICYA; MTCW 1; SAAS 26; SATA 1, 65; SATA-Obit 46
Cicero, Marcus Tullius 106B.C.-43B.C. **CMLC 3**
Cimino, Michael 1943-   CLC 16
See also CA 105
Cioran, E(mil) M. 1911-1995   CLC 64
See also CA 25-28R; 149
Cisneros, Sandra 1954- CLC 69; **DAM MULT; HLC; SSC 32**
See also AAYA 9; CA 131; CANR 64; DLB 122, 152; HW
Cixous, Helene 1937-   CLC 92
See also CA 126; CANR 55; DLB 83; MTCW 1
Clair, Rene   CLC 20
See also Chomette, Rene Lucien

Clampitt, Amy 1920-1994   **CLC 32; PC 19**
See also CA 110; 146; CANR 29; DLB 105
Clancy, Thomas L., Jr. 1947-
See Clancy, Tom
See also CA 125; 131; CANR 62; INT 131; MTCW 1
Clancy, Tom   **CLC 45, 112; DAM NOV, POP**
See also Clancy, Thomas L., Jr.
See also AAYA 9; BEST 89:1, 90:1
Clare, John 1793-1864 NCLC 9; **DAB; DAM POET; PC 23**
See also DLB 55, 96
Clarin
See Alas (y Urena), Leopoldo (Enrique Garcia)
Clark, Al C.
See Goines, Donald
Clark, (Robert) Brian 1932-   CLC 29
See also CA 41-44R; CANR 67
Clark, Curt
See Westlake, Donald E(dwin)
Clark, Eleanor 1913-1996   CLC 5, 19
See also CA 9-12R; 151; CANR 41; DLB 6
Clark, J. P.
See Clark, John Pepper
See also DLB 117
Clark, John Pepper 1935- CLC 38; **BLC 1; DAM DRAM, MULT; DC 5**
See also Clark, J. P.
See also BW 1; CA 65-68; CANR 16, 72
Clark, M. R.
See Clark, Mavis Thorpe
Clark, Mavis Thorpe 1909-   CLC 12
See also CA 57-60; CANR 8, 37; CLR 30; MAICYA; SAAS 5; SATA 8, 74
Clark, Walter Van Tilburg 1909-1971 CLC 28
See also CA 9-12R; 33-36R; CANR 63; DLB 9; SATA 8
Clark Bekederemo, J(ohnson) P(epper)
See Clark, John Pepper
Clarke, Arthur C(harles) 1917- CLC 1, 4, 13, 18, 35; **DAM POP; SSC 3**
See also AAYA 4; CA 1-4R; CANR 2, 28, 55, 74; JRDA; MAICYA; MTCW 1; SATA 13, 70
Clarke, Austin 1896-1974   **CLC 6, 9; DAM POET**
See also CA 29-32; 49-52; CAP 2; DLB 10, 20
Clarke, Austin C(hesterfield) 1934- CLC 8, 53; **BLC 1; DAC; DAM MULT**
See also BW 1; CA 25-28R; CAAS 16; CANR 14, 32, 68; DLB 53, 125
Clarke, Gillian 1937-   CLC 61
See also CA 106; DLB 40
Clarke, Marcus (Andrew Hislop) 1846-1881 **NCLC 19**
Clarke, Shirley 1925-   CLC 16
Clash, The
See Headon, (Nicky) Topper; Jones, Mick; Simonon, Paul; Strummer, Joe
Claudel, Paul (Louis Charles Marie) 1868-1955 **TCLC 2, 10**
See also CA 104; 165; DLB 192
Clavell, James (duMaresq) 1925-1994 CLC 6, 25, 87; **DAM NOV, POP**
See also CA 25-28R; 146; CANR 26, 48; MTCW 1
Cleaver, (Leroy) Eldridge 1935-1998 CLC 30; **BLC 1; DAM MULT**
See also BW 1; CA 21-24R; 167; CANR 16
Cleese, John (Marwood) 1939-   CLC 21
See also Monty Python
See also CA 112; 116; CANR 35; MTCW 1
Cleishbotham, Jebediah

Cooke, M. E.
    See Creasey, John
Cooke, Margaret
    See Creasey, John
Cook-Lynn, Elizabeth 1930- **CLC 93; DAM MULT**
    See also CA 133; DLB 175; NNAL
Cooney, Ray   **CLC 62**
Cooper, Douglas 1960-   **CLC 86**
Cooper, Henry St. John
    See Creasey, John
Cooper, J(oan) California   **CLC 56; DAM MULT**
    See also AAYA 12; BW 1; CA 125; CANR 55
Cooper, James Fenimore 1789-1851 **NCLC 1, 27, 54**
    See also AAYA 22; CDALB 1640-1865; DLB 3; SATA 19
Coover, Robert (Lowell) 1932- **CLC 3, 7, 15, 32, 46, 87; DAM NOV; SSC 15**
    See also CA 45-48; CANR 3, 37, 58; DLB 2; DLBY 81; MTCW 1
Copeland, Stewart (Armstrong) 1952- **CLC 26**
Copernicus, Nicolaus 1473-1543   **LC 45**
Coppard, A(lfred) E(dgar) 1878-1957 **TCLC 5; SSC 21**
    See also CA 114; 167; DLB 162; YABC 1
Coppee, Francois 1842-1908   **TCLC 25**
    See also CA 170
Coppola, Francis Ford 1939-   **CLC 16**
    See also CA 77-80; CANR 40; DLB 44
Corbiere, Tristan 1845-1875   **NCLC 43**
Corcoran, Barbara 1911-   **CLC 17**
    See also AAYA 14; CA 21-24R; CAAS 2; CANR 11, 28, 48; CLR 50; DLB 52; JRDA; SAAS 20; SATA 3, 77
Cordelier, Maurice
    See Giraudoux, (Hippolyte) Jean
Corelli, Marie 1855-1924   **TCLC 51**
    See Mackay, Mary
    See also DLB 34, 156
Corman, Cid 1924-   **CLC 9**
    See also Corman, Sidney
    See also CAAS 2; DLB 5, 193
Corman, Sidney 1924-
    See Corman, Cid
    See also CA 85-88; CANR 44; DAM POET
Cormier, Robert (Edmund) 1925- **CLC 12, 30; DA; DAB; DAC; DAM MST, NOV**
    See also AAYA 3, 19; CA 1-4R; CANR 5, 23; CDALB 1968-1988; CLR 12; DLB 52; INT CANR-23; JRDA; MAICYA; MTCW 1; SATA 10, 45, 83
Corn, Alfred (DeWitt III) 1943-   **CLC 33**
    See also CA 104; CAAS 25; CANR 44; DLB 120; DLBY 80
Corneille, Pierre 1606-1684   **LC 28; DAB; DAM MST**
Cornwell, David (John Moore) 1931- **CLC 9, 15; DAM POP**
    See also le Carre, John
    See also CA 5-8R; CANR 13, 33, 59; MTCW 1
Corso, (Nunzio) Gregory 1930-   **CLC 1, 11**
    See also CA 5-8R; CANR 41; DLB 5, 16; MTCW 1
Cortazar, Julio 1914-1984 **CLC 2, 3, 5, 10, 13, 15, 33, 34, 92; DAM MULT, NOV; HLC; SSC 7**
    See also CA 21-24R; CANR 12, 32; DLB 113; HW; MTCW 1
CORTES, HERNAN 1484-1547   **LC 31**
Corvinus, Jakob
    See Raabe, Wilhelm (Karl)

Corwin, Cecil
    See Kornbluth, C(yril) M.
Cosic, Dobrica 1921-   **CLC 14**
    See also CA 122; 138; DLB 181
Costain, Thomas B(ertram) 1885-1965 **C L C 30**
    See also CA 5-8R; 25-28R; DLB 9
Costantini, Humberto 1924(?)-1987 **CLC 49**
    See also CA 131; 122; HW
Costello, Elvis 1955-   **CLC 21**
Cotes, Cecil V.
    See Duncan, Sara Jeannette
Cotter, Joseph Seamon Sr. 1861-1949 **T C L C 28; BLC 1; DAM MULT**
    See also BW 1; CA 124; DLB 50
Couch, Arthur Thomas Quiller
    See Quiller-Couch, SirArthur (Thomas)
Coulton, James
    See Hansen, Joseph
Couperus, Louis (Marie Anne) 1863-1923 **TCLC 15**
    See also CA 115
Coupland, Douglas 1961- **CLC 85; DAC; DAM POP**
    See also CA 142; CANR 57
Court, Wesli
    See Turco, Lewis (Putnam)
Courtenay, Bryce 1933-   **CLC 59**
    See also CA 138
Courtney, Robert
    See Ellison, Harlan (Jay)
Cousteau, Jacques-Yves 1910-1997   **CLC 30**
    See also CA 65-68; 159; CANR 15, 67; MTCW 1; SATA 38, 98
Coventry, Francis 1725-1754   **LC 46**
Cowan, Peter (Walkinshaw) 1914-   **SSC 28**
    See also CA 21-24R; CANR 9, 25, 50
Coward, Noel (Peirce) 1899-1973 **CLC 1, 9, 29, 51; DAM DRAM**
    See also AITN 1; CA 17-18; 41-44R; CANR 35; CAP 2; CDBLB 1914-1945; DLB 10; MTCW 1
Cowley, Abraham 1618-1667   **LC 43**
    See also DLB 131, 151
Cowley, Malcolm 1898-1989   **CLC 39**
    See also CA 5-8R; 128; CANR 3, 55; DLB 4, 48; DLBY 81, 89; MTCW 1
Cowper, William 1731-1800 **NCLC 8; DAM POET**
    See also DLB 104, 109
Cox, William Trevor 1928-   **CLC 9, 14, 71; DAM NOV**
    See also Trevor, William
    See also CA 9-12R; CANR 4, 37, 55; DLB 14; INT CANR-37; MTCW 1
Coyne, P. J.
    See Masters, Hilary
Cozzens, James Gould 1903-1978 **CLC 1, 4, 11, 92**
    See also CA 9-12R; 81-84; CANR 19; CDALB 1941-1968; DLB 9; DLBD 2; DLBY 84, 97; MTCW 1
Crabbe, George 1754-1832   **NCLC 26**
    See also DLB 93
Craddock, Charles Egbert
    See Murfree, Mary Noailles
Craig, A. A.
    See Anderson, Poul (William)
Craik, Dinah Maria (Mulock) 1826-1887 **NCLC 38**
    See also DLB 35, 163; MAICYA; SATA 34
Cram, Ralph Adams 1863-1942   **TCLC 45**
    See also CA 160

Crane, (Harold) Hart 1899-1932 **TCLC 2, 5, 80; DA; DAB; DAC; DAM MST, POET; PC 3; WLC**
    See also CA 104; 127; CDALB 1917-1929; DLB 4, 48; MTCW 1
Crane, R(onald) S(almon) 1886-1967 **CLC 27**
    See also CA 85-88; DLB 63
Crane, Stephen (Townley) 1871-1900 **T C L C 11, 17, 32; DA; DAB; DAC; DAM MST, NOV, POET; SSC 7; WLC**
    See also AAYA 21; CA 109; 140; CDALB 1865-1917; DLB 12, 54, 78; YABC 2
Cranshaw, Stanley
    See Fisher, Dorothy (Frances) Canfield
Crase, Douglas 1944-   **CLC 58**
    See also CA 106
Crashaw, Richard 1612(?)-1649   **LC 24**
    See also DLB 126
Craven, Margaret 1901-1980 **CLC 17; DAC**
    See also CA 103
Crawford, F(rancis) Marion 1854-1909 **TCLC 10**
    See also CA 107; 168; DLB 71
Crawford, Isabella Valancy 1850-1887 **N C L C 12**
    See also DLB 92
Crayon, Geoffrey
    See Irving, Washington
Creasey, John 1908-1973   **CLC 11**
    See also CA 5-8R; 41-44R; CANR 8, 59; DLB 77; MTCW 1
Crebillon, Claude Prosper Jolyot de (fils) 1707-1777   **LC 1, 28**
Credo
    See Creasey, John
Credo, Alvaro J. de
    See Prado (Calvo), Pedro
Creeley, Robert (White) 1926- **CLC 1, 2, 4, 8, 11, 15, 36, 78; DAM POET**
    See also CA 1-4R; CAAS 10; CANR 23, 43; DLB 5, 16, 169; DLBD 17; MTCW 1
Crews, Harry (Eugene) 1935- **CLC 6, 23, 49**
    See also AITN 1; CA 25-28R; CANR 20, 57; DLB 6, 143, 185; MTCW 1
Crichton, (John) Michael 1942- **CLC 2, 6, 54, 90; DAM NOV, POP**
    See also AAYA 10; AITN 2; CA 25-28R; CANR 13, 40, 54; DLBY 81; INT CANR-13; JRDA; MTCW 1; SATA 9, 88
Crispin, Edmund   **CLC 22**
    See also Montgomery, (Robert) Bruce
    See also DLB 87
Cristofer, Michael 1945(?)-   **CLC 28; DAM DRAM**
    See also CA 110; 152; DLB 7
Croce, Benedetto 1866-1952   **TCLC 37**
    See also CA 120; 155
Crockett, David 1786-1836   **NCLC 8**
    See also DLB 3, 11
Crockett, Davy
    See Crockett, David
Crofts, Freeman Wills 1879-1957   **TCLC 55**
    See also CA 115; DLB 77
Croker, John Wilson 1780-1857   **NCLC 10**
    See also DLB 110
Crommelynck, Fernand 1885-1970   **CLC 75**
    See also CA 89-92
Cromwell, Oliver 1599-1658   **LC 43**
Cronin, A(rchibald) J(oseph) 1896-1981 **C L C 32**
    See also CA 1-4R; 102; CANR 5; DLB 191; SATA 47; SATA-Obit 25
Cross, Amanda

See also CA 108

Diaz del Castillo, Bernal 1496-1584 **LC 31**

di Bassetto, Corno
See Shaw, George Bernard

Dick, Philip K(indred) 1928-1982**CLC 10, 30, 72; DAM NOV, POP**
See also AAYA 24; CA 49-52; 106; CANR 2, 16; DLB 8; MTCW 1

Dickens, Charles (John Huffam) 1812-1870 **NCLC 3, 8, 18, 26, 37, 50; DA; DAB; DAC; DAM MST, NOV; SSC 17; WLC**
See also AAYA 23; CDBLB 1832-1890; DLB 21, 55, 70, 159, 166; JRDA; MAICYA; SATA 15

Dickey, James (Lafayette) 1923-1997 **CLC 1, 2, 4, 7, 10, 15, 47, 109; DAM NOV, POET, POP**
See also AITN 1, 2; CA 9-12R; 156; CABS 2; CANR 10, 48, 61; CDALB 1968-1988; DLB 5, 193; DLBD 7; DLBY 82, 93, 96, 97; INT CANR-10; MTCW 1

Dickey, William 1928-1994   **CLC 3, 28**
See also CA 9-12R; 145; CANR 24; DLB 5

Dickinson, Charles 1951-   **CLC 49**
See also CA 128

Dickinson, Emily (Elizabeth) 1830-1886 **NCLC 21; DA; DAB; DAC; DAM MST, POET; PC 1; WLC**
See also AAYA 22; CDALB 1865-1917; DLB 1; SATA 29

Dickinson, Peter (Malcolm) 1927-**CLC 12, 35**
See also AAYA 9; CA 41-44R; CANR 31, 58; CLR 29; DLB 87, 161; JRDA; MAICYA; SATA 5, 62, 95

Dickson, Carr
See Carr, John Dickson

Dickson, Carter
See Carr, John Dickson

Diderot, Denis 1713-1784   **LC 26**

Didion, Joan 1934-**CLC 1, 3, 8, 14, 32; DAM NOV**
See also AITN 1; CA 5-8R; CANR 14, 52; CDALB 1968-1988; DLB 2, 173, 185; DLBY 81, 86; MTCW 1

Dietrich, Robert
See Hunt, E(verette) Howard, (Jr.)

Difusa, Pati
See Almodovar, Pedro

Dillard, Annie 1945-   **CLC 9, 60, 115; DAM NOV**
See also AAYA 6; CA 49-52; CANR 3, 43, 62; DLBY 80; MTCW 1; SATA 10

Dillard, R(ichard) H(enry) W(ilde) 1937-**CLC 5**
See also CA 21-24R; CAAS 7; CANR 10; DLB 5

Dillon, Eilis 1920-1994   **CLC 17**
See also CA 9-12R; 147; CAAS 3; CANR 4, 38; CLR 26; MAICYA; SATA 2, 74; SATA-Obit 83

Dimont, Penelope
See Mortimer, Penelope (Ruth)

Dinesen, Isak   **CLC 10, 29, 95; SSC 7**
See also Blixen, Karen (Christentze Dinesen)

Ding Ling   **CLC 68**
See also Chiang, Pin-chin

Diphusa, Patty
See Almodovar, Pedro

Disch, Thomas M(ichael) 1940-   **CLC 7, 36**
See also AAYA 17; CA 21-24R; CAAS 4; CANR 17, 36, 54; CLR 18; DLB 8; MAICYA; MTCW 1; SAAS 15; SATA 92

Disch, Tom

See Disch, Thomas M(ichael)

d'Isly, Georges
See Simenon, Georges (Jacques Christian)

Disraeli, Benjamin 1804-1881   **NCLC 2, 39**
See also DLB 21, 55

Ditcum, Steve
See Crumb, R(obert)

Dixon, Paige
See Corcoran, Barbara

Dixon, Stephen 1936-   **CLC 52; SSC 16**
See also CA 89-92; CANR 17, 40, 54; DLB 130

Doak, Annie
See Dillard, Annie

Dobell, Sydney Thompson 1824-1874 **N C L C 43**
See also DLB 32

Doblin, Alfred   **TCLC 13**
See also Doeblin, Alfred

Dobrolyubov, Nikolai Alexandrovich 1836-1861 **NCLC 5**

Dobson, Austin 1840-1921   **TCLC 79**
See also DLB 35; 144

Dobyns, Stephen 1941-   **CLC 37**
See also CA 45-48; CANR 2, 18

Doctorow, E(dgar) L(aurence) 1931- **CLC 6, 11, 15, 18, 37, 44, 65, 113; DAM NOV, POP**
See also AAYA 22; AITN 2; BEST 89:3; CA 45-48; CANR 2, 33, 51; CDALB 1968-1988; DLB 2, 28, 173; DLBY 80; MTCW 1

Dodgson, Charles Lutwidge 1832-1898
See Carroll, Lewis
See also CLR 2; DA; DAB; DAC; DAM MST, NOV, POET; MAICYA; SATA 100; YABC 2

Dodson, Owen (Vincent) 1914-1983 **CLC 79; BLC 1; DAM MULT**
See also BW 1; CA 65-68; 110; CANR 24; DLB 76

Doeblin, Alfred 1878-1957   **TCLC 13**
See also Doblin, Alfred
See also CA 110; 141; DLB 66

Doerr, Harriet 1910-   **CLC 34**
See also CA 117; 122; CANR 47; INT 122

Domecq, H(onorio) Bustos
See Bioy Casares, Adolfo; Borges, Jorge Luis

Domini, Rey
See Lorde, Audre (Geraldine)

Dominique
See Proust, (Valentin-Louis-George-Eugene-) Marcel

Don, A
See Stephen, SirLeslie

Donaldson, Stephen R. 1947- **CLC 46; DAM POP**
See also CA 89-92; CANR 13, 55; INT CANR-13

Donleavy, J(ames) P(atrick) 1926-**CLC 1, 4, 6, 10, 45**
See also AITN 2; CA 9-12R; CANR 24, 49, 62; DLB 6, 173; INT CANR-24; MTCW 1

Donne, John 1572-1631**LC 10, 24; DA; DAB; DAC; DAM MST, POET; PC 1**
See also CDBLB Before 1660; DLB 121, 151

Donnell, David 1939(?)-   **CLC 34**

Donoghue, P. S.
See Hunt, E(verette) Howard, (Jr.)

Donoso (Yanez), Jose 1924-1996**CLC 4, 8, 11, 32, 99; DAM MULT; HLC**
See also CA 81-84; 155; CANR 32, 73; DLB 113; HW; MTCW 1

Donovan, John 1928-1992   **CLC 35**
See also AAYA 20; CA 97-100; 137; CLR 3; MAICYA; SATA 72; SATA-Brief 29

Don Roberto

See Cunninghame Graham, R(obert) B(ontine)

Doolittle, Hilda 1886-1961**CLC 3, 8, 14, 31, 34, 73; DA; DAC; DAM MST, POET; PC 5; WLC**
See also H. D.
See also CA 97-100; CANR 35; DLB 4, 45; MTCW 1

Dorfman, Ariel 1942-   **CLC 48, 77; DAM MULT; HLC**
See also CA 124; 130; CANR 67, 70; HW; INT 130

Dorn, Edward (Merton) 1929-   **CLC 10, 18**
See also CA 93-96; CANR 42; DLB 5; INT 93-96

Dorris, Michael (Anthony) 1945-1997   **C L C 109; DAM MULT, NOV**
See also AAYA 20; BEST 90:1; CA 102; 157; CANR 19, 46; DLB 175; NNAL; SATA 75; SATA-Obit 94

Dorris, Michael A.
See Dorris, Michael (Anthony)

Dorsan, Luc
See Simenon, Georges (Jacques Christian)

Dorsange, Jean
See Simenon, Georges (Jacques Christian)

Dos Passos, John (Roderigo) 1896-1970 **C L C 1, 4, 8, 11, 15, 25, 34, 82; DA; DAB; DAC; DAM MST, NOV; WLC**
See also CA 1-4R; 29-32R; CANR 3; CDALB 1929-1941; DLB 4, 9; DLBD 1, 15; DLBY 96; MTCW 1

Dossage, Jean
See Simenon, Georges (Jacques Christian)

Dostoevsky, Fedor Mikhailovich 1821-1881 **NCLC 2, 7, 21, 33, 43; DA; DAB; DAC; DAM MST, NOV; SSC 2; WLC**

Doughty, Charles M(ontagu) 1843-1926 **TCLC 27**
See also CA 115; DLB 19, 57, 174

Douglas, Ellen   **CLC 73**
See also Haxton, Josephine Ayres; Williamson, Ellen Douglas

Douglas, Gavin 1475(?)-1522   **LC 20**
See also DLB 132

Douglas, George
See Brown, George Douglas

Douglas, Keith (Castellain) 1920-1944 **T C L C 40**
See also CA 160; DLB 27

Douglas, Leonard
See Bradbury, Ray (Douglas)

Douglas, Michael
See Crichton, (John) Michael

Douglas, (George) Norman 1868-1952 **T C L C 68**
See also CA 119; 157; DLB 34, 195

Douglas, William
See Brown, George Douglas

Douglass, Frederick 1817(?)-1895**NCLC 7, 55; BLC 1; DA; DAC; DAM MST, MULT; WLC**
See also CDALB 1640-1865; DLB 1, 43, 50, 79; SATA 29

Dourado, (Waldomiro Freitas) Autran 1926- **CLC 23, 60**
See also CA 25-28R; CANR 34

Dourado, Waldomiro Autran
See Dourado, (Waldomiro Freitas) Autran

Dove, Rita (Frances) 1952-**CLC 50, 81; BLCS; DAM MULT, POET; PC 6**
See also BW 2; CA 109; CAAS 19; CANR 27, 42, 68; DLB 120

Doveglion

See Villa, Jose Garcia

Dowell, Coleman 1925-1985   **CLC 60**
   See also CA 25-28R; 117; CANR 10; DLB 130

Dowson, Ernest (Christopher) 1867-1900
   TCLC 4
   See also CA 105; 150; DLB 19, 135

Doyle, A. Conan
   See Doyle, Arthur Conan

Doyle, Arthur Conan 1859-1930**TCLC 7; DA;**
   DAB; DAC; DAM MST, NOV; SSC 12;
   WLC
   See also AAYA 14; CA 104; 122; CDBLB 1890-
   1914; DLB 18, 70, 156, 178; MTCW 1;
   SATA 24

Doyle, Conan
   See Doyle, Arthur Conan

Doyle, John
   See Graves, Robert (von Ranke)

Doyle, Roddy 1958(?)-   **CLC 81**
   See also AAYA 14; CA 143; CANR 73; DLB
   194

Doyle, Sir A. Conan
   See Doyle, Arthur Conan

Doyle, Sir Arthur Conan
   See Doyle, Arthur Conan

Dr. A
   See Asimov, Isaac; Silverstein, Alvin

Drabble, Margaret 1939-**CLC 2, 3, 5, 8, 10, 22,**
   53; DAB; DAC; DAM MST, NOV, POP
   See also CA 13-16R; CANR 18, 35, 63; CDBLB
   1960 to Present; DLB 14, 155; MTCW 1;
   SATA 48

Drapier, M. B.
   See Swift, Jonathan

Drayham, James
   See Mencken, H(enry) L(ouis)

Drayton, Michael 1563-1631   **LC 8; DAM**
   POET
   See also DLB 121

Dreadstone, Carl
   See Campbell, (John) Ramsey

Dreiser, Theodore (Herman Albert) 1871-1945
   TCLC 10, 18, 35, 83; DA; DAC; DAM
   MST, NOV; SSC 30; WLC
   See also CA 106; 132; CDALB 1865-1917;
   DLB 9, 12, 102, 137; DLBD 1; MTCW 1

Drexler, Rosalyn 1926-   **CLC 2, 6**
   See also CA 81-84; CANR 68

Dreyer, Carl Theodor 1889-1968   **CLC 16**
   See also CA 116

Drieu la Rochelle, Pierre(-Eugene) 1893-1945
   TCLC 21
   See also CA 117; DLB 72

Drinkwater, John 1882-1937   **TCLC 57**
   See also CA 109; 149; DLB 10, 19, 149

Drop Shot
   See Cable, George Washington

Droste-Hulshoff, Annette Freiin von 1797-1848
   NCLC 3
   See also DLB 133

Drummond, Walter
   See Silverberg, Robert

Drummond, William Henry 1854-1907**TCLC**
   25
   See also CA 160; DLB 92

Drummond de Andrade, Carlos 1902-1987
   CLC 18
   See also Andrade, Carlos Drummond de
   See also CA 132; 123

Drury, Allen (Stuart) 1918-1998   **CLC 37**
   See also CA 57-60; 170; CANR 18, 52; INT
   CANR-18

Dryden, John 1631-1700**LC 3, 21; DA; DAB;**

DAC; DAM DRAM, MST, POET; DC 3;
   WLC
   See also CDBLB 1660-1789; DLB 80, 101, 131

Duberman, Martin (Bauml) 1930-   **CLC 8**
   See also CA 1-4R; CANR 2, 63

Dubie, Norman (Evans) 1945-   **CLC 36**
   See also CA 69-72; CANR 12; DLB 120

Du Bois, W(illiam) E(dward) B(urghardt) 1868-
   1963   **CLC 1, 2, 13, 64, 96; BLC 1; DA;**
   DAC; DAM MST, MULT, NOV; WLC
   See also BW 1; CA 85-88; CANR 34; CDALB
   1865-1917; DLB 47, 50, 91; MTCW 1; SATA
   42

Dubus, Andre 1936- **CLC 13, 36, 97; SSC 15**
   See also CA 21-24R; CANR 17; DLB 130; INT
   CANR-17

Duca Minimo
   See D'Annunzio, Gabriele

Ducharme, Rejean 1941-   **CLC 74**
   See also CA 165; DLB 60

Duclos, Charles Pinot 1704-1772   **LC 1**

Dudek, Louis 1918-   **CLC 11, 19**
   See also CA 45-48; CAAS 14; CANR 1; DLB
   88

Duerrenmatt, Friedrich 1921-1990 **CLC 1, 4,**
   8, 11, 15, 43, 102; DAM DRAM
   See also CA 17-20R; CANR 33; DLB 69, 124;
   MTCW 1

Duffy, Bruce (?)-   **CLC 50**

Duffy, Maureen 1933-   **CLC 37**
   See also CA 25-28R; CANR 33, 68; DLB 14;
   MTCW 1

Dugan, Alan 1923-   **CLC 2, 6**
   See also CA 81-84; DLB 5

du Gard, Roger Martin
   See Martin du Gard, Roger

Duhamel, Georges 1884-1966   **CLC 8**
   See also CA 81-84; 25-28R; CANR 35; DLB
   65; MTCW 1

Dujardin, Edouard (Emile Louis) 1861-1949
   TCLC 13
   See also CA 109; DLB 123

Dulles, John Foster 1888-1959   **TCLC 72**
   See also CA 115; 149

Dumas, Alexandre (pere)
   See Dumas, Alexandre (Davy de la Pailleterie)

Dumas, Alexandre (Davy de la Pailleterie)
   1802-1870   **NCLC 11; DA; DAB; DAC;**
   DAM MST, NOV; WLC
   See also DLB 119, 192; SATA 18

Dumas, Alexandre (fils) 1824-1895**NCLC 71;**
   DC 1
   See also AAYA 22; DLB 192

Dumas, Claudine
   See Malzberg, Barry N(athaniel)

Dumas, Henry L. 1934-1968   **CLC 6, 62**
   See also BW 1; CA 85-88; DLB 41

du Maurier, Daphne 1907-1989**CLC 6, 11, 59;**
   DAB; DAC; DAM MST, POP; SSC 18
   See also CA 5-8R; 128; CANR 6, 55; DLB 191;
   MTCW 1; SATA 27; SATA-Obit 60

Dunbar, Paul Laurence 1872-1906 **TCLC 2,**
   12; BLC 1; DA; DAC; DAM MST, MULT,
   POET; PC 5; SSC 8; WLC
   See also BW 1; CA 104; 124; CDALB 1865-
   1917; DLB 50, 54, 78; SATA 34

Dunbar, William 1460(?)-1530(?)   **LC 20**
   See also DLB 132, 146

Duncan, Dora Angela
   See Duncan, Isadora

Duncan, Isadora 1877(?)-1927   **TCLC 68**
   See also CA 118; 149

Duncan, Lois 1934-   **CLC 26**

See also AAYA 4; CA 1-4R; CANR 2, 23, 36;
   CLR 29; JRDA; MAICYA; SAAS 2; SATA
   1, 36, 75

Duncan, Robert (Edward) 1919-1988 **CLC 1,**
   2, 4, 7, 15, 41, 55; DAM POET; PC 2
   See also CA 9-12R; 124; CANR 28, 62; DLB
   5, 16, 193; MTCW 1

Duncan, Sara Jeannette 1861-1922 **TCLC 60**
   See also CA 157; DLB 92

Dunlap, William 1766-1839   **NCLC 2**
   See also DLB 30, 37, 59

Dunn, Douglas (Eaglesham) 1942- **CLC 6, 40**
   See also CA 45-48; CANR 2, 33; DLB 40;
   MTCW 1

Dunn, Katherine (Karen) 1945-   **CLC 71**
   See also CA 33-36R; CANR 72

Dunn, Stephen 1939-   **CLC 36**
   See also CA 33-36R; CANR 12, 48, 53; DLB
   105

Dunne, Finley Peter 1867-1936   **TCLC 28**
   See also CA 108; DLB 11, 23

Dunne, John Gregory 1932-   **CLC 28**
   See also CA 25-28R; CANR 14, 50; DLBY 80

Dunsany, Edward John Moreton Drax Plunkett
   1878-1957
   See Dunsany, Lord
   See also CA 104; 148; DLB 10

Dunsany, Lord   **TCLC 2, 59**
   See also Dunsany, Edward John Moreton Drax
   Plunkett
   See also DLB 77, 153, 156

du Perry, Jean
   See Simenon, Georges (Jacques Christian)

Durang, Christopher (Ferdinand) 1949-**CLC**
   27, 38
   See also CA 105; CANR 50

Duras, Marguerite 1914-1996**CLC 3, 6, 11, 20,**
   34, 40, 68, 100
   See also CA 25-28R; 151; CANR 50; DLB 83;
   MTCW 1

Durban, (Rosa) Pam 1947-   **CLC 39**
   See also CA 123

Durcan, Paul 1944-**CLC 43, 70; DAM POET**
   See also CA 134

Durkheim, Emile 1858-1917   **TCLC 55**

Durrell, Lawrence (George) 1912-1990 **CLC**
   1, 4, 6, 8, 13, 27, 41; DAM NOV
   See also CA 9-12R; 132; CANR 40; CDBLB
   1945-1960; DLB 15, 27; DLBY 90; MTCW
   1

Durrenmatt, Friedrich
   See Duerrenmatt, Friedrich

Dutt, Toru 1856-1877   **NCLC 29**

Dwight, Timothy 1752-1817   **NCLC 13**
   See also DLB 37

Dworkin, Andrea 1946-   **CLC 43**
   See also CA 77-80; CAAS 21; CANR 16, 39;
   INT CANR-16; MTCW 1

Dwyer, Deanna
   See Koontz, Dean R(ay)

Dwyer, K. R.
   See Koontz, Dean R(ay)

Dwyer, Thomas A. 1923-   **CLC 114**
   See also CA 115

Dye, Richard
   See De Voto, Bernard (Augustine)

Dylan, Bob 1941-   **CLC 3, 4, 6, 12, 77**
   See also CA 41-44R; DLB 16

Eagleton, Terence (Francis) 1943-
   See Eagleton, Terry
   See also CA 57-60; CANR 7, 23, 68; MTCW 1

Eagleton, Terry   **CLC 63**
   See also Eagleton, Terence (Francis)

Early, Jack
See Scoppettone, Sandra
East, Michael
See West, Morris L(anglo)
Eastaway, Edward
See Thomas, (Philip) Edward
Eastlake, William (Derry) 1917-1997 **CLC 8**
See also CA 5-8R; 158; CAAS 1; CANR 5, 63;
DLB 6; INT CANR-5
Eastman, Charles A(lexander) 1858-1939
TCLC 55; DAM MULT
See also DLB 175; NNAL; YABC 1
Eberhart, Richard (Ghormley) 1904- CLC 3,
11, 19, 56; DAM POET
See also CA 1-4R; CANR 2; CDALB 1941-
1968; DLB 48; MTCW 1
Eberstadt, Fernanda 1960-   **CLC 39**
See also CA 136; CANR 69
Echegaray (y Eizaguirre), Jose (Maria Waldo)
1832-1916   **TCLC 4**
See also CA 104; CANR 32; HW; MTCW 1
Echeverria, (Jose) Esteban (Antonino) 1805-
1851   **NCLC 18**
Echo
See Proust, (Valentin-Louis-George-Eugene-)
Marcel
Eckert, Allan W. 1931-   **CLC 17**
See also AAYA 18; CA 13-16R; CANR 14, 45;
INT CANR-14; SAAS 21; SATA 29, 91;
SATA-Brief 27
Eckhart, Meister 1260(?)-1328(?)   **CMLC 9**
See also DLB 115
Eckmar, F. R.
See de Hartog, Jan
Eco, Umberto 1932- CLC 28, 60; DAM NOV,
POP
See also BEST 90:1; CA 77-80; CANR 12, 33,
55; DLB 196; MTCW 1
Eddison, E(ric) R(ucker) 1882-1945TCLC 15
See also CA 109; 156
Eddy, Mary (Morse) Baker 1821-1910 T C L C
71
See also CA 113
Edel, (Joseph) Leon 1907-1997   **CLC 29, 34**
See also CA 1-4R; 161; CANR 1, 22; DLB 103;
INT CANR-22
Eden, Emily 1797-1869   **NCLC 10**
Edgar, David 1948-   **CLC 42; DAM DRAM**
See also CA 57-60; CANR 12, 61; DLB 13;
MTCW 1
Edgerton, Clyde (Carlyle) 1944-   **CLC 39**
See also AAYA 17; CA 118; 134; CANR 64;
INT 134
Edgeworth, Maria 1768-1849   **NCLC 1, 51**
See also DLB 116, 159, 163; SATA 21
Edmonds, Paul
See Kuttner, Henry
Edmonds, Walter D(umaux) 1903-1998 C L C
35
See also CA 5-8R; CANR 2; DLB 9; MAICYA;
SAAS 4; SATA 1, 27; SATA-Obit 99
Edmondson, Wallace
See Ellison, Harlan (Jay)
Edson, Russell   **CLC 13**
See also CA 33-36R
Edwards, Bronwen Elizabeth
See Rose, Wendy
Edwards, G(erald) B(asil) 1899-1976CLC 25
See also CA 110
Edwards, Gus 1939-   **CLC 43**
See also CA 108; INT 108
Edwards, Jonathan 1703-1758   **LC 7; DA;**
DAC; DAM MST

See also DLB 24
Efron, Marina Ivanovna Tsvetaeva
See Tsvetaeva (Efron), Marina (Ivanovna)
Ehle, John (Marsden, Jr.) 1925-   **CLC 27**
See also CA 9-12R
Ehrenbourg, Ilya (Grigoryevich)
See Ehrenburg, Ilya (Grigoryevich)
Ehrenburg, Ilya (Grigoryevich) 1891-1967
CLC 18, 34, 62
See also CA 102; 25-28R
Ehrenburg, Ilyo (Grigoryevich)
See Ehrenburg, Ilya (Grigoryevich)
Ehrenreich, Barbara 1941-   **CLC 110**
See also BEST 90:4; CA 73-76; CANR 16, 37,
62; MTCW 1
Eich, Guenter 1907-1972   **CLC 15**
See also CA 111; 93-96; DLB 69, 124
Eichendorff, Joseph Freiherr von 1788-1857
NCLC 8
See also DLB 90
Eigner, Larry   **CLC 9**
See also Eigner, Laurence (Joel)
See also CAAS 23; DLB 5
Eigner, Laurence (Joel) 1927-1996
See Eigner, Larry
See also CA 9-12R; 151; CANR 6; DLB 193
Einstein, Albert 1879-1955   **TCLC 65**
See also CA 121; 133; MTCW 1
Eiseley, Loren Corey 1907-1977   **CLC 7**
See also AAYA 5; CA 1-4R; 73-76; CANR 6;
DLBD 17
Eisenstadt, Jill 1963-   **CLC 50**
See also CA 140
Eisenstein, Sergei (Mikhailovich) 1898-1948
TCLC 57
See also CA 114; 149
Eisner, Simon
See Kornbluth, C(yril) M.
Ekeloef, (Bengt) Gunnar 1907-1968 CLC 27;
DAM POET; PC 23
See also CA 123; 25-28R
Ekelof, (Bengt) Gunnar
See Ekeloef, (Bengt) Gunnar
Ekelund, Vilhelm 1880-1949   **TCLC 75**
Ekwensi, C. O. D.
See Ekwensi, Cyprian (Odiatu Duaka)
Ekwensi, Cyprian (Odiatu Duaka) 1921-C L C
4; BLC 1; DAM MULT
See also BW 2; CA 29-32R; CANR 18, 42, 74;
DLB 117; MTCW 1; SATA 66
Elaine   **TCLC 18**
See also Leverson, Ada
El Crummo
See Crumb, R(obert)
Elder, Lonne III 1931-1996   **DC 8**
See also BLC 1; BW 1; CA 81-84; 152; CANR
25; DAM MULT; DLB 7, 38, 44
Elia
See Lamb, Charles
Eliade, Mircea 1907-1986   **CLC 19**
See also CA 65-68; 119; CANR 30, 62; MTCW
1
Eliot, A. D.
See Jewett, (Theodora) Sarah Orne
Eliot, Alice
See Jewett, (Theodora) Sarah Orne
Eliot, Dan
See Silverberg, Robert
Eliot, George 1819-1880 NCLC 4, 13, 23, 41,
**49; DA; DAB; DAC; DAM MST, NOV; PC
20; WLC**
See also CDBLB 1832-1890; DLB 21, 35, 55
Eliot, John 1604-1690   **LC 5**

See also DLB 24
Eliot, T(homas) S(tearns) 1888-1965CLC 1, 2,
**3, 6, 9, 10, 13, 15, 24, 34, 41, 55, 57, 113;
DA; DAB; DAC; DAM DRAM, MST,
POET; PC 5; WLC**
See also CA 5-8R; 25-28R; CANR 41; CDALB
1929-1941; DLB 7, 10, 45, 63; DLBY 88;
MTCW 1
Elizabeth 1866-1941   **TCLC 41**
Elkin, Stanley L(awrence) 1930-1995 CLC 4,
**6, 9, 14, 27, 51, 91; DAM NOV, POP; SSC
12**
See also CA 9-12R; 148; CANR 8, 46; DLB 2,
28; DLBY 80; INT CANR-8; MTCW 1
Elledge, Scott   **CLC 34**
Elliot, Don
See Silverberg, Robert
Elliott, Don
See Silverberg, Robert
Elliott, George P(aul) 1918-1980   **CLC 2**
See also CA 1-4R; 97-100; CANR 2
Elliott, Janice 1931-   **CLC 47**
See also CA 13-16R; CANR 8, 29; DLB 14
Elliott, Sumner Locke 1917-1991   **CLC 38**
See also CA 5-8R; 134; CANR 2, 21
Elliott, William
See Bradbury, Ray (Douglas)
Ellis, A. E.   **CLC 7**
Ellis, Alice Thomas   **CLC 40**
See also Haycraft, Anna
See also DLB 194
Ellis, Bret Easton 1964-CLC 39, 71, 117; DAM
POP
See also AAYA 2; CA 118; 123; CANR 51, 74;
INT 123
Ellis, (Henry) Havelock 1859-1939 TCLC 14
See also CA 109; 169; DLB 190
Ellis, Landon
See Ellison, Harlan (Jay)
Ellis, Trey 1962-   **CLC 55**
See also CA 146
Ellison, Harlan (Jay) 1934-   CLC 1, 13, 42;
DAM POP; SSC 14
See also CA 5-8R; CANR 5, 46; DLB 8; INT
CANR-5; MTCW 1
Ellison, Ralph (Waldo) 1914-1994 CLC 1, 3,
**11, 54, 86, 114; BLC 1; DA; DAB; DAC;
DAM MST, MULT, NOV; SSC 26; WLC**
See also AAYA 19; BW 1; CA 9-12R; 145;
CANR 24, 53; CDALB 1941-1968; DLB 2,
76; DLBY 94; MTCW 1
Ellmann, Lucy (Elizabeth) 1956-   **CLC 61**
See also CA 128
Ellmann, Richard (David) 1918-1987CLC 50
See also BEST 89:2; CA 1-4R; 122; CANR 2,
28, 61; DLB 103; DLBY 87; MTCW 1
Elman, Richard (Martin) 1934-1997 CLC 19
See also CA 17-20R; 163; CAAS 3; CANR 47
Elron
See Hubbard, L(afayette) Ron(ald)
Eluard, Paul   **TCLC 7, 41**
See also Grindel, Eugene
Elyot, Sir Thomas 1490(?)-1546   **LC 11**
Elytis, Odysseus 1911-1996 CLC 15, 49, 100;
DAM POET; PC 21
See also CA 102; 151; MTCW 1
Emecheta, (Florence Onye) Buchi 1944-C L C
14, 48; BLC 2; DAM MULT
See also BW 2; CA 81-84; CANR 27; DLB 117;
MTCW 1; SATA 66
Emerson, Mary Moody 1774-1863 NCLC 66
Emerson, Ralph Waldo 1803-1882 NCLC 1,
38; DA; DAB; DAC; DAM MST, POET;

PC 18; WLC
See also CDALB 1640-1865; DLB 1, 59, 73
Eminescu, Mihail 1850-1889   **NCLC 33**
Empson, William 1906-1984**CLC 3, 8, 19, 33, 34**
See also CA 17-20R; 112; CANR 31, 61; DLB 20; MTCW 1
Enchi, Fumiko (Ueda) 1905-1986   **CLC 31**
See also CA 129; 121
Ende, Michael (Andreas Helmuth) 1929-1995
CLC 31
See also CA 118; 124; 149; CANR 36; CLR 14; DLB 75; MAICYA; SATA 61; SATA-Brief 42; SATA-Obit 86
Endo, Shusaku 1923-1996 **CLC 7, 14, 19, 54, 99; DAM NOV**
See also CA 29-32R; 153; CANR 21, 54; DLB 182; MTCW 1
Engel, Marian 1933-1985   **CLC 36**
See also CA 25-28R; CANR 12; DLB 53; INT CANR-12
Engelhardt, Frederick
See Hubbard, L(afayette) Ron(ald)
Enright, D(ennis) J(oseph) 1920-**CLC 4, 8, 31**
See also CA 1-4R; CANR 1, 42; DLB 27; SATA 25
Enzensberger, Hans Magnus 1929-   **CLC 43**
See also CA 116; 119
Ephron, Nora 1941-   **CLC 17, 31**
See also AITN 2; CA 65-68; CANR 12, 39
Epicurus 341B.C.-270B.C.   **CMLC 21**
See also DLB 176
Epsilon
See Betjeman, John
Epstein, Daniel Mark 1948-   **CLC 7**
See also CA 49-52; CANR 2, 53
Epstein, Jacob 1956-   **CLC 19**
See also CA 114
Epstein, Joseph 1937-   **CLC 39**
See also CA 112; 119; CANR 50, 65
Epstein, Leslie 1938-   **CLC 27**
See also CA 73-76; CAAS 12; CANR 23, 69
Equiano, Olaudah 1745(?)-1797 **LC 16; BLC 2; DAM MULT**
See also DLB 37, 50
ER   **TCLC 33**
See also CA 160; DLB 85
Erasmus, Desiderius 1469(?)-1536   **LC 16**
Erdman, Paul E(mil) 1932-   **CLC 25**
See also AITN 1; CA 61-64; CANR 13, 43
Erdrich, Louise 1954-   **CLC 39, 54; DAM MULT, NOV, POP**
See also AAYA 10; BEST 89:1; CA 114; CANR 41, 62; DLB 152, 175; MTCW 1; NNAL; SATA 94
Erenburg, Ilya (Grigoryevich)
See Ehrenburg, Ilya (Grigoryevich)
Erickson, Stephen Michael 1950-
See Erickson, Steve
See also CA 129
Erickson, Steve 1950-   **CLC 64**
See also Erickson, Stephen Michael
See also CANR 60, 68
Ericson, Walter
See Fast, Howard (Melvin)
Eriksson, Buntel
See Bergman, (Ernst) Ingmar
Ernaux, Annie 1940-   **CLC 88**
See also CA 147
Erskine, John 1879-1951   **TCLC 84**
See also CA 112; 159; DLB 9, 102
Eschenbach, Wolfram von
See Wolfram von Eschenbach

Eseki, Bruno
See Mphahlele, Ezekiel
Esenin, Sergei (Alexandrovich) 1895-1925
TCLC 4
See also CA 104
Eshleman, Clayton 1935-   **CLC 7**
See also CA 33-36R; CAAS 6; DLB 5
Espriella, Don Manuel Alvarez
See Southey, Robert
Espriu, Salvador 1913-1985   **CLC 9**
See also CA 154; 115; DLB 134
Espronceda, Jose de 1808-1842   **NCLC 39**
Esse, James
See Stephens, James
Esterbrook, Tom
See Hubbard, L(afayette) Ron(ald)
Estleman, Loren D. 1952-**CLC 48; DAM NOV, POP**
See also AAYA 27; CA 85-88; CANR 27, 74; INT CANR-27; MTCW 1
Euclid 306B.C.-283B.C.   **CMLC 25**
Eugenides, Jeffrey 1960(?)-   **CLC 81**
See also CA 144
Euripides c. 485B.C.-406B.C.**CMLC 23; DA; DAB; DAC; DAM DRAM, MST; DC 4; WLCS**
See also DLB 176
Evan, Evin
See Faust, Frederick (Schiller)
Evans, Caradoc 1878-1945   **TCLC 85**
Evans, Evan
See Faust, Frederick (Schiller)
Evans, Marian
See Eliot, George
Evans, Mary Ann
See Eliot, George
Evarts, Esther
See Benson, Sally
Everett, Percival L. 1956-   **CLC 57**
See also BW 2; CA 129
Everson, R(onald) G(ilmour) 1903-   **CLC 27**
See also CA 17-20R; DLB 88
Everson, William (Oliver) 1912-1994 **CLC 1, 5, 14**
See also CA 9-12R; 145; CANR 20; DLB 5, 16; MTCW 1
Evtushenko, Evgenii Aleksandrovich
See Yevtushenko, Yevgeny (Alexandrovich)
Ewart, Gavin (Buchanan) 1916-1995**CLC 13, 46**
See also CA 89-92; 150; CANR 17, 46; DLB 40; MTCW 1
Ewers, Hanns Heinz 1871-1943   **TCLC 12**
See also CA 109; 149
Ewing, Frederick R.
See Sturgeon, Theodore (Hamilton)
Exley, Frederick (Earl) 1929-1992 **CLC 6, 11**
See also AITN 2; CA 81-84; 138; DLB 143; DLBY 81
Eynhardt, Guillermo
See Quiroga, Horacio (Sylvestre)
Ezekiel, Nissim 1924-   **CLC 61**
See also CA 61-64
Ezekiel, Tish O'Dowd 1943-   **CLC 34**
See also CA 129
Fadeyev, A.
See Bulgya, Alexander Alexandrovich
Fadeyev, Alexander   **TCLC 53**
See also Bulgya, Alexander Alexandrovich
Fagen, Donald 1948-   **CLC 26**
Fainzilberg, Ilya Arnoldovich 1897-1937
See Ilf, Ilya
See also CA 120; 165

Fair, Ronald L. 1932-   **CLC 18**
See also BW 1; CA 69-72; CANR 25; DLB 33
Fairbairn, Roger
See Carr, John Dickson
Fairbairns, Zoe (Ann) 1948-   **CLC 32**
See also CA 103; CANR 21
Falco, Gian
See Papini, Giovanni
Falconer, James
See Kirkup, James
Falconer, Kenneth
See Kornbluth, C(yril) M.
Falkland, Samuel
See Heijermans, Herman
Fallaci, Oriana 1930-   **CLC 11, 110**
See also CA 77-80; CANR 15, 58; MTCW 1
Faludy, George 1913-   **CLC 42**
See also CA 21-24R
Faludy, Gyoergy
See Faludy, George
Fanon, Frantz 1925-1961   **CLC 74; BLC 2; DAM MULT**
See also BW 1; CA 116; 89-92
Fanshawe, Ann 1625-1680   **LC 11**
Fante, John (Thomas) 1911-1983   **CLC 60**
See also CA 69-72; 109; CANR 23; DLB 130; DLBY 83
Farah, Nuruddin 1945-**CLC 53; BLC 2; DAM MULT**
See also BW 2; CA 106; DLB 125
Fargue, Leon-Paul 1876(?)-1947   **TCLC 11**
See also CA 109
Farigoule, Louis
See Romains, Jules
Farina, Richard 1936(?)-1966   **CLC 9**
See also CA 81-84; 25-28R
Farley, Walter (Lorimer) 1915-1989 **CLC 17**
See also CA 17-20R; CANR 8, 29; DLB 22; JRDA; MAICYA; SATA 2, 43
Farmer, Philip Jose 1918-   **CLC 1, 19**
See also CA 1-4R; CANR 4, 35; DLB 8; MTCW 1; SATA 93
Farquhar, George 1677-1707   **LC 21; DAM DRAM**
See also DLB 84
Farrell, J(ames) G(ordon) 1935-1979 **CLC 6**
See also CA 73-76; 89-92; CANR 36; DLB 14; MTCW 1
Farrell, James T(homas) 1904-1979**CLC 1, 4, 8, 11, 66; SSC 28**
See also CA 5-8R; 89-92; CANR 9, 61; DLB 4, 9, 86; DLBD 2; MTCW 1
Farren, Richard J.
See Betjeman, John
Farren, Richard M.
See Betjeman, John
Fassbinder, Rainer Werner 1946-1982**CLC 20**
See also CA 93-96; 106; CANR 31
Fast, Howard (Melvin) 1914-   **CLC 23; DAM NOV**
See also AAYA 16; CA 1-4R; CAAS 18; CANR 1, 33, 54; DLB 9; INT CANR-33; SATA 7
Faulcon, Robert
See Holdstock, Robert P.
Faulkner, William (Cuthbert) 1897-1962**CLC 1, 3, 6, 8, 9, 11, 14, 18, 28, 52, 68; DA; DAB; DAC; DAM MST, NOV; SSC 1; WLC**
See also AAYA 7; CA 81-84; CANR 33; CDALB 1929-1941; DLB 9, 11, 44, 102; DLBD 2; DLBY 86, 97; MTCW 1
Fauset, Jessie Redmon 1884(?)-1961 **CLC 19, 54; BLC 2; DAM MULT**
See also BW 1; CA 109; DLB 51

Faust, Frederick (Schiller) 1892-1944(?)
TCLC 49; DAM POP
See also CA 108; 152

Faust, Irvin 1924- CLC 8
See also CA 33-36R; CANR 28, 67; DLB 2,
28; DLBY 80

Fawkes, Guy
See Benchley, Robert (Charles)

Fearing, Kenneth (Flexner) 1902-1961 CLC
51
See also CA 93-96; CANR 59; DLB 9

Fecamps, Elise
See Creasey, John

Federman, Raymond 1928- CLC 6, 47
See also CA 17-20R; CAAS 8; CANR 10, 43;
DLBY 80

Federspiel, J(uerg) F. 1931- CLC 42
See also CA 146

Feiffer, Jules (Ralph) 1929- CLC 2, 8, 64;
DAM DRAM
See also AAYA 3; CA 17-20R; CANR 30, 59;
DLB 7, 44; INT CANR-30; MTCW 1; SATA
8, 61

Feige, Hermann Albert Otto Maximilian
See Traven, B.

Feinberg, David B. 1956-1994 CLC 59
See also CA 135; 147

Feinstein, Elaine 1930- CLC 36
See also CA 69-72; CAAS 1; CANR 31, 68;
DLB 14, 40; MTCW 1

Feldman, Irving (Mordecai) 1928- CLC 7
See also CA 1-4R; CANR 1; DLB 169

Felix-Tchicaya, Gerald
See Tchicaya, Gerald Felix

Fellini, Federico 1920-1993 CLC 16, 85
See also CA 65-68; 143; CANR 33

Felsen, Henry Gregor 1916- CLC 17
See also CA 1-4R; CANR 1; SAAS 2; SATA 1

Fenno, Jack
See Calisher, Hortense

Fenton, James Martin 1949- CLC 32
See also CA 102; DLB 40

Ferber, Edna 1887-1968 CLC 18, 93
See also AITN 1; CA 5-8R; 25-28R; CANR 68;
DLB 9, 28, 86; MTCW 1; SATA 7

Ferguson, Helen
See Kavan, Anna

Ferguson, Samuel 1810-1886 NCLC 33
See also DLB 32

Fergusson, Robert 1750-1774 LC 29
See also DLB 109

Ferling, Lawrence
See Ferlinghetti, Lawrence (Monsanto)

Ferlinghetti, Lawrence (Monsanto) 1919(?)-
CLC 2, 6, 10, 27, 111; DAM POET; PC 1
See also CA 5-8R; CANR 3, 41, 73; CDALB
1941-1968; DLB 5, 16; MTCW 1

Fernandez, Vicente Garcia Huidobro
See Huidobro Fernandez, Vicente Garcia

Ferrer, Gabriel (Francisco Victor) Miro
See Miro (Ferrer), Gabriel (Francisco Victor)

Ferrier, Susan (Edmonstone) 1782-1854
NCLC 8
See also DLB 116

Ferrigno, Robert 1948(?)- CLC 65
See also CA 140

Ferron, Jacques 1921-1985 CLC 94; DAC
See also CA 117; 129; DLB 60

Feuchtwanger, Lion 1884-1958 TCLC 3
See also CA 104; DLB 66

Feuillet, Octave 1821-1890 NCLC 45
See also DLB 192

Feydeau, Georges (Leon Jules Marie) 1862-
1921 TCLC 22; DAM DRAM
See also CA 113; 152; DLB 192

Fichte, Johann Gottlieb 1762-1814 NCLC 62
See also DLB 90

Ficino, Marsilio 1433-1499 LC 12

Fiedeler, Hans
See Doeblin, Alfred

Fiedler, Leslie A(aron) 1917- CLC 4, 13, 24
See also CA 9-12R; CANR 7, 63; DLB 28, 67;
MTCW 1

Field, Andrew 1938- CLC 44
See also CA 97-100; CANR 25

Field, Eugene 1850-1895 NCLC 3
See also DLB 23, 42, 140; DLBD 13; MAICYA;
SATA 16

Field, Gans T.
See Wellman, Manly Wade

Field, Michael 1915-1971 TCLC 43
See also CA 29-32R

Field, Peter
See Hobson, Laura Z(ametkin)

Fielding, Henry 1707-1754 LC 1, 46; DA;
DAB; DAC; DAM DRAM, MST, NOV;
WLC
See also CDBLB 1660-1789; DLB 39, 84, 101

Fielding, Sarah 1710-1768 LC 1, 44
See also DLB 39

Fields, W. C. 1880-1946 TCLC 80
See also DLB 44

Fierstein, Harvey (Forbes) 1954- CLC 33;
DAM DRAM, POP
See also CA 123; 129

Figes, Eva 1932- CLC 31
See also CA 53-56; CANR 4, 44; DLB 14

Finch, Anne 1661-1720 LC 3; PC 21
See also DLB 95

Finch, Robert (Duer Claydon) 1900- CLC 18
See also CA 57-60; CANR 9, 24, 49; DLB 88

Findley, Timothy 1930- CLC 27, 102; DAC;
DAM MST
See also CA 25-28R; CANR 12, 42, 69; DLB
53

Fink, William
See Mencken, H(enry) L(ouis)

Firbank, Louis 1942-
See Reed, Lou
See also CA 117

Firbank, (Arthur Annesley) Ronald 1886-1926
TCLC 1
See also CA 104; DLB 36

Fisher, Dorothy (Frances) Canfield 1879-1958
TCLC 87
See also CA 114; 136; DLB 9, 102; MAICYA;
YABC 1

Fisher, M(ary) F(rances) K(ennedy) 1908-1992
CLC 76, 87
See also CA 77-80; 138; CANR 44

Fisher, Roy 1930- CLC 25
See also CA 81-84; CAAS 10; CANR 16; DLB
40

Fisher, Rudolph 1897-1934 TCLC 11; BLC 2;
DAM MULT; SSC 25
See also BW 1; CA 107; 124; DLB 51, 102

Fisher, Vardis (Alvero) 1895-1968 CLC 7
See also CA 5-8R; 25-28R; CANR 68; DLB 9

Fiske, Tarleton
See Bloch, Robert (Albert)

Fitch, Clarke
See Sinclair, Upton (Beall)

Fitch, John IV
See Cormier, Robert (Edmund)

Fitzgerald, Captain Hugh
See Baum, L(yman) Frank

FitzGerald, Edward 1809-1883 NCLC 9
See also DLB 32

Fitzgerald, F(rancis) Scott (Key) 1896-1940
TCLC 1, 6, 14, 28, 55; DA; DAB; DAC;
DAM MST, NOV; SSC 6, 31; WLC
See also AAYA 24; AITN 1; CA 110; 123;
CDALB 1917-1929; DLB 4, 9, 86; DLBD 1,
15, 16; DLBY 81, 96; MTCW 1

Fitzgerald, Penelope 1916- CLC 19, 51, 61
See also CA 85-88; CAAS 10; CANR 56; DLB
14, 194

Fitzgerald, Robert (Stuart) 1910-1985 CLC 39
See also CA 1-4R; 114; CANR 1; DLBY 80

FitzGerald, Robert D(avid) 1902-1987 CLC 19
See also CA 17-20R

Fitzgerald, Zelda (Sayre) 1900-1948 TCLC 52
See also CA 117; 126; DLBY 84

Flanagan, Thomas (James Bonner) 1923-
CLC 25, 52
See also CA 108; CANR 55; DLBY 80; INT
108; MTCW 1

Flaubert, Gustave 1821-1880 NCLC 2, 10, 19,
62, 66; DA; DAB; DAC; DAM MST, NOV;
SSC 11; WLC
See also DLB 119

Flecker, Herman Elroy
See Flecker, (Herman) James Elroy

Flecker, (Herman) James Elroy 1884-1915
TCLC 43
See also CA 109; 150; DLB 10, 19

Fleming, Ian (Lancaster) 1908-1964 CLC 3,
30; DAM POP
See also AAYA 26; CA 5-8R; CANR 59;
CDBLB 1945-1960; DLB 87, 201; MTCW
1; SATA 9

Fleming, Thomas (James) 1927- CLC 37
See also CA 5-8R; CANR 10; INT CANR-10;
SATA 8

Fletcher, John 1579-1625 LC 33; DC 6
See also CDBLB Before 1660; DLB 58

Fletcher, John Gould 1886-1950 TCLC 35
See also CA 107; 167; DLB 4, 45

Fleur, Paul
See Pohl, Frederik

Flooglebuckle, Al
See Spiegelman, Art

Flying Officer X
See Bates, H(erbert) E(rnest)

Fo, Dario 1926- CLC 32, 109; DAM DRAM
See also CA 116; 128; CANR 68; DLBY 97;
MTCW 1

Fogarty, Jonathan Titulescu Esq.
See Farrell, James T(homas)

Folke, Will
See Bloch, Robert (Albert)

Follett, Ken(neth Martin) 1949- CLC 18;
DAM NOV, POP
See also AAYA 6; BEST 89:4; CA 81-84; CANR
13, 33, 54; DLB 87; DLBY 81; INT CANR-
33; MTCW 1

Fontane, Theodor 1819-1898 NCLC 26
See also DLB 129

Foote, Horton 1916- CLC 51, 91; DAM DRAM
See also CA 73-76; CANR 34, 51; DLB 26; INT
CANR-34

Foote, Shelby 1916- CLC 75; DAM NOV, POP
See also CA 5-8R; CANR 3, 45, 74; DLB 2, 17

Forbes, Esther 1891-1967 CLC 12
See also AAYA 17; CA 13-14; 25-28R; CAP 1;
CLR 27; DLB 22; JRDA; MAICYA; SATA
2, 100

Forche, Carolyn (Louise) 1950- CLC 25, 83,
86; DAM POET; PC 10

Ford, Elbur
  See Hibbert, Eleanor Alice Burford
Ford, Ford Madox 1873-1939**TCLC 1, 15, 39, 57; DAM NOV**
  See also CA 104; 132; CANR 74; CDBLB 1914-1945; DLB 162; MTCW 1
Ford, Henry 1863-1947   **TCLC 73**
  See also CA 115; 148
Ford, John 1586-(?)   **DC 8**
  See also CDBLB Before 1660; DAM DRAM; DLB 58
Ford, John 1895-1973   **CLC 16**
  See also CA 45-48
Ford, Richard 1944-   **CLC 46, 99**
  See also CA 69-72; CANR 11, 47
Ford, Webster
  See Masters, Edgar Lee
Foreman, Richard 1937-   **CLC 50**
  See also CA 65-68; CANR 32, 63
Forester, C(ecil) S(cott) 1899-1966   **CLC 35**
  See also CA 73-76; 25-28R; DLB 191; SATA 13
Forez
  See Mauriac, Francois (Charles)
Forman, James Douglas 1932-   **CLC 21**
  See also AAYA 17; CA 9-12R; CANR 4, 19, 42; JRDA; MAICYA; SATA 8, 70
Fornes, Maria Irene 1930-   **CLC 39, 61**
  See also CA 25-28R; CANR 28; DLB 7; HW; INT CANR-28; MTCW 1
Forrest, Leon (Richard) 1937-1997   **CLC 4; BLCS**
  See also BW 2; CA 89-92; 162; CAAS 7; CANR 25, 52; DLB 33
Forster, E(dward) M(organ) 1879-1970 **C L C 1, 2, 3, 4, 9, 10, 13, 15, 22, 45, 77; DA; DAB; DAC; DAM MST, NOV; SSC 27; WLC**
  See also AAYA 2; CA 13-14; 25-28R; CANR 45; CAP 1; CDBLB 1914-1945; DLB 34, 98, 162, 178, 195; DLBD 10; MTCW 1; SATA 57
Forster, John 1812-1876   **NCLC 11**
  See also DLB 144, 184
Forsyth, Frederick 1938- **CLC 2, 5, 36; DAM NOV, POP**
  See also BEST 89:4; CA 85-88; CANR 38, 62; DLB 87; MTCW 1
Forten, Charlotte L.   **TCLC 16; BLC 2**
  See also Grimke, Charlotte L(ottie) Forten
  See also DLB 50
Foscolo, Ugo 1778-1827   **NCLC 8**
Fosse, Bob   **CLC 20**
  See also Fosse, Robert Louis
Fosse, Robert Louis 1927-1987
  See Fosse, Bob
  See also CA 110; 123
Foster, Stephen Collins 1826-1864 **NCLC 26**
Foucault, Michel 1926-1984   **CLC 31, 34, 69**
  See also CA 105; 113; CANR 34; MTCW 1
Fouque, Friedrich (Heinrich Karl) de la Motte
  1777-1843   **NCLC 2**
  See also DLB 90
Fourier, Charles 1772-1837   **NCLC 51**
Fournier, Henri Alban 1886-1914
  See Alain-Fournier
  See also CA 104
Fournier, Pierre 1916-   **CLC 11**
  See also Gascar, Pierre
  See also CA 89-92; CANR 16, 40
Fowles, John (Philip) 1926- **CLC 1, 2, 3, 4, 6, 9, 10, 15, 33, 87; DAB; DAC; DAM MST**

See also CA 109; 117; CANR 50, 74; DLB 5, 193; INT 117
  to Present; DLB 14, 139; MTCW 1; SATA 22
Fox, Paula 1923-   **CLC 2, 8**
  See also AAYA 3; CA 73-76; CANR 20, 36, 62; CLR 1, 44; DLB 52; JRDA; MAICYA; MTCW 1; SATA 17, 60
Fox, William Price (Jr.) 1926-   **CLC 22**
  See also CA 17-20R; CAAS 19; CANR 11; DLB 2; DLBY 81
Foxe, John 1516(?)-1587   **LC 14**
  See also DLB 132
Frame, Janet 1924-**CLC 2, 3, 6, 22, 66, 96; SSC 29**
  See also Clutha, Janet Paterson Frame
France, Anatole   **TCLC 9**
  See also Thibault, Jacques Anatole Francois
  See also DLB 123
Francis, Claude 19(?)-   **CLC 50**
Francis, Dick 1920-**CLC 2, 22, 42, 102; DAM POP**
  See also AAYA 5, 21; BEST 89:3; CA 5-8R; CANR 9, 42, 68; CDBLB 1960 to Present; DLB 87; INT CANR-9; MTCW 1
Francis, Robert (Churchill) 1901-1987 **C L C 15**
  See also CA 1-4R; 123; CANR 1
Frank, Anne(lies Marie) 1929-1945**TCLC 17; DA; DAB; DAC; DAM MST; WLC**
  See also AAYA 12; CA 113; 133; CANR 68; MTCW 1; SATA 87; SATA-Brief 42
Frank, Bruno 1887-1945   **TCLC 81**
  See also DLB 118
Frank, Elizabeth 1945-   **CLC 39**
  See also CA 121; 126; INT 126
Frankl, Viktor E(mil) 1905-1997   **CLC 93**
  See also CA 65-68; 161
Franklin, Benjamin
  See Hasek, Jaroslav (Matej Frantisek)
Franklin, Benjamin 1706-1790 **LC 25; DA; DAB; DAC; DAM MST; WLCS**
  See also CDALB 1640-1865; DLB 24, 43, 73
Franklin, (Stella Maria Sarah) Miles (Lampe)
  1879-1954   **TCLC 7**
  See also CA 104; 164
Fraser, (Lady) Antonia (Pakenham) 1932-
CLC 32, 107
  See also CA 85-88; CANR 44, 65; MTCW 1; SATA-Brief 32
Fraser, George MacDonald 1925-   **CLC 7**
  See also CA 45-48; CANR 2, 48, 74
Fraser, Sylvia 1935-   **CLC 64**
  See also CA 45-48; CANR 1, 16, 60
Frayn, Michael 1933-**CLC 3, 7, 31, 47; DAM DRAM, NOV**
  See also CA 5-8R; CANR 30, 69; DLB 13, 14, 194; MTCW 1
Fraze, Candida (Merrill) 1945-   **CLC 50**
  See also CA 126
Frazer, J(ames) G(eorge) 1854-1941**TCLC 32**
  See also CA 118
Frazer, Robert Caine
  See Creasey, John
Frazer, Sir James George
  See Frazer, J(ames) G(eorge)
Frazier, Charles 1950-   **CLC 109**
  See also CA 161
Frazier, Ian 1951-   **CLC 46**
  See also CA 130; CANR 54
Frederic, Harold 1856-1898   **NCLC 10**
  See also DLB 12, 23; DLBD 13
Frederick, John
  See Faust, Frederick (Schiller)

Frederick the Great 1712-1786   **LC 14**
Fredro, Aleksander 1793-1876   **NCLC 8**
Freeling, Nicolas 1927-   **CLC 38**
  See also CA 49-52; CAAS 12; CANR 1, 17, 50; DLB 87
Freeman, Douglas Southall 1886-1953 **T C L C 11**
  See also CA 109; DLB 17; DLBD 17
Freeman, Judith 1946-   **CLC 55**
  See also CA 148
Freeman, Mary Eleanor Wilkins 1852-1930
  TCLC 9; SSC 1
  See also CA 106; DLB 12, 78
Freeman, R(ichard) Austin 1862-1943 **T C L C 21**
  See also CA 113; DLB 70
French, Albert 1943-   **CLC 86**
  See also CA 167
French, Marilyn 1929-**CLC 10, 18, 60; DAM DRAM, NOV, POP**
  See also CA 69-72; CANR 3, 31; INT CANR-31; MTCW 1
French, Paul
  See Asimov, Isaac
Freneau, Philip Morin 1752-1832   **NCLC 1**
  See also DLB 37, 43
Freud, Sigmund 1856-1939   **TCLC 52**
  See also CA 115; 133; CANR 69; MTCW 1
Friedan, Betty (Naomi) 1921-   **CLC 74**
  See also CA 65-68; CANR 18, 45, 74; MTCW 1
Friedlander, Saul 1932-   **CLC 90**
  See also CA 117; 130; CANR 72
Friedman, B(ernard) H(arper) 1926- **CLC 7**
  See also CA 1-4R; CANR 3, 48
Friedman, Bruce Jay 1930-   **CLC 3, 5, 56**
  See also CA 9-12R; CANR 25, 52; DLB 2, 28; INT CANR-25
Friel, Brian 1929-   **CLC 5, 42, 59, 115; DC 8**
  See also CA 21-24R; CANR 33, 69; DLB 13; MTCW 1
Friis-Baastad, Babbis Ellinor 1921-1970**C L C 12**
  See also CA 17-20R; 134; SATA 7
Frisch, Max (Rudolf) 1911-1991**CLC 3, 9, 14, 18, 32, 44; DAM DRAM, NOV**
  See also CA 85-88; 134; CANR 32, 74; DLB 69, 124; MTCW 1
Fromentin, Eugene (Samuel Auguste) 1820-1876   **NCLC 10**
  See also DLB 123
Frost, Frederick
  See Faust, Frederick (Schiller)
Frost, Robert (Lee) 1874-1963**CLC 1, 3, 4, 9, 10, 13, 15, 26, 34, 44; DA; DAB; DAC; DAM MST, POET; PC 1; WLC**
  See also AAYA 21; CA 89-92; CANR 33; CDALB 1917-1929; DLB 54; DLBD 7; MTCW 1; SATA 14
Froude, James Anthony 1818-1894 **NCLC 43**
  See also DLB 18, 57, 144
Froy, Herald
  See Waterhouse, Keith (Spencer)
Fry, Christopher 1907- **CLC 2, 10, 14; DAM DRAM**
  See also CA 17-20R; CAAS 23; CANR 9, 30, 74; DLB 13; MTCW 1; SATA 66
Frye, (Herman) Northrop 1912-1991**CLC 24, 70**
  See also CA 5-8R; 133; CANR 8, 37; DLB 67, 68; MTCW 1
Fuchs, Daniel 1909-1993   **CLC 8, 22**
  See also CA 81-84; 142; CAAS 5; CANR 40;

DLB 9, 26, 28; DLBY 93

Fuchs, Daniel 1934-   **CLC 34**
See also CA 37-40R; CANR 14, 48

Fuentes, Carlos 1928-**CLC 3, 8, 10, 13, 22, 41, 60, 113; DA; DAB; DAC; DAM MST, MULT, NOV; HLC; SSC 24; WLC**
See also AAYA 4; AITN 2; CA 69-72; CANR 10, 32, 68; DLB 113; HW; MTCW 1

Fuentes, Gregorio Lopez y
See Lopez y Fuentes, Gregorio

Fugard, (Harold) Athol 1932-**CLC 5, 9, 14, 25, 40, 80; DAM DRAM; DC 3**
See also AAYA 17; CA 85-88; CANR 32, 54; MTCW 1

Fugard, Sheila 1932-   **CLC 48**
See also CA 125

Fuller, Charles (H., Jr.) 1939-**CLC 25; BLC 2; DAM DRAM, MULT; DC 1**
See also BW 2; CA 108; 112; DLB 38; INT 112; MTCW 1

Fuller, John (Leopold) 1937-   **CLC 62**
See also CA 21-24R; CANR 9, 44; DLB 40

Fuller, Margaret   **NCLC 5, 50**
See also Ossoli, Sarah Margaret (Fuller marchesa d')

Fuller, Roy (Broadbent) 1912-1991**CLC 4, 28**
See also CA 5-8R; 135; CAAS 10; CANR 53; DLB 15, 20; SATA 87

Fulton, Alice 1952-   **CLC 52**
See also CA 116; CANR 57; DLB 193

Furphy, Joseph 1843-1912   **TCLC 25**
See also CA 163

Fussell, Paul 1924-   **CLC 74**
See also BEST 90:1; CA 17-20R; CANR 8, 21, 35, 69; INT CANR-21; MTCW 1

Futabatei, Shimei 1864-1909   **TCLC 44**
See also CA 162; DLB 180

Futrelle, Jacques 1875-1912   **TCLC 19**
See also CA 113; 155

Gaboriau, Emile 1835-1873   **NCLC 14**

Gadda, Carlo Emilio 1893-1973   **CLC 11**
See also CA 89-92; DLB 177

Gaddis, William 1922- **CLC 1, 3, 6, 8, 10, 19, 43, 86**
See also CA 17-20R; CANR 21, 48; DLB 2; MTCW 1

Gage, Walter
See Inge, William (Motter)

Gaines, Ernest J(ames) 1933- **CLC 3, 11, 18, 86; BLC 2; DAM MULT**
See also AAYA 18; AITN 1; BW 2; CA 9-12R; CANR 6, 24, 42; CDALB 1968-1988; DLB 2, 33, 152; DLBY 80; MTCW 1; SATA 86

Gaitskill, Mary 1954-   **CLC 69**
See also CA 128; CANR 61

Galdos, Benito Perez
See Perez Galdos, Benito

Gale, Zona 1874-1938**TCLC 7; DAM DRAM**
See also CA 105; 153; DLB 9, 78

Galeano, Eduardo (Hughes) 1940-   **CLC 72**
See also CA 29-32R; CANR 13, 32; HW

Galiano, Juan Valera y Alcala
See Valera y Alcala-Galiano, Juan

Galilei, Galileo 1546-1642   **LC 45**

Gallagher, Tess 1943-   **CLC 18, 63; DAM POET; PC 9**
See also CA 106; DLB 120

Gallant, Mavis 1922-   **CLC 7, 18, 38; DAC; DAM MST; SSC 5**
See also CA 69-72; CANR 29, 69; DLB 53; MTCW 1

Gallant, Roy A(rthur) 1924-   **CLC 17**
See also CA 5-8R; CANR 4, 29, 54; CLR 30;

MAICYA; SATA 4, 68

Gallico, Paul (William) 1897-1976   **CLC 2**
See also AITN 1; CA 5-8R; 69-72; CANR 23; DLB 9, 171; MAICYA; SATA 13

Gallo, Max Louis 1932-   **CLC 95**
See also CA 85-88

Gallois, Lucien
See Desnos, Robert

Gallup, Ralph
See Whitemore, Hugh (John)

Galsworthy, John 1867-1933**TCLC 1, 45; DA; DAB; DAC; DAM DRAM, MST, NOV; SSC 22; WLC 2**
See also CA 104; 141; CDBLB 1890-1914; DLB 10, 34, 98, 162; DLBD 16

Galt, John 1779-1839   **NCLC 1**
See also DLB 99, 116, 159

Galvin, James 1951-   **CLC 38**
See also CA 108; CANR 26

Gamboa, Federico 1864-1939   **TCLC 36**
See also CA 167

Gandhi, M. K.
See Gandhi, Mohandas Karamchand

Gandhi, Mahatma
See Gandhi, Mohandas Karamchand

Gandhi, Mohandas Karamchand 1869-1948
    TCLC 59; DAM MULT
See also CA 121; 132; MTCW 1

Gann, Ernest Kellogg 1910-1991   **CLC 23**
See also AITN 1; CA 1-4R; 136; CANR 1

Garcia, Cristina 1958-   **CLC 76**
See also CA 141; CANR 73

Garcia Lorca, Federico 1898-1936**TCLC 1, 7, 49; DA; DAB; DAC; DAM DRAM, MST, MULT, POET; DC 2; HLC; PC 3; WLC**
See also CA 104; 131; DLB 108; HW; MTCW 1

Garcia Marquez, Gabriel (Jose) 1928-**CLC 2, 3, 8, 10, 15, 27, 47, 55, 68; DA; DAB; DAC; DAM MST, MULT, NOV, POP; HLC; SSC 8; WLC**
See also AAYA 3; BEST 89:1, 90:4; CA 33-36R; CANR 10, 28, 50; DLB 113; HW; MTCW 1

Gard, Janice
See Latham, Jean Lee

Gard, Roger Martin du
See Martin du Gard, Roger

Gardam, Jane 1928-   **CLC 43**
See also CA 49-52; CANR 2, 18, 33, 54; CLR 12; DLB 14, 161; MAICYA; MTCW 1; SAAS 9; SATA 39, 76; SATA-Brief 28

Gardner, Herb(ert) 1934-   **CLC 44**
See also CA 149

Gardner, John (Champlin), Jr. 1933-1982
    CLC 2, 3, 5, 7, 8, 10, 18, 28, 34; DAM NOV, POP; SSC 7
See also AITN 1; CA 65-68; 107; CANR 33, 73; DLB 2; DLBY 82; MTCW 1; SATA 40; SATA-Obit 31

Gardner, John (Edmund) 1926-**CLC 30; DAM POP**
See also CA 103; CANR 15, 69; MTCW 1

Gardner, Miriam
See Bradley, Marion Zimmer

Gardner, Noel
See Kuttner, Henry

Gardons, S. S.
See Snodgrass, W(illiam) D(e Witt)

Garfield, Leon 1921-1996   **CLC 12**
See also AAYA 8; CA 17-20R; 152; CANR 38, 41; CLR 21; DLB 161; JRDA; MAICYA; SATA 1, 32, 76; SATA-Obit 90

Garland, (Hannibal) Hamlin 1860-1940
    TCLC 3; SSC 18
See also CA 104; DLB 12, 71, 78, 186

Garneau, (Hector de) Saint-Denys 1912-1943
    TCLC 13
See also CA 111; DLB 88

Garner, Alan 1934-**CLC 17; DAB; DAM POP**
See also AAYA 18; CA 73-76; CANR 15, 64; CLR 20; DLB 161; MAICYA; MTCW 1; SATA 18, 69

Garner, Hugh 1913-1979   **CLC 13**
See also CA 69-72; CANR 31; DLB 68

Garnett, David 1892-1981   **CLC 3**
See also CA 5-8R; 103; CANR 17; DLB 34

Garos, Stephanie
See Katz, Steve

Garrett, George (Palmer) 1929-**CLC 3, 11, 51; SSC 30**
See also CA 1-4R; CAAS 5; CANR 1, 42, 67; DLB 2, 5, 130, 152; DLBY 83

Garrick, David 1717-1779   **LC 15; DAM DRAM**
See also DLB 84

Garrigue, Jean 1914-1972   **CLC 2, 8**
See also CA 5-8R; 37-40R; CANR 20

Garrison, Frederick
See Sinclair, Upton (Beall)

Garth, Will
See Hamilton, Edmond; Kuttner, Henry

Garvey, Marcus (Moziah, Jr.) 1887-1940
    TCLC 41; BLC 2; DAM MULT
See also BW 1; CA 120; 124

Gary, Romain   **CLC 25**
See also Kacew, Romain
See also DLB 83

Gascar, Pierre   **CLC 11**
See also Fournier, Pierre

Gascoyne, David (Emery) 1916-   **CLC 45**
See also CA 65-68; CANR 10, 28, 54; DLB 20; MTCW 1

Gaskell, Elizabeth Cleghorn 1810-1865**NCLC 70; DAB; DAM MST; SSC 25**
See also CDBLB 1832-1890; DLB 21, 144, 159

Gass, William H(oward) 1924-**CLC 1, 2, 8, 11, 15, 39; SSC 12**
See also CA 17-20R; CANR 30, 71; DLB 2; MTCW 1

Gasset, Jose Ortega y
See Ortega y Gasset, Jose

Gates, Henry Louis, Jr. 1950-**CLC 65; BLCS; DAM MULT**
See also BW 2; CA 109; CANR 25, 53; DLB 67

Gautier, Theophile 1811-1872   **NCLC 1, 59; DAM POET; PC 18; SSC 20**
See also DLB 119

Gawsworth, John
See Bates, H(erbert) E(rnest)

Gay, Oliver
See Gogarty, Oliver St. John

Gaye, Marvin (Penze) 1939-1984   **CLC 26**
See also CA 112

Gebler, Carlo (Ernest) 1954-   **CLC 39**
See also CA 119; 133

Gee, Maggie (Mary) 1948-   **CLC 57**
See also CA 130

Gee, Maurice (Gough) 1931-   **CLC 29**
See also CA 97-100; CANR 67; SATA 46, 101

Gelbart, Larry (Simon) 1923-   **CLC 21, 61**
See also CA 73-76; CANR 45

Gelber, Jack 1932-   **CLC 1, 6, 14, 79**
See also CA 1-4R; CANR 2; DLB 7

Gellhorn, Martha (Ellis) 1908-1998 **CLC 14,**

Goldberg, Anatol 1910-1982   **CLC 34**
  See also CA 131; 117
Goldemberg, Isaac 1945-   **CLC 52**
  See also CA 69-72; CAAS 12; CANR 11, 32;
  HW
Golding, William (Gerald) 1911-1993 **CLC 1,**
  2, 3, 8, 10, 17, 27, 58, 81; DA; DAB; DAC;
  DAM MST, NOV; WLC
  See also AAYA 5; CA 5-8R; 141; CANR 13,
  33, 54; CDBLB 1945-1960; DLB 15, 100;
  MTCW 1
Goldman, Emma 1869-1940   **TCLC 13**
  See also CA 110; 150
Goldman, Francisco 1954-   **CLC 76**
  See also CA 162
Goldman, William (W.) 1931-   **CLC 1, 48**
  See also CA 9-12R; CANR 29, 69; DLB 44
Goldmann, Lucien 1913-1970   **CLC 24**
  See also CA 25-28; CAP 2
Goldoni, Carlo 1707-1793 **LC 4; DAM DRAM**
Goldsberry, Steven 1949-   **CLC 34**
  See also CA 131
Goldsmith, Oliver 1728-1774   **LC 2, 48; DA;**
  DAB; DAC; DAM DRAM, MST, NOV,
  POET; DC 8; WLC
  See also CDBLB 1660-1789; DLB 39, 89, 104,
  109, 142; SATA 26
Goldsmith, Peter
  See Priestley, J(ohn) B(oynton)
Gombrowicz, Witold 1904-1969 **CLC 4, 7, 11,**
  49; DAM DRAM
  See also CA 19-20; 25-28R; CAP 2
Gomez de la Serna, Ramon 1888-1963 **CLC 9**
  See also CA 153; 116; HW
Goncharov, Ivan Alexandrovich 1812-1891
  NCLC 1, 63
Goncourt, Edmond (Louis Antoine Huot) de
  1822-1896   **NCLC 7**
  See also DLB 123
Goncourt, Jules (Alfred Huot) de 1830-1870
  NCLC 7
  See also DLB 123
Gontier, Fernande 19(?)-   **CLC 50**
Gonzalez Martinez, Enrique 1871-1952
  TCLC 72
  See also CA 166; HW
Goodman, Paul 1911-1972   **CLC 1, 2, 4, 7**
  See also CA 19-20; 37-40R; CANR 34; CAP 2;
  DLB 130; MTCW 1
Gordimer, Nadine 1923- **CLC 3, 5, 7, 10, 18, 33,**
  51, 70; DA; DAB; DAC; DAM MST, NOV;
  SSC 17; WLCS
  See also CA 5-8R; CANR 3, 28, 56; INT CANR-
  28; MTCW 1
Gordon, Adam Lindsay 1833-1870 **NCLC 21**
Gordon, Caroline 1895-1981 **CLC 6, 13, 29, 83;**
  SSC 15
  See also CA 11-12; 103; CANR 36; CAP 1;
  DLB 4, 9, 102; DLBD 17; DLBY 81; MTCW
  1
Gordon, Charles William 1860-1937
  See Connor, Ralph
  See also CA 109
Gordon, Mary (Catherine) 1949- **CLC 13, 22**
  See also CA 102; CANR 44; DLB 6; DLBY
  81; INT 102; MTCW 1
Gordon, N. J.
  See Bosman, Herman Charles
Gordon, Sol 1923-   **CLC 26**
  See also CA 53-56; CANR 4; SATA 11
Gordone, Charles 1925-1995 **CLC 1, 4; DAM**
  DRAM; DC 8
  See also BW 1; CA 93-96; 150; CANR 55; DLB

7; INT 93-96; MTCW 1
Gore, Catherine 1800-1861   **NCLC 65**
  See also DLB 116
Gorenko, Anna Andreevna
  See Akhmatova, Anna
Gorky, Maxim 1868-1936 **TCLC 8; DAB; SSC**
  28; WLC
  See also Peshkov, Alexei Maximovich
Goryan, Sirak
  See Saroyan, William
Gosse, Edmund (William) 1849-1928 **TCLC 28**
  See also CA 117; DLB 57, 144, 184
Gotlieb, Phyllis Fay (Bloom) 1926-   **CLC 18**
  See also CA 13-16R; CANR 7; DLB 88
Gottesman, S. D.
  See Kornbluth, C(yril) M.; Pohl, Frederik
Gottfried von Strassburg fl. c. 1210- **CMLC**
  10
  See also DLB 138
Gould, Lois   **CLC 4, 10**
  See also CA 77-80; CANR 29; MTCW 1
Gourmont, Remy (-Marie-Charles) de 1858-
  1915   **TCLC 17**
  See also CA 109; 150
Govier, Katherine 1948-   **CLC 51**
  See also CA 101; CANR 18, 40
Goyen, (Charles) William 1915-1983 **CLC 5, 8,**
  14, 40
  See also AITN 2; CA 5-8R; 110; CANR 6, 71;
  DLB 2; DLBY 83; INT CANR-6
Goytisolo, Juan 1931-   **CLC 5, 10, 23; DAM**
  MULT; HLC
  See also CA 85-88; CANR 32, 61; HW; MTCW
  1
Gozzano, Guido 1883-1916   **PC 10**
  See also CA 154; DLB 114
Gozzi, (Conte) Carlo 1720-1806   **NCLC 23**
Grabbe, Christian Dietrich 1801-1836 **NCLC**
  2
  See also DLB 133
Grace, Patricia 1937-   **CLC 56**
Gracian y Morales, Baltasar 1601-1658 **LC 15**
Gracq, Julien   **CLC 11, 48**
  See also Poirier, Louis
  See also DLB 83
Grade, Chaim 1910-1982   **CLC 10**
  See also CA 93-96; 107
Graduate of Oxford, A
  See Ruskin, John
Grafton, Garth
  See Duncan, Sara Jeannette
Graham, John
  See Phillips, David Graham
Graham, Jorie 1951-   **CLC 48**
  See also CA 111; CANR 63; DLB 120
Graham, R(obert) B(ontine) Cunninghame
  See Cunninghame Graham, R(obert) B(ontine)
  See also DLB 98, 135, 174
Graham, Robert
  See Haldeman, Joe (William)
Graham, Tom
  See Lewis, (Harry) Sinclair
Graham, W(illiam) S(ydney) 1918-1986 **CLC**
  29
  See also CA 73-76; 118; DLB 20
Graham, Winston (Mawdsley) 1910- **CLC 23**
  See also CA 49-52; CANR 2, 22, 45, 66; DLB
  77
Grahame, Kenneth 1859-1932 **TCLC 64; DAB**
  See also CA 108; 136; CLR 5; DLB 34, 141,
  178; MAICYA; SATA 100; YABC 1
Grant, Skeeter
  See Spiegelman, Art

Granville-Barker, Harley 1877-1946 **TCLC 2;**
  DAM DRAM
  See also Barker, Harley Granville
  See also CA 104
Grass, Guenter (Wilhelm) 1927- **CLC 1, 2, 4, 6,**
  11, 15, 22, 32, 49, 88; DA; DAB; DAC;
  DAM MST, NOV; WLC
  See also CA 13-16R; CANR 20; DLB 75, 124;
  MTCW 1
Gratton, Thomas
  See Hulme, T(homas) E(rnest)
Grau, Shirley Ann 1929-   **CLC 4, 9; SSC 15**
  See also CA 89-92; CANR 22, 69; DLB 2; INT
  CANR-22; MTCW 1
Gravel, Fern
  See Hall, James Norman
Graver, Elizabeth 1964-   **CLC 70**
  See also CA 135; CANR 71
Graves, Richard Perceval 1945-   **CLC 44**
  See also CA 65-68; CANR 9, 26, 51
Graves, Robert (von Ranke) 1895-1985 **CLC**
  1, 2, 6, 11, 39, 44, 45; DAB; DAC; DAM
  MST, POET; PC 6
  See also CA 5-8R; 117; CANR 5, 36; CDBLB
  1914-1945; DLB 20, 100, 191; DLBD 18;
  DLBY 85; MTCW 1; SATA 45
Graves, Valerie
  See Bradley, Marion Zimmer
Gray, Alasdair (James) 1934-   **CLC 41**
  See also CA 126; CANR 47, 69; DLB 194; INT
  126; MTCW 1
Gray, Amlin 1946-   **CLC 29**
  See also CA 138
Gray, Francine du Plessix 1930-   **CLC 22;**
  DAM NOV
  See also BEST 90:3; CA 61-64; CAAS 2;
  CANR 11, 33; INT CANR-11; MTCW 1
Gray, John (Henry) 1866-1934   **TCLC 19**
  See also CA 119; 162
Gray, Simon (James Holliday) 1936- **CLC 9,**
  14, 36
  See also AITN 1; CA 21-24R; CAAS 3; CANR
  32, 69; DLB 13; MTCW 1
Gray, Spalding 1941- **CLC 49, 112; DAM POP;**
  DC 7
  See also CA 128; CANR 74
Gray, Thomas 1716-1771 **LC 4, 40; DA; DAB;**
  DAC; DAM MST; PC 2; WLC
  See also CDBLB 1660-1789; DLB 109
Grayson, David
  See Baker, Ray Stannard
Grayson, Richard (A.) 1951-   **CLC 38**
  See also CA 85-88; CANR 14, 31, 57
Greeley, Andrew M(oran) 1928-   **CLC 28;**
  DAM POP
  See also CA 5-8R; CAAS 7; CANR 7, 43, 69;
  MTCW 1
Green, Anna Katharine 1846-1935 **TCLC 63**
  See also CA 112; 159; DLB 202
Green, Brian
  See Card, Orson Scott
Green, Hannah
  See Greenberg, Joanne (Goldenberg)
Green, Hannah 1927(?)-1996   **CLC 3**
  See also CA 73-76; CANR 59
Green, Henry 1905-1973   **CLC 2, 13, 97**
  See also Yorke, Henry Vincent
  See also DLB 15
Green, Julian (Hartridge) 1900-1998
  See Green, Julien
  See also CA 21-24R; 169; CANR 33; DLB 4,
  72; MTCW 1
Green, Julien   **CLC 3, 11, 77**

See also Green, Julian (Hartridge)

Green, Paul (Eliot) 1894-1981 **CLC 25; DAM DRAM**
See also AITN 1; CA 5-8R; 103; CANR 3; DLB 7, 9; DLBY 81

Greenberg, Ivan 1908-1973
See Rahv, Philip
See also CA 85-88

Greenberg, Joanne (Goldenberg) 1932- **C L C 7, 30**
See also AAYA 12; CA 5-8R; CANR 14, 32, 69; SATA 25

Greenberg, Richard 1959(?)- **CLC 57**
See also CA 138

Greene, Bette 1934- **CLC 30**
See also AAYA 7; CA 53-56; CANR 4; CLR 2; JRDA; MAICYA; SAAS 16; SATA 8, 102

Greene, Gael **CLC 8**
See also CA 13-16R; CANR 10

Greene, Graham (Henry) 1904-1991 **CLC 1, 3, 6, 9, 14, 18, 27, 37, 70, 72; DA; DAB; DAC; DAM MST, NOV; SSC 29; WLC**
See also AITN 2; CA 13-16R; 133; CANR 35, 61; CDBLB 1945-1960; DLB 13, 15, 77, 100, 162, 201; DLBY 91; MTCW 1; SATA 20

Greene, Robert 1558-1592 **LC 41**
See also DLB 62, 167

Greer, Richard
See Silverberg, Robert

Gregor, Arthur 1923- **CLC 9**
See also CA 25-28R; CAAS 10; CANR 11; SATA 36

Gregor, Lee
See Pohl, Frederik

Gregory, Isabella Augusta (Persse) 1852-1932 **TCLC 1**
See also CA 104; DLB 10

Gregory, J. Dennis
See Williams, John A(lfred)

Grendon, Stephen
See Derleth, August (William)

Grenville, Kate 1950- **CLC 61**
See also CA 118; CANR 53

Grenville, Pelham
See Wodehouse, P(elham) G(renville)

Greve, Felix Paul (Berthold Friedrich) 1879-1948
See Grove, Frederick Philip
See also CA 104; 141; DAC; DAM MST

Grey, Zane 1872-1939 **TCLC 6; DAM POP**
See also CA 104; 132; DLB 9; MTCW 1

Grieg, (Johan) Nordahl (Brun) 1902-1943 **TCLC 10**
See also CA 107

Grieve, C(hristopher) M(urray) 1892-1978 **CLC 11, 19; DAM POET**
See also MacDiarmid, Hugh; Pteleon
See also CA 5-8R; 85-88; CANR 33; MTCW 1

Griffin, Gerald 1803-1840 **NCLC 7**
See also DLB 159

Griffin, John Howard 1920-1980 **CLC 68**
See also AITN 1; CA 1-4R; 101; CANR 2

Griffin, Peter 1942- **CLC 39**
See also CA 136

Griffith, D(avid Lewelyn) W(ark) 1875(?)-1948 **TCLC 68**
See also CA 119; 150

Griffith, Lawrence
See Griffith, D(avid Lewelyn) W(ark)

Griffiths, Trevor 1935- **CLC 13, 52**
See also CA 97-100; CANR 45; DLB 13

Griggs, Sutton Elbert 1872-1930(?) **TCLC 77**

See also CA 123; DLB 50

Grigson, Geoffrey (Edward Harvey) 1905-1985 **CLC 7, 39**
See also CA 25-28R; 118; CANR 20, 33; DLB 27; MTCW 1

Grillparzer, Franz 1791-1872 **NCLC 1**
See also DLB 133

Grimble, Reverend Charles James
See Eliot, T(homas) S(tearns)

Grimke, Charlotte L(ottie) Forten 1837(?)-1914
See Forten, Charlotte L.
See also BW 1; CA 117; 124; DAM MULT, POET

Grimm, Jacob Ludwig Karl 1785-1863 **NCLC 3**
See also DLB 90; MAICYA; SATA 22

Grimm, Wilhelm Karl 1786-1859 **NCLC 3**
See also DLB 90; MAICYA; SATA 22

Grimmelshausen, Johann Jakob Christoffel von 1621-1676 **LC 6**
See also DLB 168

Grindel, Eugene 1895-1952
See Eluard, Paul
See also CA 104

Grisham, John 1955- **CLC 84; DAM POP**
See also AAYA 14; CA 138; CANR 47, 69

Grossman, David 1954- **CLC 67**
See also CA 138

Grossman, Vasily (Semenovich) 1905-1964 **CLC 41**
See also CA 124; 130; MTCW 1

Grove, Frederick Philip **TCLC 4**
See also Greve, Felix Paul (Berthold Friedrich)
See also DLB 92

Grubb
See Crumb, R(obert)

Grumbach, Doris (Isaac) 1918- **CLC 13, 22, 64**
See also CA 5-8R; CAAS 2; CANR 9, 42, 70; INT CANR-9

Grundtvig, Nicolai Frederik Severin 1783-1872 **NCLC 1**

Grunge
See Crumb, R(obert)

Grunwald, Lisa 1959- **CLC 44**
See also CA 120

Guare, John 1938- **CLC 8, 14, 29, 67; DAM DRAM**
See also CA 73-76; CANR 21, 69; DLB 7; MTCW 1

Gudjonsson, Halldor Kiljan 1902-1998
See Laxness, Halldor
See also CA 103; 164

Guenter, Erich
See Eich, Guenter

Guest, Barbara 1920- **CLC 34**
See also CA 25-28R; CANR 11, 44; DLB 5, 193

Guest, Judith (Ann) 1936- **CLC 8, 30; DAM NOV, POP**
See also AAYA 7; CA 77-80; CANR 15; INT CANR-15; MTCW 1

Guevara, Che **CLC 87; HLC**
See also Guevara (Serna), Ernesto

Guevara (Serna), Ernesto 1928-1967
See Guevara, Che
See also CA 127; 111; CANR 56; DAM MULT; HW

Guild, Nicholas M. 1944- **CLC 33**
See also CA 93-96

Guillemin, Jacques
See Sartre, Jean-Paul

Guillen, Jorge 1893-1984 **CLC 11; DAM MULT, POET**

See also CA 89-92; 112; DLB 108; HW

Guillen, Nicolas (Cristobal) 1902-1989 **C L C 48, 79; BLC 2; DAM MST, MULT, POET; HLC; PC 23**
See also BW 2; CA 116; 125; 129; HW

Guillevic, (Eugene) 1907- **CLC 33**
See also CA 93-96

Guillois
See Desnos, Robert

Guillois, Valentin
See Desnos, Robert

Guiney, Louise Imogen 1861-1920 **TCLC 41**
See also CA 160; DLB 54

Guiraldes, Ricardo (Guillermo) 1886-1927 **TCLC 39**
See also CA 131; HW; MTCW 1

Gumilev, Nikolai (Stepanovich) 1886-1921 **TCLC 60**
See also CA 165

Gunesekera, Romesh 1954- **CLC 91**
See also CA 159

Gunn, Bill **CLC 5**
See also Gunn, William Harrison
See also DLB 38

Gunn, Thom(son William) 1929- **CLC 3, 6, 18, 32, 81; DAM POET**
See also CA 17-20R; CANR 9, 33; CDBLB 1960 to Present; DLB 27; INT CANR-33; MTCW 1

Gunn, William Harrison 1934(?)-1989
See Gunn, Bill
See also AITN 1; BW 1; CA 13-16R; 128; CANR 12, 25

Gunnars, Kristjana 1948- **CLC 69**
See also CA 113; DLB 60

Gurdjieff, G(eorgei) I(vanovich) 1877(?)-1949 **TCLC 71**
See also CA 157

Gurganus, Allan 1947- **CLC 70; DAM POP**
See also BEST 90:1; CA 135

Gurney, A(lbert) R(amsdell), Jr. 1930- **C L C 32, 50, 54; DAM DRAM**
See also CA 77-80; CANR 32, 64

Gurney, Ivor (Bertie) 1890-1937 **TCLC 33**
See also CA 167

Gurney, Peter
See Gurney, A(lbert) R(amsdell), Jr.

Guro, Elena 1877-1913 **TCLC 56**

Gustafson, James M(oody) 1925- **CLC 100**
See also CA 25-28R; CANR 37

Gustafson, Ralph (Barker) 1909- **CLC 36**
See also CA 21-24R; CANR 8, 45; DLB 88

Gut, Gom
See Simenon, Georges (Jacques Christian)

Guterson, David 1956- **CLC 91**
See also CA 132; CANR 73

Guthrie, A(lfred) B(ertram), Jr. 1901-1991 **CLC 23**
See also CA 57-60; 134; CANR 24; DLB 6; SATA 62; SATA-Obit 67

Guthrie, Isobel
See Grieve, C(hristopher) M(urray)

Guthrie, Woodrow Wilson 1912-1967
See Guthrie, Woody
See also CA 113; 93-96

Guthrie, Woody **CLC 35**
See also Guthrie, Woodrow Wilson

Guy, Rosa (Cuthbert) 1928- **CLC 26**
See also AAYA 4; BW 2; CA 17-20R; CANR 14, 34; CLR 13; DLB 33; JRDA; MAICYA; SATA 14, 62

Gwendolyn
See Bennett, (Enoch) Arnold

H. D. CLC 3, 8, 14, 31, 34, 73; PC 5
See also Doolittle, Hilda
H. de V.
See Buchan, John
Haavikko, Paavo Juhani 1931- CLC 18, 34
See also CA 106
Habbema, Koos
See Heijermans, Herman
Habermas, Juergen 1929- CLC 104
See also CA 109
Habermas, Jurgen
See Habermas, Juergen
Hacker, Marilyn 1942- CLC 5, 9, 23, 72, 91;
DAM POET
See also CA 77-80; CANR 68; DLB 120
Haeckel, Ernst Heinrich (Philipp August) 1834-
1919 TCLC 83
See also CA 157
Haggard, H(enry) Rider 1856-1925 TCLC 11
See also CA 108; 148; DLB 70, 156, 174, 178;
SATA 16
Hagiosy, L.
See Larbaud, Valery (Nicolas)
Hagiwara Sakutaro 1886-1942 TCLC 60; PC
18
Haig, Fenil
See Ford, Ford Madox
Haig-Brown, Roderick (Langmere) 1908-1976
CLC 21
See also CA 5-8R; 69-72; CANR 4, 38; CLR
31; DLB 88; MAICYA; SATA 12
Hailey, Arthur 1920- CLC 5; DAM NOV, POP
See also AITN 2; BEST 90:3; CA 1-4R; CANR
2, 36; DLB 88; DLBY 82; MTCW 1
Hailey, Elizabeth Forsythe 1938- CLC 40
See also CA 93-96; CAAS 1; CANR 15, 48;
INT CANR-15
Haines, John (Meade) 1924- CLC 58
See also CA 17-20R; CANR 13, 34; DLB 5
Hakluyt, Richard 1552-1616 LC 31
Haldeman, Joe (William) 1943- CLC 61
See also CA 53-56; CAAS 25; CANR 6, 70,
72; DLB 8; INT CANR-6
Haley, Alex(ander Murray Palmer) 1921-1992
CLC 8, 12, 76; BLC 2; DA; DAB; DAC;
DAM MST, MULT, POP
See also AAYA 26; BW 2; CA 77-80; 136;
CANR 61; DLB 38; MTCW 1
Haliburton, Thomas Chandler 1796-1865
NCLC 15
See also DLB 11, 99
Hall, Donald (Andrew, Jr.) 1928- CLC 1, 13,
37, 59; DAM POET
See also CA 5-8R; CAAS 7; CANR 2, 44, 64;
DLB 5; SATA 23, 97
Hall, Frederic Sauser
See Sauser-Hall, Frederic
Hall, James
See Kuttner, Henry
Hall, James Norman 1887-1951 TCLC 23
See also CA 123; SATA 21
Hall, Radclyffe
See Hall, (Marguerite) Radclyffe
Hall, (Marguerite) Radclyffe 1886-1943
TCLC 12
See also CA 110; 150; DLB 191
Hall, Rodney 1935- CLC 51
See also CA 109; CANR 69
Halleck, Fitz-Greene 1790-1867 NCLC 47
See also DLB 3
Halliday, Michael
See Creasey, John
Halpern, Daniel 1945- CLC 14

See also CA 33-36R
Hamburger, Michael (Peter Leopold) 1924-
CLC 5, 14
See also CA 5-8R; CAAS 4; CANR 2, 47; DLB
27
Hamill, Pete 1935- CLC 10
See also CA 25-28R; CANR 18, 71
Hamilton, Alexander 1755(?)-1804 NCLC 49
See also DLB 37
Hamilton, Clive
See Lewis, C(live) S(taples)
Hamilton, Edmond 1904-1977 CLC 1
See also CA 1-4R; CANR 3; DLB 8
Hamilton, Eugene (Jacob) Lee
See Lee-Hamilton, Eugene (Jacob)
Hamilton, Franklin
See Silverberg, Robert
Hamilton, Gail
See Corcoran, Barbara
Hamilton, Mollie
See Kaye, M(ary) M(argaret)
Hamilton, (Anthony Walter) Patrick 1904-1962
CLC 51
See also CA 113; DLB 10
Hamilton, Virginia 1936- CLC 26; DAM
MULT
See also AAYA 2, 21; BW 2; CA 25-28R;
CANR 20, 37, 73; CLR 1, 11, 40; DLB 33,
52; INT CANR-20; JRDA; MAICYA;
MTCW 1; SATA 4, 56, 79
Hammett, (Samuel) Dashiell 1894-1961 CLC
3, 5, 10, 19, 47; SSC 17
See also AITN 1; CA 81-84; CANR 42; CDALB
1929-1941; DLBD 6; DLBY 96; MTCW 1
Hammon, Jupiter 1711(?)-1800(?) NCLC 5;
BLC 2; DAM MULT, POET; PC 16
See also DLB 31, 50
Hammond, Keith
See Kuttner, Henry
Hamner, Earl (Henry), Jr. 1923- CLC 12
See also AITN 2; CA 73-76; DLB 6
Hampton, Christopher (James) 1946- CLC 4
See also CA 25-28R; DLB 13; MTCW 1
Hamsun, Knut TCLC 2, 14, 49
See also Pedersen, Knut
Handke, Peter 1942- CLC 5, 8, 10, 15, 38; DAM
DRAM, NOV
See also CA 77-80; CANR 33; DLB 85, 124;
MTCW 1
Hanley, James 1901-1985 CLC 3, 5, 8, 13
See also CA 73-76; 117; CANR 36; DLB 191;
MTCW 1
Hannah, Barry 1942- CLC 23, 38, 90
See also CA 108; 110; CANR 43, 68; DLB 6;
INT 110; MTCW 1
Hannon, Ezra
See Hunter, Evan
Hansberry, Lorraine (Vivian) 1930-1965 CLC
17, 62; BLC 2; DA; DAB; DAC; DAM
DRAM, MST, MULT; DC 2
See also AAYA 25; BW 1; CA 109; 25-28R;
CABS 3; CANR 58; CDALB 1941-1968;
DLB 7, 38; MTCW 1
Hansen, Joseph 1923- CLC 38
See also CA 29-32R; CAAS 17; CANR 16, 44,
66; INT CANR-16
Hansen, Martin A(lfred) 1909-1955 TCLC 32
See also CA 167
Hanson, Kenneth O(stlin) 1922- CLC 13
See also CA 53-56; CANR 7
Hardwick, Elizabeth (Bruce) 1916- CLC 13;
DAM NOV
See also CA 5-8R; CANR 3, 32, 70; DLB 6;

MTCW 1
Hardy, Thomas 1840-1928 TCLC 4, 10, 18, 32,
48, 53, 72; DA; DAB; DAC; DAM MST,
NOV, POET; PC 8; SSC 2; WLC
See also CA 104; 123; CDBLB 1890-1914;
DLB 18, 19, 135; MTCW 1
Hare, David 1947- CLC 29, 58
See also CA 97-100; CANR 39; DLB 13;
MTCW 1
Harewood, John
See Van Druten, John (William)
Harford, Henry
See Hudson, W(illiam) H(enry)
Hargrave, Leonie
See Disch, Thomas M(ichael)
Harjo, Joy 1951- CLC 83; DAM MULT
See also CA 114; CANR 35, 67; DLB 120, 175;
NNAL
Harlan, Louis R(udolph) 1922- CLC 34
See also CA 21-24R; CANR 25, 55
Harling, Robert 1951(?)- CLC 53
See also CA 147
Harmon, William (Ruth) 1938- CLC 38
See also CA 33-36R; CANR 14, 32, 35; SATA
65
Harper, F. E. W.
See Harper, Frances Ellen Watkins
Harper, Frances E. W.
See Harper, Frances Ellen Watkins
Harper, Frances E. Watkins
See Harper, Frances Ellen Watkins
Harper, Frances Ellen
See Harper, Frances Ellen Watkins
Harper, Frances Ellen Watkins 1825-1911
TCLC 14; BLC 2; DAM MULT, POET;
PC 21
See also BW 1; CA 111; 125; DLB 50
Harper, Michael S(teven) 1938- CLC 7, 22
See also BW 1; CA 33-36R; CANR 24; DLB
41
Harper, Mrs. F. E. W.
See Harper, Frances Ellen Watkins
Harris, Christie (Lucy) Irwin 1907- CLC 12
See also CA 5-8R; CANR 6; CLR 47; DLB 88;
JRDA; MAICYA; SAAS 10; SATA 6, 74
Harris, Frank 1856-1931 TCLC 24
See also CA 109; 150; DLB 156, 197
Harris, George Washington 1814-1869 NCLC
23
See also DLB 3, 11
Harris, Joel Chandler 1848-1908 TCLC 2;
SSC 19
See also CA 104; 137; CLR 49; DLB 11, 23,
42, 78, 91; MAICYA; SATA 100; YABC 1
Harris, John (Wyndham Parkes Lucas) Beynon
1903-1969
See Wyndham, John
See also CA 102; 89-92
Harris, MacDonald CLC 9
See also Heiney, Donald (William)
Harris, Mark 1922- CLC 19
See also CA 5-8R; CAAS 3; CANR 2, 55; DLB
2; DLBY 80
Harris, (Theodore) Wilson 1921- CLC 25
See also BW 2; CA 65-68; CAAS 16; CANR
11, 27, 69; DLB 117; MTCW 1
Harrison, Elizabeth Cavanna 1909-
See Cavanna, Betty
See also CA 9-12R; CANR 6, 27
Harrison, Harry (Max) 1925- CLC 42
See also CA 1-4R; CANR 5, 21; DLB 8; SATA
4
Harrison, James (Thomas) 1937- CLC 6, 14,

Henley, Beth   **CLC 23; DC 6**
See also Henley, Elizabeth Becker
See also CABS 3; DLBY 86

Henley, Elizabeth Becker 1952-
See Henley, Beth
See also CA 107; CANR 32, 73; DAM DRAM,
MST; MTCW 1

Henley, William Ernest 1849-1903   **TCLC 8**
See also CA 105; DLB 19

Hennissart, Martha
See Lathen, Emma
See also CA 85-88; CANR 64

Henry, O.   **TCLC 1, 19; SSC 5; WLC**
See also Porter, William Sydney

Henry, Patrick 1736-1799   **LC 25**

Henryson, Robert 1430(?)-1506(?)   **LC 20**
See also DLB 146

Henry VIII 1491-1547   **LC 10**

Henschke, Alfred
See Klabund

Hentoff, Nat(han Irving) 1925-   **CLC 26**
See also AAYA 4; CA 1-4R; CAAS 6; CANR
5, 25; CLR 1, 52; INT CANR-25; JRDA;
MAICYA; SATA 42, 69; SATA-Brief 27

Heppenstall, (John) Rayner 1911-1981 **C L C
10**
See also CA 1-4R; 103; CANR 29

Heraclitus c. 540B.C.-c. 450B.C.   **CMLC 22**
See also DLB 176

Herbert, Frank (Patrick) 1920-1986 **CLC 12,
23, 35, 44, 85; DAM POP**
See also AAYA 21; CA 53-56; 118; CANR 5,
43; DLB 8; INT CANR-5; MTCW 1; SATA
9, 37; SATA-Obit 47

Herbert, George 1593-1633   **LC 24; DAB;
DAM POET; PC 4**
See also CDBLB Before 1660; DLB 126

Herbert, Zbigniew 1924-1998   **CLC 9, 43;
DAM POET**
See also CA 89-92; 169; CANR 36, 74; MTCW
1

Herbst, Josephine (Frey) 1897-1969 **CLC 34**
See also CA 5-8R; 25-28R; DLB 9

Hergesheimer, Joseph 1880-1954   **TCLC 11**
See also CA 109; DLB 102, 9

Herlihy, James Leo 1927-1993   **CLC 6**
See also CA 1-4R; 143; CANR 2

Hermogenes fl. c. 175-   **CMLC 6**

Hernandez, Jose 1834-1886   **NCLC 17**

Herodotus c. 484B.C.-429B.C.   **CMLC 17**
See also DLB 176

Herrick, Robert 1591-1674 **LC 13; DA; DAB;
DAC; DAM MST, POP; PC 9**
See also DLB 126

Herring, Guilles
See Somerville, Edith

Herriot, James 1916-1995 **CLC 12; DAM POP**
See also Wight, James Alfred
See also AAYA 1; CA 148; CANR 40; SATA
86

Herrmann, Dorothy 1941-   **CLC 44**
See also CA 107

Herrmann, Taffy
See Herrmann, Dorothy

Hersey, John (Richard) 1914-1993 **CLC 1, 2, 7,
9, 40, 81, 97; DAM POP**
See also CA 17-20R; 140; CANR 33; DLB 6,
185; MTCW 1; SATA 25; SATA-Obit 76

Herzen, Aleksandr Ivanovich 1812-1870
NCLC 10, 61

Herzl, Theodor 1860-1904   **TCLC 36**
See also CA 168

Herzog, Werner 1942-   **CLC 16**

See also CA 89-92

Hesiod c. 8th cent. B.C.-   **CMLC 5**
See also DLB 176

Hesse, Hermann 1877-1962 **CLC 1, 2, 3, 6, 11,
17, 25, 69; DA; DAB; DAC; DAM MST,
NOV; SSC 9; WLC**
See also CA 17-18; CAP 2; DLB 66; MTCW 1;
SATA 50

Hewes, Cady
See De Voto, Bernard (Augustine)

Heyen, William 1940-   **CLC 13, 18**
See also CA 33-36R; CAAS 9; DLB 5

Heyerdahl, Thor 1914-   **CLC 26**
See also CA 5-8R; CANR 5, 22, 66, 73; MTCW
1; SATA 2, 52

Heym, Georg (Theodor Franz Arthur) 1887-
1912   **TCLC 9**
See also CA 106

Heym, Stefan 1913-   **CLC 41**
See also CA 9-12R; CANR 4; DLB 69

Heyse, Paul (Johann Ludwig von) 1830-1914
TCLC 8
See also CA 104; DLB 129

Heyward, (Edwin) DuBose 1885-1940 **T C L C
59**
See also CA 108; 157; DLB 7, 9, 45; SATA 21

Hibbert, Eleanor Alice Burford 1906-1993
CLC 7; DAM POP
See also BEST 90:4; CA 17-20R; 140; CANR
9, 28, 59; SATA 2; SATA-Obit 74

Hichens, Robert (Smythe) 1864-1950 **T C L C
64**
See also CA 162; DLB 153

Higgins, George V(incent) 1939- **CLC 4, 7, 10,
18**
See also CA 77-80; CAAS 5; CANR 17, 51;
DLB 2; DLBY 81; INT CANR-17; MTCW
1

Higginson, Thomas Wentworth 1823-1911
TCLC 36
See also CA 162; DLB 1, 64

Highet, Helen
See MacInnes, Helen (Clark)

Highsmith, (Mary) Patricia 1921-1995 **CLC 2,
4, 14, 42, 102; DAM NOV, POP**
See also CA 1-4R; 147; CANR 1, 20, 48, 62;
MTCW 1

Highwater, Jamake (Mamake) 1942(?)- **C L C
12**
See also AAYA 7; CA 65-68; CAAS 7; CANR
10, 34; CLR 17; DLB 52; DLBY 85; JRDA;
MAICYA; SATA 32, 69; SATA-Brief 30

Highway, Tomson 1951- **CLC 92; DAC; DAM
MULT**
See also CA 151; NNAL

Higuchi, Ichiyo 1872-1896   **NCLC 49**

Hijuelos, Oscar 1951- **CLC 65; DAM MULT,
POP; HLC**
See also AAYA 25; BEST 90:1; CA 123; CANR
50; DLB 145; HW

Hikmet, Nazim 1902(?)-1963   **CLC 40**
See also CA 141; 93-96

Hildegard von Bingen 1098-1179   **CMLC 20**
See also DLB 148

Hildesheimer, Wolfgang 1916-1991   **CLC 49**
See also CA 101; 135; DLB 69, 124

Hill, Geoffrey (William) 1932- **CLC 5, 8, 18,
45; DAM POET**
See also CA 81-84; CANR 21; CDBLB 1960
to Present; DLB 40; MTCW 1

Hill, George Roy 1921-   **CLC 26**
See also CA 110; 122

Hill, John

See Koontz, Dean R(ay)

Hill, Susan (Elizabeth) 1942-   **CLC 4, 113;
DAB; DAM MST, NOV**
See also CA 33-36R; CANR 29, 69; DLB 14,
139; MTCW 1

Hillerman, Tony 1925- **CLC 62; DAM POP**
See also AAYA 6; BEST 89:1; CA 29-32R;
CANR 21, 42, 65; SATA 6

Hillesum, Etty 1914-1943   **TCLC 49**
See also CA 137

Hilliard, Noel (Harvey) 1929-   **CLC 15**
See also CA 9-12R; CANR 7, 69

Hillis, Rick 1956-   **CLC 66**
See also CA 134

Hilton, James 1900-1954   **TCLC 21**
See also CA 108; 169; DLB 34, 77; SATA 34

Himes, Chester (Bomar) 1909-1984 **CLC 2, 4,
7, 18, 58, 108; BLC 2; DAM MULT**
See also BW 2; CA 25-28R; 114; CANR 22;
DLB 2, 76, 143; MTCW 1

Hinde, Thomas   **CLC 6, 11**
See also Chitty, Thomas Willes

Hindin, Nathan
See Bloch, Robert (Albert)

Hine, (William) Daryl 1936-   **CLC 15**
See also CA 1-4R; CAAS 15; CANR 1, 20; DLB
60

Hinkson, Katharine Tynan
See Tynan, Katharine

Hinton, S(usan) E(loise) 1950- **CLC 30, 111;
DA; DAB; DAC; DAM MST, NOV**
See also AAYA 2; CA 81-84; CANR 32, 62;
CLR 3, 23; JRDA; MAICYA; MTCW 1;
SATA 19, 58

Hippius, Zinaida   **TCLC 9**
See also Gippius, Zinaida (Nikolayevna)

Hiraoka, Kimitake 1925-1970
See Mishima, Yukio
See also CA 97-100; 29-32R; DAM DRAM;
MTCW 1

Hirsch, E(ric) D(onald), Jr. 1928-   **CLC 79**
See also CA 25-28R; CANR 27, 51; DLB 67;
INT CANR-27; MTCW 1

Hirsch, Edward 1950-   **CLC 31, 50**
See also CA 104; CANR 20, 42; DLB 120

Hitchcock, Alfred (Joseph) 1899-1980 **CLC 16**
See also AAYA 22; CA 159; 97-100; SATA 27;
SATA-Obit 24

Hitler, Adolf 1889-1945   **TCLC 53**
See also CA 117; 147

Hoagland, Edward 1932-   **CLC 28**
See also CA 1-4R; CANR 2, 31, 57; DLB 6;
SATA 51

Hoban, Russell (Conwell) 1925- **CLC 7, 25;
DAM NOV**
See also CA 5-8R; CANR 23, 37, 66; CLR 3;
DLB 52; MAICYA; MTCW 1; SATA 1, 40,
78

Hobbes, Thomas 1588-1679   **LC 36**
See also DLB 151

Hobbs, Perry
See Blackmur, R(ichard) P(almer)

Hobson, Laura Z(ametkin) 1900-1986 **CLC 7,
25**
See also CA 17-20R; 118; CANR 55; DLB 28;
SATA 52

Hochhuth, Rolf 1931- **CLC 4, 11, 18; DAM
DRAM**
See also CA 5-8R; CANR 33; DLB 124; MTCW
1

Hochman, Sandra 1936-   **CLC 3, 8**
See also CA 5-8R; DLB 5

Hochwaelder, Fritz 1911-1986 **CLC 36; DAM**

CMLC 29
See also DLB 148
Hsun, Lu
See Lu Hsun
Hubbard, L(afayette) Ron(ald) 1911-1986
CLC 43; DAM POP
See also CA 77-80; 118; CANR 52
Huch, Ricarda (Octavia) 1864-1947 **TCLC 13**
See also CA 111; DLB 66
Huddle, David 1942-   **CLC 49**
See also CA 57-60; CAAS 20; DLB 130
Hudson, Jeffrey
See Crichton, (John) Michael
Hudson, W(illiam) H(enry) 1841-1922 **TCLC 29**
See also CA 115; DLB 98, 153, 174; SATA 35
Hueffer, Ford Madox
See Ford, Ford Madox
Hughart, Barry 1934-   **CLC 39**
See also CA 137
Hughes, Colin
See Creasey, John
Hughes, David (John) 1930-   **CLC 48**
See also CA 116; 129; DLB 14
Hughes, Edward James
See Hughes, Ted
See also DAM MST, POET
Hughes, (James) Langston 1902-1967 **CLC 1, 5, 10, 15, 35, 44, 108; BLC 2; DA; DAB; DAC; DAM DRAM, MST, MULT, POET; DC 3; PC 1; SSC 6; WLC**
See also AAYA 12; BW 1; CA 1-4R; 25-28R; CANR 1, 34; CDALB 1929-1941; CLR 17; DLB 4, 7, 48, 51, 86; JRDA; MAICYA; MTCW 1; SATA 4, 33
Hughes, Richard (Arthur Warren) 1900-1976
CLC 1, 11; DAM NOV
See also CA 5-8R; 65-68; CANR 4; DLB 15, 161; MTCW 1; SATA 8; SATA-Obit 25
Hughes, Ted 1930- **CLC 2, 4, 9, 14, 37; DAB; DAC; PC 7**
See also Hughes, Edward James
See also CA 1-4R; CANR 1, 33, 66; CLR 3; DLB 40, 161; MAICYA; MTCW 1; SATA 49; SATA-Brief 27
Hugo, Richard F(ranklin) 1923-1982 **CLC 6, 18, 32; DAM POET**
See also CA 49-52; 108; CANR 3; DLB 5
Hugo, Victor (Marie) 1802-1885 **NCLC 3, 10, 21; DA; DAB; DAC; DAM DRAM, MST, NOV, POET; PC 17; WLC**
See also DLB 119, 192; SATA 47
Huidobro, Vicente
See Huidobro Fernandez, Vicente Garcia
Huidobro Fernandez, Vicente Garcia 1893-1948   **TCLC 31**
See also CA 131; HW
Hulme, Keri 1947-   **CLC 39**
See also CA 125; CANR 69; INT 125
Hulme, T(homas) E(rnest) 1883-1917 **TCLC 21**
See also CA 117; DLB 19
Hume, David 1711-1776   **LC 7**
See also DLB 104
Humphrey, William 1924-1997   **CLC 45**
See also CA 77-80; 160; CANR 68; DLB 6
Humphreys, Emyr Owen 1919-   **CLC 47**
See also CA 5-8R; CANR 3, 24; DLB 15
Humphreys, Josephine 1945-   **CLC 34, 57**
See also CA 121; 127; INT 127
Huneker, James Gibbons 1857-1921 **TCLC 65**
See also DLB 71
Hungerford, Pixie

See Brinsmead, H(esba) F(ay)
Hunt, E(verette) Howard, (Jr.) 1918- **CLC 3**
See also AITN 1; CA 45-48; CANR 2, 47
Hunt, Kyle
See Creasey, John
Hunt, (James Henry) Leigh 1784-1859 **NCLC 1, 70; DAM POET**
See also DLB 96, 110, 144
Hunt, Marsha 1946-   **CLC 70**
See also BW 2; CA 143
Hunt, Violet 1866(?)-1942   **TCLC 53**
See also DLB 162, 197
Hunter, E. Waldo
See Sturgeon, Theodore (Hamilton)
Hunter, Evan 1926- **CLC 11, 31; DAM POP**
See also CA 5-8R; CANR 5, 38, 62; DLBY 82; INT CANR-5; MTCW 1; SATA 25
Hunter, Kristin (Eggleston) 1931-   **CLC 35**
See also AITN 1; BW 1; CA 13-16R; CANR 13; CLR 3; DLB 33; INT CANR-13; MAICYA; SAAS 10; SATA 12
Hunter, Mollie 1922-   **CLC 21**
See also McIlwraith, Maureen Mollie Hunter
See also AAYA 13; CANR 37; CLR 25; DLB 161; JRDA; MAICYA; SAAS 7; SATA 54
Hunter, Robert (?)-1734   **LC 7**
Hurston, Zora Neale 1903-1960 **CLC 7, 30, 61; BLC 2; DA; DAC; DAM MST, MULT, NOV; SSC 4; WLCS**
See also AAYA 15; BW 1; CA 85-88; CANR 61; DLB 51, 86; MTCW 1
Huston, John (Marcellus) 1906-1987 **CLC 20**
See also CA 73-76; 123; CANR 34; DLB 26
Hustvedt, Siri 1955-   **CLC 76**
See also CA 137
Hutten, Ulrich von 1488-1523   **LC 16**
See also DLB 179
Huxley, Aldous (Leonard) 1894-1963 **CLC 1, 3, 4, 5, 8, 11, 18, 35, 79; DA; DAB; DAC; DAM MST, NOV; WLC**
See also AAYA 11; CA 85-88; CANR 44; CDBLB 1914-1945; DLB 36, 100, 162, 195; MTCW 1; SATA 63
Huxley, T(homas) H(enry) 1825-1895 **NCLC 67**
See also DLB 57
Huysmans, Joris-Karl 1848-1907 **TCLC 7, 69**
See also CA 104; 165; DLB 123
Hwang, David Henry 1957-   **CLC 55; DAM DRAM; DC 4**
See also CA 127; 132; INT 132
Hyde, Anthony 1946-   **CLC 42**
See also CA 136
Hyde, Margaret O(ldroyd) 1917-   **CLC 21**
See also CA 1-4R; CANR 1, 36; CLR 23; JRDA; MAICYA; SAAS 8; SATA 1, 42, 76
Hynes, James 1956(?)-   **CLC 65**
See also CA 164
Ian, Janis 1951-   **CLC 21**
See also CA 105
Ibanez, Vicente Blasco
See Blasco Ibanez, Vicente
Ibarguengoitia, Jorge 1928-1983   **CLC 37**
See also CA 124; 113; HW
Ibsen, Henrik (Johan) 1828-1906 **TCLC 2, 8, 16, 37, 52; DA; DAB; DAC; DAM DRAM, MST; DC 2; WLC**
See also CA 104; 141
Ibuse, Masuji 1898-1993   **CLC 22**
See also CA 127; 141; DLB 180
Ichikawa, Kon 1915-   **CLC 20**
See also CA 121
Idle, Eric 1943-   **CLC 21**

See also Monty Python
See also CA 116; CANR 35
Ignatow, David 1914-1997   **CLC 4, 7, 14, 40**
See also CA 9-12R; 162; CAAS 3; CANR 31, 57; DLB 5
Ihimaera, Witi 1944-   **CLC 46**
See also CA 77-80
Ilf, Ilya   **TCLC 21**
See also Fainzilberg, Ilya Arnoldovich
Illyes, Gyula 1902-1983   **PC 16**
See also CA 114; 109
Immermann, Karl (Lebrecht) 1796-1840
NCLC 4, 49
See also DLB 133
Inchbald, Elizabeth 1753-1821   **NCLC 62**
See also DLB 39, 89
Inclan, Ramon (Maria) del Valle
See Valle-Inclan, Ramon (Maria) del
Infante, G(uillermo) Cabrera
See Cabrera Infante, G(uillermo)
Ingalls, Rachel (Holmes) 1940-   **CLC 42**
See also CA 123; 127
Ingamells, Reginald Charles
See Ingamells, Rex
Ingamells, Rex 1913-1955   **TCLC 35**
See also CA 167
Inge, William (Motter) 1913-1973 **CLC 1, 8, 19; DAM DRAM**
See also CA 9-12R; CDALB 1941-1968; DLB 7; MTCW 1
Ingelow, Jean 1820-1897   **NCLC 39**
See also DLB 35, 163; SATA 33
Ingram, Willis J.
See Harris, Mark
Innaurato, Albert (F.) 1948(?)-   **CLC 21, 60**
See also CA 115; 122; INT 122
Innes, Michael
See Stewart, J(ohn) I(nnes) M(ackintosh)
Innis, Harold Adams 1894-1952   **TCLC 77**
See also DLB 88
Ionesco, Eugene 1909-1994 **CLC 1, 4, 6, 9, 11, 15, 41, 86; DA; DAB; DAC; DAM DRAM, MST; WLC**
See also CA 9-12R; 144; CANR 55; MTCW 1; SATA 7; SATA-Obit 79
Iqbal, Muhammad 1873-1938   **TCLC 28**
Ireland, Patrick
See O'Doherty, Brian
Iron, Ralph
See Schreiner, Olive (Emilie Albertina)
Irving, John (Winslow) 1942- **CLC 13, 23, 38, 112; DAM NOV, POP**
See also AAYA 8; BEST 89:3; CA 25-28R; CANR 28, 73; DLB 6; DLBY 82; MTCW 1
Irving, Washington 1783-1859 **NCLC 2, 19; DA; DAB; DAM MST; SSC 2; WLC**
See also CDALB 1640-1865; DLB 3, 11, 30, 59, 73, 74, 186; YABC 2
Irwin, P. K.
See Page, P(atricia) K(athleen)
Isaacs, Jorge Ricardo 1837-1895   **NCLC 70**
Isaacs, Susan 1943-   **CLC 32; DAM POP**
See also BEST 89:1; CA 89-92; CANR 20, 41, 65; INT CANR-20; MTCW 1
Isherwood, Christopher (William Bradshaw) 1904-1986   **CLC 1, 9, 11, 14, 44; DAM DRAM, NOV**
See also CA 13-16R; 117; CANR 35; DLB 15, 195; DLBY 86; MTCW 1
Ishiguro, Kazuo 1954- **CLC 27, 56, 59, 110; DAM NOV**
See also BEST 90:2; CA 120; CANR 49; DLB 194; MTCW 1

Ishikawa, Hakuhin
  See Ishikawa, Takuboku
Ishikawa, Takuboku 1886(?)-1912 **TCLC 15;**
  DAM POET; PC 10
  See also CA 113; 153
Iskander, Fazil 1929-   **CLC 47**
  See also CA 102
Isler, Alan (David) 1934-   **CLC 91**
  See also CA 156
Ivan IV 1530-1584   **LC 17**
Ivanov, Vyacheslav Ivanovich 1866-1949
  TCLC 33
  See also CA 122
Ivask, Ivar Vidrik 1927-1992   **CLC 14**
  See also CA 37-40R; 139; CANR 24
Ives, Morgan
  See Bradley, Marion Zimmer
J. R. S.
  See Gogarty, Oliver St. John
Jabran, Kahlil
  See Gibran, Kahlil
Jabran, Khalil
  See Gibran, Kahlil
Jackson, Daniel
  See Wingrove, David (John)
Jackson, Jesse 1908-1983   **CLC 12**
  See also BW 1; CA 25-28R; 109; CANR 27;
  CLR 28; MAICYA; SATA 2, 29; SATA-Obit
  48
Jackson, Laura (Riding) 1901-1991
  See Riding, Laura
  See also CA 65-68; 135; CANR 28; DLB 48
Jackson, Sam
  See Trumbo, Dalton
Jackson, Sara
  See Wingrove, David (John)
Jackson, Shirley 1919-1965   **CLC 11, 60, 87;**
  DA; DAC; DAM MST; SSC 9; WLC
  See also AAYA 9; CA 1-4R; 25-28R; CANR 4,
  52; CDALB 1941-1968; DLB 6; SATA 2
Jacob, (Cyprien-)Max 1876-1944   **TCLC 6**
  See also CA 104
Jacobs, Harriet A(nn) 1813(?)-1897 **NCLC 67**
Jacobs, Jim 1942-   **CLC 12**
  See also CA 97-100; INT 97-100
Jacobs, W(illiam) W(ymark) 1863-1943
  TCLC 22
  See also CA 121; 167; DLB 135
Jacobsen, Jens Peter 1847-1885   **NCLC 34**
Jacobsen, Josephine 1908-   **CLC 48, 102**
  See also CA 33-36R; CAAS 18; CANR 23, 48
Jacobson, Dan 1929-   **CLC 4, 14**
  See also CA 1-4R; CANR 2, 25, 66; DLB 14;
  MTCW 1
Jacqueline
  See Carpentier (y Valmont), Alejo
Jagger, Mick 1944-   **CLC 17**
Jahiz, Al- c. 776-869   **CMLC 25**
Jahiz, al- c. 780-c. 869   **CMLC 25**
Jakes, John (William) 1932-   **CLC 29; DAM**
  NOV, POP
  See also BEST 89:4; CA 57-60; CANR 10, 43,
  66; DLBY 83; INT CANR-10; MTCW 1;
  SATA 62
James, Andrew
  See Kirkup, James
James, C(yril) L(ionel) R(obert) 1901-1989
  CLC 33; BLCS
  See also BW 2; CA 117; 125; 128; CANR 62;
  DLB 125; MTCW 1
James, Daniel (Lewis) 1911-1988
  See Santiago, Danny
  See also CA 125

James, Dynely
  See Mayne, William (James Carter)
James, Henry Sr. 1811-1882   **NCLC 53**
James, Henry 1843-1916 **TCLC 2, 11, 24, 40,**
  47, 64; DA; DAB; DAC; DAM MST, NOV;
  SSC 8, 32; WLC
  See also CA 104; 132; CDALB 1865-1917;
  DLB 12, 71, 74, 189; DLBD 13; MTCW 1
James, M. R.
  See James, Montague (Rhodes)
  See also DLB 156
James, Montague (Rhodes) 1862-1936 **TCLC**
  6; SSC 16
  See also CA 104; DLB 201
James, P. D. 1920-   **CLC 18, 46**
  See also White, Phyllis Dorothy James
  See also BEST 90:2; CDBLB 1960 to Present;
  DLB 87; DLBD 17
James, Philip
  See Moorcock, Michael (John)
James, William 1842-1910   **TCLC 15, 32**
  See also CA 109
James I 1394-1437   **LC 20**
Jameson, Anna 1794-1860   **NCLC 43**
  See also DLB 99, 166
Jami, Nur al-Din 'Abd al-Rahman 1414-1492
  LC 9
Jammes, Francis 1868-1938   **TCLC 75**
Jandl, Ernst 1925-   **CLC 34**
Janowitz, Tama 1957-   **CLC 43; DAM POP**
  See also CA 106; CANR 52
Japrisot, Sebastien 1931-   **CLC 90**
Jarrell, Randall 1914-1965 **CLC 1, 2, 6, 9, 13,**
  49; DAM POET
  See also CA 5-8R; 25-28R; CABS 2; CANR 6,
  34; CDALB 1941-1968; CLR 6; DLB 48, 52;
  MAICYA; MTCW 1; SATA 7
Jarry, Alfred 1873-1907   **TCLC 2, 14; DAM**
  DRAM; SSC 20
  See also CA 104; 153; DLB 192
Jarvis, E. K.
  See Bloch, Robert (Albert); Ellison, Harlan
  (Jay); Silverberg, Robert
Jeake, Samuel, Jr.
  See Aiken, Conrad (Potter)
Jean Paul 1763-1825   **NCLC 7**
Jefferies, (John) Richard 1848-1887 **NCLC 47**
  See also DLB 98, 141; SATA 16
Jeffers, (John) Robinson 1887-1962 **CLC 2, 3,**
  11, 15, 54; DA; DAC; DAM MST, POET;
  PC 17; WLC
  See also CA 85-88; CANR 35; CDALB 1917-
  1929; DLB 45; MTCW 1
Jefferson, Janet
  See Mencken, H(enry) L(ouis)
Jefferson, Thomas 1743-1826   **NCLC 11**
  See also CDALB 1640-1865; DLB 31
Jeffrey, Francis 1773-1850   **NCLC 33**
  See also DLB 107
Jelakowitch, Ivan
  See Heijermans, Herman
Jellicoe, (Patricia) Ann 1927-   **CLC 27**
  See also CA 85-88; DLB 13
Jen, Gish   **CLC 70**
  See also Jen, Lillian
Jen, Lillian 1956(?)-
  See Jen, Gish
  See also CA 135
Jenkins, (John) Robin 1912-   **CLC 52**
  See also CA 1-4R; CANR 1; DLB 14
Jennings, Elizabeth (Joan) 1926-   **CLC 5, 14**
  See also CA 61-64; CAAS 5; CANR 8, 39, 66;
  DLB 27; MTCW 1; SATA 66

Jennings, Waylon 1937-   **CLC 21**
Jensen, Johannes V. 1873-1950   **TCLC 41**
  See also CA 170
Jensen, Laura (Linnea) 1948-   **CLC 37**
  See also CA 103
Jerome, Jerome K(lapka) 1859-1927 **TCLC 23**
  See also CA 119; DLB 10, 34, 135
Jerrold, Douglas William 1803-1857 **NCLC 2**
  See also DLB 158, 159
Jewett, (Theodora) Sarah Orne 1849-1909
  TCLC 1, 22; SSC 6
  See also CA 108; 127; CANR 71; DLB 12, 74;
  SATA 15
Jewsbury, Geraldine (Endsor) 1812-1880
  NCLC 22
  See also DLB 21
Jhabvala, Ruth Prawer 1927- **CLC 4, 8, 29, 94;**
  DAB; DAM NOV
  See also CA 1-4R; CANR 2, 29, 51, 74; DLB
  139, 194; INT CANR-29; MTCW 1
Jibran, Kahlil
  See Gibran, Kahlil
Jibran, Khalil
  See Gibran, Kahlil
Jiles, Paulette 1943-   **CLC 13, 58**
  See also CA 101; CANR 70
Jimenez (Mantecon), Juan Ramon 1881-1958
  TCLC 4; DAM MULT, POET; HLC; PC
  7
  See also CA 104; 131; CANR 74; DLB 134;
  HW; MTCW 1
Jimenez, Ramon
  See Jimenez (Mantecon), Juan Ramon
Jimenez Mantecon, Juan
  See Jimenez (Mantecon), Juan Ramon
Jin, Ha 1956-   **CLC 109**
  See also CA 152
Joel, Billy   **CLC 26**
  See also Joel, William Martin
Joel, William Martin 1949-
  See Joel, Billy
  See also CA 108
John, Saint 7th cent. -   **CMLC 27**
John of the Cross, St. 1542-1591   **LC 18**
Johnson, B(ryan) S(tanley William) 1933-1973
  CLC 6, 9
  See also CA 9-12R; 53-56; CANR 9; DLB 14,
  40
Johnson, Benj. F. of Boo
  See Riley, James Whitcomb
Johnson, Benjamin F. of Boo
  See Riley, James Whitcomb
Johnson, Charles (Richard) 1948- **CLC 7, 51,**
  65; BLC 2; DAM MULT
  See also BW 2; CA 116; CAAS 18; CANR 42,
  66; DLB 33
Johnson, Denis 1949-   **CLC 52**
  See also CA 117; 121; CANR 71; DLB 120
Johnson, Diane 1934-   **CLC 5, 13, 48**
  See also CA 41-44R; CANR 17, 40, 62; DLBY
  80; INT CANR-17; MTCW 1
Johnson, Eyvind (Olof Verner) 1900-1976
  CLC 14
  See also CA 73-76; 69-72; CANR 34
Johnson, J. R.
  See James, C(yril) L(ionel) R(obert)
Johnson, James Weldon 1871-1938 **TCLC 3,**
  19; BLC 2; DAM MULT, POET; PC 24
  See also BW 1; CA 104; 125; CDALB 1917-
  1929; CLR 32; DLB 51; MTCW 1; SATA 31
Johnson, Joyce 1935-   **CLC 58**
  See also CA 125; 129
Johnson, Lionel (Pigot) 1867-1902 **TCLC 19**

See also CA 117; DLB 19

Johnson, Marguerite (Annie)
See Angelou, Maya

Johnson, Mel
See Malzberg, Barry N(athaniel)

Johnson, Pamela Hansford 1912-1981CLC 1, 7, 27
See also CA 1-4R; 104; CANR 2, 28; DLB 15; MTCW 1

Johnson, Robert 1911(?)-1938   **TCLC 69**

Johnson, Samuel 1709-1784LC 15; DA; DAB; DAC; DAM MST; WLC
See also CDBLB 1660-1789; DLB 39, 95, 104, 142

Johnson, Uwe 1934-1984   **CLC 5, 10, 15, 40**
See also CA 1-4R; 112; CANR 1, 39; DLB 75; MTCW 1

Johnston, George (Benson) 1913-   **CLC 51**
See also CA 1-4R; CANR 5, 20; DLB 88

Johnston, Jennifer 1930-   **CLC 7**
See also CA 85-88; DLB 14

Jolley, (Monica) Elizabeth 1923-CLC 46; SSC 19
See also CA 127; CAAS 13; CANR 59

Jones, Arthur Llewellyn 1863-1947
See Machen, Arthur
See also CA 104

Jones, D(ouglas) G(ordon) 1929-   **CLC 10**
See also CA 29-32R; CANR 13; DLB 53

Jones, David (Michael) 1895-1974CLC 2, 4, 7, 13, 42
See also CA 9-12R; 53-56; CANR 28; CDBLB 1945-1960; DLB 20, 100; MTCW 1

Jones, David Robert 1947-
See Bowie, David
See also CA 103

Jones, Diana Wynne 1934-   **CLC 26**
See also AAYA 12; CA 49-52; CANR 4, 26, 56; CLR 23; DLB 161; JRDA; MAICYA; SAAS 7; SATA 9, 70

Jones, Edward P. 1950-   **CLC 76**
See also BW 2; CA 142

Jones, Gayl 1949-   **CLC 6, 9; BLC 2; DAM MULT**
See also BW 2; CA 77-80; CANR 27, 66; DLB 33; MTCW 1

Jones, James 1921-1977   **CLC 1, 3, 10, 39**
See also AITN 1, 2; CA 1-4R; 69-72; CANR 6; DLB 2, 143; DLBD 17; MTCW 1

Jones, John J.
See Lovecraft, H(oward) P(hillips)

Jones, LeRoi   **CLC 1, 2, 3, 5, 10, 14**
See also Baraka, Amiri

Jones, Louis B. 1953-   **CLC 65**
See also CA 141; CANR 73

Jones, Madison (Percy, Jr.) 1925-   **CLC 4**
See also CA 13-16R; CAAS 11; CANR 7, 54; DLB 152

Jones, Mervyn 1922-   **CLC 10, 52**
See also CA 45-48; CAAS 5; CANR 1; MTCW 1

Jones, Mick 1956(?)-   **CLC 30**

Jones, Nettie (Pearl) 1941-   **CLC 34**
See also BW 2; CA 137; CAAS 20

Jones, Preston 1936-1979   **CLC 10**
See also CA 73-76; 89-92; DLB 7

Jones, Robert F(rancis) 1934-   **CLC 7**
See also CA 49-52; CANR 2, 61

Jones, Rod 1953-   **CLC 50**
See also CA 128

Jones, Terence Graham Parry 1942- CLC 21
See also Jones, Terry; Monty Python
See also CA 112; 116; CANR 35; INT 116

Jones, Terry
See Jones, Terence Graham Parry
See also SATA 67; SATA-Brief 51

Jones, Thom 1945(?)-   **CLC 81**
See also CA 157

Jong, Erica 1942- CLC 4, 6, 8, 18, 83; DAM NOV, POP
See also AITN 1; BEST 90:2; CA 73-76; CANR 26, 52; DLB 2, 5, 28, 152; INT CANR-26; MTCW 1

Jonson, Ben(jamin) 1572(?)-1637   **LC 6, 33; DA; DAB; DAC; DAM DRAM, MST, POET; DC 4; PC 17; WLC**
See also CDBLB Before 1660; DLB 62, 121

Jordan, June 1936-CLC 5, 11, 23, 114; BLCS; DAM MULT, POET
See also AAYA 2; BW 2; CA 33-36R; CANR 25, 70; CLR 10; DLB 38; MAICYA; MTCW 1; SATA 4

Jordan, Neil (Patrick) 1950-   **CLC 110**
See also CA 124; 130; CANR 54; INT 130

Jordan, Pat(rick M.) 1941-   **CLC 37**
See also CA 33-36R

Jorgensen, Ivar
See Ellison, Harlan (Jay)

Jorgenson, Ivar
See Silverberg, Robert

Josephus, Flavius c. 37-100   **CMLC 13**

Josipovici, Gabriel 1940-   **CLC 6, 43**
See also CA 37-40R; CAAS 8; CANR 47; DLB 14

Joubert, Joseph 1754-1824   **NCLC 9**

Jouve, Pierre Jean 1887-1976   **CLC 47**
See also CA 65-68

Jovine, Francesco 1902-1950   **TCLC 79**

Joyce, James (Augustine Aloysius) 1882-1941 TCLC 3, 8, 16, 35, 52; DA; DAB; DAC; DAM MST, NOV, POET; PC 22; SSC 3, 26; WLC
See also CA 104; 126; CDBLB 1914-1945; DLB 10, 19, 36, 162; MTCW 1

Jozsef, Attila 1905-1937   **TCLC 22**
See also CA 116

Juana Ines de la Cruz 1651(?)-1695LC 5; PC 24

Judd, Cyril
See Kornbluth, C(yril) M.; Pohl, Frederik

Julian of Norwich 1342(?)-1416(?)   **LC 6**
See also DLB 146

Junger, Sebastian 1962-   **CLC 109**
See also CA 165

Juniper, Alex
See Hospital, Janette Turner

Junius
See Luxemburg, Rosa

Just, Ward (Swift) 1935-   **CLC 4, 27**
See also CA 25-28R; CANR 32; INT CANR-32

Justice, Donald (Rodney) 1925-   CLC 6, 19, 102; DAM POET
See also CA 5-8R; CANR 26, 54, 74; DLBY 83; INT CANR-26

Juvenal   **CMLC 8**
See also Juvenalis, Decimus Junius

Juvenalis, Decimus Junius 55(?)-c. 127(?)
See Juvenal

Juvenis
See Bourne, Randolph S(illiman)

Kacew, Romain 1914-1980
See Gary, Romain
See also CA 108; 102

Kadare, Ismail 1936-   **CLC 52**
See also CA 161

Kadohata, Cynthia   **CLC 59**
See also CA 140

Kafka, Franz 1883-1924TCLC 2, 6, 13, 29, 47, 53; DA; DAB; DAC; DAM MST, NOV; SSC 5, 29; WLC
See also CA 105; 126; DLB 81; MTCW 1

Kahanovitsch, Pinkhes
See Der Nister

Kahn, Roger 1927-   **CLC 30**
See also CA 25-28R; CANR 44, 69; DLB 171; SATA 37

Kain, Saul
See Sassoon, Siegfried (Lorraine)

Kaiser, Georg 1878-1945   **TCLC 9**
See also CA 106; DLB 124

Kaletski, Alexander 1946-   **CLC 39**
See also CA 118; 143

Kalidasa fl. c. 400-   **CMLC 9; PC 22**

Kallman, Chester (Simon) 1921-1975 CLC 2
See also CA 45-48; 53-56; CANR 3

Kaminsky, Melvin 1926-
See Brooks, Mel
See also CA 65-68; CANR 16

Kaminsky, Stuart M(elvin) 1934-   **CLC 59**
See also CA 73-76; CANR 29, 53

Kane, Francis
See Robbins, Harold

Kane, Paul
See Simon, Paul (Frederick)

Kane, Wilson
See Bloch, Robert (Albert)

Kanin, Garson 1912-   **CLC 22**
See also AITN 1; CA 5-8R; CANR 7; DLB 7

Kaniuk, Yoram 1930-   **CLC 19**
See also CA 134

Kant, Immanuel 1724-1804   **NCLC 27, 67**
See also DLB 94

Kantor, MacKinlay 1904-1977   **CLC 7**
See also CA 61-64; 73-76; CANR 60, 63; DLB 9, 102

Kaplan, David Michael 1946-   **CLC 50**

Kaplan, James 1951-   **CLC 59**
See also CA 135

Karageorge, Michael
See Anderson, Poul (William)

Karamzin, Nikolai Mikhailovich 1766-1826 NCLC 3
See also DLB 150

Karapanou, Margarita 1946-   **CLC 13**
See also CA 101

Karinthy, Frigyes 1887-1938   **TCLC 47**
See also CA 170

Karl, Frederick R(obert) 1927-   **CLC 34**
See also CA 5-8R; CANR 3, 44

Kastel, Warren
See Silverberg, Robert

Kataev, Evgeny Petrovich 1903-1942
See Petrov, Evgeny
See also CA 120

Kataphusin
See Ruskin, John

Katz, Steve 1935-   **CLC 47**
See also CA 25-28R; CAAS 14, 64; CANR 12; DLBY 83

Kauffman, Janet 1945-   **CLC 42**
See also CA 117; CANR 43; DLBY 86

Kaufman, Bob (Garnell) 1925-1986 CLC 49
See also BW 1; CA 41-44R; 118; CANR 22; DLB 16, 41

Kaufman, George S. 1889-1961CLC 38; DAM DRAM
See also CA 108; 93-96; DLB 7; INT 108

Kaufman, Sue   **CLC 3, 8**

See also Barondess, Sue K(aufman)

Kavafis, Konstantinos Petrou 1863-1933
See Cavafy, C(onstantine) P(eter)
See also CA 104

Kavan, Anna 1901-1968 **CLC 5, 13, 82**
See also CA 5-8R; CANR 6, 57; MTCW 1

Kavanagh, Dan
See Barnes, Julian (Patrick)

Kavanagh, Patrick (Joseph) 1904-1967 **C L C 22**
See also CA 123; 25-28R; DLB 15, 20; MTCW 1

Kawabata, Yasunari 1899-1972 **CLC 2, 5, 9, 18, 107; DAM MULT; SSC 17**
See also CA 93-96; 33-36R; DLB 180

Kaye, M(ary) M(argaret) 1909- **CLC 28**
See also CA 89-92; CANR 24, 60; MTCW 1; SATA 62

Kaye, Mollie
See Kaye, M(ary) M(argaret)

Kaye-Smith, Sheila 1887-1956 **TCLC 20**
See also CA 118; DLB 36

Kaymor, Patrice Maguilene
See Senghor, Leopold Sedar

Kazan, Elia 1909- **CLC 6, 16, 63**
See also CA 21-24R; CANR 32

Kazantzakis, Nikos 1883(?)-1957 **TCLC 2, 5, 33**
See also CA 105; 132; MTCW 1

Kazin, Alfred 1915- **CLC 34, 38**
See also CA 1-4R; CAAS 7; CANR 1, 45; DLB 67

Keane, Mary Nesta (Skrine) 1904-1996
See Keane, Molly
See also CA 108; 114; 151

Keane, Molly **CLC 31**
See also Keane, Mary Nesta (Skrine)
See also INT 114

Keates, Jonathan 1946(?)- **CLC 34**
See also CA 163

Keaton, Buster 1895-1966 **CLC 20**

Keats, John 1795-1821**NCLC 8, 73; DA; DAB; DAC; DAM MST, POET; PC 1; WLC**
See also CDBLB 1789-1832; DLB 96, 110

Keene, Donald 1922- **CLC 34**
See also CA 1-4R; CANR 5

Keillor, Garrison **CLC 40, 115**
See also Keillor, Gary (Edward)
See also AAYA 2; BEST 89:3; DLBY 87; SATA 58

Keillor, Gary (Edward) 1942-
See Keillor, Garrison
See also CA 111; 117; CANR 36, 59; DAM POP; MTCW 1

Keith, Michael
See Hubbard, L(afayette) Ron(ald)

Keller, Gottfried 1819-1890 **NCLC 2; SSC 26**
See also DLB 129

Keller, Nora Okja **CLC 109**

Kellerman, Jonathan 1949- **CLC 44; DAM POP**
See also BEST 90:1; CA 106; CANR 29, 51; INT CANR-29

Kelley, William Melvin 1937- **CLC 22**
See also BW 1; CA 77-80; CANR 27; DLB 33

Kellogg, Marjorie 1922- **CLC 2**
See also CA 81-84

Kellow, Kathleen
See Hibbert, Eleanor Alice Burford

Kelly, M(ilton) T(erry) 1947- **CLC 55**
See also CA 97-100; CAAS 22; CANR 19, 43

Kelman, James 1946- **CLC 58, 86**
See also CA 148; DLB 194

Kemal, Yashar 1923- **CLC 14, 29**
See also CA 89-92; CANR 44

Kemble, Fanny 1809-1893 **NCLC 18**
See also DLB 32

Kemelman, Harry 1908-1996 **CLC 2**
See also AITN 1; CA 9-12R; 155; CANR 6, 71; DLB 28

Kempe, Margery 1373(?)-1440(?) **LC 6**
See also DLB 146

Kempis, Thomas a 1380-1471 **LC 11**

Kendall, Henry 1839-1882 **NCLC 12**

Keneally, Thomas (Michael) 1935- **CLC 5, 8, 10, 14, 19, 27, 43, 117; DAM NOV**
See also CA 85-88; CANR 10, 50, 74; MTCW 1

Kennedy, Adrienne (Lita) 1931-**CLC 66; BLC 2; DAM MULT; DC 5**
See also BW 2; CA 103; CAAS 20; CABS 3; CANR 26, 53; DLB 38

Kennedy, John Pendleton 1795-1870**NCLC 2**
See also DLB 3

Kennedy, Joseph Charles 1929-
See Kennedy, X. J.
See also CA 1-4R; CANR 4, 30, 40; SATA 14, 86

Kennedy, William 1928- **CLC 6, 28, 34, 53; DAM NOV**
See also AAYA 1; CA 85-88; CANR 14, 31; DLB 143; DLBY 85; INT CANR-31; MTCW 1; SATA 57

Kennedy, X. J. **CLC 8, 42**
See also Kennedy, Joseph Charles
See also CAAS 9; CLR 27; DLB 5; SAAS 22

Kenny, Maurice (Francis) 1929- **CLC 87; DAM MULT**
See also CA 144; CAAS 22; DLB 175; NNAL

Kent, Kelvin
See Kuttner, Henry

Kenton, Maxwell
See Southern, Terry

Kenyon, Robert O.
See Kuttner, Henry

Kepler, Johannes 1571-1630 **LC 45**

Kerouac, Jack **CLC 1, 2, 3, 5, 14, 29, 61**
See also Kerouac, Jean-Louis Lebris de
See also AAYA 25; CDALB 1941-1968; DLB 2, 16; DLBD 3; DLBY 95

Kerouac, Jean-Louis Lebris de 1922-1969
See Kerouac, Jack
See also AITN 1; CA 5-8R; 25-28R; CANR 26, 54; DA; DAB; DAC; DAM MST, NOV, POET, POP; MTCW 1; WLC

Kerr, Jean 1923- **CLC 22**
See also CA 5-8R; CANR 7; INT CANR-7

Kerr, M. E. **CLC 12, 35**
See also Meaker, Marijane (Agnes)
See also AAYA 2, 23; CLR 29; SAAS 1

Kerr, Robert **CLC 55**

Kerrigan, (Thomas) Anthony 1918-**CLC 4, 6**
See also CA 49-52; CAAS 11; CANR 4

Kerry, Lois
See Duncan, Lois

Kesey, Ken (Elton) 1935- **CLC 1, 3, 6, 11, 46, 64; DA; DAB; DAC; DAM MST, NOV, POP; WLC**
See also AAYA 25; CA 1-4R; CANR 22, 38, 66; CDALB 1968-1988; DLB 2, 16; MTCW 1; SATA 66

Kesselring, Joseph (Otto) 1902-1967**CLC 45; DAM DRAM, MST**
See also CA 150

Kessler, Jascha (Frederick) 1929- **CLC 4**
See also CA 17-20R; CANR 8, 48

Kettelkamp, Larry (Dale) 1933- **CLC 12**
See also CA 29-32R; CANR 16; SAAS 3; SATA 2

Key, Ellen 1849-1926 **TCLC 65**

Keyber, Conny
See Fielding, Henry

Keyes, Daniel 1927-**CLC 80; DA; DAC; DAM MST, NOV**
See also AAYA 23; CA 17-20R; CANR 10, 26, 54, 74; SATA 37

Keynes, John Maynard 1883-1946 **TCLC 64**
See also CA 114; 162, 163; DLBD 10

Khanshendel, Chiron
See Rose, Wendy

Khayyam, Omar 1048-1131 **CMLC 11; DAM POET; PC 8**

Kherdian, David 1931- **CLC 6, 9**
See also CA 21-24R; CAAS 2; CANR 39; CLR 24; JRDA; MAICYA; SATA 16, 74

Khlebnikov, Velimir **TCLC 20**
See also Khlebnikov, Viktor Vladimirovich

Khlebnikov, Viktor Vladimirovich 1885-1922
See Khlebnikov, Velimir
See also CA 117

Khodasevich, Vladislav (Felitsianovich) 1886-1939 **TCLC 15**
See also CA 115

Kielland, Alexander Lange 1849-1906 **T C L C 5**
See also CA 104

Kiely, Benedict 1919- **CLC 23, 43**
See also CA 1-4R; CANR 2; DLB 15

Kienzle, William X(avier) 1928- **CLC 25; DAM POP**
See also CA 93-96; CAAS 1; CANR 9, 31, 59; INT CANR-31; MTCW 1

Kierkegaard, Soren 1813-1855 **NCLC 34**

Killens, John Oliver 1916-1987 **CLC 10**
See also BW 2; CA 77-80; 123; CAAS 2; CANR 26; DLB 33

Killigrew, Anne 1660-1685 **LC 4**
See also DLB 131

Kim
See Simenon, Georges (Jacques Christian)

Kincaid, Jamaica 1949- **CLC 43, 68; BLC 2; DAM MULT; NOV**
See also AAYA 13; BW 2; CA 125; CANR 47, 59; DLB 157

King, Francis (Henry) 1923-**CLC 8, 53; DAM NOV**
See also CA 1-4R; CANR 1, 33; DLB 15, 139; MTCW 1

King, Kennedy
See Brown, George Douglas

King, Martin Luther, Jr. 1929-1968 **CLC 83; BLC 2; DA; DAB; DAC; DAM MST, MULT; WLCS**
See also BW 2; CA 25-28; CANR 27, 44; CAP 2; MTCW 1; SATA 14

King, Stephen (Edwin) 1947-**CLC 12, 26, 37, 61, 113; DAM NOV, POP; SSC 17**
See also AAYA 1, 17; BEST 90:1; CA 61-64; CANR 1, 30, 52; DLB 143; DLBY 80; JRDA; MTCW 1; SATA 9, 55

King, Steve
See King, Stephen (Edwin)

King, Thomas 1943- **CLC 89; DAC; DAM MULT**
See also CA 144; DLB 175; NNAL; SATA 96

Kingman, Lee **CLC 17**
See also Natti, (Mary) Lee
See also SAAS 3; SATA 1, 67

Kingsley, Charles 1819-1875 **NCLC 35**

See also DLB 21, 32, 163, 190; YABC 2
Kingsley, Sidney 1906-1995 **CLC 44**
   See also CA 85-88; 147; DLB 7
Kingsolver, Barbara 1955-CLC **55, 81; DAM POP**
   See also AAYA 15; CA 129; 134; CANR 60; INT 134
Kingston, Maxine (Ting Ting) Hong 1940-**CLC 12, 19, 58; DAM MULT, NOV; WLCS**
   See also AAYA 8; CA 69-72; CANR 13, 38, 74; DLB 173; DLBY 80; INT CANR-13; MTCW 1; SATA 53
Kinnell, Galway 1927- **CLC 1, 2, 3, 5, 13, 29**
   See also CA 9-12R; CANR 10, 34, 66; DLB 5; DLBY 87; INT CANR-34; MTCW 1
Kinsella, Thomas 1928- **CLC 4, 19**
   See also CA 17-20R; CANR 15; DLB 27; MTCW 1
Kinsella, W(illiam) P(atrick) 1935- **CLC 27, 43; DAC; DAM NOV, POP**
   See also AAYA 7; CA 97-100; CAAS 7; CANR 21, 35, 66; INT CANR-21; MTCW 1
Kipling, (Joseph) Rudyard 1865-1936 **TCLC 8, 17; DA; DAB; DAC; DAM MST, POET; PC 3; SSC 5; WLC**
   See also CA 105; 120; CANR 33; CDBLB 1890-1914; CLR 39; DLB 19, 34, 141, 156; MAICYA; MTCW 1; SATA 100; YABC 2
Kirkup, James 1918- **CLC 1**
   See also CA 1-4R; CAAS 4; CANR 2; DLB 27; SATA 12
Kirkwood, James 1930(?)-1989 **CLC 9**
   See also AITN 2; CA 1-4R; 128; CANR 6, 40
Kirshner, Sidney
   See Kingsley, Sidney
Kis, Danilo 1935-1989 **CLC 57**
   See also CA 109; 118; 129; CANR 61; DLB 181; MTCW 1
Kivi, Aleksis 1834-1872 **NCLC 30**
Kizer, Carolyn (Ashley) 1925-CLC **15, 39, 80; DAM POET**
   See also CA 65-68; CAAS 5; CANR 24, 70; DLB 5, 169
Klabund 1890-1928 **TCLC 44**
   See also CA 162; DLB 66
Klappert, Peter 1942- **CLC 57**
   See also CA 33-36R; DLB 5
Klein, A(braham) M(oses) 1909-1972CLC **19; DAB; DAC; DAM MST**
   See also CA 101; 37-40R; DLB 68
Klein, Norma 1938-1989 **CLC 30**
   See also AAYA 2; CA 41-44R; 128; CANR 15, 37; CLR 2, 19; INT CANR-15; JRDA; MAICYA; SAAS 1; SATA 7, 57
Klein, T(heodore) E(ibon) D(onald) 1947- **CLC 34**
   See also CA 119; CANR 44
Kleist, Heinrich von 1777-1811 **NCLC 2, 37; DAM DRAM; SSC 22**
   See also DLB 90
Klima, Ivan 1931- **CLC 56; DAM NOV**
   See also CA 25-28R; CANR 17, 50
Klimentov, Andrei Platonovich 1899-1951
   See Platonov, Andrei
   See also CA 108
Klinger, Friedrich Maximilian von 1752-1831 **NCLC 1**
   See also DLB 94
Klingsor the Magician
   See Hartmann, Sadakichi
Klopstock, Friedrich Gottlieb 1724-1803 **NCLC 11**

See also DLB 97
Knapp, Caroline 1959- **CLC 99**
   See also CA 154
Knebel, Fletcher 1911-1993 **CLC 14**
   See also AITN 1; CA 1-4R; 140; CAAS 3; CANR 1, 36; SATA 36; SATA-Obit 75
Knickerbocker, Diedrich
   See Irving, Washington
Knight, Etheridge 1931-1991CLC **40; BLC 2; DAM POET; PC 14**
   See also BW 1; CA 21-24R; 133; CANR 23; DLB 41
Knight, Sarah Kemble 1666-1727 **LC 7**
   See also DLB 24, 200
Knister, Raymond 1899-1932 **TCLC 56**
   See also DLB 68
Knowles, John 1926- **CLC 1, 4, 10, 26; DA; DAC; DAM MST, NOV**
   See also AAYA 10; CA 17-20R; CANR 40, 74; CDALB 1968-1988; DLB 6; MTCW 1; SATA 8, 89
Knox, Calvin M.
   See Silverberg, Robert
Knox, John c. 1505-1572 **LC 37**
   See also DLB 132
Knye, Cassandra
   See Disch, Thomas M(ichael)
Koch, C(hristopher) J(ohn) 1932- **CLC 42**
   See also CA 127
Koch, Christopher
   See Koch, C(hristopher) J(ohn)
Koch, Kenneth 1925- **CLC 5, 8, 44; DAM POET**
   See also CA 1-4R; CANR 6, 36, 57; DLB 5; INT CANR-36; SATA 65
Kochanowski, Jan 1530-1584 **LC 10**
Kock, Charles Paul de 1794-1871 **NCLC 16**
Koda Shigeyuki 1867-1947
   See Rohan, Koda
   See also CA 121
Koestler, Arthur 1905-1983CLC **1, 3, 6, 8, 15, 33**
   See also CA 1-4R; 109; CANR 1, 33; CDBLB 1945-1960; DLBY 83; MTCW 1
Kogawa, Joy Nozomi 1935- **CLC 78; DAC; DAM MST, MULT**
   See also CA 101; CANR 19, 62; SATA 99
Kohout, Pavel 1928- **CLC 13**
   See also CA 45-48; CANR 3
Koizumi, Yakumo
   See Hearn, (Patricio) Lafcadio (Tessima Carlos)
Kolmar, Gertrud 1894-1943 **TCLC 40**
   See also CA 167
Komunyakaa, Yusef 1947-CLC **86, 94; BLCS**
   See also CA 147; DLB 120
Konrad, George
   See Konrad, Gyoergy
Konrad, Gyoergy 1933- **CLC 4, 10, 73**
   See also CA 85-88
Konwicki, Tadeusz 1926- **CLC 8, 28, 54, 117**
   See also CA 101; CAAS 9; CANR 39, 59; MTCW 1
Koontz, Dean R(ay) 1945- **CLC 78; DAM NOV, POP**
   See also AAYA 9; BEST 89:3, 90:2; CA 108; CANR 19, 36, 52; MTCW 1; SATA 92
Kopernik, Mikolaj
   See Copernicus, Nicolaus
Kopit, Arthur (Lee) 1937-CLC **1, 18, 33; DAM DRAM**
   See also AITN 1; CA 81-84; CABS 3; DLB 7; MTCW 1
Kops, Bernard 1926- **CLC 4**

See also CA 5-8R; DLB 13
Kornbluth, C(yril) M. 1923-1958 **TCLC 8**
   See also CA 105; 160; DLB 8
Korolenko, V. G.
   See Korolenko, Vladimir Galaktionovich
Korolenko, Vladimir
   See Korolenko, Vladimir Galaktionovich
Korolenko, Vladimir G.
   See Korolenko, Vladimir Galaktionovich
Korolenko, Vladimir Galaktionovich 1853-1921 **TCLC 22**
   See also CA 121
Korzybski, Alfred (Habdank Skarbek) 1879-1950 **TCLC 61**
   See also CA 123; 160
Kosinski, Jerzy (Nikodem) 1933-1991CLC **1, 2, 3, 6, 10, 15, 53, 70; DAM NOV**
   See also CA 17-20R; 134; CANR 9, 46; DLB 2; DLBY 82; MTCW 1
Kostelanetz, Richard (Cory) 1940- **CLC 28**
   See also CA 13-16R; CAAS 8; CANR 38
Kostrowitzki, Wilhelm Apollinaris de 1880-1918
   See Apollinaire, Guillaume
   See also CA 104
Kotlowitz, Robert 1924- **CLC 4**
   See also CA 33-36R; CANR 36
Kotzebue, August (Friedrich Ferdinand) von 1761-1819 **NCLC 25**
   See also DLB 94
Kotzwinkle, William 1938- **CLC 5, 14, 35**
   See also CA 45-48; CANR 3, 44; CLR 6; DLB 173; MAICYA; SATA 24, 70
Kowna, Stancy
   See Szymborska, Wislawa
Kozol, Jonathan 1936- **CLC 17**
   See also CA 61-64; CANR 16, 45
Kozoll, Michael 1940(?)- **CLC 35**
Kramer, Kathryn 19(?)- **CLC 34**
Kramer, Larry 1935-CLC **42; DAM POP; DC 8**
   See also CA 124; 126; CANR 60
Krasicki, Ignacy 1735-1801 **NCLC 8**
Krasinski, Zygmunt 1812-1859 **NCLC 4**
Kraus, Karl 1874-1936 **TCLC 5**
   See also CA 104; DLB 118
Kreve (Mickevicius), Vincas 1882-1954TCLC **27**
   See also CA 170
Kristeva, Julia 1941- **CLC 77**
   See also CA 154
Kristofferson, Kris 1936- **CLC 26**
   See also CA 104
Krizanc, John 1956- **CLC 57**
Krleza, Miroslav 1893-1981 **CLC 8, 114**
   See also CA 97-100; 105; CANR 50; DLB 147
Kroetsch, Robert 1927- CLC **5, 23, 57; DAC; DAM POET**
   See also CA 17-20R; CANR 8, 38; DLB 53; MTCW 1
Kroetz, Franz
   See Kroetz, Franz Xaver
Kroetz, Franz Xaver 1946- **CLC 41**
   See also CA 130
Kroker, Arthur (W.) 1945- **CLC 77**
   See also CA 161
Kropotkin, Peter (Aleksieevich) 1842-1921 **TCLC 36**
   See also CA 119
Krotkov, Yuri 1917- **CLC 19**
   See also CA 102
Krumb
   See Crumb, R(obert)

Krumgold, Joseph (Quincy) 1908-1980 **C L C 12**
See also CA 9-12R; 101; CANR 7; MAICYA; SATA 1, 48; SATA-Obit 23

Krumwitz
See Crumb, R(obert)

Krutch, Joseph Wood 1893-1970 **CLC 24**
See also CA 1-4R; 25-28R; CANR 4; DLB 63

Krutzch, Gus
See Eliot, T(homas) S(tearns)

Krylov, Ivan Andreevich 1768(?)-1844**N C L C 1**
See also DLB 150

Kubin, Alfred (Leopold Isidor) 1877-1959 **TCLC 23**
See also CA 112; 149; DLB 81

Kubrick, Stanley 1928- **CLC 16**
See also CA 81-84; CANR 33; DLB 26

Kumin, Maxine (Winokur) 1925- **CLC 5, 13, 28; DAM POET; PC 15**
See also AITN 2; CA 1-4R; CAAS 8; CANR 1, 21, 69; DLB 5; MTCW 1; SATA 12

Kundera, Milan 1929- **CLC 4, 9, 19, 32, 68, 115; DAM NOV; SSC 24**
See also AAYA 2; CA 85-88; CANR 19, 52, 74; MTCW 1

Kunene, Mazisi (Raymond) 1930- **CLC 85**
See also BW 1; CA 125; DLB 117

Kunitz, Stanley (Jasspon) 1905-**CLC 6, 11, 14; PC 19**
See also CA 41-44R; CANR 26, 57; DLB 48; INT CANR-26; MTCW 1

Kunze, Reiner 1933- **CLC 10**
See also CA 93-96; DLB 75

Kuprin, Aleksandr Ivanovich 1870-1938 **TCLC 5**
See also CA 104

Kureishi, Hanif 1954(?)- **CLC 64**
See also CA 139; DLB 194

Kurosawa, Akira 1910-1998 **CLC 16; DAM MULT**
See also AAYA 11; CA 101; 170; CANR 46

Kushner, Tony 1957(?)-**CLC 81; DAM DRAM**
See also CA 144; CANR 74

Kuttner, Henry 1915-1958 **TCLC 10**
See also Vance, Jack
See also CA 107; 157; DLB 8

Kuzma, Greg 1944- **CLC 7**
See also CA 33-36R; CANR 70

Kuzmin, Mikhail 1872(?)-1936 **TCLC 40**
See also CA 170

Kyd, Thomas 1558-1594**LC 22; DAM DRAM; DC 3**
See also DLB 62

Kyprianos, Iossif
See Samarakis, Antonis

La Bruyere, Jean de 1645-1696 **LC 17**

Lacan, Jacques (Marie Emile) 1901-1981 **CLC 75**
See also CA 121; 104

Laclos, Pierre Ambroise Francois Choderlos de 1741-1803 **NCLC 4**

Lacolere, Francois
See Aragon, Louis

La Colere, Francois
See Aragon, Louis

La Deshabilleuse
See Simenon, Georges (Jacques Christian)

Lady Gregory
See Gregory, Isabella Augusta (Persse)

Lady of Quality, A
See Bagnold, Enid

La Fayette, Marie (Madelaine Pioche de la

Vergne Comtes 1634-1693 **LC 2**

Lafayette, Rene
See Hubbard, L(afayette) Ron(ald)

Laforgue, Jules 1860-1887**NCLC 5, 53; PC 14; SSC 20**

Lagerkvist, Paer (Fabian) 1891-1974 **CLC 7, 10, 13, 54; DAM DRAM, NOV**
See also Lagerkvist, Par
See also CA 85-88; 49-52; MTCW 1

Lagerkvist, Par **SSC 12**
See also Lagerkvist, Paer (Fabian)

Lagerloef, Selma (Ottiliana Lovisa) 1858-1940 **TCLC 4, 36**
See also Lagerlof, Selma (Ottiliana Lovisa)
See also CA 108; SATA 15

Lagerlof, Selma (Ottiliana Lovisa)
See Lagerloef, Selma (Ottiliana Lovisa)
See also CLR 7; SATA 15

La Guma, (Justin) Alex(ander) 1925-1985 **CLC 19; BLCS; DAM NOV**
See also BW 1; CA 49-52; 118; CANR 25; DLB 117; MTCW 1

Laidlaw, A. K.
See Grieve, C(hristopher) M(urray)

Lainez, Manuel Mujica
See Mujica Lainez, Manuel
See also HW

Laing, R(onald) D(avid) 1927-1989 **CLC 95**
See also CA 107; 129; CANR 34; MTCW 1

Lamartine, Alphonse (Marie Louis Prat) de 1790-1869**NCLC 11; DAM POET; PC 16**

Lamb, Charles 1775-1834 **NCLC 10; DA; DAB; DAC; DAM MST; WLC**
See also CDBLB 1789-1832; DLB 93, 107, 163; SATA 17

Lamb, Lady Caroline 1785-1828 **NCLC 38**
See also DLB 116

Lamming, George (William) 1927- **CLC 2, 4, 66; BLC 2; DAM MULT**
See also BW 2; CA 85-88; CANR 26; DLB 125; MTCW 1

L'Amour, Louis (Dearborn) 1908-1988 **C L C 25, 55; DAM NOV, POP**
See also AAYA 16; AITN 2; BEST 89:2; CA 1-4R; 125; CANR 3, 25, 40; DLBY 80; MTCW 1

Lampedusa, Giuseppe (Tomasi) di 1896-1957 **TCLC 13**
See also Tomasi di Lampedusa, Giuseppe
See also CA 164; DLB 177

Lampman, Archibald 1861-1899 **NCLC 25**
See also DLB 92

Lancaster, Bruce 1896-1963 **CLC 36**
See also CA 9-10; CANR 70; CAP 1; SATA 9

Lanchester, John **CLC 99**

Landau, Mark Alexandrovich
See Aldanov, Mark (Alexandrovich)

Landau-Aldanov, Mark Alexandrovich
See Aldanov, Mark (Alexandrovich)

Landis, Jerry
See Simon, Paul (Frederick)

Landis, John 1950- **CLC 26**
See also CA 112; 122

Landolfi, Tommaso 1908-1979 **CLC 11, 49**
See also CA 127; 117; DLB 177

Landon, Letitia Elizabeth 1802-1838 **N C L C 15**
See also DLB 96

Landor, Walter Savage 1775-1864 **NCLC 14**
See also DLB 93, 107

Landwirth, Heinz 1927-
See Lind, Jakov
See also CA 9-12R; CANR 7

Lane, Patrick 1939- **CLC 25; DAM POET**
See also CA 97-100; CANR 54; DLB 53; INT 97-100

Lang, Andrew 1844-1912 **TCLC 16**
See also CA 114; 137; DLB 98, 141, 184; MAICYA; SATA 16

Lang, Fritz 1890-1976 **CLC 20, 103**
See also CA 77-80; 69-72; CANR 30

Lange, John
See Crichton, (John) Michael

Langer, Elinor 1939- **CLC 34**
See also CA 121

Langland, William 1330(?)-1400(?) **LC 19; DA; DAB; DAC; DAM MST, POET**
See also DLB 146

Langstaff, Launcelot
See Irving, Washington

Lanier, Sidney 1842-1881 **NCLC 6; DAM POET**
See also DLB 64; DLBD 13; MAICYA; SATA 18

Lanyer, Aemilia 1569-1645 **LC 10, 30**
See also DLB 121

Lao-Tzu
See Lao Tzu

Lao Tzu fl. 6th cent. B.C.- **CMLC 7**

Lapine, James (Elliot) 1949- **CLC 39**
See also CA 123; 130; CANR 54; INT 130

Larbaud, Valery (Nicolas) 1881-1957**TCLC 9**
See also CA 106; 152

Lardner, Ring
See Lardner, Ring(gold) W(ilmer)

Lardner, Ring W., Jr.
See Lardner, Ring(gold) W(ilmer)

Lardner, Ring(gold) W(ilmer) 1885-1933 **TCLC 2, 14; SSC 32**
See also CA 104; 131; CDALB 1917-1929; DLB 11, 25, 86; DLBD 16; MTCW 1

Laredo, Betty
See Codrescu, Andrei

Larkin, Maia
See Wojciechowska, Maia (Teresa)

Larkin, Philip (Arthur) 1922-1985**CLC 3, 5, 8, 9, 13, 18, 33, 39, 64; DAB; DAM MST, POET; PC 21**
See also CA 5-8R; 117; CANR 24, 62; CDBLB 1960 to Present; DLB 27; MTCW 1

Larra (y Sanchez de Castro), Mariano Jose de 1809-1837 **NCLC 17**

Larsen, Eric 1941- **CLC 55**
See also CA 132

Larsen, Nella 1891-1964 **CLC 37; BLC 2; DAM MULT**
See also BW 1; CA 125; DLB 51

Larson, Charles R(aymond) 1938- **CLC 31**
See also CA 53-56; CANR 4

Larson, Jonathan 1961-1996 **CLC 99**
See also CA 156

Las Casas, Bartolome de 1474-1566 **LC 31**

Lasch, Christopher 1932-1994 **CLC 102**
See also CA 73-76; 144; CANR 25; MTCW 1

Lasker-Schueler, Else 1869-1945 **TCLC 57**
See also DLB 66, 124

Laski, Harold 1893-1950 **TCLC 79**

Latham, Jean Lee 1902-1995 **CLC 12**
See also AITN 1; CA 5-8R; CANR 7; CLR 50; MAICYA; SATA 2, 68

Latham, Mavis
See Clark, Mavis Thorpe

Lathen, Emma **CLC 2**
See also Hennissart, Martha; Latsis, Mary J(ane)

Lathrop, Francis
See Leiber, Fritz (Reuter, Jr.)

50; DAM NOV
See also CA 41-44R; CANR 29, 67; CLR 7;
DLB 14, 161; JRDA; MAICYA; MTCW 1;
SATA 7, 60, 101
Livesay, Dorothy (Kathleen) 1909-CLC 4, 15,
79; DAC; DAM MST, POET
See also AITN 2; CA 25-28R; CAAS 8; CANR
36, 67; DLB 68; MTCW 1
Livy c. 59B.C.-c. 17   **CMLC 11**
Lizardi, Jose Joaquin Fernandez de 1776-1827
NCLC 30
Llewellyn, Richard
See Llewellyn Lloyd, Richard Dafydd Vivian
See also DLB 15
Llewellyn Lloyd, Richard Dafydd Vivian 1906-
1983   **CLC 7, 80**
See also Llewellyn, Richard
See also CA 53-56; 111; CANR 7, 71; SATA
11; SATA-Obit 37
Llosa, (Jorge) Mario (Pedro) Vargas
See Vargas Llosa, (Jorge) Mario (Pedro)
Lloyd, Manda
See Mander, (Mary) Jane
Lloyd Webber, Andrew 1948-
See Webber, Andrew Lloyd
See also AAYA 1; CA 116; 149; DAM DRAM;
SATA 56
Llull, Ramon c. 1235-c. 1316   **CMLC 12**
Lobb, Ebenezer
See Upward, Allen
Locke, Alain (Le Roy) 1886-1954 **TCLC 43;**
BLCS
See also BW 1; CA 106; 124; DLB 51
Locke, John 1632-1704   **LC 7, 35**
See also DLB 101
Locke-Elliott, Sumner
See Elliott, Sumner Locke
Lockhart, John Gibson 1794-1854 **NCLC 6**
See also DLB 110, 116, 144
Lodge, David (John) 1935-CLC 36; DAM POP
See also BEST 90:1; CA 17-20R; CANR 19,
53; DLB 14, 194; INT CANR-19; MTCW 1
Lodge, Thomas 1558-1625   **LC 41**
See also DLB 172
Lodge, Thomas 1558-1625   **LC 41**
Loennbohm, Armas Eino Leopold 1878-1926
See Leino, Eino
See also CA 123
Loewinsohn, Ron(ald William) 1937-CLC 52
See also CA 25-28R; CANR 71
Logan, Jake
See Smith, Martin Cruz
Logan, John (Burton) 1923-1987   **CLC 5**
See also CA 77-80; 124; CANR 45; DLB 5
Lo Kuan-chung 1330(?)-1400(?)   **LC 12**
Lombard, Nap
See Johnson, Pamela Hansford
London, Jack TCLC 9, 15, 39; SSC 4; WLC
See also London, John Griffith
See also AAYA 13; AITN 2; CDALB 1865-
1917; DLB 8, 12, 78; SATA 18
London, John Griffith 1876-1916
See London, Jack
See also CA 110; 119; CANR 73; DA; DAB;
DAC; DAM MST, NOV; JRDA; MAICYA;
MTCW 1
Long, Emmett
See Leonard, Elmore (John, Jr.)
Longbaugh, Harry
See Goldman, William (W.)
Longfellow, Henry Wadsworth 1807-1882
NCLC 2, 45; DA; DAB; DAC; DAM MST,
POET; WLCS

See also CDALB 1640-1865; DLB 1, 59; SATA
19
Longinus c. 1st cent. -   **CMLC 27**
See also DLB 176
Longley, Michael 1939-   **CLC 29**
See also CA 102; DLB 40
Longus fl. c. 2nd cent. -   **CMLC 7**
Longway, A. Hugh
See Lang, Andrew
Lonnrot, Elias 1802-1884   **NCLC 53**
Lopate, Phillip 1943-   **CLC 29**
See also CA 97-100; DLBY 80; INT 97-100
Lopez Portillo (y Pacheco), Jose 1920-CLC 46
See also CA 129; HW
Lopez y Fuentes, Gregorio 1897(?)-1966C L C
32
See also CA 131; HW
Lorca, Federico Garcia
See Garcia Lorca, Federico
Lord, Bette Bao 1938-   **CLC 23**
See also BEST 90:3; CA 107; CANR 41; INT
107; SATA 58
Lord Auch
See Bataille, Georges
Lord Byron
See Byron, George Gordon (Noel)
Lorde, Audre (Geraldine) 1934-1992CLC 18,
71; BLC 2; DAM MULT, POET; PC 12
See also BW 1; CA 25-28R; 142; CANR 16,
26, 46; DLB 41; MTCW 1
Lord Houghton
See Milnes, Richard Monckton
Lord Jeffrey
See Jeffrey, Francis
Lorenzini, Carlo 1826-1890
See Collodi, Carlo
See also MAICYA; SATA 29, 100
Lorenzo, Heberto Padilla
See Padilla (Lorenzo), Heberto
Loris
See Hofmannsthal, Hugo von
Loti, Pierre   **TCLC 11**
See also Viaud, (Louis Marie) Julien
See also DLB 123
Louie, David Wong 1954-   **CLC 70**
See also CA 139
Louis, Father M.
See Merton, Thomas
Lovecraft, H(oward) P(hillips) 1890-1937
TCLC 4, 22; DAM POP; SSC 3
See also AAYA 14; CA 104; 133; MTCW 1
Lovelace, Earl 1935-   **CLC 51**
See also BW 2; CA 77-80; CANR 41, 72; DLB
125; MTCW 1
Lovelace, Richard 1618-1657   **LC 24**
See also DLB 131
Lowell, Amy 1874-1925   **TCLC 1, 8; DAM**
POET; PC 13
See also CA 104; 151; DLB 54, 140
Lowell, James Russell 1819-1891   **NCLC 2**
See also CDALB 1640-1865; DLB 1, 11, 64,
79, 189
Lowell, Robert (Traill Spence, Jr.) 1917-1977
CLC 1, 2, 3, 4, 5, 8, 9, 11, 15, 37; DA; DAB;
DAC; DAM MST, NOV; PC 3; WLC
See also CA 9-12R; 73-76; CABS 2; CANR 26,
60; DLB 5, 169; MTCW 1
Lowndes, Marie Adelaide (Belloc) 1868-1947
TCLC 12
See also CA 107; DLB 70
Lowry, (Clarence) Malcolm 1909-1957T C L C
6, 40; SSC 31
See also CA 105; 131; CANR 62; CDBLB

1945-1960; DLB 15; MTCW 1
Lowry, Mina Gertrude 1882-1966
See Loy, Mina
See also CA 113
Loxsmith, John
See Brunner, John (Kilian Houston)
Loy, Mina   **CLC 28; DAM POET; PC 16**
See also Lowry, Mina Gertrude
See also DLB 4, 54
Loyson-Bridet
See Schwob, Marcel (Mayer Andre)
Lucas, Craig 1951-   **CLC 64**
See also CA 137; CANR 71
Lucas, E(dward) V(errall) 1868-1938 **T C L C**
73
See also DLB 98, 149, 153; SATA 20
Lucas, George 1944-   **CLC 16**
See also AAYA 1, 23; CA 77-80; CANR 30;
SATA 56
Lucas, Hans
See Godard, Jean-Luc
Lucas, Victoria
See Plath, Sylvia
Ludlam, Charles 1943-1987   **CLC 46, 50**
See also CA 85-88; 122; CANR 72
Ludlum, Robert 1927-CLC 22, 43; DAM NOV,
POP
See also AAYA 10; BEST 89:1, 90:3; CA 33-
36R; CANR 25, 41, 68; DLBY 82; MTCW
1
Ludwig, Ken   **CLC 60**
Ludwig, Otto 1813-1865   **NCLC 4**
See also DLB 129
Lugones, Leopoldo 1874-1938   **TCLC 15**
See also CA 116; 131; HW
Lu Hsun 1881-1936   **TCLC 3; SSC 20**
See also Shu-Jen, Chou
Lukacs, George   **CLC 24**
See also Lukacs, Gyorgy (Szegeny von)
Lukacs, Gyorgy (Szegeny von) 1885-1971
See Lukacs, George
See also CA 101; 29-32R; CANR 62
Luke, Peter (Ambrose Cyprian) 1919-1995
CLC 38
See also CA 81-84; 147; CANR 72; DLB 13
Lunar, Dennis
See Mungo, Raymond
Lurie, Alison 1926-   **CLC 4, 5, 18, 39**
See also CA 1-4R; CANR 2, 17, 50; DLB 2;
MTCW 1; SATA 46
Lustig, Arnost 1926-   **CLC 56**
See also AAYA 3; CA 69-72; CANR 47; SATA
56
Luther, Martin 1483-1546   **LC 9, 37**
See also DLB 179
Luxemburg, Rosa 1870(?)-1919   **TCLC 63**
See also CA 118
Luzi, Mario 1914-   **CLC 13**
See also CA 61-64; CANR 9, 70; DLB 128
Lyly, John 1554(?)-1606LC 41; DAM DRAM;
DC 7
See also DLB 62, 167
L'Ymagier
See Gourmont, Remy (-Marie-Charles) de
Lynch, B. Suarez
See Bioy Casares, Adolfo; Borges, Jorge Luis
Lynch, David (K.) 1946-   **CLC 66**
See also CA 124; 129
Lynch, James
See Andreyev, Leonid (Nikolaevich)
Lynch Davis, B.
See Bioy Casares, Adolfo; Borges, Jorge Luis
Lyndsay, Sir David 1490-1555   **LC 20**

Lynn, Kenneth S(chuyler) 1923-   **CLC 50**
See also CA 1-4R; CANR 3, 27, 65
Lynx
See West, Rebecca
Lyons, Marcus
See Blish, James (Benjamin)
Lyre, Pinchbeck
See Sassoon, Siegfried (Lorraine)
Lytle, Andrew (Nelson) 1902-1995   **CLC 22**
See also CA 9-12R; 150; CANR 70; DLB 6;
DLBY 95
Lyttelton, George 1709-1773   **LC 10**
Maas, Peter 1929-   **CLC 29**
See also CA 93-96; INT 93-96
Macaulay, Rose 1881-1958   **TCLC 7, 44**
See also CA 104; DLB 36
Macaulay, Thomas Babington 1800-1859
    NCLC 42
See also CDBLB 1832-1890; DLB 32, 55
MacBeth, George (Mann) 1932-1992**CLC 2, 5,**
9
See also CA 25-28R; 136; CANR 61, 66; DLB
40; MTCW 1; SATA 4; SATA-Obit 70
MacCaig, Norman (Alexander) 1910-**CLC 36;**
DAB; DAM POET
See also CA 9-12R; CANR 3, 34; DLB 27
MacCarthy, Sir(Charles Otto) Desmond 1877-
1952   **TCLC 36**
See also CA 167
MacDiarmid, Hugh**CLC 2, 4, 11, 19, 63; PC 9**
See also Grieve, C(hristopher) M(urray)
See also CDBLB 1945-1960; DLB 20
MacDonald, Anson
See Heinlein, Robert A(nson)
Macdonald, Cynthia 1928-   **CLC 13, 19**
See also CA 49-52; CANR 4, 44; DLB 105
MacDonald, George 1824-1905   **TCLC 9**
See also CA 106; 137; DLB 18, 163, 178;
MAICYA; SATA 33, 100
Macdonald, John
See Millar, Kenneth
MacDonald, John D(ann) 1916-1986 **CLC 3,**
27, 44; DAM NOV, POP
See also CA 1-4R; 121; CANR 1, 19, 60; DLB
8; DLBY 86; MTCW 1
Macdonald, John Ross
See Millar, Kenneth
Macdonald, Ross   **CLC 1, 2, 3, 14, 34, 41**
See also Millar, Kenneth
See also DLBD 6
MacDougal, John
See Blish, James (Benjamin)
MacEwen, Gwendolyn (Margaret) 1941-1987
    CLC 13, 55
See also CA 9-12R; 124; CANR 7, 22; DLB
53; SATA 50; SATA-Obit 55
Macha, Karel Hynek 1810-1846   **NCLC 46**
Machado (y Ruiz), Antonio 1875-1939**T C L C**
3
See also CA 104; DLB 108
Machado de Assis, Joaquim Maria 1839-1908
    TCLC 10; BLC 2; SSC 24
See also CA 107; 153
Machen, Arthur   **TCLC 4; SSC 20**
See also Jones, Arthur Llewellyn
See also DLB 36, 156, 178
Machiavelli, Niccolo 1469-1527**LC 8, 36; DA;**
DAB; DAC; DAM MST; WLCS
MacInnes, Colin 1914-1976   **CLC 4, 23**
See also CA 69-72; 65-68; CANR 21; DLB 14;
MTCW 1
MacInnes, Helen (Clark) 1907-1985 **CLC 27,**
39; DAM POP

See also CA 1-4R; 117; CANR 1, 28, 58; DLB
87; MTCW 1; SATA 22; SATA-Obit 44
Mackay, Mary 1855-1924
See Corelli, Marie
See also CA 118
Mackenzie, Compton (Edward Montague)
1883-1972   **CLC 18**
See also CA 21-22; 37-40R; CAP 2; DLB 34,
100
Mackenzie, Henry 1745-1831   **NCLC 41**
See also DLB 39
Mackintosh, Elizabeth 1896(?)-1952
See Tey, Josephine
See also CA 110
MacLaren, James
See Grieve, C(hristopher) M(urray)
Mac Laverty, Bernard 1942-   **CLC 31**
See also CA 116; 118; CANR 43; INT 118
MacLean, Alistair (Stuart) 1922(?)-1987**C L C**
3, 13, 50, 63; DAM POP
See also CA 57-60; 121; CANR 28, 61; MTCW
1; SATA 23; SATA-Obit 50
Maclean, Norman (Fitzroy) 1902-1990 **C L C**
78; DAM POP; SSC 13
See also CA 102; 132; CANR 49
MacLeish, Archibald 1892-1982**CLC 3, 8, 14,**
68; DAM POET
See also CA 9-12R; 106; CANR 33, 63; DLB
4, 7, 45; DLBY 82; MTCW 1
MacLennan, (John) Hugh 1907-1990 **CLC 2,**
14, 92; DAC; DAM MST
See also CA 5-8R; 142; CANR 33; DLB 68;
MTCW 1
MacLeod, Alistair 1936-**CLC 56; DAC; DAM**
MST
See also CA 123; DLB 60
Macleod, Fiona
See Sharp, William
MacNeice, (Frederick) Louis 1907-1963 **C L C**
1, 4, 10, 53; DAB; DAM POET
See also CA 85-88; CANR 61; DLB 10, 20;
MTCW 1
MacNeill, Dand
See Fraser, George MacDonald
Macpherson, James 1736-1796   **LC 29**
See also Ossian
See also DLB 109
Macpherson, (Jean) Jay 1931-   **CLC 14**
See also CA 5-8R; DLB 53
MacShane, Frank 1927-   **CLC 39**
See also CA 9-12R; CANR 3, 33; DLB 111
Macumber, Mari
See Sandoz, Mari(e Susette)
Madach, Imre 1823-1864   **NCLC 19**
Madden, (Jerry) David 1933-   **CLC 5, 15**
See also CA 1-4R; CAAS 3; CANR 4, 45; DLB
6; MTCW 1
Maddern, Al(an)
See Ellison, Harlan (Jay)
Madhubuti, Haki R. 1942-**CLC 6, 73; BLC 2;**
DAM MULT, POET; PC 5
See also Lee, Don L.
See also BW 2; CA 73-76; CANR 24, 51, 73;
DLB 5, 41; DLBD 8
Maepenn, Hugh
See Kuttner, Henry
Maepenn, K. H.
See Kuttner, Henry
Maeterlinck, Maurice 1862-1949   **TCLC 3;**
DAM DRAM
See also CA 104; 136; DLB 192; SATA 66
Maginn, William 1794-1842   **NCLC 8**
See also DLB 110, 159

Mahapatra, Jayanta 1928-   **CLC 33; DAM**
MULT
See also CA 73-76; CAAS 9; CANR 15, 33, 66
Mahfouz, Naguib (Abdel Aziz Al-Sabilgi)
1911(?)-
See Mahfuz, Najib
See also BEST 89:2; CA 128; CANR 55; DAM
NOV; MTCW 1
Mahfuz, Najib   **CLC 52, 55**
See also Mahfouz, Naguib (Abdel Aziz Al-
Sabilgi)
See also DLBY 88
Mahon, Derek 1941-   **CLC 27**
See also CA 113; 128; DLB 40
Mailer, Norman 1923-**CLC 1, 2, 3, 4, 5, 8, 11,**
14, 28, 39, 74, 111; DA; DAB; DAC; DAM
MST, NOV, POP
See also AITN 2; CA 9-12R; CABS 1; CANR
28, 74; CDALB 1968-1988; DLB 2, 16, 28,
185; DLBD 3; DLBY 80, 83; MTCW 1
Maillet, Antonine 1929-   **CLC 54; DAC**
See also CA 115; 120; CANR 46, 74; DLB 60;
INT 120
Mais, Roger 1905-1955   **TCLC 8**
See also BW 1; CA 105; 124; DLB 125; MTCW
1
Maistre, Joseph de 1753-1821   **NCLC 37**
Maitland, Frederic 1850-1906   **TCLC 65**
Maitland, Sara (Louise) 1950-   **CLC 49**
See also CA 69-72; CANR 13, 59
Major, Clarence 1936-**CLC 3, 19, 48; BLC 2;**
DAM MULT
See also BW 2; CA 21-24R; CAAS 6; CANR
13, 25, 53; DLB 33
Major, Kevin (Gerald) 1949- **CLC 26; DAC**
See also AAYA 16; CA 97-100; CANR 21, 38;
CLR 11; DLB 60; INT CANR-21; JRDA;
MAICYA; SATA 32, 82
Maki, James
See Ozu, Yasujiro
Malabaila, Damiano
See Levi, Primo
Malamud, Bernard 1914-1986**CLC 1, 2, 3, 5,**
8, 9, 11, 18, 27, 44, 78, 85; DA; DAB; DAC;
DAM MST, NOV, POP; SSC 15; WLC
See also AAYA 16; CA 5-8R; 118; CABS 1;
CANR 28, 62; CDALB 1941-1968; DLB 2,
28, 152; DLBY 80, 86; MTCW 1
Malan, Herman
See Bosman, Herman Charles; Bosman, Herman
Charles
Malaparte, Curzio 1898-1957   **TCLC 52**
Malcolm, Dan
See Silverberg, Robert
Malcolm X   **CLC 82, 117; BLC 2; WLCS**
See also Little, Malcolm
Malherbe, Francois de 1555-1628   **LC 5**
Mallarme, Stephane 1842-1898 **NCLC 4, 41;**
DAM POET; PC 4
Mallet-Joris, Francoise 1930-   **CLC 11**
See also CA 65-68; CANR 17; DLB 83
Malley, Ern
See McAuley, James Phillip
Mallowan, Agatha Christie
See Christie, Agatha (Mary Clarissa)
Maloff, Saul 1922-   **CLC 5**
See also CA 33-36R
Malone, Louis
See MacNeice, (Frederick) Louis
Malone, Michael (Christopher) 1942-**CLC 43**
See also CA 77-80; CANR 14, 32, 57
Malory, (Sir) Thomas 1410(?)-1471(?)**LC 11;**
DA; DAB; DAC; DAM MST; WLCS

See also CDBLB Before 1660; DLB 146; SATA
 59; SATA-Brief 33
Malouf, (George Joseph) David 1934-**CLC 28,
 86**
 See also CA 124; CANR 50
Malraux, (Georges-)Andre 1901-1976**CLC 1,
 4, 9, 13, 15, 57; DAM NOV**
 See also CA 21-22; 69-72; CANR 34, 58; CAP
 2; DLB 72; MTCW 1
Malzberg, Barry N(athaniel) 1939-   **CLC 7**
 See also CA 61-64; CAAS 4; CANR 16; DLB 8
Mamet, David (Alan) 1947-**CLC 9, 15, 34, 46,
 91; DAM DRAM; DC 4**
 See also AAYA 3; CA 81-84; CABS 3; CANR
 15, 41, 67, 72; DLB 7; MTCW 1
Mamoulian, Rouben (Zachary) 1897-1987
 CLC 16
 See also CA 25-28R; 124
Mandelstam, Osip (Emilievich) 1891(?)-1938(?)
 TCLC 2, 6; PC 14
 See also CA 104; 150
Mander, (Mary) Jane 1877-1949   **TCLC 31**
 See also CA 162
Mandeville, John fl. 1350-   **CMLC 19**
 See also DLB 146
Mandiargues, Andre Pieyre de   **CLC 41**
 See also Pieyre de Mandiargues, Andre
 See also DLB 83
Mandrake, Ethel Belle
 See Thurman, Wallace (Henry)
Mangan, James Clarence 1803-1849**NCLC 27**
Maniere, J.-E.
 See Giraudoux, (Hippolyte) Jean
Mankiewicz, Herman (Jacob) 1897-1953
 TCLC 85
 See also CA 120; 169; DLB 26
Manley, (Mary) Delariviere 1672(?)-1724 **L C
 1, 42**
 See also DLB 39, 80
Mann, Abel
 See Creasey, John
Mann, Emily 1952-   **DC 7**
 See also CA 130; CANR 55
Mann, (Luiz) Heinrich 1871-1950   **TCLC 9**
 See also CA 106; 164; DLB 66
Mann, (Paul) Thomas 1875-1955 **TCLC 2, 8,
 14, 21, 35, 44, 60; DA; DAB; DAC; DAM
 MST, NOV; SSC 5; WLC**
 See also CA 104; 128; DLB 66; MTCW 1
Mannheim, Karl 1893-1947   **TCLC 65**
Manning, David
 See Faust, Frederick (Schiller)
Manning, Frederic 1887(?)-1935   **TCLC 25**
 See also CA 124
Manning, Olivia 1915-1980   **CLC 5, 19**
 See also CA 5-8R; 101; CANR 29; MTCW 1
Mano, D. Keith 1942-   **CLC 2, 10**
 See also CA 25-28R; CAAS 6; CANR 26, 57;
 DLB 6
Mansfield, KatherineTCLC 2, 8, 39; DAB; SSC
 9, 23; WLC
 See also Beauchamp, Kathleen Mansfield
 See also DLB 162
Manso, Peter 1940-   **CLC 39**
 See also CA 29-32R; CANR 44
Mantecon, Juan Jimenez
 See Jimenez (Mantecon), Juan Ramon
Manton, Peter
 See Creasey, John
Man Without a Spleen, A
 See Chekhov, Anton (Pavlovich)
Manzoni, Alessandro 1785-1873   **NCLC 29**
Mapu, Abraham (ben Jekutiel) 1808-1867

NCLC 18
Mara, Sally
 See Queneau, Raymond
Marat, Jean Paul 1743-1793   **LC 10**
Marcel, Gabriel Honore 1889-1973   **CLC 15**
 See also CA 102; 45-48; MTCW 1
Marchbanks, Samuel
 See Davies, (William) Robertson
Marchi, Giacomo
 See Bassani, Giorgio
Margulies, Donald   **CLC 76**
Marie de France c. 12th cent. - **CMLC 8; PC
 22**
Marie de l'Incarnation 1599-1672   **LC 10**
Marier, Captain Victor
 See Griffith, D(avid Lewelyn) W(ark)
Mariner, Scott
 See Pohl, Frederik
Marinetti, Filippo Tommaso 1876-1944**TCLC
 10**
 See also CA 107; DLB 114
Marivaux, Pierre Carlet de Chamblain de 1688-
 1763   **LC 4; DC 7**
Markandaya, Kamala   **CLC 8, 38**
 See also Taylor, Kamala (Purnaiya)
Markfield, Wallace 1926-   **CLC 8**
 See also CA 69-72; CAAS 3; DLB 2, 28
Markham, Edwin 1852-1940   **TCLC 47**
 See also CA 160; DLB 54, 186
Markham, Robert
 See Amis, Kingsley (William)
Marks, J
 See Highwater, Jamake (Mamake)
Marks-Highwater, J
 See Highwater, Jamake (Mamake)
Markson, David M(errill) 1927-   **CLC 67**
 See also CA 49-52; CANR 1
Marley, Bob   **CLC 17**
 See also Marley, Robert Nesta
Marley, Robert Nesta 1945-1981
 See Marley, Bob
 See also CA 107; 103
Marlowe, Christopher 1564-1593 **LC 22, 47;
 DA; DAB; DAC; DAM DRAM, MST; DC
 1; WLC**
 See also CDBLB Before 1660; DLB 62
Marlowe, Stephen 1928-
 See Queen, Ellery
 See also CA 13-16R; CANR 6, 55
Marmontel, Jean-Francois 1723-1799 **LC 2**
Marquand, John P(hillips) 1893-1960**CLC 2,
 10**
 See also CA 85-88; CANR 73; DLB 9, 102
Marques, Rene 1919-1979   **CLC 96; DAM
 MULT; HLC**
 See also CA 97-100; 85-88; DLB 113; HW
Marquez, Gabriel (Jose) Garcia
 See Garcia Marquez, Gabriel (Jose)
Marquis, Don(ald Robert Perry) 1878-1937
 TCLC 7
 See also CA 104; 166; DLB 11, 25
Marric, J. J.
 See Creasey, John
Marryat, Frederick 1792-1848   **NCLC 3**
 See also DLB 21, 163
Marsden, James
 See Creasey, John
Marsh, (Edith) Ngaio 1899-1982 **CLC 7, 53;
 DAM POP**
 See also CA 9-12R; CANR 6, 58; DLB 77;
 MTCW 1
Marshall, Garry 1934-   **CLC 17**
 See also AAYA 3; CA 111; SATA 60

Marshall, Paule 1929-   **CLC 27, 72; BLC 3;
 DAM MULT; SSC 3**
 See also BW 2; CA 77-80; CANR 25, 73; DLB
 157; MTCW 1
Marshallik
 See Zangwill, Israel
Marsten, Richard
 See Hunter, Evan
Marston, John 1576-1634**LC 33; DAM DRAM**
 See also DLB 58, 172
Martha, Henry
 See Harris, Mark
Marti, Jose 1853-1895**NCLC 63; DAM MULT;
 HLC**
Martial c. 40-c. 104   **PC 10**
Martin, Ken
 See Hubbard, L(afayette) Ron(ald)
Martin, Richard
 See Creasey, John
Martin, Steve 1945-   **CLC 30**
 See also CA 97-100; CANR 30; MTCW 1
Martin, Valerie 1948-   **CLC 89**
 See also BEST 90:2; CA 85-88; CANR 49
Martin, Violet Florence 1862-1915 **TCLC 51**
Martin, Webber
 See Silverberg, Robert
Martindale, Patrick Victor
 See White, Patrick (Victor Martindale)
Martin du Gard, Roger 1881-1958 **TCLC 24**
 See also CA 118; DLB 65
Martineau, Harriet 1802-1876   **NCLC 26**
 See also DLB 21, 55, 159, 163, 166, 190; YABC
 2
Martines, Julia
 See O'Faolain, Julia
Martinez, Enrique Gonzalez
 See Gonzalez Martinez, Enrique
Martinez, Jacinto Benavente y
 See Benavente (y Martinez), Jacinto
Martinez Ruiz, Jose 1873-1967
 See Azorin; Ruiz, Jose Martinez
 See also CA 93-96; HW
Martinez Sierra, Gregorio 1881-1947**TCLC 6**
 See also CA 115
Martinez Sierra, Maria (de la O'LeJarraga)
 1874-1974   **TCLC 6**
 See also CA 115
Martinsen, Martin
 See Follett, Ken(neth Martin)
Martinson, Harry (Edmund) 1904-1978 **C L C
 14**
 See also CA 77-80; CANR 34
Marut, Ret
 See Traven, B.
Marut, Robert
 See Traven, B.
Marvell, Andrew 1621-1678   **LC 4, 43; DA;
 DAB; DAC; DAM MST, POET; PC 10;
 WLC**
 See also CDBLB 1660-1789; DLB 131
Marx, Karl (Heinrich) 1818-1883 **NCLC 17**
 See also DLB 129
Masaoka Shiki   **TCLC 18**
 See also Masaoka Tsunenori
Masaoka Tsunenori 1867-1902
 See Masaoka Shiki
 See also CA 117
Masefield, John (Edward) 1878-1967**CLC 11,
 47; DAM POET**
 See also CA 19-20; 25-28R; CANR 33; CAP 2;
 CDBLB 1890-1914; DLB 10, 19, 153, 160;
 MTCW 1; SATA 19
Maso, Carole 19(?)-   **CLC 44**

See also SATA 2

McInerney, Jay 1955-**CLC 34, 112; DAM POP**
See also AAYA 18; CA 116; 123; CANR 45, 68; INT 123

McIntyre, Vonda N(eel) 1948- **CLC 18**
See also CA 81-84; CANR 17, 34, 69; MTCW 1

McKay, Claude TCLC 7, 41; BLC 3; DAB; PC 2
See also McKay, Festus Claudius
See also DLB 4, 45, 51, 117

McKay, Festus Claudius 1889-1948
See McKay, Claude
See also BW 1; CA 104; 124; CANR 73; DA; DAC; DAM MST, MULT, NOV, POET; MTCW 1; WLC

McKuen, Rod 1933- **CLC 1, 3**
See also AITN 1; CA 41-44R; CANR 40

McLoughlin, R. B.
See Mencken, H(enry) L(ouis)

McLuhan, (Herbert) Marshall 1911-1980 **CLC 37, 83**
See also CA 9-12R; 102; CANR 12, 34, 61; DLB 88; INT CANR-12; MTCW 1

McMillan, Terry (L.) 1951- **CLC 50, 61, 112; BLCS; DAM MULT, NOV, POP**
See also AAYA 21; BW 2; CA 140; CANR 60

McMurtry, Larry (Jeff) 1936-**CLC 2, 3, 7, 11, 27, 44; DAM NOV, POP**
See also AAYA 15; AITN 2; BEST 89:2; CA 5-8R; CANR 19, 43, 64; CDALB 1968-1988; DLB 2, 143; DLBY 80, 87; MTCW 1

McNally, T. M. 1961- **CLC 82**

McNally, Terrence 1939- **CLC 4, 7, 41, 91; DAM DRAM**
See also CA 45-48; CANR 2, 56; DLB 7

McNamer, Deirdre 1950- **CLC 70**

McNeile, Herman Cyril 1888-1937
See Sapper
See also DLB 77

McNickle, (William) D'Arcy 1904-1977 **C L C 89; DAM MULT**
See also CA 9-12R; 85-88; CANR 5, 45; DLB 175; NNAL; SATA-Obit 22

McPhee, John (Angus) 1931- **CLC 36**
See also BEST 90:1; CA 65-68; CANR 20, 46, 64, 69; DLB 185; MTCW 1

McPherson, James Alan 1943- **CLC 19, 77; BLCS**
See also BW 1; CA 25-28R; CAAS 17; CANR 24, 74; DLB 38; MTCW 1

McPherson, William (Alexander) 1933- **C L C 34**
See also CA 69-72; CANR 28; INT CANR-28

Mead, Margaret 1901-1978 **CLC 37**
See also AITN 1; CA 1-4R; 81-84; CANR 4; MTCW 1; SATA-Obit 20

Meaker, Marijane (Agnes) 1927-
See Kerr, M. E.
See also CA 107; CANR 37, 63; INT 107; JRDA; MAICYA; MTCW 1; SATA 20, 61, 99

Medoff, Mark (Howard) 1940- **CLC 6, 23; DAM DRAM**
See also AITN 1; CA 53-56; CANR 5; DLB 7; INT CANR-5

Medvedev, P. N.
See Bakhtin, Mikhail Mikhailovich

Meged, Aharon
See Megged, Aharon

Meged, Aron
See Megged, Aharon

Megged, Aharon 1920- **CLC 9**

See also CA 49-52; CAAS 13; CANR 1

Mehta, Ved (Parkash) 1934- **CLC 37**
See also CA 1-4R; CANR 2, 23, 69; MTCW 1

Melanter
See Blackmore, R(ichard) D(oddridge)

Melies, Georges 1861-1938 **TCLC 81**

Melikow, Loris
See Hofmannsthal, Hugo von

Melmoth, Sebastian
See Wilde, Oscar (Fingal O'Flahertie Wills)

Meltzer, Milton 1915- **CLC 26**
See also AAYA 8; CA 13-16R; CANR 38; CLR 13; DLB 61; JRDA; MAICYA; SAAS 1; SATA 1, 50, 80

Melville, Herman 1819-1891**NCLC 3, 12, 29, 45, 49; DA; DAB; DAC; DAM MST, NOV; SSC 1, 17; WLC**
See also AAYA 25; CDALB 1640-1865; DLB 3, 74; SATA 59

Menander c. 342B.C.-c. 292B.C. **CMLC 9; DAM DRAM; DC 3**
See also DLB 176

Mencken, H(enry) L(ouis) 1880-1956 **T C L C 13**
See also CA 105; 125; CDALB 1917-1929; DLB 11, 29, 63, 137; MTCW 1

Mendelsohn, Jane 1965(?)- **CLC 99**
See also CA 154

Mercer, David 1928-1980**CLC 5; DAM DRAM**
See also CA 9-12R; 102; CANR 23; DLB 13; MTCW 1

Merchant, Paul
See Ellison, Harlan (Jay)

Meredith, George 1828-1909 **TCLC 17, 43; DAM POET**
See also CA 117; 153; CDBLB 1832-1890; DLB 18, 35, 57, 159

Meredith, William (Morris) 1919-**CLC 4, 13, 22, 55; DAM POET**
See also CA 9-12R; CAAS 14; CANR 6, 40; DLB 5

Merezhkovsky, Dmitry Sergeyevich 1865-1941 **TCLC 29**
See also CA 169

Merimee, Prosper 1803-1870**NCLC 6, 65; SSC 7**
See also DLB 119, 192

Merkin, Daphne 1954- **CLC 44**
See also CA 123

Merlin, Arthur
See Blish, James (Benjamin)

Merrill, James (Ingram) 1926-1995**CLC 2, 3, 6, 8, 13, 18, 34, 91; DAM POET**
See also CA 13-16R; 147; CANR 10, 49, 63; DLB 5, 165; DLBY 85; INT CANR-10; MTCW 1

Merriman, Alex
See Silverberg, Robert

Merriman, Brian 1747-1805 **NCLC 70**

Merritt, E. B.
See Waddington, Miriam

Merton, Thomas 1915-1968 **CLC 1, 3, 11, 34, 83; PC 10**
See also CA 5-8R; 25-28R; CANR 22, 53; DLB 48; DLBY 81; MTCW 1

Merwin, W(illiam) S(tanley) 1927- **CLC 1, 2, 3, 5, 8, 13, 18, 45, 88; DAM POET**
See also CA 13-16R; CANR 15, 51; DLB 5, 169; INT CANR-15; MTCW 1

Metcalf, John 1938- **CLC 37**
See also CA 113; DLB 60

Metcalf, Suzanne
See Baum, L(yman) Frank

Mew, Charlotte (Mary) 1870-1928 **TCLC 8**
See also CA 105; DLB 19, 135

Mewshaw, Michael 1943- **CLC 9**
See also CA 53-56; CANR 7, 47; DLBY 80

Meyer, June
See Jordan, June

Meyer, Lynn
See Slavitt, David R(ytman)

Meyer-Meyrink, Gustav 1868-1932
See Meyrink, Gustav
See also CA 117

Meyers, Jeffrey 1939- **CLC 39**
See also CA 73-76; CANR 54; DLB 111

Meynell, Alice (Christina Gertrude Thompson) 1847-1922 **TCLC 6**
See also CA 104; DLB 19, 98

Meyrink, Gustav **TCLC 21**
See also Meyer-Meyrink, Gustav
See also DLB 81

Michaels, Leonard 1933- **CLC 6, 25; SSC 16**
See also CA 61-64; CANR 21, 62; DLB 130; MTCW 1

Michaux, Henri 1899-1984 **CLC 8, 19**
See also CA 85-88; 114

Micheaux, Oscar 1884-1951 **TCLC 76**
See also DLB 50

Michelangelo 1475-1564 **LC 12**

Michelet, Jules 1798-1874 **NCLC 31**

Michels, Robert 1876-1936 **TCLC 88**

Michener, James A(lbert) 1907(?)-1997 **C L C 1, 5, 11, 29, 60, 109; DAM NOV, POP**
See also AAYA 27; AITN 1; BEST 90:1; CA 5-8R; 161; CANR 21, 45, 68; DLB 6; MTCW 1

Mickiewicz, Adam 1798-1855 **NCLC 3**

Middleton, Christopher 1926- **CLC 13**
See also CA 13-16R; CANR 29, 54; DLB 40

Middleton, Richard (Barham) 1882-1911 **TCLC 56**
See also DLB 156

Middleton, Stanley 1919- **CLC 7, 38**
See also CA 25-28R; CAAS 23; CANR 21, 46; DLB 14

Middleton, Thomas 1580-1627 **LC 33; DAM DRAM, MST; DC 5**
See also DLB 58

Migueis, Jose Rodrigues 1901- **CLC 10**

Mikszath, Kalman 1847-1910 **TCLC 31**
See also CA 170

Miles, Jack **CLC 100**

Miles, Josephine (Louise) 1911-1985**CLC 1, 2, 14, 34, 39; DAM POET**
See also CA 1-4R; 116; CANR 2, 55; DLB 48

Militant
See Sandburg, Carl (August)

Mill, John Stuart 1806-1873 **NCLC 11, 58**
See also CDBLB 1832-1890; DLB 55, 190

Millar, Kenneth 1915-1983 **CLC 14; DAM POP**
See also Macdonald, Ross
See also CA 9-12R; 110; CANR 16, 63; DLB 2; DLBD 6; DLBY 83; MTCW 1

Millay, E. Vincent
See Millay, Edna St. Vincent

Millay, Edna St. Vincent 1892-1950 **TCLC 4, 49; DA; DAB; DAC; DAM MST, POET; PC 6; WLCS**
See also CA 104; 130; CDALB 1917-1929; DLB 45; MTCW 1

Miller, Arthur 1915-**CLC 1, 2, 6, 10, 15, 26, 47, 78; DA; DAB; DAC; DAM DRAM, MST; DC 1; WLC**
See also AAYA 15; AITN 1; CA 1-4R; CABS

3; CANR 2, 30, 54; CDALB 1941-1968;
DLB 7; MTCW 1
Miller, Henry (Valentine) 1891-1980**CLC 1, 2,
4, 9, 14, 43, 84; DA; DAB; DAC; DAM
MST, NOV; WLC**
See also CA 9-12R; 97-100; CANR 33, 64;
CDALB 1929-1941; DLB 4, 9; DLBY 80;
MTCW 1
Miller, Jason 1939(?)-   **CLC 2**
See also AITN 1; CA 73-76; DLB 7
Miller, Sue 1943-   **CLC 44; DAM POP**
See also BEST 90:3; CA 139; CANR 59; DLB
143
Miller, Walter M(ichael, Jr.) 1923-**CLC 4, 30**
See also CA 85-88; DLB 8
Millett, Kate 1934-   **CLC 67**
See also AITN 1; CA 73-76; CANR 32, 53;
MTCW 1
Millhauser, Steven (Lewis) 1943-**CLC 21, 54,
109**
See also CA 110; 111; CANR 63; DLB 2; INT
111
Millin, Sarah Gertrude 1889-1968   **CLC 49**
See also CA 102; 93-96
Milne, A(lan) A(lexander) 1882-1956**TCLC 6,
88; DAB; DAC; DAM MST**
See also CA 104; 133; CLR 1, 26; DLB 10, 77,
100, 160; MAICYA; MTCW 1; SATA 100;
YABC 1
Milner, Ron(ald) 1938-**CLC 56; BLC 3; DAM
MULT**
See also AITN 1; BW 1; CA 73-76; CANR 24;
DLB 38; MTCW 1
Milnes, Richard Monckton 1809-1885 **N C L C
61**
See also DLB 32, 184
Milosz, Czeslaw 1911- **CLC 5, 11, 22, 31, 56,
82; DAM MST, POET; PC 8; WLCS**
See also CA 81-84; CANR 23, 51; MTCW 1
Milton, John 1608-1674 **LC 9, 43; DA; DAB;
DAC; DAM MST, POET; PC 19; WLC**
See also CDBLB 1660-1789; DLB 131, 151
Min, Anchee 1957-   **CLC 86**
See also CA 146
Minehaha, Cornelius
See Wedekind, (Benjamin) Frank(lin)
Miner, Valerie 1947-   **CLC 40**
See also CA 97-100; CANR 59
Minimo, Duca
See D'Annunzio, Gabriele
Minot, Susan 1956-   **CLC 44**
See also CA 134
Minus, Ed 1938-   **CLC 39**
Miranda, Javier
See Bioy Casares, Adolfo
Mirbeau, Octave 1848-1917   **TCLC 55**
See also DLB 123, 192
Miro (Ferrer), Gabriel (Francisco Victor) 1879-
1930   **TCLC 5**
See also CA 104
Mishima, Yukio 1925-1970**CLC 2, 4, 6, 9, 27;
DC 1; SSC 4**
See also Hiraoka, Kimitake
See also DLB 182
Mistral, Frederic 1830-1914   **TCLC 51**
See also CA 122
Mistral, Gabriela   **TCLC 2; HLC**
See also Godoy Alcayaga, Lucila
Mistry, Rohinton 1952-   **CLC 71; DAC**
See also CA 141
Mitchell, Clyde
See Ellison, Harlan (Jay); Silverberg, Robert
Mitchell, James Leslie 1901-1935

See Gibbon, Lewis Grassic
See also CA 104; DLB 15
Mitchell, Joni 1943-   **CLC 12**
See also CA 112
Mitchell, Joseph (Quincy) 1908-1996**CLC 98**
See also CA 77-80; 152; CANR 69; DLB 185;
DLBY 96
Mitchell, Margaret (Munnerlyn) 1900-1949
TCLC 11; DAM NOV, POP
See also AAYA 23; CA 109; 125; CANR 55;
DLB 9; MTCW 1
Mitchell, Peggy
See Mitchell, Margaret (Munnerlyn)
Mitchell, S(ilas) Weir 1829-1914   **TCLC 36**
See also CA 165; DLB 202
Mitchell, W(illiam) O(rmond) 1914-1998**CLC
25; DAC; DAM MST**
See also CA 77-80; 165; CANR 15, 43; DLB
88
Mitchell, William 1879-1936   **TCLC 81**
Mitford, Mary Russell 1787-1855   **NCLC 4**
See also DLB 110, 116
Mitford, Nancy 1904-1973   **CLC 44**
See also CA 9-12R; DLB 191
Miyamoto, Yuriko 1899-1951   **TCLC 37**
See also CA 170; DLB 180
Miyazawa, Kenji 1896-1933   **TCLC 76**
See also CA 157
Mizoguchi, Kenji 1898-1956   **TCLC 72**
See also CA 167
Mo, Timothy (Peter) 1950(?)-   **CLC 46**
See also CA 117; DLB 194; MTCW 1
Modarressi, Taghi (M.) 1931-   **CLC 44**
See also CA 121; 134; INT 134
Modiano, Patrick (Jean) 1945-   **CLC 18**
See also CA 85-88; CANR 17, 40; DLB 83
Moerck, Paal
See Roelvaag, O(le) E(dvart)
Mofolo, Thomas (Mokopu) 1875(?)-1948
TCLC 22; BLC 3; DAM MULT
See also CA 121; 153
Mohr, Nicholasa 1938-**CLC 12; DAM MULT;
HLC**
See also AAYA 8; CA 49-52; CANR 1, 32, 64;
CLR 22; DLB 145; HW; JRDA; SAAS 8;
SATA 8, 97
Mojtabai, A(nn) G(race) 1938- **CLC 5, 9, 15,
29**
See also CA 85-88
Moliere 1622-1673**LC 10, 28; DA; DAB; DAC;
DAM DRAM, MST; WLC**
Molin, Charles
See Mayne, William (James Carter)
Molnar, Ferenc 1878-1952   **TCLC 20; DAM
DRAM**
See also CA 109; 153
Momaday, N(avarre) Scott 1934- **CLC 2, 19,
85, 95; DA; DAB; DAC; DAM MST,
MULT, NOV, POP; WLCS**
See also AAYA 11; CA 25-28R; CANR 14, 34,
68; DLB 143, 175; INT CANR-14; MTCW
1; NNAL; SATA 48; SATA-Brief 30
Monette, Paul 1945-1995   **CLC 82**
See also CA 139; 147
Monroe, Harriet 1860-1936   **TCLC 12**
See also CA 109; DLB 54, 91
Monroe, Lyle
See Heinlein, Robert A(nson)
Montagu, Elizabeth 1720-1800   **NCLC 7**
Montagu, Mary (Pierrepont) Wortley 1689-
1762   **LC 9; PC 16**
See also DLB 95, 101
Montagu, W. H.

See Coleridge, Samuel Taylor
Montague, John (Patrick) 1929- **CLC 13, 46**
See also CA 9-12R; CANR 9, 69; DLB 40;
MTCW 1
Montaigne, Michel (Eyquem) de 1533-1592
LC 8; DA; DAB; DAC; DAM MST; WLC
Montale, Eugenio 1896-1981**CLC 7, 9, 18; PC
13**
See also CA 17-20R; 104; CANR 30; DLB 114;
MTCW 1
Montesquieu, Charles-Louis de Secondat 1689-
1755   **LC 7**
Montgomery, (Robert) Bruce 1921-1978
See Crispin, Edmund
See also CA 104
Montgomery, L(ucy) M(aud) 1874-1942
TCLC 51; DAC; DAM MST
See also AAYA 12; CA 108; 137; CLR 8; DLB
92; DLBD 14; JRDA; MAICYA; SATA 100;
YABC 1
Montgomery, Marion H., Jr. 1925-   **CLC 7**
See also AITN 1; CA 1-4R; CANR 3, 48; DLB
6
Montgomery, Max
See Davenport, Guy (Mattison, Jr.)
Montherlant, Henry (Milon) de 1896-1972
CLC 8, 19; DAM DRAM
See also CA 85-88; 37-40R; DLB 72; MTCW
1
Monty Python
See Chapman, Graham; Cleese, John
(Marwood); Gilliam, Terry (Vance); Idle,
Eric; Jones, Terence Graham Parry; Palin,
Michael (Edward)
See also AAYA 7
Moodie, Susanna (Strickland) 1803-1885
NCLC 14
See also DLB 99
Mooney, Edward 1951-
See Mooney, Ted
See also CA 130
Mooney, Ted   **CLC 25**
See also Mooney, Edward
Moorcock, Michael (John) 1939-**CLC 5, 27, 58**
See also AAYA 26; CA 45-48; CAAS 5; CANR
2, 17, 38, 64; DLB 14; MTCW 1; SATA 93
Moore, Brian 1921- **CLC 1, 3, 5, 7, 8, 19, 32,
90; DAB; DAC; DAM MST**
See also CA 1-4R; CANR 1, 25, 42, 63; MTCW
1
Moore, Edward
See Muir, Edwin
Moore, George Augustus 1852-1933**TCLC 7;
SSC 19**
See also CA 104; DLB 10, 18, 57, 135
Moore, Lorrie   **CLC 39, 45, 68**
See also Moore, Marie Lorena
Moore, Marianne (Craig) 1887-1972**CLC 1, 2,
4, 8, 10, 13, 19, 47; DA; DAB; DAC; DAM
MST, POET; PC 4; WLCS**
See also CA 1-4R; 33-36R; CANR 3, 61;
CDALB 1929-1941; DLB 45; DLBD 7;
MTCW 1; SATA 20
Moore, Marie Lorena 1957-
See Moore, Lorrie
See also CA 116; CANR 39
Moore, Thomas 1779-1852   **NCLC 6**
See also DLB 96, 144
Morand, Paul 1888-1976   **CLC 41; SSC 22**
See also CA 69-72; DLB 65
Morante, Elsa 1918-1985   **CLC 8, 47**
See also CA 85-88; 117; CANR 35; DLB 177;
MTCW 1

Moravia, Alberto 1907-1990CLC **2, 7, 11, 27, 46; SSC 26**
See also Pincherle, Alberto
See also DLB 177
More, Hannah 1745-1833   **NCLC 27**
See also DLB 107, 109, 116, 158
More, Henry 1614-1687   **LC 9**
See also DLB 126
More, Sir Thomas 1478-1535   **LC 10, 32**
Moreas, Jean   **TCLC 18**
See also Papadiamantopoulos, Johannes
Morgan, Berry 1919-   **CLC 6**
See also CA 49-52; DLB 6
Morgan, Claire
See Highsmith, (Mary) Patricia
Morgan, Edwin (George) 1920-   **CLC 31**
See also CA 5-8R; CANR 3, 43; DLB 27
Morgan, (George) Frederick 1922-   **CLC 23**
See also CA 17-20R; CANR 21
Morgan, Harriet
See Mencken, H(enry) L(ouis)
Morgan, Jane
See Cooper, James Fenimore
Morgan, Janet 1945-   **CLC 39**
See also CA 65-68
Morgan, Lady 1776(?)-1859   **NCLC 29**
See also DLB 116, 158
Morgan, Robin (Evonne) 1941-   **CLC 2**
See also CA 69-72; CANR 29, 68; MTCW 1;
SATA 80
Morgan, Scott
See Kuttner, Henry
Morgan, Seth 1949(?)-1990   **CLC 65**
See also CA 132
Morgenstern, Christian 1871-1914 TCLC **8**
See also CA 105
Morgenstern, S.
See Goldman, William (W.)
Moricz, Zsigmond 1879-1942   **TCLC 33**
See also CA 165
Morike, Eduard (Friedrich) 1804-1875NCLC **10**
See also DLB 133
Moritz, Karl Philipp 1756-1793   **LC 2**
See also DLB 94
Morland, Peter Henry
See Faust, Frederick (Schiller)
Morley, Christopher (Darlington) 1890-1957
TCLC 87
See also CA 112; DLB 9
Morren, Theophil
See Hofmannsthal, Hugo von
Morris, Bill 1952-   **CLC 76**
Morris, Julian
See West, Morris L(anglo)
Morris, Steveland Judkins 1950(?)-
See Wonder, Stevie
See also CA 111
Morris, William 1834-1896   **NCLC 4**
See also CDBLB 1832-1890; DLB 18, 35, 57,
156, 178, 184
Morris, Wright 1910-1998CLC **1, 3, 7, 18, 37**
See also CA 9-12R; 167; CANR 21; DLB 2;
DLBY 81; MTCW 1
Morrison, Arthur 1863-1945   **TCLC 72**
See also CA 120; 157; DLB 70, 135, 197
Morrison, Chloe Anthony Wofford
See Morrison, Toni
Morrison, James Douglas 1943-1971
See Morrison, Jim
See also CA 73-76; CANR 40
Morrison, Jim   **CLC 17**
See also Morrison, James Douglas

Morrison, Toni 1931-CLC **4, 10, 22, 55, 81, 87;
BLC 3; DA; DAB; DAC; DAM MST,
MULT, NOV, POP**
See also AAYA 1, 22; BW 2; CA 29-32R;
CANR 27, 42, 67; CDALB 1968-1988; DLB
6, 33, 143; DLBY 81; MTCW 1; SATA 57
Morrison, Van 1945-   **CLC 21**
See also CA 116; 168
Morrissy, Mary 1958-   **CLC 99**
Mortimer, John (Clifford) 1923- CLC **28, 43;
DAM DRAM, POP**
See also CA 13-16R; CANR 21, 69; CDBLB
1960 to Present; DLB 13; INT CANR-21;
MTCW 1
Mortimer, Penelope (Ruth) 1918-   **CLC 5**
See also CA 57-60; CANR 45
Morton, Anthony
See Creasey, John
Mosca, Gaetano 1858-1941   **TCLC 75**
Mosher, Howard Frank 1943-   **CLC 62**
See also CA 139; CANR 65
Mosley, Nicholas 1923-   **CLC 43, 70**
See also CA 69-72; CANR 41, 60; DLB 14
Mosley, Walter 1952- CLC **97; BLCS; DAM
MULT, POP**
See also AAYA 17; BW 2; CA 142; CANR 57
Moss, Howard 1922-1987 CLC **7, 14, 45, 50;
DAM POET**
See also CA 1-4R; 123; CANR 1, 44; DLB 5
Mossgiel, Rab
See Burns, Robert
Motion, Andrew (Peter) 1952-   **CLC 47**
See also CA 146; DLB 40
Motley, Willard (Francis) 1909-1965 CLC **18**
See also BW 1; CA 117; 106; DLB 76, 143
Motoori, Norinaga 1730-1801   **NCLC 45**
Mott, Michael (Charles Alston) 1930-CLC **15,
34**
See also CA 5-8R; CAAS 7; CANR 7, 29
Mountain Wolf Woman 1884-1960   **CLC 92**
See also CA 144; NNAL
Moure, Erin 1955-   **CLC 88**
See also CA 113; DLB 60
Mowat, Farley (McGill) 1921-CLC **26; DAC;
DAM MST**
See also AAYA 1; CA 1-4R; CANR 4, 24, 42,
68; CLR 20; DLB 68; INT CANAR-24;
JRDA; MAICYA; MTCW 1; SATA 3, 55
Mowatt, Anna Cora 1819-1879   **NCLC 74**
Moyers, Bill 1934-   **CLC 74**
See also AITN 2; CA 61-64; CANR 31, 52
Mphahlele, Es'kia
See Mphahlele, Ezekiel
See also DLB 125
Mphahlele, Ezekiel 1919-1983 CLC **25; BLC
3; DAM MULT**
See also Mphahlele, Es'kia
See also BW 2; CA 81-84; CANR 26
Mqhayi, S(amuel) E(dward) K(rune Loliwe)
1875-1945TCLC **25; BLC 3; DAM MULT**
See also CA 153
Mrozek, Slawomir 1930-   **CLC 3, 13**
See also CA 13-16R; CAAS 10; CANR 29;
MTCW 1
Mrs. Belloc-Lowndes
See Lowndes, Marie Adelaide (Belloc)
Mtwa, Percy (?)-   **CLC 47**
Mueller, Lisel 1924-   **CLC 13, 51**
See also CA 93-96; DLB 105
Muir, Edwin 1887-1959   **TCLC 2, 87**
See also CA 104; DLB 20, 100, 191
Muir, John 1838-1914   **TCLC 28**
See also CA 165; DLB 186

Mujica Lainez, Manuel 1910-1984   **CLC 31**
See also Lainez, Manuel Mujica
See also CA 81-84; 112; CANR 32; HW
Mukherjee, Bharati 1940-CLC **53, 115; DAM
NOV**
See also BEST 89:2; CA 107; CANR 45, 72;
DLB 60; MTCW 1
Muldoon, Paul 1951-CLC **32, 72; DAM POET**
See also CA 113; 129; CANR 52; DLB 40; INT
129
Mulisch, Harry 1927-   **CLC 42**
See also CA 9-12R; CANR 6, 26, 56
Mull, Martin 1943-   **CLC 17**
See also CA 105
Muller, Wilhelm   **NCLC 73**
Mulock, Dinah Maria
See Craik, Dinah Maria (Mulock)
Munford, Robert 1737(?)-1783   **LC 5**
See also DLB 31
Mungo, Raymond 1946-   **CLC 72**
See also CA 49-52; CANR 2
Munro, Alice 1931- CLC **6, 10, 19, 50, 95;
DAC; DAM MST, NOV; SSC 3; WLCS**
See also AITN 2; CA 33-36R; CANR 33, 53;
DLB 53; MTCW 1; SATA 29
Munro, H(ector) H(ugh) 1870-1916
See Saki
See also CA 104; 130; CDBLB 1890-1914; DA;
DAB; DAC; DAM MST, NOV; DLB 34, 162;
MTCW 1; WLC
Murasaki, Lady   **CMLC 1**
Murdoch, (Jean) Iris 1919-CLC **1, 2, 3, 4, 6, 8,
11, 15, 22, 31, 51; DAB; DAC; DAM MST,
NOV**
See also CA 13-16R; CANR 8, 43, 68; CDBLB
1960 to Present; DLB 14, 194; INT CANR-
8; MTCW 1
Murfree, Mary Noailles 1850-1922   **SSC 22**
See also CA 122; DLB 12, 74
Murnau, Friedrich Wilhelm
See Plumpe, Friedrich Wilhelm
Murphy, Richard 1927-   **CLC 41**
See also CA 29-32R; DLB 40
Murphy, Sylvia 1937-   **CLC 34**
See also CA 121
Murphy, Thomas (Bernard) 1935- CLC **51**
See also CA 101
Murray, Albert L. 1916-   **CLC 73**
See also BW 2; CA 49-52; CANR 26, 52; DLB
38
Murray, Judith Sargent 1751-1820 NCLC **63**
See also DLB 37, 200
Murray, Les(lie) A(llan) 1938-CLC **40; DAM
POET**
See also CA 21-24R; CANR 11, 27, 56
Murry, J. Middleton
See Murry, John Middleton
Murry, John Middleton 1889-1957 TCLC **16**
See also CA 118; DLB 149
Musgrave, Susan 1951-   **CLC 13, 54**
See also CA 69-72; CANR 45
Musil, Robert (Edler von) 1880-1942 T C L C
12, 68; SSC 18
See also CA 109; CANR 55; DLB 81, 124
Muske, Carol 1945-   **CLC 90**
See also Muske-Dukes, Carol (Anne)
Muske-Dukes, Carol (Anne) 1945-
See Muske, Carol
See also CA 65-68; CANR 32, 70
Musset, (Louis Charles) Alfred de 1810-1857
NCLC 7
See also DLB 192
My Brother's Brother

See Chekhov, Anton (Pavlovich)

Myers, L(eopold) H(amilton) 1881-1944
TCLC 59
See also CA 157; DLB 15

Myers, Walter Dean 1937- **CLC 35; BLC 3;**
DAM MULT, NOV
See also AAYA 4, 23; BW 2; CA 33-36R;
CANR 20, 42, 67; CLR 4, 16, 35; DLB 33;
INT CANR-20; JRDA; MAICYA; SAAS 2;
SATA 41, 71; SATA-Brief 27

Myers, Walter M.
See Myers, Walter Dean

Myles, Symon
See Follett, Ken(neth Martin)

Nabokov, Vladimir (Vladimirovich) 1899-1977
CLC 1, 2, 3, 6, 8, 11, 15, 23, 44, 46, 64;
DA; DAB; DAC; DAM MST, NOV; SSC
11; WLC
See also CA 5-8R; 69-72; CANR 20; CDALB
1941-1968; DLB 2; DLBD 3; DLBY 80, 91;
MTCW 1

Nagai Kafu 1879-1959 **TCLC 51**
See also Nagai Sokichi
See also DLB 180

Nagai Sokichi 1879-1959
See Nagai Kafu
See also CA 117

Nagy, Laszlo 1925-1978 **CLC 7**
See also CA 129; 112

Naidu, Sarojini 1879-1943 **TCLC 80**

Naipaul, Shiva(dhar Srinivasa) 1945-1985
CLC 32, 39; DAM NOV
See also CA 110; 112; 116; CANR 33; DLB
157; DLBY 85; MTCW 1

Naipaul, V(idiadhar) S(urajprasad) 1932-
CLC 4, 7, 9, 13, 18, 37, 105; DAB; DAC;
DAM MST, NOV
See also CA 1-4R; CANR 1, 33, 51; CDBLB
1960 to Present; DLB 125; DLBY 85;
MTCW 1

Nakos, Lilika 1899(?)- **CLC 29**

Narayan, R(asipuram) K(rishnaswami) 1906-
CLC 7, 28, 47; DAM NOV; SSC 25
See also CA 81-84; CANR 33, 61; MTCW 1;
SATA 62

Nash, (Frediric) Ogden 1902-1971 **CLC 23;**
DAM POET; PC 21
See also CA 13-14; 29-32R; CANR 34, 61; CAP
1; DLB 11; MAICYA; MTCW 1; SATA 2,
46

Nashe, Thomas 1567-1601(?) **LC 41**
See also DLB 167

Nashe, Thomas 1567-1601 **LC 41**

Nathan, Daniel
See Dannay, Frederic

Nathan, George Jean 1882-1958 **TCLC 18**
See also Hatteras, Owen
See also CA 114; 169; DLB 137

Natsume, Kinnosuke 1867-1916
See Natsume, Soseki
See also CA 104

Natsume, Soseki 1867-1916 **TCLC 2, 10**
See also Natsume, Kinnosuke
See also DLB 180

Natti, (Mary) Lee 1919-
See Kingman, Lee
See also CA 5-8R; CANR 2

Naylor, Gloria 1950- **CLC 28, 52; BLC 3; DA;**
DAC; DAM MST, MULT, NOV, POP;
WLCS
See also AAYA 6; BW 2; CA 107; CANR 27,
51, 74; DLB 173; MTCW 1

Neihardt, John Gneisenau 1881-1973 **CLC 32**

See also CA 13-14; CANR 65; CAP 1; DLB 9,
54

Nekrasov, Nikolai Alekseevich 1821-1878
NCLC 11

Nelligan, Emile 1879-1941 **TCLC 14**
See also CA 114; DLB 92

Nelson, Willie 1933- **CLC 17**
See also CA 107

Nemerov, Howard (Stanley) 1920-1991 **CLC 2,**
6, 9, 36; DAM POET; PC 24
See also CA 1-4R; 134; CABS 2; CANR 1, 27,
53; DLB 5, 6; DLBY 83; INT CANR-27;
MTCW 1

Neruda, Pablo 1904-1973 **CLC 1, 2, 5, 7, 9, 28,**
62; DA; DAB; DAC; DAM MST, MULT,
POET; HLC; PC 4; WLC
See also CA 19-20; 45-48; CAP 2; HW; MTCW
1

Nerval, Gerard de 1808-1855 **NCLC 1, 67; PC**
13; SSC 18

Nervo, (Jose) Amado (Ruiz de) 1870-1919
TCLC 11
See also CA 109; 131; HW

Nessi, Pio Baroja y
See Baroja (y Nessi), Pio

Nestroy, Johann 1801-1862 **NCLC 42**
See also DLB 133

Netterville, Luke
See O'Grady, Standish (James)

Neufeld, John (Arthur) 1938- **CLC 17**
See also AAYA 11; CA 25-28R; CANR 11, 37,
56; CLR 52; MAICYA; SAAS 3; SATA 6,
81

Neville, Emily Cheney 1919- **CLC 12**
See also CA 5-8R; CANR 3, 37; JRDA;
MAICYA; SAAS 2; SATA 1

Newbound, Bernard Slade 1930-
See Slade, Bernard
See also CA 81-84; CANR 49; DAM DRAM

Newby, P(ercy) H(oward) 1918-1997 **CLC 2,**
13; DAM NOV
See also CA 5-8R; 161; CANR 32, 67; DLB
15; MTCW 1

Newlove, Donald 1928- **CLC 6**
See also CA 29-32R; CANR 25

Newlove, John (Herbert) 1938- **CLC 14**
See also CA 21-24R; CANR 9, 25

Newman, Charles 1938- **CLC 2, 8**
See also CA 21-24R

Newman, Edwin (Harold) 1919- **CLC 14**
See also AITN 1; CA 69-72; CANR 5

Newman, John Henry 1801-1890 **NCLC 38**
See also DLB 18, 32, 55

Newton, (Sir) Isaac 1642-1727 **LC 35**

Newton, Suzanne 1936- **CLC 35**
See also CA 41-44R; CANR 14; JRDA; SATA
5, 77

Nexo, Martin Andersen 1869-1954 **TCLC 43**

Nezval, Vitezslav 1900-1958 **TCLC 44**
See also CA 123

Ng, Fae Myenne 1957(?)- **CLC 81**
See also CA 146

Ngema, Mbongeni 1955- **CLC 57**
See also BW 2; CA 143

Ngugi, James T(hiong'o) **CLC 3, 7, 13**
See also Ngugi wa Thiong'o

Ngugi wa Thiong'o 1938- **CLC 36; BLC 3;**
DAM MULT, NOV
See also Ngugi, James T(hiong'o)
See also BW 2; CA 81-84; CANR 27, 58; DLB
125; MTCW 1

Nichol, B(arrie) P(hillip) 1944-1988 **CLC 18**
See also CA 53-56; DLB 53; SATA 66

Nichols, John (Treadwell) 1940- **CLC 38**
See also CA 9-12R; CAAS 2; CANR 6, 70;
DLBY 82

Nichols, Leigh
See Koontz, Dean R(ay)

Nichols, Peter (Richard) 1927- **CLC 5, 36, 65**
See also CA 104; CANR 33; DLB 13; MTCW
1

Nicolas, F. R. E.
See Freeling, Nicolas

Niedecker, Lorine 1903-1970 **CLC 10, 42;**
DAM POET
See also CA 25-28; CAP 2; DLB 48

Nietzsche, Friedrich (Wilhelm) 1844-1900
TCLC 10, 18, 55
See also CA 107; 121; DLB 129

Nievo, Ippolito 1831-1861 **NCLC 22**

Nightingale, Anne Redmon 1943-
See Redmon, Anne
See also CA 103

Nightingale, Florence 1820-1910 **TCLC 85**
See also DLB 166

Nik. T. O.
See Annensky, Innokenty (Fyodorovich)

Nin, Anais 1903-1977 **CLC 1, 4, 8, 11, 14, 60;**
DAM NOV, POP; SSC 10
See also AITN 2; CA 13-16R; 69-72; CANR
22, 53; DLB 2, 4, 152; MTCW 1

Nishida, Kitaro 1870-1945 **TCLC 83**

Nishiwaki, Junzaburo 1894-1982 **PC 15**
See also CA 107

Nissenson, Hugh 1933- **CLC 4, 9**
See also CA 17-20R; CANR 27; DLB 28

Niven, Larry **CLC 8**
See also Niven, Laurence Van Cott
See also AAYA 27; DLB 8

Niven, Laurence Van Cott 1938-
See Niven, Larry
See also CA 21-24R; CAAS 12; CANR 14, 44,
66; DAM POP; MTCW 1; SATA 95

Nixon, Agnes Eckhardt 1927- **CLC 21**
See also CA 110

Nizan, Paul 1905-1940 **TCLC 40**
See also CA 161; DLB 72

Nkosi, Lewis 1936- **CLC 45; BLC 3; DAM**
MULT
See also BW 1; CA 65-68; CANR 27; DLB 157

Nodier, (Jean) Charles (Emmanuel) 1780-1844
NCLC 19
See also DLB 119

Noguchi, Yone 1875-1947 **TCLC 80**

Nolan, Christopher 1965- **CLC 58**
See also CA 111

Noon, Jeff 1957- **CLC 91**
See also CA 148

Norden, Charles
See Durrell, Lawrence (George)

Nordhoff, Charles (Bernard) 1887-1947
TCLC 23
See also CA 108; DLB 9; SATA 23

Norfolk, Lawrence 1963- **CLC 76**
See also CA 144

Norman, Marsha 1947- **CLC 28; DAM DRAM;**
DC 8
See also CA 105; CABS 3; CANR 41; DLBY
84

Normyx
See Douglas, (George) Norman

Norris, Frank 1870-1902 **SSC 28**
See also Norris, (Benjamin) Frank(lin, Jr.)
See also CDALB 1865-1917; DLB 12, 71, 186

Norris, (Benjamin) Frank(lin, Jr.) 1870-1902
TCLC 24

Pineda, Cecile 1942- **CLC 39**
See also CA 118
Pinero, Arthur Wing 1855-1934 **TCLC 32;**
DAM DRAM
See also CA 110; 153; DLB 10
Pinero, Miguel (Antonio Gomez) 1946-1988
·**CLC 4, 55**
See also CA 61-64; 125; CANR 29; HW
Pinget, Robert 1919-1997 **CLC 7, 13, 37**
See also CA 85-88; 160; DLB 83
Pink Floyd
See Barrett, (Roger) Syd; Gilmour, David; Mason, Nick; Waters, Roger; Wright, Rick
Pinkney, Edward 1802-1828 **NCLC 31**
Pinkwater, Daniel Manus 1941- **CLC 35**
See also Pinkwater, Manus
See also AAYA 1; CA 29-32R; CANR 12, 38;
CLR 4; JRDA; MAICYA; SAAS 3; SATA 46,
76
Pinkwater, Manus
See Pinkwater, Daniel Manus
See also SATA 8
Pinsky, Robert 1940-**CLC 9, 19, 38, 94; DAM**
POET
See also CA 29-32R; CAAS 4; CANR 58;
DLBY 82
Pinta, Harold
See Pinter, Harold
Pinter, Harold 1930-**CLC 1, 3, 6, 9, 11, 15, 27,**
58, 73; DA; DAB; DAC; DAM DRAM,
MST; WLC
See also CA 5-8R; CANR 33, 65; CDBLB 1960
to Present; DLB 13; MTCW 1
Piozzi, Hester Lynch (Thrale) 1741-1821
NCLC 57
See also DLB 104, 142
Pirandello, Luigi 1867-1936**TCLC 4, 29; DA;**
DAB; DAC; DAM DRAM, MST; DC 5;
SSC 22; WLC
See also CA 104; 153
Pirsig, Robert M(aynard) 1928-**CLC 4, 6, 73;**
DAM POP
See also CA 53-56; CANR 42, 74; MTCW 1;
SATA 39
Pisarev, Dmitry Ivanovich 1840-1868 **NCLC**
25
Pix, Mary (Griffith) 1666-1709 **LC 8**
See also DLB 80
Pixerecourt, (Rene Charles) Guilbert de 1773-
1844 **NCLC 39**
See also DLB 192
Plaatje, Sol(omon) T(shekisho) 1876-1932
TCLC 73; BLCS
See also BW 2; CA 141
Plaidy, Jean
See Hibbert, Eleanor Alice Burford
Planche, James Robinson 1796-1880**NCLC 42**
Plant, Robert 1948- **CLC 12**
Plante, David (Robert) 1940- **CLC 7, 23, 38;**
DAM NOV
See also CA 37-40R; CANR 12, 36, 58; DLBY
83; INT CANR-12; MTCW 1
Plath, Sylvia 1932-1963 **CLC 1, 2, 3, 5, 9, 11,**
14, 17, 50, 51, 62, 111; DA; DAB; DAC;
DAM MST, POET; PC 1; WLC
See also AAYA 13; CA 19-20; CANR 34; CAP
2; CDALB 1941-1968; DLB 5, 6, 152;
MTCW 1; SATA 96
Plato 428(?)B.C.-348(?)B.C. **CMLC 8; DA;**
DAB; DAC; DAM MST; WLCS
See also DLB 176
Platonov, Andrei **TCLC 14**
See also Klimentov, Andrei Platonovich

Platt, Kin 1911- **CLC 26**
See also AAYA 11; CA 17-20R; CANR 11;
JRDA; SAAS 17; SATA 21, 86
Plautus c. 251B.C.-184B.C. **CMLC 24; DC 6**
Plick et Plock
See Simenon, Georges (Jacques Christian)
Plimpton, George (Ames) 1927- **CLC 36**
See also AITN 1; CA 21-24R; CANR 32, 70;
DLB 185; MTCW 1; SATA 10
Pliny the Elder c. 23-79 **CMLC 23**
Plomer, William Charles Franklin 1903-1973
CLC 4, 8
See also CA 21-22; CANR 34; CAP 2; DLB
20, 162, 191; MTCW 1; SATA 24
Plowman, Piers
See Kavanagh, Patrick (Joseph)
Plum, J.
See Wodehouse, P(elham) G(renville)
Plumly, Stanley (Ross) 1939- **CLC 33**
See also CA 108; 110; DLB 5, 193; INT 110
Plumpe, Friedrich Wilhelm 1888-1931**TCLC**
53
See also CA 112
Po Chu-i 772-846 **CMLC 24**
Poe, Edgar Allan 1809-1849 **NCLC 1, 16, 55;**
DA; DAB; DAC; DAM MST, POET; PC
1; SSC 1, 22; WLC
See also AAYA 14; CDALB 1640-1865; DLB
3, 59, 73, 74; SATA 23
Poet of Titchfield Street, The
See Pound, Ezra (Weston Loomis)
Pohl, Frederik 1919- **CLC 18; SSC 25**
See also AAYA 24; CA 61-64; CAAS 1; CANR
11, 37; DLB 8; INT CANR-11; MTCW 1;
SATA 24
Poirier, Louis 1910-
See Gracq, Julien
See also CA 122; 126
Poitier, Sidney 1927- **CLC 26**
See also BW 1; CA 117
Polanski, Roman 1933- **CLC 16**
See also CA 77-80
Poliakoff, Stephen 1952- **CLC 38**
See also CA 106; DLB 13
Police, The
See Copeland, Stewart (Armstrong); Summers,
Andrew James; Sumner, Gordon Matthew
Polidori, John William 1795-1821 **NCLC 51**
See also DLB 116
Pollitt, Katha 1949- **CLC 28**
See also CA 120; 122; CANR 66; MTCW 1
Pollock, (Mary) Sharon 1936-**CLC 50; DAC;**
DAM DRAM, MST
See also CA 141; DLB 60
Polo, Marco 1254-1324 **CMLC 15**
Polonsky, Abraham (Lincoln) 1910- **CLC 92**
See also CA 104; DLB 26; INT 104
Polybius c. 200B.C.-c. 118B.C. **CMLC 17**
See also DLB 176
Pomerance, Bernard 1940- **CLC 13; DAM**
DRAM
See also CA 101; CANR 49
Ponge, Francis (Jean Gaston Alfred) 1899-1988
CLC 6, 18; DAM POET
See also CA 85-88; 126; CANR 40
Pontoppidan, Henrik 1857-1943 **TCLC 29**
See also CA 170
Poole, Josephine **CLC 17**
See also Helyar, Jane Penelope Josephine
See also SAAS 2; SATA 5
Popa, Vasko 1922-1991 **CLC 19**
See also CA 112; 148; DLB 181
Pope, Alexander 1688-1744 **LC 3; DA; DAB;**

DAC; DAM MST, POET; WLC
See also CDBLB 1660-1789; DLB 95, 101
Porter, Connie (Rose) 1959(?)- **CLC 70**
See also BW 2; CA 142; SATA 81
Porter, Gene(va Grace) Stratton 1863(?)-1924
TCLC 21
See also CA 112
Porter, Katherine Anne 1890-1980**CLC 1, 3, 7,**
10, 13, 15, 27, 101; DA; DAB; DAC; DAM
MST, NOV; SSC 4, 31
See also AITN 2; CA 1-4R; 101; CANR 1, 65;
DLB 4, 9, 102; DLBD 12; DLBY 80; MTCW
1; SATA 39; SATA-Obit 23
Porter, Peter (Neville Frederick) 1929-**CLC 5,**
13, 33
See also CA 85-88; DLB 40
Porter, William Sydney 1862-1910
See Henry, O.
See also CA 104; 131; CDALB 1865-1917; DA;
DAB; DAC; DAM MST; DLB 12, 78, 79;
MTCW 1; YABC 2
Portillo (y Pacheco), Jose Lopez
See Lopez Portillo (y Pacheco), Jose
Post, Melville Davisson 1869-1930 **TCLC 39**
See also CA 110
Potok, Chaim 1929- **CLC 2, 7, 14, 26, 112;**
DAM NOV
See also AAYA 15; AITN 1, 2; CA 17-20R;
CANR 19, 35, 64; DLB 28, 152; INT CANR-
19; MTCW 1; SATA 33
Potter, (Helen) Beatrix 1866-1943
See Webb, (Martha) Beatrice (Potter)
See also MAICYA
Potter, Dennis (Christopher George) 1935-1994
CLC 58, 86
See also CA 107; 145; CANR 33, 61; MTCW 1
Pound, Ezra (Weston Loomis) 1885-1972**CLC**
1, 2, 3, 4, 5, 7, 10, 13, 18, 34, 48, 50, 112;
DA; DAB; DAC; DAM MST, POET; PC
4; WLC
See also CA 5-8R; 37-40R; CANR 40; CDALB
1917-1929; DLB 4, 45, 63; DLBD 15;
MTCW 1
Povod, Reinaldo 1959-1994 **CLC 44**
See also CA 136; 146
Powell, Adam Clayton, Jr. 1908-1972**CLC 89;**
BLC 3; DAM MULT
See also BW 1; CA 102; 33-36R
Powell, Anthony (Dymoke) 1905-**CLC 1, 3, 7,**
9, 10, 31
See also CA 1-4R; CANR 1, 32, 62; CDBLB
1945-1960; DLB 15; MTCW 1
Powell, Dawn 1897-1965 **CLC 66**
See also CA 5-8R; DLBY 97
Powell, Padgett 1952- **CLC 34**
See also CA 126; CANR 63
Power, Susan 1961- **CLC 91**
Powers, J(ames) F(arl) 1917-**CLC 1, 4, 8, 57;**
SSC 4
See also CA 1-4R; CANR 2, 61; DLB 130;
MTCW 1
Powers, John J(ames) 1945-
See Powers, John R.
See also CA 69-72
Powers, John R. **CLC 66**
See also Powers, John J(ames)
Powers, Richard (S.) 1957- **CLC 93**
See also CA 148
Pownall, David 1938- **CLC 10**
See also CA 89-92; CAAS 18; CANR 49; DLB
14
Powys, John Cowper 1872-1963**CLC 7, 9, 15,**
46

See also CA 85-88; DLB 15; MTCW 1

Powys, T(heodore) F(rancis) 1875-1953
    TCLC 9
    See also CA 106; DLB 36, 162

Prado (Calvo), Pedro 1886-1952   **TCLC 75**
    See also CA 131; HW

Prager, Emily 1952-   **CLC 56**

Pratt, E(dwin) J(ohn) 1883(?)-1964 **CLC 19;**
    DAC; DAM POET
    See also CA 141; 93-96; DLB 92

Premchand   **TCLC 21**
    See also Srivastava, Dhanpat Rai

Preussler, Otfried 1923-   **CLC 17**
    See also CA 77-80; SATA 24

Prevert, Jacques (Henri Marie) 1900-1977
    CLC 15
    See also CA 77-80; 69-72; CANR 29, 61;
    MTCW 1; SATA-Obit 30

Prevost, Abbe (Antoine Francois) 1697-1763
    LC 1

Price, (Edward) Reynolds 1933-**CLC 3, 6, 13,**
    43, 50, 63; DAM NOV; SSC 22
    See also CA 1-4R; CANR 1, 37, 57; DLB 2;
    INT CANR-37

Price, Richard 1949-   **CLC 6, 12**
    See also CA 49-52; CANR 3; DLBY 81

Prichard, Katharine Susannah 1883-1969
    CLC 46
    See also CA 11-12; CANR 33; CAP 1; MTCW
    1; SATA 66

Priestley, J(ohn) B(oynton) 1894-1984**CLC 2,**
    5, 9, 34; DAM DRAM, NOV
    See also CA 9-12R; 113; CANR 33; CDBLB
    1914-1945; DLB 10, 34, 77, 100, 139; DLBY
    84; MTCW 1

Prince 1958(?)-   **CLC 35**

Prince, F(rank) T(empleton) 1912-   **CLC 22**
    See also CA 101; CANR 43; DLB 20

Prince Kropotkin
    See Kropotkin, Peter (Alekseievich)

Prior, Matthew 1664-1721   **LC 4**
    See also DLB 95

Prishvin, Mikhail 1873-1954   **TCLC 75**

Pritchard, William H(arrison) 1932- **CLC 34**
    See also CA 65-68; CANR 23; DLB 111

Pritchett, V(ictor) S(awdon) 1900-1997 **C L C**
    5, 13, 15, 41; DAM NOV; SSC 14
    See also CA 61-64; 157; CANR 31, 63; DLB
    15, 139; MTCW 1

Private 19022
    See Manning, Frederic

Probst, Mark 1925-   **CLC 59**
    See also CA 130

Prokosch, Frederic 1908-1989   **CLC 4, 48**
    See also CA 73-76; 128; DLB 48

Prophet, The
    See Dreiser, Theodore (Herman Albert)

Prose, Francine 1947-   **CLC 45**
    See also CA 109; 112; CANR 46; SATA 101

Proudhon
    See Cunha, Euclides (Rodrigues Pimenta) da

Proulx, Annie
    See Proulx, E(dna) Annie

Proulx, E(dna) Annie 1935-   **CLC 81; DAM**
    POP
    See also CA 145; CANR 65

Proust, (Valentin-Louis-George-Eugene-)
    Marcel 1871-1922 **TCLC 7, 13, 33; DA;**
    DAB; DAC; DAM MST, NOV; WLC
    See also CA 104; 120; DLB 65; MTCW 1

Prowler, Harley
    See Masters, Edgar Lee

Prus, Boleslaw 1845-1912   **TCLC 48**

Pryor, Richard (Franklin Lenox Thomas) 1940-
    CLC 26
    See also CA 122

Przybyszewski, Stanislaw 1868-1927**TCLC 36**
    See also CA 160; DLB 66

Pteleon
    See Grieve, C(hristopher) M(urray)
    See also DAM POET

Puckett, Lute
    See Masters, Edgar Lee

Puig, Manuel 1932-1990**CLC 3, 5, 10, 28, 65;**
    DAM MULT; HLC
    See also CA 45-48; CANR 2, 32, 63; DLB 113;
    HW; MTCW 1

Pulitzer, Joseph 1847-1911   **TCLC 76**
    See also CA 114; DLB 23

Purdy, A(lfred) W(ellington) 1918- **CLC 3, 6,**
    14, 50; DAC; DAM MST, POET
    See also CA 81-84; CAAS 17; CANR 42, 66;
    DLB 88

Purdy, James (Amos) 1923- **CLC 2, 4, 10, 28,**
    52
    See also CA 33-36R; CAAS 1; CANR 19, 51;
    DLB 2; INT CANR-19; MTCW 1

Pure, Simon
    See Swinnerton, Frank Arthur

Pushkin, Alexander (Sergeyevich) 1799-1837
    NCLC 3, 27; DA; DAB; DAC; DAM
    DRAM, MST, POET; PC 10; SSC 27;
    WLC
    See also SATA 61

P'u Sung-ling 1640-1715   **LC 3; SSC 31**

Putnam, Arthur Lee
    See Alger, Horatio, Jr.

Puzo, Mario 1920-**CLC 1, 2, 6, 36, 107; DAM**
    NOV, POP
    See also CA 65-68; CANR 4, 42, 65; DLB 6;
    MTCW 1

Pygge, Edward
    See Barnes, Julian (Patrick)

Pyle, Ernest Taylor 1900-1945
    See Pyle, Ernie
    See also CA 115; 160

Pyle, Ernie 1900-1945   **TCLC 75**
    See also Pyle, Ernest Taylor
    See also DLB 29

Pyle, Howard 1853-1911   **TCLC 81**
    See also CA 109; 137; CLR 22; DLB 42, 188;
    DLBD 13; MAICYA; SATA 16, 100

Pym, Barbara (Mary Crampton) 1913-1980
    CLC 13, 19, 37, 111
    See also CA 13-14; 97-100; CANR 13, 34; CAP
    1; DLB 14; DLBY 87; MTCW 1

Pynchon, Thomas (Ruggles, Jr.) 1937-**CLC 2,**
    3, 6, 9, 11, 18, 33, 62, 72; DA; DAB; DAC;
    DAM MST, NOV, POP; SSC 14; WLC
    See also BEST 90:2; CA 17-20R; CANR 22,
    46, 73; DLB 2, 173; MTCW 1

Pythagoras c. 570B.C.-c. 500B.C. **CMLC 22**
    See also DLB 176

Q
    See Quiller-Couch, SirArthur (Thomas)

Qian Zhongshu
    See Ch'ien Chung-shu

Qroll
    See Dagerman, Stig (Halvard)

Quarrington, Paul (Lewis) 1953-   **CLC 65**
    See also CA 129; CANR 62

Quasimodo, Salvatore 1901-1968   **CLC 10**
    See also CA 13-16; 25-28R; CAP 1; DLB 114;
    MTCW 1

Quay, Stephen 1947-   **CLC 95**

Quay, Timothy 1947-   **CLC 95**

Queen, Ellery   **CLC 3, 11**
    See also Dannay, Frederic; Davidson, Avram;
    Lee, Manfred B(ennington); Marlowe,
    Stephen; Sturgeon, Theodore (Hamilton);
    Vance, John Holbrook

Queen, Ellery, Jr.
    See Dannay, Frederic; Lee, Manfred
    B(ennington)

Queneau, Raymond 1903-1976 **CLC 2, 5, 10,**
    42
    See also CA 77-80; 69-72; CANR 32; DLB 72;
    MTCW 1

Quevedo, Francisco de 1580-1645   **LC 23**

Quiller-Couch, SirArthur (Thomas) 1863-1944
    TCLC 53
    See also CA 118; 166; DLB 135, 153, 190

Quin, Ann (Marie) 1936-1973   **CLC 6**
    See also CA 9-12R; 45-48; DLB 14

Quinn, Martin
    See Smith, Martin Cruz

Quinn, Peter 1947-   **CLC 91**

Quinn, Simon
    See Smith, Martin Cruz

Quiroga, Horacio (Sylvestre) 1878-1937
    TCLC 20; DAM MULT; HLC
    See also CA 117; 131; HW; MTCW 1

Quoirez, Francoise 1935-   **CLC 9**
    See also Sagan, Francoise
    See also CA 49-52; CANR 6, 39, 73; MTCW 1

Raabe, Wilhelm (Karl) 1831-1910 **TCLC 45**
    See also CA 167; DLB 129

Rabe, David (William) 1940-   **CLC 4, 8, 33;**
    DAM DRAM
    See also CA 85-88; CABS 3; CANR 59; DLB 7

Rabelais, Francois 1483-1553**LC 5; DA; DAB;**
    DAC; DAM MST; WLC

Rabinovitch, Sholem 1859-1916
    See Aleichem, Sholom
    See also CA 104

Rachilde 1860-1953   **TCLC 67**
    See also DLB 123, 192

Racine, Jean 1639-1699 **LC 28; DAB; DAM**
    MST

Radcliffe, Ann (Ward) 1764-1823**NCLC 6, 55**
    See also DLB 39, 178

Radiguet, Raymond 1903-1923   **TCLC 29**
    See also CA 162; DLB 65

Radnoti, Miklos 1909-1944   **TCLC 16**
    See also CA 118

Rado, James 1939-   **CLC 17**
    See also CA 105

Radvanyi, Netty 1900-1983
    See Seghers, Anna
    See also CA 85-88; 110

Rae, Ben
    See Griffiths, Trevor

Raeburn, John (Hay) 1941-   **CLC 34**
    See also CA 57-60

Ragni, Gerome 1942-1991   **CLC 17**
    See also CA 105; 134

Rahv, Philip 1908-1973   **CLC 24**
    See also Greenberg, Ivan
    See also DLB 137

Raimund, Ferdinand Jakob 1790-1836**N C L C**
    69
    See also DLB 90

Raine, Craig 1944-   **CLC 32, 103**
    See also CA 108; CANR 29, 51; DLB 40

Raine, Kathleen (Jessie) 1908-   **CLC 7, 45**
    See also CA 85-88; CANR 46; DLB 20; MTCW
    1

Rainis, Janis 1865-1929   **TCLC 29**
    See also CA 170

Rakosi, Carl 1903- **CLC 47**
See also Rawley, Callman
See also CAAS 5; DLB 193

Raleigh, Richard
See Lovecraft, H(oward) P(hillips)

Raleigh, Sir Walter 1554(?)-1618 **LC 31, 39**
See also CDBLB Before 1660; DLB 172

Rallentando, H. P.
See Sayers, Dorothy L(eigh)

Ramal, Walter
See de la Mare, Walter (John)

Ramana Maharshi 1879-1950 **TCLC 84**

Ramon, Juan
See Jimenez (Mantecon), Juan Ramon

Ramos, Graciliano 1892-1953 **TCLC 32**
See also CA 167

Rampersad, Arnold 1941- **CLC 44**
See also BW 2; CA 127; 133; DLB 111; INT 133

Rampling, Anne
See Rice, Anne

Ramsay, Allan 1684(?)-1758 **LC 29**
See also DLB 95

Ramuz, Charles-Ferdinand 1878-1947 **TCLC 33**
See also CA 165

Rand, Ayn 1905-1982 **CLC 3, 30, 44, 79; DA; DAC; DAM MST, NOV, POP; WLC**
See also AAYA 10; CA 13-16R; 105; CANR 27, 73; MTCW 1

Randall, Dudley (Felker) 1914- **CLC 1; BLC 3; DAM MULT**
See also BW 1; CA 25-28R; CANR 23; DLB 41

Randall, Robert
See Silverberg, Robert

Ranger, Ken
See Creasey, John

Ransom, John Crowe 1888-1974 **CLC 2, 4, 5, 11, 24; DAM POET**
See also CA 5-8R; 49-52; CANR 6, 34; DLB 45, 63; MTCW 1

Rao, Raja 1909- **CLC 25, 56; DAM NOV**
See also CA 73-76; CANR 51; MTCW 1

Raphael, Frederic (Michael) 1931- **CLC 2, 14**
See also CA 1-4R; CANR 1; DLB 14

Ratcliffe, James P.
See Mencken, H(enry) L(ouis)

Rathbone, Julian 1935- **CLC 41**
See also CA 101; CANR 34, 73

Rattigan, Terence (Mervyn) 1911-1977 **CLC 7; DAM DRAM**
See also CA 85-88; 73-76; CDBLB 1945-1960; DLB 13; MTCW 1

Ratushinskaya, Irina 1954- **CLC 54**
See also CA 129; CANR 68

Raven, Simon (Arthur Noel) 1927- **CLC 14**
See also CA 81-84

Ravenna, Michael
See Welty, Eudora

Rawley, Callman 1903-
See Rakosi, Carl
See also CA 21-24R; CANR 12, 32

Rawlings, Marjorie Kinnan 1896-1953 **TCLC 4**
See also AAYA 20; CA 104; 137; DLB 9, 22, 102; DLBD 17; JRDA; MAICYA; SATA 100; YABC 1

Ray, Satyajit 1921-1992 **CLC 16, 76; DAM MULT**
See also CA 114; 137

Read, Herbert Edward 1893-1968 **CLC 4**
See also CA 85-88; 25-28R; DLB 20, 149

Read, Piers Paul 1941- **CLC 4, 10, 25**
See also CA 21-24R; CANR 38; DLB 14; SATA 21

Reade, Charles 1814-1884 **NCLC 2, 74**
See also DLB 21

Reade, Hamish
See Gray, Simon (James Holliday)

Reading, Peter 1946- **CLC 47**
See also CA 103; CANR 46; DLB 40

Reaney, James 1926- **CLC 13; DAC; DAM MST**
See also CA 41-44R; CAAS 15; CANR 42; DLB 68; SATA 43

Rebreanu, Liviu 1885-1944 **TCLC 28**
See also CA 165

Rechy, John (Francisco) 1934- **CLC 1, 7, 14, 18, 107; DAM MULT; HLC**
See also CA 5-8R; CAAS 4; CANR 6, 32, 64; DLB 122; DLBY 82; HW; INT CANR-6

Redcam, Tom 1870-1933 **TCLC 25**

Reddin, Keith **CLC 67**

Redgrove, Peter (William) 1932- **CLC 6, 41**
See also CA 1-4R; CANR 3, 39; DLB 40

Redmon, Anne **CLC 22**
See also Nightingale, Anne Redmon
See also DLBY 86

Reed, Eliot
See Ambler, Eric

Reed, Ishmael 1938- **CLC 2, 3, 5, 6, 13, 32, 60; BLC 3; DAM MULT**
See also BW 2; CA 21-24R; CANR 25, 48, 74; DLB 2, 5, 33, 169; DLBD 8; MTCW 1

Reed, John (Silas) 1887-1920 **TCLC 9**
See also CA 106

Reed, Lou **CLC 21**
See also Firbank, Louis

Reeve, Clara 1729-1807 **NCLC 19**
See also DLB 39

Reich, Wilhelm 1897-1957 **TCLC 57**

Reid, Christopher (John) 1949- **CLC 33**
See also CA 140; DLB 40

Reid, Desmond
See Moorcock, Michael (John)

Reid Banks, Lynne 1929-
See Banks, Lynne Reid
See also CA 1-4R; CANR 6, 22, 38; CLR 24; JRDA; MAICYA; SATA 22, 75

Reilly, William K.
See Creasey, John

Reiner, Max
See Caldwell, (Janet Miriam) Taylor (Holland)

Reis, Ricardo
See Pessoa, Fernando (Antonio Nogueira)

Remarque, Erich Maria 1898-1970 **CLC 21; DA; DAB; DAC; DAM MST, NOV**
See also AAYA 27; CA 77-80; 29-32R; DLB 56; MTCW 1

Remizov, A.
See Remizov, Aleksei (Mikhailovich)

Remizov, A. M.
See Remizov, Aleksei (Mikhailovich)

Remizov, Aleksei (Mikhailovich) 1877-1957 **TCLC 27**
See also CA 125; 133

Renan, Joseph Ernest 1823-1892 **NCLC 26**

Renard, Jules 1864-1910 **TCLC 17**
See also CA 117

Renault, Mary **CLC 3, 11, 17**
See also Challans, Mary
See also DLBY 83

Rendell, Ruth (Barbara) 1930- **CLC 28, 48; DAM POP**
See also Vine, Barbara

See also CA 109; CANR 32, 52, 74; DLB 87; INT CANR-32; MTCW 1

Renoir, Jean 1894-1979 **CLC 20**
See also CA 129; 85-88

Resnais, Alain 1922- **CLC 16**

Reverdy, Pierre 1889-1960 **CLC 53**
See also CA 97-100; 89-92

Rexroth, Kenneth 1905-1982 **CLC 1, 2, 6, 11, 22, 49, 112; DAM POET; PC 20**
See also CA 5-8R; 107; CANR 14, 34, 63; CDALB 1941-1968; DLB 16, 48, 165; DLBY 82; INT CANR-14; MTCW 1

Reyes, Alfonso 1889-1959 **TCLC 33**
See also CA 131; HW

Reyes y Basoalto, Ricardo Eliecer Neftali
See Neruda, Pablo

Reymont, Wladyslaw (Stanislaw) 1868(?)-1925 **TCLC 5**
See also CA 104

Reynolds, Jonathan 1942- **CLC 6, 38**
See also CA 65-68; CANR 28

Reynolds, Joshua 1723-1792 **LC 15**
See also DLB 104

Reynolds, Michael Shane 1937- **CLC 44**
See also CA 65-68; CANR 9

Reznikoff, Charles 1894-1976 **CLC 9**
See also CA 33-36; 61-64; CAP 2; DLB 28, 45

Rezzori (d'Arezzo), Gregor von 1914-1998 **CLC 25**
See also CA 122; 136; 167

Rhine, Richard
See Silverstein, Alvin

Rhodes, Eugene Manlove 1869-1934 **TCLC 53**

Rhodius, Apollonius c. 3rd cent. B.C.- **CMLC 28**
See also DLB 176

R'hoone
See Balzac, Honore de

Rhys, Jean 1890(?)-1979 **CLC 2, 4, 6, 14, 19, 51; DAM NOV; SSC 21**
See also CA 25-28R; 85-88; CANR 35, 62; CDBLB 1945-1960; DLB 36, 117, 162; MTCW 1

Ribeiro, Darcy 1922-1997 **CLC 34**
See also CA 33-36R; 156

Ribeiro, Joao Ubaldo (Osorio Pimentel) 1941- **CLC 10, 67**
See also CA 81-84

Ribman, Ronald (Burt) 1932- **CLC 7**
See also CA 21-24R; CANR 46

Ricci, Nino 1959- **CLC 70**
See also CA 137

Rice, Anne 1941- **CLC 41; DAM POP**
See also AAYA 9; BEST 89:2; CA 65-68; CANR 12, 36, 53, 74

Rice, Elmer (Leopold) 1892-1967 **CLC 7, 49; DAM DRAM**
See also CA 21-22; 25-28R; CAP 2; DLB 4, 7; MTCW 1

Rice, Tim(othy Miles Bindon) 1944- **CLC 21**
See also CA 103; CANR 46

Rich, Adrienne (Cecile) 1929- **CLC 3, 6, 7, 11, 18, 36, 73, 76; DAM POET; PC 5**
See also CA 9-12R; CANR 20, 53, 74; DLB 5, 67; MTCW 1

Rich, Barbara
See Graves, Robert (von Ranke)

Rich, Robert
See Trumbo, Dalton

Richard, Keith **CLC 17**
See also Richards, Keith

Richards, David Adams 1950- **CLC 59; DAC**
See also CA 93-96; CANR 60; DLB 53

Richards, I(vor) A(rmstrong) 1893-1979**C L C
14, 24**
See also CA 41-44R; 89-92; CANR 34, 74; DLB
27
Richards, Keith 1943-
See Richard, Keith
See also CA 107
Richardson, Anne
See Roiphe, Anne (Richardson)
Richardson, Dorothy Miller 1873-1957**TCLC
3**
See also CA 104; DLB 36
Richardson, Ethel Florence (Lindesay) 1870-
1946
See Richardson, Henry Handel
See also CA 105
Richardson, Henry Handel **TCLC 4**
See also Richardson, Ethel Florence (Lindesay)
See also DLB 197
Richardson, John 1796-1852 **NCLC 55; DAC**
See also DLB 99
Richardson, Samuel 1689-1761**LC 1, 44; DA;
DAB; DAC; DAM MST, NOV; WLC**
See also CDBLB 1660-1789; DLB 39
Richler, Mordecai 1931-**CLC 3, 5, 9, 13, 18, 46,
70; DAC; DAM MST, NOV**
See also AITN 1; CA 65-68; CANR 31, 62; CLR
17; DLB 53; MAICYA; MTCW 1; SATA 44,
98; SATA-Brief 27
Richter, Conrad (Michael) 1890-1968**CLC 30**
See also AAYA 21; CA 5-8R; 25-28R; CANR
23; DLB 9; MTCW 1; SATA 3
Ricostranza, Tom
See Ellis, Trey
Riddell, Charlotte 1832-1906 **TCLC 40**
See also CA 165; DLB 156
Riding, Laura **CLC 3, 7**
See also Jackson, Laura (Riding)
Riefenstahl, Berta Helene Amalia 1902-
See Riefenstahl, Leni
See also CA 108
Riefenstahl, Leni **CLC 16**
See also Riefenstahl, Berta Helene Amalia
Riffe, Ernest
See Bergman, (Ernst) Ingmar
Riggs, (Rolla) Lynn 1899-1954 **TCLC 56;
DAM MULT**
See also CA 144; DLB 175; NNAL
Riis, Jacob A(ugust) 1849-1914 **TCLC 80**
See also CA 113; 168; DLB 23
Riley, James Whitcomb 1849-1916**TCLC 51;
DAM POET**
See also CA 118; 137; MAICYA; SATA 17
Riley, Tex
See Creasey, John
Rilke, Rainer Maria 1875-1926**TCLC 1, 6, 19;
DAM POET; PC 2**
See also CA 104; 132; CANR 62; DLB 81;
MTCW 1
Rimbaud, (Jean Nicolas) Arthur 1854-1891
**NCLC 4, 35; DA; DAB; DAC; DAM MST,
POET; PC 3; WLC**
Rinehart, Mary Roberts 1876-1958 **TCLC 52**
See also CA 108; 166
Ringmaster, The
See Mencken, H(enry) L(ouis)
Ringwood, Gwen(dolyn Margaret) Pharis
1910-1984 **CLC 48**
See also CA 148; 112; DLB 88
Rio, Michel 19(?)- **CLC 43**
Ritsos, Giannes
See Ritsos, Yannis
Ritsos, Yannis 1909-1990 **CLC 6, 13, 31**

See also CA 77-80; 133; CANR 39, 61; MTCW
1
Ritter, Erika 1948(?)- **CLC 52**
Rivera, Jose Eustasio 1889-1928 **TCLC 35**
See also CA 162; HW
Rivers, Conrad Kent 1933-1968 **CLC 1**
See also BW 1; CA 85-88; DLB 41
Rivers, Elfrida
See Bradley, Marion Zimmer
Riverside, John
See Heinlein, Robert A(nson)
Rizal, Jose 1861-1896 **NCLC 27**
Roa Bastos, Augusto (Antonio) 1917-**CLC 45;
DAM MULT; HLC**
See also CA 131; DLB 113; HW
Robbe-Grillet, Alain 1922-**CLC 1, 2, 4, 6, 8, 10,
14, 43**
See also CA 9-12R; CANR 33, 65; DLB 83;
MTCW 1
Robbins, Harold 1916-1997 **CLC 5; DAM
NOV**
See also CA 73-76; 162; CANR 26, 54; MTCW
1
Robbins, Thomas Eugene 1936-
See Robbins, Tom
See also CA 81-84; CANR 29, 59; DAM NOV,
POP; MTCW 1
Robbins, Tom **CLC 9, 32, 64**
See also Robbins, Thomas Eugene
See also BEST 90:3; DLBY 80
Robbins, Trina 1938- **CLC 21**
See also CA 128
Roberts, Charles G(eorge) D(ouglas) 1860-1943
TCLC 8
See also CA 105; CLR 33; DLB 92; SATA 88;
SATA-Brief 29
Roberts, Elizabeth Madox 1886-1941 **TCLC
68**
See also CA 111; 166; DLB 9, 54, 102; SATA
33; SATA-Brief 27
Roberts, Kate 1891-1985 **CLC 15**
See also CA 107; 116
Roberts, Keith (John Kingston) 1935-**CLC 14**
See also CA 25-28R; CANR 46
Roberts, Kenneth (Lewis) 1885-1957**TCLC 23**
See also CA 109; DLB 9
Roberts, Michele (B.) 1949- **CLC 48**
See also CA 115; CANR 58
Robertson, Ellis
See Ellison, Harlan (Jay); Silverberg, Robert
Robertson, Thomas William 1829-1871**NCLC
35; DAM DRAM**
Robeson, Kenneth
See Dent, Lester
Robinson, Edwin Arlington 1869-1935**T C L C
5; DA; DAC; DAM MST, POET; PC 1**
See also CA 104; 133; CDALB 1865-1917;
DLB 54; MTCW 1
Robinson, Henry Crabb 1775-1867**NCLC 15**
See also DLB 107
Robinson, Jill 1936- **CLC 10**
See also CA 102; INT 102
Robinson, Kim Stanley 1952- **CLC 34**
See also AAYA 26; CA 126
Robinson, Lloyd
See Silverberg, Robert
Robinson, Marilynne 1944- **CLC 25**
See also CA 116
Robinson, Smokey **CLC 21**
See also Robinson, William, Jr.
Robinson, William, Jr. 1940-
See Robinson, Smokey
See also CA 116

Robison, Mary 1949- **CLC 42, 98**
See also CA 113; 116; DLB 130; INT 116
Rod, Edouard 1857-1910 **TCLC 52**
Roddenberry, Eugene Wesley 1921-1991
See Roddenberry, Gene
See also CA 110; 135; CANR 37; SATA 45;
SATA-Obit 69
Roddenberry, Gene **CLC 17**
See also Roddenberry, Eugene Wesley
See also AAYA 5; SATA-Obit 69
Rodgers, Mary 1931- **CLC 12**
See also CA 49-52; CANR 8, 55; CLR 20; INT
CANR-8; JRDA; MAICYA; SATA 8
Rodgers, W(illiam) R(obert) 1909-1969**CLC 7**
See also CA 85-88; DLB 20
Rodman, Eric
See Silverberg, Robert
Rodman, Howard 1920(?)-1985 **CLC 65**
See also CA 118
Rodman, Maia
See Wojciechowska, Maia (Teresa)
Rodriguez, Claudio 1934- **CLC 10**
See also DLB 134
Roelvaag, O(le) E(dvart) 1876-1931**TCLC 17**
See also CA 117; DLB 9
Roethke, Theodore (Huebner) 1908-1963**CLC
1, 3, 8, 11, 19, 46, 101; DAM POET; PC 15**
See also CA 81-84; CABS 2; CDALB 1941-
1968; DLB 5; MTCW 1
Rogers, Samuel 1763-1855 **NCLC 69**
See also DLB 93
Rogers, Thomas Hunton 1927- **CLC 57**
See also CA 89-92; INT 89-92
Rogers, Will(iam Penn Adair) 1879-1935
TCLC 8, 71; DAM MULT
See also CA 105; 144; DLB 11; NNAL
Rogin, Gilbert 1929- **CLC 18**
See also CA 65-68; CANR 15
Rohan, Koda **TCLC 22**
See also Koda Shigeyuki
Rohlfs, Anna Katharine Green
See Green, Anna Katharine
Rohmer, Eric **CLC 16**
See also Scherer, Jean-Marie Maurice
Rohmer, Sax **TCLC 28**
See also Ward, Arthur Henry Sarsfield
See also DLB 70
Roiphe, Anne (Richardson) 1935- **CLC 3, 9**
See also CA 89-92; CANR 45, 73; DLBY 80;
INT 89-92
Rojas, Fernando de 1465-1541 **LC 23**
Rolfe, Frederick (William Serafino Austin
Lewis Mary) 1860-1913 **TCLC 12**
See also CA 107; DLB 34, 156
Rolland, Romain 1866-1944 **TCLC 23**
See also CA 118; DLB 65
Rolle, Richard c. 1300-c. 1349 **CMLC 21**
See also DLB 146
Rolvaag, O(le) E(dvart)
See Roelvaag, O(le) E(dvart)
Romain Arnaud, Saint
See Aragon, Louis
Romains, Jules 1885-1972 **CLC 7**
See also CA 85-88; CANR 34; DLB 65; MTCW
1
Romero, Jose Ruben 1890-1952 **TCLC 14**
See also CA 114; 131; HW
Ronsard, Pierre de 1524-1585 **LC 6; PC 11**
Rooke, Leon 1934- **CLC 25, 34; DAM POP**
See also CA 25-28R; CANR 23, 53
Roosevelt, Theodore 1858-1919 **TCLC 69**
See also CA 115; 170; DLB 47, 186
Roper, William 1498-1578 **LC 10**

Roquelaure, A. N.
See Rice, Anne

Rosa, Joao Guimaraes 1908-1967 **CLC 23**
See also CA 89-92; DLB 113

Rose, Wendy 1948-**CLC 85; DAM MULT; PC 13**
See also CA 53-56; CANR 5, 51; DLB 175; NNAL; SATA 12

Rosen, R. D.
See Rosen, Richard (Dean)

Rosen, Richard (Dean) 1949- **CLC 39**
See also CA 77-80; CANR 62; INT CANR-30

Rosenberg, Isaac 1890-1918 **TCLC 12**
See also CA 107; DLB 20

Rosenblatt, Joe **CLC 15**
See also Rosenblatt, Joseph

Rosenblatt, Joseph 1933-
See Rosenblatt, Joe
See also CA 89-92; INT 89-92

Rosenfeld, Samuel
See Tzara, Tristan

Rosenstock, Sami
See Tzara, Tristan

Rosenstock, Samuel
See Tzara, Tristan

Rosenthal, M(acha) L(ouis) 1917-1996 **C L C 28**
See also CA 1-4R; 152; CAAS 6; CANR 4, 51; DLB 5; SATA 59

Ross, Barnaby
See Dannay, Frederic

Ross, Bernard L.
See Follett, Ken(neth Martin)

Ross, J. H.
See Lawrence, T(homas) E(dward)

Ross, John Hume
See Lawrence, T(homas) E(dward)

Ross, Martin
See Martin, Violet Florence
See also DLB 135

Ross, (James) Sinclair 1908- **CLC 13; DAC; DAM MST; SSC 24**
See also CA 73-76; DLB 88

Rossetti, Christina (Georgina) 1830-1894 **NCLC 2, 50, 66; DA; DAB; DAC; DAM MST, POET; PC 7; WLC**
See also DLB 35, 163; MAICYA; SATA 20

Rossetti, Dante Gabriel 1828-1882 **NCLC 4; DA; DAB; DAC; DAM MST, POET; WLC**
See also CDBLB 1832-1890; DLB 35

Rossner, Judith (Perelman) 1935-**CLC 6, 9, 29**
See also AITN 2; BEST 90:3; CA 17-20R; CANR 18, 51, 73; DLB 6; INT CANR-18; MTCW 1

Rostand, Edmond (Eugene Alexis) 1868-1918 **TCLC 6, 37; DA; DAB; DAC; DAM DRAM, MST**
See also CA 104; 126; DLB 192; MTCW 1

Roth, Henry 1906-1995 **CLC 2, 6, 11, 104**
See also CA 11-12; 149; CANR 38, 63; CAP 1; DLB 28; MTCW 1

Roth, Philip (Milton) 1933-**CLC 1, 2, 3, 4, 6, 9, 15, 22, 31, 47, 66, 86; DA; DAB; DAC; DAM MST, NOV, POP; SSC 26; WLC**
See also BEST 90:3; CA 1-4R; CANR 1, 22, 36, 55; CDALB 1968-1988; DLB 2, 28, 173; DLBY 82; MTCW 1

Rothenberg, Jerome 1931- **CLC 6, 57**
See also CA 45-48; CANR 1; DLB 5, 193

Roumain, Jacques (Jean Baptiste) 1907-1944 **TCLC 19; BLC 3; DAM MULT**
See also BW 1; CA 117; 125

Rourke, Constance (Mayfield) 1885-1941 **TCLC 12**
See also CA 107; YABC 1

Rousseau, Jean-Baptiste 1671-1741 **LC 9**

Rousseau, Jean-Jacques 1712-1778**LC 14, 36; DA; DAB; DAC; DAM MST; WLC**

Roussel, Raymond 1877-1933 **TCLC 20**
See also CA 117

Rovit, Earl (Herbert) 1927- **CLC 7**
See also CA 5-8R; CANR 12

Rowe, Elizabeth Singer 1674-1737 **LC 44**
See also DLB 39, 95

Rowe, Nicholas 1674-1718 **LC 8**
See also DLB 84

Rowley, Ames Dorrance
See Lovecraft, H(oward) P(hillips)

Rowson, Susanna Haswell 1762(?)-1824 **NCLC 5, 69**
See also DLB 37, 200

Roy, Arundhati 1960(?)- **CLC 109**
See also CA 163; DLBY 97

Roy, Gabrielle 1909-1983 **CLC 10, 14; DAB; DAC; DAM MST**
See also CA 53-56; 110; CANR 5, 61; DLB 68; MTCW 1

Royko, Mike 1932-1997 **CLC 109**
See also CA 89-92; 157; CANR 26

Rozewicz, Tadeusz 1921- **CLC 9, 23; DAM POET**
See also CA 108; CANR 36, 66; MTCW 1

Ruark, Gibbons 1941- **CLC 3**
See also CA 33-36R; CAAS 23; CANR 14, 31, 57; DLB 120

Rubens, Bernice (Ruth) 1923- **CLC 19, 31**
See also CA 25-28R; CANR 33, 65; DLB 14; MTCW 1

Rubin, Harold
See Robbins, Harold

Rudkin, (James) David 1936- **CLC 14**
See also CA 89-92; DLB 13

Rudnik, Raphael 1933- **CLC 7**
See also CA 29-32R

Ruffian, M.
See Hasek, Jaroslav (Matej Frantisek)

Ruiz, Jose Martinez **CLC 11**
See also Martinez Ruiz, Jose

Rukeyser, Muriel 1913-1980**CLC 6, 10, 15, 27; DAM POET; PC 12**
See also CA 5-8R; 93-96; CANR 26, 60; DLB 48; MTCW 1; SATA-Obit 22

Rule, Jane (Vance) 1931- **CLC 27**
See also CA 25-28R; CAAS 18; CANR 12; DLB 60

Rulfo, Juan 1918-1986 **CLC 8, 80; DAM MULT; HLC; SSC 25**
See also CA 85-88; 118; CANR 26; DLB 113; HW; MTCW 1

Rumi, Jalal al-Din 1297-1373 **CMLC 20**

Runeberg, Johan 1804-1877 **NCLC 41**

Runyon, (Alfred) Damon 1884(?)-1946**T C L C 10**
See also CA 107; 165; DLB 11, 86, 171

Rush, Norman 1933- **CLC 44**
See also CA 121; 126; INT 126

Rushdie, (Ahmed) Salman 1947- **CLC 23, 31, 55, 100; DAB; DAC; DAM MST, NOV, POP; WLCS**
See also BEST 89:3; CA 108; 111; CANR 33, 56; DLB 194; INT 111; MTCW 1

Rushforth, Peter (Scott) 1945- **CLC 19**
See also CA 101

Ruskin, John 1819-1900 **TCLC 63**
See also CA 114; 129; CDBLB 1832-1890; DLB 55, 163, 190; SATA 24

Russ, Joanna 1937- **CLC 15**
See also CANR 11, 31, 65; DLB 8; MTCW 1

Russell, George William 1867-1935
See Baker, Jean H.
See also CA 104; 153; CDBLB 1890-1914; DAM POET

Russell, (Henry) Ken(neth Alfred) 1927-**C L C 16**
See also CA 105

Russell, William Martin 1947- **CLC 60**
See also CA 164

Rutherford, Mark **TCLC 25**
See also White, William Hale
See also DLB 18

Ruyslinck, Ward 1929- **CLC 14**
See also Belser, Reimond Karel Maria de

Ryan, Cornelius (John) 1920-1974 **CLC 7**
See also CA 69-72; 53-56; CANR 38

Ryan, Michael 1946- **CLC 65**
See also CA 49-52; DLBY 82

Ryan, Tim
See Dent, Lester

Rybakov, Anatoli (Naumovich) 1911-**CLC 23, 53**
See also CA 126; 135; SATA 79

Ryder, Jonathan
See Ludlum, Robert

Ryga, George 1932-1987**CLC 14; DAC; DAM MST**
See also CA 101; 124; CANR 43; DLB 60

S. H.
See Hartmann, Sadakichi

S. S.
See Sassoon, Siegfried (Lorraine)

Saba, Umberto 1883-1957 **TCLC 33**
See also CA 144; DLB 114

Sabatini, Rafael 1875-1950 **TCLC 47**
See also CA 162

Sabato, Ernesto (R.) 1911-**CLC 10, 23; DAM MULT; HLC**
See also CA 97-100; CANR 32, 65; DLB 145; HW; MTCW 1

Sa-Carniero, Mario de 1890-1916 **TCLC 83**

Sacastru, Martin
See Bioy Casares, Adolfo

Sacher-Masoch, Leopold von 1836(?)-1895 **NCLC 31**

Sachs, Marilyn (Stickle) 1927- **CLC 35**
See also AAYA 2; CA 17-20R; CANR 13, 47; CLR 2; JRDA; MAICYA; SAAS 2; SATA 3, 68

Sachs, Nelly 1891-1970 **CLC 14, 98**
See also CA 17-18; 25-28R; CAP 2

Sackler, Howard (Oliver) 1929-1982 **CLC 14**
See also CA 61-64; 108; CANR 30; DLB 7

Sacks, Oliver (Wolf) 1933- **CLC 67**
See also CA 53-56; CANR 28, 50; INT CANR-28; MTCW 1

Sadakichi
See Hartmann, Sadakichi

Sade, Donatien Alphonse Francois, Comte de 1740-1814 **NCLC 47**

Sadoff, Ira 1945- **CLC 9**
See also CA 53-56; CANR 5, 21; DLB 120

Saetone
See Camus, Albert

Safire, William 1929- **CLC 10**
See also CA 17-20R; CANR 31, 54

Sagan, Carl (Edward) 1934-1996**CLC 30, 112**
See also AAYA 2; CA 25-28R; 155; CANR 11, 36, 74; MTCW 1; SATA 58; SATA-Obit 94

Sagan, Francoise **CLC 3, 6, 9, 17, 36**
See also Quoirez, Francoise

Author Index

See also CA 29-32R; CAAS 4; CANR 12, 33, 52, 61; DLB 105

Simmel, Georg 1858-1918   **TCLC 64**
See also CA 157

Simmons, Charles (Paul) 1924-   **CLC 57**
See also CA 89-92; INT 89-92

Simmons, Dan 1948-   **CLC 44; DAM POP**
See also AAYA 16; CA 138; CANR 53

Simmons, James (Stewart Alexander) 1933-
CLC 43
See also CA 105; CAAS 21; DLB 40

Simms, William Gilmore 1806-1870 **NCLC 3**
See also DLB 3, 30, 59, 73

Simon, Carly 1945-   **CLC 26**
See also CA 105

Simon, Claude 1913-1984   **CLC 4, 9, 15, 39; DAM NOV**
See also CA 89-92; CANR 33; DLB 83; MTCW 1

Simon, (Marvin) Neil 1927-**CLC 6, 11, 31, 39, 70; DAM DRAM**
See also AITN 1; CA 21-24R; CANR 26, 54; DLB 7; MTCW 1

Simon, Paul (Frederick) 1941(?)-   **CLC 17**
See also CA 116; 153

Simonon, Paul 1956(?)-   **CLC 30**

Simpson, Harriette
See Arnow, Harriette (Louisa) Simpson

Simpson, Louis (Aston Marantz) 1923-**CLC 4, 7, 9, 32; DAM POET**
See also CA 1-4R; CAAS 4; CANR 1, 61; DLB 5; MTCW 1

Simpson, Mona (Elizabeth) 1957-   **CLC 44**
See also CA 122; 135; CANR 68

Simpson, N(orman) F(rederick) 1919-**CLC 29**
See also CA 13-16R; DLB 13

Sinclair, Andrew (Annandale) 1935-   **CLC 2, 14**
See also CA 9-12R; CAAS 5; CANR 14, 38; DLB 14; MTCW 1

Sinclair, Emil
See Hesse, Hermann

Sinclair, Iain 1943-   **CLC 76**
See also CA 132

Sinclair, Iain MacGregor
See Sinclair, Iain

Sinclair, Irene
See Griffith, D(avid Lewelyn) W(ark)

Sinclair, Mary Amelia St. Clair 1865(?)-1946
See Sinclair, May
See also CA 104

Sinclair, May 1863-1946   **TCLC 3, 11**
See also Sinclair, Mary Amelia St. Clair
See also CA 166; DLB 36, 135

Sinclair, Roy
See Griffith, D(avid Lewelyn) W(ark)

Sinclair, Upton (Beall) 1878-1968 **CLC 1, 11, 15, 63; DA; DAB; DAC; DAM MST, NOV; WLC**
See also CA 5-8R; 25-28R; CANR 7; CDALB 1929-1941; DLB 9; INT CANR-7; MTCW 1; SATA 9

Singer, Isaac
See Singer, Isaac Bashevis

Singer, Isaac Bashevis 1904-1991**CLC 1, 3, 6, 9, 11, 15, 23, 38, 69, 111; DA; DAB; DAC; DAM MST, NOV; SSC 3; WLC**
See also AITN 1, 2; CA 1-4R; 134; CANR 1, 39; CDALB 1941-1968; CLR 1; DLB 6, 28, 52; DLBY 91; JRDA; MAICYA; MTCW 1; SATA 3, 27; SATA-Obit 68

Singer, Israel Joshua 1893-1944   **TCLC 33**
See also CA 169

Singh, Khushwant 1915-   **CLC 11**
See also CA 9-12R; CAAS 9; CANR 6

Singleton, Ann
See Benedict, Ruth (Fulton)

Sinjohn, John
See Galsworthy, John

Sinyavsky, Andrei (Donatevich) 1925-1997
CLC 8
See also CA 85-88; 159

Sirin, V.
See Nabokov, Vladimir (Vladimirovich)

Sissman, L(ouis) E(dward) 1928-1976**CLC 9, 18**
See also CA 21-24R; 65-68; CANR 13; DLB 5

Sisson, C(harles) H(ubert) 1914-   **CLC 8**
See also CA 1-4R; CAAS 3; CANR 3, 48; DLB 27

Sitwell, Dame Edith 1887-1964 **CLC 2, 9, 67; DAM POET; PC 3**
See also CA 9-12R; CANR 35; CDBLB 1945-1960; DLB 20; MTCW 1

Siwaarmill, H. P.
See Sharp, William

Sjoewall, Maj 1935-   **CLC 7**
See also CA 65-68; CANR 73

Sjowall, Maj
See Sjoewall, Maj

Skelton, Robin 1925-1997   **CLC 13**
See also AITN 2; CA 5-8R; 160; CAAS 5; CANR 28; DLB 27, 53

Skolimowski, Jerzy 1938-   **CLC 20**
See also CA 128

Skram, Amalie (Bertha) 1847-1905 **TCLC 25**
See also CA 165

Skvorecky, Josef (Vaclav) 1924- **CLC 15, 39, 69; DAC; DAM NOV**
See also CA 61-64; CAAS 1; CANR 10, 34, 63; MTCW 1

Slade, Bernard   **CLC 11, 46**
See also Newbound, Bernard Slade
See also CAAS 9; DLB 53

Slaughter, Carolyn 1946-   **CLC 56**
See also CA 85-88

Slaughter, Frank G(ill) 1908-   **CLC 29**
See also AITN 2; CA 5-8R; CANR 5; INT CANR-5

Slavitt, David R(ytman) 1935-   **CLC 5, 14**
See also CA 21-24R; CAAS 3; CANR 41; DLB 5, 6

Slesinger, Tess 1905-1945   **TCLC 10**
See also CA 107; DLB 102

Slessor, Kenneth 1901-1971   **CLC 14**
See also CA 102; 89-92

Slowacki, Juliusz 1809-1849   **NCLC 15**

Smart, Christopher 1722-1771   **LC 3; DAM POET; PC 13**
See also DLB 109

Smart, Elizabeth 1913-1986   **CLC 54**
See also CA 81-84; 118; DLB 88

Smiley, Jane (Graves) 1949-**CLC 53, 76; DAM POP**
See also CA 104; CANR 30, 50, 74; INT CANR-30

Smith, A(rthur) J(ames) M(arshall) 1902-1980
CLC 15; DAC
See also CA 1-4R; 102; CANR 4; DLB 88

Smith, Adam 1723-1790   **LC 36**
See also DLB 104

Smith, Alexander 1829-1867   **NCLC 59**
See also DLB 32, 55

Smith, Anna Deavere 1950-   **CLC 86**
See also CA 133

Smith, Betty (Wehner) 1896-1972   **CLC 19**

See also CA 5-8R; 33-36R; DLBY 82; SATA 6

Smith, Charlotte (Turner) 1749-1806 **NCLC 23**
See also DLB 39, 109

Smith, Clark Ashton 1893-1961   **CLC 43**
See also CA 143

Smith, Dave   **CLC 22, 42**
See also Smith, David (Jeddie)
See also CAAS 7; DLB 5

Smith, David (Jeddie) 1942-
See Smith, Dave
See also CA 49-52; CANR 1, 59; DAM POET

Smith, Florence Margaret 1902-1971
See Smith, Stevie
See also CA 17-18; 29-32R; CANR 35; CAP 2; DAM POET; MTCW 1

Smith, Iain Crichton 1928-   **CLC 64**
See also CA 21-24R; DLB 40, 139

Smith, John 1580(?)-1631   **LC 9**
See also DLB 24, 30

Smith, Johnston
See Crane, Stephen (Townley)

Smith, Joseph, Jr. 1805-1844   **NCLC 53**

Smith, Lee 1944-   **CLC 25, 73**
See also CA 114; 119; CANR 46; DLB 143; DLBY 83; INT 119

Smith, Martin
See Smith, Martin Cruz

Smith, Martin Cruz 1942-   **CLC 25; DAM MULT, POP**
See also BEST 89:4; CA 85-88; CANR 6, 23, 43, 65; INT CANR-23; NNAL

Smith, Mary-Ann Tirone 1944-   **CLC 39**
See also CA 118; 136

Smith, Patti 1946-   **CLC 12**
See also CA 93-96; CANR 63

Smith, Pauline (Urmson) 1882-1959**TCLC 25**

Smith, Rosamond
See Oates, Joyce Carol

Smith, Sheila Kaye
See Kaye-Smith, Sheila

Smith, Stevie   **CLC 3, 8, 25, 44; PC 12**
See also Smith, Florence Margaret
See also DLB 20

Smith, Wilbur (Addison) 1933-   **CLC 33**
See also CA 13-16R; CANR 7, 46, 66; MTCW 1

Smith, William Jay 1918-   **CLC 6**
See also CA 5-8R; CANR 44; DLB 5; MAICYA; SAAS 22; SATA 2, 68

Smith, Woodrow Wilson
See Kuttner, Henry

Smolenskin, Peretz 1842-1885   **NCLC 30**

Smollett, Tobias (George) 1721-1771**LC 2, 46**
See also CDBLB 1660-1789; DLB 39, 104

Snodgrass, W(illiam) D(e Witt) 1926-**CLC 2, 6, 10, 18, 68; DAM POET**
See also CA 1-4R; CANR 6, 36, 65; DLB 5; MTCW 1

Snow, C(harles) P(ercy) 1905-1980 **CLC 1, 4, 6, 9, 13, 19; DAM NOV**
See also CA 5-8R; 101; CANR 28; CDBLB 1945-1960; DLB 15, 77; DLBD 17; MTCW 1

Snow, Frances Compton
See Adams, Henry (Brooks)

Snyder, Gary (Sherman) 1930-**CLC 1, 2, 5, 9, 32; DAM POET; PC 21**
See also CA 17-20R; CANR 30, 60; DLB 5, 16, 165

Snyder, Zilpha Keatley 1927-   **CLC 17**
See also AAYA 15; CA 9-12R; CANR 38; CLR 31; JRDA; MAICYA; SAAS 2; SATA 1, 28,

75

Soares, Bernardo
   See Pessoa, Fernando (Antonio Nogueira)
Sobh, A.
   See Shamlu, Ahmad
Sobol, Joshua   **CLC 60**
Socrates 469B.C.-399B.C.   **CMLC 27**
Soderberg, Hjalmar 1869-1941   **TCLC 39**
Sodergran, Edith (Irene)
   See Soedergran, Edith (Irene)
Soedergran, Edith (Irene) 1892-1923 **T C L C 31**
Softly, Edgar
   See Lovecraft, H(oward) P(hillips)
Softly, Edward
   See Lovecraft, H(oward) P(hillips)
Sokolov, Raymond 1941-   **CLC 7**
   See also CA 85-88
Solo, Jay
   See Ellison, Harlan (Jay)
Sologub, Fyodor   **TCLC 9**
   See also Teternikov, Fyodor Kuzmich
Solomons, Ikey Esquir
   See Thackeray, William Makepeace
Solomos, Dionysios 1798-1857   **NCLC 15**
Solwoska, Mara
   See French, Marilyn
Solzhenitsyn, Aleksandr I(sayevich) 1918-
   CLC 1, 2, 4, 7, 9, 10, 18, 26, 34, 78; DA; DAB; DAC; DAM MST, NOV; SSC 32; WLC
   See also AITN 1; CA 69-72; CANR 40, 65; MTCW 1
Somers, Jane
   See Lessing, Doris (May)
Somerville, Edith 1858-1949   **TCLC 51**
   See also DLB 135
Somerville & Ross
   See Martin, Violet Florence; Somerville, Edith
Sommer, Scott 1951-   **CLC 25**
   See also CA 106
Sondheim, Stephen (Joshua) 1930- **CLC 30, 39; DAM DRAM**
   See also AAYA 11; CA 103; CANR 47, 68
Song, Cathy 1955-   **PC 21**
   See also CA 154; DLB 169
Sontag, Susan 1933-**CLC 1, 2, 10, 13, 31, 105; DAM POP**
   See also CA 17-20R; CANR 25, 51, 74; DLB 2, 67; MTCW 1
Sophocles 496(?)B.C.-406(?)B.C.   **CMLC 2; DA; DAB; DAC; DAM DRAM, MST; DC 1; WLCS**
   See also DLB 176
Sordello 1189-1269   **CMLC 15**
Sorel, Julia
   See Drexler, Rosalyn
Sorrentino, Gilbert 1929-**CLC 3, 7, 14, 22, 40**
   See also CA 77-80; CANR 14, 33; DLB 5, 173; DLBY 80; INT CANR-14
Soto, Gary 1952- **CLC 32, 80; DAM MULT; HLC**
   See also AAYA 10; CA 119; 125; CANR 50, 74; CLR 38; DLB 82; HW; INT 125; JRDA; SATA 80
Soupault, Philippe 1897-1990   **CLC 68**
   See also CA 116; 147; 131
Souster, (Holmes) Raymond 1921-**CLC 5, 14; DAC; DAM POET**
   See also CA 13-16R; CAAS 14; CANR 13, 29, 53; DLB 88; SATA 63
Southern, Terry 1924(?)-1995   **CLC 7**
   See also CA 1-4R; 150; CANR 1, 55; DLB 2

Southey, Robert 1774-1843   **NCLC 8**
   See also DLB 93, 107, 142; SATA 54
Southworth, Emma Dorothy Eliza Nevitte 1819-1899   **NCLC 26**
Souza, Ernest
   See Scott, Evelyn
Soyinka, Wole 1934-**CLC 3, 5, 14, 36, 44; BLC 3; DA; DAB; DAC; DAM DRAM, MST, MULT; DC 2; WLC**
   See also BW 2; CA 13-16R; CANR 27, 39; DLB 125; MTCW 1
Spackman, W(illiam) M(ode) 1905-1990**C L C 46**
   See also CA 81-84; 132
Spacks, Barry (Bernard) 1931-   **CLC 14**
   See also CA 154; CANR 33; DLB 105
Spanidou, Irini 1946-   **CLC 44**
Spark, Muriel (Sarah) 1918-**CLC 2, 3, 5, 8, 13, 18, 40, 94; DAB; DAC; DAM MST, NOV; SSC 10**
   See also CA 5-8R; CANR 12, 36; CDBLB 1945-1960; DLB 15, 139; INT CANR-12; MTCW 1
Spaulding, Douglas
   See Bradbury, Ray (Douglas)
Spaulding, Leonard
   See Bradbury, Ray (Douglas)
Spence, J. A. D.
   See Eliot, T(homas) S(tearns)
Spencer, Elizabeth 1921-   **CLC 22**
   See also CA 13-16R; CANR 32, 65; DLB 6; MTCW 1; SATA 14
Spencer, Leonard G.
   See Silverberg, Robert
Spencer, Scott 1945-   **CLC 30**
   See also CA 113; CANR 51; DLBY 86
Spender, Stephen (Harold) 1909-1995**CLC 1, 2, 5, 10, 41, 91; DAM POET**
   See also CA 9-12R; 149; CANR 31, 54; CDBLB 1945-1960; DLB 20; MTCW 1
Spengler, Oswald (Arnold Gottfried) 1880-1936 **TCLC 25**
   See also CA 118
Spenser, Edmund 1552(?)-1599**LC 5, 39; DA; DAB; DAC; DAM MST, POET; PC 8; WLC**
   See also CDBLB Before 1660; DLB 167
Spicer, Jack 1925-1965 **CLC 8, 18, 72; DAM POET**
   See also CA 85-88; DLB 5, 16, 193
Spiegelman, Art 1948-   **CLC 76**
   See also AAYA 10; CA 125; CANR 41, 55, 74
Spielberg, Peter 1929-   **CLC 6**
   See also CA 5-8R; CANR 4, 48; DLBY 81
Spielberg, Steven 1947-   **CLC 20**
   See also AAYA 8, 24; CA 77-80; CANR 32; SATA 32
Spillane, Frank Morrison 1918-
   See Spillane, Mickey
   See also CA 25-28R; CANR 28, 63; MTCW 1; SATA 66
Spillane, Mickey   **CLC 3, 13**
   See also Spillane, Frank Morrison
Spinoza, Benedictus de 1632-1677   **LC 9**
Spinrad, Norman (Richard) 1940- **CLC 46**
   See also CA 37-40R; CAAS 19; CANR 20; DLB 8; INT CANR-20
Spitteler, Carl (Friedrich Georg) 1845-1924 **TCLC 12**
   See also CA 109; DLB 129
Spivack, Kathleen (Romola Drucker) 1938- **CLC 6**
   See also CA 49-52

Spoto, Donald 1941-   **CLC 39**
   See also CA 65-68; CANR 11, 57
Springsteen, Bruce (F.) 1949-   **CLC 17**
   See also CA 111
Spurling, Hilary 1940-   **CLC 34**
   See also CA 104; CANR 25, 52
Spyker, John Howland
   See Elman, Richard (Martin)
Squires, (James) Radcliffe 1917-1993**CLC 51**
   See also CA 1-4R; 140; CANR 6, 21
Srivastava, Dhanpat Rai 1880(?)-1936
   See Premchand
   See also CA 118
Stacy, Donald
   See Pohl, Frederik
Stael, Germaine de 1766-1817
   See Stael-Holstein, Anne Louise Germaine Necker Baronn
   See also DLB 119
Stael-Holstein, Anne Louise Germaine Necker Baronn 1766-1817   **NCLC 3**
   See also Stael, Germaine de
   See also DLB 192
Stafford, Jean 1915-1979**CLC 4, 7, 19, 68; SSC 26**
   See also CA 1-4R; 85-88; CANR 3, 65; DLB 2, 173; MTCW 1; SATA-Obit 22
Stafford, William (Edgar) 1914-1993 **CLC 4, 7, 29; DAM POET**
   See also CA 5-8R; 142; CAAS 3; CANR 5, 22; DLB 5; INT CANR-22
Stagnelius, Eric Johan 1793-1823 **NCLC 61**
Staines, Trevor
   See Brunner, John (Kilian Houston)
Stairs, Gordon
   See Austin, Mary (Hunter)
Stannard, Martin 1947-   **CLC 44**
   See also CA 142; DLB 155
Stanton, Elizabeth Cady 1815-1902**TCLC 73**
   See also DLB 79
Stanton, Maura 1946-   **CLC 9**
   See also CA 89-92; CANR 15; DLB 120
Stanton, Schuyler
   See Baum, L(yman) Frank
Stapledon, (William) Olaf 1886-1950 **TCLC 22**
   See also CA 111; 162; DLB 15
Starbuck, George (Edwin) 1931-1996**CLC 53; DAM POET**
   See also CA 21-24R; 153; CANR 23
Stark, Richard
   See Westlake, Donald E(dwin)
Staunton, Schuyler
   See Baum, L(yman) Frank
Stead, Christina (Ellen) 1902-1983 **CLC 2, 5, 8, 32, 80**
   See also CA 13-16R; 109; CANR 33, 40; MTCW 1
Stead, William Thomas 1849-1912 **TCLC 48**
   See also CA 167
Steele, Richard 1672-1729   **LC 18**
   See also CDBLB 1660-1789; DLB 84, 101
Steele, Timothy (Reid) 1948-   **CLC 45**
   See also CA 93-96; CANR 16, 50; DLB 120
Steffens, (Joseph) Lincoln 1866-1936 **T C L C 20**
   See also CA 117
Stegner, Wallace (Earle) 1909-1993**CLC 9, 49, 81; DAM NOV; SSC 27**
   See also AITN 1; BEST 90:3; CA 1-4R; 141; CAAS 9; CANR 1, 21, 46; DLB 9; DLBY 93; MTCW 1
Stein, Gertrude 1874-1946**TCLC 1, 6, 28, 48;**

See Traven, B.

Tournier, Michel (Edouard) 1924-**CLC 6, 23, 36, 95**
See also CA 49-52; CANR 3, 36, 74; DLB 83; MTCW 1; SATA 23

Tournimparte, Alessandra
See Ginzburg, Natalia

Towers, Ivar
See Kornbluth, C(yril) M.

Towne, Robert (Burton) 1936(?)- **CLC 87**
See also CA 108; DLB 44

Townsend, Sue **CLC 61**
See also Townsend, Susan Elaine
See also SATA 55, 93; SATA-Brief 48

Townsend, Susan Elaine 1946-
See Townsend, Sue
See also CA 119; 127; CANR 65; DAB; DAC; DAM MST

Townshend, Peter (Dennis Blandford) 1945-
CLC 17, 42
See also CA 107

Tozzi, Federigo 1883-1920 **TCLC 31**
See also CA 160

Traill, Catharine Parr 1802-1899 **NCLC 31**
See also DLB 99

Trakl, Georg 1887-1914 **TCLC 5; PC 20**
See also CA 104; 165

Transtroemer, Tomas (Goesta) 1931-**CLC 52, 65; DAM POET**
See also CA 117; 129; CAAS 17

Transtromer, Tomas Gosta
See Transtroemer, Tomas (Goesta)

Traven, B. (?)-1969 **CLC 8, 11**
See also CA 19-20; 25-28R; CAP 2; DLB 9, 56; MTCW 1

Treitel, Jonathan 1959- **CLC 70**

Tremain, Rose 1943- **CLC 42**
See also CA 97-100; CANR 44; DLB 14

Tremblay, Michel 1942- **CLC 29, 102; DAC; DAM MST**
See also CA 116; 128; DLB 60; MTCW 1

Trevanian **CLC 29**
See also Whitaker, Rod(ney)

Trevor, Glen
See Hilton, James

Trevor, William 1928-**CLC 7, 9, 14, 25, 71, 116; SSC 21**
See also Cox, William Trevor
See also DLB 14, 139

Trifonov, Yuri (Valentinovich) 1925-1981
CLC 45
See also CA 126; 103; MTCW 1

Trilling, Lionel 1905-1975 **CLC 9, 11, 24**
See also CA 9-12R; 61-64; CANR 10; DLB 28, 63; INT CANR-10; MTCW 1

Trimball, W. H.
See Mencken, H(enry) L(ouis)

Tristan
See Gomez de la Serna, Ramon

Tristram
See Housman, A(lfred) E(dward)

Trogdon, William (Lewis) 1939-
See Heat-Moon, William Least
See also CA 115; 119; CANR 47; INT 119

Trollope, Anthony 1815-1882NCLC 6, 33; DA; DAB; DAC; DAM MST, NOV; SSC 28; WLC
See also CDBLB 1832-1890; DLB 21, 57, 159; SATA 22

Trollope, Frances 1779-1863 **NCLC 30**
See also DLB 21, 166

Trotsky, Leon 1879-1940 **TCLC 22**
See also CA 118; 167

Trotter (Cockburn), Catharine 1679-1749L C 8
See also DLB 84

Trout, Kilgore
See Farmer, Philip Jose

Trow, George W. S. 1943- **CLC 52**
See also CA 126

Troyat, Henri 1911- **CLC 23**
See also CA 45-48; CANR 2, 33, 67; MTCW 1

Trudeau, G(arretson) B(eekman) 1948-
See Trudeau, Garry B.
See also CA 81-84; CANR 31; SATA 35

Trudeau, Garry B. **CLC 12**
See also Trudeau, G(arretson) B(eekman)
See also AAYA 10; AITN 2

Truffaut, Francois 1932-1984 **CLC 20, 101**
See also CA 81-84; 113; CANR 34

Trumbo, Dalton 1905-1976 **CLC 19**
See also CA 21-24R; 69-72; CANR 10; DLB 26

Trumbull, John 1750-1831 **NCLC 30**
See also DLB 31

Trundlett, Helen B.
See Eliot, T(homas) S(tearns)

Tryon, Thomas 1926-1991 **CLC 3, 11; DAM POP**
See also AITN 1; CA 29-32R; 135; CANR 32; MTCW 1

Tryon, Tom
See Tryon, Thomas

Ts'ao Hsueh-ch'in 1715(?)-1763 **LC 1**

Tsushima, Shuji 1909-1948
See Dazai Osamu
See also CA 107

Tsvetaeva (Efron), Marina (Ivanovna) 1892-1941 **TCLC 7, 35; PC 14**
See also CA 104; 128; CANR 73; MTCW 1

Tuck, Lily 1938- **CLC 70**
See also CA 139

Tu Fu 712-770 **PC 9**
See also DAM MULT

Tunis, John R(oberts) 1889-1975 **CLC 12**
See also CA 61-64; CANR 62; DLB 22, 171; JRDA; MAICYA; SATA 37; SATA-Brief 30

Tuohy, Frank **CLC 37**
See also Tuohy, John Francis
See also DLB 14, 139

Tuohy, John Francis 1925-
See Tuohy, Frank
See also CA 5-8R; CANR 3, 47

Turco, Lewis (Putnam) 1934- **CLC 11, 63**
See also CA 13-16R; CAAS 22; CANR 24, 51; DLBY 84

Turgenev, Ivan 1818-1883 **NCLC 21; DA; DAB; DAC; DAM MST, NOV; DC 7; SSC 7; WLC**

Turgot, Anne-Robert-Jacques 1727-1781 **L C 26**

Turner, Frederick 1943- **CLC 48**
See also CA 73-76; CAAS 10; CANR 12, 30, 56; DLB 40

Tutu, Desmond M(pilo) 1931-**CLC 80; BLC 3; DAM MULT**
See also BW 1; CA 125; CANR 67

Tutuola, Amos 1920-1997**CLC 5, 14, 29; BLC 3; DAM MULT**
See also BW 2; CA 9-12R; 159; CANR 27, 66; DLB 125; MTCW 1

Twain, MarkTCLC 6, 12, 19, 36, 48, 59; SSC 6, 26; WLC
See also Clemens, Samuel Langhorne
See also AAYA 20; DLB 11, 12, 23, 64, 74

Tyler, Anne 1941- **CLC 7, 11, 18, 28, 44, 59, 103; DAM NOV, POP**
See also AAYA 18; BEST 89:1; CA 9-12R; CANR 11, 33, 53; DLB 6, 143; DLBY 82; MTCW 1; SATA 7, 90

Tyler, Royall 1757-1826 **NCLC 3**
See also DLB 37

Tynan, Katharine 1861-1931 **TCLC 3**
See also CA 104; 167; DLB 153

Tyutchev, Fyodor 1803-1873 **NCLC 34**

Tzara, Tristan 1896-1963 **CLC 47; DAM POET**
See also CA 153; 89-92

Uhry, Alfred 1936- **CLC 55; DAM DRAM, POP**
See also CA 127; 133; INT 133

Ulf, Haerved
See Strindberg, (Johan) August

Ulf, Harved
See Strindberg, (Johan) August

Ulibarri, Sabine R(eyes) 1919-**CLC 83; DAM MULT**
See also CA 131; DLB 82; HW

Unamuno (y Jugo), Miguel de 1864-1936
TCLC 2, 9; DAM MULT, NOV; HLC; SSC 11
See also CA 104; 131; DLB 108; HW; MTCW 1

Undercliffe, Errol
See Campbell, (John) Ramsey

Underwood, Miles
See Glassco, John

Undset, Sigrid 1882-1949TCLC 3; DA; DAB; DAC; DAM MST, NOV; WLC
See also CA 104; 129; MTCW 1

Ungaretti, Giuseppe 1888-1970CLC 7, 11, 15
See also CA 19-20; 25-28R; CAP 2; DLB 114

Unger, Douglas 1952- **CLC 34**
See also CA 130

Unsworth, Barry (Forster) 1930- **CLC 76**
See also CA 25-28R; CANR 30, 54; DLB 194

Updike, John (Hoyer) 1932-**CLC 1, 2, 3, 5, 7, 9, 13, 15, 23, 34, 43, 70; DA; DAB; DAC; DAM MST, NOV, POET, POP; SSC 13, 27; WLC**
See also CA 1-4R; CABS 1; CANR 4, 33, 51; CDALB 1968-1988; DLB 2, 5, 143; DLBD 3; DLBY 80, 82, 97; MTCW 1

Upshaw, Margaret Mitchell
See Mitchell, Margaret (Munnerlyn)

Upton, Mark
See Sanders, Lawrence

Upward, Allen 1863-1926 **TCLC 85**
See also CA 117; DLB 36

Urdang, Constance (Henriette) 1922-**CLC 47**
See also CA 21-24R; CANR 9, 24

Uriel, Henry
See Faust, Frederick (Schiller)

Uris, Leon (Marcus) 1924- **CLC 7, 32; DAM NOV, POP**
See also AITN 1, 2; BEST 89:2; CA 1-4R; CANR 1, 40, 65; MTCW 1; SATA 49

Urmuz
See Codrescu, Andrei

Urquhart, Jane 1949- **CLC 90; DAC**
See also CA 113; CANR 32, 68

Ustinov, Peter (Alexander) 1921- **CLC 1**
See also AITN 1; CA 13-16R; CANR 25, 51; DLB 13

U Tam'si, Gerald Felix Tchicaya
See Tchicaya, Gerald Felix

U Tam'si, Tchicaya
See Tchicaya, Gerald Felix

Vachss, Andrew (Henry) 1942- **CLC 106**

See also CA 118; CANR 44

Vachss, Andrew H.
See Vachss, Andrew (Henry)

Vaculik, Ludvik 1926-   **CLC 7**
See also CA 53-56; CANR 72

Vaihinger, Hans 1852-1933   **TCLC 71**
See also CA 116; 166

Valdez, Luis (Miguel) 1940-   **CLC 84; DAM MULT; HLC**
See also CA 101; CANR 32; DLB 122; HW

Valenzuela, Luisa 1938- **CLC 31, 104; DAM MULT; SSC 14**
See also CA 101; CANR 32, 65; DLB 113; HW

Valera y Alcala-Galiano, Juan 1824-1905 **TCLC 10**
See also CA 106

Valery, (Ambroise) Paul (Toussaint Jules) 1871-1945   **TCLC 4, 15; DAM POET; PC 9**
See also CA 104; 122; MTCW 1

Valle-Inclan, Ramon (Maria) del 1866-1936 **TCLC 5; DAM MULT; HLC**
See also CA 106; 153; DLB 134

Vallejo, Antonio Buero
See Buero Vallejo, Antonio

Vallejo, Cesar (Abraham) 1892-1938**TCLC 3, 56; DAM MULT; HLC**
See also CA 105; 153; HW

Vallette, Marguerite Eymery
See Rachilde

Valle Y Pena, Ramon del
See Valle-Inclan, Ramon (Maria) del

Van Ash, Cay 1918-   **CLC 34**

Vanbrugh, Sir John 1664-1726 **LC 21; DAM DRAM**
See also DLB 80

Van Campen, Karl
See Campbell, John W(ood, Jr.)

Vance, Gerald
See Silverberg, Robert

Vance, Jack   **CLC 35**
See also Kuttner, Henry; Vance, John Holbrook
See also DLB 8

Vance, John Holbrook 1916-
See Queen, Ellery; Vance, Jack
See also CA 29-32R; CANR 17, 65; MTCW 1

Van Den Bogarde, Derek Jules Gaspard Ulric Niven 1921-
See Bogarde, Dirk
See also CA 77-80

Vandenburgh, Jane   **CLC 59**
See also CA 168

Vanderhaeghe, Guy 1951-   **CLC 41**
See also CA 113; CANR 72

van der Post, Laurens (Jan) 1906-1996**CLC 5**
See also CA 5-8R; 155; CANR 35

van de Wetering, Janwillem 1931-   **CLC 47**
See also CA 49-52; CANR 4, 62

Van Dine, S. S.   **TCLC 23**
See also Wright, Willard Huntington

Van Doren, Carl (Clinton) 1885-1950 **TCLC 18**
See also CA 111; 168

Van Doren, Mark 1894-1972   **CLC 6, 10**
See also CA 1-4R; 37-40R; CANR 3; DLB 45; MTCW 1

Van Druten, John (William) 1901-1957**TCLC 2**
See also CA 104; 161; DLB 10

Van Duyn, Mona (Jane) 1921- **CLC 3, 7, 63, 116; DAM POET**
See also CA 9-12R; CANR 7, 38, 60; DLB 5

Van Dyne, Edith
See Baum, L(yman) Frank

van Itallie, Jean-Claude 1936-   **CLC 3**
See also CA 45-48; CAAS 2; CANR 1, 48; DLB 7

van Ostaijen, Paul 1896-1928   **TCLC 33**
See also CA 163

Van Peebles, Melvin 1932- **CLC 2, 20; DAM MULT**
See also BW 2; CA 85-88; CANR 27, 67

Vansittart, Peter 1920-   **CLC 42**
See also CA 1-4R; CANR 3, 49

Van Vechten, Carl 1880-1964   **CLC 33**
See also CA 89-92; DLB 4, 9, 51

Van Vogt, A(lfred) E(lton) 1912-   **CLC 1**
See also CA 21-24R; CANR 28; DLB 8; SATA 14

Varda, Agnes 1928-   **CLC 16**
See also CA 116; 122

Vargas Llosa, (Jorge) Mario (Pedro) 1936- **CLC 3, 6, 9, 10, 15, 31, 42, 85; DA; DAB; DAC; DAM MST, MULT, NOV; HLC**
See also CA 73-76; CANR 18, 32, 42, 67; DLB 145; HW; MTCW 1

Vasiliu, Gheorghe 1881-1957
See Bacovia, George
See also CA 123

Vassa, Gustavus
See Equiano, Olaudah

Vassilikos, Vassilis 1933-   **CLC 4, 8**
See also CA 81-84

Vaughan, Henry 1621-1695   **LC 27**
See also DLB 131

Vaughn, Stephanie   **CLC 62**

Vazov, Ivan (Minchov) 1850-1921 **TCLC 25**
See also CA 121; 167; DLB 147

Veblen, Thorstein B(unde) 1857-1929 **TCLC 31**
See also CA 115; 165

Vega, Lope de 1562-1635   **LC 23**

Venison, Alfred
See Pound, Ezra (Weston Loomis)

Verdi, Marie de
See Mencken, H(enry) L(ouis)

Verdu, Matilde
See Cela, Camilo Jose

Verga, Giovanni (Carmelo) 1840-1922 **TCLC 3; SSC 21**
See also CA 104; 123

Vergil 70B.C.-19B.C.   **CMLC 9; DA; DAB; DAC; DAM MST, POET; PC 12; WLCS**

Verhaeren, Emile (Adolphe Gustave) 1855-1916 **TCLC 12**
See also CA 109

Verlaine, Paul (Marie) 1844-1896**NCLC 2, 51; DAM POET; PC 2**

Verne, Jules (Gabriel) 1828-1905**TCLC 6, 52**
See also AAYA 16; CA 110; 131; DLB 123; JRDA; MAICYA; SATA 21

Very, Jones 1813-1880   **NCLC 9**
See also DLB 1

Vesaas, Tarjei 1897-1970   **CLC 48**
See also CA 29-32R

Vialis, Gaston
See Simenon, Georges (Jacques Christian)

Vian, Boris 1920-1959   **TCLC 9**
See also CA 106; 164; DLB 72

Viaud, (Louis Marie) Julien 1850-1923
See Loti, Pierre
See also CA 107

Vicar, Henry
See Felsen, Henry Gregor

Vicker, Angus
See Felsen, Henry Gregor

Vidal, Gore 1925-**CLC 2, 4, 6, 8, 10, 22, 33, 72;**

DAM NOV, POP
See also AITN 1; BEST 90:2; CA 5-8R; CANR 13, 45, 65; DLB 6, 152; INT CANR-13; MTCW 1

Viereck, Peter (Robert Edwin) 1916- **CLC 4**
See also CA 1-4R; CANR 1, 47; DLB 5

Vigny, Alfred (Victor) de 1797-1863**NCLC 7; DAM POET**
See also DLB 119, 192

Vilakazi, Benedict Wallet 1906-1947**TCLC 37**
See also CA 168

Villa, Jose Garcia 1904-1997   **PC 22**
See also CA 25-28R; CANR 12

Villaurrutia, Xavier 1903-1950   **TCLC 80**
See also HW

Villiers de l'Isle Adam, Jean Marie Mathias Philippe Auguste, Comte de 1838-1889 **NCLC 3; SSC 14**
See also DLB 123

Villon, Francois 1431-1463(?)   **PC 13**

Vinci, Leonardo da 1452-1519   **LC 12**

Vine, Barbara   **CLC 50**
See also Rendell, Ruth (Barbara)
See also BEST 90:4

Vinge, Joan (Carol) D(ennison) 1948-**CLC 30; SSC 24**
See also CA 93-96; CANR 72; SATA 36

Violis, G.
See Simenon, Georges (Jacques Christian)

Virgil
See Vergil

Visconti, Luchino 1906-1976   **CLC 16**
See also CA 81-84; 65-68; CANR 39

Vittorini, Elio 1908-1966   **CLC 6, 9, 14**
See also CA 133; 25-28R

Vivekenanda, Swami 1863-1902   **TCLC 88**

Vizenor, Gerald Robert 1934-**CLC 103; DAM MULT**
See also CA 13-16R; CAAS 22; CANR 5, 21, 44, 67; DLB 175; NNAL

Vizinczey, Stephen 1933-   **CLC 40**
See also CA 128; INT 128

Vliet, R(ussell) G(ordon) 1929-1984 **CLC 22**
See also CA 37-40R; 112; CANR 18

Vogau, Boris Andreyevich 1894-1937(?)
See Pilnyak, Boris
See also CA 123

Vogel, Paula A(nne) 1951-   **CLC 76**
See also CA 108

Voigt, Cynthia 1942-   **CLC 30**
See also AAYA 3; CA 106; CANR 18, 37, 40; CLR 13, 48; INT CANR-18; JRDA; MAICYA; SATA 48, 79; SATA-Brief 33

Voigt, Ellen Bryant 1943-   **CLC 54**
See also CA 69-72; CANR 11, 29, 55; DLB 120

Voinovich, Vladimir (Nikolaevich) 1932-**CLC 10, 49**
See also CA 81-84; CAAS 12; CANR 33, 67; MTCW 1

Vollmann, William T. 1959- **CLC 89; DAM NOV, POP**
See also CA 134; CANR 67

Voloshinov, V. N.
See Bakhtin, Mikhail Mikhailovich

Voltaire 1694-1778 **LC 14; DA; DAB; DAC; DAM DRAM, MST; SSC 12; WLC**

von Daeniken, Erich 1935-   **CLC 30**
See also AITN 1; CA 37-40R; CANR 17, 44

von Daniken, Erich
See von Daeniken, Erich

von Heidenstam, (Carl Gustaf) Verner
See Heidenstam, (Carl Gustaf) Verner von

von Heyse, Paul (Johann Ludwig)

See also CA 9-10; 25-28R; CAP 1; DLB 20
Watson, Irving S.
See Mencken, H(enry) L(ouis)
Watson, John H.
See Farmer, Philip Jose
Watson, Richard F.
See Silverberg, Robert
Waugh, Auberon (Alexander) 1939-   **CLC 7**
See also CA 45-48; CANR 6, 22; DLB 14, 194
Waugh, Evelyn (Arthur St. John) 1903-1966
    CLC 1, 3, 8, 13, 19, 27, 44, 107; DA; DAB;
    DAC; DAM MST, NOV, POP; WLC
See also CA 85-88; 25-28R; CANR 22; CDBLB
    1914-1945; DLB 15, 162, 195; MTCW 1
Waugh, Harriet 1944-   **CLC 6**
See also CA 85-88; CANR 22
Ways, C. R.
See Blount, Roy (Alton), Jr.
Waystaff, Simon
See Swift, Jonathan
Webb, (Martha) Beatrice (Potter) 1858-1943
    TCLC 22
See also Potter, (Helen) Beatrix
See also CA 117; DLB 190
Webb, Charles (Richard) 1939-   **CLC 7**
See also CA 25-28R
Webb, James H(enry), Jr. 1946-   **CLC 22**
See also CA 81-84
Webb, Mary (Gladys Meredith) 1881-1927
    TCLC 24
See also CA 123; DLB 34
Webb, Mrs. Sidney
See Webb, (Martha) Beatrice (Potter)
Webb, Phyllis 1927-   **CLC 18**
See also CA 104; CANR 23; DLB 53
Webb, Sidney (James) 1859-1947   **TCLC 22**
See also CA 117; 163; DLB 190
Webber, Andrew Lloyd   **CLC 21**
See also Lloyd Webber, Andrew
Weber, Lenora Mattingly 1895-1971 **CLC 12**
See also CA 19-20; 29-32R; CAP 1; SATA 2;
    SATA-Obit 26
Weber, Max 1864-1920   **TCLC 69**
See also CA 109
Webster, John 1579(?)-1634(?)   **LC 33; DA;**
    DAB; DAC; DAM DRAM, MST; DC 2;
    WLC
See also CDBLB Before 1660; DLB 58
Webster, Noah 1758-1843   **NCLC 30**
Wedekind, (Benjamin) Frank(lin) 1864-1918
    TCLC 7; DAM DRAM
See also CA 104; 153; DLB 118
Weidman, Jerome 1913-   **CLC 7**
See also AITN 2; CA 1-4R; CANR 1; DLB 28
Weil, Simone (Adolphine) 1909-1943**TCLC 23**
See also CA 117; 159
Weininger, Otto 1880-1903   **TCLC 84**
Weinstein, Nathan
See West, Nathanael
Weinstein, Nathan von Wallenstein
See West, Nathanael
Weir, Peter (Lindsay) 1944-   **CLC 20**
See also CA 113; 123
Weiss, Peter (Ulrich) 1916-1982**CLC 3, 15, 51;**
    DAM DRAM
See also CA 45-48; 106; CANR 3; DLB 69, 124
Weiss, Theodore (Russell) 1916-**CLC 3, 8, 14**
See also CA 9-12R; CAAS 2; CANR 46; DLB
    5
Welch, (Maurice) Denton 1915-1948**TCLC 22**
See also CA 121; 148
Welch, James 1940-   **CLC 6, 14, 52; DAM**
    MULT, POP

See also CA 85-88; CANR 42, 66; DLB 175;
    NNAL
Weldon, Fay 1931-   **CLC 6, 9, 11, 19, 36, 59;**
    DAM POP
See also CA 21-24R; CANR 16, 46, 63; CDBLB
    1960 to Present; DLB 14, 194; INT CANR-
    16; MTCW 1
Wellek, Rene 1903-1995   **CLC 28**
See also CA 5-8R; 150; CAAS 7; CANR 8; DLB
    63; INT CANR-8
Weller, Michael 1942-   **CLC 10, 53**
See also CA 85-88
Weller, Paul 1958-   **CLC 26**
Wellershoff, Dieter 1925-   **CLC 46**
See also CA 89-92; CANR 16, 37
Welles, (George) Orson 1915-1985**CLC 20, 80**
See also CA 93-96; 117
Wellman, John McDowell 1945-
See Wellman, Mac
See also CA 166
Wellman, Mac 1945-   **CLC 65**
See also Wellman, John McDowell; Wellman,
    John McDowell
Wellman, Manly Wade 1903-1986   **CLC 49**
See also CA 1-4R; 118; CANR 6, 16, 44; SATA
    6; SATA-Obit 47
Wells, Carolyn 1869(?)-1942   **TCLC 35**
See also CA 113; DLB 11
Wells, H(erbert) G(eorge) 1866-1946**TCLC 6,**
    12, 19; DA; DAB; DAC; DAM MST, NOV;
    SSC 6; WLC
See also AAYA 18; CA 110; 121; CDBLB 1914-
    1945; DLB 34, 70, 156, 178; MTCW 1;
    SATA 20
Wells, Rosemary 1943-   **CLC 12**
See also AAYA 13; CA 85-88; CANR 48; CLR
    16; MAICYA; SAAS 1; SATA 18, 69
Welty, Eudora 1909-   **CLC 1, 2, 5, 14, 22, 33,**
    105; DA; DAB; DAC; DAM MST, NOV;
    SSC 1, 27; WLC
See also CA 9-12R; CABS 1; CANR 32, 65;
    CDALB 1941-1968; DLB 2, 102, 143;
    DLBD 12; DLBY 87; MTCW 1
Wen I-to 1899-1946   **TCLC 28**
Wentworth, Robert
See Hamilton, Edmond
Werfel, Franz (Viktor) 1890-1945   **TCLC 8**
See also CA 104; 161; DLB 81, 124
Wergeland, Henrik Arnold 1808-1845 **NCLC**
    5
Wersba, Barbara 1932-   **CLC 30**
See also AAYA 2; CA 29-32R; CANR 16, 38;
    CLR 3; DLB 52; JRDA; MAICYA; SAAS 2;
    SATA 1, 58
Wertmueller, Lina 1928-   **CLC 16**
See also CA 97-100; CANR 39
Wescott, Glenway 1901-1987   **CLC 13**
See also CA 13-16R; 121; CANR 23, 70; DLB
    4, 9, 102
Wesker, Arnold 1932-   **CLC 3, 5, 42; DAB;**
    DAM DRAM
See also CA 1-4R; CAAS 7; CANR 1, 33;
    CDBLB 1960 to Present; DLB 13; MTCW 1
Wesley, Richard (Errol) 1945-   **CLC 7**
See also BW 1; CA 57-60; CANR 27; DLB 38
Wessel, Johan Herman 1742-1785   **LC 7**
West, Anthony (Panther) 1914-1987 **CLC 50**
See also CA 45-48; 124; CANR 3, 19; DLB 15
West, C. P.
See Wodehouse, P(elham) G(renville)
West, (Mary) Jessamyn 1902-1984**CLC 7, 17**
See also CA 9-12R; 112; CANR 27; DLB 6;
    DLBY 84; MTCW 1; SATA-Obit 37

West, Morris L(anglo) 1916-   **CLC 6, 33**
See also CA 5-8R; CANR 24, 49, 64; MTCW 1
West, Nathanael 1903-1940   **TCLC 1, 14, 44;**
    SSC 16
See also CA 104; 125; CDALB 1929-1941;
    DLB 4, 9, 28; MTCW 1
West, Owen
See Koontz, Dean R(ay)
West, Paul 1930-   **CLC 7, 14, 96**
See also CA 13-16R; CAAS 7; CANR 22, 53;
    DLB 14; INT CANR-22
West, Rebecca 1892-1983   **CLC 7, 9, 31, 50**
See also CA 5-8R; 109; CANR 19; DLB 36;
    DLBY 83; MTCW 1
Westall, Robert (Atkinson) 1929-1993**CLC 17**
See also AAYA 12; CA 69-72; 141; CANR 18,
    68; CLR 13; JRDA; MAICYA; SAAS 2;
    SATA 23, 69; SATA-Obit 75
Westermarck, Edward 1862-1939   **TCLC 87**
Westlake, Donald E(dwin) 1933-   **CLC 7, 33;**
    DAM POP
See also CA 17-20R; CAAS 13; CANR 16, 44,
    65; INT CANR-16
Westmacott, Mary
See Christie, Agatha (Mary Clarissa)
Weston, Allen
See Norton, Andre
Wetcheek, J. L.
See Feuchtwanger, Lion
Wetering, Janwillem van de
See van de Wetering, Janwillem
Wetherald, Agnes Ethelwyn 1857-1940**TCLC**
    81
See also DLB 99
Wetherell, Elizabeth
See Warner, Susan (Bogert)
Whale, James 1889-1957   **TCLC 63**
Whalen, Philip 1923-   **CLC 6, 29**
See also CA 9-12R; CANR 5, 39; DLB 16
Wharton, Edith (Newbold Jones) 1862-1937
    TCLC 3, 9, 27, 53; DA; DAB; DAC; DAM
    MST, NOV; SSC 6; WLC
See also AAYA 25; CA 104; 132; CDALB 1865-
    1917; DLB 4, 9, 12, 78, 189; DLBD 13;
    MTCW 1
Wharton, James
See Mencken, H(enry) L(ouis)
Wharton, William (a pseudonym) **CLC 18, 37**
See also CA 93-96; DLBY 80; INT 93-96
Wheatley (Peters), Phillis 1754(?)-1784**LC 3;**
    BLC 3; DA; DAC; DAM MST, MULT,
    POET; PC 3; WLC
See also CDALB 1640-1865; DLB 31, 50
Wheelock, John Hall 1886-1978   **CLC 14**
See also CA 13-16R; 77-80; CANR 14; DLB
    45
White, E(lwyn) B(rooks) 1899-1985 **CLC 10,**
    34, 39; DAM POP
See also AITN 2; CA 13-16R; 116; CANR 16,
    37; CLR 1, 21; DLB 11, 22; MAICYA;
    MTCW 1; SATA 2, 29, 100; SATA-Obit 44
White, Edmund (Valentine III) 1940-**CLC 27,**
    110; DAM POP
See also AAYA 7; CA 45-48; CANR 3, 19, 36,
    62; MTCW 1
White, Patrick (Victor Martindale) 1912-1990
    CLC 3, 4, 5, 7, 9, 18, 65, 69
See also CA 81-84; 132; CANR 43; MTCW 1
White, Phyllis Dorothy James 1920-
See James, P. D.
See also CA 21-24R; CANR 17, 43, 65; DAM
    POP; MTCW 1
White, T(erence) H(anbury) 1906-1964   **CLC**

30
See also AAYA 22; CA 73-76; CANR 37; DLB
160; JRDA; MAICYA; SATA 12

White, Terence de Vere 1912-1994   **CLC 49**
See also CA 49-52; 145; CANR 3

White, Walter F(rancis) 1893-1955 **TCLC 15**
See also White, Walter
See also BW 1; CA 115; 124; DLB 51

White, William Hale 1831-1913
See Rutherford, Mark
See also CA 121

Whitehead, E(dward) A(nthony) 1933-**CLC 5**
See also CA 65-68; CANR 58

Whitemore, Hugh (John) 1936-   **CLC 37**
See also CA 132; INT 132

Whitman, Sarah Helen (Power) 1803-1878
    NCLC 19
See also DLB 1

Whitman, Walt(er) 1819-1892   **NCLC 4, 31;**
DA; DAB; DAC; DAM MST, POET; PC
3; WLC
See also CDALB 1640-1865; DLB 3, 64; SATA
20

Whitney, Phyllis A(yame) 1903-   **CLC 42;**
DAM POP
See also AITN 2; BEST 90:3; CA 1-4R; CANR
3, 25, 38, 60; JRDA; MAICYA; SATA 1, 30

Whittemore, (Edward) Reed (Jr.) 1919-**CLC 4**
See also CA 9-12R; CAAS 8; CANR 4; DLB 5

Whittier, John Greenleaf 1807-1892**NCLC 8,**
59
See also DLB 1

Whittlebot, Hernia
See Coward, Noel (Peirce)

Wicker, Thomas Grey 1926-
See Wicker, Tom
See also CA 65-68; CANR 21, 46

Wicker, Tom   **CLC 7**
See also Wicker, Thomas Grey

Wideman, John Edgar 1941- **CLC 5, 34, 36,**
67; BLC 3; DAM MULT
See also BW 2; CA 85-88; CANR 14, 42, 67;
DLB 33, 143

Wiebe, Rudy (Henry) 1934-   **CLC 6, 11, 14;**
DAC; DAM MST
See also CA 37-40R; CANR 42, 67; DLB 60

Wieland, Christoph Martin 1733-1813**N C L C**
17
See also DLB 97

Wiene, Robert 1881-1938   **TCLC 56**

Wieners, John 1934-   **CLC 7**
See also CA 13-16R; DLB 16

Wiesel, Elie(zer) 1928- **CLC 3, 5, 11, 37; DA;**
DAB; DAC; DAM MST, NOV; WLCS 2
See also AAYA 7; AITN 1; CA 5-8R; CAAS 4;
CANR 8, 40, 65; DLB 83; DLBY 87; INT
CANR-8; MTCW 1; SATA 56

Wiggins, Marianne 1947-   **CLC 57**
See also BEST 89:3; CA 130; CANR 60

Wight, James Alfred 1916-1995
See Herriot, James
See also CA 77-80; SATA 55; SATA-Brief 44

Wilbur, Richard (Purdy) 1921-**CLC 3, 6, 9, 14,**
53, 110; DA; DAB; DAC; DAM MST,
POET
See also CA 1-4R; CABS 2; CANR 2, 29; DLB
5, 169; INT CANR-29; MTCW 1; SATA 9

Wild, Peter 1940-   **CLC 14**
See also CA 37-40R; DLB 5

Wilde, Oscar (Fingal O'Flahertie Wills)
1854(?)-1900**TCLC 1, 8, 23, 41; DA; DAB;**
DAC; DAM DRAM, MST, NOV; SSC 11;
WLC

See also CA 104; 119; CDBLB 1890-1914;
DLB 10, 19, 34, 57, 141, 156, 190; SATA 24

Wilder, Billy   **CLC 20**
See also Wilder, Samuel
See also DLB 26

Wilder, Samuel 1906-
See Wilder, Billy
See also CA 89-92

Wilder, Thornton (Niven) 1897-1975**CLC 1, 5,**
6, 10, 15, 35, 82; DA; DAB; DAC; DAM
DRAM, MST, NOV; DC 1; WLC
See also AITN 2; CA 13-16R; 61-64; CANR
40; DLB 4, 7, 9; DLBY 97; MTCW 1

Wilding, Michael 1942-   **CLC 73**
See also CA 104; CANR 24, 49

Wiley, Richard 1944-   **CLC 44**
See also CA 121; 129; CANR 71

Wilhelm, Kate   **CLC 7**
See also Wilhelm, Katie Gertrude
See also AAYA 20; CAAS 5; DLB 8; INT
CANR-17

Wilhelm, Katie Gertrude 1928-
See Wilhelm, Kate
See also CA 37-40R; CANR 17, 36, 60; MTCW
1

Wilkins, Mary
See Freeman, Mary Eleanor Wilkins

Willard, Nancy 1936-   **CLC 7, 37**
See also CA 89-92; CANR 10, 39, 68; CLR 5;
DLB 5, 52; MAICYA; MTCW 1; SATA 37,
71; SATA-Brief 30

Williams, C(harles) K(enneth) 1936-**CLC 33,**
56; DAM POET
See also CA 37-40R; CAAS 26; CANR 57; DLB
5

Williams, Charles
See Collier, James L(incoln)

Williams, Charles (Walter Stansby) 1886-1945
TCLC 1, 11
See also CA 104; 163; DLB 100, 153

Williams, (George) Emlyn 1905-1987**CLC 15;**
DAM DRAM
See also CA 104; 123; CANR 36; DLB 10, 77;
MTCW 1

Williams, Hank 1923-1953   **TCLC 81**

Williams, Hugo 1942-   **CLC 42**
See also CA 17-20R; CANR 45; DLB 40

Williams, J. Walker
See Wodehouse, P(elham) G(renville)

Williams, John A(lfred) 1925-**CLC 5, 13; BLC**
3; DAM MULT
See also BW 2; CA 53-56; CAAS 3; CANR 6,
26, 51; DLB 2, 33; INT CANR-6

Williams, Jonathan (Chamberlain) 1929-
CLC 13
See also CA 9-12R; CAAS 12; CANR 8; DLB
5

Williams, Joy 1944-   **CLC 31**
See also CA 41-44R; CANR 22, 48

Williams, Norman 1952-   **CLC 39**
See also CA 118

Williams, Sherley Anne 1944-**CLC 89; BLC 3;**
DAM MULT, POET
See also BW 2; CA 73-76; CANR 25; DLB 41;
INT CANR-25; SATA 78

Williams, Shirley
See Williams, Sherley Anne

Williams, Tennessee 1911-1983**CLC 1, 2, 5, 7,**
8, 11, 15, 19, 30, 39, 45, 71, 111; DA; DAB;
DAC; DAM DRAM, MST; DC 4; WLC
See also AITN 1, 2; CA 5-8R; 108; CABS 3;
CANR 31; CDALB 1941-1968; DLB 7;
DLBD 4; DLBY 83; MTCW 1

Williams, Thomas (Alonzo) 1926-1990**CLC 14**
See also CA 1-4R; 132; CANR 2

Williams, William C.
See Williams, William Carlos

Williams, William Carlos 1883-1963**CLC 1, 2,**
5, 9, 13, 22, 42, 67; DA; DAB; DAC; DAM
MST, POET; PC 7; SSC 31
See also CA 89-92; CANR 34; CDALB 1917-
1929; DLB 4, 16, 54, 86; MTCW 1

Williamson, David (Keith) 1942-   **CLC 56**
See also CA 103; CANR 41

Williamson, Ellen Douglas 1905-1984
See Douglas, Ellen
See also CA 17-20R; 114; CANR 39

Williamson, Jack   **CLC 29**
See also Williamson, John Stewart
See also CAAS 8; DLB 8

Williamson, John Stewart 1908-
See Williamson, Jack
See also CA 17-20R; CANR 23, 70

Willie, Frederick
See Lovecraft, H(oward) P(hillips)

Willingham, Calder (Baynard, Jr.) 1922-1995
CLC 5, 51
See also CA 5-8R; 147; CANR 3; DLB 2, 44;
MTCW 1

Willis, Charles
See Clarke, Arthur C(harles)

Willy
See Colette, (Sidonie-Gabrielle)

Willy, Colette
See Colette, (Sidonie-Gabrielle)

Wilson, A(ndrew) N(orman) 1950-   **CLC 33**
See also CA 112; 122; DLB 14, 155, 194

Wilson, Angus (Frank Johnstone) 1913-1991
CLC 2, 3, 5, 25, 34; SSC 21
See also CA 5-8R; 134; CANR 21; DLB 15,
139, 155; MTCW 1

Wilson, August 1945-**CLC 39, 50, 63; BLC 3;**
DA; DAB; DAC; DAM DRAM, MST,
MULT; DC 2; WLCS
See also AAYA 16; BW 2; CA 115; 122; CANR
42, 54; MTCW 1

Wilson, Brian 1942-   **CLC 12**

Wilson, Colin 1931-   **CLC 3, 14**
See also CA 1-4R; CAAS 5; CANR 1, 22, 33;
DLB 14, 194; MTCW 1

Wilson, Dirk
See Pohl, Frederik

Wilson, Edmund 1895-1972**CLC 1, 2, 3, 8, 24**
See also CA 1-4R; 37-40R; CANR 1, 46; DLB
63; MTCW 1

Wilson, Ethel Davis (Bryant) 1888(?)-1980
CLC 13; DAC; DAM POET
See also CA 102; DLB 68; MTCW 1

Wilson, John 1785-1854   **NCLC 5**

Wilson, John (Anthony) Burgess 1917-1993
See Burgess, Anthony
See also CA 1-4R; 143; CANR 2, 46; DAC;
DAM NOV; MTCW 1

Wilson, Lanford 1937- **CLC 7, 14, 36; DAM**
DRAM
See also CA 17-20R; CABS 3; CANR 45; DLB
7

Wilson, Robert M. 1944-   **CLC 7, 9**
See also CA 49-52; CANR 2, 41; MTCW 1

Wilson, Robert McLiam 1964-   **CLC 59**
See also CA 132

Wilson, Sloan 1920-   **CLC 32**
See also CA 1-4R; CANR 1, 44

Wilson, Snoo 1948-   **CLC 33**
See also CA 69-72

Wilson, William S(mith) 1932-   **CLC 49**

See also CA 81-84

Wilson, (Thomas) Woodrow 1856-1924**TCLC 79**
See also CA 166; DLB 47

Winchilsea, Anne (Kingsmill) Finch Counte 1661-1720
See Finch, Anne

Windham, Basil
See Wodehouse, P(elham) G(renville)

Wingrove, David (John) 1954- **CLC 68**
See also CA 133

Wintergreen, Jane
See Duncan, Sara Jeannette

Winters, Janet Lewis **CLC 41**
See also Lewis, Janet
See also DLBY 87

Winters, (Arthur) Yvor 1900-1968 **CLC 4, 8, 32**
See also CA 11-12; 25-28R; CAP 1; DLB 48; MTCW 1

Winterson, Jeanette 1959-**CLC 64; DAM POP**
See also CA 136; CANR 58

Winthrop, John 1588-1649 **LC 31**
See also DLB 24, 30

Wiseman, Frederick 1930- **CLC 20**
See also CA 159

Wister, Owen 1860-1938 **TCLC 21**
See also CA 108; 162; DLB 9, 78, 186; SATA 62

Witkacy
See Witkiewicz, Stanislaw Ignacy

Witkiewicz, Stanislaw Ignacy 1885-1939 **TCLC 8**
See also CA 105; 162

Wittgenstein, Ludwig (Josef Johann) 1889-1951 **TCLC 59**
See also CA 113; 164

Wittig, Monique 1935(?)- **CLC 22**
See also CA 116; 135; DLB 83

Wittlin, Jozef 1896-1976 **CLC 25**
See also CA 49-52; 65-68; CANR 3

Wodehouse, P(elham) G(renville) 1881-1975 **CLC 1, 2, 5, 10, 22; DAB; DAC; DAM NOV; SSC 2**
See also AITN 2; CA 45-48; 57-60; CANR 3, 33; CDBLB 1914-1945; DLB 34, 162; MTCW 1, SATA 22

Woiwode, L.
See Woiwode, Larry (Alfred)

Woiwode, Larry (Alfred) 1941- **CLC 6, 10**
See also CA 73-76; CANR 16; DLB 6; INT CANR-16

Wojciechowska, Maia (Teresa) 1927-**CLC 26**
See also AAYA 8; CA 9-12R; CANR 4, 41; CLR 1; JRDA; MAICYA; SAAS 1; SATA 1, 28, 83

Wolf, Christa 1929- **CLC 14, 29, 58**
See also CA 85-88; CANR 45; DLB 75; MTCW 1

Wolfe, Gene (Rodman) 1931- **CLC 25; DAM POP**
See also CA 57-60; CAAS 9; CANR 6, 32, 60; DLB 8

Wolfe, George C. 1954- **CLC 49; BLCS**
See also CA 149

Wolfe, Thomas (Clayton) 1900-1938**TCLC 4, 13, 29, 61; DA; DAB; DAC; DAM MST, NOV; WLC**
See also CA 104; 132; CDALB 1929-1941; DLB 9, 102; DLBD 2, 16; DLBY 85, 97; MTCW 1

Wolfe, Thomas Kennerly, Jr. 1930-
See Wolfe, Tom

See also CA 13-16R; CANR 9, 33, 70; DAM POP; DLB 185; INT CANR-9; MTCW 1

Wolfe, Tom **CLC 1, 2, 9, 15, 35, 51**
See also Wolfe, Thomas Kennerly, Jr.
See also AAYA 8; AITN 2; BEST 89:1; DLB 152

Wolff, Geoffrey (Ansell) 1937- **CLC 41**
See also CA 29-32R; CANR 29, 43

Wolff, Sonia
See Levitin, Sonia (Wolff)

Wolff, Tobias (Jonathan Ansell) 1945- **CLC 39, 64**
See also AAYA 16; BEST 90:2; CA 114; 117; CAAS 22; CANR 54; DLB 130; INT 117

Wolfram von Eschenbach c. 1170-c. 1220 **CMLC 5**
See also DLB 138

Wolitzer, Hilma 1930- **CLC 17**
See also CA 65-68; CANR 18, 40; INT CANR-18; SATA 31

Wollstonecraft, Mary 1759-1797 **LC 5**
See also CDBLB 1789-1832; DLB 39, 104, 158

Wonder, Stevie **CLC 12**
See also Morris, Steveland Judkins

Wong, Jade Snow 1922- **CLC 17**
See also CA 109

Woodberry, George Edward 1855-1930 **TCLC 73**
See also CA 165; DLB 71, 103

Woodcott, Keith
See Brunner, John (Kilian Houston)

Woodruff, Robert W.
See Mencken, H(enry) L(ouis)

Woolf, (Adeline) Virginia 1882-1941**TCLC 1, 5, 20, 43, 56; DA; DAB; DAC; DAM MST, NOV; SSC 7; WLC**
See also CA 104; 130; CANR 64; CDBLB 1914-1945; DLB 36, 100, 162; DLBD 10; MTCW 1

Woolf, Virginia Adeline
See Woolf, (Adeline) Virginia

Woollcott, Alexander (Humphreys) 1887-1943 **TCLC 5**
See also CA 105; 161; DLB 29

Woolrich, Cornell 1903-1968 **CLC 77**
See also Hopley-Woolrich, Cornell George

Wordsworth, Dorothy 1771-1855 **NCLC 25**
See also DLB 107

Wordsworth, William 1770-1850 **NCLC 12, 38; DA; DAB; DAC; DAM MST, POET; PC 4; WLC**
See also CDBLB 1789-1832; DLB 93, 107

Wouk, Herman 1915-**CLC 1, 9, 38; DAM NOV, POP**
See also CA 5-8R; CANR 6, 33, 67; DLBY 82; INT CANR-6; MTCW 1

Wright, Charles (Penzel, Jr.) 1935-**CLC 6, 13, 28**
See also CA 29-32R; CAAS 7; CANR 23, 36, 62; DLB 165; DLBY 82; MTCW 1

Wright, Charles Stevenson 1932- **CLC 49; BLC 3; DAM MULT, POET**
See also BW 1; CA 9-12R; CANR 26; DLB 33

Wright, Frances 1795-1852 **NCLC 74**
See also DLB 73

Wright, Jack R.
See Harris, Mark

Wright, James (Arlington) 1927-1980**CLC 3, 5, 10, 28; DAM POET**
See also AITN 2; CA 49-52; 97-100; CANR 4, 34, 64; DLB 5, 169; MTCW 1

Wright, Judith (Arandell) 1915- **CLC 11, 53; PC 14**

See also CA 13-16R; CANR 31; MTCW 1; SATA 14

Wright, L(aurali) R. 1939- **CLC 44**
See also CA 138

Wright, Richard (Nathaniel) 1908-1960 **C L C 1, 3, 4, 9, 14, 21, 48, 74; BLC 3; DA; DAB; DAC; DAM MST, MULT, NOV; SSC 2; WLC**
See also AAYA 5; BW 1; CA 108; CANR 64; CDALB 1929-1941; DLB 76, 102; DLBD 2; MTCW 1

Wright, Richard B(ruce) 1937- **CLC 6**
See also CA 85-88; DLB 53

Wright, Rick 1945- **CLC 35**

Wright, Rowland
See Wells, Carolyn

Wright, Stephen 1946- **CLC 33**

Wright, Willard Huntington 1888-1939
See Van Dine, S. S.
See also CA 115; DLBD 16

Wright, William 1930- **CLC 44**
See also CA 53-56; CANR 7, 23

Wroth, Lady Mary 1587-1653(?) **LC 30**
See also DLB 121

Wu Ch'eng-en 1500(?)-1582(?) **LC 7**

Wu Ching-tzu 1701-1754 **LC 2**

Wurlitzer, Rudolph 1938(?)- **CLC 2, 4, 15**
See also CA 85-88; DLB 173

Wycherley, William 1641-1715**LC 8, 21; DAM DRAM**
See also CDBLB 1660-1789; DLB 80

Wylie, Elinor (Morton Hoyt) 1885-1928 **TCLC 8; PC 23**
See also CA 105; 162; DLB 9, 45

Wylie, Philip (Gordon) 1902-1971 **CLC 43**
See also CA 21-22; 33-36R; CAP 2; DLB 9

Wyndham, John **CLC 19**
See also Harris, John (Wyndham Parkes Lucas) Beynon

Wyss, Johann David Von 1743-1818**NCLC 10**
See also JRDA; MAICYA; SATA 29; SATA-Brief 27

Xenophon c. 430B.C.-c. 354B.C. **CMLC 17**
See also DLB 176

Yakumo Koizumi
See Hearn, (Patricio) Lafcadio (Tessima Carlos)

Yanez, Jose Donoso
See Donoso (Yanez), Jose

Yanovsky, Basile S.
See Yanovsky, V(assily) S(emenovich)

Yanovsky, V(assily) S(emenovich) 1906-1989 **CLC 2, 18**
See also CA 97-100; 129

Yates, Richard 1926-1992 **CLC 7, 8, 23**
See also CA 5-8R; 139; CANR 10, 43; DLB 2; DLBY 81, 92; INT CANR-10

Yeats, W. B.
See Yeats, William Butler

Yeats, William Butler 1865-1939**TCLC 1, 11, 18, 31; DA; DAB; DAC; DAM DRAM, MST, POET; PC 20; WLC**
See also CA 104; 127; CANR 45; CDBLB 1890-1914; DLB 10, 19, 98, 156; MTCW 1

Yehoshua, A(braham) B. 1936- **CLC 13, 31**
See also CA 33-36R; CANR 43

Yep, Laurence Michael 1948- **CLC 35**
See also AAYA 5; CA 49-52; CANR 1, 46; CLR 3, 17, 54; DLB 52; JRDA; MAICYA; SATA 7, 69

Yerby, Frank G(arvin) 1916-1991 **CLC 1, 7, 22; BLC 3; DAM MULT**
See also BW 1; CA 9-12R; 136; CANR 16, 52; DLB 76; INT CANR-16; MTCW 1

Literary Criticism Series
Cumulative Topic Index

This index lists all topic entries in Gale's *Classical and Medieval Literature Criticism, Contemporary Literary Criticism, Literature Criticism from 1400 to 1800, Nineteenth-Century Literature Criticism,* and *Twentieth-Century Literary Criticism.*

Topic Index

Topic Index

Topic Index

LC Cumulative Nationality Index

AFGHAN
Babur 18

AMERICAN
Bradstreet, Anne 4, 30
Edwards, Jonathan 7
Eliot, John 5
Franklin, Benjamin 25
Hathorne, John 38
Hopkinson, Francis 25
Knight, Sarah Kemble 7
Mather, Cotton 38
Mather, Increase 38
Munford, Robert 5
Penn, William 25
Sewall, Samuel 38
Stoughton, William 38
Taylor, Edward 11
Washington, George 25
Wheatley (Peters), Phillis 3
Winthrop, John 31

BENINESE
Equiano, Olaudah 16

CANADIAN
Marie de l'Incarnation 10

CHINESE
Lo Kuan-chung 12
P'u Sung-ling 3
Ts'ao Hsueh-ch'in 1
Wu Ch'eng-en 7
Wu Ching-tzu 2

DANISH
Brahe, Tycho 45
Holberg, Ludvig 6

Wessel, Johan Herman 7

DUTCH
Erasmus, Desiderius 16
Lipsius, Justus 16
Spinoza, Benedictus de 9

ENGLISH
Addison, Joseph 18
Andrewes, Lancelot 5
Arbuthnot, John 1
Aubin, Penelope 9
Bacon, Francis 18, 32
Barker, Jane 42
Beaumont, Francis 33
Behn, Aphra 1, 30, 42
Boswell, James 4
Bradstreet, Anne 4, 30
Brooke, Frances 6
Bunyan, John 4
Burke, Edmund 7, 36
Butler, Samuel 16, 43
Carew, Thomas 13
Cary, Elizabeth, Lady Falkland 30
Cavendish, Margaret Lucas 30
Caxton, William , 17
Chapman, George 22
Charles I 13
Chatterton, Thomas 3
Chaucer, Geoffrey 17
Churchill, Charles 3
Cleland, John 2
Collier, Jeremy 6
Collins, William 4, 40
Congreve, William 5, 21
Coventry, Francis 46
Cowley, Abraham 43
Crashaw, Richard 24

Cromwell, Oliver 43
Daniel, Samuel 24
Davys, Mary 1, 46
Day, Thomas 1
Dee, John 20
Defoe, Daniel 1, 42
Dekker, Thomas 22
Delany, Mary (Granville Pendarves) 12
Deloney, Thomas 41
Dennis, John 11
Devenant, William 13
Donne, John 10, 24
Drayton, Michael 8
Dryden, John 3, 21
Elyot, Sir Thomas 11
Equiano, Olaudah 16
Fanshawe, Ann 11
Farquhar, George 21
Fielding, Henry 1, 46
Fielding, Sarah 1, 44
Fletcher, John 33
Foxe, John 14
Garrick, David 15
Gray, Thomas 4, 40
Greene, Robert 41
Hakluyt, Richard 31
Hawes, Stephen 17
Haywood, Eliza (Fowler) 1, 44
Henry VIII 10
Herbert, George 24
Herrick, Robert 13
Hobbes, Thomas 36
Howell, James 13
Hunter, Robert 7
Johnson, Samuel 15
Jonson, Ben(jamin) 6, 33
Julian of Norwich 6
Kempe, Margery 6

LC Cumulative Title Index

Title Index

Title Index

Title Index

Title Index

Title Index

Title Index

23
"An Excellente Balade of Charitie as wroten bie the gode Prieste Thomas Rowley, 1464" (Chatterton) **3**:123-24, 127, 135
Exclamations (Teresa de Jesus) **18**:392
The Excursion (Brooke) **6**:107-08, 110-11, 115, 117, 119, 121-22
"Execration upon Vulcan" (Jonson) **33**:175
Exemplary Novels (Cervantes)
　See *Novelas exemplares*
Exemplary Stories (Cervantes)
　See *Novelas exemplares*
Exemplary Tales (Cervantes)
　See *Novelas exemplares*
Exercitia spiritualia (Kempis) **11**:411
"The Exhibition" (Chatterton) **3**:126, 132
"Exhorta a Lisi efectos semejantes de la vibora" (Quevedo) **23**:196
Exhortation for all Christians Warming Them Against Insurrection and Rebillion (*Sincere Admonition*) (Luther) **37**:263, 303
Exhortation to Emperor Charles V (Hutten) **16**:234
Exhortation to Penitence (Machiavelli) **36**:223
Exhortation to the German Princes to Undertake War against the Turks (Hutten) **16**:235
Exhortatorium (Hutten)
　See *Ad Caesarem Maximilianum ut bellum in Venetos coeptum prosequatur exhortatorium*
Exilius; or, the Banish'd Roman (Barker) **42**:61-3, 65-6, 68-9, 77-9
"Existence" (Turgot) **26**:350, 355-56, 357, 381
Exodus (Towneley) **34**:250
"Exorcising Against Jealousy" (P'u Sung-ling) **3**:346
"Exorcism, or The Spectater" (Erasmus) **16**:194-95
"Expansibilitie" (Turgot) **26**:356
The Expedition of Humphry Clinker (*Humphry Clinker*) (Smollett) **2**:319-20, 322-26, 329-30, 332, 336-37, 341-44, 347-51, 353, 357, 359, 362-66; **46**:190-93, 195, 197-200, 204, 224-33, 235, 237, 252, 260-69, 277-88
"An Expedition to Fife and the Island of May" (Fergusson) **29**:231
"The Experience" (Taylor) **11**:359, 363, 384, 389, 396
"Experience" (Winthrop) **31**:342, 352
Experiences nouvelles touchant le vide (Pascal) **35**:389
Experimental Philosophy (Campanella)
　See *Philosophia sensibus demonstrata*
Experiments and Observations on Electricity, Made at Philadelphia (Franklin) **25**:111
"The Expiration" ("So, so breake off this last lamenting kisse") (Donne) **10**:36; **24**:150
Explanation of the Christian Faith (*Christianae Fidei Expositio; An Exposition of the Faith; Fidei Christianae Expositio; Fiendly Exposition*) (Zwingli) **37**:352, 356, 391
An Explanation of the San-kuo-chih, Done in the Popular Style (Lo Kuan-chung)
　See *San-kuo-chih yeni-i*
Explanation on the New System (Leibniz) **35**:166
Explanations of the 95 Theses (Luther)
　See *Resolutiones disputationum de indulgentiarum*
Explicatio triginita sigillorum (Bruno) **27**:94, 100
The Exploits of Garcilaso de la Vega and the Moor Tarfe (Vega)
　See *Los hechos de Garcilaso de la Vega y Moro Tarfe*
Expositio passionis Christi (More)

See *Expositio passionis Domini*
Expositio passionis Domini (*Expositio passionis Christi*) (More) **10**:365, 413-14
Exposition des origines des connaissances humaines (Condillac)
　See *Essai sur l'origine des connaissances humaines*
An Exposition of the Faith (Zwingli)
　See *Explanation of the Christian Faith*
Expostulatio (Hutten) **16**:232, 234-35
Expostulation (Agrippa von Nettesheim) **27**:13
"An Expostulation with Inigo Jones" (Jonson) **6**:350
Expulsion from the Garden (York) **34**:359
The Expulsion of the Triumphant Beast (Bruno)
　See *Lo spaccio de la bestia trionfante*
"The Exstasie" ("The Ecstasy") (Donne) **10**:13, 18, 26, 33, 35-6, 46, 51-2, 55, 81-2, 85, 87, 103; **24**:154, 162, 194-97
"The Exstasy: A Pindarique Ode to Her Majesty the Queen" (Aubin) **9**:4
"Extemporaneous Effusion on Being Appointed to the Excise" (Burns) **6**:89; **29**:47
"Extempore-to Mr. Gavin Hamilton" (Burns) **40**:87-8
Extraccio Animarum (Towneley) (*The Harrowing* (Towneley)) **34**:251, 291, 308
Extrait des sentiments de Jean Meslier (Voltaire) **14**:370
"Eyes and Tears" (Marvell) **4**:397, 403, 439
Eyn Sermon von Ablass und Gnade (*Sermon on Indulgences and Grace*) (Luther) **9**:91, 146
"Fable of the Cock and the Fox" (Chaucer)
　See "Nun's Priest's Tale"
Fables Ancient and Modern; Translated into Verse, from Homer, Ovid, Boccace, & Chaucer (Dryden) **3**:184, 187, 190, 204-05, 216, 221, 237-38, 242-43; **21**:118-19
Les fâcheux (*The Bores*) (Moliere) **10**:275, 277, 281, 283, 291, 299, 302, 310; **28**:255, 257, 267
The Faerie Queene, Disposed into Twelve Bookes Fashioning XII Morall Vertues (Spenser) **5**:295, 297, 299-302, 304-05, 307-25, 328, 331, 333-37, 341-42, 349, 355-56, 360, 364-66; **39**:303-14, 317, 320-29, 329-42, 342-47, 351-53, 354-62, 373-87, 388-95
The Fair Captive (Haywood) **44**:150
"Fair copy of my Celia's face" (Carew) **13**:20
"Fair Daffodils" (Herrick)
　See "To Daffadills"
The Fair Favorite (Davenant) **13**:175, 181-82, 196
"The Fair Hypocrite" (Manley) **1**:306, 308
The Fair Jilt; or, The History of Prince Tarquin and Miranda (Behn) **1**:30-1, 42-3, 46, 49-53, 55; **30**:87, 89; **42**:109, 117, 136, 145-46
The Fair Penitent (Rowe) **8**:285, 287, 291-300, 302-05, 307, 312-14, 316-17
A Fair Quarrel (Middleton) **33**:264, 270, 276, 280, 282, 321, 323-26
"Fair Recluse" (Smart) **3**:399
"The Fair Singer" (Marvell) **4**:403, 409, 436
The Fair Vow-Breaker (Behn)
　See *The History of the Nun; or, The Fair Vow-Breaker*
"The Faire Begger" (Lovelace) **24**:306-07
"The Fairie Temple: or, Oberons Chappell. Dedicated to Mr. John Merrifield, Counsellor at Law" ("Oberon's Chappell"; "The Temple") (Herrick) **13**:351, 372-73
"The Fairies" (Perrault)
　See "Les Fées"

The Fairies (Garrick) **15**:95-6, 128
"The Fairy Feast" (Parnell) **3**:255
"A Fairy Tale in the Ancient English Style" (Parnell) **3**:251, 254, 256-57
"Faith" (Herbert) **24**:259, 268
"Faith" (Vaughan) **27**:383
Faith Encouraged (Mather) **38**:229
A Faithful Account of the Discipline Professed and Practised in the Churches of New England (Mather)
　See *Ratio Disciplinae*
Faithful Admonition to the Professors of God's Truth in England (Knox) **37**:200-01
A Faithful Narrative of the Surprizing Work of God in the Conversion of Many Hundred Souls in Northampton, and the Neighboring Towns and Villages (Edwards) **7**:101, 118
Faithful Shepard (Calderon de la Barca) **23**:63
The Faithful Shepherdess (Fletcher) **33**:45, 53, 63-71, 75-6, 78, 81-83, 91
The Faithful Wife (Marivaux)
　See *The Faithful Wife*
"The Falcon" (Lovelace) **24**:302, 315, 330, 336-40, 346, 348
Fall of Lucifer (Chester) **34**:105-6, 123, 126, 128-9, 131-5
Fall of Man (Chester)
　See *Creation and Fall* (Chester)
Fall of Man (York)
　See *Man's Disobedience and Fall* (York)
Fall of the Angels (Chester) **34**:138
The False Alarm (Johnson) **15**:202, 208
False Confidences (Marivaux)
　See *False Confidences*
The False Count; or, A New Way to Play an Old Game (Behn) **1**:34, 37; **30**:81,
The False Friend (Vanbrugh) **21**:295, 319
The False Friend; or, The Fate of Disobedience (Pix) **8**:259, 261-63, 268-70, 272, 276, 278
"False Knight" (Erasmus) **16**:114
The False Maid (Marivaux)
　See *The False Maid*
De falso credita et ementita Donatione Constatini Magni (*Constantine Donation; On the Pretended Donation of Constantine*) (Hutten) **16**:212, 224, 231, 234, 245
Fama Fraternitatis (Andreae) **32**:22, 67, 71, 85, 87
La famiglia dell' antiquario (*The Antiquarian's Family*) (Goldoni) **4**:250, 260, 266
Familiar Letters (Howell)
　See *Epistolae Ho-Elianae: Familiar Letters Domestic and Forren*
Familiar Letters between the Principal Characters in "David Simple" (Fielding) **1**:270-73; **44**:68, 72-3, 100
Familiar Letters betwixt a Gentleman and a Lady (Davys) **1**:101-02; **46**:19-20, 23-8, 33-7
Familiar Letters on Important Occasions (*Letters*) (Richardson) **1**:398, 416-17; **44**:229-31, 234-5, 244-5, 248
"Familier" (Marmontel) **2**:221
Familiorum Colloquiorum (*Colloquia, Familiar Colloquies, Colloquies, Colloquiorum Opus*) (Erasmus) **16**:113-14, 116-17, 121-24, 128, 132, 139-40, 142-43, 146, 152, 154-57, 162, 174, 176, 192-95
The Family Instructor (Defoe) **1**:122, 170, 176; **42**:177, 184, 201-02, 205
The Family of Love (Middleton) **33**:262, 275, 277, 310
Family Religion Excited (Mather) **38**:167
"A Famous Prediction of Merlin" (Swift) **1**:516-

Title Index

(Penn) **25**:283, 287-88, 334

"Guiltless Lady Imprisoned, after Penanced" (Lovelace) **24**:307, 334-35

The Guise (Webster) **33**:340

Gulliver's Travels (Swift)
See *Travels into Several Remote Nations of the World, in Four Parts; By Lemuel Gulliver*

Gull's Horn-Book (Dekker) **22**:96, 106

Gustavus, King of Swithland (Dekker) **22**:88

Gustavus Vasa, the Deliverer of His Country (Brooke) **1**:62, 67

"Das Gute Leben eines recht schaffenen Dieners Gottes" (Andreae) **32**:92

Der gute Rat (Schlegel) **5**:278-79

Guy, Earl of Warwick (Dekker) **22**:88

Guzman the Valiant (Vega) **23**:347

Gwydonius **41**:156, 176

The Gypsies Metamorphosed (*The Metamorphosed Gipsies*) (Jonson) **6**:317, 337

"The Gypsy Maid" (Cervantes)
See "La gitanilla"

"H. Scriptures" ("Holy Scriptures") (Vaughan) **27**:341, 354, 392

"H:W: in Hiber: `belligeranti'" (Donne) **10**:39

"Habbakuk" (Parnell) **3**:255

"Had I the Wyte" (Burns) **29**:20; **40**:85

Haft Aurang (*The Constellation of the Great Bear*) (Jami) **9**:59, 62, 65-8, 71

"The Hag Is Astride" (Herrick) **13**:331, 336

Hakluyt's Voyages (Hakluyt)
See *The Principal Navigations, Voyages, Traffiques and Discoveries of theEnglish Nation*

"Hallelujah" (Winchilsea) **3**:451

"Hallow Fair" (Fergusson) **29**:172, 179, 181, 189-93, 107, 204-05, 210, 224, 227, 237-39

"Hallowe'en" (Burns) **3**:48, 52, 54, 56, 65, 67, 72-3, 84, 86; **29**:4, 6-9, 13-16, 18, 28, 64, 72-4; **40**:82, 96, 103-4

Hamburg Dramaturgy (Lessing)
See *Die Hamburgische Dramaturgie*

Die Hamburgische Dramaturgie (*Hamburg Dramaturgy*) (Lessing) **8**:61-3, 65, 67-9, 71, 73-4, 76-8, 80-7, 94, 98-104, 107, 110-11, 114-16

"Hame Content: A Satire" (Fergusson) **29**:189, 210, 217-18

"The Hamlet" (Warton)
See "Hamlet, an Ode written in Whichwood Forest"

Hamlet (Kyd)
See *The Tragedie of Soliman and Perseda*

"Hamlet, an Ode written in Whichwood Forest" ("The Hamlet") (Warton) **15**:432, 434, 443

"Han Fang" (P'u Sung-ling) **3**:344

Handbook of the Militant Christian (Erasmus)
See *Enchiridion militis christiani*

"The Handsome and the Deformed Leg" (Franklin) **25**:141, 147

"Handsome Nell" (Burns) **40**:93

The Hanging of Judas (Towneley)
See *Suspencio Jude* (Towneley)

"Hannah" (Parnell) **3**:255

Hannibal (Marivaux)
See *Hannibal*

"Hans Carvel" (Prior) **4**:455, 461, 467

Hans Frandsen (Holberg)
See *Jean de France; eller, Hans Frandsen*

"Happiness" (Philips) **30**:279, 287

"The Happy Fugitives" (Manley) **1**:306-08

Happy Homecoming (Conde)
See *Hérémakhonon: On doit attendre le bonheur*

"The Happy Lover's Reflections" (Ramsay) **29**:329

"An Haranguer" (Butler) **16**;53

Harlequin Refined by Love (Marivaux)
See *Harlequin Refined by Love*

Harlequin's Invasion (Garrick) **15**:100, 104, 114, 124

The Harmonie of the Church. Containing the Spirituall Songes and Holy Hymnes, of Godley Men, Patriarkes and Prophetes: All, Sweetly Sounding, to the Praise and Glory of the Highest **8**:19, 29

Harmonies of the World (Kepler)
See *Hormonice Mundi*

"Harmony" (Kochanowski)
See "Zgoda"

"Harriet's Birth Day" (Smart) **3**:366

"The Harrow" (Franklin) **25**:141

The Harrowing of Hell, and the Resurrection (N-Town) **34**:172-3, 178, 187-8

Harrowing of Hell (Chester) **34**:109, 120, 124-5, 130, 138

Harrowing of Hell (N-Town) **34**:180

Harrowing of Hell (York) **34**:334, 353, 374, 387

The Harrowing (Towneley)
See *Extraccio Animarum* (Towneley)

Le hasard du coin du feu (*The Opportunities of the Fireside*) (Crebillon) **1**:76-7, 79; **28**:69-72, 79, 87, 91-3

"Hassan; or, The Camel-Driver" (Collins) **4**:210

The Haunch of Venison (Goldsmith) **2**:74, 104

The Hawk-Eyed Sentinel (Cervantes) **6**:190

Hazañas del Cid (Castro)
See *Las mocedades del Cid II*

"he Apostacy of One, and But One Lady" (Lovelace) **24**:307

"He Expresses Joy at Finding...Her Whom He Had Loved as a Mere Boy" (More) **10**:427

"He that loves a rosy cheek" (Carew)
See "Disdaine Returned"

"He that loves a rosy lip" (Carew) **13**:20

"Heads of an Answer to Rymer" (Dryden) **3**:236-37; **21**:114-15

"Health" (Ramsay) **29**:309, 353

"The Heart" **8**:9, 30

"Heart of Oak" (Garrick) **15**:114, 124

Heat (Marat) **10**:222

"Heaven" (Herbert) **24**:269, 273

The Heavenly Footman (Bunyan) **4**:172, 177

Heavens Alarm to the World (Mather) **38**:283, 294

Heaven's Favourite (Marvell) **43**:297

Hebrides Journal (Boswell)
See *Journal of a Tour to the Hebrides with Samuel Johnson, LL. D.*

Los hechos de Garcilaso de la Vega y Moro Tarfe (*The Exploits of Garcilaso de la Vega and the Moor Tarfe*) (Vega) **23**:362, 400

Heedless Hopalong (Grimmelshausen)
See *Der seltsame Springinsfeld*

"Heilrædauísur" ("Good Counsel") (Petursson) **8**:253

Heinrich der Löws (Schlegel) **5**:273

Hekuba (Schlegel) **5**:280

"Helter Skelter; or, The Hue and Cry after the Attorneys Going to Ride the Circuit" (Swift) **1**:459

"The Henpecked Husband" (Burns) **29**:24; **40**:89

La Henriade (Marmontel) **2**:222-23

La henriade (Voltaire) **14**:328, 338, 342, 349, 358, 379, 382, 391, 414

Henrich and Pernille (Holberg)
See *Henrik og Pernille*

Henrik og Pernille (*Henrich and Pernille*) (Holberg) **6**:277, 283

Henry (Lyttelton)
See *The History of the Life of King Henry the Second and of the Age in Which He Lived*

Henry II. (Lyttelton)
See *The History of the Life of King Henry the Second and of the Age in Which He Lived*

"Henry and Emma" ("Nut-brown Maid") (Prior) **4**:455, 458, 460, 467, 474-79

Heptaplus (*Discourse on the seven days of the creation; Septiform Narration of the Six Days of Creation*) (Pico della Mirandola) **15**:319, 324, 329-30, 334, 338, 340-41, 345, 350-57, 359-60

"Her Man Described by Her Own Dictamen" (Jonson) **6**:305

"Her Muffe" (Lovelace) **24**:347

"Her Right Name" (Prior) **4**:460-61, 466

Les Héraclides (Marmontel) **2**:213, 216

Heráclito cristiano y Segunda harpa a imitación de la de David (Quevedo) **23**:176-77

"Heraclitus" (Prior)
See "Democritus and Heraclitus"

Heraclius (Corneille)
See *Héraclius*

Héraclius (*Heraclius*) (Corneille) **28**:4-5, 21, 28-9, 34-5, 41, 57

Herbarius (Paracelsus) **14**:198

Hercule Chrestien (Ronsard) **6**:437

Herculis christiani luctae (Andreae) **32**:92

"Here she lies, a pretty bud" (Herrick)
See "Upon a Child That Died"

Hérémakhonon: On doit attendre le bonheur (*Happy Homecoming*) (Conde)

"Here's a Health to them that's awa'" (Burns) **40**:102

"Here's his health in water" (Burns) **29**:54

L'héritier du village (Marivaux) **4**:367

Hermann (*Herrmann*) (Schlegel) **5**:273, 280-81

The Hermetic and Alchmical Writings (Paracelsus) **14**:185

"An Hermetic Philosopher" (Butler) **16**:28, 52

Hermetical Physick (Vaughan) **27**:324

"The Hermit" (Parnell) **3**:252-54, 256-58

The Hermit (Goldsmith) **2**:68

Hermosura de Angelica (Vega) **23**:340

The Hero (Gracian y Morales)
See *El Héroe*

Hero and Leander (Chapman) **22**:8, 14, 19, 22-4, 26, 28, 69, 71, 73

Hero and Leander (Marlowe) **22**:334, 337, 340, 370

Herod and the Three Kings (N-Town) **34**:208

Herod the Great (Towneley)
See *Magnus Herodes* (Towneley)

El Héroe (*The Hero*) (Gracian y Morales) **15**:135-36, 143-45, 165

The Heroic Frenzies (Bruno)
See *De gli eroici furori*

Heroic Piety of Don Fernando Cortés, Marqués del Valle (Siguenza y Gongora) **8**:343

"Heroical Epistle" (Butler)
See "Heroical Epistle of Hudibras to his Lady"

"Heroical Epistle of Hudibras to his Lady" ("Heroical Epistle") (Butler) **16**:24, 39, 49; **43**:68

"The Heroine" (P'u Sung-ling)
See "Hsieh-nü"

"Heroique Stanzas to the Glorious Memory of Cromwell" (Dryden) **3**:223-26; **21**:85

Héros (Gracian y Morales) **15**:142

Les héros de Roman (Boileau-Despreaux)

Title Index

Title Index

Title Index

Title Index

Title Index